STATUTORY INSTRUMENTS 1972

PART II
(in two Sections)

SECTION 2

Published by Authority

LONDON
HER MAJESTY'S STATIONERY OFFICE
1972

2a

© *Crown copyright* 1972

PRINTED AND PUBLISHED BY HER MAJESTY'S STATIONERY OFFICE

To be purchased from
49 High Holborn, LONDON, WC1V 6HB
13a Castle Street, EDINBURGH, EH2 3AR   109 St. Mary Street, CARDIFF, CF1 1JW
Brazennose Street, MANCHESTER, M60 8AS   50 Fairfax Street, BRISTOL, BS1 3DE
258 Broad Street, BIRMINGHAM, B1 2HE   80 Chichester Street, BELFAST, BT1 4JY

or through booksellers

1972

Price for the two Sections: £12·75 net

PRINTED IN ENGLAND

SBN 11 840113 0*

Contents of the Volume

STATUTORY INSTRUMENTS

1972 No. 1088

WAGES COUNCILS

The Wages Regulation (Stamped or Pressed Metal-Wares) (Holidays) Order 1972

Made - - -		*20th July* 1972
Coming into Operation		*16th August* 1972

Whereas the Secretary of State has received from the Stamped or Pressed Metal-Wares Wages Council (Great Britain) the wages regulation proposals set out in the Schedule hereto ;

Now, therefore, the Secretary of State in exercise of his powers under section 11 of the Wages Councils Act 1959(a), and of all other powers enabling him in that behalf, hereby makes the following Order :—

1. This Order may be cited as the Wages Regulation (Stamped or Pressed Metal-Wares) (Holidays) Order 1972.

2.—(1) In this Order the expression "the specified date" means the 16th August 1972, provided that where, as respects any worker who is paid wages at intervals not exceeding seven days, that date does not correspond with the beginning of the period for which the wages are paid, the expression "the specified date" means, as respects that worker, the beginning of the next such period following that date.

(2) The Interpretation Act 1889(b) shall apply to the interpretation of this Order as it applies to the interpretation of an Act of Parliament and as if this Order and the Order hereby revoked were Acts of Parliament.

3. The wages regulation proposals set out in the Schedule hereto shall have effect as from the specified date and as from that date the Wages Regulation (Stamped or Pressed Metal-Wares) (Holidays) Order 1971(c) shall cease to have effect.

Signed by order of the Secretary of State.
20th July 1972.

R. R. D. McIntosh,
Deputy Secretary,
Department of Employment.

(a) 1959 c. 69.   (b) 1889 c. 63.
(c) S.I. 1971/1089 (1971 II, p. 3238).

Article 3

SCHEDULE

The following provisions as to holidays and holiday remuneration shall be substituted for the provisions as to holidays and holiday remuneration set out in the Wages Regulation (Stamped or Pressed Metal-Wares) (Holidays) Order 1971 (hereinafter referred to as "Order Q. (106) ").

PART I

APPLICATION

1. This Schedule applies to every worker for whom statutory minimum remuneration has been fixed.

PART II

CUSTOMARY HOLIDAYS

2.—(1) An employer shall allow to every worker to whom this Schedule applies a holiday (hereinafter referred to as a "customary holiday") in each year on the days specified in the following sub-paragraph, provided that the worker has been in his employment for a period of not less than four weeks immediately preceding the customary holiday and has worked for the employer during the whole or part of that period and (unless excused by the employer or absent by reason of the proved illness of the worker) has worked for the employer throughout the last seven working days on which work was available to him immediately prior to the customary holiday.

(2) The said customary holidays are:—

(a) (i) In England and Wales—

Christmas Day (or, if Christmas Day falls on a Sunday, such week day as may be appointed by national proclamation, or, if none is so appointed, the next following Tuesday), Boxing Day, Good Friday, Easter Monday, Whit Monday (or where another day is substituted therefor by national proclamation, that day), August Bank Holiday, and two other days (being days of the week on which the worker normally works for the employer) in the course of a calendar year to be fixed by the employer and notified to the worker not less than three weeks before the holiday ;

(ii) In Scotland—

New Year's Day (or, if New Year's Day falls on a Sunday, the following Monday) ;

the local Spring holiday ;

the local Autumn holiday ; and

five other days (being days of the week on which the worker normally works for the employer) in the course of a calendar year to be fixed by the employer and notified to the worker not less than three weeks before the holiday ;

or (b) in the case of each of the said days (other than a day fixed by the employer in Scotland and notified to the worker as aforesaid) such week day as may be substituted therefor, being a day recognised by local custom as a day of holiday in substitution for the said day or a day agreed between the employer and the worker or his representative.

(3) Notwithstanding the preceding provisions of this paragraph, an employer may (except where in the case of a woman or young person such a requirement would be unlawful) require a worker who is otherwise entitled to any customary holiday under the foregoing provisions of this Schedule to work thereon, and, in lieu of any customary holiday on which he so works, the worker shall be entitled to be allowed a day's holiday (hereinafter referred to as a "holiday in lieu of a customary holiday") on a week day on which he would normally work for the employer within the period of four weeks next ensuing.

(4) A worker who is required to work on a customary holiday shall be paid:—

> (a) for all time worked thereon, the statutory minimum remuneration then appropriate to the worker for work on a customary holiday ; and

> (b) in respect of the holiday in lieu of the customary holiday, holiday remuneration in accordance with paragraph 6.

PART III

ANNUAL HOLIDAY

3.—(1) Subject to the provisions of paragraph 4, in addition to the holidays specified in Part II of this Schedule an employer shall, between the date on which the provisions of this Schedule become effective and 30th September 1972, and in each succeeding year between 1st May and 30th September, allow a holiday (hereinafter referred to as an "annual holiday") to every worker in his employment to whom this Schedule applies who has been employed by him during the 12 months immediately preceding the commencement of the holiday season for any of the periods set out in the table below and the duration of the annual holiday shall, in the case of each such worker, be related to his period of employment during that 12 months as follows:—

Period of employment	Duration of annual holiday for workers with a normal working week of—			
	Six days	Five days	Four days	Three days or less
At least 48 weeks	12 days	10 days	8 days	6 days
„ „ 44 „	11 „	9 „	7 „	6 „
„ „ 40 „	10 „	8 „	6 „	5 „
„ „ 36 „	9 „	7 „	6 „	5 „
„ „ 32 „	8 „	6 „	5 „	4 „
„ „ 28 „	7 „	5 „	4 „	4 „
„ „ 24 „	6 „	5 „	4 „	3 „
„ „ 20 „	5 „	4 „	3 „	3 „
„ „ 16 „	4 „	3 „	2 „	2 „
„ „ 12 „	3 „	2 „	2 „	1 day
„ „ 8 „	2 „	1 day	1 day	1 „
„ „ 4 „	1 day	1 „	—	—

(2) Notwithstanding the provisions of the last foregoing sub-paragraph—

> (a) the number of days of annual holiday which an employer is required to allow to a worker in any holiday season shall not exceed in the aggregate twice the number of days constituting the worker's normal working week.

(*b*) the duration of the worker's annual holiday during the holiday season ending on 30th September 1972, shall be reduced by any days of annual holiday duly allowed to him by the employer under the provisions of Order Q.(106), between 1st May 1972 and the date on which this Schedule becomes effective.

(3) In this Schedule the expression "holiday season" means in relation to an annual holiday during the year 1972, the period commencing on 1st May 1972, and ending on 30th September 1972, and in relation to each subsequent year, the period commencing on 1st May and ending on 30th September in that year.

4.—(1) An annual holiday under this Schedule shall be allowed on consecutive working days, being days on which the worker is normally called upon to work for the employer, and days of annual holiday shall be treated as consecutive notwithstanding that a Sunday, a customary holiday on which the worker is not required to work for the employer or a holiday in lieu of a customary holiday intervenes :

Provided that—

(i) Where the duration of an annual holiday which an employer is required to allow to a worker exceeds the number of days constituting the worker's normal working week the said holiday may be allowed in two separate periods of such consecutive working days, and in that event, notwithstanding the foregoing provisions of this Schedule, the annual holiday shall be allowed as follows : —

(*a*) as to one period, not being less than the number of days constituting the worker's normal working week, during the holiday season, and

(*b*) as to the other period, during the holiday season or within the period ending on 30th April immediately following the holiday season.

(ii) One day of the annual holiday may be allowed on a non-consecutive working day (other than the worker's weekly short day) falling within the holiday season (or after the holiday season in the circumstances specified in sub-paragraph (1)(i)(*b*) of this paragraph) where the annual holiday or, as the case may be, such separate period, is allowed immediately after a customary holiday on which the worker is not required to work or so that such a holiday intervenes.

(2) Subject to the provisions of sub-paragraph (1) of this paragraph, any day of annual holiday under this Schedule may be allowed on a day on which the worker is entitled to a day of holiday or to a half-holiday under any enactment other than the Wages Councils Act 1959.

5. An employer shall give to a worker reasonable notice of the commencing date or dates and duration of the period or periods of his annual holiday. Such notice may be given individually to the worker or by the posting of a notice in the place where the worker is employed.

PART IV

HOLIDAY REMUNERATION

A—CUSTOMARY HOLIDAYS AND HOLIDAYS IN LIEU OF CUSTOMARY HOLIDAYS

6.—(1) Subject to the provisions of this paragraph, for each day of holiday to which a worker is entitled under Part II of this Schedule he shall be paid by the employer holiday remuneration equal to the amount, *calculated at the appropriate rate of statutory minimum remuneration, increased by one third* to which he would have been entitled if the day had not been a day of holiday and he had worked on that day on work for which statutory minimum remuneration is payable for the time usually worked by him on that day of the week :

Provided, however, that payment of the said holiday remuneration is subject to the condition that the worker presents himself for employment at the usual starting hour on the first working day following the holiday and works throughout his normal working hours on that day or, if he fails to do so, failure is by reason of the proved illness of the worker or with the consent of the employer.

(2) The holiday remuneration in respect of any customary holiday shall be paid by the employer to the worker not later than the pay day on which the wages are paid for the pay week including the first working day following the customary holiday.

(3) The holiday remuneration in respect of any holiday in lieu of a customary holiday shall be paid not later than the pay day on which the wages are paid for the pay week including the first working day following the holiday in lieu of a customary holiday:

Provided that the said payment shall be made immediately upon the termination of the worker's employment in the case where he ceases to be employed before being allowed a holiday in lieu of a customary holiday to which he is entitled, and in that case the proviso to sub-paragraph (1) of this paragraph shall not apply.

B—ANNUAL HOLIDAY

7.—(1) Subject to the provisions of paragraph 8, a worker qualified to be allowed an annual holiday under this Schedule shall be paid by his employer in respect thereof, on the last pay day preceding such annual holiday, one day's holiday pay (as defined in paragraph 11) in respect of each day thereof.

(2) Where under the provisions of paragraph 4 an annual holiday is allowed in more than one period, the holiday remuneration shall be apportioned accordingly.

8. Where any accrued holiday remuneration has been paid by the employer to the worker in accordance with paragraph 9 of this Schedule, or in accordance with Order Q. (106), in respect of employment during any of the periods referred to in that paragraph or that Order respectively, the amount of holiday remuneration payable by the employer in respect of any annual holiday for which the worker has qualified by reason of employment during the said period shall be reduced by the amount of the said accrued holiday remuneration unless that remuneration has been deducted from a previous payment of holiday remuneration made under the provisions of this Schedule or of Order Q. (106).

ACCRUED HOLIDAY REMUNERATION PAYABLE ON TERMINATION OF EMPLOYMENT

9. Where a worker ceases to be employed by an employer after the provisions of this Schedule become effective the employer shall, immediately on the termination of the employment, pay to the worker as accrued holiday remuneration:—

(1) in respect of employment in the 12 months up to the 30th day of the preceding April, a sum equal to the holiday remuneration for any days of annual holiday for which he has qualified, except days of annual holiday which he has been allowed or has become entitled to be allowed before leaving the employment ; and

(2) in respect of any employment since the 30th day of the preceding April, a sum equal to the holiday remuneration which would have been payable to him if he could have been allowed an annual holiday in respect of that employment at the time of leaving it.

Part V

GENERAL

10. For the purposes of calculating any period of employment qualifying a worker for an annual holiday or for any accrued holiday remuneration under this Schedule, the worker shall be treated: —

(1) as if he were employed for a week in respect of any week in which—

    (a) he has worked for the employer for not less than 10 hours and has performed some work for which statutory minimum remuneration is payable ;

    (b) he has been absent throughout the week solely by reason of the proved illness of, or accident to, the worker, provided that the number of weeks which may be treated as weeks of employment for such reason shall not exceed six in the aggregate in the period of 12 months immediately preceding the commencement of the holiday season ;

    (c) he is absent from work throughout the week owing to suspension due to shortage of work, provided that the number of weeks which may be treated as weeks of employment for such reason shall not exceed four in the aggregate in any such period as aforesaid, and

(2) as if he were employed on any day of holiday allowed under the provisions of this Schedule or of Order Q. (106), and for the purposes of the provisions of sub-paragraph (1) of this paragraph, a worker who is absent on such a holiday shall be treated as having worked thereon for the employer for the number of hours ordinarily worked by him on that day of the week on work for which statutory minimum remuneration is payable.

11. In this Schedule, unless the context otherwise requires, the following expressions have the meanings hereby respectively assigned to them, that is to say: —

"appropriate rate of statutory minimum remuneration" means—

    (a) in the case of a time worker, the rate of statutory minimum remuneration which would be applicable to the worker *if a minimum overtime rate did not apply* and

    (b) in the case of a piece worker, the rate of statutory minimum remuneration which would be applicable to the worker if he were a time worker *and a minimum overtime rate did not apply.*

"normal working week" means the number of days on which it has been usual for the worker to work in a week in the employment of the employer during the 12 months immediately preceding the commencement of the holiday season or, where under paragraph 9 accrued holiday remuneration is payable on the termination of the employment, during the 12 months immediately preceding the date of the termination of the employment:

Provided that—

    (i) part of a day shall count as a day ;

    (ii) no account shall be taken of any week in which the worker did not perform any work for which statutory minimum remuneration has been fixed.

"one day's holiday pay" means—

(1) *Up to and including 30th April 1973* the appropriate proportion of the remuneration which the worker would be entitled to receive from his employer at the date of the annual holiday (or where the holiday is allowed in more than one period at the date of the first period) or at the termination of the employment, as the case may require, for one week's work if working his normal working week and the number of daily hours normally worked by him (exclusive of overtime), and if paid at the

appropriate rate of statutory minimum remuneration for work for which statutory minimum remuneration is payable and at the same rate for any work for which such remuneration is not payable, and "appropriate rate of statutory minimum remuneration" means—

(a) in the case of a time worker, the rate or rates of statutory minimum remuneration applicable to the worker, and

(b) in the case of a piece worker, the rate or rates of statutory minimum remuneration which would be applicable to the worker if he were a time worker.

(2) *On and after 1st May 1973* the appropriate proportion of the remuneration which the worker would be entitled to receive from his employer at the date of the annual holiday (or where the holiday is allowed in more than one period at the date of the first period) or at the termination of the employment, as the case may require, for one week's work if working his normal working week and the number of daily hours normally worked by him (exclusive of overtime) and if paid at the appropriate rate of statutory minimum remuneration for work for which statutory minimum remuneration is payable, *increased by one third,* and at the same rate (*increased as aforesaid*) for any work for which such remuneration is not payable,

and in this definition "appropriate proportion" means—

where the worker's normal working week is six days ...	one-sixth
where the worker's normal working week is five days ...	one-fifth
where the worker's normal working week is four days ...	one-quarter
where the worker's normal working week is three days or less	one-third

"statutory minimum remuneration" means statutory minimum remuneration (other than holiday remuneration) fixed by a wages regulation order made by the Secretary of State to give effect to proposals submitted to him by the Stamped or Pressed Metal-Wares Wages Council (Great Britain).

"week" in paragraphs 3 and 10 means "pay week".

12. The provisions of this Schedule are without prejudice to any agreement for the allowance of any further holidays with pay or for the payment of additional holiday remuneration.

EXPLANATORY NOTE

(*This Note is not part of the Order.*)

This Order, which has effect from 16th August 1972, sets out the holidays which an employer is required to allow to workers and the remuneration to be paid to such workers for those holidays, in substitution for the holidays and holiday remuneration fixed by the Wages Regulation (Stamped or Pressed Metal-Wares) (Holidays) Order 1971 (Order Q.(106)), which Order is revoked.

New provisions are printed in italics.

STATUTORY INSTRUMENTS

1972 No. 1089

INDUSTRIAL TRAINING

The Industrial Training Levy (Rubber and Plastics Processing) (No. 2) Order 1972

Made - - -	*20th July* 1972
Laid before Parliament	*31st July* 1972
Coming into Operation	*22nd August* 1972

The Secretary of State after approving proposals submitted by the Rubber and Plastics Processing Industry Training Board for the imposition of a further levy on employers in the rubber and plastics processing industry and in exercise of his powers under section 4 of the Industrial Training Act 1964(**a**) and of all other powers enabling him in that behalf hereby makes the following Order: —

Title and commencement

1. This Order may be cited as the Industrial Training Levy (Rubber and Plastics Processing) (No. 2) Order 1972 and shall come into operation on 22nd August 1972.

Interpretation

2.—(1) In this Order unless the context otherwise requires: —

(*a*) "agriculture" has the same meaning as in section 109(3) of the Agriculture Act 1947(**b**) or, in relation to Scotland, as in section 86(3) of the Agriculture (Scotland) Act 1948(**c**);

(*b*) "an appeal tribunal" means an industrial tribunal established under section 12 of the Industrial Training Act 1964;

(*c*) "assessment" means an assessment of an employer to the levy;

(*d*) "the Board" means the Rubber and Plastics Processing Industry Training Board;

(*e*) "business" means any activities of industry or commerce;

(*f*) "charity" has the same meaning as in section 360 of the Income and Corporation Taxes Act 1970(**d**);

(**a**) 1964 c. 16. (**b**) 1947 c. 48.
(**c**) 1948 c. 45. (**d**) 1970 c. 10.

(*g*) "emoluments" means all emoluments assessable to income tax under Schedule E (other than pensions), being emoluments from which tax under that Schedule is deductible, whether or not tax in fact falls to be deducted from any particular payment thereof;

(*h*) "employer" means a person who is an employer in the rubber and plastics processing industry at any time in the fifth levy period;

(*i*) "the fifth base period" means the period of twelve months that commenced on 6th April 1971;

(*j*) "the fifth levy period" means the period commencing with the day upon which this Order comes into operation and ending on 31st March 1973;

(*k*) "the industrial training order" means the Industrial Training (Rubber and Plastics Processing Board) Order 1967(**a**);

(*l*) "the levy" means the levy imposed by the Board in respect of the fifth levy period;

(*m*) "notice" means a notice in writing;

(*n*) "rubber and plastics processing establishment" means an establishment in Great Britain engaged in the fifth base period wholly or mainly in the rubber and plastics processing industry for a total of twenty-seven or more weeks or, being an establishment that commenced to carry on business in the fifth base period, for a total number of weeks exceeding one half of the number of weeks in the part of the said period commencing with the day on which business was commenced and ending on the last day thereof;

(*o*) "the rubber and plastics processing industry" means any one or more of the activities which, subject to the provisions of paragraph 2 of Schedule 1 to the industrial training order, are specified in paragraph 1 of that Schedule as the activities of the rubber and plastics processing industry.

(2) Any reference in this Order to a person employed at or from a rubber and plastics processing establishment shall in any case where the employer is a company be construed as including a reference to any director of the company (or any person occupying the position of director by whatever name he is called) who is required to devote substantially the whole of his time to the service of the company.

(3) In the case where a rubber and plastics processing establishment is taken over (whether directly or indirectly) by an employer in succession to, or jointly with, another person, a person employed at any time in the fifth base period at or from the establishment shall be deemed, for the purposes of this Order, to have been so employed by the employer carrying on the said establishment on the day upon which this Order comes into operation and any reference in this Order to persons employed by an employer in the fifth base period at or from a rubber and plastics processing establishment shall be contrued accordingly.

(4) Any reference in this Order to an establishment that commences to carry on business or that ceases to carry on business shall not be taken to

---

(**a**) S.I. 1967/1062 (1967 II, p. 3151).

apply where the location of the establishment is changed but its business is continued wholly or mainly at or from the new location, or where the suspension of activities is of a temporary or seasonal nature.

(5) The Interpretation Act 1889(a) shall apply to the interpretation of this Order as it applies to the interpretation of an Act of Parliament.

Imposition of the levy

3.—(1) The levy to be imposed by the Board on employers in respect of the fifth levy period shall be assessed in accordance with the provisions of this Article.

(2) The levy shall be assessed by the Board separately in respect of each rubber and plastics processing establishment of an employer (not being an employer who is exempt from the levy by virtue of paragraph (5) of this Article), but in agreement with the employer one assessment may be made in respect of any number of such establishments, in which case those establishments shall be deemed for the purposes of that assessment to constitute one establishment.

(3) Subject to the provisions of this Article, the levy assessed in respect of a rubber and plastics processing establishment of an employer shall be an amount equal to 0·75 per cent. of the sum of the emoluments of all the persons employed by the employer at or from that establishment in the fifth base period.

(4) The amount of the levy imposed in respect of a rubber and plastics processing establishment that ceases to carry on business in the fifth levy period shall be in the same proportion to the amount that would otherwise be due under paragraph (3) of this Article as the number of days between the commencement of the said levy period and the date of cessation of business (both dates inclusive) bears to the number of days in the said levy period.

(5) There shall be exempt from the levy—

    (a) an employer in whose case the number of all the persons employed by him on 5th April 1972 at or from the rubber and plastics processing establishment or establishments of the employer was less than twenty-six;

    (b) a charity.

(6) For the purposes of this Article no regard shall be had to any person wholly engaged in agriculture or in the supply of food or drink for immediate consumption.

Assessment notices

4.—(1) The Board shall serve an assessment notice on every employer assessed to the levy, but one notice may comprise two or more assessments.

(2) The amount of any assessment payable under an assessment notice shall be rounded down to the nearest £1.

(3) An assessment notice shall state the Board's address for the service of a notice of appeal or of an application for an extension of time for appealing.

(a) 1889 c. 63.

(4) An assessment notice may be served on the person assessed to the levy either by delivering it to him personally or by leaving it, or sending it to him by post, at his last known address or place of business in the United Kingdom or, if that person is a corporation, by leaving it, or sending it by post to the corporation, at such address or place of business or at its registered or principal office.

Payment of the levy

5.—(1) Subject to the provisions of this Article and of Articles 6 and 7, the amount of the levy payable under an assessment notice served by the Board shall be payable to the Board in two instalments equal to three-tenths and seven-tenths of the said amount respectively, and the said instalments shall be due respectively on 1st December 1972 and 1st September 1973.

(2) An instalment of an assessment shall not be recoverable by the Board until there has expired the time allowed for appealing against the assessment by Article 7(1) of this Order and any further period or periods of time that the Board or an appeal tribunal may have allowed for appealing under paragraph (2) or (3) of that Article or, where an appeal is brought, until the appeal is decided or withdrawn.

Withdrawal of assessment

6.—(1) The Board may, by a notice served on the person assessed to the levy in the same manner as an assessment notice, withdraw an assessment if that person has appealed against that assessment under the provisions of Article 7 of this Order and the appeal has not been entered in the Register of Appeals kept under the appropriate Regulations specified in paragraph (5) of that Article.

(2) The withdrawal of an assessment shall be without prejudice to the power of the Board to serve a further assessment notice in respect of any establishment to which that assessment related.

Appeals

7.—(1) A person assessed to the levy may appeal to an appeal tribunal against the assessment within one month from the date of the service of the assessment notice or within any further period or periods of time that may be allowed by the Board or an appeal tribunal under the following provisions of this Article.

(2) The Board by notice may for good cause allow a person assessed to the levy to appeal to an appeal tribunal against the assessment at any time within the period of four months from the date of the service of the assessment notice or within such further period or periods as the Board may allow before such time as may then be limited for appealing has expired.

(3) If the Board shall not allow an application for extension of time for appealing, an appeal tribunal shall upon application made to the tribunal by the person assessed to the levy have the like powers as the Board under the last foregoing paragraph.

(4) In the case of an establishment that ceases to carry on business in the fifth levy period on any day after the date of the service of the relevant assessment notice, the foregoing provisions of this Article shall have effect as

if for the period of four months from the date of the service of the assessment notice mentioned in paragraph (2) of this Article there were substituted the period of six months from the date of the cessation of business.

(5) An appeal or an application to an appeal tribunal under this Article shall be made in accordance with the Industrial Tribunals (England and Wales) Regulations 1965(a) as amended by the Industrial Tribunals (England and Wales) (Amendment) Regulations 1967(b) except where the establishment to which the relevant assessment relates is wholly in Scotland in which case the appeal or application shall be made in accordance with the Industrial Tribunals (Scotland) Regulations 1965(c) as amended by the Industrial Tribunals (Scotland) (Amendment) Regulations 1967(d).

(6) The powers of an appeal tribunal under paragraph (3) of this Article may be exercised by the President of the Industrial Tribunals (England and Wales) or by the President of the Industrial Tribunals (Scotland) as the case may be.

Evidence

8.—(1) Upon the discharge by a person assessed to the levy of his liability under an assessment the Board shall if so requested issue to him a certificate to that effect.

(2) The production in any proceedings of a document purporting to be certified by the Secretary of the Board to be a true copy of an assessment or other notice issued by the Board or purporting to be a certificate such as is mentioned in the foregoing paragraph of this Article shall, unless the contrary is proved, be sufficient evidence of the document and of the facts stated therein.

Signed by order of the Secretary of State.

20th July 1972.

R. Chichester-Clark,
Minister of State,
Department of Employment.

EXPLANATORY NOTE

(This Note is not part of the Order.)

This Order gives effect to proposals submitted to the Secretary of State for Employment by the Rubber and Plastics Processing Industry Training Board for the imposition of a further levy on employers in the rubber and plastics processing industry for the purpose of raising money towards the expenses of the Board.

The levy is to be imposed in respect of the fifth levy period commencing with the day upon which this Order comes into operation and ending on 31st March 1973. The levy will be assessed by the Board and there will be a right of appeal against an assessment to an industrial tribunal.

(a) S.I. 1965/1101 (1965 II, p. 2085).   (b) S.I. 1967/301 (1967 I, p. 1040).
(c) S.I. 1965/1157 (1965 II, p. 3266).   (d) S.I. 1967/302 (1967 I, p. 1050).

STATUTORY INSTRUMENTS

1972 No. 1090 (S.76)

LOCAL GOVERNMENT, SCOTLAND

The Rate Support Grant (Scotland) (Amendment) Regulations 1972

Made - - -	*17th July* 1972
Laid before Parliament	*28th July* 1972
Coming into Operation	16th August 1972

In exercise of the powers conferred on me by section 6(1) of and paragraph 5 of Part I of Schedule 1 to the Local Government (Scotland) Act 1966(a), and of all other powers enabling me in that behalf, and after consultation with such associations of local authorities as appear to me to be concerned, I hereby make the following regulations: —

1. These regulations may be cited as the Rate Support Grant (Scotland) (Amendment) Regulations 1972 and shall come into operation on 16th August 1972.

2.—(1) In these regulations any reference to "the principal regulations" is a reference to the Rate Support Grant (Scotland) Regulations 1967(b) as amended (c).

(2) The Interpretation Act 1889(d) shall apply for the interpretation of these regulations as it applies for the interpretation of an Act of Parliament.

3. In regulation 2(2) of the principal regulations, for the definition of "expenditure" there shall be substituted the following definition: —

"expenditure" means net expenditure after deducting from gross expenditure all receipts, other than charges for further education vocational courses and for courses sponsored by Industrial Training Boards, specifically applicable towards meeting such expenditure.

4. In regulation 4 of the principal regulations: —

(*a*) after paragraph (5) there shall be inserted the following paragraph: —

(5A) the provision of education for children within the meaning of the Education (Scotland) Act 1962(e) who—

(i) suffer from emotional instability or psychological disturbance;

(ii) an education authority have decided require special education; and

(iii) are in attendance at a residential school at which special education is provided;

(a) 1966 c. 51.   (b) S.I. 1967/715 (1967 II, p. 2162).
(c) The amending regulations are not relevant to the subject matter of these regulations.
(d) 1889 c. 63.   (e) 1962 c. 47.

(*b*) after paragraph (9) there shall be inserted the following paragraphs:—

(10) the provision for the purposes of the Social Work (Scotland) Act 1968(**a**) of residential establishments for children, established on or after 16th August 1972, providing education or long-term care in conditions of security;

(11) the provision for the purposes of the Social Work (Scotland) Act 1968 of residential establishments for persons specified in section 27(1)(*b*)(i) and (ii) of the said Act of 1968 (being persons subject to probation or subject to supervision following on release from detention) or for persons who are former offenders; and

(12) the training of persons undertaking approved courses of youth and community service training.

Gordon Campbell,
One of Her Majesty's Principal
Secretaries of State.

St. Andrew's House,
Edinburgh.
17th July 1972.

EXPLANATORY NOTE

(This Note is not part of the Regulations.)

These Regulations amend existing Regulations dealing with the pooling of expenditure incurred by certain local authorities, among all authorities by means of adjustments to rate support grants. For pooling purposes expenditure on further education will not be subject to deduction of receipts from charges for further education vocational courses and for courses sponsored by Industrial Training Boards. Pooling arrangements will extend to expenditure relating to the provision of residential education for maladjusted children and of certain residential establishments for the purposes of the Social Work (Scotland) Act 1968 and to the training of youth and community workers.

(**a**) 1968 c. 49.

STATUTORY INSTRUMENTS

1972 No. 1092

EDUCATION, ENGLAND AND WALES

The Teachers' Superannuation (Financial Provisions and Family Benefits) (Amendment) Regulations 1972

Made - - -	*24th July* 1972
Laid before Parliament	*2nd August* 1972
Coming into Operation	*25th August* 1972

The Secretary of State for Education and Science, with the consent of the Minister for the Civil Service and after consultation with representatives of local education authorities and of teachers and with such representatives of other persons likely to be affected as appear to her to be appropriate, in exercise of the powers conferred on her by section 9 of the Superannuation Act 1972(a) hereby makes the following regulations:—

Citation, commencement and interpretation

1.—(1) These regulations may be cited as the Teachers' Superannuation (Financial Provisions and Family Benefits) (Amendment) Regulations 1972.

(2) These regulations shall come into operation on 25th August 1972 and shall have effect as from 1st April 1972.

(3) These regulations—

(a) in so far as they amend the Teachers' Superannuation (Financial Provisions) Regulations 1972(b) (in these regulations called "the Financial Provisions Regulations") shall be construed as one with the Teachers' Superannuation Regulations 1967 to 1972 and shall be included among the regulations which may be cited together under that title;

(b) in so far as they amend the Teachers' Superannuation (Family Benefits) Regulations 1970 to 1972(c) shall be construed as one with those regulations and shall be included among the regulations which may be cited together under that title.

(4) The Interpretation Act 1889(d) shall apply for the interpretation of these regulations as it applies for the interpretation of an Act of Parliament.

(a) 1972 c. 11. (b) S.I. 1972/568 (1972 I, p. 1892).
(c) S.I. 1970/862, 1971/679, 1972/360 (1970 II, p. 2736; 1971 I, p. 1787; 1972 I, p. 1425).
(d) 1889 c. 63.

Calculation of Average Salary

2.—(1) Regulation 4 of the Financial Provisions Regulations shall have effect subject to the substitution for paragraphs (1) and (2) of the following paragraphs: —

"(1) For the purposes of the Teachers' Regulations the average salary of a teacher shall be taken, subject as in this regulation provided, to be—

(*a*) in the case of a teacher who has been continuously employed in reckonable service throughout the period of his terminal service, the highest amount of his full salary for any year in that period;

(*b*) in the case of a teacher who has not been continuously employed in reckonable service throughout that period, the highest amount of his full salary for any 365 successive days of reckonable service in that period.

(2) If a teacher has been employed in reckonable service for less than one year, his average salary shall, except as in regulation 56 of the principal Teachers' Regulations provided, be taken to be the average annual rate of his full salary during his reckonable service.

(2A)(*a*) In paragraph (1) above the expression "terminal service" means, as respects any teacher who has been employed in reckonable service for three years or more, the three years of such service (whether continuous or not) next preceding the commencement of any annual superannuation allowance or the payment of an additional superannuation allowance or gratuity under the Teachers' Regulations and, as respects any teacher who has not been employed in reckonable service for three years or more but has been employed for one year or more, the period of such service.

(*b*) In paragraph (1) above references to a teacher's full salary are to be construed as references to his salary as calculated under paragraph (1) of regulation 3 above.

(*c*) In paragraph (1)(*a*) above the word "year" means a period of twelve calendar months beginning on any day of any month."

(2) The definition in regulation 4(1) of the Teachers' Superannuation Regulations 1967(**a**) (definitions) of the expression "average salary" shall be construed as a reference to average salary as calculated under regulation 4(1) of the Financial Provisions Regulations as amended by these regulations.

(3) In respect of any teacher to whom superannuation allowances became payable before 1st April 1972 regulation 49(1) of the Teachers' Superannuation Regulations 1967 (supplementary death gratuity) shall have effect as if after the words "average salary" there were inserted the words "calculated in accordance with regulation 4(1) of the Teachers' Superannuation (Financial Provisions) Regulation 1972"; and in the interpretation of that regulation as so amended the provisions of paragraph (1) of this regulation shall be disregarded.

(**a**) S.I. 1967/489 (1967 I, p. 1562).

Increase in contributions

3. Regulation 5 of the Financial Provisions Regulations (financing of benefits) shall have effect subject to the substitution—

(*a*) in paragraph (2) (teacher's contribution), for the words "six per cent." of the words "six and three quarters per cent."; and

(*b*) in paragraph (3) (employer's contribution) for the words "six per cent. of the teacher's salary for the time being" of the words—

"the aggregate of—

(*a*) six and three quarters per cent. of the teacher's salary for the time being; and

(*b*) the balance of the new entrant contribution calculated in accordance with regulation 7A(2)"

New entrant contribution

4. After regulation 7 of the Financial Provisions Regulations there shall be inserted as a new regulation—

"New entrant contribution

7A—(1) In these regulations the expression "new entrant contribution" means the amount determined by the Government Actuary as the rate per cent. of the salary of teachers who became employed in reckonable service on 1st April 1972 at which contributions paid to the Secretary of State would in his opinion defray the costs of the benefits likely to be payable in respect of their service.

(2) For the purposes of paragraph (3)(*b*) of regulation 5 above the balance of the new entrant contribution shall be calculated by deducting from the rate per cent. so determined the sum of thirteen and one half per cent. (being the aggregate of the rates per cent. specified in paragraphs (2) and (3)(*a*) of that regulation).

(3) Where a determination made by the Government Actuary under this regulation is expressed to be provisional the references in these regulations to the new entrant contribution shall be construed as references to the contribution so determined until that determination is superseded by a determination expressed to be final.

(4) The report of the actuarial inquiry held in pursuance of section 5 of the Teachers' Superannuation Act 1967(**a**) shall specify any determination made by the Government Actuary under this regulation."

General Account A

5. All sums payable to the Secretary of State in respect of contributions so payable after 31st March 1972 under the Teachers' Superannuation (Family Benefits) Regulations 1970 to 1972 shall be paid into a part of the General Account, to be called General Account A, which shall be kept separate from the rest of that Account; and the provisions of those regulations which relate to payment out of the General Account shall have no application in respect of General Account A.

(**a**) 1967 c. 12.

Discontinuance of normal contributions under the Teachers', Widows' and Children's Pension Scheme

6.—(1) Subject to paragraph (2) below, normal contributions under regulations 26(*a*) and 27(1) of the Teachers' Superannuation (Family Benefits) Regulations 1970 as amended shall cease to be payable to the Secretary of State and accordingly—

(*a*) in regulation 26(*a*), the words "normal contributions in respect of reckonable service after the Scheme becomes applicable to him and"; and

(*b*) in regulation 27, paragraph (1)—

shall cease to have effect and are hereby revoked.

(2) The provisions of paragraph (1) above shall not affect any liability to pay normal contributions under paragraphs (2) and (3) of regulation 27 of the Teachers' Superannuation (Family Benefits) Regulations 1970 as amended.

Given under the Official Seal of the Secretary of State for Education and Science on 19th July 1972.

(L.S.)

Margaret H. Thatcher,
Secretary of State for Education
and Science.

Consent of the Minister for the Civil Service given under his Official Seal on 24th July 1972.

(L.S.)

K. H. McNeill,
Authorised by the Minister for the
Civil Service.

EXPLANATORY NOTE

(This Note is not part of the Regulations.)

These regulations amend the provisions of the Teachers' Superannuation Regulations 1967 to 1972 for the calculation of the benefits payable to or in respect of a teacher and increase the contributions payable by the teacher and his employer under those regulations.

The regulations amend the Teachers' Superannuation (Family Benefits) Regulations 1970 to 1972 by providing for the discontinuance of normal contributions and the payment of additional contributions into, and their retention in, a separate account.

The regulations have retrospective effect by virtue of section 12(1) of the Superannuation Act 1972.

STATUTORY INSTRUMENTS

1972 No. 1093

SEA FISHERIES

BOATS AND METHODS OF FISHING

The Herring (North Yorkshire Coast) (Prohibition of Fishing) Order 1972

Made - - -	24*th July* 1972
Laid before Parliament	28*th July* 1972
Coming into Operation	20*th August* 1972

The Minister of Agriculture, Fisheries and Food, and the Secretaries of State respectively concerned with the sea fishing industry in Scotland and Northern Ireland in exercise of the powers conferred on them by sections 5(1) and (2) and 15 of the Sea Fish (Conservation) Act 1967(a) as the latter section is amended by section 22(1) of, and paragraph 38 of Part II of Schedule I to, the Sea Fisheries Act 1968(b) and of all other powers enabling them in that behalf, hereby make the following Order:—

Citation and Commencement

1. This Order may be cited as the Herring (North Yorkshire Coast) (Prohibition of Fishing) Order 1972 and shall come into operation on 20th August 1972.

Interpretation

2. The Interpretation Act 1889(c) shall apply to the interpretation of this Order as it applies to the interpretation of an Act of Parliament.

Prohibition

3. During the period 20th August 1972 to 30th September 1972, both days inclusive, fishing for herring (Clupea harengus) within the area of sea specified in the Schedule to this Order is hereby prohibited.

4. In accordance with the provisions of section 5(3) of the Sea Fish (Conservation) Act 1967 it is hereby declared that this Order is not made for the sole purpose of giving effect to such a convention or agreement as is mentioned in section 5(1) of the Act.

Enforcement

5. For the purpose of the enforcement of the provisions of this Order, there are hereby conferred on every British sea-fishery officer the powers of a British sea-fishery officer under sections 8(2) to (4) of the Sea Fisheries Act 1968.

(a) 1967 c. 84.   (b) 1968 c. 77.
(c) 1889 c. 63.

In Witness whereof the Official Seal of the Minister of Agriculture, Fisheries and Food is hereunto affixed on 20th July 1972.

(L.S.)   *J. M. L. Prior,*
                                 Minister of Agriculture, Fisheries and Food.

                                                  Gordon Campbell,
24th July 1972.   Secretary of State for Scotland.

                                                 W. S. I. Whitelaw,
21st July 1972.   Secretary of State for Northern Ireland.

SCHEDULE

The area of sea adjacent to England within the fishery limits of the British Islands which lies between a line drawn in a north east (true) direction from The Heugh Lighthouse and a line drawn in an east (true) direction from The Flamborough Head Lighthouse.

EXPLANATORY NOTE

(This Note is not part of the Order.)

This Order which is made under section 5 of the Sea Fish (Conservation) Act 1967, prohibits fishing for herring in an area of sea adjacent to the North Yorkshire coast within the fishery limits of the British Islands for the period 20th August 1972 to 30th September 1972, both dates inclusive.

By virtue of section 5(8) of the Act the Order applies to all fishing boats including foreign vessels.

STATUTORY INSTRUMENTS

1972 No. 1094 (S.77)

TRANSPORT

The Greater Glasgow Passenger Transport Area (Designation) Order 1972

Made - - -	*21st July* 1972
Laid before Parliament	*31st July* 1972
Coming into Operation	*1st September* 1972

In exercise of the powers conferred upon me by sections 9, 22 and 157 of, and Schedule 5 to, the Transport Act 1968(a) and of all other powers enabling me in that behalf, and after consultation with such local authorities as are mentioned in section 9(2) of the said Act, and after being satisfied that a reasonable opportunity to make representations with respect to the area to be designated by this order has been afforded to all persons providing road passenger transport services by stage carriages within or to and from that area and after considering all representations made by such persons, I hereby make the following order:—

Commencement and citation

1. This order shall come into operation on the 1st September 1972 and may be cited as the Greater Glasgow Passenger Transport Area (Designation) Order 1972.

Interpretation

2.—(1) In this order—

"the Act of 1947" means the Local Government (Scotland) Act 1947(b);

"the Act of 1968" means the Transport Act 1968;

"the appointed day" means the 1st October 1972;

"the Authority" means the Passenger Transport Authority for the designated area established in accordance with this order;

"Glasgow Corporation" means the Corporation of the City of Glasgow;

"the constituent councils" means all the county councils and town councils whose areas fall wholly or partly within the designated area;

"the designated area" means the Greater Glasgow Passenger Transport Area designated by Article 3;

"the Executive" means the Passenger Transport Executive for the designated area established in accordance with this order;

"a casual vacancy" means a vacancy arising before the end of a term of office.

(a) 1968 c. 73.   (b) 1947 c. 43.

(2) Except where the context otherwise requires, in this order—

(*a*) references to Articles and Schedules are references to the relevant Articles and Schedules of this order, and

(*b*) references to any enactment shall be construed as references to that enactment as amended by or under any subsequent enactment.

(3) Any provision in this order requiring or authorising any town clerk or county clerk of a constituent council to do any act or thing shall be construed as a provision authorising that act or thing to be done by any deputy of his or by an officer or servant of his council duly authorised in that behalf by him or by his deputy.

(4) The Interpretation Act 1889(**a**) shall apply for the interpretation of this order as it applies for the interpretation of an Act of Parliament.

Designation of the Greater Glasgow Passenger Transport Area

3. The area described in Schedule 1 is hereby designated for the purposes of Part II of the Act of 1968 by the name of the Greater Glasgow Passenger Transport Area.

Establishment of the Authority

4.—(1) As from the appointed day, there shall be established in accordance with the following provisions of this order a Passenger Transport Authority for the designated area which, subject to the provisions of the Act of 1968 and of this order, shall consist of—

(*a*) 26 members to be appointed by the constituent councils in accordance with the following provisions of this order, and

(*b*) such number of members as may be appointed by the Secretary of State in accordance with paragraph 1 of Part I of Schedule 5 to the Act of 1968.

(2) The Authority shall be a body corporate by the name of the Greater Glasgow Passenger Transport Authority and shall have perpetual succession and a common seal.

Appointment and tenure of office of members of the Authority

5.—(1) Subject to the provisions of the Act of 1968 and of this order—

(*a*) each constituent council named in column 1 of Part I of Schedule 2 shall on or before the appointed day appoint such number of persons to be a member or members of the Authority as is specified in relation to that council in column 2 of the said Part I, and

(*b*) the constituent councils in each of the groups of such councils which are specified in column 1 of Part II of Schedule 2 shall on or before the appointed day jointly appoint such number of persons to be a member or members of the Authority as is specified in relation to that group in column 2 of the said Part II.

(**a**) 1889 c. 63.

(2) Subject to the provisions of the Act of 1968 and of this order, each member of the Authority appointed under paragraph (1) of this Article or by the Secretary of State on or before the appointed day shall come into office on the appointed day, and a member appointed by the Secretary of State after that day but before the meeting mentioned in paragraph (3) of this Article shall come into office on such day as may be fixed by his appointment, and of the members holding office at the date of the said meeting—

    (a) 15 shall retire on the 31st May 1974, and

    (b) the remainder shall retire on the 31st May 1975.

(3) For the purposes of paragraph (2) of this Article, the members who are to hold office until the dates respectively specified in that paragraph shall be determined in default of agreement by lot at a meeting of the Authority held within four months after the appointed day, the lots being drawn under the direction of the person presiding at the meeting.

(4) Subject to the provisions of the Act of 1968 and of this order, every vacancy, other than a casual vacancy, arising in the office of a member of the Authority, whether appointed under any of the foregoing provisions of this Article or under this paragraph or under any of the following provisions of this Article, shall be filled by the appointment, on or before the date on which that vacancy will occur, of a person to fill the vacancy and that appointment shall be made by the constituent council or group of constituent councils by whom the person vacating office was appointed or by the Secretary of State if that person was appointed by him, and every person appointed under this paragraph shall come into office on the said date and shall continue in office for a period of three years from that date.

(5) Subject to the provisions of the Act of 1968 and of this order, where for any reason the office of any member of the Authority becomes vacant before the end of his term of office, the casual vacancy so arising—

    (a) shall, if the unexpired portion of his term of office is four months or more, be filled by the appointment under this paragraph of a new member, and

    (b) may be so filled in any other case,

and every appointment under this paragraph in respect of any such vacancy shall be made by the constituent council or group of constituent councils by whom the member vacating office was appointed or, if he was appointed by the Secretary of State, by the Secretary of State.

(6) Subject to the provisions of the Act of 1968 and of this order, a person appointed under paragraph (5) of this Article to fill a casual vacancy shall hold office so long only as the vacating member would have held office.

(7) Any member of the Authority shall, subject to the provisions of the Act of 1968 and of this order, be eligible to be re-appointed as such a member for a further term of office beginning on or after the expiration of his current term.

(8) Notwithstanding anything contained in the foregoing provisions of this Article, if a constituent council or group of constituent councils have not been able to appoint a member or members of the Authority by the date on or before which they are required under those provisions to make that appointment, they may make that appointment as soon as practicable thereafter unless the Secretary of State has previously made the appointment on behalf of that council or those councils under paragraph 5 of Part I of Schedule 5 to the Act of 1968. Subject to the provisions of the Act of 1968 and of this

order, a person appointed to be a member by an appointment made under this paragraph shall come into office forthwith and shall hold office until the date on which he would have held office if he had been appointed by an appointment made on or before the date by which the appointment was required to be made as aforesaid.

(9) Subject to the provisions of the Act of 1968 and of this order, where the Secretary of State has under paragraph 5 of Part I of Schedule 5 to the Act of 1968 appointed a member or members of the Authority on behalf of any constituent council or group of constituent councils, the member or members so appointed shall come into office on such date as may be fixed by that appointment and shall hold office until the date on which he or they would under the foregoing provisions of this Article have held office if he or they had been appointed by the constituent council or group of constituent councils on whose behalf the Secretary of State has made the appointment, and, for the purposes of the application of the foregoing provisions of this Article with respect to the filling of vacancies in the membership of the Authority, the member or members so appointed shall be treated as if he or they had been appointed by that constituent council or those constituent councils.

(10) Subject to the following provisions of this Article, a person appointed as a member of the Authority by any one of the appointing authorities, that is to say, the Secretary of State, a constituent council or a group of constituent councils may not be appointed as such a member by any other of the appointing authorities for any term of office which coincides with, or falls partly within, his term of office under the first mentioned appointment.

(11) If it happens that a person is appointed as a member of the Authority by more than one of the said appointing authorities for a term which coincides or overlaps as mentioned in paragraph (10) above, that person shall within one month of the making of the last of those appointments choose under which appointment he will serve as a member and give notice in writing of his choice to the Secretary of the Authority, or, if no such Secretary has been appointed, to the town clerk mentioned in paragraph 1(1) of Schedule 3, and thereupon the other appointment or appointments shall be deemed void.

(12) If a person who should have given notice of his choice under paragraph (11) above fails to do so within the period specified in that paragraph, he shall be deemed to have chosen to serve under the appointment first made and to have given notice of his choice under that paragraph immediately before the end of that period.

(13) Where an appointment is deemed void under the provisions of paragraph (11) above, a further appointment shall be made as if a casual vacancy in the Authority had arisen.

Notices to be given of appointments of members of the Authority

6.—(1) As soon as practicable after each appointment of a member or members of the Authority has been made by a constituent council or a group of constituent councils, notice in writing of that appointment, specifying the name, address and designation of each person appointed, shall be given in accordance with the following provisions of this paragraph, that is to say—

    (a) in the case of an appointment made before the date of the first annual meeting of the Authority by a constituent council named in column 1 of Part I of Schedule 2 (other than by Glasgow Corporation) the notice shall be given by the town clerk or county clerk of the constituent council making the appointment to the Town Clerk of the City of Glasgow and in the case of an appointment made before the date of the said first annual meeting by Glasgow Corporation notice shall be given by the Town Clerk of the City of Glasgow to the Secretary of State and to all other constituent councils.

(b) in the case of an appointment made on or after the date of the said first annual meeting by a constituent council named in column 1 of Part I of Schedule 2 the notice shall be given by the town clerk or county clerk of the constituent council making the appointment to the Secretary of the Authority.

(c) in the case of a joint appointment by a group of constituent councils specified in column 1 of Part II of Schedule 2 the notice shall be given by the town clerk or county clerk of the first named constituent council in that group in the said column 1 to the Town Clerk of the City of Glasgow where the joint appointment is made before the date of the said first annual meeting and to the Secretary of the Authority in any other case.

(2) As soon as practicable after each appointment of a member or members of the Authority has been made by the Secretary of State, notice in writing of that appointment, specifying the name, address and designation of each person appointed shall be given by the Secretary of State—

(a) to the Town Clerk of the City of Glasgow in the case of an appointment made before the date of the said first annual meeting and

(b) to the Secretary of the Authority in all other cases.

(3) The Town Clerk of the City of Glasgow shall give notice in writing

(a) to the Secretary of State (except where the appointment in question was made by the Secretary of State) and to all the constituent councils (other than the particular constituent council or group of constituent councils making the appointment in question) as to all appointments of members of the Authority of which he receives notice under the preceding provisions of this Article specifying in each case the Secretary of State, the constituent council or group of constituent councils by whom or by which the appointment was made and the name, address and designation of the person so appointed, and

(b) to the Secretary of the Authority of any appointment made before the date of the said first annual meeting by Glasgow Corporation and also of all appointments of such members of which he has received notice under the preceding provisions of this Article.

(4) The Secretary of the Authority shall give notice in writing to the Secretary of State of all appointments of members of the Authority from time to time made under this order by any constituent council or group of constituent councils, specifying the names, addresses and designations of the persons so appointed, and shall keep all constituent councils notified of all appointments of members of the Authority from time to time made under this order, whether by a constituent council or a group of constituent councils or by the Secretary of State.

Notification of establishment of the Authority

7. The Authority shall as soon as practicable after the appointed day cause notice of their establishment to be published in such local newspapers circulating in the designated area as they may think appropriate for informing persons appearing to them to be likely to be concerned.

Vacation of office by members of the Authority

8.—(1) A member of the Authority may resign his office at any time by notice in writing under his hand given to the Secretary of the Authority, and his resignation shall take effect upon receipt of such notice by the said Secretary.

(2) A member of the Authority who becomes disqualified for being such a member shall vacate his office immediately upon becoming so disqualified.

(3) A member of the Authority shall also vacate his office if he has throughout a period of six consecutive months failed to attend any meeting of the Authority, unless the failure was due to illness or some other reason approved before or during that period by the Authority, but for the purposes of this paragraph attendance as a member at a meeting of any committee or sub-committee of the Authority shall be regarded as attendance at a meeting of the Authority.

(4) Whenever a casual vacancy arises in the office of a member of the Authority (whether by reason of any of the foregoing provisions of this Article or by reason of paragraph 3 or 4 of Part I of Schedule 5 to the Act of 1968 or otherwise howsoever), the Secretary of the Authority shall forthwith notify the vacancy so arising to the constituent council or group of constituent councils responsible for appointing a member to fill that vacancy or, where the vacating member was appointed by the Secretary of State otherwise than under paragraph 5 of Part I of Schedule 5 to the Act of 1968, to the Secretary of State.

Disqualification for membership of the Authority

9. A person shall be disqualified for being a member of the Authority at any time if at that time—

(*a*) he holds any paid office (other than that of Chairman of the Authority) of or under the Authority, or

(*b*) he is precluded by virtue of the provisions of paragraph 3 of Part I of Schedule 5 to the Act of 1968 from being appointed to be such a member, or

(*c*) he is disqualified for being a member of a local authority by virtue of the provisions contained in section 52(1)(*b*) or (*c*) of the Act of 1947.

Appointment of deputies

10.—(1) Each constituent council or group of constituent councils appointing a member of the Authority may, at the same time or at any time while any member so appointed holds office, appoint a person to act as a deputy for that member by attending and voting at any meeting of the Authority from which that member is absent.

(2) A person who is appointed to be a deputy for a member may not, so long as his appointment continues, be appointed to act as a deputy for any other member.

(3) A person appointed to be a deputy may, subject to the provisions of this order, be so appointed for such period and on such terms and conditions as may be specified in the appointment, but any person so appointed may at

any time resign his office by notice in writing given to the town clerk or county clerk of the constituent council by whom he was appointed or in the case of a person so appointed by a group of constituent councils specified in column 1 of Part II of Schedule 2 by notice in writing given to the town clerk or county clerk of the first named constituent council in that group in the said column 1, and the town clerk or county clerk of the council in question shall, upon receipt of such notice, forthwith notify the Secretary of the Authority of the resignation.

(4) A person shall cease to be entitled to act as a deputy or a member if—

(a) the member for whom that person acts as deputy vacates his office or

(b) the person appointed to be a deputy for a member is himself appointed a member of the Authority.

(5) A person appointed to be a deputy for a member may also attend and vote at any meeting of any committee of the Authority, being a meeting of the committee at which the member for whom he is deputy was entitled to attend and vote and from which that member was absent.

(6) The provisions of this order relating to the giving of notices of the appointment of members of the Authority and to the disqualification of a person for being such a member shall apply in relation to any deputy as they apply in relation to the member for whom he is appointed to act as a deputy.

Meetings and proceedings of the Authority

11. The provisions contained in Schedule 3 shall have effect with respect to the meetings and proceedings of the Authority.

Remuneration of the Chairman of the Authority

12. There may be paid to the Chairman of the Authority such sum by way of remuneration as the Authority think reasonable.

Allowances to the Chairman and members of the Authority

13.—(1) Sections 112 to 115 and 117, as read with section 118 of the Local Government Act 1948(a), and any regulations for the time being having effect under the said section 117 shall apply, with the necessary modifications, to the Authority and their members as if the Authority were a body in Scotland to which Part VI of that Act applies, for the purposes of regulating the allowances which members of the Authority are to be entitled to be paid or which they may be paid in respect of loss suffered or expenditure incurred for the purposes of enabling them to perform any approved duty as defined in the said section 115 as applied to the Authority as aforesaid.

(2) The following expenses of members of the Authority, or of any committee or sub-committee thereof, that is to say—

(a) any reasonable expenses incurred in attending a conference or meeting convened for the purpose of discussing any matter connected with the discharge of the functions of the Authority or the Executive,

---

(a) 1948 c. 26.

(b) subject to paragraph (3) of this Article, any travelling or other expenses properly incurred in making official or courtesy visits (whether inside or outside the United Kingdom) on behalf of the Authority,

(c) any expenses incurred in the reception or entertainment by way of official courtesy of—

(i) distinguished persons residing in the designated area or visiting that area, or

(ii) persons representative of, or connected with, associations or organisations concerned with public passenger transport, whether inside or outside the United Kingdom,

shall be defrayed by the Executive.

(3) The amount to be defrayed by the Executive under paragraph (2)(b) of this Article in respect of expenses incurred by a member of the Authority in connection with a visit within the United Kingdom shall not exceed the payments which the member would have been entitled to receive by way of travelling allowance or subsistence allowance under section 113 of the Local Government Act 1948, if the making of the visit had been an approved duty of the member within the meaning of that section as applied to the Authority and their members by paragraph (1) of this Article.

(4) The provisions of this Article shall apply in relation to deputies for members of the Authority, when acting as deputies, as they apply in relation to the members themselves.

Appointment and remuneration of officers and servants of the Authority

14. The Authority shall appoint a Secretary and may appoint such other officers and servants as they may think fit and there may be paid to the officers and servants of the Authority such remuneration as the Authority may think fit.

The Executive to pay the expenses of and provide accommodation for the Authority

15.—(1) Without prejudice to section 15(5) of the Act of 1968, the Executive shall defray the remuneration and allowances payable to the Chairman and any other member of the Authority or to any officer or servant of the Authority and also all expenses incurred by any officer or servant of Glasgow Corporation in performing any functions conferred or imposed on him by this order.

(2) The Executive shall provide all such accommodation and other facilities as the Authority may require to enable them and any officer or servant of theirs to exercise their functions under the Act of 1968 or this order.

Establishment of the Executive

16.—(1) The Authority shall establish a Passenger Transport Executive for the designated area which shall consist of—

(a) a Director General to be appointed in accordance with the provisions of Part II of Schedule 5 to the Act of 1968 by the Authority, and

(b) not less than two nor more than eight other members to be so appointed by the Authority after consultation with the Director General.

(2) The Executive shall be established on such date as may be fixed by the Authority, being the earliest practicable date after the Director General and at least two other members of the Executive have been appointed as aforesaid and the Authority shall cause notice of the establishment of the Executive on that date to be published in such local newspapers circulating in the designated area as they may think appropriate for informing persons appearing to them to be likely to be concerned.

(3) As soon as may be after their establishment as aforesaid the Executive shall appoint a Secretary.

Proceedings of the Executive

17.—(1) The application of the seal of the Executive shall be authenticated by the signature of the Secretary of the Executive or by some other person authorised by the Executive, either generally or specially, to act for that purpose.

(2) The provisions of paragraphs 4 to 8 of Part IV of Schedule 3 of the Act of 1947 (which provide as to the conduct of business at meetings) shall apply to the Executive as if the Executive were a local authority and as if for the references therein to that Act and to the clerk of the authority there were substituted respectively references to this order and to the Secretary of the Executive but nothing in those paragraphs shall derogate from the power of the Executive to delegate to their Director General under Article 21.

(3) The Executive may fix their quorum and may, subject to the foregoing provisions of this Article, regulate their own procedure.

Application of certain enactments relating to local authorities etc.

18.—(1) The provisions of the following enactments which relate to the disability of members of local authorities for taking part in the consideration or discussion of, or for voting on any question with respect to contracts, proposed contracts or other matters in which they have a pecuniary interest, that is to say—

> section 73 of the Act of 1947,
>
> section 126 of the Act of 1947, and
>
> section 1 of the Local Government (Pecuniary Interests) (Scotland) Act 1966(a)

shall apply as they apply to members of local authorities or of any committees or sub-committees of such authorities—

> (a) to members of the Authority and their deputies and to members of any committee or sub-committee of the Authority, but so that in such application the said provisions shall have effect as if in the said section 73 of the Act of 1947 there were substituted for the references therein to the clerk of the local authority references to the Secretary of the Authority, and

---

(a) 1966 c. 7.

(*b*) to members of the Executive or of any committee or sub-committee of the Executive, but so that in such application the said provisions shall have effect as if—

(i) they referred only to contracts and proposed contracts and did not extend to other matters,

(ii) subsection (8) was omitted from section 73 of the Act of 1947,

(iii) subsections (5) and (6) were omitted from section 1 of the Local Government (Pecuniary Interests) (Scotland) Act 1966, and

(iv) in section 73 of the Act of 1947 there were substituted for the references therein to the clerk of the local authority references to the Secretary of the Executive.

(2) The provisions of section 102 of the Act of 1947 and of section 2 of the Local Government (Pecuniary Interests) (Scotland) Act 1966 (which relate to the disclosure by officers of local authorities of their interest in contracts or proposed contracts) shall apply in relation to officers and servants of the Authority or the Executive as they apply in relation to officers and servants of local authorities.

(3) Section 101 of the Act of 1947 (which prohibits a local authority etc. appointing to any paid office a person who is or who has within 6 months prior to the appointment been a member of the authority etc.) shall apply

(*a*) in relation to the Authority as it applies in relation to a local authority but as if any reference therein to any paid office included a reference to any paid office of or under the Authority (except the office of Chairman of the Authority), and to the office of Director General or other member of the Executive, and

(*b*) in relation to the Executive or to any subsidiary thereof as it applies in relation to a local authority but as if any reference therein to any paid office included a reference to any office, appointment or employment under or with the Executive or any subsidiary thereof as the case might be.

(4) Section 351 of the Act of 1947 (which relates to the manner of giving public notices which are required to be given by a local authority) shall apply in relation to public notices which are required to be given by the Authority under this order as it applies in relation to public notices required to be given by a local authority, but as if any reference therein to the area of the authority were a reference to the designated area.

(5) Section 130 of the Local Government Act 1948 (which empowers a local authority to effect insurance against accidents to members) shall apply to the Authority and the Executive as it applies to a local authority.

(6) Section 202(2)(*a*) of the Road Traffic Act 1960(**a**) (which provides that the requirements of section 201 of that Act as to users of motor vehicles being insured or secured against third party risks are not to apply to a vehicle owned by any such local authority as is mentioned in the said subsection (2)(*a*)) shall apply to a vehicle owned by the Executive, or by any subsidiary of the Executive, as it applies to a vehicle owned by any local authority so mentioned.

(**a**) 1960 c. 16.

(7) Section 263 of the Act of 1947 (which relates to the repayment of sums borrowed by a local authority under any statutory borrowing power) and section 345 of the said Act (which relates to the appearance on behalf of local authorities in legal proceedings) shall respectively apply in relation to the Executive as they apply in relation to a local authority but as if any reference in the said section 345 to a clerk of a local authority included a reference to the Secretary of the Executive.

Designation of superannuation fund and application of the Glasgow Corporation Superannuation Scheme 1955

19.—(1) The superannuation fund maintained by Glasgow Corporation (which fund is in this Article referred to as "the Glasgow Corporation Superannuation Fund") shall be the fund in the benefits of which persons who are or have been employed by the Authority, the Executive or a subsidiary of the Executive are entitled to participate.

(2) The persons to participate in the Glasgow Corporation Superannuation Fund as persons who are or have been so employed are—

(*a*) the persons who, as officers or servants of the Authority, members, officers or servants of the Executive or directors, officers or servants of a subsidiary of the Executive, have by resolution of the Executive been specified as contributors to the said fund, and

(*b*) the persons who, as officers or servants of the Authority, the Executive or a subsidiary of the Executive, belong to a class or description of such officers or servants which has by resolution of the Executive been specified as a class or description the members of or persons falling within which are to be contributors to the said Fund,

and all such persons who have been so specified by resolution of the Executive or who are members of, or fall within, a class or description so specified are in this Article referred to as "the Passenger Transport Executive contributors".

(3) The provisions of the Glasgow Corporation Superannuation Scheme 1955(**a**) and of any enactments and instruments for the time being in force thereunder affecting the said Scheme (including the provisions of the Local Government Superannuation (Scotland) Acts 1937 to 1953(**b**) and of any relevant instruments thereunder so far as applicable to the Glasgow Corporation Superannuation Fund) (all which provisions are hereafter in this Article referred to as "the superannuation provisions") shall, subject as hereafter provided in this Article, apply to the Passenger Transport Executive contributors as they apply to persons who are or have been employees of Glasgow Corporation, and the superannuation provisions shall, subject as aforesaid have effect in relation to the Passenger Transport Executive contributors as if the references therein to employees of Glasgow Corporation or to service of or under Glasgow Corporation included references to officers or servants of the Authority, to members, officers or servants of the Executive and to directors, officers or servants of a subsidiary of the Executive and to service as such a member, director, officer or servant, as the case may be, but nothing in this Article shall have the effect of conferring or imposing upon the Executive the functions of Glasgow Corporation under the superannuation provisions with respect to the making of a scheme or to the valuation, investment or general administration of the Glasgow Corporation Superannuation Fund.

(a) Approved by S.I. 1955/1411.   (b) 1937 c. 69; 1939 c. 18; 1953 c. 25.

(4) In their application to those of the Passenger Transport Executive contributors who are or have been officers or servants of the Authority or directors, officers or servants of a subsidiary of the Executive, the superannuation provisions shall have effect as if the Authority or the subsidiary (as the case may be) were the Executive, so that for the purposes of the superannuation provisions the Executive shall have the responsibilities and the functions of the employer of those persons.

(5) The Executive shall in relation to the Passenger Transport Executive contributors—

(*a*) deduct, or cause to be deducted, from the salaries or other remuneration of those contributors the contributions which those contributors would be required by the superannuation provisions to make to the Glasgow Corporation Superannuation Fund if they were officers or servants of Glasgow Corporation, and

(*b*) pay, or cause to be paid, to Glasgow Corporation those payments (including the amount of the deductions aforesaid and the appropriate amount required by any scheme made in accordance with Article 33 of the Glasgow Corporation Superannuation Scheme 1955 for making good any deficiency) which that Corporation would be required by the superannuation provisions to pay into the said Fund if those contributors were officers or servants of Glasgow Corporation.

(6) Any discretion, or any right or duty to form an opinion, vested under the superannuation provisions in Glasgow Corporation in relation to employees of Glasgow Corporation shall in relation to the Passenger Transport Executive contributors be exercised or performed, subject to the provisions of this Article, by the Executive, but the Executive shall, as soon as may be after the exercise or performance by them of any such discretion, right or duty, give notice in writing thereof to Glasgow Corporation.

(7) The Executive shall not, without the consent of the Authority—

(*a*) resolve that a member of the Executive shall be a contributor to the Glasgow Corporation Superannuation Fund, or

(*b*) exercise or perform under the superannuation provisions in relation to a person who is or has been a member of the Executive, as respects his service as such a member, any such discretion, or any such right or duty to form an opinion, as is mentioned in paragraph (6) of this Article.

(8) The Executive shall not resolve that—

(*a*) a member of the Executive, or a director of a subsidiary of the Executive shall be a contributor to Glasgow Corporation Superannuation Fund unless his service as such a member or director is whole time service, that is to say, service to which he is required by the terms of his appointment to devote substantially the whole of his time and

(*b*) an officer or servant of the Authority, the Executive or a subsidiary of the Executive shall be a contributor to the Glasgow Corporation Superannuation Fund unless he is employed as a whole time officer within the meaning of the Local Government Superannuation (Scotland) Act 1937 or is employed whole time as a servant within the meaning of the Glasgow Corporation Superannuation Scheme 1955.

(9) The Executive shall pay to Glasgow Corporation a contribution towards the cost of the administration of the Glasgow Corporation Superannuation Fund of such annual amount as may be agreed between the Executive and that Corporation.

(10) The references in this Article to the Local Government Superannuation (Scotland) Act 1937 and to the Local Government Superannuation (Scotland) Acts 1937 to 1953 and any relevant instruments thereunder shall be read as references to the said Acts and instruments as extended by paragraph 5(1) of Schedule 7 to the Superannuation Act 1972(**a**).

(11) This Article shall be without prejudice to section 10(1)(xxx) of, and paragraph 4 of Part II of Schedule 5 to, the Act of 1968.

Appointment of committees by the Authority and the Executive

20.—(1) The Authority and the Executive may each appoint committees for any such purposes as in the opinion of the Authority or the Executive would be better regulated and managed by means of a committee and, except as provided in paragraph (2) of this Article, any such committee shall consist wholly of members of the Authority or the Executive, as the case may be.

(2) Where a committee is appointed by the Authority or the Executive for the exercise of functions which are advisory only, the committee may consist wholly or partly of persons who are not members of the Authority or the Executive, as the case may be, but so however that a member of the Executive shall not be appointed to a committee of the Authority.

(3) The Authority and the Executive may delegate to any committee appointed by them, with or without restrictions or conditions as they think fit, the exercise of any of their functions except—

    (*a*) in the case of a delegation by the Authority, their power to issue requisitions or to give any such approval as is mentioned in section 15(2) of the Act of 1968, and

    (*b*) in the case of a delegation by the Executive—

        (i) their power to borrow money, and

        (ii) their power to pass a resolution under Article 19(2).

(4) The Authority and the Executive may make rules with respect to the meetings and proceedings of any committee appointed by them (including quorum, place of meeting, notices to be given at meetings and the appointment of a Chairman or Vice Chairman) but subject to any rules so made any such committee may regulate their own procedure.

Delegation of functions to the Director General of the Executive

21. The Executive may delegate to their Director General, subject to such restrictions or conditions as they may think fit, the exercise of any functions of the Executive which under Article 20 may be delegated by them to a committee.

(**a**) 1972 c. 11.

Validity of Acts of the Authority and the Executive

22. The validity of anything done by the Authority or the Executive or any committee thereof shall not be affected by any vacancy in their membership or by any defect in the appointment, or the qualification for appointment, of the Chairman of the Authority or of the Director General of the Executive or of any other member of the Authority or the Executive or of any member of any such committee.

Authentication of documents

23. Every document purporting to be an instrument issued by the Authority or the Executive and to be sealed with the seal of the Authority or the Executive and authenticated in accordance with the provisions of paragraph 11 of Schedule 3 or of Article 17(1) or to be signed on behalf of the Authority or the Executive by their Secretary or by some other person authorised by the Authority or the Executive, either generally or specially, to act for that purpose shall be received in evidence and shall be sufficient evidence of the facts stated therein.

> *Gordon Campbell,*
> One of Her Majesty's Principal
> Secretaries of State.

St. Andrew's House,
Edinburgh.

21st July 1972.

SCHEDULE 1

DESCRIPTION OF THE DESIGNATED AREA

The designated area is the area which consists of all the following local authority areas or parts of such areas, that is to say—

(*a*) the County of the City of Glasgow;

(*b*) the large burghs of Paisley, Motherwell and Wishaw, Coatbridge, Airdrie, Clydebank, East Kilbride, Hamilton and Rutherglen;

(*c*) the small burgh of Bishopbriggs and so much of the landward area of the county of Lanark as is comprised in the Fourth, Sixth, Seventh, Eighth and Ninth Districts;

(*d*) the small burghs of Johnstone, Renfrew and Barrhead and so much of the landward area of the county of Renfrew as is comprised in the First, Second, Third and Fourth Districts;

(*e*) the small burghs of Bearsden, Kirkintilloch, Cumbernauld and Milngavie and so much of the landward area of the county of Dunbarton as is comprised in the Kirkintilloch and Cumbernauld District and in the Old Kilpatrick District excluding the electoral divisions of Bowling and Dumbarton;

(*f*) the small burgh of Kilsyth and so much of the landward area of the county of Stirling as is comprised in Western No. 3 District, the Strathblane electoral division of Western No. 2 District and the Kilsyth East and Kilsyth West electoral divisions of Central No. 2 District.

SCHEDULE 2

CONSTITUENT COUNCILS ENTITLED TO APPOINT MEMBERS OF THE AUTHORITY

PART I

Councils each entitled to appoint a member and the number of members they are to appoint

(1) Name of Council	(2) Number of Members
Glasgow Corporation	13
Paisley Town Council	1
Motherwell and Wishaw Town Council	1
Clydebank Town Council	1
East Kilbride Town Council	1
Lanark County Council	3
Renfrew County Council	1

PART II

THE GROUPS OF COUNCILS ENTITLED JOINTLY TO APPOINT A MEMBER AND THE NUMBER OF MEMBERS TO BE APPOINTED BY EACH GROUP

(1) Groups	(2) Number of Members to be appointed by each group
Coatbridge Town Council Airdrie Town Council	1
Hamilton Town Council Rutherglen Town Council	1
Johnstone Town Council Renfrew Town Council Barrhead Town Council	1
Kirkintilloch Town Council Bearsden Town Council Milngavie Town Council Bishopbriggs Town Council	1
Cumbernauld Town Council Kilsyth Town Council Dunbarton County Council Stirling County Council	1

SCHEDULE 3

PROVISIONS AS TO MEETINGS AND PROCEEDINGS OF THE AUTHORITY

1.—(1) The first meeting of the Authority shall be convened by the Town Clerk of the City of Glasgow for such day (not being later than one month after the appointed day) and at such time and place as may be fixed by the said town clerk who shall, not less than 14 days before the day fixed for that meeting, send notice of that meeting by post to each member of the Authority of whose appointment the said town clerk has been notified by that time.

(2) The said town clerk shall, until such time as the Authority have appointed their Secretary, exercise all such functions on behalf of the Authority as are imposed by this order on the said Secretary or as might be expected to be exercised by a person appointed to be the Secretary of such a body as the Authority, and as respects anything occurring or falling to be done under or in relation to this order before such appointment has been made the references in this order to the Secretary of the Authority shall be construed as references to the said town clerk.

(3) The first business to be transacted at the first meeting of the Authority shall be the appointment in accordance with the provisions of this Schedule of a person to act as Chairman of the Authority, and, for the purposes of the transaction of this business, the chair at that meeting shall be taken by the Lord Provost of the City of Glasgow or, if he is unable to be present at that meeting, by such person (not being a member of the Authority) as has been nominated to do so by the said Lord Provost, but no person taking the chair at that meeting by virtue of this sub-paragraph shall be entitled to cast any vote in connection with the transaction of the business aforesaid.

(4) A certificate purporting to be signed by the Town Clerk of the City of Glasgow that any person has been nominated by the Lord Provost of that City as mentioned in sub-paragraph (3) above shall be conclusive evidence of the inability of the said Lord Provost to be present at the said first meeting of the Authority and of the fact of the nomination of that person.

2.—(1) The first meeting of the Authority after their establishment shall be the annual meeting of the Authority for the year 1972 and the first meeting of the Authority after the 31 May in any subsequent year shall be the annual meeting for that year.

(2) In every year after 1972 the Authority shall hold their annual meeting as soon as possible after the 31 May and in any event before the 31 July in that year.

(3) The Authority shall between each annual meeting hold at least three other meetings for the transaction of general business and such other meetings shall be held as nearly as may be at regular intervals.

3.—(1) Subject to paragraph 5 of this Schedule, the Authority shall at their annual meeting in each year appoint one of their members to be Chairman of the Authority and the person so appointed shall come into office forthwith and continue in office until his successor becomes entitled to act as Chairman: provided that, subject to the provisions of this Schedule, any Chairman shall be eligible for re-appointment at the expiration of the term for which he is to hold office and, if so re-appointed, shall continue in office accordingly.

(2) The Authority may at each annual meeting appoint one of their number to be Vice Chairman and the provisions of the last foregoing sub-paragraph shall apply in relation to a Vice Chairman as they apply in relation to a Chairman.

(3) The appointment of a Chairman of the Authority shall be the first business to be transacted at each annual meeting of the Authority.

4.—(1) Subject to paragraph 5 of this Schedule, on a casual vacancy occurring in the office of Chairman or Vice Chairman, the vacancy shall be filled by the appointment by the Authority of one of their members at a meeting to be held as soon as practicable after the vacancy occurs. Where the office so becoming vacant is that of Chairman, such a meeting may be convened by the Secretary of the Authority.

(2) A person appointed under this paragraph to fill a vacancy shall hold office for the period for which the person in whose place he is appointed would have held office and shall then vacate his office but shall be eligible for re-appointment.

5.—(1) A person appointed to be Chairman of the Authority may act as such only for the purpose of presiding at the meeting at which he is appointed unless his appointment is approved by the Secretary of State.

(2) If in the case of a person appointed to be Chairman of the Authority the Secretary of State decides not to approve the appointment, then, as from the date on which the Secretary of State notifies his decision to the Authority, there shall for the purposes of paragraph 4 of this Schedule be deemed to be a casual vacancy in the office of Chairman, but this provision shall be without prejudice to the right of a previous Chairman to continue in office under paragraph 3 of this Schedule until his successor becomes entitled to act as Chairman.

6.—(1) The Chairman of the Authority may call a meeting of the Authority at any time.

(2) If the Chairman refuses to call a meeting of the Authority after a requisition for that purpose signed by 5 members of the Authority has been presented to him or if, without so refusing, the Chairman does not call a meeting within 14 days after such requisition has been presented to him, any 5 members of the Authority may forthwith call a meeting of the Authority.

(3) At least 7 clear days before a meeting of the Authority—

(a) notice of the time and place of the intended meeting shall be published at the offices of the Executive or at such other place as is fixed for the meeting of the Authority, and

(b) a summons to attend the meeting specifying the business proposed to be transacted thereat shall be left at or sent by post to the usual place of residence of every member of the Authority.

(4) In a case where the meeting is called by members of the Authority under sub-paragraph (2) above the notice referred to in sub-paragraph (3)(a) above shall be signed by those members and shall specify the business proposed to be transacted thereat, and no business other than that specified in the said notice shall be transacted at a meeting so called.

(5) Want of service on a member of the Authority of the summons referred to in sub-paragraph (3)(b) above shall not affect the validity of the meeting.

7. The provisions of paragraphs 4 to 8 of Part IV of Schedule 3 to the Act of 1947 (which provide as to the conduct of business at meetings) shall apply to the Authority as if the Authority were a local authority and as if for the references therein to that Act and to the clerk of the authority there were substituted respectively references to this order and to the Secretary of the Authority.

8. Copies of the minutes kept of the proceedings of each meeting of the Authority shall be sent by the Secretary of the Authority to the town clerk or county clerk of every constituent council and to the Director General and each other member of the Executive not later than 21 days after the meeting.

9. There shall be sent to every deputy of a member of the Authority copies of all notices of meetings and other papers which are sent to that member in connection with any such meeting.

10. Subject to the foregoing provisions of this Schedule, the Authority may make rules with respect to the meetings and proceedings of the Authority (including quorum, place of meeting and notices to be given of meetings) and subject as aforesaid and to any rules so made the Authority may regulate their own procedure.

11. The application of the seal of the Authority shall be authenticated by the signature of the Secretary of the Authority, or some other person authorised by the Authority, either generally or specially, to act for the purpose.

EXPLANATORY NOTE

(This Note is not part of the Order.)

This Order designates the passenger transport area for Greater Glasgow and provides for the establishment of the Passenger Transport Authority and the Passenger Transport Executive for that area under Part II of the Transport Act 1968.

The area designated is specified in Schedule 1 to the Order and Article 4 and Schedule 2 provide for the constitution of the Passenger Transport Authority and specify the constituent councils by whom members of the Authority are to be appointed.

By Articles 5, 6, 8, 9 and 10 provision is made for the appointment and tenure of office of members of the Authority, for their vacation of office and their disqualification for office in certain circumstances and for the appointment of deputies for members of the Authority.

Article 11 and Schedule 3 make provision as to meetings and proceedings of the Authority.

In Articles 12 to 15 provision is made for the remuneration of the Chairman of the Authority, for the payment of allowances to the Chairman and members of the Authority, for the appointment and remuneration of officers and servants of the Authority and for requiring the Executive to pay the expenses of, and to provide accommodation for, the Authority.

Articles 16 and 17 provide for the establishment of the Passenger Transport Executive and for the proceedings of the Executive.

Certain enactments relating to local authorities are applied to the Authority and the Executive by Article 18.

Provision is made in Article 19 for enabling persons employed by the Authority the Executive or subsidiaries of the Executive to participate in the Glasgow Corporation Superannuation Fund.

Articles 20 to 23 deal with the appointment of committees, the delegation of functions to the Director General of the Executive, the validity of acts of the Authority and the Executive and the authentication of documents.

STATUTORY INSTRUMENTS

1972 No. 1095 (L.11)

MATRIMONIAL CAUSES

SUPREME COURT OF JUDICATURE, ENGLAND

COUNTY COURTS

The Matrimonial Causes (Amendment) Rules 1972

Made - - - -	*20th July* 1972
Laid before Parliament	*3rd August* 1972
Coming into Operation	*1st September* 1972

We, the authority having power to make rules of court for the purposes mentioned in section 7(1) of the Matrimonial Causes Act 1967**(a)**, hereby exercise that power as follows:—

1.—(1) These Rules may be cited as the Matrimonial Causes (Amendment) Rules 1972 and shall come into operation on 1st September 1972.

(2) In these Rules a rule referred to by number means the rule so numbered in the Matrimonial Causes Rules 1971**(b)**, as amended **(c)**, and Form 6 means the form so numbered in Appendix 2 to those Rules.

(3) The Interpretation Act 1889**(d)** shall apply to the interpretation of these Rules as it applies to the interpretation of an Act of Parliament.

2. In rule 2(2) before the definition of "the Act of 1965" there shall be inserted the following definition:—

" "section 17 of the Act of 1882" means section 17 of the Married Women's Property Act 1882**(e)**, as originally enacted, or as extended by section 7 of the Matrimonial Causes (Property and Maintenance) Act 1958**(f)** or by section 2 of the Law Reform (Miscellaneous Provisions) Act 1970**(g)** or by section 39 of the Matrimonial Proceedings and Property Act 1970".

3. Rule 16 shall be amended as follows:—

(1) For the title there shall be substituted the words "*Consent to the grant of a decree*".

(a) 1967 c. 56.
(c) S.I. 1971/1923 (1971 III, p. 5243).
(e) 1882 c. 75.
(g) 1970 c. 33.

(b) S.I. 1971/953 (1971 II, p. 2713).
(d) 1889 c 63.
(f) 1958 c. 35.

(2) At the beginning of the rule there shall be inserted the following paragraph:—

> "(1) Where, before the hearing of a petition alleging any such fact as is mentioned in section 2(1)(*d*) of the Act of 1969, the respondent wishes to indicate to the court that he consents to the grant of a decree, he must do so by giving the registrar a notice to that effect signed by the respondent personally.
>
> For the purposes of this paragraph an acknowledgement of service containing a statement that the respondent consents to the grant of a decree shall be treated as such a notice if the acknowledgement is signed—
>
> (*a*) in the case of a respondent acting in person, by the respondent, or
>
> (*b*) in the case of a respondent represented by a solicitor, by the respondent as well as by the solicitor."

(3) Paragraph (1) shall stand as paragraph (2) and the figure "(2)" at the beginning of the existing paragraph (2) shall be deleted.

4. The following rule shall be inserted after rule 37:—

"Taking of affidavit in county court proceedings

37A. In relation to matrimonial proceedings pending or treated as pending in a divorce county court, section 87(1) of the County Courts Act 1959 shall have effect as if after paragraph (*c*) there were inserted the following words:—

> "or
>
> (*d*) a registrar of the divorce registry; or
>
> (*e*) any officer of the divorce registry authorised by the President under section 2 of the Commissioners for Oaths Act 1889**(a)**; or
>
> (*f*) any clerk in the Central Office of the Royal Courts of Justice authorised to take affidavits for the purpose of proceedings in the Supreme Court."

5. Rule 46 shall be amended as follows:—

(1) For the heading there shall be substituted the words *"Lists at divorce towns and exercise of registrar's jurisdiction"*.

(2) In paragraph (3) after the words "set down for trial" there shall be inserted the words "or, in the case of a cause set down for trial at the Royal Courts of Justice, a registrar of the divorce registry".

6. For paragraph (3) of rule 65 there shall be substituted the following paragraph:—

> "(3) In the following cases an application for a decree nisi to be made absolute shall be made to a judge, that is to say—
>
> (*a*) where, within six weeks after a decree nisi has been pronounced, the Queen's Proctor gives to the registrar and to the party in whose favour the decree was pronounced a notice that he requires more time to decide whether to show cause against the decree being made absolute and the notice has not been withdrawn, or

---

(**a**) 1889 c. 10.

(*b*) where there are other circumstances which ought to be brought to the attention of the court before a decree nisi is made absolute.

Unless otherwise directed, the summons by which the application is made (or, where the cause is pending in a divorce county court, notice of the application) shall be served on every party to the cause (other than the applicant) and, in a case to which sub-paragraph (*a*) applies, on the Queen's Proctor."

7. Rule 80 shall be amended as follows:—

(1) In paragraph (3) for the words from "the court may" to "divorce county court" there shall be substituted the words "the court in which an application for ancillary relief is pending may, if it is a divorce county court, order the transfer of the application to the High Court or, if it is the High Court, order the transfer of the application to a divorce county court".

(2) In paragraph (5) for the words "to the High Court" there shall be substituted the words "from a divorce county court to the High Court or from the High Court to a divorce county court".

8. The following paragraph shall be added to rule 86:—

"(5) The Attachment of Earnings Act 1971(**a**) and Part VII of C.C.R. Order 25 (which deals with attachment of earnings) shall apply to the enforcement of an order made in matrimonial proceedings in the divorce registry which are treated as pending in a divorce county court as if the order were an order made by such a court."

9. Rule 97 shall be amended as follows:—

(1) In paragraph (1) the words "pending in a divorce county court" shall be omitted.

(2) In paragraph (2) after the words "application" and "such proceedings" and in paragraph (3) after the word "application" there shall in each case be inserted the words "pending in a divorce county court".

10. After rule 104 there shall be inserted the following rules:—

"*Transfer of proceedings under section* 15 *of the Act of* 1970, *etc.*

104A.—(1) The court in which an application under section 15 of the Act of 1970, section 26 of the Act of 1965 or section 17 of the Act of 1882 is pending may, if it is a county court, order the transfer of the application to the High Court or, if it is the High Court, order the transfer of the application to a divorce county court, where the transfer appears to the court to be desirable.

(2) In considering whether an application should be transferred under paragraph (1) from a county court to the High Court or from the High Court to a divorce county court the court shall have regard to all relevant considerations, including the nature and value of the property involved, and, in the case of an application under section 15 of the Act of 1970 or section 26 of the Act of 1965, the limits for the time being of the jurisdiction of county courts under section 7 of the Family Provision Act 1966(**b**).

(3) Rule 80(10) shall apply to an order under paragraph (1) of this rule as it applies to an order under paragraph (3) of that rule.

(**a**) 1971 c. 32. (**b**) 1966 c. 35.

Exercise in divorce registry of county court jurisdiction under section 17 of the Act of 1882, etc.

104B.—(1) Where any proceedings for divorce, nullity of marriage or judicial separation pending in the divorce registry are treated as pending in a divorce county court, an application under section 17 of the Act of 1882 by one of the parties to the marriage may be made to the divorce registry as if it were a county court.

(2) In relation to proceedings begun in the divorce registry under paragraph (1) of this rule or transferred to the divorce registry under rule 104A(1)—

   (*a*) section 4 of the Act of 1967 and the rules made thereunder shall have effect, with the necessary modifications, as they have effect in relation to proceedings begun in or transferred to the divorce registry under that section;

   (*b*) C.C.R. Order 2, Rule 13 (which relates to venue), and C.C.R. Order 46, Rule 11(2) (which deals with reference to the registrar), shall not apply, and a registrar may exercise the jurisdiction conferred on a county court judge by the said section 17."

11. The following paragraph shall be added to rule 120:—

"(4) Where by virtue of any provision of these Rules a county court has power to order that any proceedings pending in the court be transferred to the High Court, the High Court shall have power, exercisable in the like circumstances, to order the removal of the proceedings into the High Court, and the foregoing paragraphs of this rule shall apply as if the power conferred by this paragraph were conferred by the said section 115."

12. In Form 6 before the word "*Signed*" where it first appears there shall be inserted the words "[*If a solicitor is instructed, he will sign below on your behalf* [*but if the answer to question 5 is Yes, you must also sign here*]]", and the words "*Or, if a solicitor is instructed*" shall be omitted.

Dated 20th July 1972.

Hailsham of St. Marylebone, C.
George Baker, P.
John Latey, J.
Ifor Lloyd.
Irvon Sunderland.
W. D. S. Caird.
J. L. Williams.
Joseph Jackson.
Harold Law.
J. D. Clarke.
D. E. Morris.

EXPLANATORY NOTE

(This Note is not part of the Rules.)

These Rules make a number of miscellaneous amendments in the Matrimonial Causes Rules 1971. Under the extended rule-making powers conferred by section 45 of the Courts Act 1971 (C. 23) provision is made for the transfer of ancillary proceedings from the High Court to a divorce county court (rules 7 and 9) and for the transfer of proceedings under section 17 of the Married Women's Property Act 1882, section 26 of the Matrimonial Causes Act 1965 (C. 72) or section 15 of the Matrimonial Proceedings and Property Act 1970 (C. 45) from a county court to the High Court and from the High Court to a divorce county court (rule 10); an application under section 17 of the Act of 1882 may be made to the divorce registry as if it were a county court, where county court proceedings for divorce, nullity of marriage or judicial separation are pending between the same parties in the divorce registry (rule 10). A respondent who consents to a divorce after two years' separation may give notice to that effect in his acknowledgment of service if the form is signed by him as well as by any solicitor acting for him (rules 3 and 12). Clerks in the Central Office of the Supreme Court are empowered to take affidavits in matrimonial proceedings pending or treated as pending in a divorce county court (rule 4). Registrars of the divorce registry are authorised to exercise the powers of the district registrar in a district registry cause set down for hearing at the Royal Courts of Justice (rule 5). The normal period between decree nisi and absolute having been reduced from three months to six weeks by General Order of the High Court, the Queen's Proctor is enabled, where he desires more time to decide whether to show cause against the decree, to file a notice having the effect of preventing the decree being made absolute except on application to a judge (rule 6). Provision is made for the divorce registry to act as a county court for the purposes of the Attachment of Earnings Act 1971 in relation to maintenance orders treated as having been made in a divorce county court (rule 8).

STATUTORY INSTRUMENTS

1972 No. 1096 (L.12)

TRUSTEES

The Judicial Trustee Rules 1972

Made - - -	*20th July* 1972
Laid before Parliament	*3rd August* 1972
Coming into Operation	*1st September* 1972

The Lord Chancellor, in exercise of the powers conferred on him by section 4 of the Judicial Trustees Act 1896(**a**), and with the consent of the Treasury and of the authority for making orders under section 56 of the Solicitors Act 1957(**b**), hereby makes the following Rules:—

Citation and commencement

1. These Rules may be cited as the Judicial Trustee Rules 1972 and shall come into operation on 1st September 1972.

Interpretation

2. The Interpretation Act 1889(**c**) shall apply to the interpretation of these Rules as it applies to the interpretation of an Act of Parliament.

3.—(1) In these Rules, unless the context otherwise requires—

"the Act" means the Judicial Trustees Act 1896;

"the Court" and "master" have the same meaning as in the Rules of the Supreme Court;

"district registrar" means a registrar of a district registry of the High Court;

"judicial trustee" means a sole judicial trustee or two or more judicial trustees appointed to act together;

"official of the Court" means the holder of any paid office in or connected with the Supreme Court and includes the Official Solicitor;

"Official Solicitor" means the Official Solicitor to the Supreme Court;

"qualified accountant" means a person who is a member or a firm all the partners in which are members of the Institute of Chartered Accountants in England and Wales or of the Association of Certified and Corporate Accountants;

"Rules of the Supreme Court" mean rules made under section 99 of the Supreme Court of Judicature (Consolidation) Act 1925(**d**).

(2) Subject to the provisions of these Rules and of any enactment, the Rules of the Supreme Court shall apply with the necessary modification to proceedings under the Act and these Rules.

(**a**) 1896 c. 35.   (**b**) 1957 c. 27.   (**c**) 1889 c. 63.   (**d**) 1925 c. 49.

(3) Without prejudice to section 56(1) of the Supreme Court of Judicature (Consolidation) Act 1925 (which provides for the assignment to the Chancery Division of proceedings for the execution of trusts) proceedings under the Act shall be assigned to the Chancery Division.

APPOINTMENT OF JUDICIAL TRUSTEE

Making of application

4.—(1) An application to the Court to appoint a judicial trustee must be made by originating summons or, if it is made in a pending cause or matter, by summons in the cause or matter.

(2) The evidence in support of such an application must include an affidavit by the applicant exhibiting and verifying a statement containing the following particulars so far as the applicant can gain information with regard to them: —

(a) a short description of the trust and instrument by which it is, or is to be, created;

(b) short particulars of the trust property, with an approximate estimate of its income, and capital value;

(c) short particulars of the incumbrances (if any) affecting the trust property;

(d) particulars as to the persons who are in possession of the documents relating to the trust; and

(e) the names and addresses of the beneficiaries and short particulars of their respective interests.

(3) Where the applicant cannot gain the information required on any point he must mention his inability in the statement.

Service of summons and notice

5.—(1) Subject to any direction of the Court—

(a) the summons shall be served on every existing trustee who is not an applicant and on such of the beneficiaries as the applicant thinks fit; but

(b) a summons issued by or on behalf of a person creating or intending to create a trust need not be served on any person.

(2) The Court may give such directions as it thinks fit for the service of the summons or the dispensing with service of the summons on any person.

(3) Where an application is made to appoint an official of the Court to be a judicial trustee, that official need not be made a party to the proceedings but shall be given by the applicant not less than four days' notice of the hearing of the application and shall be entitled to attend the hearing.

Appointment of trustee

6.—(1) The Court may appoint as a judicial trustee—

(a) any fit and proper person (whether nominated in the application or not) including—

(i) an existing trustee of the trust;

(ii) an executor or administrator of the estate of a deceased person the administration of whose property constitutes the trust;

    (iii) a beneficiary;

    (iv) a solicitor of the trust or to a trustee or to a beneficiary;

    (v) a qualified accountant; and

    (vi) a person standing in any special position with regard to the trust;
       or

  (*b*) the Official Solicitor or, if for special reasons the Court sees fit to do so, some other official of the Court.

(2) On the appointment of any person to be a judicial trustee, the Court shall make such vesting or other orders and exercise such other powers as may be necessary for vesting the trust property in the judicial trustee either as sole trustee or jointly with other trustees as the case requires.

ADMINISTRATION OF THE TRUST

Statement of trust property

7. As soon as may be after his appointment a judicial trustee shall (unless the Court considers it unnecessary) provide the Court with a complete statement of the trust property and any charges thereon with an estimate of the capital value and annual income of each item and shall thereafter give sufficient information to the Court to enable the Court to keep the statement up to date.

Security

8.—(1) This rule shall apply where the judicial trustee is not an official of the Court.

(2) Subject to paragraph (3) below, the Court may in any case and at any time require a judicial trustee to give security for the due application of the trust property under or to be under his control.

(3) The Court shall not, except for special reasons, require security to be given when the application is made by a person creating or intending to create a trust.

(4) Any security required by the Court shall be given by guarantee or otherwise as the Court may direct.

(5) In any case where security is required—

  (*a*) the Court may allow the judicial trustee to act before his security is completed;

  (*b*) the guarantee shall be filed in the Central Office or, if the matter is proceeding in a district registry, in that registry and it shall be kept as of record until duly vacated;

  (*c*) any premium payable by a judicial trustee on account of his security may, in the Court's discretion, be paid out of the trust;

  (*d*) the security may be enforced only with the leave of the Court; and

  (*e*) the Court may at any time require the security to be varied or permit it to be discharged.

Trust account

9.—(1) This rule shall apply where the judicial trustee is not the Official Solicitor.

(2) The judicial trustee shall open and keep with a bank approved by the

Court a trust account and may use it for the purposes of the trust and shall pay in to it without delay all money coming into his hands on account of the trust.

(3) The Court may give such directions as it thinks fit for securing the safety of the trust property, including a direction limiting the amount which the judicial trustee may authorise the bank to pay out of the trust account at any one time without the countersignature of the master or district registrar.

10. If the Court considers that a judicial trustee has kept trust money in his hands longer than necessary it may require him to pay interest on it at a rate not exceeding 6 per cent. per annum.

Custody of documents

11.—(1) This rule shall apply where the judicial trustee is not the Official Solicitor.

(2) The judicial trustee shall deposit or cause to be deposited in his name either with the bank where the trust account is kept or in such other custody as the Court may direct all the title deeds, certificates and other documents which are evidence of the title of the trustee to any of the trust property.

(3) In any case where such a deposit is made the judicial trustee shall—

(*a*) instruct the body or person with whom it is made that—

(i) no deed, certificate or other document deposited is to be delivered to any person except on a written request signed by the judicial trustee and countersigned by the master or district registrar; and

(ii) any person authorised in writing by the Court is to be entitled to inspect any such deed, certificate or document during business hours; and

(*b*) provide the Court with a list of all such deeds, certificates and documents and inform the Court from time to time of any variation to be made in the list.

Directions to judicial trustees

12.—(1) A judicial trustee may at any time request the Court to give him directions as to the trust or its administration.

(2) The request shall set out in writing the facts with regard to which directions are required, and shall be accompanied by the prescribed fee.

(3) The Court may require the trustee or any other person to attend at chambers (if it appears that such an attendance is necessary or convenient) or may direct a summons to be issued in the proceedings.

ACCOUNTS AND AUDIT

Accounts and audit

13.—(1) Subject to any direction of the Court to the contrary, a judicial trustee shall make up his accounts (in such form as the Court shall require) in each year to the anniversary of his appointment and shall deliver them to the Court for audit within one calendar month after such anniversary.

(2) A judicial trustee shall endorse on his accounts a certificate of the approximate capital value of the trust property at the commencement of the year of account.

(3) The accounts shall be audited by the Court unless it considers that the accounts are likely to involve questions of difficulty and refers them to a qualified accountant for report, in which case the Court may order payment to him out of the trust of such amount in respect of his report as it thinks proper.

Deductions

14.—(1) A judicial trustee shall, unless the Court otherwise directs, be allowed on the audit of his accounts deductions made on account of any—

(a) premium paid under rule 8(5)(c),

(b) report obtained under rule 13(3),

(c) remuneration allowed or directed under rule 16.

(d) fees paid by the judicial trustee under Schedule 2, and

(e) money expended pursuant to a power given to trustees by law.

(2) Subject to paragraph (1) above, deductions shall not be allowed on the audit on account of—

(a) the expenses of professional or other assistance, or

(b) the judicial trustee's own work or personal outlay,

unless one or more of the conditions in paragraph (3) is fulfilled.

(3) The conditions referred to in paragraph (2) above are that—

(a) the deduction has been authorised by the Court under rule 16(2)(a);

(b) the deduction has been directed by the Court under rule 16(2)(b);

(c) the deduction is attributable to a direction given under rule 12 or under section 1(4) of the Act;

(d) the deduction has been authorised under section 1(5) of the Act, and

(e) the Court is satisfied that the deduction is justified by the necessity of the case.

Filing and inspection of accounts

15.—(1) When the accounts have been audited they shall be filed together with a note of any corrections made on the audit, as the Court may direct.

(2) The judicial trustee shall send a copy of the accounts, or, if the Court thinks fit, of a summary of the accounts, of the trust to such beneficiaries or other persons as the Court may direct.

(3) If an application is made by any person to inspect the filed accounts, the Court may, if it thinks fit, having regard to the nature of the relation of the applicant to the trust, allow them to be inspected on giving reasonable notice.

Remuneration

16.—(1) Subject to paragraph (3) of this rule the Court may on the appointment of a judicial trustee or at any time thereafter make an order that the judicial trustee is to be remunerated.

(2) An order under paragraph (1) of this rule may provide that—

(a) in a case where the judicial trustee is the Official Solicitor or any other practising solicitor, the trustee is to be at liberty to act as solicitor to the trust and to be allowed as part of his remuneration under these Rules all proper costs in respect of professional work done by him in that capacity as though he were not a trustee, and

(b) in that or in any other case, the remuneration payable to the judicial trustee shall be of such amounts and payable at such times and in such manner as the Court may from time to time direct, having regard to the duties imposed upon him by the trust.

(3) Remuneration allowed or directed under this rule shall not, in any year of account, exceed 10 per cent. of the capital value of the trust property.

(4) For the purposes of paragraph (3) of this rule the capital value shall be ascertained from the certificate under rule 13(2) in respect of the year of account, or, if the court sees fit in the case of a final account, from the certificate in respect of the preceding year.

(5) Any remuneration allowed or directed under this rule in respect of an official of the Court on account of his services as trustee shall be paid into the Exchequer and applied in such manner as the Treasury may direct.

ENFORCEMENT

Forfeiture of remuneration

17.—(1) If the Court is satisfied that a judicial trustee has failed to comply with the Act, or with these Rules, or with any direction of the Court made in accordance with the Act or these Rules, or has otherwise misconducted himself in relation to the trust, the Court may, after having given the trustee an opportunity of being heard, order that the whole or any part of his remuneration be forfeited.

(2) This rule shall not affect any liability of the judicial trustee for breach of trust or the power of the Court to remove or suspend him under rule 18 below.

Removal and suspension of judicial trustee

18.—(1) If at any time, whether or not on the application of any person appearing to be interested in the trust, the Court considers that it is expedient in the interests of the trust to do so, it may suspend a judicial trustee or may remove a judicial trustee.

(2) When a judicial trustee is suspended—

(a) he shall have no power to act as a trustee, and

(b) the Court shall cause notice of the suspension to be given to such of the persons appearing to be interested in the trust as the Court directs, and to any person having the custody of the trust property, and shall give such other directions as may appear necessary for securing the safety of the trust property.

(3) A judicial trustee shall not be removed by the Court unless—

(a) there has been an application for that purpose made by summons, or

(b) notice has been given to him by the Court of the grounds on which it is proposed to remove him, and of the time and place at which the matter will be heard.

(4) A copy of any notice to the trustee under paragraph (3)(b) above shall be sent to such of the persons appearing to be interested in the trust as the Court may direct, and the same procedure shall so far as possible be followed in the matter as on a summons to remove a judicial trustee.

(5) Where the Court removes a sole judicial trustee it shall at the same time appoint one or more new judicial trustees and rules 6(2) and 20(2) shall apply.

Inquiry into conduct of judicial trustee

19. Where an inquiry is ordered into the administration of any trust by, or into any dealing or transaction of, a judicial trustee, the inquiry shall, unless the Court otherwise directs, be conducted by the master or district registrar who shall have the same powers in relation thereto as he has in relation to any other inquiry directed by the Court.

RESIGNATION AND DISCONTINUANCE OF JUDICIAL TRUSTEE

Resignation of judicial trustee

20.—(1) A judicial trustee who desires to be discharged from his trust shall give notice to the Court of the arrangements proposed for the appointment of a successor.

(2) Where no fit and proper person appears available to replace the judicial trustee, or where the Court considers it convenient or expedient in the interests of the trust so to do, the Court may appoint an official of the Court to be a judicial trustee in place of the former judicial trustee.

Discontinuance

21.—(1) Where an application is made by summons by a person appearing to the Court to be interested in the trust, the Court (having ascertained as far as may be the wishes of all persons so appearing) may, and if all persons so appearing concur shall, order that there shall cease to be a judicial trustee of the trust.

(2) An order may be made under this rule whether the person who is judicial trustee continues as trustee or not, and the Court shall make such vesting or other orders and exercise such powers as may be required, including those necessary for vesting the trust property in the new trustee either as sole trustee or, as the case may be, jointly with other trustees.

SPECIAL PROVISIONS RELATING TO OFFICIALS OF THE COURT

22.—(1) Schedule 1 to these Rules shall apply only where the Official Solicitor is a sole judicial trustee.

(2) Where there are several judicial trustees of whom one is the Official Solicitor, they shall comply with such directions as the Court may give as to the manner in which, and the conditions subject to which—

    (*a*) the trust fund is to be held;

    (*b*) any title deeds, certificates or other documents which are evidence of their title to the trust property are to be disposed of; and

    (*c*) any payments received or made on behalf of the trust are to be dealt with and accounts thereof are to be kept.

23. An official of the Court shall not be appointed or act as judicial trustee—

    (*a*) for any persons in their capacity as members or debenture holders of, or being in any other relation to, any corporation or unincorporated body, or any club, or

    (*b*) of a trust which involves the carrying on of any trade or business unless the Court, with or without special conditions to ensure the proper supervision of the trade or business, specifically directs.

24.—(1) The appointment of an official of the Court as a judicial trustee shall be an appointment of the holder of that office for the time being, and no further order or appointment shall be necessary by reason only of the person appointed dying or ceasing to hold office.

(2) Any property vested in an official of the Court as a judicial trustee shall, on his dying or ceasing to hold office, without any conveyance, assignment or transfer, become vested in his successor in like manner as it was vested in him.

FEES

25.—(1) The fees specified in column 2 of Schedule 2 to these Rules shall be paid in respect of the matters specified in column 1 of that Schedule.

(2) All fees payable under these Rules shall, except as otherwise provided, be subject to similar provision as to payment, account and application as other fees payable in the Supreme Court.

INFORMALITY

26.—(1) The Court may dispense with formal proof of facts in any case where it is satisfied, without such proof, that there is no reasonable doubt of any fact which affects the administration of a trust by a judicial trustee.

(2) Except where a summons is required by these Rules, that is to say under rule 4(1), 18(3) or 21(1), or where the Court otherwise directs, no summons shall be required for any purpose under the Act or these Rules, and accordingly—

(i) a judicial trustee may by letter make an application or request to or communicate with the Court in the administration of his trust;

(ii) the Court may by letter give directions or notices to the judicial trustee;

(iii) the master or district registrar may by letter make or cause to be made such appointments as he thinks fit for the attendance at chambers of the trustee or any other person connected with the trust;

(iv) any fees payable may be remitted by post;

(v) any other thing required to be done in relation to the administration of the trust may be done in a simple and informal manner.

DISTRICT REGISTRIES

27.—(1) Notwithstanding any provisions contained in the Rules of the Supreme Court, an originating summons may be issued out of a district registry for the purpose of an application to appoint a judicial trustee.

(2) Where a judicial trustee is appointed on a summons or in a cause or matter proceeding in a district registry all proceedings with respect to the trust and the administration thereof under the Act or these Rules shall, subject to paragraph (3) of this rule, be taken in the district registry.

(3) The Court may transfer any trust of which there is a judicial trustee from a district registry to London, or from London to a district registry, or

from one district registry to another, according as it appears convenient for the administration of the trust.

28. The rules specified in Schedule 3 to these Rules are hereby revoked, so however that the provisions of those rules in force immediately before the commencement of these Rules shall continue to apply to proceedings taken before that date in a county court.

Dated 19th July 1972.

Hailsham of St. Marylebone, C.

We consent,
Dated 19th July 1972.

Widgery, C.J.
Denning, M.R.
Desmond Heap.
G. P. Atkinson.

Dated 20th July 1972.

Tim Fortescue,
V. H. Goodhew,
Two of the Lords Commissioners
of Her Majesty's Treasury.

SCHEDULE 1

Rule 22(1)

Administration by Official Solicitor

1.—(1) In this Schedule "the Account" means the account maintained at the Law Courts Branch of the Bank of England, entitled "The Official Solicitor to the Supreme Court of Judicature No. 26083000" or any other account maintained at any other bank by the Official Solicitor with the authorisation and approval of the Treasury.

(2) The Official Solicitor may open a separate trust account, at any bank approved by the Court, for the temporary deposit of money or for any other purpose approved by the Court.

(3) The Official Solicitor shall transfer either to the credit of the Account or to the credit of the appropriate trust account—

    (*a*) all lodgments of cash,

    (*b*) all dividends and interest on securities and rents and payments received by him.

2.—(1) All registered stocks, shares and securities other than mortgages on real or leasehold property shall be registered in the sole name of the Official Solicitor.

(2) Real and leasehold property and mortgages thereon shall be vested in the Official Solicitor.

(3) All registered securities registered in the sole name of the Official Solicitor shall be designated in the books of the bank, company or other body in whose books such securities are registered in such manner as will identify them with the trust for which they are held.

Deposit of documents

3. All title deeds and certificates and other documents which are evidence of the title of the Official Solicitor to any of the trust property, or which represent security for such property, shall be held in safe custody by the Official Solicitor.

Financial dealings

4.—(1) The Official Solicitor shall keep separate accounts in his books in respect of each trust of all funds received, paid or transferred by him in relation to the administration of the trust.

(2) The Official Solicitor may make payments from trust funds either by payable order or by pre-authenticated order as authorised by the Treasury.

(3) The Official Solicitor may make purchases and sales of stocks, shares and securities through the Supreme Court Brokers or such other brokers as he may choose.

SCHEDULE 2

Rule 25

No. of Fee	Column 1	Column 2
1	On any matter for which a fee is provided under the orders for the time being in force relating to Supreme Court fees.	The fee so provided

2	On a request to the Court for—
	  (*a*) directions, or
	  (*b*) approval of any step taken, or to be taken, in relation to the administration of a trust. .. ..
		p
		
		50

3	On filing a statement of trust property, for every £100 or fraction of £100 of the estimated value of the property then in possession (subject to a minimum fee of £1).	13

4   On filing an amended statement of trust property, for every £100 or fraction of £100 of the estimated value of the property in possession shown therein (subject to a minimum fee of 50p): ..   13

Provided that, in estimating the value of the property for the purpose of calculating this fee, there shall be excluded any asset (or the proceeds thereof or any property acquired with such proceeds) on which Fee No. 3 has been paid.

5   On filing—

     (*a*) the accounts of a trust, ...   50

     (*b*) any other document relating to a trust.   25

6   On (*a*) auditing the account of a trust when audited by an officer of the Court, or

     (*b*) referring the accounts of a trust to a qualified accountant for report,

for every £100 or fraction of £100 of the gross amount of the income without allowing for any deduction therefrom.   13

7   On the inspection of filed accounts, for each hour or part of an hour occupied (subject to a maximum fee of £1·50 in respect of any one day).   25

SCHEDULE 3

Rule 28

RULES REVOKED

Title	Reference
The Judicial Trustee Rules 1897	S.R. & O. 1897/708 (Rev. 1903, XII, p. 911: 1897, p. 634)
The Additional Rule 1899	S.R. & O. 1899/315 (Rev. 1903, XII, p. 922: 1899, p. 1392)
The Judicial Trustee Rule (April) 1900	S.R. & O. 1900/332 (Rev. 1903, XII, p. 923: 1900, p. 921)
The Judicial Trustee (Amendment) Rules 1962	S.I. 1962/163 (1962 I, p. 163)

EXPLANATORY NOTE

(This Note is not part of the Rules.)

These Rules consolidate with amendments the rules made under the Judicial Trustees Act 1896. The principal changes made are:—

(1) the formalities of application are simplified (Rule 4);

(2) security need not necessarily be required of a judicial trustee (Rule 8);

(3) a judicial trustee who is a practising solicitor or the Official Solicitor may be allowed professional costs for work done (Rule 16);

(4) county courts will no longer accept the control and supervision of further judicial trusts (Rule 28).

STATUTORY INSTRUMENTS

1972 No. 1097 (C.19)

TRANSPORT

The Transport (London) Act 1969 (Commencement No. 4) Order 1972

Made - - - *21st July* 1972

The Secretary of State for the Environment in exercise of his powers under section 47 of the Transport (London) Act 1969(a) and of all other enabling powers hereby makes the following Order:—

1. This Order may be cited as the Transport (London) Act 1969 (Commencement No. 4) Order 1972.

2. Section 32 of the Transport (London) Act 1969 (under which the Greater London Council assumes sole responsibility for the establishment of pedestrian crossings on roads in Greater London other than trunk roads) shall come into force on 1st October 1972.

Signed by authority of the Secretary of State.

21st July 1972.

F. J. Ward,
An Under Secretary in the
Department of the Environment.

(a) 1969 c. 35.

STATUTORY INSTRUMENTS

1972 No. 1098

EDUCATION, ENGLAND AND WALES
The Provision of Milk and Meals (Amendment) Regulations 1972

Made - - - -	*24th July* 1972
Laid before Parliament	*3rd August* 1972
Coming into Operation	*1st September* 1972

The Secretary of State for Education and Science and the Secretary of State for Wales, in joint exercise of their powers under section 49 of the Education Act 1944(a) as amended by section 1 of the Education (Milk) Act 1971(b), hereby make the following regulations:—

Citation, commencement and interpretation

1.—(1) These regulations may be cited as the Provision of Milk and Meals (Amendment) Regulations 1972 and these regulations and the Provision of Milk and Meals Regulations 1969 to 1971 may be cited together as the Provision of Milk and Meals Regulations 1969 to 1972.

(2) These regulations shall come into operation on 1st September 1972.

(3) The Interpretation Act 1889(c) shall apply for the interpretation of these regulations as it applies for the interpretation of an Act of Parliament.

Amendment of regulations

2. Schedule 1 to the Provision of Milk and Meals Regulations 1969(d) as amended (e) (determination of financial hardship) shall have effect subject to—

(*a*) the substitution for the table and the first note in paragraph 1 (net income scale) of the following table and note:—

"PART A	PART B					
Size of Family	Net Weekly Income in £p					
	1	2	3	4	5	6
1	14·80					
2	18·20	17·60				
3	21·60	21·00	20·40			
4	25·00	24·40	23·80	23·20		
5	28·40	27·80	27·20	26.60	26·00	
6	31·80	31·20	30·60	30·00	29·40	28·80

(**a**) 1944 c. 31. (**b**) 1971 c. 74.
(**c**) 1889 c. 63. (**d**) S.I. 1969/483 (1969 I, p. 1382).
(**e**) The relevant amending instrument is S.I. 1971/1368 (1971 II, p. 3844).

For larger families, in respect of each child—

    (*a*) £3·40 is to be added at each incremental point in every additional line.

    (*b*) £0·60 is to be subtracted at each incremental point in every additional column"; and

    (*b*) the addition at the end of paragraph 3 (resources to be disregarded) as a new sub-paragraph of—

        "(13) Any attendance allowance under section 4 of the National Insurance (Old persons' and widows' pensions and attendance allowance) Act 1970**(a)**".

Given under the Official Seal of the Secretary of State for Education and Science on 19th July 1972.

(L.S.)

                                Margaret H. Thatcher,
                                  Secretary of State for
                                Education and Science.

Given under my hand on 24th July 1972.

                                Peter Thomas,
                                Secretary of State for Wales.

EXPLANATORY NOTE

(This Note is not part of the Regulations.)

These regulations amend the provisions of the Provision of Milk and Meals Regulations 1969 to 1971 for the calculation of a parent's income for the purposes of determining his entitlement to remission of the charge for school dinner in a nursery school or a county or voluntary school.

(a) 1970 c. 51.

STATUTORY INSTRUMENTS

1972 No. 1099

ROAD TRAFFIC

The Pedestrian Crossings Schemes (Adaptation of Enactment) (Greater London) Order 1972

Made - - -	*22nd July* 1972
Laid before Parliament	*2nd August* 1972
Coming into Operation	*1st October* 1972

The Secretary of State for the Environment in exercise of his powers under section 21(9) of the Road Traffic Regulation Act 1967(**a**) and of all other enabling powers hereby makes the following Order:—

1. This Order may be cited as the Pedestrian Crossings Schemes (Adaptation of Enactment) (Greater London) Order 1972 and shall come into operation on 1st October 1972.

2. The Interpretation Act 1889(**b**) shall apply for the interpretation of this Order as it applies for the interpretation of an Act of Parliament.

3. In its application to Greater London section 21(3) of the Road Traffic Regulation Act 1967 is hereby adapted and shall have effect as though for the words "and the number proposed for any length of road or area" there were substituted the words "and the number proposed for any length of road or the maximum and minimum numbers proposed for any area".

Signed by authority of the Secretary of State.

John Peyton,
Minister for Transport Industries,
Department of the Environment.

22nd July 1972.

EXPLANATORY NOTE

(This Note is not part of the Order.)

Section 21 of the Road Traffic Regulation Act 1967 relates to schemes for the establishment of pedestrian crossings on roads other than trunk roads. By virtue of section 21(9) of the Act the Secretary of State is empowered to adapt section 21 in its application to Greater London. This Order adapts section 21(3) of the Act so that a scheme in relation to Greater London may specify the *maximum and minimum* number of pedestrian crossings proposed for any area.

(**a**) 1967 c. 76.   (**b**) 1889 c. 63.

STATUTORY INSTRUMENTS

1972 No. 1101

CARIBBEAN AND NORTH ATLANTIC TERRITORIES

The Cayman Islands (Constitution) Order 1972

Made - - - -	26*th July* 1972
Laid before Parliament	1*st August* 1972
Coming into Operation	22*nd August* 1972

At the Court at Buckingham Palace, the 26th day of July 1972

Present,

The Queen's Most Excellent Majesty in Council

Her Majesty, by virtue of the powers conferred upon Her by section 5 of the West Indies Act 1962(**a**) and of all other powers enabling Her in that behalf, is pleased, by and with the advice of Her Privy Council, to order, and it is hereby ordered as follows: —

Citation, commencement, revocation and interpretation.

1.—(1) This Order may be cited as the Cayman Islands (Constitution) Order 1972 and shall come into operation on 22nd August 1972.

(2) The instruments mentioned in Schedule I to this Order are revoked on the coming into operation of this Order:

Provided that Part III of the Schedule to the Cayman Islands (Constitution) Order 1965(**b**) as amended by the Cayman Islands (Constitution) (Amendment) Order 1967(**c**) shall be revoked on the day notified by the Governor under section 2(1) of this Order.

(3) The Interpretation Act 1889(**d**) shall apply with the necessary adaptations for the purpose of interpreting and otherwise in relation to this Order as it applies for the purpose of interpreting and in relation to an Act of Parliament.

Constitution of Cayman Islands.

2.—(1) Schedule 2 to this Order shall have effect as the Constitution of the Cayman Islands as from the date on which the Legislative Assembly of the Cayman Islands is next dissolved after the coming into operation of this Order:

Provided that Part II of the said Schedule shall have effect from such later day as may be notified by the Governor of the Cayman Islands by a Cayman Islands Government Notice.

(2) Schedule 2 to this Order may be cited as the Constitution of the Cayman Islands, and references in any law made before this Order to the Cayman Islands (Constitution) Order 1965 or to any particular provision thereof shall be construed, as from the commencement of this Order, as references to the Constitution of the Cayman Islands and to the corresponding provision thereof.

W. G. Agnew.

(**a**) 1962 c. 19.   (**b**) S.I. 1965/1860 (1965 III, p. 5588).
(**c**) S.I. 1967/970 (1967 II, p. 2933).   (**d**) 1889 c. 63.

SCHEDULE 1

INSTRUMENTS REVOKED BY THIS ORDER

Instrument	Reference
The Cayman Islands (Constitution) Order 1965	S.I. 1965/1860 (1965 III, p. 5588).
The Cayman Islands (Constitution) (Amendment) Order 1967	S.I. 1967/970 (1967 II, p. 2933).
The Cayman Islands (Constitution) (Amendment) Order 1971	S.I. 1971/1737 (1971 III, p. 4733).
The Cayman Islands (Legislative Assembly—Extension of Duration) Order 1971	S.I. 1971/2100 (1971 III, p. 6190).
The Cayman Islands Constitution (Amendment) Order 1972	S.I. 1972/808 (1972 II, p. 2600).

SCHEDULE 2

The Constitution of the Cayman Islands

ARRANGEMENT OF SECTIONS

PART I

The Governor

PART II

Executive Council

PART III

Legislative Assembly

PART I

The Governor

1.—(1) There shall be a Governor of the Cayman Islands who shall The Governor. be appointed by Her Majesty by Commission under Her Sign Manual and Signet and shall hold office during Her Majesty's pleasure.

(2) The Governor shall, for the purpose of administering the government of the Islands, have such powers and duties as are conferred or imposed on him by this Constitution or any other law and such other powers as Her Majesty may from time to time be pleased to assign to him, and, subject to the provisions of this Constitution and of any other law by which any such powers or duties are conferred or imposed, shall do and execute all things that belong to his office according to such Instructions, if any, as Her Majesty may from time to time see fit to give him ; but no court shall enquire whether or not he has complied with any such Instructions.

(3) A person appointed to the office of Governor shall, before entering upon the functions of that office, make oaths of allegiance and for the due execution of that office in the forms set out in the Schedule to this Constitution.

2. The Governor shall receive such emoluments as may be fixed by Emoluments a Secretary of State, and those emoluments are hereby charged upon of Governor. the revenues of the Islands.

3.—(1) During any period when the office of Governor is vacant or Acting the Governor is absent from the Islands or is for any other reason un- Governor. able to perform the functions of his office those functions shall, during Her Majesty's pleasure, be assumed and performed by—

(*a*) such person as Her Majesty may designate in that behalf by Instructions given under Her Sign Manual and Signet or through a Secretary of State ; or

(*b*) if there is no person in the Islands so designated and able to perform those functions, such public officer as the Governor, acting in his discretion, shall by writing under his hand appoint.

(2) Before assuming the functions of the office of Governor, any such person as aforesaid shall make the oaths directed by section 1 of this Constitution to be made by the Governor.

(3) Any such person as aforesaid shall not continue to perform the functions of the office of Governor after the Governor or some other person having a prior right to perform the functions of that office has notified him that he is about to resume or assume those functions.

4.—(1) Whenever the Governor—   Governor's

(*a*) has occasion to be absent from the seat of government but not deputy. from the Islands ; or

(*b*) has occasion to be absent from the Islands for a period which he has reason to believe will be of short duration ; or

(*c*) is suffering from an illness which he has reason to believe will be of short duration,

he may, by instrument under the public seal, acting in his discretion, appoint any person in the Islands to be his deputy during such absence or illness and in that capacity to perform on his behalf such of the functions of the office of Governor as may be specified in that instrument.

(2) The power and authority of the Governor shall not be abridged, altered or in any way affected by the appointment of a deputy under this section, and a deputy shall conform to and observe all instructions that the Governor, acting in his discretion, may from time to time address to him ; but no court shall enquire whether or not he has complied with any such instructions.

(3) A person appointed as a deputy under this section shall hold that appointment for such period as may be specified in the instrument by which he is appointed, and his appointment may be revoked at any time by Her Majesty by instructions given through a Secretary of State, or by the Governor, acting in his discretion.

PART II

Executive Council

Executive Council.   **5.** There shall be an Executive Council in and for the Islands which, subject to section 10 of this Constitution, shall consist of—

    (a) three official members, who shall be appointed by the Governor, acting in pursuance of instructions given to him by Her Majesty through a Secretary of State, by instrument under the public seal, from among persons holding public office ; and

    (b) four elected members, who shall be elected by the elected members of the Assembly from among the elected members of the Assembly.

Tenure of office of members of Council.   **6.**—(1) The official members of the Executive Council shall hold their seats in the Council during Her Majesty's pleasure :

Provided that the seat of an official member shall in any case become vacant—

    (a) if he resigns his seat in the Council by writing under his hand addressed to the Governor and the Governor, acting in his discretion, accepts the resignation ;

    (b) if he is absent from the Islands without the written permission of the Governor, acting in his discretion ; or

    (c) if he ceases to hold public office.

(2) The seat of an elected member of the Executive Council shall become vacant—

    (a) if he resigns his seat in the Council by writing under his hand addressed to and received by the Governor ;

    (b) when the Assembly first meets after a dissolution thereof ;

    (c) if he ceases to be a member of the Assembly for any reason other than a dissolution thereof ;

    (d) if he is absent from the Islands without the written permission of the Governor ;

    (e) if, without the written permission of the Governor, he is absent from three consecutive meetings of the Executive Council ; or (*f*) if his election to the Executive Council is revoked by a resolution of the Assembly in favour of which there are cast the votes of not less than two-thirds of all the elected members of the Assembly :

Provided that a motion for the revocation of the election of an elected member under this paragraph on the ground that he has contravened the provisions of section 9(2) of this Constitution shall not be introduced except by a member of the Executive Council.

7.—(1) The Governor shall, subject to the following provisions of this section, consult with the Executive Council in the formulation of policy and in the exercise of all powers conferred upon him by this Constitution or by any other law for the time being in force in the Islands, except in the exercise of— *Governor to consult Council.*

(*a*) any power conferred upon him by this Constitution which he is empowered to exercise in his discretion or in pursuance of Instructions given to him by Her Majesty ;

(*b*) any power conferred by any law other than this Constitution which he is empowered or directed, either expressly or by necessary implication, by that or any other law to exercise without consulting the Council ; or

(*c*) any power that in his opinion relates to—

    (i) defence ;

    (ii) external affairs ;

    (iii) internal security ;

    (iv) the police ; or

    (v) the appointment (including the appointment on promotion or transfer, appointment on contract and appointment to act in an office) of any person to any public office, the suspension, termination of employment, dismissal, or retirement of any public officer or taking of disciplinary action in respect of such an officer, the application to any public officer of the terms or conditions of employment of the public service (including salary scales, allowances, leave, passages or pensions) for which financial provision has been made, or the organisation of the public service to the extent that it does not involve new financial provision :

Provided that in exercising his powers in relation to the matters mentioned in this paragraph (*c*) the Governor shall keep the Executive Council informed of any matters that in his judgment may involve the economic or financial interests of the Cayman Islands or the enactment of laws under Part IV of this Constitution.

(2) The Governor shall not be required to consult with the Executive Council in any case in which, in his judgement—

(*a*) the service of Her Majesty would sustain material prejudice thereby ;

(*b*) the matters to be decided are too unimportant to require such consultation ; or

(*c*) the urgency of the matter requires him to act before the Council can be consulted.

(3) In every case falling within paragraph (c) of the last foregoing subsection the Governor shall, as soon as practicable, communicate to the Executive Council the measures which he has adopted and the reasons for those measures.

(4) The question whether the Governor has exercised any power after consultation with or in accordance with the advice of the Executive Council shall not be enquired into by any court.

Governor may act contrary to advice of Council.

8.—(1) Subject to the provisions of this Constitution, in any case where the Governor is required by the last foregoing section to consult with the Executive Council, he shall act in accordance with the advice given him by the Council unless he considers it inexpedient in the interests of public order, public faith or good government to do so:

Provided that he shall not so act against the advice of the Council without first obtaining the approval of a Secretary of State, unless in his judgment the matter is so urgent that it is necessary for him to act before obtaining such approval, in which case he shall forthwith report his action to a Secretary of State with the reasons therefor.

(2) Whenever the Governor acts otherwise than in accordance with the advice given to him by the Council, any member of the Council may require that there be recorded in the minutes the grounds of any advice or opinion which he may have given on the question.

Assignment of responsibility.

9.—(1) Subject to any instructions given to him by Her Majesty through a Secretary of State, the Governor acting in his discretion shall to the extent that he deems appropriate charge members of the Executive Council with responsibility for any business of the Government (other than a matter mentioned in section 7(1)(c) of this Constitution) or any Department of the Government.

(2) It shall be the duty of a member so charged with responsibility to act in the exercise thereof in accordance with the policies of the Government as decided in the Council and in accordance with the principles of collective responsibility, and to support in the Legislative Assembly any measure decided upon in the Council, unless he has received the prior permission of the Governor to act otherwise or not to support such a measure.

Temporary members of Council.

10.—(1) Whenever a member of the Executive Council is by reason of his illness or absence from the Islands or for any other reason incapable of performing the functions of his office, then—

(a) in the case of the incapacity of an official member, the Governor acting in his discretion may, by instrument under the public seal, appoint any public officer to be temporarily a member of the Council ; or

(b) in the case of the incapacity of an elected member, the elected members of the Assembly, if the Governor informs the Assembly that that is desirable, may elect a person from among the elected members of the Assembly to be temporarily a member of the Council.

(2) The Governor shall forthwith report to Her Majesty through a Secretary of State any appointment made under this section.

(3) A person appointed or elected under this section to be temporarily a member of the Executive Council shall vacate his seat—

(a) when he is informed by the Governor that the circumstances giving rise to the appointment or election have ceased to exist ; or (*b*) in the case of a person appointed in place of an official member, if his appointment is revoked by Her Majesty through a Secretary of State or by the Governor, acting in his discretion.

(4) Subject to the provisions of this section, the provisions of this Constitution shall apply in relation to a person appointed or elected to be temporarily a member of the Executive Council as they apply to the member in whose place he was appointed or elected.

11. Any question whether a person is a member of the Executive Council shall be determined by the Governor acting in his discretion.

Determination of questions as to membership.

12. Before assuming the functions of his office a member of the Executive Council shall make before the Governor, or some other person authorised in that behalf by the Governor, acting in his discretion, an oath for the due execution of his office in the form set out in the Schedule to this Constitution.

Oath by members of Council.

13.—(1) The Executive Council shall not be summoned except by the authority of the Governor, acting in his discretion.

(2) No business shall be transacted at any meeting of the Executive Council unless there are four members present besides the Governor or other person presiding.

Summoning of Council and transaction of business.

(3) Subject to the provisions of the last foregoing subsection, the Executive Council shall not be disqualified for the transaction of business by reason of any vacancy in the membership of the Council (including any vacancy not filled when the Council is first constituted or is reconstituted at any time) and the validity of the transaction of business in the Council shall not be affected by reason only of the fact that some person who was not entitled to do so took part therein.

14.—(1) The Governor shall, so far as is practicable, attend and preside at meetings of the Executive Council.

Presiding in Council.

(2) In the absence of the Governor there shall preside at any meeting of the Executive Council such member of the Council as the Governor, acting in his discretion, may appoint.

15. No question shall be submitted to the Executive Council for their advice except by and with the approval of the Governor, acting in his discretion ; but if the Governor declines to submit any question to the Council when requested in writing by any member of the Council to do so, that member may require that there be recorded in the minutes his written application, together with the answer given thereto by the Governor.

Submission of questions to Council.

16. The person presiding may, when in his opinion the business before the Executive Council makes it desirable, summon any person to a meeting of the Council, notwithstanding that that person is not a member of the Council.

Summoning of persons to Council.

PART III

Legislative Assembly

Legislative Assembly.

17.—(1) There shall be a Legislative Assembly for the Islands.

(2) Subject to the provisions of this Constitution, the Assembly shall consist of—

(*a*) the Governor, or at any time when there is a person holding the office of Speaker, the Speaker;

(*b*) three official members, who shall be appointed by the Governor acting in pursuance of instructions given to him by Her Majesty through a Secretary of State, by instrument under the public seal, from among persons holding public office; and

(*c*) twelve elected members, who shall be persons qualified for election in accordance with the provisions of this Constitution and elected in the manner provided by any law in force in the Islands.

Qualifications for elected membership.

18. Subject to the provisions of the next following section, a person shall be qualified to be elected as a member of the Assembly if, and shall not be qualified to be so elected unless, he—

(*a*) is a British subject of the age of twenty-one years or over; and

(*b*) has resided in the Islands for a period or periods totalling not less than five years out of the seven years immediately preceding the date of his nomination for election and is resident therein at that date; and either

(*c*) was born in the Islands or of parents one of whom at the time of his birth was domiciled or ordinarily resident in the Islands; or

(*d*) is domiciled in the Islands at the date of his nomination for election.

Disqualifications for elected membership.

19.—(1) No person shall be qualified to be elected as a member of the Assembly who—

(*a*) is, by virtue of his own act, under any acknowledgement of allegiance, obedience or adherence to a foreign power or state;

(*b*) holds, or is acting in, any public office;

(*c*) has been adjudged or otherwise declared bankrupt under any law in force in any part of the Commonwealth and has not been discharged;

(*d*) is a person certified to be insane or otherwise adjudged to be of unsound mind under any law in force in the Islands;

(*e*) subject to the provisions of the next following subsection, is under sentence of death imposed on him by a court in any part of the Commonwealth, or is serving a sentence of imprisonment (by whatever name called) exceeding twelve months imposed on him by such a court or substituted by competent authority for some other sentence imposed on him by such a court, or is under such a sentence of imprisonment the execution of which has been suspended;

(*f*) is disqualified for election by any law in force in the Islands by reason of his holding, or acting in, any office the functions of which involve—

(i) any responsibility for, or in connection with, the conduct of any election; or

(ii) any responsibility for the compilation or revision of any electoral register ;

(*g*) is a party to, or a partner in a firm or a director or manager of a company which is a party to, any contract with the Government of the Islands for or on account of the public service and has not, in the case of a contested election, caused to be published, at least one month before the day of the poll, a Government Notice setting out the nature of such contract and his interest, or the interest of any such firm or company, therein ; or

(*h*) is disqualified for membership of the Assembly by any law in force in the Islands relating to offences connected with elections.

(2) For the purposes of paragraph (*e*) of the last foregoing subsection—

(*a*) where a person is serving two or more sentences of imprisonment that are required to be served consecutively he shall, throughout the whole time during which he so serves, be regarded as serving a sentence exceeding twelve months if (but not unless) any one of those sentences exceeds that term ; and

(*b*) no account shall be taken of a sentence of imprisonment imposed as an alternative to or in default of the payment of a fine.

20.—(1) Subject to the provisions of this Constitution, an official member of the Assembly shall hold his seat in the Assembly during Her Majesty's pleasure.

Tenure of office of members of Assembly.

(2) The seat of an official member of the Assembly shall become vacant—

(*a*) if he ceases to hold a public office ;

(*b*) upon a dissolution of the Assembly ; or

(*c*) if he resigns his seat by writing under his hand addressed to the Governor, and the Governor, acting in his discretion, accepts his resignation.

(3) The seat of an elected member of the Assembly shall become vacant—

(*a*) upon a dissolution of the Assembly ;

(*b*) if, without the written permission of the Governor, he is absent from three consecutive meetings of the Assembly ;

(*c*) if he ceases to be a British subject ;

(*d*) if he ceases to be resident in the Islands ;

(*e*) if he resigns his seat by writing under his hand addressed to the Governor ;

(*f*) if he becomes a party to any contract with the Government of the Islands for or on account of the public service, or if any firm in which he is a partner or any company of which he is a director or manager becomes a party to any such contract, or if he becomes a partner in a firm or a director or manager of a company which is a party to any such contract :

Provided that, if in the circumstances it appears to him to be just to do so, the Governor may exempt any elected member from vacating his seat under the provisions of this paragraph, if the member, before or as soon as practicable after becoming a party to the contract, or before or as soon as practicable after becoming otherwise interested in the contract (whether as a partner in a firm or as a director or manager of a company), discloses to the Governor the nature of the contract and his interest or the interest of the firm or company therein ;

(g) if any of the circumstances arise that, if he were not a member of the Assembly, would cause him to be disqualified for election thereto by virtue of paragraph (a), (b), (c), (d), (f) or (h) of sub-section (1) of the last foregoing section ; or

(h) in the circumstances specified in the next following section.

Vacation of seat on sentence.

21.—(1) Subject to the provisions of this section, if an elected member of the Assembly is sentenced by a court in any part of the Commonwealth to death or to imprisonment (by whatever name called) for a term exceeding twelve months, he shall forthwith cease to perform his functions as a member of the Assembly, and his seat in the Assembly shall become vacant at the expiration of a period of thirty days thereafter:

Provided that the Governor may, at the request of the member, from time to time extend that period for thirty days to enable the member to pursue any appeal in respect of his conviction or sentence, so however that extensions of time exceeding in the aggregate three hundred and thirty days shall not be given without the approval of the Assembly signified by resolution.

(2) If at any time before the member vacates his seat he is granted a free pardon or his conviction is set aside or his sentence is reduced to a term of imprisonment of less than twelve months or a punishment other than imprisonment is substituted, his seat in the Assembly shall not become vacant under the provisions of the last foregoing subsection, and he may again perform his functions as a member of the Assembly.

(3) For the purposes of this section—

(a) where a person is sentenced to two or more terms of imprisonment that are required to be served consecutively, account shall be taken only of any of those terms that exceeds twelve months ; and

(b) no account shall be taken of a sentence of imprisonment imposed as an alternative to or in default of the payment of a fine.

Temporary members of Assembly.

22.—(1) Whenever an official member of the Assembly is by reason of his illness or absence from the Islands or for any other reason incapable of performing the functions of his office, the Governor acting in his discretion may, by instrument under the public seal, appoint any public officer to be temporarily a member of the Assembly in his place.

(2) A person appointed under this section to be temporarily a member of the Assembly—

(a) shall hold his seat in the Assembly during Her Majesty's pleasure ; and

(b) shall vacate his seat when he is informed by the Governor that the member on account of whose incapacity he was appointed is again able to perform his functions as a member of the Assembly, or when the seat of that member becomes vacant.

(3) The Governor shall forthwith report to Her Majesty through a Secretary of State any appointment made under this section.

(4) Subject to the provisions of this section, the provisions of this Constitution shall apply to a person appointed to be temporarily a member of the Assembly as they apply to the member on account of whose incapacity he was appointed.

23.—(1) Any question whether a person has been validly appointed as an official member of the Assembly, or whether an official member of the Assembly has vacated his seat therein, shall be determined by the Governor acting in his discretion. *Determination of questions as to membership of Assembly.*

(2) Any question whether a person has been validly elected as a member of the Assembly, or whether an elected member of the Assembly has vacated his seat therein, shall be determined by the Grand Court, whose decision shall be final and not subject to any appeal.

(3) (*a*) An application to the Grand Court for the determination of any question whether a person has been validly elected as a member of the Assembly may be made by—

(i) a person who voted or had the right to vote at the election to which the application relates ;

(ii) a person claiming to have had the right to be returned at such election ;

(iii) a person alleging himself to have been a candidate at such election ; or

(iv) the Attorney-General.

(*b*) An application to the Grand Court for the determination of any question whether an elected member of the Assembly has vacated his seat therein may be made by—

(i) any elected member of the Assembly ; or

(ii) the Attorney-General.

(*c*) If any application referred to in paragraph (*a*) or (*b*) of this subsection is made by a person other than the Attorney-General, the Attorney-General may intervene and may then appear or be represented in the proceedings.

24.—(1) Any person who sits or votes in the Assembly knowing or having reasonable grounds for knowing that he is not entitled to do so shall be liable to a penalty not exceeding twenty pounds for each day upon which he so sits or votes. *Penalty for sitting or voting in Assembly when unqualified.*

(2) Any such penalty shall be recoverable by civil action in the Grand Court at the suit of the Governor.

25. Subject to the provisions of the next following section, a person shall be entitled to be registered as an elector in one electoral district only, but he shall not be entitled to be registered as an elector for elections to the Assembly unless he— *Qualifications of electors.*

(*a*) is a British subject of the age of eighteen years or over ; and

(*b*) either has been ordinarily resident in the Islands for a period or periods amounting to at least five years out of the seven years immediately preceding the date of registration and is resident therein at that date, or is domiciled and resident therein at that date.

Disqualifi-
cations of
electors.

26.—(1) A person shall not be entitled to be registered as an elector in any electoral district who—

    (a) subject to the provisions of the next following subsection, is under sentence of death imposed on him by a court in any part of the Commonwealth, or is serving a sentence of imprisonment (by whatever name called) exceeding twelve months imposed on him by such a court or substituted by competent authority for some other sentence imposed on him by such a court, or is under such a sentence of imprisonment the execution of which has been suspended ;

    (b) is a person certified to be insane or otherwise adjudged to be of unsound mind under any law in force in the Islands ; or

    (c) is disqualified for registration as an elector by any law in force in the Islands relating to offences connected with elections.

(2) The provisions of subsection (2) of section 19 of this Constitution shall apply for the purposes of the last foregoing subsection as they apply for the purposes of paragraph (e) of subsection (1) of the said section 19.

Right to
vote at
elections.

27.—(1) Any person who is registered as an elector in an electoral district shall, while so registered, be entitled to vote at any election for that district unless he is prohibited from so voting by any law in force in the Islands—

    (a) because he is a returning officer ; or

    (b) because he has been concerned in any offence connected with elections.

(2) No person shall vote at any election for any electoral district who—

    (a) is not registered as an elector in that district ;

    (b) has voted in another electoral district at the same election ;

    (c) is in lawful custody ; or

    (d) is for any other reason unable to attend to vote in person (except in so far as it may be provided by law that such persons may vote).

Law as to
elections.

28. Subject to the provisions of this Constitution, a law enacted under this Constitution may provide for the election of members of the Assembly, including (without prejudice to the generality of the foregoing power) the following matters, that is to say : —

    (a) the qualifications and disqualifications of electors ;

    (b) the registration of electors ;

    (c) the ascertainment of the qualifications of electors and of candidates for election ;

    (d) the division of the Islands into electoral districts for the purpose of elections ;

    (e) the holding of elections :

    (f) the determination of any question whether any person has been validly elected a member of the Assembly or whether the seat of any elected member in the Assembly has become vacant ;

(g) the definition and trial of offences connected with elections and the imposition of penalties therefor, including the disqualification for membership of the Assembly, or for registration as an elector, or for voting at elections, of any person concerned in any such offence ; and

(h) the disqualification for election as members of the Assembly of persons holding or acting in any office the functions of which involve any responsibility for, or in connection with, the conduct of any election or the compilation or revision of any electoral register.

Part IV

Powers and Procedure in Legislative Assembly

29. Subject to the provisions of this Constitution, the Governor, with the advice and consent of the Assembly, may make laws for the peace, order and good government of the Islands.

Power to make laws.

30. Subject to the provisions of this Constitution, the Governor and the Assembly shall, in the transaction of business and the making of laws, conform as nearly as may be to the directions contained in any Instructions under Her Majesty's Sign Manual and Signet which may from time to time be addressed to the Governor in that behalf.

Royal Instructions.

31.—(1) Subject to the provisions of this Constitution and of any Instructions under Her Majesty's Sign Manual and Signet, the Assembly may from time to time make, amend and revoke Standing Orders for the regulation and orderly conduct of its own proceedings and the despatch of business, and for the passing, intituling and numbering of Bills and for the presentation thereof to the Governor for assent ; but no such Standing Orders or amendment or revocation thereof shall have effect unless they have been approved by the Governor.

Standing Orders.

(2) The first Standing Orders of the Assembly shall, subject to the provisions of this Constitution, be the Standing Orders of the Legislative Assembly constituted by the Order of 1965 as in force immediately before the appointed day, with such adaptations and modifications as may be necessary, and those Standing Orders may be amended or revoked by Standing Orders made under the last foregoing subsection.

32.—(1) At sittings of the Assembly there shall preside—

Presiding in Assembly.

(a) the Governor ; or

(b) at any time when there is a person holding the office of Speaker, the Speaker ; or

(c) in the absence of the Governor or, as the case may be, of the Speaker, the senior official member of the Assembly.

(2) The Governor, acting in his discretion, may appoint a Speaker of the Legislative Assembly, who shall be a person, whether or not a member of the Assembly, who is qualified and not disqualified to be a member of the Assembly :

Provided that this sub-section shall not come into force until the Legislative Assembly has passed a resolution that there shall be an office of Speaker.

Assembly may transac business notwithstanding vacancies.

33. The Assembly shall not be disqualified for the transaction of business by reason of any vacancy in the membership thereof (including any vacancy not filled when the Assembly is first constituted or is reconstituted at any time) and any proceedings therein shall be valid notwithstanding that some person who was not entitled to do so sat or voted in the Assembly or otherwise took part in those proceedings.

Quorum.

34.—(1) If at any sitting of the Assembly a quorum is not present and any member of the Assembly who is present objects on that account to the transaction of business and, after such interval as may be prescribed in the Standing Orders of the Assembly, the person presiding at the sitting ascertains that a quorum is still not present, he shall adjourn the Assembly.

(2) For the purposes of this section a quorum shall consist of seven members of the Assembly in addition to the person presiding.

Voting.

35.—(1) Save as otherwise provided in this Constitution, all questions proposed for decision in the Assembly shall be determined by a majority of votes of the members present and voting.

(2) The Governor or other member presiding shall not vote unless on any question the votes are equally divided, in which case he shall have and exercise a casting vote.

Summoning of persons to assist Assembly.

36.—(1) The Governor or other person presiding may, when in his opinion the business before the Assembly makes it desirable, summon any person to a meeting of the Assembly notwithstanding that that person is not a member of the Assembly.

(2) Any person so summoned shall be entitled to take part as if he were a member in the proceedings of the Assembly relating to the matter in respect of which he was summoned, except that he may not vote.

Introduction of Bills.

37.—(1) Subject to the provisions of this Constitution and of the Standing Orders of the Assembly, any member may introduce any Bill or propose any motion for debate in, or may present any petition to, the Assembly, and the same shall be debated and disposed of according to the Standing Orders of the Assembly.

(2) Except on the recommendation of the Governor the Assembly shall not—

(*a*) proceed upon any Bill (including any amendment to a Bill) which, in the opinion of the person presiding in the Assembly, makes provision for imposing or increasing any tax, for imposing or increasing any charge on the revenues or other funds of the Islands or for altering any such charge otherwise than by reducing it or for compounding or remitting any debt due to the Islands ;

(*b*) proceed upon any motion (including any amendment to a motion) the effect of which, in the opinion of the person presiding in the Assembly, is that provision would be made for any of the purposes aforesaid ; or

(*c*) receive any petition which, in the opinion of the person presiding in the Assembly, requests that provision be made for any of the purposes aforesaid.

38.—(1) If the Governor considers that it is expedient— Governor's reserved power.

(*a*) in the interests of public order, public faith or good government (which expressions shall, without prejudice to their generality, include the responsibility of the Islands as a territory within the Commonwealth and all matters pertaining to the creation or abolition of any public office or to the salary or other conditions of service of any public officer) ; or

(*b*) in order to secure detailed control of the finances of the Islands during such time as, by virtue of the receipt of financial assistance by the Islands from Her Majesty's Exchequer in the United Kingdom for the purpose of balancing the annual budget or otherwise, such control rests with Her Majesty's Government,

that any Bill introduced, or any motion proposed, in the Assembly should have effect, then, if the Assembly fail to pass the Bill or to carry the motion within such time and in such form as the Governor thinks reasonable and expedient, the Governor may, at any time that he thinks fit, and notwithstanding any provision of this Constitution or of any other law in force in the Islands or of any Standing Orders of the Assembly, declare that the Bill or motion shall have effect as if it had been passed or carried by the Assembly either in the form in which it was introduced or proposed or with such amendments as the Governor thinks fit which have been moved or proposed in the Assembly or any committee thereof ; and the Bill or the motion shall be deemed thereupon to have been so passed or carried, and the provisions of this Constitution, and in particular the provisions relating to assent to Bills and disallowance of laws, shall have effect accordingly:

Provided that the Governor shall not exercise his powers under this subsection without having first consulted a Secretary of State, unless in his judgment the matter is so urgent that it is necessary for him to do so before having so consulted.

(2) The Governor shall forthwith report to a Secretary of State every case in which he makes any such declaration and the reasons therefor.

(3) If any member of the Assembly objects to any declaration made under this section, he may, within fourteen days of the making thereof, submit to the Governor a statement in writing of his reasons for so objecting, and a copy of the statement shall, if furnished by the member, be forwarded by the Governor as soon as practicable to a Secretary of State.

(4) Any declaration made under this section other than a declaration relating to a Bill may be revoked by a Secretary of State and the Governor shall forthwith cause notice of the revocation to be published by Government Notice ; and from the date of such publication any motion that is deemed to have been carried by virtue of the declaration shall cease to have effect and the provisions of sub-section (2) of section 38 of the Interpretation Act 1889 shall apply to the revocation as they apply to the repeal of an Act of Parliament.

(5) The powers of the Governor under this section shall be exercised by him acting in his discretion.

Assent to Bills.

39.—(1) A Bill shall not become a law until—

(a) the Governor has assented to it in Her Majesty's name and on Her Majesty's behalf and has signed it in token of his assent ; or

(b) Her Majesty has given Her assent to it through a Secretary of State and the Governor has signified Her assent by Proclamation.

(2) When a Bill is presented to the Governor for his assent, he shall, subject to the provisions of this Constitution and of any Instructions addressed to him under Her Majesty's Sign Manual and Signet or through a Secretary of State, declare that he assents, or refuses to assent, to it, or that he reserves the Bill for the signification of Her Majesty's pleasure :

Provided that the Governor shall reserve for the signification of Her Majesty's pleasure—

(a) any Bill which is in any way repugnant to, or inconsistent with, the provisions of this Constitution ; and

(b) any Bill which determines or regulates the privileges, immunities or powers of the Assembly or of its members ;

unless he has been authorized by a Secretary of State to assent to it.

(3) This section shall have effect in relation to any Bill passed by the Legislative Assembly subsisting immediately before the appointed day but not assented to before that day as it has effect in relation to Bills passed after the appointed day.

Return of Bills by Governor.

40. The Governor may return to the Assembly any Bill presented to him for his assent, transmitting therewith any amendments which he may recommend, and the Assembly shall deal with such recommendation.

Disallowance of laws.

41.—(1) Any law to which the Governor has given his assent may be disallowed by Her Majesty through a Secretary of State.

(2) Whenever a law has been disallowed by Her Majesty the Governor shall, as soon as practicable, cause notice of the disallowance to be published by Government Notice and the law shall be annulled with effect from the date of the publication of that notice.

(3) The provisions of subsection (2) of section 38 of the Interpretation Act 1889, shall apply to the annulment of any law under this section as they apply to the repeal of an Act of Parliament, save that any enactment repealed or amended by or in pursuance of that law shall have effect as from the date of the annulment as if that law had not been made.

Committees of Assembly.

42.—(1) The Governor may, by directions in writing, establish one or more committees of the Assembly having such functions in relation to the conduct of the business of the Government of the Islands in relation to such matters as may be prescribed by such directions, and (without prejudice to the generality of the foregoing power) directions establishing a committee under this subsection may include provision—

(a) with respect to the tenure of office of members of the committee ;

(b) regulating the manner in which the committee shall perform its functions and the procedure of the committee.

(2) Before establishing a committee under the last foregoing subsection the Governor shall consult with the Executive Council with respect to the establishment thereof, the directions to be given thereto and the number of members thereof, but shall not be obliged to act in accordance with its advice.

(3) A committee of the Assembly established under this section shall act in accordance with the policies of the Government of the Islands and with any directions given to the committee by the Governor:

Provided that the question whether it has so acted shall not be enquired into in any court.

(4) If the Governor so directs, a committee shall cease to deal with any particular business within its competence which is under consideration by the committee.

(5) The functions of a committee of the Assembly established under this section shall not include functions in relation to the conduct of business in respect of any matter referred to in section 7(1)(c) of this Constitution.

(6) The provisions of this section shall be without prejudice to the establishment, by or under the rules of procedure of the Assembly, of committees of the Assembly for the purpose of the exercise of its function under Part IV of this Constitution or the establishment by the Governor of committees of the Assembly for special purposes relating to any of the matters mentioned in the last foregoing subsection.

43.—(1) A committee established under section 42(1) of this Constitution shall consist of a chairman and such number of other members as the Governor may decide: **Membership of committees.**

Provided that the majority of the members of such a committee shall be elected members of the Assembly, appointed by the Governor in accordance with the advice of the elected members of the Assembly.

(2) The Chairman of a committee established under section 42(1) of this Constitution shall be a member of the Executive Council who has been charged with responsibility under section 9 of this Constitution and whose responsibility corresponds as nearly as maybe to the functions of such committee.

(3) The members of a committee who are not members of the Assembly shall be appointed by the Governor acting in his discretion.

44. Except for the purpose of enabling this section to be complied with, no official or elected member of the Assembly shall be permitted to take part in its proceedings until he has made before the Governor, or some other person authorized in that behalf by the Governor, acting in his discretion, an oath of allegiance in the form set out in the Schedule to this Constitution. **Oath of Allegiance.**

45. A law enacted under this Constitution may determine and regulate the privileges, immunities and powers of the Assembly and its members, but no such privileges, immunities or powers shall exceed those of the Commons' House of Parliament of the United Kingdom or of the members thereof. **Privileges of Assembly and members.**

Sessions.   **46.**—(1) Subject to the provisions of this Constitution, the sessions of the Assembly shall be held at such places and begin at such times as the Governor may from time to time by Proclamation appoint.

(2) The first session of the Assembly shall begin within twelve months after the appointed day; and thereafter there shall be at least one session of the Assembly in every year, so however that there shall be an interval of less than twelve months between the last sitting in one session and the first sitting in the next session.

Prorogation and dissolution.   **47.**—(1) The Governor may at any time, by Proclamation, prorogue or dissolve the Assembly.

(2) The Governor shall dissolve the Assembly at the expiration of four years from the date when the Assembly first meets after any general election unless it has been sooner dissolved.

General elections.   **48.** There shall be a general election at such time within two months after every dissolution of the Assembly as the Governor shall by Proclamation appoint.

PART V

Appeals from the Grand Court

Appeals to Court of Appeal for Jamaica; saving.   **49.**—(1) Subject to the provisions of this section, the Court of Appeal for Jamaica shall have such jurisdiction to hear and determine appeals (including reserved questions of law and cases stated) from the Grand Court of the Islands and, in connection with such appeals, such powers and authorities as may be conferred upon it by any law for the time being in force in the Islands.

(2) The foregoing subsection shall not apply to appeals relating to any matter in respect of which this Constitution or any other law provides that the decision of the Grand Court of the Islands is to be final.

PART VI

Miscellaneous

Interpretation.   **50.**—(1) In this Constitution unless it is otherwise provided or required by the context—

" appointed day " means the date as from which this Constitution (other than Part II thereof) has effect under section 2 (1) of the Cayman Islands (Constitution) Order 1972 ;

" Assembly " means the Legislative Assembly of the Islands established by this Constitution ;

" functions " includes jurisdictions, powers and duties ;

" Government Notice " means a Cayman Islands Government Notice ;

" Governor " means the person for the time being holding the office of Governor of the Islands, and includes any person for the time being lawfully performing the functions of that office and, to the extent to which a deputy appointed under section 4 of this Constitution is authorised to act, that deputy ;

" the Islands " means the Cayman Islands ;

" law " includes any instrument having the force of law made in exercise of a power conferred by a law ;

" the Order of 1965 " means the Cayman Islands (Constitution) Order 1965 as amended by subsequent Orders in Council ;

" public office " means, subject to the provisions of the next following subsection, an office of emolument in the public service ;

" public officer " means the holder of any public office, and includes a person appointed to act in any public office ;

" the public service " means the service of the Crown in a civil capacity in respect of the government of the Islands ;

" session " means the meetings of the Assembly commencing when the Assembly first meets after being constituted under this Constitution, or after its prorogation or dissolution at any time, and terminating when the Assembly is prorogued or is dissolved without having been prorogued ;

" sitting " means a period during which the Assembly is sitting continuously without adjournment and includes any period during which the Assembly is in committee.

(2) For the purposes of this Constitution, a person shall not be considered to hold a public office by reason only that he—

(a) is in receipt of any remuneration or allowance as a member of the Executive Council or the Assembly ;

(b) is in receipt of a pension or other like allowance in respect of service under the Crown ; or

(c) holds an office the holder of which is declared by any law in force in the Islands not to be disqualified for election as a member of the Assembly.

(3) Any person who has vacated his seat in any body, or has vacated any office established by this Constitution may, if qualified, again be appointed or elected as a member of that body or to that office, as the case may be, from time to time.

(4) A reference in this Constitution to the holder of an office by the term designating his office shall be construed as a reference to any person for the time being lawfully performing the functions of that office.

(5) Without prejudice to the last foregoing subsection—

(a) where the holder of any office constituted by or under this Constitution is on leave of absence pending the relinquishment of that office, the person or authority having power to make appointments to that office may appoint another person thereto ; and

(b) where two or more persons concurrently hold the same office by virtue of the foregoing paragraph, the person last appointed shall in respect of any function conferred on the holder of that office be deemed to be the sole holder thereof.

(6) Any power conferred by this Constitution to make any Proclamation or order or to give any directions shall be construed as including a power exercisable in like manner to amend or revoke any such Proclamation, order or directions.

(7) Where a person is required by this Constitution to make an oath he shall if he so desires be permitted to comply with that requirement by making an affirmation in accordance with the provisions of the Schedule to this Constitution.

(8) For the purposes of this Constitution the resignation of a member of any body or holder of any office thereby established that is required to be addressed to any person shall, unless otherwise expressly provided, be deemed to have effect from the time at which it is received by that person.

(9) For the purposes of this Constitution a person shall not be regarded as absent from the Islands or as unable to perform any of his functions thereunder by reason only that he is in passage between any one of the Islands and another or from one part of any Island to another part.

Public Seal.   **51.** The Governor shall keep and use the public seal for sealing all things that should pass that seal.

Grants of land.   **52.** Subject to the provisions of any law for the time being in force in the Islands, the Governor or any person duly authorised by him in writing under his hand may, in Her Majesty's name and on Her behalf, make and execute under the public seal grants and dispositions of any land or other immovable property within the Islands that may be lawfully granted or disposed of by Her Majesty.

Governor's power of pardon.   **53.** Subject to any Instructions given to him by Her Majesty under Her Sign Manual and Signet, the Governor may, in Her Majesty's name and on Her behalf—

(a) grant to any person concerned in the commission of any offence for which he may be tried in the Islands, or to any person convicted of any offence under any law in force in the Islands, a pardon, either free or subject to lawful conditions ;

(b) grant to any person so convicted a respite, either indefinite or for a specified period, of the execution of any sentence passed on him in respect of the conviction ;

(c) substitute a less severe form of punishment for that imposed on any such person by any such sentence ; or

(d) remit the whole or any part of any such sentence or of any penalty or forfeiture due to Her Majesty by reason of the conviction.

Offices and appointments.   **54.** The Governor, in Her Majesty's name and on Her behalf, may constitute such offices for the Islands as may lawfully be constituted by Her Majesty and, subject to the provisions of any law in force in the Islands, may make appointments (including appointments on promotion and transfer) to any such office ; and any person so appointed shall, unless it is otherwise provided by any such law, hold office during Her Majesty's pleasure.

Discipline.   **55.**—(1) Subject to the provisions of any law in force in the Islands, the Governor may for cause shown to his satisfaction dismiss or suspend from the exercise of his office any person holding a public office, or take such disciplinary action as may seem to him to be desirable.

(2) The reference in this section to the power to dismiss any person holding a public office shall be construed as including a reference to any power to require or permit a person to retire.

56.—(1) Subject to the provisions of this section, all offices and authorities established by or under the Order of 1965 and existing immediately before the appointed day shall on and after that day, so far as consistent with the provisions of this Constitution, continue as if they had been established by or under this Constitution ; and any person who immediately before that day is holding or acting in any such office or as a member of any such authority shall on and after that day continue to hold or act in that office or to be such a member as if he had been appointed thereto or as the case may be elected as such in accordance with this Constitution and had made any oath thereby required. *Existing offices and authorities.*

(2) The provisions of this section shall be without prejudice to any powers conferred by or under this Constitution upon any person or authority to make provision for any matter, including (but without prejudice to the generality of the foregoing words) the establishment and abolition of offices, courts of law and authorities and the appointment, election or selection of persons to hold or act in any office or to be members of any court or authority and their removal from office.

57.—(1) All Acts, Ordinances, rules, regulations, orders and other instruments made under or having effect by virtue of the Order of 1965 and having effect as part of the law of the Islands immediately before the appointed day shall on and after the appointed day have effect as if they had been made under or by virtue of this Constitution. *Existing laws.*

(2) Subject to the provisions of the next following subsection, the existing laws shall on and after the appointed day be construed with such modifications, adaptations, qualifications and exceptions as are necessary to bring them into conformity with this Constitution.

(3) Subject to the provisions of this Constitution, the Governor may by regulations at any time within eighteen months from the appointed day make such amendments to any existing law as appear to him to be necessary or expedient for bringing that law into conformity with the provisions of this Constitution or otherwise for giving effect or enabling effect to be given to those provisions.

(4) In this section the expression " existing laws " means laws and instruments (other than Acts of the Parliament of the United Kingdom and instruments made thereunder) having effect as part of the law of the Islands immediately before the appointed day.

58. Her Majesty hereby reserves to Herself power, with the advice of Her Privy Council, to make laws for the peace, order and good government of the Islands. *Power reserved to Her Majesty.*

Sections
1(3), 3(2),
12 and 44.

SCHEDULE TO THE CONSTITUTION

FORMS OF OATHS AND AFFIRMATIONS

1. *Oath of Allegiance*

I .... do swear that I will be faithful and bear true allegiance to Her Majesty Queen Elizabeth the Second, Her Heirs and Successors, according to law. So help me God.

2. *Oath for due execution of office*

I .... do swear that I will well and truly serve Her Majesty Queen Elizabeth the Second, Her Heirs and Successors, in the office (*here insert the description of the office*). So help me God.

3. *Affirmations.* In the forms above respectively set forth, for the word " swear " there shall be substituted the words " solemnly and sincerely affirm and declare ", and the words " So help me God " shall be omitted.

EXPLANATORY NOTE

(*This Note is not part of the Order.*)

This Order, which is made under section 5 of the West Indies Act 1962, confers a new constitution on the Cayman Islands, and supersedes the Cayman Islands (Constitution) Order 1965, which is revoked.

The Constitution contains provision with regard to the office of Governor, the Executive Council, the Legislature and appeals from the Grand Court.

While the constitution requires the Governor, in general, to exercise his functions in accordance with the advice of the Executive Council, it provides for him to be responsible in his discretion for defence, external affairs, internal security, the police and certain matters relating to the public service.

Provision is made for the assignment of responsibility for business or departments of the Government to members of the Executive Council.

The composition of the Legislative Assembly is altered by abolition of the three seats of nominated members.

There is provision whereby a Speaker can be appointed by the Governor if the Legislative Assembly resolve that such an appointment be made.

1972 No. 1102

FUGITIVE CRIMINAL

The Extradition (Hijacking) (Amendment) Order 1972

Made - - - -	*26th July* 1972
Laid before Parliament	*1st August* 1972
Coming into Operation	*22nd August* 1972

At the Court at Buckingham Palace, the 26th day of July 1972

Present,

The Queen's Most Excellent Majesty in Council

Her Majesty, in exercise of the powers conferred upon Her by sections 2, 17 and 21 of the Extradition Act 1870(**a**) and sections 3(2), 6(1) and 6(3) of the Hijacking Act 1971(**b**), or otherwise in Her Majesty vested, is pleased, by and with the advice of Her Privy Council, to order, and it is hereby ordered, as follows:—

1. This Order may be cited as the Extradition (Hijacking) (Amendment) Order 1972 and shall come into operation on 22nd August 1972.

2. The Interpretation Act 1889(**c**) shall apply for the interpretation of this Order as it applies for the interpretation of an Act of Parliament.

3. The Extradition (Hijacking) Order 1971(**d**) shall be amended by adding to Schedule 2 (which names the foreign States with which the United Kingdom has extradition treaties in force and which are parties to the Convention for the Suppression of Unlawful Seizure of Aircraft signed at The Hague on 16th December 1970(**e**)) the following entries:—

State	Date of Extradition Treaty	Date of Entry into force of Convention for the State concerned
Chile	26th January 1897	3rd March 1972
Finland... ...	30th May 1924	14th January 1972
Paraguay ...	12th September 1908	5th March 1972
Iraq	2nd May 1932	29th January 1972
Poland	11th January 1932	20th April 1972

(**a**) 1870 c. 52.   (**b**) 1971 c. 70.   (**c**) 1889 c. 63.
(**d**) S.I. 1971/2102 (1971 III, p. 6193).   (**e**) Cmnd. 4956.

4. The Extradition (Hijacking) Order 1971 shall be amended by adding to Part I of Schedule 3 (which names the foreign States with which the United Kingdom has no extradition treaties in force and which are parties to the Convention for the Suppression of Unlawful Seizure of Aircraft signed at The Hague on 16th December 1970) the following entries:—

State	Date of Entry into force of Convention for the State concerned
Brazil	13th February 1972
Byelorussia	29th January 1972
Iran	24th February 1972
Ukraine	20th March 1972

W. G. Agnew.

EXPLANATORY NOTE

(This Note is not part of the Order.)

This Order applies the Extradition Acts 1870 to 1935, as amended, so as to make the offence of hijacking extraditable in respect of Chile, Finland, Paraguay, Iraq, Poland, Brazil, Byelorussia, Iran and Ukraine.

STATUTORY INSTRUMENTS

1972 No. 1103 (L.13)

COUNTY COURTS

The County Courts (Administration Order Jurisdiction) Order 1972

Made - - -	26*th July* 1972
Laid before Parliament	1*st August* 1972
Coming into Operation	2*nd October* 1972

At the Court at Buckingham Palace, the 26th day of July 1972

Present,

The Queen's Most Excellent Majesty in Council

Her Majesty, in exercise of the powers conferred on Her by section 20(2) of the Administration of Justice Act 1965(**a**), is pleased, by and with the advice of Her Privy Council, to order, and it is hereby ordered, as follows:—

1.—(1) This Order may be cited as the County Courts (Administration Order Jurisdiction) Order 1972 and shall come into operation on 2nd October 1972.

(2) The Interpretation Act 1889(**b**) shall apply to the interpretation of this Order as it applies to the interpretation of an Act of Parliament.

2. The County Courts (Administration Order Jurisdiction) Order 1970(**c**) shall be varied by increasing from £500 to £1,000 the sum which, by virtue of article 2 of that Order, is to be substituted for the sum specified in section 148(1) and (3) of the County Courts Act 1959(**d**) as amended by section 20(1) of the Administration of Justice Act 1965.

W. G. Agnew.

EXPLANATORY NOTE

(This Note is not part of the Order.)

This Order increases the jurisdiction of county courts to make administration orders by raising from £500 to £1,000 the limit on the total indebtedness of a debtor in respect of whom an order may be made.

(**a**) 1965 c. 2.
(**c**) S.I. 1970/1441 (1970 III, p. 4700).

(**b**) 1889 c. 63.
(**d**) 1959 c. 22.

STATUTORY INSTRUMENTS

1972 No. 1104

JUDGES

The Judges' Remuneration Order 1972

Laid before Parliament in draft

Made   - - -   26th July 1972

At the Court at Buckingham Palace, the 26th day of July 1972

Present,

The Queen's Most Excellent Majesty in Council

Whereas a draft of the following Order was laid before Parliament and approved by resolution of each House:

Now, therefore, in exercise of the powers conferred on Her by section 1 of the Judges' Remuneration Act 1965(**a**) and all other powers enabling Her in that behalf Her Majesty, by and with the advice of Her Privy Council, is pleased to order, and it is hereby ordered, as follows:—

1. This Order may be cited as the Judges' Remuneration Order 1972.

2. There shall be paid to the holder of any judicial office listed in the schedule to this Order a salary at the annual rate specified in relation to that office in the second column of that schedule instead of the salary specified in the second column of the schedule to the Judges' Remuneration (No. 2) Order 1970(**b**).

3. The Judges' Remuneration (No. 2) Order 1970 is hereby revoked.

W. G. Agnew.

SCHEDULE

Judicial Office	*Salary* £
Lord of Appeal in Ordinary	17,250
Lord Chief Justice	18,500
Master of the Rolls	17,250
President of the Family Division	17,250
Lord Justice of Appeal	15,750
Puisne Judge of the High Court of Justice	15,750
Lord President of the Court of Session	15,750
Lord Justice Clerk	15,500
Ordinary Judge of the Court of Session	13,750
Lord Chief Justice of Northern Ireland	15,000
Lord Justice of Appeal in Northern Ireland	13,500
Puisne Judge of the High Court of Justice in Northern Ireland	13,500

(**a**) 1965 c. 61.   (**b**) S.I. 1970/1950 (1970 III, p. 6387).

EXPLANATORY NOTE

(This Note is not part of the Order.)

This Order increases the salaries of the holders of the high judicial offices mentioned in the schedule to the amounts there specified.

STATUTORY INSTRUMENTS

1972 No. 1105

MERCHANT SHIPPING

MASTERS AND SEAMEN

The Merchant Shipping (Certificates of Competency as A.B.) (Gilbert and Ellice Islands Colony) Order 1972

Made - - -	*26th July* 1972
Laid before Parliament	*1st August* 1972
Coming into Operation	*1st September* 1972

At the Court at Buckingham Palace, the 26th day of July 1972

Present,

The Queen's Most Excellent Majesty in Council

Whereas provision is made by the law of the Gilbert and Ellice Islands Colony for the grant of certificates of competency as A.B.:

And whereas the Secretary of State has reported to Her Majesty that he is satisfied that the conditions under which such certificates are granted require standards of competency not lower than those required for the grant of a certificate in pursuance of regulations made under section 5 of the Merchant Shipping Act 1948(a):

Now, therefore, Her Majesty, in pursuance of the powers vested in Her by section 5(4) of the Merchant Shipping Act 1948 and of all other powers enabing Her in that behalf, is pleased, by and with the advice of Her Privy Council, to order, and it is hereby ordered, as follows: —

1.—(1) This Order may be cited as the Merchant Shipping (Certificates of Competency as A.B.) (Gilbert and Ellice Islands Colony) Order 1972 and shall come into operation on 1st September 1972.

(2) In this Order "the Act" means the Merchant Shipping Act 1948.

(3) The Interpretation Act 1889(b) shall apply to the interpretation of this Order as it applies to the interpretation of an Act of Parliament.

2. Certificates of competency as A.B. granted in the Gilbert and Ellice Islands Colony shall have the same effect for the purposes of section 5 of the Act as if they had been granted in pursuance of regulations made under that section.

3. Any of the provisions of the regulations made under section 5 of the Act applying section 104 of the Merchant Shipping Act 1894(c) to certificates of competency as A.B. granted under those regulations shall apply in relation

---

(a) 1948 c. 44.　　　　(b) 1889 c. 63.　　　　(c) 1894 c. 60.

to certificates of competency as A.B. granted in the Gilbert and Ellice Islands Colony.

W. G. Agnew.

EXPLANATORY NOTE

(This Note is not part of the Order.)

This Order provides for the recognition in the United Kingdom of certificates of competency as A.B. granted to seamen in the Gilbert and Ellice Islands Colony.

STATUTORY INSTRUMENTS

1972 No. 1116

WAGES COUNCILS

The Wages Regulation (Retail Furnishing and Allied Trades) Order 1972

Made - - - -	24*th July* 1972
Coming into Operation	4*th September* 1972

Whereas the Secretary of State has received from the Retail Furnishing and Allied Trades Wages Council (Great Britain) the wages regulation proposals set out in the Schedule hereto;

Now, therefore, the Secretary of State in exercise of his powers under section 11 of the Wages Councils Act 1959(a), and of all other powers enabling him in that behalf, hereby makes the following Order:—

1. This Order may be cited as the Wages Regulation (Retail Furnishing and Allied Trades) Order 1972.

2.—(1) In this Order the expression "the specified date" means the 4th September 1972, provided that where, as respects any worker who is paid wages at intervals not exceeding seven days, that date does not correspond with the beginning of the period for which the wages are paid, the expression "the specified date" means, as respects that worker, the beginning of the next such period following that date.

(2) The Interpretation Act 1889(b) shall apply to the interpretation of this Order as it applies to the interpretation of an Act of Parliament and as if this Order and the Order hereby revoked were Acts of Parliament.

3. The wages regulation proposals set out in the Schedule hereto shall have effect as from the specified date and as from that date the Wages Regulation (Retail Furnishing and Allied Trades) Order 1971(c) shall cease to have effect.

Signed by order of the Secretary of State.
24th July 1972.

R. R. D. McIntosh,
Deputy Secretary,
Department of Employment.

(a) 1959 c. 69.   (b) 1889 c. 63.
(c) S.I. 1971/1518 (1971 III, p. 4220).

ARRANGEMENT OF SCHEDULE

Part I : STATUTORY MINIMUM REMUNERATION

Part II: ANNUAL HOLIDAY AND HOLIDAY REMUNERATION

Part III : GENERAL

SCHEDULE   Article 3

The following minimum remuneration and provisions as to holidays and holiday remuneration shall be substituted for the statutory minimum remuneration and the provisions as to holidays and holiday remuneration fixed by the Wages Regulation (Retail Furnishing and Allied Trades) Order 1971 (hereinafter referred to as "Order R.F.A. (56)").

Part I : STATUTORY MINIMUM REMUNERATION
APPLICATION

1. Subject to the provisions of paragraphs 2, 2A, 7 and 10, the minimum remuneration payable to workers to whom this Schedule applies shall be the remuneration set out in paragraphs 3, 3A, 4, 5, 5A, 5B and 6: Provided that any increase in remuneration payable under the provisions of paragraphs 5, 5A, 5B or 6 shall become effective on the first day of the first full pay week following the date upon which the increase would otherwise become payable under those provisions.

HOURS ON WHICH REMUNERATION IS BASED

2.—(1) *Up to and including 30th September 1972* the minimum remuneration specified in this Part of this Schedule relates to a week of *41* hours exclusive of overtime and, except in the case of guaranteed weekly remuneration under paragraph 10, is subject to a proportionate reduction according as the number of hours worked is less than *41*.

(2) In calculating the remuneration for the purpose of this Schedule recognised breaks for meal times shall, subject to the provisions of paragraph 8, be excluded.

2A.—(1) *On and after 1st October 1972* the minimum remuneration specified in this Part of this Schedule relates to a week of *40* hours exclusive of overtime and, except in the case of guaranteed weekly remuneration under paragraph 10, is subject to a proportionate reduction according as the number of hours worked is less than *40*.

(2) In calculating the remuneration for the purpose of this Schedule recognised breaks for meal times shall, subject to the provisions of paragraph 8, be excluded.

SHOP MANAGERS AND SHOP MANAGERESSES

3. *Up to and including 3rd September 1973* and subject to the provisions of this paragraph, the minimum remuneration payable to Shop Managers and Shop Manageresses employed in the areas specified in Column 2 of the next following table shall be the amount appearing in the said Column 2 against the amount of weekly trade shown in Column 1.

Column 1	Column 2					
	LONDON AREA per week		PROVINCIAL A AREA per week		PROVINCIAL B AREA per week	
	Male	Female	Male	Female	Male	Female
WEEKLY TRADE	£	£	£	£	£	£
Under £175 ...	18·90	18·00	18·50	17·60	17·90	17·10
£175 and under £200	19·15	18·25	18·75	17·85	18·15	17·35
£200 „ „ £240	19·35	18·45	18·95	18·05	18·35	17·55
£240 „ „ £280	19·55	18·65	19·15	18·25	18·55	17·75
£280 „ „ £320	19·75	18·85	19·35	18·45	18·75	17·95
£320 „ „ £360	19·95	19·05	19·55	18·65	18·95	18·15
£360 „ „ £400	20·15	19·25	19·75	18·85	19·15	18·35
£400 „ „ £440	20·35	19·45	19·95	19·05	19·35	18·55
£440 „ „ £480	20·55	19·65	20·15	19·25	19·55	18·75
£480 „ „ £520	20·75	19·85	20·35	19·45	19·75	18·95
£520 „ „ £560	20·95	20·05	20·55	19·65	19·95	19·15
£560 „ „ £600	21·15	20·25	20·75	19·85	20·15	19·35
£600 „ „ £640	21·35	20·45	20·95	20·05	20·35	19·55
£640 „ „ £680	21·55	20·65	21·15	20·25	20·55	19·75
£680 „ „ £720	21·75	20·85	21·35	20·45	20·75	19·95
£720 „ „ £760	21·95	21·05	21·55	20·65	20·95	20·15
£760 „ „ £800	22·15	21·25	21·75	20·85	21·15	20·35
£800 „ „ £840	22·35	21·45	21·95	21·05	21·35	20·55
£840 „ „ £880	22·55	21·65	22·15	21·25	21·55	20·75
£880 „ „ £920	22·75	21·85	22·35	21·45	21·75	20·95
£920 „ „ £960	22·95	22·05	22·55	21·65	21·95	21·15
£960 „ „ £1000	23·15	22·25	22·75	21·85	22·15	21·35
£1,000 and over ...	23·35	22·45	22·95	22·05	22·35	21·55

For the purposes of this paragraph "weekly trade" shall be calculated half-yearly and based on the period of 12 months immediately preceding the commencement of each half-year in the following manner:—

For the period of 26 weeks beginning (1) with the fifth week or (2) with the 31st week following the accounting date in any year, the weekly trade of a shop shall be one fifty-second of the amount of the total receipts for goods sold at that shop during the 52 weeks immediately preceding the accounting date (in the case of (1) hereof) or the 26th week following the accounting date (in the case of (2) hereof).

Except as provided as aforesaid, the weekly trade in respect of any week shall be the amount of the total receipts for goods sold at the shop in the preceding week.

In this paragraph—

(*a*) "accounting date" means that date in each year on which the books of accounts of a shop are closed for the purpose of preparing the annual accounts in respect of that shop, or, in the absence of any such date, the 5th April in any year;

(*b*) the expression "receipts for goods sold" includes receipts in respect of hire purchase transactions;

(c) "shop" includes any part of the shop not engaged in the retail furnishing and allied trades.

3A. *On and after 4th September 1973* and subject to the provisions of this paragraph, the minimum remuneration payable to Shop Managers and Shop Manageresses employed in the areas specified in Column 2 of the next following table shall be the amount appearing in the said Column 2 against the amount of weekly trade shown in Column 1.

Column 1	Column 2		
	LONDON AREA per week	PROVINCIAL A AREA per week	PROVINCIAL B AREA per week
	£	£	£
WEEKLY TRADE			
Under £175	18·90	18·50	17·90
£175 and under £200	19·15	18·75	18·15
£200 ,, ,, £240	19·35	18·95	18·35
£240 ,, ,, £280	19·55	19·15	18·55
£280 ,, ,, £320	19·75	19·35	18·75
£320 ,, ,, £360	19·95	19·55	18·95
£360 ,, ,, £400	20·15	19·75	19·15
£400 ,, ,, £440	20·35	19·95	19·35
£440 ,, ,, £480	20·55	20·15	19·55
£480 ,, ,, £520	20·75	20·35	19·75
£520 ,, ,, £560	20·95	20·55	19·95
£560 ,, ,, £600	21·15	20·75	20·15
£600 ,, ,, £640	21·35	20·95	20·35
£640 ,, ,, £680	21·55	21·15	20·55
£680 ,, ,, £720	21·75	21·35	20·75
£720 ,, ,, £760	21·95	21·55	20·95
£760 ,, ,, £800	22·15	21·75	21·15
£800 ,, ,, £840	22·35	21·95	21·35
£840 ,, ,, £880	22·55	22·15	21·55
£880 ,, ,, £920	22·75	22·35	21·75
£920 ,, ,, £960	22·95	22·55	21·95
£960 ,, ,, £1,000	23·15	22·75	22·15
£1,000 and over	23·35	22·95	22·35

For the purposes of this paragraph "weekly trade" shall be calculated half-yearly and based on the period of 12 months immediately preceding the commencement of each half-year in the following manner:—

For the period of 26 weeks beginning (1) with the fifth week or (2) with the 31st week following the accounting date in any year, the weekly trade of a shop shall be one fifty-second of the amount of the total receipts for goods sold at that shop during the 52 weeks immediately preceding the accounting date (in the case of (1) hereof) or the 26th week following the accounting date (in the case of (2) hereof).

Except as provided as aforesaid, the weekly trade in respect of any week shall be the amount of the total receipts for goods sold at the shop in the preceding week.

In this paragraph—

(a) "accounting date" means that date in each year on which the books of accounts of a shop are closed for the purposes of preparing the annual accounts in respect of that shop, or, in the absence of any such date, the 5th April in any year;

(b) the expression "receipts for goods sold" includes receipts in respect of hire purchase transactions;

(c) "shop" includes any part of the shop not engaged in the retail furnishing and allied trades.

TEMPORARY SHOP MANAGERS AND
TEMPORARY SHOP MANAGERESSES

4.—(1) Subject to the provisions of this paragraph, the minimum remuneration payable to Temporary Shop Managers and Temporary Shop Manageresses, for each continuous period of employment as Temporary Shop Manager or Temporary Shop Manageress (reckoned in accordance with the provisions of sub-paragraph (2) of this paragraph), shall be the appropriate minimum remuneration for a Shop Manager or Shop Manageress, as the case may be, under the provisions of paragraphs 3 or 3A.

(2) In reckoning any continuous period of employment as Temporary Shop Manager or Temporary Shop Manageress for the purposes of sub-paragraph (1) of this paragraph, no account shall be taken of any period of employment:—

(a) not exceeding two consecutive working days; or

(b) not exceeding a total of two weeks in any year, being a period when the Shop Manager or Shop Manageress is absent on holiday:

Provided that for the purposes of this paragraph where in any year a worker is employed by the same employer as a Temporary Shop Manager or Temporary Shop Manageress at more than one shop during the absence on holiday of the Shop Manager or Shop Manageress, the first period of such employment and any subsequent periods of such employment in the same year shall be treated as a continuous period of employment.

(3) The minimum remuneration payable to Temporary Shop Managers and Temporary Shop Manageresses for any period of employment mentioned in (a) or (b) of sub-paragraph (2) of this paragraph, shall be not less than the appropriate minimum remuneration for a *Sales Supervisor* under the provisions of this Schedule.

(4) For the purposes of this paragraph "year" means the 12 months commencing with 1st January and ending with 31st December.

WORKERS OTHER THAN SHOP MANAGERS, SHOP MANAGERESSES, TEMPORARY SHOP MANAGERS, TEMPORARY SHOP MANAGERESSES OR TRANSPORT WORKERS

5. *Up to and including 3rd March 1973* and subject to the provisions of paragraph 1, the minimum remuneration payable to male or female workers of the classes specified in Column 1 of the next following table employed in the London Area, Provincial A Area or Provincial B Area, as the case may be, shall be the appropriate amount set out in Column 2.

Column 1	Column 2					
	LONDON AREA per week		PROVINCIAL A AREA per week		PROVINCIAL B AREA per week	
	Male	Female	Male	Female	Male	Female
	£	£	£	£	£	£
(1) *SALES SUPERVISOR* ...	17·00	15·25	16·50	15·00	15·90	14·50
(2) CLERK GRADE I	16·50	14·75	16·00	14·50	15·40	14·00
(3) CLERK GRADE II, *SALES ASSISTANT,* CASHIER, CENTRAL WAREHOUSE WORKER, STOCKHAND OR VAN SALESMAN:—						
Aged *21* years or over	15·50	13·75	15·00	13·50	14·40	13·00
„ 20 and under 21 years ...	13·20	11·70	12·75	11·50	12·25	11·05
„ 19 „ „ 20 „ ...	12·40	11·00	12·00	10·80	11·50	10·40
„ 18 „ „ 19 „ ...	11·65	10·30	11·25	10·15	10·80	9·75
„ 17 „ „ 18 „ ...	10·10	8·95	9·75	8·80	9·35	8·45
„ 16 „ „ 17 „ ...	9·30	8·25	9·00	8·10	8·65	7·80
„ under 16 years	8·55	7·55	8·25	7·45	7·90	7·15
(4) *SHOP WORKER, PORTER OR GENERAL WORKER:—*						
Aged *21* years or over	15·00	13·25	14·50	13·00	13·90	12·50
„ 20 and under 21 years ...	12·75	11·25	12·35	11·05	11·80	10·65
„ 19 „ „ 20 „ ...	12·00	10·60	11·60	10·40	11·10	10·00
„ 18 „ „ 19 „ ...	11·25	9·95	10·90	9·75	10·45	9·40
„ 17 „ „ 18 „ ...	9·75	8·60	9·45	8·45	9·05	8·15
„ 16 „ „ 17 „ ...	9·00	7·95	8·70	7·80	8·35	7·50
„ under 16 years	8·25	7·30	8·00	7·15	7·65	6·90

5A. *On and after 4th March 1973 and up to and including 3rd September 1973* and subject to the provisions of paragraph 1, the minimum remuneration payable to male or female workers of the classes specified in Column 1 of the next following table employed in the London Area, Provincial A Area or Provincial B Area, as the case may be, shall be the appropriate amount set out in Column 2.

Column 1	Column 2					
	LONDON AREA per week		PROVINCIAL A AREA per week		PROVINCIAL B AREA per week	
	Male	Female	Male	Female	Male	Female
	£	£	£	£	£	£
(1) *SALES SUPERVISOR* ...	17·00	16·15	16·50	15·70	15·90	15·10
(2) CLERK GRADE I	16·50	15·70	16·00	15·20	15·40	14·65
(3) CLERK GRADE II, *SALES ASSISTANT,* CASHIER, CENTRAL WAREHOUSE WORKER, STOCKHAND OR VAN SALESMAN:—						
Aged *21* years or over ...	15·50	14·75	15·00	14·25	14·40	13·70
„ 20 and under 21 years ...	13·20	12·55	12·75	12·10	12·25	11·65
„ 19 „ „ 20 „ ...	12·40	11·80	12·00	11·40	11·50	10·95
„ 18 „ „ 19 „ ...	11·65	11·05	11·25	10·70	10·80	10·25
„ 17 „ „ 18 „ ...	10·10	9·60	9·75	9·25	9·35	8·90
„ 16 „ „ 17 „ ...	9·30	8·85	9·00	8·55	8·65	8·20
„ under 16 years	8·55	8·10	8·25	7·85	7·90	7·50
(4) *SHOP WORKER, PORTER OR GENERAL WORKER:—*						
Aged *21* years or over ...	15·00	14·25	14·50	13·80	13·90	13·20
„ 20 and under 21 years ...	12·75	12·10	12·35	11·75	11·80	11·20
„ 19 „ „ 20 „ ...	12·00	11·40	11·60	11·00	11·10	10·55
„ 18 „ „ 19 „ ...	11·25	10·70	10·90	10·35	10·45	9·95
„ 17 „ „ 18 „ ...	9·75	9·25	9·45	9·00	9·05	8·60
„ 16 „ „ 17 „ ...	9·00	8·55	8·70	8·25	8·35	7·95
„ under 16 years	8·25	7·85	8·00	7·60	7·65	7·25

5B. *On and after 4th September 1973* and subject to the provisions of paragraph 1, the minimum remuneration payable to workers of the classes specified in Column 1 of the next following table employed in the London Area, Provincial A Area or Provincial B Area, as the case may be, shall be the appropriate amount set out in Column 2.

Column 1	Column 2		
	LONDON AREA per week	PROVINCIAL A AREA per week	PROVINCIAL B AREA per week
	£	£	£
(1) *SALES SUPERVISOR* ...	*17·00*	*16·50*	*15·90*
(2) CLERK GRADE I	*16·50*	*16·00*	*15·40*
(3) CLERK GRADE II, *SALES ASSISTANT*, CASHIER, CENTRAL WAREHOUSE WORKER, STOCKHAND OR VAN SALESMAN:—			
Aged *21* years or over	*15·50*	*15·00*	*14·40*
„ 20 and under 21 years ...	*13·20*	*12·75*	*12·25*
„ 19 „ „ 20 „ ...	*12·40*	*12·00*	*11·50*
„ 18 „ „ 19 „ ...	*11·65*	*11·25*	*10·80*
„ 17 „ „ 18 „ ...	*10·10*	*9·75*	*9·35*
„ 16 „ „ 17 „ ...	*9·30*	*9·00*	*8·65*
„ under 16 years	*8·55*	*8·25*	*7·90*
(4) *SHOP WORKER, PORTER OR GENERAL WORKER:—*			
Aged *21* years or over	*15·00*	*14·50*	*13·90*
„ 20 and under 21 years ...	*12·75*	*12·35*	*11·80*
„ 19 „ „ 20 „ ...	*12·00*	*11·60*	*11·10*
„ 18 „ „ 19 „ ...	*11·25*	*10·90*	*10·45*
„ 17 „ „ 18 „ ...	*9·75*	*9·45*	*9·05*
„ 16 „ „ 17 „ ...	*9·00*	*8·70*	*8·35*
„ under 16 years	*8·25*	*8·00*	*7·65*

TRANSPORT WORKERS

6. Subject to the provisions of paragraph 1, the minimum remuneration payable to Transport Workers employed in the London Area, Provincial A Area or Provincial B Area, as the case may be, shall be the appropriate amount set out in Column 3 of the next following table:—

Column 1	Column 2	Column 3		
Age of transport worker	Mechanically propelled vehicle with carrying capacity of	LONDON AREA per week	PROVINCIAL A AREA per week	PROVINCIAL B AREA per week
		£	£	£
21 years or over ...	} 1 ton or less {	*16·50*	*16·00*	*15·40*
Under 21 years ...		*14·75*	*14·50*	*13·90*
All ages ... {	Over 1 ton and up to 5 tons	*17·00*	*16·50*	*15·90*
	Over 5 tons	*17·70*	*17·20*	*16·60*

MINIMUM OVERTIME RATES

7. Overtime shall be payable at the following minimum rates:—

(1) To any worker, for work on a Sunday or customary holiday,

    (a) where time worked does not exceed 4½ hours ... double time for 4½ hours

    (b) where time worked exceeds 4½ hours but does not exceed 8 hours ... ... double time for 8 hours

    (c) where time worked exceeds 8 hours ... ... double time for all time worked

Provided that—

    (i) Where a worker performs work on a customary holiday which is a day fixed by the employer, being a day on which the worker would normally work, during the period commencing on the last day on which the worker would normally work before Christmas Day and ending on the next following 9th January, overtime rates in accordance with the provisions of this sub-paragraph shall be payable to that worker only if—

        (a) he is a worker who normally works for the employer for more than 9 hours in a week; and

        (b) he has been in the employment of the employer throughout the period of 8 weeks immediately preceding the week in which Christmas Day falls.

    (ii) Overtime rates in accordance with the foregoing provisions of this paragraph shall be payable to a Shop Manager, Temporary Shop Manager, Shop Manageress or Temporary Shop Manageress only if the overtime worked is specifically authorised in writing by the employer or his representative.

    (iii) Where it is or becomes the practice in a Jewish undertaking for the employer to require the worker's attendance on Sunday instead of Saturday, the provisions of this paragraph shall apply as if in such provisions the word "Saturday" were substituted for "Sunday", except where such attendance on Sunday is unlawful.

(2) To any worker, on the weekly short day in any week during which, under sub-section (3) of section 40 of the Shops Act 1950(a), the employer is relieved of his obligation to allow the worker a weekly half-day,

    for any time worked after 1.30 p.m. ... ... double time

(3) To any worker, other than a Shop Manager, Temporary Shop Manager, Shop Manageress or Temporary Shop Manageress—

    (a) on the weekly short day (not being a weekly short day to which sub-paragraph (2) of this paragraph applies)

    for any time worked after 1.30 p.m. ... ... time-and-a-half

    (b) in any week, exclusive of any time in respect of which a minimum overtime rate is payable under the foregoing provisions of this paragraph,

    for all time worked in excess of *41* hours *up to and including 30th September 1972* and in excess of *40* hours *on and after 1st October 1972* ... ... time-and-a-half

(a) 1950 c. 28.

Provided that—

    (i) *up to and including 30th September 1972* in any week which includes one customary holiday "35 hours" shall be substituted for "*41* hours" and in any week which includes two customary holidays "28 hours" shall be substituted for the said "*41* hours";

    (ii) *on and after 1st October 1972* in any week which includes one customary holiday "35 hours" shall be substituted for "*40* hours" and in any week which includes two customary holidays "28 hours" shall be substituted for the said "*40* hours".

WAITING TIME

8. A worker shall be entitled to payment of the minimum remuneration specified in this Schedule for all the time during which he is present on the premises of the employer unless he is present thereon in any of the following circumstances, that is to say—

    (1) without the employer's consent, express or implied;

    (2) for some purpose unconnected with his work, and other than that of waiting for work to be given to him to perform;

    (3) by reason only of the fact that he is resident thereon; or

    (4) during normal meal times, and he is not waiting for work to be given to him to perform.

WORKERS WHO ARE NOT REQUIRED TO WORK ON A CUSTOMARY HOLIDAY

9.—(1) Subject to the provisions of sub-paragraph (2) and sub-paragraph (3) of this paragraph, a worker who is not required to work on a customary holiday shall be paid for that holiday not less than the amount to which he would have been entitled under the foregoing provisions had the day not been a customary holiday and had he worked the number of hours ordinarily worked by him on that day of the week.

(2) A worker shall not be entitled to any payment under this paragraph unless he—

    (*a*) worked for the employer throughout the last working day on which work was available for him preceding the holiday; and

    (*b*) presents himself for employment at the usual starting time on the first working day after the holiday:

Provided that (*a*) or (*b*), as the case may be, of this sub-paragraph shall be deemed to be complied with where the worker is excused by his employer or is prevented by his proved illness or injury from working or presenting himself for employment as aforesaid.

(3) A worker shall not be entitled to any payment under this paragraph in respect of a customary holiday which is a day fixed by the employer, being a day on which the worker would normally work, during the period commencing on the last day on which the worker would normally work before Christmas Day and ending on the next following 9th January unless—

    (*a*) he is a worker who normally works for the employer for more than 9 hours in a week; and

    (*b*) he has been in the employment of the employer throughout the period of 8 weeks immediately preceding the week in which Christmas Day falls.

GUARANTEED WEEKLY REMUNERATION PAYABLE TO A FULL-TIME WORKER

10.—(1) Notwithstanding the other provisions of this Schedule, where in respect of any week the total remuneration (including holiday remuneration but excluding remuneration in respect of overtime) payable to a full-time worker under those other provisions is less than the guaranteed weekly remuneration provided under this paragraph, the minimum remuneration payable to that worker for that week shall be that guaranteed weekly remuneration with the addition of any amount excluded as aforesaid.

(2) The guaranteed weekly remuneration payable in respect of any week to a full-time worker is the remuneration to which he would be entitled under paragraph 3, 3A, 5, 5A, 5B or 6 for *41* hours' work in his normal occupation *up to and including 30th September 1972 or for 40* hours' work in his normal occupation *on and after 1st October 1972*:

Provided that—

(a) where the worker normally works for the employer on work to which this Schedule applies for less than *41* hours in the week *up to and including 30th September 1972 or* for less than *40* hours in the week *on and after 1st October 1972* by reason only of the fact that he does not hold himself out as normally available for work for more than the number of hours he normally works in the week and the worker has informed the employer in writing that he does not so hold himself out, the guaranteed weekly remuneration shall be the remuneration to which the worker would be entitled (calculated as in paragraph 2 or 2A) for the number of hours in the week normally worked by the worker for the employer on work to which this Schedule applies;

(b) where in any week a worker at his request and with the written consent of his employer is absent from work during any part of his normal working hours on any day (other than a holiday allowed under Part II of this Schedule or a customary holiday or a holiday allowed to all persons employed in the undertaking or branch of an undertaking in which the worker is employed), the guaranteed weekly remuneration payable in respect of that week shall be reduced in respect of each day on which he is absent as aforesaid by one-sixth where the worker's normal working week is six days or by one-fifth where his normal working week is five days.

(3) Guaranteed weekly remuneration is not payable in respect of any week unless the worker throughout his normal working hours in that week (excluding any time allowed to him as a holiday or during which he is absent from work in accordance with proviso (b) to sub-paragraph (2) of this paragraph) is—

(a) capable of and available for work; and

(b) willing to perform such duties outside his normal occupation as the employer may reasonably require if his normal work is not available in the establishment in which he is employed.

(4) Guaranteed weekly remuneration is not payable in respect of any week if the worker's employment is terminated before the end of that week.

(5) If the employer is unable to provide the worker with work by reason of a strike or other circumstances beyond his control and gives the worker four clear days' notice to that effect, guaranteed weekly remuneration shall not be payable after the expiry of such notice in respect of any week during which or during part of which the employer continues to be unable to provide work as aforesaid:

Provided that in respect of the week in which the said notice expires there shall be paid to the worker, in addition to any remuneration payable in respect of time worked in that week, any remuneration that would have been payable if the worker had worked his normal hours of work on every day in the week prior to the expiry of the notice.

BENEFITS AND ADVANTAGES

11. The following benefits or advantages, being benefits or advantages provided, in pursuance of the terms and conditions of the employment of the worker, by the employer or by some other person under arrangements with the employer and not being benefits or advantages the provision of which is illegal by virtue of the Truck Acts 1831 to 1940(a), or of any other enactment, are authorised to be reckoned as payment of wages by the employer in lieu of payment in cash in the following manner:—

(1) board and lodging for seven days a week, as the appropriate amount set out in the following table—

In the case of a worker aged	LONDON AREA per week	PROVINCIAL A AREA per week	PROVINCIAL B AREA per week
	£	£	£
21 years or over	1·80	1·60	1·35
20 and under 21 years	1·70	1·50	1·25
19 „ „ 20 „	1·60	1·40	1·15
18 „ „ 19 „	1·50	1·30	1·05
17 „ „ 18 „	1·40	1·20	0·95
under 17 years	1·25	1·05	0·80

or, where board and lodging is not so provided,

(2) dinner of good and sufficient quality and quantity provided on each day on which the worker normally works in the week, other than the weekly short day, as an amount of £0.45 per week;

(3) tea of good and sufficient quality and quantity provided as aforesaid, as an amount of £0.15 per week.

PART II : ANNUAL HOLIDAY AND HOLIDAY REMUNERATION

ANNUAL HOLIDAY

12.—(1) Subject to the provisions of sub-paragraph (2) of this paragraph and of paragraph 13, an employer shall, between the date on which the provisions of this Schedule become effective and 31st October 1972, and in each succeeding year between 1st April and 31st October, allow a holiday (hereinafter referred to as an "annual holiday") to every worker in his employment to whom this Schedule applies who has been employed by him during the 12 months immediately preceding the commencement of the holiday season for any one of the periods of employment (calculated in accordance with the provisions of paragraph 19) set out in the first column of the table below and the duration of the annual holiday shall in the case of each such worker be related to that period as follows:—

(a) 1831 c. 37; 1887 c. 46; 1896 c. 44; 1940 c. 38.

Period of employment	Duration of annual holiday			
	Where the worker's normal working week is			
	Six days	Five days	Four days	Three days or less
12 months	12 days	10 days	8 days	6 days
Not less than 11 months but less than 12 months	11 ,,	9 ,,	7 ,,	5 ,,
,, ,, ,, 10 ,, ,, ,, ,, 11 ,, ...	10 ,,	8 ,,	7 ,,	5 ,,
,, ,, ,, 9 ,, ,, ,, ,, 10 ,, ...	9 ,,	7 ,,	6 ,,	4 ,,
,, ,, ,, 8 ,, ,, ,, ,, 9 ,, ...	8 ,,	7 ,,	5 ,,	4 ,,
,, ,, ,, 7 ,, ,, ,, ,, 8 ,, ...	7 ,,	6 ,,	5 ,,	3 ,,
,, ,, ,, 6 ,, ,, ,, ,, 7 ,, ...	6 ,,	5 ,,	4 ,,	3 ,,
,, ,, ,, 5 ,, ,, ,, ,, 6 ,, ...	5 ,,	4 ,,	3 ,,	2 ,,
,, ,, ,, 4 ,, ,, ,, ,, 5 ,, ...	4 ,,	3 ,,	3 ,,	2 ,,
,, ,, ,, 3 ,, ,, ,, ,, 4 ,, ...	3 ,,	2 ,,	2 ,,	1 day
,, ,, ,, 2 ,, ,, ,, ,, 3 ,, ...	2 ,,	2 ,,	1 day	1 ,,
,, ,, ,, 1 month ,, ,, ,, 2 ,, ...	1 day	1 day	1 ,,	nil

(2) Notwithstanding the provisions of the last foregoing sub-paragraph—

(a) the number of days of annual holiday which an employer is required to allow to a worker in any holiday season shall not exceed in the aggregate twice the number of days constituting the worker's normal working week;

(b) where the worker does not wish to take his annual holiday or part thereof during the holiday season in any year and, before the expiration of such holiday season, enters into an agreement in writing with his employer that the annual holiday or part thereof shall be allowed, at a date or dates to be specified in that agreement, after the expiration of the holiday season but before the first day of January in the following year, then any day or days of annual holiday so allowed shall be treated as having been allowed during the holiday season;

(c) the duration of the workers' annual holiday during the holiday season ending on 31st October 1972 shall be reduced by any days of annual holiday duly allowed to him by the employer under the provisions of Order R.F.A. (56) between 1st April 1972 and the date on which this Schedule becomes effective.

(3) In this Schedule the expression "holiday season" means in relation to the year 1972 the period commencing on 1st April 1972, and ending on 31st October 1972, and, in each succeeding year, the period commencing on 1st April and ending on 31st October of the same year.

13. Where at the written request of the worker at any time during the three months immediately preceding the commencement of the holiday season in any year, his employer allows him any day or days of annual holiday and pays him holiday remuneration in respect thereof calculated in accordance with the provisions of paragraphs 16 and 17, then

(1) the annual holiday to be allowed in accordance with paragraph 12 in the holiday season in that year shall be reduced by the day or days of annual holiday so allowed prior to the commencement of that holiday season; and

(2) for the purpose of calculating accrued holiday remuneration under paragraph 18 any day or days of annual holiday deducted in accordance with sub-paragraph (1) hereof shall be treated as if they had been allowed in the holiday season.

14.—(1) An annual holiday shall be allowed on consecutive working days, being days on which the worker is normally called upon to work for the employer.

(2) Where the number of days of annual holiday for which a worker has qualified exceeds the number of days constituting his normal working week, the holiday may be allowed in two periods of consecutive working days; so however that when a holiday is so allowed, one of the periods shall consist of a number of such days not less than the number of days constituting the worker's normal working week.

(3) For the purposes of this paragraph, days of annual holiday shall be treated as consecutive notwithstanding that a customary holiday on which the worker is not required to work for the employer or a day on which he does not normally work for the employer intervenes.

(4) Where a customary holiday on which the worker is not required to work for the employer immediately precedes a period of annual holiday or occurs during such a period and the total number of days of annual holiday required to be allowed in the period under the foregoing provisions of this paragraph, together with any customary holiday, exceeds the number of days constituting the worker's normal working week, then, notwithstanding the foregoing provisions of this paragraph, the duration of that period of annual holiday may be reduced by one day and in such a case one day of annual holiday may be allowed on a day on which the worker normally works for the employer (not being the worker's weekly short day) in the holiday season or after the holiday season in the circumstances specified in sub-paragraph (2)(*b*) of paragraph 12.

(5) No day of annual holiday shall be allowed on a customary holiday.

(6) A day of annual holiday under this Schedule may be allowed on a day on which the worker is entitled to a day of holiday (not being a customary holiday) or to a half-holiday under any enactment other than the Wages Councils Act 1959:

Provided that where the total number of days of annual holiday allowed to a worker under this Schedule is less than the number of days in his normal working week, the said annual holiday shall be in addition to the said day of holiday or the said half-holiday.

15. An employer shall give to a worker reasonable notice of the commencing date or dates and of the duration of his annual holiday. Such notice may be given individually to the worker or by the posting of a notice in the place where the worker is employed.

REMUNERATION FOR ANNUAL HOLIDAY

16.—(1) Subject to the provisions of paragraph 17, a worker qualified to be allowed an annual holiday under this Schedule shall be paid by his employer, on the last pay day preceding such holiday, one day's holiday pay in respect of each day thereof.

(2) Where an annual holiday is taken in more than one period the holiday remuneration shall be apportioned accordingly.

17. Where any accrued holiday remuneration has been paid by the employer to the worker (in accordance with paragraph 18 of this Schedule or with Order R.F.A. (56)), in respect of employment during any of the periods referred to in that paragraph, the amount of holiday remuneration payable by the employer in respect of any annual holiday for which the worker has qualified by reason of employment during the said period shall be reduced by the amount of the said accrued holiday remuneration, unless that remuneration has been deducted from a previous payment of holiday remuneration made under the provisions of this Schedule or of Order R.F.A. (56).

ACCRUED HOLIDAY REMUNERATION PAYABLE ON
TERMINATION OF EMPLOYMENT

18. Where a worker ceases to be employed by an employer after the provisions of this Schedule become effective, the employer shall, immediately on the termination of the employment (hereinafter referred to as the "termination date"), pay to the worker as accrued holiday remuneration:—

(1) in respect of employment occurring in the 12 months up to 1st April immediately preceding the termination date, a sum equal to the holiday remuneration for any days of annual holiday for which he has qualified except days of annual holiday which he has been allowed or has become entitled to be allowed before leaving the employment; and

(2) in respect of any employment since the said 1st April, a sum equal to the holiday remuneration which would have been payable to him if he could have been allowed an annual holiday in respect of that employment at the time of leaving it:

Provided that—

(a) no worker shall be entitled to the payment by his employer of accrued holiday remuneration if he is dismissed on the grounds of misconduct and is so informed by the employer at the time of dismissal;

(b) where a worker is employed under a contract of service under which he is required to give not less than one week's notice before terminating his employment and the worker, without the consent of his employer, terminates his employment without having given not less than one week's notice, or before one week has expired from the beginning of such notice, the amount of accrued holiday remuneration payable to the worker shall be the amount payable under the foregoing provisions of this paragraph less an amount equal to the statutory minimum remuneration which would be payable to him at the termination date for one week's work if working his normal working week and the normal number of daily hours worked by him;

(c) where during the period or periods in respect of which the said accrued holiday remuneration is payable the worker has at his written request been allowed any day or days of holiday (other than days of holiday allowed by the employer under paragraph 13) for which he has not qualified under the provisions of this Schedule, any accrued holiday remuneration payable as aforesaid may be reduced by the amount of any sum paid by the employer to the worker in respect of such day or days of holiday.

CALCULATION OF EMPLOYMENT

19. For the purpose of calculating any period of employment qualifying a worker for an annual holiday or for any accrued holiday remuneration, the worker shall be treated as if he were employed for a month in respect of any month throughout which he has been in the employment of the employer.

Part III : GENERAL

DEFINITIONS

20. For the purposes of this Schedule—

"BOARD" means not less than three meals a day, of good and sufficient quality and quantity, one of which shall be dinner; and "LODGING" means clean and adequate accommodation and clean and adequate facilities for eating, sleeping, washing and leisure.

"CARRYING CAPACITY" means the weight of the maximum load normally carried by the vehicle, and such carrying capacity when so established shall not be affected either by variations in the weight of the load resulting from collections or deliveries or emptying of containers during the course of the journey, or by the fact that on any particular journey a load greater or less than the established carrying capacity is carried.

"CASHIER" means a worker employed in a shop and engaged wholly or mainly in receiving cash or giving change.

"CENTRAL WAREHOUSE WORKER" means a worker wholly or mainly employed in a central warehouse, that is to say, a warehouse from which an undertaking in the retail furnishing and allied trades supplies its shops.

"CLERK GRADE I" means a worker engaged wholly or mainly on clerical work which includes responsibility for maintaining ledgers or wages books or for preparing financial accounts of the undertaking or of a branch or department thereof.

"CLERK GRADE II" means a worker, other than a Clerk Grade I, engaged wholly or mainly on clerical work.

"CUSTOMARY HOLIDAY" means

(1) (*a*) In England and Wales—

Christmas Day (or, if Christmas Day falls on a Sunday, such week-day as may be appointed by national proclamation, or, if none is so appointed, the next following Tuesday), Boxing Day, Good Friday, Easter Monday, Whit Monday (or where another day is substituted therefor by national proclamation, that day), August Bank Holiday and any day proclaimed as a public holiday throughout England and Wales; and

(*b*) one other day (being a day on which the worker would normally work) during the period commencing on the last day on which the worker would normally work before Christmas Day and ending on the next following 9th January to be fixed by the employer and notified to the worker not less than three weeks before the holiday;

(*c*) in Scotland—

New Year's Day (or, if New Year's Day falls on a Sunday, the following Monday);
the local Spring holiday;
the local Autumn holiday;
Christmas Day (when Christmas Day falls on any day other than a Sunday); two other days or, when Christmas Day falls on a Sunday, three other days (being days on which the worker would normally work) in the course of a calendar year, to be fixed by the employer and notified to the worker not less than three weeks before the holiday and any day proclaimed as a public holiday throughout Scotland; and

(*d*) one other day (being a day on which the worker would normally work) during the period commencing on the last day on which the worker would normally work before Christmas Day and ending on the next following 9th January to be fixed by the employer and notified to the worker not less than three weeks before the holiday; or

(2) where in any undertaking it is not the custom or practice to observe such days as are specified in (1)(*a*) or (1)(*c*) above as holidays, such other days, not fewer in number, as may by agreement between the employer or his representative and the worker or his representative be substituted for the specified days.

"FULL-TIME-WORKER" means a worker who normally works for the employer for at least 36 hours in the week on work to which this Schedule applies.

"GENERAL WORKER" means a worker employed in a shop or in a warehouse operated in connection with a shop and engaged in general duties.

"LONDON AREA", "PROVINCIAL A AREA" and "PROVINCIAL B AREA" have the meanings respectively assigned to them in paragraph 21.

"MONTH" means the period commencing on a date of any number in one month and ending on the day before the date of the same number in the next month or, if the commencing date is the 29th, 30th or 31st day of a month and there is no date of the same number in the next month, then on the last day of that month.

"NORMAL WORKING WEEK" means the number of days on which it has been usual for the worker to work in a week while in the employment of the employer during the 12 months immediately preceding the commencement of the holiday season or, where under paragraph 18 accrued holiday remuneration is payable on the termination of the employment, during the 12 months immediately preceding the date of the termination of the employment:

Provided that—

(1) part of a day shall count as a day;

(2) no account shall be taken of any week in which the worker did not perform any work for which statutory minimum remuneration has been fixed.

"ONE DAY'S HOLIDAY PAY" means the appropriate proportion of the remuneration which the worker would be entitled to receive from his employer at the date of the annual holiday (or where the holiday is taken in more than one period at the date of the first period) or at the termination date, as the case may be, for one week's work—

(1) if working his normal working week, and the number of daily hours normally worked by him (exclusive of overtime),

(2) if the employer were not providing him with meals or board and lodging, and

(3) if he were paid at the appropriate rate of statutory minimum remuneration for work for which statutory minimum remuneration is payable and at the same rate for any work for the same employer for which such remuneration is not payable,

and in this definition "appropriate proportion" means—

						where the worker's normal working week is six days	... one-sixth
,,	,,	,,	,,	,,	,,	,, five days	... one-fifth
,,	,,	,,	,,	,,	,,	,, four days	... one-quarter
,,	,,	,,	,,	,,	,,	,, three days	... one-third
,,	,,	,,	,,	,,	,,	,, two days	... one-half
,,	,,	,,	,,	,,	,,	,, one day	... the whole.

"PORTER" means a worker employed wholly or mainly upon one or more of the operations of packing, unpacking, moving, loading, or unloading merchandise or materials.

"SALES ASSISTANT" means a worker who is wholly or mainly engaged in the serving of customers and is normally expected to advise customers on the choice or use of merchandise.

"SALES SUPERVISOR" means a sales assistant other than a shop manager or a shop manageress who either (a) exercises general supervision over not less than 6 sales assistants or (b) exercises supervisory authority under a shop manager or a shop manageress and performs the duties of the shop manager or shop manageress in his or her absence.

"SHOP MANAGER", "SHOP MANAGERESS" means a worker who is employed at, and is normally immediately in charge of the operation of, an undertaking or branch (but not of a department of an undertaking or branch), including the custody of cash and stock, and, if employed in the London Area or in Provincial A Area, has immediate control of staff, if any, or, if employed in Provincial B Area, has immediate control of at least one full-time or two part-time staff; and for the purpose of this definition a worker shall not be deemed not to be immediately in charge of the operation of an undertaking or branch by reason only of being subject to the supervision of the employer or some person acting on his behalf, being in either case a person who is not normally, during the hours when the undertaking or branch is open to the public, wholly or mainly engaged in work at the undertaking or branch.

"*SHOP WORKER*" *means a worker other than a sales assistant, a sales supervisor, a shop manager or a shop manageress who (a) is wholly or mainly engaged in the serving of customers but is not normally expected to advise them in the choice or use of merchandise, or (b) is otherwise wholly or mainly employed in or about a shop in duties other than the serving of customers but involving assistance in the making of sales.*

"STOCKHAND" means a worker employed in a shop or in a warehouse operated in connection with a shop, and wholly or mainly engaged in the reception, checking and re-issuing of goods together with the keeping of records in connection therewith.

"TEMPORARY SHOP MANAGER", "TEMPORARY SHOP MANAGERESS" means a worker who, in the absence of the Shop Manager or Shop Manageress, as the case may be, is employed at and is temporarily immediately in charge of the operation of an undertaking or branch (but not of a department of an undertaking or branch) including the custody of cash and stock, whilst the worker is so in charge; and for the purpose of this definition a worker shall not be deemed not to be immediately in charge of the operation of an undertaking or branch by reason only of being subject to the supervision of the employer or some person acting on his behalf, being in either case a person who is not normally, during the hours when the undertaking or branch is open to the public, wholly or mainly engaged in work at the undertaking or branch.

"TIME-AND-A-HALF" and "DOUBLE TIME" mean, respectively, one and a half times and twice the hourly rate obtained by dividing the minimum weekly remuneration to which the worker is entitled under the provisions of paragraphs 3, 3A, 4, 5, 5A, 5B or 6—

(a) *by 41 up to and including 30th September 1972; and*

(b) *by 40 on and after 1st October 1972.*

"TRANSPORT WORKER" means a male worker (other than a van salesman) engaged wholly or mainly in driving a mechanically propelled road vehicle for the transport of goods and on work in connection with the vehicle and its load (if any) while on the road.

"VAN SALESMAN" means a worker wholly or mainly employed in the sale of goods to customers from a van or other vehicle.

"WATCHMAN" means a worker wholly or mainly engaged in guarding the employer's premises for the prevention of theft, fire, damage or trespass.

"WEEK" means "pay week".

"WEEKLY SHORT DAY" means:—

(1) that day in any week on which the worker is, in accordance with the provisions of section 17 of the Shops Act 1950, required not to be employed about the business of a shop after half-past one o'clock in the afternoon, or,

(2) where there is no such day, or where the day falls on a customary holiday, a working day in the week not being a customary holiday, fixed by the employer and notified to the worker not later than the Saturday preceding the week during which it is to have effect; or, failing such notification, the last working day in the week which is not a customary holiday:

Provided that where the day specified in (1) of this definition falls on Christmas Day or Boxing Day in England and Wales or Christmas Day or New Year's Day in Scotland the employer may fix as the weekly short day for that week a working day in the following week not being either a customary holiday or the weekly short day for that following week.

AREAS

21. In this Schedule:—

(1) "LONDON AREA" means the Metropolitan Police District, as defined in the London Government Act 1963(a), the City of London, the Inner Temple and the Middle Temple.

(a) 1963 c. 33.

(2) "PROVINCIAL A AREA" means

(a) in Scotland

(i) the following burghs:—

ABERDEEN COUNTY
  Aberdeen (including
  part in Kincardine
    County)
  Fraserburgh
  Peterhead

ANGUS COUNTY
  Arbroath
  Brechin
  Dundee
  Forfar
  Montrose

ARGYLL COUNTY
  Dunoon

AYR COUNTY
  Ardrossan
  Ayr
  Irvine
  Kilmarnock
  Largs
  Prestwick
  Saltcoats
  Stevenston
  Troon

BANFF COUNTY
  Buckie

BUTE COUNTY
  Rothesay

CLACKMANNAN
          COUNTY
  Alloa

DUMFRIES COUNTY
  Dumfries

DUNBARTON
          COUNTY
  Bearsden
  Clydebank
  Dumbarton
  Helensburgh
  Kirkintilloch
  Milngavie

EAST LOTHIAN
          COUNTY
  North Berwick

FIFE COUNTY
  Buckhaven and Methil
  Burntisland
  Cowdenbeath
  Dunfermline
  Kirkcaldy
  Leven
  Lochgelly
  St. Andrews

INVERNESS COUNTY
  Inverness

KINCARDINE
          COUNTY
  Stonehaven

LANARK COUNTY
  Airdrie
  Coatbridge
  Glasgow
  Hamilton
  Lanark
  Motherwell and
          Wishaw
  Rutherglen

MIDLOTHIAN
          COUNTY
  Dalkeith
  Edinburgh
  Musselburgh

MORAY COUNTY
  Elgin

ORKNEY COUNTY
  Kirkwall

PERTH COUNTY
  Perth

RENFREW COUNTY
  Barrhead
  Gourock
  Greenock
  Johnstone
  Paisley
  Port Glasgow
  Renfrew

ROSS AND
  CROMARTY COUNTY
  Stornaway

ROXBURGH COUNTY
  Hawick

SELKIRK COUNTY
  Galashiels

STIRLING COUNTY
  Denny and Dunipace
  Falkirk
  Grangemouth
  Kilsyth
  Stirling

WEST LOTHIAN
          COUNTY
  Armadale
  Bathgate
  Bo'ness

WIGTOWN COUNTY
  Stranraer

ZETLAND COUNTY
  Lerwick

(ii) the following Special Lighting Districts, the boundaries of which have been defined, namely, Vale of Leven and Renton in the County of Dunbarton, and Larbert and Airth in the County of Stirling, and

(iii) the following areas the boundaries of which were defined as Special Lighting Districts prior to 10th March 1943, namely, Bellshill and Mossend, Blantyre, Cambuslang, Larkhall and Holytown, New Stevenston and Carfin, all in the County of Lanark.

(b) In England and Wales, the areas administered by County Borough, Municipal Borough or Urban District Councils, except where they are included in the London area or are listed in (3)(b) of this paragraph.

(3) "PROVINCIAL B AREA" means

(a) In Scotland, all areas other than those listed in (2)(a) of this paragraph;

(b) In England and Wales, all areas not included in the London area administered by Rural District Councils, and the areas administered by the following Municipal Borough and Urban District Councils:—

ENGLAND (excluding Monmouthshire)

BEDFORDSHIRE
Ampthill
Sandy

BERKSHIRE
Wallingford
Wantage

BUCKINGHAMSHIRE
Buckingham
Linslade
Marlow
Newport Pagnell

CHESHIRE
Alsager
Longdendale

CORNWALL
Bodmin
Bude Stratton
Fowey
Helston
Launceston
Liskeard
Looe
Lostwithiel
Padstow
Penryn
St. Just
Torpoint

DERBYSHIRE
Bakewell
Whaley Bridge
Wirksworth

DEVON
Ashburton
Buckfastleigh
Budleigh Salterton
Crediton
Dartmouth
Great Torrington
Holsworthy
Honiton
Kingsbridge
Lynton
Northam
Okehampton
Ottery St. Mary
Salcombe
Seaton
South Molton
Tavistock
Totnes

DORSET
Blandford Forum
Lyme Regis
Shaftesbury
Sherborne
Wareham
Wimborne Minster

DURHAM
Barnard Castle
Tow Law

ELY, ISLE OF
Chatteris

ESSEX
Brightlingsea
Burnham-on-Crouch
Saffron Walden
West Mersea
Wivenhoe

GLOUCESTERSHIRE
Nailsworth
Tewkesbury

HEREFORDSHIRE
Bromyard
Kington
Ledbury

HERTFORDSHIRE
Baldock
Chorleywood
Royston
Sawbridgeworth

HUNTINGDONSHIRE
Huntingdon and
Godmanchester
Ramsey
St. Ives
St. Neots

KENT
Lydd
New Romney
Queenborough
Sandwich
Tenterden

LANCASHIRE
Carnforth
Grange

LINCOLNSHIRE
Alford
Barton-upon-Humber
Bourne
Brigg
Horncastle
Mablethorpe and Sutton
Market Rasen
Woodhall Spa

NORFOLK
Cromer
Diss
Downham Market
Hunstanton
North Walsham
Sheringham
Swaffham
Thetford
Wells-next-the-Sea
Wymondham

NORTHAMPTON-
SHIRE
Brackley
Burton Latimer
Higham Ferrers
Oundle

NORTHUMBERLAND
Alnwick
Amble

OXFORDSHIRE
Bicester
Chipping Norton
Thame
Woodstock

RUTLAND
Oakham

SHROPSHIRE
Bishop's Castle
Church Stretton
Ellesmere
Market Drayton
Newport
Wem

SOMERSET
Chard
Crewkerne
Glastonbury
Ilminster
Portishead
Shepton Mallet
Street
Watchet
Wellington

SUFFOLK
Aldeburgh
Beccles
Bungay
Eye
Hadleigh
Halesworth
Haverhill

SUFFOLK—*cont.*
Leiston-cum-Sizewell
Saxmundham
Southwold
Sudbury
Stowmarket
Woodbridge

SUSSEX
Arundel
Rye

WESTMORLAND
Appleby
Lakes

WILTSHIRE
Bradford-on-Avon
Calne

WILTSHIRE—*cont.*
Malmesbury
Marlborough
Melksham
Westbury
Wilton

WORCESTERSHIRE
Bewdley
Droitwich

YORKSHIRE
Hedon
Hornsea
Malton
Norton
Pickering
Richmond
Tickhill
Withernsea

WALES AND MONMOUTHSHIRE

ANGLESEY
Amlwch
Beaumaris
Llangefni
Menai Bridge

BRECONSHIRE
Builth Wells
Hay
Llanwrtyd Wells

CAERNARVONSHIRE
Bethesda
Betws-y-Coed
Criccieth
Llanfairfechan
Penmaenmawr
Portmadoc
Pwllheli

CARDIGANSHIRE
Aberayron
Cardigan
Lampeter
New Quay

CARMARTHENSHIRE
Cwmamman
Kidwelly
Llandeilo
Llandovery
Newcastle Emlyn

DENBIGHSHIRE
Llangollen
Llanrwst
Ruthin

FLINTSHIRE
Buckley
Mold

GLAMORGAN
Cowbridge

MERIONETHSHIRE
Bala
Barmouth
Dolgellau
Towyn

MONMOUTHSHIRE
Caerleon
Chepstow
Usk

MONTGOMERYSHIRE
Llanfyllin
Llanidloes
Machynlleth
Montgomery
Newtown and
   Llanllwchaiarn
Welshpool

PEMBROKESHIRE
Fishguard and
   Goodwick
Narberth
Neyland
Tenby

RADNORSHIRE
Knighton
Llandrindod Wells
Presteigne

(4)   Any reference to a local government area shall be construed as a reference to that area as it was on 23rd April 1961, unless otherwise stated.

WORKERS TO WHOM THIS SCHEDULE APPLIES

22.—(1)(i) Subject to the provisions of sub-paragraph (2) of this paragraph the workers to whom this Schedule applies are all workers employed in Great Britain in any undertaking or any branch or department of an undertaking, being an undertaking, branch or department engaged—

(*a*) wholly or mainly in the retail furnishing and allied trades; or

(*b*) wholly or mainly in those trades and one or more of the groups of retail distributive trades set out in the Appendix to this paragraph, and to a greater extent in the retail furnishing and allied trades than in any one of those groups:

Provided that if a branch or department of an undertaking is not so engaged this Schedule shall not apply to workers employed in that branch or department (notwithstanding that the undertaking as a whole is so engaged), except in the case of workers as respects their employment in a department of that branch if that department is so engaged.

(ii) For the purposes of this sub-paragraph

(a) in determining the extent to which an undertaking or branch or department of an undertaking is engaged in a group of trades, regard shall be had to the time spent in the undertaking, branch or department on work in that group of trades;

(b) an undertaking or branch or department of an undertaking which is engaged in any operation in a group of trades shall be treated as engaged in that group of trades.

(2) This Schedule does not apply to any of the following workers in respect of their employment in any of the following circumstances, that is to say:—

(i) workers in relation to whom the Road Haulage Wages Council operates in respect of any employment which is within the field of operation of that Council;

(ii) workers employed on post office business;

(iii) workers employed on the maintenance or repair of buildings, plant, equipment or vehicles (but not including workers employed as cleaners);

(iv) workers employed on the installation, maintenance or repair of radio or television sets;

(v) workers employed on the repair or renovation of furniture (including mattresses), the making up, planning or laying of carpets, linoleum or similar floor coverings, or the measuring, cutting, sewing, making up or fixing of blinds, curtains, pelmets or loose covers;

(vi) workers employed on the packing, storing or removal of furniture or other household effects in connection with a household removal;

(vii) workers employed in the assembling, installation, maintenance, alteration or repair of electrical or gas appliances and apparatus of all kinds;

(viii) workers employed by a Gas or Electricity Supply Undertaking;

(ix) workers employed as watchmen.

(3) For the purpose of this Schedule the retail furnishing and allied trades consist of:—

(i) the sale by retail of:—

(a) household and office furniture, including garden furniture, mattresses, floor coverings and mirrors, but excluding billiard tables, clocks, pianos, gramophones and pictures;

(b) ironmongery, turnery and hardware, of kinds commonly used for household purposes, including gardening implements;

(c) hand tools;

(d) woodware, basketware, glassware, potteryware, chinaware, brassware, plasticware and ceramic goods, being articles or goods of kinds commonly used for household purposes or as household ornaments;

(e) electrical and gas appliances and apparatus, of kinds commonly used for household purposes (excluding clocks), and accessories and component parts thereof;

(f) heating, lighting and cooking appliances and apparatus, of kinds commonly used for household purposes, and accessories and component parts thereof;

(g) radio and television sets and their accessories and component parts;

(*h*) pedal cycles and their accessories and component parts;

(*i*) perambulators, push chairs and invalid carriages;

(*j*) toys, indoor games, requisites for outdoor games, gymnastics and athletics, but excluding billiard tables and sports clothing;

(*k*) saddlery, leather goods (other than articles of wearing apparel), travel goods and ladies' handbags;

(*l*) paint, distemper and wallpaper and oils of kinds commonly used for household purposes (excluding petrol and lubricating oils);

(*m*) brushes, mops and brooms, used for household purposes, and similar articles;

(*n*) disinfectants, chemicals, candles, soaps and polishes, of kinds commonly used for household purposes;

(ii) operations in or about the shop or other place where any of the articles specified in (i) of this sub-paragraph are sold by retail, being operations carried on for the purpose of such sale or otherwise in connection with such sale;

(iii) operations in connection with the warehousing or storing of any of the articles specified in (i) of this sub-paragraph for the purpose of the sale thereof by retail, or otherwise in connection with such sale, where the warehousing or storing takes place at a warehouse or store carried on in conjunction with one or more shops or other places where the said articles are sold by retail;

(iv) operations in connection with the transport of any of the articles specified in (i) of this sub-paragraph when carried on in conjunction with their sale by retail or with the warehousing or storing operations specified in (iii) of this sub-paragraph; and

(v) clerical or other office work carried on in conjunction with the sale by retail of any of the articles specified in (i) of this sub-paragraph and relating to such sale or to any of the operations specified in (ii) to (iv) of this sub-paragraph;

and for the purpose of this definition the sale by retail of any of the articles specified in (i) of this sub-paragraph does not include sale by auction (except where the auctioneer sells articles by retail which are his property or the property of his master) but includes the sale of any of the articles therein specified to a person for use in connection with a trade or business carried on by him if such sale takes place at or in connection with a shop engaged in the retail sale to the general public of any of the said articles.

APPENDIX TO PARAGRAPH 22

GROUPS OF RETAIL DISTRIBUTIVE TRADES

Group 1.—The Retail Food Trades, that is to say, the sale by retail of food or drink for human consumption and operations connected therewith including:—

(i) operations in or about the shop or other place where the food or drink aforesaid is sold, being operations carried on for the purpose of such sale or otherwise in connection with such sale;

(ii) operations in connection with the warehousing or storing of such food or drink for the purpose of sale by retail, or otherwise in connection with such sale, where the warehousing or storing takes place at a warehouse or store carried on in conjunction with one or more shops or other places where such food or drink is sold by retail;

(iii) operations in connection with the transport of such food or drink when carried on in conjunction with its sale by retail or with the warehousing or storing operations specified in (ii) above; and

(iv) clerical or other office work carried on in conjunction with the sale by retail aforesaid and relating to such sale or to any of the operations in (i) to (iii) above;

but not including

the sale by retail of bread, pastry or flour confectionery (other than biscuits or meat pastries) or the sale by retail of meat (other than bacon, ham, pressed beef, sausages, or meat so treated as to be fit for human consumption without further preparation or cooking) or the sale by retail of milk (other than dried or condensed milk) or the sale by retail of ice-cream, aerated waters, chocolate confectionery or sugar confectionery, or the sale of food or drink for immediate consumption.

For the purpose of this definition "sale by retail" includes any sale of food or drink to a person for use in connection with a catering business carried on by him, when such sale takes place at or in connection with a shop engaged in the retail sale of food or drink to the general public.

Group 2.—The Retail Drapery, Outfitting and Footwear Trades, that is to say—

(1) the sale by retail of

(*a*) wearing apparel of all kinds (including footwear, headwear and hand-wear) and accessories, trimmings and adornments for wearing apparel (excluding jewellery and imitation jewellery);

(*b*) haberdashery;

(*c*) textile fabrics, in the piece, leather cloth, plastic cloth and oil cloth (but not including carpets, linoleum and other kinds of floor covering);

(*d*) knitting, rug, embroidery, crochet and similar wools or yarns;

(*e*) made-up household textiles (but excluding mattresses and floor coverings);

(*f*) umbrellas, sunshades, walking sticks, canes and similar articles;

(2) operations in or about the shop or other place where any of the articles included in (1) above are sold by retail, being operations carried on for the purpose of such sale or otherwise in connection with such sale;

(3) operations in connection with the warehousing or storing of any of the articles included in (1) above for the purpose of the sale thereof by retail, or otherwise in connection with such sale, where the warehousing or storing takes place at a warehouse or store carried on in conjunction with one or more shops or other places where the said articles are sold by retail;

(4) operations in connection with the transport of any of the articles included in (1) above when carried on in conjunction with their sale by retail or with the warehousing or storing operations specified in (3) above; and

(5) clerical or other office work carried on in conjunction with the sale by retail of any of the articles included in (1) above and relating to such sale or to any of the operations specified in (2) to (4) above;

and for the purpose of this definition the sale by retail of any of the articles in (1) above includes the sale of that article to a person for use in connection with a trade or business carried on by him if such sale takes place at or in connection with a shop engaged in the retail sale to the general public of any of the articles included in (1) above.

Group 3.—The Retail Bookselling and Stationery Trades, that is to say—

(1) the sale by retail of the following articles:—

(*a*) books (excluding printed music and periodicals);

(*b*) all kinds of stationery including printed forms, note books, diaries and similar articles, and books of kinds used in an office or business for the purpose of record;

(*c*) pens, pencils, ink, blotting paper and similar articles;

(*d*) maps and charts;

(*e*) wrapping and adhesive paper, string, paste and similar articles;

(2) operations in or about the shop or other place where any of the articles specified in (1) above are sold by retail, being operations carried on for the purpose of such sale or otherwise in connection with such sale;

(3) operations in connection with the warehousing or storing of any of the articles specified in (1) above for the purpose of the sale thereof by retail, or otherwise in connection with such sale, where the warehousing or storing takes place at a warehouse or store carried on in conjunction with one or more shops or other places where the said articles are sold by retail;

(4) operations in connection with the transport of any of the articles specified in (1) above when carried on in conjunction with their sale by retail or with the warehousing or storing operations specified in (3) above; and

(5) clerical or other office work carried on in conjunction with the sale by retail of any of the articles specified in (1) above and relating to such sale or to any of the operations specified in (2) to (4) above;

Group 4.—The Retail Newsagency, Tobacco and Confectionery Trades, that is to say—

(1) the sale by retail of the following articles:—

     (*a*) newspapers, magazines and other periodicals;

     (*b*) tobacco, cigars, cigarettes, snuff and smokers' requisites;

     (*c*) articles of sugar confectionery and chocolate confectionery and ice-cream;

(2) operations in or about the shop or other place where any of the articles specified in (1) above are sold by retail, being operations carried on for the purpose of such sale or otherwise in connection with such sale;

(3) operations in connection with the warehousing or storing of any of the articles specified in (1) above for the purpose of the sale thereof by retail, or otherwise in connection with such sale, where the warehousing or storing takes place at a warehouse or store carried on in conjunction with one or more shops or other places where the said articles are sold by retail;

(4) operations in connection with the transport of any of the articles specified in (1) above when carried on in conjunction with their sale by retail or with the warehousing or storing operation specified in (3) above; and

(5) clerical or other office work carried on in conjunction with the sale by retail of any of the articles specified in (1) above and relating to such sale or to any of the operations specified in (2) to (4) above.

EXPLANATORY NOTE

(This Note is not part of the Order.)

This Order, which has effect from 4th September 1972, sets out the statutory minimum remuneration payable and the holidays to be allowed to workers in substitution for the statutory minimum remuneration fixed, and holidays provided for, by the Wages Regulation (Retail Furnishing and Allied Trades) Order 1971 (Order R.F.A. (56)), which Order is revoked.

New provisions are printed in italics.

STATUTORY INSTRUMENTS

1972 No. 1117

FOOD AND DRUGS

MILK AND DAIRIES

The Milk (Special Designation) (Amendment) Regulations 1972

Made - - -		*25th July* 1972
Laid before Parliament		*2nd August* 1972
Coming into Operation		*1st October* 1972

The Minister of Agriculture, Fisheries and Food and the Secretary of State for Social Services, acting jointly, in exercise of the powers conferred on them by sections 35, 43(3), 87 and 123 of the Food and Drugs Act 1955**(a)**, as read with the Secretary of State for Social Services Order 1968**(b)**, and of all other powers enabling them in that behalf, hereby make the following regulations after consultation with such organisations as appear to them to be representative of interests substantially affected by the regulations:—

Citation, commencement and interpretation

1.—(1) These regulations may be cited as the Milk (Special Designation) (Amendment) Regulations 1972, and shall come into operation on 1st October 1972.

(2) The Interpretation Act 1889**(c)** applies to the interpretation of these regulations as it applies to the interpretation of an Act of Parliament.

Amendment of principal regulations

2. The Milk (Special Designation) Regulations 1963**(d)** as amended**(e)**, shall be further amended as follows:—

(*a*) by inserting immediately before paragraph 1 of Part IV of Schedule 2 thereto the following words:—

"A. *Conditions applicable whether or not the treatment of the milk includes the direct application of steam*";

(*b*) by adding at the end of the said Part IV the conditions set out in Schedule 1 to these regulations;

(*c*) by adding thereto, as Schedule 6, Schedule 2 to these regulations.

(a) 4 & 5 Eliz. 2. c. 16. (b) S.I. 1968/1699 (1968 III, p. 4585).
(c) 1889 c. 63. (d) S.I. 1963/1571 (1963 III, p. 2937).
(e) S.I. 1965/1555 (1965 II, p. 4543).

In Witness whereof the Official Seal of the Minister of Agriculture, Fisheries and Food is hereunto affixed on 24th July 1972.

(L.S.) *J. M. L. Prior,*
Minister of Agriculture, Fisheries and Food.

Keith Joseph,
25th July 1972. Secretary of State for Social Services.

SCHEDULE 1

Regulation 2(*b*)

B. *Additional conditions applicable when the treatment of the milk includes the direct application of steam*

1. In the following paragraphs of this Part of this Schedule—

"input temperature" means the temperature of the milk immediately before the application of the steam;

"licensing authority "means the licensing authority for the licensing area in which the treatment is carried out;

"operational change" means any change in the site, layout or construction of equipment for treating milk by the ultra high temperature method by the direct application of steam, or any change in the steam supply or in the particular temperature used for treating the milk as aforesaid;

"output temperature" means the temperature of the vapour or of the milk in either case at the point of leaving the evaporative cooling expansion vessel.

2. Any treatment of milk by the ultra high temperature method by the direct application of steam shall be so carried out that both the percentage of the milk consisting of milk fat and the percentage of the milk consisting of milk solids other than milk fat are the same after that treatment as before it.

3.—(1) Any equipment for treating milk as aforesaid shall be provided with control apparatus which, when calibrated as required by subparagraph (2) of this paragraph, will ensure compliance with the last preceding paragraph providing no operational change is made or takes place.

(2) Before the equipment is used for treating milk as aforesaid either initially or after any operational change is made or takes place, the control apparatus shall be calibrated in relation to the particular temperature to be used for treating milk as aforesaid so as to determine the control temperatures (being the input temperature, the output temperature and the difference between them which, if respectively maintained, will ensure compliance with the last preceding paragraph providing no operational change is made or takes place).

(3) A note of the control temperatures currently applying and of the particular temperature used for treating milk as aforesaid when those control temperatures were determined shall be kept with such equipment and be available at all reasonable times for inspection by any person duly authorised by the licensing authority.

4. The holder of the licence shall forthwith notify the licensing authority of any operational change which is made or takes place.

5.—(1) For each occasion on which such equipment is in operation—

(*a*) the input temperature and the output temperature shall be indicated by indicating thermometers; and

(*b*) either both of these temperatures or one of them and the difference between them shall be continuously recorded on charts marked with graduations at intervals of 0·5F. adequately spaced to give clear readings.

(2) The records on such charts shall be dated and shall be preserved for a period of not less than three months.

6. Any treatment of milk as aforesaid or calibration of control apparatus in compliance with paragraph B3 of this Part of this Schedule shall be carried out only with dry saturated steam.

7. In connection with the treatment of milk as aforesaid, apparatus shall be provided which automatically and continuously ensures that water is separated from the steam and does not enter the milk heating equipment.

8. The treatment shall be so carried out as to secure that no foreign matter other than steam enters the milk and that there is no adulteration of the milk at the commencement or termination of the treatment or at any time when the treatment is interrupted.

9. The water used for generating the steam which is to be applied to the milk—

(*a*) shall be wholesome; and

(*b*) may be treated with any water treatment compound necessary to make it wholesome and with any boiler feed water treatment compound specified in Schedule 6 to these regulations, but otherwise shall not be treated with any water treatment compound.

10. The equipment for treating the milk shall be so constructed that the steam can be sampled immediately before it is applied to the milk and the holder of the licence shall permit any- person duly authorised by the licensing authority so to sample the steam.

SCHEDULE 2
Regulation 2(*c*)

Permitted Boiler Feed Water Treatment Compounds

Potassium alginate
Sodium alginate
Potassium carbonate
Sodium carbonate
Sodium hydroxide
Monosodium dihydrogen orthophosphate
Disodium monohydrogen orthophosphate
Trisodium orthophosphate
Sodium tripolyphosphate
Sodium hexametaphosphate
Tetrasodium pyrophosphate
Sodium silicate
Sodium metasilicate
Sodium sulphate
Magnesium sulphate
Neutral or alkaline sodium sulphite
Unmodified starch
Sodium aluminate
Polyoxyethylene glycol (minimum molecular weight, 1000)

EXPLANATORY NOTE

(This Note is not part of the regulations.)

These amending regulations come into operation on 1st October 1972. They prescribe additional conditions subject to which licences are granted to use the special designation "Ultra Heat Treated" in relation to milk which has been treated by the ultra high temperature method. These conditions are applicable when the treatment of milk includes the direct application of steam.

STATUTORY INSTRUMENTS

1972 No. 1124

EDUCATION, ENGLAND AND WALES

The Awards (First Degree, etc. Courses) (Amendment) Regulations 1972

Made - - -	*25th July* 1972
Laid before Parliament	*4th August* 1972
Coming into Operation	*1st September* 1972

The Secretary of State for Education and Science, in exercise of her powers under section 1 of the Education Act 1962(a), hereby makes the following regulations:—

Citation, commencement and interpretation

1.—(1) These regulations may be cited as the Awards (First Degree, etc. Courses) (Amendment) Regulations 1972 and shall come into operation on 1st September 1972.

(2) In these regulations "the principal regulations" means the Awards (First Degree, etc. Courses) Regulations 1971(b).

(3) The Interpretation Act 1889(c) shall apply for the interpretation of these regulations as it applies for the interpretation of an Act of Parliament.

Definitions

2. In the definition of the word "year" in regulation 2 of the principal regulations there shall be inserted after the word "means" the words "as regards any course".

Members of religious orders

3. For paragraph (3) of regulation 19 of the principal regulations there shall be substituted—

"(3) The sum referred to in paragraphs (1) and (2) above is—

if the student resides at his parent's home or in a house of the order of which he is a member £195

if the student resides elsewhere—

in the case of a student attending a course at the university of Oxford or Cambridge, at an establishment within the area comprising the City of London and the Metropolitan Police District or an institution outside the United Kingdom ... £265

in the case of a student attending a course elsewhere ... ... £245".

(a) 1962 c. 12.
(c) 1889 c. 63.

(b) S I. 1971/1297 (1971 II, p. 3722).

Suspension, etc. of payments

4. In paragraph (3) of regulation 24 of the principal regulations, after the word "is" there shall be inserted the words "in the case of a student in respect of whom apart from this paragraph a minimum payment would be payable, the appropriate proportion of the minimum payment, and in the case of any other student".

Requirements for maintenance, etc.

5. The provisions of schedule 1 to the principal regulations specified in the first column below shall have effect subject to the substitution for the amounts in the second column of the amounts in the third column.

Paragraph 1(*b*)	£400	£325
Paragraph 3(1)	£465	£480
(2)	£430	£445
(3)	£345	£355
(4)	£465	£480
Paragraph 14(2)(*b*)	£430	£445

Resources

6. In paragraph 6(12) (payments under covenant) of schedule 2 to the principal regulations after the word "not" there shall be inserted the words "in the case of any beneficiary".

Given under the Official Seal of the Secretary of State for Education and Science on 25th July 1972.

(L.S.)   *Margaret H. Thatcher,*
Secretary of State for Education and Science.

EXPLANATORY NOTE

(This Note is not part of the Regulations.)

These regulations increase the rates of ordinary maintenance prescribed by, and make minor amendments to, the Awards (First Degree, etc. Courses) Regulations 1971.

STATUTORY INSTRUMENTS

1972 No. 1126

ACQUISITION OF LAND

COMPENSATION

The Acquisition of Land (Rate of Interest after Entry) (No. 2) Regulations 1972

Made - - -		*26th July* 1972
Laid before Parliament		*7th August* 1972
Coming into Operation		*8th August* 1972

The Treasury, in exercise of the powers conferred upon them by section 32(1) of the Land Compensation Act 1961(a), and of all other powers enabling them in that behalf, hereby make the following Regulations:—

1. These Regulations may be cited as the Acquisition of Land (Rate of Interest after Entry) (No. 2) Regulations 1972, and shall come into operation on 8th August 1972.

2. The Interpretation Act 1889(b) shall apply for the interpretation of these Regulations as it applies for the interpretation of an Act of Parliament.

3. The rate of interest on any compensation in respect of the compulsory acquisition of an interest in any land on which entry has been made before the payment of the compensation shall be $8\frac{1}{2}$ per cent. per annum.

4. The Acquisition of Land (Rate of Interest after Entry) Regulations 1972(c) are hereby revoked.

Hugh Rossi,
Oscar Murton,
Two of the Lords Commissioners
of Her Majesty's Treasury.

26th July 1972.

EXPLANATORY NOTE

(This Note is not part of the Regulations.)

These Regulations increase from $7\frac{1}{2}$ per cent. to $8\frac{1}{2}$ per cent. per annum, in respect of any period after the coming into operation of these Regulations, the rate of interest payable where entry is made, before payment of compensation, on land in England and Wales which is being purchased compulsorily, and revoke the Acquisition of Land (Rate of Interest after Entry) Regulations 1972.

(a) 1961 c. 33.   (b) 1889 c. 63.   (c) S.I. 1972/949 (1972 I, p.2970).

STATUTORY INSTRUMENTS

1972 No. 1127

ACQUISITION OF LAND

COMPENSATION

The Acquisition of Land (Rate of Interest after Entry) (Scotland) (No. 2) Regulations 1972

Made - - -		*26th July* 1972
Laid before Parliament		*7th August* 1972
Coming into Operation		*8th August* 1972

The Treasury, in exercise of the powers conferred upon them by section 40(1) of the Land Compensation (Scotland) Act 1963(a), and of all other powers enabling them in that behalf, hereby make the following Regulations:—

1.—(1) These Regulations may be cited as the Acquisition of Land (Rate of Interest after Entry) (Scotland) (No. 2) Regulations 1972, and shall come into operation on 8th August 1972.

(2) These Regulations shall extend to Scotland only.

2. The Interpretation Act 1889(b) shall apply for the interpretation of these Regulations as it applies for the interpretation of an Act of Parliament.

3. The rate of interest on any compensation in respect of the compulsory acquisition of an interest in any land on which entry has been made before the payment of the compensation shall be 8½ per cent. per annum.

4. The Acquisition of Land (Rate of Interest after Entry) (Scotland) Regulations 1972(c) are hereby revoked.

Hugh Rossi,

Oscar Murton,

Two of the Lords Commissioners
of Her Majesty's Treasury.

26th July 1972.

EXPLANATORY NOTE

(This Note is not part of the Regulations.)

These Regulations increase from 7½ per cent. to 8½ per cent. per annum, in respect of any period after the coming into operation of these Regulations, the rate of interest payable where entry is made, before payment of compensation, on land in Scotland which is being purchased compulsorily, and revoke the Acquisition of Land (Rate of Interest after Entry) (Scotland) Regulations 1972.

(a) 1963 c. 51.   (b) 1889 c. 63.   (c) S.I. 1972/950 (1972 I, p.2971).

STATUTORY INSTRUMENTS

1972 No. 1130 (C.20) (S.79)

HOUSING, SCOTLAND

The Housing (Financial Provisions) (Scotland) Act 1972 (Commencement) Order 1972

Made - - - *28th July* 1972

In exercise of the powers conferred on me by section 81(3) of the Housing (Financial Provisions) (Scotland) Act 1972(**a**) and of all other powers enabling me in that behalf, I hereby make the following Order: —

1. This Order may be cited as the Housing (Financial Provisions) (Scotland) Act 1972 (Commencement) Order 1972.

2. Except as otherwise expressly provided in the Act, the whole Act shall come into force on 3rd August 1972, with the exception of—

(*a*) Part V (Controlled and regulated tenancies);

(*b*) Sections 60 to 67 (Rent limit for dwellinghouses let by Housing Associations and the Housing Corporation);

(*c*) In Schedule 9 paragraphs 23, 25 and 27 to 31 (Consequential amendments to the Rent (Scotland) Act 1971(**b**) and the Fire Precautions Act 1971(**c**);

(*d*) In Schedule 10, paragraph 4 (Transitional provisions);

(*e*) In Schedule 11, Part V so far as relating to the Rent (Scotland) Act 1971 and the Fire Precautions Act 1971 (Repeals).

Gordon Campbell,
One of Her Majesty's Principal
Secretaries of State.

St. Andrew's House,
Edinburgh.
28th July 1972.

(**a**) 1972 c. 46.   (**b**) 1971 c. 28.   (**c**) 1971 c. 40.

EXPLANATORY NOTE

(This Note is not part of the Order.)

Section 81(3) of the Housing (Financial Provisions) (Scotland) Act 1972 provides that (except where otherwise expressly provided) the Act shall come into operation one month after it is passed or on such earlier date as the Secretary of State may by Order provide.

This Order brings into force on 3rd August 1972 all the provisions of the Act with the exception of those specified in the Order and those other provisions in respect of which provision has been made in the Act for specific dates for their commencement.

STATUTORY INSTRUMENTS

1972 No. 1131

INCOME TAX

The Share Option and Share Incentive Schemes Regulations 1972

Made - - -	*28th July* 1972
Laid before the House of Commons	*4th August* 1972
Coming into Operation	*25th August* 1972

The Commissioners of Inland Revenue, in exercise of the powers conferred upon them by paragraphs 3 of Part I and 4 of Part VII of Schedule 12 to the Finance Act 1972(**a**), hereby make the following Regulations:—

1.—(1) The Regulations may be cited as the Share Option and Share Incentive Schemes Regulations 1972 and shall come into operation on 25th August 1972.

(2) The Interpretation Act 1889(**b**) shall apply for the interpretation of these Regulations as it applies for the interpretation of an Act of Parliament.

(3) In these Regulations

"the Board" means the Commissioners of Inland Revenue;

"the Schedule" means Schedule 12 to the Finance Act 1972;

other expressions have the same meaning as in the Schedule.

Application for approval

2. An application for approval of a share option or share incentive scheme shall be made in writing to the Board and shall be accompanied by two copies of any information relevant to the scheme including:—

(1) the name and registered office of the company in which shares or an interest in shares may be acquired by participants;

(2) the memorandum and articles of association of that company and any relevant amendments;

(3) the announcement to shareholders of the proposal of the scheme;

(4) the resolution of the shareholders authorising the introduction of the scheme;

(5) the rules of the scheme;

(**a**) 1972 c. 41. (**b**) 1889 c. 63.

(6) the agreement, if any, to be entered into by the participants;

(7) the trust deed, if any;

(8) any other documents relating to, or having a bearing on, the scheme which have been issued or approved for issue to shareholders and/or participants;

(9) a statement whether the shares to be used for the purposes of the scheme are quoted on a recognised stock exchange and, if so, the name(s) of the stock exchange(s);

(10) the name(s) and registered office(s) of the company or companies whose directors and/or employees will be entitled to participate in the scheme.

3. If approval is given subject to the condition referred to in paragraph 2 of Part I of the Schedule being satisfied, the company shall, whenever a person obtains a right to acquire shares, or acquires shares or an interest in shares, under the scheme, notify to the Board in writing the price at which shares may be acquired by the exercise of the right or, as the case may be, the price at which shares or an interest in shares have been or may be acquired.

4. Any alteration in or relevant addition to the information furnished under Regulation 2 in connection with the application for approval shall be notified forthwith by the company to the Board in writing.

5. Where

(1) the price at which shares may be acquired by the exercise of a right obtained under an approved share option scheme is varied as provided for in paragraph 6 of Part III of the Schedule, or

(2) the price at which shares are acquired under an approved share incentive scheme is reduced as provided for in paragraph 5(2) of Part IV of the Schedule,

the company shall forthwith notify the revised price to the Board in writing, together with details of any variation in the share capital of the body issuing the shares since the rights were obtained or the shares were acquired and, where paragraph (2) above applies, the market value at that time of shares of the same class to which no other restrictions attach than restrictions attaching to all shares of that class.

Furnishing of information concerning participants in approved schemes

6. After each year of assessment the Inspector may give notice to the company or to the body from which rights are to be obtained or shares or interests in shares are to be acquired requiring it to provide, within 30 days of the date of the notice, in respect of each person participating in the scheme during that year of assessment, information as follows: —

(1) his name and address;

(2) if his address is in Scotland, his national insurance number;

(3) the Inspector by whom deduction cards are ordinarily issued;

(4) if he has obtained during the year a right to acquire shares under the scheme, the consideration, if any, given for the right, the number of shares which may be acquired by its exercise and the price at which they may be acquired, together with the amount, if any, for which shares remain to be acquired under rights obtained by him earlier;

(5) if he has during the year exercised, assigned or released a right obtained under the scheme, the date of the exercise, assignment or release and the number and price of any shares acquired;

(6) if he has acquired shares or an interest in shares under the scheme during the year, the number of shares or particulars of the interest and the price at which they were acquired, together with the amount or value of shares or interests acquired by him earlier (and remaining subject to restrictions not attaching to all shares of the same class);

(7) his relevant emoluments for that or the preceding year of assessment;

(8) any other relevant information.

7. If the company or body mentioned in Regulation 6 is not resident in the United Kingdom, the notice mentioned in that Regulation may be given to the manager of any branch or to any agent of the company or body in the United Kingdom.

By Order of the Commissioners of Inland Revenue.

A. H. Dalton,
Secretary.

28th July 1972.

EXPLANATORY NOTE

(This Note is not part of the Regulations.)

Schedule 12 to the Finance Act 1972, which supplements sections 78 and 79 of the Act, makes provision for the approval by the Board of Inland Revenue of employees' share option and share incentive schemes. Approval carries tax benefits for participants. In order to obtain approval of a scheme, the company concerned must satisfy the Board that the scheme complies with the conditions laid down in Schedule 12. Paragraph 3 of Part I of the Schedule empowers the Board to make regulations prescribing the particulars and evidence which must be provided in support of an application for approval of a scheme. Paragraph 4 of Part VII of the Schedule empowers the Board to make regulations requiring information to be given about the persons participating in approved schemes, the shares issued and rights acquired in pursuance of such schemes, and the exercise, assignment or release of such rights as appears to them to be necessary to enable them to give effect to the provisions of the Act. These Regulations are made under those powers.

The Regulations will come into effect on 25th August 1972.

STATUTORY INSTRUMENTS

1972 No. 1132

IRON AND STEEL

The Iron and Steel (Pension Schemes) (Transfer) (No. 3) Regulations 1972

Made - - -	*27th July* 1972
Laid before Parliament	*8th August* 1972
Coming into Operation	*1st September* 1972

The Secretary of State in exercise of his powers under section 40 of the Iron and Steel Act 1949(**a**), as revived and amended by section 31 of the Iron and Steel Act 1967(**b**), and all other powers in that behalf enabling him, after consultation with the British Steel Corporation and such organisations as appear to him to be representative of persons concerned, hereby makes the following regulations: —

Citation and commencement

1.—(1) These regulations may be cited as the Iron and Steel (Pension Schemes) (Transfer) (No. 3) Regulations 1972, shall come into operation on 1st September 1972 and, subject to paragraph (2) hereof, shall have effect from that date.

(2) Regulation 5 shall have effect from the dates specified therein.

2.—(1) In these regulations—

"pension" has the meaning assigned thereto by the Iron and Steel Act 1949;

"pension fund" in relation to a scheduled scheme means all investments and moneys which, or the income from which, can be applied at the date of the coming into operation of these regulations for the purposes of paying pensions;

"pension rights" has the meaning assigned thereto by the Iron and Steel Act 1949;

"the principal scheme" means the British Steel Corporation Staff Superannuation Scheme approved by the Minister of Power on 7th July 1969;

"scheduled scheme" means a pension scheme specified in the Schedule hereto.

(2) The Interpretation Act 1889(**c**) shall apply to the interpretation of these regulations as it applies to the interpretation of an Act of Parliament.

Transfer of Pension Funds of, and Policies of Assurance relating to, scheduled schemes

3.—(1) The pension fund of each of the scheduled schemes, and every right

(**a**) 1949 c. 72.　　　　　　(**b**) 1967 c. 17.
(**c**) 1889 c. 63.

of trustees of a scheduled scheme to receive moneys on the occurrence of certain events by virtue of a policy of assurance held for the purposes of that scheme together with every obligation of the trustees under that policy, shall on these regulations coming into operation be transferred by virtue of these regulations and without further assurance to the trustees of the principal scheme.

(2) The pension funds aforesaid and the moneys received in respect of the said rights together with the pension fund constituted under the principal scheme shall be invested and managed as one fund in accordance with the provisions of the principal scheme relating to the investment and management of the pension fund established under the principal scheme.

4.—(1) A certificate, signed by a trustee of the principal scheme and by any person in whom the pension fund or any part thereof or a right as aforesaid transferred by these regulations was vested, that the pension fund or that part or that right was so transferred, or a copy of the said certificate certified by a trustee of the principal scheme to be a true copy thereof, shall be received by all persons responsible for the registration or inscription of the title to the pension fund or that part thereof or by the assurers, as the case may be, as evidence that it was transferred as aforesaid.

(2) Every person in whom was vested the pension fund or any part thereof or a right transferred as aforesaid shall do all things necessary, or which the trustees of the principal scheme may require to be done, for the purpose of ensuring—

(a) the due registration or inscription of the title of the trustees of the principal scheme to the pension fund or transfer of the right, as the case may be;

(b) the delivery to the said trustees of any document constituting evidence of the said registration, inscription or transfer; and

(c) the receipt by the said trustees of all dividends or interest in respect of the pension fund so transferred due for payment after the date of the coming into operation of these regulations.

Provisions of scheduled scheme

5.—(1) The provisions of a scheduled scheme which relate to eligibility for the payment of benefits and which provide for the payment of contributions shall continue in effect, except that all payments of benefits due under those provisions (including in respect of each such scheme those outstanding immediately before the date specified opposite that Scheme in the Schedule hereto) shall be made by the trustees of the principal scheme from the fund constituted by regulation 3 and all contributions due under those provisions (including in respect of each such scheme those outstanding immediately before the date specified opposite that Scheme in the Schedule hereto) shall be made to the said trustees for payment into the said fund.

(2) Any power or discretion to pay a benefit conferred by the provisions of a scheduled scheme on any person shall be exercisable by the trustees of the principal scheme in place of the person invested with that power or discretion by the scheduled scheme.

(3) Any trustee of a scheduled scheme who would but for the operation of these regulations have been entitled to payment of a sum by way of an indemnity from the pension fund of that scheme shall be so entitled from the

fund constituted by regulation 3, and the trustees of the principal scheme shall accordingly pay him that sum.

(4) Except as provided by this regulation the provisions of a scheduled scheme shall cease to have effect.

Elections under principal scheme

6.—(1) This regulation applies to an election made by a member of a scheduled scheme under a provision of the principal scheme to receive benefits provided for in the principal scheme instead of benefits provided for in the scheduled scheme.

(2) The trustees of the principal scheme shall ensure that an election to which this regulation applies shall not operate so as to place any person (other than the person exercising the election) having pension rights under the scheduled scheme in any worse position by reason of the exercise of the election, and the said trustees shall make such payments to that person as may be necessary to secure that result.

Dated 27th July 1972.

Tom Boardman,
Minister for Industry,
Department of Trade and Industry.

SCHEDULE

Regulations 2(1) and 5

The McCall and Company (Sheffield) Limited Pension Scheme	1st July 1970
Owen and Dyson Limited Pension Scheme	1st July 1970
G. R. Turner Limited Pension and Assurance Scheme ..	1st July 1970
G. R. Turner Limited Pension Fund	1st July 1970
Stewarts and Lloyds and Stanton Staff Pension Fund and Group Life Assurance Scheme	1st January 1971
Stewarts and Lloyds Limited Staff Assurance Scheme No. 1	1st January 1971
Stewarts and Lloyds Limited Staff Assurance Scheme No. 2	1st January 1971
Stewarts and Lloyds Limited Life Assurance Equalisation Scheme	1st January 1971
Stewarts and Lloyds Limited Additional Life Assurance Scheme	1st January 1971
The Staveley Company's Superannuation Fund	1st January 1971
The Staveley Company's Senior Officials Pension Scheme	1st January 1971
The Stanton Ironworks Male Staff Superannuation Fund	1st January 1971
The Stanton Ironworks Female Staff Superannuation Fund	1st January 1971
The Sheepbridge Company Pension Scheme	1st January 1971

The publicly owned company's part of the Thomas W.
Ward Limited Supplementary Retirement Benefits Scheme   1st January 1971

English Steel Corporation Group Staff Pension Fund and
Life Assurance Scheme   ..   ..   1st March 1971

English Steel Corporation Limited Staff Pension Fund and
Life Assurance Scheme   ..   ..   1st March 1971

Supplementary Pension Scheme for the English Steel Cor-
poration Group of Companies Scheme A   ..   ..   1st March 1971

Supplementary Pension Scheme for the English Steel Cor-
poration Group of Companies Scheme B   ..   ..   1st March 1971

Taylor Bros and Company Limited Pension Fund and Life
Assurance Scheme   ..   ..   1st March 1971

The Darlington Forge Limited Pension Fund and Life
Assurance Scheme   ..   ..   1st March 1971

Vickers Staff Association for Life Assurance and Pensions   1st March 1971

The Whitehead Iron and Steel Company Limited Staff
Pension and Life Assurance Scheme   ..   ..   3rd April 1971

The Whitehead Iron and Steel Staff Superannuation Fund   3rd April 1971

The Whitehead Iron and Steel Company Limited Staff Life
Insurance Scheme   ..   ..   3rd April 1971

The Consett Iron Company's Superannuation Fund   ..   1st May 1971

Dorman Long and Co. Pension Fund ..   ..   ..   1st May 1971

Dorman Long and Co. Q Scheme (in respect of staff em-
ployees only)   ..   ..   1st May 1971

Dorman Long Group Senior Executives Pension Scheme   1st May 1971

The Teesside Bridge and Engineering Works Pension Fund   1st May 1971

The Teesside Bridge and Engineering Works Q Scheme (in
respct of staff employees only)   ..   ..   ..   1st May 1971

Redpath Brown and Company Pension Fund ..   ..   1st May 1971

Redpath Brown and Company Q Scheme (in respect of
staff employees only)   ..   ..   1st May 1971

The South Durham and Cargo Fleet Pension Scheme   ..   1st June 1971

The South Durham Steel and Iron Company Limited Supplementary Pension Scheme (in respect of staff employ-
ees only)   ..   ..   1st June 1971

Skinningrove Iron Company Limited Staff Pension Scheme   1st September 1971

Skinningrove Iron Company Limited Staff Assurance Fund   1st September 1971

EXPLANATORY NOTE

(This Note is not part of the Regulations.)

These regulations provide for the transfer to the trustees of the British Steel
Corporation Staff Superannuation Scheme of the assets and liabilities of those
pension schemes listed in the Schedule.

All the pension funds relating to the scheduled schemes, and the rights of
the trustees to receive payments under assurance policies held for the purposes
of the schemes, are to be transferred to the trustees of the Corporation's
scheme and the pension funds and moneys received under those policies, together with the Corporation's scheme pension fund, are to be administered as
one fund (regulation 3). Transfer certificates are to be given to those responsible for effecting the transfers and all documents relating to the scheduled

schemes are to be delivered to the trustees of the Corporation's scheme (regulation 4). The provisions of the scheduled schemes which relate to eligibility for the payment of benefits and contributions are, with the exceptions specified, to continue to have effect from the dates specified in the Schedule but the other provisions are to cease to have effect from those dates (regulation 5). A member of a scheduled scheme may elect to receive benefits provided under the Corporation's scheme instead of those provided under his old scheme. The trustees of the Corporation's scheme are required to ensure that no person other than the member making such an election is placed in a worse position as a result of that election (regulation 6).

STATUTORY INSTRUMENTS

1972 No. 1134

SUGAR

The Sugar (Distribution Payments) (No. 15) Order 1972

Made - - - -	*28th July* 1972
Laid before Parliament -	*31st July* 1972
Coming into Operation -	*1st August* 1972

The Minister of Agriculture, Fisheries and Food, in exercise of the powers conferred upon him by sections 14(5) and 33(4) of the Sugar Act 1956(a), having effect subject to the provisions of section 3 of, and Part II of Schedule 5 to, the Finance Act 1962(b), section 22 of the Finance Act 1964(c) and section 52 of the Finance Act 1966(d) and of all other powers enabling him in that behalf, with the concurrence of the Treasury, and on the advice of the Sugar Board hereby makes the following order:—

1.—(1) This order may be cited as the Sugar (Distribution Payments) (No. 15) Order 1972, and shall come into operation on 1st August 1972.

(2) The Interpretation Act 1889(e) shall apply for the interpretation of this order as it applies for the interpretation of an Act of Parliament.

2. Notwithstanding the provisions of article 2 of the Sugar (Distribution Payments) (No. 14) Order 1972(f), the rates of distribution payments payable under and in accordance with the provisions of section 14 of the Sugar Act 1956, having effect as aforesaid, in respect of sugar and invert sugar imported or home produced or used in the manufacture of imported composite sugar products shall on and after 1st August 1972 be those rates specified in the Schedule to this order; and section 10 of the Finance Act 1901(g) (which relates to new or altered customs or excise duties and their effect upon contracts) shall apply accordingly.

In Witness whereof the Official Seal of the Minister of Agriculture, Fisheries and Food is hereunto affixed on 27th July 1972.

(L.S.)

F. M. Kearns,
Authorised by the Minister.

We concur.
28th July 1972.

Tim Fortescue,
Hugh Rossi,
Two of the Lords Commissioners of
Her Majesty's Treasury.

(a) 1956 c. 48.	(b) 1962 c.44.	(c) 1964 c. 49	(d) 1966 c. 18.
(e) 1889 c. 63.	(f) S.I. 1972/1079 (1972 II, p. 3187).		(g) 1901 c. 7.

SCHEDULE
PART I
RATES OF DISTRIBUTION PAYMENT FOR SUGAR

Polarisation	Rate of Distribution Payment per ton
Exceeding—	£
99°	2·000
98° but not exceeding 99°	1·886
97° ,, ,, ,, 98°	1·840
96° ,, ,, ,, 97°	1·792
95° ,, ,, ,, 96°	1·744
94° ,, ,, ,, 95°	1·696
93° ,, ,, ,, 94°	1·648
92° ,, ,, ,, 93°	1·600
91° ,, ,, ,, 92°	1·552
90° ,, ,, ,, 91°	1·504
89° ,, ,, ,, 90°	1·456
88° ,, ,, ,, 89°	1·408
87° ,, ,, ,, 88°	1·368
86° ,, ,, ,, 87°	1·328
85° ,, ,, ,, 86°	1·292
84° ,, ,, ,, 85°	1·256
83° ,, ,, ,, 84°	1·220
82° ,, ,, ,, 83°	1·184
81° ,, ,, ,, 82°	1·152
80° ,, ,, ,, 81°	1·120
79° ,, ,, ,, 80°	1·088
78° ,, ,, ,, 79°	1·056
77° ,, ,, ,, 78°	1·024
76° ,, ,, ,, 77°	0·992
Not exceeding 76°	0·960

PART II
RATES OF DISTRIBUTION PAYMENT FOR INVERT SUGAR

Sweetening matter content by weight	Rate of Distribution Payment per cwt.
	£
70 per cent. or more	0·06
Less than 70 per cent. and more than 50 per cent.	0·04
Not more than 50 per cent.	0·02

EXPLANATORY NOTE
(*This Note is not part of the Order.*)

This order provides for reductions equivalent to £4 per ton of refined sugar in the rates of distribution payment in respect of sugar and invert sugar which become eligible for such payments on and after 1st August 1972.

STATUTORY INSTRUMENTS

1972 No. 1135

SUGAR

The Sugar (Distribution Repayments) (Amendment) (No. 14) Order 1972

Made - - - -	28*th July* 1972
Laid before Parliament	31*st July* 1972
Coming into Operation	1*st August* 1972

The Minister of Agriculture, Fisheries and Food, in exercise of the powers conferred upon him by sections 15 and 33(4) of the Sugar Act 1956(a), having effect subject to the provisions of section 3 of, and Part II of Schedule 5 to, the Finance Act 1962(b), section 22 of the Finance Act 1964(c) and section 52 of the Finance Act 1966(d) and of all other powers enabling him in that behalf, an order (e) having been made under section 14 of the said Act, hereby makes the following order:—

1.—(1) This order may be cited as the Sugar (Distribution Repayments) (Amendment) (No. 14) Order 1972, and shall come into operation on 1st August 1972.

(2) The Interpretation Act 1889(f) shall apply for the interpretation of this order as it applies for the interpretation of an Act of Parliament.

2.—(1) Notwithstanding the provisions of article 2(1) of the Sugar (Distribution Repayments) (Amendment) (No. 13) Order 1972(g) the amount of distribution repayment payable in respect of invert sugar, if the relevant drawback is payable thereon as being invert sugar produced in the United Kingdom from materials on which sugar duty has been paid on or after 1st August 1972, shall be calculated thereon at the rate applicable to the invert sugar in accordance with the rates prescribed in the Schedule to this order.

(2) Article 2(1) of the Sugar (Distribution Repayments) Order 1972(h) shall apply for the interpretation of this article.

In Witness whereof the Official Seal of the Minister of Agriculture, Fisheries and Food is hereunto affixed on 28th July 1972.

(L.S.)

F. M. Kearns,
Authorised by the Minister.

(a) 1956 c. 48. (b) 1962 c. 44. (c) 1964 c. 49.
(d) 1966 c. 18. (e) S.I. 1972/1134 (1972 II, p. 3340). (f) 1889 c. 63.
(g) S.I. 1972/1080 (1972 II, p. 3189). (h) S.I. 1972/67 (1972 I, p. 162).

THE SCHEDULE

RATES OF DISTRIBUTION REPAYMENT FOR INVERT SUGAR

Sweetening matter content by weight	Rate of Distribution Repayment per cwt.
	£
More than 80 per cent.	0·07
More than 70 per cent. but not more than 80 per cent.	0·06
More than 60 per cent. but not more than 70 per cent.	0·04
More than 50 per cent. but not more than 60 per cent.	0·03
Not more than 50 per cent. and the invert sugar not being less in weight than 14 lb. per gallon	0·02

EXPLANATORY NOTE

(This Note is not part of the Order.)

This order, which is consequent upon the Sugar (Distribution Payments) (No. 15) Order 1972 (S.I. 1972/1134), provides for reductions equivalent to £4 per ton of refined sugar in the rates of distribution repayment, in respect of sugar and invert sugar produced in the United Kingdom from materials which become eligible for distribution payments on or after 1st August 1972.

STATUTORY INSTRUMENTS

1972 No. 1136

SUGAR

The Composite Sugar Products (Distribution Payments— Average Rates) (No. 15) Order 1972

Made	-	-	-	28*th July* 1972
Laid before Parliament-				31*st July* 1972
Coming into Operation				1*st August* 1972

Whereas the Minister of Agriculture, Fisheries and Food (hereinafter called " the Minister ") has on the recommendation of the Sugar Board made an order (a) pursuant to the powers conferred upon him by section 9(1) of the Sugar Act 1956(b) having effect subject to section 14(8) of that Act and to the provisions of section 3 of, and Part II of Schedule 5 to, the Finance Act 1962 (c), section 22 of the Finance Act 1964(d) and section 52 of the Finance Act 1966(e), providing that in the case of certain descriptions of composite sugar products distribution payments shall be calculated on the basis of an average quantity of sugar or invert sugar taken to have been used in the manufacture of the products and that certain other descriptions shall be treated as not containing any sugar or invert sugar:

And whereas the Minister has by the Sugar (Distribution Payments) (No.15) Order 1972(f) provided for a change in the rates of distribution payments in respect of sugar and invert sugar which became eligible for such payments on and after 1st August 1972.

Now, therefore, the Minister on the recommendation of the Sugar Board, and in exercise of the powers conferred upon him by sections 9(1) and 33(4) of the Sugar Act 1956, having effect as aforesaid, and of all other powers enabling him in that behalf, hereby makes the following order:—

1.—(1) This order may be cited as the Composite Sugar Products (Distribution Payments—Average Rates) (No.15) Order 1972, and shall come into operation on 1st August 1972.

(2) The Interpretation Act 1889(g) shall apply to the interpretation of this order as it applies to the interpretation of an Act of Parliament.

2. Distribution payments payable on or after 1st August 1972 under and in accordance with section 14 of the Sugar Act 1956, having effect as aforesaid, in respect of sugar and invert sugar used in the manufacture of the descriptions of imported composite sugar products specified in the second column of Schedule 1 to this order, being goods which are classified in the tariff headings indicated in relation to them in the first column of the said Schedule shall, notwithstanding the provisions of the Sugar (Distribution Payments) (No. 15) Order 1972 and the Composite Sugar Products (Distribution Payments—Average Rates) (No. 14) Order 1972(a) be calculated by reference to the weight of the products and the rates specified in relation thereto in the third column of the said Schedule.

3. Imported composite sugar products other than those of a description specified in Schedules 1 and 2 to this order shall be treated as not containing any sugar or invert sugar for the purposes of distribution payments.

(a) S.I. 1972/1081 (1972 II, p. 3191).   (b) 1956 c. 48.   (c) 1962 c. 44.   (d) 1964 c. 49.
(e) 1966 c. 18.   (f) S.I. 1972/1134 (1972 II, p. 3340).   (g) 1889 c. 63.

In Witness whereof the Official Seal of the Minister of Agriculture, Fisheries and Food is hereunto affixed on 28th July 1972.

(L.S.)

F. M. Kearns,
Authorised by the Minister.

SCHEDULE 1

In this Schedule:—

" Tariff heading " means a heading or, where the context so requires, a subheading of the Customs Tariff 1959 (see paragraph (1) of Article 2 of the Import Duties (General) (No. 7) Order 1971)(a).

Tariff heading	Description of Composite Sugar Products	Rate of Distribution Payment
		Per cwt. £
04.02 ..	Milk and cream, preserved, concentrated or sweetened, containing more than 10 per cent. by weight of added sugar	0·04
17.02 (B) (2) and 17.05 (B)	Syrups containing sucrose sugar, whether or not flavoured or coloured, but not including fruit juices containing added sugar in any proportion:—	
	Containing 70 per cent. or more by weight of sweetening matter	0·06
	Containing less than 70 per cent., and more than 50 per cent. by weight of sweetening matter	0·04
	Containing not more than 50 per cent. by weight of sweetening matter	0·02
17.02 (F) ..	Caramel:—	
	Solid	0·10
	Liquid	0·06
17.04 ..	Sugar confectionery, not containing cocoa ..	0·08
18.06 ..	Chocolate and other food preparations containing cocoa and added sugar:—	
	Chocolate couverture not prepared for retail sale; chocolate milk crumb, liquid ..	0·04
	Chocolate milk crumb, solid	0·05
	Solid chocolate bars or blocks, milk or plain, with or without fruit or nuts; other chocolate confectionery consisting wholly of chocolate or of chocolate and other ingredients not containing added sugar :.	0·04
	Other	0·05

(a) S.I. 1971/1971 (1971 III, p. 5330).

SCHEDULE 1—*continued*

Tariff heading	Description of Composite Sugar Products	Rate of Distribution Payment
		Per cwt. £
19.08 ..	Pastry, biscuits, cakes and other fine bakers' wares containing added sugar:—	
	Biscuits, wafers and rusks containing more than 12½ per cent. by weight of added sugar, and other biscuits, wafers and rusks included in retail packages with such goods.. ..	0·02
	Cakes with covering or filling containing added sugar; meringues	0·03
	Other	0·01
20.01 ..	Vegetables and fruit, prepared or preserved by vinegar or acetic acid, containing added sugar:—	
	Containing 10 per cent. or more by weight of added sugar	0·03
	Other	0·00½
20.03 ..	Fruit preserved by freezing, containing added sugar	0·01
20.04 ..	Fruit, fruit-peel and parts of plants, preserved by sugar (drained, glacé or crystallised)	0·06
20.05 ..	Jams, fruit jellies, marmalades, fruit puree and fruit pastes, being cooked preparations, containing added sugar	0·06
20.06 ..	Fruit otherwise prepared or preserved, containing added sugar:—	
	Ginger	0·05
	Other	0·01

SCHEDULE 2

Tariff heading	Description of Composite Sugar Products
17.05 (A) and (B)	Sugar and invert sugar, flavoured or coloured.

EXPLANATORY NOTE

(This Note is not part of the Order.)

This order provides for reductions in the average rates of distribution payments payable in respect of imported composite sugar products of the descriptions specified in Schedule 1 on and after 1st August 1972. These correspond to reductions in the rates of distribution payment effected by the Sugar (Distribution Payments) (No. 15) Order 1972 (S.I. 1972/1134). Provision is also made for certain imported composite sugar products to be treated as not containing any sugar or invert sugar.

STATUTORY INSTRUMENTS

1972 No. 1137

AGRICULTURE

The Price Stability of Imported Products (Rates of Levy) (Cereals) (No. 18) Order 1972

Made -	-	-	-	*28th July* 1972
Coming into Operation				*1st August* 1972

The Minister of Agriculture, Fisheries and Food, in exercise of the powers conferred upon him by section 1(2), (4), (5), (6) and (7) of the Agriculture and Horticulture Act 1964(a) and of all other powers enabling him in that behalf, hereby makes the following order:—

1. This order may be cited as the Price Stability of Imported Products (Rates of Levy) (Cereals) (No. 18) Order 1972, and shall come into operation on 1st August 1972.

2.—(1) In this order—

" the Principal Order " means the Price Stability of Imported Products (Levy Arrangements) (Cereals) Order 1971(b), as amended by any subsequent order and if any such order is replaced by any subsequent order the expression shall be construed as a reference to such subsequent order;

AND other expressions have the same meaning as in the Principal Order.

(2) The Interpretation Act 1889(c) shall apply to the interpretation of this order as it applies to the interpretation of an Act of Parliament and as if this order and the order hereby revoked were Acts of Parliament.

3. In accordance with and subject to the provisions of Part II of the Principal Order (which provides for the charging of levies on imports of certain specified commodities) the rate of levy for such imports into the United Kingdom of any specified commodity as are described in column 2 of the Schedule to this order in relation to a tariff heading indicated in column 1 of that Schedule shall be the rate set forth in relation thereto in column 3 of that Schedule.

4. The Price Stability of Imported Products (Rates of Levy) (Cereals) (No. 17) Order 1972(d) is hereby revoked.

In Witness whereof the Official Seal of the Minister of Agriculture, Fisheries and Food is hereunto affixed on 28th July 1972.

(L.S.)

M. E. Johnston,
Authorised by the Minister.

(a) 1964 c. 28.   (b) S.I. 1971/631 (1971 I, p. 1660).   (c) 1889 c. 63.
(d) S.I. 1972/991 (1972 II, p.3076).

SCHEDULE

1. Tariff Heading	2. Description of Imports	3. Rate of Levy
	Imports of:—	per ton £
10.01	Denatured wheat	4·00
	Wheat (other than denatured wheat)..	9·00
10.03	Barley other than barley having a potential diastatic activity of not less than 170 degrees	5·75
10.04	Oats	3·25
10.05	Maize (other than sweet corn on the cob)	5·50
10.07	Grain sorghum	4·75

11.02	Cereal groats, meals, kibbled or cut cereals, rolled, flaked, crushed or bruised cereals and other processed cereals—
	  of barley .. ..
	  of maize .. ..
		
		4·50
		5·50

EXPLANATORY NOTE

(This Note is not part of the Order.)

This order, which comes into operation on 1st August 1972, supersedes the Price Stability of Imported Products (Rates of Levy) (Cereals) (No. 17) Order 1972.

It—

(a) reduces the rate of levy to be charged on imports of—

   (i) barley other than barley having a potential diastatic activity of not less than 170 degrees to £5·75 per ton;

   (ii) oats to £3·25 per ton; and

(b) reimposes unchanged the remaining rates of levy in force immediately before the commencement of the order.

STATUTORY INSTRUMENTS

1972 No. 1138 (S.80)

RATING AND VALUATION

The Electricity Boards (Standard Amount) (Scotland) Order 1972

Made - - -	*7th July* 1972
Laid before the Commons House of Parliament	*14th July* 1972
Coming into Operation	*28th July* 1972

In exercise of the powers conferred on me by section 17(1) as read with section 45(2) of the Local Government (Scotland) Act 1966(**a**) and of all other powers enabling me in that behalf, I hereby make the following order: —

1.—(1) This order may be cited as the Electricity Boards (Standard Amount) (Scotland) Order 1972 and shall come into operation on the day following the day on which it is approved by a resolution of the Commons House of Parliament.

(2) The Interpretation Act 1889(**b**) shall apply for the interpretation of this order as it applies for the interpretation of an Act of Parliament and as if this order and the order hereby revoked were Acts of Parliament.

2. For the purpose of calculating the payments which are, under the provisions of Part V of the Local Government Act 1948(**c**), to be made year by year by the South of Scotland Electricity Board and the North of Scotland Hydro-Electric Board respectively for the benefit of local authorities in Scotland for the year 1972-73 and subsequent years, the standard amount referred to in sections 96 to 98 of that Act (which relate to payments by the South of Scotland Board) shall be £5,137,000; and the standard amount referred to in section 99 of that Act (which relates to payments by the Hydro-Electric Board) shall be £1,378,000.

3. The Electricity Boards (Standard Amount) (Scotland) Order 1967(**d**) in its application to years subsequent to the year 1971-72 is hereby revoked.

Gordon Campbell,
One of Her Majesty's
Principal Secretaries of State.

St. Andrew's House,
Edinburgh.

7th July 1972.

(**a**) 1966 c. 51.	(**b**) 1889 c. 63.
(**c**) 1948 c. 26.	(**d**) S.I. 1967/1163 (1967 II, p. 3405).

EXPLANATORY NOTE

(This Note is not part of the Order.)

This Order provides for an increase for the year 1972-73 and subsequent years in the standard amounts on which payments in lieu of rates to Scottish local authorities by the South of Scotland Electricity Board and the North of Scotland Hydro-Electric Board are based, to take account of the general increase in valuations following the 1971 revaluation.

STATUTORY INSTRUMENTS

1972 No. 1139 (L.14)

SOLICITORS

The Solicitors' Remuneration Order 1972

Made - - -	*27th July* 1972
Laid before Parliament	*7th August* 1972
Coming into Operation	*1st January* 1973

We, Quintin McGarel, Baron Hailsham of Saint Marylebone, Lord High Chancellor of Great Britain, John Passmore, Baron Widgery, Lord Chief Justice of England, Alfred Thompson, Baron Denning, Master of the Rolls, Sir Desmond Heap, President of The Law Society and George Pownall Atkinson, Esquire, President of the Bristol Law Society (being the persons authorised by section 56 of the Solicitors Act 1957(a) to make general orders prescribing and regulating the remuneration of solicitors in respect of non-contentious business generally) and Theodore Burton Fox Ruoff, Esquire, C.B., C.B.E., Chief Land Registrar (being a person so authorised in respect of business under the Land Registration Act 1925(b)) do hereby make the following Order in exercise of the powers vested in us by the said section:—

1.—(1) This Order may be cited as the Solicitors' Remuneration Order 1972.

(2) The Interpretation Act 1889(c) shall apply to the interpretation of this Order as it applies to the interpretation of an Act of Parliament.

(3) This Order shall come into operation on 1st January 1973 and shall apply to all business for which instructions are accepted on or after that date.

2. A solicitor's remuneration for non-contentious business (including business under the Land Registration Act 1925) shall be such sum as may be fair and reasonable having regard to all the circumstances of the case and in particular to—

  (i) the complexity of the matter or the difficulty or novelty of the questions raised;
  (ii) the skill, labour, specialised knowledge and responsibility involved;
  (iii) the time spent on the business;
  (iv) the number and importance of the documents prepared or perused, without regard to length;
  (v) the place where and the circumstances in which the business or any part thereof is transacted;
  (vi) the amount or value of any money or property involved;
  (vii) whether any land involved is registered land within the meaning of the Land Registration Act 1925; and
  (viii) the importance of the matter to the client.

(a) 1957 c. 27. (b) 1925 c. 21. (c) 1889 c. 63.

3.—(1) Without prejudice to the provisions of sections 69, 70 and 71 of the Solicitors Act 1957 (which relate to taxation of costs) the client may require the solicitor to obtain a certificate from The Law Society stating that in their opinion the sum charged is fair and reasonable or, as the case may be, what other sum would be fair and reasonable, and in the absence of taxation the sum stated in the certificate, if less than that charged, shall be the sum payable by the client.

(2) Before the solicitor brings proceedings to recover costs on a bill for non-contentious business he must, unless the costs have been taxed, have informed the client in writing—

    (i) of his right under paragraph (1) of this article to require the solicitor to obtain a certificate from The Law Society, and

    (ii) of the provisions of the Solicitors Act 1957 relating to taxation of costs.

(3) The client shall not be entitled to require the solicitor to obtain a certificate from The Law Society under paragraph (1) of this article—

    (i) after the expiry of one month from the date on which the client was given the information required by paragraph (2) of this article;

    (ii) after a bill has been delivered and paid; or

    (iii) after the High Court has ordered the bill to be taxed.

4.—(1) On the taxation of any bill delivered under this Order it shall be the duty of the solicitor to satisfy the taxing officer as to the fairness and reasonableness of the sum charged.

(2) If the taxing officer allows less than one half of the sum charged, he shall bring the facts of the case to the attention of The Law Society.

5.—(1) After the expiry of one month from the delivery of any bill for non-contentious business a solicitor may charge interest on the amount of the bill (including any disbursements) at a rate not exceeding the rate for the time being payable on judgment debts, so, however, that before interest may be charged the client must have been given the information required by article 3(2) of this Order.

(2) If an application is made for the bill to be taxed or the solicitor is required to obtain a certificate from The Law Society, interest shall be calculated by reference to the amount finally ascertained.

6. A solicitor may take from his client security for the payment of any remuneration, including the amount of any interest to which the solicitor may become entitled under article 5 of this Order.

7. The Orders specified in the schedule hereto are hereby revoked except in their application to business for which instructions are accepted before this Order comes into operation.

Dated 27th July 1972.

> *Hailsham of St. Marylebone,* C.
> *Widgery,* C. J.
> *Denning,* M. R.
> *Desmond Heap.*
> *G. P. Atkinson.*
> *Theodore B. F. Ruoff.*

SCHEDULE

Article 7

ORDERS REVOKED

Title	Reference
Solicitors' Remuneration Order 1883	Rev. XXI, p.205
Solicitors' Remuneration Act General Order 1925	S. R. & O. 1925/755 (Rev. XXI, p.213: 1925, p.1440)
Solicitors' Remuneration (Registered Land) Order 1925	S. R. & O. 1926/2 (Rev. XXI, p.221: 1926, p.1224)
Solicitors' Remuneration Order 1936	S. R. & O. 1936/326 (Rev. XXI, p.215: 1936 II, p.2512)
Solicitors' Remuneration (Registered Land) Order 1936	S. R. & O. 1936/327 (1936 II, p.2513)
Solicitors' Remuneration Order 1944	S. R. & O. 1944/203 (Rev. XXI, p.217: 1944 I, p.915)
Solicitors' Remuneration Order 1953	S.I. 1953/117 (1953 II, p.1946)
Solicitors' Remuneration (Registered Land) Order 1953	S.I. 1953/118 (1953 II, p.1951)
Solicitors' Remuneration Order 1970	S.I. 1970/2021 (1970 III, p.6591)
Solicitors' Remuneration (Registered Land) Order 1970	S.I. 1970/2022 (1970 III, p.6595)

EXPLANATORY NOTE

(This Note is not part of the Order.)

This Order provides that in place of the scale charges prescribed by the Remuneration Orders listed in the schedule solicitors may charge for non-contentious business such sum as may be fair and reasonable in all the circumstances, having regard in particular to the considerations mentioned in article 2.   Without prejudice to his right to have a bill taxed by the court, a client may, if he wishes, apply to The Law Society for a certificate stating whether in their opinion the sum charged by the solicitor is fair and reasonable or, as the case may be, what other sum would be fair and reasonable: the latter, if less than the sum charged, will, in the absence of taxation, be the sum payable by the client.

The Order applies to business for which instructions are accepted on or after the 1st January 1973.

STATUTORY INSTRUMENTS

1972 No. 1145

SOCIAL SECURITY

The Supplementary Benefit (Determination of Requirements) Regulations 1972

Laid before Parliament in draft

Made - - -		*28th July* 1972
Coming into Operation—		
Regulations 1, 2(1), (2), (3)(i), (4), 3		*2nd October* 1972
Regulation 2(3)(ii)		*4th June* 1973

Whereas a draft of the following regulations was laid before Parliament and approved by resolution of each House of Parliament:

Now, therefore, the Secretary of State for Social Services, with the consent of the Treasury, in exercise of the powers conferred by section 5 of the Ministry of Social Security Act 1966(a), and of all other powers enabling him in that behalf, hereby makes the following regulations:—

Citation, commencement and interpretation

1.—(1) These regulations may be cited as the Supplementary Benefit (Determination of Requirements) Regulations 1972 and shall come into operation except regulation 2(3)(ii) on 2nd October 1972, and in the case of regulation 2(3)(ii) on 4th June 1973.

(2) In these regulations, unless the context otherwise requires, "the Act" means the Ministry of Social Security Act 1966 and other expressions have the same meaning as in the Act.

(3) The rules for the construction of Acts of Parliament contained in the Interpretation Act 1889(b) shall apply for the purpose of the interpretation of these regulations as they apply for the purpose of the interpretation of an Act of Parliament.

Amendment of provisions for calculating requirements

2.—(1) Part II (calculation of requirements) of Schedule 2 to the Act (provisions for determining right to and amount of benefit) shall be varied in accordance with the following provisions of this regulation.

(a) 1966 c. 20.   (b) 1889 c. 63.

(2) For paragraph 9 (normal requirements) and paragraph 10 (blind persons' requirements), as varied (**a**), there shall be substituted the following paragraphs—

"Normal requirements

           £

9. Requirements of persons other than blind persons—

    (*a*) husband and wife or other persons falling within paragraph 3(1) of this Schedule ...   .   10·65

    (*b*) person living alone or householder not falling within sub-paragraph (*a*) of this paragraph who is directly responsible for household necessities and rent (if any)   ...   6·55

    (*c*) any other person aged—

        (i) not less than 18 years ...   .   5·20

        (ii) less than 18 but not less than 16 years   ...   ...   4·05

        (iii) less than 16 but not less than 13 years   ...   ...   3·40

        (iv) less than 13 but not less than 11 years   ...   2·75

        (v) less than 11 but not less than 5 years   ...   ...   2·25

        (vi) less than 5 years   ...   .   1·90

Blind Persons

10. Requirements of persons who are or include blind persons—

           £

    (*a*) husband and wife or other persons falling within paragraph 3(1) of this Schedule—

        (i) if one of them is blind ...   .   11·90

        (ii) if both of them are blind   ...   ...   12·70

    (*b*) any other blind person aged—

        (i) not less than 18 years ...   .   7·80

        (ii) less than 18 but not less than 16 years   ...   ...   4·95

        (iii) less than 16 but not less than 13 years   ...   ...   3·40

        (iv) less than 13 but not less than 11 years   ...   ...   2·75

        (v) less than 11 but not less than 5 years   ...   ...   2·25

        (vi) less than 5 years   ...   .   1·90"

(3) In paragraph 12A (attendance requirements)(**b**)—

    (i) for the references in sub-paragraph (1) to £4·80 there shall be substituted references to £5·40.

    (ii) at the end of the paragraph there shall be added the following sub-paragraph:

        "(4) Where in respect of a severely disabled person (other than one to whom sub-paragraph (1) applies) there is entitlement to attendance allowance at the rate of £3·60 a week sub-paragraph (1) shall have effect as if for the references to £5·40 there were substituted references to £3·60 and for the reference to attendance requirements there were substituted a reference to such person's requirements for attendance by virtue of which that entitlement arises."

(a) The relevant amending instrument is S.I. 1971/1054 (1971 II, p. 3141).
(b) Inserted by S.I. 1971/1054 (1971 II, p. 3141).

(4) For paragraph 13(1)(*b*) (increase on account of rent of the amount speci-fied for requirements where the beneficiary is a non-householder aged 18 years or over), as varied (**a**), there shall be substituted the following—

"(*b*) in any other case by £0·70."

Additional provisions relating to persons in receipt of long-term addition to supplementary benefit

3.—(1) The said Part II of Schedule 2 to the Act shall be further varied in accordance with the following provisions of this regulation.

(2) Immediately after paragraph 12A there shall be inserted the following paragraph—

"*Persons in receipt of long-term addition to supplementary benefit*

12B. The amounts applicable under the preceding paragraphs shall be increased by £0·10 in the case of a person whose requirements include an amount specified in either paragraph 11 or paragraph 12 of this Schedule."

(3) In paragraph 17 (persons paying for board and lodging), as varied (**a**), for the reference to paragraphs 9 to 12A there shall be substituted a refer-ence to paragraphs 9 to 12B.

Keith Joseph,
Secretary of State for Social Services.

26th July 1972.

We consent.

Tim Fortescue,

Hugh Rossi,

Two of the Lords Commissioners
of Her Majesty's Treasury.

28th July 1972.

(**a**) The relevant amending instrument is S.I. 1971/1054 (1971 II, p. 3141).

EXPLANATORY NOTE
(This Note is not part of the Regulations.)

These Regulations vary the provisions of Part II (calculation of requirements) of Schedule 2 (determination of right to and amount of benefit) to the Ministry of Social Security Act 1966.

Regulation 1 is formal. Regulation 2 increases certain weekly amounts allowed for requirements; paragraph (2) relates to normal and blind persons' requirements; paragraph (3)(i) increases the present weekly amount for attendance requirements and paragraph (3)(ii) provides for an increase of amounts applicable in other cases of severe disablement where the person has title (or underlying title) to attendance allowance at a lower rate; paragraph (4) increases the rent addition for non-householders under paragraph 13(1)(*b*) of the Schedule and removes the present age qualification. Regulation 3 provides for an increase of amounts applicable where a person's requirements include an amount specified in paragraph 11 or paragraph 12 of the Schedule (long-term addition to supplementary benefit). The Regulations have effect from 2nd October 1972 except regulation 2(3)(ii) which comes into operation on 4th June 1973.

STATUTORY INSTRUMENTS

1972 No. 1146

PURCHASE TAX

The Purchase Tax (Terminal Provisions) Regulations 1972

Made - - -	*1st August* 1972
Laid before the House of Commons	*9th August* 1972
Coming into Operation— *Regulations* 1, 2, 3, 4	*1st October* 1972
Regulation 5	*1st April* 1973
Regulation 6	*1st May* 1973

The Commissioners of Customs and Excise by virtue of the powers conferred on them by section 31 of the Purchase Tax Act 1963(**a**) and section 54(7) of the Finance Act 1972(**b**) and of all other powers enabling them in that behalf hereby make the following Regulations—

1.—(1) These Regulations may be cited as the Purchase Tax (Terminal Provisions) Regulations 1972.

(2) These Regulations shall come into operation on the following dates: —

Regulations 1, 2, 3 and 4	1st October 1972
Regulation 5	1st April 1973
Regulation 6	1st May 1973

(3) The Interpretation Act 1889(**c**) shall apply for the interpretation of these Regulations as it applies for the interpretation of an Act of Parliament.

2. On and after 1st October 1972 every person having in his possession chargeable goods in circumstances where the delivery of the goods is liable, under section 40(4) of the Purchase Tax Act 1963, to be treated as a delivery under a chargeable purchase : —

(*a*) shall keep records in the form and containing the particulars set out in Regulation 3 of these Regulations of such goods and of his purchases of such goods and shall preserve those records for a period of two years and shall produce them for inspection by any officer or other person authorised in that behalf by the Commissioners of Customs and Excise at such time and at such place as that officer or person may require;

(**a**) 1963 c. 9.   (**b**) 1972 c. 41.
(**c**) 1889 c. 63.

(b) shall furnish at the time and place specified in Regulation 4 of these Regulations to the persons who have delivered such goods statements in the form and containing the particulars specified in that Regulation of such goods remaining in his possession and of any purchase he has made of such goods. Every such statement shall contain a declaration signed by the person to whom the goods were delivered that the statement is to the best of his knowledge correct and complete.

3. The records required to be kept by Regulation 2 of these Regulations shall be in the form of a separate record of goods supplied by each supplier and shall contain the following particulars: —

(a) the name and address of that supplier;

(b) the quantity and description of goods delivered at any particular time with sufficient particulars to enable the goods to be identified;

(c) the date of delivery; and

(d) the date when any of those goods are purchased from the supplier by the person required to keep the record.

4.—(1) Every statement required by Regulation 2 of these Regulations shall be in the form of a separate statement for each of the periods 1st October 1972 to 31st December 1972 and 1st January 1973 to 31st March 1973 but, if there is any change in purchase tax whereby any class of goods to which the statement relates ceases to be chargeable with purchase tax or becomes chargeable at a lower or a higher rate of purchase tax, there shall be instead statements for the part of such period before that change and for the part of such period after that change.

For the purpose of this Regulation "rate of purchase tax" includes the amount of any adjustment thereto under section 9(2) of the Finance Act 1961(a).

(2) Every such statement shall contain the following particulars: —

(a) the period or part of a period to which it relates;

(b) the name and address of the person to whom it is furnished;

(c) the name and address of the person by whom it is furnished; and

(d) the quantity and description of the following goods with sufficient particulars to enable them to be identified: —

(i) goods purchased by that person during the period or part of a period; and

(ii) goods not so purchased which at the end of the period or part of a period remain in the possession of the person furnishing the statement,

and shall be furnished not later than fifteen days after the period or part of a period to which it relates to the person supplying the goods to which it relates at his address.

5. The Purchase Tax Regulations 1965(b) are revoked to the extent specified in the third column of Part I of the Schedule to these Regulations.

(a) 1961 c. 36.   (b) S.I. 1965/1050 (1965 I, p. 2551).

6. The Purchase Tax Regulations 1965 are further revoked to the extent specified in the third column of Part II of the Schedule to these Regulations.

1st August 1972.

K. B. Pepper,
Commissioner of Customs and Excise.

King's Beam House,
Mark Lane,
London, EC3R 7HE.

THE SCHEDULE

PART I

REGULATIONS REVOKED ON 1ST APRIL 1973

Instrument	Reference	Extent of Revocation
The Purchase Tax Regulations 1965.	S.I. 1965/1050 (1965 I, p. 2551).	Regulations 1, 2, 4, 6 and 10.
		In the Schedule, the Forms numbered 1 and 2.

PART II

REGULATIONS REVOKED ON 1ST MAY 1973

Instrument	Reference	Extent of Revocation
The Purchase Tax Regulations 1965.	S.I. 1965/1050 (1965 I, p. 2551).	Regulations 7 and 12.
		In the Schedule, the Form numbered 3.

EXPLANATORY NOTE

(*This Note is not part of the Regulations*)

These Regulations provide that from 1st October 1972 until the tax is removed persons having in their possession chargeable goods on which purchase tax does not become due until they purchase them (as under sale or return arrangements) shall keep records of all such goods and shall furnish periodical statements to their suppliers of such goods remaining in their possession and of those purchased by them.

These Regulations also provide for the revocation of the Purchase Tax Regulations 1965 by stages, consequent upon the termination of the tax. Provisions revoked include those which regulate purchase tax registration, declarations by importers, and representations as to the purpose of a purchase or importation (with effect from 1st April 1973) and the furnishing of returns of tax (with effect from 1st May 1973).

STATUTORY INSTRUMENTS

1972 No. 1147

VALUE ADDED TAX

The Value Added Tax (General) Regulations 1972

Made - - - -	*1st August* 1972
Laid before the House of Commons	*9th August* 1972
Coming into Operation:	
as to Parts I and II	*1st October* 1972
as to the remainder	*1st April* 1973

The Commissioners of Customs and Excise, in exercise of the powers conferred on them by sections 3(3), (4) and (5), 7(8), 12(7), 16(2) and (3), 17(1), 18, 23(2) and (3), 27(3), 30(1), (2), (4), (5) and (6), 33(3) and (4) and 35(1) of, and Paragraph 13 of Schedule 1 to, the Finance Act 1972(a) and of all other powers enabling them in that behalf, hereby make the following Regulations:—

PART I

PRELIMINARY

Citation and commencement

1.—(1) These Regulations may be cited as the Value Added Tax (General) Regulations 1972.

(2) They shall come into operation as to Parts I and II on 1st October 1972 and as to the remainder on 1st April 1973.

Interpretation

2.—(1) In these Regulations:—

"the Act" means the Finance Act 1972;

"Controller" means the Controller, Customs and Excise, Value Added Tax Central Unit;

"prescribed accounting period" means a period as referred to in Regulation 46 of these Regulations;

"registered person" means a person registered by the Commissioners under Schedule 1 to the Act;

"registration number" means the number allocated by the Commissioners to a taxable person in the certificate of registration issued to him.

(a) 1972 c. 41.

(2) In these Regulations any reference to a form prescribed in the Schedule to these Regulations shall include a reference to a form to the like effect which has been approved by the Commissioners.

(3) The Interpretation Act 1889(a) shall apply for the interpretation of these Regulations at it applies for the interpretation of an Act of Parliament.

PART II

REGISTRATION AND NOTIFICATION

3.—(1) Any person required under paragraph 3, 5 or 6 of Schedule 1 to the Act to notify the Commissioners of his liability to be registered or who wishes to register under paragraph 7 of the said Schedule shall do so on the form numbered 1 in the Schedule to these Regulations.

(2) Where the notification referred to in this Regulation is made for or on behalf of a partnership, the person so notifying shall furnish the particulars of the names and addresses of all the partners, whether or not actively engaged in the day-to-day business of the partnership, on the form numbered 2 in the Schedule to these Regulations.

4. Every registered person except one to whom paragraph 8, 9 or 10 of Schedule 1 to the Act applies shall, within 21 days after any change has been made in the name, constitution or ownership of his business, or after any other event has occurred which may necessitate the variation of the register or cancellation of his registration, notify the Commissioners in writing of such change or event and furnish them with full particulars thereof.

5.—(1) Where any notice is to be given for the purposes of the Act or these Regulations by or on behalf of a partnership, such notice shall be given by the precedent partner.

(2) The precedent partner is the partner who, being resident in the United Kingdom—

(a) is first named in the agreement of partnership; or

(b) if there is no agreement, is named singly or with precedence to the other partners in the usual name of the firm; or

(c) is the precedent acting partner, if the person named with precedence is not an acting one;

provided that, where there is no precedent partner, it shall be the duty of all the partners to give such notification as may be required; and, in such a case, all the partners shall give that notification in one document; but notification by any partner on behalf of the partnership shall be deemed to be notification by all of them.

(3) Where, in Scotland, a body of persons carrying on a business which includes the making of taxable supplies is a partnership required to be registered, any notice shall be given and signed in the manner indicated in section 6 of the Partnership Act 1890(b).

(a) 1889 c. 63.   (b) 1890 c. 39.

6. Where any notice is to be given for the purposes of the Act or these Regulations by or on behalf of a club or an association the affairs of which are managed by its members or a committee or committees of its members, such notice shall be given by a responsible officer of the club or association who shall be named in the notice.

7.—(1) If a registered person dies or becomes bankrupt or otherwise incapacitated, the Commissioners may, from the date on which he died or became bankrupt or incapacitated until some other person is registered in his stead or the incapacity ceases, as the case may be, treat as a registered person any person acting or purporting to act as a personal representative, trustee, receiver or committee; and the provisions of the Act and of any Regulations made thereunder shall apply to any person so treated as though he were a registered person.

(2) Any person acting or purporting to act as aforesaid shall, within 21 days of being appointed, or of commencing so to act, whichever is the earlier, inform the Commissioners in writing of the date of the death or of the nature of the incapacity and the date on which it began.

PART III

TAX INVOICES

8.—(1) Save as otherwise provided in these Regulations, a taxable person making a taxable supply to another taxable person shall provide him with a tax invoice.

(2) The particulars of the tax chargeable on a supply of goods described in paragraph 2 of Schedule 2 to the Act shall be provided by the person selling them on a document containing the particulars prescribed in Regulation 9(1); and such a document issued to the buyer shall be treated for the purposes of paragraph (1) of this Regulation as a tax invoice provided by the person by whom the goods are deemed to be supplied in accordance with the said paragraph 2.

(3) Where a taxable person provides a document to himself which purports to be a tax invoice in respect of a supply of goods or services to him by another taxable person, that document may, with the approval of the Commissioners, be treated as the tax invoice required to be provided by the supplier under paragraph (1) of this Regulation.

9.—(1) Subject to Regulation 11 and save as the Commissioners may otherwise allow, a registered taxable person providing a tax invoice in accordance with Regulation 8 shall state thereon the following particulars—

(*a*) an identifying number;

(*b*) the date of the supply;

(*c*) the name, address and registration number of the supplier;

(*d*) the name and address of the person to whom the goods or services are supplied;

(*e*) the type of supply by reference to the following categories—

(i) a supply by sale,

(ii) a supply on hire-purchase or any similar transaction,

(iii) a supply by loan,

(iv) a supply by way of exchange,

(v) a supply on hire, lease or rental,

(vi) a supply of goods made from customer's materials,

(vii) a supply by sale on commission,

(viii) a supply on sale or return or similar terms, or

(ix) any other type of supply which the Commissioners may at any time by notice specify;

(*f*) a description sufficient to identify the goods or services supplied;

(*g*) the quantity of the goods or the extent of the services and the amount, excluding tax, payable for each description;

(*h*) the gross total amount payable excluding tax;

(*i*) the rate of any cash discount offered; and

(*j*) the rate and amount of tax chargeable.

(2) Where a taxable supply takes place as described in section 7(2)(*c*) or (5) of the Act, any consignment or delivery note or similar document or any copy thereof issued by the supplier before the time of supply shall not, notwithstanding that it may contain all the particulars set out in paragraph (1) of this Regulation, be treated as a tax invoice provided it is so endorsed.

10. Where a taxable person provides an invoice containing the particulars prescribed in Regulation 9 and specifies thereon any goods or services which are the subject of an exempt or zero-rated supply, he shall distinguish on the invoice between the goods or services which are the subject of an exempt, zero-rated or other supply and state separately the gross total amount payable in respect of each.

11. A taxable person who is a retailer shall not be required to provide a tax invoice, except that he shall provide such an invoice at the request of a customer who is a taxable person in respect of any supply to him; but, in that event, if, but only if, the value of the supply, including tax, does not exceed £10, the tax invoice need contain only the following particulars—

(*a*) the name, address and registration number of the retailer;

(*b*) the date of the supply;

(*c*) a description sufficient to identify the goods or services supplied;

(*d*) the total amount payable including tax; and

(*e*) the rate of tax in force at the time of the supply,

but shall not contain any reference to any zero-rated or exempt supply.

12. Regulations 8 to 11 shall not apply to—

(*a*) any zero-rated supply;

(*b*) any supply to which an order made under section 3(6) of the Act applies;

(*c*) any gift of goods by a registered taxable person in the course of a business carried on by him; or

(*d*) any supply to which an order made under section 14 of the Act applies.

2f

PART IV

TIME OF SUPPLY

Interpretation

13. In this Part of these Regulations—

"agreement to hire" means an agreement for the bailment of goods for hire and includes leases of goods and rental agreements, but does not include an agreement under which the bailee has an option to buy the goods or under which the property in the goods passes to the bailee, nor does it include hire-purchase agreements, credit-sale agreements or conditional sale agreements, as defined in the Hire-Purchase Act 1965**(a)**, the Hire-Purchase (Scotland) Act 1965**(b)** or the Hire-Purchase Act (Northern Ireland) 1966**(c)**.

Supplies of goods on hire, lease or rental

14.—(1) Subject to paragraph (2) of this Regulation, where goods are or have been supplied under an agreement to hire, they shall be treated as being successively supplied on hire for successive parts of the period of the agreement, and each of the successive supplies shall be treated as taking place when a payment under the agreement is received or a tax invoice relating to the supply is issued by the supplier, whichever is the earlier.

(2) Where goods are suppplied under an agreement to hire which provides for periodical payments and the supplier at or about the beginning of any period not exceeding 1 year issues a tax invoice containing the following particulars—

(a) the date on which each payment is to become due in the period;

(b) the amount payable (excluding tax) on each date; and

(c) the rate of tax in force at the time of the issue of the tax invoice and the amount of tax chargeable in accordance with that rate on each payment,

they shall be treated as being successively supplied on hire for successive parts of the period of the agreement, and each of the successive supplies shall be treated as taking place when a payment becomes due or is received, whichever is the earlier.

Supplies of any form of power, heat, refrigeration or ventilation

15. Supplies such as are described in section 5(4) of the Act shall be treated as taking place whenever a payment is received or a tax invoice relating to the supply is issued by the supplier, whichever is the earlier.

Supplier's goods in possession of buyer

16.—(1) Where goods are supplied under an agreement whereby the supplier retains the property therein until the goods or part of them are appropriated under the agreement by the buyer and in circumstances where the whole or part of the consideration is determined at that time, a supply of any of the goods shall be treated as taking place at the earliest of the following dates—

(a) the date of such appropriation by the buyer;

(b) the date when a tax invoice is issued by the supplier; and

(c) the date when a payment is received by the supplier.

(a) 1965 c. 66.   **(b)** 1965 c. 67.
(c) 1966 c. 42 (N.I.).

(2) If, within 14 days after such appropriation of the goods or part of them by the buyer as is mentioned in paragraph (1) of this Regulation, the supplier issues a tax invoice in respect of goods appropriated, the provisions of section 7(5) of the Act shall apply to that supply.

(3) Paragraph (1) of this Regulation shall not apply to a supply such as is mentioned in section 7(2)(c) of the Act.

Retention payments

17. Where any contract for the supply of goods or services after 1st April 1973 provides for the retention of any part of the consideration by one party pending full and satisfactory performance of the contract, or of any part of it, by the other party, a supply shall be treated as taking place whenever a payment is received in respect of it or a tax invoice is issued by the supplier, whichever is the earlier.

Continuous supplies of services

18. Where services are supplied for any period for a consideration the whole or part of which is determined or payable periodically, they shall be treated as being successively supplied for successive parts of the period, and each of the successive supplies shall be treated as taking place when a payment is received or a tax invoice relating to the supply is issued by the supplier, whichever is the earlier.

19. Where services are supplied as described in Regulation 18 under an agreement which provides for periodical payments and the supplier, at or about the beginning of any period not exceeding 1 year, issues a tax invoice containing the following additional particulars—

(a) the date on which each payment is to become due in the period;

(b) the amount payable (excluding tax) on each date; and

(c) the rate of tax in force at the time of the issue of the tax invoice and the amount of tax chargeable in accordance with that rate on each payment,

they shall be treated as being successively supplied for successive parts of the period of the agreement, and each of the successive supplies shall be treated as taking place when a payment becomes due or is received, whichever is the earlier.

Supplies of services by barristers and advocates

20. If a fee in respect of services supplied by a barrister or advocate is not ascertained or ascertainable at or before the time when the service is supplied, the supply of that service shall be treated as taking place when the fee is received or a tax invoice is issued, whichever is the earlier.

Supplies in the construction industry

21.—(1) Where services, or services together with goods, are supplied in the course of the construction, alteration, demolition, repair or maintenance of a building or of any civil engineering work under a contract which provides for periodical payments for such supplies, a supply shall be treated as taking place at the earlier of the following times—

(a) when a payment is received by the supplier where the consideration for the contract is wholly in money; or

(b) when the supplier issues a tax invoice.

(2) For the purposes of this Regulation an authenticated receipt by the supplier containing the particulars required under Regulation 9(1) to be contained in a tax invoice shall be treated as a tax invoice on condition that no tax invoice or similar document which was intended to be or could be construed as being a tax invoice for the supply to which the receipt relates is issued.

General

22.—(1) Where under this Part of these Regulations a supply is treated as taking place when a tax invoice is issued by the supplier or when any payment is received by him, tax on that supply shall be chargeable only to the extent covered by the invoice or payment.

(2) Where, before any of the dates of payment specified on an invoice issued as described in Regulation 14(2) or in Regulation 19 there is a change in the tax charged on the supply to which the invoice relates, that invoice shall cease to be treated as a tax invoice in respect of any payment due after the change.

PART V

INPUT TAX

23. In this Part of these Regulations "method" means any method which is referred to in Regulation 24 or the use of which may be allowed or directed by the Commissioners pursuant to that Regulation.

24.—(1) Subject to paragraph (2) of this Regulation, the proportion of input tax to be attributed to taxable supplies by any taxable person who makes exempt supplies shall be determined in any prescribed accounting period by either of the following methods—

Method 1

Subject to Regulation 25 he may deduct such part of his input tax as bears the same ratio to his total input tax as the value of taxable supplies by him bears to the value of all supplies by him.

Method 2

Subject to Regulation 25 he may deduct input tax on the supply to him of goods, or paid or payable by him on imported goods, which are shown to the satisfaction of the Commissioners to have been acquired by him for supply by him in the same state and otherwise apply method 1.

(2) The Commissioners may allow or direct the use of a method other than one specified in paragraph (1) of this Regulation.

25. There shall be excluded from any calculation made by any person for the purpose of using a method—

   (*a*) all capital sums receivable in respect of the grant, assignment or surrender of an interest in land which he has occupied in the course of carrying on a business;

   (*b*) input tax on supplies to him or paid by him on imported goods which is specified as non-deductible in any order made by the Treasury under section 3(6) of the Act;

   (*c*) that part of the value of any supply on which output tax is not chargeable by virtue of any order made by the Treasury under section 3(6) of the Act; and (*d*) any transactions such as are mentioned in Item 4 of Group 5 of Schedule 5 to the Act except where the person whose business is wholly or mainly the negotiation or undertaking of, or the making of arrangements for, such transactions is himself the person using the method.

26.—(1) The Commissioners may, in respect of any period of not less than 1 year or such other period as they may approve ending on 31st March in any year or on such other date as they may approve, adjust the proportional attribution of input tax by a taxable person to taxable supplies so as to obtain the correct attribution for that period.

(2) After the date upon which a person ceases to be taxable the Commissioners may adjust his proportional attribution of input tax to taxable supplies so as to obtain the correct attribution for a period not exceeding 2 years before that date.

(3) Any amount due from or to a taxable person after an adjustment under paragraph (1) or (2) of this Regulation shall be notified in writing to that person who shall within 28 days inform the Commissioners in writing of his agreement or disagreement with the adjusted amount, and where he does not so inform them within that time the adjustment shall be deemed to be agreed.

(4) Any amount agreed or deemed to be agreed under paragraph (3) of this Regulation shall be accounted for as the Commissioners may direct.

(5) Any disagreement notified to the Commissioners under paragraph (3) of this Regulation shall be resolved either by an agreed further adjustment or by the assessed adjustment being confirmed by the Commissioners.

27.—(1) Where, in any prescribed accounting period or in any period of less than 2 years ending on 31st March in any year or on such other date as the Commissioners may approve, a person's only exempt supplies are such as are mentioned in Regulation 25(*a*) or (*d*), all his supplies in that period shall be treated as taxable supplies.

(2) Where, in any prescribed accounting period or in any period of less than 2 years ending on 31st March in any year or on such other date as the Commissioners may approve, the value of a taxable person's exempt supplies amounts to less than either—

(*a*) £100 per month on average, or

(*b*) 5 per cent of the value of all his supplies,

all his supplies in that period shall be treated as taxable supplies; and for the purpose of any calculation made under this paragraph all exempt supplies such as are mentioned in Regulation 25(*a*) or (*d*) shall be disregarded.

28. A person using any method shall—

(*a*) use it for at least 2 years save as the Commissioners may otherwise allow or direct;

(*b*) if he elects to change from one method to another, make any such change as from 1st April in any year or such other date as the Commissioners may approve.

29.—(1) Subject to paragraph (2) of this Regulation, if any taxable person makes a claim on the form numbered 3 in the Schedule to these Regulations within 6 months of the date with effect from which he was registered, supported by such evidence as the Commissioners may require, they may authorise him to deduct, as if it were input tax, tax on the supply of goods to him before that date, or paid by him on imported goods before that date, for the purpose of a business which either was carried on or was to be carried on by him at the time of such supply or payment.

(2) No input tax may be deducted under paragraph (1) of this Regulation in respect of goods which had been supplied by the taxable person making the claim before the date with effect from which he was registered or otherwise than is prescribed in this Part of these Regulations.

PART VI

IMPORTATION, EXPORTATION AND REMOVAL FROM WAREHOUSE

Interpretation

30.—(¹) In Regulation 41 "export house" means any taxable person not being a manufacturer who in the course of his business in the United Kingdom arranges or finances the export of goods from the United Kingdom.

(2) In Regulation 41 "approved inland clearance depot" means any inland premises approved by the Commissioners for the clearance of goods for customs purposes.

(3) In Regulations 42 and 43 "goods" does not include motor vehicles.

(4) In Regulations 42 and 43 "ship" includes a hovercraft within the meaning of the Hovercraft Act 1968(a).

(5) In Regulations 44 and 45 "manufacturer" means a person who manufactures motor vehicles in the United Kingdom and includes the person nominated by a manufacturer of motor vehicles abroad as his sole agent for the United Kingdom for the purposes of tax-free sales under these Regulations.

(6) In this Part of these Regulations "overseas visitor" means a person who, during the 2 years immediately preceding the date of the supply mentioned in Regulations 42 and 43 or the date of the application mentioned in Regulation 44, has not been in the United Kingdom for more than 365 days; or, who, for the purposes of Regulation 44, during the 6 years immediately preceding the date of the application has not been in the United Kingdom for more than 1,095 days.

Exception of application of customs enactments

31. The following provisions of the Customs and Excise Act 1952(b), that is to say—

   (a) section 111 (remission of duty on spirits for use in art or manufacture);

   (b) section 122 (remission of duty on spirits for methylation);

   (c) sections 137 and 138 (drawback on exportation and warehousing of beer); and

   (d) sections 182 and 183 (exemptions from duty of tobacco products and drawback on tobacco),

shall be excepted from the enactments which are to have effect as mentioned in section 17(1) of the Act.

(a) 1968 c. 59.   **(b)** 1952 c. 44.

32. The following Regulations made under section 40 of the Customs and Excise Act 1952, that is to say—

(*a*) The Process (Temporary Importations) Regulations 1958**(a)**;

(*b*) The Temporary Importation (Equipment on Hire or Loan) Regulations 1970**(b)**; and

(*c*) The Temporary Importation (Magnetic Tapes) Regulations 1971**(c)**, shall be excepted from the enactments which are to have effect as mentioned in section 17(1) of the Act.

Removal on importation or from warehouse

33. Goods imported by a taxable person in the course of a business carried on by him may, with the authority of the proper officer, be delivered or removed without payment of tax provided that—

(*a*) where entry is made, the particulars in the entry include his registration number; or

(*b*) where goods are imported by post and entry is not required to be made, his registration number is shown on the customs declaration attached to or accompanying the package; or

(*c*) in any other case, the Commissioners have permitted the goods to be removed without entry.

34. Goods may, with the authority of the proper officer, be removed from warehouse without payment of tax by a taxable person in the course of a business carried on by him provided that the particulars in the entry made on removal include his registration number.

35. Save as the Commissioners may otherwise allow, a taxable person shall account for tax chargeable on goods on their importation or removal from warehouse by him together with any tax chargeable on the supply of goods or services by him in a return furnished by him in accordance with these Regulations for the prescribed accounting period during which the goods were imported or removed from warehouse, as the case may be.

36. If a taxable person fails to comply with Regulation 35, the Commissioners may direct that Regulations 33 and 34 shall not apply to subsequent deliveries and removals by him.

Temporary importations

37.—(1) The Commissioners, having regard to the tax chargeable on the supply of like goods in the United Kingdom, may permit any goods imported otherwise than on hire or loan to be delivered without payment of tax if they are satisfied—

(*a*) that it is intended to re-export the imported goods or goods incorporating them or manufactured or produced from them; and

(*b*) that the provisions of this Regulation and such conditions as may be imposed by the Commissioners are complied with,

and tax shall not be payable so long as they continue to be so satisfied.

(a) S.I. 1958/1642 (1958 I, p. 811).   (b) S.I. 1970/423 (1970 I, p. 1458).
(c) S.I. 1971/1356 (1971 II, p. 3835).

(2) The importer shall at the time of importation—

(*a*) produce the goods for examination to the proper officer if so required; and

(*b*) deposit such sum of money or give such other security as the proper officer may require to ensure compliance with this Regulation and any conditions imposed thereunder.

(3) Save as the Commissioners may otherwise allow, the goods shall not be used by or supplied to any person in the United Kingdom.

(4) The proper officer may require the goods or any goods incorporating them or manufactured or produced from them to be produced to him at any time.

(5) The importer or other person having charge of the goods shall—

(*a*) keep such resords relating to the goods as the proper officer may require;

(*b*) on demand produce those records to the proper officer and furnish him with such information relating to the goods as he may require.

(6) The goods shall be exported within 6 months of the date of importation or within such longer period as the Commissioners may allow.

(7) The importer or other person having charge of the goods shall produce to the proper officer such evidence of exportation as he may require.

38. Where goods are imported, and

(*a*) the Commissioners are satisfied that the goods are on hire or loan to the importer from an overseas supplier; and

(*b*) the proper officer is satisfied that the goods are to be re-exported; and

(*c*) such conditions as the Commissioners may impose are complied with,

they may remit such amount of tax as represents the difference between the tax ordinarily payable on importation and such tax as would have been payable had the charge made for the hire or loan been the value of the goods:

provided that if in the opinion of the Commissioners such charge is less than would normally be made or if no charge is made, the Commissioners may assess that value having regard to charges made for the hiring of similar goods for a similar period in the United Kingdom.

Relief on the reimportation of certain goods

39. Subject to such conditions as the Commissioners may impose, the tax chargeable on the importation of goods which have been previously exported from the United Kingdom shall not be payable if the Commissioners are satisfied that—

(*a*) the importer is not a taxable person or, if he is, the goods are imported otherwise than in the course of his business;

(*b*) the goods were last exported by him or on his behalf;

(*c*) the goods were supplied in the United Kingdom before their export, and any purchase tax or tax due on that supply was paid and neither has been, nor will be, refunded;

(*d*) the goods were not exported free of tax under a scheme provided for in these Regulations or free of purchase tax;

(*e*) the goods have not been subject to process or repair abroad; and

(*f*) the goods

(i) were at the time of exportation intended to be reimported, or

(ii) have been returned for repair or replacement or after rejection by an overseas customer or because it was not possible to deliver them to an overseas customer, or

(iii) were in private use and possession in the United Kingdom before they were exported.

Partial relief on the reimportation of goods exported for process or repair

40. Goods which have been exported from the United Kingdom by or on behalf of the person reimporting them and which have undergone any process or repair abroad shall be chargeable with tax on reimportation as if the amount of any increase in the value of the goods, since their exportation, attributable to the process or repair were the whole value thereof.

Supplies to export houses

41. Where goods are supplied to an export house and—

(*a*) the goods are delivered by the supplier direct to a port, Customs airport or approved inland clearance depot for immediate shipment; and

(*b*) the goods are exported,

the supply, subject to such conditions as the Commissioners may impose, shall be zero-rated.

Supplies to persons departing from the United Kingdom

42. Where the Commissioners are satisfied that—

(*a*) goods have been supplied direct to a ship or aircraft on behalf of an overseas visitor or a resident of the United Kingdom who at the time of the supply intended to depart from and remain outside the United Kingdom for a period of at least 12 months;

(*b*) the goods were produced to the proper officer on exportation; and

(*c*) unless they have otherwise allowed, the goods were exported in that ship or aircraft,

the supply, subject to such conditions as they may impose, shall be zero-rated.

43.—(1) Where the Commissioners are satisfied that—

(*a*) goods have been supplied to an overseas visitor who, at the time of the supply, intended to depart from the United Kingdom within 3 months from that date and that the goods should accompany him;

(*b*) the goods were capable of being carried on the person or in the hand baggage of the exporter or, if he intended to depart from the United Kingdom with a motor vehicle, in that vehicle;

(*c*) the goods were produced to the proper officer on exportation; and

(*d*) the goods have been exported,

the supply, subject to such conditions as they may impose, shall be zero-rated.

(2) This Regulation shall not apply to any person who is a member of the crew of any ship or aircraft departing from the United Kingdom.

44. The Commissioners may, on application by an overseas visitor who intends to depart from the United Kingdom and remain outside the United Kingdom for a period of at least 12 months, permit him to acquire a new motor vehicle from a manufacturer without payment of tax for subsequent export, and its supply, subject to such conditions as they may impose, shall be zero-rated.

45. The Commissioners may, on application by any person who intends to depart from the United Kingdom within 6 months and remain outside the United Kingdom for at least 12 months, permit him to acquire a new motor vehicle from a manufacturer without payment of tax for subsequent export, and its supply, subject to such conditions as they may impose, shall be zero-rated.

PART VII

ACCOUNTING AND PAYMENT

46.—(1) Every registered person shall, on the form numbered 4 in the Schedule to these Regulations, furnish the Controller with a return showing the amount of tax payable by or to him in respect of each period of 3 months ending on dates notified in the certificate of registration issued to him, or otherwise, and containing full information in respect of all other matters specified in the said form; and shall furnish such a return not later than the last day of the month next following the end of the period to which it relates: provided that—

(a) the Commissioners may direct or allow a registered person to furnish returns in respect of periods of 1 month and to furnish those returns within 1 month of the periods to which they relate;

(b) the Commissioners may direct that any period commencing on 1st April 1973 shall comprise 3, 4 or 5 months as may be appropriate; and

(c) where the Commissioners are satisfied that, in order to meet the circumstances of any particular case, it is necessary to vary the length of any period or the date on which any period begins or ends or the date on which any return shall be furnished, they may direct or allow a registered person to furnish returns accordingly.

(2) Any person to whom the Commissioners give any direction in pursuance of the proviso to paragraph (1) shall comply therewith.

(3) Where a return is furnished by a body corporate acting as a representative member of a group as provided by section 21 of the Act, the return shall, unless the Commissioners otherwise allow, be accompanied by a document in the form numbered 5 in the Schedule to these Regulations giving such information about the group as is specified therein.

(4) Any person who ceases to be liable to be registered shall, not later than 1 month after so ceasing, furnish to the Controller a final return on the form numbered 6 in the Schedule to these Regulations in respect of that part of the last period during which he was registered.

(5) The Commissioners may allow tax chargeable in any period to be treated as being chargeable in such later period as they may specify.

47. Where goods are deemed to be supplied by a taxable person by virtue of paragraph 2 of Schedule 2 to the Act, the person selling the goods, whether or not he is registered under the Act, shall within 21 days of the sale—

(*a*) furnish to the Controller a statement showing—

    (i) his name and address and, if registered, his registration number,

    (ii) the name, address and registration number of the person whose goods were sold,

    (iii) the date of the sale,

    (iv) the description and quantity of the goods sold, and

    (v) the amount for which they were sold and the amount of tax chargeable;

(*b*) pay the amount of tax due; and

(*c*) send to the person whose goods were sold a copy of the statement referred to in (*a*) above,

and the person selling the goods and the person whose goods were sold shall exclude from any return which either or both may be required to furnish under these Regulations the tax chargeable on that supply of those goods.

48. Save as the Commissioners may otherwise allow, a registered person furnishing a return in accordance with Regulation 46 shall account therein for all his output tax and all tax for which he is accountable by virtue of Part VI of these Regulations in respect of the period to which the return relates and at the same time pay any amount of tax appearing by that return to be due.

49. The Commissioners may allow a person to estimate a part of his output tax for any period in cases where they are satisfied that he is not able to account for the exact amount of output tax chargeable in that period, provided that any such estimated amount shall be adjusted and exactly accounted for as tax chargeable in the next period thereafter.

50.—(1) Any registered person claiming deduction of input tax in relation to any period shall do so on the return furnished by him for that period, or for any subsequent period.

(2) The Commissioners may allow a person to estimate a part of his deductible input tax for any period in cases where they are satisfied that he is not able to claim the exact amount to be deducted by him for that period, provided that any such estimated amount shall be adjusted and exactly accounted for as tax deductible in the next period thereafter.

51. If a registered person makes an error in accounting for tax or in any return furnished under these Regulations he shall correct it as the Commissioners may require but in no case later than on the return funished next after its discovery.

Part VIII

Distress and Diligence

Distress

52.—(1) If upon demand made by a Collector of Customs and Excise a person neglects or refuses to pay tax which he is required to pay under the Act or any Regulation made thereunder, the Collector may distrain on the goods and chattels of that person and by warrant signed by him direct any authorised person to levy such distress, provided that where an amount of tax is due under section 31(6) of the Act no distress shall be levied until 21 days after that amount became due.

(2) For the purpose of levying any such distress an authorised person may after obtaining a warrant for the purpose signed by a Collector of Customs and Excise break open, in the daytime, any house or premises.

(3) A levy or warrant to break open shall be executed by or under the direction of, and in the presence of, the authorised person.

(4) A distress levied by the authorised person shall be kept for 5 days, at the costs and charges of the person neglecting or refusing to pay.

(5) If the person aforesaid does not pay the sum due, together with the costs and charges, within the said 5 days, the distress shall be independently appraised and shall be sold by public auction by the authorised person for payment of the sums due and all costs and charges; and costs and charges of taking, keeping and selling the distress shall be retained by the authorised person, and any surplus remaining after the deduction of the costs and charges and of the sum due shall be restored to the owner of the goods distrained.

Diligence

53. In Scotland, the following provisions shall have effect—

(*a*) Upon certificate made to him by a Collector of Customs and Excise that any tax is due under the Act or under Regulations made thereunder and has not been paid the sheriff or sheriff substitute for the county shall issue a warrant for the Collector recovering the said tax by poinding the goods and effects of any person entered in the certificate as being a defaulter:

(*b*) The warrant shall be executed by the sheriff officers of the county:

(*c*) The goods and effects so poinded shall be detained and kept on the ground, or at the house where the same were poinded, or in such other place of which the owner shall have notice, near to the said ground or house, as the officer so poinding the same shall think proper, for the space of 5 days, during which time the said goods and effects shall remain in the custody of the said officer, and liable to the payment of the whole tax in arrear and to the costs to be paid to the officer who poinded the same as hereinafter directed, unless the owner from whom the same were poinded shall redeem the same, within the said space of 5 days, by payment to the officer of the said tax in arrear and costs, to be settled in the same manner as if the said goods and effects had been sold as hereinafter directed:

(*d*) The goods and effects so poinded shall, after the expiration of the said 5 days, be valued and appraised by any 2 persons to be appointed by the officer and shall be sold and disposed of, at a sum not less than the value, by the officer who does poind the same:

(*e*) The value shall be applied, in the first place to the satisfaction and payment of the tax owing by the person whose goods are so poinded, and, in the second place, to the payment for the trouble of the officer so poinding, at the rate of 10 pence per pound of the tax for which the goods shall be so poinded unless the owner from whom the same were poinded shall redeem the same by payment of the appraised value, within the space of 5 days after the valuation, to the officer who poinded the same:

(*f*) In case any surplus remains of the price or value, after payment of the said tax, and after payment of what is allowed to be retained by the officer in manner herein directed, such surplus shall be returned to the owner from whom the goods were poinded:

(*g*) In case no purchaser appears at the said sale, then the said goods and effects, so poinded, shall be consigned and lodged in the hands of the sheriff of the county, or his substitute, and if not redeemed by the owner within the space of 5 days after the consignment in the hands of the said sheriff or sheriff substitute, the same shall be rouped, sold, and disposed of by order of the sheriff, in such manner, and at such time and place, as he shall appoint, he always being liable to the payment of the tax to the authorised person, and to payment to the officer who shall have poinded the same, for his trouble and expense, as before stated, and to the fees due to the officer, and being, in the third place, entitled to 5 pence per pound of the value of the goods so disposed of, for his own pains and trouble, after preference and allowance of the said tax, and of what is appointed to be paid to the officer for his trouble:

(*h*) There shall also be allowed, to the officer so poinding, the expense of maintaining or preserving the said goods and effects from the time of poinding the same, during the period allowed to the owner to redeem them, and also the expense of the sale; and in like manner the expense shall be allowed to the sheriff or sheriff substitute, for maintaining or preserving the goods poinded, during the period that the owner is allowed to redeem, after consignment in his hands, and until the sale thereof, and also the expense of the sale:

(*i*) Every auctioneer, or seller by commission, selling by auction, in Scotland, any goods or effects whatsoever by any mode of sale at auction, shall, at least 3 days before he begins any sale by way of auction, deliver or cause to be delivered to the authorised person a notice in writing, signed by such auctioneer or seller by auction, specifying therein the particular day when such sale is to begin, and the name and surname of the person whose goods and effects are to be sold, with his place of residence.

R. W. Radford,
Commissioner of Customs and Excise.

1st August 1972.
King's Beam House,
Mark Lane,
London,EC3R 7HE.

Regulation 3(1)   **SCHEDULE**

Form No. 1

**Notification of taxable business for
Value Added Tax**

1 Full name
(company, sole
proprietor, firm,
public corporation,
government depart-
ment, local authority
or responsible
officer)

2 Trading style if
different from 1

3 Status of business ....

4 Address of 1
(registered address of
company, business
address of proprietor
or firm, head office
address, private address
of responsible officer)

Postcode   Telephone No. ....

5 Address of the principal
place where the business
is carried on if different
from 4

Postcode   Telephone No. ....

6 Address of the place at
which the principal
accounts of the business
are kept if different from
4 or 5

Postcode   .... Telephone No. ....

7 Enter the code number corresponding to the trade
classification of the business.

8 *If you are applying for voluntary registration under
15 below DO NOT complete this item.*

State whether the taxable turnover of the business,
including self-supplies, is likely to exceed £5,000 in the
next twelve months.   *Yes/No
If answer is NO indicate which of the following limits
has been exceeded by ticking in the appropriate box
or boxes (a) – (d).

(a) £1,750 in the last calendar quarter

(b) a total of £3,000 in the last two calendar quarters

(c) a total of £4,250 in the last three calendar quarters

(d) a total of £5,000 in the last four calendar quarters

9 Say what you expect the approximate taxable turnover
of the business to be in the next twelve months.   £............................

10 Do you expect to make any exempt supplies?   *Yes/No
If YES enter the approximate amount for the next
twelve months.   £............................

11 Do you expect your input tax to exceed your output
tax regularly?   *Yes/No
If YES
(a) give your reasons here (e.g. exporter), ...
and
(b) enter the estimated value of your zero-rated
outputs in the next twelve months.   £............................

12 Are your VAT accounts to be kept on a computer?   *Yes/Partly/No

13 If you intend to pay VAT by means of credit transfer
through Bank Giro or National Giro tick the
appropriate box.   Bank Giro   National Giro

14 Enter for VAT repayment purposes
EITHER   Bank sorting code No.   Bank account No.
your Bank sorting code No. and your Bank account No.
OR
your National Giro account No.
National Giro account No.

Applications

15 *[I apply for the person named at 1 to be treated exceptionally as a taxable person for the reasons
given in the accompanying letter]

16 *[I apply for the person named at 1 to be treated exceptionally as not being a taxable person for the
reasons given in the accompanying letter]

Declaration

17 I [*full name of signatory in BLOCK CAPITALS*] ....
declare that the particulars and statements in this form
*[the accompanying letter] and
*[details of partners' names and addresses shown on the attached form VAT 2 initialled by me]
are true and complete.

Dated................................Signed..

18 List in order the identifying numbers of the Customs and Excise
VAT Notices which you hold or have asked for (other than
Notices No. 700 and 701)

Regulation 3(2)
Form No. 2

Value Added Tax
Notification of Details of all Partners

Full name ....

Address
including postcode ....

....

....

Full name ....

Address
including postcode ....

....

Full name ....

Address
including postcode ....

....

Initials...

Date ....

Form No. 3

Regulation 29(1)

Value Added Tax
Claim for Relief
Goods which have borne VAT and are on hand at time of registration

Name of person or ....
firm making claim

Registration number

....

Address ....

....

Description of goods on which relief is claimed	Quantities on hand on the effective date of registration		Name and address of taxable person who supplied the goods (Place of importation or name of warehouse if goods were imported by the applicant or VAT-paid ex warehouse)	Date of invoice from taxable person (or number and date of import entry or warehouse warrant)	Amount of tax on the actual quantities on hand, columns (2) and (3), calculated from the relevant invoices (or) import documents or warehouse warrants)
	In the same state	Already used in making other goods, the goods so made being still on hand			
(1)	(2)	(3)	(4)	(5)	(6)
					£ p

Declaration by Claimant

I declare that the above is a true account of the goods which have borne VAT remaining on hand on...........................
and of the tax paid on their supply or importation. The account is based on the attached documentary evidence
of payment of tax and I undertake to produce any further records to an officer of Customs and Excise on request.

Date...   Signed ....

Regulation 46(1)
Form No. 4

Return of Value Added Tax
For the period to

Registration No.	Period No.

PART A. Account of tax payable or repayable

Tax due for this period:	Output tax	1 £	
	Tax due on imported goods and goods from bonded warehouses	2 £	
Underdeclarations and/or underpayments of tax in respect of previous periods:	Notified by Customs and Excise	3 £	
	Other	4 £	
Total tax due:	Sum of boxes 1 to 4	5 £	
Deductible input tax for this period:		6 £	
Overdeclarations and/or overpayments of tax in respect of previous periods:	Notified by Customs and Excise	7 £	
	Other	8 £	
Total tax deductible:	Sum of boxes 6 to 8	9 £	
Net tax payable or repayable:	Payable to Customs and Excise	10 £	
	Repayable by Customs and Excise		

Method of payment to Customs and Excise: National Giro ☐   Bank Giro ☐   Remittance enclosed ☐

PART B. Value of outputs and inputs (excluding any Value Added Tax)

Pounds only

Outputs:	Outputs chargeable at the standard rate of tax	11 £	
	Exports	12 £	
	Other zero-rated taxable outputs	13 £	
	Total taxable outputs (sum of boxes 11, 12 and 13)	14 £	
	Exempt outputs	15 £	
	Total outputs (sum of boxes 14 and 15)	16 £	
Inputs:	Total taxable inputs including zero-rated inputs	17 £	

PART C. Retailers' special schemes

Enter in the box(es):   1 if you have used scheme 1

2, 3 or 4 if you have used any of these schemes   18

PART D. Calculation of deductible input tax

Enter 1, 2 or 3 in this box to show which method you have used	19

Amount of any input tax wholly attributable to taxable supplies	20	£

Amount of input tax partly attributable to taxable supplies   21 £

Percentage used to attribute input tax $\left(\dfrac{\text{box } 14 \times 100}{\text{box } 16} \right)$ 22

That part of the amount in box 21 which is deductible for the period $\left(\dfrac{\text{box } 21 \times \text{box } 22}{100} \right)$ 23 £

Total deductible input tax for the period (sum of boxes 20 and 23); this total should also be entered at box 6 overleaf   24 £

PART E.   Declaration by the signatory

I ....

declare that   (i)   the information given in this return is true and complete in respect of all business or businesses carried on by the registered person except in so far as he is separately registered if so required and, except as notified, none of the changes listed in Notice No. 700 has occurred during the period covered by the return,

(ii)   the amounts shown as deductible input tax in this return relate to tax which may be deducted by virtue of Section 3 of the Finance Act 1972 and Regulations made under that section, and I claim deduction of input tax accordingly,

(iii)   where I have used one of the retailers' special schemes I have complied with Notice No. 707.

Signed   ....

Date   ....

Form No. 5

Regulation 46(3)

Value Added Tax
Trading Figures for Associated Businesses in a Group Registration

Registration number of Representative Member.....................................

Reference number	Total turnover £	Total purchases £	Net Tax payment £	Net Tax repayment £
Representative Member				

Regulation 46(4)
Form No. 6

Final Return of Value Added Tax
For the period to

Registration No.

PART A.   Account of tax payable or repayable

Tax due for this period:	Output tax	1 £	
	Tax due on imported goods and goods from bonded warehouses	2 £	
Underdeclarations and/or underpayments of tax in respect of previous periods:	Notified by Customs and Excise	3 £	
	Other	4 £	
Total tax due:	Sum of boxes 1 to 4	5 £	
Deductible input tax for this period:		6 £	
Overdeclarations and/or overpayments of tax in respect of previous periods:	Notified by Customs and Excise	7 £	
	Other	8 £	
Total tax deductible:	Sum of boxes 6 to 8	9 £	
Net tax payable or repayable:	Payable to Customs and Excise		10 £
	Repayable by Customs and Excise		

Method of payment to Customs and Excise: National Giro ☐   Bank Giro ☐   Remittance enclosed ☐

PART B.   Value of outputs and inputs (excluding any Value Added Tax)

Pounds only

Outputs:	Outputs chargeable at the standard tate of tax	11 £	
	Exports	12 £	
	Other zero-rated taxable outputs	13 £	
	Total taxable outputs (sum of boxes 11, 12 and 13)	14 £	
	Exempt outputs	15 £	
	Total output (sum of boxes 14 and 15)	16 £	
Inputs:	Total taxable inputs including zero-rated inputs	17 £	

PART C.   Retailers' special schemes

Enter in the box(es):   1 if you have used scheme 1

                       2, 3 or 4 if you have used any of these schemes   18

PART D.   Calculation of deductible input tax

Enter 1, 2 or 3 in this box to show which method you have used	19
Amount of any input tax wholly attritutabe to taxable supplies	20 £
Amount of input tax partly attributable to taxable supplies	21 £
Percentage used to attribute input tax $\left(\dfrac{\text{box } 14 \times 100}{\text{box } 16} \right)$	22
That part of the amount in box 21 which is deductible for the period $\left(\dfrac{\text{box } 21 \times \text{box } 22}{100} \right)$	23 £
Total deductible input tax for the period (sum of boxes 20 and 23); this total should also be entered at box 6 overleaf	24 £

PART E.   Declaration by the signatory

....

declare that   (i) the information given in this return is true and complete in respect of all business or businesses carried on by the registered person except in so far as he is separately registered if so required and, except as notified, none of the changes listed in Notice No. 700 has occurred during the period covered by the return,

(ii) the amounts shown as deductible input tax in this return relate to tax which may be deducted by virtue of Section 3 of the Finance Act 1972 and Regulations made under that section, and I claim deduction of input tax accordingly,

(iii) where I have used one of the retailers' special schemes I have complied with Notice No. 707,

(iv) the total tax due as stated in this return includes the amount of £...........................representing tax due on all goods in stock or forming part of the assets of the business (including capital goods) at the close of business on..

Signed   ....

Date   ....

EXPLANATORY NOTE

(This Note is not part of the Regulations.)

These Regulations, made under various provisions of the Finance Act 1972, prescribe various practical arrangements required for the introduction of the value added tax.

Part I is formal.

Part II deals with the notification of taxable businesses to Customs and Excise and the setting up and maintenance of a register of taxable persons.

Part III provides for the issue of invoices, to be known as tax invoices, in respect of taxable supplies of goods and services, and for the particulars to be contained in such invoices.

Part IV determines the time when certain supplies of goods and services are to be treated as taking place for the purposes of the charge to tax.

Part V deals with the deduction of input tax, including its attribution where necessary either to taxable or to exempt supplies.

Part VI deals with the treatment for tax purposes of, and the collection of tax on, imported goods and goods removed from bonded warehouses; and also with the zero-rating of certain specified supplies of goods that have been or are to be exported.

Part VII prescribes how tax is to be accounted for and paid to Customs and Excise.

Part VIII makes detailed provision for the levying of distress (or in Scotland the doing of diligence) on the goods and chattels of persons refusing or neglecting to pay tax due.

STATUTORY INSTRUMENTS

1972 No. 1148

VALUE ADDED TAX

The Value Added Tax (Supplies by Retailers) Regulations 1972

Made - - -	*1st August* 1972
Laid before the House of Commons	*9th August* 1972
Coming into Operation	*1st April* 1973

The Commissioners of Customs and Excise, by virtue of the powers conferred on them by section 30 of the Finance Act 1972(**a**) and of all other powers enabling them in that behalf, hereby make the following Regulations: —

1.—(1) These Regulations may be cited as the Value Added Tax (Supplies by Retailers) Regulations 1972 and shall come into operation on 1st April 1973.

(2) In these Regulations: —

"the Act" means the Finance Act 1972;

"notice" means any notice published pursuant to these Regulations;

"prescribed accounting period" means any period such as is mentioned in Regulation 46 of the Value Added Tax (General) Regulations 1972(**b**); and

"scheme" means any method such as is mentioned in Regulation 2.

(3) The Interpretation Act 1889(**c**) shall apply for the interpretation of these Regulations as it applies for the interpretation of an Act of Parliament.

2.—(1) The Commissioners may permit the value which is to be taken as the value, in any prescribed accounting period or part thereof, of supplies by a retailer which are taxable at other than the zero-rate to be determined by a method agreed with a retailer or by any method described in a notice published by them for that purpose; and they may publish any notice accordingly.

(2) The Commissioners may vary the terms of any method either by publishing a fresh notice or by adapting any method by agreement with any retailer.

3. The Commissioners may refuse to permit the value of taxable supplies to be determined in accordance with a scheme and in particular may do so in any case where it appears to them that the retailer could reasonably be expected to account for tax in accordance with Regulations made under section 30(1) of the Act.

4. No retailer may at any time use more than one scheme except as provided for in any notice or as the Commissioners may otherwise allow.

(**a**) 1972 c. 41.   (**b**) S.I. 1972/1147 (1972 II, p. 3362).   (**c**) 1889 c. 63.

5. Any retailer using any scheme shall notify the Commissioners in writing on every return of tax furnished by him in compliance with Regulation 46 of the Value Added Tax (General) Regulations 1972 which scheme he is using.

6. Save as the Commissioners may otherwise allow, a retailer who accounts for tax on the basis of taxable supplies valued in accordance with any scheme shall, so long as he remains a taxable person, continue to do so for a period of not less than 1 year from the adoption of that scheme by him, and any change by a retailer from one scheme to another shall be made at the end of any complete year reckoned from the beginning of the tax period in which he first adopted the scheme.

7.—(1) A retailer shall notify the Commissioners before ceasing to account for tax on the basis of taxable supplies valued in accordance with these Regulations.

(2) A retailer may be required to pay tax on such proportion as the Commissioners may consider fair and reasonable of any sums due to him at the end of the period in which he last used a scheme.

8. A retailer registered in the Register of Pharmaceutical Chemists kept under the Pharmacy Act 1954(**a**) or the Pharmacy and Poisons Act (Northern Ireland) 1925(**b**) shall, in making any calculations in order to use any scheme pursuant to these Regulations, —

(*a*) disregard any monies received by him from whatever source in respect of any supply described in Group 14 of Schedule 4 to the Act; and,

(*b*) if he is using a scheme which involves apportioning gross takings as described therein on the basis of goods supplied to him, exclude from those supplies any goods dispensed by him as mentioned in the said Group 14.

9. Where the rate of tax chargeable on any supplies is varied pursuant to any enactment, a retailer using any scheme shall take such steps relating to that scheme as are directed in any notice applicable to him.

10.—(1) Where the supplies by any retailer include both supplies of food which are zero-rated under Group 1 of Schedule 4 to the Act and supplies of food in the course of catering, he shall either—

(*a*) keep such records as will enable the proportion of the value of such supplies which is to be attributed to zero-rated and all other supplies to be determined to the satisfaction of the Commissioners; or

(*b*) where he can satisfy the Commissioners that it is impracticable to keep such records make an estimate of the proportion of the value of such supplies which is to be attributed to zero-rated and all other supplies.

(2) Where any retailer makes an estimate in accordance with paragraph (1)(*b*) of this Regulation, tax shall be accounted for on the basis of that estimate; but, if at any time he has evidence or the Commissioners are satisfied that the estimate is no longer accurate, he shall thereupon make a further estimate in accordance with paragraph (1)(*b*) of this Regulation and shall inform the Commissioners accordingly, and tax shall be accounted for on the basis of such further estimate from such date as the Commissioners may direct.

(**a**) 1954 c. 61.   (**b**) 1925 c. 8 (N.I.).

(3) Where the Commissioners are not satisfied with any further estimate made under the preceding paragraph, they may determine the proportion of the value of supplies which is to be attributed to the various descriptions of supplies and tax shall be accounted for in accordance with such determination from such date as the Commissioners shall direct.

R. W. Radford,
Commissioner of Customs and Excise.

1st August 1972.

King's Beam House,
Mark Lane,
London, EC3R 7HE.

EXPLANATORY NOTE

(This Note is not part of the Regulations.)

These Regulations make general provision for special schemes by which a retailer may calculate value added tax on his outputs. The detailed schemes are to be as described in a notice published by the Commissioners of Customs and Excise or as determined by agreement with the retailer. Regulation 8 contains special provisions in regard to pharmaceutical supplies, and Regulation 10 describes the method of determining the proportion of outputs on which tax is chargeable in cases where the retailer supplies both zero-rated food and food in the course of catering.

STATUTORY INSTRUMENTS

1972 No. 1149 (C.21)

SOCIAL SECURITY

The National Insurance Act 1971 (Commencement No. 3) Order 1972

Made - - -	31*st July* 1972
Laid before Parliament	8*th August* 1972
Coming into Operation	28*th August* 1972

The Secretary of State for Social Services in exercise of powers conferred by section 16(3) of and paragraph 1 of Schedule 6 to the National Insurance Act 1971(a) and of all other powers enabling him in that behalf, hereby makes the following Order:—

Citation and commencement

1. This Order may be cited as the National Insurance Act 1971 (Commencement No. 3) Order 1972 and shall come into operation on 28th August 1972.

Appointed day

2. The day appointed for the coming into force of any provision of the National Insurance Act 1971 specified in column 1 of the Schedule to this Order, so far as that provision relates to any subject matter specified in column 2 of that Schedule, shall be 28th August 1972.

Keith Joseph,
Secretary of State for Social Services.

31st July 1972.

(a) 1971 c. 50.

SCHEDULE   Article 2

Provisions of the National Insurance Act 1971	Subject Matter
Section 12	Polygamous Marriages
Section 16(3) and Schedule 7	Repeals affecting— the National Insurance Act 1965(a)— section 113(1)
	the National Insurance (Industrial Injuries) Act 1965(b)— section 86(5)
	the Family Allowances Act 1965(c)— section 17(9)
	the National Insurance Act 1969(d)— section 6(1) and Schedule 5 in the cases of— (a) maximum under s.29(1)(a) of aggregate of weekly benefits payable for successive accidents (b) maximum disablement gratuity under s.12(3) section 6(2) section 10(1)

EXPLANATORY NOTE

(This Note is not part of the Order.)

This Order brings into force on 28th August 1972 those provisions of the National Insurance Act 1971 which are not already in operation, namely section 12, which relates to polygamous marriages, and other provisions which are of a minor or consequential nature.

(a) 1965 c. 51.   **(b)** 1965 c. 52.
(c) 1965 c. 53.   **(d)** 1969 c. 44.

STATUTORY INSTRUMENTS

1972 No. 1150

SOCIAL SECURITY

The National Insurance, Industrial Injuries and Family Allowances (Polygamous Marriages) Regulations 1972

Made - - - -	*31st July* 1972
Laid before Parliament	*8th August* 1972
Coming into Operation	*28th August* 1972

The Secretary of State for Social Services, in exercise of his powers under section 12 of the National Insurance Act 1971(a), hereby makes the following regulations:—

Citation, commencement and interpretation

1.—(1) These regulations may be cited as the National Insurance, Industrial Injuries and Family Allowances (Polygamous Marriages) Regulations 1972 and shall come into operation on 28th August 1972.

(2) In these regulations, unless the context otherwise requires—

" the Insurance Act " means the National Insurance Act 1965(b) ;

" the Industrial Injuries Act " means the National Insurance (Industrial Injuries) Act 1965(c) ;

" the Family Allowances Act " means the Family Allowances Act 1965(d) ;

" polygamous marriage " means a marriage celebrated under a law which, as it applies to the particular ceremony and to the parties thereto, permits polygamy ;

" monogamous marriage " means a marriage celebrated under a law which does not permit polygamy ;

and other expressions shall, as appropriate, have the same meanings as in the Insurance Act, the Industrial Injuries Act and the Family Allowances Act.

(3) References in these regulations to any enactment or regulation shall, except in so far as the context otherwise requires, be construed as references to that enactment or regulation as amended or extended by or under any other enactment, order or regulation.

(4) The rules for the construction of Acts of Parliament contained in the Interpretation Act 1889(e) shall apply for the purposes of the interpretation of these regulations as they apply for the purposes of the interpretation of an Act of Parliament.

(a) 1971 c. 50. (b) 1965 c. 51. (c) 1965 c. 52. (d) 1965 c. 53. (e) 1889 c. 63.

General rule as to the consequences of a polygamous marriage for the purpose of the Insurance Act, the Industrial Injuries Act and the Family Allowances Act

2.—(1) Subject to the following provisions of these regulations, a polygamous marriage shall, for the purpose of the Insurance Act, the Industrial Injuries Act and the Family Allowances Act and any enactment construed as one with those Acts, be treated as having the same consequences as a monogamous marriage for any day, but only for any day, throughout which the polygamous marriage is in fact monogamous.

(2) In this and the next following regulation—

(*a*) a polygamous marriage is referred to as being in fact monogamous when neither party to it has any spouse additional to the other ; and

(*b*) the day on which a polygamous marriage is contracted, or on which it terminates for any reason, shall be treated as a day throughout which that marriage was in fact monogamous if at all times on that day after it was contracted, or, as the case may be, before it terminated, it was in fact monogamous.

Special rules for particular purposes and circumstances of the Insurance Act

3.—(1) Subject to the provisions of paragraphs (2) and (3) of this regulation, where on or after the date on which she attained pensionable age a woman was a married woman by virtue of a polygamous marriage and either—

(*a*) throughout a day, falling on or after the date on which both she and her spouse have attained pensionable age and retired from regular employment, that marriage was in fact monogamous, or

(*b*) throughout the day on which her spouse died that marriage was in fact monogamous,

that marriage, whether or not it has at all times been or continues to be in fact monogamous, shall, for the purposes of determining her right to and the rate of a retirement pension under the Insurance Act or under section 1 of the National Insurance Act 1970(**a**) be treated as having the same consequences as a monogamous marriage from and including the date on which she attained pensionable age or, if the marriage was contracted after that date, from and including the date of the marriage.

(2) Paragraph (1) of this regulation shall not operate so as to entitle a woman to a retirement pension for any period before the first such day as is referred to in sub-paragraph (*a*) of that paragraph or, in a case where that sub-paragraph does not apply, the day referred to in sub-paragraph (*b*) of that paragraph.

(3) Where the marriage of a woman is a polygamous marriage which was contracted—

(*a*) before she attained pensionable age and—
  (i) was not in fact monogamous when she attained that age, but
  (ii) became in fact monogamous on a date after she attained that age ; or

(*b*) on or after the day on which she attained pensionable age and—
  (i) was not in fact monogamous when it was contracted, but
  (ii) became in fact monogamous on a date after it was contracted ;

(**a**) 1970 c. 51.

that marriage shall be treated as having the same consequences as a monogamous marriage for the purposes of section 34(1)(*a*) of the Insurance Act (increase in woman's retirement pension in certain circumstances) only with effect from the date referred to in sub-paragraph (*a*)(ii) or, as the case may be, sub-paragraph (*b*)(ii) of this paragraph.

(4) In a case where section 33(3) of the Insurance Act (retirement pensions for certain widows who were widowed before attaining pensionable age) or regulation 8C of the National Insurance (Married Women) Regulations 1948(**a**) as amended(**b**) (retirement pensions for certain women whose marriages were dissolved before attaining pensionable age), applies and the relevant marriage for the purposes of that section or regulation was a polygamous marriage, for the purposes of paragraph (*b*) of the said section 33(3) and of paragraph (1)(*b*) of the said regulation 8C the polygamous marriage shall, notwithstanding that it has not at all times been in fact monogamous, be treated as having the same consequences as if it had been a monogamous marriage.

(5) Where a woman is a married woman by virtue of a polygamous marriage which is in fact monogamous on the date as from which she becomes entitled to a retirement pension under section 5 of the National Insurance Act 1971(**c**) (retirement pensions for persons over age 80), that marriage, notwithstanding that it ceases to be in fact monogamous, shall, for the purpose of determining the rate of retirement pension payable to her under the said section 5, thereafter be treated as having the same consequences as a monogamous marriage.

Transitory provision

4. Nothing in these regulations shall entitle a person—

(*a*) to benefit under the Insurance Act or the Industrial Injuries Act, or to an allowance under the Family Allowances Act, for any period before the date on which the regulations come into operation, or

(*b*) to a maternity or death grant under the Insurance Act payable in respect of a confinement or death which occurred before that date.

Keith Joseph,

Secretary of State for Social Services.

31st July 1972.

EXPLANATORY NOTE

(This Note is not part of the Regulations.)

These Regulations, made under the power conferred by section 12 of the National Insurance Act 1971, apply in place of the provisions of section 113(1) of the National Insurance Act 1965, section 86(5) of the National Insurance (Industrial Injuries) Act 1965 and section 17(9) of the Family Allowances Act 1965. Those provisions, under which a marriage celebrated

---

(**a**) S.I. 1948/1470 (Rev. XVI, p. 123: 1948 I, p. 2795).
(**b**) The relevant amending instrument is S.I. 1971/906 (1971 II, p. 2626).   (**c**) 1971 c. 50.

under a law which permits polygamy was only valid for the purposes of those Acts if and so long as it had at all times been in fact monogamous, are repealed by the said Act of 1971.

Regulation 1 relates to the citation, commencement and interpretation of these Regulations ; regulation 2 lays down the general rule for National Insurance, Industrial Injuries and Family Allowances purposes, namely, that a polygamous marriage shall have the same consequences as a monogamous marriage for any period during which it is in fact monogamous ; regulation 3 contains additional rules for particular purposes and circumstances of the National Insurance legislation ; and regulation 4 contains a transitory provision making benefit under the National Insurance and Industrial Injuries legislation and allowances under the Family Allowances legislation not payable by virtue of the provisions of the Regulations for any period before they come into operation.

STATUTORY INSTRUMENTS

1972 No. 1151 (C.22)

TOWN AND COUNTRY PLANNING,

ENGLAND AND WALES

The Town and Country Planning Act 1971 (Commencement No. 2) (South Hampshire) Order 1972

Made - - - *31st July* 1972

The Secretary of State for the Environment in exercise of the power conferred on him by section 21 of the Town and Country Planning Act 1971(a) hereby makes the following order:—

1.—(1) This order may be cited as the Town and Country Planning Act 1971 (Commencement No. 2) (South Hampshire) Order 1972.

(2) In this order:—

"the Act" means the Town and Country Planning Act 1971; and
"the Order area" means the area described in Schedule 1 to this order.

2. The provisions of the Act specified in the first column of Schedule 2 hereto (which relate to the matters specified in the second column of the said Schedule) shall come into operation in the Order area on 21st August 1972.

SCHEDULE 1

THE ORDER AREA

The county boroughs of Portsmouth and Southampton.

In the administrative county of Hampshire:—

The boroughs of Eastleigh, Gosport and Romsey.

The urban districts of Fareham and Havant and Waterloo.

In the rural district of Droxford, the whole of the following parishes:—

Bishops Waltham
Boarhunt
Curdridge
Denmead
Droxford
Durley
Hambledon
Shedfield
Soberton
Southwick and Widley
Swanmore
Upham
Wickham

(a) 1971 c. 78.

In the rural district of New Forest, the whole of the following parishes: —

Copythorne
Dibden
Eling
Fawley
Marchwood
Netley Marsh

In the rural district of Petersfield, the whole of the following parishes: —

Clanfield
Horndean
Rowlands Castle

In the rural district of Romsey and Stockbridge, the whole of the following parishes: —

Ampfield
Chilworth
North Baddesley
Nursling and Rownhams
Romsey Extra

In the rural district of Winchester, the whole of the following parishes: —

Botley	Hound
Bursledon	Hursley
Coldon Common	Twyford
Compton	Olivers Battery
Fair Oak	Otterbourne
Hamble	Owslebury
Hedge End	West End

SCHEDULE 2

PROVISIONS COMING INTO OPERATION IN THE ORDER AREA ON 21ST AUGUST 1972

Provisions of the Act	Subject matter of provisions
In Part II: section 9(3) and (5) to (8)	Amended provisions relating to approval of structure plans by Secretary of State.
section 10A	Provision for joint surveys, reports and structure plans.
section 10B	Provision for withdrawal of structure plans, and as to effect of steps taken in connection with plans withdrawn or not submitted.
section 14(4)	Provisions relating to approval of local plans submitted to the Secretary of State.

Peter Walker,
Secretary of State for the Environment.

31st July 1972.

EXPLANATORY NOTE

(This Note is not part of the Order.)

This Order brings into force for the county boroughs of Portsmouth and Southampton and certain adjacent areas of the administrative county of Hampshire as described in Schedule 1 to the Order those provisions of Part II of the Town and Country Planning Act 1971 (inserted into that Act by sections 1, 2 and 3 of the Town and Country Planning (Amendment) Act 1972 (1972 c. 42)) which are set out in Schedule 2. By virtue of the Town and Country Planning Act 1968 (Commencement No. 7) (South Hampshire) Order 1971 (S.I. 1971/2079 (C. 54)), the remaining provisions of Part II of the Act, which relate to structure and local plans, are already in operation in the area concerned.

The provisions which are brought into force by the present Order are—

(*a*) new substantive provisions empowering any two or more local planning authorities, with the consent of the Secretary of State, to carry out their duties under Part II of the Act of 1971 to institute surveys, prepare reports and prepare and submit structure plans for their areas by instituting a joint survey, preparing a joint report and preparing and submitting a joint structure plan for a combined area consisting of their areas or any part of their areas;

(*b*) new substantive provisions for the withdrawal of structure plans after submission to the Secretary of State;

(*c*) provisions specifying an amended procedure for the consideration and approval by the Secretary of State of structure plans and proposals for the amendment of structure plans (under this new procedure, the Secretary of State will no longer be required to afford objectors to the structure plan or to the proposals an opportunity of being heard at an inquiry but he will still be required to consider all valid objections and will, in addition, be required to hold an examination in public of matters affecting his consideration of the plan or proposals);

(*d*) the provisions now set out in section 14(4) of the Act of 1971 for the procedure to be adopted where the Secretary of State has directed that a local plan be submitted to him for approval.

1972 No. 1152 (C.23)

TOWN AND COUNTRY PLANNING,

ENGLAND AND WALES

The Town and Country Planning Act 1971 (Commencement No. 3) (Leicester-Leicestershire) Order 1972

Made - - - *31st July* 1972

The Secretary of State for the Environment in exercise of the power conferred on him by section 21 of the Town and Country Planning Act 1971(a) hereby makes the following order: —

1.—(1) This order may be cited as the Town and Country Planning Act 1971 (Commencement No. 3) (Leicester-Leicestershire) Order 1972.

(2) In this order: —
"the Act" means the Town and Country Planning Act 1971; and
"the Order area" means the area described in Schedule 1 to this order.

2. The provisions of the Act specified in the first column of Schedule 2 hereto (which relate to the matters specified in the second column of the said Schedule) shall come into operation in the Order area on 21st August 1972.

SCHEDULE 1

THE ORDER AREA

The county borough of Leicester.
The administrative county of Leicestershire.

SCHEDULE 2

PROVISIONS COMING INTO OPERATION IN THE ORDER AREA ON 21ST AUGUST 1972

Provisions of the Act	Subject matter of provisions
In Part II: section 9(3) and (5) to (8)	Amended provisions relating to approval of structure plans by Secretary of State.
section 10A	Provision for joint surveys, reports and structure plans.
section 10B	Provision for withdrawal of structure plans, and as to effect of steps taken in connection with plans withdrawn or not submitted.
section 14(4)	Provisions relating to approval of local plans submitted to the Secretary of State.

(a) 1971 c. 78.

Peter Walker,
Secretary of State for the Environment.

31st July 1972.

EXPLANATORY NOTE

(This Note is not part of the Order.)

This Order brings into force for the county borough of Leicester and the administrative county of Leicestershire those provisions of Part II of the Town and Country Planning Act 1971 (inserted into that Act by sections 1, 2 and 3 of the Town and Country Planning (Amendment) Act 1972 (1972 c. 42)) which are set out in Schedule 2. By virtue of the Town and Country Planning Act 1968 (Commencement No. 8) (Leicester-Leicestershire) Order 1971 (S.I. 1971/2080 (C. 55)), the remaining provisions of Part II of the Act, which relate to structure and local plans, are already in operation in the area concerned.

The provisions which are brought into force by the present Order are—

(*a*) new substantive provisions empowering any two or more local planning authorities, with the consent of the Secretary of State, to carry out their duties under Part II of the Act of 1971 to institute surveys, prepare reports and prepare and submit structure plans for their areas by instituting a joint survey, preparing a joint report and preparing and submitting a joint structure plan for a combined area consisting of their areas or any part of their areas;

(*b*) new substantive provisions for the withdrawal of structure plans after submission to the Secretary of State;

(*c*) provisions specifying an amended procedure for the consideration and approval by the Secretary of State of structure plans and proposals for the amendment of structure plans (under this new procedure, the Secretary of State will no longer be required to afford objectors to the structure plan or to the proposals an opportunity of being heard at an inquiry but he will still be required to consider all valid objections and will, in addition, be required to hold an examination in public of matters affecting his consideration of the plan or proposals);

(*d*) the provisions now set out in section 14(4) of the Act of 1971 for the procedure to be adopted where the Secretary of State has directed that a local plan be submitted to him for approval.

STATUTORY INSTRUMENTS

1972 No. 1153 (C. 24)

TOWN AND COUNTRY PLANNING,

ENGLAND AND WALES

The Town and Country Planning Act 1971 (Commencement No. 4) (Teesside, etc.) Order 1972

Made - - - 31st July 1972

The Secretary of State for the Environment in exercise of the power conferred on him by section 21 of the Town and Country Planning Act 1971(a) hereby makes the following order: —

1.—(1) This order may be cited as the Town and Country Planning Act 1971 (Commencement No. 4) (Teesside, etc.) Order 1972.

(2) In this order: —
   "the Act" means the Town and Country Planning Act 1971; and
   "the Order area" means the area described in Schedule 1 to this order.

2. The provisions of the Act specified in the first column of Schedule 2 hereto (which relate to the matters specified in the second column of the said Schedule) shall come into operation in the Order area on 21st August 1972.

(a) 1971 c. 78.

SCHEDULE 1

THE ORDER AREA

The county borough of Teesside.

In the administrative county of the North Riding of Yorkshire, the urban districts of Guisborough, Loftus, Saltburn and Marske-by-the-Sea and Skelton and Brotton and the rural district of Stokesley.

In the administrative county of Durham, in the rural district of Stockton, the whole of the following parishes:—

> Newsham
> Aislaby
> Egglescliffe
> Longnewton
> Preston-on-Tees
> Elton
> Redmarshall
> Carlton
> Whitton
> Grindon
> Wolviston
> Newton Bewley
> Greatham

and that part of the parish of Elwick Hall which is to the south or west of Close Beck.

SCHEDULE 2

PROVISIONS COMING INTO OPERATION IN THE ORDER AREA ON 21ST AUGUST 1972

Provisions of the Act	Subject matter of Provisions
In Part II: section 9(3) and (5) to (8)	Amended provisions relating to approval of structure plans by Secretary of State.
section 10A	Provision for joint surveys, reports and structure plans.
section 10B	Provision for withdrawal of structure plans, and as to effect of steps taken in connection with plans withdrawn or not submitted.
section 14(4)	Provisions relating to approval of local plans submitted to the Secretary of State.

Peter Walker,
Secretary of State for the Environment.

31st July 1972.

EXPLANATORY NOTE
(This Note is not part of the Order.)

This Order brings into force for the county borough of Teesside and certain adjacent areas in the administrative counties of Durham and the North Riding of Yorkshire as described in Schedule 1 to the Order those provisions of Part II of the Town and Country Planning Act 1971 (inserted into that Act by sections 1, 2 and 3 of the Town and Country Planning (Amendment) Act 1972 (1972 c. 42)) which are set out in Schedule 2. By virtue of the Town and Country Planning Act 1968 (Commencement No. 6) (Teesside, etc.) Order 1971 (S.I. 1971/1108 (C.25), the remaining provisions of Part II of the Act, which relate to structure and local plans, are already in operation in the area concerned.

The provisions which are brought into force by the present Order are—

(a) new substantive provisions empowering any two or more local planning authorities, with the consent of the Secretary of State, to carry out their duties under Part II of the Act of 1971 to institute surveys, prepare reports and prepare and submit structure plans for their areas by instituting a joint survey, preparing a joint report and preparing and submitting a joint structure plan for a combined area consisting of their areas or any part of their areas;

(b) new substantive provisions for the withdrawal of structure plans after submission to the Secretary of State;

(c) provisions specifying an amended procedure for the consideration and approval by the Secretary of State of structure plans and proposals for the amendment of structure plans (under this new procedure, the Secretary of State will no longer be required to afford objectors to the structure plan or to the proposals an opportunity of being heard at an inquiry but he will still be required to consider all valid objections and will, in addition, be required to hold an examination in public of matters affecting his consideration of the plan or proposals);

(d) the provisions now set out in section 14(4) of the Act of 1971 for the procedure to be adopted where the Secretary of State has directed that a local plan be submitted to him for approval.

STATUTORY INSTRUMENTS

1972 No. 1154

TOWN AND COUNTRY PLANNING, ENGLAND AND WALES

The Town and Country Planning (Structure and Local Plans) Regulations 1972

Made - - -	*31st July* 1972
Laid before Parliament	*1st August* 1972
Coming into Operation	*22nd August* 1972

ARRANGEMENT OF REGULATIONS

PART I

APPLICATION, CITATION, COMMENCEMENT AND INTERPRETATION

PART II

PUBLICITY IN CONNECTION WITH THE PREPARATION OF STRUCTURE OR LOCAL PLANS: SALE OF DOCUMENTS AND PRESCRIBED PERIOD FOR MAKING REPRESENTATIONS

PART III

CONSULTATION

PART IV

FORM AND CONTENT OF STRUCTURE PLANS

Part V

Form and Content of Local Plans

Part VI

Procedure for the Approval, Withdrawal or Rejection of Structure Plans

Part VII

Procedure for the Adoption, Abandonment, Approval or Rejection of Local Plans

Part VIII

Structure and Local Plans: Availability and Sale of Documents, Register and Index Map

Part IX

Alteration of Structure Plans and Alteration, Repeal or Replacement of Local Plans

43. Alteration of structure plans.
44. Alteration, repeal or replacement of local plans.

Part X

Preparation and Making, etc., of Structure or Local Plans by the Secretary of State

45. Preparation and making, etc., of structure or local plans by the Secretary of State.

Part XI

Structure and Local Plans: Reconciliation of Contradictions

46. Reconciliation of contradictions in structure plans.
47. Reconciliation of contradictions in local plans.
48. Reconciliation of contradictions between local plans.
49. Revocation and savings.

Schedule 1

Structure Plans

Part I.   Matters to which policy is required to relate by regulation 9(1).
Part II. Matters required by regulation 10 to be contained in written statement.

Schedule 2

Local Plans

Part I.   Matters to which proposals are required to relate by regulation 16(1).
Part II. Matters required by regulation 17 to be contained in written statement.

Schedule 3

Forms of Notices

The Secretary of State for the Environment (as respects England, except Monmouthshire) and the Secretary of State for Wales (as respects Wales and Monmouthshire) in exercise of their powers under sections 7(3) and (6), 8(1), (2) and (3), 9(3)(a), 11(3), (5) and (9), 12(1), (2) and (3), 18(1) and (2) and 287 of the Town and Country Planning Act 1971(a), and of all other powers enabling them in that behalf, hereby make the following regulations:—

(a) 1971 c. 78.

Part I

Application, Citation, Commencement and Interpretation

Application

1. These regulations shall apply to England (except Greater London) and Wales.

Citation and commencement

2. These regulations may be cited as the Town and Country Planning (Structure and Local Plans) Regulations 1972, and shall come into operation on 22nd August 1972.

Interpretation

3.—(1) In these regulations—

"the Act" means the Town and Country Planning Act 1971;

"action area" has the meaning assigned to it by section 7(5) of the Act;

"an area of a new town" means an area designated by an order made or having effect as if made under section 1 of the New Towns Act 1965(**a**);

"an area of town development" means an area (comprising one or more parts defined on one occasion) in the whole of which town development within the meaning of the Town Development Act 1952(**b**) is to be carried out;

"certified copy" means a copy certified by the clerk of the local planning authority or, in the case of a structure plan for a combined area, by the clerk of any of the local planning authorities concerned as being a true copy;

"county" means an administrative county;

"document" includes a map, diagram, illustration or other descriptive matter in any form, and also includes, where appropriate, a copy of a document;

"duly made", in relation to objections, means duly made in accordance with a notice given or served under these regulations;

"examination in public" means an examination in public within the meaning of section 9(3)(*b*) of the Act;

"local plan" means a local plan within the meaning of section 11 of the Act;

"notice by advertisement" means a notice published in the London Gazette and in each of two successive weeks in at least one local newspaper circulating in the locality in which the land to which the notice relates is situated;

"structure plan" means a structure plan within the meaning of section 7 of the Act;

"written statement" means, as respects a structure plan, the written statement required by section 7(3) of the Act, and, as respects a local plan, the written statement required by section 11(3) of the Act.

(**a**) 1965 c. 59.　　　　　(**b**) 1952 c. 54.

(2) In relation to a structure plan for a combined area, references in these regulations (except in this regulation and in regulations 7, 23, 39 and 40) to a local planning authority shall be read as references to the local planning authorities concerned.

(3) A regulation or schedule referred to in these regulations only by number means the regulation or schedule so numbered in these regulations.

(4) The Interpretation Act 1889(a) shall apply for the interpretation of these regulations as it applies for the interpretation of an Act of Parliament.

Part II

Publicity in Connection with the Preparation of Structure or Local Plans: Sale of Documents and Prescribed Period for Making Representations

Sale of copies of documents made public for the purpose mentioned in section 8(1)(a) or 12(1)(a) of the Act

4. The local planning authority shall, in such particular cases as the Secretary of State may direct, provide persons making a request in that behalf with copies of any plan or other document which has been made public for the purpose mentioned in section 8(1)(a) or 12(1)(a) of the Act, subject to the payment of a reasonable charge therefor.

Prescribed period for making representations

5. The prescribed period for the purposes of section 8(1) or 12(1) of the Act shall be such period (not being less than six weeks) as shall be specified by an authority when giving publicity thereunder to the matters proposed to be included in a structure or local plan.

Part III

Consultation

Consultation

6.—(1) Before finally determining the content of a structure or local plan, the local planning authority shall consult with respect to the matters they propose to include in the plan the following authorities or bodies, namely:—

  (a) where the plan relates to any land in a county district, the council of that district;

  (b) where the area of land to which the plan relates includes land within the area of a new town, the new town development corporation;

  (c) such other authorities or bodies as the local planning authority think appropriate or the Secretary of State may direct.

(2) The local planning authority shall give to any authority or body whom they consult under paragraph (1) above an adequate opportunity of expressing views with respect to the matters proposed to be included in the plan and shall consider any such views before finally determining the content of the plan.

_____

(a) 1889 c. 63.

Part IV

Form and Content of Structure Plans

Title

7. A structure plan shall be given a title which shall include the name of the local planning authority or, in the case of a structure plan for a combined area, the names of the local planning authorities concerned, and, where the plan relates to part only of the authority's area, or, as the case may be, to a combined area, an indication of the area to which the plan relates; and each document contained in or accompanying a structure plan shall bear the title of the plan.

Treatment of certain urban or proposed urban areas

8.—(1) As respects any part of the area to which a structure plan (other than a structure plan relating only to the whole or any part of a county borough) relates, being a part which is, or which it is proposed should become, urban or predominantly urban, the local planning authority may with the consent of the Secretary of State, and shall, if the Secretary of State so directs, as well as formulating their policy and general proposals for that part as part of the whole area to which the plan relates, formulate policy and general proposals for that part in a separate part of the plan.

(2) A separate part of a structure plan prepared under paragraph (1) above shall be prepared as if it were itself a structure plan.

Policy and general proposals

9.—(1) The policy formulated in a structure plan written statement shall relate to such of the matters specified in Part I of Schedule 1 as the local planning authority may think appropriate.

(2) The policy and general proposals formulated in a structure plan written statement shall be set out so as to be readily distinguishable from the other contents thereof.

(3) A structure plan written statement shall include a reasoned justification of the policy and general proposals formulated therein.

Matters to be contained in written statement

10. In addition to the other matters required to be contained therein by the Act and by these regulations, a structure plan written statement shall contain the following matters, namely, such indications as the local planning authority may think appropriate of the items set out in Part II of Schedule 1.

Action areas: prescribed period

11. The prescribed period for the purposes of section 7(5) of the Act (indication of an action area in the general proposals in a structure plan) shall be ten years from the date on which the particular structure plan is submitted to the Secretary of State.

Diagrams and insets

12.—(1) A structure plan shall contain or be accompanied by a diagram, called the key diagram, showing, so far as the local planning authority may think practicable, the policy and general proposals formulated in the written statement:

Provided that the policy and general proposals for any part of the area to which a structure plan relates may, instead of being shown on the key diagram, be shown on an inset; and the location of any inset shall be shown on the key diagram.

(2) No diagram or inset contained in, or accompanying, a structure plan shall be on a map base.

Explanation of notation on diagrams

13. Any diagram contained in, or accompanying, a structure plan shall include an explanation of the notation used thereon.

PART V

FORM AND CONTENT OF LOCAL PLANS

Title

14. A local plan shall be given a title which shall include the name of the local planning authority, the name given to the particular plan by or under regulation 15, and an indication of the area to which the plan relates; and each document contained in or accompanying a local plan shall bear the title of the plan.

District, action area and subject plans

15.—(1) A local plan based on a comprehensive consideration of matters affecting the development and other use of land in the area to which it relates shall, unless it is a local plan for an action area, be called a district plan.

(2) A local plan for an action area shall be called an action area plan.

(3) A local plan which is based on a consideration of a particular description or descriptions of development or other use of land in the area to which it relates shall be called by the name of the subject or subjects to which it relates.

Proposals

16.—(1) The proposals formulated in a local plan written statement shall relate to such of the matters specified in Part I of Schedule 2 as the local planning authority may think appropriate.

(2) The proposals formulated in a local plan written statement shall be set out so as to be readily distinguishable from the other contents thereof.

(3) A local plan written statement shall contain a reasoned justification of the proposals formulated therein.

Matters to be contained in written statement

17. In addition to the other matters required to be contained therein by the Act and by these regulations, a local plan written statement shall contain the following matters, namely, such indications as the local planning authority may think appropriate of the items set out in Part II of Schedule 2.

Maps, insets and diagrams

18.—(1) The map comprised in a local plan in compliance with section 11(3) of the Act shall be called the proposals map, and shall—

(*a*) be prepared on a map base reproduced from, or based on, the Ordnance Survey map, and showing National Grid lines and numbers;

(*b*) subject as hereinafter mentioned, be prepared to such scale as the local planning authority may think appropriate, or the Secretary of State may direct:

Provided that the proposals for any part of the area to which a local plan relates may be shown to a larger scale on an inset prepared in accordance with sub-paragraph (*a*) above; and the proposals shown on an inset may be shown on the proposals map by showing thereon the boundary of the inset.

(2) A proposals map or inset which defines land as the site of a proposed road for the purposes of section 21 of the Highways Act 1959(**a**), or which defines land as the site of a proposed road or as land required for the widening of an existing road and designates that land as land to which section 206 of the Highways Act 1959 applies, shall be to a scale of not less than 1/2500.

(3) Any map forming part of a local plan shall show the scale to which it has been prepared; and any map or diagram contained in, or accompanying, a local plan shall include such explanation as the local planning authority may think necessary of the notation used thereon.

(4) In addition to the other matters shown thereon, a proposals map shall show the boundary of any area of town development.

Part VI

Procedure for the Approval, Withdrawal or Rejection of Structure Plans

Submission of structure plan to the Secretary of State

19. A structure plan shall be prepared in duplicate. One duplicate shall be submitted to the Secretary of State, together with two certified copies thereof and a statement giving particulars of the matters specified in section 8(3)(*a*) and (*b*) of the Act.

Notice of submission of structure plan

20. On the submission of a structure plan to the Secretary of State the local planning authority shall give notice by advertisement in the appropriate form (Form 1) specified in Schedule 3, or a form substantially to the like effect.

(**a**) 1959 c. 25.

Notice of return of structure plan

21. Where, under section 8(4) of the Act, the Secretary of State returns a structure plan to the local planning authority, the authority shall give notice by advertisement in the appropriate form (Form 2) specified in Schedule 3, or a form substantially to the like effect.

Notice of resubmission of structure plan

22. On the resubmission of a structure plan to the Secretary of State the local planning authority shall give notice by advertisement in the appropriate form (Form 3) specified in Schedule 3, or a form substantially to the like effect, and shall serve a notice in the same terms on any person who made objections to the plan to the Secretary of State when it was originally submitted to him.

Notice of withdrawal of structure plan

23. Where a local planning authority, or in relation to a structure plan for a combined area all or any of the local planning authorities concerned, has or have given notice to the Secretary of State of withdrawal of a structure plan in accordance with section 10B of the Act the local planning authority, or in relation to a structure plan for a combined area the local planning authority or authorities, withdrawing the structure plan shall give notice of such withdrawal, and of the withdrawal of the copies of the plan made available for inspection as required by section 8(2) of the Act, by advertisement in the appropriate form (Form 4) specified in Schedule 3, or a form substantially to the like effect, and for the purpose of complying with section 10B(2) of the Act shall serve a notice in the same terms on any person by whom objections to the plan have been duly made and not withdrawn.

Notice of examination in public

24. When the Secretary of State causes an examination in public to be held into matters affecting his consideration of a structure plan he shall at least six weeks before the date of the examination give notice by advertisement of his intention to hold such an examination.

Proposed modifications

25. Where the Secretary of State proposes to modify a structure plan he shall, except as respects any modification which he is satisfied will not materially affect the content of the plan—

(*a*) notify the local planning authority of the proposed modifications, and the authority shall give notice by advertisement in the appropriate form (Form 5) specified in Schedule 3, or a form substantially to the like effect, and shall serve a notice in the same terms on such persons as the Secretary of State may direct; and

(*b*) consider any objections duly made to the proposed modifications.

Notification of the Secretary of State's decision

26. The Secretary of State shall notify the local planning authority in writing of his decision on a structure plan and the authority shall forthwith give notice by advertisement in the appropriate form (Form 6) specified in Schedule 3, or a form substantially to the like effect, and shall serve a notice in the same terms on any person who, in accordance with a notice given or served under this part of these regulations, has requested the authority to notify him of the decision on the plan and on such other persons as the Secretary of State may direct.

Copies of notices and certificates as to notices to be sent to the Secretary of State

27. On first giving notice by advertisement in accordance with any provision in this part of these regulations, the local planning authority shall send the Secretary of State a certified copy of the notice; and, after complying with the requirements of any provision in this part of these regulations relating to the giving or giving and serving of notices, the authority shall send the Secretary of State a certificate to that effect.

PART VII

PROCEDURE FOR THE ADOPTION, ABANDONMENT, APPROVAL OR REJECTION OF LOCAL PLANS

Preparation of local plan

28. A local plan shall be prepared in duplicate.

Notice of preparation of local plan

29. A local planning authority who have prepared and deposited a local plan shall give notice by advertisement in the appropriate form (Form 7) specified in Schedule 3, or a form substantially to the like effect.

Notice of withdrawal of copies of local plan and subsequent action

30.—(1) A local planning authority who are given directions by the Secretary of State under section 12(4) of the Act and who, in accordance with section 12(5)(a) of the Act, withdraw the copies of a local plan made available for inspection as required by section 12(2) of the Act, shall give notice by advertisement in the appropriate form (Form 8) specified in Schedule 3, or a form substantially to the like effect, and, for the purpose of complying with section 12(5)(b) of the Act, shall serve a notice in the same terms on any person by whom objections to the plan have been made to the authority.

(2) After satisfying the Secretary of State as mentioned in section 12(4) of the Act and before taking any further steps for the adoption of the plan, the authority shall again make copies of the plan available for inspection at the places where they were previously available for inspection, and shall give notice by advertisement in the appropriate form (Form 9) specified in Schedule 3, or a form substantially to the like effect, and shall serve a notice in the same terms on any person who made objections to the plan to the authority when copies were previously available for inspection.

Local inquiry to be a public local inquiry

31. A local inquiry held for the purpose of considering objections made to a local plan shall be a public local inquiry.

Notice of local inquiry or other hearing

32. Where a local planning authority cause a local inquiry to be held for the purpose of considering objections made to a local plan, they shall, at least six weeks before the date of the inquiry, give notice by advertisement in the appropriate form (Form 10) specified in Schedule 3, or a form substantially to the like effect, and shall serve a notice in the same terms on any person whose objections have been duly made and are not withdrawn and on such other persons as they think fit; and, where the authority cause a hearing (other than a local inquiry) to be held for the said purpose, they shall, at least six weeks before the date of the hearing, serve a notice in the appropriate form (Form 10) specified in Schedule 3, or a form substantially to the like effect, on any person whose objections have been duly made and are not withdrawn and on such other persons as they think fit.

Report of local inquiry or other hearing

33.—(1) Where, for the purpose of considering objections made to a local plan, a local inquiry or other hearing is held, the local planning authority shall, as part of the consideration of those objections, consider the report of the person appointed to hold the inquiry or other hearing and decide whether or not to take any action as respects the plan in the light of the report and each recommendation, if any, contained therein; and the authority shall prepare a statement of their decisions, giving their reasons therefor.

(2) The authority shall make certified copies of the report, and of the statement prepared under paragraph (1) above, available for inspection not later than the date on which notice is first given under regulation 35.

Proposed modifications

34.—(1) Where the local planning authority propose to modify a local plan, they shall—

    (*a*) prepare a list of the proposed modifications, giving their reasons for proposing them;

    (*b*) give notice by advertisement in the appropriate form (Form 11) specified in Schedule 3, or a form substantially to the like effect, and shall serve a notice in the same terms on any person whose objections to the plan have been duly made and are not withdrawn and on such other persons as they think fit;

    (*c*) consider any objections duly made to the proposed modifications;

    (*d*) decide whether or not to afford to persons whose objections so made are not withdrawn, or to any of them, an opportunity of appearing before, and being heard by, a person appointed by the Secretary of State for the purpose; and

    (*e*) if a local inquiry or other hearing is held, also afford the like opportunity to such other persons as they think fit;

Provided that, unless the Secretary of State directs them to do so, the authority shall not be obliged to cause a local inquiry or other hearing to be held for the purpose of considering objections made to proposed modifications; but, if a local inquiry is held, it shall be a public local inquiry.

(2) Regulations 32 and 33 shall apply in relation to proposed modifications as they apply in relation to a local plan.

Action following decision to adopt local plan

35.—(1) Where a local planning authority decide to adopt a local plan, they shall, before adopting the plan, give notice by advertisement in the appropriate form (Form 12) specified in Schedule 3, or a form substantially to the like effect, and shall serve a notice in the same terms on any person whose objections to the plan have been duly made and are not withdrawn, and on such other persons as they think fit.

(2) After complying with paragraph (1) above, the authority shall send the Secretary of State by recorded delivery service a certificate that they have complied therewith; and, subject as mentioned in section 14(3) of the Act, the authority shall not adopt the plan until the expiration of twenty-eight days from the date on which the certificate is sent:

Provided that, if, before the plan is adopted, the Secretary of State directs the authority not to adopt the plan until he notifies them that he has decided not to give a direction under section 14(3) of the Act, the authority shall not adopt the plan until they receive such notification.

Notice of adoption or abandonment of local plan

36. Where the local planning authority adopt or abandon a local plan, they shall give notice by advertisement in the appropriate form (Form 13) specified in Schedule 3, or a form substantially to the like effect, and shall serve a notice in the same terms on any person who, in accordance with a notice given or served under this part of these regulations, has requested the authority to notify him of the adoption, abandonment, approval or rejection of the plan, and on such other persons as they think fit.

Documents to be sent to the Secretary of State

37. In addition to the document mentioned in regulation 35(2), the local planning authority shall send to the Secretary of State—

(*a*) not later than the date on which notice is first given under regulation 29, two certified copies of the local plan prepared by them and a statement giving particulars of the matters specified in section 12(3)(*a*) and (*b*) of the Act;

(*b*) not later than the date on which notice of the adoption of a local plan is first given under regulation 36, two certified copies of the plan adopted;

(*c*) not later than the date on which notice is first given or served under any provision in this part of these regulations, a copy of each document (other than a document mentioned in paragraph (*a*) or (*b*) above) referred to in the notice as having been deposited;

(*d*) on first giving or serving notice under any provision in this part of these regulations, a certified copy of the notice; and

(*e*) any other relevant document the Secretary of State may at any time require.

Notice of approval, modification or rejection of local plan by the Secretary of State

38.—(1) Where a local planning authority are required by a direction under section 14(3) of the Act to submit a local plan to the Secretary of State for his approval and the Secretary of State causes a local inquiry to be held for the purpose of considering objections duly made to the local plan, he shall, at least six weeks before the date of the inquiry, give notice by advertisement in the appropriate form (Form 10) specified in Schedule 3, or a form substantially to the like effect, and shall serve a notice in the same terms on any person whose objections have been duly made and are not withdrawn and on such other persons as he thinks fit; and when the Secretary of State causes a hearing (other than a local inquiry) to be held for the said purpose, he shall, at least six weeks before the date of the hearing, serve a notice in the appropriate form (Form 10) specified in Schedule 3, or a form substantially to the like effect, on any person whose objections have been duly made and are not withdrawn and on such other persons as he thinks fit.

(2) A local inquiry held for the purposes of paragraph (1) above shall be a public local inquiry.

(3) Where the Secretary of State proposes to modify a local plan he shall, except as respects any modification which he is satisfied will not materially affect the content of the plan—

(*a*) notify the local planning authority of the proposed modifications, and the authority shall give notice by advertisement in the appropriate form (Form 5) specified in Schedule 3, or a form substantially to the like effect, and shall serve a notice in the same terms on such persons as the Secretary of State may direct;

(*b*) consider any objections duly made to the proposed modifications;

(*c*) decide whether or not to afford to persons whose objections so made are not withdrawn, or to any of them, an opportunity of appearing before, and being heard by, a person appointed by him for the purpose; and

(*d*) if a local inquiry or other hearing is held, also afford the like opportunity to the local planning authority and to such other persons as he thinks fit:

Provided that the Secretary of State shall not be obliged to cause a local inquiry or other hearing to be held for the purpose of considering objections made to proposed modifications; but if a local inquiry is held it shall be a public local inquiry.

(4) Regulations 26 and 27 shall apply in relation to a local plan as they apply in relation to a structure plan.

Part VIII

Structure and Local Plans: Availability and Sale of Documents, Register and Index Map

Availability of documents referred to in notices

39.—(1) Where a notice given or served under these regulations refers to a deposited document, the local planning authority, or, in the case of a structure plan for a combined area, each of the local planning authorities concerned shall make the document available for inspection at their office, at a place in each county district which is within their area and is wholly or partly comprised in the area to which the relevant plan relates, and at such other places as the authority think convenient to the public having regard to the area to which the plan relates.

(2) Any document made available for inspection under paragraph (1) above shall, unless it is withdrawn in accordance with sect.on 8(6) or 12(5)(a) of the Act, or unless the relevant plan is rejected or abandoned, be available for inspection free of charge at all reasonable hours from a date not later than the date on which the notice is given or served until the expiration of six weeks from the date of the publication of the first notice of the approval or adoption of the plan required by these regulations.

Availability of operative structure and local plans

40.—(1) Except in the case of a structure plan for a combined area, the local planning authority shall make any operative structure or local plan available for inspection at their office: and, in the case of an operative structure plan for a combined area, the local planning authorities concerned shall make the plan available for inspection at the office of one of them and shall make certified copies of the plan available for inspection at the office of each of the others.

(2) The local planning authority, or in the case of a structure plan for a combined area each of the local planning authorities concerned, shall make certified copies of any operative structure or local plan available for inspection at a place in each county district which is within their area and is wholly or partly comprised in the area to which the plan relates.

(3) Any document made available for inspection under paragraph (1) or (2) above shall be accompanied by a statement setting out the provisions of section 244(1) and (2) of the Act, and that statement shall remain on deposit until the expiration of the period specified in the said section 244(1).

(4) Any document made available for inspection under this regulation shall be available for inspection free of charge at all reasonable hours.

Sale of documents

41.—(1) The local planning authority shall provide persons making a request in that behalf with copies of any plan or other document which has been made available for inspection under section 8(2) or 12(2) of the Act, subject to the payment of a reasonable charge therefor.

(2) As soon as possible after a structure or local plan becomes operative the local planning authority shall arrange for the printing of the plan, and thereafter at such times as the authority think fit, or the Secretary of State may direct, shall arrange for the reprinting of the plan; and printed copies of the plan shall be made available for sale to the public at a reasonable charge:

Provided that. unless the Secretary of State otherwise directs, it shall suffice in relation to the application of this paragraph to any operative alteration, repeal or replacement of a structure or local plan, if the alteration, repeal or replacement is taken into account when the plan is next reprinted.

Register and index map

42.—(1) The local planning authority shall prepare and keep up-to-date a register containing the following information in respect of their area, namely—

> (a) brief particulars of any structure or local plan copies of which have been made available for inspection under section 8(2) or 12(2) of the Act, and of any action taken in connection with any such plan, including, in the case of an operative plan, the date on which the plan became operative and a reference to the boundary of the plan as shown on the index map prepared under paragraph (2) below;

> (b) brief particulars of any proposals for the alteration, repeal or replacement of any structure or local plan copies of which have been made available for inspection under section 8(2) of the Act as applied by section 10(2) or section 12(2) of the Act as applied by section 15(3) and of any action taken in connection with any such proposals, including, in the case of an operative alteration, repeal or replacement, the date on which it became operative.

(2) The authority shall also prepare and keep up-to-date an index map for their area showing the boundary of any operative structure or local plan, together with a reference to the appropriate entry in the register prepared under paragraph (1) above.

(3) The authority shall make the register and index map available for inspection with any operative structure or local plan made available for inspection under regulation 40, and shall make certified copies of the register and index map available for inspection with copies of any structure or local plan made available for inspection under the provisions of the Act or of these regulations; and documents made available for inspection under this paragraph shall be available for inspection free of charge at all reasonable hours.

PART IX

ALTERATION OF STRUCTURE PLANS AND ALTERATION, REPEAL OR REPLACEMENT OF LOCAL PLANS

Alteration of structure plans

43. The provisions of these regulations relating to structure plans shall apply, with any necessary modifications, in relation to proposals for alterations to a structure plan as they apply in relation to a structure plan.

Alteration, repeal or replacement of local plans

44. The provisions of these regulations relating to local plans shall apply, with any necessary modifications, in relation to proposals for the alteration, repeal or replacement of a local plan as they apply in relation to a local plan.

PART X

PREPARATION AND MAKING, ETC., OF STRUCTURE OR LOCAL PLANS BY THE SECRETARY OF STATE

Preparation and making, etc., of structure or local plans by the Secretary of State

45. The provisions of these regulations shall apply, with any necessary modifications, in relation to the preparation and making of a structure plan or local plan or, as the case may be, the alteration, repeal or replacement of a structure or local plan, by the Secretary of State under section 17 of the Act:

Provided that the local planning authority shall, unless the Secretary of State otherwise directs, give and serve such notices as are required by these regulations and comply with Part VIII hereof.

PART XI

STRUCTURE AND LOCAL PLANS: RECONCILIATION OF CONTRADICTIONS

Reconciliation of contradictions in structure plans

46.—(1) In the case of any contradiction in a structure plan between a separate part prepared under regulation 8 and the rest of the plan, the provisions of the separate part shall prevail.

(2) Subject to paragraph (1) above, in the case of any contradiction in a structure plan between the written statement and any other document forming part of the plan, the provisions of the written statement shall prevail.

Reconciliation of contradictions in local plans

47. In the case of any contradiction between the written statement and any other document forming part of a local plan, the provisions of the written statement shall prevail.

Reconciliation of contradictions between local plans

48. In the case of any contradiction between local plans for the same part of any area, the provisions which are more recently adopted, approved or made shall prevail.

Revocation and Savings

49. The Town and Country Planning (Structure and Local Plans) Regulations 1971(**a**) are hereby revoked: provided that in so far as these regulations contain a corresponding provision anything done under the regulations hereby revoked shall be deemed to have been done under the corresponding provision of these regulations.

(a) S.I. 1971/1109 (1971 II, p. 3291).

SCHEDULE 1

STRUCTURE PLANS

PART I

MATTERS TO WHICH POLICY IS REQUIRED TO RELATE BY REGULATION 9(1)

The matters to which the policy formulated in a structure plan written statement is required to relate by regulation 9(1) are such of the following matters as the local planning authority may think appropriate:

  (i) Population.

  (ii) Employment.

  (iii) Housing.

  (iv) Industry and commerce.

  (v) Transportation.

  (vi) Shopping.

  (vii) Education.

  (viii) Other social and community services.

  (ix) Recreation and leisure.

  (x) Conservation, townscape and landscape.

  (xi) Utility services.

  (xii) Any other relevant matters.

PART II

MATTERS REQUIRED BY REGULATION 10 TO BE CONTAINED IN WRITTEN STATEMENT

The matters required by regulation 10 to be contained in a structure plan written statement are such indications as the local planning authority may think appropriate of the following:

  (i) The existing structure of the area to which the plan relates and the present needs and opportunities for change.

  (ii) Any changes already projected, or likely to occur, which may materially affect matters dealt with in the plan, and the effect those changes are likely to have.

  (iii) The effect (if any) on the area of the plan of any proposal to make an order under section 1 of the New Towns Act 1965 (designation of sites of new towns) or of any order made or having effect as if made under section 1 of the New Towns Act 1965 or of any known intentions of a development corporation established in pursuance of such an order.

  (iv) The extent (if any) to which town development within the meaning of the Town Development Act 1952 is being, or is to be, carried out in the area to which the plan relates.

  (v) The size, composition and distribution of population, and the state of employment and industry (and the assumptions on which estimates are based) in the area to which the plan relates, both at the time the plan is prepared and at such future times as the local planning authority think appropriate for the purposes of the plan.

  (vi) The regard the local planning authority have had to the current policies with respect to the economic planning and development of the region as a whole.

  (vii) The regard the local planning authority have had to social policies and considerations.

(viii) The regard the local planning authority have had to the resources likely to be available for carrying out the policy and general proposals formulated in the plan.

(ix) The broad criteria to be applied as respects the control of development in the area, or any part of the area, to which the plan relates.

(x) The extent and nature of the relationship between the policies formulated in the plan.

(xi) The considerations underlying any major items of policy formulated in the plan as respects matters of common interest to the local planning authority by whom the plan is prepared and the local planning authorities for neighbouring areas, and the extent to which those major items have been agreed by the authorities concerned.

(xii) Any other relevant matters.

SCHEDULE 2

Local Plans

Part I

Matters to which Proposals are Required to Relate by Regulation 16(1)

The matters to which the proposals formulated in a local plan written statement are required to relate by regulation 16(1) are such of the following matters as the local planning authority may think appropriate:

(i) Population.

(ii) Employment.

(iii) Housing.

(iv) Industry and commerce.

(v) Transportation.

(vi) Shopping.

(vii) Education.

(viii) Other social and community services.

(ix) Recreation and leisure.

(x) Conservation, townscape and landscape.

(xi) Utility services.

(xii) Any other relevant matters.

Part II

Matters Required by Regulation 17 to be Contained in Written Statement

The matters required by regulation 17 to be contained in a local plan written statement are such indications as the local planning authority may think appropriate of the following:

(i) The character, pattern and function of the existing development and other use of land in the area to which the plan relates and the present needs and opportunities for change.

(ii) Any changes already projected, or likely to occur, which may materially affect matters dealt with in the plan, and the effect those changes are likely to have, including when the area to which the plan relates is within the area of a new town, the effect of any development proposed by the new town development corporation;

(iii) The regard the local planning authority have had to social policies and considerations.

(iv) The regard the local planning authority have had to the resources likely to be available for carrying out the proposals formulated in the plan.

(v) The criteria to be applied as respects the control of development in the area, or any part of the area, to which the plan relates.

(vi) The extent and nature of the relationship between the proposals formulated in the plan.

(vii) Any other relevant matters.

SCHEDULE 3

Regulation 20   FORMS OF NOTICES

Form 1: Form of notice of submission of structure plan

NOTICE OF SUBMISSION OF STRUCTURE PLAN

Town and Country Planning Act 1971
(Title of structure plan)

(1) submitted the above-named structure plan to the Secretary of State [for the Environment] [for Wales] (2) on   19   for his approval. [The plan relates to land in the following county district(s): (3)](2)

Certified copies of the plan, of the report of survey and of the statement mentioned in section 8(3) of the Act have been deposited at (4).

The deposited documents are available for inspection free of charge (5).

Objections to the plan should be sent in writing to the Secretary, [Department of the Environment, 2 Marsham Street, London, SWIP 3EB] [Welsh Office, Summit House, Windsor Place, Cardiff, CF1 3BX] (2) before (6). Objections should state the matters to which they relate and the grounds on which they are made*. A person making objections may send a written request (stating his name and the address to which notice is to be sent) to (7) to be notified of the decision on the plan.

19   .

(Signature)

*Forms for making objections are obtainable at the places where documents have been deposited.

Regulation 21

Form 2: Form of notice of return of structure plan

NOTICE OF RETURN OF STRUCTURE PLAN

Town and Country Planning Act 1971
(Title of structure plan)

The above-named structure plan has been returned to (1) by the Secretary of State [for the Environment] [for Wales] (2) and the council have been directed to take certain further action as respects publicity in connection with the plan, and, after doing so, to resubmit the plan to the Secretary of State with such modifications, if any, as the authority then consider appropriate [within (8)] (2).

When the plan is resubmitted objections made to the plan as originally submitted will be considered, and there will be an opportunity to make objections to the plan as resubmitted.

19

(Signature)

Regulation 22

Form 3: Form of notice of resubmission of structure plan

NOTICE OF RESUBMISSION OF STRUCTURE PLAN

Town and County Planning Act 1971
(Title of structure plan)

[To:] (9)

(1) resubmitted the above-named structure plan [with modifications] [without modification] (2) to the Secretary of State [for the Environment] [for Wales] (2) on
19   for his approval.   [The plan relates to land in the following county district(s):
(3)] (2).

Certified copies of the plan, of the report of survey and of the statement mentioned in section 8(3) of the Act have been deposited at (4).

The deposited documents are available for inspection free of charge (5).

Objections to the plan should be sent in writing to the Secretary, [Department of the Environment, 2 Marsham Street, London, SWIP 3EB] [Welsh Office, Summit House, Windsor Place, Cardiff, CF1 3BX] (2) before (6).   Objections should state the matters to which they relate and the grounds on which they are made*.   A person making objections may send a written request (stating his name and the address to which notice is to be sent) to (7) to be notified of the decision on the plan.   Objections made to the plan when it was originally submitted to the Secretary of State will be considered by him.

19   .

(Signature)

*Forms for making objections are obtainable at the places where documents have been deposited.

Regulation 23

*Form 4: Form of notice of withdrawal of structure plan and of copies
thereof made available for public inspection*

NOTICE OF WITHDRAWAL OF STRUCTURE PLAN AND OF COPIES THEREOF MADE AVAILABLE
FOR PUBLIC INSPECTION

Town and Country Planning Act 1971
(Title of structure plan)

Notice is hereby given that the above-named structure plan submitted to the Secretary of State for approval on (16) together with copies thereof made available for public inspection has been withdrawn by (1).

19   .

Signature.

Regulations 25 and 38

Form 5: Form of notice of proposed modifications to [structure] [local] plan

NOTICE OF PROPOSED MODIFICATIONS TO [STRUCTURE] [LOCAL] (2) PLAN

Town and County Planning Act 1971
(Title of [structure] [local] plan)

[To :] (9)

The Secretary of State [for the Environment] [for Wales] (2) proposes to modify the above-named plan.

Certified copies of the plan and of the list of proposed modifications (other than modifications which the Secretary of State is satisfied will not materially affect the content of the plan) have been deposited at (4).

The deposited documents are available for inspection free of charge (5).

Objections to the proposed modifications should be sent in writing to the Secretary, [Department of the Environment, 2 Marsham Street, London, SWIP 3EB] [Welsh Office, Summit House, Windsor Place, Cardiff, CFI 3BX] (2) before (6).   Objections should state the matters to which they relate and the grounds on which they are made*.   A person making objections may send a written request (stating his name and the address to which notice is to be sent) to (7) to be notified of the decision on the plan.

19   .

(Signature)

*Forms for making objections are obtainable at the places where documents have been deposited.

Regulation 26

Form 6: Form of notice of approval or rejection of structure plan

NOTICE OF [APPROVAL] [REJECTION] (2) OF STRUCTURE PLAN

Town and Country Planning Act 1971
(Title of structure plan)

[To:] (9)

On   19   the Secretary of State [for the Environment] [for Wales] [approved] [rejected](2) the above-named structure plan [so far as it relates to (12)] [with modifications] [and] [with reservations] (2).

Certified copies of the plan and of the Secretary of State's letter notifying his decision have been deposited at (4).

The deposited documents are available for inspection free of charge (5).

[The plan became operative on (13), but if any person aggrieved by the plan desires to question its validity on the ground that it is not within the powers conferred by Part II of the Town and Country Planning Act 1971, or that any requirement of the said Part II or of any regulations made thereunder has not been complied with in relation to the approval of the plan, he may, within six weeks from (14) make an application to the High Court under section 244 of the Town and Country Planning Act 1971] (15).

19   .

(Signature)

Footnotes to forms 1 *to* 6

1. Insert name of local planning authority or authorities.
2. Insert as appropriate.
3. Insert name(s) of county district(s).
4. Insert address of local planning authority's office and addresses of other places at which documents deposited.
5. Specify days and hours during which deposited documents are available for inspection.
6. Specify date not less than six weeks after date on which notice first published in local newspaper.
7. State appropriate officer and name and address of local planning authority.
8. State period specified in directions.
9. Insert, together with name and address of addressee, in personal notice.
10. State name of person appointed to hold local inquiry or hearing.
11. State time and date of local inquiry or other hearing and address at which it is to be held.
12. Give indication of area.
13. Insert date appointed in Secretary of State's letter.
14. Insert date of first publication of the notice.
15. Insert paragraph only if the plan is approved.
16. Insert date of submission of plan.

Regulation 29

Form 7: *Form of notice of preparation of local plan*

NOTICE OF PREPARATION OF LOCAL PLAN

Town and Country Planning Act 1971
(Title of local plan)

(1) have prepared the above-named local plan.   [The plan relates to land in the following county district(s):—(2)] (3).

Certified copies of the plan, of the report of survey and of the statement mentioned in section 12(3) of the Act have been deposited at (4).

The deposited documents are available for inspection free of charge (5).

Objections to the plan should be sent in writing to (6) before (7).   Objections should state the matters to which they relate and the grounds on which they are made*, and may include a request (stating the address to which notice is to be sent) to be notified of the decision on the plan.

19   .

(Signature)

*Forms for making objections are obtainable at the places where documents have been deposited.

Regulation 30(1)

Form 8: Form of notice of withdrawal of copies of local plan

NOTICE OF WITHDRAWAL OF COPIES OF LOCAL PLAN

Town and Country Planning Act 1971
(Title of local plan)

[To:](8)

The Secretary of State [for the Environment] [for Wales] (3) has directed (1) not to take any further steps for the adoption of the above-named local plan without taking certain further action as respects publicity in connection with the plan and satisfying him that they have done so.

The copies of the plan made available for inspection have been withdrawn.   Before (1) take further steps for the adoption of the plan, copies of the plan will again be made available for inspection at the places where they were previously available for inspection.   Objections made to the plan when copies were previously available for inspection will be considered, and there will be a further opportunity to make objections to the plan.

19   .

(Signature)

Regulation 30(2)

Form 9: Form of notice of re-deposit of copies of local plan

NOTICE OF RE-DEPOSIT OF COPIES OF LOCAL PLAN

Town and Country Planning Act 1971
(Title of local plan)

[To:](8)

(1) have decided to take further steps for the adoption of the above-named local plan.   [The plan relates to land in the following county district(s):—(2)](3).

Certified copies of the plan, of the report of survey and of the statement mentioned in section 12(3) of the Act have been deposited at (4).

The deposited documents are available for inspection free of charge (5).

Objections to the plan should be sent in writing to (6) before (7).   Objections should state the matters to which they relate and the grounds on which they are made*, and may include a request (stating the address to which notice is to be sent) to be notified of the decision on the plan.   Objections made to the plan when copies were previously available for inspection will be considered.

19   .

(Signature)

*Forms for making objections are obtainable at the places where documents have been deposited.

Regulation 32

Form 10*: Form of notice of local inquiry or other hearing*

NOTICE OF [PUBLIC LOCAL INQUIRY] [HEARING] (3)

Town and Country Planning Act 1971
(Title of local plan)

(9) WILL HOLD A [PUBLIC LOCAL INQUIRY] [HEARING] (3) AT (10) INTO OBJECTIONS MADE [TO PROPOSED MODIFICATIONS] (3) TO THE ABOVE-NAMED LOCAL PLAN.

19 .

(Signature)

Regulation 34

Form 11*: Form of notice of proposal to modify local plan*

NOTICE OF PROPOSAL TO MODIFY LOCAL PLAN

Town and Country Planning Act 1971
(Title of local plan)

[To:](8)

(1) propose to modify the above-named local plan.

Certified copies of the plan, of the report of the [inquiry into] [hearing of] (3) objections, of the council's statement prepared following the consideration of the report and of the list of proposed modifications have been deposited at (4).

The deposited documents are available for inspection free of charge (5).

Objections to the proposed modifications should be sent in writing to (6) before (7). Objections should state the matters to which they relate and the grounds on which they are made*, and may include a request (stating the address to which notice is to be sent) to be notified of the decision on the plan.

19 .

(Signature)

*Forms for making objections are obtainable at the places where documents have been deposited.

Regulation 35

Form 12*: Form of notice of decision to adopt local plan*

NOTICE OF DECISION TO ADOPT LOCAL PLAN

Town and Country Planning Act 1971
(Title of local plan)

[To:] (8)

(1) have decided to adopt the above-named local plan [as modified by them] (3) on or after (11), unless, before the plan has been adopted, the Secretary of State [for the Environment] [for Wales] (3) directs that the plan shall not be adopted until further notice or shall not have effect unless approved by him.

Certified copies of the plan [together with certified copies of the reports of all local inquiries or other hearings held and of the council's statements prepared following the consideration of such reports] (12) have been deposited at (4).

The deposited documents are available for inspection free of charge (5).

19 .

(Signature)

Regulation 36

Form 13: Form of notice of adoption or abondonment of local plan

NOTICE OF [ADOPTION] [ABANDONMENT] (3) OF LOCAL PLAN

Town and Country Planning Act 1971
(Title of local plan)

[To:] (8)

On   19   (1) by resolution [adopted] [abandoned] (3) the above-named local plan [as modified by the council] (3).

Certified copies of the plan and of the resolution [together with certified copies of the reports of all local inquiries or other hearings held and of the council's statements prepared following the consideration of such reports] (12) have been deposited at (4).

The deposited documents are available for inspection free of charge (5).

[The plan became operative on (13), but if any person aggrieved by the plan desires to question its validity on the ground that it is not within the powers conferred by Part II of the Town and Country Planning Act 1971, or that any requirement of the said Part II or of any regulations made thereunder has not been complied with in relation to the adoption of the plan, he may, within six weeks from (14), make an application to the High Court under section 244 of the Town and Country Planning Act 1971] (15).

19   .

(Signature)

Footnotes to forms 7 to 13

1. Insert name of local planning authority.
2. Insert name(s) of county district(s).
3. Insert as appropriate.
4. Insert address of local planning authority's office and addresses of other places at which documents deposited.
5. Specify days and hours during which deposited documents are available for inspection by public.
6. State appropriate officer and name and address of local planning authority.
7. Specify date not less than six weeks after date on which notice first published in local newspaper.
8. Insert, together with name and address of addressee, in personal notice.
9. Insert name of person appointed to hold local inquiry or hearing.
10. State time and date of local inquiry or other hearing and address at which it is to be held.
11. Specify date taking account of the period of 28 days specified in regulation 35(2).
12. Modify as necessary or omit where inappropriate.
13. Insert date appointed in the resolution.
14. Insert date of first publication of the notice.
15. Insert paragraph only if plan is adopted.

Peter Walker,
Secretary of State for the Environment.

31st July 1972.

Peter Thomas,
Secretary of State for Wales.

28th July 1972.

EXPLANATORY NOTE

(*This Note is not part of the Regulations.*)

These regulations revoke and re-enact the Town and Country Planning (Structure and Local Plans) Regulations 1971, with the substitution of references to the provisions of the Town and Country Planning Act 1971 for references to the provisions of the enactments consolidated by that Act and with amendments which take into account the provisions of the Town and Country Planning (Amendment) Act 1972 (c.42). They make provision with respect to the form and content of structure and local plans prepared under Part II of the Town and Country Planning Act 1971 and with respect to the procedure to be followed in connection with their preparation, submission and approval or adoption, as the case may be. There is also provision for the procedure to be followed in connection with the withdrawal of structure plans, with the alteration of structure plans and with the alteration, repeal or replacement of local plans.

The substance of the former regulations is reproduced, with the following differences:

(*a*) the provisions relating to the procedure to be followed in connection with structure plans include provisions relating to joint structure plans made under section 10A of the Act of 1971 in respect of combined areas;

(*b*) there are additional provisions (regulation 23) relating to the procedure to be followed in connection with the withdrawal of structure plans;

(*c*) the former provisions relating to the holding of local inquiries for the purpose of considering objections made to a structure plan have been replaced by a provision (regulation 24) referring to the examination in public which the Secretary of State is now required to hold by virtue of the provisions of section 9(3) of the Act of 1971 (as amended by section 3 of the Act of 1972);

(*d*) there is a new requirement (regulation 6(1)(*b*)) for the local planning authority to consult with the New Town Development Corporation before finally determining the content of a structure or local plan where any land to which the plan relates is included in the area of a new town.

STATUTORY INSTRUMENTS

1972 No. 1156 (L.15)

COUNTY COURTS

PROCEDURE

The County Court (Amendment No. 2) Rules 1972

Made - - - -		*27th July* 1972
Coming into Operation		*1st September* 1972

1.—(1) These Rules may be cited as the County Court (Amendment No. 2) Rules 1972.

(2) In these Rules an Order and Rule referred to by number means the Order and Rule so numbered in the County Court Rules 1936(**a**), as amended (**b**), and a form referred to by number means the form so numbered in Appendix A to those Rules.

(3) The Interpretation Act 1889(**c**) shall apply for the interpretation of these Rules as it applies for the interpretation of an Act of Parliament.

2. Order 1, Rule 2, shall be amended as follows:—

    (1) For paragraph (2) there shall be substituted the following paragraph:—

      "(2) Every office shall be closed on the following days—

        (*a*) Sundays;

        (*b*) bank holidays;

        (*c*) the day before Good Friday (from noon) and Good Friday;

        (*d*) the Friday before the spring holiday;

        (*e*) Christmas Eve or—

          (i) if that day is a Saturday, then 23rd December,

          (ii) if that day is a Sunday or Tuesday, then 27th December; and

        (*f*) Christmas Day and, if that day is a Friday or Saturday, then 28th December."

    (2) The following paragraph shall be added at the end:—

      "(4) In this Rule a "bank holiday" means a bank holiday in England and Wales under the Banking and Financial Dealings Act 1971(**d**), and "the spring holiday" means the bank holiday on the last Monday in May or any day appointed instead of that day under section 1(2) of the said Act."

(**a**) S.R. & O. 1936/626 (1936 I, p. 282).

(**b**) The relevant amending instruments are S.I. 1958/2226, 1963/403, 1967/276, 1969/585, 1971/836 (1958 I, p. 372; 1963 I, p. 475; 1967 I, p. 990; 1969 I, p. 1551; 1971 II, p. 2393).

(**c**) 1889 c. 63.   (**d**) 1971 c. 80.

3. Order 5 shall be amended as follows:—

(1) In the heading to Part IV, after the words "TRUSTS" there shall be added the word "ETC".

(2) Rules 33 and 34 shall be renumbered and shall stand as Rules 34 and 33 respectively.

(3) In Rules 26, 29, 30, 31 and 32 and in Rule 34 as so renumbered for the word "judge" wherever it appears there shall be substituted the word "court".

(4) In Rules 29 and 32 for the word "he" wherever it appears there shall be substituted the word "it"

(5) Immediately before Rule 34 as so renumbered there shall be inserted the following heading:—

"PART V—REPRESENTATION OF ESTATE".

(6) After Rule 34 as so renumbered there shall be inserted the following Rule:—

"34A.—(1) Where any person against whom an action would have lain has died but the cause of action survives, the action may, if no grant of probate or administration has been made, be brought against the estate of the deceased. *[Proceedings against estates]*

(2) Without prejudice to the generality of paragraph (1), an action brought against "the personal representatives of A.B. deceased" shall be treated, for the purposes of that paragraph, as having been brought against his estate.

(3) An action purporting to have been commenced against a defendant who has died shall, if the cause of action survives and no grant of probate or administration has been made, be treated as having been brought against his estate in accordance with paragraph (1).

(4) In any such action as is referred to in paragraph (1) or (3)—

(*a*) the plaintiff shall, in the case of an ordinary action, on or before the return day, or, in the case of a default action, within the time allowed for service of the summons, apply to the court for an order appointing a person to represent the deceased's estate for the purpose of the proceedings or, if a grant of probate or administration has been made since the commencement of the action, for an order that the personal representative of the deceased be made a party to the proceedings, and in either case for an order that the proceedings be carried on against the person so appointed or, as the case may be, against the personal representative, as if he had been substituted for the estate;

(*b*) the court may, at any stage of the proceedings and on such terms as it thinks just and either of its own motion or on application, make any such order as is mentioned in sub-paragraph (*a*) and allow such amendments (if any) to be made and make such other order as the court thinks necessary in order to ensure that all matters in dispute in the proceedings may be effectually and completely determined and adjudicated upon.

(5) Before making an order under paragraph (4) the court may require notice to be given to any insurer of the deceased who has an interest in the proceedings and to such (if any) of the persons having an interest in the estate as it thinks fit.

(6) Where an order is made under paragraph (4), the person against whom the proceedings are to be carried on shall be served with a copy of the order, together with a copy of the summons in the action, in accordance with the rules applicable to the service of such a summons on a defendant.

(7) Where no grant of probate or administration has been made, any judgment or order given or made in the proceedings shall bind the estate to the same extent as it would have been bound if a grant had been made and a personal representative of the deceased had been · a party to the proceedings."

(7) Part V shall be renumbered and shall stand as Part VI.

4. The following Rule shall be added at the end of Order 13:—

Application under s.21 of Administration of Justice Act 1969 or s.31 or 32 of Administration of Justice Act 1970
1969 c. 58
1970 c. 31

"15.—(1) Subject to the following paragraphs of this Rule, the provisions of the Rules of the Supreme Court relating to applications under section 21 of the Administration of Justice Act 1969 or section 31 or 32 of the Administration of Justice Act 1970 shall apply with the necessary modifications in relation to proceedings or subsequent proceedings in a county court as they apply to proceedings or subsequent proceedings in the High Court.

(2) For the references in the said provisions to a summons there shall be substituted, in the case of an originating summons, a reference to an originating application or, in the case of any other summons, a reference to notice under Rule 1 of this Order, and notice of an application made after the commencement of proceedings shall be served on the person against whom the order is sought, in accordance with the rules applicable to service of the process by which the proceedings were commenced.

(3) The affidavit in support of an application made before the commencement of proceedings shall show that the proceedings are such that the court to which the application is made has jurisdiction to hear and determine."

5. Order 25 shall be amended as follows:—

(1) In Rule 79(2) after the word "Wales" there shall be inserted the words "or the creditor does not know where he resides".

(2) The following paragraph shall be added to Rule 83:—

"(4) An attachment of earnings order may be made to secure the payment of a judgment debt if the debt is—

(*a*) of not less than £5, or

(*b*) for the amount remaining payable under a judgment for a sum of not less than £5."

(3) In Rule 94(9) the words "or an attachment of earnings order made by the High Court designates the registrar of a county court as the collecting officer," shall be omitted.

(4) In Rule 94(11) for the word "Rule" there shall be substituted the words "Rules 83(4) and".

6. Order 46 shall be amended as follows:—

(1) In Rule 7(2), for the words from "paragraphs (3) to (8)" to the end there shall be substituted the words "for the purpose of such consideration the registrar shall, if he has not already done so, fix a day for the preliminary consideration of the action under Order 21.".

(2) Rule 17 shall be amended as follows:—

(*a*) In paragraph (1A) the words "or for an attachment of earnings order" shall be omitted.

(*b*) In paragraph (2)(*b*)(iv) after the word "order" there shall be inserted the words "the date to which those arrears have been calculated and the date on which the next payment under the order falls due."

(*c*) In paragraph (3) after the words "application is granted" there shall be inserted the following sub-paragraph:—

"(*a*) the applicant shall, if the application is granted on the making of the maintenance order or an order varying the maintenance order, lodge in the court office a statement signed by the applicant or his solicitor, and a copy thereof, giving the address of the person entitled to receive payments under the maintenance order and the particulars mentioned in paragraph (2)(*b*)(ii), (iv) and (vii)".

(*d*) Sub-paragraphs (*a*), (*b*) and (*c*) of paragraph (3) shall be re-lettered as (*b*), (*c*) and (*d*) respectively.

(*e*) In sub-paragraph (3)(*c*), as so re-lettered, for the words "if any" there shall be substituted the words "or statement".

7. Form 402 shall be amended by substituting for the words "Balance of judgment debt" to the end the words—

"To be completed by the court

Balance of judgment debt and costs	£	
Court fee on application	£	
Sum on payment of which this matter will be satisfied	£	
[Unsatisfied costs of execution not included in above	£	] ".

8. In Form 404 after the words "Do not leave blanks." there shall be inserted the words "The answers you give may be checked with your employer.".

9. Notwithstanding anything in Rules 7 and 8 of these Rules, Forms 402 and 404 may continue to be used in the form hitherto prescribed until the Lord Chancellor otherwise directs.

We, the undersigned members of the Rule Committee appointed by the Lord Chancellor under section 102 of the County Courts Act 1959(a) having by virtue of the powers vested in us in this behalf made the foregoing Rules, do hereby certify the same under our hands and submit them to the Lord Chancellor accordingly.

D. O. McKee.
Conolly H. Gage.
H. S. Ruttle.
David Pennant.
W. Granville Wingate.
W. Ralph Davies.
E. A. Everett.
K. W. Mellor.
Arnold Russell Vick.
D. A. Marshall.
E. W. Sankey.

I allow these Rules, which shall come into operation on 1st September 1972.

Dated 27th July 1972.

Hailsham of St. Marylebone, C.

EXPLANATORY NOTE

(This Note is not Part of the Rules.)

These Rules amend the County Court Rules so as to make provision for the matters mentioned in section 2 of the Proceedings Against Estates Act 1970(c.17) (Rule 3) and for the disclosure of documents and the inspection etc. of property under section 21 of the Administration of Justice Act 1969 and sections 31 and 32 of the Administration of Justice Act 1970 (Rule 4). The days on which county court offices are to be closed are redefined in view of the Banking and Financial Dealings Act 1971 (Rule 2). A number of minor amendments are made in relation to attachment of earnings (Rules 5, 7 and 8) and other matters.

(a) 1959 c. 22.

STATUTORY INSTRUMENTS

1972 No. 1157

INDUSTRIAL TRAINING

The Industrial Training Levy (Furniture and Timber) Order 1972

Made - - -	1st *August* 1972
Laid before Parliament	9th *August* 1972
Coming into Operation	1st *September* 1972

The Secretary of State after approving proposals submitted by the Furniture and Timber Industry Training Board for the imposition of a further levy on employers in the furniture and timber industry and in exercise of his powers under section 4 of the Industrial Training Act 1964(**a**) and of all other powers enabling him in that behalf hereby makes the following Order: —

Title and commencement

1. This Order may be cited as the Industrial Training Levy (Furniture and Timber) Order 1972 and shall come into operation on 1st September 1972.

Interpretation

2.—(1) In this Order unless the context otherwise requires: —

(*a*) "agriculture" has the same meaning as in section 109(3) of the Agriculture Act 1947(**b**) or, in relation to Scotland, as in section 86(3) of the Agriculture (Scotland) Act 1948(**c**);

(*b*) "an appeal tribunal" means an industrial tribunal established under section 12 of the Industrial Training Act 1964;

(*c*) "assessment" means an assessment of an employer to the levy;

(*d*) "the Board" means the Furniture and Timber Industry Training Board;

(*e*) "business" means any activities of industry or commerce;

(*f*) "charity" has the same meaning as in section 360 of the Income and Corporation Taxes Act 1970(**d**);

(*g*) "dock work" and "registered dock worker" have the same meanings as in the Docks and Harbours Act 1966(**e**);

(*h*) "emoluments" means all emoluments assessable to income tax under Schedule E (other than pensions), being emoluments from which tax under that Schedule is deductible, whether or not tax in fact falls to be deducted from any particular payment thereof;

(**a**) 1964 c. 16.   (**b**) 1947 c. 48.
(**c**) 1948 c. 45.   (**d**) 1970 c. 10.
(**e**) 1966 c. 28.

(*i*) "employer" means a person who is an employer in the furniture and timber industry at any time in the sixth levy period;

(*j*) "furniture and timber establishment" means an establishment in Great Britain engaged in the sixth base period wholly or mainly in the furniture and timber industry for a total of twenty-seven or more weeks or, being an establishment that commenced to carry on business in the sixth base period, for a total number of weeks exceeding one half of the number of weeks in the part of the said period commencing with the day on which business was commenced and ending on the last day thereof;

(*k*) "the furniture and timber industry" means any one or more of the activities which, subject to the provisions of paragraph 2 of the Schedule to the industrial training order, are specified in paragraph 1 of that Schedule as the activities of the furniture and timber industry;

(*l*) "the industrial training order" means the Industrial Training (Furniture and Timber Industry Board) Order 1969(**a**) as amended by the Industrial Training (Furniture and Timber Industry Board) Order 1969 (Amendment) Order 1970(**b**);

(*m*) "the levy" means the levy imposed by the Board in respect of the sixth levy period;

(*n*) "notice" means a notice in writing;

(*o*) "the sixth base period" means the period of twelve months that commenced on 6th April 1971;

(*p*) "the sixth levy period" means the period commencing with the day upon which this Order comes into operation and ending on 5th April 1973;

(2) In the case where a furniture and timber establishment is taken over (whether directly or indirectly) by an employer in succession to, or jointly with, another person, a person employed at any time in the sixth base period at or from the establishment shall be deemed, for the purposes of this Order, to have been so employed by the employer carrying on the said establishment on the day upon which this Order comes into operation, and any reference in this Order to persons employed by an employer at or from a furniture and timber establishment in the sixth base period shall be construed accordingly.

(3) Any reference in this Order to an establishment that commences to carry on business or that ceases to carry on business shall not be taken to apply where the location of the establishment is changed but its business is continued wholly or mainly at or from the new location, or where the suspension of activities is of a temporary or seasonal nature.

(4) The Interpretation Act 1889(**c**) shall apply to the interpretation of this Order as it applies to the interpretation of an Act of Parliament.

Imposition of the levy

3.—(1) The levy to be imposed by the Board on employers in respect of the sixth levy period shall be assessed in accordance with the provisions of this Article.

(2) The levy shall be assessed by the Board separately in respect of each furniture and timber establishment of an employer (not being an employer

---

(**a**) S.I. 1969/1290 (1969 III, p. 3820).   (**b**) S.I. 1970/1634 (1970 III, p. 5372).
(**c**) 1889 c. 63.

who is exempt from the levy by virtue of paragraph (5) of this Article) but in agreement with the employer one assessment may be made in respect of any number of such establishments, in which case those establishments shall be deemed for the purposes of that assessment to constitute one establishment.

(3) Subject to the provisions of this Article, the levy assessed in respect of a furniture and timber establishment of an employer shall be an amount equal to—

(a) 0·5 per cent. of the sum of the emoluments of all the persons employed by the employer at or from the establishment in the sixth base period or of the first £20,000 of that sum where it exceeds £20,000; and

(b) 1·1 per cent. of the amount (if any) of the said sum of emoluments in excess of £20,000.

(4) The amount of the levy imposed in respect of an establishment that ceases to carry on business in the sixth levy period shall be in the same proportion to the amount that would otherwise be due under paragraph (3) of this Article as the number of days between the commencement of the said levy period and the date of cessation of business (both dates inclusive) bears to the number of days in the said levy period.

(5) There shall be exempt from the levy—

(a) an employer in whose case the sum of the emoluments of all the persons employed by him in the sixth base period at or from the furniture and timber establishment or establishments of the employer is less than £10,000;

(b) a charity.

(6) For the purposes of this Article no regard shall be had to the emoluments of any person wholly employed—

(a) in agriculture;

(b) as a registered dock worker in dock work; or

(c) in the supply of food or drink for immediate consumption.

Assessment notices

4.—(1) The Board shall serve an assessment notice on every employer assessed to the levy, but one notice may comprise two or more assessments.

(2) An assessment notice shall state the amount (rounded down, where necessary to the nearest £1) of the levy payable thereunder, and where the notice comprises two or more assessments the said amount shall, before any such rounding down, be equal to the total amount of the levy assessed by the Board under Article 3 of this Order in respect of each establishment included in the notice.

(3) An assessment notice shall state the Board's address for the service of a notice of appeal or of an application for an extension of time for appealing.

(4) An assessment notice may be served on the person assessed to the levy either by delivering it to him personally or by leaving it, or sending it to him by post, at his last known address or place of business in the United Kingdom or, if that person is a corporation, by leaving it, or sending it by post to the corporation, at such address or place of business or at its registered or principal office.

Payment of levy

5.—(1) Subject to the provisions of this Article and of Articles 6 and 7, the amount of the levy payable under an assessment notice served by the Board shall be due and payable to the Board on 30th November 1972 except where the date of the assessment notice is later than 31st October 1972 in which case the said amount shall be due and payable one month after the date of the notice.

(2) The amount of an assessment shall not be recoverable by the Board until there has expired the time allowed for appealing against the assessment by Article (1) of this Order and any further period or periods of time that the Board or an appeal tribunal may have allowed for appealing under paragraph (2) or (3) of that Article or, where an appeal is brought, until the appeal is decided or withdrawn.

Withdrawal of assessment

6.—(1) The Board may, by a notice served on the person assessed to the levy in the same manner as an assessment notice, withdraw an assessment if that person has appealed against that assessment under the provisions of Article 7 of this Order and the appeal has not been entered in the Register of Appeals kept under the appropriate Regulations specified in paragraph (5) of that Article.

(2) The withdrawal of an assessment shall be without prejudice—

(*a*) to the power of the Board to serve a further assessment notice in respect of any establishment to which that assessment related;

(*b*) to any other assessment included in the original assessment notice, and such notice shall thereupon have effect as if any assessment withdrawn by the Board had not been included therein.

Appeals

7.—(1) A person assessed to the levy may appeal to an appeal tribunal against the assessment within one month from the date of the service of the assessment notice or within any further period or periods of time that may be allowed by the Board or an appeal tribunal under the following provisions of this Article.

(2) The Board by notice may for good cause allow a person assessed to the levy to appeal to an appeal tribunal against the assessment at any time within the period of four months from the date of the service of the assessment notice or within such further period or periods as the Board may allow before such time as may then be limited for appealing has expired.

(3) If the Board shall not allow an application for extension of time for appealing, an appeal tribunal shall upon application made to the tribunal by the person assessed to the levy have the like powers as the Board under the last foregoing paragraph.

(4) In the case of an establishment that ceases to carry on business in the sixth levy period on any day after the date of the service of the relevant assessment notice, the foregoing provisions of this Article shall have effect as if for the period of four months from the date of the service of the assessment notice mentioned in paragraph (2) of this Article there were substituted the period of six months from the date of the cessation of business.

(5) An appeal or an application to an appeal tribunal under this Article shall be made in accordance with the Industrial Tribunals (England and Wales) Regulations 1965(**a**) as amended by the Industrial Tribunals (England and Wales) (Amendment) Regulations 1967(**b**) except where the establishment to which the relevant assessment relates is wholly in Scotland in which case the appeal or application shall be made in accordance with the Industrial Tribunals (Scotland) Regulations 1965(**c**) as amended by the Industrial Tribunals (Scotland) (Amendment) Regulations 1967(**d**).

(6) The powers of an appeal tribunal under paragraph (3) of this Article may be exercised by the President of the Industrial Tribunals (England and Wales) or by the President of the Industrial Tribunals (Scotland) as the case may be.

Evidence

8.—(1) Upon the discharge by a person assessed to the levy of his liability under an assessment the Board shall if so requested issue to him a certificate to that effect.

(2) The production in any proceedings of a document purporting to be certified by the Secretary of the Board to be a true copy of an assessment or other notice issued by the Board or purporting to be a certificate such as is mentioned in the foregoing paragraph of this Article shall, unless the contrary is proved, be sufficient evidence of the document and of the facts stated therein.

Signed by order of the Secretary of State.

1st August 1972.

R. Chichester-Clark,
Minister of State,
Department of Employment.

EXPLANATORY NOTE

(*This Note is not part of the Order.*)

This Order gives effect to proposals submitted to the Secretary of State for Employment by the Furniture and Timber Industry Training Board for the imposition of a further levy upon employers in the furniture and timber industry for the purpose of raising money towards the expenses of the Board.

The levy is to be imposed in respect of the sixth levy period commencing with the day upon which this Order comes into operation and ending on 5th April 1973. The levy will be assessed by the Board and there will be a right of appeal against an assessment to an industrial tribunal.

(**a**) S.I. 1965/1101 (1965 II, p. 2805).   (**b**) S.I. 1967/301 (1967 I, p. 1040).
(**c**) S.I. 1965/1157 (1965 II, p. 3266).   (**d**) S.I. 1967/302 (1967 I, p. 1050).

STATUTORY INSTRUMENTS

1972 No. 1161 (C. 25)

LANDLORD AND TENANT

The Small Tenements Recovery Act 1838 (Repeal) (Appointed Day) Order 1972

Made - - -	*2nd August* 1972
Laid before Parliament	*8th August* 1972
Coming into Operation	*1st October* 1972

The Secretary of State for the Environment, in exercise of his powers under section 35(5) of the Rent Act 1965(a), and of all other powers enabling him in that behalf, hereby makes the following order:—

Citation, commencement and interpretation

1.—(1) This order may be cited as the Small Tenements Recovery Act 1838 (Repeal) (Appointed Day) Order 1972, and shall come into operation on 1st October 1972.

(2) The Interpretation Act 1889(b) shall apply for the interpretation of this order as it applies for the interpretation of an Act of Parliament.

Appointed day

2. The appointed day for the purposes of section 35(5) of the Rent Act 1965 is 1st October 1972.

Transitional

3. Without prejudice to the operation of section 38(2) of the Interpretation Act 1889, where a complaint has been made before 1st October 1972 to a magistrates' court under the Small Tenements Recovery Act 1838(c) in so far as it has been applied by any other Act or under section 22(2), 45(3), 73(2) or 85(2) of the Housing Act 1957(d) the proceedings may be continued and any warrant issued may be executed as if this order had not been made.

Peter Walker,
Secretary of State for the Environment.

2nd August 1972.

(a) 1965 c. 75.   (b) 1889 c. 63.
(c) 1838 c. 74.   (d) 1957 c. 56.

EXPLANATORY NOTE
(This Note is not part of the Order.)

This Order applies to England and Wales.

The Small Tenements Recovery Act 1838 enables a landlord, on bringing to an end the tenancy of a house let at £20 a year or less, to obtain an order for possession from a magistrates' court. Part III of the Rent Act 1965 requires all actions for the possession of dwellings to be brought in the county court or the High Court. However, section 35(5) of the 1965 Act preserves, until a day to be appointed, the 1838 Act only in so far as that Act has been applied by other legislation and also the use of certain parallel powers contained in sections 22(2), 45(3), 73(2) and 85(2) of the Housing Act 1957.

This Order fixes 1st October 1972 as the appointed day for the purposes of section 35(5) of the 1965 Act. By virtue of section 52(1) of, and Part II of Schedule 7 to, that Act the 1838 Act is repealed from this day and consequential repeals take effect in the various Acts which apply the 1838 Act, and by virtue of section 51 and paragraph 10 of Schedule 6 consequential amendments are effected to sections 22(2), 45(3), 73(2) and 85(2) of the Housing Act 1957. Amongst the enactments repealed from the appointed day is section 158(2) of the Housing Act 1957 which allows a local authority, for the purpose of exercising their housing powers, to use the 1838 Act to obtain possession (when the tenancy has come to an end) of a house or other building, regardless of the amount of the rent.

STATUTORY INSTRUMENTS

1972 No. 1162

SEA FISHERIES

The White Fish Authority (Research and Development Grants) Order 1972

Made - - -	*30th June* 1972
Laid before the House of Commons	*7th July* 1972
Coming into Operation	*2nd August* 1972

The Minister of Agriculture, Fisheries and Food and the Secretaries of State respectively concerned with the sea fishing industry in Scotland and Northern Ireland in exercise of the powers conferred upon them by section 23(2) of the Sea Fish Industry Act 1970(**a**) and of all other powers enabling them in that behalf, with the approval of the Treasury, hereby make the following Order:—

1.—(1) This Order, which may be cited as the White Fish Authority (Research and Development Grants) Order 1972, shall come into operation on the day following the day on which it is approved by the Commons House of Parliament.

(2) The Interpretation Act 1889(**b**) shall apply for the interpretation of this Order as it applies for the interpretation of an Act of Parliament.

2. The limit of £2 million imposed by section 23(2) of the Sea Fish Industry Act 1970 for the aggregate amount of any grants made under subsection (1) of that section and any grants made under section 17 of the Sea Fish Industry Act 1951(**c**) (grants to the White Fish Authority in relation to expenditure on research or experiment or in providing, etc. plants for processing white fish or making ice) shall be raised by the sum of £1 million.

In witness whereof the Official Seal of the Minister of Agriculture, Fisheries and Food is hereunto affixed on 27th June 1972.

(L.S.)

J. M. L. Prior,
Minister of Agriculture, Fisheries and Food.

Gordon Campbell,
28th June 1972.   Secretary of State for Scotland.

(**a**) 1970 c. 11.   (**b**) 1889 c. 63.
(**c**) 1951 c. 30.

W. S. I. Whitelaw,
Secretary of State for Northern Ireland.

29th June 1972.

Approved on 30th June 1972.

Tim Fortescue,
V. H. Goodhew,
Two of the Lords Commissioners
of Her Majesty's Treasury.

EXPLANATORY NOTE

(This Note is not part of the Order.)

This Order is made under section 23 of the Sea Fish Industry Act 1970.

It raises by £1 million the limit of £2 million imposed in relation to the aggregate amount of any grants payable to the White Fish Authority for the purposes of research or experiment or in providing, etc. plants for processing white fish or making ice.

This Order was approved by a resolution of the House of Commons on 1st August 1972 and came into operation on 2nd August 1972.

STATUTORY INSTRUMENTS

1972 No. 1164

EMERGENCY POWERS

The Emergency (No. 2) Regulations 1972

Made - - - -	*3rd August* 1972
Laid before Parliament	*3rd August* 1972
Coming into Operation	*4th August* 1972

ARRANGEMENT OF REGULATIONS

At the Court at H.M. Yacht Britannia, the 3rd day of August 1972

Present,

The Queen's Most Excellent Majesty in Council

Whereas a proclamation of emergency has this day been made under section 1 of the Emergency Powers Act 1920(a), as amended by the Emergency Powers Act 1964(b), and that proclamation is now in force:

Now, therefore, Her Majesty, in pursuance of section 2 of the said Act of 1920, is pleased, by and with the advice of Her Privy Council, to order, and it is hereby ordered, as follows:—

PRELIMINARY

Title and commencement

1.—(1) These Regulations may be cited as the Emergency (No. 2) Regulations 1972.

(2) These Regulations shall come into operation on 4th August 1972.

(a) 1920 c. 55.   (b) 1964 c. 38.

Interpretation

2.—(1) In these Regulations, except so far as the context otherwise requires, the following expressions have the meanings hereby respectively assigned to them, that is to say:—

" air service licence " and " air transport service " have the same meanings as in the Civil Aviation (Licensing) Act 1960(**a**) ;

" animal feeding stuffs " includes any substance used in the composition or preparation of animal feeding stuffs ;

" Area Gas Board " means an Area Board within the meaning of the Gas Act 1948(**b**) ;

" chattel ", in relation to Scotland, means corporeal moveable ;

" district ", in relation to a sewerage authority, includes any area in which the authority exercise functions with respect to the reception of foul or surface water into their sewers ;

" Electricity Board " has the same meaning as in the Electricity Act 1947(**c**) ;

" essential goods " means food, water, fuel and other necessities ;

" essential services " means services essential to the life of the community ;

" food " includes any substance used in the composition or preparation of food ;

" hovercraft " has the same meaning as in the Hovercraft Act 1968(**d**) ;

" land " includes (without prejudice to any of the provisions of section 3 of the Interpretation Act 1889(**e**)) parts of houses or buildings ;

" liquid fuel " means any liquid used as fuel, whether for the propulsion of vehicles or for industrial, domestic or any other purposes ;

" port " includes any dock, harbour, pier, quay, wharf, mooring, anchorage or other similar place ;

" port authority " means the authority or person having the control or management of a port ;

" regional water board " has the same meaning as in the Water (Scotland) Act 1967(**f**) ;

" requisition " means, in relation to any chattle, take possession of the chattel or require the chattel to be placed at the disposal of the requisitioning authority ;

" river authority " includes—

    (*a*) the Conservators of the River Thames,

    (*b*) the Lee Conservancy Catchment Board, and

    (*c*) the Isle of Wight River and Water Authority ;

" sewerage authority " means an authority which is a sewerage authority for the purposes of Part II of the Public Health Act 1936(**g**), the Common Council of the City of London, the council of a county in Scotland, the town council of a burgh, any combination of such county or town councils constituted for the purposes of the provision

---

(**a**) 1960 c. 38.   (**b**) 1948 c. 67.   (**c**) 1947 c. 54.   (**d**) 1968 c. 59.
    (**e**) 1889 c. 63.   (**f**) 1967 c. 78.   (**g**) 1936 c. 49.

of sewerage works or sewage disposal services, a development corporation established under the New Towns Act 1946(a), the New Towns Act 1965(b), or the New Towns (Scotland) Act 1968(c), and the Commission for the New Towns ;

" solid fuel " means coal, anthracite and coke and other manufactured fuel of which coal or anthracite is the principal constituent ;

" statutory water undertakers " has the same meaning as in the provisions of the Water Act 1945(d) other than Part II of that Act ;

" water development board " has the same meaning as in the Water (Scotland) Act 1967.

(2) The Interpretation Act 1889 shall apply to the interpretation of these Regulations as it applies to the interpretation of an Act of Parliament.

(3) Any reference in these Regulations to the doing of any act shall, unless the context otherwise requires, be construed as including a reference to the making of any statement.

(4) Any reference in these Regulations to any enactment shall, without prejudice to any specific provision in that behalf, be construed as a reference thereto as amended or extended, and as including a reference thereto as applied, by or under any other enactment.

(5) Any reference in any document to these Regulations or to any of them shall, unless the contrary intention appears, be construed as a reference to these Regulations or to that Regulation as amended by any subsequent Regulations made under the Emergency Powers Act 1920.

REGULATION OF PORTS

Control of port traffic

3.—(1) The Secretary of State may, in the case of any port, give such directions to the port authority or any other person as appear to him to be necessary or expedient for securing that the most advantageous use is made in the public interest of the facilities provided at the port, and such directions may, in particular, make provision for excluding or removing from the port ships of any class or a specified ship and for all or any of the following matters, that is to say :—

(*a*) the berthing and movement of ships ;

(*b*) the movement and use of tugs, lighters, barges, floating cranes and elevators and other floating apparatus ;

(*c*) the loading and unloading of ships and the use of appliances therefor ;

(*d*) the movement and use of vehicles ;

(*e*) the prevention of entry by unauthorised persons ; and

(*f*) in connection with the loading and unloading of ships or the storage and warehousing of goods, the priority that should be given to particular cargoes or to particular operations ;

and such directions shall have effect notwithstanding any lease or appropriation of berths and storage or warehouse accommodation.

(2) The Secretary of State may give directions under the foregoing paragraph requiring goods lying at the port to be removed within such period as may be specified in the directions, and, in default of compliance with those directions and without prejudice to the taking of proceedings in

---

(a) 1946 c. 68.　　(b) 1965 c. 59.　　(c) 1968 c. 16.　　(d) 1945 c. 42.

respect of the default, the Secretary of State may remove, or authorise the removal of, the goods to such place, and by such means, as he thinks fit, and the owner or consignee of the goods shall pay to the Secretary of State such reasonable charges in respect of the removal and storage thereof by or on the authority of the Secretary of State as may be agreed or as may, in default of agreement, be determined by arbitration.

(3) All occupiers of public warehouses at or in the neighbourhood of the port shall, if so required by directions given by the Secretary of State, furnish to the Secretary of State from time to time information of vacant accommodation at their warehouses, and shall, to the extent of the accommodation available, accept for storage any goods removed by or on the authority of the Secretary of State under the last foregoing paragraph:

Provided that the Secretary of State shall, in exercising his power to require the storage of goods removed as aforesaid, have regard to the suitability of the accommodation for storing those goods.

(4) The Secretary of State may appoint for any port or group of ports a body of persons, to be known as the Port Emergency Committee for the port or, as the case may be, the group, and may authorise that Committee and persons designated by them for the purpose to exercise on his behalf in relation to the port or, as the case may be, each port comprised in the group all or any of his functions under this Regulation.

(5) Where the Secretary of State appoints a Port Emergency Committee under paragraph (4) of this Regulation, he—

(a) may appoint a member of the Committee to be chairman of the Committee, and

(b) may give (whether in the instrument of appointment of the Committee or otherwise) any general or special instructions as to the proceedings of the Committee and as to the exercise by the Committee of such of his functions under this Regulation as the Committee are authorised to exercise ; and any such Committee, and any person designated by them under that paragraph, shall comply with any instructions of the Secretary of State given under this paragraph.

(6) Paragraphs (1) to (5) of this Regulation shall have effect in relation to hovercraft as they have effect in relation to ships, and any reference in those paragraphs to ships shall be construed accordingly.

Default powers relating to port traffic

4.—(1) Where any directions have been given under paragraph (1) of the foregoing Regulation, other than any such directions as are mentioned in paragraph (2) of that Regulation, and those directions are not complied with within the time specified in the directions or, if no time is so specified, are not complied with within a reasonable time, the Secretary of State may take, or may authorise any other person to take, such steps as the Secretary of State may consider appropriate in the circumstances for effecting anything which would have been effected if the directions had been complied with.

(2) Without prejudice to the generality of the foregoing paragraph, the steps which may be taken by virtue of this Regulation in respect of any directions shall include entering upon, taking possession of, moving or using any ship, hovercraft or other vessel, apparatus, vehicle, premises or other property to which the directions related by such means as the Secretary of State or other person taking those steps may determine to be appropriate.

(3) Where any steps are taken by virtue of this Regulation in respect of any directions, the person to whom the directions were given shall pay to the Secretary of State or other person taking those steps such reasonable charges in respect of expenses incurred by the Secretary of State or person in taking those steps, or in consequence of having taken them, as may be agreed or as may, in default of agreement, be determined by arbitration.

(4) In Part VIII of the Merchant Shipping Act 1894(a) (liability of ship-owners) " owner ", in relation to any ship, shall be construed as including the Secretary of State or other person by whom any steps are taken in relation to the ship by virtue of this Regulation.

In this paragraph " ship " has the same meaning as in Part VIII of that Act.

(5) The provisions of this Regulation shall have effect without prejudice to any power exercisable by virtue of paragraph (2) or paragraph (3) of the foregoing Regulation ; and the exercise of any power by virtue of this Regulation in respect of any directions shall be without prejudice to the taking of proceedings in respect of any contravention of, or failure to comply with, the directions.

(6) Paragraphs (4) and (5) of the foregoing Regulation shall have effect in relation to functions under this Regulation as they have effect in relation to functions under that Regulation.

Employment in ports

5.—(1) This Regulation shall apply to any port, or part of a port, specified in a direction given by the Secretary of State for Employment and for the time being in force, but not otherwise.

(2) Notwithstanding anything in any dock labour scheme or in section 1 of the Docks and Harbours Act 1966(b) (additional control of employment of dock workers), any employer, whether registered under such a scheme or not, and whether he holds a licence under that Act or not, may at any port—

(a) employ on dock work any person whom he has been requested by the Secretary of State to employ on such work ;

(b) employ any person on any such dock work, or dock work of any such class, as may be approved by the Secretary of State for the purposes of this Regulation ;

and such employment shall not constitute a contravention, either on the part of the employer or of the person employed, of any provision of any dock labour scheme or section 1 of that Act.

(3) Where the Secretary of State gives to an employer notice in writing that this paragraph is to apply to him, all earnings properly due to any person employed by that employer in the circumstances mentioned in sub-paragraph (a) of the last foregoing paragraph shall be paid to him by the Secretary of State as agent of the employer, and the employer shall, in such manner and at such time and place as may be directed by the Secretary of State,—

(a) furnish a statement of the gross wages (including overtime and allow-ances and without deductions of any kind) due to that person from the employer and of the period in respect of which they are due ; and

---

(a) 1894 c. 60.   (b) 1966 c. 28.

(*b*) pay to the Secretary of State the total amount of the gross wages so due, and such further amount, calculated either by way of percentage of the gross wages or otherwise, as the Secretary of State may by notice require as a contribution towards the administrative expenses of the Secretary of State under this Regulation.

(4) If under Regulation 3 of these Regulations the Secretary of State appoints a Port Emergency Committee for a port to which this Regulation applies in whole or in part or for a group of ports of which that port is one, he may authorise that Committee to exercise on his behalf in relation to that port all or any of his functions under this Regulation ; and paragraph (5) of that Regulation shall have effect in relation to functions under this Regulation as it has effect in relation to functions under that Regulation.

(5) Where any person employed by the National Dock Labour Board for the purpose of the administration of a dock labour scheme performs services for the Secretary of State or a Port Emergency Committee under this Regulation, the performance of those services shall be deemed to have been authorised by the Board as part of his employment, and the Secretary of State shall pay to the Board such sums as may, in default of agreement, be determined by arbitration in respect of—

(*a*) the remuneration and allowances payable to that person by the Board for the period during which that person performs such services for the Secretary of State or Committee ;

(*b*) the amount of the employer's contribution in respect of that person for that period and in respect of payments of his remuneration for that period ; and

(*c*) the amount of any selective employment tax payable by the Board in respect of that person for that period.

(6) The Secretary of State, and, if any of his functions under this Regulation are delegated to a Port Emergency Committee for a port or for a group of ports, that Committee, shall be furnished by the National Dock Labour Board with such office accommodation and equipment as appears to the Secretary of State to be requisite for the proper exercise and performance of his functions under this Regulation, and the Secretary of State shall pay to the Board in respect of the use of that accommodation and equipment such sums as may, in default of agreement, be determined by arbitration.

(7) A direction given by the Secretary of State for Employment with respect to any port under paragraph (1) of this Regulation may be revoked by a subsequent direction given by him, and thereupon this Regulation shall cease to apply to that port, without prejudice to the giving of a new direction in relation thereto:

Provided that the revocation of such a direction with respect to any port or part thereof shall not affect the previous operation of this Regulation in relation to that port or part thereof, or the validity of any action taken thereunder, or any penalty or punishment incurred in respect of any contravention or failure to comply therewith, or any proceeding or remedy in respect of any such punishment or penalty.

(8) In this Regulation " dock labour scheme " means a scheme for the time being in force under the Dock Workers (Regulation of Employment)

Act 1946(a), "dock work", in relation to a port, means work which is treated for the purposes of a dock labour scheme as dock work at that port, and "the employer's contribution" means the employer's contribution (including any graduated contribution) under the National Insurance Act 1965(b), the National Insurance (Industrial Injuries) Act 1965(c), the National Health Service Contributions Act 1965(d) and section 27 of the Redundancy Payments Act 1965(e).

RELAXATION OF RESTRICTIONS AS TO USE OF
ROAD VEHICLES

Goods vehicle licences

6. A goods vehicle with respect to which an operator's licence under Part V of the Transport Act 1968(f) is required, but no such licence is in force, may, notwithstanding anything in that Act, be used on a road for the carriage of goods for hire or reward, or for or in connection with any trade or business carried on by any person, so long as the use of the vehicle is under, and in accordance with, any general or special authority granted for the purposes of this paragraph by or on behalf of the Secretary of State.

Public service vehicle licences, road service licences, &c.

7.—(1) Notwithstanding anything in section 127 of the Road Traffic Act 1960(g), no public service vehicle licence shall be necessary for the use of a motor vehicle on a road as a stage carriage, an express carriage or a contract carriage so long as the use of the vehicle is under, and in accordance with, any general or special authority granted for the purposes of this paragraph by or on behalf of the Secretary of State.

(2) Notwithstanding anything in section 134 of the Road Traffic Act 1960, a vehicle may be used as a stage carriage or an express carriage otherwise than under a road service licence or a permit granted under section 30 of the Transport Act 1968, so long as the use of the vehicle is under, and in accordance with, any general or special authority granted for the purposes of this paragraph by or on behalf of the Secretary of State.

(3) So much of section 101 of the Road Traffic Act 1930(h) as requires the consent of a dock authority or a harbour authority to the running by a local authority of a public service vehicle on a road vested in a dock authority or harbour authority shall not apply so long as the running of the vehicle is under, and in accordance with, any general or special authority granted for the purposes of this paragraph by or on behalf of the Secretary of State.

(4) Notwithstanding anything in section 23 of the Transport (London) Act 1969(i), a vehicle may be used to provide a London bus service (as defined by subsection (7) of that section) otherwise than in pursuance of an agreement with, or consent granted by, the London Transport Executive, so long as the use of the vehicle is under, and in accordance with, any general or special authority granted for the purposes of this paragraph by or on behalf of the Secretary of State.

(a) 1946 c. 22. (b) 1965 c. 51. (c) 1965 c. 52. (d) 1965 c. 54. (e) 1965 c. 62.
(f) 1968 c. 73. (g) 1960 c. 16. (h) 1930 c. 43. (i) 1969 c. 35.

Other provisions as to road passenger vehicles

8.—(1) Nothing in section 144 of the Road Traffic Act 1960, in section 10 of the London Hackney Carriages Act 1843(**a**), in section 8 of the Metropolitan Public Carriage Act 1869(**b**), in section 48 of the Tramways Act 1870(**c**) or any rules or regulations thereunder, in Schedule 5 to the Burgh Police (Scotland) Act 1892(**d**) or in any local Act or any regulations or other instrument made or issued under any local Act shall apply so as to prevent any person from driving or acting as conductor of a vehicle although he is not licensed for the purpose so long as he is doing so under, and in accordance with, any general or special authority granted for the purposes of this paragraph by or on behalf of the Secretary of State.

(2) Notwithstanding anything in any enactment (whether public general or local) or in any regulations or other instrument made or issued under any enactment (whether public general or local) or in any condition of any road service licence—

(*a*) passengers may be carried (whether standing or otherwise) on any public service vehicle, tramcar or trolley vehicle without limit of number, and

(*b*) any public service vehicle, tramcar or trolley vehicle may be operated without a conductor's being carried thereon,

so long as the carriage of the passengers or, as the case may be, the operation of the vehicle is under, and in accordance with, any general or special authority granted for the purposes of this paragraph by or on behalf of the Secretary of State.

Construction and use regulations

9. Notwithstanding anything in section 40 of the Road Traffic Act 1972(**e**), a person may use on a road, or cause or permit to be so used, a motor vehicle or trailer which does not comply with regulations having effect as if made under the said section 40 so long as the use of the vehicle is under, and in accordance with, a special authority granted for the purposes of this Regulation by or on behalf of the Secretary of State.

Test and plating certificates

10.—(1) Notwithstanding anything in section 44 of the Road Traffic Act 1972, a person may use on a road, or cause or permit to be so used, a motor vehicle to which that section applies, and in respect of which no test certificate has been issued as therein mentioned, so long as the use of the vehicle is under, and in accordance with, any general or special authority granted for the purposes of this paragraph by or on behalf of the Secretary of State.

(2) Nothing in regulations having effect as if made under section 52(1) of the Road Traffic Act 1972 (which require the production of an effective test certificate or the making of a prescribed declaration on application for a vehicle excise licence for a vehicle) shall apply where the Secretary of State is satisfied that the vehicle is being used, or is to be used, under and in accordance with any general or special authority granted for the purposes of paragraph (1) of this Regulation.

(3) Notwithstanding anything in section 46 of the Road Traffic Act 1972, a person may use on a road, or cause or permit to be so used,—

(*a*) a goods vehicle which is of a class required by regulations under section 45 of that Act to have been submitted for examination for plating, and in respect of which no plating certificate is for the time being in force, or

---

(**a**) 1843 c. 86. (**b**) 1869 c. 115. (**c**) 1870 c. 78. (**d**) 1892 c. 55. (**e**) 1972 c. 20.

(*b*) a goods vehicle which is of a class required by such regulations to have been submitted for a goods vehicle test, and in respect of which no goods vehicle test certificate is for the time being in force,

so long as (in either case) the use of that vehicle is under, and in accordance with, any general or special authority granted for the purposes of this paragraph by or on behalf of the Secretary of State.

(4) Notwithstanding anything in section 51 of the Road Traffic Act 1972, a person may use a goods vehicle on a road for drawing a trailer, or cause or permit a goods vehicle to be so used, where the plating certificate issued for the goods vehicle does not specify a maximum laden weight for the vehicle together with any trailer which may be drawn by it, so long as the use of the vehicle for drawing the trailer is under, and in accordance with, any general or special authority granted for the purposes of this paragraph by the Secretary of State.

(5) Nothing in regulations having effect as if made under section 52(2) of the Road Traffic Act 1972 (which require the production of an effective goods vehicle test certificate, or a certificate of temporary exemption, or the making of a prescribed declaration, on application for a vehicle excise licence for a vehicle) shall apply where the Secretary of State is satisfied that the vehicle is being used, or is to be used, under and in accordance with any general or special authority granted for the purposes of paragraph (3) of this Regulation.

(6) Section 162(1) of the Road Traffic Act 1972 (which imposes requirements with respect to the production of certain documents) shall not, so far as it relates to the production of a test certificate, a plating certificate or a goods vehicle test certificate, apply in the case of a motor vehicle used under, and in accordance with, any general or special authority granted under this Regulation.

(7) In this Regulation " test certificate " has the meaning assigned to it by section 43(2) of the Road Traffic Act 1972, and " plating certificate " and " goods vehicle test certificate " have the meanings assigned to them by section 45(1) of that Act.

Drivers' hours

11.—(1) Nothing in subsections (1) to (6) of section 96 of the Transport Act 1968 (which relate to a driver's permitted hours and periods of duty and rest) shall apply to a driver so long as he is acting under, and in accordance with, any general or special authority granted for the purposes of this paragraph by or on behalf of the Secretary of State.

(2) Nothing in regulations under section 98 of the said Act—

(*a*) which concerns the entering of a current record in a driver's record book, or

(*b*) which requires a driver to have such a book in his possession,

shall apply to a driver so long as he is acting under, and in accordance with, any general or special authority granted for the purposes of this paragraph by or on behalf of the Secretary of State.

(3) An authority under paragraph (1) or paragraph (2) above may, instead of conferring all of the exemptions specified in the paragraph, confer only such exemptions as are specified in the authority.

Drivers' licences

12.—(1) Notwithstanding anything in section 4 of the Road Traffic Act 1972 or in Part III or Part IV of that Act, a person who holds a valid licence granted under Part III of that Act authorising him to drive a motor car may drive on a road, and may be employed by another person so to drive, a vehicle to which this Regulation applies, so long as he drives it under, and in accordance with, a general or special authority granted for the purposes of this Regulation by or on behalf of the Secretary of State.

(2) The vehicles to which this Regulation applies are—

(a) heavy locomotives ;

(b) light locomotives ;

(c) motor tractors ;

(d) heavy motor cars ; and

(e) motor cars so constructed that a trailer may by partial superimposition be attached thereto in such a manner as to cause a substantial part of the weight of the trailer to be borne thereby.

(3) So much of any regulations for the time being in force and having effect as if made under section 119 of the Road Traffic Act 1972 as requires any person, or enables any person to be required, to produce a heavy goods vehicle driver's licence shall not apply in the case of a vehicle driven under, and in accordance with, any general or special authority granted under this Regulation.

(4) In this Regulation " heavy goods vehicle driver's licence " means a licence under Part IV of the Road Traffic Act 1972, and any expression which is defined in section 190 of that Act has the meaning assigned to it by that section.

Excise licences

13.—(1) Notwithstanding anything in the Vehicles (Excise) Act 1971(**a**), a person may use or keep on a public road a mechanically propelled vehicle without there being in force and fixed to and exhibited on that vehicle a licence issued under that Act for or in respect of the use of that vehicle, so long as the use or keeping of the vehicle is under, and in accordance with, any general or special authority granted for the purposes of this paragraph by or on behalf of the Secretary of State.

(2) Where an excise licence issued or having effect under the Vehicles (Excise) Act 1971 is in force with respect to any mechanically propelled vehicle, the uses of that vehicle which are authorised by the licence shall be deemed to extend to any use made of the vehicle under, and in accordance with, any general or special authority granted for the purposes of this paragraph by or on behalf of the Secretary of State, and the provisions of section 18 of that Act shall not apply to any use of any vehicle in respect of which such a licence is in force so long as that use of that vehicle is under, and in accordance with, any such general or special authority.

Third-party insurance

14.—(1) Notwithstanding anything in section 143(1) of the Road Traffic Act 1972, a person may use, or cause or permit another person to use, a motor vehicle on a road without there being in force in relation to the use thereof by that person or that other person, as the case may be, a policy of insurance or security in respect of third-party risks issued or given for the purposes of Part VI of that Act so long as—

(a) there is in force in relation to some other use of the vehicle a policy of insurance or security issued or given for those purposes and the use of the vehicle by that person or that other person, as the case may be,—

(a) 1971 c. 10.

(i) is one to which, as respects the period of the emergency, the policy or security is, by arrangement between the Secretary of State and the issuer or giver of the policy or security or some person acting on his behalf, treated as also relating, and

(ii) is under, and in accordance with, any general or special authority granted for the purposes of this paragraph by or on behalf of the Secretary of State ; or

(b) the use of the vehicle by that person or that other person, as the case may be, is under, and in accordance with, any such general or special authority and there is in force in relation to the use of the vehicle such an agreement to insure or make good failures to discharge liability in respect of third-party risks as may be specified in the authority ;

and sections 162(1) and 166(1) of the said Act of 1972 (which impose requirements with respect to the furnishing of the names and addresses of the driver and the owner of a motor vehicle and to the production of certificates of insurance or security) shall not, so far as they relate to the production of such certificates, apply in the case of a motor vehicle driven under, and in accordance with, any such general or special authority.

(2) So much of any regulations having effect as if made by virtue of section 153 of the Road Traffic Act 1972 as, on an application for a vehicle excise licence require the production of a certificate of insurance, or evidence that the necessary security has been given or that the vehicle is exempt from the provisions of section 143 of the said Act, shall not apply where the Secretary of State is satisfied that the vehicle is being used, or is to be used, under, and in accordance with, any general or special authority granted for the purposes of paragraph (1) of this Regulation.

Transport of petroleum-spirit and other substances

15.—(1) Regulations made under section 6 of the Petroleum (Consolidation) Act 1928(a) (regulations as to the conveyance of petroleum-spirit by road) shall not have effect in relation to any vehicle, so long as the use of the vehicle is under, and in accordance with, any general or special authority granted for the purposes of this paragraph by or on behalf of the Secretary of State.

(2) Without prejudice to the foregoing paragraph, regulations made under that section, in so far as they are made for any of the purposes specified in subsection (1)(d) of that section, shall not have effect in relation to the loading or unloading of vehicles at any place, so long as that place is used under, and in accordance with, any general or special authority granted for the purposes of this paragraph by or on behalf of the Secretary of State.

(3) In this Regulation any reference to section 6 of the Petroleum (Consolidation) Act 1928 shall be construed as including a reference to that section as read with section 19 of that Act (which confers power to apply the Act to substances other than petroleum-spirit) and any Order in Council made thereunder which is for the time being in force, and any reference in this Regulation to regulations under section 6 of that Act shall be construed accordingly.

PUBLIC SERVICES AND FACILITIES

Transport services and facilities

16. The British Railways Board and the London Transport Executive may respectively, to such extent as appears to them to be necessary or expedient for providing or maintaining railway services and facilities in a manner

(a) 1928 c. 32.

best calculated to promote the public interest, disregard any obligation imposed by or under any enactment—

(a) to carry goods or passengers or to provide transport services or facilities ;

(b) to employ or provide a person for any particular purpose or to perform any particular duty ; or

(c) to keep gates on a level crossing over a public road closed across the road ;

so long as, in so doing, they are acting under, and in accordance with, any general or special authority granted for the purposes of this Regulation by or on behalf of the Secretary of State.

Electricity supply

17.—(1) Any Electricity Board may, to such extent as appears to them to be necessary or expedient for maintaining or making the best use of supplies of electricity available for distribution or for conserving and making the best use of supplies of fuel or power available for the generation of electricity, disregard or fall short in discharging any obligation imposed by or under any enactment, or any contractual obligation—

(a) to give or continue to give supplies of electricity ; or

(b) to supply electricity in accordance with standards prescribed by or under the enactment or contract in question ;

so long as, in so doing, they are acting under, and in accordance with, any general or special authority granted for the purposes of this Regulation by or on behalf of the Secretary of State.

(2) If and so far as it appears to the Secretary of State necessary or expedient for maintaining or making the best use of supplies of electricity available for distribution—

(a) he may give to the person carrying on business at, or appearing to be in charge of, or occupying, any premises, directions for regulating or prohibiting consumption of electricity on the premises ; and

(b) he may take, or authorise any person acting on his behalf to take, such steps as appear appropriate to cut off any supply of electricity.

(3) Without prejudice to the generality of the provisions of Regulation 40(2) below, the power of giving directions conferred by paragraph (2)(a) above may be exercised by means of an order—

(a) applicable to premises of any class or description specified in the order, or premises used for purposes of any class or description specified in the order, or

(b) where previous directions have been given otherwise than by order, applicable to the persons or premises as respects which the previous directions had effect, or such of them as may be specified in the order.

(4) If any person, without authority duly given by or on behalf of the Secretary of State, reconnects a supply cut off in pursuance of this Regulation, he shall be guilty of an offence against this Regulation.

(5) The Secretary of State may authorise any person acting on his behalf to enter any premises, if necessary by force, for the purpose—

(a) of ascertaining whether there has been any contravention of a direction under this Regulation, or

(b) of cutting off any supply of electricity in pursuance of this Regulation, or of ascertaining whether it remains duly cut off.

(6) The provisions of this Regulation are without prejudice to the generality of Regulation 21 below (regulation of consumption and supply of electricity and other products).

(7) The powers of the Secretary of State under paragraph (2) of this Regulation shall also be exercisable by such persons, being either servants of the Crown or persons acting on behalf of Her Majesty, as may be authorised in that behalf by the Secretary of State.

Gas supply

18.—(1) The Gas Council or any Area Gas Board may, to such extent as appears to them to be necessary or expedient—

(a) for maintaining or making the best use of supplies of gas available for distribution ; or

(b) for conserving and making the best use of supplies of fuel or other material available for the manufacture of gas ; or

(c) for preserving public safety ;

disregard or fall short in discharging any obligation imposed by or under any enactment, or any contractual obligation—

(i) to give or continue to give supplies of gas ; or

(ii) to supply gas in accordance with standards prescribed by or under the enactment or contract in question ;

so long as, in so doing, they are acting under, and in accordance with, any general or special authority granted for the purposes of this paragraph by or on behalf of the Secretary of State.

(2) If and so far as it appears to the Secretary of State necessary or expedient for any of the purposes set out in sub-paragraphs (a), (b) and (c) of paragraph (1) above—

(a) he may give to the person carrying on business at, or appearing to be in charge of, or occupying, any premises, directions for regulating or prohibiting the consumption of gas on the premises ; and

(b) he may take, or authorise any person acting on his behalf to take, such steps as appear appropriate to cut off any supply, or means of supply, of gas by disconnecting any service pipe or by any other means.

(3) If any person, without authority duly given by or on behalf of the Secretary of State, reconnects a supply, or means of supply, cut off in pursuance of this Regulation, he shall be guilty of an offence against this Regulation.

(4) The Secretary of State may authorise any person acting on his behalf to enter any premises, if necessary by force, for the purpose—

(a) of ascertaining whether there has been any contravention of a direction under this Regulation,

(b) of cutting off any supply, or means of supply, of gas in pursuance of this Regulation, or of ascertaining whether it remains duly cut off, or

(c) of inspecting, examining or testing any plant or equipment for the supply or consumption of gas with a view to ensuring the preservation of public safety.

(5) The provisions of this Regulation are without prejudice to the generality of Regulation 21 below (regulation of consumption and supply of gas and other products).

(6) The powers of the Secretary of State under this Regulation, other than his powers under paragraph (1), shall also be exercisable by such persons, being either servants of the Crown or persons acting on behalf of Her Majesty, as may be authorised in that behalf by the Secretary of State.

Water supply and resources

19.—(1) Any statutory water undertakers, regional water board or water development board may, for the purpose of maintaining supplies of water in any locality, disregard any restriction imposed by or under any enactment or rule of law with respect to the taking of water from any source or any obligation so imposed with respect to the discharge of compensation water, and may for that purpose take water from any source, so long as, in either case, in so doing, they are acting under, and in accordance with, any general or special authority granted for the purposes of this paragraph by or on behalf of the Secretary of State.

(2) Any statutory water undertakers, regional water board or water development board may, to such extent as appears to them to be necessary or expedient for conserving and making the best use of supplies of water in any locality, disregard or fall short in discharging any obligation imposed by or under any enactment or rule of law with respect to the provision by them of supplies of water (including, in particular, but without prejudice to the generality of the foregoing words, any obligation with respect to the filtration or other treatment of water or the pressure at which water is to be supplied) so long as, in so doing, they are acting under, and in accordance with, any general or special authority granted for the purposes of this paragraph by or on behalf of the Secretary of State.

(3) In the exercise of their new functions under the Water Resources Act 1963(a), any river authority may, for the purpose of maintaining supplies of water in any locality, disregard any restriction or obligation imposed by or under any enactment or rule of law with respect to—

   (a) the taking or impounding of water from any source,

   (b) the discharge of water into any inland water or underground strata, or

   (c) in connection with their functions, the construction or alteration of any works,

and may for that purpose take or impound water from any source, or discharge water into any inland water or underground strata ; but the powers conferred by this paragraph shall only be exercisable so long as in exercising them the authority are acting under, and in accordance with, any general or special authority granted for the purposes of this paragraph by or on behalf of the Secretary of State.

Sewerage and sewage disposal

20. Any sewerage authority may, for the purpose of effectively draining their district and dealing with the contents of their sewers, disregard any prohibition or restriction imposed by or under any enactment or rule of law with respect to the discharge of foul or surface water into any natural or artificial stream, watercourse, canal, pond or lake, so long as, in so doing, they are acting under, and in accordance with, any general or special authority granted for the purposes of this Regulation by or on behalf of the Secretary of State.

CONSUMPTION AND SUPPLY

Supply, &c., of fuel, refinery products, electricity and gas

21. The Secretary of State may by order provide for regulating or prohibiting the supply or acquisition, or the consumption (whether for domestic or industrial purposes or for any other purposes whatsoever) of solid or liquid fuel or refinery products, or the supply or the consumption (whether for domestic or industrial purposes or for any other purposes whatsoever) of electricity or gas.

Directions as to solid or liquid fuel or refinery products

22.—(1) The Secretary of State—

   (a) may give to any person carrying on business as a supplier of liquid

(a) 1963 c. 38.

fuel or as a supplier of solid fuel directions as to the supply by him of any such solid or liquid fuel as may be specified in the directions, and

(b) may give to any person carrying on business as a refiner of liquid fuel directions as to the production of any liquid fuel, or other refinery products, or as to the use, disposal or supply of any refinery products, including those forming part of any stock held by him for the purposes of his business.

(2) Directions under paragraph (1) of this Regulation may in particular—

(a) require any fuel or refinery product to be supplied, in accordance with such requirements as may be specified in the directions, to such persons as may be so specified, or

(b) prohibit or restrict the supply of any fuel or refinery product to persons so specified, or to persons other than those to be supplied in accordance with the directions,

and directions may be given under paragraph (1)(b) of this Regulation for securing that the liquid fuel produced is, or is to any extent, of a description specified in the direction.

(3) Where any fuel or refinery product is supplied to any person in pursuance of a direction under this Regulation, that person shall pay such price in respect thereof as may be reasonable.

(4) The foregoing provisions of this Regulation shall apply in relation to any person carrying on a trade or business (otherwise than as a supplier of fuel) for the purposes of which he is in possession of a stock of solid fuel, as if, in respect of that fuel, he were carrying on business as such a supplier ; and any directions to such a person under this Regulation may include directions prohibiting the consumption of such fuel by him :

Provided that in relation to any such person any reference in this Regulation to supply shall be construed as a reference to delivery at the place where the fuel is kept.

Maximum prices for food and animal feeding stuffs

23. The Minister of Agriculture, Fisheries and Food may by order provide for regulating, to such extent and in such manner as may be specified in the order, the maximum prices which may be charged for such foods or animal feeding stuffs as may be so specified.

Distribution of food and animal feeding stuffs

24.—(1) The Minister of Agriculture, Fisheries and Food may give to any person carrying on business as a supplier of food or animal feeding stuffs directions as to the persons to whom he is to supply any such food or animal feeding stuffs as may be specified in the directions ; and any such directions may in particular require any food or animal feeding stuffs to be supplied to such persons as may be specified in the directions in accordance with such requirements as may be so specified or may, to such extent as may be specified in the directions, prohibit the supply of food or animal feeding stuffs to persons so specified.

(2) Where anything is supplied to any person in pursuance of directions under this Regulation, that person shall pay such price in respect thereof as may be reasonable.

Supply of medicines

25.—(1) The restrictions and prohibitions imposed by or under the following provisions of the Medicines Act 1968(a), that is to say—

(a) Part II (licences and certificates relating to medicinal products),

_____

(a) 1968 c. 67.

(*b*) Part III (dealings with medicinal products), and

(*c*) Part V (containers, packages and identification of medicinal products),

shall not apply to a person so long as he is acting under, and in accordance with, any general or special authority granted for the purposes of this paragraph by or on behalf of the Secretary of State, or the Minister of Agriculture, Fisheries and Food.

(2) Nothing in any regulations made, or having effect, under the Medicines Act 1971(a) shall require the payment of a fee on an application made under, and in accordance with, any general or special authority granted for the purposes of this paragraph by or on behalf of the Secretary of State, or the Minister of Agriculture, Fisheries and Food.

(3) An authority under paragraph (1) above may, instead of conferring exemptions from all the restrictions and prohibitions specified in the paragraph, confer only such exemptions as are specified in the authority.

REGULATION OF TRANSPORT SERVICES

Transport of goods by road or rail

26.—(1) The Secretary of State may give to any person carrying on business as a carrier of goods by road or by rail for hire or reward directions as to the goods which are to be carried by him ; and any such directions may in particular require any essential goods to be carried for such persons, from and to such places, and in accordance with such requirements, as may be specified in the directions or may, to such extent as may be so specified, prohibit the carriage of goods for persons, or from or to places, so specified.

(2) Where in pursuance of directions given under this Regulation any goods are carried for the benefit of any person, that person shall pay such charge in respect of the carriage as may be reasonable.

(3) The powers of the Secretary of State under this Regulation shall also be exercisable by such persons, being either servants of the Crown or persons acting on behalf of Her Majesty, as may be authorised in that behalf by the Secretary of State.

(4) The foregoing provisions of this Regulation shall apply in relation to any person carrying on a trade or business (otherwise than as a carrier of goods by road for hire or reward) for or in connection with which he uses any goods vehicles, as if, in respect of those vehicles, he were carrying on business as such a carrier of goods ; and any directions to such a person under this Regulation may include directions prohibiting the carriage of goods in the course of his own trade or business.

Transport of passengers by road or rail

27.—(1) The Secretary of State may give to any person carrying on the business of operating public service vehicles directions as to the passengers who are to be carried, or the road services which are to be provided, by him ; and any such directions may in particular require persons to be carried from and to places specified in the directions or may, to such extent as may be so specified, prohibit the carriage of persons from or to places so specified and may also specify requirements in accordance with which passengers are to be carried or, as the case may be, road services are to be provided.

(2) The Secretary of State may give to any person carrying on business as a carrier of passengers by rail directions as to the passengers who are

(a) 1971 c. 69.

to be carried by him, and any such directions may in particular require persons to be carried from and to places specified in the directions or may, to such extent as may be so specified, prohibit the carriage of persons from or to places so specified.

(3) Where in pursuance of directions given under this Regulation any passengers are carried for the benefit of any other person otherwise than at separate fares, that person shall pay such charge in respect of the carriage as may be reasonable.

(4) The powers of the Secretary of State under this Regulation shall also be exercisable by such persons, being either servants of the Crown or persons acting on behalf of Her Majesty, as may be authorised in that behalf by the Secretary of State.

(5) The reference in this Regulation to public service vehicles shall be construed in accordance with sections 117 and 118 of the Road Traffic Act 1960.

Air transport

28.—(1) The Secretary of State may give to any person providing air transport services (being a person whose sole or principal place of business is in Great Britain) directions as to the passengers or cargo which are to be carried by him ; and any such directions in particular—

(a) may require any persons engaged in the performance of essential services to be carried from and to such places, and in accordance with such requirements, as may be specified in the directions or may, to such extent as may be so specified, prohibit the carriage of passengers from or to places so specified ;

(b) may require any essential goods to be carried for such persons, from and to such places, and in accordance with such requirements, as may be so specified or may, to such extent as may be so specified, prohibit the carriage of goods for persons, or from or to places, so specified.

(2) No air service licence shall be required for a flight undertaken for the purpose of complying with directions given under this Regulation.

(3) Where in pursuance of directions given under this Regulation any passenger is carried, he (or, if he is carried for the benefit of any other person, that person) shall pay such charge in respect of the carriage as may be reasonable ; and where in pursuance of any such directions any goods are carried for the benefit of any person, that person shall pay such charge in respect of the carriage as may be reasonable.

(4) The powers of the Secretary of State under this Regulation shall also be exercisable by such persons, being either servants of the Crown or persons acting on behalf of Her Majesty, as may be authorised in that behalf by the Secretary of State.

Transport by sea

29.—(1) The Secretary of State may give to any person having the management of a ship to which this Regulation applies (being a person in Great Britain or a person whose sole or principal place of business is in Great Britain) directions prohibiting that ship from proceeding to sea from any port in Great Britain except upon such voyages, or subject to such conditions as to the cargoes or classes of cargoes which may be carried in the ship, or as to the passengers who may be so carried, as may be specified in the directions.

(2) This Regulation applies to any ship registered in the United Kingdom, the Channel Islands or the Isle of Man.

(3) The powers of the Secretary of State under this Regulation shall also be exercisable by such persons, being either servants of the Crown or persons acting on behalf of Her Majesty, as may be authorised in that behalf by the Secretary of State.

REQUISITIONING OF CHATTELS AND TAKING POSSESSION OF LAND

Requisitioning of chattels

30.—(1) A competent authority, if it appears to that authority to be necessary or expedient so to do for any of the purposes specified in section 2(1) of the Emergency Powers Act 1920, may requisition any chattel in Great Britain (including any vehicle, vessel or aircraft or anything on board a vehicle, vessel or aircraft and including also any detachable part of any vehicle or aircraft) and may give such directions as appear to the competent authority to be necessary or expedient in connection with the requisition.

(2) Where a competent authority requisitions any chattel under this Regulation, the competent authority may use or deal with, or authorise the use of, or dealing with, the chattel for such purpose and in such manner as the competent authority thinks expedient for any of the purposes specified in the said section 2(1) and may hold, or sell or otherwise dispose of, the chattel as if the competent authority were the owner thereof and as if the chattel were free from any mortgage, pledge, lien or other similar obligation.

(3) The powers conferred by the foregoing provisions of this Regulation on a competent authority shall also be exercisable by such persons, being either servants of the Crown or persons acting on behalf of Her Majesty, as may be authorised in that behalf by the competent authority.

(4) Where a chattel is requisitioned under this Regulation, the competent authority shall pay to the owner of the chattel and to any other person interested in the chattel who suffers damage owing to the requisition such compensation as may be agreed or as may, in default of agreement, be determined by arbitration to be just having regard to all the circumstances of the particular case, so, however, that in assessing the compensation no account shall be taken of any appreciation of the value of the chattel due to the emergency.

(5) For the purposes of this Regulation, any of the following Ministers and authorities shall be a competent authority, that is to say, a Secretary of State, the Minister of Agriculture, Fisheries and Food and the Minister of Posts and Telecommunications.

Taking possession of land

31.—(1) A Secretary of State, if it appears to him to be necessary or expedient so to do for any of the purposes specified in section 2(1) of the Emergency Powers Act 1920, may take possession of any land in Great Britain, and may give such directions as appear to him to be necessary or expedient in connection with the taking of possession of that land.

(2) While any land is in the possession of a Secretary of State by virtue of this Regulation, the land may, notwithstanding any restriction imposed on the use thereof (whether by any Act or other instrument or otherwise), be used by, or under the authority of, the Secretary of State for such purpose, and in such manner, as he thinks expedient for any of the purposes specified in the said section 2(1).

(3) Without prejudice to the last foregoing paragraph, a Secretary of State may, so far as appears to him to be necessary or expedient in connection with the taking of possession of any land in pursuance of this Regulation, or with the use of any land in the possession of the Secretary of State by virtue of this Regulation, do, or authorise persons using the land under the authority of the Secretary of State to do, in relation to the land anything which any person having an interest in the land would be entitled to do by virtue of that interest.

(4) In respect of land of which possession is taken under this Regulation, the Secretary of State shall pay to the person who would otherwise be entitled to possession of the land, and to any other person having an estate or interest in the land who suffers damage by reason of the taking of possession or of anything done in relation to the land while in the possession of the Secretary of State, such compensation as may be agreed or as may, in default of agreement, be determined by arbitration to be just having regard to all the circumstances of the particular case.

OFFENCES

Sabotage

32.—(1) No person shall do any act with intent to impair the efficiency or impede the working or movement of any vessel, aircraft, hovercraft, vehicle, machinery, apparatus or other thing used or intended to be used in the performance of essential services, or to impair the usefulness of any works, structure or premises used or intended to be used as aforesaid.

(2) The foregoing provisions of this Regulation shall apply in relation to any omission on the part of a person to do anything which he is under a duty, either to the public or to any person, to do, as they apply in relation to the doing of any act by a person.

Trespassing and loitering

33.—(1) No person shall trespass on, or on premises in the vicinity of, any premises used or appropriated for the purposes of essential services ; and if any person is found trespassing on any premises in contravention of this paragraph, then, without prejudice to any proceedings which may be taken against him, he may be removed by the appropriate person from the premises.

(2) No person shall, for any purpose prejudicial to the public safety, be in, or in the vicinity of, any premises used or appropriated for the purposes of essential services ; and where, in any proceedings taken against a person by virtue of this paragraph, it is proved that at the material time he was present in, or in the vicinity of, the premises concerned, the prosecution may thereupon adduce such evidence of the character of that person (including evidence of his having been previously convicted of any offence) as tends to show that he was so present for a purpose prejudicial to the public safety.

(3) No person loitering in the vicinity of any premises used or appropriated for the purposes of essential services shall continue to loiter in that vicinity after being requested by the appropriate person to leave it.

(4) In this Regulation the expression " the appropriate person " means—

(*a*) any person acting on behalf of Her Majesty,

(*b*) any constable,

(*c*) the occupier of the premises or any person authorised by the occupier.

Interference with Her Majesty's forces, constables and other persons performing essential services

34.—(1) No person shall do any act having reasonable cause to believe that it would be likely to endanger the safety of any member of Her Majesty's forces or of any constable or of any person who is charged with the exercise or performance of any power or duty under any of these Regulations or is performing essential services.

(2) No person shall—

(*a*) wilfully obstruct any person acting in the course of his duty as a constable, or exercising or performing any power or duty under any of these Regulations, or performing essential services ; or

(*b*) do any act having reasonable cause to believe that it would be likely to prevent any person from, or mislead or interfere with any person in, performing his duty as a constable, or exercising or performing any power or duty under any of these Regulations, or performing essential services.

Inducing persons to withhold services

35. No person shall—

(*a*) do any act calculated to induce any member of Her Majesty's forces or constable to withhold his services or commit breaches of discipline ; or

(*b*) with intent to contravene, or to aid, abet, counsel or procure a contravention of, paragraph (*a*) of this Regulation, have in his possession or under his control any document of such a nature that the dissemination of copies thereof among members of Her Majesty's forces or constables would constitute such a contravention.

SUPPLEMENTAL

Power to arrest without warrant

36. Where a constable, with reasonable cause, suspects that an offence against any of these Regulations has been committed, he may arrest without warrant anyone whom he, with reasonable cause, suspects to be guilty of the offence.

Attempts to commit offences and assisting offenders

37.—(1) Without prejudice to the operation of section 8 of the Accessories and Abettors Act 1861(**a**) and section 35 of the Magistrates' Courts Act 1952(**b**), any person who attempts to commit, conspires with any other person to commit, or does any act preparatory to the commission of, an offence against any of these Regulations shall be guilty of an offence against that Regulation.

(2) Any person who, knowing or having reasonable cause to believe that another person is guilty of an offence against any of these Regulations, gives that other person any assistance with intent thereby to prevent, hinder or interfere with the apprehension, trial or punishment of that person for the said offence shall be guilty of an offence against that Regulation.

(3) This Regulation shall, in its application to Scotland, have effect as if, for the references to section 8 of the Accessories and Abettors Act 1861 and section 35 of the Magistrates' Courts Act 1952, there were substituted a reference to any rule of law relating to art and part guilt.

(**a**) 1861 c. 94.   (**b**) 1952 c. 55.

Penalties and place of trial

38.—(1) If any person contravenes or fails to comply with any of these Regulations or any order made, direction given or requirement imposed under any of these Regulations, he shall be guilty of an offence against that Regulation ; and a person guilty of an offence against any of these Regulations shall, on summary conviction, be liable to imprisonment for a term not exceeding three months or to a fine not exceeding £100, or to both :

Provided that a person shall not be guilty of an offence against any of these Regulations by reason only of his taking part in, or peacefully persuading any other person or persons to take part in, a strike.

(2) Proceedings in respect of an offence alleged to have been committed by a person against any of these Regulations may be taken before the appropriate court in Great Britain having jurisdiction in the place where that person is for the time being.

Arbitrations

39. An arbitration under these Regulations shall, unless otherwise agreed, be the arbitration, in England and Wales, of a single arbitrator to be appointed by the Lord Chancellor and, in Scotland, of a single arbiter to be appointed by the Lord President of the Court of Session.

Provisions as to orders and directions

40.—(1) Any power conferred by these Regulations to make an order includes power to revoke or vary the order by a subsequent order.

(2) Any power of giving directions conferred by any provision of these Regulations may be exercised by means of an order applicable to all persons to whom directions may be given under that provision, or to such of them as fall within any class or description specified in the order.

W. G. Agnew.

STATUTORY INSTRUMENTS

1972 No. 1165

VALUE ADDED TAX

The Input Tax (Exceptions) (No. 1) Order 1972

Made - - - -	1st *August* 1972
Laid before the House of Commons	9th *August* 1972
Coming into Operation	1st *April* 1973

The Treasury, in exercise of the powers conferred on them by section 3(6) of the Finance Act 1972(**a**) hereby make the following Order:—

1. This Order may be cited as the Input Tax (Exceptions) (No. 1) Order 1972 and shall come into operation on 1st April 1973.

2.—(1) The Interpretation Act 1889(**b**) shall apply for the interpretation of this Order as it applies for the interpretation of an Act of Parliament.

(2) In this Order " tax ", " taxable person " and " input tax " have the same meanings as in Part I of the Finance Act 1972 and " major interest " has the same meaning as in section 5(6) of that Act.

3. Where a taxable person constructing a building for the purpose of granting a major interest in it or in any part of it incorporates in any part of the building or its site which is used for the purposes of a dwelling goods other than materials, builder's hardware, sanitary ware or other articles of a kind ordinarily installed by builders as fixtures, tax on the supply or importation of the goods shall not be deducted by him as input tax under section 3 of the Finance Act 1972.

Tim Fortescue,
Hugh Rossi,
Two of the Lords Commissioners
of Her Majesty's Treasury

1st August 1972.

EXPLANATORY NOTE

(This Note is not part of the Order)

This Order disallows deduction of input tax by builders on certain fittings incorporated as fixtures in dwelling accommodation in which they own a major interest.

(**a**) 1972 c. 41.	(**b**) 1889 c. 63.

STATUTORY INSTRUMENTS

1972 No. 1166

VALUE ADDED TAX

The Input Tax (Exceptions) (No. 2) Order 1972

Made - - - -	*1st August* 1972
Laid before the House of Commons	*9th August* 1972
Coming into Operation	*1st April* 1973

The Treasury, in exercise of the powers conferred on them by section 3(6) of the Finance Act 1972(**a**) hereby make the following Order:—

1. This Order may be cited as the Input Tax (Exceptions) (No. 2) Order 1972 and shall come into operation on 1st April 1973.

2.—(1) The Interpretation Act 1889(**b**) shall apply for the interpretation of this Order as it applies for the interpretation of an Act of Parliament.

(2) In this Order " tax ", " taxable person " and " input tax " have the same meanings as in Part I of the Finance Act 1972.

(3) In this Order " motor car " means, subject to paragraph (4) below, any motor vehicle of a kind normally used on public roads which has three or more wheels and either—

(*a*) is constructed or adapted solely or mainly for the carriage of passengers; or

(*b*) has to the rear of the driver's seat roofed accommodation which is fitted with side windows or which is constructed or adapted for the fitting of side windows.

(4) The following are not included in the definition of " motor car "—

(*a*) vehicles capable of accommodating only one person or suitable for carrying twelve or more persons;

(*b*) vehicles of not less than three tons unladen weight;

(*c*) caravans, ambulances and prison vans;

(*d*) vehicles of a type approved by the Assistant Commissioner of Police of the Metropolis as conforming to the conditions of fitness for the time being laid down by him for the purposes of the London Cab Order 1934(**c**);

(*e*) vehicles constructed for a special purpose other than the carriage of persons and having no other accommodation for carrying persons than such as is incidental to that purpose.

3. Tax on the supply or importation of a motor car shall not be deducted as input tax under section 3 of the Finance Act 1972 unless the motor car is supplied or imported for the purpose of its sale or the application to it of any treatment or process.

(**a**) 1972 c. 41. (**b**) 1889 c. 63. (**c**) S.R. & O. 1934 1346. (Rev. XIV, p. 795: 1934 I, p. 1221).

4. Where a motor car is supplied to or imported by a taxable person, and—

(*a*) tax on the supply or importation cannot be deducted as input tax by virtue of Article 3 of this Order; and

(*b*) the motor car is subsequently supplied by the taxable person and is so supplied otherwise than by being let on hire;

tax on the supply by the taxable person shall not be charged except to the extent (if any) that it exceeds the amount that could have been deducted as input tax but for Article 3 of this Order.

Tim Fortescue,

Hugh Rossi,

Two of the Lords Commissioners
of Her Majesty's Treasury

1st August 1972.

EXPLANATORY NOTE

(This Note is not part of the Order)

This Order disallows deduction of input tax on certain motor cars acquired by taxable persons for use in their business. The Order provides for consequential relief from output tax when the motor-car is finally disposed of by the business. The disallowance of deduction of input tax does not apply to cars acquired for sale or for treatment or process.

STATUTORY INSTRUMENTS

1972 No. 1167

VALUE ADDED TAX

The Input Tax (Exceptions) (No. 3) Order 1972

Made - - - -	*1st August* 1972
Laid before the House of Commons	*9th August* 1972
Coming into Operation	*1st April* 1973

The Treasury, in exercise of the powers conferred on them by section 3(6) of the Finance Act 1972(**a**) hereby make the following Order:—

1. This Order may be cited as the Input Tax (Exceptions) (No. 3) Order 1972 and shall come into operation on 1st April 1973.

2.—(1) The Interpretation Act 1889(**b**) shall apply for the interpretation of this Order as it applies for the interpretation of an Act of Parliament.

(2) In this Order " business ", " services ", " tax ", " taxable person " and " input tax " have the same meanings as in Part I of the Finance Act 1972.

(3) In this Order " business entertainment " means entertainment (including hospitality of any kind) provided by a taxable person in connection with a business carried on by him, but does not include the provision of anything for persons employed by the taxable person unless its provision for them is incidental to its provision for others.

(4) For the purposes of paragraph (3) above directors of a company or persons engaged in the management of a company shall be deemed to be persons employed by the company.

(5) In this Order " overseas customer ", in relation to a taxable person, means—

(*a*) any person who is not ordinarily resident nor carrying on a business in the United Kingdom and avails himself, or may be expected to avail himself, in the course of a business carried on by him outside the United Kingdom, of any goods or services the supply of which forms part of the taxable person's business; and

(*b*) any person who is not ordinarily resident in the United Kingdom and is acting, in relation to such goods or services, on behalf of an overseas customer as defined in paragraph (*a*) above or on behalf of any government or public authority of a country outside the United Kingdom.

3. Tax on the supply to a taxable person of goods or services used by him for the purpose of business entertainment shall not be deducted as input tax

---

(**a**) 1972 c. 41.   (**b**) 1889 c. 63.

under section 3 of the Finance Act 1972 unless the entertainment is provided for an overseas customer of his and is of a kind and on a scale which is reasonable, having regard to all the circumstances.

Tim Fortescue,
Hugh Rossi,
Two of the Lords Commissioners
of Her Majesty's Treasury

1st August 1972.

EXPLANATORY NOTE
(This note is not part of the Order)

This Order disallows deduction of input tax on business entertaining expenses (other than the expenses of entertaining overseas customers).

STATUTORY   INSTRUMENTS

1972 No. 1168

VALUE ADDED TAX

The Value Added Tax (Self-Supply) (No. 1) Order 1972

Made - - - -	*1st August* 1972
Laid before the House of Commons	*9th August* 1972
Coming into Operation	*1st April* 1973

The Treasury, in exercise of the powers conferred on them by sections 6(1) and 21(2) of the Finance Act 1972(a) hereby make the following Order:—

1. This Order may be cited as the Value Added Tax (Self-Supply) (No. 1) Order 1972 and shall come into operation on 1st April 1973.

2.—(1) The Interpretation Act 1889(b) shall apply for the interpretation of this Order as it applies for the interpretation of an Act of Parliament.

(2) In this Order " business ", " input tax ", " tax ", " taxable person " and " the Commissioners " have the same meanings as in Part I of the Finance Act 1972.

(3) In this Order " motor car " means, subject to paragraph (4) below, any motor vehicle of a kind normally used on public roads which has three or more wheels and either—

(*a*) is constructed or adapted solely or mainly for the carriage of passengers; or

(*b*) has to the rear of the driver's seat roofed accommodation which is fitted with side windows or which is constructed or adapted for the fitting of side windows.

(4) The following are not included in the definition of " motor car "—

(*a*) vehicles capable of accommodating only one person or suitable for carrying twelve or more persons;

(*b*) vehicles of not less than three tons unladen weight;

(*c*) caravans, ambulances and prison vans;

(*d*) vehicles of a type approved by the Assistant Commissioner of Police of the Metropolis as conforming to the conditions of fitness for the time being laid down by him for the purposes of the London Cab Order 1934(c);

(*e*) vehicles constructed for a special purpose other than the carriage of persons and having no other accommodation for carrying persons than such as is incidental to that purpose.

3.—(1) This Article applies to the following motor cars produced or acquired by a taxable person in the course of a business carried on by him, that is to say—

(*a*) any motor car produced by him otherwise than by the conversion of a vehicle acquired by him; and

(*b*) any motor car produced by him by the conversion of another vehicle (whether a motor car or not) with respect to which the conditions specified in paragraph (2) below are satisfied; and

---

(**a**) 1972 c. 41.   (**b**) 1889 c. 63.   (**c**) S.R. & O. 1934 1346.(Rev. XIV, p. 795: 1934 I, p. 1221).

(c) any motor car acquired by him with respect to which those conditions are satisfied.

(2) The conditions mentioned in paragraph (1) above are—

(a) that the motor car or other vehicle was imported by the taxable person or supplied to him under a taxable supply; and

(b) that tax on the importation or supply has been or may be deducted as input tax under section 3 of the Finance Act 1972.

(3) Where a motor car to which this Article applies—

(a) is neither supplied by the taxable person in the course of the business carried on by him nor converted into another vehicle (whether a motor car or not) in the course of that business; but

(b) is used by him for the purpose of that business;

the motor car shall be treated for the purposes of Part I of the Finance Act 1972 as both supplied to him for the purpose of that business and supplied by him in the course of that business, except where the motor car is one to which this Article applies by virtue of paragraph (1)(a) above and the Commissioners are satisfied that it is used solely for the purpose of research or development.

(4) The preceding provisions of this Article shall apply in relation to any bodies corporate which are treated for the purposes of section 21 of the Finance Act 1972 as members of a group as if those bodies were one person, but any motor car which would fall to be treated as supplied to and by that person shall be treated as supplied to and by the representative member.

Tim Fortescue,
Hugh Rossi,
Two of the Lords Commissioners
of Her Majesty's Treasury.

1st August 1972.

EXPLANATORY NOTE
(This Note is not part of the Order)

This Order (which is consequential on the Input Tax (Exceptions) (No. 2) Order 1972 (S.I. 1972/1166)) brings within the tax certain motor cars which are self-supplied by taxable persons for their own use. The effect of the Order is to bring such cars within the scope of the Input Tax (Exceptions) (No. 2) Order 1972, and places them in the same position as regards disallowance of input tax, as other cars.

STATUTORY INSTRUMENTS

1972 No. 1169

VALUE ADDED TAX

The Value Added Tax (Self-Supply) (No. 2) Order 1972

Made - - - -	*1st August* 1972
Laid before the House of	
Commons - -	*9th August* 1972
Coming into Operation -	*1st April* 1973

The Treasury, in exercise of the powers conferred on them by sections 6(1) and 21(2) of the Finance Act 1972(a) hereby make the following Order:—

1. This Order may be cited as the Value Added Tax (Self-Supply) (No. 2) Order 1972 and shall come into operation on 1st April 1973.

2.—(1) The Interpretation Act 1889(b) shall apply for the interpretation of this Order as it applies for the interpretation of an Act of Parliament.

(2) In this Order " business ", " input tax ", " tax ", " taxable supply " and " the Commissioners " have the same meanings as in Part I of the Finance Act 1972.

(3) In this Order " printed matter " includes printed stationery but does not include anything produced by typing, duplicating or photocopying.

3.—(1) Where a person, in the course of a business carried on by him, produces printed matter and the printed matter—

(a) is not supplied to another person or incorporated in other goods produced in the course of that business; but

(b) is used by him for the purpose of a business carried on by him;
then, subject to paragraph (2) below, the printed matter shall be treated for the purposes of Part I of the Finance Act 1972 as both supplied to him for the purpose of that business and supplied by him in the course of that business.

(2) Paragraph (1) above does not apply if—

(a) all the supplies made by that person in the United Kingdom in the course of a business carried on by him are taxable supplies or are treated as taxable supplies by virtue of regulations under section 3(3) of the Finance Act 1972; or

(b) the open market value of the supplies falling to be treated as made by and to that person would not exceed £5,000 a year; or

(c) the Commissioners have directed that that paragraph is not to apply and have not withdrawn the direction;
but the Commissioners shall not so direct unless they are satisfied that the tax (if any) that would be attributable to the supplies, after allowing for any deduction of input tax, would be negligible.

(a) 1972 c. 41.   (b) 1889 c. 63.

(3) For the purposes of this Article the open market value of the supplies shall be determined as for the purposes of Part I of the Finance Act 1972, except that no allowance shall be made for tax.

(4) The preceding provisions of this Article shall apply in relation to any bodies corporate which are treated for the purposes of section 21 of the Finance Act 1972 as members of a group as if those bodies were one person, but any printed matter which would fall to be treated as supplied to and by that person shall be treated as supplied to and by the representative member.

Tim Fortescue,

Hugh Rossi,

Two of the Lords Commissioners
of Her Majesty's Treasury.

1st August 1972.

EXPLANATORY NOTE

(This Note is not part of the Order)

This Order brings within the tax certain self-supplies of stationery and other printed matter produced by an exempt or partly-exempt person for his own use, thus preventing possible distortion of competition.

STATUTORY INSTRUMENTS

1972 No. 1170

VALUE ADDED TAX

The Value Added Tax (Treatment of Transactions) (No. 1) Order 1972

Made - - -	*1st August* 1972
Laid before the House of Commons	*9th August* 1972
Coming into Operation	*1st April* 1973

The Treasury, in exercise of the powers conferred on them by section 5(7)(*c*) of the Finance Act 1972(**a**), hereby make the following Order: —

1. This Order may be cited as the Value Added Tax (Treatment of Transactions) (No. 1) Order 1972 and shall come into operation on 1st April 1973.

2. The Interpretation Act 1889(**b**) shall apply for the interpretation of this Order as it applies for the interpretation of an Act of Parliament.

3. The following description of transaction shall be treated as neither a supply of goods nor a supply of services—

a gratuitous loan of goods by a taxable person in the normal course of and for the purpose of a business carried on by him.

> *Tim Fortescue,*
> *Hugh Rossi,*
> Two of the Lords Commissioners
> of Her Majesty's Treasury.

1st August 1972.

EXPLANATORY NOTE
(*This Note is not part of the Order.*)

This Order removes from the scope of the value added tax any free loan of goods which is made by a taxable person in the ordinary course of a business carried on by him and for the purpose of that business. Any such loan would otherwise be a supply of goods by virtue of section 5(2) of the Finance Act 1972 and would be chargeable with tax unless the supply was zero-rated or exempt.

(**a**) 1972 c. 41.　　　　　　(**b**) 1889 c. 63.

STATUTORY INSTRUMENTS

1972 No. 1171

SEA FISHERIES

The White Fish (Inshore Vessels) and Herring Subsidies (United Kingdom) Scheme 1972

Made - - -	*6th July* 1972
Laid before Parliament	*12th July* 1972
Coming into Operation	*1st August* 1972

The Minister of Agriculture, Fisheries and Food, and the Secretaries of State for Scotland and Wales (being the Secretaries of State respectively concerned with the sea fishing industry in Scotland and Wales) in exercise of the powers conferred upon them by section 49 of the Sea Fish Industry Act 1970(a) and of all other powers enabling them in that behalf, with the approval of the Treasury, hereby make the following scheme:—

Citation, extent, commencement and interpretation

1.—(1) This scheme, which may be cited as the White Fish (Inshore Vessels) and Herring Subsidies (United Kingdom) Scheme 1972, shall apply to the United Kingdom and shall come into operation on 1st August 1972.

(2) In this scheme, unless the context otherwise requires—

"the appropriate Minister"—

(*a*) in relation to England and Northern Ireland, means the Minister of Agriculture, Fisheries and Food;

(*b*) in relation to Scotland, means the Secretary of State concerned with the sea fishing industry in Scotland;

(*c*) in relation to Wales, means—

(i) for the purpose of the actual making of any payment under this scheme, the Minister of Agriculture, Fisheries and Food, and

(ii) for all the other purposes of this scheme, the said Minister and the Secretary of State concerned with the sea fishing industry in Wales acting jointly;

"approved" means approved by the appropriate Minister;

"gross proceeds" in relation to a voyage means the proceeds from the first hand sale of all fish (including white fish, herring, salmon, migratory trout and shellfish) taken by the vessel on that voyage together with any other proceeds which the appropriate Minister may consider as referable to the voyage less such deductions as may be determined by the appropriate Minister in respect of the part of such proceeds which forms the perquisite of the crew of the vessel on that voyage;

(a) 1970 c. 11.

"herring stonage payment" means any grant payable in accordance with the provisions of paragraph 3(1)(c);

"herring voyage payment" means any grant payable in accordance with the provisions of paragraph 3(1)(d);

"length" in relation to a vessel, means the length in relation to which its tonnage was calculated for the purposes of registration under Part IV of the Merchant Shipping Act 1894(**a**);

"month" means a calendar month;

"paragraph" means a paragraph of this scheme;

"vessel" means a vessel registered in the United Kingdom as a fishing vessel;

"white fish" means fish of any kind found in the sea, except herring, salmon, migratory trout and shellfish;

"white fish stonage payment" means any grant payable in accordance with the provisions of paragraph 3(1)(a);

"white fish voyage payment" means any grant payable in accordance with the provisions of paragraph 3(1)(b).

(3) For the purpose of this scheme the trans-shipment of white fish or herring in a port in the United Kingdom or within the exclusive fishery limits of the British Islands other than the waters within the fishery limits of the British Islands which are adjacent to the Isle of Man or any of the Channel Islands shall be treated as the landing of white fish or herring in the United Kingdom.

(4) The Interpretation Act 1889(**b**) shall apply for the interpretation of this scheme as it applies for the interpretation of an Act of Parliament and as if this scheme and the schemes hereby revoked were Acts of Parliament.

Revocation of previous scheme

2. The White Fish and Herring Subsidies (United Kingdom) Scheme 1969(**c**) is hereby revoked.

General conditions of grant

3.—(1) A grant may be paid in accordance with the following provisions of this scheme to the owner (or his agent) or, where there is a charter-party, to the charterer (or his agent), of a vessel, in respect of—

(a) white fish landed from the vessel in the United Kingdom during the period beginning with 1st August 1972 and ending with 31st July 1973;

(b) a voyage made by the vessel during the period last hereinbefore referred to for the purpose of catching white fish and landing them in the United Kingdom;

(c) herring landed from the vessel in the United Kingdom during the period beginning with 1st August 1972 and ending with 31st July 1973; or

(d) a voyage made by the vessel during the period last hereinbefore referred to for the purpose of catching herring and landing them in the United Kingdom:

Provided that no grant shall be payable by virtue of this sub-paragraph in any case where the white fish or herring are landed in the Isle of Man or Channel Islands.

(a) 1894 c. 60.   (b) 1889 c. 63.
(c) S.I. 1969/1015 (1969 II, p. 2956).

(2) Whether or not a grant is payable by virtue of sub-paragraph (1) of this paragraph, a grant may be paid as aforesaid in respect of herring landed from the vessel in the United Kingdom during the period beginning with 1st August 1972 and ending with 31st July 1973 and sold for conversion into oil, meal or other approved product, if the appropriate Minister is satisfied that the said herring could not have been sold for purposes other than such conversion:

Provided that no grant shall be payable by virtue of this sub-paragraph in respect of—

(i) herring landed at any port not specified in Part I of Schedule 1 to this scheme;

(ii) more than 20% of the total landings of herring in any month at any port specified as aforesaid or, where such port is comprised in any group of ports specified in Part II of the said Schedule, at any such group of ports, as the case may be.

4. The owner or charterer of a vessel (or his duly authorised agent) who applies for payment of a grant under this scheme or any person acting on behalf of such owner or charterer and appointed by him for the purpose shall, within such time in such form and for such period as may be specified by the appropriate Minister, supply such information and make such returns concerning fishing operations, costs and trading results as may be required by the appropriate Minister, including detailed accounts of the financial results of the operation of all vessels to which this scheme applies owned or chartered by such owner or charterer, and shall when required at any time during the period comprising the remainder of the calendar year current when an application for grant is made in respect of any such vessel and the two years immediately following that year, make any relevant books and records open to examination by any person authorised by the appropriate Minister.

5. Application for payment of a grant under this scheme shall be made by the owner or charterer (or his duly authorised agent) in such form as the appropriate Minister may from time to time require and shall be completed and certified in all respects as so required and shall be delivered to the appropriate Minister at such address as he may specify for the purpose.

6. Application for payment of a grant under this scheme shall be made not later than one month after the landing of the white fish or herring or the completion of the voyage, as the case may be, or such longer period as the appropriate Minister may allow.

7. Notice that a person is authorised to make application for and receive payment of grants under this scheme on behalf of an owner or charterer shall be given in writing signed by the owner or charterer in such form as the appropriate Minister may from time to time require and shall be sent to the address specified by the appropriate Minister for the purpose of paragraph 5:

Provided that not more than one person shall be authorised as aforesaid at any time at a port in respect of grants payable under either paragraph 3(1) or paragraph 3(2) in relation to a vessel.

8. Without prejudice to the discretion of the appropriate Minister in the payment of grants under this scheme—

(*a*) if any owner or charterer or any person acting on his behalf makes a statement or produces a document which is false in a material particular or fails, without reasonable cause, or refuses to supply any information, make any return or produce any document in respect of any of the matters required to be disclosed either in connection with an application for payment of grant under this scheme or in accordance with the provisions of paragraph 4; or

(b) if any of the conditions of grant or conditions relating to the payment of grants under this scheme are not complied with by any owner or charterer or any person acting on behalf of an owner or charterer,

payment of grants to that owner, charterer or person at any time may be refused.

9.—(1) For the purpose of determining the grant, if any, which may be paid under this scheme in the case of two or more vessels jointly operating the same gear, the weight of white fish or herring landed from the combined voyage, the proceeds from the sale of such white fish or herring and the gross proceeds of such voyage shall be deemed to be divided equally between the vessels concerned whether they are of the same length or of different lengths, and the grant, if any, shall be calculated separately for each vessel in accordance with the provisions of this scheme.

(2) Notwithstanding the provisions of paragraphs 10, 13 and 14 any grant under this scheme shall be paid, if at any time after 1st September 1963 any structural alteration shall have been made to any vessel which has increased or decreased its length, at the rate appropriate to the length of the vessel before such alteration unless in any such case the appropriate Minister is satisfied that the alteration was likely to be conducive to the increased fishing efficiency of the vessel.

Conditions relating to payments for voyages

10. Subject to the provisions of this scheme—

(a) a white fish voyage payment may be made in respect of each voyage made by a vessel falling within one of the categories specified in Part I of Schedule 2 to this scheme;

(b) a herring voyage payment may be made in respect of each voyage made by a vessel falling within one of the categories specified in Part II of Schedule 2 to this scheme,

such payment being, in each case, an amount equal to the appropriate rate of grant per day at sea set out in Part I, or as the case may be Part II, of Schedule 2 to this scheme multiplied by such number of days as the appropriate Minister is satisfied are to be taken into account for the purposes of this scheme as days at sea on that voyage.

11.—(1) Subject to sub-paragraph (2) of this paragraph, and without prejudice to the generality of the provisions of paragraph 10, in computing for the purposes of that paragraph the length of a voyage—

(a) the day of departure and the day of arrival of the vessel may each be reckoned as one day at sea so however that if the day of arrival is also the day of departure upon a subsequent voyage whether made for the catching and landing in the United Kingdom of white fish or of herring, then that day shall not be reckoned with the subsequent voyage;

(b) each period of 24 hours which is spent during a voyage in any port shall be excluded.

(2) Where reference is made in this scheme to a voyage made during a specified period the reference shall be construed, in the case of a voyage only part of which is made during that period, as a reference to that part.

12.—(1) In a case where, in respect of a voyage, both a white fish voyage payment and a herring voyage payment might otherwise have been made only one such payment shall be made, being, in a case where the proceeds from the sale of the white fish exceed the proceeds from the sale of the herring, a white fish voyage payment, and in a case where the proceeds from the sale of the herring exceed the proceeds from the sale of the white fish, a herring voyage payment.

(2) No white fish voyage payment or herring voyage payment shall be made if the proceeds from the sale of white fish and herring landed in consequence of the voyage, taken together, amount to less than half the gross proceeds of the voyage.

(3) Where by virtue of the last preceding sub-paragraph neither a white fish voyage payment nor a herring voyage payment may be made, a claim may be made for a white fish stonage payment or for a herring stonage payment or for both in respect of white fish or herring landed in consequence of the voyage, notwithstanding that the vessel falls within one of the categories specified in Part I or Part II of Schedule 2 to this scheme:

Provided that a payment made in pursuance of this sub-paragraph shall in no case exceed the payment which would have been made but for the operation of the last preceding sub-paragraph.

(4) In this paragraph "proceeds", in relation to the sale of white fish, or, as the case may be herring, means the total proceeds from the first-hand sale thereof.

Conditions relating to payments for white fish and herring landed

13.—(1) Subject to the provisions of this scheme a white fish stonage payment may be made in the case of a vessel under 60 feet in length, not being a vessel falling within Category A of Part I of Schedule 2 to this scheme, in respect of white fish landed and sold at first-hand otherwise than by retail, at the appropriate rate set out in Part I of Schedule 3 to this scheme.

(2) No white fish stonage payment shall be made—

(*a*) in respect of fish (other than filleted fish, wings of ray and skate, skinned dogfish and monkfish tails) landed without heads or tails or from which any portion of the head or tail has been removed; or

(*b*) in respect of fish which is determined by the appropriate Minister to form part of the perquisite of the crew of the vessel from which the fish were landed; or

(*c*) in respect of white fish which are subject to the prohibitions contained in section 1(1) of the Sea Fish (Conservation) Act 1967(**a**).

14.—(1) Subject to the provisions of this scheme a herring stonage payment may be made, in the case of a vessel under 40 feet in length, not being a vessel falling within Category C of Part II of Schedule 2 to this scheme, in respect of herring landed, at the rate set out in Part II of Schedule 3 to this scheme;

(**a**) 1967 c. 84.

(2) Subject to the provisions of this scheme a grant may be paid at the rate set out in Part III of Schedule 3 to this scheme in respect of herring landed from a vessel and sold for conversion into oil, meal or other approved product.

15.—(1) For the purpose of computing the amount of a white fish stonage payment or a herring stonage payment which may be made under paragraphs 13(1) and 14(1) of this scheme the weight of the white fish or herring, as the case may be, shall be the weight determined at the time of the first-hand sale.

(2) No white fish stonage payment shall be made in consequence of a voyage where a claim for a herring voyage payment is made in respect of the same voyage and no herring stonage payment shall be made in consequence of a voyage where a claim for a white fish voyage payment is made in respect of the same voyage.

(3) No white fish stonage payment shall be made in respect of white fish landed from a vessel where the voyage on which the fish was caught commences and terminates on one day, that day being also the day of arrival of the vessel from a voyage, or the day of the departure of the vessel upon a voyage, in respect of which a claim for a herring voyage payment is made.

In Witness whereof the official seal of the Minister of Agriculture, Fisheries and Food is hereunto affixed on 5th July 1972.

(L.S.)

James Prior,
Minister of Agriculture,
Fisheries and Food.

5th July 1972.

Gordon Campbell,
Secretary of State for Scotland.

5th July 1972.

Peter Thomas,
Secretary of State for Wales.

Approved on 6th July 1972.

Tim Fortescue,
P. L. Hawkins,
Two of the Lords Commissioners of
Her Majesty's Treasury.

Paragraph 3

SCHEDULE 1

PART I

Ports

Aberdeen	Girvan	Oban
Annalong	Gourock	Peterhead
Anstruther	Greenock	Portavogie
Arbroath	Grimsby	Portpatrick
Ardglass	Hartlepool	Scalloway
Ayr	Inverness	Scarborough
Berwick on Tweed	Kilkeel	Seahouses
Bridlington	Kyle of Lochalsh	Stornoway
Buckie	Leith	Tarbert (Harris)
Eyemouth	Lerwick	Tarbert (Loch Fyne)
Fleetwood	Lowestoft	Ullapool
Fort William	Mallaig	Warrenpoint
Fraserburgh	Milford Haven	Whitby
Gairloch	Newhaven	Whitehaven
	North Shields	Yarmouth

PART II

Groups of Ports

1

Aberdeen
Fraserburgh
Peterhead

5

Berwick on Tweed
Hartlepool
North Shields
Seahouses

9

Kyle of Lochalsh
Mallaig
Oban

2

Anstruther
Arbroath
Eyemouth
Leith
Newhaven

6

Bridlington
Scarborough
Whitby

10

Lerwick
Scalloway

3

Annalong
Ardglass
Kilkeel
Portavogie
Warrenpoint

7

Gairloch
Stornoway
Tarbert (Harris)
Ullapool

11

Lowestoft
Yarmouth

4

Ayr
Girvan
Gourock
Greenock
Tarbert (Loch Fyne)

8

Fleetwood
Whitehaven

Paragraph 10

SCHEDULE 2

PART I

CATEGORIES OF VESSELS AND RATES OF GRANT IN RESPECT OF VOYAGES FOR THE CATCHING AND LANDING OF WHITE FISH

Category A

Vessels of 35 feet in length or over but under 60 feet in length, provided, in relation to any such vessel registered in the United Kingdom as a fishing vessel before 1st January 1972 that the appropriate Minister is satisfied that the total of any grants payable in respect of:—

(*a*) white fish or herring landed from the vessel (not being grants in respect of herring landed and sold for conversion into oil, meal or other approved product), or

(*b*) voyages made by the vessel for the catching and landing of white fish or herring

amounted, or would but for special circumstances beyond the control of the owner or charterer have amounted, in the year 1971 to at least £250.

		Rate of grant per day at sea £p
Vessels of 35 feet in length or over but under 40 feet in length	...	3.10
Vessels of 40 feet in length or over but under 45 feet in length	...	3.30
Vessels of 45 feet in length or over but under 55 feet in length	...	3.70
Vessels of 55 feet in length or over but under 60 feet in length	...	4.00

Category B

Vessels of 60 feet in length or over but under 80 feet in length.

		Rate of grant per day at sea £p
Vessels of 60 feet in length or over but under 65 feet in length	...	4.00
Vessels of 65 feet in length or over but under 80 feet in length	...	4.60

PART II

CATEGORIES OF VESSELS AND RATES OF GRANT IN RESPECT OF VOYAGES FOR THE CATCHING AND LANDING OF HERRING

Category C

Vessels of 35 feet in length or over but under 40 feet in length, provided, in relation to any such vessel registered in the United Kingdom as a fishing vessel before 1st January 1972, that the appropriate Minister is satisfied that the total of any grants payable in respect of:—

(*a*) white fish or herring landed from the vessel (not being grants in respect of herring landed and sold for conversion into oil, meal or other approved product), or

(*b*) voyages made by the vessel for the catching and landing of white fish or herring

amounted, or would but for special circumstances beyond the control of the owner or charterer have amounted, in the year 1971 to at least £250.

	Rate of grant per day at sea £p
Vessels of 35 feet in length or over but under 40 feet in length ...	2.80

Category D

Vessels of 40 feet in length or over.

	Rate of grant per day at sea £p
Vessels of 40 feet in length or over but under 60 feet in length ...	3.70
Vessels of 60 feet in length or over but under 80 feet in length ...	4.20
Vessels of 80 feet in length or over	5.20

Paragraph 13

SCHEDULE 3

PART I

RATES OF GRANT IN RESPECT OF WHITE FISH LANDED

Kind of Fish

	Rate of grant per stone p
All whole gutted white fish and filleted white fish of a kind normally sold for human consumption (including roes and chitlings), wings of ray and skate, skinned dogfish and monkfish tails	4
Ungutted bass, dogfish, eels, mackerel, mullet (red and grey) and pilchards	4
All other whole ungutted white fish, if the appropriate Minister is satisfied that such fish has been sold for human consumption ...	3
All other whole white fish...	1

Paragraph 14

PART II

RATE OF GRANT IN RESPECT OF HERRING LANDED

	Rate of grant per stone p
Herring landed	1.2

Paragraph 14

PART III

RATE OF GRANT IN RESPECT OF HERRING LANDED AND SOLD FOR CONVERSION INTO OIL, MEAL OR OTHER APPROVED PRODUCT

	Rate of grant per cran £p
Herring landed from vessels and sold for conversion into oil, meal or other approved product	90

EXPLANATORY NOTE

(This Note is not part of the Scheme.)

The Sea Fish Industry Act 1970 (c. 11) provides that schemes may be made for the payment of grants to the owners or charterers of fishing vessels engaged in catching and landing of white fish and herring.

This scheme provides for the payment of grants in respect of the catching and landing of white fish by vessels under 80 feet and of catching and landing of herring, such grants being calculated by reference either to voyages made by vessels or to fish landed from them. The period in respect of which grants are payable is from the 1st August 1972 to the 31st July 1973.

This scheme succeeds the White Fish (Inshore Vessels) and Herring Subsidies (United Kingdom) Scheme 1971 (S.I. 1971/1295).

1972 No. 1173

ANIMALS

DISEASES OF ANIMALS

The Brucellosis (Area Eradication) (England and Wales) (Amendment) Order 1972

Made - - -	*3rd August* 1972
Coming into Operation	*24th August* 1972

The Minister of Agriculture, Fisheries and Food, in pursuance of the powers conferred on him by sections 1, 5 and 85(1) of the Diseases of Animals Act 1950(a), as read with the Diseases of Animals (Extension of Definitions) Order 1971(b), and, as respects section 5 of the Diseases of Animals Act 1950, as extended by section 106(3) of the Agriculture Act 1970(c), and of all his other enabling powers, hereby makes the following order:—

Citation and commencement

1. This order, which may be cited as the Brucellosis (Area Eradication) (England and Wales) (Amendment) Order 1972, shall come into operation on 24th August 1972.

Interpretation

2.—(1) In this order, "the principal order" means the Brucellosis (Area Eradication) (England and Wales) Order 1971(d).

(2) Unless the context otherwise requires, expressions used in this order have the same meanings as in the principal order.

(3) The Interpretation Act 1889(e) applies to the interpretation of this order as it applies to the interpretation of an Act of Parliament.

Amendment of principal order

3.—(1) After sub-paragraph (b) of paragraph (2) of Article 4 of the principal order (movement of cattle into or through Eradication Areas or Attested Areas) there shall be inserted:—

"or

(c) the movement of cattle (otherwise than on foot) which have not been certified by a veterinary inspector or other officer of the Ministry as

---

(a) 1950 c. 36. For change of title of the Minister see S.I. 1955/554 (1955 I, p. 1200).
(b) S.I. 1971/531 (1971 I, p. 1530).   (c) 1970 c. 40.
(d) S.I. 1971/1717 (1971 III, p. 4673).   (e) 1889 c. 63.

having reacted to a diagnostic test for brucellosis into an Eradication Area from a place outside that Area direct to any premises used in connection with the holding of a market, being premises in respect of which the licence issued under Article 15 of this order, and for the time being in force, permits the use thereof for the purpose of selling cattle intended for immediate slaughter, or

(*d*) the movement of cattle under six months of age (otherwise than on foot) into an Eradication Area from a place outside that Area direct to any premises used in connection with the holding of a market in respect of which a licence has been issued under Article 15 of this order,".

(2) In subparagraph (*a*) of the proviso to paragraph (1) of Article 5 of the principal order (movement of cattle within an Eradication Area or Attested Area) there shall be substituted for the words "subparagraph (*b*)" the words "subparagraphs (*b*) to (*d*)".

In Witness whereof the Official Seal of the Minister of Agriculture, Fisheries and Food is hereunto affixed on 3rd August 1972.

(L.S.)

J. M. L. Prior,
Minister of Agriculture, Fisheries and Food.

EXPLANATORY NOTE

(This Note is not part of the Order.)

The Brucellosis (Area Eradication) (England and Wales) Order 1971 sets out the various controls to be applied to cattle in areas designated by the Minister of Agriculture, Fisheries and Food as Eradication or Attested Areas for purposes connected with the eradication of brucellosis. Article 4 of the order imposes a general prohibition on the movement of cattle into or through an Eradication or Attested Area and Article 5 of the order imposes a general prohibition on the movement of cattle within such areas, otherwise, in both cases, than in accordance with the terms of a licence issued by an officer of the Minister subject to certain exceptions which are specified in paragraph (2) of Article 4 and paragraph (1) of Article 5. The present order amends Articles 4(2) and 5(1) of the 1971 order by adding two further categories of cattle to those which are exempted from the licensing provisions of those Articles.

The first group consists of cattle which have not reacted to a diagnostic test for brucellosis, and which are being taken direct to a market, or a section of a market, in an Eradication Area which has been licensed by the Ministry for the sale of cattle intended for slaughter. The second group comprises cattle under the age of six months which are being taken direct to a market in an Eradication Area.

STATUTORY INSTRUMENTS

1972 No. 1174

ANIMALS

DISEASES OF ANIMALS

The Brucellosis (Area Eradication) (England and Wales) (Extension) Order 1972

Made - - -	*3rd August* 1972
Coming into Operation	*24th August* 1972

The Minister of Agriculture, Fisheries and Food, in exercise of the powers conferred on him by section 5 of the Diseases of Animals Act 1950(a), as extended by section 106(3) of the Agriculture Act 1970(b), and of all his other enabling powers, hereby makes the following order:—

Citation and commencement

1. This order, which may be cited as the Brucellosis (Area Eradication) (England and Wales) (Extension) Order 1972, shall come into operation on 24th August 1972.

Interpretation

2.—(1) Unless the context otherwise requires, expressions used in this order have the same meanings as in the Brucellosis (Area Eradication) (England and Wales) Order 1971(c), as amended(d).

(2) The Interpretation Act 1889(e) applies to the interpretation of this order as it applies to the interpretation of an Act of Parliament.

Application of Area Eradication Order to additional Eradication Areas

3. The provisions of the Brucellosis (Area Eradication) (England and Wales) Order 1971, as amended, shall apply to, and have effect in,—

(*a*) the Area designated in the Schedule to the Brucellosis (Eradication Areas) (England and Wales) Order 1971(f) as the Wales No. 2 Eradication Area, as from 1st January 1973, and

(*b*) the Area designated in the said Schedule as the North-West England No. 2 Eradication Area, as from 1st November 1973.

In Witness whereof the Official Seal of the Minister of Agriculture, Fisheries and Food is hereunto affixed on 3rd August 1972.

(L.S.)   *J. M. L. Prior*,
Minister of Agriculture, Fisheries and Food.

(a) 1950 c. 36.
(b) 1970 c. 40.
(c) S.I. 1971/1717 (1971 III, p. 4673).
(d) S.I. 1972/1173 (1972 II, p. 3486).
(e) 1889 c. 63.
(f) S.I. 1971/533.

EXPLANATORY NOTE

(This Note is not part of the Order.)

Under the Brucellosis (Eradication Areas) (England and Wales) Order 1971, certain areas of England and Wales were designated by the Minister of Agriculture, Fisheries and Food as Eradication Areas for purposes connected with the eradication of brucellosis.

The present order applies to two of those Areas (namely, those designated in the Schedule to the 1971 order as the Wales No. 2 and the North-West England No. 2 Eradication Areas) the provisions of the Brucellosis (Area Eradication) (England and Wales) Order 1971, as amended. Those provisions will take effect in the Wales No. 2 Area on 1st January 1973, and in the North-West England No. 2 Area on 1st November 1973.

STATUTORY INSTRUMENTS

1972 No. 1176 (C.26)

SOCIAL SECURITY

The National Insurance (Amendment) Act 1972 Commencement Order 1972

Made - - - *3rd August* 1972

The Secretary of State for Social Services, in exercise of powers conferred by section 3(2) of the National Insurance (Amendment) Act 1972(a), hereby makes the following Order:—

Citation

1. This Order may be cited as the National Insurance (Amendment) Act 1972 Commencement Order 1972.

Appointed day

2. The day appointed for the coming into force of the National Insurance (Amendment) Act 1972(a), as it applies to Great Britain, shall be 2nd October 1972.

Keith Joseph,
Secretary of State for Social Services.

3rd August 1972.

(a) 1972 c. 36.

STATUTORY INSTRUMENTS

1972 No. 1177

PENSIONS

The Personal Injuries (Civilians) (Amendment) Scheme 1972

Made - - -	*2nd August* 1972
Laid before Parliament	*15th August* 1972
Coming into Operation	*2nd October* 1972

The Secretary of State for Social Services, with the consent of the Treasury, in exercise of the powers conferred upon him by section 2 of the Personal Injuries (Emergency Provisions) Act 1939(a), and of all other powers enabling him in that behalf, hereby makes the following Scheme:—

Citation, interpretation and commencement

1. This Scheme, which may be cited as the Personal Injuries (Civilians) (Amendment) Scheme 1972, amends the Personal Injuries (Civilians) Scheme 1964(b), as amended (c), (hereinafter referred to as "the principal Scheme"), and shall come into operation on 2nd October 1972 so, however, that in relation to any award payable weekly the foregoing reference to 2nd October 1972, where this is not the normal weekly pay day for that award, shall be construed as a reference to the first normal weekly pay day for that award following 2nd October 1972.

Higher rates of pensions and allowances under the principal Scheme

2. For Schedules 3 and 4 to the principal Scheme (rates of pensions and allowances payable in respect of disablement or death) there shall be substituted the Schedules set out in Part I of the Schedule hereto and numbered 3 and 4 respectively.

Amendment of Articles of the principal Scheme

3. In Articles 17 (unemployability allowances), 21 (treatment allowances) and 28 (rent allowance to widows who have children) of the principal Scheme there shall be made the amendments set out in Part II of the Schedule hereto.

(a) 2 & 3 Geo. 6. c. 82.　　　　(b) S.I. 1964/2077 (1964 III, p. 5187).
(c) The relevant amending Schemes are S.I. 1966/163, 648, 1967/1250, 1968/1206, 1969/1035, 1971/1178 (1966 I, p. 299; II, p. 1454; 1967 II, p. 3617; 1968 II, p. 3228; 1969 II, p. 3055; 1971 II, p. 3468).

Revocation of Article 25 of the principal Scheme

4. Article 25 of the principal Scheme (general condition applicable to awards under Part IV) is hereby revoked.

Substitution of Article 63 of the principal Scheme

5. For Article 63 of the principal Scheme (pensioners admitted to institutions) there shall be substituted the Article set out in Part III of the Schedule hereto.

Keith Joseph,
Secretary of State for Social Services.

31st July 1972.

We consent.

P. L. Hawkins,
Oscar Murton,
Two of the Lords Commissioners of
Her Majesty's Treasury.

2nd August 1972.

SCHEDULE

PART I

Schedules to be substituted in the principal Scheme by Article 2 of this Scheme

SCHEDULE 3

RATES OF PENSIONS AND ALLOWANCES PAYABLE IN RESPECT OF DISABLEMENT

Description of Pension or Allowance	*Rate*
1. Pension for 100 per cent disablement under Article 11.	£11·20 per week
2. Education allowance under Article 13.	£120·00 per annum (maximum)
3. Constant attendance allowance—	
(*a*) under the proviso to Article 14	£9·00 per week (maximum)
(*b*) in any other case under that Article	£4·50 per week (maximum)
3A. Exceptionally severe disablement allowance under Article 14A.	£4·50 per week
4. Severe disablement occupational allowance under Article 15.	£2·00 per week
5. Allowance for wear and tear of clothing—	
(*a*) under Article 16(1)(*a*)	£12·00 per annum
(*b*) under Article 16(1)(*b*) and 16(2)	£19·00 per annum
6. Unemployability allowances—	
(*a*) personal allowance under Article 17(1)(*i*)	£7·35 per week
(*b*) additional allowances for dependants by way of—	
(i) increase or further increase of allowance in respect of a wife or dependent husband under Article 17(4)(*c*)	£3·65 per week (maximum)
(ii) allowance in respect of an adult dependant under Article 17(4)(*d*)	£4·15 per week (maximum)
(iii) increased allowance under Article 17(4)(*f*)—	
(*a*) in respect of the child, or the elder or eldest of the children, of a disabled person	£3·30 per week
(*b*) in respect of the second child of a disabled person	£2·40 per week
(*c*) in respect of each other child of a disabled person	£2·30 per week

2j

Description of Pension or Allowance	*Rate*

6A. Invalidity allowance payable under Article 17A—

    (*a*) if on the relevant date the disabled person was under the age of 35 or if that date fell before 5th July 1948 — £1·15 per week

    (*b*) if head (*a*) does not apply and on the relevant date the disabled person was under the age of 45 — £0·70 per week

    (*c*) if heads (*a*) and (*b*) do not apply and on the relevant date the disabled person was a man under the age of 60, or a woman under the age of 55 — £0·35 per week

7. Comforts allowance—

    (*a*) under Article 18(1)(*a*) — £1·70 per week

    (*b*) under Article 18(1)(*b*) or 44(1) — £0·85 per week

8. Allowance for lowered standard of occupation under Article 19 — £4·48 per week (maximum)

9. Age allowance under Article 20 where the degree of pensioned disablement is—

    (*a*) 40 or 50 per cent — £0·55 per week

    (*b*) 60 or 70 per cent — £0·80 per week

    (*c*) 80 or 90 per cent — £1·15 per week

    (*d*) 100 per cent — £1·60 per week

10. Treatment allowances—

    (*a*) increase of personal allowance under Article 21(2) — £1·60 per week (maximum)

    (*b*) increase of personal allowance under Article 21(3)—

        (i) under sub-paragraph (*a*) — £6·75 per week

        (ii) under sub-paragraph (*c*)—

            (*a*) if on the relevant date the disabled person was under the age of 35 or if that date fell before 5th July 1948 — £1·15 per week

            (*b*) if head (*a*) does not apply and on the relevant date the disabled person was under the age of 45 — £0·70 per week

            (*c*) if heads (*a*) and (*b*) do not apply and on the relevant date the disabled person was a man under the age of 60, or a woman under the age of 55 — £0·35 per week

    (*c*) increased additional allowance under Article 21(4) proviso (*a*) — £4·15 per week

    (*d*) increased additional allowance under Article 21 (4) proviso (*b*)—

        (i) in respect of the child, or the elder or eldest of the children, of a disabled person — £2·10 per week

Description of Pension or Allowance	Rate
(ii) in respect of the second child of a disabled person	£1·20 per week
(iii) in respect of each other child of a disabled person	£1·10 per week
(e) higher rate of additional allowance under Article 21(4A)—	
(i) in respect of the child, or the elder or eldest of the children, of a disabled person	£3·30 per week
(ii) in respect of the second child of a disabled person	£2·40 per week
(iii) in respect of each other child of a disabled person	£2·30 per week
(f) additional allowance under Article 21(5)	£4·15 per week
11. Part-time treatment allowance under Article 23	£4·75 a day (maximum)

SCHEDULE 4

RATES OF PENSIONS AND ALLOWANCES PAYABLE IN RESPECT OF DEATH

Description of Pension or Allowance	Rate
1. Pension to widow—	
(a) under Article 26(1)(a)	£8·80 per week
(b) under Article 26(1)(b)	£2·03 per week
2. Rent allowance under Article 28	£3·40 per week (maximum)
3. Allowance under Article 29 or 49 to an elderly widow—	
(a) if age 65 but under age 70	£0·50 per week
(b) if age 70 or over	£1·00 per week
4. Pension under Article 30 to unmarried dependant who lived as wife	£1·00 per week (maximum)
5. Pension to dependent widower under Article 32	£8·80 per week (maximum)
6. Allowances under Article 33 in respect of children under the age of 15—	
(a) in respect of the child, or the elder or eldest of the children, of a deceased person	£3·50 per week
(b) in respect of each other child of a deceased person—	
(i) where the child qualifies for a family allowance under the Family Allowances Act 1965 or under any legislation in Northern Ireland or the Isle of Man corresponding to that Act	£3·00 per week
(ii) where the child does not so qualify	£3·35 per week

Description of Pension or Allowance	*Rate*
7. Pensions under Article 34(1) to motherless or fatherless children under the age of 15—	
(*a*) in respect of the child, or the elder or eldest of the children, of a deceased person, and in respect of each other child of a deceased person who does not qualify for a family allowance as aforesaid	£3·50 per week
(*b*) in respect of each other child of a deceased person who qualifies for a family allowance as aforesaid	£3·00 per week
8. Pension or allowance under Article 35(3) to or in respect of a child over the age of 15—	
(*a*) where the child has attained the age of 18 and is incapable of self-support by reason of an infirmity which arose before he attained the age of 15	£6·75 per week (maximum)
(*b*) any other case	£5·00 per week (maximum)
9. Education allowance under Article 36	£120·00 per annum (maximum)
10. Pensions to parents—	
(*a*) minimum rate under Article 38(4)	£0·25 per week
(*b*) maximum rate under Article 38(4)—	
(i) where there is only one eligible parent	£1·00 per week
(ii) where there is more than one eligible parent	£1·38 per week
(*c*) increase under the proviso to Article 38(4)	(i) where there is only one eligible parent—£0·38 per week (maximum)
	(ii) where there is more than one eligible parent—£0·62 per week (maximum)
11. Pensions to other dependants—	
(*a*) for each juvenile dependant under Article 39(4)	£0·30 per week (maximum)
(*b*) aggregate rate under Article 39(4)	£1·00 per week (maximum)
(*c*) under Article 39(5)	£1·00 per week (maximum)
12. Funeral grant under Article 40(1)	£30·00 (maximum)

Part II

Amendment of Articles of the principal Scheme

1. In Article 17 (unemployability allowances) in paragraph (2) for the words "£104 a year" there shall be substituted the words "£234 a year".

2. In Article 21 (treatment allowances) for paragraph (4A) there shall be substituted the following paragraph:—

"(4A) The rate of an additional allowance awarded under paragraph (4) of this Article in respect of a child or children of a disabled person may be further increased to the appropriate rate specified in Schedule 3 paragraph 10(*e*) if the disabled person—

(*a*) is in receipt of an increase of his personal allowance under paragraph (3)(*c*) of this Article or, but for his age on the relevant date, would be in receipt of such an increase; or

(*b*) is in receipt of an allowance under Article 17(1)(*i*); or

(*c*) having reached the age of 65 years or, in the case of a woman, 60 years is not eligible for retirement pension under the National Insurance Acts 1965 to 1972, or any benefit similar thereto as is referred to in paragraph (6) of this Article, solely by reason of his failure to satisfy any contribution conditions.".

3. In Article 28 (rent allowance to widows who have children) in paragraph (1) for the words "having regard to the amount by which her weekly rent and rates exceed 6s." there shall be substituted the words "having regard to her weekly rent and rates".

PART III

Substitution of Article 63 of the principal Scheme

For Article 63 (pensioners admitted to institutions) there shall be substituted the following Article:—

"63. *Maintenance in hospital or an institution.*—(1) Where any person to or in respect of whom a pension or gratuity may be or has been awarded is receiving or has received free in-patient treatment, or is being or has been maintained in an institution (otherwise than for the purpose of undergoing medical or other treatment) which is supported wholly or partly out of public funds, or in which he is being or has been maintained pursuant to arrangements made by the Secretary of State, the Secretary of State may deduct such amount as he may think fit having regard to all the circumstances of the case from the pension or gratuity payable in respect of the period during which such treatment is received or during which the person is being so maintained, as the case may be, and may apply the amount so deducted, or any part thereof, in such proportions and subject to such conditions as he may determine having regard to all the circumstances of the case, in a payment or payments to the person upon his discharge following a period of free in-patient treatment, or in or towards paying or repaying the cost of maintaining the person incurred by any appropriate authority.

(2) For the purposes of this Article, a person shall be regarded as receiving or having received free in-patient treatment for any period for which he is or has been maintained free of charge while undergoing medical or other treatment as an in-patient—

(*a*) in a hospital or similar institution maintained or administered under the National Health Service Acts 1946 to 1968, the National Health Service (Scotland) Acts 1947 to 1968 or the Health Services Act (Northern Ireland) 1971, or by or on behalf of the Secretary of State, or by or on behalf of the Defence Council; or

(*b*) pursuant to arrangements made by the Secretary of State or by a Hospital Board or a Regional Hospital Board constituted under the National Health Service Acts 1946 to 1968, the National Health Service (Scotland) Acts 1947 to 1968 or the Health Services Act (Northern Ireland) 1971 in a hospital or similar institution not so maintained or administered;

and, for this purpose, a person shall only be regarded as not being maintained free of charge in a hospital or similar institution for any period if he is paying or has paid, in respect of his maintenance, charges which are designed to cover the whole cost of the accommodation or services (other than services by way of treatment) provided for him in the hospital or similar institution for that period."

EXPLANATORY NOTE

(This Note is not part of the Scheme.)

1. This Scheme further amends the Personal Injuries (Civilians) Scheme 1964, which provides for compensation to or in respect of civilians injured or killed in the 1939-45 War.

2. Article 2 makes amendments relating to the rates of pensions or allowances in the principal Scheme which are increased as follows:—

(*a*) the rates of pensions in respect of 100 per cent disablement from £10·00 a week to £11·20 a week with proportionate increases where the degree of disablement is less than 100 per cent;

(*b*) the rates of pensions for certain widows from £7·80 a week to £8·80 a week, and for dependent widowers from a maximum of £7·80 a week to a maximum of £8·80 a week;

(*c*) the normal maximum rate of an allowance payable for constant attendance from £4·00 a week to £4·50 a week and the maximum rate for exceptional cases of very severe disablement from £8·00 a week to £9·00 a week;

(*d*) the exceptionally severe disablement allowance from £4·00 a week to £4·50 a week;

(*e*) the allowance for unemployable pensioners from £6·55 a week to £7·35 a week;

(*f*) the total additional allowance payable in respect of the wife or adult dependant of an unemployable pensioner and of a pensioner receiving treatment as defined in Article 21(8) from £3·70 a week to £4·15 a week;

(*g*) the allowances payable in respect of children of unemployable pensioners in respect of the first or only child from £2·95 a week to £3·30 a week, in respect of the second child from £2·05 a week to £2·40 a week, and in respect of any other child from £1·95 a week to £2·30 a week;

(*h*) the maximum allowance for lowered standard of occupation from £4·00 a week to £4·48 a week;

(*i*) the allowances payable in respect of children of pensioners receiving treatment as defined in Article 21(8) in respect of the first or only child from £1·85 a week to £2·10 a week, in respect of the second child from £0·95 a week to £1·20 a week, and in respect of any other child from £0·85 a week to £1·10 a week;

(*j*) the allowances payable to pensioners who have attained the age of 65 and whose pensioned disablement is assessed at 40 per cent or over from between £0·50 a week and £1·40 a week to between £0·55 a week and £1·60 a week respectively;

(*k*) the maximum of the additional personal treatment allowance payable to a pensioner who is not entitled to full sickness benefit or invalidity pension and allowance under national insurance provisions from £6·00 a week to £6·75 a week;

(*l*) the maximum rent allowance payable to certain widows from £3·00 a week to £3·40 a week;

(*m*) the allowances payable in respect of children in the care of widows in respect of the first or only child from £3·15 a week to £3·50 a week, and in respect of each other child from £2·65 a week to £3·00 a week where the child qualifies for a family allowance, and from £3·00 a week to £3·35 a week where the child does not so qualify;

(*n*) the rates of pensions and allowances payable for motherless or fatherless children in respect of the first or only child or any other child who does not qualify for a family allowance from £3·15 a week or a maximum of £4·65 a week to £3·50 a week or a maximum of £5·00 a week according to the age of the child, and in respect of each other child under the age of 15 who qualifies for a family allowance from £2·65 a week to £3·00 a week;

(*o*) the maximum rates of pensions payable to motherless or fatherless children who, having attained the age of 18 years, are incapable of self-support by reason of infirmity which arose before they became 15 years of age, from £6·00 a week to £6·75 a week.

3. Article 3 makes amendments the effects of which are: —

(*a*) to raise the maximum amount of earnings which may be received by a disabled person while deemed to be unemployable for the purposes of an award of unemployability allowance from £104 a year to £234 a year;

(*b*) to enable the maximum rate of additional allowances payable in respect of the children of a disabled person receiving treatment as defined in Article 21(8) to be awarded in cases where the disabled person would not otherwise qualify for such an award solely by reason of his age, in cases where the disabled person is in receipt of an unemployability allowance and in certain cases where the disabled person is not eligible for retirement pension;

(*c*) to enable the rate of rent allowance to be determined by reference to the amount of weekly rent and rates instead of as hitherto the amount by which the weekly rent and rates exceed 30p.

4. Article 4 removes a restriction under which no award could be made in respect of the death of a person, occurring more than 7 years after the date of the qualifying injury, unless he had been in receipt of a pension in respect of disablement.

5. Article 5 extends the Secretary of State's discretionary power to make deductions from awards in respect of maintenance in an institution supported out of public funds to all cases where the pensioner is maintained free of charge in a National Health Service hospital or similar institution for the purpose of receiving treatment and provides for payments out of such deductions to be made to the pensioner for his resettlement following a period of such treatment.

STATUTORY INSTRUMENTS

1972 No. 1178

GAS

The Gas Safety Regulations 1972

Made - - -	*2nd August* 1972
Laid before Parliament	*8th August* 1972
Coming into Operation	*1st December* 1972

The Secretary of State, in exercise of powers conferred by section 67 of the Gas Act 1948(a) and now vested in him (b), hereby makes the following regulations: —

PART I

GENERAL

Citation and commencement

1. These regulations may be cited as the Gas Safety Regulations 1972 and shall come into operation on 1st December 1972.

Interpretation

2.—(1) In these regulations—

"building regulations" means regulations under section 4 of the Public Health Act 1961(c);

"building standards regulations" has the same meaning as in section 3(1) of the Building (Scotland) Act 1959(d);

"factory" has the same meaning as in the Factories Act 1961(e);

"gas appliance" means an appliance designed for use by consumers of gas to be used for lighting, heating, motive power or any other purpose for which gas can be used;

"governor" means a device for regulating the pressure of gas;

"heat input" means the gas consumption of an appliance expressed in terms of the quantity of heat supplied to the appliance in a specific time;

"installation pipe" means any pipe not being a service pipe for the use of gas on the premises of a consumer and includes any valve or cock inserted therein;

"meter bypass" means any pipes (including valves or cocks inserted therein) through which a supply of gas may pass direct from a service pipe to an installation pipe without passing through a meter;

(a) 1948 c. 67.   (b) S.I. 1969/1498, 1970/1537 (1969 III, p. 4797; 1970 III, p. 5293).
(c) 1961 c. 64.   (d) 1959 c. 24.   (e) 1961 c. 34.

"meter control" means a valve or cock adjacent to and on the inlet side of a meter controlling the supply of gas from the Area Board to the consumer;

"meter governor" means an outlet pressure governor fitted between the meter control and the meter which is designed to operate at an inlet pressure which could not be such as to balance a column of water exceeding 30 inches in height;

"operating pressure" means the pressure of gas at which a gas appliance operates;

"outlet pressure governor" means a governor for automatic control of pressure of gas at a point on its outlet;

"pressure test point" means a fitting to which a pressure gauge can be connected;

"primary meter" means a meter connected to a service pipe, the index reading of which constitutes the basis of charge by the Area Board for gas used on the premises;

"purging" means the removal from a service pipe, meter or installation pipe or other gas fitting of all air and gas other than the gas to be supplied;

"secondary meter" means a meter which is not a primary meter;

"services" means pipes, drains, sewers, cables, conduits and electrical apparatus serving any premises;

"service governor" means an outlet pressure governor installed in a service pipe;

"service pipe" means the pipe between the gas main of the Area Board and a primary meter control for the use of gas on the premises of a consumer;

"service valve" means a valve or cock inserted in the service pipe outside a building for shutting off the supply of gas;

"sleeve" means a tubular case inserted in a prepared hole in a structure for the reception of a service pipe or installation pipe;

"temporary continuity bonding" means an electrical connection made to bridge a gap caused by the temporary absence of a continuous single gas pipe or any gas fitting to safeguard against the risk of fire, explosion or electric shock caused by contact with other services;

"thermal cut-off device" means a device designed to cut off automatically the flow of gas in the event of the temperature exceeding 203 degrees Fahrenheit;

"venting" means the removal of gas from a service governor to the external air.

(2) References in these regulations to the supply of gas shall be construed as references to gas supplied by an Area Board to a consumer and references to the use of gas shall be construed as references to the use of gas so supplied.

(3) The Interpretation Act 1889(a) shall apply to the interpretation of these regulations as it applies to the interpretation of an Act of Parliament.

(a) 1889 c. 63.

Part II

Installation of Service Pipes

3.—(1) No person shall install a service pipe, service pipe fitting, service valve or service governor on any premises unless he is employed by an Area Board under a contract of service, a person approved in writing by an Area Board for the purpose or a person employed by such a person under a contract of service.

(2) Any person who installs a service pipe, service pipe fitting, service valve or service governor on any premises shall comply in so doing with the following provisions in this Part of these regulations.

(3) Where such a person carries out the installation in the performance of a contract of service his employer shall ensure that the following provisions in this Part of these regulations are duly complied with.

4.—(1) All service pipes, service pipe fittings, service valves and service governors installed shall be of good construction and sound material and of adequate strength and size to secure safety.

(2) All service pipes, service pipe fittings, service valves and service governors shall be installed and jointed in a sound and workmanlike manner and so as to be gastight.

5. Where—

(a) a service pipe is installed of internal diameter of 2 inches or more; or

(b) a service pipe is installed for the supply of gas to any premises where the nature of the premises or of any activity carried on or to be carried on upon the premises is such that the person who installs the service pipe knows or has reason to suspect that there is a special risk of personal injury, fire, explosion or other dangers arising from the use of gas; or

(c) a service pipe is installed which supplies more than one primary meter in a building,

a service valve shall be fixed in the service pipe in a readily accessible position as near as practicable to the boundary of the premises through or to which the service pipe is laid and the position of the service valve shall be clearly indicated.

6. A service pipe shall not be installed in any position in which it cannot be used with safety having regard to the position of other nearby services and to such parts of the structure of any building through which it is laid as might affect its safe use.

7.—(1) No service pipe shall be installed in a cavity wall nor so as to pass through a cavity wall otherwise than by the shortest practicable route.

(2) Where a service pipe is installed so as to pass through any wall or is installed so as to pass through any floor of solid construction—

(a) the service pipe shall be enclosed in a sleeve; and

(b) the service pipe and sleeve shall be so constructed and installed as to prevent gas passing along the spaces between the pipe and the sleeve and between the sleeve and the wall or floor and so as to allow normal movement of the pipe.

(3) No service pipe shall be installed in an unventilated void space.

(4) No service pipe shall be installed under the foundations of a building or under the base of walls or footings.

8. All service pipes installed shall be constructed of material which is inherently resistant to corrosion or shall be protected against corrosion externally and, unless there is no risk of internal corrosion, internally.

9.—(1) No service pipe shall be connected to the gas main except by a suitable connector.

(2) Every service pipe installed shall be of such diameter as will permit it to be connected to the main without causing damage to the main.

10. All service pipes installed underground shall be installed in accordance with the following conditions—

(*a*) the pipes shall be bedded on firm ground throughout their length;

(*b*) the pipes shall be laid at such a depth as to ensure that there is no undue risk of accidental damage to the pipes or of damage by frost;

(*c*) the pipes shall not be laid in the same trench as other services unless the authorities responsible for those other services have first been consulted;

(*d*) where condensation of water is likely to occur the pipes shall be laid, where practicable, with a fall of at least one inch in ten feet from the meter to the gas main; and

(*e*) where condensation of water is likely to occur and such a fall is not practicable—

(i) a suitable vessel for the reception of any condensate which may form in any pipe shall be fixed to the pipe in a conspicuous and readily accessible position and means shall be provided for the removal of the condensate; and

(ii) a notice in permanent form to the effect that there is a vessel for the collection of condensate shall be fixed to the service pipe adjacent to the meter control.

11. All service pipes installed above ground shall be properly supported and so placed or protected as to ensure that there is no undue risk of accidental damage to the pipes.

12. No service pipe shall be installed in such a way as to impair the structure of any building nor so as to impair the fire resistance of any part of its structure.

13. Where both a service governor and a bypass to the governor are installed a governor shall be fitted on the bypass.

14. Where a service governor is installed and the pressure at which the gas will be supplied at the inlet of the governor could be such as to balance a column of water not less than 30 inches in height a relief valve or seal and vent pipe of adequate size and capable of venting safely shall be installed in the outlet of the governor.

15. A person who has installed a service governor shall forthwith after installation adequately seal the governor to prevent unauthorised persons interfering with it without breaking the seal.

16. A person who has installed a service pipe, service pipe fitting, service valve or service governor shall ensure—

    (*a*) that it is forthwith after installation adequately tested to verify that it is gastight and examined to verify that it has been installed in accordance with the foregoing provisions of this Part of these regulations;

    (*b*) that after such testing any necessary protective coating is applied to the joints of all service pipes installed;

    (*c*) that after complying with the provisions of sub-paragraphs (*a*) and (*b*) purging is carried out throughout every service pipe installed to the external air and throughout any gas fitting installed on a previous occasion through which gas could not flow at the time of installation; and

    (*d*) that immediately after such purging every service pipe which has been installed and is not to be put into immediate use is temporarily sealed off, capped or plugged at the meter control with the appropriate pipe fitting.

Part III

Installation of Meters

17.—(1) No person shall install a meter, meter control, meter bypass, meter governor or other gas fitting to be used in connection with a meter on any premises unless he is employed by an Area Board under a contract of service, a person approved in writing by an Area Board for the purpose or a person employed by such a person under a contract of service.

(2) Any person who installs a meter, meter control, meter bypass, meter governor or other gas fitting to be used in connection with a meter on any premises shall comply in so doing with the following provisions in this Part of these regulations.

(3) Where such a person carries out the installation in the performance of a contract of service his employer shall ensure that the following provisions in this Part of these regulations are duly complied with.

(4) In paragraph (1) of this regulation "meter" means primary meter.

(5) Where a person installs a secondary meter or a meter control, meter bypass, meter governor or other gas fitting to be used in connection with a secondary meter on any premises forming part of a factory, the occupier shall ensure that the following provisions in this Part of these regulations are duly complied with.

18.—(1) Every meter, meter control, meter bypass, meter governor and other gas fitting to be used in connection with a meter installed shall be of good construction and sound material.

(2) Every meter, meter control, meter bypass, meter governor and other gas fitting to be used in connection with a meter shall be installed and jointed in a sound and workmanlike manner and so as to be gastight.

19.—(1) Every meter, meter control, meter bypass, meter governor and other gas fitting to be used in connection with a meter shall be installed in a readily accessible position for inspection and maintenance, and, in the case of the meter control, for operation by the consumer.

(2) Every meter installed shall be so placed as to ensure that there is no undue risk of accidental damage to the meter.

20.—(1) Every meter installed shall be provided with a suitable meter control as near as practicable to the inlet connection to the meter.

(2) Where the meter control has a detachable key or lever, which is not so attached as to move only horizontally, it shall be so attached to the meter control that when it has been moved as far as possible in a downward direction gas cannot be supplied to an installation pipe.

(3) Every detachable key or lever of the meter control shall be securely held in place.

21. No meter or meter control shall be installed in contact with, or close to, any floor, wall or ceiling in such a manner as to be liable to be affected by corrosion.

22.—(1) No meter shall be installed in a building, which has two or more floors above the ground floor of the building, on or under a stairway or elsewhere, where the stairway or other part of the building provides the only means of escape in case of fire.

(2) Every meter and its connections installed in a building other than one mentioned in paragraph (1) on or under a stairway or elsewhere, where the stairway or other part of the building provides the only means of escape in case of fire, shall either be of fire-resistant construction or be housed in a compartment of which the enclosing sides, top and bottom including the doors have a fire resistance of not less than half an hour and of which the doors shall be fitted with automatic self-closing devices or the meter shall be connected to a service pipe which incorporates a thermal cut-off device near the meter.

23. Where a meter is installed, a notice in permanent form shall be prominently mounted on or near the meter indicating that the consumer should—

(*a*) shut off the supply of gas immediately in the event of an escape of gas in the consumer's premises;

(*b*) where any gas continues to escape after the supply has been shut off, as soon as practicable give notice to the Area Board of the escape; and

(*c*) not re-open the supply until all necessary steps have been taken to prevent the gas from again escaping.

24. Where a service pipe is installed which supplies more than one primary meter installed in the same premises or in different premises, a notice in permanent form shall be prominently mounted on or near each primary meter indicating this fact.

25. Where secondary meters are installed, a notice in permanent form shall be prominently mounted on or near the primary meter indicating the number of secondary meters installed.

26. Where a secondary meter is installed no primary meter through which gas passes to the secondary meter shall be a prepayment meter.

27.—(1) Every meter installed shall be supported.

(2) Where a meter is installed having bosses or side pipes attached to the meter by a soldered joint only, rigid pipe connections shall not be made to the meter.

28. Every meter installed shall be so placed as to ensure that there is no risk of damage to the meter from a nearby electricity meter or other electrical apparatus.

29. An electrical connection shall be maintained while a meter is being installed between the service pipe and installation pipe by a suitable temporary continuity bonding, except when the inlet and outlet of the meter form a continuous single pipe.

30. Where both a meter governor and a meter bypass are installed a governor shall be fitted on the bypass.

31. Where a meter governor is installed—

  (i) the governor shall be so constructed and installed as to cut off the supply of gas automatically in the event of the pressure at the outlet of the governor exceeding the pressure to which the installation pipes and the gas appliances connected thereto are designed to be subject;

  (ii) the person who installs the governor shall, if he has reason to suspect that foreign matter may block or otherwise interfere with the safe operation of the governor, fit to the governor a suitable filter or other suitable protection.

32. A person who has installed a meter governor shall forthwith after installation adequately seal the governor to prevent unauthorised persons interfering with it without breaking the seal.

33. A person who has installed a meter, meter control, meter bypass, meter governor or any other gas fitting to be used in connection with a meter shall ensure—

  (*a*) that it is forthwith after installation adequately tested to verify that it is gastight and examined to verify that it has been installed in accordance with the foregoing provisions of this Part of these regulations; and

  (*b*) that immediately after such testing and examination purging is carried out throughout the meter and every other gas fitting installed through which gas can then flow including gas fittings installed on a previous occasion through which gas could not flow at the time of installation.

PART IV

INSTALLATION OF INSTALLATION PIPES

34.—(1) Any person who installs an installation pipe or installation pipe fitting on any premises shall comply in so doing with the following provisions in this Part of these regulations.

(2) Where such a person carries out the installation in the performance of a contract of service his employer shall ensure that the following provisions in this Part of these regulations are duly complied with.

(3) Where a person installs an installation pipe or installation pipe fitting on any premises forming part of a factory, the occupier shall ensure that the following provisions in this Part of these regulations are duly complied with.

35.—(1) All installation pipes and installation pipe fittings installed shall be of good construction and sound material and of adequate strength and size to secure safety.

(2) All installation pipes and installation pipe fittings shall be installed and jointed by competent persons in a sound and workmanlike manner and so as to be gastight.

36.—(1) An installation pipe shall not be installed in any position in which it cannot be used with safety having regard to the position of other nearby services and to such parts of the structure of any building through which it is laid as might affect its safe use.

(2) A person who installs an installation pipe shall ensure that any necessary electrical bonding is carried out by a competent person so as to connect the pipe electrically to any other nearby services.

37.—(1) No installation pipe shall be installed in a cavity wall nor so as to pass through a cavity wall otherwise than by the shortest practicable route.

(2) Where an installation pipe is installed so as to pass through any wall or is installed so as to pass through any floor of solid construction—

(*a*) the installation pipe shall be enclosed in a sleeve; and

(*b*) the installation pipe and sleeve shall be so constructed and installed as to prevent gas passing along the spaces between the pipe and the sleeve and between the sleeve and the wall or floor and so as to allow normal movement of the pipe.

(3) No installation pipe shall be installed under the foundations of a building or under the base of walls or footings.

38. Every installation pipe installed, which passes through or is in contact with or is likely to be exposed to any material liable to cause the corrosion of the pipe, shall be constructed of material which is inherently resistant to corrosion or shall be protected against corrosion.

39. Where installation pipes are installed with changes in pipe levels and condensation of water is likely to occur, a suitable vessel for the reception of any condensate which may form in any pipe shall be fixed to the pipe in a conspicuous and readily accessible position and means shall be provided for the removal of the condensate.

40. All installation pipes installed shall be properly supported and so placed or protected as to ensure that there is no undue risk of accidental damage to the pipes.

41. No installation pipe shall be installed in such a way as to impair the structure of any building nor so as to impair the fire resistance of any part of its structure.

42. Where installation pipes supplied from primary meters are installed in a building for the supply of gas to which a service pipe of internal diameter of more than 2 inches is installed and the supply of gas is required for purposes other than domestic use—

(a) a valve or cock shall be properly fixed in a conspicuous and readily accessible position in the following cases:—

(i) in the case of a building having two or more floors to which gas is supplied, in the incoming installation pipe to each such floor; and

(ii) in the case of a floor of a building having self-contained areas to which gas is supplied (whether or not the building has more than one floor), in the incoming installation pipe to each such self-contained area;

(b) a line diagram shall be attached to the building in a readily accessible position as near as practicable to the primary meter indicating the position of all installation pipes, meters, meter controls, valves or cocks, pressure test points, condensate receivers and electrical bonding.

43. A person who has installed an installation pipe or installation pipe fitting shall ensure—

(a) that it is forthwith after installation adequately tested to verify that it is gastight and examined to verify that it has been installed in accordance with the foregoing provisions of this Part of these regulations;

(b) that after such testing any necessary protective coating is applied to the joints of all installation pipes installed;

(c) that after complying with the provisions of sub-paragraphs (a) and (b) purging is carried out throughout every installation pipe installed through which gas can then flow; and

(d) that immediately after such purging every installation pipe which has been installed and is not to be put into immediate use is temporarily sealed off, capped or plugged at every outlet of it with the appropriate pipe fitting.

PART V

INSTALLATION OF GAS APPLIANCES

44.—(1) Any person who installs a gas appliance on any premises shall comply in so doing with the following provisions in this Part of these regulations.

(2) Where such a person carries out the installation in the performance of a contract of service his employer shall ensure that the following provisions in this Part of these regulations are duly complied with.

(3) Where a person installs a gas appliance on any premises forming part of a factory, the occupier shall ensure that the following provisions in this Part of these regulations are duly complied with.

45.—(1) All gas appliances shall be installed by competent persons.

(2) No gas appliance shall be installed unless—

(a) the appliance and the gas fittings and other works for the supply of gas to be used in connection with the appliance,

(b) the means of removal of the products of combustion from the appliance,

(c) the availability of sufficient supply of air for the appliance for proper combustion,

(d) the means of ventilation to the room or internal space in which the appliance is to be used, and

(e) the general conditions of installation including the connection of the appliance to any other gas fitting,

are such as to ensure that the appliance can be used without constituting a danger to any person or property.

46.—(1) A person shall not install a gas appliance if the appliance and the gas fittings and any flue or means of ventilation to be used in connection with the appliance do not—

(a) if in Greater London, other than an outer London borough, comply with any such provisions of the London Building Acts and any byelaws made thereunder,

(b) if in any other part of England or Wales, comply with any such provisions of the building regulations, or

(c) if in Scotland, comply with any such provisions of the building standards regulations,

as are in force at the date of installation of the appliance.

(2) A person who has installed a gas appliance shall forthwith after installation test its connection to the installation pipe to verify that it is gastight and examine the appliance and the gas fittings and other works for the supply of gas and any flue or means of ventilation to be used in connection with the appliance and make any necessary adjustments in order to ensure—

(a) that the appliance has been installed in accordance with the foregoing provisions of this Part of these regulations;

(b) that the heat input and operating pressure are as recommended by the manufacturer;

(c) that all gas safety controls are in proper working order; and

(d) that, without prejudice to the generality of sub-paragraph (a), any flue system or means of removal of the products of combustion from the appliance and any means of ventilation and of supply of combustion air provided in connection with the use of the appliance are in safe working order.

PART VI

USE OF GAS

47. No person shall use or permit a gas appliance to be used if at any time he knows or has reason to suspect—

(a) that there is insufficient supply of air available for the appliance for proper combustion at the point of combustion;

(b) that the removal of the products of combustion from the appliance is not safely being carried out;

(*c*) that the room or internal space in which the appliance is situated is not adequately ventilated for the purpose of providing air containing a sufficiency of oxygen for the persons present in the room, or in, or in the vicinity of, the internal space while the appliance is in use;

(*d*) that any gas is escaping from the appliance or from any gas fitting used in connection with the appliance; or

(*e*) that the appliance or any part of it or any gas fitting or other works for the supply of gas used in connection with the appliance is so faulty or maladjusted that it cannot be used without constituting a danger to any person or property.

48.—(1) If at any time any person supplied with gas by an Area Board knows or has reason to suspect that any gas is escaping in the premises supplied with gas he shall immediately shut off the supply of gas at such place as may be requisite to prevent the gas from escaping.

(2) Where any gas continues to escape in any premises after the supply of gas has been shut off, the person supplied with gas shall as soon as practicable give notice to the Area Board of the escape.

(3) Where any gas escapes in any premises supplied with gas and the supply of gas is shut off, the supply shall not be opened until all necessary steps have been taken to prevent the gas from again escaping.

PART VII

REMOVAL, DISCONNECTION, ALTERATION, REPLACEMENT AND MAINTENANCE OF GAS FITTINGS, ETC.

49. An electrical connection shall be maintained by means of temporary continuity bonding while a gas pipe, pipe fitting or meter is being removed or replaced until the work of disconnecting or connecting the gas pipe, pipe fitting or meter, as the case may be, has been completed, except, in the case of a meter, when its inlet and outlet form a continuous single pipe.

50. A person who disconnects a gas fitting or any part of the gas supply system on any premises shall seal it off, cap it or plug it at every outlet of every pipe to which it is connected with the appropriate pipe fitting.

51.—(1) No alteration shall be made to a gas fitting or to any part of the gas supply system on any premises (whether it has been installed before or after the date of coming into operation of these regulations) if as a result of such alteration there would have been a contravention of or failure to comply with any provision of Parts II to V of these regulations if the gas fitting or part of the gas supply system in question had been installed at the date of the alteration.

(2) On every replacement of a gas fitting or of any part of the gas supply system on any premises (whether it has been installed before or after the date of coming into operation of these regulations) the provisions of Part II, III, IV or V (as the case may be) of these regulations shall apply to its replacement as they apply to its installation after the said date:

Provided that where, in the case of the replacement of a meter in a building having two or more floors above the ground floor of the building, the said meter was installed on or under a stairway or in any other part of the building, where the stairway or other part of the building provided the only means of escape in case of fire, the replacement meter may be placed in the former position if the meter and its connections would comply with the requirements of regulation 22(2) relating to meters installed in buildings having less than two floors above the ground floor or the replacement meter may be placed in another position if the meter would not contravene the provisions of regulation 22(1).

(3) A person who makes any alteration to or replacement of a gas fitting or any part of the gas supply system on any premises subsequent to installation shall ensure that it is forthwith adequately tested to verify that it is gastight.

(4) A person who makes any such alteration of a gas fitting or of any part of the gas supply system on any premises shall ensure that it is forthwith after such testing examined to verify that there would have been no such contravention of or failure to comply with any provision of Parts II to V of these regulations as is referred to in paragraph (1).

(5) A person who makes any such replacement of a gas fitting or of any part of the gas supply system on any premises shall ensure that it is forthwith after such testing examined to verify that it complies with such requirements of Parts II to V of these regulations as apply to the replacement by virtue of paragraph (2).

52. An Area Board supplying gas to any building shall at all times at their own expense keep all service valves inserted in the service pipes in proper working order.

Part VIII

Penalties

53. Any person offending against these regulations shall be liable on summary conviction to a fine not exceeding £100.

Dated 2nd August 1972.

Tom Boardman,
Minister for Industry,
Department of Trade and Industry.

EXPLANATORY NOTE

(This Note is not part of the Regulations)

These regulations made by the Secretary of State for Trade and Industry under Section 67 of the Gas Act 1948 will apply generally throughout Great Britain and, except in the Inner London Boroughs, are wholly new. In the Inner London Boroughs they take the place of certain provisions of the London Gas Undertakings Regulations 1954 made under the London Gas Undertakings (Regulations) Act 1939. Any provisions of those regulations which are inconsistent with or rendered redundant by these regulations cease to have effect from the date when these regulations come into operation, that is to say from 1st December 1972.

Parts II to V lay down certain requirements to be observed by persons installing gas pipes, meters, appliances and other fittings on consumers' premises. These are designed to ensure that the basic standards necessary to secure safety from the installation are maintained. Part VI imposes certain requirements on the use of gas appliances supplied by Area Gas Boards largely designed to prevent the public being put at risk by the continued use of gas appliances where such use is known to be dangerous or there is reason to believe so. Part VII provides requirements for work done on gas fittings after first installation and Part VIII provides penalties for contraventions.

These regulations do not affect any obligation arising under the building regulations and byelaws which apply in different parts of Great Britain, and both sets of provisions should be consulted where gas appliances are installed or other gas installation work or alterations done which affect the structure.

STATUTORY INSTRUMENTS

1972 No. 1186

INCOME TAX

The Income Tax (Employments) (No. 11) Regulations 1972

Made - - - -	*4th August* 1972
Laid before the House of Commons	11*th August* 1972
Coming into Operation	15th *September* 1972

The Commissioners of Inland Revenue, in exercise of the powers conferred upon them by section 204 of the Income and Corporation Taxes Act 1970(a) hereby make the following Regulations:—

1.—(1) These Regulations shall come into operation on 15th September 1972 in so far as they apply to codes for use from 6th April 1973, but otherwise not until 6th April 1973; and these Regulations may be cited as the Income Tax (Employments) (No. 11) Regulations 1972.

(2) The Interpretation Act 1889(b) shall apply for the interpretation of these Regulations as it applies for the interpretation of an Act of Parliament.

(3) In these Regulations the expression "the Principal Regulations" means the Income Tax (Employments) Regulations 1965(c) as amended(d), and the expression "the Seamen's Regulations" means the Income Tax (Employments) (No. 6) (Seamen) Regulations 1970(e).

2. The definitions in paragraph (1) of Regulation 2 of the Principal Regulations shall be varied as follows:—

(i) To the definition of code there shall be added the words "and references to code include any designation thereof by numbers and letters, alone or in combination".

(ii) The definition of "emoluments" shall be deleted and the following definition substituted:

"emoluments" means the full amount of any income to be taken into account in assessing liability under Schedule E after the deduction of allowable superannuation contributions and references to payments of emoluments include references to payments on account of emoluments.

(iii) There shall be deleted from the definition of "free emoluments" the words "including earned income relief thereon, but excluding reduced rate relief".

(iv) The definition of "reliefs from income tax" shall be varied to "include allowances and deductions but not allowable superannuation contributions".

(a) 1970 c. 10.   (b) 1889 c. 63.
(c) S.I. 1965/516 (1965 I, p. 1321).
(d) The relevant amending instruments are S.I. 1966/1373; 1969/170, 688; 1970/666, 1142; 1972/552: (1966 III, p. 3691; 1969 I, p. 440, II, p. 1859; 1970 II, p. 2166, II, p. 3878; 1972 I, p. 1860).
(e) S.I. 1970/1142 (1970 II, p. 3878).

3. The following definitions shall be added to paragraph (1) of Regulation 2 of the Principal Regulations.

"Allowable superannuation contributions" means any sum paid by an employee by way of contribution towards a superannuation fund or scheme which is allowed to be deducted as an expense under Schedule E.

"Gross emoluments" means emoluments before the deduction of allowable superannuation contributions.

"Higher rate" means one of the higher rates of income tax specified in the Income Tax Acts.

4. Regulation 7 of the Principal Regulations shall be varied by deleting paragraph (2).

5. Regulation 8 of the Principal Regulations shall be varied as follows:—

(1) Paragraph (1) shall be deleted and the following paragraph substituted—

The Inspector may determine that tax shall be deducted at an appropriate higher rate from the whole of any emoluments if he has reason to believe that the employee will be chargeable at one or more of the higher rates on some part of his total income.

(2) Paragraph (3) shall be varied by deleting the words "the Inspector has determined that tax shall be deducted at the standard rate, or that no tax shall be deducted, he" and substituting the words "paragraphs (1) or (2) of this Regulation apply, the Inspector".

6. Regulation 9 of the Principal Regulations shall be varied by deleting the second sub-paragraph and substituting—

"Provided that no such notice need be given when the change in the code is due to an alteration or alterations in the rates of any of the personal reliefs allowable under section 8 Income and Corporation Taxes Act 1970 or in the tax tables, but the other matters referred to in Regulation 7 are not different from those for the preceding year".

7. Paragraph 2 of Regulation 11 of the Principal Regulations shall be varied by deleting "Regulation 12" and substituting "Regulation 12(1)" and adding at the end—

"Provided that no such notice need be given when the change in the code is due to an alteration or alterations in the rates of any of the personal reliefs allowable under section 8 Income and Corporation Taxes Act 1970 or in the tax tables, but the other matters referred to in Regulation 7 have not changed".

8. Regulation 12 of the Principal Regulations shall be varied by numbering the existing paragraph "(1)" and adding a new paragraph (2) as follows:—

"Where there is a change in the rates of any of the personal reliefs allowable under section 8 of the Income and Corporation Taxes Act 1970, the Inspector may give notice requiring the employer, with effect from the date specified in the notice, to amend specified codes as directed and a code so amended shall be the appropriate code and all the provisions of these Regulations which relate to objections and appeals against the Inspector's determination, or to deduction of tax by reference to the appropriate code or to the specification of the appropriate code in any Deduction Card, return or certificate, shall, with the necessary modifications, have effect accordingly."

9.—(1) Paragraph 6(*b*) of Regulation 13 shall be varied by deleting the word "gross".

(2) Paragraph 7 of Regulation 13 shall be varied by deleting the whole of the first sub-paragraph and substituting—

"Where in accordance with Regulation 8 the Inspector determines that tax shall be deducted from any emoluments wholly at one of the higher rates of tax or that no tax shall be deducted therefrom, the foregoing provisions of this Regulation shall not apply but the employer shall deduct tax at the appropriate higher rate, or shall deduct no tax, as the case may require without regard to the employee's cumulative emoluments or the corresponding cumulative tax, and where tax is deductible at a higher rate, shall record the date of payment, the amount of the emoluments and the amount of tax deducted therefrom."

10. Regulation 16 of the Principal Regulations shall be varied as follows:—

(1) Paragraph (1) sub-paragraph (b) shall be deleted.

(2) From paragraph (2) there shall be deleted the words "or, where the employee has ceased to be employed by him and no Deduction Card is held, by reference to the code prescribed by the Commissioners of Inland Revenue under paragraph (2) of Regulation 19".

(3) From paragraph (3) there shall be deleted the word "gross" and the whole of the proviso.

11.—(1) Where an employer makes any payment of emoluments to an employee after he has ceased to be employed by him and the payments have not been included in the certificate issued to the employee in accordance with Regulation 17(2) of the Principal Regulations, Regulation 13 of the Principal Regulations shall not apply and on making any such payment the employer shall deduct tax at the basic rate of tax for the year in which the payment is made.

(2) On making any such payment as aforesaid the employer shall record on the Deduction Card, or in such form as may be authorised by the Commissioners of Inland Revenue, the date of payment, the amount of the emoluments, and the amount of tax deducted on making the payment.

12. Regulations 19 and 29 of the Principal Regulations shall have effect, as regards payments of emoluments made on or after 6th April 1973, as if for any reference to a rate of £11 or more a week there were substituted a reference to a rate of more than £11·50 a week, and as if for any reference to a rate of £47 or more a month there were substituted a reference to a rate of more than £50 a month.

13. Paragraph 2 of Regulation 19 of the Principal Regulations shall be varied by deleting the words "with the exception that the amounts of the free emoluments and taxable emoluments shall not be recorded on the Deduction Card".

14. Paragraph 1 of Regulation 25 of the Principal Regulations shall be varied by deleting the existing first paragraph and substituting: "After the end of the year the employer shall give the employee a certificate in a form prescribed or authorised by the Commissioners of Inland Revenue showing the total of gross emoluments paid by the employer to the employee during the year and—".

15. Paragraph (1) of Regulation 29 of the Principal Regulations shall be varied by deleting the sub-paragraph (a) and substituting the following:—

"(a) in respect of each employee, a return showing the total amount of emoluments, and the total amount of gross emoluments, paid by him to the employee during the year, the appropriate code, and the total net tax deducted from the emoluments; and".

16. Paragraph 2 of Regulation 52 of the Principal Regulations shall be varied by deleting the word "gross".

17. The definition of "wages" in paragraph 3 of Regulation 2 of the Seamen's Regulations shall be deleted and the following definition substituted:—

"wages" means the full amount of the emoluments after the deduction of allowable superannuation contributions and includes all pay at the monthly or weekly rates stated in the agreement with the seaman, leave pay, pay in lieu of leave, leave subsistence allowance, pay in respect of overtime, ship-wreck unemployment indemnity, special payment while sick abroad (as defined by the National Maritime Board) and any other emoluments paid to a seaman which arise out of his service as such, not being sick pay while sick in the United Kingdom.

18. The following definition shall be added to paragraph 3 of Regulation 2 of the Seamen's Regulations:—

"gross wages" means wages before the deduction of allowable superannuation contributions.

19. Paragraph 6 of Regulation 3 of the Seamen's Regulations shall be varied by adding a second paragraph as follows:—

"Where there is a change in the rates of any of the personal reliefs allowable under section 8 of the Income and Corporation Taxes Act 1970, the Inspector may give notice requiring the employer, with effect from the date specified in the notice, to amend specified codes as directed and a code so amended shall be the authorised code and all the provisions of the Principal Regulations which relate to objections and appeals against the Inspector's determination and the provisions of those Regulations which relate to the deduction of tax by reference to the authorised code or to the specification of the authorised code in any return, code card or discharge book, shall, with the necessary modifications, have effect accordingly."

20. Paragraph 2 of Regulation 7 of the Seamen's Regulations shall be varied by altering (*f*) to (*g*) and adding the following:—

(*f*) the gross wages paid to him by the employer for the period to which the return relates.

By Order of the Commissioners of Inland Revenue.

J. M. Green,
Secretary.

4th August 1972.

EXPLANATORY NOTE
(This Note is not part of the Regulations.)

These Regulations further amend the Income Tax (Employments) Regulations 1965 and the Income Tax (Employments) (No. 6) (Seamen) Regulations 1970. They affect 1973-74 and subsequent tax years and provide for:

(1) the application of PAYE after the introduction by the Finance Act 1972 of basic and higher rates of income tax in place of the standard rate of income tax and of surtax (Regulations 5 and 9(2), with a consequential change in the definition of "free emoluments");

(2) the calculation by employers of PAYE tax by reference to emoluments after instead of before deducting allowable superannuation contributions. (The changes are effected by amendments in definitions [Regulations 2 and 3, 17 and 18] with consequential changes in Regulations 9(1), 10(3), 14, 15, 16 and 20);

(3) future changes in PAYE codes following alterations in the rates of any of the personal allowances (Regulations 6, 7, 8 and 19 with an addition to the definition of "code");

(4) the increase in the limit of weekly or monthly pay above which PAYE has to be operated (Regulation 12); and minor changes in the arrangements for the deduction of tax in some circumstances eg where no deduction card is held, where the employee has left his employment (Regulations 4, 10, 11 and 13).

STATUTORY INSTRUMENTS

1972 No. 1187

INDUSTRIAL TRAINING

The Industrial Training Levy (Wool, Jute and Flax) Order 1972

Made - - -	*3rd August* 1972
Laid before Parliament	*14th August* 1972
Coming into Operation	*6th September* 1972

The Secretary of State after approving proposals submitted by the Wool, Jute and Flax Industry Training Board for the imposition of a further levy on employers in the wool, jute and flax industry and in exercise of his powers under section 4 of the Industrial Training Act 1964(**a**) and of all other powers enabling him in that behalf hereby makes the following Order:—

Title and commencement

1. This Order may be cited as the Industrial Training Levy (Wool, Jute and Flax) Order 1972 and shall come into operation on 6th September 1972.

Interpretation

2.—(1) In this Order unless the context otherwise requires:—

(*a*) "agriculture" has the same meaning as in section 109(3) of the Agriculture Act 1947(**b**), or, in relation to Scotland, as in section 86(3) of the Agriculture (Scotland) Act 1948(**c**);

(*b*) "an appeal tribunal" means an industrial tribunal established under section 12 of the Industrial Training Act 1964;

(*c*) "assessment" means an assessment of an employer to the levy;

(*d*) "the Board" means the Wool, Jute and Flax Industry Training Board;

(*e*) "business" means any activities of industry or commerce;

(*f*) "charity" has the same meaning as in section 360 of the Income and Corporation Taxes Act 1970(**d**);

(*g*) "emoluments" means all emoluments assessable to income tax under Schedule E (other than pensions), being emoluments from which tax under that Schedule is deductible, whether or not tax in fact falls to be deducted from any particular payment thereof;

(*h*) "employer" means a person who is an employer in the wool, jute and flax industry at any time in the eighth levy period;

(*i*) "the eighth base period" means the period commencing on 1st April 1971 and ending on 31st March 1972;

(*j*) "the eighth levy period" means the period commencing with the day upon which this Order comes into operation and ending on 5th April 1973;

(*k*) "the industrial training order" means the Industrial Training (Wool, Jute and Flax Board) Order 1968(**e**);

(**a**) 1964 c. 16. (**b**) 1947 c. 48.
(**c**) 1948 c. 45. (**d**) 1970 c. 10.
(**e**) S.I. 1968/898 (1968 II, p. 2376).

(*l*) "the levy" means the levy imposed by the Board in respect of the eighth levy period;

(*m*) "notice" means a notice in writing;

(*n*) "related or administrative activities" means (subject to the provisions of this Order) activities of a kind to which paragraph 1(*r*) of the Schedule to the industrial training order applies;

(*o*) "wool, jute and flax establishment" means an establishment in Great Britain engaged in the eighth base period wholly or mainly in the wool, jute and flax industry for a total of twenty-seven or more weeks or, being an establishment that commenced to carry on business in the eighth base period, for a total number of weeks exceeding one-half of the number of weeks in the part of the said period commencing with the day on which business was commenced and ending on the last day thereof;

(*p*) "the wool, jute and flax industry" means any one or more of the activities which, subject to the provisions of paragraph 2 of the Schedule to the industrial training order, are specified in paragraph 1 of that Schedule as the activities of the wool, jute and flax industry, but does not include the activities of an establishment engaged wholly or mainly in the activities following or any of them, that is to say—

   (i) dealing in fleeces, textile fibres (not being jute, flax, hemp or similar fibres) or tops; or

   (ii) any related or administrative activities carried on only in connection with the activities specified in (i) of this sub-paragraph.

(2) In the case where a wool, jute and flax establishment is taken over (whether directly or indirectly) by an employer in succession to, or jointly with, another person, a person employed at any time in the eighth base period at or from the establishment shall be deemed, for the purposes of this Order, to have been so employed by the employer carrying on the said establishment on the day upon which this Order comes into operation, and any reference in this Order to persons employed by an employer at or from a wool, jute and flax establishment in the eighth base period shall be construed accordingly.

(3) Any reference in this Order to an establishment that commences to carry on business or that ceases to carry on business shall not be taken to apply where the location of the establishment is changed but its business is continued wholly or mainly at or from the new location, or where the suspension of activities is of a temporary or seasonal nature.

(4) The Interpretation Act 1889(**a**) shall apply to the interpretation of this Order as it applies to the interpretation of an Act of Parliament.

Imposition of the Levy

3.—(1) The levy to be imposed by the Board on employers in respect of the eighth levy period shall be assessed in accordance with the provisions of this Article and of the Schedule to this Order.

(**a**) 1889 c. 63.

(2) The levy shall be assessed by the Board separately in respect of each wool, jute and flax establishment of an employer (not being an employer who is exempt from the levy by virtue of paragraph 3 of the said Schedule), but in agreement with the employer one assessment may be made in respect of any number of such establishments, in which case those establishments shall be deemed for the purposes of that assessment to constitute one establishment.

Assessment Notices

4.—(1) The Board shall serve an assessment notice on every employer assessed to the levy, but one notice may comprise two or more assessments.

(2) An assessment notice shall state the amount (rounded down, where necessary, to the nearest £1) of the levy payable by the person assessed thereto, and where the notice comprises two or more assessments the said amount shall, before any such rounding down, be equal to the total amount of the levy assessed by the Board under Article 3 of this Order in respect of each establishment included in the notice.

(3) An assessment notice shall state the Board's address for the service of a notice of appeal or of an application for an extension of time for appealing.

(4) An assessment notice may be served on the person assessed to the levy either by delivering it to him personally or by leaving it, or sending it to him by post, at his last known address or place of business in the United Kingdom or, if that person is a corporation, by leaving it, or sending it by post to the corporation, at such address or place of business or at its registered or principal office.

Payment of the Levy

5.—(1) Subject to the provisions of this Article and of Articles 6 and 7, the amount of the levy payable under an assessment notice served by the Board shall be due and payable to the Board one month after the date of the notice.

(2) The amount of an assessment shall not be recoverable by the Board until there has expired the time allowed for appealing against the assessment by Article 7(1) of this Order and any further period or periods of time that the Board or an appeal tribunal may have allowed for appealing under paragraph (2) or (3) of that Article or, where an appeal is brought, until the appeal is decided or withdrawn.

Withdrawal of Assessment

6.—(1) The Board may, by notice served on the person assessed to the levy in the same manner as an assessment notice, withdraw an assessment if that person has appealed against that assessment under the provisions of Article 7 of this Order and the appeal has not been entered in the Register of Appeals kept under the appropriate Regulations specified in paragraph (5) of that Article.

(2) The withdrawal of an assessment shall be without prejudice—

　　(a) to the power of the Board to serve a further assessment notice in respect of any establishment to which that assessment related; or

　　(b) to any other assessment included in the original assessment notice, and such notice shall thereupon have effect as if any assessment withdrawn by the Board had not been included therein.

Appeals

7.—(1) A person assessed to the levy may appeal to an appeal tribunal against the assessment within one month from the date of the service of the assessment notice or within any further period or periods of time that may be allowed by the Board or an appeal tribunal under the following provisions of this Article.

(2) The Board by notice may for good cause allow a person assessed to the levy to appeal to an appeal tribunal against the assessment at any time within the period of four months from the date of the service of the assessment notice or within such further period or periods as the Board may allow before such time as may then be limited for appealing has expired.

(3) If the Board shall not allow an application for extension of time for appealing, an appeal tribunal shall upon application made to the tribunal by the person assessed to the levy have the like powers as the Board under the last foregoing paragraph.

(4) In the case of an establishment that ceases to carry on business in the eighth levy period on any day after the date of the service of the relevant assessment notice, the foregoing provisions of this Article shall have effect as if for the period of four months from the date of the service of the assessment notice mentioned in paragraph (2) of this Article there were substituted the period of six months from the date of the cessation of business.

(5) An appeal or an application to an appeal tribunal under this Article shall be made in accordance with the Industrial Tribunals (England and Wales) Regulations 1965(**a**) as amended by the Industrial Tribunals (England and Wales) (Amendment) Regulations 1967(**b**) except where the establishment to which the relevant assessment relates is wholly in Scotland in which case the appeal or application shall be made in accordance with the Industrial Tribunals (Scotland) Regulations 1965(**c**) as amended by the Industrial Tribunals (Scotland) (Amendment) Regulations 1967(**d**).

(6) The powers of an appeal tribunal under paragraph (3) of this Article may be exercised by the President of the Industrial Tribunals (England and Wales) or by the President of the Industrial Tribunals (Scotland) as the case may be.

Evidence

8.—(1) Upon the discharge by a person assessed to the levy of his liability under an assessment the Board shall if so requested issue to him a certificate to that effect.

(2) The production in any proceedings of a document purporting to be certified by the Secretary of the Board to be a true copy of an assessment or other notice issued by the Board or purporting to be a certificate such as is mentioned in the foregoing paragraph of this Article shall, unless the contrary is proved, be sufficient evidence of the document and of the facts stated therein.

Signed by order of the Secretary of State.

3rd August 1972.

R. Chichester-Clark,

Minister of State,

Department of Employment.

(**a**) S.I. 1965/1101 (1965 II, p. 2805).   (**b**) S.I. 1967/301 (1967 I, p. 1040).
(**c**) S.I. 1965/1157 (1965 II, p. 3266).   (**d**) S.I. 1967/302 (1967 I, p. 1050).

Article 3

SCHEDULE

1.—(1) In this Schedule unless the context otherwise requires—

(a) "the appropriate percentage" means, in relation to the emoluments of persons employed at or from a wool, jute and flax establishment that was engaged wholly or mainly in any one or more of the activities comprised in one of the two groups of activities specified in the first and second columns of the Appendix to this Schdule, the percentage specified in relation to that group in the third column of that Appendix;

(b) "arranging for the carrying out on commission" in relation to any activities mentioned in the Appendix to this Schedule means arranging for the carrying out by another person in pursuance of a contract of work or labour (with or without the provision of materials) of those activities wholly or mainly upon or from materials owned in the course of this business by the person for whom such activities are to be carried out;

(c) "production" in relation to any yarn includes any of the processes mentioned in sub-paragraphs (d), (e), (f) and (g) of paragraph 1 of the Schedule to the industrial training order;

(d) other expressions have the meanings assigned to them respectively by paragraph 3 or 4 of the Schedule to the industrial training order or by Article 2 of this Order.

(2) The activities in either Group specified in the first and second columns of the Appendix to this Schedule include the activities of arranging either directly or through another person for the carrying out on commission of any activities comprised in that Group, and include also any related or administrative activities undertaken in relation to any activities comprised in such Group.

(3) In reckoning any sum of emoluments for the purposes of this Schedule no regard shall be had to the emoluments of any person wholly engaged in agriculture or in the supply of food or drink for immediate consumption.

2. Subject to the provisions of this Schedule, the amount of levy to be imposed on an employer in respect of a wool, jute and flax establishment shall be equal to the appropriate percentage of the sum of the emoluments of all the persons employed by the employer in the eighth base period at or from the establishment.

3. There shall be exempt from the levy : —

(a) an employer in whose case—

(i) the sum of the emoluments of all the persons employed by him in the eighth base period at or from the wool, jute and flax establishment or establishments of the employer (including any persons employed at or from a wool, jute and flax establishment by an associated company of the employer) did not exceed £15,000; or

(ii) the number of employees employed by him (or by an associated company of the employer) at or from such establishment or establishments on the 31st day of March 1972 did not exceed 15;

(b) a charity.

4. The amount of the levy imposed in respect of a wool, jute and flax establishment that ceases to carry on business in the eighth levy period shall be in the same proportion to the amount that would otherwise be due in accordance with the foregoing provisions of this Schedule as the number of days between the commencement of the said levy period and the date of cessation of business (both dates inclusive) bears to the number of days in the said levy period.

APPENDIX

Group No.	Description of Activities	Appropriate Percentage
1.	The activities following or any of them—	
	(a) the production of yarn from jute;	0.88%
	(b) the manufacture of any woven fabric from such yarn; or	
	(c) the production of any other yarn or the manufacture of any other woven fabric, being production or manufacture in a textile factory from any textile fibres, yarn or continuous filament and, in any case, by a system commonly employed in the production of jute yarn or in the manufacture of jute fabric or by a system similar thereto.	
2.	Any other activities of the wool, jute and flax industry not being activities comprised in Group 1 in this Appendix.	0.75%

EXPLANATORY NOTE

(This Note is not part of the Order.)

This Order gives effect to proposals submitted to the Secretary of State for Employment by the Wool, Jute and Flax Industry Training Board for the imposition of a further levy upon employers in the wool, jute and flax industry for the purpose of raising money towards the expenses of the Board.

The levy is to be imposed in respect of the eighth levy period commencing with the day upon which this Order comes into operation and ending on 5th April 1973. The levy will be assessed by the Board and there will be a right of appeal to an industrial tribunal.

STATUTORY INSTRUMENTS

1972 No. 1188 (L.16)

OATHS

The Commissioners for Oaths (Fees) Order 1972

Made - - -		*28th July* 1972
Coming into Operation		*2nd October* 1972

The Lord Chancellor, in exercise of the powers conferred on him by section 216 of the Supreme Court of Judicature (Consolidation) Act 1925(**a**) and with the concurrence of the Lord Chief Justice and the Master of the Rolls, hereby makes the following Order:—

1. This Order may be cited as the Commissioners for Oaths (Fees) Order 1972 and shall come into operation on 2nd October 1972.

2. The following fees shall be charged by commissioners for oaths in respect of the administration of oaths and taking of affidavits:—

	£
For taking an affidavit or a declaration or an affirmation or an attestation upon honour, for each person making the same	0.50
And in addition thereto for each exhibit therein referred to and required to be marked or for each schedule required to be marked	0.20

3. The Commissioners for Oaths (Fees) Order 1959 (**b**) is hereby revoked.

Dated 26th July 1972.

Hailsham of St. Marylebone, C.

We concur,

Dated 28th July 1972.

Widgery, C.J.
Denning, M.R.

(**a**) 1925 c. 49.   (**b**) S.I. 1959/2255 (1959 II, p. 1977).

EXPLANATORY NOTE
(This Note is not part of the Order.)

This Order increases the fee which commissioners for oaths are to charge for taking affidavits and similar declarations from 25p to 50p and the fee for marking exhibits from 10p to 20p.

STATUTORY INSTRUMENTS

1972 No. 1189 (L. 17)

BANKRUPTCY, ENGLAND

The Bankruptcy Fees (Amendment No. 2) Order 1972

Made - - -	31*st July* 1972
Coming into Operation	2*nd October* 1972

The Lord Chancellor and the Treasury, in exercise of the powers conferred on them by section 133 of the Bankruptcy Act 1914(**a**) and sections 2 and 3 of the Public Offices Fees Act 1879(**b**), hereby make, sanction and consent to the following Order:—

1.—(1) This Order may be cited as the Bankruptcy Fees (Amendment No. 2) Order 1972 and shall come into operation on 2nd October 1972.

(2) The Interpretation Act 1889(**c**) shall apply to the interpretation of this Order as it applies to the interpretation of an Act of Parliament.

2. The Bankruptcy Fees Order 1970(**d**), as amended (**e**), shall have effect subject to the following amendments:—

In Fee No. 22 and Fee No. 39 of Table A in the Schedule to that Order, for the figures "£0 5s. 0d." and "£0.25", and "£0 2s. 0d." and "£0.10" there shall be substituted the figures "£0 10s. 0d." and "£0.50", and "£0 4s. 0d." and "£0.20" respectively.

Dated 26th July 1972.

Hailsham of St. Marylebone, C.

Dated 31st July 1972.

Tim Fortescue,
Hugh Rossi,
Two of the Lords Commissioners
of Her Majesty's Treasury.

(**a**) 1914 c. 59.   (**b**) 1879 c. 58.   (**c**) 1889 c. 63.
(**d**) S.1. 1970/2007 (1970 III, p. 6524).   (**e**) There is no relevant amending Order.

EXPLANATORY NOTE

(This Note is not part of the Order.)

This Order amends the Bankruptcy Fees Order 1970 by increasing the fees payable for taking affidavits and marking exhibits.

STATUTORY INSTRUMENTS

1972 No. 1190 (L. 18)

SUPREME COURT OF JUDICATURE, ENGLAND

FEES AND STAMPS

The Supreme Court Fees (Amendment) Order 1972

Made - - -	*31st July* 1972
Coming into Operation	*2nd October* 1972

The Lord Chancellor, the Judges of the Supreme Court and the Treasury, in exercise of the powers and authorities vested in them respectively by section 213 of the Supreme Court of Judicature (Consolidation) Act 1925(**a**), section 365(3) of the Companies Act 1948(**b**) and sections 2 and 3 of the Public Offices Fees Act 1879(**c**), do hereby, according as the provisions of the said enactments respectively authorise and require them, make, advise, concur in, sanction and consent to the following Order:—

1.—(1) This Order may be cited as the Supreme Court Fees (Amendment) Order 1972 and shall come into operation on 2nd October 1972.

(2) The Interpretation Act 1889(**d**) shall apply to the interpretation of this Order as it applies to the interpretation of an Act of Parliament.

2. The Supreme Court Fees Order 1970(**e**), as amended (**f**), shall be further amended as follows:—

(1) In Article 3, the words "(1) Subject to the provisions of sub-paragraph (2) of this Article" and paragraph (2) shall be omitted.

(2) The Note immediately preceding section 1 of the Schedule shall be omitted.

(3) In the Schedule, column 2A shall be omitted and column 2B shall stand as column 2.

(**a**) 1925 c. 49. (**b**) 1948 c. 38.
(**c**) 1879 c. 58. (**d**) 1889 c. 63.
(**e**) S.I. 1970/1870 (1970 III, p. 6135). (**f**) S.I 1971/1245 (1971 II, p. 3615).

(4) In the Schedule, in Fee No. 91 for the figures "0·25" and "0·10" in column 2 there shall be substituted the figures "0.50" and "0.20" respectively.

Dated 26th July 1972.

Hailsham of St. Marylebone, C.

Dated 28th July 1972.

Widgery, C.J.
Denning, M.R.
George Baker, P.

Dated 31st July 1972.

Tim Fortescue,
Hugh Rossi,
Two of the Lords Commissioners
of Her Majesty's Treasury.

EXPLANATORY NOTE

(This Note is not part of the Order.)

This Order increases the fees payable in the Supreme Court for taking affidavits and marking exhibits.   References to the currency in use before decimalization are removed from the Supreme Court Fees Order 1970.

STATUTORY INSTRUMENTS

1972 No. 1191 (L.19)

SUPREME COURT OF JUDICATURE, ENGLAND

FEES AND STAMPS

The Supreme Court (Non-Contentious Probate) Fees (Amendment) Order 1972

Made - - -	*31st July* 1972
Coming into Operation	*2nd October* 1972

The Lord Chancellor, the Judges of the Supreme Court, and the Treasury, in exercise of the powers and authorities vested in them respectively by section 213 of the Supreme Court of Judicature (Consolidation) Act 1925(**a**), and sections 2 and 3 of the Public Offices Fees Act 1879(**b**), do hereby, according as the provisions of the said enactments respectively authorise and require them, make, advise, consent to and concur in the following Order:—

1.—(1) This Order may be cited as the Supreme Court (Non-Contentious Probate) Fees (Amendment) Order 1972 and shall come into operation on 2nd October 1972.

(2) The Interpretation Act 1889(**c**) shall apply to the interpretation of this Order as it applies to the interpretation of an Act of Parliament.

2.—The Supreme Court (Non-Contentious Probate) Fees Order 1970(**d**) shall have effect subject to the following amendment:—

For Fee No. 20 in the Schedule to that Order there shall be substituted the following fee:—

	£ s. d.	£
"20. Save in a personal application for a grant—		
(*a*) for administering an oath, for each deponent to each affidavit	0 10 0	0·50

(**a**) 1925 c. 49.
(**c**) 1889 c. 63.
(**b**) 1879 c. 58.
(**d**) S.I. 1970/1869 (1970 III, p. 6128).

(*b*) for marking each exhibit	0	4	0	0·20
(*c*) for superintending and attesting execution of a guarantee, for each surety	0	10	0	0·50 "

Dated 26th July 1972.

Hailsham of St. Marylebone, C.

Dated 28th July 1972.

Widgery, C.J.
Denning, M.R.
George Baker, P.

Dated 31st July 1972.

Tim Fortescue,
Hugh Rossi,
Two of the Lords Commissioners
of Her Majesty's Treasury.

EXPLANATORY NOTE

(This Note is not part of the Order.)

This Order amends the Supreme Court (Non-Contentious Probate) Fees Order 1970 by increasing the fees for taking affidavits and guarantees from 25p to 50p and the fee for marking exhibits from 10p to 20p.

STATUTORY INSTRUMENTS

1972 No. 1194 (L.20)

SUPREME COURT OF JUDICATURE, ENGLAND
PROCEDURE

The Rules of the Supreme Court (Amendment No. 2) 1972

Made - - - -	1*st August* 1972
Laid before Parliament	14*th August* 1972
Coming into Operation	1*st October* 1972

We, the Rule Committee of the Supreme Court, being the authority having for the time being power under section 99(4) of the Supreme Court of Judicature (Consolidation) Act 1925**(a)** to make, amend or revoke rules regulating the practice and procedure of the Supreme Court of Judicature, hereby exercise those powers and all other powers enabling us in that behalf as follows:—

1.—(1) These Rules may be cited as the Rules of the Supreme Court (Amendment No. 2) 1972 and shall come into operation on 1st October 1972.

(2) In these Rules an Order referred to by number means the Order so numbered in the Rules of the Supreme Court 1965**(b)**, as amended**(c)**.

(3) The Interpretation Act 1889**(d)** shall apply to the interpretation of these Rules as it applies to the interpretation of an Act of Parliament.

2. In Order 1, rule 4(1), after the definition of "senior master" there shall be inserted the following definition:—

" "vacation" means the interval between the end of any of the sittings mentioned in Order 64, rule 1, and the beginning of the next sittings."

3. Order 59 shall be amended as follows:—

(1) In rule 5(1)(*b*) the words "impressed with the appropriate judicature fee stamp or" shall be omitted.

(2) In rule 5(5), sub-paragraphs (*c*) and (*d*) shall be omitted and sub-paragraphs (*e*) and (*f*) shall be re-lettered accordingly.

(3) The following paragraph shall be substituted for paragraph (2A) of rule 16:—

"(2A) The notice of appeal shall be served on the appropriate registrar as well as on the party or parties required to be served under rule 3."

(4) In rule 16(3) for the words from "leave with" to "fee stamp or" there shall be substituted the words "produce to the chief registrar of the Chancery Division a sealed copy of the decree appealed against and leave with him a copy of that decree and two copies of the notice of appeal (one of which shall be".

(a) 1925 c. 49.   (b) S.I. 1965/1776 (1965 III, p. 4995).
(c) The relevant amending instruments are S.I. 1968/1244, 1971/1269, 1955, 1972/813 (1968 II, p. 3360; 1971 II, 3634; III, p. 5274; 1972 II, p. 2618).
(d) 1889 c. 63.

(5) In rule 16(4) the words from the beginning to "registrar; and" shall be omitted.

(6) In rule 16(5) for the words "the clerk of the rules" there shall be substituted the words "the appropriate registrar".

(7) For paragraph (6) of rule 16 there shall be substituted the following paragraph:—

"(6) In this rule "the appropriate registrar" means—

(*a*) in relation to a cause pending in a county court, the registrar of that court,

(*b*) in relation to a cause proceeding in the principal registry of the Family Division, the principal registrar of that Division, and

(*c*) in relation to a cause proceeding in a district registry, the registrar of that registry."

(8) At the end of rule 19 there shall be added the following paragraph:—

"(7) In relation to any proceedings in the principal registry of the Family Division which by virtue of matrimonial causes rules are treated as pending in a county court, paragraphs (1) to (5) shall have effect with the necessary modifications as if the principal registry were a county court."

4. Order 62 shall be amended as follows:—

(1) In rule 12(4), sub-paragraph (*b*) shall be omitted and sub-paragraph (*c*) shall stand as sub-paragraph (*b*).

(2) In rule 12(5), the letter "(*a*)" and the words from "and (*b*)" to the end shall be omitted.

(3) After rule 20 there shall be inserted the following rule:—

"*Powers of district registrars under Part III of Solicitors Act* 1957

20A.—(1) An originating summons for an order under any provision of Part III of the Solicitors Act 1957**(a)** for the taxation of a bill of costs may be issued out of a district registry if, but only if—

(*a*) the costs are for contentious business done in a cause or matter which proceeded in that registry, or

(*b*) the costs are for non-contentious business and that registry is one specified in paragraph (3).

In this paragraph "contentious business" and "non-contentious business" have the same meanings respectively as in the said Act of 1957.

(2) Where an originating summons is issued out of a district registry pursuant to paragraph (1), the registrar of that registry shall have power to make the order sought by the summons and to tax the costs to which the order relates.

(a) 1957 c. 27.

(3) The district registries referred to in paragraph (1)(*b*) are the following:—

Birmingham	Exeter	Norwich
Bournemouth	Ipswich	Nottingham
Brighton	Kingston upon Hull	Oxford
Bristol	Leeds	Plymouth
Caernarvon	Lincoln	Preston
Cambridge	Liverpool	Reading
Cardiff	Manchester	Sheffield
Carlisle	Middlesbrough	Southampton
Chester	Newcastle upon Tyne	Swansea
		Truro."

5. Order 64 shall be amended as follows:—

(1) In the heading to rule 1 the words "*and vacations*" shall be omitted.

(2) Rule 1(1) shall be amended as follows:—

(*a*) In sub-paragraph (*a*) for the words "the day appointed for that purpose by Order in Council made under section 53 of the Act" there shall be substituted the words "1st October".

(*b*) In sub-paragraphs (*c*) and (*d*) for the words "Whit Sunday" there shall in each case be substituted the words "the spring holiday".

(3) For paragraphs (2) and (3) of Rule 1 there shall be substituted the following paragraph:—

"(2) In this rule "spring holiday" means the bank holiday falling on the last Monday in May or any day appointed instead of that day under section 1(2) of the Banking and Financial Dealings Act 1971**(a)**."

(4) In rule 6(1), the words "and the vacations to be observed by them" shall be omitted.

(5) For paragraph (1) of rule 7, there shall be substituted the following paragraph:—

"(1) The offices of the Supreme Court shall be open on every day of the year except—

(*a*) Saturdays and Sundays,

(*b*) Good Friday and the day after Easter Monday,

(*c*) Christmas Eve or—

(i) if that day is a Saturday, then 23rd December,

(ii) if that day is a Sunday or Tuesday, then 27th December,

(*d*) Christmas Day and, if that day is a Friday or Saturday, then 28th December,

(*e*) bank holidays in England and Wales under the Banking and Financial Dealings Act 1971, and

(*f*) such other days as the Lord Chancellor, with the concurrence of the Lord Chief Justice, the Master of the Rolls and the President of the Family Division, may direct."

6. In Order 104, rule 8(2), after the words "paragraph (1)(*b*)(i)" there shall be inserted the figure "(iii)".

(a) 1971 c. 80.

7. Order 106, rule 2, shall be amended as follows:—

(1) In paragraph (2) the words "subject to the following provisions of this rule" shall be omitted and after the words "Division and" there shall be inserted the words "subject to Order 62, rule 20A".

(2) Paragraphs (3) to (6) shall be omitted.

Dated 1st August 1972.

Hailsham of St. Marylebone, C.

Widgery, C. J.

Denning, M. R.

George Baker, P.

John Pennycuick, V-C.

Eustace Roskill, L. J.

Nigel Bridge, J.

S. B. R. Cooke, J.

James Fox-Andrews,

Donald K. Rattee.

William Carter.

H. Montgomery-Campbell.

EXPLANATORY NOTE
(This Note is not part of the Rules.)

These Rules amend the provisions of the Rules of the Supreme Court relating to vacations and the closing of the court offices so as to take account of the Supreme Court (Spring Holiday) Order 1972 (S.I. 1972/968) and the Banking and Financial Dealings Act 1971 (Rules 2 and 5). They also require all appeals in matrimonial causes to be set down with the chief registrar of the Chancery Division (Rule 3), enable proceedings for the taxation of the costs of non-contentious business to be brought in a number of additional district registries (Rules 4 and 7) and make a minor amendment with regard to the registration of maintenance orders in magistrates' courts (Rule 6).

STATUTORY INSTRUMENTS

1972 No. 1195

POLICE

The Police (Amendment) (No. 3) Regulations 1972

Made - - -	*4th August* 1972
Laid before Parliament	*11th August* 1972
Coming into Operation	*1st September* 1972

In exercise of the powers conferred upon me by section 33 of the Police Act 1964(**a**), and after consulting the Police Council for the United Kingdom in accordance with section 4(4) of the Police Act 1969(**b**) and the Police Advisory Board for England and Wales in accordance with section 4(6) of the said Act of 1969, I hereby make the following Regulations:—

PART I

CITATION, OPERATION ETC.

1. These Regulations may be cited as the Police (Amendment) (No. 3) Regulations 1972.

2. These Regulations shall come into operation on 1st September 1972 and shall have effect as from that date except that for the purposes of Part II thereof they shall have effect as from 1st April 1972.

3. In these Regulations any reference to the principal Regulations is a reference to the Police Regulations 1971(**c**), as amended (**d**).

PART II

PROVISIONS HAVING EFFECT FROM 1ST APRIL 1972

4. For the Table in Schedule 7 to the principal Regulations (subsistence, refreshment and lodging allowances) there shall be substituted the Table set out in Appendix 1 to these Regulations.

PART III

PROVISIONS HAVING EFFECT FROM 1ST SEPTEMBER 1972

5. In Regulation 6(1) of the principal Regulations (meanings assigned to certain expressions) for the definitions of the expressions "sergeant" and "superintendent" there shall be substituted the following definitions:—

' "sergeant" includes station sergeant and first class sergeant (C.I.D.) in the metropolitan police force;

"superintendent" includes chief superintendent;'.

(**a**) 1964 c. 48.   (**b**) 1969 c. 63.
(**c**) S.I. 1971/156 (1971 I, p. 439).
(**d**) The relevant amending instruments are S.I. 1971/1901, 1972/74 (1971 III, p. 5156; 1972 I, p. 203).

6. For Regulation 8(1) of the principal Regulations (ranks) there shall be substituted the following provision: —

"8.—(1) The ranks of a police force shall be known by the following designations: —

Chief Constable
Assistant Chief Constable or Commander
Chief Superintendent
Superintendent
Chief Inspector
Inspector
Sergeant
Constable.".

7. For paragraph (1)(b) of Regulation 13 of the principal Regulations (qualifications for appointment to a police force) there shall be substituted the following provision: —

"(b) must have attained the age of 19 years and, unless he has previous service as a member of a police force or by reason of other experience or his personal qualities is specially suitable for appointment, must not have attained the age of—

(i) in the case of a man, 30 years or, if he has previous whole-time service in the armed forces or previous service as a seaman, 40 years;

(ii) in the case of a woman, 35 years or, if she has such previous service as aforesaid, 40 years;".

8. For the proviso to Regulation 18(2) of the principal Regulations (personal records) there shall be subsituted the following proviso: —

"Provided that, if the member so requests—

(i) a punishment of a fine or of a reprimand shall be expunged after 3 years free from punishment, other than a caution;

(ii) any other punishment shall be expunged after 5 years free from punishment other than a caution.".

9. In Regulation 24(3) of the principal Regulations (normal daily period of duty) for the words "Where the normal daily period of duty is performed in one tour of duty" there shall be substituted the words "The normal daily period of duty shall, so far as the exigencies of duty permit, be performed in one tour of duty and, in such case,".

10.—(1) At the end of paragraph (1) of Regulation 47 of the principal Regulations (removal allowance) there shall be added the following sub-paragraph: —

"(d) shall reimburse the member his payments in connection with his former home by way of mortgage interest, rent or rates (within the meaning of Regulation 42(6)) payable in respect of the first 13 weeks following the move up to an amount equal to that which would have been payable to him by way of rent allowance in respect of that period had he not moved but had continued to be entitled to a rent allowance payable at the rate at which such an allowance was payable immediately before the move so, however, that where the police authority are of opinion that the member has not taken all reasonable steps to reduce or terminate his liability to make such payments as aforesaid they may restrict the reimbursement to payments which the member would have been liable to make had he taken all such steps.".

(2) At the end of paragraph (2) of the said Regulation 47 there shall be added the following sub-paragraph: —

"(*d*) may, subject to the conditions mentioned in paragraph (1)(*d*), reimburse the expenses there mentioned.".

11.—(1) In Part I of Schedule 5 to the principal Regulations (scales of pay for men) for Tables A and B there shall be substituted, respectively, the Tables A and B set out in Appendix 2 to these Regulations.

(2) For paragraph 1(4) of the said Part I there shall be substituted the following provision: —

"(4) Where a superintendent has completed 4 years of service in the rank of chief inspector and the Secretary of State approves the application of this sub-paragraph in his case, his annual pay before completing 1 year of service in the rank of superintendent shall be—

(*a*) in the case of a member of the City of London or metropolitan police force, £3,372 instead of £3,276;

(*b*) in any other case, £3,015 instead of £2,919.".

12.—(1) In Part II of Schedule 5 to the principal Regulations (scales of pay for women) for Tables A, B, C and D there shall be substituted, respectively, the Tables A, B, C and D set out in Appendix 3 to these Regulations.

(2) For paragraph 1(3) of the said Part II there shall be substituted the following provision: —

"(3) Where a superintendent has completed 4 years of service in the rank of chief inspector and the Secretary of State approves the application of this sub-paragraph in her case, her annual pay before completing 1 year of service in the rank of superintendent shall be—

(*a*) in the case of a member of the City of London or metropolitan police force, £3,204 instead of £3,111;

(*b*) in any other case, £2,865 instead of £2,772.".

(3) In paragraph 2(6) of the said Part II for the sums "£1,148", "£1,098", "£1,199" and "£1,149" there shall be substituted, respectively, the sums "£1,211", "£1,161", "£1,265" and "£1,215".

13. In Schedule 6 to the principal Regulations (detective duty and supplementary detective allowances) for Tables A and B there shall be substituted, respectively, the Tables A and B set out in Appendix 4 to these Regulations.

14.—(1) Nothing in Regulation 8(1) of the principal Regulations, as amended by Regulation 6 of these Regulations, shall be construed as affecting the right of a person who, immediately before 1st September 1972, was a reversionary member of a home police force or a central police officer (within the meaning of the principal Regulations) to revert to his former force in a rank not mentioned therein.

(2) For the purposes of Regulation 32(2) of the principal Regulations and Schedule 5 thereto, as amended by Regulations 11 and 12 of these Regulations—

(*a*) service in the rank of superintendent, class I or class II, shall be treated as if it had been service in the rank of superintendent, and

(*b*) service in the rank of station sergeant, or of first or second class sergeant (C.I.D.) shall be treated as service in the rank of sergeant.

(3) In the case of a superintendent who, immediately before 1st September 1972, held the rank of superintendent, class I, Schedule 5 to the principal Regulations, as amended as aforesaid, shall have effect as if for the entries relating to the rank of superintendent in Table B of Part I thereof and in Tables A and B of Part II thereof there were substituted, respectively, the entries in the Table set out in Appendix 5 to these Regulations.

Robert Carr,
One of Her Majesty's Principal
Secretaries of State.

Home Office,
Whitehall.

4th August 1972.

APPENDIX 1

TABLE SUBSTITUTED FOR TABLE IN SCHEDULE 7 TO THE PRINCIPAL REGULATIONS

TABLE

Description of allowance	Superin-tendents	Inspectors, Sergeants and Constables
Refreshment Allowance:	£	£
(i) for one meal	0·54	0·50
(ii) for two meals	0·78	0·70
Subsistence Allowance:		
Period of retention or engagement on duty—		
(i) over 5 hours and not exceeding 8 hours	0·78	0·70
(ii) over 8 hours and not exceeding 12 hours	1·11	1·00
(iii) over 12 hours and not exceeding 24 hours	1·90	1·65
(iv) over 24 hours—at the rate under (iii) above for each complete period of 24 hours' retention or engagement, together with whichever is the appropriate amount under the preceding provisions of this Table for any excess over the aggregate of each complete period.		
Lodging Allowance—for each night	3·25	2·80

APPENDIX 2

TABLES SUBSTITUTED FOR TABLES A AND B IN PART I OF SCHEDULE 5 TO THE PRINCIPAL REGULATIONS

TABLE A

MEMBERS OF CITY OF LONDON AND METROPOLITAN POLICE FORCES

Rank	Annual pay			
	Before completing 1 year of service in the rank	After 1 year of service in the rank	After 2 years of service in the rank	After 3 years of service in the rank
	£	£	£	£
Chief superintendent	3,846	3,975	4,101	4,230
Superintendent	3,276	3,372	3,468	3,561
Chief inspector in the City of London police force	2,831	2,927	3,020	3,116
Chief inspector in the metropolitan police force	2,591	2,669	2,750	2,831
Inspector	2,279	2,360	2,441	2,519
Station sergeant or first class sergeant (C.I.D.)	2,129	2,129	2,201	2,201
Sergeant	1,877	1,949	2,018	2,087

TABLE B

MEMBERS OF OTHER POLICE FORCES

Rank	Annual pay			
	Before completing 1 year of service in the rank	After 1 year of service in the rank	After 2 years of service in the rank	After 3 years of service in the rank
	£	£	£	£
Chief superintendent	3,630	3,738	3,846	3,846
Superintendent	2,919	3,015	3,111	3,207
Chief inspector	2,460	2,541	2,619	2,700
Inspector	2,151	2,229	2,310	2,391
Sergeant	1,827	1,899	1,968	2,037

APPENDIX 3

TABLES SUBSTITUTED FOR TABLES A, B, C AND D IN PART II OF SCHEDULE 5 TO THE PRINCIPAL REGULATIONS

TABLE A

MEMBERS OF CITY OF LONDON AND METROPOLITAN POLICE FORCES

Rank	Annual pay			
	Before completing 1 year of service in the rank	After 1 year of service in the rank	After 2 years of service in the rank	After 3 years of service in the rank
	£	£	£	£
Chief superintendent	3,654	3,777	3,897	4,020
Superintendent	3,111	3,204	3,294	3,384
Chief inspector	2,465	2,537	2,615	2,693
Inspector	2,168	2,246	2,321	2,396
Sergeant	1,787	1,853	1,919	1,985

TABLE B

MEMBERS OF OTHER POLICE FORCES

Rank	Annual pay			
	Before completing 1 year of service in the rank	After 1 year of service in the rank	After 2 years of service in the rank	After 3 years of service in the rank
	£	£	£	£
Chief superintendent	3,450	3,552	3,654	3,654
Superintendent	2,772	2,865	2,955	3,048
Chief inspector	2,337	2,415	2,487	2,565
Inspector	2,043	2,118	2,196	2,271
Sergeant	1,737	1,803	1,869	1,935

TABLE C

MEMBERS OF THE CITY OF LONDON AND METROPOLITAN POLICE FORCES

Reckonable service	Standard scale of annual pay	Transitional scales of annual pay			
		Aged 19 on entry	Aged 20 on entry	Aged 21 on entry	Aged 22 or over on entry
	£	£	£	£	£
Before completing 1 year of service ...	1,085	1,085	1,109	1,154	1,205
After 1 year of service	1,142	1,142	1,160	1,211	1,262
After 2 years of service	1,259	1,259	1,259	1,316	1,352
After 3 years of service	1,316	1,316	1,316	1,373	1,409
After 4 years of service	1,373	1,373	1,373	1,448	1,466
After 5 years of service	1,448	1,448	1,448	1,448	1,526
After 6 years of service	1,526	1,526	1,526	1,526	1,601
After 7 years of service	1,526	1,526	1,526	1,601	1,601
After 8 years of service	1,526	1,526	1,601	1,601	1,601
After 9 years of service	1,601	1,601	1,601	1,601	1,601
After 13 years of service	1,676	1,676	1,676	1,676	1,676
After 17 years of service	1,751	1,751	1,751	1,751	1,751

TABLE D

MEMBERS OF OTHER POLICE FORCES

Reckonable service	Standard scale of annual pay	Transitional scales of annual pay			
		Aged 19 on entry	Aged 20 on entry	Aged 21 on entry	Aged 22 or over on entry
	£	£	£	£	£
Before completing 1 year of service ...	1,035	1,035	1,059	1,104	1,155
After 1 year of service	1,092	1,092	1,110	1,161	1,212
After 2 years of service	1,209	1,209	1,209	1,266	1,302
After 3 years of service	1,266	1,266	1,266	1,323	1,359
After 4 years of service	1,323	1,323	1,323	1,398	1,416
After 5 years of service	1,398	1,398	1,398	1,398	1,476
After 6 years of service	1,476	1,476	1,476	1,476	1,551
After 7 years of service	1,476	1,476	1,476	1,551	1,551
After 8 years of service	1,476	1,476	1,551	1,551	1,551
After 9 years of service	1,551	1,551	1,551	1,551	1,551
After 13 years of service	1,626	1,626	1,626	1,626	1,626
After 17 years of service	1,701	1,701	1,701	1,701	1,701

APPENDIX 4

TABLES SUBSTITUTED FOR TABLES A AND B IN SCHEDULE 6 TO THE PRINCIPAL REGULATIONS

TABLE A

DETECTIVE DUTY ALLOWANCE

Rank	Men	Women
	£	£
Superintendent	300	285
Chief inspector in the City of London police force	297	—
Chief inspector in the metropolitan police force	270	258
Chief inspector in any other police force	258	246
Inspector in the City of London and metropolitan police forces ...	240	228
Inspector in any other police force	228	216
First class sergeant (C.I.D.)	216	—
Sergeant in the City of London and metropolitan police forces ...	198	189
Sergeant in any other police force	192	183
Constable in the City of London and metropolitan police forces ...	150	144
Constable in any other police force	144	138

TABLE B

SUPPLEMENTARY DETECTIVE ALLOWANCE

Rank	8 to 12 hours qualifying overtime		12 or more hours qualifying overtime	
	Men	Women	Men	Women
	£	£	£	£
Chief inspector in the City of London police force ...	246	—	444	—
Chief inspector in the metropolitan police force ...	225	213	405	384
Chief inspector in any other police force	213	201	384	366
Inspector in the City of London and metropolitan police forces	198	189	357	339
Inspector in any other police force	189	180	339	321
First class sergeant (C.I.D.)	180	—	324	—
Sergeant in the City of London and metropolitan police forces	165	156	297	282
Sergeant in any other police force	159	150	285	270
Constable in the City of London and metropolitan police forces	126	120	228	216
Constable in any other police force	120	114	216	204

APPENDIX 5

TABLE

SCALES OF PAY FOR FORMER SUPERINTENDENTS, CLASS I

	Annual pay			
	Before completing 1 year of service in the rank	After 1 year of service in the rank	After 2 years of service in the rank	After 3 years of service in the rank
	£	£	£	£
Men Superintendent in a police force other than the City of London or metropolitan police force ...	3,276	3,372	3,468	3,561
Women Superintendent in the City of London or metropolitan police force	3,285	3,378	3,468	3,468
Superintendent in any other police force	3,111	3,204	3,294	3,384

EXPLANATORY NOTE

(This Note is not part of the Regulations.)

These Regulations amend the Police Regulations 1971, save in the case of Regulation 4, with effect from 1st September 1972.

Regulation 4 increases the rates of subsistence, refreshment and lodging allowances with effect from 1st April 1972 (retrospective increases are authorised by section 33(4) of the Police Act 1964).

Regulation 6 simplifies the rank structure of police forces other than the metropolitan police force. A single rank of superintendent is substituted for the two ranks of superintendent, class I, and superintendent, class II, and the ranks of station sergeant, first class sergeant (C.I.D.) and second class sergeant (C.I.D.) are abolished. Regulations 5, 11, 12 and 14 contain incidental, consequential and transitional provisions including, in Regulation 14(3), provision securing that a superintendent who had been a superintendent, class I, does not suffer a reduction in pay. (Additionally, these Regulations contemplate changes in the metropolitan police force rank structure and provide for increases in the pay of women members of police forces as mentioned below.)

Regulation 7 relaxes the qualifications for appointment to a police force by permitting the appointment of a person over the normal age limit if he is specially suitable for appointment by reason of his experience or personal qualities.

Regulation 8 reduces the periods after which punishments must, on request, be expunged from a policeman's personal records, except in the case of punishments for which the period is only 3 years.

Regulation 9 provides that a policeman shall normally perform his duties each day in a single tour of duty.

Regulation 10, in the case of a policeman to whom a removal allowance is payable, provides for the reimbursement, within specified limits and for the first 13 weeks following his move, of his continuing outgoings on his former home by way of mortgage interest, rent or rates.

Regulation 12 (apart from making provision consequential on Regulation 6) narrows the gap between the pay of a woman and that of a man holding the same rank. Regulation 13 makes related increases in detective allowances payable to women.

STATUTORY INSTRUMENTS

1972 No. 1198

MEDICINES

The Medicines (Termination of Transitional Exemptions) (No. 1) Order 1972

Made - - - *4th August* 1972

The Secretaries of State respectively concerned with health in England and in Wales, the Secretary of State concerned with health and with agriculture in Scotland, the Secretary of State for Northern Ireland and the Minister of Agriculture, Fisheries and Food, acting jointly, in exercise of their powers under sections 17 and 37(3) of the Medicines Act 1968(a) (as having effect subject to the provisions of Article 2(2) of, and Schedule 1 to the Transfer of Functions (Wales) Order 1969(b) and section 1(1)(a) of the Northern Ireland (Temporary Provisions) Act 1972(c)) and of all other powers enabling them in that behalf, after consulting such organisations as appear to them to be representative of interests likely to be substantially affected by the following Order, hereby make the following Order:—

Citation and interpretation

1.—(1) This order may be cited as the Medicines (Termination of Transitional Exemptions) (No. 1) Order 1972.

(2) In this order, unless the context otherwise requires "the Act" means the Medicines Act 1968 and other expressions have the same meaning as in the Act.

(3) The Interpretation Act 1889(d) applies for the purpose of the interpretation of this order as it applies for the purpose of the interpretation of an Act of Parliament.

Termination of transitional exemptions from licences

2. The 1st September 1972 shall be the day appointed for the purposes of subsections (2) to (5) of section 16 of the Act (transitional exemptions) as being the day upon which those subsections shall cease to have effect in relation to anything done on or after that day in so far as it does not either—

(*a*) relate to a substance that is a medicinal product by virtue only of the provisions of section 130(1)(*b*) of the Act (ingredients), or

(*b*) consist of the sale or offer for sale by way of wholesale dealing of a medicinal product, other than a veterinary drug, which may be lawfully sold by retail otherwise than in accordance with a prescription given by a doctor or dentist, or from premises other than a registered pharmacy

---

(a) 1968 c. 67.   (b) S.I. 1969/388 (1969 I, p. 1070).
(c) 1972 c. 22.   (d) 1889 c. 63.

(within the meaning of the Act but as modified for the purposes of section 10 of the Act by Article 4 of the Medicines (Retail Pharmacists—Exemptions from Licensing Requirements) Order 1971(a)).

Termination of transitional exemptions from clinical trials and animal test certificates

3. The date appointed for the purposes of section 37 of the Act (transitional provisions as to clinical trials and medicinal tests on animals) shall be 1st December 1972.

Keith Joseph,
Secretary of State for Social Services.

28th July 1972.

Peter Thomas,
Secretary of State for Wales.

1st August 1972.

Gordon Campbell,
Secretary of State for Scotland.

3rd August 1972.

W. S. I. Whitelaw,
Secretary of State for Northern Ireland.

3rd August 1972.

In witness whereof the official seal of the Minister of Agriculture, Fisheries and Food is hereunto affixed on 4th August 1972.

(L.S.)   *J. M. L. Prior,*
Minister of Agriculture, Fisheries and Food.

(a) S.I. 1971/1445 (1971 III, p. 4078).

EXPLANATORY NOTE

(This Note is not part of the Order.)

This Order appoints the 1st September 1972 as the day upon which the transitional exemptions under section 16 of the Medicines Act 1968 whereby since 1st September 1971 (see The Medicines (First Appointed Day) Order 1971 S.I. 1971/1153) dealings in certain medicinal products have been exempt from the licensing requirements of the Act, shall cease to have effect in relation to anything done on or after that day other than in relation to ingredients, or to wholesale dealing in medicinal products which are for human use only and which may be lawfully sold by a retailer without a practitioner's prescription or which may be sold from premises which are not those of authorised sellers of poisons or which are not pharmacy premises registered under the Medicines Act 1968. This Order also appoints the 1st December 1972 as the date upon which the transitional exemptions relating to clinical trials and medicinal tests on animals shall cease to have effect. By virtue of section 37(4) of that Act, this latter date is also the date before which applications for clinical trial and animal test certificates of right may be made.

STATUTORY INSTRUMENTS

1972 No. 1199

MEDICINES

The Medicines (Exemption from Licences) (Manufacture and Assembly Temporary Provisions) Order 1972

Made - - -	*4th August* 1972
Laid before Parliament	*11th August* 1972
Coming into Operation	*1st September* 1972

The Secretaries of State respectively concerned with health in England and in Wales, the Secretary of State concerned with health and with agriculture in Scotland, the Secretary of State for Northern Ireland and the Minister of Agriculture, Fisheries and Food, acting jointly, in exercise of their powers under sections 15(1) and 129(4) of the Medicines Act 1968(**a**) (as having effect subject to the provisions of Article 2(2) of, and Schedule 1 to the Transfer of Functions (Wales) Order 1969(**b**) and section 1(1)(*a*) of the Northern Ireland (Temporary Provisions) Act 1972(**c**)) and of all other powers enabling them in that behalf, after consulting such organisations as appear to them to be representative of interests likely to be substantially affected by the following order, hereby make the following order:—

Citation, commencement and interpretation

1.—(1) This order may be cited as the Medicines (Exemption from Licences) (Manufacture and Assembly Temporary Provisions) Order 1972 and shall come into operation on 1st September 1972.

(2) In this order, unless the context otherwise requires—
"the Act" means the Medicines Act 1968;

"medicinal product" includes substances or articles specified in orders made under section 104 or section 105 of the Act which are for the time being in force and which direct that Part II of the Act shall have effect in relation to such substances or articles as that Part has effect in relation to medicinal products within the meaning of the Act;

and other expressions have the same meaning as in the Act.

(3) Except in so far as the context otherwise requires, any reference in this order to any enactment, regulation or order shall be construed as a reference to that enactment, regulation or order, as the case may be, amended or extended by any other enactment, regulation or order.

(4) The Interpretation Act 1889(**d**) applies for the purpose of the interpretation of this order as it applies for the purpose of the interpretation of an Act of Parliament.

(**a**) 1968 c. 67.	(**b**) S.I. 1969/388 (1969 I, p. 1070).
(**c**) 1972 c. 22.	(**d**) 1889 c. 63.

Temporary exemption from manufacturer's licences

2.—(1) Subject to the provisions of paragraphs (3) (4) (5) and (6) of this Article the restrictions imposed by section 8(2) of the Act (restrictions as to manufacture and assembly) shall not apply to the manufacture or assembly of any medicinal product if and so long as the conditions specified in paragraph (2) of this Article are satisfied.

(2) The conditions referred to in the preceding paragraph are—

   (i) that the person who manufactures or assembles the medicinal product (in this order referred to as "the manufacturer") is, in respect of those activities, a person in relation to whom section 16(4) of the Act (transitional exemptions) has effect;

   (ii) that in respect of such manufacture or assembly an application for the grant of a manufacturer's licence, other than a licence of right, has been made before 1st July 1972 and that application has not been determined by the licensing authority and its determination by the licensing authority has not been deferred;

   (iii) that the whole or any instalment of any fees that are payable in connection with that application have been paid;

   (iv) that the manufacturer manufactures or assembles the medicinal product in accordance with—

      (*a*) the particulars contained in or which accompany that application,

      (*b*) any product licence required under the provisions of the Act which is applicable to medicinal products of the same description, and

      (*c*) such standard provisions, prescribed under section 47 of the Act, as are applicable to manufacturer's licences(**a**);

   (v) that the licensing authority has directed that the provisions of this Article may apply to such manufacture or assembly by the manufacturer and the manufacturer has been notified in writing of that direction;

   (vi) that such manufacture is not the manufacture of a product to which Article 2 of the Medicines (Exemption from Licences) (Special and Transitional Cases) Order 1971(**b**) (exemption from product licences for certain special manufactured products) relates.

(3) For the purposes of this order an application shall be taken as deferred when any information requested by the licensing authority under section 44(1) of the Act has not been furnished and it has not been shown to the reasonable satisfaction of the licensing authority that the applicant for that manufacturer's licence is unable to furnish that information and where the licensing authority has indicated in writing to the manufacturer that by virtue of that section that application is not being determined because of that failure to furnish that information.

(**a**) See Schedule 2 to the Medicines (Standard Provisions for Licences and Certificates) Regulations 1971, S.I. 1971/972 (1971 II, p. 2809).
(**b**) S.I. 1971/1450 (1971 III, p. 4118).

(4) If by an interim order made under section 107(3)(*a*) of the Act the operation of the decision of the licensing authority on that application is suspended, the provisions of this order shall apply as if that application has not been determined, so long as the operation of the decision continues to be suspended by the order.

(5) Where the application for the manufacturer's licence has not been made before 1st July 1972 but has been made before such relevant day as is appointed under section 17 of the Act (termination of transitional exemptions), the licensing authority may direct that the provisions of this order may apply as if the application had been made before 1st July 1972.

(6) Where after a direction under sub-paragraph (v) of paragraph (2) of this Article has been notified, it appears to the licensing authority that in the interests of safety the provisions of this Article ought not to apply, the licensing authority may notify the manufacturer in writing that that direction is no longer effective, whereupon the provisions of this Article will cease to apply to the manufacturer.

Application of exemption orders under section 15 of the Act during temporary period of exemption from manufacturer's licences

3.—(1) For the purposes of Article 3 of the Medicines (Exemption from Licences) (Special and Transitional Cases) Order 1971(**a**) the manufacturer shall be treated as the holder of a manufacturer's licence if and so long as the restrictions imposed by section 8(2) of the Act do not apply to him by virtue of the application to him of the preceding Article of this order.

(2) For the purposes of Article 2 of the Medicines (Exemption from Licences) (Wholesale Dealing) Order 1972(**b**) the authorised premises, in relation to the manufacturer who is exempt from the need to be the holder of a manufacturer's licence by virtue of this order, shall be the premises specified in the application for a manufacturer's licence as being the premises which the manufacturer proposes to use for the manufacture, assembly, storage or distribution of the medicinal products to which the application relates.

Keith Joseph,
Secretary of State for Social Services.

28th July 1972.

Peter Thomas,
Secretary of State for Wales.

1st August 1972.

Gordon Campbell,
Secretary of State for Scotland.

3rd August 1972.

W. S. I. Whitelaw,
Secretary of State for Northern Ireland.

3rd August 1972.

In witness whereof the official seal of the Minister of Agriculture, Fisheries and Food is hereunto affixed on 4th August 1972.

(L.S.)   *J. M. L. Prior,*
Minister of Agriculture, Fisheries and Food.

(**a**) S.I. 1971/1450 (1971 III, p. 4118).   (**b**) S.I. 1972/640 (1972 I, p. 2081).

EXPLANATORY NOTE

(This Note is not part of the Order.)

This Order exempts from the restrictions imposed by section 8(2) of the Medicines Act 1968 as to manufacture and assembly of medicinal products except in accordance with a manufacturer's licence granted under Part II of the Act, the manufacture or assembly of certain medicinal products by manufacturers who are entitled to manufacturer's licences of right but who have applied for ordinary licences before 1st July 1972.

The exemption only applies during the period until the application for ordinary licences has been determined.

STATUTORY INSTRUMENTS

1972 No. 1200

MEDICINES

The Medicines (Exemption from Licences) (Special Cases and Miscellaneous Provisions) Order 1972

Made - - -	*4th August* 1972
Laid before Parliament	*11th August* 1972
Coming into Operation	*1st September* 1972

The Secretaries of State respectively concerned with health in England and in Wales, the Secretary of State concerned with health and with agriculture in Scotland, the Secretary of State for Northern Ireland and the Minister of Agriculture, Fisheries and Food, acting jointly, in exercise of their powers under sections 13(2), 15(1), 23(4), 35(8) and 129(4) of the Medicines Act 1968**(a)** (as having effect subject to the provisions of Article 2(2) of and Schedule 1 to the Transfer of Functions (Wales) Order 1969**(b)** and section 1(1)(*a*) of the Northern Ireland (Temporary Provisions) Act 1972**(c)**) and of all other powers enabling them in that behalf, after consulting such organisations as appear to them to be representative of interests likely to be substantially affected by the following order, hereby make the following order:—

Citation, commencement and interpretation

1.—(1) This order may be cited as the Medicines (Exemption from Licences) (Special Cases and Miscellaneous Provisions) Order 1972 and shall come into operation on 1st September 1972.

(2) In this order, unless the context otherwise requires—

"the Act "means the Medicines Act 1968;

"medicinal product" shall not include substances or articles specified in orders made under section 104 or section 105(1)(*b*) of the Act which are for the time being in force unless such order specifically directs that this Order shall have effect in relation to such substances or articles as this Order has effect in relation to medicinal products within the meaning of the Act;

"the Special Cases Order" means the Medicines (Exemption from Licences) (Special and Transitional Cases) Order 1971**(d)**;

and other expressions have the same meaning as in the Act.

(a) 1968 c. 67.	**(b)** S.I. 1969/388 (1969 I, p. 1070).
(c) 1972 c. 22.	**(d)** S.I. 1971/1450 (1971 III, p. 4118).

(3) Except in so far as the context otherwise requires, any reference in this order to any enactment or order shall be construed as a reference to that enactment or order, as the case may be, amended or extended by any other enactment or order.

(4) The Interpretation Act 1889**(a)** applies for the purpose of the interpretation of this order as it applies for the purpose of the interpretation of an Act of Parliament.

Exemption from licences for procuring the manufacture of certain products for stock

2.—(1) Subject to the following paragraphs of this Article, the restrictions imposed by section 7 of the Act (licences for dealings in medicinal products) shall not apply to anything done—

(*a*) by a doctor or dentist which relates to a medicinal product specially prepared by him, or to his order for administration to one or more patients of his or where that doctor or dentist is a member of a group of doctors or dentists working together to provide general medical or dental services, to one or more patients of any other doctor or dentist of that group, and consists of procuring the manufacture or assembly, of a stock of the product with a view to administering the product to such patients;

(*b*) by a veterinary surgeon or veterinary practitioner which relates to a medicinal product specially prepared by him or to his order for administration to one or more animals under his care or, where that veterinary surgeon or veterinary practitioner is a member of a group of veterinary surgeons or veterinary practitioners working together to provide general veterinary services, to one or more animals under the care of any other veterinary surgeon or veterinary practitioner of that group and consists of procuring the manufacture or assembly of a stock of the product with a view to administering it to such animals;

(*c*) in a registered pharmacy, a hospital or a health centre and is done there by or under the supervision of a pharmacist and consists of procuring the manufacture or assembly, of a stock of medicinal products with a view to dispensing them in accordance with a prescription given by—

(i) a particular doctor or dentist, or, where that particular doctor or dentist is a member of a group of doctors or dentists working together to provide general medical or dental services, or is a member of a particular group of doctors or dentists working together in a hospital in the treatment of the same patient or category of patients, any other doctor or dentist of that group, or

(ii) a particular veterinary surgeon or veterinary practitioner or, where that particular veterinary surgeon or veterinary practitioner is a member of a group of such veterinary surgeons or veterinary practitioners working together to provide general veterinary services, any other veterinary surgeon or veterinary practitioner of that group, or

(iii) a practitioner for administration to a particular patient of his, or as the case may be, to a particular animal or herd which is under his care.

(a) 1889 c. 63.

(2) The exemption conferred by the preceding paragraph shall not apply to procuring the manufacture of medicinal products unless the products are to be manufactured by the holder of a manufacturer's licence which staisfies the condition specified in Article 2(2)(v) of the Special Cases Order as amended by Article 5 of this Order.

(3) Paragraphs (1)(*a*) and (1)(*b*) of this Article shall not have effect so as to exempt from the restrictions imposed by section 7 of the Act anything done by a practitioner in relation to a stock held by him of such medicinal products in excess of a total of 5 litres of fluid and 2.5 kilograms of solids of all medicinal products to which those paragraphs relate.

(4) Paragraph (1) of this Article shall not have effect so as to exempt from the restrictions imposed by section 7 of the Act anything done—

(*a*) in relation to a vaccine specially prepared for administration to poultry, or

(*b*) in relation to any other vaccine, unless the vaccine is specially prepared for administration to the animal from which it is derived, or

(*c*) in relation to plasma, or a serum, unless the plasma or serum is specially prepared for administration to one or more animals in the herd from which it is derived.

(5) So long as section 12 of the Pharmacy and Poisons Act 1933(**a**) remains in force in its application to Great Britain, paragraph (1)(*c*) of this Article in so far as that paragraph relates to a registered pharmacy, shall apply to anything done in the premises of an authorised seller of poisons within the meaning of that Act, being premises that are entered in the register kept under the said section 12.

(6) So long as section 17 of the Pharmacy and Poisons Act (Northern Ireland) 1925(**b**) remains in force, paragraph (1)(*c*) of this Article, in so far as that paragraph relates to a registered pharmacy, shall apply to anything that is done on premises for which an annual licence is in force under the said section 17.

Further exemptions from product licences for certain special manufactured products

3.—(1) The restrictions imposed by section 7 of the Act (restriction as to dealings with medicinal products) shall not apply to the sale, supply, or procuring the manufacture or assembly of any medicinal product to which this Article relates if the conditions specified in paragraph (3) of this Article are satisfied.

(2) The medicinal products to which this Article relates are medicinal products which are for use by being administered to one or more human beings and which may be lawfully sold by retail or supplied in circumstances corresponding to retail sale, otherwise than in accordance with a prescription given by a doctor or dentist.

(3) The conditions referred to in paragraph (1) of this Article are—

(i) that the medicinal product is sold or supplied to a person exclusively for use by him in the course of a business carried on by him for the purpose of administering it or causing it to be administered to one or more human beings otherwise than by selling it;

(**a**) 1933 c. 25.   (**b**) 1925 c. 8. (N.I.).

(ii) that, if sold or supplied through a holder of a wholesale dealer's licence or a person entitled to such a licence by virtue of that person's entitlement to a licence of right, the medicinal product is sold or supplied to such person, and for such use by him, as described in sub-paragraph (i) of this paragraph;

(iii) that, where the manufacture or assembly of the medicinal product is procured, it is procured by such person, and for such use by him, as described in sub-paragraph (i) of this paragraph;

(iv) that no advertisement or representation (within the meaning of section 92 of the Act) relating to the medicinal product is issued with a view to it being seen generally by the public in the United Kingdom, that no advertisement relating to that product, by means of any catalogue, price list or circular letter is issued by, at the request or with the consent of, the person selling that product by retail or by way of wholesale or supplying it in circumstances corresponding to retail sale, or the person who manufactures it, and that the sale or supply as aforesaid is in response to a bona fide unsolicited order;

(v) that the medicinal product is prepared by or under the supervision of a pharmacist; and

(vi) that the medicinal product is manufactured by the holder of a manufacturer's licence which relates specifically to the manufacture of medicinal products to which Article 2 of the Special Cases Order and this Article relate, in the latter case by specifying the description of medicinal products in question or by way of an appropriate general classification (including classification by reference to the persons to whom the product is to be sold or supplied).

(4) In respect of medicinal products to which the preceding paragraphs of this Article relate the provisions of subsection (1) of section 23 of the Act (special provisions as to effect of manufacturer's licences) shall have effect as if the holder of the manufacturer's licence in respect of any such products was also the holder of a product licence in respect of such products or as if such products were manufactured or assembled to the order of a person who is the holder of such a product licence.

Exemptions in respect of clinical trials and medicinal tests on animals

4.—(1) Subject to paragraph (4) of this Article, the restrictions imposed by sections 7, 31(2) and 32 of the Act (restrictions as to dealings with medicinal products for clinical trials or medicinal tests on animals) shall not apply to anything done in relation to a medicinal product when—

(*a*) it consists of selling or supplying, or procuring the sale or supply of, medicinal products for the purposes of a clinical trial or, as the case may be, a medicinal test on animals, or

(*b*) it is done by a person in the course of a business carried on by him and consists of administering a medicinal product to an animal by way of a medicinal test on animals, or procuring such medicinal product to be so administered,

provided the conditions specified in paragraph (2) of this Article are satisfied.

(2) The conditions referred to in the preceding paragraph are—

  (i) that either (*a*) the person selling or supplying the medicinal product is selling or supplying that product exclusively for the purposes of a clinical trial or, as the case may be, for a medicinal test on animals, or (*b*) where he is not selling or supplying that product exclusively as aforesaid, that in so far as he is selling or supplying the product for other purposes, such sale or supply is in accordance with a product licence, or clinical trial or animal test certificate or in circumstances which enable such sale or supply to be carried out otherwise than in accordance with such licence or certificate,

  (ii) that, in relation to medicinal tests on animals, the manufacture or assembly of the medicinal product in question is procured by a veterinary surgeon or a veterinary practitioner for the purpose of its being administered to one or more animals which are under his care,

  (iii) that the clinical trial or, as the case may be, medicinal test on animals in question is not to be carried out under arrangements made by or on behalf of the person who manufactured that medicinal product, the person responsible for its composition (within the meaning of section 7(6) of the Act) or the person selling or supplying it unless such person is the doctor or dentist or one of the doctors or dentists, by whom, or under whose direction that medicinal product is to be administered in that trial or, as the case may be, the person by whom or under whose direction that medicinal product is to be administered in that test,

  (iv) that the doctor or dentist or one of the doctors or dentists by whom or under whose direction the medicinal product is to be administered in the clinical trial or as the case may be, that the person by whom or under whose direction the medicinal product is to be administered in the medicinal test on animals has notified the licensing authority of the trial, or, as the case may be the test, in question, specifying the product and the use of the product that is to be administered and the name and address of the supplier of that product, and

  (v) that the licensing authority has not, within the period of 21 days of the date of such notification, or within such extended period as the licensing authority may in a particular case allow, directed that the provisions of this Article shall not apply to the medicinal product in question.

(3) Without prejudice to the preceding paragraphs of this Article, the restrictions imposed by sections 7(3) and 31(4) of the Act (restrictions as to importation of medicinal products for clinical trials) shall not apply to the importation of a medicinal product, exclusively for the purpose of a clinical trial, provided that the conditions specified in sub-paragraph (ii), (iii), (iv) and (v) of the preceding paragraph are satisfied in relation to the medicinal product and the clinical trial in question.

(4) Paragraph (1) of this Article shall not have effect in relation to a veterinary surgeon or veterinary practitioner where the medicinal test in question is to be carried out under arrangements made by, or at the request of, another person, and (where the arrangements are made by the veterinary surgeon or veterinary practitioner and not at the request of any other person) shall not have effect so as to exempt from the restrictions in question anything done—

(*a*) in relation to a vaccine specially prepared for administration to poultry, or

(*b*) in relation to any other vaccine, unless the vaccine is specially prepared for administration to the animal from which it is derived, or

(*c*) in relation to plasma or a serum, unless the plasma or serum is specially prepared for administration to one or more animals in the herd from which it is derived.

Variation of Article 2 of the Special Cases Order

5. Article 2 of the Special Cases Order (exemption from product licences for certain special manufactured products) shall be varied as follows:—

(*a*) in paragraph (2)(i)(*a*) after the word "Act" there shall be inserted the words "or Article 2(1)(*a*) of the Medicines (Exemption from Licences) (Special Cases and Miscellaneous Provisions) Order 1972";

(*b*) in paragraph (2)(i)(*b*) after the word "Act" there shall be inserted the words "or Article 2(1)(*b*) of the said Order of 1972";

(*c*) for sub-paragraph (i)(c) of paragraph (2) there shall be substituted the following:—

"(*c*) for use in a registered pharmacy, a hospital or a health centre under the supervision of a pharmacist either in circumstances to which section 10 of the Act (as modified by the Medicines (Retail Pharmacists—Exemption from Licensing Requirements) Order 1971(**a**)) or Article 2(1)(*c*) of the said Order of 1972 relates, or, as respects a substance that is a medicinal product by virtue of its use as an ingredient in accordance with the provisions of section 130(1)(*b*) of the Act, where such substance is to be used only as such an ingredient in the preparation or dispensing of a medicinal product in accordance with a prescription given by a practitioner, being a prescription which relates to a medicinal product which is for administration to a particular patient of that practitioner or as the case may by to a particular animal or herd which is under his care.";

(*d*) for sub-paragraph (ii) of paragraph (2) there shall be substituted the following:—

"(ii) that no advertisement (within the meaning of section 92 of the Act) relating to the medicinal product is issued with a view to it being seen generally by the public in the United Kingdom, that no advertisement relating to that product by means of any catalogue, price list or circular letter is issued by, at the request or with the consent of, the person selling that product by retail or by way of wholesale dealing or supplying it in circumstances corresponding

---

(**a**) S.I. 1971/1445 (1971 III, p. 4078).

to retail sale, or the person who manufactures it, and that the sale or supply as aforesaid is in response to a bona fide unsolicited order;".

Keith Joseph,
Secretary of State for Social Services.

28th July 1972.

Peter Thomas,
Secretary of State for Wales.

1st August 1972.

Gordon Campbell,
Secretary of State for Scotland.

3rd August 1972.

W. S. I. Whitelaw,
Secretary of State for Northern Ireland.

3rd August 1972.

In witness whereof the official seal of the Minister of Agriculture, Fisheries and Food is hereunto affixed on 4th August 1972.

(L.S.)   *J. M. L. Prior,*
Minister of Agriculture, Fisheries and Food.

EXPLANATORY NOTE

(This Note is not part of the Order.)

This Order exempts from the restrictions imposed by Part II of the Medicines Act 1968 certain dealings and activities concerned with medicinal products. Article 2 provides for procuring the manufacture of stocks of certain medicinal products by practitioners and pharmacists without the need of a product licence. Article 3 exempts from the requirements to hold a product licence in the case of the sale or supply of certain medicinal products the persons who in the course of their business will not resell those products but will use them exclusively for the purpose of administering them to other persons. Article 4 provides for certain exemptions from the need to hold certificates or product licences in relation to clinical trials or medicinal tests on animals. The Order (in Article 5) also varies the provisions of Article 2 of the Medicines (Exemption from Licences) (Special and Transitional Cases) Order 1971 consequential upon the exemptions conferred by Article 2 of this Order. The other variation in Article 5 is of a minor character.

STATUTORY INSTRUMENTS

1972 No. 1201

MEDICINES

The Medicines (Applications for Product Licences and Clinical Trial and Animal Test Certificates) Amendment Regulations 1972

Made - - -	*4th August* 1972
Laid before Parliament	*11th August* 1972
Coming into Operation	*1st September* 1972

The Secretaries of State respectively concerned with health in England and in Wales, the Secretary of State concerned with health and with agriculture in Scotland, the Secretary of State for Northern Ireland and the Minister of Agriculture, Fisheries and Food, acting jointly, in exercise of their powers under sections 18, 36 and 129(1) of the Medicines Act 1968(a) (as having effect subject to the provisions of Article 2(2) of and Schedule 1 to the Transfer of Functions (Wales) Order 1969(b) and section 1(1)(a) of the Northern Ireland (Temporary Provisions) Act 1972(c)) and of all other powers enabling them in that behalf, after consulting such organisations as appear to them to be representative of interests likely to be substantially affected by the following regulations, hereby make the following regulations:—

Citation, interpretation and commencement

1. These regulations, which may be cited as the Medicines (Applications for Product Licences and Clinical Trial and Animal Test Certificates) Amendment Regulations 1972 shall be read as one with the Medicines (Applications for Product Licences and Clinical Trial and Animal Test Certificates) Regulations 1971(d) (hereinafter referred to as "the principal regulations"), and shall come into operation on 1st September 1972.

Amendment of regulation 3 of the principal regulations

2.—(1) Regulation 3(1) of the principal regulations shall be amended as follows:—

    (a) for paragraph (c) of the proviso there shall be substituted the following paragraph:—

        "(c) in the case of homoeopathic products and products using similar attenuations, in respect of

            (i) two or more attenuations of the same mother tinctures or other solutions or of the same triturations, or

            (ii) two or more attenuations of any mother tinctures or other solutions or triturations having the same specification and pharmaceutical form apart from the tinctures, solutions, or triturations,";

(a) 1968 c. 67.
(c) 1972 c. 22.
(b) S.I. 1969/388 (1969 I, p. 1070).
(d) S.I. 1971/973 (1971 II, p. 2816).

(b) at the end of the proviso there shall be added the following paragraphs:—

"(f) in respect of two or more medicinal products to be administered to one or more patients in the course of the same clinical trial;

(g) in respect of two or more medicinal products, substances or articles to be administered to one or more animals in the course of the same medicinal test on animals; and

(h) in respect of two or more medicinal products manufactured outside the United Kingdom which are to be imported, and which are identified in the application by their monograph name, or which are for use as ingredients as described in paragraph (b) section 130(1) of the Act, in the circumstances to which that paragraph applies, where the applicant satisfies the licensing authority that products of the same description and manufactured by the same manufacturer outside the United Kingdom have been imported into the United Kingdom within the period of 12 months ending with the date of the application.".

(2) After paragraph (4) of regulation 3 of the principal regulations there shall be added the following paragraph:—

"(5) Subject to the requirements of paragraph (1), an applicant, being the proposed licensee, may furnish to the licensing authority in the form of a single document signed by him any number of applications, which need not be signed separately as required by paragraph (4), where such applications are in respect of medicinal products for which product licences, including product licences of right, are held by a person other than the applicant and the right to all dealings to which the applications relate in those medicinal products have been assigned, sold or otherwise transferred by that other person to the applicant.".

Keith Joseph,
Secretary of State for Social Services.

28th July 1972.

Peter Thomas,
Secretary of State for Wales.

1st August 1972.

Gordon Campbell,
Secretary of State for Scotland.

3rd August 1972.

W. S. I. Whitelaw,
Secretary of State for Northern Ireland.
3rd August 1972.

In witness whereof the official seal of the Minister of Agriculture, Fisheries and Food is hereunto affixed on 4th August 1972.

(L.S.)   *J. M. L. Prior,*
Minister of Agriculture, Fisheries and Food.

EXPLANATORY NOTE
(This Note is not part of the Regulations.)

These Regulations amend regulation 3 of the Medicines (Applications for Product Licences and Clinical Trial and Animal Test Certificates) Regulations 1971 by extending the circumstances in which one application may be furnished for the grant of product licences or clinical trial or animal test certificates in respect of more than one medicinal product, substance or article, and specifying the circumstances in which more than one application for a product licence may be included in a single document.

STATUTORY INSTRUMENTS

1972 No. 1203

HOUSING, ENGLAND AND WALES

The Rent Rebate and Rent Allowance (Services etc.) Regulations 1972

Made - - -	*7th August* 1972
Laid before Parliament	*7th August* 1972
Coming into Operation	*10th August* 1972

The Secretary of State for the Environment as respects England (excluding Monmouthshire) and the Secretary of State for Wales as respects Wales and Monmouthshire, in exercise of their powers under section 25(3) of the Housing Finance Act 1972(**a**) and of all other powers enabling them in that behalf, hereby make the following regulations : —

1.—(1) These regulations may be cited as the Rent Rebate and Rent Allowance (Services etc.) Regulations 1972 and shall come into operation on 10th August 1972.

(2) The Interpretation Act 1889(**b**) shall apply for the interpretation of these regulations as it applies for the interpretation of an Act of Parliament.

(3) In these regulations—
"the Act" means the Housing Finance Act 1972; and
"section 25" means section 25 of the Act.

(4) Any reference in these regulations to a numbered regulation shall be construed as a reference to the regulation bearing that number in these regulations.

2. Subject to regulation 3, the circumstances set out in the Schedule to these regulations are hereby prescribed as those in which amounts are not to be reckoned for the purposes of section 25 as payable for the provision of services.

3.—(1) Where amounts fairly attributable to the use of furniture and the provision of services in aggregate constitute a negligible proportion of the rent, these amounts are not to be reckoned for the purposes of section 25 as payable for the use of furniture or the provision of services, as the case may be.

(**a**) 1972 c.47.   (**b**) 1889 c.63

(2) In this regulation—

"the provision of services" excludes any matter falling within regulation 2; and

"rent" excludes any sum attributable to rates and includes amounts which by virtue of regulation 4 are to be treated for the purposes of section 25 as rent and also amounts fairly attributable to the use of furniture and the provision of services which are not to be so treated.

4. Where amounts payable by the tenant are expressed to be something other than rent but they are not to be reckoned as payable for the use of furniture or the provision of services by virtue of the foregoing provisions of these regulations, those amounts are to be treated for the purposes of section 25 as rent.

Regulation 2

SCHEDULE

PART I

CIRCUMSTANCES RELATING TO THE PROVISION OF SERVICES

1. Where the tenant enjoys any general communal facility.

2. Where the tenant, being a qualifying person, enjoys any special communal facility with other qualifying persons.

3. Where there is provided any privilege or facility connected with the occupancy of a dwelling which is not a communal facility, but which is requisite for the purposes of access, cold water supply or sanitary accommodation.

4.—(1) In this Schedule—

"communal facility" means any privilege or facility connected with the occupancy of a dwelling which is enjoyed by the tenant in common with other tenants by reason of the said occupancy and not as the result of the exercise of any option on his part;

"general communal facility" means a communal facility listed in Part II of this Schedule;

"qualifying person" means a person of pensionable age or a person registered in pursuance of arrangements under section 29(1) of the National Assistance Act 1948(**a**) (welfare arrangements for handicapped persons); and

"special communal facility" means a communal facility listed in Part III of this Schedule.

(2) In this Schedule any reference to access or to premises requisite for the purposes of access includes passenger lifts, halls, corridors and staircases.

PART II

GENERAL COMMUNAL FACILITIES

1. Access (including the lighting and cleaning of premises requisite for the purposes of access).

2. Cold water supply.

3. Sanitary accommodation.

(**a**) 1948 c.29.

4. Service lifts.

5. Laundry and drying facilities.

6. Gardens and play areas.

7. Garaging or parking of motor cars or other vehicles.

8. Removal of refuse.

9. Storage of articles belonging to any tenant or any member of his household.

10. Radio or television relay (excluding any television or radio receiver).

11. Caretaking.

PART III

SPECIAL COMMUNAL FACILITIES

1. Warden services.

2. Communal telephone service.

3. Communal rooms.

4. Space heating of communal rooms and premises requisite for the purposes of access.

Peter Walker,
Secretary of State for the Environment.

7th August 1972.

Peter Thomas,
Secretary of State for Wales.

7th August 1972.

EXPLANATORY NOTE

(This Note is not part of the Regulations.)

Section 25 of the Housing Finance Act 1972 defines rent which is eligible to be met by a rent rebate or rent allowance. Where no part of a dwelling is sub-let it means the occupational element of the rent, that is the amount of the rent exclusive of any sum attributable to rates (including water rates and charges) and subject to any regulations made under section 25, exclusive of any sum attributable to the use of furniture or the provision of services.

These regulations, which are made under section 25, prescribe circumstances in which amounts are not to be reckoned for the purposes of that section as payable for the use of furniture or the provision of services and in which amounts which are expressed to be something other than rent are to be treated for the purposes of that section as rent. In the circumstances prescribed amounts will be regarded as part of the occupational element of the rent and therefore will be part of the rent eligible to be met by a rent rebate or rent allowance.

The circumstances prescribed relate mainly to the provision of services which are regarded as general communal facilities, with the addition in the case of persons of pensionable age and certain handicapped persons of other special communal facilities (including in particular warden services). Amounts payable for the provision of services relating to access, cold water supply and sanitary accommodation, although not communal facilities, are additionally not to be reckoned for the purposes of section 25 as so payable. Disregarded also are amounts payable for the use of furniture and the provision of other services where those amounts in total form only a negligible proportion of the rent.

STATUTORY INSTRUMENTS

1972 No. 1204

HOUSING, ENGLAND AND WALES

The Isles of Scilly (Housing) Order 1972

Made - - -	*7th August* 1972
Laid before Parliament	*7th August* 1972
Coming into Operation	*10th August* 1972

The Secretary of State for the Environment, in exercise of his powers under section 103 of the Housing Finance Act 1972(a) and of all other powers enabling him in that behalf, hereby makes the following order:—

1. This order may be cited as the Isles of Scilly (Housing) Order 1972 and shall come into operation on 10th August 1972.

2.—(1) The Interpretation Act 1889(b) shall apply for the interpretation of this order as it applies for the interpretation of an Act of Parliament.

(2) In this order—

"the Act of 1972" means the Housing Finance Act 1972;

"the Council" means the Council of the Isles; and

"the Isles" means the Isles of Scilly.

(3) Any reference in this order to a numbered Schedule shall be construed, except where the context otherwise requires, as a reference to the Schedule bearing that number in this order.

(4) Any reference in this order to any enactment shall be construed, except where the context otherwise requires, as a reference to that enactment as amended, and as including references thereto as extended or applied by or under any other enactment, including any provision of this order.

(5) Any reference in this order to any instrument includes a reference thereto as amended by any other instrument.

3.—(1) The enactments specified in Schedule 1 shall extend to the Isles subject to the adaptations and modifications specified in Schedule 2.

(2) Nothing in this article shall apply to any provision contained in Part III or Part IV of the Act of 1972, or to any provision of Part IX of that Act if and so far as that provision of the said Part IX relates to controlled or regulated tenancies or to the Rent Act 1968(c).

(a) 1972 c. 47. (b) 1889 c. 63.
(c) 1968 c. 23.

4.—(1) The orders specified in Schedule 3 are hereby revoked.

(2) The revocation of the said orders in so far as they relate to payments made or to be made by the Secretary of State thereunder, shall have effect only as respects payments for the year 1972-73 and subsequent years, and have effect subject to Schedule 8 to the Act of 1972.

Article 3

SCHEDULE 1

Housing Enactments extended to the Isles

The Housing Act 1957(**a**)

The Housing (Financial Provisions) Act 1958(**b**)

The Housing (Underground Rooms) Act 1959(**c**)

The House Purchase and Housing Act 1959(**d**)

The Housing Act 1961(**e**)

The Housing Act 1964(**f**)

The Housing Subsidies Act 1967(**g**)

The Housing Act 1969(**h**)

The Housing Act 1971(**i**)

The Housing Finance Act 1972.

Article 3

SCHEDULE 2

Adaptations and Modifications of the Enactments specified
in Schedule 1

1. Any reference in the enactments specified in Schedule 1 to a local authority or to a housing authority shall, unless the context otherwise requires, include the Council.

2. Any reference in the said enactments to the general rate fund shall be construed as a reference to the General Fund of the Council.

3. In the Housing Act 1957, section 173 shall apply as though the Council were the council of a county borough.

4. In section 14(1) of the Housing Subsidies Act 1967, for the words "before the commencement of this Act" there shall be substituted the words "before 19th May 1969 (being the date on which the Isles of Scilly (Housing) Order 1969(**j**) came into operation)".

(**a**) 1957 c. 56.
(**c**) 1959 c. 34.
(**e**) 1961 c. 65.
(**g**) 1967 c. 29.
(**i**) 1971 c. 76.

(**b**) 1958 c. 42.
(**d**) 1959 c. 33.
(**f**) 1964 c. 56.
(**h**) 1969 c. 33.
(**j**) S.I. 1969/638 (1969 II, p. 1759).

5. In the Housing Act 1969, in section 33 (conversion of highway into footpath or bridle-way)—

   (i) in subsection (1), the words from "whether" onwards shall be omitted; and

   (ii) in subsection (2), the words "who are not the local planning authority" and, in paragraph (*a*), the words "instead of by the local planning authority" shall be omitted and, in paragraph (*b*), for the words from "by" onwards there shall be substituted the words "under section 213 of that Act by a competent authority".

6. In the Housing Finance Act 1972—

   (*a*) in section 2, "the authority's subsidies for the year 1971-72" means the payments described in subsection (4) of that section with the addition of any payments made or to be made to the Council for the year 1971-72 in respect of property within their Housing Revenue Account under any of the orders specified in Schedule 3;

   (*b*) in Schedule 8—

      (i) in paragraph 10, the sums referred to shall include any sums paid to the Council before the coming into force of this order under any of the orders specified in Schedule 3; and

      (ii) in paragraph 14, the sums referred to shall include any sums payable to the Council under any of the orders specified in Schedule 3.

Article 4

SCHEDULE 3

INSTRUMENTS REVOKED

The Isles of Scilly (Housing) Order 1946(**a**)

The Isles of Scilly (Housing) Order 1961(**b**)

The Isles of Scilly (Housing) (Amendment) Order 1963(**c**)

The Isles of Scilly (Housing) (Amendment) Order 1969(**d**)

The Isles of Scilly (Housing) Order 1969(**e**).

Peter Walker,
Secretary of State for the Environment.

7th August 1972.

EXPLANATORY NOTE

(This Note is not part of the Order.)

This Order is made under section 103 of the Housing Finance Act 1972 ("the Act of 1972"). This section provides a comprehensive power to extend housing enactments by order to the Isles of Scilly. It replaces a number of

---

(**a**) S.R. & O. 1946/2105 (Rev. XII, p. 572: 1946 I, p. 980).
(**b**) S.I. 1961/136 (1961 I, p. 189). (**c**) S.I. 1963/1722 (1963 III, p. 3342).
(**d**) S.I. 1969/637 (1969 II, p. 1758). (**e**) S.I. 1969/638 (1969 II, p. 1759).

existing provisions (set out in section 103(6) of the Act of 1972), which together enabled certain housing provisions to be extended to the Isles by order subject to exceptions, adaptations and modifications and financial provision to be made for new dwellings provided by the Council. The Order revokes all existing housing orders relating to the Isles (listed in Schedule 3).

The Order extends general housing legislation (specified in Schedule 1) to the Isles, subject to the adaptations and modifications (which are set out in Schedule 2). These adaptations and modifications take account of the special position of the Council of the Isles. The Order does not, however, apply to Part III or IV of the Act of 1972, or to Part IX of that Act in so far as it applies to controlled or regulated tenancies or to the Rent Act 1968 (which will extend to the Isles when those provisions come into operation).

STATUTORY INSTRUMENTS

1972 No. 1205

STATUTORY INSTRUMENTS

The Statutory Instruments (Amendment) Regulations 1972

Made - - -	*7th August* 1972
Laid before Parliament	*9th August* 1972
Coming into Operation	*30th August* 1972

The Minister for the Civil Service, in exercise of the powers conferred by section 8(1) of the Statutory Instruments Act 1946(**a**) and now vested in him (**b**) and of all other powers enabling him in that behalf, and with the concurrence of the Lord Chancellor and the Speaker of the House of Commons, hereby makes the following Regulations: —

1. These Regulations may be cited as the Statutory Instruments (Amendment) Regulations 1972, and shall come into operation on 30th August 1972.

2. The Interpretation Act 1889(**c**) shall apply for the interpretation of these Regulations as it applies for the interpretation of an Act of Parliament.

3. The Statutory Instruments Regulations 1947(**d**) shall be amended by substituting for the proviso to Regulation 10(1)(*a*) the following proviso: —

"Provided that copies of—

(i) instruments which have ceased to be in operation at the time of the completion of the annual edition,

(ii) local instruments, and

(iii) Orders in Council under section 1(3) of the Northern Ireland (Temporary Provisions) Act 1972(**e**),

may be omitted;".

Given under the official seal of the Minister for the Civil Service on 7th August 1972.

(L.S.)

Neil Burton,
Authorised by the Minister
for the Civil Service.

I concur.

Hailsham of St. Marylebone, C.
Lord Chancellor.

7th August 1972.

I concur.

Selwyn Lloyd,
Speaker of the
House of Commons.

7th August 1972.

(**a**) 1946 c. 36.   (**b**) S.I. 1968/1656 (1968 III, p. 4485).   (**c**) 1889 c. 63.
(**d**) S.I. 1948/1 (Rev. XXI, p. 498: 1948 I, p. 4002).   (**e**) 1972 c. 22.

EXPLANATORY NOTE

(This Note is not part of the Regulations.)

These Regulations amend Regulation 10 of the Statutory Instruments Regulations 1947, which provides for the preparation of the annual edition of Statutory Instruments. Under the amended provision it will not be necessary to include in the annual edition Orders in Council under section 1(3) of the Northern Ireland (Temporary Provisions) Act 1972. These Orders in Council will be included in the annual volumes of Northern Ireland Statutes.

1972 No. 1206 (S.83)

POLICE

The Police (Scotland) Amendment (No. 2) Regulations 1972

Made - - - -	*3rd August* 1972
Laid before Parliament	*11th August* 1972
Coming into Operation	*1st September* 1972

In exercise of the powers conferred on me by sections 7 and 26 of the Police (Scotland) Act 1967**(a)**, and of all other powers enabling me in that behalf, and after consulting (i) the Police Council for the United Kingdom in accordance with section 4(4) of the Police Act 1969**(b)** and (ii) the Police Advisory Board for Scotland in accordance with section 26(9) of the said Act of 1967 as amended by section 4(6) of the said Act of 1969, I hereby make the following regulations:—

PART I

Citation, Commencement and Interpretation

1. These regulations may be cited as the Police (Scotland) Amendment (No.2) Regulations 1972.

2. These regulations shall come into operation on 1st September 1972 and shall have effect as follows, that is to say—

(*a*) for the purposes of regulation 5 thereof, as from 22nd June 1972;

(*b*) for the purposes of regulation 6 thereof, as from 6th April 1964;

(*c*) for the purposes of regulations 7, 9, 10 and 12 to 16 thereof, as from 1st September 1972;

(*d*) for the purposes of regulation 8 thereof, as from 1st April 1964; and

(*e*) for the purposes of regulation 11 thereof, as from 1st April 1972.

3. In these regulations any reference to the principal regulations is a reference to the Police (Scotland) Regulations 1972**(c)**.

4. The Interpretation Act 1889**(d)** shall apply for the interpretation of these regulations as it applies for the interpretation of an Act of Parliament.

(**a**) 1967 c. 77.   (**b**) 1969 c. 63.
(**c**) S.I. 1972/777 (1972 II, p. 2490).   (**d**) 1889 c. 63.

Part II

Surtax liability on rent allowance and provided accommodation

5. For regulation 42 of the principal regulations (which relates to compensatory grant) there shall be substituted the following regulation:—

"*Compensatory grant*

42.—(1) In each fiscal year, a constable of a police force, who, during the preceding fiscal year, has paid income tax or surtax attributable to the inclusion of a rent allowance or compensatory grant in his emoluments in respect of service as a constable of that force shall be paid a compensatory grant.

(2) The amount of the compensatory grant made to a constable of a police force in any year shall be the aggregate of—

> (a) the amount by which the income tax in fact deducted from his emoluments in respect of service as a constable of that force during the preceding year, according to the tax tables prepared or prescribed by the Commissioners of Inland Revenue, is increased by the inclusion in such emoluments of a rent allowance or any compensatory grant, and

> (b) the amount by which he satisfies the police authority that any surtax paid by him during the preceding year for any earlier year beginning on or after 6th April 1963 is increased by the inclusion in his emoluments in respect of such service during that earlier year of a rent allowance or any compensatory grant.

(3) The compensatory grant may, except in the circumstances described in paragraph (4), be paid by such instalments throughout the year in which it is payable as the police authority may determine.

(4) Where, in the course of a fiscal year, a constable of a police force leaves the force or dies whilst serving therein, he or his personal representative, as the case may be, shall be paid the whole of the compensatory grant due to the constable during that year and, in addition, shall be paid a further compensatory grant equal to that which, had he not left the force or died, would have been due to him in a subsequent year by reason of income tax deducted from, or surtax paid on, his emoluments while in fact a constable of the police force.

(5) For the purposes of the preceding provisions of this regulation—

> (a) the expression "year" or "fiscal year" means a year commencing on 6th April and ending on the following 5th April;

> (b) the expression "income tax" means income tax other than surtax;

> (c) in the case of a constable of a police force whose total income for any year which is chargeable to surtax includes income other than his emoluments in respect of service as a constable of that force, any reference to the amount of surtax paid for that year shall be construed as a reference to the amount which would have been so paid had his total chargeable income for that year not included such other income; and

> (d) where a constable of a police force has served more than once in the same force, references in this regulation to service in the force shall be construed as references to his service therein since his last appointment thereto.".

6.—(1) Where the compensatory grant made to a constable of a police force in any fiscal year beginning on or after 6th April 1964 but before the coming into operation of the principal regulations was less than it would have been if the regulation substituted for regulation 42 of the principal regulations by the preceding regulation had been substituted—

(*a*) with effect from 6th April 1964, for regulation 40 of the Police (Scotland) Regulations 1956**(a)**, (which applied in respect of the period 6th April 1964 to 17th May 1968); and

(*b*) with effect from 17th May 1968, for regulation 40 of the Police (Scotland) Regulations 1968**(b)**, (which applied in respect of the period 17th May 1968 to 22nd June 1972 when the principal regulations came into operation),

then the constable in question shall be entitled to the difference by way of an increase in compensatory grant for the fiscal year in question.

(2) In this regulation the expression "fiscal year" means a year commencing 6th April and ending on the following 5th April.

7. For regulation 43 of the principal regulations (which relates to discharge of tax liability in respect of police house or quarters) there shall be substituted the following regulation:—

"*Discharge of tax liability in respect of police house or quarters*

43.—(1) Where a constable of a police force is provided with a house or quarters free of rent and rates and his liability to pay income tax or surtax is increased—

(*a*) in consequence thereof, by virtue of section 185 of the Income and Corporation Taxes Act 1970**(c)** or otherwise, or

(*b*) in consequence of any payment required to be made by this regulation, that liability shall be discharged by the police authority in accordance with, and to the extent hereinafter provided in, this regulation.

(2) A constable of a police force shall be reimbursed the amount by which the income tax in fact deducted from his emoluments in respect of service as a constable of that force, according to the tax tables prepared or prescribed by the Commissioners of Inland Revenue, is increased—

(*a*) in consequence of his being provided with a house or quarters free of rent and rates, or

(*b*) in consequence of any payment under this regulation.

(3) Where any surtax becomes due and payable for any year by a constable of a police force, the liability therefor shall be discharged by the police authority to the extent that he satisfies them that the amount thereof is increased—

(*a*) in consequence of his having been provided with a house or quarters free of rent and rates during his service as a constable of that force or, where he transferred thereto from some other force, during his service as a constable of that other force, or

(*b*) in consequence of any payment under this regulation by the police authority or, where he transferred as aforesaid, by the police authority maintaining the force from which he transferred, not being a payment under paragraph (4).

(a) S.I. 1956/1999 (1956 II, p. 1766).   (b) S.I. 1968/716 (1968 II, p. 2024).
(c) 1970 c. 10.

(4) Where any liability to surtax would fall to be discharged by a police authority under the preceding paragraph but for the fact that the person concerned has left the police force maintained by them, otherwise than on transfer to another police force, or has died, that liability shall be discharged by the police authority and, to the extent that, in consequence of the discharge of that liability, any further surtax becomes due and payable, liability for that further surtax shall be also so discharged.

(5) For the purposes of the preceding provisions of this regulation—

    (a) the expression "income tax" means income tax other than surtax; and

    (b) in the case of a constable of a police force whose total income for any year which is chargeable to surtax includes income other than emoluments in respect of his service as a constable of that force or, where he transferred thereto from some other force, as a constable of that other force, any reference to surtax due and payable for that year shall be construed as a reference to the surtax which would have been so due and payable had his total chargeable income for that year not included such other income.".

8.—(1) Where before the coming into operation of these regulations a constable of a police force has paid any income tax (including surtax) which arose in consequence of any house or quarters with which he was provided, free of rent, on or after 1st April 1964, being provided also free of rates, then, to the extent that liability therefor would have fallen to be discharged by a police authority under a regulation hereinafter mentioned if in paragraph (a) of each such regulation there had been inserted the words "or otherwise" after the words "section 47 of the Finance Act 1963"—

    (a) with effect from 1st April 1964, in the case of regulation 40A of the Police (Scotland) Regulations 1956, as amended **(a)**, (which applied in respect of the period 1st April 1964 to 17th May 1968);

    (b) with effect from 17th May 1968, in the case of regulation 41 of the Police (Scotland) Regulations 1968, (which applied in respect of the period 17th May 1968 to 22nd June 1972); and

    (c) with effect from 22nd June 1972, in the case of regulation 43 of the principal regulations as originally made, (which applied in respect of the period 22nd June 1972 to 1st September 1972 when regulation 7 of these regulations takes effect),

then that police authority shall reimburse the constable in question the amount of tax so paid by him.

(2) For the purposes of regulation 43(1)(b) and (2)(b) of the principal regulations, as amended by regulation 7 of these regulations, any payment under this regulation shall be treated as if it were a payment under the said regulation 43.

PART III

Other Provisions

9. In regulation 21(3) of the principal regulations (which relates to normal daily period of duty) for the words "Where the normal daily period of duty is

---

(a) The relevant amending regulation is S.I. 1964/461 (1964 I, p. 742).

performed in one tour of duty" there shall be substituted the words "The normal daily period of duty shall, so far as the exigencies of duty permit, be performed in one tour of duty and, in such case,".

10.—(1) For paragraph 1(c) of regulation 44 of the principal regulations (which relates to removal allowance) there shall be substituted the following provisions:—

"(c) shall, where the constable is the owner of his new home, reimburse expenses reasonably incurred by him in connection with the acquisition thereof if—

(i) he was the owner of his former home, or

(ii) the police authority, after consulting the chief constable, are satisfied that he could neither have been provided with a suitable house or quarters nor have been reasonably expected to find suitable rented accommodation within a reasonable distance of his normal place of duty,

so, however, that where the police authority are of opinion that the constable could have acquired a suitable home for a consideration less than that actually paid, they may restrict the reimbursement of expenses directly related to the consideration paid by him to expenses which would have been reasonably incurred had he paid that lesser consideration;

(d) shall reimburse the constable his payments in connection with his former home by way of rates (within the meaning of regulation 39(6)) and mortgage interest or rent payable in respect of the first 13 weeks following the move up to an amount equal to that which would have been payable to him by way of rent allowance in respect of that period had he not moved but had continued to be entitled to a rent allowance payable at the rate at which such an allowance was payable immediately before the move so, however, that where the police authority are of opinion that the constable has not taken all reasonable steps to reduce or terminate his liability to make such payments as aforesaid they may restrict the reimbursement to payments which the constable would have been liable to make had he taken all such steps.".

(2) For paragraph 2(c) of the said regulation 44 there shall be substituted the following provisions:—

"(c) may, in the circumstances and subject to the conditions mentioned in paragraph (1)(c), reimburse the expenses there mentioned;

(d) may, subject to the conditions mentioned in paragraph (1)(d), reimburse the expenses there mentioned.".

11. In Schedule 5 of the principal regulations (which relates to refreshment, subsistence and lodging allowances) for the Table in paragraph 1 there shall be substituted the following Table:—

"TABLE

Description of Allowance	Superin- tendents	Inspectors, Sergeants and Constables
	£	£
Refreshment Allowance:		
(i) for one meal...	0·540	0·500
(ii) for two meals	0·780	0·700
Subsistence Allowance:		
Period of retention or engagement on duty—		
(i) over 5 hours and not exceeding 8 hours ...	0·780	0·700
(ii) over 8 hours and not exceeding 12 hours ...	1·110	1·000
(iii) over 12 hours and not exceeding 24 hours ...	1·900	1·650
(iv) over 24 hours—at the rate under (iii) above for each complete period of 24 hours' retention or engagement, together with whichever is the appropriate amount under the preceding provisions of this Table for any excess over the aggregate of such complete periods		
Lodging Allowance—for each night	3·250	2·800

"

12. In regulation 1(1)(g) of the principal regulations (which relates to meanings assigned to certain expressions) for the definition of the expression "superintendent" there shall be substituted the following definition:—

" "superintendent" includes chief superintendent;".

13. For regulation 2 of the principal regulations (which relates to ranks) there shall be substituted the following regulation:—

"**2.** The ranks of a police force which may be held by constables shall be known by the following designations:—

Chief Constable,
Assistant Chief Constable,
Chief Superintendent,
Superintendent,
Chief Inspector,
Inspector,
Sergeant,
Constable.".

14.—(1) Nothing in regulation 2 of the principal regulations as amended by regulation 13 of these regulations, shall be construed as affecting the right of a constable who, immediately before 1st September 1972, was a reversionary member of a home police force or a central police officer (within the meaning of the principal regulations) to revert to his former force in a rank not mentioned therein.

(2) For the purposes of regulation 29(2) of the principal regulations (which relates to rates of pay) service in the rank of superintendent, Grade I or Grade II, shall be treated as if it had been service in the rank of superintendent.

(3) In the case of a superintendent who, immediately before 1st September 1972, held the rank of superintendent, Grade I, regulation 29 of the principal regulations shall have effect as if he had continued to hold that rank and regulations 12, 13, 14(1) and 14(2) of these regulations had not been made.

15.—(1) For the Tables designated A and B in Part II of Schedule 3 to the principal regulations (scales of pay for women) there shall be substituted, respectively, the Tables so designated and set out in Schedule 1 to these regulations.

(2) For paragraph 2(6) of Part II of the said Schedule 3 there shall be substituted the following provision:—

"(6) The annual pay of a woman to whom sub-paragraph (5) applies who, by virtue thereof, is treated as having completed 2 years of reckonable service shall be restricted until she in fact completes 2 years of such service—

(*a*) if she had not attained the age of 21 years on or before the date on which she first became a constable, to £1,161;

(*b*) subject as aforesaid, to £1,215.".

16. For the Tables designated A and B in Schedule 4 to the principal regulations (which relates to detective duty and supplementary detective allowances) there shall be substituted, respectively, the Tables so designated and set out in Schedule 2 to these regulations.

Gordon Campbell,
One of Her Majesty's Principal
Secretaries of State.

St Andrew's House,
Edinburgh.
3rd August 1972.

SCHEDULE 1

TABLES SUBSTITUTED FOR TABLES IN PART II OF SCHEDULE 3 TO THE PRINCIPAL REGULATIONS (SCALES OF PAY FOR WOMEN) WITH EFFECT FROM 1ST SEPTEMBER 1972

"TABLE A

Rank	Before completing 1 year of service in the rank	After 1 year of service in the rank	After 2 years of service in the rank	After 3 years of service in the rank
	£ a year	£ a year	£ a year	£ a year
Chief Inspector ...	2,337	2,415	2,487	2,565
Inspector ...	2,043	2,118	2,196	2,271
Sergeant ...	1,737	1,803	1,869	1,935

TABLE B

Rank	Standard scale of annual pay	Transitional scales of annual pay			
		Aged 19 on entry	Aged 20 on entry	Aged 21 on entry	Aged 22 or over on entry
	£	£	£	£	£
Before completing 1 year of service	1,035	1,035	1,059	1,104	1,155
After 1 year of service	1,092	1,092	1,110	1,161	1,212
After 2 years of service	1,209	1,209	1,209	1,266	1,302
After 3 years of service	1,266	1,266	1,266	1,323	1,359
After 4 years of service	1,323	1,323	1,323	1,398	1,416
After 5 years of service	1,398	1,398	1,398	1,398	1,476
After 6 years of service	1,476	1,476	1,476	1,476	1,551
After 7 years of service	1,476	1,476	1,476	1,551	1,551
After 8 years of service	1,476	1,476	1,551	1,551	1,551
After 9 years of service	1,551	1,551	1,551	1,551	1,551
After 13 years of service	1,626	1,626	1,626	1,626	1,626
After 17 years of service	1,701	1,701	1,701	1,701	1,701

"

SCHEDULE 2

TABLES SUBSTITUTED FOR TABLES IN SCHEDULE 4 TO THE PRINCIPAL REGULATIONS (DETECTIVE DUTY AND SUPPLEMENTARY DETECTIVE ALLOWANCES) WITH EFFECT FROM 1ST SEPTEMBER 1972

"TABLE A

Rank	Men	Women
	£	£
Superintendent	300	285
Chief Inspector	258	246
Inspector	228	216
Sergeant	192	183
Constable	144	138

TABLE B

Rank	8 to 12 hours qualifying overtime		12 or more hours qualifying overtime	
	Men	Women	Men	Women
	£	£	£	£
Chief Inspector	213	201	384	366
Inspector	189	180	339	321
Sergeant	159	150	285	270
Constable	120	114	216	204

"

EXPLANATORY NOTE

(This Note is not part of the Regulations.)

These Regulations, first, amend the Police (Scotland) Regulations 1972, which came into operation on 22nd June 1972, and, secondly, contain related provisions in respect of periods before that date.

Regulation 5 amends, with effect from 22nd June 1972, the provisions of the regulations of 1972 relating to compensatory grant. It provides that in calculating such grant account shall be taken not only of income tax deducted under the P.A.Y.E. system but also of surtax, so far as it is referable to police emoluments. Regulation 6 contains corresponding provision in respect of the period 6th April 1964 to 22nd June 1972.

Regulation 7 amends, with effect from 1st September 1972, the provisions of the regulations of 1972 relating to the discharge of a policeman's tax liability in respect of a police house provided free of rent and rates. First, it ensures that the tax liability to be discharged by the police authority includes not only the policeman's liability in respect of the annual value of the house but also that arising from the house being provided free of rates. Regulation 8 contains corresponding provision in respect of the period 1st April 1964 to 1st September 1972. Secondly, regulation 7 distinguishes between income tax deducted under the P.A.Y.E. system and income tax by way of surtax; surtax liability to be discharged by the police authority is limited to liability referable to police emoluments. (Regulation 8 contains no corresponding provision in this regard.)

In Part III, regulation 9 provides that, subject to the exigencies of duty, the normal daily period of duty should be performed in one tour; regulation 10 provides for the reimbursement after transfer of certain continuing expenditure concerning an officer's former home; regulation 11 provides for increases in the rates of refreshment, subsistence and lodging allowances with effect from 1st April 1972; regulations 12, 13 and 14 provide for the replacement of the ranks of superintendent Grade I and superintendent Grade II by the rank of superintendent; regulation 15 provides for increases in pay for policewomen; regulation 16 provides for increases in detective duty and supplementary detective allowances for policewomen.

In so far as regulation 2 provides that the regulations shall have retrospective effect (as mentioned above), they are made in exercise of the power conferred by section 26(3) of the Police (Scotland) Act 1967.

STATUTORY INSTRUMENTS

1972 No. 1207

AGRICULTURE

The Agriculture (Notices to Quit) (Miscellaneous Provisions) Order 1972

Made - - - -	*31st July* 1972
Laid before Parliament	*14th August* 1972
Coming into Operation	*6th September* 1972

The Lord Chancellor, in exercise of the powers conferred on him by section 73 of the Agriculture Act 1947**(a)**, as amended**(b)**, section 26 of the Agricultural Holdings Act 1948**(c)**, as amended**(d)**, section 21(6) of the Reserve and Auxiliary Forces (Protection of Civil Interests) Act 1951**(e)**, as amended **(d)**, section 19(2) of the Agriculture (Miscellaneous Provisions) Act 1963**(f)** and of all other powers enabling him in that behalf, and after consultation with the Council on Tribunals in accordance with section 10 of the Tribunals and Inquiries Act 1971**(g)**, hereby makes the following Order:—

1. This Order may be cited as the Agriculture (Notices to Quit) (Miscellaneous Provisions) Order 1972 and shall come into operation on 6th September 1972.

2. In this Order—

"the 1948 Act" means the Agricultural Holdings Act 1948 as amended;

"the 1951 Act" means the Reserve and Auxiliary Forces (Protection of Civil Interests) Act 1951 as amended;

"the 1959 Order" means the Agricultural Land Tribunals and Notices to Quit Order 1959**(h)** as amended**(i)**;

"the 1964 Order" means the Agriculture (Notices to Remedy and Notices to Quit) Order 1964**(j)**;

"tribunal" means an Agricultural Land Tribunal.

3. The Interpretation Act 1889**(k)** shall apply to the interpretation of this Order as it applies to the interpretation of an Act of Parliament.

(a) 1947 c. 48.
(b) By sections 5 and 8 of, and Schedules 1 and 2 to the Agriculture Act 1958 (c. 71).
(c) 1948 c. 63.   (d) By section 8 of, and Schedule 1 to the Agriculture Act 1958.
(e) 1951 c. 65.   (f) 1963 c. 11.   (g) 1971 c. 62.
(h) S.I. 1959/81 (1959 I, p. 91).   (i) The relevant amending instrument is the 1964 Order.
(j) S.I. 1964/706 (1964 II, p. 1358).   (k) 1889 c. 63.

4. The 1959 Order shall be amended as follows:—

(1) For rule 11 in the Schedule there shall be substituted the following rule:

"Where a tenant makes an application to postpone the termination of his tenancy under Article 12 of the Agriculture (Notices to Remedy and Notices to Quit) Order 1964, other than at the arbitration or at the hearing before the tribunal, his application shall be made substantially in accordance with Form 11."

(2) Form 11 in the Appendix shall be amended—

(a) by substituting for the words "Article 9 of the Agricultural Land Tribunals and Notices to Quit Order 1959" the words "Article 12 of the Agriculture (Notices to Remedy and Notices to Quit) Order 1964", and

(b) by adding at the end of footnote (1) the words "A written notice is required (by Article 12(2) of the 1964 Order referred to above) to be given at the same time to the landlord.".

5. The 1964 Order shall be amended as follows:—

(1) In Article 5(2) the words "the grounds on which and" shall be omitted;

(2) For Article 10 there shall be substituted the following Article:—

"10. Where there has been an arbitration under Article 9 above in respect of a notice to quit which is capable of taking effect as a notice to quit to which sub-section (1) of section 24 of the 1948 Act applies and, in consequence of the arbitration, the notice to quit takes effect accordingly, the time within which a counter-notice may be served by the tenant on the landlord under that sub-section shall be one month from the termination of the arbitration."

6.—(1) The Agriculture (Control of Notices to Quit) (Service Men) Order 1959(a) is hereby revoked.

(2) In any case to which, notwithstanding the existence of any such circumstances as are mentioned in sub-section (2) of section 24 of the 1948 Act, sub-section (1) thereof applies by virtue of the modification of that section by section 21 of the 1951 Act, paragraph (3) of this Article shall have effect, the 1959 Order shall have effect subject to the modifications specified in paragraph 1 of the Schedule hereto, and the 1964 Order as amended by this Order shall have effect subject to the modifications specified in paragraphs 2 and 3 of that Schedule.

(3) Where, on an application by the landlord for the consent of the tribunal to the operation of a notice to quit, it appears to the tribunal that the notice to quit was given for one or more of the reasons specified in paragraphs (b), (d) and (e) of section 24(2) of the 1948 Act, and that it is expedient that any question arising out of those reasons should be determined by arbitration between the landlord and tenant under the 1948 Act before the tribunal consider whether to grant or withhold consent to the operation of the notice to quit, they may require that the question be determined accordingly.

(4) This article shall not apply in relation to proceedings arising from a notice to quit served before the coming into operation of this Order.

Dated 31st July 1972.

Hailsham of St. Marylebone, C.

(a) S.I. 1959/82 (1959 I, p. 121).

SCHEDULE

Article 6(2)

MODIFICATIONS TO THE 1959 AND 1964 ORDERS

1. Where a notice to quit has been given for one or more of the reasons specified in paragraphs (b), (d) and (e) of section 24(2) of the 1948 Act, and the tenant has duly served a counter-notice under section 24(1) thereof, the form of application by the landlord for the tribunal's consent to the operation of the notice to quit prescribed by paragraph (3) of Rule 2 of the Schedule to the 1959 Order, and numbered Form 1, shall be deemed to include a requirement to state, as far as practicable, for which of the reasons notice to quit was given, and, if any question arising out of them has been determined by arbitration, the determination.

2. At the end of Article 9 of the 1964 Order there shall be added the following words:—

"so however that the tenant's failure to serve such a notice shall not affect his right to contest the reason in proceedings before an Agricultural Land Tribunal consequent upon the service of a counter-notice under section 24(1) of that Act or in any arbitration by which the tribunal may require any question arising out of the reason to be determined."

3. For Article 10 of the 1964 Order there shall be substituted the following Article:—

"10. Where a tenant requires a question to be determined by arbitration in pursuance of Article 9 above, the time within which a counter-notice under section 24(1) of the 1948 Act may be served by the tenant on the landlord under that sub-section shall be one month from the termination of the arbitration."

EXPLANATORY NOTE

(This Note is not part of the Order.)

This Order makes a number of amendments and modifications to instruments relating to notices to quit agricultural holdings. Article 4 corrects two re-ferences in the Agricultural Land Tribunals and Notices to Quit Order 1959 to provisions revoked in 1964, and makes provision for reminding the tenant of the obligation introduced in 1964 to serve a notice on the landlord. Article 5 amends the Agriculture (Notices to Remedy and Notices to Quit) Order 1964—

(a) by making it unnecessary for a tenant requiring arbitration on an issue of liability to do work to specify the grounds of objection as well as the items objected to, and

(b) by making more plain the effect of Article 10.

Article 6, with the schedule, revokes and re-enacts, with drafting amendments, the Agriculture (Control of Notices to Quit) (Service Men) Order 1959.

STATUTORY INSTRUMENTS

1972 No. 1208

PROBATION AND AFTER-CARE
The Probation (Amendment) Rules 1972

Made - - -	*5th August* 1972
Coming into Operation	*1st September* 1972

In exercise of the power conferred upon me by Schedule 5 to the Criminal Justice Act 1948**(a)**, I hereby make the following Rules:—

1. These Rules may be cited as the Probation (Amendment) Rules 1972 and shall come into operation on 1st September 1972.

2. For Rule 28(1) of the Probation Rules 1965**(b)**, as amended **(c)**, there shall be substituted the following paragraphs:—

"(1) A probation committee may appoint such number of persons to such of the following ranks as the Secretary of State may approve:—

Principal Probation Officer,

Deputy Principal Probation Officer,

Assistant Principal Probation Officer,

Senior Probation Officer.

(1A) The appointment of a person to the post of—

Principal Probation Officer,

Deputy Principal Probation Officer,

Assistant Principal Probation Officer,

Senior Probation Officer in charge of a probation area,

shall be subject to the approval of the Secretary of State.".

3. At the end of Rule 52 of the said Rules of 1965, as amended **(c)**, there shall be added the following paragraph:—

"(5) Any reference in these Rules to a probation area shall be construed as a reference to a probation and after-care area.".

Robert Carr,

One of Her Majesty's Principal
Secretaries of State.

Home Office,
   Whitehall.

5th August 1972.

(a) 1948 c. 58.   (b) S.I. 1965/723 (1965 I, p. 2236).
(c) The relevant amending instrument is S.I. 1967/1884 (1967 III, p. 5121).

EXPLANATORY NOTE

(This Note is not part of the Rules.)

These Rules amend the Probation Rules 1965.

Rule 2 reproduces the effect of Rule 28(1) of the 1965 Rules (power of the Secretary of State to approve senior ranks and also to approve the appointment of particular persons to fill particular posts in such ranks), but with the modification that his approval is no longer required where a person is appointed to the post of senior probation officer except where that person is to be in charge of a probation and after-care area.

Rule 3 provides for the construction of references to a probation area.

STATUTORY INSTRUMENTS

1972 No. 1209

CUSTOMS AND EXCISE

The Import Duties (Temporary Exemptions) (No. 9) Order 1972

Made - - - -	7th August 1972
Laid before the House of Commons	11th August 1972
Coming into Operation	1st September 1972

The Lords Commissioners of Her Majesty's Treasury, by virtue of the powers conferred on them by sections 3(6) and 13 of the Import Duties Act 1958(a), and of all other powers enabling them in that behalf, on the recommendation of the Secretary of State, hereby make the following Order:—

1.—(1) This Order may be cited as the Import Duties (Temporary Exemptions) (No. 9) Order 1972.

(2) The Interpretation Act 1889(b) shall apply for the interpretation of this Order as it applies for the interpretation of an Act of Parliament.

(3) This Order shall come into operation on 1st September 1972.

2.—(1) Until the beginning of 1st January 1973 or, in the case of goods in relation to which an earlier day is specified in Schedule 1 to this Order, until the beginning of that day, any import duty which is for the time being chargeable on goods of a heading of the Customs Tariff 1959 specified in that Schedule shall not be chargeable in respect of goods of any description there specified in relation to that heading.

(2) The period for which goods of the headings of the Customs Tariff 1959 and descriptions specified in Schedule 2 to this Order are exempt from import duty shall be extended until the beginning of 1st January 1973 or, in the case of goods in relation to which an earlier day is specified in that Schedule, until the beginning of that day.

(3) Any entry in column 2 in Schedule 1 or Schedule 2 to this Order shall be taken to comprise all goods which would be classified under an entry in the same terms constituting a subheading (other than the final subheading) in the relevant heading in the Customs Tariff 1959.

(4) For the purposes of classification under the Customs Tariff 1959, in so far as that depends on the rate of duty, any goods to which paragraph (1) or paragraph (2) above applies shall be treated as chargeable with the same duty as if this Order had not been made.

3. In article 3 of the Import Duties (Temporary Exemptions) (No. 3) Order 1972(c) (certain monolithic integrated circuit linear amplifiers exempt from, or subject to a reduced rate of, import duty until 1st September 1972) in paragraph (1) for the words " 1st September 1972 " there shall be substituted the words " 1st January 1973 ".

V. H. Goodhew,
P. L. Hawkins,

Two of the Lords Commissioners of Her Majesty's Treasury.

7th August 1972.

(a) 1958 c. 6.   (b) 1889 c. 63.   (c) S.I. 1972/648 (1972 I, p. 2122).

SCHEDULE 1

GOODS TEMPORARILY EXEMPT FROM IMPORT DUTY

Tariff Heading	Description
28.30	Barium chloride (until 2nd November 1972)
29.03	Benzene-1,3-disulphonic acid
29.07	3-Nitrophenol
29.10	4-Hydroxymethyl-2-(iodoethyl)-1,3-dioxolan, mixed isomers
29.15	Sodium 3,5-di(methoxycarbonyl)benzenesulphonate
29.16	Calcium lactate which, on ignition at 120° centigrade, loses not less than 25 per cent. of its weight and which contains

(1) not more than $0\cdot0002$ per cent. by weight of arsenic expressed as As,

(2) not more than $0\cdot07$ per cent. by weight of chlorides expressed as Cl, and

(3) not more than $0\cdot12$ per cent. by weight of sulphates expressed as SO_4,

all being calculated on the pentahydrate, $C_6H_{10}CaO_6.5H_2O$

*tri*Sodium ($\pm$)-*iso*citrate

29.21	1,3-Di-(4-methyl-1,3,2-dioxaborinan-2-yloxy)butane Di-(4,4,6-trimethyl-1,3,2-dioxaborinan-2-yl) oxide
29.22	Amantadine hydrochloride
29.23	Metaraminol hydrogen (+)-tartrate Potassium 4-aminobenzoate of which an aqueous solution containing 100 grammes per litre has a pH not greater than $8\cdot5$
29.25	1,3-Di-(2-hydroxyethyl)-5,5-dimethylhydantoin Diphenamid
29.29	3-Diethylaminopropiophenone *O*-(4-methoxyphenylcarbamoyl)oxime hydrochloride
29.31	2-(Ethylthio)ethanol
29.35	Adenosine 5'-(trilithium pyrophosphate) *NN*-Diethyl-2-[3-(1-naphthyl)-2-tetrahydrofurfurylpropionyloxy]-ethylammonium hydrogen oxalate Imidazolidin-2-one 1-Methylimidazole (until 2nd November 1972) Oxazepam Tetrahydrofurfuryl methacrylate
29.36	*N*-(1-Ethylpyrrolidin-2-ylmethyl)-2-methoxy-5-sulphamoylbenzamide
29.38	Sodium ascorbate Tocopherol, mixed isomers, containing not less than 50 per cent. by weight of (+)-α-tocopherol
29.39	17β-Hydroxy-17α-methylandrost-4-en-3-one
30.05	Plates bearing a reagent for the detection of Australian antigen (Au plates)

Tariff Heading	Description
48.07	Paper, coated, of a substance not less than 50 nor more than 80 grammes per square metre, being resistant to toluene solvent on the one coated side which, when subjected for 24 hours to 50 per cent. relative humidity at 17° centigrade, has an apparent surface resistance of not less than 10 megaohms and not more than 5,000 megaohms, measured under the same conditions between two electrodes 1 inch wide and 1 inch apart and using a Keithley model 600B electrometer (until 2nd November 1972)
70.08	Curved eyepieces of toughened glass not being coloured, tinted or otherwise shaded, with parallel faces and ground edges, having a maximum dimension of not less than 56 millimetres
74.02	Copper alloy ingots containing not less than 3·5 per cent. by weight of beryllium as the major alloying element
74.06	Copper powder containing not less than 5 per cent. nor more than 9 per cent. by weight of iron, not less than 1 per cent. nor more than 3 per cent. by weight of manganese, not less than 0·2 per cent. nor more than 1 per cent. by weight of nickel, as the other major metallic constituents (until 2nd November 1972)
91.03	Electric clocks of the instrument panel type designed to be permanently mounted in a motor vehicle with the power source provided by the battery of the vehicle (until 2nd November 1972)

SCHEDULE 2

GOODS FOR WHICH EXEMPTION FROM IMPORT DUTY IS EXTENDED

Tariff Heading	Description
25.19	Magnesite, dead-burned, containing (a) not less than 94 per cent. by weight of magnesium compounds expressed as MgO, (b) a total of not more than 1·0 per cent. by weight of aluminium compounds and iron compounds expressed as Al_2O_3 and Fe_2O_3, (c) a total of not less than 2·5 per cent. by weight and not more than 5·0 per cent. by weight of calcium compounds and silicon compounds expressed as CaO and SiO_2, and in which the weight of calcium compounds expressed as CaO is not less than 1·5 times the weight of silicon compounds expressed as SiO_2 (until 2nd November 1972)
28.18	Magnesium oxide, dead-burned but not fused, of a purity not less than 96 per cent., which contains (a) not more than 0·05 per cent. by weight of boron compounds expressed as B_2O_3, (b) a total of not more than 0·5 per cent. by weight of aluminium compounds and iron compounds expressed as Al_2O_3 and Fe_2O_3, and (c) a total of not less than 1·0 per cent. by weight and not more than 3·5 per cent. by weight of calcium compounds and silicon compounds expressed as CaO and SiO_2, the weight of calcium compounds being not less than 1·5 times and not more than 2·5 times the weight of silicon compounds; and (d) of which not less than 35 per cent. by weight is retained by a sieve having a nominal width of aperture of $\frac{3}{16}$ inch (until 2nd November 1972)
29.06	4-Ethylphenol Resorcinol 2,4-Xylenol
29.07	4-Chloro-2-cyclopentylphenol

Tariff Heading	*Description*

29.16   Cyclandelate

29.25   *N*-(Hydroxymethyl)acrylamide

29.26   Di-[2-(1,3-dimethylbutylideneamino)ethyl]amine
         1-(Di-[2-(1,3-dimethylbutylideneamino)ethyl]amino)-
         3-phenoxypropan-2-ol

29.27   Dichlobenil

29.31   Diethyl sulphide
         Dimethyl sulphide
         2-Mercaptoethanol
         2-Methylpropane-2-thiol

29.32   4-Hydroxy-3-nitrophenylarsonic acid

29.35   Acriflavine
         1,4-Butyrolactone (until 2nd November 1972)
         Cyanuric acid
         6-[2-(5-Nitro-2-furyl)vinyl]pyridazin-3-ylammonium chloride

29.39   Thyrocalcitonin, porcine

37.01   Photographic plates on a glass base of flatness 0·001 inch or less per linear inch, of thickness between 0·058 inch and 0·092 inch, of a length and width between 2 and 4 inches, with an emulsion on one side and an anti-halation layer either incorporated in the emulsion or on the reverse side: the emulsion being between 5 and 7 micrometres thick, having a spectral sensitivity peak at about 520 nanometres and capable of resolving in excess of 2,000 line pairs per millimetre, and having an average surface contamination per square centimetre of less than 5 particles of a diameter greater than 2 micrometres

39.01   Polyimide film, not exceeding 46 centimetres in width, uncoated or coated with fluorocarbon resin and having a total thickness not greater than 0·2 millimetre
         Resins, being products of the condensation of adipic acid with a mixture of propane-1,2-diol and ethanediol of which the ethanediol content is not less than 50 per cent. by weight, and having:—
         (*a*) an acetyl value not less than 34 and not more than 38,
         (*b*) an acid value not more than 1,
         (*c*) a colour not deeper than 50 Hazen units, and
         (*d*) a viscosity at 40° centigrade of not less than 70 seconds and not more than 125 seconds, for a free fall of 20 centimetres of a steel sphere $\frac{1}{8}$ inch in diameter, in a tube of internal diameter 3·5 centimetres, when determined by the method of British Standard 188:1957, part 3 as amended up to and including September 1964
         (until 2nd November 1972)

39.03   Cellulose acetate propionate in the forms covered by Note 3(*b*) of Chapter 39
         Regenerated cellulose in the form of sheets not exceeding 430 millimetres by 1,020 millimetres in size, 18 grammes per square metre in weight or 12 micrometres in thickness

51.01   Yarn wholly of polytetrafluoroethylene

Tariff Heading	Description

51.02   Monofil wholly of fluorocarbon polymer

59.17   Yarn or tow of polytetrafluoroethylene fibre impregnated with poly-tetrafluoroethylene dispersion whether or not treated with a lubricant

70.20   Glass fibre continuous filament yarn of low alkali borosilicate glass (E glass) (until 2nd November 1972)

73.15   Alloy steel coils for re-rolling, which contain not less than 14 per cent. nor more than 18 per cent. by weight of chromium as the major alloying element, and not more than 0·5 per cent. by weight of nickel, and having a width exceeding 500 millimetres but not more than 1,372 millimetres, and a thickness of not less than 3 millimetres nor more than 6 millimetres

Heat resisting wire, not plated, coated or covered, of metal alloy containing by weight the following:

	Not less than (per cent.)	Not more than (per cent.)
Chromium	19·0	26·0
Aluminium ...	4·0	5·5
Manganese ...	0·10	0·50
Iron	Balance	Balance

and not more than a total of 2 per cent. by weight of substances other than chromium, aluminium and manganese

Hot rolled alloy steel strip in coils, containing not less than 14 per cent. by weight nor more than 18 per cent. by weight of chromium as the major alloying element, and not more than 0·5 per cent. by weight of nickel, of a width of not less than 400 millimetres nor more than 500 millimetres and of a thickness of not less than 3 millimetres nor more than 6 millimetres

74.01   Copper alloy containing not less than 99·8 per cent. by weight of copper and not less than 0·08 per cent. nor more than 0·11 per cent. by weight of silver as the major alloying element in the form of billets of a diameter of not less than 149 millimetres nor more than 156 millimetres and of a length of not less than 1,358 millimetres nor more than 2,480 millimetres

81.02   Molybdenum alloy sheet containing not less than 98 per cent. by weight of molybdenum and not more than 1 per cent. by weight of titanium as the major alloying element, of a thickness not less than 1 millimetre nor more than 5 millimetres, and of such dimensions that the top surface area of the sheet is not less than 7,000 square millimetres and not more than 185,000 square millimetres (until 2nd November 1972)

Molybdenum alloy slabs containing not less than 98 per cent. by weight of molybdenum and not more than 1 per cent. by weight of titanium as the major alloying element, of a thickness of not less than 12 millimetres nor more than 51 millimetres, and of such dimensions that the top surface area of the slab is not less than 7,000 square millimetres and not more than 185,000 square millimetres (until 2nd November 1972)

81.04   Titanium alloy containing not less than 5 per cent. nor more than 7 per cent. by weight of aluminium, not less than 3 per cent. nor more than 5 per cent. by weight of vanadium as the major alloying elements, being in the form of blooms not less than 152 centimetres nor more than 191 centimetres in length, not less than 38 centimetres nor more than 41 centimetres in width and not less than 30 centimetres nor more than 36 centimetres in thickness (until 2nd November 1972)

Tariff Heading	*Description*

83.13   Tinplate caps for sealing jars, of an internal diameter on the rim of not less than 1·580 inches and not more than 1·610 inches and a maximum depth of not less than 0·415 inch and not more than 0·425 inch stamped from tinplate of nominal thickness of 0·0055 inch or of 0·0066 inch, with an internal curl, a vinyl coating applied to the internal surface and a plasticised lining compound deposited on the internal side wall and top sealing panel to form a sealing gasket

85.15   The following apparatus for use in aircraft:

(*a*) automatic radio direction finding apparatus covering a frequency range of at least 200 KHz to 850 KHz;

(*b*) distance measuring apparatus for determining the slant range from aircraft to ground transponder and operating within the frequency range of 960 MHz to 1,215 MHz;

(*c*) very high frequency omni-directional radio range apparatus (VOR), instrument landing system localiser apparatus (ILS/LOC), instrument landing system glide path apparatus (ILS/G.PATH);

(*d*) very high frequency communication apparatus (VHF/COM) (transmitters, receivers, or combined transmitter/receivers) covering a frequency band of at least 118 to 135·95 MHz, with not less than 180 channels and capable of operating in areas where 50 kHz channel spacing is in force;

(*e*) apparatus combining the functions and capabilities of any of the apparatus specified in (*c*) and (*d*) above but excluding apparatus combining any of those functions and capabilities with any other function or capability;

being in each case apparatus of a type approved by the Civil Aviation Authority, at the date of this Order, under Article 14(5) of the Air Navigation Order 1972, for use in aircraft of not more than 5,700 kilogrammes maximum total weight authorised, flying in controlled airspace in accordance with the Instrument Flight Rules as defined in the said Air Navigation Order, but not for use in other aircraft (until 2nd November 1972)

EXPLANATORY NOTE

(This Note is not part of the Order)

This Order provides that the goods listed in Schedule 1 shall be temporarily exempt from import duty, and those listed in Schedule 2 shall continue to be exempt from import duty, both until 1st January 1973 or, in the case of certain items, until such earlier day as is specified.

The Order also continues the reduction, until 1st January 1973, in the duty chargeable on certain monolithic integrated circuit linear amplifiers under heading 85.21: this temporary reduction is from 10 per cent. to 3 per cent. in the full rate of duty and from 7 per cent. to nil in the Commonwealth rate.

As regards the exemption for equipment for use in aircraft under heading 85.15, apparatus of a type approved by the Civil Aviation Authority is listed in Civil Aviation Publication CAP 208, Airborne Radio Apparatus Vol. 2, published by Her Majesty's Stationery Office. This publication is subject to amendment, and confirmation that apparatus is of a type approved at the date of this Order should be obtained from the Civil Aviation Authority, Controllerate of National Air Traffic Services, Tels. N2(c), 19–29 Woburn Place, London WC1H 0LX.

STATUTORY INSTRUMENTS

1972 No. 1210

TRIBUNALS AND INQUIRIES

The Tribunals and Inquiries (Value Added Tax Tribunals) Order 1972

Made - - -	*7th August* 1972
Laid before Parliament	*15th August* 1972
Coming into Operation	*8th September* 1972

The Lord Chancellor and the Secretary of State for Scotland, in exercise of the powers conferred on them by section 15(1), (3) and (4) of the Tribunals and Inquiries Act 1971(**a**), hereby make the following Order: —

1.—(1) This Order may be cited as the Tribunals and Inquiries (Value Added Tax Tribunals) Order 1972 and shall come into operation on 8th September 1972.

(2) The Interpretation Act 1889(**b**) shall apply to the interpretation of this Order as it applies to the interpretation of an Act of Parliament.

(3) In this Order: —

"the Act of 1971" means the Tribunals and Inquiries Act 1971; and

"value added tax tribunals" means the tribunals established under section 40 of, and Schedule 6 to, the Finance Act 1972(**c**).

2. Schedule 1 to the Act of 1971 shall have effect as if there were specified therein—

(*a*) in Part I, value added tax tribunals for England and Wales and for Northern Ireland; and

(*b*) in Part II, value added tax tribunals for Scotland.

3. Section 13 of the Act of 1971 shall apply to value added tax tribunals.

4. Section 10 of the Act of 1971 shall have effect as if, for the words "or the Commissioners of Inland Revenue", there were substituted the words "the Commissioners of Inland Revenue or the Commissioners of Customs and Excise."

Dated 4th August 1972.

Hailsham of St. Marylebone, C.

Dated 7th August 1972.

Gordon Campbell,
One of Her Majesty's Principal
Secretaries of State.

(**a**) 1971 c. 62.   (**b**) 1889 c. 63.   (**c**) 1972 c. 41.

EXPLANATORY NOTE

(This Note is not part of the Order.)

This Order brings under the supervision of the Council on Tribunals the value added tax tribunals established under the Finance Act 1972. It also confers on parties to proceedings before those tribunals a right of appeal on a point of law to the High Court, the Court of Session or the High Court in Northern Ireland and requires the Commissioners of Customs and Excise to consult the Council before making procedural rules governing such proceedings.

STATUTORY INSTRUMENTS

1972 No. 1211 (S.84)

LANDLORD AND TENANT

RENT CONTROL, ETC (SCOTLAND)

The Cancellation of Registration (Procedure) (Scotland) Regulations 1972

Made - - -	*7th August* 1972
Laid before Parliament	*14th August* 1972
Coming into Operation	*4th September* 1972

In exercise of the powers conferred on me by section 46 of the Rent (Scotland) Act 1971(**a**), as read with section 44A(4) of that Act as inserted by section 39 of the Housing (Financial Provisions) (Scotland) Act 1972(**b**), and of all other powers enabling me in that behalf, I hereby make the following regulations:—

Citation and commencement

1. These regulations may be cited as the Cancellation of Registration (Procedure) (Scotland) Regulations 1972 and shall come into operation on 4th September 1972.

Interpretation

2.—(1) In these regulations,

'the Act' means the Rent (Scotland) Act 1971;

'application' means an application for the cancellation of a registration which is made to the rent officer under section 44A of the Act jointly by the landlord and tenant under a rent agreement;

'rent agreement' means a rent agreement within the meaning of section 44A of the Act, of which a copy accompanies an application, and

'registration' means the rent registered for the dwellinghouse under Part IV of the Act which it is sought to cancel by the application.

(2) The Interpretation Act 1889(**c**) shall apply for the interpretation of these regulations as it applies for the interpretation of an Act of Parliament.

Procedure on applications to rent officer

3. On receiving an application, the rent officer may, by notice in writing served on the landlord or the tenant or on both the landlord and the tenant require him or them to give to the rent officer, within such period of not less than 14 days from the service of the notice as may be specified in the notice, such information as he may reasonably require regarding such of the particulars contained in the application or such of the terms of the rent agreement as may be specified in the notice.

(**a**) 1971 c. 28.   (**b**) 1972 c.46   (**c**) 1889 c. 63

4. Where it appears to the rent officer, after making such inquiry, if any, as he thinks fit, and considering any information supplied to him in pursuance of regulation 3 above, that the rent payable under the rent agreement does not exceed a fair rent for the dwellinghouse, he may, subject to section 44A(6) of the Act, cancel the registration without further proceedings.

5. Where the rent officer, in carrying out his functions under these regulations, inspects a dwellinghouse, he shall explain to the tenant or to his spouse, if either is present at the inspection, the procedure upon an application.

6.—(1) Where the rent officer does not cancel the registration in pursuance of regulation 4 above, he shall serve a notice under this regulation.

(2) A notice under this regulation shall be served on the landlord and the tenant informing them that the rent officer proposes, at a time (which shall not be earlier than 7 days after the service of the notice) and place specified in the notice to consider in consultation with the landlord and tenant, or such of them as may appear at that time and place, whether the registration ought to be cancelled.

(3) At any such consultation, the landlord and the tenant may each be represented by a person authorised by him in that behalf, whether or not that person is an advocate or a solicitor.

Notices

7. Any notice required to be served under these regulations and any notification required to be given under section 44A(8) of the Act (notification of rent officer's decision) may be sent by post in a pre-paid letter or delivered—

(*a*) to the landlord and to the tenant at their respective addresses given in the application; or

(*b*) where the application is made on behalf of the landlord or the tenant by an agent acting on his behalf, to that agent at the address of the agent given in the application.

Gordon Campbell,
One of Her Majesty's Principal
Secretaries of State.

St Andrew's House,
Edinburgh.

7th August 1972.

EXPLANATORY NOTE

(This Note is not part of the Regulations.)

These Regulations prescribe the procedure to be followed where a rent has been registered for a dwellinghouse under Part IV of the Rent (Scotland) Act 1971 and a landlord and tenant apply to the rent officer, under section 44A of that Act, for the cancellation of the registration.

STATUTORY   INSTRUMENTS

1972 No. 1215

CUSTOMS AND EXCISE

The Import Duties (Temporary Exemptions) (No. 10) Order 1972

Made - - - -	*8th August* 1972
Laid before the House of Commons - -	*9th August* 1972
Coming into Operation -	*13th August* 1972

The Lords Commissioners of Her Majesty's Treasury, by virtue of the powers conferred on them by sections 3(6) and 13 of the Import Duties Act 1958(**a**), and of all other powers enabling them in that behalf, on the recommendation of the Secretary of State, hereby make the following Order:—

1.—(1) This Order may be cited as the Import Duties (Temporary Exemptions) (No. 10) Order 1972.

(2) The Interpretation Act 1889(**b**) shall apply for the interpretation of this Order as it applies for the interpretation of an Act of Parliament.

(3) This Order shall come into operation on 13th August 1972.

2.—(1) With respect to goods falling within heading 02.01(A)(1) (beef and veal) of the Customs Tariff 1959, the period for which, by virtue of the Import Duties (Temporary Exemptions) (No. 5) Order 1972(**c**) and the Import Duties (Temporary Exemptions) (No. 7) Order 1972(**d**), there is exemption from import duty shall be extended until the beginning of 10th September 1972.

(2) For the purposes of classification under the Customs Tariff 1959, in so far as that depends on the rate of duty, any goods to which paragraph (1) above applies shall be treated as chargeable with the same duty as if this Order had not been made.

> *P. L. Hawkins,*
> *Oscar Murton,*
> Two of the Lords Commissioners
> of Her Majesty's Treasury.

8th August 1972.

EXPLANATORY NOTE

(This Note is not part of the Order.)

This Order continues, until 10th September 1972, the temporary exemption from import duty of fresh, chilled or frozen beef and veal.

(**a**) 1958 c. 6.   (**b**) 1889 c. 63.   (**c**) S.I. 1972/849 (1972 II, p. 2698).
(**d**) S.I. 1972/1042 (1972 II, p. 3143).

STATUTORY INSTRUMENTS

1972 No. 1216

COAL INDUSTRY

The Opencast Coal (Rate of Interest on Compensation) (No. 2) Order 1972

Made - - -	*7th August* 1972
Laid before Parliament	*15th August* 1972
Coming into Operation	*16th August* 1972

The Treasury, in exercise of the powers conferred upon them by sections 35(8) and 49(4) of the Opencast Coal Act 1958(**a**) and of all other powers enabling them in that behalf, hereby make the following Order:—

1. This Order may be cited as the Opencast Coal (Rate of Interest on Compensation) (No. 2) Order 1972, and shall come into operation on 16th August 1972.

2. The Interpretation Act 1889(**b**) shall apply for the interpretation of this Order as it applies for the interpretation of an Act of Parliament.

3. The rate of interest for the purposes of section 35 of the Opencast Coal Act 1958 shall be $7\frac{1}{2}$ per cent. per annum.

4. The Opencast Coal (Rate of Interest on Compensation) Order 1972(**c**) is hereby revoked.

Hugh Rossi,
Oscar Murton,
Two of the Lords Commissioners
of Her Majesty's Treasury.

7th August 1972.

EXPLANATORY NOTE

(*This Note is not part of the Order.*)

Section 35 of the Opencast Coal Act 1958 provides that interest shall be payable in addition to compensation in certain circumstances. This Order increases the rate of interest from $5\frac{1}{4}$ per cent. to $7\frac{1}{2}$ per cent. per annum and revokes the Opencast Coal (Rate of Interest on Compensation) Order 1972.

(**a**) 1958 c. 69.   (**b**) 1889 c. 63.   (**c**) S.I. 1972/373 (1972 I, p. 1448).

STATUTORY INSTRUMENTS

1972 No. 1217

ROAD TRAFFIC

The Motor Vehicles (Third Party Risks) Regulations 1972

Made - - - -	1*st August* 1972
Laid before Parliament	15*th August* 1972
Coming into Operation	1*st November* 1972

The Secretary of State for the Environment in exercise of his powers under sections 147, 157 and 162 of the Road Traffic Act 1972(a), and under section 37 of the Vehicles (Excise) Act 1971(b), as extended by section 153 of the Road Traffic Act 1972, and of all other enabling powers, and after consultation with representative organisations in accordance with the provisions of section 199(2) of the Road Traffic Act 1972, hereby makes the following Regulations:—

Commencement and citation

1. These Regulations shall come into operation on 1st November 1972 and may be cited as the Motor Vehicles (Third Party Risks) Regulations 1972.

2. The Motor Vehicles (Third Party Risks) Regulations 1961(c) and the Motor Vehicles (Third Party Risks) (Amendment) Regulations 1969(d) are hereby revoked.

Temporary use of existing forms

3. Nothing in these Regulations shall affect the validity of any certificate which has been issued before these Regulations came into force in a form prescribed by the Motor Vehicles (Third Party Risks) Regulations 1961, as amended by the Motor Vehicles (Third Party Risks) (Amendment) Regulations 1969, as in force immediately before the coming into operation of these Regulations, and any certificate in such a form may continue to be issued until the expiration of three years from the coming into force of these Regulations.

Interpretation

4.—(1) In these Regulations, unless the context otherwise requires, the following expressions have the meanings hereby respectively assigned to them:—

"the Act" means the Road Traffic Act 1972;

(a) 1972 c. 20. (b) 1971 c. 10.
(c) S.I. 1961/1465 (1961 II, p. 2967). (d) S.I. 1969/1733 (1969 III, p. 5445).

"company" means an authorised insurer within the meaning of Part VI of the Act or a body of persons by whom a security may be given in pursuance of the said Part VI;

"motor vehicle" has the meaning assigned to it by sections 190, 192 and 193 of the Act, but excludes any invalid carriage, tramcar or trolley vehicle to which Part VI of the Act does not apply;

"policy" means a policy of insurance in respect of third party risks arising out of the use of motor vehicles which complies with the requirements of Part VI of the Act and includes a covering note;

"security" means a security in respect of third party risks arising out of the use of motor vehicles which complies with the requirements of Part VI of the Act;

"specified body" means—

(a) any of the local authorities referred to in paragraph (a) of section 144(2) of the Act; or

(b) a Passenger Transport Executive established under an order made under section 9 of the Transport Act 1968(a), or a subsidiary of that Executive, being an Executive or subsidiary to whose vehicles section 144(2)(a) of the Act has been applied; or

(c) the London Transport Executive or a wholly-owned subsidiary of that Executive referred to in paragraph (e) of section 144(2) of the Act.

(2) Any reference in these Regulations to a certificate in Form A, B, C, D, E or F shall be construed as a reference to a certificate in the form so headed and set out in Part 1 of the Schedule to these Regulations which has been duly made and completed subject to and in accordance with the provisions set out in Part 2 of the said Schedule.

(3) Any reference in these Regulations to any enactment shall be construed as a reference to that enactment as amended by any subsequent enactment.

(4) The Interpretation Act 1889(b) shall apply for the interpretation of these Regulations as it applies for the interpretation of an Act of Parliament, and as if for the purposes of section 38 of that Act these Regulations were an Act of Parliament and the Regulations revoked by Regulation 2 of these Regulations were Acts of Parliament thereby repealed.

Issue of certificates of insurance or security

5.—(1) A company shall issue to every holder of a security or of a policy other than a covering note issued by the company:—

(a) in the case of a policy or security relating to one or more specified vehicles a certificate of insurance in Form A or a certificate of security in Form D in respect of each such vehicle;

(b) in the case of a policy or security relating to vehicles other than specified vehicles such number of certificates in Form B or Form D as may be necessary for the purpose of complying with the requirements of section 162(1) of the Act and of these Regulations as to the production of evidence that a motor vehicle is not being driven in contravention of section 143 of the Act:

(a) 1968 c. 73.　　　　　　(b) 1889 c. 63.

Provided that where a security is intended to cover the use of more than ten motor vehicles at one time the company by whom it was issued may, subject to the consent of the Secretary of State, issue one certificate only, and where such consent has been given the holder of the security may issue duplicate copies of such certificate duly authenticated by him up to such number and subject to such conditions as the Secretary of State may determine.

(2) Notwithstanding the foregoing provisions of this Regulation, where as respects third party risks a policy or security relating to a specified vehicle extends also to the driving by the holder of other motor vehicles, not being specified vehicles, the certificate may be in Form A or Form D, as the case may be, containing a statement in either case that the policy or security extends to such driving of other motor vehicles. Where such a certificate is issued by a company they may, and shall in accordance with a demand made to them by the holder, issue to him a further such certificate or a certificate in Form B.

(3) Every policy in the form of a covering note issued by a company shall have printed thereon or on the back thereof a certificate of insurance in Form C.

6. Every certificate of insurance or certificate of security shall be issued not later than four days after the date on which the policy or security to which it relates is issued or renewed.

Production of evidence as alternatives to certificates

7. The following evidence that a motor vehicle is not or was not being driven in contravention of section 143 of the Act may be produced in pursuance of section 162 of the Act as an alternative to the production of a certificate of insurance or a certificate of security:—

(1) a duplicate copy of a certificate of security issued in accordance with the proviso to sub-paragraph (*b*) of paragraph (1) of Regulation 5 of these Regulations;

(2) in the case of a motor vehicle of which the owner has for the time being deposited with the Accountant-General of the Supreme Court the sum of fifteen thousand pounds in accordance with the provisions of section 144(1) of the Act, a certificate in Form E signed by the owner of the motor vehicle or by some person authorised by him in that behalf that such sum is on deposit;

(3) in the case of a motor vehicle owned by a specified body, a police authority or the Receiver for the metropolitan police district, a certificate in Form F signed by some person authorised in that behalf by such specified body, police authority or Receiver as the case may be that the said motor vehicle is owned by the said specified body, police authority or Receiver.

8. Any certificate issued in accordance with paragraph (2) or (3) of the preceding Regulation shall be destroyed by the owner of the vehicle to which it relates before the motor vehicle is sold or otherwise disposed of.

Production of evidence of insurance or security on application for excise licences

9.—(1) Any person applying for a vehicle licence under the Vehicles (Excise) Act 1971 shall, except as hereinafter provided and subject to the provisions of Regulation 8 of the Motor Vehicles (International Motor Insurance Card) Regulations 1971**(a)**, produce to the Secretary of State either:—

(a) S.I. 1971/792 (1971 II, p. 2256).

(*a*) a certificate of insurance, certificate of security or duplicate copy of a certificate of security issued in accordance with these Regulations indicating that on the date when the licence comes into operation there will be in force the necessary policy or the necessary security in relation to the user of the motor vehicle by the applicant or by other persons on his order or with his permission and such further evidence as may be necessary to establish that the certificate relates to such user; or

(*b*) in the case where the motor vehicle is one of more than ten motor vehicles owned by the same person in respect of which a policy or policies of insurance have been obtained by him from the same authorised insurer, a statement duly authenticated by the authorised insurer to the effect that on the date when the licence becomes operative an insurance policy which complies with Part VI of the Act will be in force in relation to the user of the motor vehicle; or

(*c*) evidence that section 143 of the Act does not apply to the motor vehicle at a time when it is being driven under the owner's control, in accordance with the following provisions—

   (i) in the case of a motor vehicle of which the owner has for the time being deposited with the Accountant-General of the Supreme Court the sum of fifteen thousand pounds in accordance with the provisions of section 144(1) of the Act, a certificate in Form E signed by the owner of the motor vehicle or by some person authorised by him in that behalf that such sum is on deposit;

   (ii) in the case of a motor vehicle owned by a specified body, a police authority or by the Receiver for the metropolitan police district, a certificate in Form F signed by some person authorised in that behalf by such specified body, police authority or Receiver as the case may be that the vehicle in respect of which the application for a licence is made is owned by the said specified body, police authority or Receiver.

(2) A person engaged in the business of letting motor vehicles on hire shall not, when applying for a licence under the Vehicles (Excise) Act 1971, be required to comply with the provisions of paragraph (1) of this Regulation if the motor vehicle in respect of which the licence is applied for is intended to be used solely for the purpose of being let on hire and driven by the person by whom the motor vehicle is hired or by persons under his control.

Keeping of records by companies

10.—(1) Every company by whom a policy or a security is issued shall keep a record of the following particulars relative thereto and of any certificates issued in connection therewith:—

(*a*) the full name and address of the person to whom the policy, security or certificate is issued;

(*b*) in the case of a policy relating to one or more specified motor vehicles the registration mark of each such motor vehicle;

(*c*) the date on which the policy or security comes into force and the date on which it expires;

(*d*) in the case of a policy the conditions subject to which the persons or classes of persons specified in the policy will be indemnified;

(e) in the case of a security the conditions subject to which the undertaking given by the company under the security will be implemented;

and every such record shall be preserved for one year from the date of expiry of the policy or security.

(2) Every specified body shall keep a record of the motor vehicles owned by them in respect of which a policy or a security has not been obtained, and of any certificates issued by them under these Regulations in respect of such motor vehicles, and of the withdrawal or destruction of any such certificates.

(3) Any person who has deposited and keeps deposited with the Accountant-General of the Supreme Court the sum of fifteen thousand pounds in accordance with the provisions of section 144(1) of the Act shall keep a record of the motor vehicles owned by him and of any certificates issued by him or on his behalf under these Regulations in respect of such motor vehicles and of the withdrawal or destruction of any such certificates.

(4) Any company, specified body or other person by whom records of documents are required by these Regulations to be kept shall without charge furnish to the Secretary of State or to any chief officer of police on request any particulars thereof.

Notification to the Secretary of State of ineffective policies or securities

11. Where to the knowledge of a company a policy or security issued by them ceases to be effective without the consent of the person to whom it was issued, otherwise than by effluxion of time or by reason of his death, the company shall forthwith notify the Secretary of State of the date on which the policy or security ceased to be effective:

Provided that such notification need not be made if the certificate relating to the policy or security has been received by the company from the person to whom the certificate was issued on or before the date on which the policy or security ceases to be effective.

Return of certificates to issuing company

12.—(1) The following provisions shall apply in relation to the transfer of a policy or security with the consent of the holder to any other person:—

(a) the holder shall, before the policy or security is transferred, return any relative certificates issued for the purposes of these Regulations to the company by whom they were issued; and

(b) the policy or security shall not be transferred to any other person unless and until the certificates have been so returned or the company are satisfied that the certificates have been lost or destroyed.

(2) In any case where with the consent of the person to whom it was issued a policy or security is suspended or ceases to be effective, otherwise than by effluxion of time, in circumstances in which the provisions of section 147(4) of the Act (relating to the surrender of certificates) do not apply, the holder of the policy or security shall within seven days from the date when it is suspended or ceases to be effective return any relative certificates issued for the purposes of these Regulations to the company by whom they were issued and the company

shall not issue a new policy or security to the said holder in respect of the motor vehicle or vehicles to which the said first mentioned policy or security related unless and until the certificates have been returned to the company or the company are satisfied that they have been lost or destroyed.

(3) Where a policy or security is cancelled by mutual consent or by virtue of any provision in the policy or security, any statutory declaration that a certificate has been lost or destroyed made in pursuance of section 147(4) (which requires any such declaration to be made within a period of seven days from the taking effect of the cancellation) shall be delivered forthwith after it has been made to the company by whom the policy was issued or the security given.

(4) The provisions of the last preceding paragraph shall be without prejudice to the provisions of paragraph (c) of subsection (2) of section 149 of the Act as to the effect for the purposes of that subsection of the making of a statutory declaration within the periods therein stated.

Issue of fresh certificates

13. Where any company by whom a certificate of insurance or a certificate of security has been issued are satisfied that the certificate has become defaced or has been lost or destroyed they shall, if they are requested to do so by the person to whom the certificate was issued, issue to him a fresh certificate. In the case of a defaced certificate the company shall not issue a fresh certificate unless the defaced certificate is returned to the company.

Signed by authority of the Secretary of State.

John Peyton,

1st August 1972.   Minister for Transport Industries, Department of the Environment.

THE SCHEDULE

PART 1

Forms of Certificates

FORM A

Certificate of Motor Insurance

Certificate No.............................   Policy No..........................(Optional)

1. Registration mark of vehicle.
2. Name of policy holder.
3. Effective date of the commencement of insurance for the purposes of the relevant law.
4. Date of expiry of insurance.
5. Persons or classes of persons entitled to drive.
6. Limitations as to use.

I/We hereby certify that the policy to which this certificate relates satisfies the requirements of the relevant law applicable in Great Britain.

....
Authorised Insurers

Note: For full details of the insurance cover reference should be made to the policy.

FORM B

Certificate of Motor Insurance

Certificate No.................................... Policy No.....................(Optional)

1. Description of vehicles.
2. Name of policy holder.
3. Effective date of the commencement of insurance for the purposes of the relevant law.
4. Date of expiry of insurance.
5. Persons or classes of persons entitled to drive.
6. Limitations as to use.

I/We hereby certify that the policy to which this certificate relates satisfies the requirements of the relevant law applicable in Great Britain.

....
Authorised Insurers

Note: For full details of the insurance cover
reference should be made to the policy.

FORM C

Certificate of Motor Insurance

I/We hereby certify that this covering note satisfies the requirements of the relevant law applicable in Great Britain.

....
Authorised Insurers

FORM D

Certificate of Security

Certificate No.................................... Security No.....................(Optional)

1. Name of holder of security.
2. Effective date of the commencement of security for the purposes of the relevant law.
3. Date of expiry of security.
4. Conditions to which security is subject.

I/We hereby certify that the security to which this certificate relates satisfies the requirements of the relevant law applicable in Great Britain.

....
Persons giving security

Note: For full details of the cover
reference should be made to the security.

Form E

Certificate of Deposit

I/We hereby certify that I am/we are the owner(s) of the vehicle of which the registration mark is.......................and that in pursuance of the relevant law applicable in Great Britain I/we have on deposit with the Accountant-General of the Supreme Court the sum of fifteen thousand pounds.

Signed ....

on behalf of.......................

Form F

Certificate of Ownership

We hereby certify that the vehicle of which the registration mark is....................

...............................is owned by..

Signed ....

on behalf of.......................

Part 2

Provisions relating to the forms and completion of certificates

1. Every certificate shall be printed and completed in black on white paper or similar material. This provision shall not apply to any reproduction of a seal or monogram or similar device referred to in paragraph 2 of this Part of this Schedule.

2. No certificate shall contain any advertising matter, either on the face or on the back thereof:

Provided that the name and address of the company by whom a certificate is issued' or a reproduction of the seal of the company or any monogram or similar device of the company, or the name and address of an insurance broker shall not be deemed to be advertising matter for the purposes of this paragraph if it is printed or stamped at the foot or on the back of such certificate.

3. The whole of each form as set out in Part 1 of this Schedule shall in each case appear on the face of the form, the items being in the order so set out and the certification being set out at the end of the form.

4. The particulars to be inserted on the said forms shall so far as possible appear on the face of the form, but where in the case of any of the numbered headings in Forms A, B, or D, this cannot conveniently be done, any part of such particulars may be inserted on the back of the form, provided that their presence on the back is clearly indicated under the relevant heading.

5. The particulars to be inserted on any of the said forms shall not include particulars relating to any exceptions purporting to restrict the insurance under the relevant policy or the operation of the relevant security which are by subsection (1) of section 148 of the Act rendered of no effect as respects the third party liabilities required by sections 145 and 146 of the Act to be covered by a policy or security.

6.—(1) In any case where it is intended that a certificate of insurance, certificate of security or a covering note shall be effective not only in Great Britain, but also in any of the following territories, that is to say Northern Ireland, the Isle of Man, the Island of Guernsey, the Island of Jersey or the Island of Alderney, Forms A, B, C and D may be modified by the addition thereto, where necessary, of a reference to the relevant legal provisions of such of those territories as may be appropriate.

(2) A certificate of insurance or a certificate of security may contain either on the face or on the back of the certificate a statement as to whether or not the policy or security to which it relates satisfies the requirements of the relevant law in any of the territories referred to in this paragraph.

7. Every certificate of insurance or certificate of security shall be duly authenticated by or on behalf of the company by whom it is issued.

8. A certificate in Form F issued by a subsidiary of a Passenger Transport Executive or by a wholly-owned subsidiary of the London Transport Executive shall indicate under the signature that the issuing body is such a subsidiary of an Executive, which shall there be specified.

EXPLANATORY NOTE

(*This Note is not part of the Regulations.*)

These Regulations consolidate with amendments the Regulations revoked by Regulation 2. The Regulations relate to the issue of certificates of insurance or security (Regulations 5 and 6 and the Schedule), evidence which may be produced to show that a motor vehicle is not being driven in contravention of the compulsory third party insurance requirements (Regulation 7), the duty to destroy certain certificates (Regulation 8), the production of evidence of insurance or security on application for a vehicle excise licence (Regulation 9), the keeping of records by insurance companies and certain other persons relating to certificates (Regulation 10), the notification to the Secretary of State of ineffective policies or securities (Regulation 11), the duty to return certificates to the issuing company (Regulation 12), and the issue of fresh certificates (Regulation 13). The amendments are for the most part of a minor character and include the following:—

(*a*) references to enactments are brought up to date;

(*b*) the evidence specified in Regulation 7 is no longer restricted to being produced by the driver of a motor vehicle in pursance of section 162 of the Road Traffic Act 1972;

(*c*) the evidence which may be required from a person applying for a licence for a motor vehicle is extended in the case when he presents a certificate of insurance or security to such further evidence as may be necessary to connect the certificate to the applicant and his vehicle;

(*d*) an explanatory note is added to some of the prescribed certificates making it clear that they do not contain a full summary of the policy or security; and

(*e*) reference in certificates to specific enactments is no longer required.

STATUTORY INSTRUMENTS

1972 No. 1218

BORROWING CONTROL

The Control of Borrowing (Amendment) Order 1972

Made - - -	*8th August* 1972
Laid before Parliament	*10th August* 1972
Coming into Operation	*1st September* 1972

The Treasury, in exercise of the powers conferred upon them by sections 1 and 3(4) of the Borrowing (Control and Guarantees) Act 1946(**a**) and of all other powers enabling them in that behalf, hereby make the following Order:—

1. This Order may be cited as the Control of Borrowing (Amendment) Order 1972, and shall come into operation on 1st September 1972.

2. The Interpretation Act 1889(**b**) shall apply for the interpretation of this Order as it applies for the interpretation of an Act of Parliament.

3. Article 8A of the Control of Borrowing Order 1958(**c**), as substituted by the Control of Borrowing (Amendment) Order 1970(**d**), shall be amended, in paragraph (2)(*b*) thereof, by the substitution, for the words "£1 million", of the words "£3 million".

P. L. Hawkins,
Oscar Murton,
Two of the Lords Commissioners
of Her Majesty's Treasury.

8th August 1972.

(**a**) 1946 c. 58.   (**b**) 1889 c. 63.
(**c**) S.I. 1958/1208 (1958 I, p. 203).   (**d**) S.I. 1970/708 (1970 II, p. 2256).

EXPLANATORY NOTE

(This Note is not part of the Order.)

This Order further amends the Control of Borrowing Order 1958.

Article 8A of the Control of Borrowing Order 1958, as amended, confers a general exemption from the controls contained in Part I of that Order. The exemption does not apply to the issue of sterling securities of £1 million or more, unless the timing of the issue has been approved by the Bank of England. The Order raises the limit of £1 million to £3 million.

STATUTORY INSTRUMENTS

1972 No. 1219 (S.85)

ANIMALS

DISEASES OF ANIMALS

The Brucellosis (Area Eradication) (Scotland) Amendment (No. 2) Order 1972

Made - - -		*1st August* 1972
Coming into Operation		*24th August* 1972

In exercise of the powers conferred upon me by sections 1, 5 and 85(1) of the Diseases of Animals Act 1950(a) as read with the Transfer of Functions (Animal Health) Order 1955(b) and the Diseases of Animals (Extension of Definitions) Order 1971(c), and as respects the said section 5 as extended by section 106(3) of the Agriculture Act 1970(d), and of all other powers enabling me in that behalf, I hereby make the following order:—

Citation and commencement

1. This order, which may be cited as the Brucellosis (Area Eradication) (Scotland) Amendment (No. 2) Order 1972, shall come into operation on 24th August 1972.

Interpretation

2.—(1) In this order, "the principal order" means the Brucellosis (Area Eradication) (Scotland) Order 1971(e).

(2) Unless the context otherwise requires, expressions used in this order have the same meaning as in the principal order.

(3) The Interpretation Act 1889(f) applies for the interpretation of this order as it applies for the interpretation of an Act of Parliament.

Amendment of the principal order

3.—(1) After sub-paragraph (*b*) of paragraph (2) of Article 4 of the principal order (movement of cattle into or through Eradication Areas or Attested Areas) there shall be inserted:—

"*or*

(*c*) the movement of cattle (otherwise than on foot) which have not been certified by a veterinary inspector or other officer of the Ministry or of the Secretary of State as having reacted to a diagnostic test for brucellosis into an Eradication Area from a place outside that Area direct to any premises used in connection with the holding of a market, being premises in respect of which the licence issued under Article 15 of this order, and for the time being in force, permits the use thereof for the purpose of selling cattle intended for immediate slaughter, or

---

(a) 1950 c. 36.
(b) S.I. 1955/958 (1955 I, p. 1184).
(c) S.I. 1971/531 (1971 I, p. 1530).
(d) 1970 c. 40.
(e) S.I. 1971/1752 (1971 III, p. 4769).
(f) 1889 c. 63.

(*d*) the movement of cattle under six months of age (otherwise than on foot) into an Eradication Area from a place outside that Area direct to any premises used in connection with the holding of a market in respect of which a licence has been issued under Article 15 of this Order:".

(2) In sub-paragraph (*a*) of the proviso to paragraph (1) of Article 5 of the principal order (movement of cattle within an Eradication Area or Attested Area) there shall be substituted for the words "sub-paragraph (*b*)" the words "sub-paragraphs (*b*) to (*d*)".

Gordon Campbell,
One of Her Majesty's
Principal Secretaries of State.

St Andrew's House,
Edinburgh.

1st August 1972.

EXPLANATORY NOTE

(This Note is not part of the Order.)

The Brucellosis (Area Eradication) (Scotland) Order 1971 sets out the various controls to be applied to cattle in areas designated by the Secretary of State as Eradication or Attested Areas for purposes connected with the eradication of brucellosis. Article 4 of the order imposes a general prohibition on the movement of cattle into or through an Eradication or Attested area and Article 5 of the order imposes a general prohibition on the movement of cattle within such areas otherwise, in both cases, than in accordance with the terms of a licence issued by a veterinary inspector or other officer of the Ministry or an officer of the Secretary of State subject to certain exceptions which are specified in paragraph (2) of Article 4 and paragraph (1) of Article 5. The present order amends Articles 4(2) and 5(1) of the 1971 order by adding two further categories of cattle to those which are exempted from the licensing provisions of those Articles.

The first group consists of cattle which have not reacted to a diagnostic test for brucellosis, and which are being taken direct to a market, or a section of a market, in an Eradication Area which has been licensed by a veterinary inspector or other officer of the Ministry or of the Secretary of State for the sale of cattle intended for slaughter. The second group comprises cattle under the age of six months which are being taken direct to a market in an Eradication Area.

STATUTORY INSTRUMENTS

1972 No. 1220 (S.86)

EDUCATION, SCOTLAND

Milk and Meals (Education) (Scotland) Amendment Regulations 1972

Made - - - -	*7th August* 1972
Laid before Parliament	*15th August* 1972
Coming into Operation	*22nd August* 1972

In exercise of the powers conferred on me by sections 53(3) and 144(5) of the Education (Scotland) Act 1962**(a)**, and of all other powers enabling me in that behalf, I hereby make the following regulations:—

Citation, commencement and interpretation

1.—(1) These regulations may be cited as the Milk and Meals (Education) (Scotland) Amendment Regulations 1972 and these regulations and the Milk and Meals (Education) (Scotland) Regulations 1971**(b)** may be cited together as the Milk and Meals (Education) (Scotland) Regulations 1971 and 1972.

(2) These regulations shall come into operation on 22nd August 1972.

(3) The Interpretation Act 1889**(c)** shall apply for the interpretation of these regulations as it applies for the interpretation of an Act of Parliament.

Amendment of principal regulations

2. The Schedule to the Milk and Meals (Education) (Scotland) Regulations 1971 (determination of financial hardship) shall have effect subject to—

    (*a*) the substitution for the table and first note of the following table and note—

(**a**) 1962 c. 47.   (**b**) S.I. 1971/1537 (1971 III, p. 4340).
(**c**) 1889 c. 63.

"Part A   Part B

Size of family	Net weekly income in £p					
	1	2	3	4	5	6
1	14·80					
2	18·20	17·60				
3	21·60	21·00	20·40			
4	25·00	24·40	23·80	23·20		
5	28·40	27·80	27·20	26·60	26·00	
6	31·80	31·20	30·60	30·00	29·40	28·80

For larger families, in respect of each child—

    (a) £3·40 is to be added at each incremental point in every additional line;

    (b) £0·60 is to be subtracted at each incremental point in every additional column.";

    and

(b) the addition in the second note after the word "rates" at the end of the definition of "net weekly income" of the following words—

"and disregarding any attendance allowance under section 4 of the National Insurance (Old persons' and widows' pensions and attendance allowance) Act 1970".

Gordon Campbell,
One of Her Majesty's Principal
Secretaries of State.

St. Andrew's House,
Edinburgh.
7th August 1972.

EXPLANATORY NOTE

(This Note is not part of the Regulations.)

These Regulations amend the provisions of the Milk and Meals (Education) (Scotland) Regulations 1971 for the calculation of a parent's income for the purpose of determining his entitlement to remission of the charge for school midday meals.

STATUTORY INSTRUMENTS

1972 No. 1221 (S. 87)

LANDLORD AND TENANT

RENT CONTROL, ETC. (SCOTLAND)

The Rent Regulation (Forms etc.) (Scotland) Regulations 1972

Made - - - -	*8th August* 1972
Laid before Parliament	*23rd August* 1972
Coming into Operation	*28th August* 1972

In exercise of the powers conferred upon me by sections 35, 46(1)(*a*) and (*c*) and 81(1)(*a*) and (*c*) of the Rent (Scotland) Act 1971(**a**) and sections 35 and 46(1)(*a*) and (*c*) of that Act as read with sections 50 and 61 respectively of the Housing (Financial Provisions) (Scotland) Act 1972(**b**), and of all other powers enabling me in that behalf, I hereby make the following regulations:—

1. These regulations may be cited as the Rent Regulation (Forms etc) (Scotland) Regulations 1972 and shall come into operation on 28th August 1972.

2.—(1) In these regulations, unless the context otherwise requires—

"the Act of 1971" means the Rent (Scotland) Act 1971;

"the Act of 1972" means the Housing (Financial Provisions) (Scotland) Act 1972;

"rent agreement" means a rent agreement with a tenant having security of tenure within the meaning of section 42(1) of the Act of 1972 to which section 43 of that Act applies; and

"the register" means the register kept by the Rent Officer for the purposes of Part IV of the Act of 1971 and includes the separate part of the register under that Part of that Act kept for the purposes of section 61 of the Act of 1972.

(2) The Interpretation Act 1889(**c**) shall apply for the interpretation of these regulations as it applies for the interpretation of an Act of Parliament.

3.—(1) The Rent Regulation (Forms etc.) (Scotland) Regulations 1969(**d**) and the Rent Regulation (Forms etc.) (Scotland) (Amendment) Regulations 1969(**e**) are hereby revoked, except insofar as the forms therein prescribed are required to be used in connection with proceedings after the date on which these regulations come into force and consequent upon action taken before that date.

(2) Section 38 of the Interpretation Act 1889 shall apply as if these regulations were an Act of Parliament and as if the regulations hereby revoked by these regulations were Acts of Parliament repealed by an Act of Parliament.

(**a**) 1971 c. 28.   (**b**) 1972 c. 46.   (**c**) 1889 c. 63.
(**d**) S.I. 1969/1419 (1969 III, p. 4478).   (**e**) S.I. 1969/1846 (1969 III, p. 5774).

4. The particulars set out in Schedule 1 to these regulations shall be the particulars with regard to the tenancy which the register is required to contain in pursuance of section 39(2)(*a*) of the Act of 1971 or that section as applied by section 61(2) of the Act of 1972.

5. The particulars set out in Schedule 2 to these regulations shall be the particulars which a rent agreement is required to contain in pursuance of section 43(5)(*a*) of the Act of 1972.

6. The forms set out in Schedule 3 to these regulations, or forms as near thereto as circumstances admit, shall be the forms to be used for the purposes of the Act of 1971 and the Act of 1972 in the cases to which those forms are applicable.

7. For the purposes of section 39(3) of the Act of 1971 and of section 43(13) of the Act of 1972, the fee to be paid for a certified copy of an entry in the register or for a certified copy of a rent agreement shall be 12p.

Gordon Campbell,
One of Her Majesty's Principal
Secretaries of State.

St. Andrew's House,
Edinburgh.
8th August 1972.

Section 39
(2)(a) of the
Act of 1971.

SCHEDULE 1

PARTICULARS WITH REGARD TO THE TENANCY WHICH THE REGISTER IS
REQUIRED TO CONTAIN

1. The name and address of the landlord and the tenant and of their respective agents (if any).

2. The nature of the tenancy, that is
   (*a*) whether it is a tenancy to which sections 60 to 66 of the Act of 1972 apply, or
   (*b*) whether it is, or is due to become converted from being a controlled tenancy into, a regulated tenancy and, whether it is a protected or a statutory tenancy.

3. The date of commencement and the duration of the contractual tenancy or, if the tenancy is a statutory tenancy, the date upon which it became a statutory tenancy.

4. The rental period under the tenancy.

5. An inventory of any furniture provided by the landlord.

6. A list of any services provided by the landlord.

7. The respective liability of the landlord and the tenant for
   (*a*) the maintenance and repair of the dwellinghouse, and
   (*b*) the rates in respect of the dwellinghouse.

8. A description of any part of the premises comprised in the dwellinghouse which is used as a shop or office, or for business, trade or professional purposes.

9. Any other terms of the tenancy taken into consideration in determining a fair rent for the dwellinghouse.

Section 43
(5)(a) of the
Act of 1972.

SCHEDULE 2

PARTICULARS WHICH A RENT AGREEMENT IS REQUIRED TO CONTAIN.

1. Declare that the tenant's attention has been drawn specifically to Notes 1 to 10 before he has entered into the rent agreement.

2. Name and address of landlord and tenant and of their respective agents (if any).

3. Address and description of the dwellinghouse (Note 11).

4. Current gross annual value of the dwellinghouse.

5. If the tenancy has become a regulated tenancy by virtue of Part VI of the Rent (Scotland) Act 1971 (i.e. following upon the issue of a qualification certificate), state the date upon which the qualification certificate was issued.

6. If the tenancy is or is due to become a regulated tenancy under section 34 of the Housing (Financial Provisions) (Scotland) Act 1972, state the rateable value of the dwellinghouse on 27 August 1972 (Note 12).

7. State the rent which is at present payable and whether it is exclusive/

inclusive of rates borne by the landlord and, if inclusive, state the amount of rates included in the rent.

8. The date of commencement and duration of the tenancy.

9. The rental period.

10. State the respective liability of the landlord and the tenant for the maintenance and repair of the dwellinghouse.

11. State the proposed rent which is agreed and the instalments (if any) in which that rent is payable.

12. If the proposed rent is inclusive of rates borne by the landlord, state the amount of rates included in the rent.

13. State whether any services or furniture are provided by the landlord and the amount of the proposed rent which is considered to be fairly attributable to each of them.

14. If any part of the dwellinghouse is used as a shop or office, or for business, trade or professional purposes, state the amount of the proposed rent which is considered to be fairly attributable to that part.

15. State whether any change has occurred during the present tenancy in the condition of the dwellinghouse (Note 2) which is considered to be due to

(a) any disrepair or other defect attributable to a failure by the tenant (including a former holder of the present tenancy) to comply with the terms of the tenancy, or

(b) any improvement, including the replacement of any fixture or fitting, carried out by the tenant, (including a former holder of the present tenancy) other than under the terms of the tenancy.

16. State whether any improvement or standard grant has been obtained in respect of the dwellinghouse.

NOTES

(To be incorporated with the Particulars in any rent Agreement and any Copy Thereof)

1. After the controlled tenancy has become converted into a regulated tenancy, the tenant is protected to ensure that the controlled rent may not be increased above the fair rent for the dwellinghouse.

2. In determining what is a fair rent for the dwellinghouse, section 42 of the Rent (Scotland) Act 1971 (referred to hereafter as "the Act of 1971") provides that regard should be had to all the circumstances (except personal circumstances) and in particular to the age, character and locality of the dwellinghouse and to its state of repair. There requires to be disregarded any scarcity element and any changes in the condition of the dwellinghouse which are mentioned in paragraph 15 of the particulars.

3. There are in general two main ways in which the controlled rent may be increased after the tenancy has become a regulated tenancy (other than for rates, services and improvements). These are either

(a) the landlord or the tenant or both may apply to the rent officer for the registration of a fair rent for the dwellinghouse, in which case any increase in rent up to the registered rent would be payable in three equal annual instalments, with a minimum increase each year of 50p per week; or

(b) the landlord and the tenant may enter into a rent agreement which may be either an agreement increasing the rent payable under the existing contractual tenancy or the grant of another regulated tenancy at a higher rent than under the previous tenancy.

4. If after the landlord and tenant enter into a rent agreement, then, before it can take effect, it is, as is explained in the following paragraphs, subject to the tacit approval of the rent officer to ensure that the rent agreed between the parties does not take effect if it exceeds what, in his opinon, is a fair rent for the dwellinghouse.

5. Section 43(6) of the Housing (Financial Provisions) (Scotland) Act 1972 (referred to hereafter as "the Act of 1972") provides that a rent agreement cannot take effect earlier than 28 days after it has been lodged by the landlord with the rent officer. At the same time as it is lodged with the rent officer, the landlord is required to serve a copy of the agreement on his tenant.

6. The rent agreement may only take effect after the expiry of that 28 day period if the rent officer does not, within that period, notify both the landlord and the tenant in writing that he proposes to treat it as a joint application for the registration of a fair rent for the dwellinghouse because he is satisfied that the rent payable under the agreement exceeds a fair rent for the dwellinghouse.

7. If the rent agreement takes effect, the rent officer is required to make it available for public inspection without charge and a certified copy of it may be obtained upon payment of the prescribed fee.

8. If the landlord fails to comply with any of the requirements of sections 42, 43 or 44 of the Act of 1972 in connection with the rent agreement, the increase in rent may be recovered by the tenant.

9. If the landlord and tenant agree upon any further increases in rent, then, unless either the increase is solely on account of an increase in rates borne by the landlord or the new rent agreement takes effect more than three years after the first such agreement took effect, the rent agreement must also contain these particulars and be subject to the tacit approval of the rent officer as explained above.

10. If, after a rent agreement has become effective, a rent is registered for the dwellinghouse and that registration is the first after the conversion of the tenancy into a regulated tenancy, any increase in rent from the rent now payable (i.e. not taking into account the rent agreed under the rent agreement) up to the amount of the registered rent may be payable in annual instalments if the rent agreement took effect less than two years before the date of registration.

11. The description of the dwellinghouse should include:—

(a) the location of the flat, if the dwellinghouse is situated in tenement property;

(b) the number of rooms comprised in the dwellinghouse and the use which is made of them;

(c) any accommodation of which the tenant has shared use and state whether the sharing is with the landlord or with another tenant; and

(d) a description of any part of the premises comprised in the dwellinghouse which is used as a shop or office, or for business, trade or professional purposes.

12. The date of conversion of the controlled tenancy into a regulated tenancy depends upon the rateable value of the dwellinghouse on 27 August 1972, as follows namely:—

Rateable value	*Date of conversion*
£50 or more	1st January 1973
£25 or less than £50	1st January 1974
Less than £25	1st January 1975

(The Secretary of State has power, by order, to advance or retard the relevant date of conversion).

SCHEDULE 3

LIST OF FORMS

Form No.	*Purpose*	*Statutory references*
1	Notice of increase of unregistered rent under a regulated tenancy on account of an increase in rates borne by the landlord.	ss. 22(2) & 25 of the Act of 1971.
2	Notice of increase of unregistered rent under a regulated tenancy on account of improvements completed after the commencement of the regulated tenancy.	ss. 24(2) & 25 of the Act of 1971.
3	Notice of increase of unregistered rent under a regulated tenancy on account of improvements completed before the tenancy became converted into a regulated tenancy.	s. 36(2) of the Act of 1972 and s. 25 of the Act of 1971.
4	Notice of increase of rent under a regulated tenancy up to the amount of the registered rent, where there are no restrictions on rent increases.	s. 21(2) & 25 of the Act of 1971.
5	Notice of increase of rent under a regulated tenancy where a rent has been registered after the completion of grant-aided improvements and there are restrictions on rent increases.	ss. 21(2), 25 and 79 of and Schedule 13 to the Act of 1971, as amended by s.48 of and Schedule 7 to the Act of 1972.
6	Notice of increase of rent under a regulated tenancy where a rent has been registered after the conversion of the tenancy into a regulated tenancy following upon the issue of a qualification certificate and there are restrictions on rent increases with respect to any year beginning before 1st January 1973.	ss. 21(2), 25 and 79 of and Schedule 13 to the Act of 1971.
7	Notice of increase of rent under a regulated tenancy where a rent has been registered after the conversion of the tenancy into a regulated tenancy following upon the issue of a qualification certificate and there are restrictions on rent increases with respect to any year beginning on or after 1st January 1973.	ss. 21(2), 25 and 79 of and Schedule 13 to the Act of 1971, as amended by s.48 of and Schedule 7 to the Act of 1972.

Form No.	Purpose	Statutory references
8	Notice of increase of rent under a regulated tenancy where a rent has been registered after the conversion of the tenancy into a regulated tenancy under section 34 of the Housing (Financial Provisions) (Scotland) Act 1972 and there are restrictions on rent increases.	ss. 21(2) and 25 of the Act of 1971 and s.36 of and Schedule 6 to the Act of 1972.
9	Application for the registration of a rent, unsupported by a certificate of fair rent, where the dwelling-house is or is to be let under a regulated tenancy.	s. 40 of the Act of 1971.
10	Application for the registration of a rent, unsupported by a certificate of fair rent, where the dwelling-house is let under a tenancy to which sections 60 to 66 of the Housing (Financial Provisions) (Scotland) Act 1972 apply.	s. 40 of the Act of 1971 and s.61 of the Act of 1972.
11	Application for a certificate of fair rent where the dwelling-house is or is to be let under a regulated tenancy.	ss. 41(1) and 73(2) of the Act of 1971.
12	Application for a certificate of fair rent where the dwellinghouse is or is to be let under a tenancy to which sections 60 to 66 of the Housing (Financial Provisions) (Scotland) Act 1972 apply.	s. 41(1) of the Act of 1971 and s. 61 of the Act of 1972.
13	Application for the registration of a rent, supported by a certificate of fair rent, where the dwelling-house is or is to be let under a regulated tenancy.	ss. 41(4) and 74 of the Act of 1971.
14	Application for the registration of a rent, supported by a certificate of fair rent, where the dwelling-house is or is to be let under a tenancy to which sections 60 to 66 of the Housing (Financial Provisions) (Scotland) Act 1972 apply.	s. 41(4) of the Act of 1971 and s.61 of the Act of 1972.
15	Application for the cancellation of a registration.	s.44A of the Act of 1971.
16	Notice requiring further information to be given to a rent assessment committee.	Paragraph 7 of Schedule 6 to the Act of 1971 and s.61 of the Act of 1972.
17	Notice of grant of a regulated tenancy.	Paragraph 13 of Schedule 6 to the Act of 1971.
18	Notice of grant of a tenancy to which sections 60 to 66 of the Housing (Financial Provisions) (Scotland) Act 1972 apply.	Paragraph 13 of Schedule 6 to the Act of 1971 and s.61 of the Act of 1971.

Form No.	Purpose	Statutory references
19	Application for a qualification certificate where dwelling-house is considered to satisfy the qualifying conditions.	s. 71(1) of the Act of 1971.
20	Application for a qualification certificate where dwelling-house does not satisfy the qualifying conditions.	s.71(2) of the Act of 1971.
21	Notice by a local authority to a tenant under section 72(1) of the Rent (Scotland) Act 1971.	s.72(1) of the Act of 1971.
22	Qualification certificate where application was made when dwelling-house is considered to satisfy the qualifying conditions.	s.72(2) of the Act of 1971.
23	Notice of refusal of a qualification certificate, where application was made when dwelling-house is considered to satisfy the qualifying conditions.	s.72(2) of the Act of 1971.
24	Certificate of provisional approval.	s.73(1) of the Act of 1971.
25	Notice of refusal of a certificate of provisional approval.	s.73(1) of the Act of 1971.
26	Qualification certificate where application was made when dwelling-house did not satisfy the qualifying conditions.	s.73(3) of the Act of 1971.
27	Notice of refusal of a qualification certificate where application was made when dwelling-house did not satisfy the qualifying conditions.	s. 73(3) of the Act of 1971.

FORM NO. 1

RENT (SCOTLAND) ACTS 1971 AND 1972

Notice of increase of unregistered rent under a regulated tenancy on account of an increase in rates borne by the landlord (Note 1)

Date.....................................

To.....................................

1. The amount of the rent which is, at present, lawfully recoverable from you as tenant of the dwellinghouse situated at..
is £.............................per.................................

2. The rates in respect of the dwellinghouse are borne by the landlord and the amount of rates, as ascertained in accordance with Schedule 4 to the Rent (Scotland) Act 1971 (Note 2), which is included in the above rent, is £...............
per...............(Note 3).

3. The rates for the dwellinghouse have been increased from £...............per annum to £...............per annum with effect as from............................ and therefore the amount of the rates borne by the landlord, as ascertained in accordance with the said Schedule 4 (Note 2), is £...............for a rental period of.............................

4. The landlord is entitled, in terms of section 22(1) of the Rent (Scotland) Act 1971, to increase the recoverable rent for any statutory period of the tenancy to take account of any increase in rates borne by the landlord for that period.

5. Accordingly I hereby give you notice that the rent lawfully recoverable from you as tenant of the dwellinghouse is hereby increased by £...............per
...............(Note 4) to £...............per..............., with effect as from.........
.....................(Note 5).

Delete words in square brackets if they do not apply

[6. The new rent of £...............per...............will be payable for the dwellinghouse as from..............., the beginning of the first rental period after the service of this notice.

In addition, the sum of £..............,being the arrears of the above increase from the date when it took effect, will be due from you on the day after the service of this notice.]

....
(Signature of Landlord/Landlord's Agents)

....
(Address of Landlord/Landlord's Agents)

NOTES

(To be incorporated in the notice)

1. This notice of increase is required where:

    (a) the tenancy of the dwellinghouse is a regulated tenancy within the meaning of the Rent (Scotland) Act 1971 (referred to hereafter as "the Act of 1971");

(*b*) the tenancy of the dwellinghouse is a statutory tenancy within the meaning of the Act of 1971 or will become one as a result of the operation of this notice (Note 7);

(*c*) no rent has been registered for the dwellinghouse, and

(*d*) the rent payable for the dwellinghouse is inclusive of rates borne by the landlord.

In these circumstances section 22(1) of the Act of 1971 provides that the rent recoverable for any statutory period of the tenancy may, upon service of this notice, be increased to take account of any increase in rates borne by the landlord for that period.

2. Schedule 4 of the Act of 1971 provides that the amount of rates for any rental period should be ascertained by dividing the total rates payable for the whole rating period, in which the rent for that rental period is payable, by the number which is obtained by dividing the length of that rating period by the length of the rental period.

Until the local authority make their first demand for, or for an instalment of, the rates for a rating period, the amount of the rates for any rental period is to be calculated on the basis that the rates for that rating period continue to be the same as for the previous rating period.

When the local authority have made their first such demand or when they have made any subsequent demand during the rating period, the amount of the rates for any rental period must, if necessary, be recalculated, but any such recalculation cannot effect the ascertainment of rates for any rental period beginning more than six months before the date of service of the demand which gives rise to the recalculation.

3. If this is the first notice of increase of rent on account of rates which has been served for a stautory period of the regulated tenancy, insert the amount of the rates borne by the landlord for the last contractual period, that is, the last rental period beginning before the protected (i.e. contractual) tenancy came to an end and the tenancy became a statutory tenancy.

If this is the first such notice of increase which has been served for a statutory period of a tenancy which has been converted from being a controlled into a regulated tenancy, insert the amount of the rates borne by the landlord for the last rental period beginning before the conversion.

If this is not the first such notice of increase, insert the amount of the rates borne by the landlord for the rental period(s) to which the last previous notice of increase related.

4. Insert the amount of the difference between the amount of the rates included in the rent at present lawfully recoverable from the tenant and the amount of the rates borne by the landlord for the rental period(s) to which this notice of increase relates. This should be the difference between the amounts specified in paragraphs 2 and 3 of the notice.

Section 34 of the Act of 1971 provides that where, in ascertaining the amount of any difference with respect to rates, the rental periods to be compared are not of equal length, a period of one month is to be treated as equivalent to one-twelfth of a year and a period of a week as equivalent to one-fifty-second of a year.

5. The date to be inserted cannot be earlier than six months before the service of this notice of increase.

If this notice is served during a contractual period of the tenancy (that is, a rental period beginning before the protected tenancy comes to an end) the date to be inserted must be later than the date on which the tenancy could be brought to an end by a notice to quit served by the landlord at the same time as this notice (Note 7).

6. Paragraph 6 of the notice will only be required if the date from which the increase is to take effect is earlier than the date of service of this notice.

In that case, section 22(3) of the Act of 1971 provides that any rent unpaid shall become due on the day after the service of the notice.

7. If this notice is served during a contractual period of the regulated tenancy and the landlord, by serving a notice to quit at the same time as this notice, could bring the tenancy to an end before the date specified in this notice for the increased rent to take effect, section 25(3) of the Act of 1971 provides that this notice will operate to convert the tenancy into a statutory tenancy as from that date.

Form No. 2

Rent (Scotland) Acts 1971 and 1972

Notice of increase of unregistered rent under a regulated tenancy on account of improvements completed after the commencement of the regulated tenancy (Note 1)

Date..................................

To...

1. The amount of the rent which is, at present, lawfully recoverable from you as tenant of the dwellinghouse situated at...is £..................per...................

2. The following improvement has been effected in the dwellinghouse........... (Note 2) and the amount expended on the improvement by the landlord is £..................(Note 3).

3. The landlord is entitled, in terms of section 24 of the Rent (Scotland) Act 1971, to increase the recoverable rent for any statutory period by an annual amount of £.............................being $12\frac{1}{2}\%$ of the amount expended on the improvement.

4. Accordingly, I hereby give you notice that the rent lawfully recoverable from you as tenant of the dwellinghouse will be increased by £..................per ....to £..................per..................with effect from.................. ....(Note 4).

5. If you consider that the improvement was unnecessary or that a greater amount was expended on it than was reasonable, you may, in certain circumstances, apply to the sheriff for an order cancelling or reducing the increase (Note 5).

....
(Signature of Landlord/Landlord's Agents)

....
(Address of Landlord/Landlord's Agents)

Notes

(To be incorporated in the notice)

1. This notice of increase is required where:
   (*a*) the tenancy of the dwellinghouse is a regulated tenancy within the meaning of the Rent (Scotland) Act 1971 (referred to hereafter as "the Act of 1971");
   (*b*) the tenancy of the dwellinghouse is a statutory tenancy within the meaning of the Act of 1971 or will become one as a result of the operation of this notice (Note 6);
   (*c*) no rent has been registered for the dwellinghouse and,
   (*d*) an improvement has been effected in the dwellinghouse and the improvement was completed on or after 8th December 1965 and after the time as from which the rent under the regulated tenancy was agreed.

In these circumstances, section 24(1) of the Act of 1971 provides that the rent recoverable for any statutory period of the tenancy may, upon service of this notice, be increased by 12½% per annum of the amount expended on the improvement by the landlord or superior landlord or any person from whom the landlord or superior landlord derives title.

No increase in rent may be obtained under section 24(1) on account of

    (*a*) any improvement with respect to which a grant under Part II of the Housing (Financial Provisions) (Scotland) Act 1968 (improvement or standard grant) is payable on or after 25th August 1969, or

    (*b*) any improvement completed before the tenancy was converted from being a controlled tenancy into a regulated tenancy.

2. Insert a description of the improvement effected in the dwellinghouse.

Improvement is defined under section 36(1) of the Act of 1971 as including structural alteration, extension or addition and the provision of additional fixtures or fittings, but not anything done by way of decoration or repair.

Under section 30 of the Act of 1971, where the dwellinghouse has access to a street on which works have been carried out under any of the enactments referred to in section 1 of the Local Government (Street Works) (Scotland) Act 1956 or the corresponding provisions of any local Act, any expenditure or liability incurred on or after 8th December 1965 by the landlord in connection with the carrying out of those works is to be treated as expenditure incurred by the landlord on an improvement effected in the dwellinghouse. Where this section applies, a description of the improvement effected in the dwellinghouse should include a description of the street works in question.

3. Where, in respect of an improvement

    (*a*) a grant has been made under section 15 of the Airports Authority Act 1965 (grants towards the cost of soundproofing)

    (*b*) a grant has been made under section 27 or 40 of the Housing (Financial Provisions) (Scotland) Act 1968 (improvement or standard grants) in pursuance of an application made before 25th August 1969 or

    (*c*) a repayment has been made under section 12 of the Clean Air Act 1956 (adaptation of fireplaces in private dwellings),

the amount to be inserted as the amount expended on the improvement must be that amount as diminished by the amount of the grant or repayment.

Where an improvement consists of the street works referred to in Note 2 above and benefit accrues from the carrying out of the works not only to the dwellinghouse but also to other premises of the landlord, the amount to be treated as expenditure on an improvement effected in the dwellinghouse shall be so much only of the expenditure or liability incurred by the landlord as may be determined by agreement in writing between the landlord and the tenant or by the sheriff. The amount of any expenditure must also be diminished by the amount of any contribution made in respect of that expenditure under any enactment.

4. This notice cannot be retrospective and, therefore, the date to be inserted here should be a date after the date of the service of this notice.

If this notice is served during a contractual period of the tenancy (i.e. a rental period beginning before the protected tenancy comes to an end) the date to be inserted must be later than the date on which the tenancy could be brought to an end by a notice to quit served by the landlord at the same time as this notice (Note 6).

5. The tenant upon whom this notice is served may, not later than one month after the service of this notice, or such longer time as the sheriff may allow, apply to the sheriff for an order cancelling or reducing the increase on the ground that the improvement was unnecessary or that a greater amount was expended on it than was reasonable.

No such application may be made in respect of an improvement where

 (a) a grant has been made under section 15 of the Airports Authority Act 1965 (grants towards the cost of soundproofing) or

 (b) a grant has been made under section 27 or 40 of the Housing (Financial Provisions) (Scotland) Act 1968 (improvement or standard grants) in pursuance of an application made before 25th August 1969 or

 (c) the improvement consists of the street works referred to in Note 2 above or

 (d) the tenant has, in writing, consented to the improvement and acknowledged (in whatever terms) that the rent can be increased on account of the improvement.

6. If this notice is served during a contractual period of the regulated tenancy and the landlord, by serving a notice to quit at the same time as this notice, could bring the tenancy to an end before the date specified in this notice for the increased rent to take effect, section 25(3) of the Act of 1971 provides that this notice will operate to convert the tenancy into a statutory tenancy as from that date.

FORM NO. 3

RENT (SCOTLAND) ACTS 1971 AND 1972

Notice of increase of unregistered rent under a regulated tenancy on account of improvements completed before the tenancy became converted into a regulated tenancy (Note 1)

Date.....................................

To...

1. The amount of the rent which is, at present, lawfully recoverable from you as tenant of the dwellinghouse situated at.. is £.................per...................

2. The following improvement of the dwellinghouse, namely.................... (Note 2), was completed on................................(Note 3) before the date when the controlled tenancy of the dwellinghouse was converted into a regulated tenancy on..................................(Note 3), and the landlord has incurred £.....................(Note 4) as expenditure upon that improvement.

3. The landlord is entitled, by virtue of section 36(2) of the Housing (Financial Provisions) (Scotland) Act 1972, to increase the recoverable rent for any rental period of the regulated tenancy by the amount to which he could have increased (but did not increase) the recoverable rent for a rental period of the controlled tenancy, under paragraph 1(3)(*a*) or that paragraph as applied by paragraph 2(3) of Schedule 8 to the Rent (Scotland) Act 1971, namely by an annual amount of £...............being $12\frac{1}{2}\%$ per cent of the amount of his expenditure incurred upon the improvement.

4. Accordingly I hereby give you notice that the rent lawfully recoverable from you as tenant of the dwellinghouse will be increased by £................. per.................to £.................per.................with effect from.............. ....(Note 5).

....
(Signature of Landlord/Landlord's Agents)

....
(Address of Landlord/Landlord's Agents)

NOTES

(*To be incorporated in the notice*)

1. This notice of increase is required where:
   (*a*) the tenancy of the dwellinghouse has become a regulated tenancy within the meaning of the Rent (Scotland) Act 1971 (referred to hereafter as "the Act of 1971") by conversion from being a controlled tenancy by virtue of
      (i) section 34 of the Housing (Financial Provisions) (Scotland) Act 1972 (referred to hereafter as "the Act of 1972") or
      (ii) Part VI of the Act of 1971 (following upon the issue of a qualification certificate) or
      (iii) paragraph 5 of Schedule 2 to the Act of 1971 (conversion on death of first successor);

(*b*) the rent recoverable for the last rental period of the controlled tenancy beginning before the conversion was less than it would have been if the landlord had increased the rent on account of an improvement of the dwellinghouse completed before the conversion; and

(*c*) no rent has been registered for the dwellinghouse.

In these circumstances, section 36(2) of the Act of 1972 provides that the rent recoverable for any rental period of the regulated tenancy may be increased, by the service of this notice, above the rent recoverable for the last rental period beginning before the conversion by the amount to which the landlord could have increased that rent on account of the improvement.

2. Insert a description of the improvement of the dwellinghouse.

Improvement includes structural alteration of the dwellinghouse and the provision of additional or improved fixtures and fittings but does not include anything done by way of decoration or repair.

Where the dwellinghouse has access to a street on which works have been carried out under any of the enactments referred to in section 1 of the Local Government (Street Works) (Scotland) Act 1956 or the corresponding provisions of any local Act, paragraph 5 of Schedule 8 to the Act of 1971 provides that the amount of any expenditure or liability incurred by the landlord after 5th July 1957 in connection with the carrying out of those works shall be treated as expenditure incurred by the landlord on an improvement of the dwellinghouse. Where this provision applies therefore, a description of the improvement of the dwellinghouse should include a description of the street works in question.

3. Insert relevant date.

4. Insert amount expended by the landlord on the improvement.

The amount of any repayment under section 12(1) of the Clean Air Act 1956 (adaptation of fireplaces in private dwellings) should not be included as the amount expended by the landlord on the improvement.

Where an improvement consists of the street works referred to in Note 2 above, and benefit accrues from the carrying out of the works not only to the dwellinghouse but also to other premises of the landlord, the amount to be treated as the amount expended by the landlord on the improvement shall be so much only of the expenditure or liability incurred by the landlord as may be determined by agreement in writing between the landlord and the tenant or by the sheriff, to be properly apportionable to the dwellinghouse, having regard to the benefit accruing, from the carrying out of the works, to the dwellinghouse and to the other premises. The amount of any expenditure must also be diminished by the amount of any contribution made in respect of that expenditure under any enactment.

5. By virtue of the proviso to section 36(2) of the Act of 1972, the date from which the increase is to take effect may be any date after the service of this notice.

If this notice is served during a contractual period of the regulated tenancy (i.e. a rental period beginning before the protected tenancy comes to an end), and the landlord by serving a notice to quit at the same time as this notice, could bring the tenancy to an end before the date specified in the notice for the increase to take effect, section 25(3) of the Act of 1971 provides that this notice will operate to convert the tenancy into a statutory tenancy as from that date. In this case, the date to be inserted as the date upon which the increase is to take effect must be later than the date upon which the tenancy could be brought to an end by such a notice to quit.

FORM No. 4

RENT (SCOTLAND) ACTS 1971 AND 1972

Notice of increase of rent under a regulated tenancy, up to the amount of the registered rent where there are no restrictions on rent increases (Note 1)

Date...

To..

1. The amount of the rent which is at present lawfully recoverable from you as tenant of the dwellinghouse situated at..............................is £.............. per...................

2. A rent of £..................per...................was registered on..................... as the fair rent for the dwellinghouse (Note 4).

3. The landlord is entitled, in terms of section 21(2)(*b*) of the Rent (Scotland) Act 1971, to increase the rent recoverable for any statutory period of the tenancy up to the amount of the registered rent.

4. Accordingly I hereby give you notice that the rent lawfully recoverable from you as tenant of the dwellinghouse will be increased by £.............. per.................. to £..................per..................with effect as from......... ....(Note 5).

Delete words in square brackets if they do not apply

[5. It is noted in the register that the rates in respect of the dwellinghouse are borne by the landlord and, in terms of section 43(3) of the Rent (Scotland) Act 1971, the amount of rates for any rental period ascertained in accordance with Schedule 4 to that Act (Note 6), is recoverable from you in addition to the above rent for any statutory period of the tenancy, without service of any notice of increase. The amount of the rates which is at present lawfully recoverable from you, in addition to the above rent, is £..................per..................].

....
(Signature of Landlord/Landlord's Agents)

....
(Address of Landlord/Landlord's Agents)

NOTES

(*To be incorporated in the notice*)

1. This notice of increase is required where;
    (*a*) the tenancy of the dwellinghouse is a regulated tenancy within the meaning of the Rent (Scotland) Act 1971 (referred to hereafter as "the Act of 1971");
    (*b*) the tenancy of the dwellinghouse is a statutory tenancy within the meaning of the Act of 1971 or will become one as a result of the operation of this notice (Note 2);
    (*c*) a rent has been registered for the dwellinghouse which is higher than the rent at present recoverable; and
    (*d*) the increase in rent up to the amount of the registered rent is not subject to phasing under section 79 of and Schedule 13 to the Act of 1971 or

under section 37 of and Schedule 6 to the Housing (Financial Provisions) (Scotland) Act 1972 (referred to hereafter as "the Act of 1972") (Note 3).

In these circumstances, section 21(2)(*b*) of the Act of 1971 provides that the rent may be increased up to the amount of the registered rent by the service of this notice.

2. If the tenancy is a protected tenancy, (that is, if the regulated tenancy is a contractual tenancy) the registration of a fair rent for the dwellinghouse, which is higher than the rent at present recoverable, does not allow the landlord to increase the rent up to the amount registered, unless there is a provision to that effect in the tenancy contract.

If the protected tenancy has come to an end and the tenant is retaining possession of the dwellinghouse as a statutory tenant, the landlord may increase the rent recoverable for a rental period of the statutory tenancy up to the amount of the registered rent by the service of this notice.

Even although the notice of increase relates to statutory periods, section 25(3) of the Act of 1971 provides that it may be served during a contractual period (i.e. a rental period beginning before the protected tenancy comes to an end) and, if the landlord, by serving a notice to quit at the same time as this notice, could bring the tenancy to an end before the date specified in this notice for the increase to take effect, this notice will operate to convert the tenancy into a statutory tenancy as from that date.

3. Section 79 of and Schedule 13 to the Act of 1971 and section 37 of and Schedule 6 to the Act of 1972 provide in general for the phasing of any increase in rent, before the full amount of the registered rent may be obtained, where a rent is first registered for the dwellinghouse

(*a*) under a tenancy which has been converted into a regulated tenancy under Part VI of the Act of 1971 (i.e. following upon the issue of a qualification certificate) or under section 34 of the Act of 1972 or

(*b*) under a regulated tenancy after the completion, during the existence of the tenancy, of works towards the cost of which a grant was payable under Part II of the Housing (Financial Provisions) (Scotland) Act 1968 (improvement or standard grants),

and in certain circumstances, where a rent is subsequently registered for the dwellinghouse.

4. The rent register may be inspected at the office of the rent officer.

5. The date to be inserted cannot be earlier than the date upon which the rent was registered for the dwellinghouse nor earlier than four weeks before the date of service of this notice.

If this notice is served during a contractual period of the tenancy, the date to be inserted must be later than the date on which the tenancy could be brought to an end by a notice to quit served by the landlord at the same time as this notice (Note 2).

6. Schedule 4 of the Act of 1971 provides that the amount of rates for any rental period should be ascertained by dividing the total rates payable for the whole rating period, in which the rent for that rental period is payable, by the number which is obtained by dividing the length of that rating period by the length of the rental period.

Until the local authority make their first demand for, or for an instalment of, the rates for a rating period, the amount of the rates for any rental period is to be calculated on the basis that the rates for that rating period continue to be the same as for the previous rating period.

When the local authority have made their first such demand or when they have made any subsequent demand during the rating period, the amount of the rates for any rental period must, if necessary, be recalculated, but any such recalculation cannot affect the ascertainment of rates for any rental period beginning more than six months before the date of service of the demand which gives rise to the recalculation.

FORM No. 5

RENT (SCOTLAND) ACTS 1971 AND 1972

Notice of increase of rent under a regulated tenancy where a rent has been registered after the completion of grant-aided improvements and there are restrictions on rent increases (Note 1).

Date....................................

To...

1. A rent of £..................per..................was registered on..................
(Note 3) as the fair rent for the dwellinghouse situated at............................
...................................., of which you are the tenant (Note 4).

2. (*a*) The registration is, or is treated as if it is (Note 5), the first after the completion, during the existence of the regulated tenancy, of works towards the cost of which a grant was payable after 25th August 1969 under Part II of the Housing (Financial Provisions) (Scotland) Act 1968 (improvement or standard grants) [or

(*b*) Where there has been such a registration as is mentioned in sub-paragraph (*a*) above, the registration is any subsequent registration which occurs at any time during the period of delay of two years specified in paragraph 3 below, and details of the former registration are as follows:—

Delete words in square brackets if they do not apply

   (i) the amount of rent then registered............................

   (ii) the amount (if any) then noted in the register
      as the amount apportioned to services
      (Note 6)..]

3. By virtue of section 79 of and Schedule 13 to the Rent (Scotland) Act 1971, there is a period of delay of two years imposed as from..................(being the date which is referred to in Note 7 [(*a*)] [(*b*)] [(*c*)]) before the full amount of the registered rent may be recovered and the rent may only be increased by this notice for any statutory period beginning in any year of that period of delay to the extent permitted under the said Schedule 13 (Note 8).

4. This is a notice increasing the rent payable for a statutory period of the tenancy beginning in the [first] [second] year of the period of delay and the amount of the increase is calculated as follows:—

Add   £ per ....

   (*a*) The amount of the previous limit
      (Note 8)   £...............

   [(*b*) The amount (if any) noted in the
      register as the amount apportioned
      to services (Note 6)   £...............]

   (*c*) Whichever is the greater of—

      (i) the minimum amount to which
         the rent may be increased
         (Note 8); or

      (ii) [one-third] [two-thirds] of
         £...............being the appro-
         priate proportion of the total
         increase (Note 8)   £...............

[(*d*) If the registration referred to in paragraph 1 above is such a registration as is mentioned in paragraph 2(*b*) above, add where appropriate, the amount of the difference between the new registration and the former registration (Note 9)   £...............]

£ ....

Deduct   £ ....
The amount of the rent which is at present lawfully recoverable from you as tenant of the dwellinghouse £ ....

The amount of the increase per........................is £ ....

5. Accordingly, I hereby give you notice that your rent will be increased from your present rent of £...............per...............by an increase of £.............. per...............to the new rent of £............per...............and the date from which such increase is to take effect is..................(Note 10).

[6. It is noted in the register that the rates in respect of the dwellinghouse are borne by the landlord and, in terms of section 43(3) of the Rent (Scotland) Act 1971, the amount of the rates for any rental period, ascertained in accordance with Schedule 4 to that Act (Note 11), is recoverable from you in addition to the above rent for any statutory period of the tenancy, without service of any notice of increase. The amount of the rates which is at present lawfully recoverable from you, in addition to the above rent, is £..................per..................]

....
(Signature of Landlord/landlord's agents)

....
(Address of landlord/landlord's agents)

NOTES

(To be incorporated in the notice)

1. This notice of increase is required where:—

(*a*) the tenancy of the dwellinghouse is a regulated tenancy within the meaning of the Rent (Scotland) Act 1971 (referred to hereafter as "the Act of 1971");

(*b*) the tenancy of the dwellinghouse is a stautory tenancy or will become one as a result of the operation of this notice (Note 2);

(*c*) a rent has been registered for the dwellinghouse which is higher than the rent at present recoverable; and

(*d*) the registration is one of those mentioned in paragraph 2 of this notice

In these circumstances, section 79 of and Schedule 13 to the Act of 1971 provide that the rent may only be increased by a notice of increase under section 21(2)(*b*) of that Act to the extent (if any) permitted under that Schedule.

2. If the tenancy is a protected tenancy (that is, if the regulated tenancy is a contractual tenancy) the registration of a fair rent for the dwellinghouse, which is higher than the rent at present recoverable, does not allow the landlord to increase the rent up to the amount registered, unless there is a provision to that effect in the tenancy contract.

If the protected tenancy has come to an end, and the tenant is retaining posse-ssion of the dwellinghouse as a statutory tenant, section 21(2)(b) of the Act of 1971 provides that the landlord may, subject to section 79 of and Schedule 13 to that Act, increase the rent up to the amount of the registered rent by the service of this notice.

Even although this notice of increase relates to statutory periods, section 25(3) of the Act of 1971 provides that it may be served during a contractual period (i.e. a rental period beginning before the protected tenancy comes to an end) and, if the landlord, by serving a notice to quit at the same time as this notice, could bring the tenancy to an end before the date specified in this notice for the increase to take effect, this notice will operate to convert the tenancy into a statutory tenancy as from that date.

The restrictions on rent increases imposed by section 79 of and Schedule 13 to the Act of 1971 cannot be evaded, either by the landlord and the tenant entering into an agreement increasing the rent payable under the tenancy or by the land-lord granting to the tenant or to any of his potential statutory successors a new tenancy of the dwellinghouse, whether before or during the period of delay of two years specified in paragraph 3 of this notice.

3. Insert the date upon which the rent determined by the rent officer or by the rent assessment committee was registered for the dwellinghouse.

4. The rent register may be inspected at the office of the rent officer.

5. Where
   (a) a new regulated tenancy has been granted to the tenant or to any of his potential statutory successors after the completion of the works referred to in paragraph 2(a) of this notice; and
   (b) a rent has then been registered for the dwellinghouse, which, had the new tenancy not been granted, would have been such a registration as is mentioned in the said paragraph 2(a),

paragraph 8 of Schedule 13 to the Act of 1971 provides that the amount to which the rent may be increased after the date of registration for any rental period of the new tenancy is, subject to Note 7(c) below, the amount to which the rent could have been increased for a statutory period of the previous tenancy, had that tenancy continued. Where that provision applies, the registration is, for the purposes of this notice, treated as if it had been such a registration as is mentioned in paragraph 2(a) of this notice.

6. Where the rent is registered before 1st January 1973, there may be an amount noted in the register as the amount apportioned to services and, if so, this amount is excluded from the restrictions on rent increases with respect to any year of the period of delay which begins before 1st January 1973 (Note 8).

7. (a) Insert the date of registration of the rent mentioned in paragraph 2(a) of this notice.

(b) Where a rent determined by a rent assessment committee is registered in substitution for a rent determined by the rent officer, the date of registration is deemed for the purposes of Schedule 13 to the Act of 1971 to be the date on which the rent determined by the rent officer was registered.

(c) Where
   (i) between the time of the completion of the works referred to in paragraph 2(a) of this notice and the registration of the rent specified in that paragraph, there has been an agreement increasing the rent payable under the tenancy or a new regulated tenancy granted to the tenant or to any of his potential statutory successors; and
   (ii) that agreement or new tenancy is a rent agreement with a tenant

having security of tenure within the meaning of Part V of the Housing (Financial Provisions) (Scotland) Act 1972 (referred to hereafter as "the Act of 1972"); and

(iii) the requirements of sections 42 and 44 of that Act have been observed as respects the rent agreement,

paragraph 8B of Schedule 13 to the Act of 1971 provides that the provisions of that Schedule should apply, as respects the period after the actual date when the rent was registered for the dwellinghouse, as if the date of registration had been on the date when the agreement took effect. For the purposes of this notice, therefore, the date of registration should be deemed to be the date on which the rent agreement took effect.

8. Under Schedule 13 to the Act of 1971, the amount to which the rent may be increased for any statutory period beginning in any year of the period of delay is the appropriate proportion, namely one-third or two-thirds, of the total increase in rent, according as to whether the statutory period begins in the first or the second year of the period of delay.

The total increase in rent is the difference between the amount of the registration which is referred to in paragraph 2(a) of this notice and the amount of the previous limit (that is, the amount, exclusive of rates, which at the date of registration (Note 7) was recoverable by way of rent or would have been so recoverable if all authorised notices of increase had been served), but with respect to any year of the period of delay which begins before 1st January 1973, the total increase in rent is the difference between the amount of that registered rent and the sum of—

(a) the amount of the previous limit; and

(b) the amount, if any, which is noted on the register as the amount apportioned to services (Note 6).

The minimum amount to which the rent may be increased however (but not above the amount of the registered rent) for each year of the period of delay is—

(a) 37½p per week with respect to any year of the period of delay which begins before 1st January 1973; or

(b) 50p per week with respect to any year of the period of delay which begins on or after that date.

In other words, with respect to any year of the period of delay which begins before 1st January 1973, if the total increase exceeds £1·12½p per week, the rent may be increased in three equal annual instalments, each of one-third of the increase; but, if it does not exceed £1·12½p per week, the rent may be increased by annual instalments of 37½p per week up to the registered rent. With respect to any year of the period of delay which begins, on or after a registration, on or after 1st January 1973, if the total increase exceeds £1·50p per week the rent may be increased in three equal annual instalments, each of one-third of the increase; but if it does not exceed £1·50p per week, the rent may be increased by annual instalments of 50p per week up to the registered rent.

In addition to this amount of the increase, the previous limit, and where appropriate, the amount apportioned to services may also be recovered.

9. Where the registration referred to in paragraph 1 of this notice is not the first registration after the completion of the works referred to in paragraph 2(a) of this notice (i.e. where it is such a registration as is mentioned in paragraph 2(b) of this notice) and it exceeds the rent for the time being recoverable under the regulated tenancy, the rent payable for any statutory period beginning before the end of the period of delay may be increased only to the same extent as if the rent first registered has remained registered.

Where the new rent is lower than the rent first registered, the rent payable may not however exceed the amount of the new rent registered.

Where the new rent is higher than the rent first registered, the difference between them may

(a) where the date of registration of the new rent is before 1st January 1973, be added in full in any statutory period beginning in the year after the year of the period of delay in which the new rent is registered; or (*b*) where the date of registration of the new rent is on or after 1st January 1973, be added in full for any statutory period beginning after the date of registration of the new rent.

10. The date to be inserted here must be a date which is not earlier than

(*a*) the date of registration which is specified in paragraph 1 of this notice; or

(*b*) four weeks before the date of service of this notice; or

(*c*) the commencement of the first rental period beginning in the relevant year of the period of delay to which this notice relates.

If this notice is served during a contractual period of the tenancy, the date to be inserted must also be later than the date on which the tenancy could be brought to an end by a notice to quit served by the landlord at the same time as this notice (Note 2).

11. Schedule 4 of the Act of 1971 provides that the amount of rates for any rental period should be ascertaned by dividing the total rates payable for the whole rating period, in which the rent for that rental is payable, by the number which is obtained by dividing the length of that rating period by the length of the rental period.

Until the local authority make their first demand for, or for an instalment of, the rates for a rating period, the amount of the rates for any rental period is to be calculated on the basis that the rates for that rating period continue to be the same as for the previous rating period.

When the local authority have made their first such demand or when they have made any subsequent demand during the rating period, the amount of the rates for any rental period must, if necessary, be recalculated, but any such recalculation cannot affect the ascertainment of rates for any rental period beginning more than six months before the date of service of the demand which gives rise to the recalculation.

FORM NO. 6

RENT (SCOTLAND) ACTS 1971 AND 1972

Notice of increase of rent under a regulated tenancy where a rent has been registered after the conversion of the tenancy into a regulated tenancy following upon the issue of a qualification certificate and there are restrictions on rent increases with respect to any year beginning before 1 *January* 1973 *(Note* 1).

Date.....................................

To..

1. A rent of £.................per.................was registered on.................
(Note 3) as the fair rent for the dwellinghouse situated at............................,
of which you are the tenant (Note 4).

Delete words
in square
brackets if
they do not
apply

2. (*a*) The registration is, or is treated as if it is (Note 5), the first after the conversion of the tenancy into a regulated tenancy under Part VI of the Rent (Scotland) Act 1971 (following upon the issue of a qualification certificate) [or

(*b*) Where there has been such a registration as is mentioned in sub-paragraph (*a*) above, the registration is any subsequent registration which occurs at any time during the period of delay of four years specified in paragraph 3 below, and, details of the former registration are as follows:—

    (i) the amount of rent then registered.............................

    (ii) the amount (if any) then noted in the register as the amount apportioned to services (Note 6)...............]

3. By virtue of section 79 of and Schedule 13 to the Rent (Scotland) Act 1971, there is a period of delay of four years imposed as from.....................(Note 7) before the full amount of the registered rent may be recovered, and the rent may only be increased, by this notice, for any statutory period beginning in any year of that period of delay which begins before 1st January 1973 to the extent permitted under the said Schedule 13 as originally enacted (Note 8).

4. This is a notice increasing the rent payable for a statutory period of the tenancy beginning in the [first] [second] [third] [fourth] year of the period of delay and the amount of the increase is calculated as follows:—

Add   £   per....................

    (*a*) The amount of the previous limit
        (Note 8)   £...............

    (*b*) The amount (if any) noted in the
        register as the amount apportioned
        to services (Note 6)   £...............

    (*c*) Whichever is the greater of—

        (i) the minimum amount to which
           the rent may be increased (i.e.
           $37\frac{1}{2}$p per week for each year of
           the period of delay); or

        (ii) [one-fifth] [two-fifths] [three-
           fifths] [four-fifths] of £...........
           being the appropriate propor-
           tion of the difference between
           the registered rent and the sum
           of (*a*) and (*b*) (Note 8).   £...............

[(*d*) If the registration referred to in paragraph 1 above is such a registration as is mentioned in paragraph 2(*b*) above, add, where appropriate, the amount of the difference between the new registration and the former registration (Note 9) £...............] £..............

Deduct　　　　　　　　　　　　　　　　　　　£.........................

The amount of the rent which is at present lawfully recoverable from you as tenant of the dwellinghouse　　　　　　　　　　　　　　　　　　£.........................

The amount of the increase per....................is　£

5. Accordingly, I hereby give you notice that your rent will be increased from your present rent of £.................per..................by an increase of £...........
......per..................to the new rent of £.................per..................and the date from which such increase is to take effect is.........................(Note 10).

[6. It is noted in the register that the rates in respect of the dwellinghouse are borne by the landlord and, in terms of section 43(3) of the Rent (Scotland) Act 1971, the amount of the rates for any rental period, ascertained in accordance with Schedule 4 to that Act (Note 11), is recoverable from you in addition to the above rent for any statutory period of the tenancy, without service of any notice of increase. The amount of the rates which is at present lawfully recoverable from you in addition to the above rent, is £.................per..................]

....

(Signature of landlord/landlord's agents)

....

(Address of landlord/landlords's agents)

NOTES

(To be incorporated in the notice)

1. This notice of increase is required where:—

(*a*) the tenancy of the dwelling house is a regulated tenancy within the meaning of the Rent (Scotland) Act 1971 (referred to hereafter as "the Act of 1971");

(*b*) the tenancy of the dwellinghouse is a statutory tenancy or will become one as a result of the operation of this notice (Note 2);

(*c*) a rent has been registered for the dwellinghouse which is higher than the rent at present recoverable; and

(*d*) the registration is one of those mentioned in paragraph 2 of this notice.

In these circumstances, section 79 of and Schedule 13 to the Act of 1971 provide that the rent may only be increased by a notice of increase under section 21(2)(*b*) of that Act to the extent (if any) permitted under that Schedule.

2. If the tenancy is a protected tenancy (that is, if the regulated tenancy is a contractual tenancy) the registration of a fair rent for the dwellinghouse, which is higher than the rent at present recoverable, does not allow the landlord to increase the rent up to the amount registered, unless there is a provision to that effect in the tenancy contract.

If the protected tenancy has come to an end, and the tenant is retaining possession of the dwellinghouse as a statutory tenant, section 21(2)(*b*) of the Act of 1971 provides that the landlord may, subject to section79 of and Schedule 13 to that Act, increase the rent up to the amount of the registered rent by the service of this notice. Even although this notice of increase relates to statutory periods, section 25(3) of the Act of 1971 provides that it may be served during a contractual period (i.e. a rental period beginning before the protected tenancy comes to an end) and, if the landlord, by serving a notice to quit at the same time as this notice, could bring the tenancy to an end before the date specified in this notice for the increase to take effect, this notice will operate to convert the tenancy into a statutory tenancy as from that date.

The restrictions on rent increases imposed by section 79 of and Schedule 13 to the Act of 1971 cannot be evaded, either by the landlord and the tenant entering into an agreement increasing the rent payable under the tenancy or by the landlord granting to the tenant or to any of his potential statutory successors a new tenancy of the dwellinghouse, whether before or during the period of delay of four years specified in paragraph 3 of this notice.

3. Insert the date upon which the rent determined by the rent officer or the rent determined or designated by the rent assessment committee was registered for the dwellinghouse.

4. The rent register may be inspected at the office of the rent officer.

5. Where

    (*a*) a new regulated tenancy has been granted to the tenant or to any of his potential statutory successors after the conversion of the tenancy into a regulated tenancy; and

    (*b*) a rent has then been registered for the dwellinghouse, which, had the new tenancy not been granted, would have been such a registration as is mentioned in the said paragraph 2(*a*),

paragraph 8 of Schedule 13 to the Act of 1971 provides that the amount to which the rent may be increased after the date of registration for any rental period of the new tenancy is the amount to which the rent could have been increased for a statutory period of the previous tenancy, had that tenancy continued. Where that provision applies, the registration is, for the purposes of this notice, treated as if it had been such a registration as is mentioned in paragraph 2(*a*) of this notice.

6. Where the rent is registered before 1st January 1973, there may be an amount noted in the register as the amount apportioned to services and, if so, this amount is excluded from the restrictions on rent increases with respect to any year of the period of delay which begins before 1st January 1973 (Note 8).

7. Insert the date of registration of rent mentioned in paragraph 2(*a*) of this notice.

Where a rent determined or designated by a rent assessment committee is registered in substitution for a rent determined by the rent officer, the date of registration is deemed for the purposes of Schedule 13 to the Act of 1971 to be the date on which the rent determined by the rent officer was registered.

8. Under Schedule 13 to the Act of 1971, as originally enacted, the amount to which the rent may be increased for any statutory period beginning in any year of the period of delay which begins before 1st January 1973 is the appropriate proportion, namely one-fifth, two-fifths, three-fifths or four-fifths according as to whether the statutory period begins in the first, second, third or fourth year of the period of delay, of the difference between the amount of the registration which is referred to in paragraph 2(*a*) of this notice and the sum of—

(a) the amount of the previous limit (that is, the amount, exclusive of rates, which at the date of registration (Note 7) was recoverable by way of rent or would have been so recoverable if all authorised notices of increase had been served); and

(b) the amount, if any, which is noted on the register as the amount apportioned to services (Note 6).

The minimum amount to which the rent may be increased however (but not above the amount of the registered rent) for each year of the period of delay is 37½p per week.

In other words, with respect to any year of the period of delay which begins before 1st January 1973, if the increase (that is the difference between registered rent and the sum of (a) and (b) above) exceeds £1·87½p per week, the rent may be increased in five equal annual instalments, each of one-fifth of the increase; but, if it does not exceed £1·87½p per week, the rent may be increased by annual instalments of 37½p per week up to the registered rent.

In addition to this amount of the increase, the previous limit and, where appropriate the amount apportioned to services may also be recovered.

9. Where the registration referred to in paragraph 1 of this notice is not the first registration after the conversion of the tenancy into a regulated tenancy (i.e. where it is such a registration as is mentioned in paragraph 2(b) of this notice) and it exceeds the rent for the time being recoverable under the regulated tenancy, the rent payable for any statutory period beginning before the end of the period of delay may be increased only to the same extent as if the rent first registered had remained registered.

Where the new rent is lower than the rent first registered, the rent payable may not however exceed the amount of the new rent registered.

Where the new rent is higher than the rent first registered, the difference between them may

(a) where the date of registration of the new rent is before 1st January 1973, be added in full in any statutory period beginning in the year after the year of the period of delay in which the new rent is registered; or

(b) where the date of registration of the new rent is on or after 1st January 1973, be added in full for any statutory period beginning after the date of registration of the new rent.

10. The date to be inserted here must be a date which is not earlier than

(a) the date of registration which is specified in paragraph 1 of this notice; or

(b) four weeks before the date of service of this notice; or

(c) the commencement of the first rental period beginning in the relevant year of the period of delay to which this notice relates.

If this notice is served during a contractual period of the tenancy, the date to be inserted must also be later than the date on which the tenancy could be brought to and end by a notice to quit served by the landlord at the same time as this notice (Note 2).

11. Schedule 4 of the Act of 1971 provides that the amount of rates for any rental period should be ascertained by dividing the total rates payable for the whole rating period, in which the rent for that rental period is payable, by the number which is obtained by dividing the length of that rating period by the length of the rental period.

Until the local authority make their first demand for, or for an instalment of, the rates for a rating period, the amount of the rates for any rental period is to be calculated on the basis that the rates for that rating period continue to be the same as for the previous rating period.

When the local authority have made their first such demand or when they have made any subsequent demand during the rating period, the amount of the rates for any rental period must, if necessary, be recalculated, but any such recalculation cannot affect the ascertainment of rates for any rental period beginning more than six months before the date of service of the demand which gives rise to the recalculation.

FORM NO. 7

RENT (SCOTLAND) ACTS 1971 AND 1972

Notice of increase of rent under a regulated tenancy where a rent has been registered after the conversion of the tenancy into a regulated tenancy following upon the issue of a qualification certificate and there are restrictions on rent increases with respect to any year beginning on or after 1 *January* 1973 (*Note* 1).

Date...................................

To...

1. A rent of £..................per..................was registered on..................
(Note 3) as the fair rent for the dwellinghouse situated at............................
of which you are the tenant (Note 4).

2. (*a*) The registration is, or is treated as if it is (Note 5) the first after the conversion of the tenancy into a regulated tenancy under Part VI of the Rent (Scotland) Act 1971 (following upon the issue of a qualification certificate) [or

(*b*) Where there has been such a registration as is mentioned in sub-paragraph (*a*) above, the registration is any subsequent registration which occurs at any time during the period of delay specified in paragraph 3 below and the amount of the former registration was £..................per..................]   Delete words in square brackets if they do not apply

3. By virtue of section 79 of and Schedule 13 to the Rent (Scotland) Act 1971, as amended by Schedule 7 to the Housing (Financial Provisions) (Scotland) Act 1972, there is a period of delay of [two] [three] years (Note 6) imposed as from........................(being the date which is referred to in Note 7 [(*a*)] [(*b*)] [(*c*)]) before the full amount of the registered rent may be recovered and the rent may only be increased by this notice for any statutory period beginning in a year of that period of delay which begins on or after 1st January 1973 to the extent permitted under the said Schedule 13, as so amended.

4. This is a notice increasing the rent payable for a statutory period of the tenancy beginning in the [first] [second] [third] year of the period of delay which begins on or after 1st January 1973 and the amount of the increase is calculated as follows:—

Add   £   per....................

(*a*) The amount of the previous limit
(Note 8)   £...............

(*b*) Whichever is the greater of—

(i) the minimum amount to which the rent may be increased (Note 8); or

(ii) ....of £...............,
being the appropriate proportion of the difference between the registered rent and the amount of the previous limit (Note 8)   £...............

[(*c*) If the registration referred to in paragraph 1 above is such a registration as is mentioned in paragraph 2(*b*) above, add, where appropriate, the amount of the difference between the new registration and the former registration (Note 9)   £...............]   £.......................

Deduct

The amount of the rent which is at
present lawfully recoverable from
you as tenant of the dwellinghouse   £.........................

The amount of the increase per......is   £.........................

5. Accordingly, I hereby give you notice that your rent will be increased from your present rent of £.................per.................by an increase of £........... per.................to the new rent of £.................per.................and the date from which such increase is to take effect is........................(Note 10).

[6. It is noted in the register that the rates in respect of the dwellinghouse are borne by the landlord and, in terms of section 43(3) of the Rent (Scotland) Act 1971, the amount of the rates for any rental period, ascertained in accordance with Schedule 4 to that Act (Note 11), is recoverable from you in addition to the above rent for any statutory period of the tenancy, without service of any notice of increase. The amount of the rates which is at present lawfully recoverable from you, in addition to the above rent, is £.................per.................]

....
(Signature of landlord/landlord's agent)

....
(Address of landlord/landlord's agents)

NOTES

(To be incorporated in the notice)

1. This notice of increase is required where:—

   (*a*) the tenancy of the dwellinghouse is a regulated tenancy within the meaning of the Rent (Scotland) Act 1971 (referred to hereafter as "the Act of 1971");

   (*b*) the tenancy of the dwellinghouse is a statutory tenancy or will become one as a result of the operation of this notice (Note 2);

   (*c*) a rent has been registered for the dwellinghouse which is higher than the rent at present recoverable; and

   (*d*) the registration is one of those mentioned in paragraph 2 of this notice.

In these circumstances, section 79 of and Schedule 13 to the Act of 1971 provide that the rent may only be increased by a notice of increase under section 21(2)(*b*) of that Act to the extent (if any) permitted under that Schedule.

2. If the tenancy is a protected tenancy (that is, if the regulated tenancy is a contractual tenancy), the registration of a fair rent for the dwellinghouse, which is higher than the rent at present recoverable, does not allow the landlord to increase the rent up to the amount registered, unless there is a provision to that effect in the tenancy contract.

If the protected tenancy has come to an end, and the tenant is retaining possession of the dwellinghouse as a statutory tenant, section 21(2)(*b*) of the Act of 1971 provides that the landlord may, subject to section 79 of and Schedule 13 to that Act, increase the rent up to the amount of the registered rent by the service of this notice.

Even although this notice of increase relates to statutory periods, section 25(3) of the Act of 1971 provides that it may be served during a contractual period (i.e. a rental period beginning before the protected tenancy comes to an end) and, if the landlord, by serving a notice to quit at the same time as this notice, could bring the tenancy to an end before the date specified in this notice for the increase to take effect, this notice will operate to convert the tenancy into a statutory tenancy as from that date.

The restrictions on rent increases imposed by section 79 of and Schedule 13 to the Act of 1971 cannot be evaded, either by the landlord and the tenant entering into an agreement increasing the rent payable under the tenancy or by the landlord granting to the tenant or to any of his potential statutory successors a new tenancy of the dwellinghouse, whether before or during the period of delay specified in paragraph 3 of this notice.

3. Insert the date upon which the rent determined by the rent officer or the rent determined or designated by the rent assessment committee was registered for the dwellinghouse.

4. The rent register may be inspected at the office of the rent officer.

5. Where
  (a) a new regulated tenancy has been granted to the tenant or to any of his potential statutory successors after the conversion of the tenancy into a regulated tenancy; and
  (b) a rent has then been registered for the dwellinghouse, which, had the new tenancy not been granted, would have been such a registration as is mentioned in paragraph 2(a) of this notice,

paragraph 8 of Schedule 13 to the Act of 1971 provides that the amount to which the rent may be increased after the date of registration for any rental period of the new tenancy is, subject to Note 7(c) below, the amount to which the rent could have been increased for a statutory period of the previous tenancy, had that tenancy continued. Where that provision applies, the registration is, for the purposes of this notice, treated as if it had been such a registration as is mentioned in paragraph 2(a) of this notice.

6. Where a rent for the dwellinghouse is registered on or after 1st January 1973, paragraph 2 of Schedule 13 to the Act of 1971, as amended by paragraph 11 of Schedule 7 to the Housing (Financial Provisions) (Scotland) Act 1972 (referred to hereafter as "the Act of 1972") provides for a period of delay of two years from the date of registration (Note 7) before the full amount of the registered rent may be obtained.

Where a rent for the dwellinghouse has been registered before 1st January 1973 and there is a period of delay of four years imposed by paragraph 2 of Schedule 13 to the Act of 1971, as originally enacted, paragraph 12 of Schedule 7 to the Act of 1972 provides for the reduction of the length of that period of delay as from 1st January 1973. The extent of that reduction depends upon what year of the period of delay begins on or after 1st January 1973 as follows:—
  (a) if the second year of a period of delay of four years begins on or after 1st January 1973 (i.e. if the rent was registered in 1972) the period of delay is reduced to two years;
  (b) if the third year of a period of delay of four years begins on or after 1st January 1973 (i.e. if the rent was registered in 1971) the period of delay is reduced to three years; and
  (c) if the fourth year of a period of delay of four years begins on or after 1st January 1973 (i.e. if the rent was registered in 1970) the period of delay is terminated at the end of the third year.

The length of the reduced period of delay should, where appropriate, be inserted.

7. (a) Insert the date of registration of the rent mentioned in paragraph 2(a) of this notice.

(*b*) Where a rent determined or designated by a rent assessment committee is registered in substitution for a rent determined by the rent officer, the date of registration is deemed for the purposes of Schedule 13 to the Act of 1971 to be the date on which the rent determined by the rent officer was registered.

(*c*) Where

    (i) between the date of the conversion of the tenancy into a regulated tenancy and the registration of the rent specified in paragraph 2(*a*) of this notice, there has been an agreement increasing the rent payable under the tenancy or a new regulated tenancy granted to the tenant or to any of his potential statutory successors; and

    (ii) that agreement or new tenancy is a rent agreement with a tenant having security of tenure within the meaning of Part V of the Act of 1972; and

    (iii) the requirements of sections 42 and 43 of that Act have been observed as respects the rent agreement,

paragraph 8B of Schedule 13 to the Act of 1971 provides that the provisions of that Schedule should apply, as respects the period after the actual date when the rent was registered for the dwellinghouse, as if the date of registration had been on the date when the agreement took effect. For the purposes of this notice, therefore, the date of registration should be deemed to be the date on which the rent agreement took effect.

8. Under Schedule 13 to the Act of 1971, as amended, the amount to which the rent may be increased for any statutory period beginning in any year of the period of delay which begins on or after 1st January 1973 is the appropriate proportion of the increase, that is of the difference between the amount of the registration which is referred to in paragraph 2(*a*) of this notice and the amount of the previous limit (i.e. the amount, exclusive of rates, which at the date of registration (Note 7) was recoverable by way of rent or would have been so recoverable if all authorised notices of increase had been served).

Where a rent has been registered on or after 1st January 1973, and there is a two year period of delay imposed as from the date of registration (Note 6), the appropriate proportion is one-third or two-thirds of the increase according as to whether the statutory period begins in the first or the second year of the period of delay, but the minimum amount to which the rent may be increased (but not above the amount of the registered rent) for each year of the period of delay is 50p per week. Accordingly, in this case, if the total increase exceeds £1·50p per week, the rent may be increased in three equal annual instalments, each of one-third of the increase; but if it does not exceed £1·50p per week the rent may be increased by annual instalments of 50p per week up to the registered rent.

Where a rent has been registered before 1st January 1973 and the period of delay of four years is reduced in accordance with paragraph 12 of Schedule 7 to the Act of 1972 (Note 6), the appropriate proportion is ascertained as follows:—

    (*a*) if the second year of the period of delay of four years begins on or after 1st January 1973 and the period of delay has been reduced to two years, the appropriate proportion of the increase which may be recovered for any statutory period beginning in the second year of the period of delay is three-fifths; and

    (*b*) if the third year of the period of delay of four years begins on or after 1st January 1973 and that period of delay has been reduced to three years, the appropriate proportion of the increase which may be recovered for any statutory period beginning in the third year of the period of delay is four-fifths.

In the case where a rent has been registered before 1st January 1973, the minimum amount to which the rent may be increased (but not above the amount of the registered rent) for each year of the period of delay is

    (*a*) 37½p per week with respect to any year of the period of delay which begins before 1st January 1973; and (*b*) 50p per week with respect to any year of the period of delay which begins on or after that date.

9. Where the registration referred to in paragraph 1 of this notice is not the first registration after the conversion of the tenancy into a regulated tenancy, (i.e. where it is such a registration is mentioned in paragraph 2(*b*) of the notice) and it exceeds the rent for the time being recoverable under the regulated tenancy, the rent payable for any statutory period beginning before the end of the period of delay may be increased only to the same extent as if the rent first registered had remained registered.

Where the new rent is lower than the rent first registered the rent payable may not however exceed the amount of the new rent registered.

Where the new rent is higher than the rent first registered, the difference between them may

(*a*) where the date of registration of the new rent is before 1st January 1973, be added in full in any statutory period beginning in the year after the year of the period of delay in which the new rent is registered; or

(*b*) where the date of registration of the new rent is on or after 1st January 1973, be added in full for any statutory period beginning after the date of registration of the new rent.

10. The date to be inserted here must be a date which is not earlier than

(*a*) the date of registration which is specified in paragraph 1 of this notice; or

(*b*) four weeks before the date of service of this notice; or

(*c*) the commencement of the first rental period beginning in the relevant year of the period of delay to which this notice relates.

If this notice is served during a contractual period of the tenancy, the date to be inserted must also be later than the date on which the tenancy could be brought to an end by a notice to quit served by the landlord at the same time as this notice (Note 2).

11. Schedule 4 of the Act of 1971 provides that the amount of rates for any rental period should be ascertained by dividing the total rates payable for the whole rating period, in which the rent for that rental period is payable, by the number which is obtained by dividing the length of that rating period by the length of the rental period.

Until the local authority make their first demand for, or for an instalment of, the rates for a rating period, the amount of the rates for any rental period is to be calculated on the basis that the rates for that rating period continue to be the same as for the previous rating period.

When the local authority have made their first such demand or when they have made any subsequent demand during the rating period, the amount of the rates for any rental period must, if necessary, be recalculated, but any such recalculation cannot affect the ascertainment of rates for any rental period beginning more than six months before the date of service of the demand which gives rise to the recalculation.

FORM NO. 8

RENT (SCOTLAND) ACTS 1971 AND 1972

Notice of increase of rent under a regulated tenancy where a rent has been registered after the conversion of the tenancy into a regulated tenancy under section 34 of the Housing (Financial Provisions) (Scotland) Act 1972 and there are restrictions on rent increases (Note 1).

Date....................................

To...

1. A rent of £.................per.................was registered on.................
(Note 3) as the fair rent for the dwellinghouse situated at.................,of which you are the tenant (Note 4).

2.(*a*) The registration is, or is treated as if it is (Note 5), the first to take effect after the conversion of the tenancy into a regulated tenancy under section 34 of the Housing (Financial Provisions) (Scotland) Act 1972, [or

Delete words in square brackets if they do not apply

(*b*) Where there has been such a registration as is mentioned in sub-paragraph (*a*) above, the registration is any subsequent registration which occurs at any time during the period of delay of two years specified in paragraph 3 below, and the amount of the former registration was £.................per....................]

3. By virtue of section 37 of and Schedule 6 to the Housing (Financial Provisions) (Scotland) Act 1972 there is a period of delay of two years imposed as from.........................(being the date which is referred to in Note 6 [(*a*)] [(*b*)] [(*c*)]) before the full amount of the registered rent may be recovered and the rent may only be increased by this notice for any statutory period beginning in any year of that period of delay to the extent permitted under the said Schedule 6 (Note 7).

4. This is a notice increasing the rent payable for a statutory period of the tenancy beginning in the [first] [second] year of the period of delay and the amount of the increase is calculated as follows:—

Add   £   per....................
  (*a*) The amount of the previous limit
    (Note 7)   £...............
  (*b*) Whichever is the greater of—
    (i) the minimum amount to which
      the rent may be increased, (i.e.
      50p per week for each year of
      the period of delay); or
    (ii) [one-third] [two-thirds] of
      £...............being the appro-
      priate proportion of the differ-
      ence between the registered rent
      and the previous limit (Note 7) £...............
  [(*c*) If the registration referred to in
    paragraph 1 above is such a registra-
    tion as is mentioned in paragraph
    2(*b*) above, add, where appropriate,
    the amount of the difference between
    the new registration and the former
    registration (Note 8)   £...............]   £........................

Deduct

The amount of the rent which is at
present lawfully recoverable from
you as tenant of the dwellinghouse £............................

The amount of the increase per......is £............................

5. Accordingly, I hereby give you notice that your rent will be increased from
your present rent of £.................per.................by an increase of £............
per.................to the new rent of £.....................per.................and the
date from which such increase is to take effect is.................(Note 9).

[6. It is noted in the register that the rates in respect of the dwellinghouse
are borne by the landlord and, in terms of section 43(3) of the Rent (Scotland)
Act 1971, the amount of the rates for any rental period, ascertained in accordance with Schedule 4 to that Act (Note 10), is recoverable from you in addition
to the above rent for any statutory period of the tenancy, without service of
any notice of increase. The amount of the rates which is at present lawfully
recoverable from you, in addition to the above rent, is £.................per.........]

....
(Signature of landlord/landlord's agents)

....
(Address of landlord/landlord's agents)

NOTES

(*To be incorporated in the notice*)

1. This notice of increase is required where:—

   (*a*) the tenancy of the dwellinghouse is a regulated tenancy within the
   meaning of the Rent (Scotland) Act 1971 (referred to hereafter as "the
   Act of 1971");

   (*b*) the tenancy of the dwellinghouse is a statutory tenancy or will become
   one as a result of the operation of this notice (Note 2);

   (*c*) a rent has been registered for the dwellinghouse which is higher than the
   rent at present recoverable; and

   (*d*) the registration is one of those mentioned in paragraph 2 of this notice.

In these circumstances, section 37 of and Schedule 6 to the Housing (Financial
Provisions) (Scotland) Act 1972 (referred to hereafter as "the Act of 1972")
provide that the rent may only be increased by a notice of increase under section
21(2)(*b*) of the Act of 1971 to the extent (if any) permitted under the said Schedule
6.

2. If the tenancy is a protected tenancy (that is, if the regulated tenancy is
a contractual tenancy), the registration of a fair rent for the dwellinghouse, which
is higher than the rent at present recoverable, does not allow the landlord to
increase the rent up to the amount registered, unless there is a provision to that
effect in the tenancy contract.

If the protected tenancy has come to an end, and the tenant is retaining possession of the dwellinghouse as a statutory tenant, section 21(2)(*b*) of the Act of
1971 provides that the landlord may, subject to section 37 of and Schedule 6 to
the Act of 1972, increase the rent up to the amount of the registered rent by the
service of this notice.

Even although this notice of increase relates to statutory periods, section 25(3) of the Act of 1971 provides that it may be served during a contractual period (i.e. a rental period beginning before the protected tenancy comes to an end) and, if the landlord, by serving a notice to quit at the same time as this notice, could bring the tenancy to an end before the date specified in this notice for the increase to take effect, this notice will operate to convert the tenancy into a statutory tenancy as from that date.

The restrictions on rent increases imposed by section 37 of and Schedule 6 to the Act of 1972 cannot be evaded, either by the landlord and the tenant entering into an agreement increasing the rent payable under the tenancy or by the landlord granting to the tenant or to any of his potential statutory successors a new tenancy of the dwellinghouse, whether before or during the period of delay of two years specified in paragraph 3 of this notice.

3. Insert the date upon which the rent determined by the rent officer or by the rent assessment committee was registered for the dwellinghouse. Where the rent is registered before the date when the tenancy became converted into a regulated tenancy, the date of registration is, by virtue of section 38(3) of the Act of 1972, deemed to be the date when the registration takes effect.

4. The rent register may be inspected at the office of the rent officer.

5. Where
    (a) a new regulated tenancy has been granted to the tenant or to any of his potential statutory successors after the conversion of the tenancy into a regulated tenancy; and
    (b) a rent has then been registered for the dwellinghouse, which, had the new tenancy not been granted, would have been such a registration as is mentioned in paragraph 2(a) of this notice,

paragraph 7 of Schedule 6 to the Act of 1972 provides that the amount to which the rent may be increased after the date of registration for any rental period of the new tenancy is, subject to Note 6(c) below, the amount to which the rent could have been increased for a statutory period of the previous tenancy, had that tenancy continued. Where that provision applies, the registration is, for the purposes of this notice, treated as if it had been such a registration as is mentioned in paragraph 2(a) of this notice.

6. (a) Insert the date of registration of the rent mentioned in paragraph 2(a) of this notice. Where that rent was registered before the date when the tenancy became converted into a regulated tenancy, the date of registration is deemed to be the date when the registration took effect.

(b) Where a rent determined by a rent assessment committee is registered in substitution for a rent determined by the rent officer, the date of registration is deemed for the purposes of Schedule 6 to the Act of 1972 to be the date on which the rent determined by the rent officer was registered.

    (c) Where
       (i) between the date of the conversion of the tenancy into a regulated tenancy and the registration of the rent specified in paragraph 2(a) of this notice, there has been an agreement increasing the rent payable under the tenancy or a new regulated tenancy granted to the tenant or to any of his potential statutory successors; and
      (ii) that agreement or new tenancy is a rent agreement with a tenant having security of tenure within the meaning of Part V of the Act of 1972; and
      (iii) the requirements of sections 42 and 43 of that Act have been observed as respects the rent agreement,

paragraph 9 of Schedule 6 to the Act of 1972 provides that the provisions of that Schedule should apply, as respects the period after the actual date when the rent was registered for the dwellinghouse, as if the date of registration had been on the date when the agreement took effect. For the purposes of this notice, therefore, the date of registration should be deemed to be the date on which the rent agreement took effect.

7. Under Schedule 6 to the Act of 1972, the amount to which the rent may be increased for any statutory period beginning in any year of the period of delay is the appropriate proportion, namely one-third, or two-thirds, according as to whether the statutory period begins in the first or the second year of the period of delay, of the difference between the amount of the registration which is referred to in paragraph 2(*a*) of this notice and the amount of the previous limit (that is the amount, exclusive of rates, which, at the date of registration (Note 6) was recoverable by way of rent or would have been so recoverable if all authorised notices of increase had been served). The minimum amount to which the rent may be increased however (but not above the amount of the registered rent) for each year of the period of delay is 50p per week.

In other words if the total increase (i.e. the difference between the registered rent and the amount of the previous limit) exceeds £1·50p per week the rent may be increased in three equal annual instalments, each of one-third of the increase; but if it does not exceed £1·50p per week the rent may be increased by annual instalments of 50p per week up to the registered rent.

8. Where the registration referred to in paragraph 1 of this notice is not the first registration after the conversion of the tenancy into a regulated tenancy (i.e. where it is such a registration as is mentioned in paragraph 2(*b*) of this notice) and it exceeds the rent for the time being recoverable under the regulated tenancy, the rent payable for any statutory period beginning before the end of the period of delay may be increased only to the same extent as if the rent first registered has remained registered.

Where the new rent is lower than the rent first registered, the rent payable may not however exceed the amount of the new rent registered.

Where the new rent is higher than the rent first registered, the difference between them may be added in full for any statutory period beginning after the date of registration of the new rent.

9. The date to be inserted here must be a date which is not earlier than

(*a*) the date of registration which is specified in paragraph 1 of this notice; or

(*b*) four weeks before the date of service of this notice; or

(*c*) the commencement of the first rental period beginning in the relevant year of the period of delay to which this notice relates.

If this notice is served during a contractual period of the tenancy, the date to be inserted must also be later than the date on which the tenancy could be brought to an end by a notice to quit served by the landlord at the same time as this notice (Note 2).

10. Schedule 4 of the Act of 1971 provides that the amount of rates for any rental period should be ascertained by dividing the total rates payable for the whole rating period, in which the rent for that rental period is payable, by the number which is obtained by dividing the length of that rating period by the length of the rental period.

Until the local authority make their first demand for, or for an instalment of, the rates for a rating period, the amount of the rates for any rental period is to be calculated on the basis that the rates for that rating period continue to be the same as for the previous rating period. When the local authority have made their first such demand or when they have made any subsequent demand during the rating period, the amount of the rates for any rental period must, if necessary, be recalculated, but any such recalculation cannot affect the ascertainment of rates for any rental period beginning more than six months before the date of service of the demand which gives rise to the recalculation.

FORM No. 9

RENT (SCOTLAND) ACTS 1971 AND 1972

Application for the registration of a rent unsupported by a certificate of fair rent where the dwellinghouse is or is to be let under a regulated tenancy (Note 1)

Date..

To the Rent Officer

Delete words
in square
brackets if
they do not
apply

[I,] [We, jointly, (Note 2)] hereby apply, under section 40 of the Rent (Scotland) Act 1971, for the registration of a fair rent for the dwellinghouse situated at ...., under a regulated tenancy.

    The rent which it is proposed should be registered for the dwellinghouse is £   per   (Note 3).

The following particulars are submitted.

Signed...
[Landlord/Landlord's agents]

....
[Tenant/Tenant's agents]

THE PARTICULARS

(*Please write in block letters or type and strike out words which do not apply*)

1. Name and address of landlord and of his agents (if any).

2. Name and address of tenant and of his agents (if any).

3. Description of the dwellinghouse (Note 4).

4. Current gross annual value of the dwellinghouse.

5. Rateable value of the dwellinghouse on 23rd March 1965 (or upon such later date as the rateable value of the dwellinghouse was first shown on the valuation roll) (Note 5).

6. If the tenancy has become a regulated tenancy by virtue of Part VI of the Rent (Scotland) Act 1971 (i.e. following upon the issue of a qualification certificate),

    (*a*) state the date upon which the tenancy became a regulated tenancy (Note 6) and

    (*b*) enclose a copy of the qualification certificate (Note 7).

7. If the tenancy has or is due to become a regulated tenancy under section 34 of the Housing (Financial Provisions) (Scotland) Act 1972, state the rateable value of the dwellinghouse on 27 August 1972 (Notes 5 and 8).

8. The rent at present payable is £   per   , exclusive/inclusive of rates borne by the landlord and, if inclusive, state the amount of the rates included in the rent.

9. State the particulars of the tenancy (Note 9).

10. State whether any change has occurred during the present tenancy in the condition of the dwellinghouse (Note 10) which is claimed by the applicant(s) to be due to

(a) any disrepair or other defect attributable to a failure by the tenant (including a former holder of the present tenancy) to comply with the terms of the tenancy, or

(b) any improvement, including the replacement of any fixture or fitting, carried out by the tenant (including a former holder of the present tenancy) other than under the terms of the tenancy.

11. State whether an improvement or standard grant has been obtained from the local authority.

12. If a rent has already been registered for the dwellinghouse, specify whichever is the later date

(i) the date upon which the registration took effect, or

(ii) where, upon an application for the registration of a different rent the registered rent has been confirmed, the date of that application (or the last of them),

and, if the application is made by the landlord or the tenant alone within 3 years of that date, state the grounds upon which the application is made (Note 11).

13. Specify the amount, if any, of the rent proposed to be registered which it is considered should be noted in the register as the amount fairly attributable to

(a) the use of part of the premises comprised in the dwellinghouse as a shop or office or for business trade or professional purposes;

(b) the use of furniture provided by the landlord; or

(c) the provision of any service by the landlord.

NOTES

(To be incorporated in the application and any copy thereof)

1. This form of application is required where

(a) the tenancy of the dwellinghouse

(1) is or has become converted into a regulated tenancy within the meaning of the Rent (Scotland) Act 1971 (referred to hereafter as "the Act of 1971") or

(2) is due to become a regulated tenancy under section 34 of the Housing (Financial Provisions) (Scotland) Act 1972 (referred to hereafter as "the Act of 1972") and the application is made not earlier than six months before the relevant date of conversion (Note 8) and

(b) either the landlord or the tenant or both the landlord and the tenant jointly wish to apply to the rent officer for the registration of a rent for the dwellinghouse under the regulated tenancy, and

(c) the application is not, nor is required to be (Note 7), supported by a certificate of fair rent.

An application for the registration of a rent cannot be entertained at a time when there is in operation, with respect to the dwellinghouse, a condition relating to rent imposed under any of the enactments specified in section 40(5) of the Act of 1971.

2. Where an application is made jointly by the landlord and the tenant, there is no right to have the matter referred to a rent assessment committee if the rent officer is satisfied that the rent proposed to be registered is a fair rent.

3. The rent specified should be a rent exclusive of any rates borne by the landlord but inclusive of any sums payable by the tenant for the use of furniture or for services provided by the landlord, (s. 43 of the Act of 1971).

4. The description of the dwellinghouse should include

    (*a*) the location of the flat, if the dwellinghouse is situated in tenement property;

    (*b*) the number of rooms comprised in the dwellinghouse and the use which is made of them;

    (*c*) any accommodation of which the tenant has shared use and state whether the sharing is with the landlord or with another tenant, and

    (*d*) a description of any part of the premises comprised in the dwellinghouse which is used as a shop or office or for business, trade, or professional purposes.

5. If, on the appropriate date, the dwellinghouse forms part only of lands and heritages for which a rateable value is then shown on the valuation roll, its rateable value is, by virtue of section 6 of the Act of 1971, taken to be such value as is found by the sheriff to be a proper apportionment of the rateable value so shown. Where paragraph 7 of the particulars applies, the proper apportionment of the rateable value may be determined, by virtue of section 34(5) of the Act of 1972, by agreement in writing between the landlord and tenant.

6. Under section 70 of the Act of 1971, the date upon which such a tenancy becomes a regulated tenancy is the date of issue of the qualification certificate, unless that certificate was issued under section 72(2) of that Act and its date of issue was before

    (*a*) 1st January 1971 in the case of a dwellinghouse of a rateable value of £45 or more on 25th August 1969 or

    (*b*) 1st July 1971 in the case of a dwellinghouse of a rateable value of less than £45 on 25th August 1969,

in which case it is the relevant date specified above.

7. It is only necessary to enclose a copy of the qualification certificate if it is an application by the landlord for the first registration of a rent after the tenancy has become a regulated tenancy (s. 74(1) of the Act of 1971).

After a certificate of fair rent has been issued on an application under Part I of Schedule 12 to the Act of 1971 (i.e. after the issue of a certificate of provisional approval), this form of application cannot be used and the appropriate form may be obtained from the rent officer.

8. Paragraph 7 of the particulars only applies if the tenancy of the dwellinghouse has been or is due to be converted from being a controlled tenancy into a regulated tenancy under section 34 of the Act of 1972. The date of conversion depends upon the rateable value of the dwellinghouse on 27 August 1972, as follows namely:—

Rateable value	Date of Conversion
£50 or more	1st January 1973
£25 or less than £50	1st January 1974
less than £25	1st January 1975

(The Secretary of State has power, by order, to advance or retard the relevant date of conversion)

9. The particulars of the tenancy which should be given are
- (i) the nature of the tenancy, that is whether it is a contractual/statutory tenancy;
- (ii) the date of commencement of the contractual/statutory tenancy;
- (iii) the duration of the contractual tenancy;
- (iv) the rental period;
- (v) any services or furniture provided by the landlord and the amount (if any) of the rent which is apportioned to them under the tenancy agreement;
- (vi) the respective liability of the landlord and tenant for the maintenance and repair of the dwellinghouse;
- (vii) any other terms of the tenancy (if these cannot be briefly stated, a copy of the tenancy agreement may be attached).

10. Any such changes in the condition of the dwellinghouse are required, by section 42(3) of the Act of 1971, to be disregarded in determining a fair rent for the dwellinghouse.

11. In these circumstances, section 40(3) of the Act of 1971 provides that the rent officer can only entertain the application on the grounds that "since that date, there has been such a change in the condition of the dwellinghouse (including the making of any improvement therein), the terms of the tenancy or any other circumstances taken into consideration when the rent was registered or confirmed as to make the registered rent no longer a fair rent".

FORM NO. 10

RENT (SCOTLAND) ACTS 1971 AND 1972

Application for the registration of a rent unsupported by a certificate of fair rent where the dwellinghouse is let under a tenancy to which sections 60 to 66 of the Housing (Financial Provisions) (Scotland) Act 1972 apply (Note 1)

Date.................................

To the Rent Officer

Delete words in square brackets if they do not apply
   [I,] [We, jointly, (Note 2)] hereby apply, under section 40 of the Rent (Scotland) Act 1971, as applied by section 61 of the Housing (Financial Provisions) (Scotland) Act 1972, for the registration of a fair rent for the dwellinghouse situated at ...., under a housing association tenancy (Note 1).

   The rent which it is proposed should be registered for the dwellinghouse is £...............per................................(Note 3).

   The following particulars are submitted.

Signed...
[Landlord/Landlord's agents]

....
[Tenant/Tenant's agents]

THE PARTICULARS

(*Please write in block letters or type and strike out words which do not apply*)

1. Name and address of landlord and of his agents (if any).

2. Name and address of tenant and of his agents (if any).

3. Description of the dwellinghouse (Note 4).

4. Current gross annual value of the dwellinghouse.

5. The rent at present payable is £   per exclusive/inclusive of rates borne by the landlord and, if inclusive, state the amount of the rates included in the rent.

6. State the particulars of tenancy (Note 5).

7. State whether any change has occurred during the present tenancy in the condition of the dwellinghouse (Note 6) which is claimed by the applicant(s) to be due to

   (*a*) any disrepair or other defect attributable to a failure by the tenant (including a former holder of the present tenancy) to comply with the terms of the tenancy, or

   (*b*) any improvement, including the replacement of any fixture or fitting, carried out by the tenant (including a former holder of the present tenancy) other than under the terms of the tenancy.

8. If a rent has already been registered for the dwellinghouse, specify whichever is the later date

(i) the date upon which the registration took effect (Note 7), or

(ii) where, upon an application for the registration of a different rent, the registered rent has been confirmed, the date of that application (or the last of them), and

if the application is made by the landlord or the tenant alone within 3 years of that date, state the grounds upon which the application is made (Note 8).

9. Specify the amount, if any, of the rent proposed to be registered which it is considered should be noted in the register as the amount fairly attributable to the provision of any furniture or any service by the landlord.

NOTES

(To be incorporated in the application and any copy thereof)

1. This form of application is required where

(a) the tenancy of the dwellinghouse is one to which sections 60 to 66 of the Housing (Financial Provisions) (Scotland) Act 1972 (referred to hereafter as "the Act of 1972") apply, that is a tenancy (referred to as "a housing association tenancy") where

(i) the interest of the landlord under that tenancy belongs to a housing association or to the Housing Corporation and

(ii) the tenancy would be a protected tenancy but for section 5 of the Rent (Scotland) Act 1971 (referred to hereafter as "the Act of 1971"); and

(b) either the landlord or the tenant or both the landlord and the tenant jointly wish to apply to the rent officer for the registration of a rent for the dwellinghouse under the tenancy, and

(c) the application is not supported by a certificate of fair rent.

The application for the registration of a rent cannot be entertained at a time when there is in operation, with respect to the dwellinghouse, a condition relating to rent imposed under any of the enactments specified in section 40(5) of the Act of 1971.

2. Where an application is made jointly by the landlord and the tenant, there is no right to have the matter referred to a rent assessment committee if the rent officer is satisfied that the rent proposed to be registered is a fair rent.

3. The rent specified should be a rent exclusive of any rates borne by the landlord but inclusive of any sums payable by the tenant for the use of furniture or for services provided by the landlord (s. 43 of the Act of 1971, as applied by section 61 of the Act of 1972).

4. The description of the dwellinghouse should include:

(a) the location of the flat if the dwellinghouse is situated in tenement property;

(b) the number of rooms comprised in the dwellinghouse and the use which is made of them; and

(c) any accommodation of which the tenant has shared use and state whether the sharing is with the landlord or with another tenant.

5. The particulars of the tenancy which should be given are:—

(i) the date of commencement and duration of the tenancy;

(ii) the rental period;

(iii) any services or furniture provided by the landlord and the amount (if any) of the rent which is apportioned to them under the tenancy agreement;

(iv) the respective liability of the landlord and tenant for the maintenance and repair of the dwellinghouse; and

(v) any other terms of the tenancy (if these cannot be briefly stated a copy of the tenancy agreement may be attached).

6. In determining what is a fair rent for the dwellinghouse, any such changes in the condition of the dwellinghouse are required to be disregarded (s. 42(3) of the Act of 1971, as applied by section 61 of the Act of 1972).

7. Section 61(3) of the Act of 1972 provides that the registration of a rent for a housing association tenancy takes effect on the date of registration. Where however the registration is, by virtue of section 64 of that Act, provisional (Note 9), it is provided that, for the purposes of this provision, a reference to the date upon which the registered rent took effect should be deemed to be a reference to the date of the provisional registration.

8. In these circumstances, section 40(3) of the Act of 1971, as applied by section 61 of the Act of 1972, provides that the rent officer can only entertain the application on the grounds that "since that date, there has been such a change in the condition of the dwellinghouse (including the making of any improvement therein), the terms of the tenancy or any other circumstances taken into consideration when the rent was registered or confirmed as to make the registered rent no longer a fair rent".

9. Section 61(3) of the Act of 1972 provides that the registration of a fair rent before 1st January 1973 is provisional only until that date.

Where the rent limit of the dwellinghouse immediately before the date of registration exceeds the rent registered, the registration is provisional only until it takes effect in accordance with section 64 of the Act of 1972.

FORM NO. 11

RENT (SCOTLAND) ACTS 1971 AND 1972

Application for a certificate of fair rent where the dwellinghouse is or is to be let under a regulated tenancy.

Date.................................

To the Rent Officer

I hereby apply under [section 41(1) of] [section 73(2) of and Part I of Schedule 12 to] the Rent (Scotland) Act 1971 (Note 1), for a certificate of fair rent specifying a fair rent under a regulated tenancy of the dwellinghouse [to be] situated at..[after the completion of the works shown in the plans and specifications which accompany this application (Note 2)] [after the completion of the works shown in the plans and specifications which accompanied the application for a qualification certificate. I enclose copies of these plans and specifications and also of the certificate of provisional approval (Note 3)].

Delete words in square brackets if they do not apply

I propose that the rent to be specified in the certificate of fair rent should be £   per   (Note 4).

The following particulars are submitted.

Signed...
Applicant/Applicant's agents

THE PARTICULARS

(*Please write in block letters or type and strike out words which do not apply*)

1. Name and address of applicant and of his agents, (if any).

2. If the dwellinghouse is not subject to a controlled tenancy, state the grounds upon which the application is made, that is whether the applicant is intending

(*a*) to provide a dwellinghouse by the erection or conversion of any premises,

(*b*) to make any improvements in the dwellinghouse, or

(*c*) to let on a regulated tenancy a dwellinghouse which is not at present subject to such a tenancy and, if a rent has been registered for such a dwellinghouse, specify whichever is the later date (Note 5)

(i) the date upon which the registration took effect or,

(ii) where, upon an application for the registration of a different rent, the last of them).

3. If the dwellinghouse is subject to a controlled tenancy or if the grounds of the application are as stated in paragraphs 2(*a*) or (*b*) above, give a brief description of the proposed works shown in the accompanying plans and specifications and state

(*a*) the estimated cost of the works and,

(*b*) whether an application has been or will be made to the local authority for an improvement or standard grant.

4. In the case of an existing dwellinghouse, give a brief description of the dwellinghouse (Note 6) and state

(*a*) its current gross annual value and,

(*b*) its rateable value on 23rd March 1965 (or upon such later date as its rateable value was first shown on the valuation roll).

5. Where the dwellinghouse is already subject to a regulated tenancy or to a controlled tenancy which is due to become a regulated tenancy on the date of issue of a qualification certificate, state

(*a*) the name of the tenant;

(*b*) the rent at present payable, £   per   exclusive/inclusive of rates borne by the landlord and, if inclusive, state the amount of rates included in the rent;

(*c*) the particulars of the tenancy (Note 7);

(*d*) whether any change has occurred during the present tenancy in the condition of the dwellinghouse (Note 8) which is claimed by the applicant to be due to

(i) any disrepair or other defect attributable to a failure by the tenant (including a former holder of the present tenancy) to comply with the terms of the tenancy or,

(ii) any improvement, including the replacement of any fixture or fitting carried out by the tenant (including a former holder of the present tenancy) other than under the terms of the tenancy.

6. Where paragraph 5 does not apply and it is proposed to grant a regulated tenancy, state (Note 9)

(*a*) the proposed duration of the tenancy;

(*b*) the proposed rental period;

(*c*) the proposed respective liability of the landlord and the tenant for the maintenance and repair of the dwellinghouse;

(*d*) any service or furniture to be provided by the landlord;

(*e*) whether the rates will be borne by the landlord, and

(*f*) any other terms (a separate sheet may be attached if necessary).

7. State the amount, if any, of the rent proposed to be specified in the certificate of fair rent which it is considered should be noted on the certificate of fair rent as the amount fairly attributable to:—

(*a*) the use of part of the premises comprised in the dwellinghouse as a shop or office or for business, trade or professional purposes;

(*b*) the use of furniture provided or to be provided by the landlord; and

(*c*) the provision of any service by the landlord.

NOTES

(To be incorporated in the application and any copy thereof)

1. The reference to section 73(2) of and Part I of Schedule 12 to the Rent (Scotland) Act 1971 (referred to hereafter as "the Act of 1971") is only required where—

(*a*) the application for a certificate of fair rent is made when the dwelling-house is subject to a controlled tenancy;

(*b*) an application for a qualification certificate has been made to the local authority; and

(*c*) the local authority have issued a certificate of provisional approval.

A certificate of fair rent which is issued in pursuance of such an application, specifies the rent which would be a fair rent under the regulated tenancy that might arise when a qualification certificate might be issued, if the works shown in the plans and specifications which accompanied the application for the qualification certificates were carried out.

2. These words are only required if the application is not made under section 73(2) of and Part I of Schedule 12 to the Act of 1971 and if the grounds of the application are as stated in paragraph 2(*a*) or (*b*) of the submitted particulars.

3. These words are required if the application is made under section 73(2) of and Part I of Schedule 12 to the Act of 1971 (Note 1).

4. The rent specified should be a rent exclusive of rates borne by the landlord but inclusive of any sums payable by the tenant for the use of furniture or for services provided or to be provided by the landlord (section 43 of the Act of 1971).

5. The application cannot be entertained until three years after the date (if any) which is specified.

6. The description of the dwellinghouse should include
   (*a*) the location of the flat, if the dwellinghouse is situated in tenement property;
   (*b*) the number of rooms comprised in the dwellinghouse and the use which is or is to be made of them;
   (*c*) any accommodation of which the tenant has or is to have shared use and state whether sharing is or is to be with the landlord or with another tenant and,
   (*d*) a description of any part of the premises comprised in the dwellinghouse which is used as a shop or office or for business, trade or professional purposes.

7. The particulars of the tenancy which should be given are:—
   (i) the nature of the tenancy, that is whether it is a contractual/statutory tenancy;
   (ii) the date of commencement of the contractual/statutory tenancy;
   (iii) the duration of the contractual tenancy;
   (iv) the rental period;
   (v) any services or furniture provided by the landlord and the amount (if any) of the rent which is apportioned to them under the tenancy agreement;
   (vi) the respective liability of the landlord and tenant for the maintenance and repair of the dwellinghouse; and
   (vii) any other terms of the tenancy (if these cannot be briefly stated, a copy of the tenancy agreement may be attached).

8. In determining what is a fair rent for the dwellinghouse, any such changes in the condition of the dwellinghouse are required to be disregarded (section 42(3) of the Act of 1971).

9. Except in so far as other terms are specified, it will be assumed that the tenant will be liable for internal decorative repairs but for no others and that no services or furniture will be provided for him.

FORM No. 12

RENT (SCOTLAND) ACTS 1971 AND 1972

Application for a certificate of fair rent where the dwellinghouse is, or is to be, let under a tenancy to which sections 60 to 66 of the Housing (Financial Provisions) (Scotland) Act 1972 apply (Note 1)

Date.....................................

To the Rent Officer

I hereby apply, under section 41(1) of the Rent (Scotland) Act 1971, as applied by section 61 of the Housing (Financial Provisions) (Scotland) Act 1972, for a certificate of fair rent specifying a fair rent under a housing association tenancy (Note 1) of the dwellinghouse [to be] situated at.....................................
[after the completion of the works shown in the plans and specifications which accompany this application (Note 2)].

Delete words in square brackets if they do not apply

I propose that the rent to be specified in the certificate of fair rent should be £   per   (Note 3).

The following particulars are submitted.

Signed ....
Applicant/Applicant's agents

THE PARTICULARS

(Please write in block letters or type and strike out words which do not apply)

1. Name and address of applicant and of his agents (if any).

2. State the grounds upon which the application is made, that is whether the applicant is intending
    (a) to provide a dwellinghouse by the erection or conversion of any premises,
    (b) to make any improvements in the dwellinghouse, or
    (c) to let on a housing association tenancy a dwellinghouse which is not at present subject to such a tenancy and, if a rent has been registered for such a dwellinghouse, specify whichever is the later date (Note 4)
        (i) the date upon which the registration took effect (Note 5), or
        (ii) where, upon an application for the registration of a different rent, the registered rent was confirmed, the date of that application (or the last of them).

3. If the grounds of the application are as stated in paragraphs 2(a) or (b) above, give a brief description of the proposed works shown in the accompanying plans and specifications and specify the estimated cost of the works.

4. In the case of an existing dwellinghouse, give a brief description of the dwellinghouse (Note 6) and state its current gross annual value.

5. Where the dwellinghouse is already subject to a housing association tenancy, state
    (a) the name of the tenant;
    (b) the rent at present payable, £   per   exclusive/inclusive of rates borne by the landlord, and, if inclusive, state the amount of rates included in the rent;

(c) the particulars of the tenancy (Note 7); and

(d) whether any change has occurred during the present tenancy in the condition of the dwellinghouse (Note 8) which is claimed by the applicant to be due to

    (i) any disrepair or other defect attributable to a failure by the tenant (including a former holder of the present tenancy) to comply with the terms of the tenancy or,

    (ii) any improvement, including the replacement of any fixture or fitting, carried out by the tenant (including a former holder of the present tenancy) other than under the terms of the tenancy.

6. Where paragraph 5 does not apply and it is proposed to grant a housing association tenancy, state (Note 9)

(a) the proposed duration of the tenancy;

(b) the proposed rental period;

(c) the proposed respective liability of the landlord and the tenant for the maintenance and repair of the dwellinghouse;

(d) any service or furniture to be provided by the landlord;

(e) whether the rates will be borne by the landlord; and

(f) any other terms (a separate sheet may be attached if necessary).

7. State the amount, if any, of the rent proposed to be specified in the certificate of fair rent which it is considered should be noted on the certificate of fair rent as the amount fairly attributable to any services or furniture provided or to be provided by the landlord.

Notes

(To be incorporated in the application and any copy thereof.)

1. A tenancy to which sections 60 to 66 of the Housing (Financial Provisions) (Scotland) Act 1972 (referred to hereafter as "the Act of 1972") apply is a tenancy (referred to as a "housing association tenancy") where

(a) the interest of the landlord under that tenancy belongs to a housing association or to the Housing Corporation; and

(b) the tenancy would be a protected tenancy but for section 5 of the Rent (Scotland) Act 1971 (referred to hereafter as "the Act of 1971").

2. These words are only required if the grounds of the application are as stated in paragraph 2(a) or (b) of the submitted particulars.

3. The rent specified should be a rent exclusive of rates borne by the landlord but inclusive of any sums payable by the tenant for the use of furniture or for services provided or to be provided by the landlord (section 43 of the Act of 1971).

4. The application cannot be entertained until three years after the date (if any) which is specified.

5. Section 61(3) of the Act of 1972 provides that the registration of a rent for a housing association tenancy takes effect on the date of registration. Where however the registration is, by virtue of section 64 of that Act, provisional, it is provided that, for the purposes of this provision, a reference to the date upon which the registered rent took effect should be deemed to be a reference to the date of the provisional registration.

6. The description of the dwellinghouse should include—

(*a*) the location of the flat, if the dwellinghouse is situated in tenement property;

(*b*) the number of rooms comprised in the dwellinghouse and the use which is, or is to be, made of them; and

(*c*) any accommodation of which the tenant has, or is to have, shared use and state whether sharing is or is to be with the landlord or with another tenant.

7. The particulars of the tenancy which should be given are—

(*a*) the date of commencement and duration of the tenancy;

(*b*) the rental period;

(*c*) any services or furniture provided by the landlord and the amount (if any) of the rent which is apportioned to them under the tenancy agreement;

(*d*) the respective liability of the landlord and tenant for the maintenance and repair of the dwellinghouse; and

(*e*) any other terms of the tenancy (if this cannot be briefly stated, a copy of the tenant's agreement may be attached).

8. In determining what is a fair rent for the dwellinghouse, any such changes in the condition of the dwellinghouse are required to be disregarded (section 42(3) of the Act of 1971).

9. Except in so far as other terms are specified, it will be assumed that the tenant will be liable for internal decorative repairs but for no others and that no services or furniture will be provided for him.

FORM NO. 13

RENT (SCOTLAND) ACTS 1971 AND 1972

Application for the registration of a rent, supported by a certificate of fair rent, where the dwellinghouse is or is to be let under a regulated tenancy.

Date.....................................

To the Rent Officer

I hereby apply, under section 41(4) [and section 74(1) (Note 1)] of the Rent (Scotland) Act 1971, for the registration of a rent for the dwellinghouse situated at...in accordance with the certificate of fair rent issued in repect of the dwellinghouse under a regulated tenancy on   (Note 2). I enclose a copy of the certificate of fair rent.

Delete words in square brackets if they do not apply

[I also enclose a copy of the qualification certificate (Note 1).]

The following particulars are submitted.

Signed ....
Applicant/Applicant's Agents

THE PARTICULARS

(*Please write in block letters or type and strike out words which do not apply*)

1. Name and address of applicant and of his agents (if any).

2. State the current gross annual value of the dwellinghouse.

3. If the dwellinghouse was not subject to a controlled or a regulated tenancy when the certificate of fair rent was issued, has a regulated tenancy now been granted (Note 3) and, if so, state—

    (*a*) the name of the tenant;

    (*b*) the date of commencement of the tenancy;

    (*c*) the duration of the tenancy and the rental period; and

    (*d*) whether the terms of the tenancy are shown as in the certificate of fair rent.

4. Where proposed works are specified in the certificate of fair rent,

    (*a*) have those works been carried out in accordance with the plans and specifications which accompanied the application for the certificate of fair rent; and

    (*b*) has an improvement or standard grant been obtained from the local authority.

5. Where proposed works are not specified in the certificate of fair rent, is the condition of the dwellinghouse the same as at the date of the certificate of fair rent.

6. Where any services or furniture are or are to be provided by the landlord, state the amount of the rent specified in the certificate of fair rent which the applicant considers is fairly attributable to such services or furniture, unless such amount is already noted on the certificate of fair rent.

NOTES

(To be incorporated in the application and any copy thereof)

1. The reference to section 74(1) of the Rent (Scotland) Act 1971 (referred to hereafter as "the Act of 1971") is only required where—

 (a) this is an application by the landlord for the first registration of a rent for the dwellinghouse after the tenancy has become a regulated tenancy following upon the issue of a qualification certificate; and

 (b) the certificate of fair rent has been issued on an application under Part I of Schedule 12 to that Act (i.e. after the issue of a certificate of provisional approval).

In these circumstances the application must be accompanied by a copy of the qualification certificate as well as by a copy of the certificate of fair rent and the procedure upon such applications is governed by Part II of Schedule 12 instead of by Part II of Schedule 6 to the Act of 1971.

2. Under section 41(4) of the Act of 1971, this application may only be made within three years of the date of the certificate of fair rent—

 (a) by the landlord under such a regulated tenancy of the dwellinghouse as is specified in the certificate; or

 (b) by a person intending to grant such a regulated tenancy.

An application for the registration of a rent cannot be entertained at a time when there is in operation, with respect to the dwellinghouse, a condition relating to rent imposed under any of the enactments specified in section 40(5) of the Act of 1971.

3. Under paragraph 13 of Schedule 6 to the Act of 1971, if a rent is registered in pursuance of this appication which is made by a person who intends to grant a regulated tenancy, the registration is provisional only until it is granted, and is of no effect unless the rent officer is notified, in the prescribed manner, within one month from the date of registration or such longer time as the rent officer may allow, that it has been granted.

Form No. 14

Rent (Scotland) Acts 1971 and 1972

Application for the registration of a rent, supported by a certificate of fair rent, where the dwellinghouse is or is to be let under a tenancy to which sections 60 to 66 of the Housing (Financial Provisions) (Scotland) Act 1972 apply (Note 1).

Date.....................................

To the Rent Officer

I hereby apply under section 41(4) of the Rent (Scotland) Act 1971, as applied by section 61 of the Housing (Financial Provisions) (Scotland) Act 1972, for the registration of a rent for the dwellinghouse situated at................................ ....in accordance with the certificate of fair rent issued in respect of the dwellinghouse under a housing association tenancy (Note 1) on ....(Note 2). I enclose a copy of the certificate of fair rent.

The following particulars are submitted.

Signed ....
Applicant/Applicant's Agents

Particulars

(*Please write in block letters or type and strike out words which do not apply*)

1. Name and address of applicant and of his agents (if any).

2. State the current gross annual value of the dwellinghouse.

3. If the dwellinghouse was not let on a housing association tenancy (Note 1) when the certificate of fair rent was issued, has such a tenancy now been granted (Note 3), and if so, state—

   (*a*) the name of the tenant;

   (*b*) the date of commencement of the tenancy;

   (*c*) the duration of the tenancy and the rental period; and

   (*d*) whether the terms of the tenancy are as shown in the certificate of fair rent.

4. Where proposed works are specified in the certificate of fair rent, have those works been carried out in accordance with the plans and specifications which accompanied the application for the certificate of fair rent.

5. Where proposed works are not specified in the certificate of fair rent, is the condition of the dwellinghouse the same as at the date of the certificate of fair rent.

Notes

(*To be incorporated in the application and any copy thereof*)

1. A tenancy to which sections 60 to 66 of the Housing (Financial Provisions) (Scotland) Act 1972 (referred to hereafter as "the Act of 1972") apply is a tenancy (referred to as "a housing association tenancy") where—

(*a*) the interest of the landlord under that tenancy belongs to a housing association or to the Housing Corporation; and

(*b*) the tenancy would be a protected tenancy but for section 5 of the Rent (Scotland) Act 1971 (referred to hereafter as "the Act of 1971")

2. Under section 41(4) of the Act of 1971, as applied by section 61 of the Act of 1972, this application may only be made within three years of the date of the certificate of fair rent—

(*a*) by the landlord under such a housing association tenancy of the dwelling-house as is specified in the certificate; or

(*b*) by a person intending to grant such a tenancy.

An application for the registration of a rent cannot be entertained at a time when there is in operation, with respect to the dwellinghouse, a condition relating to rent imposed under any of the enactments specified in section 40(5) of the Act of 1971, as applied by section 61 of the Act of 1972.

3. Under paragraph 13 of Schedule 6 to the Act of 1971, as applied by section 61 of the Act of 1972, if a rent is registered in pursuance of this application which is made by a person who intends to grant a housing association tenancy the registration is provisional only until it is granted and is of no effect unless the rent officer is notified, in the prescribed manner, within one month from the date of registration or such longer time as the rent officer may allow, that it has been granted.

4. Section 61(3) of the Act of 1972 provides that the registration of a fair rent before 1st January 1973 is provisional only until that date.

Where the rent limit of the dwellinghouse immediately before the date of registration exceeds the rent registered, the registration is provisional only until it takes effect in accordance with section 64 of the Act of 1972.

FORM NO. 15

RENT (SCOTLAND) ACTS 1971 AND 1972

Application for the cancellation of a registration.

Date.....................................

To the Rent Officer

We hereby jointly apply, under section 44A of the Rent (Scotland) Act 1971, for the cancellation of the rent registered for the dwellinghouse situated at.........
....

We enclose a copy of our rent agreement (Note 1).

The following particulars are submitted.

Signed   ....

Landlord/Landlord's Agents

....

Tenant/Tenant's Agents

PARTICULARS

(*Please write in block letters or type and strike out words which do not apply*)

1. Specify whichever is the later date (Note 2):—
   (*a*) the date upon which the registration took effect, or
   (*b*) where, upon an application for the registration of a different rent, the registered rent was confirmed, the date of that application (or the last of them).

2. Name and address of landlord and of his agents (if any).

3. Name and address of tenant and of his agents (if any).

4. Current gross annual value of the dwellinghouse.

5. State
   (*a*) whether any change has occurred in the condition of the dwellinghouse since the date of the registration and, if so,
   (*b*) whether any such change occurred during the present tenancy which is claimed to be due to
      (i) any disrepair or other defect attributable to a failure by the tenant (including a former holder of the present tenancy) to comply with the terms of the tenancy, or
      (ii) any improvement (including the replacement of any fixture or fitting), carried out by the tenant (including a former holder of the present tenancy) other than under the terms of the tenancy.

NOTES

(*To be incorporated in the application and any copy thereof*)

1. The application must be accompanied by a copy of the written rent agreement which has been made between the landlord and the tenant. A rent agreement is, by virtue of section 44A(9) of the Rent (Scotland) Act 1971, an agreement

increasing the rent payable under a contractual regulated tenancy or the grant of a new regulated tenancy at a rent higher than that under the previous regulated tenancy.

2. The application cannot be entertained until 3 years after the date which is specified.

Form No. 16

Rent (Scotland) Acts 1971 and 1972

Notice requiring further information to be given to a Rent Assessment Committee.

Date....................................

To

The application for the registration of a rent for the dwellinghouse situated at...under a [regulated tenancy] [tenancy to which sections 60 to 66 of the Housing (Financial Provisions) (Scotland) Act 1972 apply (Note 1)], which was made by.. on.., has been referred by the Rent Officer to this Rent Assessment Committee.

Delete words in square brackets if they do not apply

To enable the Committee to consider the matter referred to them they hereby, by virtue of paragraph 7(1)(*a*) of Schedule 6 to the Rent (Scotland) Act 1971, [as applied by section 61 of the Housing (Financial Provisions) (Scotland) Act 1972 (Note 2),] require you, the landlord/tenant of the dwellinghouse, to supply them, not later than.., with the following information:—

You should send this information to the Clerk of the Committee at the following address...

If you fail without reasonable cause to comply with this notice, paragraph 7(2) of the said Schedule 6, [as applied by the said section 61 (Note 2),] provides that you will be liable on summary conviction to a fine not exceeding £50 and, on a second or subsequent conviction to a fine not exceeding £100.

Signed ....
Clerk to the Committee

Notes

(*To be incorporated in the notice or any copy thereof*)

1. A tenancy to which sections 60 to 66 of the Housing (Financial Provisions) (Scotland) Act 1972 apply is a tenancy where

(*a*) the interest of the landlord under that tenancy belongs to a housing association or to the Housing Corporation; and

(*b*) the tenancy would be a protected tenancy but for section 5 of the Rent (Scotland) Act 1971.

2. These words are only required if the tenancy is one to which the said sections 60 to 66 apply (Note 1).

FORM NO. 17

RENT (SCOTLAND) ACTS 1971 AND 1972

Notice of grant of a regulated tenancy

Date...................................

To the Rent Officer

A rent was registered on..............................(Note) for the dwellinghouse situated at..and, by virtue of paragraph 13 of Schedule 6 to the Rent (Scotland) Act 1971, the registration is provisional only until a regulated tenancy is granted.

I hereby notify you that a regulated tenancy of the dwellinghouse has been granted to........................in accordance with the particulars entered in the register. The tenancy commenced on....................................

Signed   ....
Landlord/Landlord's Agents

Name and address of landlord and of his agents (if any)

....

....

....

NOTES

(To be incorporated in the notice and any copy thereof)

Where a rent is registered in pursuance of an application supported by a certificate of fair rent by a person who intends to grant a regulated tenancy, the registration is of no effect unless the rent officer is notified, within one month from the date of registration or such longer time as the rent officer may allow, that the regulated tenancy has been granted.

FORM NO. 18

RENT (SCOTLAND) ACTS 1971 and 1972

Notice of grant of a tenancy to which sections 60 to 66 of the Housing (Financial Provisions) Scotland) Act 1972 apply (Note 1)

Date...............................

To the Rent Officer

A rent was registered on........................(Note 2) for the dwellinghouse situated at...and by virtue of paragraph 13 of Schedule 6 to the Rent (Scotland) Act 1971, as applied by section 61 of the Housing (Financial Provisions) (Scotland) Act 1972, the registration is provisional only until a housing association tenancy (Note 1) is granted.

I hereby notify you that a housing association tenancy of the dwellinghouse has been granted to...in accordance with the particulars entered in the register. The tenancy commenced on.....................

Signed ....

Landlord/Landlord's Agents

Name and address of landlord and of his agents (if any)

....

....

....

NOTES

(To be incorporated in the notice and any copy thereof)

1. A tenancy to which sections 60 to 66 of the Housing (Financial Provisions) (Scotland) Act 1972 apply is a tenancy (referred to as "a housing association tenancy") where—

   (*a*) the interest of the landlord under that tenancy belongs to a housing association or to the Housing Corporation; and

   (*b*) the tenancy would be a protected tenancy but for section 5 of the Rent (Scotland) Act 1971.

2. Where a rent is registered in pursuance of an application supported by a certificate of fair rent by a person who intends to grant a housing association tenancy, the registration is of no effect unless the rent officer is notified, within one month from the date of registration or such longer time as the rent officer may allow, that the housing association tenancy has been granted.

FORM NO. 19

RENT (SCOTLAND) ACTS 1971 AND 1972

Application for a qualification certificate where the dwellinghouse is considered to satisfy the qualifying conditions (Note 1).

Date..

To   Town/County Council

I hereby apply, under section 71(1) of the Rent (Scotland) Act 1971, as amended (Note 1), for a qualification certificate in respect of the dwellinghouse situated

at...and declare that the dwellinghouse

        (i) is subject to a controlled tenancy (Note 2);

        (ii) is provided with all the standard amenities (Note 3);

        (iii) is in good repair (Note 4);

        (iv) meets the tolerable standard (Note 5).

Delete words in square brackets if they do not apply
    The name of the tenant is.................[and his address, if different from the address of the dwellinghouse, is......................................]. (Note 6).

Signed ....
Landlord/Landlord's Agents

Name and address of landlord and of his Agents (if any)

....
....
....

NOTES

(To be incorporated in the application and any copy thereof)

1. Under section 71(1) of the Rent (Scotland) Act 1971 (referred to hereafter as "the Act of 1971"), as amended by paragraph 2 of Schedule 7 to the Housing (Financial Provisions) (Scotland) Act 1972 (referred to hereafter as "the Act of 1972") an application for a qualification certificate may be made in respect of a dwellinghouse by a landlord under a controlled tenancy of the dwellinghouse, if he considers that the dwellinghouse satisfies the qualifying conditions.

The qualifying conditions are defined in section 70(4) of the Act of 1971 as meaning that the dwellinghouse:—

    (*a*) is provided with all the standard amenities (Note 3);

    (*b*) is in good repair (Note 4); and

    (*c*) meets the tolerable standard (Note 5).

2. A controlled tenancy is construed in accordance with section 7 of the Act of 1971. Generally speaking, a tenancy is controlled if

    (*a*) it is a protected or a statutory tenancy within the meaning of that Act;

    (*b*) the tenant has been in occupation of the dwellinghouse since before 6th July 1957 or has succeeded to the tenancy on the death of someone who had been a tenant on that date; and

    (*c*) the rateable value of the dwellinghouse on 7 November 1956 was £40 or less.

A controlled tenancy may already have been converted into a regulated tenancy

(a) if, upon the death of the original tenant and his first successor, the right to remain in occupation of the dwellinghouse has been passed on a second time or

(b) under section 34 of the Act of 1972.

3. The standard amenities are defined in section 39(1) of the Housing (Financial Provisions) (Scotland) Act 1968 as meaning the following amenities provided for the exclusive use of the occupants of the dwellinghouse:—

(a) a fixed bath or shower in a bathroom, or, if that is not reasonably practicable, in any part of the dwelling other than a bedroom;

(b) a wash-hand basin;

(c) a sink;

(d) a water closet;

(e) a hot and cold water supply at the fixed bath or shower, the wash-hand basin and the sink.

4. The dwellinghouse must be in good repair having regard to its age, character and locality and disregarding internal decorative repair.

5. The tolerable standard is defined in section 2 of the Housing (Scotland) Act 1969. In order to meet the tolerable standard, the dwellinghouse must:—

(a) be structurally stable;

(b) be substantially free from rising or penetrating damp;

(c) have satisfactory provision for natural and artificial lighting, for ventilation and for heating;

(d) have an adequate piped supply of wholesome water available within the house;

(e) have a sink provided with a satisfactory supply of both hot and cold water within the house;

(f) have a water closet—

(i) available for the exclusive use of the occupants of the house within the house or, where the house forms part of a building, within that building; and

(ii) readily accessible from, and suitably located, within the house or building, as the case may be;

(g) have an effective system for the drainage and disposal of foul and surface water;

(h) have satisfactory facilities for the cooking of food within the house; and

(i) have satisfactory access to all external doors and outbuildings.

(The Secretary of State may by order vary or extend the above criteria in such a way as to raise the tolerable standard).

6. A copy of this application will be sent by the local authority to the tenant who will be given an opportunity to make representations that the dwellinghouse does not satisfy the qualifying conditions.

Form No. 20

Rent (Scotland) Acts 1971 and 1972

Application for a qualification certificate where the dwellinghouse does not satisfy the qualifying conditions (Note 1).

Date................................

To   Town/County Council

1. I hereby apply, under section 71(2) of the Rent (Scotland) Act 1971, as amended (Note 1), for a qualification certificate in respect of the dwellinghouse situated at   .

Delete words in square brackets if they do not apply

2. The dwellinghouse is subject to a controlled tenancy (Note 2). The name of the tenant is   [and his address, if different from the address of the dwellinghouse, is   ] (Note 3).

3. The following works are required to be carried out to enable the dwellinghouse to satisfy the qualifying conditions (Note 4) and I enclose plans and specifications of those works (Note 5):—

4. State

    (*a*) whether any of the proposed works have begun to be carried out; and

    (*b*) whether an application for an improvement or a standard grant from the local authority has been or is to be made in respect of the cost of carrying out the proposed works (Note 6).

5. I declare that, apart from the proposed works, the dwellinghouse

    (*a*) is provided with all the standard amenities (Note 7);

    (*b*) is in good repair (Note 8); and

    (*c*) meets the tolerable standard (Note 9).

Signed   ....
                     Landlord/Landlord's Agents

Name and address of landlord and of his Agents (if any)

....
....
....

Notes

(To be incorporated in the application and any copy thereof)

1. Under section 71(2) of the Rent (Scotland) Act 1971 (referred to hereafter as "the Act of 1971"), as amended by paragraph 2 of Schedule 7 of the Housing (Financial Provisions) (Scotland) Act 1972 (referred to hereafter as "the Act of 1972"), an application for a qualification certificate may be made in respect of a dwellinghouse by a landlord under a controlled tenancy, even although at the time of the making of the application the dwellinghouse does not satisfy the qualifying conditions (Note 4).

2. A controlled tenancy is construed in accordance with section 7 of the Act of 1971. Generally speaking, a tenancy is controlled if

(a) it is a protected or a statutory tenancy within the meaning of that Act;

(b) the tenant has been in occupation of the dwellinghouse since before 6th July 1957 or has succeeded to the tenancy on the death of someone who had been a tenant on that date; and

(c) the rateable value of the dwellinghouse on 7 November 1956 was £40 or less.

A controlled tenancy may already have been converted into a regulated tenancy

(a) if, upon the death of the original tenant and his first successor, the right to remain in occupation of the dwellinghouse has been passed on a second time or

(b) under section 34 of the Act of 1972.

3. A copy of this application will be sent by the local authority to the tenant, whose attention is drawn to Note 10 below.

4. The qualifying conditions are defined under section 70(4) of the Act of 1971 as meaning that the dwellinghouse

(a) is provided with all the standard amenities (Note 7);

(b) is in good repair (Note 8); and

(c) meets the tolerable standard (Note 9).

5. If it appears to the local authority that the dwellinghouse will satisfy the qualifying conditions when the works specified in the application have been carried out, they will issue a certificate of provisional approval. If the local authority refuse to issue such a certificate, they will send the applicant a written statement of their reasons for the refusal. The applicant may then appeal to the sheriff on the ground that the certificate of provisional approval should be issued.

Where the works required to enable the dwellinghouse to satisfy the qualifying conditions cannot be carried out without the consent of the tenant and the tenant is unwilling to give his consent, then, if the tenancy is a statutory tenancy and those works are specified in this application and a certificate of provisional approval is issued, section 80 of the Act of 1971, as amended, provides that the landlord may apply to the sheriff for an order empowering him to enter and carry out the works.

6. This application may be made as part of or in conjunction with an application for an improvement or a standard grant.

7. The standard amenities are defined in section 39(1) of the Housing (Financial Provisions) (Scotland) Act 1968 as meaning the following amenities provided for the exclusive use of the occupants of the dwellinghouse:—

(a) a fixed bath or shower in a bathroom, or, if that is not reasonably practicable, in any part of the dwelling other than a bedroom;

(b) a wash-hand basin;

(c) a sink;

(d) a water closet;

(e) a hot and cold water supply at the fixed bath or shower, the wash-hand basin and the sink.

8. The dwellinghouse must be in good repair having regard to its age, character and locality and disregarding internal decorative repair.

9. The tolerable standard is defined in section 2 of the Housing (Scotland) Act 1969. In order to meet the tolerable standard, the dwellinghouse must:—

(*a*) be structurally stable;

(*b*) be substantially free from rising or penetrating damp;

(*c*) have satisfactory provision for natural and artificial lighting, for ventilation and for heating;

(*d*) have an adequate piped supply of wholesome water available within the house;

(*e*) have a sink provided with a satisfactory supply of both hot and cold water within the house;

(*f*) have a water closet—

(i) available for the exclusive use of the occupants of the house within the house, or where the house forms part of a building, within that building; and

(ii) readily asscessible from, and suitably located, within the house or building as the case may be;

(*g*) have an effective system for the drainage and disposal of foul and surface water;

(*h*) have satisfactory facilities for the cooking of food within the house; and

(*i*) have satisfactory access to all external doors and outbuildings.

(The Secretary of State may, by order, vary or extend the above criteria in such a way as to raise the tolerable standard.)

10. The following information is drawn to the attention of the tenant:—

(*a*) If it appears to the local authority that the dwellinghouse will satisfy the qualifying conditions (Note 4) when the works specified in this application have been carried out, they will issue a certificate of provisional approval. The tenant may appeal to the sheriff to have any such certificate quashed.

(*b*) After the works specified in this application have been carried out, then, if the local authority are satisfied that the dwellinghouse satisfies the qualifying conditions, they will issue a qualification certificate. The tenant may again appeal to the sheriff to have this certificate quashed.

(*c*) On the date of issue of a qualification certificate, the tenancy will be converted into a regulated tenancy.

(*d*) The right of the tenant to stay on in the dwellinghouse will not be affected by the conversion, but, when the tenancy becomes regulated, an application may be made to the rent officer for the registration of a fair rent for the dwellinghouse.

(*e*) If an application is made by the landlord for the registration of a rent, he will specify a rent which he proposes should be registered. Whatever the rent proposed by the landlord, the rent officer will, however, only register a fair rent for the dwellinghouse. The tenant will be given the opportunity to make representations against the registration of the rent proposed by the landlord and, if the tenant does so, the rent officer will give him the further opportunity of considering in consultation with him and the landlord the amount of the rent which should be registered.

(*f*) If a fair rent is registered which is higher than the rent at present payable by the tenant, any increase is payable in annual instalments.

(*g*) As an alternative to obtaining the registration of a rent, the tenant may, after the tenancy has become a regulated tenancy and after 1st January 1973, agree a rent to be paid with the landlord. Any such agreement must, however, be in writing and can only come into effect after the rent officer has been consulted to ensure that the agreed rent does not exceed a fair rent for the dwellinghouse.

(*h*) Further information is given in the booklets entitled "House Improvements and Rents" and "Controlled Tenancies—Conversion to Regulated Tenancies", which you may obtain from the local authority or from the rent officer.

FORM NO. 21

RENT (SCOTLAND) ACTS 1971 AND 1972

Notice by local authority to a tenant under section 72(1) of the Rent (Scotland) Act
1971

To   Date...................................

Delete words   1. An application for a qualification certificate in respect of the dwellinghouse
in square   situated at   has been made to the
brackets if   Town/County Council by [on behalf of]   , the landlord
they do not   of the dwellinghouse.
apply.

2. A copy of the application is attached and is sent to you as the person named
in it as being the tenant of the dwellinghouse under a controlled tenancy.

3. Before the Council can issue a qualification certificate, they must be satisfied
that the dwellinghouse satisfies the following conditions (known as "the qualifying conditions"), namely that the dwellinghouse

(*a*) must be provided with all the standard amenities (Note 1);

(*b*) must be in good repair (Note 2); and

(*c*) must meet the tolerable standard (Note 3).

4. You may, within 28 days from the service of this notice, make representations to the Council that the dwellinghouse does not satisfy the qualifying
conditions. You may send any written representations to—

5. The Council will consider any representations made by you before deciding
whether or not the dwellinghouse satisfies the qualifying conditions. A copy of
their decision will be sent to you and, if they issue a qualification certificate,
you may appeal to the sheriff.

6. The following information as to the effect of the issue of a qualification
certificate is drawn to your attention:—

(*a*) On the date of issue of a qualification certificate, your tenancy will
be converted into a regulated tenancy.

(*b*) Your right to stay on in the dwellinghouse is not affected by the conversion, but, when the tenancy becomes regulated, an application may be
made to the rent officer for the registration of a fair rent for the dwellinghouse.

(*c*) If an application is made by the landlord for the registration of a rent,
he will specify a rent which he proposes should be registered. Whatever
the rent proposed by the landlord, the rent officer will, however, only
register a fair rent for the dwellinghouse. You will be given the opportunity to make representations against the registration of the rent proposed by the landlord and, if you do, the rent officer will give you the
further opportunity of considering in consultation with him and the landlord, the amount of rent which should be registered.

(*d*) If a fair rent is registered which is higher than the rent at present payable
by you, any increase is payable in annual instalments.

(*e*) As an alternative to obtaining the registration of a rent, you may,
after the tenancy has become a regulated tenancy and after 1 January
1973, agree a rent to be paid with the landlord. Any such agreement
must however be in writing and can only come into effect if the rent officer

has been consulted to ensure that the agreed rent does not exceed a fair rent for the dwellinghouse.

(*f*) Further information is given in the booklets entitled "House Improvements and Rents" and "Controlled Tenancies—Conversion to Regulated Tenancies," which you may obtain from the local authority or from the rent officer.

Signed...

Clerk to the Council

NOTES

(To be incorporated in the notice and any copy thereof)

1. The standard amenities are defined in section 39(1) of the Housing (Financial Provisions) (Scotland) Act 1968 as meaning the following amenities provided for the exclusive use of the occupants of the dwellinghouse:—

(*a*) a fixed bath or shower in a bathroom, or, if that is not reasonably practicable, in any part of the dwellinghouse other than a bedroom;

(*b*) a wash-hand basin;

(*c*) a sink;

(*d*) a water closet;

(*e*) a hot and cold water supply at the fixed bath or shower, the wash-hand basin and the sink.

2. The dwellinghouse must be in good repair having regard to its age, character and locality and disregarding internal decorative repair.

3. The tolerable standard is defined in section 2 of the Housing (Scotland) Act 1969. In order to meet the tolerable standard, the dwellinghouse must:—

(*a*) be structurally stable;

(*b*) be substantially free from rising or penetrating damp;

(*c*) have satisfactory provision for natural and artificial lighting, for ventilation and for heating;

(*d*) have an adequate piped supply of wholesome water available within the house;

(*e*) have a sink provided with a satisfactory supply of both hot and cold water within the house;

(*f*) have a water closet—

    (i) available for the exclusive use of the occupants of the house within the house or, where the house forms part of a building, within that building; and

    (ii) readily accessible from, and suitably located, within the house or building as the case may be;

(*g*) have an effective system for the drainage and disposal of foul and surface water;

(*h*) have satisfactory facilities for the cooking of food within the house; and

(*i*) have satisfactory access to all external doors and outbuildings.

(The Secretary of State may by order vary or extend these criteria in such a way as to raise the tolerable standard.)

FORM NO. 22

RENT (SCOTLAND) ACTS 1971 AND 1972

Qualification certificate where application was made when the dwellinghouse is considered to satisfy the qualifying conditions

Date....................................

To...

The...........................Town/County Council have considered your application under section 71(1) of the Rent (Scotland) Act 1971 (as amended) for a qualification certificate in respect of the dwellinghouse situated at................. [and the representations made by the tenant under the controlled tenancy of the dwellinghouse].

Delete words in square brackets if they do not apply

This is to certify that the Council are satisfied that the dwellinghouse satisfies the qualifying conditions mentioned in section 70 of that Act.

Your attention is drawn to Note 1 below.

A copy of this qualification certificate is being sent to the tenant, who may appeal to the sheriff (Note 2).

Signed ....
Clerk to the Council

NOTES

(To be incorporated in the certificate and any copy thereof)

1. On the date of issue of the qualification certificate the controlled tenancy of the dwellinghouse is converted into a regulated tenancy (unless the tenancy has otherwise become a regulated tenancy or has ceased to exist).

The first application by the landlord to the rent officer for the registration of a fair rent for the dwellinghouse must be accompanied by a copy of this certificate.

2. The tenant may appeal to the Sheriff, within twenty eight days of the service upon him by the local authority of a copy of this certificate (or such longer period as the sheriff may allow) on either or both of the following grounds:—

(*a*) that the certificate ought not to have been issued;

(*b*) that the certificate is invalid by reason of a failure to comply with any of the requirements of Part VI of the Rent (Scotland) Act, 1971 or of some informality, defect or error.

The sheriff may confirm or quash the certificate but, if the appeal is on ground (*b*) above, the sheriff is required to confirm the certificate unless he is satisfied that the interests of the tenant have been substantially prejudiced by the facts relied on by him.

Form No. 23

Rent (Scotland) Acts 1971 and 1972

Notice of refusal of a qualification certificate where application was made when the dwellinghouse is considered to satisfy the qualification conditions.

Date....................................

To..

The......................................Town/County Council have considered your application under section 71(1) of the Rent (Scotland) Act 1971 (as amended) for a qualification certificate in respect of the dwellinghouse situated at............ ....[and the representations made by the tenant under the controlled tenancy of the dwellinghouse].

Delete words in square brackets if they do not apply

The Council are not satisfied that the dwellinghouse satisfies the qualifying conditions mentioned in section 70 of that Act, for the following reasons:—

This notice is accordingly sent of the Council's refusal of your application.

You may appeal to the sheriff, within twenty eight days of the service of this notice (or such longer period as the sheriff may allow), on the grounds that the qualification certificate ought to be issued. On any such appeal, the sheriff may confirm the refusal or order the Council to issue the certificate.

A copy of this notice of refusal is being sent to the tenant.

Signed...
Clerk to the Council

FORM No. 24

RENT (SCOTLAND) ACTS 1971 AND 1972

Certificate of provisional approval.

Date.................................

To...

The.............................Town/County Council have considered your application under section 71(2) of the Rent (Scotland) Act 1971 (as amended) for a qualification certificate in respect of the dwellinghouse situated at.................
....

It appears to the Council that the dwellinghouse will satisfy the qualifying conditions mentioned in section 70 of the Act, when the works specified in the application have been carried out.

This is to certify that the Council have accordingly approved your application provisionally.

Your attention is drawn to Notes 1 to 3 below.

A copy of this certificate of provisional approval is being sent to the tenant who may appeal to the sheriff (Note 4).

Signed ....

Clerk to the Council

NOTES

(To be incorporated in the certificate and any copy thereof)

1. After the works specified in the application for a qualification certificate have been carried out, the local authority is required to issue the qualification certificate if they are satisfied that the dwellinghouse satisfies the qualifying conditions.

If at the time the qualification certificate is issued, the state of the dwellinghouse differs in any respect from that which, at the time the application for the certificate was made, it could be expected to be in when the works specified in the application have been carried out, the local authority will specify those differences in the certificate.

2. On the date of issue of a qualification certificate, the controlled tenancy of the dwellinghouse will become converted into a regulated tenancy. An application may then be made to the Rent Officer for the registration of a fair rent for the dwellinghouse.

The applicant for a qualification certificate may, after he has obtained this certificate of provisional approval, apply to the Rent Officer for a certificate of fair rent for the dwellinghouse which will specify the rent which would be a fair rent under the regulated tenancy that might arise if a qualification certificate was issued. A copy of this certificate of provisional approval and of the plans and specifications which accompanied the application for a qualification certificate must accompany an application for a certificate of fair rent.

3. Where the works required to enable the dwellinghouse to satisfy the qualifying conditions cannot be carried out without the consent of the tenant and the tenant is unwilling to give his consent, then, if the tenancy is a statutory tenancy and those works were specified in an application for a qualification certificate and a certificate of provisional approval has been issued, section 80 of the Rent

(Scotland) Act 1971, as amended, provides that the landlord may apply to the sheriff for an order empowering him to enter and carry out the works.

4. The tenant may appeal to the sheriff, within twenty eight days of the service upon him by the local authority of a copy of this certificate (or such longer period as the sheriff may allow) on either or both of the following grounds:

(*a*) that the certificate ought not to have been issued;

(*b*) that the certificate is invalid by reason of a failure to comply with any of the requirements of Part VI of the Rent (Scotland) Act 1971 or of some informality, defect or error.

The sheriff may confirm or quash the certificate but, if the appeal is on ground (*b*) above, the sheriff is required to confirm this certificate unless he is satisfied that the interests of the tenant have been substantially prejudiced by the facts relied on by him.

FORM NO. 25

RENT (SCOTLAND) ACTS 1971 AND 1972

Notice of refusal of a certificate of provisional approval

Date....................................

To..

The.................................Town/County Council have considered your application under section 71(2) of the Rent (Scotland) Act 1971 (as amended) for a qualification certificate in respect of the dwellinghouse situated at............

....

It does not appear to the Council that the dwellinghouse will satisfy the qualifying conditions mentioned in section 70 of that Act when the works specified in the application have been carried out, for the following reasons:—

This notice is accordingly sent of the Council's refusal to issue a certificate of provisional approval.

You may appeal to the sheriff, within twenty eight days of the service of this notice (or such longer period as the sheriff may allow) on the ground that the certificate of provisional approval ought to be issued. On any such appeal, the sheriff may confirm the refusal or order the Council to issue the certificate.

A copy of this notice of refusal is being sent to the tenant.

Signed...
Clerk to the Council

FORM NO. 26

RENT (SCOTLAND) ACTS 1971 AND 1972

Qualification certificate where application was made when dwellinghouse did not satisfy the qualifying conditions.

Date...................................

To...

With reference to your application under section 71(2) of the Rent (Scotland) Act 1971 (as amended) for a qualification certificate in respect of the dwelling-house situated at....................................and to the certificate of provisional approval issued on................................, the.............................. Town/County Council are satisfied that the works specified in the application have been carried out and hereby certify that they are satisfied that the dwelling-house satisfies the qualifying conditions mentioned in section 70 of that Act.

Your attention is drawn to Note 1 below.

[The state of the dwellinghouse differs from the state which at the time the application was made, the dwellinghouse could be expected to be in when the works specified in the application had been carried out. The differences are as follows:] Delete words in square brackets if they do not apply

A copy of this qualification certificate is being sent to the tenant who may appeal to the sheriff (Note 2).

Signed..

Clerk to the Council

NOTES

(To be incorporated in the certificate and any copy thereof)

1. On the date of issue of the qualification certificate, the controlled tenancy of the dwellinghouse is converted into a regulated tenancy (unless the tenancy has otherwise become a regulated tenancy or has ceased to exist).

The first application by the landlord to the rent officer for the registration of a fair rent for the dwellinghouse must be accompanied by a copy of this certificate and also by the copy of the certificate of fair rent, if one has been obtained after the issue of the certificate of provisional approval.

2. The tenant may appeal to the sheriff, within twenty eight days of the service upon him by the local authority of a copy of this certificate (or such longer period as the sheriff may allow) on either or both of the following grounds:

  (*a*) that the certificate ought not to have been issued;

  (*b*) that the certificate is invalid by reason of a failure to comply with any of the requirements of Part VI of the Rent (Scotland) Act 1971 or of some informality, defect or error.

The sheriff may confirm or quash the certificate but, if the appeal is on ground (*b*) above, the sheriff is required to confirm this certificate unless he is satisfied that the interests of the tenant have been substantially prejudiced by the facts relied on by him.

FORM NO. 27

RENT (SCOTLAND) ACTS 1971 AND 1972

Notice of refusal of a qualification certificate where application was made when the dwellinghouse did not satisfy the qualifying conditions.

Date....................................

To...

With reference to your application under section 71(2) of the Rent (Scotland) Act 1971 (as amended) for a qualification certificate in respect of the dwelling-house situated at...and to the certificate of provisional approval issued on..................................., the........................ Town/County Council are not satisfied that the dwellinghouse satisfies the qualifying conditions for the following reasons:—

This notice is accordingly sent of the Council's refusal of your application.

You may appeal to the sheriff within twenty eight days of the service of this notice (or such longer period as the sheriff may allow) on the ground that the qualification certificate ought to be issued. On such appeal, the sheriff may confirm the refusal or order the Council to issue the certificate.

A copy of this notice of refusal is being sent to the tenant.

Signed...
Clerk to the Council

EXPLANATORY NOTE

(This Note is not part of the Regulations)

These regulations supersede the Rent Regulation (Forms etc.) (Scotland) Regulations 1969 and the Rent Regulation (Forms etc.) (Scotland) (Amendment) Regulations 1969, which are revoked by Regulation 3.

Regulation 4 and Schedule 1 prescribe the particulars of a tenancy which a rent officer is required to enter in the register when he registers a rent for a dwelling-house.

Regulation 5 and Schedule 2 prescribe the particulars which are required to be contained in a rent agreement in pursuance of section 43(5)(*a*) of the Housing (Financial Provisions) (Scotland) Act 1972.

Regulation 6 and Schedule 3 prescribe the forms, or forms as near thereto as circumstances admit, which are to be used for the purposes of the Rent (Scotland) Act 1971 and the Housing (Financial Provisions) (Scotland) Act 1972 in the cases where those forms are applicable.

Forms Nos 1 to 8 of Schedule 3 are those to be used in certain cases where a landlord increases the rent under a regulated tenancy. Forms Nos 9 to 18 of Schedule 3 are those to be used in connection with applications for the registration of a rent or for a certificate of fair rent under a regulated tenancy or under a tenancy to which sections 60 to 66 of the Housing (Financial Provisions) (Scotland) Act 1972 apply. Forms Nos 19 to 27 of Schedule 3 are those to be used by landlords of controlled tenancies applying for a qualification certificate under Part VI of the Rent (Scotland) Act 1971 and by local authorities in connection with such applications.

Regulation 7 prescribes a fee of 12p which is required to be paid to the rent officer to obtain a certified copy of an entry in the register or of a rent agreement.

STATUTORY INSTRUMENTS

1972 No. 1222

PENSIONS

The Pensions Increase (Approved Schemes) (National Health Service) Regulations 1972

Made - - - -	*8th August* 1972
Laid before Parliament	*16th August* 1972
Coming into Operation	*9th September* 1972

The Secretary of State for Social Services in exercise of his powers under section 13(2), (4) and (5) and Schedule 6 to the Pensions (Increase) Act 1971(a) and of all other powers enabling him in that behalf, with the approval of the Minister for the Civil Service, hereby makes the following regulations:—

Citation and commencement

1. These regulations may be cited as the Pensions Increase (Approved Schemes) (National Health Service) Regulations 1972 and shall come into operation on 9th September 1972.

Interpretation

2.—(1) In these regulations, unless the context otherwise requires—

"the Act of 1971" means the Pensions (Increase) Act 1971 as amended by sections 25 and 29 of, and schedules 6 and 8 to, the Superannuation Act 1972 **(b)**;

"average remuneration", in relation to a person, means the annual average of his remuneration as it would have been calculated if he had been superannuable under the Regulations in respect of his reckonable service;

"dependant", in relation to a woman, means a person who is to the satisfaction of the Secretary of State wholly or mainly supported by that woman and who either has not attained the age of 16 years or is receiving full-time instruction at an educational establishment or is undergoing training for a trade, profession or vocation in such circumstances that he is required to devote the whole of his time to that training for a period of not less than two years;

(a) 1971 c. 56.   (b) 1972 c. 11.

"employing authority" means an authority which is, or is deemed to be, an employing authority for the purposes of the Regulations;

"reckonable service", in relation to a person, has the meaning assigned to it by the schedule to these regulations;

"superannuation scheme" means the Federated Superannuation System for Universities, the Federated Superannuation Scheme for Nurses and Hospital Officers and any other scheme approved by the Minister for the Civil Service for the purposes of section 13(2)(*b*) of the Act of 1971;

"superannuable under the Regulations", in relation to a person, means entitled to participate in the superannuation benefits provided by the Regulations (other than regulations 43 and 45);

"the Regulations" means the National Health Service (Superannuation) Regulations 1961**(a)** as amended**(b)**; and

"the Secretary of State" means the Secretary of State for Social Services.

(2) The Interpretation Act 1889**(c)** shall apply to the interpretation of these regulations as it applies to the interpretation of an Act of Parliament.

(3) In these regulations, unless the context otherwise requires, references to any enactment or regulations shall be construed as references to that enactment or those regulations as amended or extended by any other enactment or regulations, or to the provisions of that enactment or those regulations as continued by any other enactment or regulations, or to that enactment or those regulations as deemed to have been made under any other enactment or regulations.

Application of these regulations

3. These regulations shall apply for the payment to persons described in regulation 4 hereof of the amounts described in regulation 6.

Persons to whom these regulations apply

4.—(1) These regulations shall apply to any person who—

(*a*) has ceased to be employed by an employing authority; and

(*b*) immediately before ceasing to be so employed—

(i) was subject to a superannuation scheme; and

(ii) had completed the minimum period of reckonable service and had satisfied any other requirements which would qualify a person for a pension under the Regulations either—

(A) immediately upon ceasing such employment; or

(B) subsequently upon reaching such age as is specified in the Regulations, and

(*c*) has received or has become entitled to receive payment of any retirement benefit under a superannuation scheme; and

---

(a) S.I. 1961/1441 (1961 II, p. 2824).   (b) S.I. 1966/1523 (1966 III, p. 4309).
(c) 1889 c. 63.

(*d*) either—

    (i) has attained the age of 60 years or the minimum age provided for by an order made under section 3(8) of the Act of 1971 and, in the case of a person to whom paragraph (1)(*b*)(ii)(B) of this regulation applies, has attained the age referred to therein; or

    (ii) has retired on account of physical or mental infirmity, or has satisfied the Secretary of State that he is disabled by physical or mental infirmity; or

    (iii) is a woman who has at least one dependant.

(2) Notwithstanding the provisions of paragraph (1)(*a*) and (*b*) of this regulation, in the case of a person to whom paragraph (1)(*b*)(ii)(B) of this regulation applies and who, within 12 months of ceasing to be employed by an employing authority, enters into any of the employments mentioned in paragraph 2 of the schedule to these regulations in respect of which the requirements of paragraph 3(*a*) of that schedule have been fulfilled, these regulations shall apply only in respect of any further termination of employment under an employing authority and not in respect of any previous termination.

Notional pension and lump sum

5.—(1) There shall be ascribed to each person to whom these regulations apply a notional pension calculated on the following basis—

    (*a*) for each year of reckonable service, one eightieth of his average remuneration; and

    (*b*) for any additional fraction of a year of reckonable service which exceeds 6 months, one one hundred and sixtieth of his average remuneration.

(2) Where a person is receiving a supplementary payment under regulation 46(3) of the Regulations (which provides for supplementary payments in the case of certain officers), the amount of his notional pension shall be reduced by such amount as the Secretary of State may determine as representing that part of the supplementary payment which is referable to employment under an employing authority on and after 5th July 1948.

(3) Where the amount of a notional pension ascribed to any person does not exceed £26 a year, these regulations shall not apply to him unless he is receiving a supplementary payment as referred to in paragraph (2) of this regulation.

(4) In calculating a notional pension in respect of a person to whom a notional pension was ascribed under the Pensions Increase (Approved Schemes) (National Health Service) Regulations 1968(**a**), as amended (**b**), any fraction of a pound shall be treated as a whole pound.

(5) Where a person to whom these regulations apply leaves employment in circumstances in which, if the Regulations had applied, he would have been awarded a lump sum retiring allowance which he would not have become entitled to receive until he

    (*a*) attained such age as is specified in the Regulations; or

    (*b*) became permanently incapacitated before attaining that age,

there shall be ascribed to him a notional lump sum retiring allowance calculated on the following basis—

    (i) for each year of reckonable service, three eightieths of his average remuneration; and

---

(**a**) S.I. 1968/1285 (1968 II, p. 3603)   (**b**) S.I. 1969/1447 (1969 III, p. 4678).

(ii) for any additional fraction of a year of reckonable service which exceeds 6 months, three one hundred and sixtieths of his average remuneration.

Payments of benefits equivalent to statutory pension increases

6. The Secretary of State shall, in respect of any period beginning on or after 1st September 1971, pay to a person to whom these regulations apply amounts equal to the benefits which would have been conferred on him by the Act of 1971 if—

(*a*) he had been eligible under the principal civil service pension scheme within the meaning of section 2 of the Superannuation Act 1972 for a pension of the same amount as his notional pension as calculated under paragraphs (1) to (4) of regulation 5 of these regulations, or a lump sum of the same amount as his notional lump sum retiring allowance as calculated under paragraph (5) of regulation 5 of these regulations, or both such pension and lump sum as the case may be, beginning on the day after the last day of his reckonable service; and

(*b*) any allowance which, but for the Act of 1971, would have been paid to him under the Pensions Increase (Approved Schemes) (National Health Service) Regulations 1968, as amended, were a relevant increase within the meaning of section 6(10) of that Act.

SCHEDULE

Regulations 2(1) and 4(2)

Meaning of reckonable service

1. Subject to the provisions of this schedule, a person's reckonable service shall be a period equivalent to the aggregate of any periods of employment which—

(*a*) have been spent in any employment described in paragraph 2 of this schedule; and

(*b*) have become reckonable under a superannuation scheme as described in paragraph 3 of this schedule.

2. The employments to which paragraph 1 of this schedule relates are—

(i) employment under an employing authority, or an authority which was, or was deemed to be, an employing authority for the purposes of the National Health Service (Superannuation) (Scotland) Regulations 1961**(a)**;

(ii) employment in which the person was subject to any regulations or scheme made under section 2 of the Local Government (Superannuation) Act (Northern Ireland) 1950**(b)** section 67 of and schedule 8 to the Health Services Act (Northern Ireland) 1971**(c)** or section 54 of the National Health Service (Isle of Man) Act 1948 (an Act of Tynwald);

(iii) employment in the civil service of the State;

(iv) employment under an employing authority or a local Act authority within the meaning of section 1(3) of the Local Government Superannuation Act 1937**(d)** or section 1(6) of the Local Government Superannuation (Scotland) Act 1937**(e)**; and

---

(**a**) S.I. 1961/1398 (1961 II, p. 2697). (**b**) 1950 c. 10. (NI)
(**c**) 1971 c. 1. (NI) (**d**) 1937 c 68.
(**e**) 1937 c. 69.

(v) employment by a county or district nursing association during any period when a local health authority had arrangements with, or paid contributions to, that association under Part III of the National Health Service Act 1946(a) or Part III of the National Health Service (Scotland) Act 1947(b) or section 10 of the Health Services and Public Health Act 1968(c).

3. For the purposes of paragraph 1 of this schedule a period of employment shall be deemed to have become reckonable under a superannuation scheme if—

(a) during such period the person was subject to a superannuation scheme and the contributions authorised or required to be paid by the employer were duly paid; or

(b) such period was taken into account in calculating a sum in the nature of a transfer value paid to that scheme under the Regulations or any corresponding provision in force in Scotland, Northern Ireland or the Isle of Man or under rules made under section 2 of the Superannuation (Miscellaneous Provisions) Act 1948(d):

Provided that—

(i) so much of any period referred to in sub-paragraph (b) as consisted of non-contributing service shall be reckonable under this paragraph at half its actual length, and

(ii) so much of any such period as consisted of part-time service shall be reckonable under this paragraph as though it were whole-time service for a proportionately reduced period.

4. For the purposes of regulation 4(1)(b)(ii) of these regulations, there may be added to the service described in paragraph 1 of this schedule any period of previous service which would have been reckonable under regulation 22 of the Regulations (which provides for the reckoning of qualifying service in certain cases) or any corresponding provision in force in Scotland, Northern Ireland or the Isle of Man.

5. For the purposes of paragraph 3(a) of this schedule no account shall be taken of any period of employment preceding a break of 12 months or more during which the person was not in employment described in paragraph 2 hereof.

Keith Joseph,
Secretary of State for Social Services.

8th August 1972.

Approval of the Minister for the Civil Service given under his Official Seal on 8th August 1972.

(L.S.)

A. W. Wyatt,
Authorised by the Minister for the Civil Service.

(a) 1946 c. 81.   (b) 1947 c. 27.
(c) 1968 c. 46.   (d) 1948 c. 33.

EXPLANATORY NOTE

(This Note is not part of the Regulations.)

These Regulations provide for payments to certain persons who retire from employment in the National Health Service having elected to secure their superannuation benefits through schemes which operate by way of insurance policies to produce lump sums or annuities, or both, upon retirement, and who would have been eligible for increases under the Pensions (Increase) Act 1971 had they been pensionable under the National Health Service superannuation scheme.

The relevant schemes are the Federated Superannuation System for Universities, the Federated Superannuation Scheme for Nurses and Hospital Officers and any other scheme approved for this purpose by the Minister for the Civil Service.

The conditions of entitlement combine, with necessary modification, those for a health service pension and those for increases under the Pensions (Increase) Act 1971. The principal conditions are that the person—

    (i) completed the necessary qualifying service in health service or local government employment or certain types of related employment or the civil service;

    (ii) would have been entitled to receive payment of a pension had he been subject to the health service scheme up to the date of his retirement; and

    (iii) has attained the age of 60 years, or any earlier age prescribed under section 3(8) of the Pensions (Increase) Act 1971, or is incapacitated, or is a woman who has a dependant.

The payments are based on a notional pension and, where appropriate, a notional lump sum (defined in regulation 5) corresponding broadly to the pension and any deferred lump sum the person would have received if he had been in the health service scheme and entitled to reckon under that scheme certain service during which he was within the Federated Superannuation Scheme for Nurses and Hospital Officers, the Federated Superannuation System for Universities or any other approved scheme.

In accordance with the power conferred by section 13(5) of the Pensions (Increase) Act 1971, the Regulations provide for the payments to take effect from 1st September 1971.

STATUTORY INSTRUMENTS

1972 No. 1223

WAGES COUNCILS

The Wages Regulation (Lace Finishing) Order 1972

Made - - -	*8th August* 1972
Coming into Operation	*30th August* 1972

Whereas the Secretary of State has received from the Lace Finishing Wages Council (Great Britain) the wages regulation proposals set out in the Schedule hereto;

Now, therefore, the Secretary of State in exercise of his powers under section 11 of the Wages Councils Act 1959(**a**), and of all other powers enabling him in that behalf, hereby makes the following Order:—

1. This Order may be cited as the Wages Regulation (Lace Finishing) Order 1972.

2.—(1) In this Order the expression "the specified date" means the 30th August 1972, provided that where, as respects any worker who is paid wages at intervals not exceeding seven days, that date does not correspond with the beginning of the period for which the wages are paid, the expression "the specified date" means, as respects that worker, the beginning of the next such period following that date.

(2) The Interpretation Act 1889(**b**) shall apply to the interpretation of this Order as it applies to the interpretation of an Act of Parliament and as if this Order and the Order hereby revoked were Acts of Parliament.

3. The wages regulation proposals set out in the Schedule hereto shall have effect as from the specified date and as from that date the Wages Regulation (Lace Finishing) Order 1970(**c**) shall cease to have effect.

Signed by order of the Secretary of State.
8th August 1972.

> *R. R. D. McIntosh,*
> Deputy Secretary,
> Department of Employment.

(**a**) 1959 c. 69. (**b**) 1889 c. 63.
(**c**) S.I. 1970/1129 (1970 II, p. 3612).

SCHEDULE

The following minimum remuneration shall be substituted for the statutory minimum remuneration fixed by the Wages Regulation (Lace Finishing) Order 1970 (Order L. (32)).

STATUTORY MINIMUM REMUNERATION
PART I
GENERAL

1. The minimum remuneration payable to a worker to whom this Schedule applies for all work except work to which a minimum overtime rate applies under Part IV of this Schedule shall be—

(1) in the case of a time worker, the general minimum time rate payable to the worker under Part II of this Schedule;

(2) in the case of a worker (other than a homeworker) employed on piece work, piece rates each of which would yield, in the circumstances of the case, to an ordinary piece worker, at least the same amount as the general minimum time rate which would be applicable to the worker if she were a time worker aged 18 years or over;

(3) in the case of a home worker

    (*a*) where a general minimum piece rate applies under Part III of this Schedule, that rate:

        Provided that no such piece rate shall apply where, before the work is started, it is agreed between the employer and the worker that special difficulty is occasioned as a result of the processing of the yarn or of any technical process of manufacture or finish;

    (*b*) where no general minimum piece rate applies, piece rates each of which would yield, in the circumstances of the case, to an ordinary piece worker, at least *25p* per hour:

        Provided that where the worker fetches her own work from the warehouse and does not receive it through a middlewoman or middleman, the appropriate rates under (*a*) or (*b*) of this sub-paragraph shall be increased by 5 per cent in the case of hair nets and by 15 per cent in the case of all other work.

2. This Schedule applies to female workers (not being middlewomen) in relation to whom the Lace Finishing Wages Council (Great Britain) operates namely workers employed in Great Britain in the branch of the lace trade specified in the Trade Boards (Lace Finishing Trade, Great Britain) (Constitution and Proceedings) Regulations, 1931**(a)**, that is to say:—

That branch of the lace trade which is engaged in machine-made lace and net finishing, other than the finishing of the produce of plain net machines but including the finishing of hair nets, veilings and quillings whether made on plain net or other machines.

PART II
GENERAL MINIMUM TIME RATES

3. The general minimum time rates payable to workers employed on time work are as follows:—

	Per hour p
Workers aged 18 years or over	*30*
Workers aged 17 years and under 18 years	*25*
Workers aged under 17 years	*22½*

(a) S.R. & O. 1931/841 (1931, p. 1355).

Provided that in the case of workers who enter or have entered the trade for the first time at or over the age of 17 years 9 months the general minimum time rate payable during the first three months of employment shall be *25p* per hour.

PART III

GENERAL MINIMUM PIECE RATES FOR HOMEWORKERS DRAWING AND ROVING

4. The general minimum piece rates payable to homeworkers for hand-drawing and hand-roving by traditional methods of Leavers laces and Raschel laces with Leavers type draw threads are as follows:—

	Per gross yards p
(1) One thread drawing (up to and including 12 ties of the draw thread per inch)	12
(2) One thread drawing (over 12 ties of the draw thread per inch)	14
(3) Two thread drawing	19
(4) For each thread over two	5
(5) Roving irrespective of number of threads (payable in addition to the drawing prices)	1½

Provided that where the lace is black lace the said rates shall be increased by *one-tenth*.

PART IV

OVERTIME AND WAITING TIME

MINIMUM OVERTIME RATES

5. Minimum overtime rates are payable to any worker whose place of work is under the control or management of the employer or of a middlewoman or middleman, as follows:—

(1) On a Sunday, for all time worked   ...   .   Double time

(2) In any week for all time worked in excess of 40 hours, exclusive of Sunday ...   .   Time-and-a-quarter

6. In this Part of this Schedule, the expressions "time-and-a-quarter" and "double time" mean respectively

(1) in the case of a time worker, one and a quarter times and twice the general minimum time rate otherwise payable to the worker;

(2) in the case of a worker employed on piece work,

(*a*) the piece rates otherwise payable to the worker, and, in addition thereto,

(*b*) one quarter and the whole respectively of the general minimum time rate that would be payable if the worker were a time worker.

WAITING TIME

7.—(1) A worker is entitled to payment of the minimum remuneration specified in this Schedule for all time during which she is present on the premises of her employer, unless she is present thereon in any of the following circumstances:—

(*a*) without the employer's consent, express or implied,

(*b*) for some purpose unconnected with her work and other than that of waiting for work to be given to her to perform,

(c) by reason only of the fact that she is resident thereon,

(d) during normal meal times in a room or place in which no work is being done, and she is not waiting for work to be given to her to perform.

(2) The minimum remuneration payable under sub-paragraph (1) of this paragraph to a piece worker when not engaged on piece work is that which would be payable if she were a time worker.

EXPLANATORY NOTE

(This Note is not part of the Order.)

This Order, which has effect from 30th August 1972, sets out the statutory minimum remuneration payable in substitution for that fixed by the Wages Regulation (Lace Finishing) Order 1970 (Order L. (32)), which Order is revoked.

New provisions are printed in italics.

STATUTORY INSTRUMENTS

1972 No. 1224

WAGES COUNCILS

The Wages Regulation (Lace Finishing) (Holidays) Order 1972

Made - - -		*8th August* 1972
Coming into Operation		*30th August* 1972

Whereas the Secretary of State has received from the Lace Finishing Wages Council (Great Britain) (hereafter in this Order referred to as the "Wages Council") the wages regulation proposals set out in the Schedule hereto;

Now, therefore, the Secretary of State in exercise of his powers under section 11 of the Wages Councils Act 1959(a), and of all other powers enabling him in that behalf, hereby makes the following Order: —

1. This Order may be cited as the Wages Regulation (Lace Finishing) (Holidays) Order 1972.

2.—(1) In this Order the expression "the specified date" means the 30th August 1972, provided that where, as respects any worker who is paid wages at intervals not exceeding seven days, that date does not correspond with the beginning of the period for which the wages are paid, the expression "the specified date" means, as respects that worker, the beginning of the next such period following that date.

(2) The Interpretation Act 1889(b) shall apply to the interpretation of this Order as it applies to the interpretation of an Act of Parliament and as if this Order and the Order hereby revoked were Acts of Parliament.

3. The wages regulation proposals set out in the Schedule hereto shall have effect as from the specified date and as from that date the Wages Regulation (Lace Finishing) (Holidays) Order 1970(c) shall cease to have effect.

Signed by order of the Secretary of State.
8th August 1972.

R. R. D. McIntosh,
Deputy Secretary,
Department of Employment.

(a) 1959 c. 69.   (b) 1889 c. 63.
(c) S.I. 1970/1130 (1970 II, p. 3616).

Article 3

SCHEDULE

The following provisions as to holidays and holiday remuneration shall be substituted for the provisions as to holidays and holiday remuneration set out in the Wages Regulation (Lace Finishing) (Holidays) Order 1970 (hereinafter referred to as "Order L. (33)").

PART I

APPLICATION

1. This Schedule applies only to those workers for whom statutory minimum remuneration has been fixed who work in premises under the control or management of the employer.

PART II

CUSTOMARY HOLIDAYS

2.—(1) An employer shall allow to every worker in his employment to whom this Schedule applies a holiday (in this Schedule referred to as a "customary holiday") in each year on the days specified in the next following sub-paragraph provided that the worker has been in his employment for a period of not less than one week immediately preceding the customary holiday.

(2) The said customary holidays are:—

(a) Christmas Day (or, if Christmas Day falls on a Sunday, such week-day as may be appointed by national proclamation, or, if none is so appointed, the next following Tuesday), Boxing Day, Good Friday, Easter Monday, *the last Monday in May and the last Monday in August (or when another day is substituted by national proclamation for either of the said days in May or August, that day)*; or

(b) in the case of each of the said days, a day substituted therefor being a day recognised by local custom as a day of holiday in substitution for the said day.

(3) *Where Christmas Day or Boxing Day (or any day substituted for any of these days under the provisions of (b) of sub-paragraph (2) of this paragraph) falls on a Saturday, the employer shall allow to a worker who normally works on each week-day except Saturday, a holiday on a day on which the worker normally works for the employer before 6th April immediately following the customary holiday;*

Provided that a worker shall not be entitled to a holiday in pursuance of this sub-paragraph:—

(i) *if she is not qualified under sub-paragraph (1) of this paragraph to be allowed the customary holiday;*

or (ii) *if she has been allowed a day of holiday (not being a customary holiday or a day of annual holiday) on a day on which she would normally work for the employer before the customary holiday and has been paid for that holiday not less than the amount to which she would have been entitled had the day been a customary holiday allowed to her under sub-paragraph (1) of this paragraph.*

PART III

ANNUAL HOLIDAY

3.—(1) Subject to the provisions of paragraph 4, in addition to the holidays specified in Part II of this Schedule an employer shall between the date on which this Schedule becomes effective and 30th September 1972, and in each succeeding year between

6th April and 30th September allow a holiday (hereinafter referred to as an "annual holiday") to every worker in his employment to whom this Schedule applies who has been employed by him during the 12 months immediately preceding the commencement of the holiday season for any of the periods of employment (calculated in accordance with the provisions of paragraph 10) set out in the appropriate column of the table below and the duration of the annual holiday shall, in the case of each such worker, be related to her period of employment during that 12 months as follows:—

Period of employment	Duration of Annual holiday for workers with a normal working week of—			
	five days or more	four days	three days	two days
At least 48 weeks	15 days	12 days	9 days	6 days
,, ,, 44 ,,	13 ,,	11 ,,	8 ,,	5 ,,
,, ,, 40 ,,	12 ,,	10 ,,	7 ,,	5 ,,
,, ,, 36 ,,	11 ,,	9 ,,	6 ,,	4 ,,
,, ,, 32 ,,	10 ,,	8 ,,	6 ,,	4 ,,
,, ,, 28 ,,	8 ,,	7 ,,	5 ,,	3 ,,
,, ,, 24 ,,	7 ,,	6 ,,	4 ,,	3 ,,
,, ,, 20 ,,	6 ,,	5 ,,	3 ,,	2 ,,
,, ,, 16 ,,	5 ,,	4 ,,	3 ,,	2 ,,
,, ,, 12 ,,	3 ,,	3 ,,	2 ,,	1 day
,, ,, 8 ,,	2 ,,	2 ,,	1 day	1 ,,

(2) Where in any holiday season a worker does not wish to take during the holiday season days of holiday not exceeding twice the number of days constituting her normal working week being all or part of the annual holiday for which she has qualified under this paragraph and before the expiration of such holiday season enters into an agreement in writing with her employer that such days of annual holiday shall be allowed, at a date or dates to be specified in that agreement, after the expiration of the holiday season but before the 6th April in the following year, then any day or days of annual holiday so allowed shall be treated as having been allowed during the holiday season.

(3) The duration of the worker's annual holiday in the holiday season ending on 30th September 1972, shall be reduced by any days of annual holiday duly allowed to her by the employer under the provisions of Order L.(33) between 6th April 1972, and the date on which the provisions of this Schedule become effective.

(4) In this Schedule the expression "holiday season" means in any year, the period commencing on 6th April and ending on 30th September of the same year.

4.—(1) Subject to the provisions of this paragraph, an annual holiday under this Schedule shall be allowed on consecutive working days and days of holiday shall be treated as consecutive notwithstanding that a day of holiday allowed to a worker under Part II of this Schedule or a day upon which she does not normally work for the employer intervenes.

(2)(a) Where the number of days of annual holiday for which a worker has qualified exceeds the number of days constituting her normal working week, but does not exceed twice that number, the holiday may be allowed in two periods of consecutive working days; so however that when a holiday is so allowed, one of the periods shall consist of a number of such days not less than the number of days constituting the worker's normal working week.

(b) Where the number of days of annual holiday for which a worker has qualified exceeds twice the number of days constituting her normal working week the holiday may be allowed as follows:—

(i) as to the period comprising twice the number of days constituting the worker's normal working week, in accordance with sub-paragraph (a) of this paragraph; and

    (ii) as to any additional days, on working days which need not be consecutive, to be fixed by the employer after consultation with the worker, either during the holiday season or before the beginning of the next following holiday season.

(3) Where a day of holiday allowed to a worker under Part II of this Schedule immediately precedes a period of annual holiday or occurs during such a period then, notwithstanding the foregoing provisions of this paragraph, the duration of that period of annual holiday may be reduced by one day and in such a case one day of annual holiday may be allowed on any working day in the holiday season, or by agreement between the employer and the worker on any working day before the beginning of the next following holiday season.

5. An employer shall give to a worker reasonable notice of the commencement date or dates and of the duration of her annual holiday. Such notice may be given individually to the worker or by the posting of a notice in the place where the worker is employed.

PART IV

HOLIDAY REMUNERATION

CUSTOMARY HOLIDAYS

6.—(1) Subject to the provisions of this paragraph, for each day of holiday to which a worker is entitled under Part II of this Schedule she shall be paid by the employer as holiday remuneration an amount equal to the sum which would be payable to her by the employer if that day were not a holiday and she worked thereon the number of hours normally worked by her (exclusive of overtime) on that day of the week and if she were paid at the agreed minimum hourly rate payable to her under her contract of employment immediately before the holiday or where in the case of a piece worker no such rate is payable, one day's holiday pay (as defined in paragraph 11).

(2) Holiday remuneration in respect of any customary holiday shall be paid by the employer to the worker on the pay-day on which the wages for the first working day following the customary holiday are paid.

ANNUAL HOLIDAY

7.—(1) Subject to the provisions of paragraph 8, a worker qualified to be allowed an annual holiday under this Schedule shall be paid as holiday remuneration by her employer on the last pay-day preceding such annual holiday—

    (a) in respect of days of annual holiday not exceeding twice the number of days constituting the worker's normal working week, whichever of the following is the greater:—

        (i) an amount equal to one twenty-sixth of the total remuneration paid by the employer to the worker during the twelve months ended on 5th April immediately preceding the commencement of the holiday season; or

        (ii) one day's holiday pay (as defined in paragraph 11) in respect of each day of annual holiday; and

    (b) in respect of any additional days of annual holiday in accordance with the provisions of paragraph 6(1) of this Schedule.

(2) Where, under the provisions of paragraphs 3 and 4, an annual holiday is allowed in more than one period, the holiday remuneration shall be apportioned accordingly.

8. Where under the provisions of paragraph 9 of this Schedule or of Order L.(33) any accrued holiday remuneration has been paid by the employer to the worker, in respect of employment during either of the periods referred to in that paragraph or that Order, the amount of holiday remuneration payable by the employer in respect of any annual holiday for which the worker has qualified by reason of employment during the said period shall be reduced by the amount of the said accrued holiday remuneration unless that remuneration has been deducted from a previous payment of holiday remuneration made under the provisions of this Schedule or of Order L.(33).

ACCRUED HOLIDAY REMUNERATION PAYABLE ON TERMINATION OF EMPLOYMENT

9. Where a worker ceases to be employed by an employer after the provisions of this Schedule becomes effective, the employer shall, immediately on the termination of the employment (hereinafter called "the termination date"), pay to the worker as accrued holiday remuneration:—

(1) in respect of employment in the 12 months up to and including 5th April immediately preceding the termination date, a sum equal to the holiday remuneration for any days of annual holiday for which she has qualified except days of annual holiday which she has been allowed or has become entitled to be allowed before leaving the employment; and

(2) in respect of any employment since 5th April immediately preceding the termination date, an amount equal to the holiday remuneration which would have been payable to her if she could have been allowed an annual holiday in respect of that employment at the time of leaving it.

Part V

GENERAL

10. For the purposes of calculating any period of employment qualifying a worker for an annual holiday, the worker shall be treated as if she were employed for a week in respect of any week in which—

(1) she has worked for the employer for not less than 10 hours and has performed some work for which statutory minimum remuneration is payable; or

(2) she has performed no work for the employer solely by reason of the proved illness of, or accident to, the worker or otherwise by permission of the employer:

Provided that the number of weeks which may be treated as weeks of employment for such reasons shall not exceed 13 in the aggregate in any such period; or

(3) she was absent on a holiday allowed under the provisions of this Schedule.

11. In this Schedule, unless the context otherwise requires, the following expressions have the meanings hereby respectively assigned to them, that is to say:—

"NORMAL WORKING WEEK" means the number of days on which it has been usual for the worker to work in a week in the employment of the employer in the twelve months immediately preceding the commencement of the holiday season:

Provided that—

(a) part of a day shall count as a day;

(b) no account shall be taken of any week in which the worker did not perform any work for which statutory minimum remuneration has been fixed.

"ONE DAY'S HOLIDAY PAY" means the appropriate proportion of the remuneration which the worker would be entitled to receive from her employer at the date of the annual holiday for one week's work if working her normal working week and the number of daily hours normally worked by her (exclusive of overtime) and if paid as a time worker at the appropriate rate of statutory minimum remuneration for work for which statutory minimum remuneration is payable and at the same rate for any work for which such remuneration is not payable, and in this definition "appropriate proportion" means—

where the worker's normal working week is five days ...	...	one-fifth
where the worker's normal working week is four days ...	...	one-quarter
where the worker's normal working week is three days	...	one-third
where the worker's normal working week is two days ...	...	one-half.

"STATUTORY MINIMUM REMUNERATION" means minimum remuneration (other than holiday remuneration) fixed by a wages regulation order.

"TOTAL REMUNERATION" means any payments paid or payable to the worker under her contract of employment for time worked or piece work done by her, holiday remuneration, any productivity, long service, or other bonus payable to the worker on a weekly, fortnightly or monthly basis and merit payments so payable but does not include any other payments.

"WEEK" (except in Part II) means "pay week".

12. The provisions of this Schedule are without prejudice to any agreement for the allowance of any further holidays with pay or for the payment of additional holiday remuneration.

EXPLANATORY NOTE

(This Note is not part of the Order.)

This Order, which has effect from 30th August 1972, sets out the holidays which an employer is required to allow to workers and the remuneration payable for those holidays in substitution for the holidays and holiday remuneration fixed by the Wages Regulation (Lace Finishing) (Holidays) Order 1970 (Order L. (33)), which Order is revoked.

New provisions are printed in italics.

STATUTORY INSTRUMENTS

1972 No. 1225 (C.27)

MEDICINES

The Medicines Act 1968 (Commencement No. 2) Order 1972

Made - - - *8th August* 1972

The Secretaries of State respectively concerned with health in England and Wales, the Secretary of State concerned with health and with agriculture in Scotland, the Secretary of State for Northern Ireland, and the Minister of Agriculture, Fisheries and Food acting jointly, in exercise of their powers under section 136(3) of the Medicines Act 1968(**a**), (as having effect subject to the provisions or Article 2(2) of, and Schedule 1 to, the Transfer of Functions (Wales) Order 1969(**b**) and section 1(1)(*a*) of the Northern Ireland (Temporary Provisions) Act 1972(**c**)) and of all other powers enabling them in that behalf, after consulting such organisations as appear to them to be representative of interests likely to be substantially affected by the following order, hereby make the following order:—

1. The day appointed for the coming into operation of the following provisions of the Medicines Act 1968, that is to say, sections 85(5), 86(3), 93 and 97, shall be 1st September 1972.

2. This Order may be cited as the Medicines Act 1968 (Commencement No. 2) Order 1972.

Keith Joseph,
Secretary of State for Social Services.

3rd August 1972.

Peter Thomas,
Secretary of State for Wales.

7th August 1972.

Gordon Campbell,
Secretary of State for Scotland.

8th August 1972.

W. S. I. Whitelaw,
Secretary of State for Northern Ireland.

7th August 1972.

In witness whereof the official seal of the Minister of Agriculture, Fisheries and Food is hereunto affixed on 4th August 1972.

(L.S.)

J. M. L. Prior,
Minister of Agriculture, Fisheries and Food.

(**a**) 1968 c. 67.   (**b**) S.I. 1969/388 (1969 I, p. 1070).   (**c**) 1972 c. 22.

EXPLANATORY NOTE

(This Note is not part of the Order.)

This Order brings into operation on 1st September 1972 four provisions of the Medicines Act 1968. These are section 85(5) which prohibits the sale, supply or possession for sale or supply, of medicinal products that are in containers or packages which have false or misleading labels or markings; section 86(3) which prohibits the supply with medicinal products, or possession for such supply, of false or misleading leaflets relating to the medicinal products (under section 91(1) of the Medicines Act 1968 any contravention of those sections is an offence); section 93 which makes it an offence to issue or cause to be issued any false or misleading advertisements or representations relating to medicinal products and section 97 which gives power to the licensing authority to require copies of advertisements relating to medicinal products.

STATUTORY INSTRUMENTS

1972 No. 1226

MEDICINES

The Medicines (Standard Provisions for Licences and Certificates) Amendment Regulations 1972

Made - - -	8th *August* 1972
Laid before Parliament	16th *August* 1972
Coming into Operation	31st *August* 1972

The Secretaries of State respectively concerned with health in England and in Wales, the Secretary of State concerned with health and with agriculture in Scotland, the Secretary of State for Northern Ireland and the Minister of Agriculture, Fisheries and Food, acting jointly, in exercise of their powers under section 47(1) of the Medicines Act 1968(**a**) (as having effect subject to the provisions of Article 2(2) of, and Schedule 1 to, the Transfer of Functions (Wales) Order 1969(**b**) and section 1(1)(*a*) of the Northern Ireland (Temporary Provisions) Act 1972(**c**)) and of all other powers enabling them in that behalf, after consulting such organisations as appear to them to be representative of interests likely to be substantially affected by the following regulations, hereby make the following regulations:—

Citation, interpretation and commencement

1. These regulations, which may be cited as the Medicines (Standard Provisions for Licences and Certificates) Amendment Regulations 1972, shall be read as one with the Medicines (Standard Provisions for Licences and Certificates) Regulations 1971(**d**) (hereinafter referred to as "the principal regulations") and shall come into operation on 31st August 1972.

Amendment of regulation 2(1) of the principal regulations

2. Regulation 2(1) of the principal regulations (definitions) shall be amended by adding immediately before the definition of "medicinal product", the following definition : —

" 'licence holder' and 'certificate holder' shall be construed in the same manner as the holder of a licence or certificate is required to be construed under section 132(4) of the Act;".

Amendment of Part II of Schedule 1 to the principal regulations

3. In Part II of Schedule 1 to the principal regulations (standard provisions for clinical trial certificates) immediately after paragraph 3 there shall be added the following paragraphs : —

(**a**) 1968 c. 67. (**b**) S.I. 1969/388 (1969 I, p. 1070).
(**c**) 1972 c. 22. (**d**) S.I. 1971/972 (1971 II, p. 2809).

"4. The clinical trial in respect of which the clinical trial certificate has been issued shall be carried out in accordance with the outline of the clinical trial contained in the application for that certificate subject to any changes thereto which the licensing authority may from time to time approve.

5.—(1) The medicinal product to which the clinical trial certificate relates shall be administered only by or under the direction of a doctor or dentist named in the application for that certificate or by or under the direction of a doctor or dentist approved by the licensing authority for this purpose.

(2) Where the medicinal product to which the clinical trial certificate relates is to be administered by or under the direction of a doctor or dentist who has not been named in the application for that certificate or where it is intended that there shall be a change of the doctor or dentist so named, the certificate holder shall seek the approval of the licensing authority and for this purpose shall notify the licensing authority in writing of the name, address and qualifications of the doctor or dentist in question.

(3) In the event of any doctor or dentist ceasing to participate in the clinical trial in respect of which the clinical trial certificate has been issued, the certificate holder shall as soon as is reasonably possible inform the licensing authority and shall give the reason for such cessation.

6. Before any administration of the medicinal product to which the clinical trial certificate relates takes place, the certificate holder shall communicate the provisions of that certificate to each and every doctor or dentist who, in the course of the clinical trial in respect of which that certificate has been issued, is to administer or to direct the administration of that medicinal product.".

Amendment of Part III of Schedule 1 to the principal regulations

4. In Part III of Schedule 1 to the principal regulations (standard provisions for animal test certificates) immediately after paragraph 6 there shall be added the following paragraphs: —

"7. The medicinal test on animals in respect of which the animal test certificate has been issued shall be carried out in accordance with the outline of the medicinal test on animals contained in the application for that certificate subject to any changes thereto which the licensing authority may from time to time approve.

8.—(1) The medicinal product to which the animal test certificate relates shall be administered only by, or under the direction of, the person named in the application for that certificate as the person by whom it was proposed that the medicinal test on animals should be carried out or by or under the direction of such other person approved by the licensing authority for this purpose.

(2) Where the medicinal product to which the animal test certificate relates is to be administered by, or under the direction of, a person who has not been named in the application for that certificate or where it is intended that there shall be a change of the person so named, the certificate holder shall seek the approval of the licensing authority and for this purpose shall notify the licensing authority in writing of the name, address and qualifications of the person in question.

(3) In the event of any such named or approved person ceasing to participate in the medicinal test on animals in respect of which the animal test certificate has been issued, the certificate holder shall as soon as is reasonably possible inform the licensing authority and shall give the reason for such cessation.

9.—(1) The medicinal test on animals in respect of which the animal test certificate has been issued shall be carried out only at the location specified in the application for that certificate.

(2) Where the medicinal test on animals to which the animal test certificate relates is to be carried out at a location that has not been specified in the application or where it is intended that there shall be a change in the location so specified, the certificate holder shall seek the approval of the licensing authority and for this purpose shall notify the licensing authority in writing of the location in question.

10. Before any administration of the medicinal product to which the animal test certificate relates takes place, the certificate holder shall arrange that the particulars relating to the administration of that medicinal product together with any relevant safety precautions be communicated to each and every person who, in the course of the medicinal test on animals in respect of which that certificate has been issued, is to administer or to direct the administration of that medicinal product.".

Amendment of Schedule 2 to the principal regulations

5. In Schedule 2 to the principal regulations (standard provisions for manufacturer's licences) immediately after paragraph 11 there shall be added the following paragraphs:—

"12.—(1) The licence holder who is not the holder of a product licence in respect of the medicinal product to which the manufacturer's licence relates, shall comply with any provisions of such a product licence that relates to the sale of that medicinal product and shall, by means of a label or otherwise, communicate the particulars of such provisions as relate to mode of sale, or restriction as to sale, to any person to whom the licence holder sells or supplies that medicinal product.

(2) Where the manufacturer's licence relates to the assembly of a medicinal product, and the licence holder sells or supplies that medicinal product at such a stage of assembly that does not fully comply with the provisions of the relevant product licence that relates to labelling, that licence holder shall communicate the particulars of those provisions to the person to whom that medicinal product has been so sold or supplied.

13. Where in his application for a manufacturer's licence the licence holder had specified a general classification of medicinal products in respect of which that licence was required or had given particulars of manufacturing operations and of substances or articles in accordance with paragraph 6 of Schedule 1 to the Medicines (Applications for Manufacturer's and Wholesale Dealer's Licences) Regulations 1971(a) and there has been, or it is proposed that there shall be, a change in such general classification or such particulars, the licence holder shall forthwith notify the licensing authority in writing of such change or proposed change.

(a) S.I. 1971/974 (1971 II, p. 2836).

14. Where the manufacturer's licence relates to the assembly of a medicinal product and that medicinal product is not manufactured by the licence holder, and where particulars as to the name and address of the manufacturer of, or of the person who imports, that medicinal product had been given by the licence holder to the licensing authority, the licence holder shall forthwith notify the licensing authority in writing of any changes in such particulars.

15. The licence holder, for the purpose of enabling the licensing authority to ascertain whether there are any grounds for suspending, revoking or varying any licence or certificate granted or issued under Part II of the Act, shall permit, and provide all necessary facilities to enable, any person duly authorised in writing by the licensing authority, on production if required of his credentials, to carry out such inspection or to take such samples or copies, in relation to things belonging to, or any business carried on by, the licence holder, as such person would have the right to carry out or take under the Act for the purpose of verifying any statement contained in an application for a licence or certificate.".

Amendment of Schedule 3 to the principal regulations

6. In Schedule 3 to the principal regulations (standard provisions for wholesale dealer's licences) immediately after paragraph 5 there shall be added the following paragraphs:-

"6.—(1) Subject to the provisions of sub-paragraph (2) of this paragraph, no medicinal product to which the wholesale dealer's licence relates shall be sold or offered for sale by way of wholesale dealing by virtue of that licence unless there has been granted in respect of that medicinal product a product licence which is for the time being in force and any sale or offer for sale shall be in conformity with the provisions of such product licence.

(2) The provisions of the preceding sub-paragraph of this paragraph shall not apply where—

    (i) by virtue of any provisions of the Act or of any order made thereunder, the sale (other than sale by way of wholesale dealing) of the medicinal product to which the wholesale dealer's licence relates is not subject to the restrictions imposed by section 7(2) of the Act, or

    (ii) the sale or offer for sale by way of wholesale dealing is of a medicinal product the dealings in which, at the time of its acquisition by the licence holder, were not subject to the said restrictions imposed by section 7(2) of the Act, or

    (iii) at the time of such sale or offer for sale, the licence holder does not know, or could not by reasonable diligence and care have known, that such sale or offer for sale is of a medicinal product, or believes, on reasonable grounds, that the provisions of sub-paragraphs (2)(i) or 2(ii) of this paragraph apply in relation to such sale or offer for sale.

7. The licence holder, for the purpose of enabling the licensing authority to ascertain whether there are any grounds for suspending, revoking or varying any licence or certificate granted or issued under Part II of the Act, shall permit, and provide all necessary facilities to enable, any person duly

authorised in writing by the licensing authority, on production if required of his credentials, to carry out such inspection or to take such samples or copies, in relation to things belonging to, or any business carried on by, the licence holder, as such person would have the right to carry out or take under the Act for the purpose of verifying any statement contained in an application for a licence or certificate.".

Keith Joseph,
Secretary of State for Social Services.

3rd August 1972.

Peter Thomas,
Secretary of State for Wales.

7th August 1972.

Gordon Campbell,
Secretary of State for Scotland.

8th August 1972.

W. S. I. Whitelaw,
Secretary of State for Northern Ireland.

7th August 1972.

In witness whereof the official seal of the Minister of Agriculture, Fisheries and Food is hereunto affixed on 4th August 1972.

(L.S.)   *J. M. L. Prior,*
Minister of Agriculture, Fisheries and Food.

EXPLANATORY NOTE

(*This Note is not part of the Regulations.*)

These Regulations amend the Medicines (Standard Provisions for Licences and Certificates) Regulations 1971 and add to the Schedules to those regulations further standard provisions which may be incorporated in any licence or certificate. Regulations 3 and 4 provide for further standard provisions which may be incorporated in clinical trial and animal test certificates, regulation 5 provides for further standard provisions which may be incorporated in manufacturer's licences and regulation 6 provides further standard provisions which may be incorporated in wholesale dealer's licences. The remaining amendment (regulation 2) is of a minor character.

STATUTORY INSTRUMENTS

1972 No. 1229 (C.28)

SOCIAL SECURITY

The National Insurance Act 1972 (Commencement No. 1) Order 1972

Made - - -	*9th August* 1972
Laid before Parliament	*10th August* 1972
Coming into Operation	*11th August* 1972

The Secretary of State for Social Services, in conjunction with the Treasury, in exercise of powers conferred by section 6(5) of, and paragraph 1 of Part I of Schedule 4 to, the National Insurance Act 1972(a), and of all other powers enabling him in that behalf, hereby makes the following Order: —

Citation and commencement

1. This Order may be cited as the National Insurance Act 1972 (Commencement No. 1) Order 1972 and shall come into operation on 11th August 1972.

Appointed days

2.—(1) Subject to the following provision of this Order, the day appointed for the coming into force of any provision of the National Insurance Act 1972 specified in column 1 of the Schedule to this Order, so far as that provision relates to any subject matter specified in column 2 of that Schedule, shall be the date specified in column 3 of that Schedule in relation to that subject matter.

(2) As respects the period beginning with 2nd October 1972 and ending with 4th October 1972, the rate of a person's unemployment benefit, sickness benefit or invalidity pension for any day in that period by virtue of section 19(3) of the National Insurance Act 1965(b) or section 3(4) of the National Insurance Act 1971(c) (rate of unemployment benefit, sickness benefit or invalidity pension for persons over pensionable age who have not retired from regular employment) shall be determined as if the day appointed for the coming into force of the provisions of the said Act of 1972 relating to higher rates of retirement pension under the said Act of 1965 were 5th October 1972.

(3) In a case where the weekly rate of retirement pension payable to a person who has retired from regular employment falls to be increased under the provisions of section 3(6) of the National Insurance Act 1971 (increase, in certain cases, of retirement pension by reference to pensioner's previous entitlement to invalidity allowance), the amount of the increase payable to that person shall be determined as if the day appointed for the coming into force of the provisions of the said Act of 1972 relating to invalidity allowance was 2nd October 1972.

(a) 1972 c. 57.   (b) 1965 c. 51.
(c) 1971 c. 50.

(4) In the case of a person to whom injury benefit under the National Insurance (Industrial Injuries) Act 1965(**a**) is payable for 4th October 1972 at a reduced weekly rate by virtue of the provisions of section 29(1) of that Act (adjustments for successive accidents), the rate of that injury benefit and of any sickness benefit under the National Insurance Act 1965 or invalidity pension under the National Insurance Act 1971 shall be determined as if the day appointed for the coming into force of the provisions of the said Act of 1972 relating to higher rates of those benefits were 4th October 1972 and, where appropriate, as if the reference to 5th October in paragraph (2) of this Article were a reference to 4th October 1972.

Signed by authority of the Secretary of State for Social Services,

Paul Dean,

Parliamentary Under Secretary of State,
Department of Health and Social Security.

9th August 1972.

Tim Fortescue,

V. H. Goodhew,

Two of the Lords Commissioners of
Her Majesty's Treasury.

9th August 1972.

Article 2   SCHEDULE

Provisions of the National Insurance Act 1972	Subject Matter	Appointed Day
Section 1 and Schedule 1	Rates of benefit under the National Insurance Act 1965 in the case of—	
	(a) unemployment, sickness and invalidity benefit	5th October 1972
	(b) maternity allowance, widow's benefit, guardian's allowance, retirement pension, age addition and child's special allowance	2nd October 1972
	(c) calculation of earnings-related supplement and widow's supplementary allowance	2nd October 1972
Section 3(1) and (2) and Schedule 2	Flat-rate contributions under the National Insurance Act 1965, any increase payable by way of Exchequer Supplement under section 7 of that Act and graduated contributions under that Act	2nd October 1972
Section 3(3)	Payments to the National Insurance Fund out of moneys provided by Parliament in addition to Exchequer Supplements	2nd October 1972
Section 4(1) and Schedule 3	Rates and amounts of benefit under the National Insurance (Industrial Injuries) Act 1965 in the case of—	
	(a) injury benefit (including increases thereof) and increases of disablement pension in respect of children and adult dependants in the case of a beneficiary receiving, as an in-patient in a hospital or similar institution, medical treatment for the relevant injury or loss of faculty	5th October 1972

(**a**) 1965 c. 52.

SCHEDULE—(*continued*)

Provisions of the National Insurance Act 1972	Subject Matter	Appointed Day
	(*b*) disablement benefit (including increases of disablement pension other than those mentioned in the preceding sub-paragraph), increase of unemployability supplement under section 13A, maximum under section 29(1)(*a*) of aggregate of weekly benefits payable for successive accidents and maximum disablement gratuity under section 12(3)	4th October 1972
	(*c*) widow's pension under section 19, widower's pension under section 20 and allowance in respect of children of deceased's family under section 21	2nd October 1972
Section 4(2)	Amendments relating to widow's pension under section 19 of the National Insurance (Industrial Injuries) Act 1965	2nd October 1972
Section 4(3)	Power to make regulations prescribing earnings level that does not disqualify for unemployability supplement	4th October 1972
Section 4(4)	Benefit under the Industrial Injuries and Diseases (Old Cases) Act 1967(**a**)	4th October 1972
Section 4(5)	Employers' contributions under the National Insurance (Industrial Injuries) Act 1965 and contributions paid out of moneys provided by Parliament under section 2(1)(*b*) of that Act	2nd October 1972
Section 6(1)	Application to invalidity benefit of provisions of section 11(1)(*a*)-(*d*) of the National Insurance Act 1966(**b**) (which, among other things, enable regulations to provide for claims and decisions relating to sickness benefit to be made or operate prospectively)	2nd October 1972
Section 6(2)	Power to vary or revoke orders made under section 12(3) of the National Insurance Act 1966(**b**) (adjustments in respect of expenses)	2nd October 1972
Section 6(3)-(4)	Financial provisions	2nd October 1972
Section 6(5) and Schedule 4 Part I	Commencement and transitory matters	11th August 1972
Section 8(1), (2) and, as it applies to Great Britain, (4)	Citation and construction	11th August 1972
Section 8(5), as it applies to Great Britain, and Schedule 6 Part I	Repeals affecting— the National Insurance (Industrial Injuries) Act 1965 section 19	2nd October 1972
	the National Insurance Act 1966 section 5(5)	2nd October 1972
	the National Insurance Act 1970(**c**) section 7(3)	2nd October 1972
	the National Insurance Act 1971— section 1(1) to (3) and (5) and Schedule 1	2nd October 1972
	section 2(1) and Schedule 2 in the case of— (*a*) unemployment, sickness and invalidity benefit	5th October 1972
	(*b*) maternity allowance, widow's benefit, guardian's allowance, retirement pension, age addition and child's special allowance	2nd October 1972

(**a**) 1967 c. 34.   (**b**) 1966 c. 6.   (**c**) 1970 c. 51.

SCHEDULE—(*continued*)

Provisions of the National Insurance Act 1972	Subject Matter	Appointed Day
	section 8(1) and Schedule 4 in the case of—	
	(*a*) injury benefit (including increases thereof) and increases of disablement pension in respect of children and adult dependants in the case of a beneficiary receiving, as an in-patient in a hospital or similar institution, medical treatment for the relevant injury or loss of faculty	5th October 1972
	(*b*) disablement benefit (including increases of disablement pension other than those mentioned in the preceding sub-paragraph), increase of unemployability supplement, maximum of aggregate of weekly benefits payable for successive accidents and maximum disablement gratuity	4th October 1972
	(*c*) widow's pension, widower's pension and allowance in respect of children of deceased's family	2nd October 1972
	section 11(1)	4th October 1972

EXPLANATORY NOTE

(This Note is not part of the Order.)

This Order brings into operation, in Great Britain, all the provisions of the National Insurance Act 1972 except section 5 (already in force) and those relating to attendance allowance.

STATUTORY INSTRUMENTS

1972 No. 1230 (C.29)

SOCIAL SECURITY

The National Insurance Act 1972 (Commencement No. 2) Order 1972

Made - - -	*9th August* 1972
Laid before Parliament	*10th August* 1972
Coming into Operation	*11th August* 1972

The Secretary of State for Social Services, in conjunction with the Treasury, in exercise of powers conferred by section 6(5) of, and Schedule 4 to, the National Insurance Act 1972(**a**), and of all other powers enabling him in that behalf, hereby makes the following Order: —

Citation and commencement

1. This Order may be cited as the National Insurance Act 1972 (Commencement No. 2) Order 1972 and shall come into operation on 11th August 1972.

Appointed days

2. The day appointed for the coming into force of any provision of the National Insurance Act 1972 specified in column 1 of the Schedule to this Order, so far as that provision relates to any subject matter specified in column 2 of that Schedule, shall be the date specified in column 3 of that Schedule in relation to that subject matter.

Signed by authority of the Secretary of State for Social Services,

Paul Dean,
Parliamentary Under Secretary of State,
Department of Health and Social Security.

9th August 1972.

Tim Fortescue,
V. H. Goodhew,
Two of the Lords Commissioners of
Her Majesty's Treasury.

9th August 1972.

(**a**) 1972 c. 57.

SCHEDULE

Article 2

Provisions of the National Insurance Act 1972	Subject Matter	Appointed Day
Section 1(1) and Schedule 1	Higher weekly rate of attendance allowance	2nd October 1972
Section 2 and Schedule 4 Part II	Provisions relating to attendance allowance except as they relate to the lower weekly rate thereof	21st August 1972
Section 8(5), as it applies to Great Britain, and Schedule 6 Part I	Repeals affecting— the National Insurance Act 1970(a)— sections 4(2) to (5) and 6(1) the National Insurance Act 1971(b)— section 2(1) and Schedule 2 as they relate to attendance allowance Schedule 5 paragraph 12(2)	21st August 1972 2nd October 1972 21st August 1972

EXPLANATORY NOTE

(This Note is not part of the Order.)

This Order brings into operation, in Great Britain, the provisions of the National Insurance Act 1972 relating to attendance allowance at the higher weekly rate.

(a) 1970 c. 51. **(b)** 1971 c. 50.

STATUTORY INSTRUMENTS

1972 No. 1231

SOCIAL SECURITY

The National Insurance (Industrial Injuries) (Increase of Benefit and Miscellaneous Provisions) Regulations 1972

Made - - -	11*th August* 1972
Laid before Parliament	11*th August* 1972
Coming into Operation—	
Regulations 1 *and* 5	12*th August* 1972
Regulation 4(1)	1*st October* 1972
Remainder	4*th October* 1972

The Industrial Injuries Joint Authority and the Secretary of State for Social Services, in exercise of the powers conferred by the provisions of the National Insurance (Industrial Injuries) Acts 1965 to 1972 set out respectively in Parts I and II of Schedule 1 to this instrument, and of all other powers enabling them in that behalf, hereby make the following regulations, which contain no provisions other than such as are made in consequence of the National Insurance Act 1972(**a**) and which accordingly, by virtue of section 6 of and paragraph 2(1)(*a*) of Schedule 4 to that Act, are exempt from the requirements of section 62(2) of the National Insurance (Industrial Injuries) Act 1965(**b**) (reference to Industrial Injuries Advisory Council): —

Citation, commencement and interpretation

1.—(1) These regulations may be cited as the National Insurance (Industrial Injuries) (Increase of Benefit and Miscellaneous Provisions) Regulations 1972 and shall come into operation, in the case of regulations 1 and 5, on 12th August 1972, in the case of regulation 4(1), on 1st October 1972 and in the case of the remainder of the regulations on 4th October 1972.

(2) In these regulations, unless the context otherwise requires—

"the principal Act" means the National Insurance (Industrial Injuries) Act 1965;

"the Act of 1972" means the National Insurance Act 1972;

"the Benefit Regulations" means the National Insurance (Industrial Injuries) (Benefit) Regulations 1964(**c**), as amended (**d**);

"the Claims and Payments Regulations" means the National Insurance (Industrial Injuries) (Claims and Payments) Regulations 1964(**e**), as amended (**f**);

and other expressions have the same meaning as in the principal Act.

(a) 1972 c. 57. (b) 1965 c. 52.
(c) S.I. 1964/504 (1964 I, p. 833).
(d) The relevant amending instruments are S.I. 1969/1168, 1970/46, 1971/1201 (1969 II, p. 3432; 1970 I, p. 243; 1971 I, p. 3514).
(e) S.I. 1964/73 (1964 I, p. 115).
(f) There is no amendment which relates expressly to the subject matter of these Regulations.

(3) References in these regulations to any enactment or regulation shall, except in so far as the context otherwise requires, include references to such enactment or regulation as amended or extended by or under any subsequent enactment, order or regulation.

(4) The rules for the construction of Acts of Parliament contained in the Interpretation Act 1889(a) shall apply in relation to this instrument and to the revocation effected by it as if this instrument and the regulation revoked by it were Acts of Parliament and as if the revocation were a repeal.

Increase in rates and amounts of benefit payable under regulations

2.—(1) The rates and amounts of benefit of the several descriptions specified in Schedule 2 to these regulations shall be increased as from the dates respectively specified in paragraph (2) of this regulation, and accordingly the provisions of the Benefit Regulations set out in column 1 of that Schedule (which provisions relate to the said rates and amounts of benefit) shall be amended as from the appropriate date by substituting for the rates and amounts set out in column 3 of that Schedule the corresponding rates and amounts set out in column 4 thereof.

(2) The said increases shall operate, in so far as they relate to injury benefit, as from 5th October 1972, and in so far as they relate to any other benefit as from 4th October 1972:

Provided that the increased amount of a disablement gratuity shall be payable only where the period taken into account by the assessment of the extent of disablement in respect of which the gratuity is awarded begins on or after 4th October 1972, but nevertheless the amendment made by this regulation to Schedule 4 of the Benefit Regulations (which Schedule, as applied by regulations 6 and 8 of those regulations, prescribes, in relation to awards of disablement gratuity, the weekly rate of pension payable in lieu thereof and the weekly amount by which increase of benefit during hospital treatment is reduced) shall have effect as from 4th October 1972, whether the period taken into account by the assessment began before or after that date.

Conditions relating to payment of additional benefit under awards made before the appointed or prescribed day

3. Where an award of any benefit under the principal Act has been made before the day appointed or prescribed for the payment of benefit of the description to which the award relates at a higher weekly rate by virtue of the Act of 1972 or of these regulations, paragraph 3(1) of Schedule 6 to the National Insurance Act 1969 (which relates to the effect of any such award) shall, if the period to which the award relates has not ended before that day, have effect subject to the condition that if the award has not been made in accordance with the provisions of sub-paragraph (2) of that paragraph (which sub-paragraph authorises the making of such an award providing for the payment of the benefit at the higher weekly rate as from that day) and a question arises as to—

    (*a*) the weekly rate at which the benefit is payable by virtue of the Act of 1972 or of these regulations, or

    (*b*) whether the conditions for the receipt of the benefit at the higher weekly rate are satisfied,

---

(a) 1889 c. 63.

the benefit shall be or continue to be payable at the weekly rate specified in the award until the said question shall have been determined in accordance with the provisions of the principal Act.

Amendments to the Benefit Regulations

4.—(1) In regulation 18 of the Benefit Regulations (widow's pension) paragraph (*b*) shall be omitted.

(2) After regulation 35 of the Eenefit Regulations there shall be inserted the following regulation : —

"Earnings level for the purposes of unemployability supplement under section 13 *of the National Insurance (Industrial Injuries) Act* 1965

35A. For the purposes of section 13(2) of the National Insurance (Industrial Injuries) Act 1965 (earnings level that does not disqualify for unemployability supplement) the prescribed amount of earnings in a year shall be £234."

Amendments to the Claims and Payments Regulations

5.—(1) In Regulation 23 of the Claims and Payments Regulations (commencement of payment on review) the words "under Part III of the Act" shall be omitted.

(2) At the end of Regulation 23 of the Claims and Payments Regulations there shall be added the following words : —

"Provided that in the case of a review pursuant to section 5(5) of the National Insurance Act 1972 of a decision that a claimant was not entitled to death benefit, benefit shall not be payable for any period earlier than 9th August 1972."

Given under the official seal of the Industrial Injuries Joint Authority.

(L.S.)

F. B. Hindmarsh,
A person authorised by the Industrial
Injuries Joint Authority to act on behalf
of the Secretary, Industrial Injuries
Joint Authority.

11th August 1972.

Signed by authority of the Secretary of State for Social Services.

Paul Dean,
Parliamentary Under Secretary of State,
Department of Health and Social Security.

11th August 1972.

SCHEDULE 1

PROVISIONS OF THE NATIONAL INSURANCE (INDUSTRIAL INJURIES) ACTS 1965 TO 1972
CONFERRING POWERS EXERCISED IN MAKING THESE REGULATIONS

PART I

Provisions conferring powers exercised by the Industrial Injuries Joint Authority

Enactment	Relevant Provisions
The National Insurance (Industrial Injuries) Act 1965(a)	Section 12(3) Section 14(7) Section 15(1) Section 19(4) Section 78(2)

PART II

Provisions conferring powers exercised by the Secretary of State for Social Services

Enactment	Relevant Provisions	Relevant Amending Enactments
The National Insurance (Industrial Injuries) Act 1965	Section 13(2) Section 16 Section 54(3)	The National Insurance Act 1972(b) section 4(3) The National Insurance Act 1966(c) section 13(1) and Schedule 3 paragraph 5(j)
The National Insurance Act 1969(d)	Schedule 6, paragraphs 3 and 4	—

(a) 1965 c. 52.   (b) 1972 c. 57.   (c) 1966 c. 6.   (d) 1969 c. 44.

SCHEDULE 2

Regulation 2

AMENDMENT OF PROVISIONS OF THE BENEFIT REGULATIONS
RELATING TO RATES AND AMOUNTS OF BENEFIT

1	2	3	4
Amended provision	Description of rates and amounts of benefit	Existing rate or amount	New rate or amount
Regulation 4(2)	Weekly rates of injury benefit in respect of children under the upper limit of compulsory school age:—		
	(a) where the employment or employments amounted to full-time or substantially full-time employment	£5·50	£6·20
	(b) in any other case	£1·85	£2·10
Regulation 7	Weekly rates of allowance in respect of constant attendance:—		
	(a) where to a substantial extent dependent on such attendance	£4·00	£4·50
	(b) maximum payable where so dependent and attendance required is greater by reason of exceptionally severe disablement	£6·00	£6·75
	(c) where entirely or almost entirely dependent on such attendance	£8·00	£9·00
Schedule 3 (applied by Regulation 3)	Amount of gratuities for degrees of disablement of:—		
	1 per cent	£66·00	£74·00
	2 per cent	£99·00	£111·00
	3 per cent	£132·00	£148·00
	4 per cent	£165·00	£185·00
	5 per cent	£198·00	£222·00
	6 per cent	£231·00	£259·00
	7 per cent	£264·00	£296·00
	8 per cent	£297·00	£333·00
	9 per cent	£330·00	£370·00
	10 per cent	£363·00	£407·00
	11 per cent	£396·00	£444·00
	12 per cent	£429·00	£481·00
	13 per cent	£462·00	£518·00
	14 per cent	£495·00	£555·00
	15 per cent	£528·00	£592·00
	16 per cent	£561·00	£629·00
	17 per cent	£594·00	£666·00
	18 per cent	£627·00	£703·00
	19 per cent	£660·00	£740·00
Schedule 4 (applied by Regulations 6 and 8)	Weekly rate of disablement pension payable in lieu of disablement gratuity for degree of disablement of:—		
	less than 20 per cent but not less than 16 per cent	£2·00	£2·24
	less than 16 per cent but not less than 11 per cent	£1·50	£1·68
	less than 11 per cent but not less than 6 per cent	£1·00	£1·12
	less than 6 per cent	£0·50	£0·56

EXPLANATORY NOTE

(This Note is not part of the Regulations.)

These Regulations increase the rates of certain benefits payable under regulations made under the National Insurance (Industrial Injuries) Act 1965 in order to bring them into conformity with the higher rates of benefit payable directly under that Act by virtue of the National Insurance Act 1972, and contain consequential and transitional provisions following upon the passing of the last-mentioned Act.

These Regulations amend the National Insurance (Industrial Injuries) (Benefit) Regulations 1964 by prescribing the earnings level which may be reached before a person is disqualified for unemployability supplement under section 13(2) of the National Insurance (Industrial Injuries) Act 1965 and by omitting regulation 18(*b*) thereof consequent upon the transfer of its provisions to section 4(2)(*a*) of the Act of 1972.

These Regulations also amend the National Insurance (Industrial Injuries) (Claims and Payments) Regulations 1964 in order to provide that on a review pursuant to section 5 of the Act of 1972 of a decision that a claimant was not entitled to death benefit, benefit shall not be payable for any period earlier than 9th August 1972. A minor consequential amendment is also made to the last-mentioned Regulations.

These Regulations are made in consequence of the National Insurance Act 1972 and in accordance with Schedule 4, paragraph 2(1), to that Act have not been referred to the Industrial Injuries Advisory Council.

STATUTORY INSTRUMENTS

1972 No. 1232

SOCIAL SECURITY

The National Insurance (Attendance Allowance) Amendment Regulations 1972

Made - - -	*9th August* 1972
Laid before Parliament	*18th August* 1972
Coming into Operation	*21st August* 1972

The Secretary of State for Social Services, in conjunction with the Treasury in so far as relates to matters with regard to which the Treasury have so directed, in exercise of his powers under section 81(3) and (4) of the National Insurance Act 1965(**a**), section 6(6) of the National Insurance Act 1970(**b**) and section 2 of the National Insurance Act 1972(**c**), and of all other powers enabling him in that behalf, hereby makes the following regulations, which relate solely to matters which have been referred to the Attendance Allowance Board in pursuance of section 5(1)(*b*) of the said Act of 1970 as extended by section 2(6) of the said Act of 1972, and which, by virtue of section 8(5) of the said Act of 1970, are exempt from the requirements of section 108 of the said Act of 1965 (consideration of regulations by the National Insurance Advisory Committee): —

Citation, commencement and interpretation

1.—(1) These regulations may be cited as the National Insurance (Attendance Allowance) Amendment Regulations 1972 and shall come into operation on 21st August 1972.

(2) In these regulations, unless the context otherwise requires, "the principal regulations" means the National Insurance (Attendance Allowance) Regulations 1971(**d**), as amended (**e**).

(3) The rules for the construction of Acts of Parliament contained in the Interpretation Act 1889(**f**) shall apply in relation to this instrument and in relation to the revocation effected by it as if this instrument and the regulation revoked by it were Acts of Parliament and as if the revocation were a repeal.

(**a**) 1965 c. 51.   (**b**) 1970 c. 51.   (**c**) 1972 c. 57.
(**d**) S.I. 1971/621 (1971 I, p. 1623).   (**e**) S.I. 1971/1854 (1971 III, p. 5089).
(**f**) 1889 c. 63.

Amendment of Part I of the principal regulations

2. In regulation 1(2) of the principal regulations (definitions), after the definition of "the Act of 1970" there shall be inserted the following definition: —

" 'the Act of 1972' means the National Insurance Act 1972(**a**);".

Amendment of Part II of the principal regulations

3. In regulation 2 of the principal regulations (entitlement conditions relating to residence and presence in Great Britain), in paragraph (1), for the words "section 4(2) of the Act of 1970" there shall be substituted the words "section 2(1) of the Act of 1972"; and in regulation 3 of the principal regulations (exception from disqualification for receipt of benefit), for the words "the Act of 1970" there shall be substituted the words "the Act of 1972".

Amendment of Part III of the principal regulations

4.—(1) For regulation 5 of the principal regulations (adults in certain accommodation other than hospitals) there shall be substituted the following regulation: —

"Adults in certain accommodation other than hospitals

5. Subject to regulation 6 of these regulations, attendance allowance shall not be payable in respect of a person who has attained the age of sixteen for any period during which he is a person living in accommodation provided for him in pursuance of, or provided for him in circumstances in which the cost of the accommodation is or may be borne wholly or partly out of public or local funds in pursuance of, any of the enactments mentioned in the Schedule to these regulations, not being, in a case where the accommodation is provided in pursuance of any provision of the Social Work (Scotland) Act 1968(**b**) referred to in the said Schedule, accommodation which, in the opinion of the Secretary of State, is analogous to the temporary accommodation referred to in section 21(1)(*b*) of the National Assistance Act 1948(**c**).".

(2) For the Schedule to the principal regulations, there shall be substituted the provisions set out in Schedule 1 to these regulations.

Amendment of Part IV of the principal regulations

5.—(1) Regulations 7 and 8 of the principal regulations (modification of section 4(2) and (4) of the Act of 1970 in its application to children) shall be amended in accordance with the following provisions of this regulation.

(2) For regulation 7(1) there shall be substituted the following regulation: —

"Modification of section 2(1) of the Act of 1972 in its application to children

7.—(1) Section 2(1) of the Act of 1972 (entitlement to attendance allowance) shall have effect in relation to a child subject to the modifications contained in the following provisions of this regulation."

(**a**) 1972 c. 57.　　　　　　　　　(**b**) 1968 c. 49.
(**c**) 1948 c. 29.

(3) For regulation 7(4) there shall be substituted the following regulation: —

"(4) Section 2(1) of the Act of 1972 shall have effect as if after the word "functions" in both places where that word appears there were inserted the words "(being attention substantially in excess of that normally required by a child of the same age and sex)"; and as if after the word "others" in both places where it appears there were inserted the words "(being supervision substantially in excess of that normally required by a child of the same age and sex)".

(4) In regulation 7(5)(*d*), for the word "paragraph" there shall be substituted the word "sub-paragraph".

(5) In regulation 8—

(*a*) for the shoulder note and the words in paragraph (1) down to "during which", there shall be substituted the following shoulder note and words: —

"Children in hospital and certain other accommodation

8.—(1) Section 2(3) and (5) of the Act of 1972 (attendance allowance not payable in certain circumstances) shall have effect in relation to a child in accordance with the following provisions of this regulation and attendance allowance shall not be payable in respect of a child for any period during which—"; and

(*b*) for sub-paragraph (*b*) of paragraph (1) there shall be substituted the following sub-paragraph: —

"(*b*) the child is a person living in accommodation provided for him in pursuance of, or provided for him in circumstances in which the cost of the accommodation is or may be borne wholly or partly out of public or local funds in pursuance of, any of the enactments mentioned in the Schedule to these regulations; or".

Amendment of Part V of the principal regulations

6. Regulation 9 of the principal regulations (claims in advance) is hereby revoked.

Amendment of Part VI of the principal regulations

7.—(1) Regulation 13 of the principal regulations (application for reviews of determinations made by the Board) shall be amended in accordance with the following provisions of this regulation and shall accordingly have effect as set out in Part I of Schedule 2 to these regulations.

(2) In paragraph (1) of the said regulation 13, there shall be inserted at the beginning the words "Subject to the provisions of paragraph (1A) of this regulation", and after the said paragraph (1) there shall be inserted the following paragraph: —

"(1A) Such an application for review as is referred to in paragraph (1) of this regulation shall not be made within 12 months of a previous such application without the leave of the Board."

(3) In paragraph (2) of the said regulation 13, after the word "application" there shall be inserted the words "in respect of which the leave of the Board has been given or is not required".

8.—(1) Regulation 14 of the principal regulations (reviews of determinations made by the Board) shall be amended in accordance with the provisions of paragraph (2) of this regulation and shall accordingly have effect as set out in Part II of Schedule 2 to these regulations.

(2) In paragraph (2) of the said regulation 14, after the word "Board" there shall be inserted the words "having where appropriate given leave under regulation 13 (1A) of these regulations".

9. Regulation 15 of the principal regulations (amendment of the National Insurance (Determination of Claims and Questions) (No. 2) Regulations 1967) shall become paragraph (1) of that regulation and shall be renumbered accordingly; and immediately after it there shall be added the following paragraph:—

"(2) In paragraph (2)(*a*), as amended (**a**), of regulation 15 of the said regulations, there shall be added at the end of head (*iii*) the word 'or' and the following additional head:—

'(*iv*) a determination on review made by the Attendance Allowance Board constituted under section 5 of the National Insurance Act 1970.'."

Signed by authority of the Secretary of State for Social Services.

Paul Dean,
Parliamentary Under Secretary of State,
Department of Health and Social Security.

9th August 1972.

Tim Fortescue,
V. H. Goodhew,
Two of the Lords Commissioners of
Her Majesty's Treasury.

9th August 1972.

(**a**) The relevant amending instrument is S.I. 1971/1419 (1971 II, p. 3964).

SCHEDULE 1   Regulation 4(2)

SCHEDULE SUBSTITUTED FOR THE SCHEDULE TO THE PRINCIPAL REGULATIONS

THE SCHEDULE   Regulations 5 and 8(1)(*b*)

ATTENDANCE ALLOWANCE NOT PAYABLE FOR ADULTS AND CHILDREN LIVING IN ACCOMMODATION PROVIDED FOR THEM IN PURSUANCE OF, OR PROVIDED FOR THEM IN CIRCUMSTANCES IN WHICH THE COST OF THE ACCOMMODATION IS OR MAY BE BORNE WHOLLY OR PARTLY OUT OF PUBLIC OR LOCAL FUNDS IN PURSUANCE OF, ANY OF THE ENACTMENTS REFERRED TO IN COLUMN 3.

Chapter	Short Title	Enactments
1933 c. 12.	The Children and Young Persons Act 1933.	Section 53.
1937 c. 37.	The Children and Young Persons (Scotland) Act 1937.	Sections 40(3), 41(1), 47(1), 57(1) and (2) and 58A.
1944 c. 10.	The Disabled Persons (Employment) Act 1944.	Section 15.
1944 c. 31.	The Education Act 1944.	Sections 9(1), 33(2), 34(4), 41, 42 and 50.
1948 c. 29.	The National Assistance Act 1948.	Part III other than section 21(1)(*b*).
1948 c. 43.	The Children Act 1948.	Sections 1, 13 and 19.
1953 c. 33.	The Education (Miscellaneous Provisions) Act 1953.	Section 6(2)(*b*).
1962 c. 47.	The Education (Scotland) Act 1962.	Sections 1 and 5.
1968 c. 46.	The Health Services and Public Health Act 1968.	Section 12.
1968 c. 49.	The Social Work (Scotland) Act 1968.	Sections 12, 15, 21, 37(2) and (3), 40(4) and (7), 43(4), 44, 45 and 59(1).
1969 c. 54.	The Children and Young Persons Act 1969.	Sections 23 and 28.

SCHEDULE 2   Regulations 7(1) and 8(1)

PART I

REGULATION 13 OF THE PRINCIPAL REGULATIONS AS AMENDED* BY THESE REGULATIONS

Application for reviews of determinations made by the Board

13.—(1) *Subject to the provisions of paragraph (1A) of this regulation*, an application for a review, in pursuance of section 6(3)(*a*) or (*b*) of the Act of 1970, of a determination may be made by the claimant or the Secretary of State and shall be made in writing to

*The words added by these regulations are shown in italics.

the Board stating the grounds of the application; any such application by the claimant shall be delivered or sent to a local office, and in the case of an application by the Secretary of State he shall send a copy of it to the claimant.

(1A) *Such an application for review as is referred to in paragraph (1) of this regulation shall not be made within 12 months of a previous such application without the leave of the Board.*

(2) On receipt of any such application *in respect of which the leave of the Board has been given or is not required,* the Board shall proceed to deal with it in accordance with the provisions of section 6 of the Act of 1970.

(3) In this regulation "a local office" means any office appointed by the Secretary of State as a local office for the purposes of the principal Act or of these regulations.

PART II

REGULATION 14 OF THE PRINCIPAL REGULATIONS AS AMENDED* BY THESE REGULATIONS

Reviews of determinations made by the Board

14.—(1) The prescribed period within which the Board may, in pursuance of section 6(3)(*b*) of the Act of 1970, review a determination on any ground, shall be a period of 3 months from the date on which notice of the determination which it is sought to have reviewed was given or sent to the claimant, so however that if an application for review is made (whether by the claimant or the Secretary of State) within 3 months from that date the prescribed period shall be extended until the application for review is determined.

(2) Where the Board, *having where appropriate given leave under regulation 13(1A) of these regulations,* have reviewed a determination or have refused to review a determination, the claimant and the Secretary of State shall be notified in writing of the determination on the review or of that refusal as the case may be and the reasons for it and the claimant shall be notified of the conditions governing an appeal to the Commissioner.

EXPLANATORY NOTE

(*This Note is not part of the Regulations.*)

These Regulations further amend the National Insurance (Attendance Allowance) Regulations 1971 ("the principal regulations"). Most of the amendments of the principal regulations made by these Regulations are consequential upon amendments to the provisions of the National Insurance Act 1970 ("the 1970 Act") relating to attendance allowance made by the National Insurance Act 1972 ("the 1972 Act").

Regulation 1 relates to the citation, commencement and interpretation of these Regulations; regulation 2 inserts a definition of the 1972 Act in Part I of the principal regulations; and regulation 3 makes minor amendments to Part II of the principal regulations consequent upon the repeal by the 1972 Act of certain provisions of the 1970 Act. Regulation 4 amends regulation 5 of the principal regulations (circumstances in which attendance allowance is not payable for adults in certain accommodation other than hospitals); regulation 5 amends Part IV of the principal regulations (modification of certain provisions relating to attendance allowance in their application to children);

---

*The words added by these regulations are shown in italics.

and regulation 6 revokes regulation 9 of the principal regulations (claims in advance) which is replaced by section 2(3) of the 1972 Act. Regulation 7 amends Part VI of the principal regulations, by making provision whereby an application for review of a determination made by the Attendance Allowance Board cannot be made within 12 months of a previous such application without the leave of the Board, and by further amending regulation 15 of the National Insurance (Determination of Claims and Questions) (No. 2) Regulations 1967 (S.I. 1967/1570) so that a review decision of the benefit authorities (insurance officer, local tribunal or the National Insurance Commissioner) based solely upon a review determination of the Board may make attendance allowance payable, or payable at the higher weekly rate, for a period more than 12 months before the application for review was made. Schedule 1 to these Regulations, which applies both to adults and children, replaces the Schedule to the principal regulations and Schedule 2 sets out regulations 13 and 14 of the principal regulations as amended by these Regulations.

STATUTORY INSTRUMENTS

1972 No. 1233

CIVIL AVIATION

The Rules of the Air and Air Traffic Control (Second Amendment) Regulations 1972

Made - - -	*7th August* 1972
Coming into Operation	*7th September* 1972

The Secretary of State, in exercise of his powers under Article 61(1) of the Air Navigation Order 1972(**a**), and of all other powers enabling him in that behalf, hereby makes the following Regulations:

1. These Regulations may be cited as the Rules of the Air and Air Traffic Control (Second Amendment) Regulations 1972 and shall come into operation on 7th September 1972.

2. The Interpretation Act 1889(**b**) applies for the purpose of the interpretation of these Regulations as it applies for the purpose of the interpretation of an Act of Parliament.

3. The Schedule to the Rules of the Air and Air Traffic Control Regulations 1972(**c**), as amended(**d**), shall be further amended as follows:

In Rule 37(13)(*a*), there shall be added at the end

"but shall not include any airspace within the said area which is within the aerodrome traffic zone of Oxford (Kidlington) Aerodrome.".

7th August 1972.

D. F. Hubback,
A Deputy Secretary,
Department of Trade and Industry.

EXPLANATORY NOTE

(This Note is not part of the Regulations.)

These Regulations further amend the Rules of the Air and Air Traffic Control Regulations 1972. The relevant airspace within which special rules for Brize Norton Aerodrome apply will not now include any airspace which is within the aerodrome traffic zone of Oxford (Kidlington) Aerodrome.

(**a**) S.I. 1972/129 (1972 I, p. 366).   (**b**) 1889 c. 63.
(**c**) S.I. 1972/321 (1972 I, p. 1258).   (**d**) 1972/699 (1972 II, p. 2232).

STATUTORY INSTRUMENTS

1972 No. 1234

INDUSTRIAL DEVELOPMENT

The Special Development Areas Order 1972

Made - - - -	10*th August* 1972
Laid before Parliament	10*th August* 1972
Coming into Operation	10*th August* 1972

The Secretary of State in exercise of his powers under section 1(4) and (6) of the Industry Act 1972**(a)** hereby makes the following Order:—

1.—(1) The Interpretation Act 1889**(b)** shall apply to the interpretation of this Order as it applies to the interpretation of an Act of Parliament.

(2) This Order may be cited as the Special Development Areas Order 1972 and shall come into operation immediately after being laid before Parliament.

2. The areas described in the Schedule to this Order are hereby designated as special development areas for the purposes of section 1 of the Industry Act 1972 and specified as such areas for the purpose of grant payable in accordance with Part I of the said Act in respect of assets provided before the passing of the said Act and before the making of this Order.

Dated 10th August 1972.

Christopher Chataway,
Minister for Industrial Development,
Department of Trade and Industry.

(a) 1972 c. 63.   **(b)** 1889 c. 63

Article 2   SCHEDULE

The Scottish Special Development Area being part of the Scottish Development Area and consisting of the area designated by the New Town (Glenrothes) Designation Order 1948(a) as the site of a proposed new town, the area designated by the New Town (Livingston) Designation Order 1962(b) as the site of a proposed new town and the employment exchange areas of:—

Airdrie
Alexandria
Barrhead
Bellshill
Blantyre
Bridgeton
Cambuslang
Carluke
Coatbridge
Clydebank
Cumbernauld
Dumbarton
Easterhouse
East Kilbride
Girvan
Glasgow (South Side)

Govan
Greenock
Hamilton
  (including the area served by
  the sub-office of Strathaven)
Helensburgh
Hillington
Irvine
  (including the area served by
  the sub-office of Dalry)

Johnstone
Kilsyth
Kilwinning
Kinning Park
Kirkintilloch
Larkhall
Lesmahagow
Leven and Methil

Maryhill
Motherwell
Paisley
Parkhead
Partick
Port Glasgow
Renfrew
Rutherglen
Saltcoats
  (excluding the Isle of Arran)
Sanquhar
Shotts
Springburn
Uddingston
Wishaw

The Northern Special Development Area, being part of the Northern Development Area and consisting of the employment exchange areas of:—

Ashington
Aspatria
Bedlington
Birtley
Bishop Auckland
  (including the area served by
  the sub-office of Evenwood)
Blaydon
Blyth
Chester-le-Street
Cleator Moor
Cockermouth
Consett
Crook
Durham
East Boldon
Felling
Gateshead
Haltwhistle
Hartlepool
Hartlepool Headland
Houghton-le-Spring
Jarrow and Hebburn
Lanchester

Maryport
Millom
Newburn
Newcastle-upon-Tyne
North Shields
Peterlee
Prudhoe
Seaham
Seaton Delaval
Shildon
South Shields
Southwick
Spennymoor
Stanley
Sunderland
Walker
Wallsend
Washington
West Moor
Whitehaven
Whitley Bay
Wingate
Workington

(a) S.I. 1948/1528.   (b) S.I. 1962/814.

The Welsh Special Development Area, being part of the Welsh Development Area and consisting of the employment exchange areas of:—

Aberdare	Merthyr Tydfil
Abertillery	Mountain Ash
Ammanford	Neath
(excluding those areas served by the	Newbridge
sub-offices of Llandeilo and Llandovery)	Pontardawe
Bargoed	Pontlottyn
Blackwood	Pontypridd
Brynmawr	Resolven
Cymmer	Tonypandy
Dowlais	Tonyrefail
Ebbw Vale	Tredegar
Ferndale	Treharris
Garnant	Treorchy
Llantrisant	Ystradgynlais
Maesteg	Ystrad Mynach

For the purposes of this Schedule the employment exchange areas referred to above are areas for which an employment exchange has been established or maintained for the purpose of the Employment and Training Act 1948(a) as those areas exist on the date on which this Order comes into force.

EXPLANATORY NOTE

(This Note is not part of the Order).

This Order designates the areas described in the Schedule as special development areas for the purposes of section 1 of the Industry Act 1972. It also in accordance with the terms of section 1(6) of the Industry Act 1972 specifies those areas as special development areas for the purpose of grant payable, in accordance with the provisions of Part I of that Act, in respect of assets provided before that Act was passed and before this Order was made.

(a) 1948 c. 46.

STATUTORY INSTRUMENTS

1972 No. 1237 (S.88)

RATING AND VALUATION

The British Railways Board (Amendment of Certified Amount) (Scotland) Order 1972

Laid before Parliament in draft

Made - - -		*7th August* 1972
Coming into Operation		*8th August* 1972

In exercise of the powers conferred on me by section 109(1) of the Local Government Act 1948(**a**) and section 11 of the Local Government (Financial Provisions) (Scotland) Act 1963(**b**) and of all other powers enabling me in that behalf, and after consultation with the British Railways Board and such associations of local authorities as appeared to me to be concerned, I hereby make the following order, in the terms of a draft approved by resolution of each House of Parliament: —

1.—(1) This order may be cited as the British Railways Board (Amendment of Certified Amount) (Scotland) Order 1972 and shall come into operation on 8th August 1972.

(2) The Interpretation Act 1889(**c**) shall apply for the interpretation of this order as it applies for the interpretation of an Act of Parliament.

2. For the purpose of determining the standard amount for the British Railways Board in Scotland under section 66(3) of the Transport Act 1962(**d**) for the year 1972-73 and subsequent years, the amount certified by the Secretary of State in accordance with the provisions of section 2(1) of the Local Government (Financial Provisions, etc.) (Scotland) Act 1962(**e**), as amended by the British Railways Board (Amendment of Certified Amount) (Scotland) Order 1967(**f**), namely £160,000 is hereby further amended to £279,000.

Gordon Campbell,
One of Her Majesty's
Principal Secretaries of State.

St. Andrew's House,
Edinburgh.

7th August 1972.

(**a**) 1948 c. 26.	(**b**) 1963 c. 12.
(**c**) 1889 c. 63.	(**d**) 1962 c. 46.
(**e**) 1962 c. 9.	(**f**) S.I. 1967/1175 (1967 II, p. 3460).

EXPLANATORY NOTE

(This Note is not part of the Order.)

The purpose of this Order is to adjust, for 1972-73 and subsequent years, the standard amount on which the payments to Scottish local authorities by the British Railways Board in lieu of rates are based, to take account of the general increase in valuations following the 1971 revaluation.

STATUTORY INSTRUMENTS

1972 No. 1239 (S.90)

EDUCATION, SCOTLAND

The Teachers Superannuation (Financial Provisions and Family Benefits) (Scotland) Regulations 1972

Made - - -		*9th August* 1972
Laid before Parliament		*18th August* 1972
Coming into Operation		*8th September* 1972

In exercise of the powers conferred upon me by section 9 of the Superannuation Act 1972(**a**) and of all other powers enabling me in that behalf, with the consent of the Minister for the Civil Service and after consultation with representatives of education authorities and of teachers and with such representatives of other persons likely to be affected as appear to me to be appropriate, I hereby make the following regulations: —

Citation, commencement and interpretation

1.—(1) These regulations may be cited as the Teachers Superannuation (Financial Provisions and Family Benefits) (Scotland) Regulations 1972.

(2) These regulations shall come into operation on 8th September 1972 and shall have effect as from 1st April 1972.

(3) These regulations—

(*a*) in so far as they amend the Teachers Superannuation (Financial Provisions) (Scotland) Regulations 1972(**b**) (in these regulations called "the Financial Provisions Regulations") shall be construed as one with the Teachers Superannuation (Scotland) Regulations 1969 to 1972(**c**) and shall be included among the regulations which may be cited together under that title;

(*b*) in so far as they amend the Teachers Superannuation (Family Benefits) (Scotland) Regulations 1971 to 1972(**d**) shall be construed as one with those regulations and shall be included among the regulations which may be cited together under that title.

(4) The Interpretation Act 1889(**e**) shall apply for the interpretation of these regulations as it applies for the interpretation of an Act of Parliament.

(a) 1972 c. 11.   (b) S.I. 1972/551 (1972 I, p. 1855).
(c) S.I. 1969/77, 659, 1971/1995, 1972/551 (1969 I, p. 133; II, p. 1820; 1971 III, p. 5683; 1972 I, p. 1855).
(d) S.I. 1971/1775; 1972/442 (1971 III, p. 4813; 1972 I, p. 1644).
(e) 1889 c. 63.

Calculation of average salary

2.—(1) Regulation 4 of the Financial Provisions Regulations shall have effect subject to the substitution for paragraphs (1) and (2) of the following paragraphs : —

"(1) For the purposes of the Teachers Regulations the average salary of a teacher shall be taken, subject as in this regulation provided, to be

(*a*) in the case of a teacher who has been continuously employed in reckonable service throughout the period of his terminal service, the highest amount of his full salary for any year in that period;

(*b*) in the case of a teacher who has not been continuously employed in reckonable service throughout that period, the highest amount of his full salary for any 365 successive days of reckonable service in that period.

(2) If a teacher has been employed in reckonable service for less than one year, his average salary shall, except as provided in regulation 55 of the Teachers Regulations, be taken to be the average annual rate of his full salary during his reckonable service.

(2A) (*a*) In paragraph (1) the expression "terminal service" means, as respects any teacher who has been employed in reckonable service for three years or more, the three years of such service (whether continuous or not) next preceding the commencement of any annual superannuation allowance or the payment of an additional superannuation allowance or gratuity under the Teachers Regulations and, as respects any teacher who has not been employed in reckonable service for three years or more but has been employed for one year or more, the period of such service.

(*b*) in paragraph (1) references to a teacher's full salary are to be construed as references to his salary as calculated under paragraph (1) of regulation 3.

(*c*) In paragraph (1)(*a*) the word "year" means a period of twelve calendar months beginning on any day of any month."

(2) The definition in regulation 5(1) (Definitions) of the Teachers Superannuation (Scotland) Regulations 1969 of the expression "average salary" shall be construed as a reference to average salary as calculated under regulation 4(1) of the Financial Provisions Regulations as amended by these regulations.

(3) In respect of any teacher to whom superannuation allowances became payable before 1st April 1972 regulation 48(1) (Supplementary Death Gratuities) of the Teachers Superannuation (Scotland) Regulations 1969 shall have effect as if after the words "average salary" there were inserted the words "calculated in accordance with regulation 4(1) of the Teachers Superannuation (Financial Provisions) (Scotland) Regulations 1972": and in the interpretation of that regulation as so amended the provisions of paragraph (1) of this regulation shall be disregarded.

Increase in contributions

3. Regulation 5 (Financing of Benefits) of the Financial Provisions Regulations shall have effect subject to the substitution—

(*a*) in paragraph (2) (teacher's contribution) for the words "6 per cent" of the words "6$\frac{1}{2}$ per cent"; and

(b) in paragraph (3) (employer's contribution) for the words "6 per cent of the teacher's salary for the time being" of the words—

"the aggregate of—

    (a) $6\frac{1}{2}$ per cent of the teacher's salary for the time being; and

    (b) the balance of the new entrant contribution calculated in accordance with regulation 7A(2)"

New entrant contribution

4. After regulation 7 of the Financial Provisions Regulations there shall be inserted as a new regulation—

"New entrant contribution

7A.—(1) In these regulations the expression "new entrant contribution" means the amount determined by the Government Actuary as the rate per cent of the salary of teachers who became employed in reckonable service on 1st April 1972 at which contributions paid to the Secretary of State would in his opinion defray the costs of the benefits likely to be payable in respect of their service.

(2) For the purposes of paragraph (3)(b) of regulation 5 the balance of the new entrant contribution shall be calculated by deducting from the rate per cent so determined the sum of 13 per cent (being the aggregate of the rates per cent specified in paragraphs (2) and (3)(a) of that regulation).

(3) Where a determination made by the Government Actuary under this regulation is expressed to be provisional the references in these regulations to the new entrant contribution shall be construed as references to the contribution so determined until that determination is superseded by a determination expressed to be final.

(4) The report of the actuarial inquiry held in pursuance of section 5 of the Teachers Superannuation (Scotland) Act 1968(**a**) shall specify any determination made by the Government Actuary under this regulation."

General Account A

5. All sums payable to the Secretary of State in respect of contributions payable after 31st March 1972 under the Teachers Superannuation (Family Benefits) (Scotland) Regulations 1971 to 1972 shall be paid into a part of the General Account, to be called General Account A, which shall be kept separate from the rest of that Account; and the provisions of those regulations which relate to payment out of the General Account shall have no application in respect of General Account A.

Discontinuance of normal contributions under the Teachers, Widows' and Children's Scheme

6.—(1) Subject to paragraph (2) below, normal contributions under regulations 24 and 25(1) of the Teachers Superannuation (Family Benefits) (Scotland) Regulations 1971 to 1972 shall cease to be payable to the Secretary of State and accordingly—

    (a) in regulation 24, the words "normal contributions in respect of his reckonable service after the Scheme becomes applicable to him and"; and

    (b) in regulation 25, paragraph (1)—

shall cease to have effect and are hereby revoked.

(**a**) 1968 c. 12.

(2) The provisions of paragraph (1) above shall not affect any liability to pay normal contributions under paragraphs (2) and (3) regulation 25 of the Teachers Superannuation (Family Benefits) (Scotland) Regulations 1971 to 1972.

Gordon Campbell,
One of Her Majesty's Principal
Secretaries of State.

St Andrew's House,
Edinburgh.
8th August 1972.

Consent of the Minister for the Civil Service
given under his Official Seal on 9th August 1972.

L.S.

W. G. Bristow,
Authorised by the Minister
for the Civil Service.

EXPLANATORY NOTE

(This Note is not part of the Regulations.)

These Regulations amend the provisions of the Teachers Superannuation (Scotland) Regulations 1969 to 1972 for the calculation of the benefits payable to or in respect of a teacher and increase the contributions payable by the teacher and his employer under those Regulations.

The Regulations amend the Teachers Superannuation (Family Benefits) (Scotland) Regulations 1971 to 1972 by providing for the discontinuance of normal contributions and the payment of additional contributions into, and their retention in, a separate account.

The Regulations have retrospective effect by virtue of section 12(1) of the Superannuation Act 1972.

STATUTORY INSTRUMENTS

1972 No. 1240

NATIONAL ASSISTANCE SERVICES

The National Assistance (Charges for Accommodation) Regulations 1972

Made - - -	*9th August* 1972
Laid before Parliament	*18th August* 1972
Coming into Operation	*2nd October* 1972

The Secretary of State for Social Services, in exercise of his powers under section 22 of the National Assistance Act 1948(**a**), and of all other powers enabling him in that behalf, hereby makes the following regulations: —

Citation and commencement

1. These regulations may be cited as the National Assistance (Charges for Accommodation) Regulations 1972, and shall come into operation on 2nd October 1972.

Interpretation

2.—(1) In these regulations unless the context otherwise requires—

"the Act of 1948" means the National Assistance Act 1948;

"the Act of 1970" means the National Insurance (Old persons' and widows' pensions and attendance allowance) Act 1970(**b**); ·

"Personal Injuries Scheme", "Service Pensions Instrument" and "1914-18 War Injuries Scheme" have the same meanings as in the National Insurance (Overlapping Benefits) Regulations 1972(**c**).

(2) Any reference in these regulations to the provisions of any enactment or instrument shall be construed, unless the context otherwise requires, as a reference to those provisions as amended by any subsequent enactment or instrument.

(3) The Interpretation Act 1889(**d**) applies to the interpretation of these regulations as it applies to the interpretation of an Act of Parliament and as if these regulations and the regulations hereby revoked were Acts of Parliament.

Revocation of existing regulations

3. The National Assistance (Charges for Accommodation) Regulations 1971(**e**) are hereby revoked.

(**a**) 1948 c. 29.	(**b**) 1970 c. 51.	(**c**) S.I. 1972/604 (1972 I, p. 1994).
(**d**) 1889 c. 63.	(**e**) S I. 1971/1404 (1971 II, p. 3938).	

Prescription of minimum charges

4. For the purposes of section 22(3) of the Act of 1948 (which relates to charges to be made for accommodation provided under Part III of the Act) the liability of a person to pay for accommodation provided in premises managed by a local authority shall in no case be reduced below the sum of £5·40 per week.

5. Where accommodation is provided for a child accompanied by a person over the age of 16, the liability of that person under section 22(7) of the Act of 1948 to pay for the accommodation of that child shall in no case be reduced below such one of the following sums as is appropriate, that is to say : —

(*a*) in respect of a child under 5 years of age, the sum of £1·90 per week;

(*b*) in respect of a child aged 5 years or over but less than 11 years, the sum of £2·25 per week;

(*c*) in respect of a child aged 11 years or over but less than 13 years, the sum of £2·75 per week;

(*d*) in respect of a child aged 13 years or over but less than 16 years, the sum of £3·40 per week.

Prescription of sum needed for personal requirements

6. For the purposes of section 22(4) of the Act of 1948 a local authority shall assume that a person to whom subsection (3) of that section applies will need for his personal requirements the sum of £1·35 per week;

Provided that if that person is someone to whom there is payable attendance allowance under the provisions of section 4(2) of the Act of 1970 as amended by section 14 of and paragraph 12(2) of Schedule 5 to the National Insurance Act 1971(**a**) or constant attendance allowance under any Personal Injuries Scheme, Service Pensions Instrument or any 1914-18 War Injuries Scheme, the aforementioned sum assumed to be needed for his personal requirements shall be increased by the amount of such attendance allowance or constant attendance allowance.

Keith Joseph,
Secretary of State for Social Services.

9th August 1972.

(**a**) 1971 c. 50.

EXPLANATORY NOTE

(This Note is not part of the Regulations.)

These Regulations supersede the National Assistance (Charges for Accommodation) Regulations 1971. The minimum weekly amount which a person is required to pay for accommodation managed by a local authority under Part III of the National Assistance Act 1948 is increased from £4·80 to £5·40. Where a person is accompanied by a child the weekly amounts payable in respect of the child are increased from £1·70 to £1·90 when the child is under 5 years, from £2 to £2·25 when the child is aged 5 years or over but less than 11 years, from £2·45 to £2·75 when the child is aged 11 years or over but less than 13 years and from £3 to £3·40 when the child is aged 13 years or over but less than 16 years. The weekly sum for personal requirements which (unless in special circumstances the local authority considers a different sum appropriate) the local authority shall allow in assessing a person's ability to pay for accommodation is increased from £1·20 to £1·35 but if the person is one to whom there is payable attendance allowance under the Act of 1970 (as amended) or constant attendance allowance under any Personal Injuries Scheme, Service Pensions Instrument or any 1914-18 War Injuries Scheme, the weekly sum for personal requirements shall be increased by that amount.

STATUTORY INSTRUMENTS

1972 No. 1241

PENSIONS

The Pensions Increase (Federated Superannuation Scheme for Nurses and Hospital Officers) (Metropolitan Civil Staffs) Regulations 1972

Made - - -	*8th August* 1972
Laid before Parliament	*17th August* 1972
Coming into Operation	*1st October* 1972

In pursuance of sections 13(2), (4) and (5) and 18(2) of the Pensions (Increase) Act 1971(**a**) as amended by sections 25(1) and 29(1) of and Schedule 6 to the Superannuation Act 1972(**b**), I hereby, with the approval of the Minister for the Civil Service, make the following Regulations:—

Citation and commencement

1. These Regulations may be cited as the Pensions Increase (Federated Superannuation Scheme for Nurses and Hospital Officers) (Metropolitan Civil Staffs) Regulations 1972 and shall come into operation on 1st October 1972.

Interpretation

2.—(1) In these Regulations, unless the context otherwise requires, the expression—

"the Act of 1971" means the Pensions (Increase) Act 1971;

"average remuneration", in relation to any person, means the average amount of the salary and emoluments of his office during the last three years of his reckonable service;

"the civil service pension scheme" means the principal civil service pension scheme within the meaning of section 2 of the Superannuation Act 1972 and for the time being in force;

"an F.S.S.N. scheme" means a superannuation scheme operated under the Federated Superannuation Scheme for Nurses and Hospital Officers;

"notional pension", in relation to any person, means the notional pension referred to in Regulation 5 of these Regulations;

(**a**) 1971 c. 56.   (**b**) 1972 c. 11.

"reckonable service", in relation to any person, means any period of relevant employment during which the person was subject to an F.S.S.N. scheme and in respect of which the contributions authorised or required to be paid under the scheme by the employer were duly paid;

"relevant employment" means employment within the meaning of paragraph (c) of Schedule 6 to the Act of 1971 (metropolitan civil staffs employment).

(2) The Interpretation Act 1889(a) shall apply for the interpretation of these Regulations as it applies for the interpretation of an Act of Parliament.

Effect of the Regulations

3. These Regulations shall apply for the payment to persons described in Regulation 4 of these Regulations of the allowances described in Regulation 6 of these Regulations, being allowances which appear to be appropriate having regard to the benefits provided by Part I of the Act of 1971 for persons whose superannuation benefits are regulated under the civil service pension scheme.

Persons to whom the Regulations apply

4. These Regulations shall apply to any person who—

(a) has retired from relevant employment after attaining the age of 60 years; and

(b) at the date of his retirement was subject to an F.S.S.N. scheme and had completed 10 years' reckonable service; and

(c) has received or become entitled to receive payment of any retirement benefit under that scheme.

Notional pension

5.—(1) There shall be ascribed to each person to whom these Regulations apply a notional pension calculated by multiplying one eightieth of his average remuneration by the number of completed years of his reckonable service.

(2) In calculating a notional pension any fraction of a pound shall be treated as a whole pound.

Payments of benefis equivalent to statutory pension increases

6.—(1) The Secretary of State may—

(a) in respect of any period beginning on or after 1st September 1971, direct payment out of the Metropolitan Police Fund to any person to whom these Regulations apply of an allowance equal to the benefits conferred by sections 1 and 6 of the Act of 1971 on persons whose superannuation benefits are regulated under the civil service pension scheme which would have been payable to him if he had been eligible under that scheme for a pension, beginning on the day after the last day of his reckonable service, the basic rate of which was of the same amount as his notional pension; and

---

(a) 1889 c. 63.

(*b*) in respect of any period beginning on or after 1st December 1972, direct payment as aforesaid to any such person of an allowance equal to the increase which would, by virtue of an Order made under section 2 of the Act of 1971, have been payable to him if he had been eligible as aforesaid.

(2) In relation to any period before the coming into operation of these Regulations, nothing in this Regulation shall affect any allowance payable by virtue of section 18(2) of the Act of 1971 (which contains transitional provisions) but any payment on account of such an allowance, so far as it could have been made on account of an allowance payable by virtue of this Regulation, shall be treated for the purposes thereof as if it had been so made.

3rd August 1972.

Robert Carr,
One of Her Majesty's Principal
Secretaries of State.

Approval of the Minister for the Civil Service given under his Official Seal on 8th August 1972.

(L.S.)

A. W. Wyatt,
Authorised by the
Minister for the Civil Service.

EXPLANATORY NOTE

(*This Note is not part of the Regulations.*)

Where a person on retirement from employment as a member of the civil staff of the Metropolitan Police was entitled to superannuation benefits under a scheme operated under the Federated Superannuation Scheme for Nurses and Hospital Officers (F.S.S.N.), those benefits will not have been increased by the Pensions (Increase) Act 1971, since they are provided by means of insurance policies. Equally, a person who was so entitled is not eligible for any increase which may be provided for by an order made under section 2 of that Act by the Minister for the Civil Service.

These Regulations enable benefits to be paid to such a person out of the Metropolitan Police Fund corresponding to the benefits for which provision is made by the 1971 Act for retired civil servants who are in receipt of pensions under the principal civil service pension scheme.

The benefit of the Regulations is made retrospective to 1st September 1971 under powers conferred by sections 13(5) and 18(2) of the 1971 Act.

STATUTORY INSTRUMENTS

1972 No. 1242

PLANT HEALTH

The Dutch Elm Disease (Local Authorities) (Amendment) Order 1972

Made - - -	10*th August* 1972
Laid before Parliament	16*th August* 1972
Coming into Operation	7*th September* 1972

The Forestry Commissioners, by virtue and in exercise of the powers vested in them by section 3(1), (2) and (4) of the Plant Health Act 1967(**a**), and of every other power enabling them in that behalf, hereby make the following Order:—

1. This Order, which may be cited as the Dutch Elm Disease (Local Authorities) (Amendment) Order 1972, shall come into operation on 7th September 1972.

2. The Interpretation Act 1889(**b**) shall apply for the interpretation of this Order as it applies for the interpretation of an Act of Parliament.

3. The Schedule to the Dutch Elm Disease (Local Authorities) Order 1971(**c**), as amended (**d**), shall be further amended by the addition thereto of the local authorities specified in the Schedule hereto.

IN WITNESS whereof the Official Seal of the Forestry Commissioners is hereunto affixed on 10th August 1972.

P. Nicholls,
Forestry Commissioner.

THE SCHEDULE
LOCAL AUTHORITIES

County Councils
  Cheshire
  Dorset
  Hampshire
  Salop
  Staffordshire

Non-county Borough Councils
  Banbury
  Crewe
  Dukinfield
  Macclesfield
  Stalybridge
  Warwick

County Borough Councils
  Birkenhead
  Dudley
  Newport
  Oxford
  Stockport
  Swansea
  Wallasey

London Borough Councils
  Barking
  Hounslow
  Lambeth

(**a**) 1967 c. 8.   (**b**) 1889 c. 63.   (**c**) S.I. 1971/1708 (1971 III, p. 4994).
(**d**) The relevant amending instruments are S.I. 1971/1823, 1963 (1971 III, pp. 4994, 5302).

EXPLANATORY NOTE

(This Note is not part of the Order.)

This Order amends the Dutch Elm Disease (Local Authorities) Order 1971 by adding further local authorities to the local authorities who are empowered by that Order as amended by the Dutch Elm Disease (Local Authorities) (Amendment) Order 1971 and the Dutch Elm Disease (Local Authorities) (Amendment) (No. 2) Order 1971 to take steps in connection with the disease of elm trees known as Dutch elm disease.

STATUTORY INSTRUMENTS

1972 No. 1243

INDUSTRIAL INVESTMENT

The Concorde (Production Financing) Order 1972

Laid before the House of Commons in draft

Made - - -	*9th August* 1972
Coming into Operation	*1st September* 1972

The Secretary of State, with the approval of the Treasury, in exercise of his powers under subsection (4) of section 8 of the Industrial Expansion Act 1968(**a**) and of all other powers enabling him in that behalf hereby makes the following Order, a draft of which has been approved by a resolution of the House of Commons in accordance with the said subsection: —

1. This Order may be cited as the Concorde (Production Financing) Order 1972 and shall come into operation on 1st September 1972.

2. The limit of £100 million specified in subsection (3) of section 8 of the Industrial Expansion Act 1968 in relation to the types of financial support for the production of the Concorde aircraft mentioned in that subsection is increased to £125 million.

Michael Heseltine,
Minister for Aerospace,
7th August 1972.   Department of Trade and Industry.

We approve the making of this Order.

V. H. Goodhew,
Oscar Murton,
9th August 1972.   Two of the Lords Commissioners of
Her Majesty's Treasury.

(**a**) 1968 c. 32.

EXPLANATORY NOTE

(This Note is not part of the Order.)

Section 8 of the Industrial Expansion Act 1968 authorises the provision of finance by the Secretary of State for the production of Concorde aircraft and sets a limit of £100 million on the aggregate of the amount of loans made by him, guarantees in respect of loans made by others and sums paid in respect of such guarantees. Subsection (4) of the section enables the Secretary of State to increase this limit by Order to an amount not exceeding £125 million. This Order increases the limit to that figure.

STATUTORY INSTRUMENTS

1972 No. 1244

AGRICULTURE

CORN CROPS

The Corn Returns Act 1882 (Amendment of Units) Order 1972

Made - - - 10*th August* 1972

Coming into Operation 1*st September* 1972

The Minister of Agriculture, Fisheries and Food, in exercise of the powers conferred on him by section 17(2) of the Agriculture (Miscellaneous Provisions) Act 1972(**a**), and of all other powers enabling him in that behalf, hereby makes the following order:—

Citation and commencement

1. This order may be cited as the Corn Returns Act 1882 (Amendment of Units) Order 1972, and shall come into operation on 1st September 1972.

Amendment of Corn Returns Act 1882

2.—(1) Sections 8 and 9(6) of the Corn Returns Act 1882(**b**) (which respectively require that computations of corn in returns under that Act shall be in hundredweights and that the annual and septennial average price published in pursuance of that Act shall be for a hundredweight of corn) shall have effect as respects England and Wales as if for any reference to the hundredweight of one hundred and twelve imperial standard pounds there were substituted a reference to the ton of two thousand two hundred and forty imperial standard pounds.

(2) In applying section 9(4) of the said Act (which provides the method of calculating weekly, quarterly and yearly average prices for British corn) to the ascertainment of the quarterly average price for the quarter ending on 29th September 1972, and to the ascertainment of the yearly average price for the year ending 25th December 1972, any weekly average price originally computed with reference to the hundredweight of one hundred and twelve imperial standard pounds shall be recalculated with reference to the ton of two thousand two hundred and forty imperial standard pounds.

(3) In applying section 9(5) of the said Act (which provides the method of calculating septennial average prices) to the ascertainment of the septennial average price for any period of seven years ending on or after 25th December 1972, any yearly average price originally computed with reference to the hundredweight of one hundred and twelve imperial standard pounds shall be recalculated with reference to the ton of two thousand two hundred and forty imperial standard pounds.

(**a**) 1972 c. 62. (**b**) 1882 c. 37.

In Witness whereof the Official Seal of the Minister of Agriculture, Fisheries and Food is hereunto affixed on 10th August 1972.

(L.S.)　　　　　　　　　　　　　　*J. M. L. Prior,*
　　　　　　　　　　Minister of Agriculture, Fisheries and Food.

EXPLANATORY NOTE

(This Note is not part of the order.)

This order amends sections 8 and 9(6) of the Corn Returns Act 1882 so that from the date of coming into operation of the order weekly returns made in pursuance of the Act, and annual and septennial prices of British corn published under it shall be in terms of the imperial ton instead of, as formerly, the imperial hundredweight. Transitional provisions are also made governing the publication of average prices which relate to a period during which returns have been made both in terms of the hundredweight and the ton.

STATUTORY INSTRUMENTS

1972 No. 1245

AGRICULTURE

CORN CROPS

The Corn Returns (Amendment) Regulations 1972

Made - - -	*10th August* 1972
Coming into Operation	*1st September* 1972

The Minister of Agriculture, Fisheries and Food in exercise of his powers under sections 4, 5 and 14 of the Corn Returns Act 1882(a) (as amended by section 2 of the Corn Sales Act 1921(b), section 18 of the Agriculture (Miscellaneous Provisions) Act 1943(c) and section 108 of the Agriculture Act 1970(d), as read with an Order in Council dated 30th July 1891(e), section 1 of the Ministry of Agriculture and Fisheries Act 1919(f) and article 3 of the Transfer of Functions (Ministry of Food) Order 1955(g), and with the Corn Returns Act 1882 (Amendment of Units) Order 1972(h)) and all other powers enabling him in that behalf, hereby makes the following regulations: —

Citation, interpretation and commencement

1. These regulations, which may be cited as the Corn Returns (Amendment) Regulations 1972, shall be construed as one with the Corn Returns Regulations 1970(i) (in these regulations referred to as "the principal regulations"), and shall come into operation on 1st September 1972.

Amendment of principal regulations

2.—(1) In regulation 2(1) (interpretation) of the principal regulations the following definition shall be inserted: —

" "denatured" in relation to wheat means rendered, before purchase, unfit for human consumption, by treatment with dye, fish oil or fish liver oil"

(2) Schedule 2 to the principal regulations (which sets out the form of return required by those regulations) shall be deleted from the principal regulations, and there shall be substituted therefor the Schedule to these regulations.

In Witness whereof the Official Seal of the Minister of Agriculture, Fisheries and Food is hereunto affixed on 10th August 1972.

(L.S.)

J. M. L. Prior,
Minister of Agriculture, Fisheries and Food.

(a) 1882 c. 37.　　　　(b) 1921 c. 35.　　　　(c) 1943 c. 16.
(d) 1970 c. 40.　　(e) S.R. & O. Rev. I, p. 614: 1891, p. 64.　　(f) 1919 c. 91.
(g) S.I. 1955/554 (1955 I, p. 1200).
(h) S.I. 1972/1244 (1972 II, p. 3752).　　　　(i) S.I. 1970/1047 (1970 II, p. 3247).

SCHEDULE

CORN RETURNS ACT 1882 (As Amended)

A return of all British corn bought from growers during the week ended midnight Thursday   19   by the undersigned buyer carrying on business in the area of

SECTION 1 (1)	For Official Use (2)	Total purchases made during week					Total Purchase Price (6)
		Quantity					
		Ex Farm (3)		Free on rail or delivered (4)		Total (5)	
		tons	cwt.	tons	cwt.	tons cwt.	£
WHEAT—other than de-natured							
WHEAT—denatured							
WHEAT—TOTAL							
BARLEY							
OATS							
RYE							
MAIZE							

SECTION 2 (7)		Ex Farm Forward Fixed Price Contracts & Ex Farm Spot Purchases made during week			
		Ex Farm Forward Fixed Price Contracts		Ex Farm Spot Purchases	
		Total Quantity (8)	Total Purchase Price (9)	Total Quantity (10)	Total Purchase Price (11)
		tons cwt.	£	tons cwt.	£
WHEAT*					
„ seed					
„ milling hard					
„ milling soft					
„ feeding—other than denatured					
„ feeding— de-natured					
BARLEY*					
„ seed					
„ malting					
„ feeding & milling					
OATS*					
„ seed					
„ milling					
„ feeding					
RYE					
MAIZE					

SECTION 3 (12)	Ex Farm Spot Prices paid for Malting Barley during week	
	Highest £..................per ton (13)	Lowest £..................per ton (14)

*WHEAT, BARLEY or OATS bought and coming within any category other than those specified should be included with feeding grain

Signed ....

Name of Firm or Company ....   Telephone ....

Address ....

....   Telex ....

....

EXPLANATORY NOTE

(This Note is not part of the Regulations.)

These regulations amend the Corn Returns Regulations 1970 by substituting a new form of return for the previous form. The principal change in this form is a change from hundredweights and pounds to tons and hundredweights as the units in terms of which quantities of corn purchased are to be listed. Provision is also made for details of transactions in denatured wheat to be separately identified within the returns.

STATUTORY INSTRUMENTS

1972 No. 1246

CUSTOMS AND EXCISE

The Import Duties (Temporary Exemptions) (No. 11) Order 1972

Made - - - -	11*th August* 1972
Laid before the *House of Commons*	11*th August* 1972
Coming into Operation	12*th August* 1972

The Lords Commissioners of Her Majesty's Treasury, by virtue of the powers conferred on them by sections 3(6) and 13 of the Import Duties Act 1958(**a**), and of all other powers enabling them in that behalf, on the recommendation of the Secretary of State(**b**), hereby make the following Order:—

1.—(1) This Order may be cited as the Import Duties (Temporary Exemptions) (No. 11) Order 1972.

(2) The Interpretation Act 1889(**c**) shall apply for the interpretation of this Order as it applies for the interpretation of an Act of Parliament.

(3) This Order shall come into operation on 12th August 1972.

2.—(1) Until the beginning of 3rd October 1972 any import duty which is for the time being chargeable on goods of heading 73.40 of the Customs Tariff 1959 shall not be chargeable in respect of circular can ends of tinplate, of a thickness of not less than $0 \cdot 15$ millimetre nor more than $0 \cdot 35$ millimetre, of an overall diameter of not less than 54 millimetres nor more than 200 millimetres, whether or not enamelled or lacquered on one or both sides, and having a curled edge.

(2) For the purposes of classification under the Customs Tariff 1959, in so far as that depends on the rate of duty, any goods to which paragraph (1) above applies shall be treated as chargeable with the same duty as if this Order had not been made.

V. H. Goodhew,

Hugh Rossi,

Two of the Lords Commissioners
of Her Majesty's Treasury.

11th August 1972.

EXPLANATORY NOTE

(This Note is not part of the Order.)

This Order provides for the temporary exemption from import duty, until 3rd October 1972, of certain can ends of tinplate.

(**a**) 1958 c. 6.   (**b**) *See* S.I. 1970/1537 (1970 III, p. 5293).   (**c**) 1889 c. 63.

STATUTORY INSTRUMENTS

1972 No. 1252

SUGAR

The Sugar (Distribution Payments) (No. 16) Order 1972

Made - - - -	11*th August* 1972
Laid before Parliament	14*th August* 1972
Coming into Operation	15*th August* 1972

The Minister of Agriculture, Fisheries and Food, in exercise of the powers conferred upon him by sections 14(5) and 33(4) of the Sugar Act 1956(a), having effect subject to the provisions of section 3 of, and Part II of Schedule 5 to, the Finance Act 1962(b), section 22 of the Finance Act 1964(c) and section 52 of the Finance Act 1966(d) and of all other powers enabling him in that behalf, with the concurrence of the Treasury, and on the advice of the Sugar Board hereby makes the following order:—

1.—(1) This order may be cited as the Sugar (Distribution Payments) (No. 16) Order 1972, and shall come into operation on 15th August 1972.

(2) The Interpretation Act 1889(e) shall apply for the interpretation of this order as it applies for the interpretation of an Act of Parliament.

2. Notwithstanding the provisions of article 2 of the Sugar (Distribution Payments) (No. 15) Order 1972(f), the rates of distribution payments payable under and in accordance with the provisions of section 14 of the Sugar Act 1956, having effect as aforesaid, in respect of sugar and invert sugar imported or home produced or used in the manufacture of imported composite sugar products shall on and after 15th August 1972 be those rates specified in the Schedule to this order; and section 10 of the Finance Act 1901(g) (which relates to new or altered customs or excise duties and their effect upon contracts) shall apply accordingly.

In Witness whereof the Official Seal of the Minister of Agriculture, Fisheries and Food is hereunto affixed on 9th August 1972.

(L.S.)

E. J. G. Smith,
Authorised by the Minister.

We concur.
11th August 1972.

V. H. Goodhew,
Oscar Murton,
Two of the Lords Commissioners of
Her Majesty's Treasury.

(a) 1956 c. 48.   (b) 1962 c. 44.   (c) 1964 c. 49.   (d) 1966 c. 18.
(e) 1889 c. 63.   (f) S.I. 1972/1134 (1972 II, p. 3340).   (g) 1901 c. 7.

SCHEDULE
PART I
RATES OF DISTRIBUTION PAYMENT FOR SUGAR

Polarisation	Rate of Distribution Payment per ton
Exceeding:—	£
99°	6·000
98° but not exceeding 99°	5·658
97° ,, ,, ,, 98°	5·520
96° ,, ,, ,, 97°	5·376
95° ,, ,, ,, 96°	5·232
94° ,, ,, ,, 95°	5·088
93° ,, ,, ,, 94°	4·944
92° ,, ,, ,, 93°	4·800
91° ,, ,, ,, 92°	4·656
90° ,, ,, ,, 91°	4·512
89° ,, ,, ,, 90°	4·368
88° ,, ,, ,, 89°	4·224
87° ,, ,, ,, 88°	4·104
86° ,, ,, ,, 87°	3·984
85° ,, ,, ,, 86°	3·876
84° ,, ,, ,, 85°	3·768
83° ,, ,, ,, 84°	3·660
82° ,, ,, ,, 83°	3·552
81° ,, ,, ,, 82°	3·456
80° ,, ,, ,, 81°	3·360
79° ,, ,, ,, 80°	3·264
78° ,, ,, ,, 79°	3·168
77° ,, ,, ,, 78°	3·072
76° ,, ,, ,, 77°	2·976
Not exceeding 76°	2·880

PART II
RATES OF DISTRIBUTION PAYMENT FOR INVERT SUGAR

Sweetening matter content by weight	Rate of Distribution Payment per cwt.
	£
70 per cent. or more	0·19
Less than 70 per cent. and more than 50 per cent.	0·13
Not more than 50 per cent.	0·06

EXPLANATORY NOTE
(This Note is not part of the Order.)

This order provides for increases equivalent to £4 per ton of refined sugar in the rates of distribution payment in respect of sugar and invert sugar which become eligible for such payments on and after 15th August 1972.

STATUTORY INSTRUMENTS

1972 No. 1253

SUGAR

The Sugar (Distribution Repayments) (Amendment) (No. 15) Order 1972

Made	-	-	-	11*th August* 1972
Laid before Parliament				14*th August* 1972
Coming into Operation				15*th August* 1972

The Minister of Agriculture, Fisheries and Food, in exercise of the powers conferred upon him by sections 15 and 33(4) of the Sugar Act 1956(**a**), having effect subject to the provisions of section 3 of, and Part II of Schedule 5 to, the Finance Act 1962(**b**), section 22 of the Finance Act 1964(**c**) and section 52 of the Finance Act 1966(**d**) and of all other powers enabling him in that behalf, an order(**e**) having been made under section 14 of the said Act, hereby makes the following order:—

1.—(1) This order may be cited as the Sugar (Distribution Repayments) (Amendment) (No. 15) Order 1972, and shall come into operation on 15th August 1972.

(2) The Interpretation Act 1889(**f**) shall apply for the interpretation of this order as it applies for the interpretation of an Act of Parliament.

2.—(1) Notwithstanding the provisions of article 2(1) of the Sugar (Distribution Repayments) (Amendment) (No. 14) Order 1972(**g**) the amount of distribution repayment payable in respect of invert sugar, if the relevant drawback is payable thereon as being invert sugar produced in the United Kingdom from materials on which sugar duty has been paid on or after 15th August 1972, shall be calculated thereon at the rate applicable to the invert sugar in accordance with the rates prescribed in the Schedule to this order.

(2) Article 2(1) of the Sugar (Distribution Repayments) Order 1972(**h**) shall apply for the interpretation of this article.

In Witness whereof the Official Seal of the Minister of Agriculture, Fisheries and Food is hereunto affixed on 11th August 1972.

(L.S.)

E. J. G. Smith,
Authorised by the Minister.

(**a**) 1956 c. 48. (**b**) 1962 c. 44. (**c**) 1964 c. 49.
(**d**) 1966 c. 18. (**e**) S.I. 1972/1252 (1972 II, p. 3758). (**f**) 1889 c. 63.
(**g**) S.I. 1972/1135 (1972 II, p. 3342). (**h**) S.I. 1972/67 (1972 I, p. 162).

THE SCHEDULE

RATES OF DISTRIBUTION REPAYMENT FOR INVERT SUGAR

Sweetening matter content by weight	Rate of Distribution Repayment per cwt.
	£
More than 80 per cent.	0 ·22
More than 70 per cent. but not more than 80 per cent.	0 ·19
More than 60 per cent. but not more than 70 per cent.	0 ·13
More than 50 per cent. but not more than 60 per cent.	0 ·10
Not more than 50 per cent. and the invert sugar not being less in weight than 14 lb. per gallon	0 ·06

EXPLANATORY NOTE

(This Note is not part of the Order.)

This order, which is consequent upon the Sugar (Distribution Payments) (No. 16) Order 1972 (S.I. 1972/1252), provides for increases equivalent to £4 per ton of refined sugar in the rates of distribution repayment, in respect of sugar and invert sugar produced in the United Kingdom from materials which become eligible for distribution payments on or after 15th August 1972.

STATUTORY INSTRUMENTS

1972 No. 1254

SUGAR

The Composite Sugar Products (Distribution Payments—Average Rates) (No. 16) Order 1972

Made - - - -	11*th August* 1972
Laid before Parliament	14*th August* 1972
Coming into Operation	15*th August* 1972

Whereas the Minister of Agriculture, Fisheries and Food (hereinafter called " the Minister ") has on the recommendation of the Sugar Board made an order(**a**) pursuant to the powers conferred upon him by section 9(1) of the Sugar Act 1956(**b**) having effect subject to section 14(8) of that Act and to the provisions of section 3 of, and Part II of Schedule 5 to, the Finance Act 1962(**c**), section 22 of the Finance Act 1964(**d**) and section 52 of the Finance Act 1966(**e**), providing that in the case of certain descriptions of composite sugar products distribution payments shall be calculated on the basis of an average quantity of sugar or invert sugar taken to have been used in the manufacture of the products and that certain other descriptions shall be treated as not containing any sugar or invert sugar:

And whereas the Minister has by the Sugar (Distribution Payments) (No. 16) Order 1972(**f**) provided for a change in the rates of distribution payments in respect of sugar and invert sugar which became eligible for such payments on and after 15th August 1972.

Now, therefore, the Minister on the recommendation of the Sugar Board, and in exercise of the powers conferred upon him by sections 9(1) and 33(4) of the Sugar Act 1956, having effect as aforesaid, and of all other powers enabling him in that behalf, hereby makes the following order:—

1.—(1) This order may be cited as the Composite Sugar Products (Distribution Payments—Average Rates) (No. 16) Order 1972, and shall come into operation on 15th August 1972.

(2) The Interpretation Act 1889(**g**) shall apply to the interpretation of this order as it applies to the interpretation of an Act of Parliament.

2. Distribution payments payable on or after 15th August 1972 under and in accordance with section 14 of the Sugar Act 1956, having effect as aforesaid, in respect of sugar and invert sugar used in the manufacture of the descriptions of imported composite sugar products specified in the second column of Schedule 1 to this order, being goods which are classified in the tariff headings indicated in relation to them in the first column of the said Schedule shall, notwithstanding the provisions of the Sugar (Distribution Payments) (No. 16) Order 1972 and the Composite Sugar Products (Distribution Payments—Average Rates) (No. 15) Order 1972(**a**) be calculated by reference to the weight of the products and the rates specified in relation thereto in the third column of the said Schedule.

3. Imported composite sugar products other than those of a description specified in Schedules 1 and 2 to this order shall be treated as not containing any sugar or invert sugar for the purposes of distribution payments.

(a) S.I. 1972/1136 (1972 II, p. 3344). (b) 1956 c. 48. (c) 1962 c. 44. (d) 1964 c. 49.
(e) 1966 c. 18. (f) S.I. 1972/1252 (1972 II, p. 3758). (g) 1889 c. 63

In Witness whereof the Official Seal of the Minister of Agriculture, Fisheries and Food is hereunto affixed on 11th August 1972.

(L.S.)

E. J. G. Smith,
Authorised by the Minister.

SCHEDULE 1

In this Schedule:—

" Tariff heading " means a heading or, where the context so requires, a subheading of the Customs Tariff 1959 (see paragraph (1) of Article 2 of the Import Duties (General) (No. 7) Order 1971)(a).

Tariff heading	Description of Composite Sugar Products	Rate of Distribution Payment
		Per cwt. £
04.02 ..	Milk and cream, preserved, concentrated or sweetened, containing more than 10 per cent. by weight of added sugar	0·13
17.02 (B) (2) and 17.05 (B)	Syrups containing sucrose sugar, whether or not flavoured or coloured, but not including fruit juices containing added sugar in any proportion:—	
	Containing 70 per cent. or more by weight of sweetening matter	0·19
	Containing less than 70 per cent., and more than 50 per cent. by weight of sweetening matter	0·13
	Containing not more than 50 per cent. by weight of sweetening matter	0·06
17.02 (F) ..	Caramel:—	
	Solid	0·30
	Liquid	0·20
17.04 ..	Sugar confectionery, not containing cocoa ..	0·24
18.06 ..	Chocolate and other food preparations containing cocoa and added sugar:—	
	Chocolate couverture not prepared for retail sale; chocolate milk crumb, liquid ..	0·13
	Chocolate milk crumb, solid	0·16
	Solid chocolate bars or blocks, milk or plain with or without fruit or nuts; other chocolate confectionery consisting wholly of chocolate or of chocolate and other ingredients not containing added sugar ..	0·13
	Other	0·17

(a) S.I. 1971/1971 (1971 III, p. 5330).

SCHEDULE 1—*continued*

Tariff heading	Description of Composite Sugar Products	Rate of Distribution Payment
		Per cwt. £
19.08 ..	Pastry, biscuits, cakes and other fine bakers' wares containing added sugar:—	
	Biscuits, wafers and rusks containing more than $12\frac{1}{2}$ per cent. by weight of added sugar, and other biscuits, wafers and rusks included in retail packages with such goods.. ..	0·07
	Cakes with covering or filling containing added sugar; meringues	0·09
	Other	0·03
20.01 ..	Vegetables and fruit, prepared or preserved by vinegar or acetic acid, containing added sugar:—	
	Containing 10 per cent. or more by weight of added sugar	0·10
	Other	0·02
20.03 ..	Fruit preserved by freezing, containing added sugar	0·03
20.04 ..	Fruit, fruit-peel and parts of plants, preserved by sugar (drained, glacé or crystallised)	0·19
20.05 ..	Jams, fruit jellies, marmalade, fruit puree and fruit pastes, being cooked preparations, containing added sugar	0·18
20.06 ..	Fruit otherwise prepared or preserved, containing added sugar:—	
	Ginger	0·15
	Other	0·03

SCHEDULE 2

Tariff heading	Description of Composite Sugar Products
17.05 (A) and (B)	Sugar and invert sugar, flavoured or coloured.

EXPLANATORY NOTE
(*This Note is not part of the Order.*)

This order provides for increases in the average rates of distribution payments payable in respect of imported composite sugar products of the descriptions specified in Schedule 1 on and after 15th August 1972. These correspond to increases in the rates of distribution payment effected by the Sugar (Distribution Payments) (No. 16) Order 1972 (S.I. 1972/1252). Provision is also made for certain imported composite sugar products to be treated as not containing any sugar or invert sugar.

STATUTORY INSTRUMENTS

1972 No. 1255

EDUCATION, ENGLAND AND WALES

The Standards for School Premises (Amendment) Regulations 1972

Made - - -	*10th August* 1972
Laid before Parliament	*21st August* 1972
Coming into Operation	*12th September* 1972

The Secretary of State for Education and Science and the Secretary of State for Wales, in joint exercise of their powers under section 10(1) of the Education Act 1944(**a**), hereby make the following regulations: —

Citation, commencement and interpretation

1.—(1) These regulations may be cited as the Standards for School Premises (Amendment) Regulations 1972 and shall come into operation on 12th September 1972.

(2) The Standards for School Premises Regulations 1959(**b**), the Standards for School Premises (Middle Schools and Minor Amendments) Regulations 1969(**c**), the Standards for School Premises (Amendment) Regulations 1971(**d**) and these regulations may be cited together as the Standards for School Premises Regulations 1959 to 1972.

(3) The Interpretation Act 1889(**e**) shall apply for the interpretation of these regulations as it applies for the interpretation of an Act of Parliament.

Amendment of 1959 Regulations

2. The Standards for School Premises Regulations 1959 as amended shall have effect subject to the insertion of the words "or such smaller area as may for special reasons be approved in the case of any school" immediately after—

    (*a*) the words "1¼ acres" in regulation 37 (playing field accommodation for special schools for educationally sub-normal day pupils); and

    (*b*) the words "5,600 square feet" in regulation 38 (teaching accommodation for special schools for educationally sub-normal pupils).

(**a**) 1944 c. 31.   (**b**) S.I. 1959/890 (1959 I, p. 1006).
(**c**) S.I. 1969/433 (1969 I, p. 1271).   (**d**) S.I. 1971/1553 (1971 III, 4364).
(**e**) 1889 c. 63.

Given under the Official Seal of the Secretary of State for Education and Science on 9th August 1972.

(L.S.)

Margaret H. Thatcher,

Secretary of State for Education and Science.

Given under my hand on 10th August 1972.

Peter Thomas,
Secretary of State for Wales.

EXPLANATORY NOTE

(This Note is not part of the Regulations.)

These regulations amend the provisions of the Standards for School Premises Regulations 1959 which prescribe a minimum area for the playing field and teaching accommodation for a special school for educationally subnormal children. They enable the Secretary of State to approve a smaller area for any particular school where there are special reasons.

STATUTORY INSTRUMENTS

1972 No. 1256 (C.30) (S.91)

NATIONAL HEALTH SERVICE, SCOTLAND

The National Health Service (Scotland) Act 1972 (Commencement No. 1) Order 1972

Made - - - 10*th August* 1972

In exercise of the powers conferred on me by section 65(1) of the National Health Service (Scotland) Act 1972(**a**), I hereby make the following Order: —

1. This Order may be cited as the National Health Service (Scotland) Act 1972 (Commencement No. 1) Order 1972.

2. Section 28 of the National Health Service (Scotland) Act 1972 shall come into operation on 21st August 1972.

Gordon Campbell,
One of Her Majesty's Principal
Secretaries of State.

St. Andrew's House,
Edinburgh.
10th August 1972.

EXPLANATORY NOTE

(*This Note is not part of the Order.*)

This Order brings into operation on 21st August 1972 section 28 of the National Health Service (Scotland) Act 1972, which relates to the appointment of the Scottish National Health Service Staff Commission.

(**a**) 1972 c. 58.

STATUTORY INSTRUMENTS

1972 No. 1258

SOCIAL SECURITY

The National Insurance (Industrial Injuries) (Prescribed Diseases) Amendment (No. 2) Regulations 1972

Made - - -	14*th August* 1972
Laid before Parliament	22*nd August* 1972
Coming into Operation	12*th September* 1972

The Secretary of State for Social Services, in exercise of his powers under sections 56 and 85 of the National Insurance (Industrial Injuries) Act 1965(**a**) and section 57 of that Act as modified by section 8 of the National Insurance Act 1966(**b**) and section 5 of the National Insurance Act 1972(**c**), and of all other powers enabling him in that behalf, hereby makes the following regulations, which contain no provision other than such as are made in consequence of the said Act of 1972 and which accordingly, by virtue of section 6 of and paragraph 2(1)(*a*) of Part I of Schedule 4 to that Act, are exempt from the requirements of section 62(2) of the said Act of 1965 (reference to Industrial Injuries Advisory Council):—

Citation, interpretation and commencement

1. These regulations, which may be cited as the National Insurance (Industrial Injuries) (Prescribed Diseases) Amendment (No. 2) Regulations 1972, shall be read as one with the National Insurance (Industrial Injuries) (Prescribed Diseases) Regulations 1959(**d**), as amended(**e**) (hereinafter referred to as "the principal regulations"), and shall come into operation on 12th September 1972.

Amendment of regulation 6 of the principal regulations

2. For the proviso to regulation 6(1) of the principal regulations (date of development) there shall be substituted the following proviso:—

"Provided that—

(*a*) subject to the provisions of section 5(3) of the National Insurance Act 1972, as modified by the Second Schedule hereto, any date of development determined for the purpose of that claim shall not preclude fresh consideration of the question whether the same person is suffering from the same disease on any subsequent claim for or award of benefit; and

(*b*) if, on the consideration of a claim, no award of benefit is made, any date of development determined for the purposes of that claim shall be disregarded for the purposes of any subsequent claim.".

(**a**) 1965 c. 52. (**b**) 1966 c. 6.
(**c**) 1972 c. 57. (**d**) S.I. 1959/467 (1959 II, p. 1943).
(**e**) The revelant amending instrument is S.I. 1966/1248 (1966 III, p. 3376).

Amendment of regulation 23 of the principal regulations

3. In regulation 23(2) of the principal regulations (application of Part III of the National Insurance (Industrial Injuries) Act 1965 and Part IV of the National Insurance Act 1965), after the words "National Insurance Act 1966" there shall be inserted the words "and by section 5 of the National Insurance Act 1972".

Amendment of the Second Schedule to the principal regulations

4.—(1) In the heading to the Second Schedule (hereinafter called "the said Schedule") to the principal regulations, after the words "NATIONAL INSURANCE ACT 1966" there shall be inserted the words "AND OF SECTION 5 OF THE NATIONAL INSURANCE ACT 1972".

(2) After paragraph 1 of the said Schedule there shall be inserted the following paragraph: —

"1A. Section 5(3) of the National Insurance Act 1972 shall have effect as if for the words 'an accident' there were substituted the words 'a prescribed disease'; as if for the words 'an injury resulted in whole or in part from the accident' there were substituted the words 'a person suffered from a prescribed disease'; as if for the words 'that accident' there were substituted the words 'that disease'; and as if for the words 'the injury did so result' there were substituted the words 'the person did so suffer'."

(3) In paragraph 2 of the said Schedule, after the words "National Insurance Act 1966" there shall be inserted the words "and by section 5 of the National Insurance Act 1972".

Signed by authority of the Secretary of State for Social Services.

Paul Dean,
Parliamentary Under-Secretary of State,
Department of Health and Social Security.

14th August 1972.

EXPLANATORY NOTE

(This Note is not part of the Regulations.)

These Regulations further amend the National Insurance (Industrial Injuries) (Prescribed Diseases) Regulations 1959 ("the principal regulations") to give effect to the provisions contained in section 5 of the National Insurance Act 1972 except in so far as those provisions relate solely to industrial accidents (see sub-section (2)).

Regulation 1 relates to citation, interpretation and commencement of these regulations; regulation 2 amends regulation 6 of the principal regulations to secure that, subject to the provisions of section 5(3) of the Act of 1972, the determination of the date of development of a disease shall not preclude fresh consideration of the diagnosis question on any subsequent claim for or award of benefit in respect of the same disease; regulation 3 applies section 5 of the Act of 1972 (finality of decisions) to the determination of claims and questions in relation to prescribed diseases as modified in the Second Schedule to the principal regulations; and regulation 4 further amends the said Second Schedule to take account of section 5 of the Act of 1972 and in particular modifies sub-section (3) thereof to give effect to the provisions therein in the context of prescribed diseases.

These Regulations are made in consequence of the said Act of 1972, and by virtue of paragraph 2(1)(a) of Part I of Schedule 4 to that Act have not been referred to the Industrial Injuries Advisory Council.

STATUTORY INSTRUMENTS

1972 No. 1259

SOCIAL SECURITY

The National Insurance (Assessment of Graduated Contributions) Amendment (No. 2) Regulations 1972

Made - - -	14th *August* 1972
Laid before Parliament	22nd *August* 1972
Coming into Operation	2nd *October* 1972

The Secretary of State for Social Services, in exercise of his powers under section 4(4), (6) and (7) of the National Insurance Act 1965(**a**), and of all other powers enabling him in that behalf, hereby makes the following regulations which contain no provisions other than such as are made in consequence of the National Insurance Act 1972(**b**) and which accordingly, by virtue of section 6(5) of, and paragraph 2(1)(*a*) of Schedule 4 to, the last aforementioned Act, are exempt from the requirements of section 108 of the said Act of 1965 (reference to the National Insurance Advisory Committee): —

Citation, commencement and interpretation

1. These regulations, which may be cited as the National Insurance (Assessment of Graduated Contributions) Amendment (No. 2) Regulations 1972, shall be read as one with the National Insurance (Assessment of Graduated Contributions) Regulations 1967(**c**), as amended (**d**) (hereinafter referred to as "the principal regulations") and shall come into operation on the 2nd October 1972.

Amendment of regulation 2 of the principal regulations

2. In regulation 2 of the principal regulations (equivalent amounts) for the sum of £24 in paragraph (2)(*a*) there shall be substituted the sum of £30 and for the sum of £104 in paragraph (2)(*c*) there shall be substituted the sum of £130.

Amendment of regulation 9 of the principal regulations

3. In regulation 9 of the principal regulations—

(1) in paragraph (*h*) for the words "any income tax year ending on or after" there shall be substituted the words "the income tax year ending on" and for the amounts "£78·41" and "£77·91" there shall be substituted the amounts "£88·67" and "£88·17" respectively;

(2) after paragraph (*h*) there shall be added the following paragraph: —

"(i) in respect of any income tax year ending on or after 5th April 1974 shall, if the graduated contributions so paid in that year amount to £98·55 or more, be £98·05."

(**a**) 1965 c. 51.   (**b**) 1972 c. 57.   (**c**) S.I. 1967/844 (1967 II, p. 2513).
(**d**) The relevant amending instruments are S.I. 1969/1133, 1970/46, 1971/1202 (1969 II, p. 3363; 1970 I, p. 243; 1971 II, p. 3522).

Substitution of Schedules 4 and 5 to the principal regulations

4. For the provisions of Schedule 4 and Schedule 5 to the principal regulations (weekly and monthly scales for calculation of graduated contributions) there shall be substituted the provisions set out in Schedule 1 and Schedule 2 to these regulations.

Keith Joseph,
Secretary of State for Social Services.

14th August 1972.

Regulation 4   SCHEDULE 1

Provisions to be substituted for those in Schedule 4 to the principal regulations.

EMPLOYMENT WHICH IS NOT A NON-PARTICIPATING
EMPLOYMENT

PART I

WEEKLY SCALE

Amount of payment	Amount of contribution
£	£
9·01	0·01
9·25	0·02
9·50	0·04
10·00	0·06
10·50	0·08
11·00	0·11
11·50	0·13
12·00	0·15
12·50	0·18
13·00	0·20
13·50	0·23
14·00	0·25
14·50	0·27
15·00	0·30
15·50	0·32
16·00	0·34
16·50	0·37
17·00	0·39
17·50	0·42
18·00	0·45
19·00	0·50
20·00	0·55
21·00	0·59
22·00	0·64

Amount of payment	Amount of contribution
£	£
23·00	0·69
24·00	0·74
25·00	0·78
26·00	0·83
27·00	0·88
28·00	0·93
29·00	0·97
30·00	1·02
31·00	1·07
32·00	1·12
33·00	1·16
34·00	1·21
35·00	1·26
36·00	1·31
37·00	1·35
38·00	1·40
39·00	1·45
40·00	1·50
41·00	1·54
42·00	1·59
43·00	1·64
44·00	1·69
45·00	1·73
46·00	1·78
47·00	1·83
48·00	1·85
or more	

PART II

MONTHLY SCALE

Amount of payment	Amount of contribution
£	£
39·02	0·02
40·00	0·09
42·00	0·19
44·00	0·28
46·00	0·38
48·00	0·47
50·00	0·57
52·00	0·66
54·00	0·76
56·00	0·85
58·00	0·95
60·00	1·04
62·00	1·14
64·00	1·23
66·00	1·33
68·00	1·42

Amount of payment	Amount of contribution
£	£
70·00	1·52
72·00	1·61
74·00	1·71
76·00	1·80
78·00	1·95
82·00	2·14
86·00	2·33
90·00	2·52
94·00	2·71
98·00	2·90
102·00	3·09
106·00	3·28
110·00	3·47
114·00	3·66
118·00	3·85
122·00	4·04
126·00	4·23
130·00	4·42
134·00	4·61
138·00	4·80
142·00	4·99
146·00	5·18
150·00	5·37
154·00	5·56
158·00	5·75
162·00	5·94
166·00	6·13
170·00	6·32
174·00	6·51
178·00	6·70
182·00	6·89
186·00	7·08
190·00	7·27
194·00	7·46
198·00	7·65
202·00	7·84
206·00	7·98
208·00 or more	8·03

SCHEDULE 2   Regulation 4

Provisions to be substituted for those in Schedule 5 to the principal regulations.

NON-PARTICIPATING EMPLOYMENT

PART I

WEEKLY SCALE

Amount of payment	Amount of contribution
£	£
9·01	0·01
12·00	0·02
15·00	0·04
18·00	0·07
19·00	0·12
20·00	0·16
21·00	0·21
22·00	0·26
23·00	0·31
24·00	0·35
25·00	0·40
26·00	0·45
27·00	0·50
28·00	0·54
29·00	0·59
30·00	0·64
31·00	0·69
32·00	0·73
33·00	0·78
34·00	0·83
35·00	0·88
36·00	0·92
37·00	0·97
38·00	1·02
39·00	1·07
40·00	1·11
41·00	1·16
42·00	1·21
43·00	1·26
44·00	1·30
45·00	1·35
46·00	1·40
47·00	1·45
48·00	1·47
or more	

PART II

MONTHLY SCALE

Amount of payment	Amount of contribution
£	£
39·01	0·01
40·00	0·03
50·00	0·08
60·00	0·13
70·00	0·17
78·00	0·29
82·00	0·48
86·00	0·67
90·00	0·86
94·00	1·05
98·00	1·24
102·00	1·43
106·00	1·62
110·00	1·81
114·00	2·00
118·00	2·19
122·00	2·38
126·00	2·57
130·00	2·76
134·00	2·95
138·00	3·14
142·00	3·33
146·00	3·52
150·00	3·71
154·00	3·90
158·00	4·09
162·00	4·28
166·00	4·47
170·00	4·66
174·00	4·85
178·00	5·04
182·00	5·23
186·00	5·42
190·00	5·61
194·00	5·80
198·00	5·99
202·00	6·18
206·00	6·32
208·00 or more	6·37

EXPLANATORY NOTE

(This Note is not part of the Regulations.)

These Regulations contain no provisions other than such as are made in consequence of the National Insurance Act 1972 and accordingly they are, by virtue of section 6(5) of, and paragraph 2(1)(*a*) of Schedule 4 to, that Act, exempt from reference to the National Insurance Advisory Committee, and no such reference has been made. The Regulations amend the provisions of the National Insurance (Assessment of Graduated Contributions) Regulations 1967 relating to the determination of graduated contributions payable where remuneration is not paid weekly, to the manner in which graduated contributions are to be calculated, and to the annual maximum of graduated contributions payable by a person in respect of remuneration from two or more employments by raising the amount of graduated contributions payable under the National Insurance Act 1965 and the maximum prescribed amounts.

STATUTORY INSTRUMENTS

1972 No. 1260 (C.31)

AGRICULTURE

The Agriculture (Miscellaneous Provisions) Act 1972 (Commencement) Order 1972

Made - - - 14*th August* 1972

The Minister of Agriculture, Fisheries and Food and the Secretary of State, acting jointly, in pursuance of section 27(3) of the Agriculture (Miscellaneous Provisions) Act 1972(**a**) and all their other enabling powers, hereby make the following order:—

1. This order may be cited as the Agriculture (Miscellaneous Provisions) Act 1972 (Commencement) Order 1972.

2. Section 18 of the Agriculture (Miscellaneous Provisions) Act 1972 (which section amends the power to obtain agricultural statistics by means of notices), and Schedule 6 to that Act so far as it relates to sections 77 and 78 of the Agriculture Act 1947(**b**), shall come into operation on 15th August 1972.

In Witness whereof the Official Seal of the Minister of Agriculture, Fisheries and Food is hereunto affixed on 10th August 1972.

(L.S.)

J. M. L. Prior,
Minister of Agriculture, Fisheries and Food.

Gordon Campbell,
Secretary of State for Scotland.

14th August 1972.

(**a**) 1972 c. 62.　　　　　　　　(**b**) 1947 c. 48.

STATUTORY INSTRUMENTS

1972 No. 1261

AGRICULTURE

LIVESTOCK INDUSTRIES

The Licensing of Bulls (England and Wales) Regulations 1972

Made - - -	*11th August* 1972
Laid before Parliament	*21st August* 1972
Coming into Operation	*1st September* 1972

The Minister of Agriculture, Fisheries and Food in pursuance of sections 1, 2, 4, 5, 6, 10 and 11 of the Improvement of Live Stock (Licensing of Bulls) Act 1931(**a**), as amended by section 6(4), 6(5) and 6(6) of the Agriculture (Miscellaneous Provisions) Act 1944(**b**) and extended by section 16(4) of the Agriculture (Miscellaneous Provisions) Act 1963(**c**), and amended and extended by section 8 of, and Schedule 3 to, the Agriculture (Miscellaneous Provisions) Act 1972(**d**), and of all his other enabling powers, with the approval of the Treasury as to fees, and on the joint recommendation of the Royal College of Veterinary Surgeons and the British Veterinary Association as to regulation 13(2) hereof, hereby makes the following regulations : —

Citation, commencement and extent

1. These regulations, which may be cited as the Licensing of Bulls (England and Wales) Regulations 1972, shall come into operation on 1st September 1972 and shall apply to England and Wales.

Revocation

2. The Licensing of Bulls (England and Wales) Regulations 1969(**e**), are hereby revoked, but such revocation shall not affect the validity of any notice duly served thereunder or any proceedings duly undertaken by virtue of those regulations, which shall have effect as if served under or undertaken by virtue of the corresponding provisions of these regulations.

Interpretation

3.—(1) In these regulations, unless the context otherwise requires—

"the Act" means the Improvement of Live Stock (Licensing of Bulls) Act 1931;

"general permit" means any permit other than a special permit;

"licence" means a licence under the Act to keep a bull for breeding purposes;

"a member of the Veterinary Panel" means a veterinary surgeon who is a member of a panel appointed for the purposes of Schedule 3 to the Agri-

---

(**a**) 1931 c. 43.   For change of title of the Minister see S.I. 1955/554 (1955 I, p. 1200).
(**b**) 1944 c. 28.   (**c**) 1963 c. 11.   (**d**) 1972 c. 62.
(**e**) S.I. 1969/1139 (1969 II, p. 3385)

culture (Miscellaneous Provisions) Act 1972 by the Royal College of Veterinary Surgeons and the British Veterinary Association acting jointly;

"the Minister" and "the Ministry" mean the Minister and the Ministry of Agriculture, Fisheries and Food respectively;

"permit" means a permit under the Act to keep a bull for any purpose other than breeding purposes;

"special permit" means a permit which, by virtue of the proviso to section 4(4) of the Act (which authorises the granting of permits in respect of bulls kept for zoological or experimental purposes), does not include a condition that the bull to which it relates shall not be allowed to serve a cow.

(2) Any reference in these regulations to a form denoted by a number shall be construed as a reference to the form so numbered in the Schedule to these regulations or a form substantially to the like effect.

(3) The Interpretation Act 1889(a) shall apply to the interpretation of these regulations as it applies to the interpretation of an Act of Parliament, and as though these regulations and the regulations hereby revoked were Acts of Parliament.

Prescribed age of bull

4. For the purposes of section 1 of the Act (which prohibits the keeping of a bull that has attained the prescribed age unless a licence or permit is in force in respect of it) the prescribed age shall be the age of ten months.

Applications for licences and permits

5. An application for a licence shall be in Form 1, shall be accompanied by a certificate in Form 2 signed by a member of the Veterinary Panel and, in the case of a bull of the Friesian breed, shall contain a sketch plan of the natural markings of the bull showing separately the bull as viewed from the left hand and right hand sides and its head as viewed from the front. An application for a permit shall be in form 3.

Time for making applications

6.—(1) Subject to the provisions of paragraph (2) hereof, the prescribed time for making an application for a licence or a permit shall be as follows—

    (*a*) in the case of a licence, not later than seven days before the bull attains the prescribed age;

    (*b*) in the case of a permit, within such time as may be applicable according to the following Table—

Where a licence or permit in respect of the bull has not at any time been applied for.	Not later than twenty-eight days before the bull attains the prescribed age.
Where a licence in respect of the bull has been refused or revoked.	Before the expiration of fourteen days from the date of the refusal or revocation or, if a referee's inspection is duly applied for, within fourteen days after the Minister notifies the applicant that he has confirmed the refusal or revocation in accordance with the referee's report.

(a) 1889 c. 63.

Where a permit in respect of the bull has been granted and has not expired.	Not later than fourteen days before the expiry of that permit.

(2) Notwithstanding the provisions of the foregoing paragraph, in the case of a bull which is or is to be imported or brought into England or Wales and which at the date of entry into England and Wales has attained or will have attained the prescribed age or will attain that age within twenty one days from that date, an application for a licence or permit shall be made not later than fourteen days after the date of entry.

Forms of licences and permits

7. A licence shall be in Form 4 and a permit shall be in Form 5.

Duplicate of licences and permits

8. Any application for a duplicate of a licence or permit that has been lost or destroyed shall be in Form 6.

Change of place at which permit bulls may be kept

9. Where it is a condition of a permit that the bull to which it relates shall be kept at a specified place, any application made under section 4(2) of the Act for the substitution in the permit of some other place for the place theretofore specified shall be made in writing by the owner of the bull.

Notice of suspension

10. Any notice of suspension served under section 4(3) of the Act (making it a condition of a licence that the bull to which it relates shall not for a specified period be allowed to serve a cow) shall be served on any person for the time being having the bull in his possession or custody.

Application for referee's inspection

11.—(1) Any application made under section 5(1) of the Act for a referee's inspection of a bull, consequent on the refusal or revocation of a licence or on the service of a notice of suspension as respects that bull, shall be in Form 7, and shall be made before the expiration of a period of fourteen days from the date of the refusal or revocation or the service of the notice, as the case may be.

(2) Any notice of the result of his application given to an applicant by the Minister shall be given in writing.

Fees

12.—(1) Fees of the following amounts shall be payable to the Minister in respect of licences, special permits, and inspections by referees—

(a) in respect of a licence to keep a bull (excluding the professional fees of the member of the Veterinary Panel for inspecting and certifying the bull payable by the applicant for a licence) ... ... £1·00

(b) in respect of a special permit ... ... £8·00

(c) in respect of a duplicate of any licence or permit ... £0·70

(d) in respect of an inspection by a referee—

(i) except as otherwise prescribed below, for each bull ... £22·00

> (ii) where two bulls owned by the same person are to be inspected by the same referee at the same premises at the same time, for each bull   ...   .   £19·00
>
> (iii) where three or more bulls owned by the same person are to be inspected by the same referee at the same premises at the same time, for each bull ...   ...   £18·00

Provided that no fee shall be payable in respect of a licence or special permit to keep a bull where at the time of application therefor a licence or special permit issued by the Secretary of State in respect of Scotland is in force in relation to the bull.

(2) The prescribed fee shall be remitted direct to the Ministry with the corresponding application except in the case of applications for a licence.

(3) If, before the inspection referred to in regulation 11(1) hereof takes place, the application for a referee's inspection is withdrawn by the applicant, the Ministry may return the fee to him.

Prescribed inspection marks

13.—(1) The provisions of paragraph 2 of this regulation shall have effect for the purposes of paragraph 1(2) of Schedule 3 to the Agriculture (Miscellaneous Provisions) Act 1972 (which provides for the marking of bulls by members of the Veterinary Panel with a prescribed mark and in a prescribed manner).

(2) The prescribed mark shall be the letter V inside a square and the bull shall be marked with it in or on the right ear, or if that is impracticable, on some other appropriate place.

Service of notices and other documents

14.—(1) Any notice required or authorised by or under the Act to be given or served by the Minister may be given or served by delivering it to the person to or on whom it is to be given or served, or by sending it to him by post in a letter addressed to him at his last known place of abode or business.

(2) Any application, notice or other document required or authorised by or under the Act to be made, given or sent by any person to the Minister or the Ministry shall be made, given, sent by post or otherwise delivered in a letter addressed to the Secretary, Ministry of Agriculture, Fisheries and Food, at an office of the Ministry in England or Wales.

Prescribed mark for identification purposes

15.—(1) This regulation shall have effect for the purposes of section 10(1)(b) of the Act (which empowers an officer of the Ministry to mark any bull with a prescribed mark in a prescribed manner).

(2) If an officer of the Ministry has reason to suppose that any bull apparently over the prescribed age is unlicenced and not the subject of any special or general permit he may mark the bull with the identification mark prescribed in the following paragraph.

(3) The mark prescribed for a bull that is being marked by an officer of the Ministry for the purpose of identification shall be a combination of any two letters of the alphabet or a combination of figures or both such combinations and the bull shall be marked with that mark in or on one of its ears or, if that is impracticable, on some other appropriate place.

Transitional provisions

16.—(1) The following provisions shall apply to the inspection, marking, licensing or rejection of a bull in respect of which an application for a licence made to the Minister before the date of commencement of the present regulations remains undetermined as at such date: —

(*a*) The bull shall be inspected by an officer of the Ministry and for this purpose the Minister may require the owner of the bull to make it available for inspection at any place or time that has been notified to the owner, and the owner shall provide all reasonable facilities and assistance for the purpose of the inspection and marking of the bull:

Provided that a bull that has previously been inspected on behalf of the Minister for any other purpose may, if the Minister thinks fit, be exempted from the inspection prescribed by this regulation.

(*b*) If, after inspection, the bull is found suitable for a licence, it shall be marked by an officer of the Ministry with a design consisting of a crown in or on its right ear, or, if that is impracticable, on some other appropriate place.

(*c*) If, after inspection, the bull is found unsuitable for a licence, it shall be marked by an officer of the Ministry with the letter R in or on its left ear or, if that is impracticable, on some other appropriate place.

(*d*) Any bull that has been inspected and marked pursuant to this article may also be marked by an officer of the Ministry for identification purposes, with the identification mark prescribed in article 15(3) of these regulations.

(2) A licence granted under these transitional provisions shall be in form 8. A licence granted as a result of a successful appeal against the refusal of the Minister to grant a licence shall, if the appeal arose out of an application for a licence made before the present regulations came into force, also be in form 8.

(3) An applicant for a licence whose application having been made before the date of commencement of the present regulations and whose bull has not been inspected by an officer of the Ministry may if he so desires withdraw his application, in which case the Minister may refund the fee paid by the applicant to the Ministry. Such withdrawal shall be without prejudice to the applicant's right to apply for a licence under and subject to the provisions of these regulations.

In Witness whereof the Official Seal of the Minister of Agriculture, Fisheries and Food is hereunto affixed on 10th August 1972.

(L.S.)   *J. M. L. Prior,*
Minister of Agriculture, Fisheries
and Food.

Approved on 11th August 1972.

V. H. Goodhew,
Hugh Rossi,
Two of the Lords Commissioners of
Her Majesty's Treasury.

Regulation 3(2)

Regulation 5

SCHEDULE

FORM 1

No.

MINISTRY OF AGRICULTURE, FISHERIES AND FOOD

Improvement of Live Stock (Licensing of Bulls) Act 1931 (as amended)
Licensing of Bulls (England and Wales) Regulations 1972

APPLICATION FOR A LICENCE TO KEEP A BULL

Date of birth   19   *Earmarks*

                day   month   year   Breed Society Mark

Breeding*   Mark allotted or approved under
                                          TB Order 1964

I hereby apply for a licence in respect of the bull described above, and I hereby certify the foregoing particulars to be correct.

I am the †owner/agent for the owner of the bull.

FULL name of applicant (in BLOCK LETTERS)

Address

Telephone number

Date   Signature

*For a pure-bred enter breed. For a cross-bred enter "cross-bred" and give the genetic make up (e.g. ½ Charolais × ½ Friesian) insofar as this is known.

†Delete as appropriate.

Form 2   Regulation 5

No.

VETERINARY CERTIFICATE

1. I have inspected this bull and to the best of my knowledge and belief the particulars given in the attached application as to date of birth and breeding are correct.

2. I hereby certify that

  (a) the earmarks quoted in the application are correct;

  (b) †the markings on the bull are in accordance with the sketch plan contained in the application;

  (c) this bull had not previously been marked with the inspection mark prescribed by the Minister on the joint recommendation of the Royal College of Veterinary Surgeons and the British Veterinary Association;

  (d) I have marked this bull with the prescribed inspection mark in the prescribed manner;

  (e) I am a member of the panel appointed jointly by the Royal College of Veterinary Surgeons and the British Veterinary Association for purposes of inspecting bulls under the Act.

3A* In my professional opinion, at the time of examination this bull was suitable for a licence under the Act as it was not:

  (a) of defective or inferior conformation and likely to beget defective or inferior progeny; or

  (b) permanently affected with any contagious or infectious disease; or

  (c) permanently affected with any other disease rendering the bull unsuitable for breeding purposes.

3B* In my professional opinion this bull is not suitable for a licence under the Act for the following reasons:

Signed   Date
        Veterinary Surgeon

FULL NAME (BLOCK LETTERS)

PRACTICE AND ADDRESS

†Delete if the bull is not of the Friesian breed.

*Delete paragraph 3A or 3B as appropriate.

Regulation 5 FORM 3

No.

MINISTRY OF AGRICULTURE, FISHERIES AND FOOD

Improvement of Live Stock (Licensing of Bulls) Act 1931 (as amended)
Licensing of Bulls (England and Wales) Regulations 1972

APPLICATION FOR A PERMIT TO KEEP AN UNLICENSED BULL

Date of birth 19 *Earmarks*
day month year Breed Society Mark

Breeding (see Note 1) Mark allotted or approved under
TB Order 1964

Full postal address of premises
at which bull is to be kept

I hereby apply for a $\frac{\text{*special permit (see Note (2))}}{\text{general permit (see Note (3))}}$ to keep the unlicensed bull described above until 19 , for the purpose of

I enclose *cheque/postal order/money order for £8 (see Note (4)) in payment of the prescribed fee.

I am the *owner/agent for the owner of the bull.

Full name of applicant (in BLOCK LETTERS)

Address

Telephone No.

Date 19 Signature

*Strike out words that do not apply.

NOTES:

1. The breeding of the bull need not be given when a general permit is applied for. When a special permit is applied for the breed of the bull should be entered if it is pure-bred; for a cross-bred the word "cross-bred" should be entered and the genetic make up (e.g. $\frac{7}{8}$ Charolais $\times \frac{1}{8}$ Friesian) should be given (insofar as this is known).

2. A special permit is a permit granted to keep a bull for zoological or experimental purposes which, by virtue of the exemption conferred by the proviso to section 4(4) of the Act, does not include a condition that the bull shall not be allowed to serve a cow or heifer.

3. A general permit is a permit which includes a condition that the bull must not be allowed to serve any cow or heifer. This type of permit is issued when a bull is to be kept entire to be fattened for slaughter.

4. The prescribed fee for a special permit is £8. A fee is not required for a general permit.

FORM 4   Regulation 7

No.

MINISTRY OF AGRICULTURE, FISHERIES AND FOOD

Improvement of Live Stock (Licensing of Bulls) Act 1931 (as amended)
Licensing of Bulls (England and Wales) Regulations 1972

BULL LICENCE

This is to certify that the bull described in the application attached is licensed under
the Improvement of Live Stock (Licensing of Bulls) Act 1931 (as amended).

Date   19 .   Secretary

FORM 5   Regulation 7

No.

MINISTRY OF AGRICULTURE, FISHERIES AND FOOD

Improvement of Live Stock (Licensing of Bulls) Act 1931 (as amended)
Licensing of Bulls (England and Wales) Regulations 1972

*SPECIAL/GENERAL PERMIT TO KEEP AN UNLICENSED BULL

Date of birth   19   *Earmarks*
         day   month   year   Breed Society Mark

Breeding
                                      Mark allotted or approved under
                                      TB Order 1964

The Minister of Agriculture, Fisheries and Food hereby permits the unlicensed bull
described above belonging to
to be kept at
until
for the purpose of
subject to the following conditions:

Date   19 .   Secretary

*Strike out words that do not apply.

NOTE:
For general permits the breeding of the bull should not be quoted.

Regulation 8   FORM 6

No.

MINISTRY OF AGRICULTURE, FISHERIES AND FOOD

Improvement of Live Stock (Licensing of Bulls) Act 1931 (as amended)
Licensing of Bulls (England and Wales) Regulations 1972

APPLICATION FOR A DUPLICATE OF A LICENCE OR PERMIT

Date of birth   19   *Earmarks*
        day   month   year   Breed Society Mark

Breeding*

                                        Mark allotted or approved under
                                        TB Order 1964

Full name of applicant (in BLOCK LETTERS)

Full postal address

    I certify that the †licence/permit numbered............................ and issued on or
about .... to keep the bull described above has
been lost or destroyed and I hereby apply for a duplicate.

    I enclose †cheque/postal order/money order for 70p in payment of the prescribed fee.

Date   19 .   Signature

    *For a pure-bred bull enter breed. For a cross-bred bull enter "cross-bred" and give the
genetic make up (e.g. ⅞ Charolais × ⅛ Friesian) insofar as this is known.

    †Strike out words that do not apply.

FORM 7 Regulation 11(1)

No.

MINISTRY OF AGRICULTURE, FISHERIES AND FOOD

Improvement of Live Stock (Licensing of Bulls) Act 1931 (as amended)
Licensing of Bulls (England and Wales) Regulations 1972

APPLICATION FOR A REFEREE'S INSPECTION

Date of birth 19 *Earmarks*

day month year *Breed Society Mark*

Breeding†

Mark allotted or approved under
TB Order 1964

Full name of applicant (in BLOCK LETTERS)

Full postal address

Whereas the Minister of Agriculture, Fisheries and Food has *refused to grant/revoked/served a notice of suspension of a licence to keep the bull described above, now therefore I require a referee's inspection of the bull in accordance with Section 5 of the Improvement of Live Stock (Licensing of Bulls) Act 1931.

The bull will be kept during the next 28 days at

I enclose *cheque/postal order/money order for $\left.\begin{array}{l} *£22\cdot00 \\ £19\cdot00 \\ £18\cdot00 \end{array}\right\}$ (see Note) in payment of

the prescribed fee.‡

Date 19 . Signature

†For a pure-bred enter breed. For a cross-bred enter "cross-bred" and give the genetic make up (e.g. $\frac{7}{8}$ Charolais $\times$ $\frac{1}{8}$ Friesian) insofar as this is known.
*Strike out words that do not apply.
‡This will be returned if the refusal, revocation or notice of suspension is not confirmed.

NOTE:

The prescribed fees payable for a referee's inspection are:—

(i) for the inspection of one bull ... ... £22·00

(ii) for the inspection of two bulls in the same ownership, provided the inspection of each bull is to be carried out by the same referee on the same premises and at the same time, for each bull ... ... £19·00

(iii) for the inspection of three or more bulls in the same ownership, provided the inspection of each bull is carried out by the same referee on the same premises and at the same time, for each bull ... ... £18·00

Regulation 16   FORM 8

No.

MINISTRY OF AGRICULTURE, FISHERIES AND FOOD

Improvement of Live Stock (Licensing of Bulls) Act 1931 (as amended)
Licensing of Bulls (England and Wales) Regulations 1972

BULL LICENCE

Date of birth   19   *Earmarks*
             day   month   year

Breeding

This is to certify that the bull described above is licensed under the Improvement of
Live Stock (Licensing of Bulls) Act 1931.

Date   19 .   Secretary

EXPLANATORY NOTE

(This Note is not part of the Regulations.)

By virtue of section 8 and of schedule 3 to the Agriculture (Miscellaneous Provisions) Act 1972 licensing of bulls by reference to pedigree and
certain other standards of suitability is abolished and the Minister of Agriculture, Fisheries and Food is empowered to make regulations requiring an
application for a licence under the Improvement of Live Stock (Licensing of
Bulls) Act 1931 to be accompanied by a veterinary certificate as to the bull's
suitability for a licence on the basis of conformation and freedom from
disease.

These regulations therefore revoke the Licensing of Bulls (England and
Wales) Regulations 1969. Applications for a bull licence must now be accompanied by a veterinary certificate in the form prescribed by the regulations.
The veterinary surgeon who gives the certificate, must be a member of the
panel defined in the regulations and must also mark the bull with the prescribed inspection mark.   The regulations prescribe an identification mark
with which an officer of the Ministry can mark a bull if it is apparently over
the prescribed age for licensing and unlicenced.   To facilitate the licensing of
bulls in respect of which applications made under the 1969 regulations had
not been determined at the date the present regulations came into force, the
regulations contain transitional provisions.   New forms of licence and application are prescribed, the provisions of the 1969 regulations relating to permits being re-enacted with some amendments.   The regulations prescribe the
fees payable in respect of applications made thereunder.

STATUTORY INSTRUMENTS

1972 No. 1262

DIPLOMATIC AND INTERNATIONAL IMMUNITIES AND PRIVILEGES

The Intergovernmental Conference on the Dumping of Wastes at Sea (Immunities and Privileges) Order 1972

Made - - - -	*14th August* 1972
Laid before Parliament	*18th August* 1972
Coming into Operation	*20th October* 1972

At the Court at Balmoral, the 14th day of August 1972

Present,

The Queen's Most Excellent Majesty in Council

Whereas the Intergovernmental Conference on the Dumping of Wastes at Sea is to be held in the United Kingdom from 30th October to 10th November 1972 and is to be attended by representatives of Her Majesty's Government in the United Kingdom and of the Governments of foreign sovereign Powers:

Now, therefore, Her Majesty, by virtue and in exercise of the powers conferred on Her by section 6 of the International Organisations Act 1968(**a**) (hereinafter referred to as the Act) or otherwise in Her Majesty vested, is pleased, by and with the advice of Her Privy Council, to order, and it is hereby ordered, as follows: —

1. This Order may be cited as the Intergovernmental Conference on the Dumping of Wastes at Sea (Immunities and Privileges) Order 1972 and shall come into operation on 20th October 1972.

2. The Interpretation Act 1889(**b**) shall apply for the interpretation of this Order as it applies for the interpretation of an Act of Parliament.

3.—(1) Except in so far as in any particular case any privilege or immunity is waived by the Governments whom they represent, representatives of the Governments of foreign sovereign Powers at the Intergovernmental Conference on the Dumping of Wastes at Sea shall enjoy: —

(*a*) immunity from suit and legal process in respect of things done or omitted to be done by them in their capacity as representatives;

(*b*) while exercising their functions and during their journeys to and from the place of meeting, the like inviolability of residence, the like immunity from personal arrest or detention and from seizure of their personal baggage, the like inviolability of all papers and documents, and the like exemption or relief from taxes (other than customs and excise duties or purchase tax) as is accorded to the head of a diplomatic mission; and

---

(**a**) 1968 c. 48.   (**b**) 1889 c. 63.

(c) while exercising their functions and during their journeys to and from the place of meeting, the like exemptions and privileges in respect of their personal baggage as in accordance with Article 36 of the Vienna Convention on Diplomatic Relations, which is set out in Schedule 1 to the Diplomatic Privileges Act 1964(a), are accorded to a diplomatic agent.

(2) Where the incidence of any form of taxation depends upon residence, a representative shall not be deemed to be resident in the United Kingdom during any period when he is present in the United Kingdom for the discharge of his duties.

(3) Part IV of Schedule 1 to the Act shall not operate so as to confer any privilege or immunity on the official staff of a representative other than delegates, deputy delegates, advisers, technical experts and secretaries of delegations.

(4) Neither this Article nor Part IV of Schedule 1 to the Act shall operate so as to confer any privilege or immunity on any person as the representative of the Government of the United Kingdom or as a member of the official staff of such a representative or on any person who is a citizen of the United Kingdom and Colonies.

W. G. Agnew.

EXPLANATORY NOTE

(This Note is not part of the Order.)

This Order confers privileges and immunities upon the representatives of the Governments of foreign sovereign Powers at the Intergovernmental Conference on the Dumping of Wastes at Sea, which is to be held in the United Kingdom from 30th October to 10th November 1972, and upon certain members of their official staffs.

(a) 1964 c. 81.

STATUTORY INSTRUMENTS

1972 No. 1266

CIVIL AVIATION

The Air Navigation (Second Amendment) Order 1972

Made - - -	14th *August* 1972
Laid before Parliament	18th *August* 1972
Coming into Operation	
(*a*) *for the purposes of Article* 3(1)	1st *October* 1972
(*b*) *for all other purposes*	7th *September* 1972

At the Court at Balmoral the 14th day of August 1972

Present,

The Queen's Most Excellent Majesty in Council

Her Majesty, in exercise of the powers conferred upon Her by sections 8, 57 and 59 of the Civil Aviation Act 1949(**a**) and of all other powers enabling Her in that behalf, is pleased, by and with the advice of Her Privy Council, to order, and it is hereby ordered, as follows:

Citation and Operation

1. This Order may be cited as the Air Navigation (Second Amendment) Order 1972 and shall come into operation for the purposes of Article 3(1) on 1st October 1972 and for all other purposes on 7th September 1972.

Interpretation

2. The Interpretation Act 1889(**b**) applies for the purpose of the interpretation of this Order as it applies for the purpose of the interpretation of an Act of Parliament.

Amendment of the Air Navigation Order 1972

3. The Air Navigation Order 1972(**c**), as amended (**d**), shall be further amended as follows:

(1) To Article 4, there shall be added at the end:

"(17) The registration of an aircraft which is the subject of an undischarged mortgage entered in the Register of Aircraft Mortgages kept by the Authority pursuant to an Order in Council made under section 16 of the Civil Aviation Act 1968(**e**) shall not become void by virtue of

---

(**a**) 1949 c. 67.
(**c**) S.I. 1972/129 (1972 I, p. 366).
(**e**) 1968 c. 61.
(**b**) 1889 c. 63.
(**d**) S.I. 1972/672 (1972 I, p. 2168).

paragraph (10) of this Article, nor shall the Authority cancel the registration of such an aircraft pursuant to paragraph (13) of this Article unless all persons shown in the Register of Aircraft Mortgages as mortgagees of that aircraft have consented to the cancellation.";

(2) In Article 14 for "apparatus" wherever it appears there shall be substituted "equipment";

(3) In Article 20(2) after sub-paragraph (*d*) there shall be inserted:

"(*dd*) the holder of a flight navigator's licence shall not be entitled to perform functions on a flight to which Article 18(4) of this Order applies unless the licence bears a valid certificate of experience;";

(4) For the side heading to Schedule 1 there shall be substituted "Articles 4(6), 23(1) and 89(7)";

(5) For the side heading to Schedule 5 there shall be substituted "Articles 11(3) and 13(2)";

(6) In Schedule 9:

(*a*) In Part A 6, in the entry relating to the Flight Navigator's Licence under the sub-heading *"Maximum Period of Validity"*, for "12 months" there shall be substituted "5 years";

(*b*) In Part C:

(i) in paragraph 1 after "proviso (*d*)" there shall be added "and proviso (*dd*)";

(ii) in paragraph 2:
(*aa*) in sub-paragraph (*b*)(ii) after "certificate of experience" there shall be inserted "for a pilot";

(*bb*) after sub-paragraph (*b*)(ii) there shall be added:—

"(iii) in the case of a certificate of experience for a flight navigator, that on the date on which the certificate was signed the holder of the licence of which it forms part produced his navigation logs, charts and workings of astronomical observations to the person signing the certificate and satisfied him that he had successfully navigated an aircraft for a total of 20 hours within the period of 13 months preceding that date, disregarding any flight of less than 1,000 nautical miles;";

(*cc*) at the beginning of sub-paragraph (*c*) there shall be added " in the case of a certificate for a pilot";

(*dd*) at the end of sub-paragraph (*d*) there shall be added "or flight navigator.";

(iii) in paragraph 5 after "functions to be performed" there shall be inserted "by pilots";

(iv) in paragraph 6(2) after the words "a certificate of experience" where they first occur, there shall be inserted "for a pilot";

(v) at the end of paragraph 7 there shall be added "A certificate of experience in the capacity of flight navigator shall be appropriate to functions performed in the capacity of flight navigator.";

(vi) in paragraph 8 after "certificate of experience" there shall be inserted "for a pilot";

(vii) in paragraph 9 for "is certifies" in the third line of paragraph (*a*) there shall be substituted "it certifies";

(viii) in paragraph 9 for paragraph (*b*) there shall be substituted:

"(*b*) A certificate of experience for a pilot shall not be valid in relation to a flight made more than 6 months after it was signed in the case of Group F or more than 13 months after it was signed in the case of any other Group, and a certificate of experience for a flight navigator shall not be valid in relation to a flight made more than 13 months after it was signed.";

(7) In Schedule 10, for paragraph 2(3) there shall be substituted:

"(3) *Approach Radar Control Rating* shall entitle the holder of the licence, at any aerodrome at which the rating is valid, to provide air traffic control service with the aid of any type of surveillance radar equipment for which the rating is valid for any aircraft which is flying within 40 nautical miles of the aerodrome traffic zone whether or not it is flying by visual reference to the surface".

W. G. Agnew.

EXPLANATORY NOTE

(*This Note is not part of the Order.*)

This Order further amends the Air Navigation Order 1972.

In addition to some minor drafting amendments the following changes are made:

(1) where an aircraft is the subject of an undischarged mortgage entered in the Register of Aircraft Mortgages, that aircraft shall not cease to be registered in the register of aircraft in the United Kingdom unless all the mortgagees of that aircraft agree;

(2) the holder of a flight navigator's licence will no longer be entitled to perform functions on a flight on which (in accordance with Article 18(4) of the Air Navigation Order 1972) a flight navigator must be carried, unless his licence bears a valid certificate of experience as such;

(3) the maximum period of validity of a flight navigator's licence will be extended from 12 months to 5 years;

(4) the approach radar control rating included in an air traffic controller's licence will now entitle the holder to provide an air traffic control service with the aid of surveillance radar equipment for aircraft flying within 40 nautical miles of the aerodrome traffic zone of the aerodrome at which the service is being provided.

STATUTORY INSTRUMENTS

1972 No. 1267

MERCHANT SHIPPING

SAFETY

The Collision Regulations (Traffic Separation Schemes) (Amendment) Order 1972

Made - - -	14*th August* 1972
Coming into Operation	1*st September* 1972

To be laid before Parliament

At the Court at Balmoral, the 14th day of August 1972

Present,

The Queen's Most Excellent Majesty in Council

Whereas, by virtue of sections 418 and 738 of the Merchant Shipping Act 1894(a), Her Majesty may by Order in Council, on the joint recommendation of the Secretary of State for Defence (b) and the Secretary of State for Trade and Industry (c), make regulations for the prevention of collisions at sea:

And whereas Her Majesty acting on the joint recommendation of the said Secretaries of State made an Order in Council (d), on the 24th May 1972, giving effect to the regulations relating to traffic separation schemes for ships set out in the Schedule to that Order and coming into operation on the 1st September 1972:

And whereas the said Secretaries of State have recommended Her Majesty to postpone the date on which one of the said traffic separation schemes shall come into operation:

Now, therefore, Her Majesty, in pursuance of the aforesaid powers and all other powers enabling Her in that behalf, is pleased by and with the advice of Her Privy Council to order, and it is hereby, ordered, as follows:—

1.—(1) This Order may be cited as the Collision Regulations (Traffic Separation Schemes) (Amendment) Order 1972 and shall come into operation on 1st September 1972.

(2) The Interpretation Act 1889(e), shall apply to the interpretation of this Order as it applies to the interpretation of an Act of Parliament.

2. Notwithstanding the provisions of the Collision Regulations (Traffic Separation Schemes) Order 1972, the traffic separation scheme "Off Kiel Lighthouse" set out in paragraph A8 of Part II of the Regulations relating to Traffic Separation Schemes for Ships set out in the Schedule to that Order shall not have effect until 1st December 1972, and that Order and those Regulations shall until 1st December 1972 have effect as if that paragraph were omitted.

W. G. Agnew.

(a) 1894 c. 60.　　　　(b) See Defence (Transfer of Functions) Act 1964 (c. 15).
(c) See S.I. 1970/1537 (1970 III, p. 5293).　　(d) S.I. 1972/809 (1972 II, p. 2602).
(e) 1889 c. 63.

EXPLANATORY NOTE

(This Note is not part of the Order.)

This Order postpones the date on which one of the traffic separation schemes set out in Part II of the Regulations scheduled to the Collision Regulations (Traffic Separation Schemes) Order 1972 comes into operation.

STATUTORY INSTRUMENTS

1972 No. 1268

CIVIL AVIATION

The Mortgaging of Aircraft Order 1972

Laid before Parliament in draft

Made -	-	-	-	*14th August* 1972
Coming into Operation				*1st October* 1972

At the Court at Balmoral, the 14th day of August 1972

Present,

The Queen's Most Excellent Majesty in Council

Her Majesty, in exercise of the powers conferred upon Her by section 16 of the Civil Aviation Act 1968(a) and of all other powers enabling Her in that behalf, is pleased, by and with the advice of Her Privy Council, to order, and it is hereby ordered, as follows:—

Citation and Commencement

1. This Order may be cited as the Mortgaging of Aircraft Order 1972 and shall come into operation on 1st October 1972.

Interpretation

2.—(1) The Interpretation Act 1889(b) applies for the interpretation of this Order as it applies for the interpretation of an Act of Parliament.

(2) In this Order:

"appropriate charge" means the charge payable under section 9 of the Civil Aviation Act 1971(c);

"the Authority" means the Civil Aviation Authority;

"mortgage of an aircraft" includes a mortgage which extends to any store of spare parts for that aircraft but does not otherwise include a mortgage created as a floating charge;

"owner" means the person shown as the owner of a mortgaged aircraft on the form of application for registration of that aircraft in the United Kingdom nationality register;

"United Kingdom nationality register" means the register of aircraft maintained by the Authority in pursuance of an Order in Council under section 8 of the Civil Aviation Act 1949(d).

(a) 1968 c. 61.	(b) 1889 c. 63.
(c) 1971 c. 75.	(d) 1949 c. 67.

Mortgage of Aircraft

3. An aircraft registered in the United Kingdom nationality register or such an aircraft together with any store of spare parts for that aircraft may be made security for a loan or other valuable consideration.

Registration of Aircraft Mortgages

4.—(1) Any mortgage of an aircraft registered in the United Kingdom nationality register may be entered in the Register of Aircraft Mortgages kept by the Authority.

(2) Applications to enter a mortgage in the Register shall be made to the Authority by or on behalf of the mortgagee in the form set out in Part I of Schedule 1 hereto, and shall be accompanied by a copy of the mortgage, which the applicant shall certify to be a true copy, and the appropriate charge.

5.—(1) A notice of intention to make an application to enter a contemplated mortgage of an aircraft in the Register (hereinafter referred to as "a priority notice") may also be entered in the Register.

(2) Applications to enter a priority notice in the Register shall be made to the Authority by or on behalf of the prospective mortgagee in the form set out in Part II of Schedule 1 hereto, and shall be accompanied by the appropriate charge.

6.—(1) Where two or more aircraft are the subject of one mortgage or where the same aircraft is the subject of two or more mortgages, separate applications shall be made in respect of each aircraft or of each mortgage, as the case may be.

(2) Where a mortgage is in a language other than English, the application to enter that mortgage in the Register shall be accompanied not only by a copy of that mortgage but also by a translation thereof, which the applicant shall certify as being, to the best of his knowledge and belief, a true translation.

7.—(1) When an application to enter a mortgage or priority notice in the Register is duly made, the Authority shall enter the mortgage or the priority notice, as the case may be, in the Register by placing the application form therein and by noting on it the date and the time of the entry.

(2) Applications duly made shall be entered in the Register in order of their receipt by the Authority.

(3) The Authority shall by notice in its Official Record specify the days on which and hours during which its office is open for registering mortgages and priority notices. Any application delivered when the office is closed for that purpose shall be treated as having been received immediately after the office is next opened.

(4) The Authority shall notify the applicant of the date and time of the entry of the mortgage or the priority notice, as the case may be, in the Register and of the register number of the entry and shall send a copy of the notification to the mortgagor and the owner.

Amendment of entries in the Register

8.—(1) Any change in the person appearing in the Register as mortgagee or as mortgagor or in the name or address of such person or in the description of the mortgaged property shall be notified to the Authority by or on behalf of the mortgagee, in the form set out in Part III of Schedule 1 hereto.

(2) On receipt of the said form, duly completed and signed by or on behalf of the mortgagor and the mortgagee and on payment of the appropriate charge, the Authority shall enter the notification in the Register and shall notify the mortgagor, the mortgagee and the owner that it has done so.

Discharge of Mortgages

9.—(1) Where a registered mortgage is discharged the mortgagor shall notify the Authority of the fact in the form set out in Part IV of Schedule 1 hereto.

(2) On receipt of the said form, duly completed and signed by or on behalf of the mortgagor and the mortgagee and of a copy of the mortgage with a discharge or receipt for the mortgage money duly endorsed thereon, or of any other document which shows, to the satisfaction of the Authority, that the mortgage has been discharged and on payment of the appropriate charge, the Authority shall enter the said form in the Register and mark the relevant entries in the Register "Discharged", and shall notify the mortgagee, the mortgagor and the owner that it has done so.

Rectification of the Register

10. Any of the following courts, that is to say the High Court of Justice in England, the Court of Session in Scotland and the High Court of Justice in Northern Ireland may order such amendments to be made to the Register as may appear to the court to be necessary or expedient for correcting any error therein. On being served with the order the Authority shall make the necessary amendment to the Register.

Inspection of Register and copies of entries

11.—(1) On such days and during such hours as the Authority may specify in its Official Record, any person may, on application to the Authority and on payment to it of the appropriate charge inspect any entry in the Register specified in the application.

(2) The Authority shall, on the application of any person and on payment by him of the appropriate charge, supply to the applicant a copy, certified as a true copy, of the entries in the Register specified in the application.

(3) The Authority shall, on the application of any person and on payment by him of the appropriate charge, notify the applicant whether or not there are any entries in the Register relating to any aircraft specified in the application by reference to its nationality and registration marks.

(4) A document purporting to be a copy of an entry in the Register shall be admissible as evidence of that entry if it purports to be certified as a true copy by the Authority.

(5) Nothing done in pursuance of paragraph (2) or (3) of this Article shall affect the priority of any mortgage.

Removal of aircraft from the United Kingdom Nationality Register

12. The removal of an aircraft from the United Kingdom nationality register shall not affect the rights of any mortgagee under any registered mortgage and entries shall continue to be made in the Register in relation to the mortgage as if the aircraft had not been removed from the United Kingdom nationality register.

Register as notice of facts appearing in it

13. All persons shall at all times be taken to have express notice of all facts appearing in the Register, but the registration of a mortgage shall not be evidence of its validity.

Priority of Mortgages

14.—(1) Subject to the following provisions of this article, a mortgage of an aircraft entered in the Register shall have priority over any other mortgage of or charge on that aircraft, other than another mortgage entered in the Register: provided that mortgages made before 1st October 1972, whether entered in the Register or not, shall up to and including 31st December 1972 have the same priority as they would have had if this Order had not been made.

(2) Subject to the following provisions of this article, where two or more mortgages of an aircraft are entered in the Register, those mortgages shall as between themselves have priority according to the times at which they were respectively entered in the Register:

Provided that:

(i) mortgages of an aircraft made before 1st October 1972 which are entered in the Register before 31st December 1972 shall have priority over any mortgages of that aircraft made on or after 1st October 1972 and shall as between themselves have the same priority as they would have had if this Order had not been made;

(ii) without prejudice to proviso (i), where a priority notice has been entered in the Register and the contemplated mortgage referred to therein is made and entered in the Register within 14 days thereafter that mortgage shall be deemed to have priority from the time when the priority notice was registered.

(3) In reckoning the period of 14 days under the preceding paragraph of this article, there shall be excluded any day which the Authority has by notice in its Official Record specified as a day on which its office is not open for registration of mortgages.

(4) The priorities provided for by the preceding provisions of this article shall have effect notwithstanding any express, implied or constructive notice affecting the mortgagee.

(5) Nothing in this article shall be construed as giving a registered mortgage any priority over any possessory lien in respect of work done on the aircraft (whether before or after the creation or registration of the mortgage) on the express or implied authority of any persons lawfully entitled to possession of the aircraft or over any right to detain the aircraft under any Act of Parliament.

Mortgage not affected by bankruptcy

15. A registered mortgage of an aircraft shall not be affected by any act of bankruptcy committed by the mortgagor after the date on which the mortgage is registered, notwithstanding that at the commencement of his bankruptcy the mortgagor had the aircraft in his possession, order or disposition, or was reputed owner thereof, and the mortgage shall be preferred to any right, claim or interest therein of the other creditors of the bankrupt or any trustee or assignee on their behalf.

Application of Bills of Sale Acts and registration provisions of the Companies Acts

16.—(1) The provisions of the Bills of Sale Acts 1878**(a)** and 1882**(b)** and the Bills of Sale (Ireland) Acts 1879**(c)** and 1883**(d)** insofar as they relate to bills of sale and other documents given by way of security for the payment of money shall not apply to any mortgage of an aircraft registered in the United Kingdom nationality register, which is made on or after 1st October 1972.

(2) Section 95(2)(*h*) of the Companies Act 1948**(e)**, section 106A (2)(*d*) of that Act as set out in the Companies (Floating Charges) (Scotland) Act 1961**(f)** or any re-enactment thereof and section 93(2)(*h*) of the Companies Act (Northern Ireland) 1960**(g)** shall have effect as if after the word "ship" where it first occurs in each case there were inserted the words "or aircraft":

Provided that nothing in this paragraph shall render invalid as against the liquidator or creditor of the company, any mortgage or charge created by a company before the date on which this Order comes into force which would not have been invalid against the liquidator or such a creditor if this Order had not been made.

False Statement and Forgery

17.—(1) If, in furnishing any information for the purpose of this Order, any person makes any statement which he knows to be false in a material particular, or recklessly makes any statement which is false in a material particular, he shall be guilty of an offence.

(2) Any person guilty of an offence under paragraph (1) of this article shall:—

(*a*) on summary conviction be liable to a fine not exceeding £400;

(*b*) on conviction on indictment be liable to a fine of such amount as the court think fit or to imprisonment for a term not exceeding 2 years or to both such a fine and such imprisonment.

(3) Without prejudice to any rule of the law of Scotland relating to forging and uttering, the Forgery Act 1913**(h)** shall apply in relation to documents forwarded to the Authority in pursuance of this Order as if such documents were included in the list of documents in section 3(3) of that Act.

Indemnity

18.—(1) Subject to paragraph (2) of this article, any person who suffers loss by reason of any error or omission in the Register or of any inaccuracy in a copy of an entry in the Register supplied pursuant to Article 11(2) of this Order or in a notification made pursuant to Article 11(3) of this Order shall be indemnified by the Authority.

(2) No indemnity shall be payable under this article:

(*a*) where the person who has suffered loss has himself caused or substantially contributed to the loss by his fraud or has derived title from a person so committing fraud;

(*b*) on account of costs or expenses incurred in taking or defending any legal proceedings without the consent of the Authority.

Application to Scotland

19. The provisions of Schedule 2 to this Order shall have effect for the purpose of the application of this Order to Scotland.

W. G. Agnew.

(a) 1878 c. 31.	**(b)** 1882 c. 43.	**(c)** 1879 c. 50.
(d) 1883 c. 7.	**(e)** 1948 c. 38.	**(f)** 1961 c. 46.
(g) 1960 c. 22 (N.I.).	**(h)** 1913 c. 27.	

SCHEDULE 1

FORMS

PART I   Article 4(2)

REGISTER OF AIRCRAFT MORTGAGES

Entry of Aircraft Mortgage

To be completed by Applicant:—

I hereby apply for the mortgage, particulars of which are given below, to be entered in the Register of Aircraft Mortgages.

1. Date of mortgage.

2. Description of the mortgaged aircraft (including its type, nationality and registration marks and aircraft serial number) and of any store of spare parts for that aircraft to which the mortgage extends.
(The description of the store of spare parts must include an indication of their character and approximate number and the place or places where they are stored must be given *1).

3. The sum secured by the mortgage *2.

4. Does the mortgage require the mortgagee to make further advances? If so, of what amount?

5. Name and address and, where applicable, company registration number of the mortgagor.

6. Register number of priority notice, if any.

---

*1 The description of the mortgaged property may, if necessary, be continued on a separate sheet, which shall be signed by the applicant.

*2 Where the sum secured is of a fluctuating amount, this should be stated and the upper and lower limits, if any, should be set out.

*3 Delete where inapplicable.

Signed ....

Name in block capitals ....

On behalf of *3 ....
(insert name and, where applicable, company registration number of mortgagee)

of ....
(insert address of mortgagee)

Article 5(2)   **PART II**

REGISTER OF AIRCRAFT MORTGAGES

Entry of Priority Notice

To be completed by Applicant:—

I hereby give notice that I am contemplating entering into a mortgage, particulars of which are given below, and that if I do enter into the said mortgage I shall apply for it to be entered in the Register of Aircraft Mortgages. I hereby apply for this notice to be entered in the said Register.

1. Description of the aircraft which is the subject of the contemplated mortgage (including its type, nationality and registration marks and aircraft serial number) and of any store of spare parts for that aircraft to which it is contemplated that the mortgage will extend.   *1

2. The sum to be secured by the contemplated mortgage.   *2

3. Is it contemplated that the mortgage will require the mortgagee to make further advances? If so, of what amount?

4. Name and address and, where applicable, company registration number of the prospective mortgagor.

---

*1 The description of the property which is the subject of the contemplated mortgage may, if necessary, be continued on a separate sheet which shall be signed by the applicant.

*2 Where the sum to be secured is of a fluctuating amount, this should be stated and the upper and lower limits, if any, should be set out.

*3 Delete where inapplicable.

Signed...

Name in block capitals.......................

on behalf of *3...............................
(insert name and, where applicable, company registration number of mortgagee)

of...
(insert address of mortgagee)

PART III

Article 8(1)

REGISTER OF AIRCRAFT MORTGAGES

Change in Particulars

We hereby give notice that the particulars shown on the Register of Aircraft Mortgages under Register number.................................should be amended as follows:—

(*a*) Signed ....
Name in block capitals.................
on behalf of *1.............................
(insert name of mortgagee)

(*b*) Signed ....
Name in block capitals.................
on behalf of *1
(insert name of person shown in the Register as the mortgagee)*2

(*c*) Signed ....
Name in block capitals.................
on behalf of *1.............................
(insert name of mortgagor)

---

*1 Delete where inapplicable

*2 Applicable only where the change in particulars is a change in the person appearing in the Register as mortgagee.

PART IV

Article 9(1)

REGISTER OF AIRCRAFT MORTGAGES

Discharge of registered mortgage

I hereby give notice that the mortgage entered in the Register of Aircraft Mortgages under register number...has been discharged.

Signed...
Name in block capitals......................
on behalf of*..................................
(insert name of mortgagor)

I agree that the aforesaid mortgage has been discharged.

Signed...
Name in block capitals......................
on behalf of*..................................
(insert name of mortgagee)

---

*Delete where inapplicable

SCHEDULE 2

Article 19

PART I

APPLICATION OF THE ORDER TO SCOTLAND

1. (*a*) In this Schedule—

"act of bankruptcy" has the meaning assigned to it in subparagraph (*b*)(ii) of this paragraph;

"aircraft mortgage" has the meaning assigned to it in paragraph 2 of this Schedule;

"mortgagee" means the creditor in an aircraft mortgage;

"mortgagor" means the person in security of whose indebtedness or obligation the aircraft mortgage is granted;

and references to an aircraft which is the subject of an aircraft mortgage include, where the mortgage so extends, a reference to a store of spare parts designated or appropriated to that aircraft.

(*b*) In the application of this Order to Scotland—

(i) in Article 14 there shall be added the following paragraph—

"6. Subject to paragraph 5 of this article, an aircraft mortgage may contain provisions regulating the order in which that mortgage shall rank with any other mortgage of that aircraft or any floating charge within the meaning of the Companies (Floating Charges) (Scotland) Act 1961(a) or any re-enactment thereof."

(ii) in Article 15 the words "act of bankruptcy" shall mean—

(*a*) in the case of a company, a winding-up order, or a resolution for voluntary winding-up (other than a members' voluntary winding-up) or the taking of possession, by or on behalf of the holders of any debentures secured by a floating charge, of any property of the company comprised in or subject to the charge;

(*b*) in the case of any other person, his notour bankruptcy, the execution of a trust deed for behoof of, or the making of a composition contract or arrangement with his creditors or in the event of his death, the appointment of a judicial factor under section 163 of the Bankruptcy (Scotland) Act 1913(b) to divide his insolvent estate among his creditors, or the making of an order for the administration of his estate according to the law of bankruptcy under section 130 of the Bankruptcy Act 1914(c) or the administration of his estate in accordance with the rules set out in Part I of Schedule 1 to the Administration of Estates Act 1925(d).

2. A security created in Scotland under Article 3 of this Order for a loan or other obligation shall be constituted by a mortgage in, or as nearly as may be in, the form specified in Part II of this Schedule which shall be known as an aircraft mortgage.

3. A mortgage registered under this Order shall have effect without any requirement of law that delivery of the aircraft shall be made to the mortgagee.

4. A mortgage so registered may be transferred, in whole or in part, by the mortgagee by a transfer in, or as nearly as may be in, the form specified in Part III of this Schedule.

5. An aircraft mortgage may be discharged, in whole or in part, by the mortgagee by a discharge in, or as nearly as may be in, the form specified in Part IV of this Schedule or by a receipt for the mortgage money duly endorsed on the aircraft mortgage.

6. The provisions of paragraphs 7 to 11 of this Schedule, with such variations as may

---

(**a**) 1961 c. 46.   (**b**) 1913 c. 20.
(**c**) 1914 c. 59.   (**d**) 1925 c. 23.

have been agreed by the parties, shall regulate the rights and powers of parties under an aircraft mortgage.

7. Where the mortgagor, or the owner, is in default within the meaning of paragraph 8 of this Schedule, the mortgagee may exercise such of the rights conferred upon him by the following provisions of this Schedule as he may consider appropriate, and any such right shall be in addition to, and not in derogation from, any other remedy arising from the aircraft mortgage or any other agreement between the parties.

8. The mortgagor or the owner shall be in default if—

(a) the mortgagee has required the discharge or performance of the debt or obligation to which the aircraft mortgage relates and the mortgagor fails to meet that requirement, or

(b) the mortgagor or the owner has failed to comply with any other condition of the aircraft mortgage, or

(c) the mortgagor or the owner has committed an act of bankruptcy.

9. Where default as aforesaid has occurred the mortgagee may sell the mortgaged aircraft in accordance with the following provisions of this paragraph:—

(a) The mortgagee who intends to sell the aircraft shall give not less than 60 days notice in writing of that intention to the mortgagor, the owner and every person shown in the Register as holding a mortgage over the aircraft, but the said period of notice may be dispensed with or shortened with the consent of all the persons to whom notice is required to be given.

(b) On the expiry of, or the dispensing with, the period of notice, or, as the case may be, of the reduced period of notice, the mortgagee may sell the aircraft with the consent in writing of every other mortgagee shown in the Register as holding a mortgage over the aircraft.

(c) In the event of any mortgagee withholding his consent the mortgagee who has served the notice may apply to the Court of Session for a warrant to sell the aircraft; any such application shall be served upon any mortgagee who has withheld his consent and may be granted by the Court, subject to such conditions as it thinks reasonable in all the circumstances.

10. Moneys received by a mortgagee from the sale of the mortgaged aircraft shall be held by him in trust to be applied in accordance with the following order of priority:—

(a) first, in payment of all expenses properly incurred by him in connection with the sale, or any prior attempted sale, of the aircraft;

(b) secondly, in payment of the whole amount of principal and interest due under any prior aircraft mortgage to which the sale is not made conditional;

(c) thirdly, in payment of the whole amount of principal and interest due under his aircraft mortgage and in payment in due proportion of the whole amount due under an aircraft mortgage, if any, ranking *pari passu* with his own mortgage;

(d) fourthly, in payment of any amounts of principal and interest due under any duly registered mortgages over the aircraft, the ranking of which is postponed to that of his own mortgage; and

(e) fifthly, in payment of any amount of principal and interest due under any mortgages over the aircraft ranked in accordance with the priorities provided for in Article 14 of this Order where the holder of any such mortgage has lodged in the hands of the mortgagee a claim in writing countersigned by the mortgagor,

and any residue of the moneys so received shall be paid to the owner or to any person authorised by the owner to give receipts therefor.

11.—(1) Where default as aforesaid has occurred the mortgagee may apply to the Court of Session for a warrant for possession of the mortgaged aircraft, and the application shall be served upon the mortgagor, the owner and every person shown in the Register as holding a mortgage over the aircraft and upon the owner or occupier of the land or premises where the aircraft is for the time being situated.

(2) Upon such an application being made the Court may—

(*a*) grant warrant to the applicant to take interim possession of the aircraft pending further consideration of the application,

(*b*) on further consideration grant the application for possession subject to such conditions as it shall consider reasonable in all the circumstances.

(3) Subject to any conditions imposed by the Court a warrant for possession shall empower the applicant to enter at any reasonable time on any land or into any premises where the mortgaged aircraft, or any part thereof, may be, and to remove the aircraft or part, to manage the aircraft and to receive all income accruing from freights or charter fees, to pay insurance premiums and expenses of such managment, to effect repairs and make replacements of parts and to recover all expenses, payments and disbursements incurred by him in relation to the exercise of these powers as sums due under his mortgage with interest thereon at the rate stipulated therein from the respective dates of payment or disbursement.

(4) A mortgagee who has obtained a warrant for possession may at any time thereafter sell the mortgaged aircraft after giving not less than 30 days notice in writing of his intention to do so to the mortgagor, the owner and every person shown in the Register as holding a mortgage over the aircraft, provided that the said period of notice may be dispensed with or shortened with the consent of all the persons to whom notice is required to be given.

12. The Court of Session shall have jurisdiction to grant an application by a mortgagee in any mortgage of an aircraft registered in the United Kingdom for a warrant for possession or sale of the aircraft while the aircraft is situated in Scotland as if the mortgage had been an aircraft mortgage created in Scotland.

13. The provisions of section 16 of the Administration of Justice (Scotland) Act 1933(a) (power to regulate procedure, etc., by Act of Sederunt) shall apply to the provisions of this Order as it applies to the provisions of an Act of Parliament.

PART II

AIRCRAFT MORTGAGE

Particulars of Aircraft

Where registered

Nationality and registration marks

Type

(*a*) Manufacturer's description

(*b*) Aircraft serial number

(*c*) Any other relevant details appearing in the United Kingdom nationality register.

We,

hereby in security of (specify the nature of the debt or obligation for which the mortgage is granted and the instrument by which it is constituted) hereby grant a mortgage in favour of the said

over the Aircraft above particularly described of which we are the Owners, [and the store of spare parts for the said Aircraft of which we are the Owners wheresoever they are situated (or otherwise as the case may be)] And we covenant with the said

that we have power to mortgage in the manner aforesaid the said Aircraft [and its store of spare parts] and that the same is [are] free from encumbrances save as appears in the Register of Aircraft Mortgages.

[To be attested]

(a) 1933 c. 41.

PART III
AIRCRAFT MORTGAGE
TRANSFER OF MORTGAGE

We

in consideration of

paid to us by

hereby transfer to the said

the benefit of an Aircraft Mortgage granted in our favour [or in favour of.................

.............................] dated

and registered in the Register of Aircraft Mortgages on..

under Register No...................................

[To be attested]

Note This Transfer may be endorsed on the original of the Aircraft Mortgage or may be a separate document.

PART IV
AIRCRAFT MORTGAGE
DISCHARGE OF MORTGAGE

We

acknowledge to have received the sum of

in [partial] discharge of an Aircraft Mortgage granted by

in our favour [or in favour of..]

dated...................................and registered in the Register of Aircraft Mortgages

on...........................under Register No...

[to which we acquired right by Transfer by the said...

(or as the case may be) in our favour dated..

and registered in the said Register on..]

[To be attested]

Note This Discharge may be endorsed on the original Aircraft Mortgage or may be a separate document.

EXPLANATORY NOTE
(This Note is not part of the Order.)

This Order makes provision with respect to the mortgaging of aircraft registered in the United Kingdom. In particular it provides for the registration of mortgages of aircraft in a Register of Aircraft Mortgages to be kept by the Civil Aviation Authority and for the priority inter se of registered mortgages.

STATUTORY INSTRUMENTS

1972 No. 1269

ROAD TRAFFIC

The London Transport (Consent Appeals) Regulations 1972

Made - - -		*14th August* 1972
Coming into Operation		*31st August* 1972

The Secretary of State for the Environment, in exercise of his powers under paragraphs 7, 8, 9, 10 and 12 of Schedule 4 to the Transport (London) Act 1969(a) and all other powers enabling him in that behalf, and after consultation with the Council on Tribunals in accordance with the requirements of section 10 of the Tribunals and Inquiries Act 1971(b), hereby makes the following Regulations.

Citation and Commencement

1. These Regulations may be cited as the London Transport (Consent Appeals) Regulation 1972 and shall come into operation on 31st August 1972

Interpretation

2.—(1) In these Regulations, unless the context otherwise requires—

"the Act" means the Transport (London) Act 1969;

"the commissioners" means the traffic commissioners for the Metropolitan Traffic Area appointed under Part III of the Road Traffic Act 1960, as amended by the Act;

"consent" means a consent continued in force or granted by the Executive under Schedule 4;

"the Executive" means the London Transport Executive established under section 4 of the Act;

"Schedule 4" means Schedule 4 to the Act.

(2) The Interpretation Act 1889(c) shall apply for the interpretation of these Regulations as it applies for the interpretation of an Act of Parliament.

Scope of Regulations

3. These Regulations shall apply to any appeal to the commissioners under paragraph 7, 8, 9, 10 or 12 of Schedule 4.

Commencement of Appeal

4. An appeal shall be begun by lodging with the commissioners within the period specified in Regulation 5 of these Regulations the notice and documents specified in Regulations 6 and 7 of these Regulations.

(a) 1969 c. 35.　　　　　　　　　　(b) 1971 c. 62.
(c) 1889 c. 63.

Period of Appeal

5.—(1) Subject to the provisions of paragraph (2) of this Regulation—

(*a*) an appeal under paragraph 7 of Schedule 4 on the ground that a consent granted by the Executive does not comply with the requirements of paragraph 2, 4 or 5 of Schedule 4 shall be begun within one month from the date on which the appellant receives notice from the Executive of the grant of such consent and of the terms thereof;

(*b*) an appeal under paragraph 8, 9 or 10 of Schedule 4 against refusal by the Executive of an application by the holder of a consent for the renewal of that consent or for the variation of any term thereof, or condition attached or deemed to be attached thereto, or of the route authorised thereby, shall be begun within one month from the date on which the appellant receives notice from the Executive of such refusal;

(*c*) an appeal under paragraph 9 or 10 of Schedule 4 against a variation made by the Executive, without application from the holder of the consent, of any term of that consent or of any condition attached or deemed to be attached thereto or of the route authorised thereby shall be begun within one month from the date on which the appellant receives notice from the Executive of that variation;

(*d*) an appeal under paragraph 12 of Schedule 4 against cancellation of a consent shall be begun within one month from the date on which the appellant receives notice from the Executive of such cancellation.

(2) Where the appellant has received from the Executive notice of any kind referred to in paragraph (1) of this Regulation before the date on which these Regulations come into operation, the period of one month during which such an appeal shall be begun shall commence on the date on which these Regulations come into operation.

(3) An appeal under paragraph 8, 9 or 10 of Schedule 4 against failure of the Executive to accede to any application of the kind specified in paragraph (1)(*b*) of this Regulation shall be begun within 10 weeks from the date on which the relevant application was lodged with the Executive and may be so begun if and only if the appellant has not within a period of 6 weeks from that date received notice from the Executive of the decision on his application:

Provided that where the said application was lodged with the Executive more than 6 weeks before the date on which these Regulations come into operation, it shall be deemed for the purposes of this paragraph to have been so lodged 6 weeks before that date.

Contents of Notice of Appeal

6.—(1) Every notice of appeal shall be in writing and shall state—

(*a*) the name and address of the appellant;

(*b*) the grounds upon which the appeal is made; and

(*c*) the nature of the Order which the appellant wishes the commissioners to make.

(2) Every notice of an appeal shall be signed by the appellant or by some person authorised to do so on his behalf and in the latter case the notice shall state in what capacity or by what authority he signs.

Documents to accompany Notice of Appeal

7. Every notice of appeal shall be accompanied by the following documents: —

(*a*) a copy of the consent to which the appeal relates;

(*b*) in the case of an appeal under paragraph 7 of Schedule 4, a copy of any consent granted under the London Passenger Transport Act 1933(**a**) or under section 58(2) of the Transport Act 1962(**b**) which relates to the service in question;

(*c*) in the case of an appeal against refusal or failure by the Executive to grant an application by the appellant, a copy of that application;

(*d*) in the case of an appeal under paragraph 8, 9, 10 or 12 of Schedule 4 a copy of any notice of refusal, variation or cancellation received from the Executive;

(*e*) copies of any correspondence between the appellant and the Executive relating to the subject matter of the appeal.

Documents to be served on Executive

8. The appellant shall, at the same time as his notice of appeal is lodged with the commissioners, or as soon as practicable thereafter, serve on the Executive a copy thereof, together with a list of all accompanying documents lodged with the commissioners (whether or not such documents are required to be so lodged by Regulation 7 of these Regulations) and a copy of any document so lodged by the appellant which is not required to be so lodged by the said Regulation 7.

Service of Documents

9. Any communications to be made to the commissioners for the purposes of these Regulations shall be addressed to the clerk to the commissioners at the office for the time being of the commissioners; and any communications to be made to the Executive for those purposes shall be addressed to the Secretary of the Executive at the principal office of the Executive for the time being.

Signed by authority of the Secretary of State.

14th August 1972.

F. J. Ward,
An Under Secretary in
the Department of the Environment.

(**a**) 1933 c. 14.   (**b**) 1962 c. 46.

EXPLANATORY NOTE

(This Note is not part of the Regulations.)

Under section 23(2) of the Transport (London) Act 1969 no person other than the London Transport Executive or a subsidiary of theirs may provide certain bus services in Greater London except in pursuance of an agreement with the Executive or under a consent continued in force or granted under Schedule 4 to the Act. Schedule 4 gives persons who hold such consents a right of appeal to the traffic commissioners for the Metropolitan Traffic Area where the consent granted does not comply with the requirements of the Schedule, where the holder's application for renewal or variation of the consent has not been granted, and where the consent is varied or cancelled by the Executive.

These Regulations prescribe the period and manner in which such appeals are to be made.

STATUTORY INSTRUMENTS

1972 No. 1272

CIVIL AVIATION

The Civil Aviation Authority (Charges) (Amendment) Regulations 1972

Made - - -	*14th August* 1972
Laid before Parliament	*17th August* 1972
Coming into Operation *for all purposes except that* *of regulation* 3 (1) *and* (3)	*7th September* 1972
for the purposes of *regulation* 3 (1) *and* (3)	*1st October* 1972

The Secretary of State, in exercise of his powers under section 9(3) of the Civil Aviation Act 1971(a) and of all other powers enabling him in that behalf, hereby makes the following Regulations:

1. These Regulations may be cited as the Civil Aviation Authority (Charges) (Amendment) Regulations 1972 and shall come into operation:

for all purposes except that of regulation 3 (1) and (3) on 7th September 1972

for the purposes of regulation 3 (1) and (3) on 1st October 1972.

2. The Interpretation Act 1889(b) shall apply for the purpose of the interpretation of these Regulations as it applies for the purpose of the interpretation of an Act of Parliament.

3. The Civil Aviation Authority (Charges) Regulations 1972(c) shall be amended as follows:

(1) there shall be added the following regulation: —

"6. The provisions of Schedule 3 to these Regulations shall have effect with respect to the charges to be paid to the Authority in connection with matters arising under an Order in Council under section 16 of the Civil Aviation Act 1968(d) (which gives power to provide for the mortgaging of aircraft).";

(a) 1971 c. 75.
(c) S.I. 1972/150 (1972 I, p. 504).

(b) 1889 c. 63.
(d) 1968 c. 61.

(2) in Schedule 1:

    (*a*) for paragraph 12(1)(*a*), there shall be substituted:

        "(*a*) a professional pilot or a flight navigator . . . .10.00";

    (*b*) in paragraph 12(1)(*b*) the words "a flight navigator or" shall be deleted;

(3) there shall be added as Schedule 3, the Schedule to these Regulations.

Michael Heseltine,
Minister for Aerospace,
14th August 1972.   Department of Trade and Industry.

SCHEDULE

CHARGES IN CONNECTION WITH THE REGISTRATION OF AIRCRAFT MORTGAGES

1. The charge to be paid upon an application for the registration of a mortgage of an aircraft or of a priority notice relating to a contemplated mortgage of an aircraft shall be in accordance with the following scale:

Where the maximum total weight of the aircraft which is the subject of the mortgage or contemplated mortgage:

(*a*) does not exceed 2,730 kg.	£4·00
(*b*) exceeds 2,730 kg. but does not exceed 5,700 kg	£8·00
(*c*) exceeds 5,700 kg but does not exceed 13,600 kg	£12·00
(*d*) exceeds 13,600 kg but does not exceed 45,500 kg	£16·00
(*e*) exceeds 45,500 kg	£20·00

Provided that:

    (i) the charge to be paid where a glider is the subject of the mortgage or contemplated mortgage shall be £4.00;

    (ii) where a priority notice has been entered in the Register of Aircraft Mortgages and the contemplated mortgage referred to in that notice is made, the charge which would otherwise be payable upon the registration of the mortgage shall be reduced by one half.

For the purposes of this Schedule "maximum total weight" has the same meaning as for purposes of paragraph 1 of Schedule 1 hereto.

2. The charge to be paid upon an application for the registration of a change in the particulars appearing in the Register shall be:

where the aircraft which is the subject of the mortgage is a glider or an aircraft (not being a glider) with a maximum total weight not exceeding 13,600 kg	£1·00
in any other case	£2·00

3. The charge to be paid upon an application for the registration of the discharge of a mortgage shall be half that which would be payable on an application to register that mortgage.

4. The charge to be paid upon an application to inspect the entries in the Register relating to any one aircraft or for notification whether there are entries in the Register relating to any one aircraft shall be 0·60p.

5. The charge to be paid upon an application for a copy of the entries in the Register relating to any one aircraft shall be:

where the application is made at the same time as an application to inspect entries in the Register relating to that aircraft or for notification whether there are entries in the Register relating to that aircraft ... 0·10p.

in any other case ... ... 0·20p.

EXPLANATORY NOTE

(This Note is not part of the Regulations.)

These Regulations amend the Civil Aviation Authority (Charges) Regulations 1972:

(1) by increasing the charge of a flight navigator's licence from £6 to £10. Under the Air Navigation (Second Amendment) Order 1972 (S.I. 1972/1266), the maximum period of validity of such a licence was increased from 12 months to 5 years;

(2) by prescribing charges payable to the Authority for matters connected with the registration of aircraft mortgages.

STATUTORY INSTRUMENTS

1972 No. 1274 (S. 92)

AGRICULTURE

CORN CROPS

The Corn Returns Act 1882 (Amendment of Units) (Scotland) Order 1972

Made - - -		*10th August* 1972
Coming into Operation		1*st September* 1972

In exercise of the powers conferred on me by section 17(2) of the Agriculture (Miscellaneous Provisions) Act 1972(a), and of all other powers enabling me in that behalf, I hereby make the following order:—

Citation, extent and commencement

1. This order may be cited as the Corn Returns Act 1882 (Amendment of Units) (Scotland) Order 1972, shall apply to Scotland only and shall come into operation on 1st September 1972.

Amendment of Corn Returns Act 1882

2.—(1) Sections 8 and 9(6) of the Corn Returns Act 1882(b) (which respectively require that computations of corn in returns under that Act shall be in hundredweights and that the annual and septennial average price published in pursuance of that Act shall be for a hundredweight of corn) shall have effect as respects Scotland as if for any reference to the hundredweight of one hundred and twelve imperial standard pounds there were substituted a reference to the ton of two thousand two hundred and forty imperial standard pounds.

(2) In applying section 9(4) of the said Act (which provides the method of calculating weekly, quarterly and yearly average prices for British corn) to the ascertainment of the quarterly average price for the quarter ending on 29th September 1972, and to the ascertainment of the yearly average price for the year ending 25th December 1972, any weekly average price originally computed with reference to the hundredweight of one hundred and twelve imperial standard pounds shall be recalculated with reference to the ton of two thousand two hundred and forty imperial standard pounds.

(3) In applying section 9(5) of the said Act (which provides the method of calculating septennial average prices) to the ascertainment of the septennial average price for any period of seven years ending on or after 25th December 1972, any yearly average price originally computed with reference to the hundred-weight of one hundred and twelve imperial standard pounds shall be recalculated

(a) 1972 c. 62.   (b) 1882 c. 37.

with reference to the ton of two thousand two hundred and forty imperial standard pounds.

Gordon Campbell,
One of Her Majesty's Principal
Secretaries of State.

St. Andrew's House,
Edinburgh.

10th August 1972.

EXPLANATORY NOTE
(This Note is not part of the Order.)

This Order amends sections 8 and 9(6) of the Corn Returns Act 1882 so that from the date of coming into operation of the order weekly returns made in pursuance of the Act and annual and septennial average prices of British corn computed and published under it shall be in terms of the imperial ton instead of, as formerly, the imperial hundredweight. Transitional provisions are also made governing the computation and publication of average prices which relate to a period during which returns have been made both in terms of the hundredweight and the ton.

STATUTORY INSTRUMENTS

1972 No. 1275 (S.93)

AGRICULTURE

CORN CROPS

The Corn Returns (Scotland) Amendment Regulations 1972

Made - - -	*10th August* 1972
Coming into Operation	*1st September* 1972

In exercise of the powers conferred on me by sections 4, 5 and 14 of the Corn Returns Act 1882(a) as amended by section 2 of the Corn Sales Act 1921(b), section 18 of the Agriculture (Miscellaneous Provisions) Act 1943(c), section 14 of the Agriculture (Miscellaneous Provisions) Act 1954(d) and section 108 of the Agriculture Act 1970 (e) and as read with the Corn Returns Act 1882 (Amendment of Units) (Scotland) Order 1972 (f), and of all other powers enabling me in that behalf, I hereby make the following regulations : —

Citation, interpretation, extent and commencement

1. These regulations, which may be cited as the Corn Returns (Scotland) Amendment Regulations 1972, shall be construed as one with the Corn Returns (Scotland) Regulations 1970(g) (in these regulations referred to as "the principal regulations"), shall apply to Scotland only and shall come into operation on 1st September 1972.

Amendment of principal regulations

2.—(1) In regulation 2(1) (interpretation) of the principal regulations the following definition shall be inserted : —

" "denatured" in relation to wheat means "rendered, before purchase, unfit for human consumption, by treatment with dye, fish oil, or fish liver oil."

(2) Schedule 2 to the principal regulations (which sets out the form of return required by those regulations) shall be deleted from the principal regulations, and there shall be substituted therefor the Schedule to these regulations.

Gordon Campbell,
One of Her Majesty's Principal
Secretaries of State.

St Andrew's House,
Edinburgh.
10th August 1972.

(a) 1882 c. 37.   (b) 1921 c. 35.   (c) 1943 c. 16.
(d) 1954 c. 39.   (e) 1970 c. 40.   (f) S.I. 1972/1274 (1972 II, p. 3817).
(g) S.I. 1970/1099 (1970 II, p. 3450).

SCHEDULE

CORN RETURNS ACT 1882 (As Amended)

A return of all British corn bought from growers during the week ended midnight Thursday.....................19.... by the undersigned buyer carrying on business in the area of.........................

SECTION 1 (1)	For Official Use (2)	Total purchases made during week			
		Quantity			Total Purchase Price (6)
		Ex Farm (3)	Free on rail or delivered (4)	Total (5)	
WHEAT—other than de-natured		tons / cwt.	tons / cwt.	tons / cwt.	£
WHEAT—denatured					
WHEAT—TOTAL					
BARLEY					
OATS					
RYE					
MAIZE					

SECTION 2 (7)		Ex Farm Forward Fixed Price Contracts & Ex Farm Spot Purchases made during week			
		Ex Farm Forward Fixed Price Contracts		Ex Farm Spot Purchases	
		Total Quantity (8)	Total Purchase Price (9)	Total Quantity (10)	Total Purchase Price (11)
WHEAT* „ seed		tons / cwt.	£	tons / cwt.	£
„ milling hard					
„ milling soft					
„ feeding other than denatured					
„ feeding— de-natured					
BARLEY* „ seed					
„ malting					
„ feeding & milling					
OATS* „ seed					
„ milling					
„ feeding					
RYE					
MAIZE					

SECTION 3 (12)		Ex Farm Spot Prices paid for Malting Barley during week	
		Highest £.................per ton (13)	Lowest £.................per ton (14)

*WHEAT, BARLEY or OATS bought and coming within any category other than those specified should be included with feeding grain

Signed ....

Name of firm or Company.. Telephone ....

Address ....

.... Telex ....

....

EXPLANATORY NOTE

(This Note is not part of the Regulations.)

These Regulations amend the Corn Returns (Scotland) Regulations 1970 by substituting a new form of return for the previous form. The principal change in this form is a change from hundredweights and pounds to tons and hundredweights as the units in terms of which quantities of corn purchased are to be listed. Additional particulars to be given of the purchases comprised in the return are prescribed in relation to denatured wheat.

STATUTORY INSTRUMENTS

1972 No. 1276

SOCIAL SECURITY

The National Insurance (Industrial Injuries) (Mariners) Amendment Regulations 1972

Made - - -	*15th August* 1972
Laid before Parliament	*23rd August* 1972
Coming into Operation	*2nd October* 1972

The Secretary of State for Social Services, in exercise of his powers under sections 67(1) and 75 of the National Insurance (Industrial Injuries) Act 1965(**a**) and of all other powers enabling him in that behalf, hereby makes the following regulations, which contain no provisions other than such as are made in consequence of the National Insurance Act 1972(**b**) and which accordingly by virtue of section 6(5) of, and paragraph 2(1)(*a*) of Schedule 4 to, that Act are exempt from the requirements of section 62(2) of the said Act of 1965 (reference to the Industrial Injuries Advisory Council), and which are made in consequence of the said Act of 1972 and which accordingly by virtue of section 6(5) of, and paragraph 2(2)(*b*) of Schedule 4 to, that Act are exempt from the requirements of section 85(4) of the said Act of 1965 (no regulations to be made wholly or partly by virtue of the provisions of section 75 of that Act unless a draft of the regulations has been approved by resolution of each House of Parliament): —

Citation, interpretation and commencement

1. These regulations, which may be cited as the National Insurance (Industrial Injuries) (Mariners) Amendment Regulations 1972, shall be read as one with the National Insurance (Industrial Injuries) (Mariners) Regulations 1948(**c**), as amended (**d**) (hereinafter referred to as "the principal regulations"), and shall come into operation on 2nd October 1972.

Amendment of regulation 6 of the principal regulations

2. In regulation 6 of the principal regulations (contributions in respect of masters or members of the crew of ships or vessels other than home trade ships), for the amounts "£0·004" and "£0·002" there shall be substituted the amounts "£0·008" and "£0·004" respectively.

Signed by authority of the Secretary of State for Social Services,

Paul Dean,
Parliamentary Under-Secretary of State,
Department of Health and Social Security.

15th August 1972.

(**a**) 1965 c. 52.　　　　　　(**b**) 1972 c. 57.
(**c**) S.I. 1948/1471 (Rev. XVI, p. 432: 1948 I, p. 2990).
(**d**) The relevant amending instrument is S.I. 1970/46 (1970 I, p. 243).

EXPLANATORY NOTE

(This Note is not part of the Regulations.)

These Regulations contain no provisions other than such as are made in consequence of the National Insurance Act 1972 and accordingly by virtue of paragraph 2 of Schedule 4 to that Act, no reference of them has been made to the Industrial Injuries Advisory Council, nor has a draft of the Regulations been laid before Parliament for approval by resolution of each House.

The Regulations amend the provisions of the National Insurance (Industrial Injuries) (Mariners) Regulations 1948 relating to contributions in respect of masters or members of the crew of ships or vessels other than home trade ships (regulation 2).

STATUTORY INSTRUMENTS

1972 No. 1277

PENSIONS

The Superannuation (Judicial Offices) (Assistant Registrar of the Lancaster Palatine Court) Rules 1972

Made - - -	*9th August* 1972
Laid before Parliament	*25th August* 1972
Coming into Operation	*2nd October* 1972

The Lord Chancellor, in exercise of the powers conferred on him by section 39A of the Superannuation Act 1965(**a**) (inserted in that Act by section 30 of the Administration of Justice Act 1969(**b**)) and by section 16 of, and paragraph 4(4) of Schedule 2 to, the Courts Act 1971(**c**), and with the consent of the Minister for the Civil Service, hereby makes the following Rules:—

1.—(1) These Rules may be cited as the Superannuation (Judicial Offices) (Assistant Registrar of the Lancaster Palatine Court) Rules 1972 and shall come into operation on 2nd October 1972.

(2) In these Rules, "the principal Rules" means the Superannuation (Judicial Offices) Rules 1970(**d**), and a rule referred to by number means the rule so numbered in those Rules.

(3) The Interpretation Act 1889(**e**) shall apply to the interpretation of these Rules as it applies to the interpretation of an Act of Parliament.

2. The principal Rules shall apply to any person who, immediately before 1st January 1972, held the office of Assistant Registrar of the Court of Chancery of the County Palatine of Lancaster as if that office were included in the Schedule to those Rules and the Duchy of Lancaster shall be an "authority" and the office of Assistant Registrar, an "office", for the purposes of rule 2(1).

Dated 3rd August 1972.

Hailsham of St. Marylebone, C.

Consent of the Minister for the Civil Service given under his Official Seal on 9th August 1972.

(L.S.)

W. G. Bristow,
Authorised by the
Minister for the Civil Service.

(**a**) 1965 c. 74. (**b**) 1969 c. 58. (**c**) 1971 c. 23.
(**d**) S.I. 1970/1021 (1970 II, p. 3171). (**e**) 1889 c. 63.

EXPLANATORY NOTE

(This Note is not part of the Rules.)

These Rules apply the provisions of the Superannuation (Judicial Offices) Rules 1970 to any person holding the office of Assistant Registrar of the Lancaster Palatine Court immediately before 1st January 1972.

STATUTORY INSTRUMENTS

1972 No. 1278

SAVINGS BANKS

The Trustee Savings Banks (Pensions) (No. 2) Order 1972

Made - - -	15*th August* 1972
Laid before Parliament	22*nd August* 1972
Coming into Operation	13*th September* 1972

The Minister for the Civil Service, in exercise of the powers conferred upon him by section 82 of the Trustee Savings Banks Act 1969(a), as amended by paragraph 76 of Schedule 6 to the Superannuation Act 1972(b), and of all other powers enabling him in that behalf, and after consulting the National Dept Commissioners, hereby makes the following Order:—

1.—(1) This Order may be cited as the Trustee Savings Banks (Pensions) (No. 2) Order 1972, and shall come into operation on 13th September 1972.

(2) This Order shall extend to Northern Ireland, the Isle of Man and the Channel Islands.

2.—(1) In this Order:—

"the Civil Service Pension Scheme 1972" means the principal civil service pension scheme made by the Minister for the Civil Service under section 1 of the Superannuation Act 1972 on 15th June 1972 and laid on that date before Parliament;

"officer" means an officer of a trustee savings bank or of the Inspection Committee;

"reckonable service" means service as computed for the purpose of determining the amount of a superannuation allowance or an allowance by way of lump sum;

"the transitional period" means that period beginning with 29th February 1972 and ending with 19th July 1972;

"the 1969 Act" means the Trustee Savings Banks Act 1969;

"the 1970 Order" means the Trustee Savings Banks (Pensions) Order 1970(c), as amended by the Trustee Savings Banks (Pensions) (Amendment) Order 1972(d).

(2) The Interpretation Act 1889(e) shall apply for the interpretation of this Order as it applies for the interpretation of an Act of Parliament.

3. In their application in relation to any officer who died or retired during the transitional period, the provisions of sections 75 and 77 of the 1969 Act, as amended by the 1970 Order, and of articles 4, 5 and 11 of the 1970 Order shall have effect as if:—

(a) 1969 c. 50.   (b) 1972 c. 11.   (c) S.I. 1970/1056 (1970 II, p. 3289).
(d) S.I. 1972/495 (1972 I, p. 1742).   (e) 1889 c. 63.

(*a*) for any reference to the average annual amount of the salary and emoluments of his office during the last three years of his service there were substituted a reference to his pensionable pay within the meaning of section 75(3) of the 1969 Act, as amended by article 3(1)(*b*) of the Trustee Savings Banks (Pensions) Order 1972(**a**);

(*b*) for any reference to each year of service there were substituted a reference to each year of service, and so in proportion for any number of days of service beyond a number of completed years each such day being treated as one three hundred and sixty fifth part of a further year;

(*c*) in section 75(1)(*b*) of the 1969 Act the words "after five years' service as such" were omitted;

(*d*) in section 77(1) of the 1969 Act for the reference to section 75(1) as amended by article 3(1) of the 1970 Order there were substituted a reference to section 75(1) as amended by article 3(1) of the 1970 Order and modified by this article;

(*e*) in relation to an officer who retired on medical grounds with not less than ten years' reckonable service, for the provisions contained in article 5 of the 1970 Order there were substituted, with the necessary adaptations, the provisions of rule 3.4 of the Civil Service Pension Scheme 1972;

(*f*) in relation to an officer who retired on medical grounds with at least two but less than ten years' reckonable service, for the provisions contained in article 4 of the 1970 Order (which provides for the grant of short service gratuities) and in section 75(1)(aa) of the 1969 Act, as amended by the 1970 Order, (which provide for the grant of lump sum allowances) there were substituted, with the necessary adaptations, the provisions of rule 3.5 of the Civil Service Pension Scheme 1972 (which provide for the making of ill-health payments), and as if the following words were added to the end of that rule: —

"If an officer is so retired with more than five years' reckonable service, the ill-health payment will be increased by the amount of one month's pensionable pay for each year of such service (and so in proportion for any further part of a year) following whichever is the later of: —

(i) the date on which he completed five years' reckonable service; or

(ii) the first date after his thirtieth birthday on which he completed an exact number of years of reckonable service."

(*g*) the provisions of article 11 of the 1970 Order (which provides for the grant of pensions to widows, children and dependants) were, with the necessary adaptations, subject to the modifications contained in rules 9.8 to 9.16 of the Civil Service Pension Scheme 1972 (which contain transitional provisions in respect of widows' and childrens' benefits).

Given under the official seal of the Minister for the Civil Service on 15th August 1972.

L.S.

W. G. Bristow,
Authorised by the Minister
for the Civil Service.

(**a**) S.I. 1972/1029 (1972 II, p. 3128).

EXPLANATORY NOTE

(This Note is not part of the Order.)

This Order applies to officers of trustee savings banks provisions corresponding to those contained in section 9 of the Principal Civil Service Pension Scheme. The provisions give additional superannuation benefits to persons whose service ended in the period from 29th February to 19th July 1972.

STATUTORY INSTRUMENTS

1972 No. 1279

WAGES COUNCILS

The Wages Regulation (Milk Distributive) (Scotland) Order 1972

Made - - -	*14th August* 1972
Coming into Operation	*13th September* 1972

Whereas the Secretary of State has received from the Milk Distributive Wages Council (Scotland) the wages regulation proposals set out in the Schedule hereto ;

Now, therefore, the Secretary of State in exercise of his powers under section 11 of the Wages Councils Act 1959(**a**) and of all other powers enabling him in that behalf, hereby makes the following Order :—

1. This Order may be cited as the Wages Regulation (Milk Distributive) (Scotland) Order 1972.

2.—(1) In this Order the expression "the specified date" means the 13th September 1972, provided that where, as respects any worker who is paid wages at intervals not exceeding seven days, that date does not correspond with the beginning of the period for which the wages are paid, the expression "the specified date" means, as respects that worker, the beginning of the next such period following that date.

(2) The Interpretation Act 1889(**b**) shall apply to the interpretation of this Order as it applies to the interpretation of an Act of Parliament and as if this Order and the Order hereby revoked were Acts of Parliament.

3. The wages regulation proposals set out in the Schedule hereto shall have effect as from the specified date and as from that date the Wages Regulation (Milk Distributive) (Scotland) (No. 2) Order 1971(**c**) shall cease to have effect.

Signed by order of the Secretary of State.

14th August 1972.

> *R. R. D. McIntosh,*
> Deputy Secretary,
> Department of Employment.

(**a**) 1959 c. 69.   (**b**) 1889 c. 63.
(**c**) S.I. 1971/1531 (1971 III, p. 4324).

ARRANGEMENT OF SCHEDULE

PART I

STATUTORY MINIMUM REMUNERATION

PART II

HOLIDAYS AND HOLIDAY REMUNERATION

PART III

GENERAL

Article 3

SCHEDULE

The following minimum remuneration and provisions as to holidays and holiday remuneration shall be substituted for the statutory minimum remuneration and the provisions as to holidays and holiday remuneration set out in the Wages Regulation (Milk Distributive) (Scotland) (No. 2) Order 1971 (hereinafter referred to as "Order M.D.S. (99)").

PART I

STATUTORY MINIMUM REMUNERATION

GENERAL

1.—(1) Subject to the provisions of paragraphs 4, 6, 7 and 8, the minimum remuneration payable to a worker to whom this Schedule applies for all work except work to which a minimum overtime rate applies under paragraph 5 is:—

(a) in the case of a time worker, the hourly general minimum time rate payable to the worker under the provisions of this Schedule;

(b) in the case of a worker employed on piece work, piece rates each of which would yield, in the circumstances of the case, to an ordinary worker at least the same amount of money as the hourly general minimum time rate which would be payable if the worker were a time worker.

(2) In this Schedule, the expression "hourly general minimum time rate" means the general minimum time rate applicable to the worker under paragraph 2 or 3 divided by 42.

GENERAL MINIMUM TIME RATES

MALE OR FEMALE WORKERS

2. The general minimum time rates applicable to male or female workers (*other than Transport Workers*) are as follows:—

	MALE WORKERS Per week £	FEMALE WORKERS Per week £
(1) Senior Foreman	22·10	20·70
(2) Foreman	21·10	19·70
(3) Chargehand, Checker, Processor and Qualified Trainer	19·85	18·45
(4) Fork Lift Truck Operator, Laboratory Assistant, Machine Operator (High Speed) Grade I and Storeman	19·35	17·95
(5) Boilerman and Machine Operator (High Speed) Grade II	19·10	17·70
(6) Clerks aged 22 years or over... ...	18·85	17·45

(7) The following workers:—

(a) All other male workers

(b) Roundswomen and female workers employed in garaging, pasteurising or milk sterilising, the said workers being aged:—

	Per week £
21 years or over	18·60
20 and under 21 years	16·74
19 „ „ 20 „	14·88
18 „ „ 19 „	13·48
17 „ „ 18 „	11·16
16 „ „ 17 „	9·76
under 16 years	8·83

(8) All other female workers (including Assistant Roundswomen, Clerks and Shop Assistants) being aged:—

	Per week £
21 years or over	17·20
20 and under 21 years	15·91
19 „ „ 20 „	14·62
18 „ „ 19 „	13·33
17 „ „ 18 „	11·61
16 „ „ 17 „	10·32
under 16 years	9·03

TRANSPORT WORKERS

3. *The general minimum time rates applicable to drivers who are 21 years or over are as follows:—*

(a) *Tanker drivers regularly engaged on the collection of milk from farms:—*
during the first year of service ... ... £22·03 *per week*
after „ „ „ „ „ ... ... £22·17 „ „

Provided that:—

(i) *an additional payment of £1 per week shall be payable to such a tanker driver who measures and samples milk at farms;*

(ii) *a subsistence allowance of 15p per day shall be payable to such a tanker driver who is required to work more than 60 miles from his depot.*

(b) *Other drivers:—*

Column 1								Column 2
Carrying capacity of vehicle (as defined in paragraph 19)								*Per week* £
Under 5 tons ...	...	...	...	...	...	...	...	*19·75*
Over 5 tons and up to and including 10 tons			...	...	...	...	...	*20·21*
„ 10 „ „ „ „ 15 „				...	...	...	...	*21·10*
„ 15 „ „ „ „ 18 „				...	...	...	...	*21·56*
„ 18 „ „ „ „ 21 „				...	...	...	...	*22·14*
Over 21 tons	...	...	...	...	...	...	...	*22·62*

EARLY OR NIGHT WORK

4.—(1) A worker who ordinarily works, wholly or partly, between the hours of 10 p.m. and 6 a.m. shall be paid:—

(a) *in the case of a worker who is engaged on retail delivery work—*

(i) *for all time worked on such work between the said hours of 10 p.m. and 6 a.m. (excluding any time worked in a depot from which the delivery is made) twice the hourly general minimum time rate otherwise applicable to him under the provisions of this Schedule;*

(ii) *for all time worked in any such depot between the said hours of 10 p.m. and 6 a.m., in addition to any hourly general minimum time rate or minimum overtime rate payable to him in respect of such work under the provisions of this Schedule, 5p in respect of each hour or part of an hour so worked:*
Provided that any time to which (i) of this sub-paragraph applies shall not be regarded as time worked for the purpose of calculating any minimum overtime rate.

For the purpose of this sub-paragraph the expression "retail delivery" means the delivery of milk wholly or mainly to households and retail establishments.

(b) *in the case of a worker engaged on any other work, in addition to any hourly general minimum time rate or minimum overtime rate payable to him in respect of such work under the provisions of this Schedule, 5p in respect of each hour or part of an hour worked by him between the said hours of 10 p.m. and 6 a.m.*

(2) A worker who is required, in addition to his usual working hours on any day, to work for any time between 12 midnight and 6 a.m. shall be paid in respect of all time worked outside his usual working hours between 12 midnight and 6 a.m. twice the hourly general minimum time rate otherwise applicable to him: Provided that such additional time worked shall not be regarded as time worked for the purpose of calculating any minimum overtime rate.

MINIMUM OVERTIME RATES

5. Subject to the provisions of paragraphs 4, 6, 7 and 8 minimum overtime rates are payable as follows:—

(1) to any worker who normally works for more than 21 hours per week—

(a) on a Sunday, not being a rest day or a customary holiday—

(i) for any time worked not exceeding 5 hours ... time-and-a-half for 5 hours

(ii) for all time worked in excess of 5 hours ... time-and-a-half

(b) on a Sunday, being also a rest day but not being a customary holiday—

(i) for any time worked not exceeding 4 hours ...	double time for 4 hours
(ii) for all time worked in excess of 4 hours ...	double time

(c) on a rest day, not being a Sunday or a customary holiday—

(i) for any time worked not exceeding 5 hours ...	time-and-a-half for 5 hours
(ii) for all time worked in excess of 5 hours ...	time-and-a-half

(2) to workers other than those referred to in sub-paragraph (1) above—

(a) for work on a customary holiday—for all time worked	double time
(b) on a rest day for all time worked	time-and-a-half

(3) to any worker in any week exclusive of any time in respect of which a minimum overtime rate is payable under the foregoing provisions of this paragraph or under the provisions of paragraph 6(3) for all time worked in excess of 42 hours:—

(a) for the first 4 hours worked	time-and-a-quarter
(b) thereafter	time-and-a-half

Provided that in the case of a rota worker whose normal hours are fixed in respect of each week of the period of rota by his employer and the hours so fixed average 42 per week over a period of rota, the preceding sub-paragraph shall apply as respects each week of the period of rota as if for the expression "42 hours" there were substituted a reference to the number of hours fixed by the employer as aforesaid in respect of that week.

REMUNERATION FOR CUSTOMARY HOLIDAYS

6.—(1) This paragraph applies to workers who normally work for the employer for more than 21 hours a week.

(2) Where a worker to whom this paragraph applies—

(a) is not required to work on a customary holiday,

(b) worked for the employer throughout the last working day on which work was available to him preceding a customary holiday, and

(c) presents himself for employment at the usual starting time on the first working day after a customary holiday,

he shall be paid for the customary holiday the amount to which he would have been entitled under paragraph 2 or 3 had the day not been a customary holiday, and had he worked on a day other than a rest day the number of hours ordinarily worked by him on that day of the week (or eight and two fifths hours in the case of a worker who does not ordinarily work on that day of the week): Provided that the condition set out in (b) or (c) of this sub-paragraph shall be deemed to be satisfied where the worker is excused by his employer or is prevented by his proved illness or injury from working or presenting himself for employment as aforesaid.

(3) Where a worker to whom this paragraph applies works on a customary holiday he shall be paid for time worked on the customary holiday as follows:—

(a) on a customary holiday, not being a rest day—

(i) for any time worked not exceeding eight and two-fifths hours	double-time for eight and two-fifths hours
(ii) for all time worked in excess of eight and two-fifths hours	double time

(b) on a customary holiday which is also a rest day—

(i) for any time worked not exceeding eight and two-fifths hours ... ...   treble time for eight and two-fifths hours

(ii) for all time worked in excess of eight and two-fifths hours ... ...   treble time;

and IN ADDITION, the worker shall be allowed a holiday in lieu of the customary holiday on a day other than a rest day or any other customary holiday, such day in lieu to be fixed by agreement between the employer and the worker or his representative, before the next following 1st March:

Provided that, in the absence of agreement between the employer and the worker or his representative, a day of holiday in lieu of each such customary holiday shall be allowed on the last day or days when the worker would otherwise work before the next following 1st March.

(4) The worker shall be paid for a holiday in lieu of a customary holiday as if it were a customary holiday on which he was not required to work.

7. In this Part of this Schedule the expressions "time-and-a-quarter", "time-and-a-half", "double time" and "treble time" mean respectively one and a quarter times, one and a half times, twice and three times the hourly general minimum time rate.

WAITING TIME

8.—(1) A worker is entitled to payment of the minimum remuneration specified in this Schedule for all time during which he is present on the premises of his employer unless he is present thereon in any of the following circumstances:—

(a) without the employer's consent, express or implied,

(b) for some purpose unconnected with his work and other than that of waiting for work to be given to him to perform,

(c) by reason only of the fact that he is resident thereon,

(d) during normal meal times in a room or place in which no work is being done, and he is not waiting for work to be given to him to perform.

(2) The minimum remuneration payable under sub-paragraph (1) of this paragraph to a piece worker when not engaged on piece work is that which would be payable if he were a time worker.

PART II

HOLIDAYS AND HOLIDAY REMUNERATION
ANNUAL HOLIDAY

9.—(1) Subject to the provisions of sub-paragraph (3) of this paragraph, an employer shall between the date on which the provisions of this Schedule become effective and 31st October 1972, and between 1st April and 31st October in each succeeding year, allow a holiday (hereinafter referred to as "an annual holiday") to every worker in his employment to whom this Schedule applies, who was employed by him during the 12 months immediately preceding the commencement of the holiday season for any of the periods of employment (calculated in accordance with the provisions of paragraph 17) specified in the table below, and the duration of the holiday shall, in the case of each such worker, be related to his period of employment during that 12 months as follows:—

Period of employment	Duration of annual holiday
At least 48 weeks	2 normal working weeks
„ „ 44 „	1 „ „ week and 4 days
„ „ 39 „	1 „ „ „ „ 3 „
„ „ 35 „	1 „ „ „ „ 2 „
„ „ 31 „	1 „ „ „ „ 1 day
„ „ 22 „	1 „ „ „
„ „ 18 „	4 days
„ „ 13 „	3 „
„ „ 4 „	1 day

(2) In this Schedule the expression "holiday season" means in relation to an annual holiday during the year 1972, the period commencing on 1st April 1972, and ending on 31st October 1972, and in relation to each subsequent year, the period commencing on 1st April and ending on 31st October in that year.

(3) Notwithstanding the provisions of sub-paragraph (1) of this paragraph:—

(a) the number of days of annual holiday which an employer is required to allow to a worker in any holiday season shall not exceed in the aggregate twice the number of days constituting the worker's normal working week;

(b) the duration of the worker's annual holiday during the holiday season ending on 31st October 1972, shall be reduced by any days of annual holiday duly allowed to him by the employer under the provisions of any previous wages regulation order or orders between 1st April 1972 and the date on which the provisions of this Schedule become effective.

10. Subject to the provisions of paragraph 12, an annual holiday shall be allowed on consecutive working days, being days on which the worker is normally called upon to work for the employer and days of annual holiday shall be treated as consecutive notwithstanding that some other holiday, a rest day or a day upon which the worker is not normally required to work for the employer intervenes.

ADDITIONAL ANNUAL HOLIDAY

11.—(1) Subject to the provisions of this paragraph, in addition to the holiday specified in paragraph 9 an employer shall, in the year commencing on 1st April 1972 and in each succeeding year commencing on 1st April, allow a further annual holiday (hereinafter referred to as an "additional annual holiday") to every worker in his employment to whom this Schedule applies who—

(a) at 31st March immediately preceding the relevant year has been continuously employed by him for not less than one year; and

(b) during the year ending on the said 31st March has worked for a period qualifying him in accordance with paragraphs 9 and 17 for an annual holiday equal in duration to twice his normal working week.

(2) The duration of the additional annual holiday shall be in accordance with the next following table:—

Period of continuous employment at 31st March immediately preceding the year in which the additional annual holiday is to be allowed.	Duration of additional annual holiday
At least 3 years	1 normal working week
„ „ 2 „	4 days
„ „ 1 year	2 „

(3) Days of additional annual holiday need not be consecutive and shall be allowed—

(a) on days on which the worker is normally called upon to work for the employer, and

(b) at any time after the holiday season but during the relevant year either on dates agreed between the employer and the worker at any time before 21st March in that period, or during the remaining days of that period:

Provided that where the employer so decides, any day or days of additional annual holiday may be allowed during the holiday season.

GENERAL

12. A day of annual holiday or additional annual holiday shall not be allowed to a worker on a rest day or on any day on which he is entitled to a holiday under any enactment other than the Wages Councils Act 1959.

13. An employer shall give to a worker reasonable notice of the commencing date and duration of his annual holiday and of any days of additional annual holiday not previously agreed. Such notice may be given individually to a worker or by the posting of a notice in the place where the worker is employed.

HOLIDAY REMUNERATION

14. Subject to the provisions of paragraph 15, a worker qualified to be allowed an annual holiday or additional annual holiday under this Schedule shall be paid by his employer in respect thereof, on the last pay day preceding such annual holiday, one day's holiday pay as defined in paragraph 19 in respect of each day thereof.

15. Where in accordance with the provisions of this or of any previous wages regulation order any accrued holiday remuneration has been paid by the employer to the worker in respect of any period of employment in the 12 months immediately preceding the holiday season within which an annual holiday or additional annual holiday is allowed by the employer to the worker in accordance with the provisions of this Schedule, the amount of holiday remuneration payable by the employer in respect of the said period under the provisions of paragraph 14 shall be reduced by the amount of the said accrued holiday remuneration.

ACCRUED HOLIDAY REMUNERATION PAYABLE ON TERMINATION OF EMPLOYMENT

16. Where a worker ceases to be employed by an employer after the provisions of this Schedule become effective the employer shall, immediately on the termination of the employment (hereinafter referrred to as "the termination date"), pay to the worker as accrued holiday remuneration:—

(1) in respect of employment in the 12 months up to the end of the preceding March, a sum equal to the holiday remuneration for any days of annual holiday or additional annual holiday for which he has qualified, except days of annual holiday or additional annual holiday which he has been allowed or has become entitled to be allowed before leaving the employment; and

(2) in respect of any employment since the end of the preceding March—

    (a) a sum equal to the holiday remuneration which would have been payable to him if he could have been allowed an annual holiday in respect of that period of employment at the time of leaving it; and

    (b) in addition, where a worker has qualified for an additional annual holiday in accordance with the provisions of paragraph 11, one day's holiday pay in respect of each of the following periods of employment occurring between the end of the preceding March and the termination date—

        (i) in the case of a worker who has qualified for an additional annual holiday of 4 days or more, each successive period of not less than 13 weeks;

        (ii) in the case of a worker who has qualified for an additional annual holiday of 2 days, each successive period of not less than 26 weeks.

Provided that no worker shall be entitled to the payment by his employer of accrued holiday remuneration if he is dismissed on the grounds of misconduct in connection with his employment and is so informed by his employer at the time of dismissal.

CALCULATION OF EMPLOYMENT

17. For the purpose of calculating any period of employment qualifying a worker for an annual holiday, additional annual holiday or for any accrued holiday remuneration under this Schedule, the worker shall be treated:—

(1) as if he were employed for a week in respect of any week in which—

    (a) he has worked for the employer for not less than 21 hours and has performed some work for which statutory minimum remuneration is payable; or (*b*) he has been absent throughout the week, or he has worked for the employer for less than 21 hours in either case solely by reason of the proved illness of, or accident to, the worker: Provided that the number of weeks which may be treated as weeks of employment for such reasons shall not exceed eight in the aggregate in the period of 12 months immediately preceding the commencement of the holiday season; or

(2) as if he were employed on any day of holiday allowed under the provisions of this or of any previous wages regulation order, and for the purposes of sub-paragraph (1) of this paragraph, a worker who is absent on such a holiday shall be treated as having worked thereon the number of hours ordinarily worked by him on that day of the week for the employer on work for which statutory minimum remuneration is payable.

OTHER HOLIDAY AGREEMENTS

18. The provisions of this Schedule are without prejudice to any agreement for the allowance of any further holidays with pay or for the payment of additional holiday remuneration.

PART III

GENERAL

DEFINITIONS

19. In this Schedule, unless the context otherwise requires, the following expressions apply to both male and female workers and have the meanings hereby respectively assigned to them, that is to say:—

"ASSISTANT ROUNDSWOMAN" means a worker wholly or mainly employed in assisting any person carrying out the duties normally performed by a rounds-woman whether or not such person is a roundswoman as defined in this Schedule.

"BOILERMAN" means a worker wholly or mainly employed on the duties of attending to boilers.

"CARRYING CAPACITY"

(*1*) *The carrying capacity of a vehicle means the weight of the maximum load normally carried by the vehicle, and such carrying capacity when so established shall not be affected either by variations in the weight of the load resulting from collections or deliveries or emptying of containers during the course of the journey, or by the fact that on any particular journey a load greater or less than the established carrying capacity is carried.*

(2) *Where a trailer is attached to the vehicle, the load shall be the loads of the vehicle and trailer combined.*

"CHARGEHAND" means a worker in charge of creamery workers not exceeding ten in number (exclusive of the Chargehand).

"CLERK" means a person employed wholly or mainly on clerical work.

"CHECKER" means a person bearing full responsibility for the checking and recording of outgoing goods and for the reconciliation of stocks.

"CUSTOMARY HOLIDAY" means New Year's Day, the local Spring holiday (Monday), the local Autumn holiday (Monday), and three other days being days locally recognised as holidays.

"FOREMAN" means a person to whom is deputed the duty of exercising super-visory authority over workers exceeding ten in number (exclusive of the Foreman).

"FORK LIFT TRUCK OPERATOR" means a person whose principal occupation is that of a Fork Lift Truck Operator.

"LABORATORY ASSISTANT" means a person required by his employer to carry out certain tests in relation to the quality of milk products.

"MACHINE OPERATOR (HIGH SPEED) GRADE I" means a person opera-ting a machine having an output from a single unit exceeding 300 containers per minute and who can operate all the other high speed equipment in the establishment.

"MACHINE OPERATOR (HIGH SPEED) GRADE II" means a person operating a machine having an output from a single unit exceeding 300 containers per minute.

"NIGHT WORKER" means a worker who is ordinarily employed on a spell of duty which starts before and ends after midnight.

"NORMAL WORKING WEEK" means:—

(a) in the case of a rota worker the total number of days (excluding rest days) on which the worker has ordinarily worked for the employer during the periods of rota during the 12 months immediately preceding the commencement of the holiday season, or where under paragraph 16 accrued holiday remuneration is payable, during the 12 months immediately preceding the termination date, divided by the total number of weeks in the said periods of rota;

(b) in the case of any other worker the number of days (excluding rest days) on which it has been usual for the worker to work for the employer in a week during the 12 months immediately preceding the commencement of the holiday season, or where under paragraph 16 accrued holiday remuneration is payable, during the 12 months immediately preceding the termination date: Provided that in either case:—

(i) for the purpose of calculating the normal working week, part of a day shall count as a day;

(ii) except in the case of a rota worker's rest days, no account shall be taken of any week in which the worker did not perform any work for which statutory minimum remuneration has been fixed;

(iii) in the case of a night worker a day is a period of 24 hours commencing at noon.

"ONE DAY'S HOLIDAY PAY" means, where the worker's normal working week is:—

5 days—one-fifth of
4 days—one-quarter of
3 days—one-third of

the remuneration which the worker would be entitled to receive from his employer at the date of the annual holiday or additional annual holiday or at the termination date, as the case may be, for work for which statutory minimum remuneration is payable, either:—

(a) for the number of hours normally worked by him for the employer in his normal working week, or
(b) for 42 hours,

whichever number of hours is the less, if paid at the appropriate hourly general minimum time rate for that number of hours' work.

"PROCESSOR" means a person to whom is deputed the duty of processing milk.

"QUALIFIED TRAINER" means a worker who is directly responsible for the instruction of trainees and their hour to hour supervision whilst they are undergoing training whether on or off the job.

"REST DAYS" means two days in each week which have been notified to the worker by the employer before the commencement of the week as rest days, or, failing such notification, the last two days in the week; and "REST DAY" means one of these days:

Provided that in the case of a rota worker "REST DAYS" means any such days calculated at the rate of two days for each week in the period of rota.

"ROTA WORKER" means a worker employed under an agreement which provides that his rest days should be taken according to a rota over a period not exceeding 12 weeks.

"ROUNDSWOMAN" means a worker wholly or mainly employed as a sales-woman on a definite or established route and responsible for keeping account of retail sales to customers and of any cash or tokens received in payment and who is not accompanied, save in exceptional circumstances, by any other person who exercises control or supervision.

"SENIOR FOREMAN" means a person to whom is deputed the duty of exercising supervisory authority over workers exceeding thirty in number (exclusive of the Senior Foreman.)

"SHOP ASSISTANT" means a person employed, wholly or mainly, in a shop as defined in sections 38 and 74 of the Shops Act 1950(a) in serving customers or in checking in and out or in both such operations.

"STATUTORY MINIMUM REMUNERATION" means minimum remuneration (other than holiday remuneration) fixed by a wages regulation order.

"STOREMAN" means a person to whom is deputed the responsibility for the receipt, storage, maintenance and issue of stores and for the accounting thereof.

"WAGES REGULATION ORDER" means a wages regulation order made by the Secretary of State to give effect to proposals submitted to him by the Milk Distributive Wages Council (Scotland).

"WEEK" means pay week.

WORKERS TO WHOM THE SCHEDULE APPLIES

20.—(1) This Schedule applies to workers in relation to whom the Milk Distributive Wages Council (Scotland) operates, that is to say workers employed in Scotland in the operations in the Milk Distributive Trade specified in the Schedule to the Trade Boards (Milk Distributive Trade, Scotland) (Constitution and Proceedings) Regulations 1933(b), namely:—

(i) the wholesale and retail sale of milk;

(ii) the sale of other goods by workers mainly employed in the sale specified in (i) of this sub-paragraph;

(iii) all work incidental to the sale specified in (i) of this sub-paragraph.

(2) Work incidental to the sale specified in sub-paragraph (1)(i) of this paragraph includes, inter alia:—

(a) collecting, delivering, despatching;

(b) pasteurising, sterilising, homogenising, humanising, cooling, separating and all work performed in connection with any other process in the preparation of milk;

(c) blending, testing and sampling of milk;

(d) cleaning of utensils, receptacles, vehicles, premises, plant, machinery;

(e) stoking, attending to boiler, plant or machinery, fire lighting, portering of coal or other fuel;

(f) horse keeping and harness cleaning;

(g) portering, lift or hoist-operating, time-keeping, storing, stock-keeping, ware-housing;

(h) boxing, parcelling, labelling, weighing, measuring, checking, bottling, packing and unpacking;

(a) 1950 c. 28.   (b) S.R. & O. 1933/1123 (Rev. XXIII, p. 484: 1933, p. 2045).

(*i*) clerical work or canvassing carried on in conjunction with the work specified in sub-paragraph (1) of this paragraph.

(3) Notwithstanding the foregoing provisions of this paragraph the Milk Distributive Trade does not include any of the following operations:—

(*a*) the wholesale sale of milk (and operations incidental thereto) from an establishment at which milk products are manufactured and from which unseparated milk is not ordinarily sold as such;

(*b*) the wholesale sale of milk direct from the farm where the milk was produced and all operations incidental thereto;

(*c*) the sale of milk in restaurants, shops or similar premises by waiters or shop assistants who are not mainly engaged upon such sale;

(*d*) the transport of goods by common carriers;

(*e*) carting and operations incidental thereto where the business carried on consists exclusively of such operations;

(*f*) work done by or on behalf of the Post Office.

(4) For the purpose of this paragraph the expression "milk" means milk other than dried or condensed milk.

EXPLANATORY NOTE

(This Note is not part of the Order.)

This Order, which has effect from 13th September 1972, sets out the statutory minimum remuneration payable and the holidays to be allowed to workers in substitution for the statutory minimum remuneration fixed and the holidays provided for by the Wages Regulation (Milk Distributive) (Scotland) (No. 2) Order 1971 (Order M.D.S. (99)), which Order is revoked.

New provisions are printed in italics.

STATUTORY   INSTRUMENTS

1972 No. 1280

INJURIES IN WAR COMPENSATION

The Injuries in War (Shore Employments) Compensation (Amendment) Scheme 1972

Made -   -   -   -   *9th August* 1972

The Defence Council, with the consent of the Minister for the Civil Service, in exercise of the powers conferred on them by section 1 of the Injuries in War Compensation Act, 1914 (Session 2)(**a**) (as amended by the Defence (Transfer of Functions) (No. 1) Order 1964(**b**)) and section 1(1) and (3) of the Defence (Transfer of Functions) Act 1964(**c**) and of all other powers enabling them in that behalf, hereby make the following Scheme:—

1. The Injuries in War (Shore Employments) Compensation Scheme 1914 as amended(**d**) shall be further amended as follows:

In paragraph (3) thereof for the figures "£10.00.", wherever they occur, there shall be substituted the figures "£11.20".

2. This Scheme shall have effect as from 2nd October 1972, so, however, that no payment shall be made thereunder in respect of any period before that date.

3. This Scheme may be cited as the Injuries in War (Shore Employments) Compensation (Amendment) Scheme 1972 and the Injuries in War (Shore Employments) Compensation Schemes 1914 to 1971 and this Scheme may be cited together as the Injuries in War (Shore Employments) Compensation Schemes 1914 to 1972.

Balniel,
Michael Carver,
Members of the Defence Council.

Dated 31st July 1972.

Consent of the Minister for the
Civil Service given under his Official Seal.

W. G. Bristow,
Authorised by the Minister for
the Civil Service.

Dated 9th August 1972.

(**a**) 5 & 6 Geo. 5. c. 18.   (**b**) S.I. 1964/488 (1964) I, p 769).
(**c**) 1964 c. 15.   (**d**) The relevant amending instrument is S.I.
                                       1971/1987 (1971, III p. 5670).

EXPLANATORY NOTE

(This Note is not part of the Scheme.)

The Injuries in War (Shore Employments) Compensation Schemes 1914 to 1971 provide for the payment of weekly allowances to small numbers of ex-members of the Women's Auxiliary Forces who suffered disablement from their service overseas during the 1914-18 war. This amending Scheme provides that the maximum weekly allowance payable shall be increased from £10.00 to £11.20 and that other allowances shall be increased proportionately . The increases will take effect as from 2nd October 1972 in accordance with section 1(5) of the Injuries in War Compensation Act, 1914 (Session 2).

STATUTORY INSTRUMENTS

1972 No. 1281 (S.94)

EDUCATION, SCOTLAND

The Remuneration of Teachers (Scotland) Amendment Order 1972

Made - - -	*14th August* 1972	
Coming into Operation	*15th August* 1972	

Whereas—

(1) under section 2(2) of the Remuneration of Teachers (Scotland) Act 1967(**a**) (hereinafter referred to as "the Act") the Scottish Teachers Salaries Committee (hereinafter referred to as "the Committee"), constituted under section 1 of the Act for the purpose of considering the remuneration of (*a*) teachers employed whole-time by education authorities in the provision of school education under the Education (Scotland) Acts 1939 to 1969 and duly qualified for appointment other than temporary appointment in terms of regulations for the time being in force under the said Acts; and (*b*) teachers employed whole-time by education authorities in the provision of further education under the said Acts, have transmitted to the Secretary of State recommendations agreed on by them with respect to the remuneration of teachers of the said descriptions;

(2) under section 3(1) of the Act there were referred to arbitration matters in respect of which agreement had not been reached in the Committee;

(3) the recommendations of the arbiters have been transmitted to the Secretary of State under section 4(1) of the Act;

(4) there are in force orders made under section 2 of the Act with respect to the remuneration of such teachers, namely, the Remuneration of Teachers (Scotland) Order 1970(**b**), the Remuneration of Teachers (Scotland) Amendment Order 1971(**c**) and the Remuneration of Teachers (Scotland) Amendment No. 2 Order 1971(**d**);

(5) it appears to the Secretary of State that effect can more conveniently be given to the recommendations mentioned at paragraphs (1) and (3) above by amending by virtue of section 2(5) of the Act the scales and other provisions set out in the memorandum referred to in the said orders, namely, the memorandum published by Her Majesty's Stationery Office under the title "SCOTTISH TEACHERS' SALARIES MEMORANDUM 1970";

(6) under section 2(5) of the Act the Secretary of State has prepared a draft order setting out the amendments to the said memorandum which, in his opinion, are requisite for giving effect to the recommendations mentioned at paragraphs (1) and (3) above; and

(7) the Secretary of State, as required by section 2(6) of the Act, has con-

---

(**a**) 1967 c. 36.   (**b**) S.I. 1970/993 (1970 II, p. 3133).
(**c**) S.I. 1971/20 (1971 I, p. 12).   (**d**) S.I. 1971/669 (1971 I, p. 1772).

sulted the Committee with respect to the draft order and the Committee have made no representations with respect thereto;

Now therefore, the Secretary of State, in exercise of the powers conferred on him by section 2(6), that section as applied by section 4(1) and section 8(3) of the Act, and of all other powers enabling him in that behalf, hereby makes the following order—

Citation and commencement

1. This order may be cited as the Remuneration of Teachers (Scotland) Amendment Order 1972 and shall come into operation on 15th August 1972.

Interpretation

2. The Interpretation Act 1889(**a**) shall apply for the interpretation of this order as it applies for the interpretation of an Act of Parliament.

Amendment of memorandum with effect from 1st April 1972

3. The provisions set out in the above-mentioned memorandum, as amended by the above-mentioned orders in force under section 2 of the Act, shall with effect from 1st April 1972 be further amended in the following manner:—

(a) In Part III:

(i) in sub-paragraph (1) of paragraph 20 "£129" shall be deleted and "£141" shall be substituted therefor;

(ii) in sub-paragraph (2) of paragraph 20 "£75" shall be deleted and "£81" shall be substituted therefor;

(iii) in sub-paragraph (1) of paragraph 21 "£75" shall be deleted and "£81" shall be substituted therefor;

(iv) in sub-paragraph (2) of paragraph 21 "£153" shall be deleted and "£168" shall be substituted therefor;

(v) in sub-paragraph (3) of paragraph 21 "£81" shall be deleted and "£129" shall be substituted therefor;

(vi) in sub-paragraph (1) of paragraph 22 "£75" shall be deleted and "£81" shall be substituted therefor;

(vii) in sub-paragraph (2) of paragraph 22 "£81" shall be deleted and "£129" shall be substituted therefor;

(viii) in sub-paragraph (1) of paragraph 23 "£75" shall be deleted and "£81" shall be substituted therefor;

(ix) in sub-paragraphs (2) and (3) of paragraph 23 "£81" shall be deleted and "£90" shall in each case be substituted therefor;

(x) at the end of the heading to paragraph 24 the words "or assistant educational psychologists" shall be added;

(xi) in sub-paragraph (1) of paragraph 24 "£93" shall be deleted and "£102" shall be substituted therefor;

(xii) in sub-paragraph (2) of paragraph 24 "£120" shall be deleted and "£132" shall be substituted therefor;

(xiii) after sub-paragraph (2) of paragraph 24 the following sub-paragraph shall be inserted:

"(2A) The appropriate basic scale shall be increased throughout by £135 for a teacher who is employed wholly or mainly as an assistant educational psychologist.".

(**a**) 1889 c. 63.

(*b*) In Part IV:

(i) in paragraph 32 "£108" shall be deleted and "£117" shall be substituted therefor;

(ii) in line 4 of paragraph 33 the words after "allowance of" shall be deleted and the following words shall be substituted therefor:
"the amount shown in column (2) opposite to the said serial number and the senior teacher shall receive a responsibility allowance of the amount shown in column (3) opposite to the said serial number.";

(iii) in sub-paragraph (1) of paragraph 34 the words "Part B of" shall be deleted;

(iv) in sub-paragraph (1) of paragraph 36 "£390" shall be deleted and "£423" shall be substituted therefor; and the words "one of the categories in Part B of Appendix VII" shall be deleted and the words "Grade I" shall be substituted therefor;

(v) in sub-paragraph (2) of paragraph 36 "£108" shall be deleted and "£117" shall be substituted therefor; and the words "one of the categories described in Part C of Appendix VII" shall be deleted and the words "Grade II" shall be substituted therefor.

(*c*) In Part V:

(i) in head (*a*) of sub-paragraph (2) of paragraph 39 "£81" shall be deleted and "£90" shall be substituted therefor;

(ii) in head (*b*) of sub-paragraph (2) of paragraph 39 "£153" shall be deleted and "£168" shall be substituted therefor;

(iii) in sub-paragraph (2) of paragraph 40 "£81" shall be deleted and "£90" shall be substituted therefor.

(*d*) In Part A of Appendix II:

(i) after the word "university" at the end of head (*d*) of sub-paragraph (2) of paragraph 1 the following heads shall be added:
", or

(*e*) a D.Mus degree, by examination, of a university in the United Kingdom, or

(*f*) the Diploma in Musical Education (honours) of the Royal Scottish Academy of Music and Drama, or

(*g*) the Fellowship Diploma of Royal College of Organists together with a B.Mus degree of a university in the United Kingdom obtained prior to the introduction by the awarding university of an honours classification.";

(ii) in sub-head (i) of head (*a*) of sub-paragraph (4) of paragraph 1 the word "Scottish" shall be deleted and after the word "university" there shall be inserted the words "in the United Kingdom";

(iii) sub-paragraph (1) of paragraph 2 shall be deleted and the following sub-paragraph shall be substituted therefor:
"(1) Where a teacher is employed wholly or mainly—

(*a*) in a secondary school, or

(*b*) in a special school in the instruction of pupils over the age of 12 years, or

(*c*) as a Head Teacher of a special school, or in a primary school with a special class attached, and there are pupils over the age of 12 years on the roll of that special school or special class, or

(*d*) otherwise in secondary education,

and his qualifications are as described in sub-paragraphs (2) or (3) following his basic salary shall be calculated by reference to Scale 2.";

(iv) in head (*a*) of sub-paragraph (2) of paragraph 2 after the words "degree of a" there shall be inserted the word "Scottish" and the words "in the United Kingdom or awarded by the Council for National Academic Awards", shall be deleted;

(v) head (*q*) of sub-paragraph (2) of paragraph 2 shall be deleted and the following head shall be substituted therefor:

"(*q*) the Diploma in Educational Handwork or in Technical Subjects of a college of education supplemented by the Higher National Certificate, or";

(vi) head (*r*) of sub-paragraph (2) of paragraph 2 shall be deleted and the following head shall be substituted therefor:

"(*r*) the Diploma in Technical Education of a college of education, or";

(vii) at the end of head (*r*) of sub-paragraph (2) of paragraph 2 the following head shall be added:

"(*s*) the Extra Master's Certificate of Competency of the Department of Trade and Industry (or Ministry of Transport) by examination passed after 1st March 1931.";

(viii) after the word "education" at the end of sub-paragraph (1) of paragraph 3 the following words shall be added:

", or as a Head Teacher of a special school, or in a primary school with a special class attached, and there are pupils over the age of 12 years on the roll of that special school or special class and where the basic salary of the teacher is not calculable by reference to Scale 2.";

(ix) in sub-head (i) of head (*f*) of sub-paragraph (5) of paragraph 3 after the words "teaching of music in schools" there shall be inserted the words "or on the theory of music"; and after the words "Licentiateship of the Trinity College of Music (Class Music Teaching)" the word ", and" shall be deleted and the following words shall be substituted therefor:

"Licentiateship (Music) of the Trinity College of Music

Licentiateship (Music) of the London College of Music

Associateship of the Royal College of Music (Musicianship and Theory)

Licentiateship of the Royal Academy of Music (Harmony, Counterpoint and Composition)

Licentiateship of the Guildhall School of Music (Composition)

Licentiateship of the Guildhall School of Music (Harmony, Counterpoint and Orchestration), and";

(x) after the word "paragraph" at the end of head (*h*) of sub-paragraph (5) of paragraph 3 the following head shall be added:

", or

(i) The Master's (foreign-going) Certificate of Competency of the

Department of Trade and Industry (or Ministry of Transport)".:

(e) PART B of Appendix II shall be deleted and the following PART shall be substituted therefor:

"PART B

Basic Salary Scales

Service Year	Scales					
	1	2	3	3A	3B	4
	£	£	£	£	£	£
1st	1,587	1,401	1,227	1,164	1,164	1,164
2nd	1,692	1,470	1,293	1,209	1,209	1,209
3rd	1,797	1,542	1,359	1,254	1,254	1,254
4th	1,902	1,611	1,425	1,299	1,299	1,299
5th	2,007	1,680	1,491	1,344	1,344	1,344
6th	2,112	1,770	1,578	1,419	1,404	1,404
7th	2,217	1,860	1,665	1,494	1,461	1,461
8th	2,358	1,950	1,752	1,566	1,518	1,518
9th	2,499	2,040	1,839	1,656	1,593	1,578
10th	2,640	2,130	1,926	1,746	1,668	1,635
11th	2,781	2,220	2,013	1,833	1,740	1,692
12th	2,781	2,331	2,112	1,923	1,815	1,752
13th	2,781	2,442	2,211	2,013	1,890	1,842
14th	2,781	2,442	2,211(1)	2,100	1,962	1,932
15th and subsequent years	2,781	2,442	2,211	2,190	2,037	2,022(2)

NOTES

(1) The basic salary shall be increased by £69 in the 14th and subsequent years of service where a teacher's qualifications are described in paragraph 3 of Part A of this Appendix and—

(a) his basic salary before 1st April 1970 was, or would have been, calculated by reference to Scale 4 or Scale 5 or extended Scale 6 of Part B of Appendix II to the Scottish Teachers' Salaries Memorandum 1968, or

(b) being a woman with a Teaching Qualification (Secondary Education) in music she began before 1st January 1956 to attend a course of training at a college of education leading to the award of a Teacher's Technical Certificate in music.

(2) The following extension to Scale 4 shall apply only to a teacher described in paragraph 4(2) of Part A of this Appendix who, before 1st January 1920, entered upon training under Chapter III of the Regulations for the Preliminary Education, Training and Certification of Teachers for Various Grades of Schools (Scotland) 1906 to 1915, or training which for the purpose of the Appendix is approved as equivalent thereto.

Service Year	Scale 4
16th	2,085
17th	2,151
18th	2,217
19th and subsequent years	2,280

".

(f) In Part A of Appendix V:

(i) in column (2) of Serial number 4 the words "deaf or partially deaf pupils" shall be deleted and the following words shall be substituted therefor:

"pupils falling within one or more of the categories defined in paragraph 2 of the Special Educational Treatment (Scotland) Regulations 1954";

(ii) in columns (2) and (3) of Serial numbers 5-12 (both inclusive) the entries shall be deleted;

(iii) in column (2) of Serial number 13 the words "any of serial numbers 4 to 12" shall be deleted and the words "serial number 4" shall be substituted therefor;

(iv) in column (3) of Serial number 19 "£153" shall be deleted and "£168" shall be substituted therefor;

(v) in column (3) of Serial number 20 "£180" shall be deleted and "£195" shall be substituted therefor;

(vi) in column (3) of Serial number 25 "£222" shall be deleted and "£243" shall be substituted therefor;

(vii) in column (3) of Serial number 26 "£153" shall be deleted and "£168" shall be substituted therefor;

(viii) in column (3) of Serial number 28 "£42", wherever it occurs, and "£114" shall be deleted and "£48" and "£126" respectively shall be substituted therefor;

(ix) in column (2) of Serial number 29 the words "any of serial numbers 4 to 12" shall be deleted and the words "serial number 4" shall be substituted therefor;
and

in column (3) of Serial number 29 "£153" shall be deleted and "£168" shall be substituted therefor;

(x) in column (3) of Serial number 30 "£48" shall be deleted and "£54" shall be substituted therefor;

(xi) in column (3) of Serial number 31 "£240" shall be deleted and "£261" shall be substituted therefor;

(xii) in column (3) of Serial number 32 "£81" shall be deleted and "£90" shall be substituted therefor;

(xiii) in column (3) of Serial numbers 33 and 34 the entry shall be deleted and the following shall in each case be substituted therefor:

"£1,041 plus £5·40 in respect of each thousand of the number of pupils in full-time education in the authority's schools and further education centres to a maximum of 100,000 pupils and £2·70 in respect of each thousand pupils in excess of 100,000. For the purpose of the calculation the said number of pupils shall be taken to be one-third of the sum of the average number of pupils in attendance during the school years that began in 1968, 1969 and 1970.";

(xiv) after the entry in columns (1), (2) and (3) in relation to Serial number 33 the following entry shall be inserted:

"33A Assistant or Depute Organiser, Supervisor or Adviser. 50 per cent of the sum that is payable to the Organiser, Supervisor or Adviser.";

(xv) in column (3) of Serial number 35 "£327" shall be deleted and "£393" shall be substituted therefor;

(xvi) the entry in columns (1), (2) and (3) of Serial number 36 shall be deleted.

(g) Part B of Appendix V shall be deleted and the following Part shall be substituted therefor:

"Part B

Scales referred to in Column (3) of Part A of this Appendix

Serial number (1)	Scale (2)	Average number of pupils in attendance according to Part C of this appendix (3)					Amount of allowance (4)
37	A	In the whole school:—					£
		50 or less	(a)	... ...			285
		51–100	(b)	... ...			366
		101–180	(c)	... ...			525
		181–300	(d)	... ...			684
		301–450	(dd)	... ...			792
		451–600	(e)	... ...			900
		601–800	(f)	... ...			1,125
		801–1,000	(g)	... ...			1,248
		1,001 or more	(h)	... ...			1,368
38	B	In secondary classes:—					
		100 or less	(a)	... ...			195
		101–180	(b)	... ...			285
		181–300	(c)	... ...			366
		301–450	(cc)	... ...			408
		451–600	(d)	... ...			450
		601–800	(e)	... ...			525
		801–1,000	(f)	... ...			561
		1,001–1,300	(g)	... ...			600
		1,301–1,700	(h)	... ...			699
		1,701–2,100	(i)	... ...			801
		2,101 or more	(j)	... ...			900
39	C	In the 4th and later years of the secondary course leading to presentation for the Scottish Certificate of Education:—					
		50 or less	(a)	... ...			261
		51–100	(b)	... ...			330
		101–200	(c)	... ...			525
		201–300	(d)	... ...			600
		301–400	(e)	... ...			684
		401–500	(f)	... ...			759
		501 or more	(g)	... ...			828
40	D	In the whole school:—					
		30 or less	(a)	... ...			324
		31–60	(b)	... ...			438
		61–100	(c)	... ...			561
		101–200	(d)	... ...			690
		201–300	(e)	... ...			801
		301–350	(f)	... ...			903
		351 or more	(g)	... ...			990
42	F	In secondary classes:—					
		450 or less	(a)	... ...			183
		451–600	(b)	... ...			231
		601–800	(c)	... ...			306
		801–1,000	(d)	... ...			387
		1,001–1,300	(e)	... ...			444
		1,301–1,700	(f)	... ...			480
		1,701–2,100	(g)	... ...			516
		2,101 or more	(h)	... ...			552

Serial number (1)	Scale (2)	Average number of pupils in attendance according to Part C of this appendix (3)					Amount of allowance (4)
							£
43	G	In the 4th and later years of the secondary course leading to presentation for the Scottish Certificate of Education:—					
		50 or less	(a)	...	...	... ...	141
		51–100	(b)	...	...	... ...	189
		101–200	(c)	...	...	... ...	243
		201–300	(d)	...	...	... ...	306
		301–400	(e)	...	...	... ...	360
		401–500	(f)	...	...	... ...	408
		501 or more	(g)	...	...	... ...	453
44	H	In a group of special classes:—					
		20 or less	(a)	...	...	... ...	108
		21–60	(b)	...	...	... ...	177
		61–100	(c)	...	...	... ...	243
		101–160	(d)	...	...	... ...	312
		161–250	(e)	...	...	... ...	387
		251 or more	(f)	...	...	... ...	483

".

(h) In Part C of Appendix V:

(i) in paragraph 1 "1966, 1967 and 1968" shall be deleted and "1968, 1969 and 1970" shall be substituted therefor;

(ii) in paragraph 4 "1966" shall be deleted and "1968" shall be substituted therefor;

(iii) in paragraph 5 "1969" and "1970", wherever it occurs, shall be deleted and "1971" and "1972" respectively shall be substituted therefor.

(i) In Section A of Appendix VI:

(i) in Part I after paragraph 8 the following paragraphs shall be inserted:

"8A Associateship of the Institute of Metallurgy by examination held after 1961 under the Revised Regulations.

8B a D.Mus degree, by examination, of a university in the United Kingdom.";

(ii) in Part II paragraph 13 shall be deleted and the following shall be substituted therefor:

"13 Licentiateship of the Institute of Metallurgy by examination held after 1961 under the Revised Regulations.";

(iii) in Part II after paragraph 40 the following paragraph shall be inserted:

"40A Diploma in Technical Subjects supplemented by the Higher National Certificate.".

(j) Section B of Appendix VI shall be deleted and the following Section shall be substituted therefor:

"Section B

(Reference Paragraph 31)

Salary Scales for Heads of Departments, Senior Teachers and Teachers

Service Year	5 Group I teachers, and other teachers in Grade I posts	6 Group II teachers in Grade II or Grade III posts and Group III teachers in Grade II posts	7 Group III teachers in Grade III posts
	£	£	£
1st	1,680	1,410	1,290
2nd	1,803	1,485	1,350
3rd	1,926	1,560	1,410
4th	2,046	1,632	1,470
5th	2,169	1,707	1,545
6th	2,313	1,797	1,620
7th	2,460	1,887	1,704
8th	2,604	1,977	1,788
9th	2,748	2,085	1,872
10th	2,904	2,193	1,956
11th	3,060	2,301	2,040
12th	3,060	2,442	2,124
13th	3,060	2,586	2,208
14th and subsequent years	3,060	2,586	2,322

".

(k) In Appendix VIII:

(i) in paragraph 2 "1968" and "1969" shall be deleted and "1970" and "1971" respectively shall be substituted therefor;

(ii) in column (2) of Serial number 45 of the Table in paragraph 4 "1968" shall be deleted and "1970" shall be substituted therefor;

(iii) in column (2) of Serial number 46 of the Table in paragraph 4 "9 or 10" and "1968" shall be deleted and "5" and "1970" respectively shall be substituted therefor;

(iv) in column (2) of Serial number 47 of the Table in paragraph 4 "11" and "1968" shall be deleted and "6" and "1970" respectively shall be substituted therefor;

(v) in column (2) of Serial number 48 of the Table in paragraph 4 "12" and "1968" shall be deleted and "7" and "1970" respectively shall be substituted therefor;

(vi) in paragraph 6 "1968" shall be deleted and "1970" shall be substituted therefor.

(l) Part B of Appendix IX shall be deleted and the following Part shall be substituted therefor:

"Part B
(Reference Paragraph 33)
Responsibility Allowances for Heads of Departments and Senior Teachers

Serial number (1)	Amount of allowance		Range of index figures (4)
	Head of Department (2)	Senior Teacher (3)	
	£	£	
49B	978	822	Over 400,000
49A	945	795	300,001–400,000
49	903	765	240,001–300,000
50	846	729	210,001–240,000
51	801	684	180,001–210,000
52	684	555	120,001–180,000
53	483	348	60,001–120,000
54	306	207	60,000 or under

".

(*m*) In Appendix X:

(i) Part A shall be deleted and the following Part shall be substituted therefor:

"Part A

Range of Index Figures (1)	Scale for Principal (2)		Scale for Depute Principal (3)	
		£		£
over 600,000	8C	5,829	10C	4,770
500,001–600,000	8B	5,727	10B	4,671
400,001–500,000	8A	5,628	10A	4,569
300,001–400,000	8	5,529	10	4,470
240,001–300,000	9	5,391	11	4,350
180,001–240,000	12		14	
120,001–180,000	13		15	
60,001–120,000	14	See Part B	16	See Part B
30,001–60,000	16		17	
30,000 or under	17		18	

".

(ii) Part B shall be deleted and the following Part shall be substituted therefor:

"Part B
Scales for Principals and Depute Principals

Year of service in post	Scales						
	12	13	14	15	16	17	18
	£	£	£	£	£	£	£
1st	4,485	3,969	3,462	3,198	2,937	2,691	2,433
2nd	4,617	4,098	3,591	3,327	3,066	2,820	2,562
3rd	4,746	4,227	3,720	3,456	3,198	2,949	2,691
4th	4,881	4,362	3,855	3,591	3,333	3,084	2,826
5th and subsequent	5,016	4,500	3,993	3,729	3,468	3,219	2,964

"

Amendment of memorandum with effect from 1st August 1972

4. The provisions set out in the above-mentioned memorandum, as amended by the above-mentioned orders in force under section 2 of the Act, shall with effect from 1st August 1972 be further amended in the following manner:—

(*a*) In Part III in head (*b*) of sub-paragraph (4) of paragraph 25 after the words "a post" there shall be inserted the words ", other than a post in a primary or secondary department of a school,";

(*b*) In Part A of Appendix V:

(i) in column (2) of Serial number 13 the words "Deputy Head Teacher, Second Master, First Assistant or Senior Woman Assistant" shall be deleted and the words "Assistant Head Teacher, or Deputy Head Teacher who occupies the post he occupied on 31st July 1972" shall be substituted therefor;

(ii) in column (3) of Serial number 13 the proviso shall be deleted;

(iii) in column (2) of Serial number 14 after the words "Infant Mistress" there shall be added the words "who occupies the post she occupied on 31st July 1972";

(iv) in column (2) of Serial number 15 the words ", Second Master, or First Assistant" shall be deleted;

(v) in column (3) of Serial number 15 "40" shall be deleted and "50" shall be substituted therefor;

(vi) the entry in columns (2) and (3) of Serial number 16 shall be deleted and the following entry shall be substituted therefor:

"Assistant Head Teacher in a school as described opposite to serial number 2 or serial number 3 of this Part of this appendix. | 40 per cent of the amount which would be payable under Scales A, B and C to the Head Teacher if the school consisted only of the part or parts in which the teacher concerned is employed.";

(vii) in column (2) of Serial numbers 17 and 18 (preamble) the words after "Principal Teacher" shall be deleted and ", or Woman Adviser who occupies the post she occupied on 31st July 1972:—" shall be substituted therefor;

(viii) in column (2) of Serial number 17 the word "being" shall be deleted and the word "in" shall be substituted therefor;

(ix) in column (2) of Serial number 18 the words "being or including" shall be deleted and the word "in" shall be substituted therefor;

(x) the entries in columns (1), (2) and (3) of Serial numbers 19 and 20 shall be deleted and the following entries shall be substituted respectively therefor:

"19 Assistant Principal Teacher in a school as described opposite to serial number 2 or serial number 3 of this Part of this appendix. | 50 per cent of the sum payable under the provisions of serial number 17 or 18 whichever is applicable, or £168 whichever is the greater." and

"20 A combined post, other than as described opposite to any other serial number of this Part of this appendix, in a secondary department where the number of pupils does not exceed 600.

The sum payable under the provisions of this Part of this appendix in respect of the higher of the two posts.";

(xi) in column (2) of Serial number 21 the words ", Second Master or First Assistant" and the words ", or serial number 19, or serial number 20" shall be deleted; and in column (3) "50" shall be deleted and "25" shall be substituted therefor; and ", 18, 19 or 20" shall be deleted and "or 18" shall be substituted therefor;

(xii) the entries in columns (1), (2) and (3) of Serial numbers 22 and 23 shall be deleted and the following entry shall be substituted therefor:

"22 A combined post as an Assistant Head Teacher as described opposite to serial number 16 of this Part of this appendix and as a Principal Teacher as described opposite to serial numbers 17 or 18 whichever is applicable.

The sum payable under the provisions of serial number 16 together with 25 per cent of the sum payable under the provisions of serial numbers 17 or 18 whichever is applicable.";

(xiii) the entry in columns (2) and (3) of Serial number 24 shall be deleted and the following entry shall be substituted therefor:

"A combined post as a Woman Adviser and as a Principal Teacher as described opposite to serial number 17 or serial number 18 of this Part of this appendix where the teacher occupies the post she occupied on 31st July 1972.

The sum payable under serial numbers 17 or 18 whichever is applicable together with 30 per cent or 20 per cent of the said sum according to whether the number of hours per week of instruction in the subject or combination of subjects of which she is Principal Teacher is not less than or is less than 40.";

(xiv) in column (2) of Serial number 25 after the word "appendix" there shall be added the words "and where the teacher occupies the post he occupied on 31st July 1972";

(xv) in column (2) of Serial number 26 after the word "appendix" there shall be added the words "and where the teacher occupies the post he occupied on 31st July 1972";

(xvi) in column (2) of Serial numbers 29 to 32 (both inclusive) the words ", Second Master, First Assistant or Senior Woman Assistant" whenever they occur (including the preamble to said numbers) shall be deleted and the words "or Assistant Head Teacher" shall be substituted therefor.

(c) In Part B of Appendix V in column (3) of Serial number 44 the words "In a group of special classes" shall be deleted and the words "As patients in hospital" shall be substituted therefor.

(d) In Appendix XII in paragraph 4 the words "equal in amount to the responsibility allowance payable to a special assistant teacher" and the words "equal in amount to the responsibility allowance payable to a principal assistant teacher" shall be deleted and the words "of £168" and "of £243" respectively shall be substituted therefor.

Amendment of memorandum with effect from 15th August 1972

5. The provisions set out in the above-mentioned memorandum, as amended by the above-mentioned orders in force under section 2 of the Act, are hereby further amended in the following manner:—

(*a*) In Part III in sub-paragraph (2) of paragraph 19 the words "Secretary of State" shall be deleted and the words "Scottish Teachers Salaries Committee" shall be substituted therefor, the words "equivalent in standard to the qualifications described" shall be deleted and the words "a qualification for inclusion" shall be substituted therefor and the words "or part of a paragraph" wherever they appear shall be deleted.

(*b*) In Section A of Appendix VI:

(i) in paragraph 9 of Part I the words "Secretary of State" shall be deleted and the words "Scottish Teachers Salaries Committee" shall be substituted therefor;

(ii) in paragraph 41 of Part II the words "Secretary of State" shall be deleted and the words "Scottish Teachers Salaries Committee" shall be substituted therefor;

(iii) in paragraph 28 of Part III the words "Secretary of State" shall be deleted and the words "Scottish Teachers Salaries Committee" shall be substituted therefor.

Given under the seal of the Secretary of State for Scotland.

(L.S.)

J. M. Fearn,
Under Secretary.

Scottish Education Department,
St. Andrew's House,
Edinburgh.
14th August 1972.

EXPLANATORY NOTE

(This Note is not part of the Order.)

This Order amends with effect from 1st April 1972 the salary scales, additions to scales, responsibility allowances and lists of qualifications in the Scottish Teachers' Salaries Memorandum 1970, as amended.

The Order also brings into operation with effect from 1st August 1972 certain revised and new allowances to take account of the introduction on that date of a new pattern of posts of special responsibility in schools.

The Order transfers from the Secretary of State to the Scottish Teachers Salaries Committee, with effect from the date on which the Order comes into operation, responsibility for the assessment, for salary purposes, of qualifications which are not listed in the above-mentioned Memorandum.

Articles 3 and 4 have been given retrospective effect by virtue of the power in section 8(3) of the Remuneration of Teachers (Scotland) Act 1967.

STATUTORY INSTRUMENTS

1972 No. 1282

SOCIAL SECURITY

The Family Income Supplements (Miscellaneous Amendments) Regulations 1972

Made	-	-	-	*15th August* 1972
Laid before Parliament			*25th August* 1972
Coming into Operation			*15th September* 1972

The Secretary of State for Social Services, in exercise of the powers conferred upon him by sections 4(2)(*a*) and (*b*) and 10(2) of the Family Income Supplements Act 1970(**a**), and of all other powers enabling him in that behalf, hereby makes the following regulations: —

Citation, commencement and interpretation

1.—(1) These regulations, which may be cited as the Family Income Supplements (Miscellaneous Amendments) Regulations 1972, shall come into operation on 15th September 1972.

(2) The rules for the construction of Acts of Parliament contained in the Interpretation Act 1889(**b**) shall apply for the purposes of the interpretation of these regulations as they apply for the purposes of the interpretation of an Act of Parliament.

Amendment of the Family Income Supplements (*General*) *Regulations* 1971

2.—(1) The Family Income Supplements (General) Regulations 1971(**c**), as amended (**d**), shall be further amended in accordance with the following provisions of this regulation.

(2) In regulation 1(2) of the said regulations (definitions), for the definition of "war disablement pension" there shall be substituted the following definition: —

" 'war disablement pension' means—

(*a*) retired pay, pension or allowance granted in respect of disablement under powers conferred by or under the Ministry of Pensions Act 1916(**e**), the Air Force (Constitution) Act 1917(**f**), the Personal Injuries (Emergency Provisions) Act 1939(**g**), the Pensions (Navy, Army, Air Force and Mercantile Marine) Act 1939(**h**), the Polish Resettlement Act 1947(**i**), the Home Guard Act 1951(**j**) or the Ulster Defence Regiment Act 1969(**k**);

(*b*) any retired pay or pension to which section 365(1) of the Income and Corporation Taxes Act 1970(**l**) applies, not being retired pay, pension or allowance to which head (*a*) of this definition applies; or

---

(**a**) 1970 c. 55. (**b**) 1889 c. 63. (**c**) S.I. 1971/226 (1971 I, p. 662).
(**d**) S.I. 1972/14 (1972 I, p. 29). (**e**) 1916 c. 65. (**f**) 1917 c. 51.
(**g**) 1939 c. 82. (**h**) 1939 c. 83. (**i**) 1947 c. 19.
(**j**) 1951 c. 8 (15 & 16 Geo. 6 & 1 Eliz. 2). (**k**) 1969 c. 65. (**l**) 1970 c. 10.

(c) any payment which the Secretary of State accepts as being analogous to any such retired pay, pension or allowance as is referred to in head (a) or head (b) of this definition;".

(3) For paragraph (5) (sums to be disregarded in calculating or estimating a person's normal gross income) of regulation 2 of the said regulations there shall be substituted the following paragraph:—

"(5) In calculating or estimating a person's normal gross income and the weekly amount thereof, there shall be deducted—

(a) the whole of any sums by way of attendance allowance;

(b) the whole of any payments made in respect of a child who is boarded out for the purposes of the Boarding-Out of Children Regulations 1955(a) or the Boarding-Out of Children (Scotland) Regulations 1959(b);

(c) the whole of any sums by way of benefit under the Act;

(d) the whole of any sums by way of benefit under the Ministry of Social Security Act 1966(c);

(e) up to £2·00 a week of any sums (other than sums payable by way of attendance allowance) payable by way of a war disablement pension; and

(f) the whole of any sums by way of a rent allowance under Part II of the Housing Finance Act 1972(d) or under Part II of the Housing (Financial Provisions) (Scotland) Act 1972(e).

Amendment of the Family Income Supplements (Claims and Payments) Regulations 1971

3.—(1) Regulation 2 (manner in which claims are to be made) of the Family Income Supplements (Claims and Payments) Regulations 1971(f) shall be amended in accordance with the following provisions of this regulation.

(2) For paragraph (1) there shall be substituted the following paragraph:—

"(1) Every claim shall be made in writing on a form approved by the Secretary of State, or in such other manner, being in writing, as the Secretary of State may accept as sufficient in the circumstances of any particular case or class of cases and shall be delivered or sent to an office of the Department."

(3) After paragraph (1) as so substituted, there shall be inserted the following paragraph:—

"(1A) The date on which a claim is made shall be the date on which it is received in an office of the Department (hereafter in this paragraph) referred to as 'the relevant date'), so however that if—

(a) a person making a claim requests the Secretary of State to treat that claim as having been made on a date earlier than the relevant date, or the Secretary of State is aware that a claim which has been sent by post has not been delivered in the ordinary course of post; and

(b) the Secretary of State is satisfied that it was through no fault on the part of that person that the claim was not made on a date earlier than the relevant date,

---

(a) S.I. 1955/1377 (1955 I, p. 286).   (b) S.I. 1959/835 (1959 I, p. 579).
(c) 1966 c. 20.   (d) 1972 c. 47.   (e) 1972 c. 46.
(f) S.I. 1971/227 (1971 I, p. 668).

the Secretary of State may treat the claim as having been made on a date earlier than the relevant date, being a date not more than three months before the relevant date.

(4) For paragraph (5) there shall be substituted the following paragraph:—

"(5) Any reference in the Act or in regulations to the date on which a claim is made shall—

(a) in the case of a claim which is treated as having been made on a date earlier than the relevant date under paragraph (1A) of this regulation, be construed as a reference to the date on which such claim is so treated as having been made; and

(b) in the case of a claim which is treated as if it had been duly made in the first instance under paragraph (3) of this regulation, be construed as a reference to the date on which such claim is so treated as having been duly made."

Signed by authority of the Secretary of State for Social Services.

Paul Dean,
Parliamentary Under-Secretary of State,
Department of Health and Social Security.

15th August 1972.

EXPLANATORY NOTE

(This Note is not part of the Regulations.)

These Regulations make minor amendments to the Family Income Supplements (General) Regulations 1971 and the Family Income Supplements (Claims and Payments) Regulations 1971.

Regulation 1 relates to the citation, commencement and interpretation of the Regulations. Regulation 2 amends the Family Income Supplements (General) Regulations 1971 by substituting for the definition of "war disablement pension" in regulation 1(2) a new definition and by substituting for regulation 2(5) a new provision whereby rent allowances under the Housing Finance Act 1972 and the Housing (Financial Provisions) (Scotland) Act 1972 and sums which hitherto fell to be disregarded for the purpose of computing a person's normal gross income will in future be deducted for that purpose. Regulation 3 amends the Family Income Supplements (Claims and Payments) Regulations 1971 so that, in certain circumstances, a claim for family income supplement may be treated as having been made before the date on which it is received in an office of the Department of Health and Social Security.

STATUTORY INSTRUMENTS

1972 No. 1287

SOCIAL SECURITY

The National Insurance and Industrial Injuries (Classification and Collection of Contributions) Amendment Regulations 1972

Made - - -	*15th August* 1972
Laid before Parliament	*25th August* 1972
Coming into Operation	*2nd October* 1972

The Secretary of State for Social Services, in conjunction with the Treasury so far as relates to matters with regard to which the Treasury have so directed, and in exercise of his powers under sections 1(3) and 8(5) of the National Insurance Act 1965(**a**) and section 3(3)(*b*) of the National Insurance (Industrial Injuries) Act 1965(**b**) and of all other powers enabling him in that behalf, hereby makes the following regulations which contain no provisions other than such as operate with reference to the amount of a person's earnings and which accordingly, by virtue of section 6(5) of, and paragraph 2(1)(*b*)(i) of Schedule 4 to, the National Insurance Act 1972(**c**) are exempt from the requirements of section 108 of the National Insurance Act 1965 and section 62(2) of the National Insurance (Industrial Injuries) Act 1965 (reference to the National Insurance Advisory Committee and the Industrial Injuries Advisory Council):—

Citation, commencement and interpretation

1.—(1) These regulations may be cited as the National Insurance and Industrial Injuries (Classification and Collection of Contributions) Amendment Regulations 1972 and shall come into operation on 2nd October 1972.

(2) Each provision of these regulations which amends other regulations shall be read as one with the regulation which it amends.

Amendment of the National Insurance (Classification) Regulations 1972

2. In Schedule 1 to the National Insurance (Classification) Regulations 1972(**d**) (classification of insured persons)—

    (*a*) in paragraphs 11 in column (B), 14 in columns (A) and (B), 37 and 38 to 57 in column (B), for the sum "£5·00" there shall be substituted the sum "£6·00", and

    (*b*) in paragraph 22 in column (A) for the words "ordinarily less than £4·00" there shall be substituted the words "ordinarily not more than £5·00".

(**a**) 1965 c. 51.   (**b**) 1965 c. 52.
(**c**) 1972 c. 57.   (**d**) S.I. 1972/555 (1972 I, p. 1861).

Amendment of the National Insurance and Industrial Injuries (Collection of Contributions) Regulations 1948

3. In regulation 10A of the National Insurance and Industrial Injuries (Collection of Contributions) Regulations 1948(**a**), as amended (**b**), (contributions in weeks in which no services are rendered and remuneration does not exceed the specified amount) and in the proviso to regulation 11 of those regulations (contributions during holidays) for the sum "£5.00" there shall be substituted the sum "£6.00".

Signed by authority of the Secretary of State for Social Services.

Paul Dean,
Parliamentary Under-Secretary of State,
Department of Health and Social Security.

10th August 1972.

V. H. Goodhew,
Hugh Rossi,
Two of the Lords Commissioners of
Her Majesty's Treasury.

15th August 1972.

EXPLANATORY NOTE

(This Note is not part of the Regulations.)

By virtue of section 6(5) of, and paragraph 2(1)(*b*)(i) of Schedule 4 to, the National Insurance Act 1972 the Regulations are exempt from reference to the National Insurance Advisory Committee and to the Industrial Injuries Advisory Council, and no such reference have been made.

These Regulations, by amending various paragraphs of Schedule 1 to the National Insurance (Classification) Regulations 1972 and regulations 10A and 11 of the National Insurance and Industrial Injuries (Collection of Contributions) Regulations 1948, raise the sum of weekly earnings in the case of certain insured persons in specified employments where classification is modified or where liability for contributions is determined by reference to their earnings.

(**a**) 1948/1274 (Rev. XVI, p. 148; 1948 I, p. 3037).

(**b**) The relevant amending instruments are S.I. 1959/207, 1969/1362, 1971/1421 (1959 II, p. 1893; 1969 III, p. 4069; 1971 II, p. 3992).

STATUTORY INSTRUMENTS

1972 No. 1288

SOCIAL SECURITY

The Workmen's Compensation (Supplementation) Amendment Scheme 1972

Made - - -	15*th August* 1972
Laid before Parliament	25*th August* 1972
Coming into Operation	4*th October* 1972

The Secretary of State for Social Services, with the consent of the Treasury, in exercise of his powers under section 2 of the Industrial Injuries and Diseases (Old Cases) Act 1967(**a**), as amended by section 4(4)(*a*) of the National Insurance Act 1972(**b**), and of all other powers enabling him in that behalf, hereby makes, in consequence of the said Act of 1972, the following Scheme : —

Citation, interpretation and commencement

1. This Scheme, which may be cited as the Workmen's Compensation (Supplementation) Amendment Scheme 1972, shall be read as one with the Workmen's Compensation (Supplementation) Scheme 1966(**c**), as amended(**d**) (hereinafter referred to as "the principal Scheme"), and shall come into operation on 4th October 1972.

Amendment of Article 10 of the principal Scheme

2. In paragraph (1)(*a*)(iii) of Article 10 of the principal Scheme (allowances in respect of two or more different injuries or diseases), for the sum "£3·65" there shall be substituted the sum "£4·10".

Amendment of Schedule 1 to the principal Scheme

3. Schedule 1 to the principal Scheme shall be amended by substituting for the sum "£8·50" and "£3·65" in the first and second columns thereof respectively the sum "£9·24½" and "£3·75", and by the addition at the end of the first and second columns thereof respectively of the sum "£9·25" and "£4·10".

(**a**) 1967 c. 34.   (**b**) 1972 c. 57.
(**c**) S.I. 1966/165 (1966 I, p. 325).
(**d**) The relevant amending instrument is S.I. 1971/1223 (1971 II, p. 3580).

Signed by authority of the Secretary of State for Social Services.

Paul Dean,
Parliamentary Under-Secretary of State,
Department of Health and Social Security.

10th August 1972.

We consent,

V. H. Goodhew,
Hugh Rossi,
Two of the Lords Commissioners of
Her Majesty's Treasury.

15th August 1972.

EXPLANATORY NOTE

(This Note is not part of the Scheme.)

This Scheme amends the Workmen's Compensation (Supplementation) Scheme 1966 so as to give effect to section 4(4)(*a*) of the National Insurance Act 1972 by increasing the weekly rate of lesser incapacity allowance payable in certain circumstances.

The Scheme is made in consequence of the Act of 1972 and accordingly, by virtue of section 6(5) of and paragraph 2(2) of Part I of Schedule 4 to that Act, no draft of the Scheme has been laid before Parliament.

STATUTORY INSTRUMENTS

1972 No. 1289

SOCIAL SECURITY

WORKMEN'S COMPENSATION

The Pneumoconiosis, Byssinosis and Miscellaneous Diseases Benefit (Amendment) Scheme 1972

Made - - -	*15th August* 1972
Laid before Parliament	*25th August* 1972
Coming into Operation	*4th October* 1972

The Secretary of State for Social Services, with the consent of the Treasury, in exercise of his powers under sections 5 and 7 of the Industrial Injuries and Diseases (Old Cases) Act 1967(**a**), as amended by section 4(4)(*b*) of the National Insurance Act 1972(**b**), and of all other powers enabling him in that behalf, hereby makes, in consequence of the said Act of 1972, the following Scheme:—

Citation, interpretation and commencement

1. This Scheme, which may be cited as the Pneumoconiosis, Byssinosis and Miscellaneous Diseases Benefit (Amendment) Scheme 1972, shall be read as one with the Pneumoconiosis, Byssinosis and Miscellaneous Diseases Benefit Scheme 1966(**c**), as amended(**d**) (hereinafter referred to as "the principal Scheme"), and shall come into operation on 4th October 1972.

Amendment of Article 4 of the principal Scheme

2. In paragraph 1(*a*)(ii) of Article 4 of the principal Scheme (allowance for partial disablement), for the sum "£3·65" there shall be substituted the sum "£4·10".

(**a**) 1967 c. 34. (**b**) 1972 c. 57.
(**c**) S.I. 1966/164 (1966 I, p. 303).
(**d**) The relevant amending instrument is S.I. 1971/1222 (1971 II, p. 3576).

Signed by authority of the Secretary of State for Social Services.

Paul Dean,
Parliamentary Under-Secretary of State,
Department of Health and Social Security.

10th August 1972.

We consent

V. H. Goodhew,
Hugh Rossi,
Two of the Lords Commissioners of
Her Majesty's Treasury.

15th August 1972.

EXPLANATORY NOTE

(This Note is not part of the Scheme.)

This Scheme amends the Pneumoconiosis, Byssinosis and Miscellaneous Diseases Benefit Scheme 1966 so as to give effect to section 4(4)(*b*) of the National Insurance Act 1972 by increasing the rate of allowance in respect of partial disablement.

The Scheme is made in consequence of the Act of 1972 and accordingly, by virtue of section 6(5) of and paragraph 2(2) of Part I of Schedule 4 to that Act, no draft of the Scheme has been laid before Parliament.

1972 No. 1294

MERCHANT SHIPPING

MASTERS AND SEAMEN

The Merchant Shipping (Disciplinary Offences) Regulations 1972

Made - - -	*17th August* 1972
Laid before Parliament	*25th August* 1972
Coming into Operation	1st January 1973

The Secretary of State, after consulting with the organisations referred to in section 99(2) of the Merchant Shipping Act 1970(**a**), in exercise of powers conferred by sections 34, 35, 38(3) and 68(2) and (5) of that Act and now vested in him (**b**), and of all other powers enabling him in that behalf, hereby makes the following Regulations: —

Citation, commencement and interpretation

1.—(1) These Regulations may be cited as the Merchant Shipping (Disciplinary Offences) Regulations 1972 and shall come into operation on 1st January 1973.

(2) In these Regulations—

"the Act" means the Merchant Shipping Act 1970;

"the 1894 Act" means the Merchant Shipping Act 1894(**c**);

"intermediate port", in relation to an appeal by a seaman to a superintendent or proper officer, means a port at which a ship calls before arriving at the port at which, or nearest to the place at which, the seaman is to be discharged;

"master" includes (except in regulation 5) any officer authorised under regulation 5(2) to exercise the powers of the master and to perform his duties in relation to a disciplinary offence;

"officer" means an officer qualified for the purposes of section 43 of the Act or duly certificated under the 1894 Act;

"seaman" does not include an officer;

"ship" means a ship registered in the United Kingdom.

(3) The Interpretation Act 1889(**d**) shall apply to the interpretation of these Regulations as it applies to the interpretation of an Act of Parliament.

(**a**) 1970 c. 36.
(**b**) See the Secretary of State for Trade and Industry Order 1970 (S.I. 1970/1537 (1970 III, p. 5293)).
(**c**) 57 & 58 Vict. c. 60.　　　(**d**) 52 & 53 Vict. c. 63.

Application

2.—(1) These Regulations apply to any seaman employed in a ship otherwise than—

(a) in a pleasure yacht;

(b) in a ship belonging to a general lighthouse authority;

(c) in a ship of less than 200 tons engaged solely on coastal voyages;

(d) solely in connection with the construction, alteration, repair or testing of the ship, its machinery or equipment, and not engaged in the navigation of the ship;

(e) in a ship engaged solely on a coastal voyage for the purpose of trials of the ship, its machinery or equipment.

(2) For the purposes of paragraph (1)(c) and (e) of this regulation—

"coastal voyage" means a voyage between places in the British Islands (including the Republic of Ireland) or from and returning to such a place during which, in either case, no call is made at any place outside those islands;

"tons" means tons gross tonnage and the gross tonnage of a ship having alternative tonnages shall be the larger of those tonnages.

PART I

Disciplinary Offences

3. It is a disciplinary offence on board a ship for a seaman to whom these Regulations apply—

(a) wilfully to strike any person;

(b) wilfully to disobey a lawful command;

(c) without reasonable cause—

(i) to fail to be available for duty at a time when he is required by the master or by a person authorised by the master to be so available; or

(ii) to fail to report or to remain at his place of duty at a time when he is so required to be at that place; or

(iii) while on duty, to be asleep at his place of duty;

(d) to be under the influence of drink or a drug (whether alone or in combination) to such an extent that he behaves in a disorderly manner or is unfit to be entrusted with his duty or with any duty which he might be called upon to perform, unless the drug was taken by him for medical purposes and either—

(i) he took it on medical advice and complied with any directions given as part of that advice; or

(ii) he had no reason to believe that the drug might have the influence it had;

(e) without the consent of the master or of any other person authorised to give it, to bring on board the ship or to have in his possession on board any offensive weapon;

(f) wilfully and without reasonable cause—

(i) to damage the ship; or

(ii) to damage any property on board the ship; or

(iii) to throw any such property overboard;

(g) without reasonable cause, to take or to be in possession of any property belonging to or in the custody of any person on board the ship;

(h) to cause or knowingly to permit to be on board the ship any person who, being neither in Her Majesty's service nor authorised by law to be on board the ship, is on board without the consent of the master or of any other person authorised to give it.

Disciplinary offences on board certain ships

4.—(1) It is a disciplinary offence on board a ship described in paragraph (3) of this regulation for a seaman to whom these Regulations apply—

(a) to smoke; or

(b) to use a naked light or mechanical lighter; or

(c) to use an electric torch which is not of a type approved by the master;

in any part of the ship in which smoking or the use of such a light, mechanical lighter or torch is prohibited by the master or the employer.

(2) It is a disciplinary offence on board a ship described in paragraph (3) of this regulation for a seaman to whom these Regulations apply, without the consent of the master or of any other person authorised to give it, to bring on board the ship or to have in his possession on board any matches or a mechanical lighter.

(3) The description of ship referred to in paragraphs (1) and (2) of this regulation is any ship in which—

(i) by reason of the cargo or stores which are or have been carried in the ship, there is a special risk of fire or explosion; and

(ii) the master or the employer has given notice to seamen in the ship (whether by means of notices displayed in the ship or otherwise) that the acts mentioned in sub-paragraphs (a), (b) and (c) of paragraph (1) of this regulation are prohibited, either in all or specified parts of the ship.

(4) In this regulation—

"mechanical lighter" includes any mechanical, chemical or electrical contrivance designed or adapted for or capable of causing fire or explosion.

Procedure relating to disciplinary offences

5.—(1) Subject to paragraph (2) of this regulation, a disciplinary offence may be dealt with only by the master of the ship on board which the offence is alleged to have occurred and the master may impose a fine (not exceeding such an amount as is specified in regulation 8) on the seaman whom he finds has committed the offence.

(2) The powers of the master in relation to a disciplinary offence may be exercised and his duties may be performed by any officer authorised for the purpose by the master; and the name of any officer so authorised shall be entered by the master in the official log book.

6. A disciplinary offence shall be dealt with within 24 hours of the time it comes to the notice of the master, unless it is not practicable to deal with it within that time, in which case it shall be dealt with as soon as practicable thereafter.

7. In dealing with a disciplinary offence, the following procedure shall be followed—

(a) A seaman charged with a disciplinary offence shall, if he so requests, be permitted at the hearing before the master to be accompanied by a friend for the purpose of advising him and the friend may speak on behalf of the seaman.

(b) The charge shall be entered by the master in the official log book and shall be read to the seaman by the master, who shall record therein that it has been so read.

(c) The seaman shall then be asked whether or not he admits the charge. If he does admit it, the admission shall be recorded by the master in the official log book. In all other cases an entry to the effect that the seaman does not admit the charge shall be recorded therein.

(d) The evidence of any witness called by the master shall be heard in the presence of the seaman, who shall be afforded reasonable opportunity to question the witness on his evidence.

(e) The seaman shall be given an opportunity to make a statement in answer to the charge, including any comments on the evidence produced against him. Particulars of the statement (or a record that the seaman declined to make one, if such should be the case) shall be entered by the master in the official log book or contained in a separate document annexed to, and referred to in an entry made by the master in, the official log book.

(f) The seaman shall be permitted to call witnesses to give evidence on his behalf, and any such witness may be questioned by the master on his evidence.

(g) The master shall, after consideration of all the evidence given before him, give his decision in the presence of the seaman as to whether he finds the seaman has committed the offence charged and—

  (i) if he does not find that the seaman has committed the offence, he shall dismiss the charge;

  (ii) if he finds that the seaman has committed the offence, he shall, after having regard to any mitigating circumstances brought to his notice, give his decision either as to the amount of the fine he is imposing or that he is imposing no fine;

and the master shall record his decisions in the official log book.

(h) The master shall—

  (i) inform a seaman on whom a fine has been imposed, of his right of appeal under section 35 of the Act and of the time within which notice of intended appeal must be given in accordance with these Regulations;

  (ii) if the seaman so requests, supply to him copies of all entries in the official log book (including any annexes thereto) referring to the disciplinary offence to which the fine relates.

Fines

8.—(1) The fine that may be imposed on a seaman for a disciplinary offence under regulation 3 shall be an amount not exceeding £2 or, in the case of a second or subsequent commission of that offence before the seaman is discharged from the ship, an amount not exceeding £5.

(2) The fine that may be imposed on a seaman for a disciplinary offence under regulation 4 shall be an amount not exceeding £10.

9. A fine imposed on a seaman for a disciplinary offence may be remitted in whole or in part by the master—

    (*a*) if the master is of the opinion that the seaman's conduct since the fine was imposed has been such as to justify the remission; or

    (*b*) if new evidence has been discovered which was not known to the master at the time he dealt with the offence and which, in his opinion, justifies the remission;

and a record of every such remission shall be entered in the official log book by the master.

10. A fine imposed on a seaman for a disciplinary offence and against which an appeal is pending at the time mentioned in section 38(2) of the Act may be provisionally deducted from the seaman's wages pending the appeal.

PART II

Appeals against a fine for a disciplinary offence

11. Subject to regulations 14 and 15, an appeal by a seaman against a fine for a disciplinary offence shall be heard by a superintendent or proper officer at the place at which the seaman is discharged.

12. Subject to regulation 14, if a seaman on whom a fine has been imposed for a disciplinary offence wishes to appeal against the decision to a superintendent or proper officer, he shall give notice of intended appeal to the master within 2 days of the decision; provided that if the decision is given within 2 days of the ship's expected time of arrival at the port at which, or nearest to the place at which, the seaman is to be discharged, the notice shall be given before the seaman is discharged.

13. Upon receipt of a notice of intended appeal from the seaman, the master shall—

    (*a*) make an entry in the official log book recording the date of receipt of the notice; and

    (*b*) subject to regulation 14, give notice of the appeal, not later than 36 hours before the ship's expected time of arrival at the port at which, or nearest to the place at which, the seaman is to be discharged, to the superintendent or proper officer for that port; provided that if it is not practicable for the notice to be given within that period, it shall be given as soon as practicable thereafter.

14.—(1) Notwithstanding anything contained in regulations 11, 12 or 13(b), an appeal by a seaman against a fine for a disciplinary offence may be heard at an intermediate port by the superintendent or proper officer for that port if—

(a) either the master or the seaman requests that superintendent or proper officer to hear the appeal; and

(b) notice of intended appeal is given by the seaman to the master and by the master to the superintendent or proper officer within a reasonable time of the ship's expected time of arrival at the intermediate port; and

(c) the superintendent or proper officer is of the opinion that it is desirable that the appeal should be heard by him.

(2) If an appeal is to be heard at an intermediate port, the master shall make an entry to that effect in the official log book.

15. Notwithstanding anything contained in regulation 11, if an appeal has not been determined at an intermediate port and either—

(a) there is no superintendent or proper officer available to hear the appeal at the place, date and time at which the seaman is discharged; or

(b) the Secretary of State is of the opinion, that, having regard to all the circumstances of the case, it is expedient that the appeal should be heard at a place other than that at which the seaman is discharged;

the appeal shall be heard at such other place as the Secretary of State may direct.

16.—(1) The superintendent or proper officer to whom a notice of intended appeal has been given shall make arrangements as to the place, date and time at which the appeal is to be heard and shall inform the master of those arrangements.

(2) The master shall, upon being informed by the superintendent or proper officer of the arrangements which have been made for hearing the appeal, inform the seaman of those arrangements.

(3) The master shall supply to the seaman copies of all entries in the official log book (including any annexes thereto) referring to the disciplinary offence to which the appeal relates, unless he has already supplied those copies in accordance with regulation 7(h)(ii).

17. The master shall, upon request, supply the superintendent or proper officer with copies of all entries in the official log book (including any annexes thereto) referring to the disciplinary offence to which the appeal relates and, if so required, produce to him the official log book.

18.—(1) In hearing an appeal, the following procedure shall be followed—

(a) The seaman shall, if he so requests, be permitted at the hearing to be accompanied by a friend for the purpose of advising him and the friend may speak on behalf of the seaman.

(b) The seaman shall be given an opportunity to state the grounds of his appeal, to produce supporting evidence and to call witnesses to give evidence on his behalf.

(c) Subject to paragraph (2) of this regulation, the master shall be given an opportunity to call witnesses and to give evidence himself.

(*d*) The evidence of any witness (whether called by the superintendent or proper officer or otherwise) shall be heard in the presence of the seaman.

(*e*) Subject to paragraph (2) of this regulation, both the seaman and the master shall be afforded reasonable opportunity to question any witness on his evidence and to comment upon it.

(*f*) The superintendent or proper officer shall notify the seaman and the employer of his decision regarding the appeal and shall record that decision in the official log book.

(2) If the master is absent from the hearing of the appeal and the superintendent or proper officer is satisfied that no injustice will result, the appeal may (notwithstanding sub-paragraphs (*c*) and (*e*) of paragraph (1) of this regulation) be heard and determined by the superintendent or proper officer in the absence of the master.

19.—(1) Where a seaman is not present at the place, date and time arranged for the hearing of his appeal—

(*a*) if the seaman so requests within 6 months from the date on which he was discharged from the ship; and

(*b*) if the seaman had not been informed of those arrangements or had other reasonable excuse for not being present;

the superintendent or proper officer shall make further arrangements for the appeal to be heard.

(2) If the superintendent or proper officer makes further arrangements for the appeal to be heard, he shall notify them to the seaman and to the employer.

(3) If the superintendent or proper officer does not make further arrangements for the appeal to be heard, he shall notify his reasons to the seaman and to the employer.

(4) It shall be sufficient compliance with the requirements of paragraphs (2) or (3) of this regulation for the notification to be sent by registered post to the last known address of the seaman and to the last known address of the employer.

20.—(1) All entries in the official log book (including annexes thereto) required to be made by the master under these Regulations shall be signed by the master and by a member of the crew.

(2) A master or the officer authorised by him under regulation 5(2) to exercise the powers of the master and to perform his duties in relation to a disciplinary offence, who fails to make an entry in an official log book required to be made by the master under these Regulations (except regulation 14(2)), shall be guilty of an offence and shall be punishable on summary conviction with a fine not exceeding £20.

Michael Heseltine,
Minister for Aerospace,
Department of Trade and Industry.

17th August 1972.

EXPLANATORY NOTE

(This Note is not part of the Regulations.)

These Regulations, made under the Merchant Shipping Act 1970, make provision for the maintenance of discipline on board ships (other than fishing vessels) registered in the United Kingdom. They apply to all seamen, except certificated officers, employed in such ships otherwise than as specified in regulation 2. The Regulations—

(*a*) specify the types of misconduct which constitute disciplinary offences on board all such ships (regulation 3);

(*b*) specify the types of misconduct which constitute disciplinary offences on board the ships described in regulation 4(3) in which there is a special risk of fire or explosion (regulation 4);

(*c*) prescribe the procedure to be followed in dealing with disciplinary offences (regulations 5-7), the fines which may be imposed (regulation 8) and make provision for matters relating to such fines (regulations 9 and 10);

(*d*) provide for appeals against fines for disciplinary offences, including the procedure to be followed on any such appeal (regulations 11-20).

STATUTORY INSTRUMENTS

1972 No. 1295

MERCHANT SHIPPING

MASTERS AND SEAMEN

The Merchant Shipping (Seamen's Documents) Regulations 1972

Made - - - -	17th *August* 1972
Laid before Parliament	25th *August* 1972
Coming into Operation	1st *January* 1973

The Secretary of State, after consulting with the organisations referred to in section 99(2) of the Merchant Shipping Act 1970(a), in exercise of powers conferred by sections 70 and 71 of that Act and now vested in him(b), and of all other powers enabling him in that behalf, hereby makes the following Regulations:—

Citation, commencement and interpretation

1.—(1) These Regulations may be cited as the Merchant Shipping (Seamen's Documents) Regulations 1972 and shall come into operation on 1st January 1973.

(2) In these Regulations—

(*a*) the expressions "British protected person", "citizen of the United Kingdom and colonies", "colony", "protected state" and "protectorate" have respectively the same meanings as they have in and for the purposes of the British Nationality Act 1948(c);

(*b*) "associated state" has the same meaning as it has in and for the purposes of the West Indies Act 1967(d);

(*c*) "the Act" means the Merchant Shipping Act 1970;

(*d*) "British Seaman's Identity Card" means a British Seaman's Identity Card issued under the British Seamen's Identity Cards Order 1942(e);

(*e*) "the Order of 1960" means the British Seamen's Cards Order 1960(f) as amended(g);

(*f*) "British seaman" has the meaning assigned to it in section 70(3) of the Act;

(*g*) a person to whom a British Seaman's Card or a discharge book has been issued is referred to as the holder of it; and

---

(**a**) 1970 c. 36.
(**b**) See the Secretary of State for Trade and Industry Order 1970 (S.I. 1970/1537 (1970 III, p. 5293)).
(**c**) 11 & 12 Geo. 6. c. 56.
(**d**) 1967 c 4.
(**e**) S.R. & O. 1942/2681 (1942 II, p. 2010).
(**f**) S.I. 1960/967 (1960 II, p. 1987).
(**g**) S.I. 1967/1610 (1967 III, p. 4431).

(*h*) "Seaman's Record Book" means a Seaman's Record Book and Certificates of Discharge issued to a seaman by the Secretary of State, the Board of Trade, the Minister of Transport, the Minister of Transport and Civil Aviation, the Minister of War Transport or the Minister of Shipping.

(3) For the purposes of these Regulations, a person shall be treated as having the right of abode if he has the right of abode in the United Kingdom under section 2 of the Immigration Act 1971(**a**) or would have that right if the whole of that Act were in force.

(4) In computing any of the periods of 7 days referred to in regulations 2(1) and 16(1) any period during which the person concerned is not present in the United Kingdom shall be disregarded.

(5) The Interpretation Act 1889(**b**) shall apply to the interpretation of these Regulations as it applies to the interpretation of an Act of Parliament.

PART I

BRITISH SEAMEN'S CARDS

Application for British Seamen's Cards

2.—(1) Subject to the provisions of regulation 3, a person who satisfies the conditions specified in paragraph (2) of this regulation (whether or not he has previously held a British Seaman's Card or a British Seaman's Identity Card)—

(*a*) shall, if he has the right of abode, apply for a British Seaman's Card within 7 days of satisfying those conditions; and

(*b*) may, if he has not that right, apply for a British Seaman's Card.

(2) The conditions referred to in paragraph (1) of this regulation are that the person—

(*a*) is present in the United Kingdom; and

(*b*) is a British seaman to whom this regulation applies; and

(*c*) is not the holder of a British Seaman's Card issued to him under regulation 5 or endorsed under regulation 8 or regulation 15.

3.—(1) Regulation 2 applies to any British seaman—

(*a*) who is employed or ordinarily employed in a ship otherwise than in an employment specified in paragraph (2) of this regulation; and

(*b*) who is not exempted by virtue of paragraph (3) of this regulation.

(2) The employments which are to be disregarded for the purposes of paragraph (1) of this regulation are—

(*a*) employment in a fishing vessel;

(*b*) employment in a ship belonging to a general lighthouse authority;

(*c*) except in the case of a person who is a cadet or who is employed in a ship solely to provide goods, personal services or entertainment on board, employment on terms under which he receives no wages or only nominal wages; and

---

(**a**) 1971 c. 77.　　　　　　　　　　(**b**) 52 & 53 Vict. c. 63.

(*d*) in the case of a person who is not a citizen of the United Kingdom and colonies or a British protected person, employment in a ship registered otherwise than in the United Kingdom, the Channel Islands, the Isle of Man or any colony, protectorate, protected state or associated state.

(3) Regulation 2 does not apply to—

(*a*) a person who is not—

(i) a citizen of the United Kingdom and colonies;

(ii) a British protected person;

(iii) a British subject without citizenship; or

(iv) a British subject by virtue of section 2(1) of the British Nationality Act 1948;

and who holds a seaman's identity document which has been issued to him by or under the authority of the government of a country specified in section 1(3) of the British Nationality Act 1948 or of any territory or trust territory under the protection of or administered by such government or of the Republic of Ireland, and of which he has not ceased to be regarded as the holder by that government;

(*b*) a person who holds a seaman's identity document—

(i) which has been issued to him by the government of any colony, protectorate, protected state or associated state, and

(ii) of which he has not ceased to be regarded as the holder by that government;

(*c*) a person in the employment of the Crown who is employed, but not ordinarily employed, as a master or seaman; and

(*d*) a member of the naval, military or air forces of the Crown or of any service administered by the Defence Council.

4.—(1) A person applying for a British Seaman's Card shall—

(*a*) make an application in accordance with regulation 30; and

(*b*) unless it has been lost or destroyed, surrender to the superintendent any British Seaman's Card or British Seaman's Identity Card previously held by him.

(2) Any person required under regulation 2(1)(*a*) to apply for a British Seaman's Card who fails to make application for a British Seaman's Card in accordance with these Regulations shall be guilty of an offence.

Issue of British Seamen's Cards

5. If a person applying for a British Seaman's Card—

(i) satisfies the conditions set out in regulation 2(2); and

(ii) has paid the fee (if any) prescribed;

in the case of a person having the right of abode, the Secretary of State shall, and, in any other case, may issue a British Seaman's Card to him.

Form of British Seamen's Cards

6. A British Seaman's Card shall be in the form set out in Schedule 1 to these Regulations and shall contain the particulars therein specified.

Validity of British Seamen's Cards

7. A British Seaman's Card shall be valid—

    (*a*) until the end of the period of 5 years from the date of its issue; and

    (*b*) if it has been endorsed in accordance with regulation 8, until the end of a further period of 5 years from the end of the period referred to in (*a*) above;

provided that, if at the end of either of such periods, the holder is not present in the United Kingdom, his British Seaman's Card shall remain valid until he first returns to the United Kingdom within 12 months thereafter.

8.—(1) The holder of a British Seaman's Card may make an application in writing to a superintendent and in accordance with regulation 30 for the British Seaman's Card to be endorsed under this regulation.

  (2) If—

    (*a*) an application is made under paragraph (1) of this regulation not less than 4 years and 9 months after the date of issue of the British Seaman's Card to which it relates nor more than 7 days after the British Seaman's Card ceases to be valid by virtue of the proviso to regulation 7; and

    (*b*) the superintendent to whom the application is made is satisfied—

      (i) that the person making the application is the holder of the British Seaman's Card;

      (ii) that the British Seaman's Card is valid at the date of the application or ceased to be valid by virtue of the proviso to regulation 7 not more than 7 days before the application was made; and

      (iii) that the person making the application has paid the fee (if any) prescribed;

in the case of a person having the right of abode, he shall and, in any other case, may endorse the British Seaman's Card with a statement that it shall be valid until the end of the period referred to in regulation 7(*b*).

  (3) If—

    (*a*) an application is made under paragraph (1) of this regulation within the period of 12 months beginning 5 years after the date of issue of the British Seaman's Card to which it relates; and

    (*b*) the superintendent to whom the application is made is satisfied—

      (i) that the person making the application is the holder of the British Seaman's Card;

      (ii) that the British Seaman's Card was valid at the end of the period of 5 years from the date of its issue; and

      (iii) that the person making the application has paid the fee (if any) prescribed;

he may endorse the British Seaman's Card with a statement that it shall be valid until the end of the period referred to in regulation 7(*b*).

9. When his British Seaman's Card is lost, destroyed, defaced or required to be surrendered a person shall cease to be regarded as the holder of a British Seaman's Card.

Production of British Seamen's Cards

10.—(1) The holder of a British Seaman's Card shall produce it to a superintendent, a proper officer, his employer or the master of his ship, on demand or within such period as the person requiring its production may allow.

(2) A person who fails to produce his British Seaman's Card in pursuance of a requirement made under this regulation shall be guilty of an offence.

Surrender of British Seamen's Cards

11.—(1) The holder of a British Seaman's Card shall surrender it to a superintendent—

(*a*) forthwith, upon his ceasing to be a British seaman or upon the card being defaced; and

(*b*) on demand, after he has ceased to have the right of abode.

(2) A person who fails to comply with the requirements of this regulation shall be guilty of an offence.

Delivery of British Seamen's Cards

12.—(1) Any person who comes into possession of a British Seaman's Card of which he is not the holder shall forthwith deliver it to the Registrar General of Shipping and Seamen or to a superintendent.

(2) Any person who fails to comply with this regulation shall be guilty of an offence.

British Seamen's Cards issued under the Order of 1960

13.—(1) This regulation applies to a British Seaman's Card issued under the Order of 1960 and which is still valid on the date these Regulations come into operation.

(2) Subject to regulations 14 and 15, a British Seaman's Card to which this regulation applies shall continue in force and shall have effect as if it were a British Seaman's Card issued under regulation 5 until—

(*a*) 31st December 1973; or

(*b*) if it is endorsed in accordance with regulation 15, until 31st December 1977;

provided that, if the holder is not present in the United Kingdom on either such date, his British Seaman's Card shall remain valid until he first returns to the United Kingdom after that date; and references in regulations 9, 10, 12, 26, 27, 28 and 29 to British Seamen's Cards or to seamen's documents shall include references to British Seamen's Cards to which this regulation applies.

14. A British Seaman's Card to which regulation 13 applies shall cease to be valid upon—

(*a*) the holder of it ceasing to be a British seaman; or

(*b*) its being lost, destroyed, or defaced; or

(*c*) its being required to be surrendered.

15.—(1) The holder of a British Seaman's Card to which regulation 13 applies shall, before the date specified in paragraph (2)(*a*) of that regulation, make an application to a superintendent for it to be endorsed under this regulation.

(2) If the superintendent to whom an application is made under this regulation is satisfied—

(*a*) that the person making the application is the holder of the British Seaman's Card; and

(*b*) that the British Seaman's Card is valid at the date of the application;

he shall endorse it with a statement that it shall be valid until 31st December 1977.

PART II

DISCHARGE BOOKS

Application for Discharge Books

16.—(1) Subject to the provisions of these Regulations, a person who satisfies the conditions specified in paragraph (2) of this regulation shall apply for a discharge book within 7 days of satisfying those conditions.

(2) The conditions referred to in paragraph (1) are that the person—

(*a*) is not exempted from the requirements of section 1 of the Act (which relates to crew agreements) by regulations made under subsection (5)(*b*) of that section; and

(*b*) either—

(i) is present in the United Kingdom while employed as a seaman in a ship registered in the United Kingdom otherwise than in an employment specified in regulation 17(3); or

(ii) being a citizen of the United Kingdom and colonies, has been discharged abroad after being so employed and has arrived in the United Kingdom within 6 months of being discharged, unless, at the time he arrived in the United Kingdom, he did not intend to take such employment; and

(*c*) is not the holder of a discharge book issued in accordance with these Regulations.

17.—(1) Regulation 16 shall not apply to a person if he holds a document—

(*a*) containing substantially the same information as a discharge book; and

(*b*) which has been issued to him by or under the authority of the government of a country specified in Schedule 3; and

(*c*) of which he has not ceased to be regarded as the holder by that government.

(2) Regulation 16 shall not apply to a person in the employment of the Crown who is not ordinarily employed as a master or seaman.

(3) For the purposes of regulation 16 no regard shall be had to employment in a fishing vessel or in a ship exempted from the requirements of section 1 of the Act (which relates to crew agreements) by regulations made under subsection (5)(*a*) of that section.

18—(1) A person applying for a discharge book shall—

(*a*) make an application in accordance with regulation 30; and

(*b*) unless it has been lost or destroyed, produce to the superintendent the latest discharge book or Seaman's Record Book previously held by him.

(2) Any person required under the provisions of regulation 16(1) to apply for a discharge book who fails to make application for a discharge book in accordance with these Regulations shall be guilty of an offence.

Issue of Discharge Books

19.—(1) If a person applying for a discharge book—

(*a*) is required under the provisions of regulation 16(1) to apply for a discharge book; and

(*b*) has paid the fee (if any) prescribed;

the Secretary of State shall issue to him a discharge book containing the particulars specified in Schedule 2 (except paragraphs 4 and 15).

(2) If a person applying for a discharge book—

(*a*) is not required under the provisions of regulation 16(1) to apply for a discharge book;

(*b*) is, or has been employed in a ship registered in the United Kingdom; and

(*c*) has paid the fee (if any) prescribed;

the Secretary of State may issue to him a discharge book containing the particulars specified in Schedule 2 (except paragraphs 4 and 15).

Form and content of Discharge Books

20. A discharge book shall be in book form and shall provide for there to be recorded in it from time to time, in relation to its holder, statements of the following particulars—

(*a*) those specified in Schedule 2 to these Regulations (except paragraphs 4 and 15);

(*b*) the name of each ship registered in the United Kingdom in which he is employed, its port of registry, official number and gross or register tonnage, the capacity in which he is employed in the ship, the date on which and the place at which he begins to be so employed, and the description of each voyage and the date and place of his discharge;

(*c*) dates of any period for which he is working or standing by, any period of paid leave, any period of unpaid leave, any period of sickness and any period of study leave, and the certificates for which the study is undertaken;

(*d*) dates and nature of training courses (including pre-sea training courses) he attends and the certificates or other qualifications (if any) obtained;

(*e*) his income tax code, the year to which it applies and the date on which it becomes effective;

(*f*) his inoculation and vaccination certificates; and

(*g*) records of tests of his eyesight.

Entries in Discharge Books

21.—(1) Entries in discharge books of the particulars—

(*a*) referred to in paragraphs (*a*), (*b*), (*d*), (*e*), (*f*) and (*g*) of regulation 20 may be made by a superintendent or the Registrar General of Shipping and Seamen;

(*b*) referred to in paragraphs (*a*), (*b*) and (*f*) of regulation 20 may be made by a proper officer;

(*c*) referred to in paragraphs (*b*) and (*c*) of regulation 20 may be made by the master of the ship in which the holder is employed or by one of the ship's officers authorised by the master in that behalf;

(*d*) referred to in regulation 20(*e*) and in paragraphs 2 and 16 of Schedule 2 may be made by the master of the ship in which the holder is employed;

(*e*) referred to in paragraphs (*c*) and (*e*) of regulation 20 and in paragraph 16 of Schedule 2 may be made by the seaman's employer;

(*f*) referred to in regulation 20(*c*) and in paragraph 10 of Schedule 2 to these Regulations may be made by an official of the Merchant Navy Establishment Administration;

and by no other person.

(2) Any person authorised by this regulation to make an entry in a discharge book shall, upon the discharge book being produced to him for that purpose, make the entry unless an entry of the same particulars appears to have been duly made in it.

22. A superintendent, a proper officer or the Registrar General of Shipping and Seamen may at any time correct any entry in a discharge book.

Production of Discharge Books

23.—(1) The holder of a discharge book shall produce it on demand at any time—

(*a*) to a superintendent, a proper officer, the Registrar General of Shipping and Seamen or an official of the Merchant Navy Establishment Administration;

(*b*) to his employer and to the master of the ship in which the holder is employed; and

(*c*) to any other person authorised by regulation 21 to make an entry in it, for the purpose of making that entry.

(2) The holder of a discharge book who fails to produce it when required to do so in accordance with this regulation shall be guilty of an offence.

Delivery of Discharge Books

24.—(1) A master having possession of a discharge book issued to a person—

(*a*) who has died, shall deliver it to the superintendent or proper officer to whom he makes a return of that person's death (in accordance with section 254 of the Merchant Shipping Act 1894**(a)** or with regulations made under section 72 of the Act), at the time he makes the return;

(a) 57 & 58 Vict. c. 60.

(*b*) who is not present when he is discharged, shall deliver it to the superintendent or proper officer for the place at which he is discharged, within 48 hours after the discharge or as soon as practicable thereafter;

(*c*) who is left behind in any country, shall deliver it to a superintendent or proper officer, within 48 hours after that person is left behind or as soon as practicable thereafter.

(2) Any person other than a master having possession of a discharge book shall, immediately after he becomes aware that the holder has died, has been discharged from any ship, or has been left behind in any country, deliver it to a superintendent or proper officer or to the Registrar General of Shipping and Seamen.

(3) A person who fails to comply with the requirements of this regulation shall be guilty of an offence.

Effect of loss, destruction, defacement or filling up of Discharge Books

25. When—

(*a*) his discharge book is lost, destroyed or defaced, or

(*b*) the space provided in it for entries of any particulars except those referred to in Schedule 2 is filled up,

a person shall cease to be regarded as the holder of a discharge book and shall, within 7 days of satisfying the conditions specified in regulation 16(2), apply for a new discharge book.

PART III

PROVISIONS RELATING TO BRITISH SEAMEN'S CARDS AND TO DISCHARGE BOOKS

26. In this Part of these Regulations "seaman's document" means a British Seaman's Card or a discharge book; and references in this Part of these Regulations to the holder of a seaman's document shall be construed accordingly.

Notification of errors in Seamen's Documents

27.—(1) If it appears to the holder thereof that any entry in a seaman's document is not correct, he shall forthwith inform a superintendent.

(2) Any person who fails to comply with the requirements of this regulation shall be guilty of an offence.

Surrender of Seamen's Documents

28.—(1) If it appears to a superintendent, a proper officer or the Registrar General of Shipping and Seamen—

(*a*) that the holder of a seaman's document was not entitled to apply for it at the time it was issued to him; or

(*b*) that the person having possession of a seaman's document is not the holder thereof;

the person (including the holder) having possession of a seaman's document shall, on demand made by a superintendent, a proper officer, or the Registrar General of Shipping and Seamen (as the case may be) surrender it to him.

(2) Any person who fails to comply with the requirements of this regulation shall be guilty of an offence.

Alterations in Seamen's Documents

29.—(1) No person other than a person authorised by regulation 5, 8, 15, 19, 21 or 22 (as the case may be) acting in accordance with the provisions of those regulations, shall make any mark or entry upon, or erase, cancel or alter any mark or entry made upon or otherwise deface or destroy a seaman's document.

(2) Any person who contravenes the provisions of this regulation shall be guilty of an offence.

Applications relating to Seamen's Documents

30. An application for the issue of a seaman's document or for the endorsement of a British Seaman's Card under regulation 8 or 15 shall be made in writing to a superintendent, and

(*a*) where—

(i) in the case of an application for a British Seaman's Card, the applicant surrenders to the superintendent a British Seaman's Card held by him; or

(ii) in the case of an application for a discharge book, the applicant produces to the superintendent a discharge book or a Seaman's Record Book held by him; or

(iii) in the case of an application for a British Seaman's Card or for a discharge book, it appears to the superintendent that the applicant has lost his latest British Seaman's Card or discharge book (as the case may be) and that the Secretary of State has in his possession particulars of any of the matters set out in Schedule 2;

shall state the applicant's name and particulars of such of the other matters set out in Schedule 2 to these Regulations as are not correctly stated in the document (if any) surrendered or produced in accordance with this paragraph or in the particulars referred to in paragraph (iii) of this paragraph; and

(*b*) in any other case, shall state particulars of the matters set out in Schedule 2;

and the applicant shall furnish to the superintendent such documents (including 3 copies of a recent head and shoulders black and white photograph of himself measuring 2 inches by 2 inches) and such other evidence as he may require for the proper consideration of the application.

Offences

31. Any offence under these Regulations shall be punishable on summary conviction with a fine not exceeding £10.

Michael Heseltine,
Minister for Aerospace,
Department of Trade and Industry.

17th August 1972.

SCHEDULE 1

FORM OF BRITISH SEAMAN'S CARD

Page 1

MERCHANT SHIPPING ACT 1970

The Merchant Shipping (Seamen's Documents) Regulations 1972.

NOTICE

1. This card is a seafarer's identity document for the purpose of the Seafarer's Identity Documents Convention, 1958, adopted by the General Conference of the International Labour Organisation on 13th May, 1958.

2. This card must be carefully preserved and produced by the Holder on demand to a Superintendent, or proper officer, his employer or the master of his ship.

3. If the card is lost the fact should be reported at once to a Superintendent.

4. The Holder must not make any entry or alteration on this card himself. If any entry requires alteration apply to a Superintendent or to the Registrar General of Shipping and Seamen.

5. If the Holder of this card ceases to be employed or ordinarily employed as a master or seaman he must surrender the card forthwith to a Superintendent.

6. Failure to observe the requirements of the Regulations under which this card is issued may render the offender liable to prosecution.

Page 2   B.S.C. 1

DECLARATION

I DECLARE (i) that the person to whom this card relates has satisfied me as to his entitlement to hold this card and (ii) that the photograph within bearing an official stamp is a true likeness of that person and that the signature and physical description of that person are true.

Date..

Office
Stamp

Signature of Issuing Officer

Note: Any person other than the person to whom this card was issued who comes into possession of it should deliver it to a Mercantile Marine Superintendent or send it to the Registrar General of Shipping and Seamen, Llantrisant Road, Cardiff, postage unpaid

---

Page 3

BRITISH
PERSONAL

All particulars to be in BLOCK CAPITALS
Surname ....
Other Names..

Birth (*a*) Date................(*b*) Place...................
Height................ft. ....ins.
Colour of Eyes...
Distinguishing Marks (if any)...........................
....
....
Discharge Book No. (if any) ....
Nationality ....
Home Address ....
....
....
....
National Insurance No. ....

Page 4

SEAMAN'S CARD
PARTICULARS   Serial No..........................
Photograph of Holder

Embossing
Stamp

Signature of Holder
(or, if Holder is unable to sign, his thumbprint stating right or left, and signature of a witness).

Page 5
PERIOD OF VALIDITY

Valid until............................19.............. or,
if he is not then present in the United King-
dom until the Holder's first return to the
United Kingdom within twelve months
thereafter.

ENDORSEMENT FOR FURTHER PERIOD OF
VALIDITY

Endorsed under the Regulations as valid until
.... 19.......... or,
if he is not then present in the United King-
dom until the Holder's first return to the
United Kingdom within twelve months
thereafter.

Signature of Endorsing Officer

Date ....

Office
stamp

Page 6
FOR USE OF H.M. GOVERNMENT

SCHEDULE 2

PARTICULARS TO BE FURNISHED IN APPLICATIONS FOR SEAMEN'S DOCUMENTS

1. the name of the person applying for the document;
2. his home address;
3. the date and place of his birth;
4. if a woman who is or has been married, her maiden surname and the date of her marriage;
5. his nationality;
6. the colour of his eyes;
7. his distinguishing marks (if any);
8. his height;
9. the number of his discharge book (if any);
10. his Merchant Navy Establishment Administration number (if any);
11. the grade, number and date of issue of any certificate of competency held by him;
12. national insurance number;
13. any pension fund of which he may be a member and his registered number therein;
14. any trades union or professional society of which he may be a member and his registered number therein;
15. in the case of a cadet, the name of his employer and whether he is a deck or engineer cadet;
16. the name, relationship and address of his next of kin.

SCHEDULE 3

COUNTRIES REFERRED TO IN REGULATION 17(1) (WHICH RELATES TO PERSONS HOLDING DOCUMENTS, CONTAINING SUBSTANTIALLY THE SAME INFORMATION AS DISCHARGE BOOKS, ISSUED BY OR UNDER THE AUTHORITY OF THE GOVERNMENTS OF CERTAIN COUNTRIES).

Barbados
Canada
Falkland Islands
Guyana
Hong Kong
India
The Republic of Ireland
Jamaica
Kenya
Malaysia
Malta
Mauritius
Nigeria
Pakistan
St Lucia
Sierra Leone
Singapore
Tanzania
Trinidad and Tobago

EXPLANATORY NOTE

(This Note is not part of the Regulations.)

These Regulations, made under the Merchant Shipping Act 1970, make provisions, which supersede existing provisions,

(*a*) in Part I, for the issue of identity documents, known as British Seamen's Cards, to the persons described in regulations 2 and 3 who, not being aliens, are employed or ordinarily employed as masters or seamen; and

(*b*) in Part II, for the issue of discharge books to contain particulars, including records of their seagoing employment, to seamen described in regulations 16 and 17 who are or have been employed in ships registered in the United Kingdom.

STATUTORY INSTRUMENTS

1972 No. 1297

WAGES COUNCILS

The Wages Regulation (Retail Drapery, Outfitting and Footwear) (No. 2) Order 1972

Made	-	-	-	*17th August* 1972
Coming into Operation			*9th October* 1972

Whereas the Secretary of State has received from the Retail Drapery, Outfitting and Footwear Trades Wages Council (Great Britain) the wages regulation proposals set out in the Schedule hereto ;

Now, therefore, the Secretary of State in exercise of powers conferred by section 11 of the Wages Councils Act 1959(a) and now vested in him (b), and of all other powers enabling him in that behalf, hereby makes the following Order : —

1. This Order may be cited as the Wages Regulation (Retail Drapery, Outfitting and Footwear) (No. 2) Order 1972.

2.—(1) In this Order the expression "the specified date" means the 9th October 1972, provided that where, as respects any worker who is paid wages at intervals not exceeding seven days, that date does not correspond with the beginning of the period for which the wages are paid, the expression "the specified date" means, as respects that worker, the beginning of the next such period following that date.

(2) The Interpretation Act 1889(c) shall apply to the interpretation of this Order, as it applies to the interpretation of an Act of Parliament and as if this Order and the Order hereby revoked were Acts of Parliament.

3. The wages regulation proposals set out in the Schedule hereto shall have effect as from the specified date and as from that date the Wages Regulation (Retail Drapery, Outfitting and Footwear) Order 1972(d) shall cease to have effect.

Signed by order of the Secretary of State.

17th August 1972.

R. R. D. McIntosh,
Deputy Secretary,
Department of Employment.

(a) 1959 c. 69.
(b) S.I. 1959/1769, 1968/729 (1959 I, p. 1795; 1968 II, p. 2108).
(c) 1889 c. 63.   (d) S.I. 1972/35 (1972 I, p. 61).

ARRANGEMENT OF SCHEDULE

PART I

STATUTORY MINIMUM REMUNERATION

PART II

ANNUAL HOLIDAY AND HOLIDAY REMUNERATION

PART III

GENERAL

Article 3 SCHEDULE

The following minimum remuneration and provisions as to holidays and holiday remuneration shall be substituted for the statutory minimum remuneration and the provisions as to holidays and holiday remuneration fixed by the Wages Regulation (Retail Drapery, Outfitting and Footwear) Order 1972 (Order R.D.O. (60)).

Part I

STATUTORY MINIMUM REMUNERATION

APPLICATION

1. Subject to the provisions of paragraphs 2, 6 and 9, the minimum remuneration payable to workers to whom this Schedule applies shall be the remuneration set out in paragraphs 3, 4 and 5.

Any increase in remuneration payable under the provisions of paragraph 3, 4 or 5 shall become effective on the first day of the first full pay week following the date upon which the increase would otherwise become payable under those provisions.

HOURS ON WHICH REMUNERATION IS BASED

2.—(1) The minimum remuneration specified in paragraphs 3, 4 and 5 relates to a week of 40 hours exclusive of overtime and, except in the case of guaranteed weekly remuneration under paragraph 9, is subject to a proportionate reduction according as the number of hours worked is less than 40.

(2) In calculating the remuneration for the purpose of this Schedule recognised breaks for meal times shall, subject to the provisions of paragraph 7, be excluded.

WORKERS OTHER THAN TEMPORARY SHOP MANAGERS, TEMPORARY SHOP MANAGERESSES AND TRANSPORT WORKERS

3.—(1) Subject to the provisions of paragraph 1, the minimum remuneration payable to male or female workers of the classes specified in column 1 of the following table employed in the London Area, Provincial A Area or Provincial B Area, as the case may be, shall be the appropriate amount set out in Column 2.

Column 1	Column 2					
	LONDON AREA Per week		PROVINCIAL A AREA Per week		PROVINCIAL B AREA Per week	
	Male £	Female £	Male £	Female £	Male £	Female £
(a) SHOP MANAGERS and SHOP MANAGERESSES where the number of staff (computed in accordance with the provisions of sub-paragraph (2) of this paragraph) is:—						
1 or 2	18·00	16·85	17·70	16·55	17·15	16·10
3	18·30	17·15	18·00	16·85	17·45	16·40
4	18·65	17·50	18·35	17·20	17·80	16·75
5	18·95	17·80	18·65	17·50	18·10	17·05
6	19·30	18·15	19·00	17·85	18·45	17·40
(b) CLERKS GRADE I, aged 22 years or over	16·70	14·50	16·30	14·25	15·65	13·70
(c) CLERKS GRADE I, aged under 22 years, CLERKS GRADE II, SALES ASSISTANTS, CASHIERS, CENTRAL WAREHOUSE WORKERS, CREDIT TRAVELLERS, STOCK HANDS—						
Aged 21 years or over	16·40	14·30	16·00	14·00	15·35	13·50
„ 20 and under 21 years	13·20	11·80	12·90	11·50	12·30	11·15
„ 19 „ 20 „	12·20	11·15	11·95	10·85	11·35	10·50
„ 18 „ 19 „	11·55	10·75	11·30	10·50	10·75	10·15
„ 17 „ 18 „	9·60	9·25	9·35	8·95	8·95	8·65
„ 16 „ 17 „	9·15	8·95	8·90	8·70	8·55	8·35
„ under 16 years	8·85	8·70	8·60	8·40	8·20	8·05
(d) ALL OTHER WORKERS (OTHER THAN THE WORKERS SPECIFIED IN PARAGRAPH 4 AND PARAGRAPH 5)—						
Aged 21 years or over	16·00	14·05	15·60	13·75	15·10	13·25
„ 20 and under 21 years	13·05	11·65	12·75	11·30	12·20	10·95
„ 19 „ 20 „	12·15	11·10	11·90	10·80	11·30	10·45
„ 18 „ 19 „	11·50	10·70	11·25	10·45	10·70	10·10
„ 17 „ 18 „	9·55	9·20	9·30	8·90	8·90	8·60
„ 16 „ 17 „	9·10	8·90	8·85	8·65	8·50	8·30
„ under 16 years	8·80	8·65	8·55	8·35	8·15	8·00

Provided that where a sales assistant enters, or has entered, the retail drapery, outfitting and footwear trades for the first time at or over the age of 20 years, the minimum remuneration payable shall be—

(i) during the first three months of the employment, £0·50 per week less, and

(ii) during the second three months of the employment, £0·25 per week less than the minimum remuneration otherwise applicable to the worker under (c) of this sub-paragraph.

(2) In the foregoing table, "number of staff" means the number of persons (including the manager or manageress) normally employed by the employer, for whose control the manager or manageress is responsible to the employer, and in computing that number both full-time workers and workers other than full-time workers shall be included, except that in the case of workers other than full-time workers the number to be counted shall be the number of such workers or the number (treating any fraction as one) obtained by dividing by 30 the aggregate of the hours normally worked in the week by all such workers whichever is the less.

TEMPORARY SHOP MANAGERS AND TEMPORARY SHOP MANAGERESSES

4.—(1) Subject to the provisions of this paragraph, the minimum remuneration payable to temporary shop managers and temporary shop manageresses, for each continuous period of employment as temporary shop manager or temporary shop manageress (reckoned in accordance with the provisions of sub-paragraph (2) of this paragraph) shall be the appropriate minimum remuneration for a shop manager or shop manageress, as the case may be, under the provisions of paragraph 3(1)(a).

(2) In reckoning any continuous period of employment as temporary shop manager or temporary shop manageress for the purposes of sub-paragraph (1) of this paragraph, no account shall be taken of any period of employment—

(a) not exceeding two consecutive working days ; or

(b) not exceeding a total of two weeks in any year, being a period when the shop manager or shop manageress is absent on holiday :

Provided that for the purposes of this paragraph where in any year a worker is employed by the same employer as a temporary shop manager or temporary shop manageress at more than one shop during the absence on holiday of the shop manager or shop manageress, the first period of such employment and any subsequent periods of such employment in the same year shall be treated as a continuous period of employment.

(3) The minimum remuneration payable to temporary shop managers and temporary shop manageresses for any period of employment mentioned in (a) or (b) of sub-paragraph (2) of this paragraph, shall be not less than the appropriate minimum remuneration for a sales assistant under the provisions of this Schedule.

(4) For the purposes of this paragraph "year" means the 12 months commencing with 1st January and ending with 31st December.

TRANSPORT WORKERS

5. Subject to the provisions of paragraph 1, the minimum remuneration payable to Transport Workers employed in the London Area, Provincial A Area or Provincial B Area, as the case may be, shall be the appropriate amount set out in Column 3 of the following table : —

Column 1	Column 2		Column 3		
	Type of Vehicle				
Age of transport worker	Mechanically propelled vehicle with carrying capacity of	Horse-drawn vehicle	LONDON AREA	PROVINCIAL A AREA	PROVINCIAL B AREA
			Per week	Per week	Per week
			£	£	£
21 years or over	1 ton or less	one-horse	16·40	16·00	15·30
20 and under 21 years			13·15	13·05	12·45
19 ,, ,, 20 ,, ...			12·65	12·55	11·95
18 ,, ,, 19 ,, ...			12·00	11·90	11·40
under 18 years			10·10	10·00	9·60
All ages	Over 1 ton and up to 2 tons	two-horse	16·60	16·20	15·50
	Over 2 tons and up to 5 tons	—	16·80	16·40	15·70
	Over 5 tons	—	17·00	16·60	15·90

MINIMUM OVERTIME RATES

6.—(1) Subject to the provisions of this paragraph, overtime shall be payable to all workers at the following minimum rates:—

(*a*) For work on a Sunday or customary holiday,

    (i) where time worked does not exceed 4½ hours—double time for 4½ hours

    (ii) where time worked exceeds 4½ hours but does not exceed 8 hours—double time for 8 hours

    (iii) where time worked exceeds 8 hours—double time for all time worked.

    Provided that—

      (i) Where a worker performs work on a customary holiday which is a day fixed by the employer, being a day on which the worker would normally work, during the period commencing on the last day on which the worker would normally work before Christmas Day and ending in England and Wales on the next following 2nd January, and in Scotland on the next following 3rd January, overtime rates in accordance with the provisions of this sub-paragraph shall be payable to that worker only if—

        (*a*) he is a worker who normally works for the employer for more than 9 hours in a week ; and

        (*b*) he has been in the employment of the employer throughout the period of 8 weeks immediately preceding the week in which Christmas Day falls.

      (ii) Where it is or becomes the practice in a Jewish undertaking for the employer to require attendance on Sunday instead of Saturday, the provisions of this paragraph shall apply as if in such provisions the word "Saturday" were substituted for "Sunday", except where such substitution is unlawful.

(*b*) On the weekly short day in any week during which, under sub-section (3) of section 40 of the Shops Act 1950(a), the employer is relieved of his obligation to allow the worker a weekly half day,

    for any time worked after 1.30 p.m.   ..   ..   ..   double time

(*c*) On the weekly short day (not being a weekly short day to which (*b*) of this sub-paragraph applies),

    for any time worked after 1.30 p.m. ..   ..   ..   time-and-a-half

(*d*) In any week, exclusive of any time in respect of which a minimum over-time rate is payable under the foregoing provisions of this paragraph,

    for all time worked in excess of 40 hours   ..   ..   time-and-a-half

    Provided that in any week which includes one customary holiday "33 hours" shall be substituted for "40 hours", in any week which includes two customary holidays "26 hours" shall be substituted for "40 hours" and in any week which includes three customary holidays "19 hours" shall be substituted for the said "40 hours".

(2) Overtime rates in accordance with provisions (*a*), (*c*) and (*d*) of sub-paragraph (1) of this paragraph shall be payable to a shop manager, temporary shop manager, shop manageress or temporary shop manageress only if the overtime worked is specifically authorised in writing by the employer or his representative.

(a) 1950 c. 28.

WAITING TIME

7. A worker is entitled to payment of the minimum remuneration specified in this Schedule for all the time during which he is present on the premises of the employer, unless he is present thereon in any of the following circumstances, that is to say—

(1) without the employer's consent, express or implied;

(2) for some purpose unconnected with his work, and other than that of waiting for work to be given to him to perform;

(3) by reason only of the fact that he is resident thereon; or

(4) during normal meal times and he is not waiting for work to be given to him to perform.

WORKERS WHO ARE NOT REQUIRED TO WORK ON A CUSTOMARY HOLIDAY

8.—(1) Subject to the provisions of sub-paragraph (2) and sub-paragraph (3) of this paragraph, a worker who is not required to work on a customary holiday shall be paid for that holiday not less than the amount to which he would have been entitled under the foregoing provisions of this Schedule had the day not been a customary holiday and had he worked the number of hours ordinarily worked by him on that day of the week.

(2) A worker shall not be entitled to any payment under this paragraph unless he—

(a) worked for the employer throughout the last working day on which work was available for him preceding the holiday; and

(b) presents himself for employment at the usual starting time on the first working day after the holiday:

Provided that (a) or (b), as the case may be, of this sub-paragraph shall be deemed to be complied with where the worker is excused by his employer or is prevented by his proved illness or injury from working or presenting himself for employment as aforesaid.

(3) A worker shall not be entitled to any payment under this paragraph in respect of a customary holiday which is a day fixed by the employer, being a day on which the worker would normally work, during the period commencing on the last day on which the worker would normally work before Christmas Day and ending in England and Wales on the next following 2nd January and in Scotland on the next following 3rd January unless—

(a) he is a worker who normally works for the employer for more than 9 hours in a week; and

(b) he has been in the employment of the employer throughout the period of 8 weeks immediately preceding the week in which Christmas Day falls.

GUARANTEED WEEKLY REMUNERATION PAYABLE TO A FULL-TIME WORKER

9.—(1) Notwithstanding the other provisions of this Schedule, where in any week the total remuneration (including holiday remuneration but excluding the amount specified in sub-paragraph (2) of this paragraph) payable under those other provisions to a full-time worker is less than the guaranteed weekly remuneration provided under this paragraph, the minimum remuneration payable to that worker for that week shall be that guaranteed weekly remuneration with the addition of any amount excluded as aforesaid.

(2) The amount to be excluded from the total remuneration referred to in the forgoing sub-paragraph is the whole of the remuneration payable in respect of overtime.

(3) The guaranteed weekly remuneration is the remuneration to which the worker would be entitled under paragraph 3, 4 or 5 for 40 hours work in his normal occupation:

Provided that—

    (a) where the worker normally works for the employer on work to which this Schedule applies for less than 40 hours in the week by reason only of the fact that he does not hold himself out as normally available for work for more than the number of hours he normally works in the week, and the worker has informed his employer in writing that he does not so hold himself out, the guaranteed weekly remuneration shall be the remuneration to which the worker would be entitled (calculated as in paragraph 2) for the number of hours in the week normally worked by the worker for the employer on work to which this Schedule applies ;

    (b) where in any week a worker at his request and with the written consent of his employer is absent from work during any part of his normal working hours on any day (other than a holiday allowed under Part II or a customary holiday or a holiday allowed to all persons employed in the undertaking or branch of an undertaking in which the worker is employed), the guaranteed weekly remuneration payable in respect of that week shall be reduced in respect of each day on which he is absent as aforesaid by one-sixth where the worker's normal working week is six days or by one-fifth where his normal working week is five days.

(4) Guaranteed weekly remuneration is not payable in respect of any week unless the worker throughout his normal working hours in that week (excluding any time allowed to him as a holiday or during which he is absent from work in accordance with proviso (b) to sub-paragraph (3) of this paragraph) is

    (a) capable of and available for work ; and

    (b) willing to perform such duties outside his normal occupation as the employer may reasonably require if his normal work is not available in the establishment in which he is employed.

(5) Guaranteed weekly remuneration is not payable in respect of any week if the worker's employment is terminated before the end of that week.

(6) If the employer is unable to provide the worker with work by reason of a strike or other circumstances beyond his control and gives the worker four clear days' notice to that effect, guaranteed weekly remuneration shall not be payable after the expiry of such notice in respect of any week during which or during part of which the employer continues to be unable to provide work as aforesaid:

Provided that in respect of the week in which the said notice expires there shall be paid to the worker in addition to any remuneration payable in respect of time worked in that week, any remuneration that would have been payable if the worker had worked his normal hours of work on every day in the week prior to the expiry of the notice.

BENEFITS OR ADVANTAGES

10.—(1) The benefits or advantages set out in (a), (b), (c) and (d) of this sub-paragraph, being benefits or advantages provided, in pursuance of the terms and conditions of the employment of a worker to whom this Schedule applies, by the employer or by some other person under arrangements with the employer, are authorised to be reckoned as payment of wages by the employer in lieu of payment in cash in the following manner:—

(a) Dinner of good and sufficient quality and quantity provided on each day on which the worker normally works in the week, other than the weekly short day, as an amount of £0·70 per week except in the circumstances provided for in (d) of this sub-paragraph.

(b) Tea of good and sufficient quality and quantity provided on each day on which the worker normally works in the week, other than the weekly short day, as an amount of £0·25 per week except in the circumstances provided for in (d) of this sub-paragraph.

(c) Full board on Sunday and customary holidays, part board only on the other days of the week and lodging for the full week, as the appropriate amount set out in the table below:—

In the case of a worker aged	LONDON AREA	PROVINCIAL A AREA	PROVINCIAL B AREA
	Per week	Per week	Per week
	£	£	£
21 years or over	2·15	1·90	1·70
20 and under 21 years	2·00	1·80	1·55
19 „ „ 20 „	1·80	1·50	1·30
18 „ „ 19 „	1·65	1·40	1·20
17 „ „ 18 „	1·50	1·25	1·05
16 „ „ 17 „	1·25	1·00	0·80
under 16 years	1·15	0·90	0·65

(d) Full board and lodging for the full week, as the appropriate amount set out in the table below:—

In the case of a worker aged	LONDON AREA	PROVINCIAL A AREA	PROVINCIAL B AREA
	Per week	Per week	Per week
	£	£	£
21 years or over	2·80	2·50	2·35
20 and under 21 years	2·70	2·40	2·20
19 „ „ 20 „	2·45	2·20	2·00
18 „ „ 19 „	2·30	2·00	1·85
17 „ „ 18 „	2·15	1·90	1·65
16 „ „ 17 „	1·90	1·65	1·45
under 16 years	1·80	1·50	1·30

Provided that where in any week the total amount which, in accordance with the foregoing provisions of this sub-paragraph, the employer would be entitled to reckon as payment of wages to a worker in lieu of payment in cash, exceeds the appropriate amount (according to the age of the worker and the area in which he is employed) set out in (d) of this sub-paragraph, then in the case of that worker the employer shall not be entitled in respect of that week, so to reckon as payment of wages as aforesaid, more than such appropriate amount set out in (d) of this sub-paragraph:

Provided also that where a worker is employed in a shop—

(i) which is registered under section 53 of the Shops Act 1950 (which relates to persons observing the Jewish Sabbath), this sub-paragraph in relation to such a worker shall have effect as if for the word "Sunday" in (c) thereof, there were substituted the word "Saturday";

(ii) situated in a district in which an order is in force under section 54 of the Shops Act 1950, authorising shops to be open for the serving of customers on Sunday and which it is the practice to keep open on Sunday, this sub-paragraph in relation to such a worker shall have effect as if for the word "Sunday" there were substituted the words "the week-day upon which the shop in which the worker is employed must be closed in pursuance of an order made under section 54 of the Shops Act 1950".

(2) In this paragraph—

"PART BOARD" means breakfast and supper, being meals of good and sufficient quality and quantity ;

"FULL BOARD" means breakfast, dinner, tea and supper, being meals of good and sufficient quality and quantity ; and

"LODGING" means clean and adequate accommodation and clean and adequate facilities for eating, sleeping, washing and leisure.

(3) Nothing in this paragraph shall be construed as authorising the making of any deduction or the giving of remuneration in any manner which is illegal by virtue of the Truck Acts 1831 to 1940(a), or of any other enactment.

PART II
ANNUAL HOLIDAY AND HOLIDAY REMUNERATION
ANNUAL HOLIDAY

11.—(1) Subject to the provisions of paragraph 12, an employer shall, between the date on which the provisions of this Schedule become effective and 31st October 1972, and in each succeeding year between 1st April and 31st October, allow a holiday (hereinafter referred to as an "annual holiday") to every worker (other than a worker who normally works for the employer for less than 9 hours in a week) in his employment to whom this Schedule applies who has been employed by him during the 12 months immediately preceding the commencement of the holiday season for any one of the periods of employment (calculated in accordance with the provisions of paragraph 18) set out in the table below and the duration of the annual holiday shall in the case of each such worker be related to that period as follows : —

Period of employment	Duration of annual holiday			
	Where the worker's normal working week is			
	Six days	Five days	Four days	Three days or less
12 months...	12 days	10 days	8 days	6 days
Not less than 11 months but less than 12 months ...	11 ,,	9 ,,	7 ,,	5 ,,
,, ,, ,, 10 ,, ,, ,, ,, ,, 11 ,, ...	10 ,,	8 ,,	7 ,,	5 ,,
,, ,, ,, 9 ,, ,, ,, ,, ,, 10 ,, ...	9 ,,	7 ,,	6 ,,	4 ,,
,, ,, ,, 8 ,, ,, ,, ,, ,, 9 ,, ...	8 ,,	7 ,,	5 ,,	4 ,,
,, ,, ,, 7 ,, ,, ,, ,, ,, 8 ,, ...	7 ,,	6 ,,	5 ,,	3 ,,
,, ,, ,, 6 ,, ,, ,, ,, ,, 7 ,, ...	6 ,,	5 ,,	4 ,,	3 ,,
,, ,, ,, 5 ,, ,, ,, ,, ,, 6 ,, ...	5 ,,	4 ,,	3 ,,	2 ,,
,, ,, ,, 4 ,, ,, ,, ,, ,, 5 ,, ...	4 ,,	3 ,,	3 ,,	2 ,,
,, ,, ,, 3 ,, ,, ,, ,, ,, 4 ,, ...	3 ,,	2 ,,	2 ,,	1 day
,, ,, ,, 2 ,, ,, ,, ,, ,, 3 ,, ...	2 ,,	2 ,,	1 day	1 ,,
,, ,, ,, 1 month ,, ,, ,, 2 ,, ...	1 day	1 day	1 ,,	nil

(2) Notwithstanding the provisions of the last foregoing sub-paragraph—

(a) the number of days of annual holiday which an employer is required to allow to a worker in any holiday season shall not exceed in the aggregate twice the number of days constituting the worker's normal working week ;

(a) 1831 c. 37; 1887 c. 46; 1896 c. 44; 1940 c. 38.

(*b*) where a worker does not wish to take his annual holiday or part thereof during the holiday season in any year and, before the expiration of such holiday season, enters into an agreement in writing with his employer that the annual holiday or part thereof shall be allowed, at a date or dates to be specified in that agreement, after the expiration of the holiday season but before the first day of January in the following year, then any day or days of annual holiday so allowed shall be treated as having been allowed during the holiday season ;

(*c*) the duration of the worker's annual holiday during the holiday season ending on 31st October 1972 shall be reduced by any days of annual holiday duly allowed to him by the employer under the provisions of Order R.D.O. (60) between 1st April 1972 and the date on which the provisions of this Schedule become effective.

(3) In this Schedule the expression "holiday season" means in relation to the year 1972 the period commencing on 1st April 1972, and ending on 31st October 1972, and, in each succeeding year, the period commencing on 1st April and ending on 31st October of the same year.

12. Where at the written request of the worker at any time during the three months immediately preceding the commencement of the holiday season in any year, his employer allows him any day or days of holiday and pays him holiday remuneration in respect thereof calculated in accordance with the provisions of paragraphs 15 and 16, then—

(1) the annual holiday to be allowed in accordance with paragraph 11 in the holiday season in that year shall be reduced by the day or days of holiday so allowed prior to the commencement of that holiday season ; and

(2) for the purpose of calculating accrued holiday remuneration under paragraph 17 any day or days of holiday deducted in accordance with sub-paragraph (1) hereof shall be treated as if they had been allowed in the holiday season.

13.—(1) Subject to the provisions of this paragraph, an annual holiday shall be allowed on consecutive working days, being days on which the worker is normally called upon to work for the employer.

(2) Where the number of days of annual holiday for which a worker has qualified exceeds the number of days constituting his normal working week, the holiday may by agreement between the employer and the worker be allowed in two periods of consecutive working days ; so however that when a holiday is so allowed, one of the periods shall consist of a number of such days not less than the number of days constituting the worker's normal working week.

(3) For the purposes of this paragraph, days of annual holiday shall be treated as consecutive notwithstanding that a customary holiday on which the worker is not required to work for the employer or a day on which he does not normally work for the employer intervenes.

(4) Where a customary holiday on which the worker is not required to work for the employer immediately precedes a period of annual holiday or occurs during such a period and the total number of days of annual holiday required to be allowed in the period under the foregoing provisions of this paragraph, together with any customary holiday, exceeds the number of days constituting the worker's normal working week then, notwithstanding the foregoing provisions of this paragraph, the duration of that period of annual holiday may be reduced by one day and in such a case one day of annual holiday may be allowed on a day on which the worker normally works for the employer (not being the worker's weekly short day) in the holiday season or after the holiday season in the circumstances specified in sub-paragraph (2)(*b*) of paragraph 11.

(5) No day of annual holiday shall be allowed on a customary holiday.

(6) A day of annual holiday under this Schedule may be allowed on a day on which the worker is entitled to a day of holiday (not being a customary holiday) or to a half-holiday under any enactment other than the Wages Councils Act 1959:

Provided that where the total number of days of annual holiday allowed to a worker under this Schedule is less than the number of days in his normal working week, the said annual holiday shall be in addition to the said day of holiday or the said half-holiday.

14. An employer shall give to a worker reasonable notice of the commencing date or dates and of the duration of his annual holiday. Such notice may be given individually to the worker or by the posting of a notice in the place where the worker is employed.

REMUNERATION FOR ANNUAL HOLIDAY

15.—(1) Subject to the provisions of paragraph 16, a worker qualified to be allowed an annual holiday under this Schedule shall be paid by his employer, on the last pay day preceding such holiday, one day's holiday pay (as defined in paragraph 19) in respect of each day thereof.

(2) Where an annual holiday is taken in more than one period the holiday remuneration shall be apportioned accordingly.

16. Where any accrued holiday remuneration has been paid by the employer to the worker (in accordance with paragraph 17 of this Schedule or with Order R.D.O. (60)) in respect of employment during any of the periods referred to in that paragraph, or that Order, the amount of holiday remuneration payable by the employer in respect of any annual holiday for which the worker has qualified by reason of employment during the said period shall be reduced by the amount of the said accrued holiday remuneration unless that remuneration has been deducted from a previous payment of holiday remuneration made under the provisions of this Schedule or of Order R.D.O. (60).

ACCRUED HOLIDAY REMUNERATION PAYABLE ON
TERMINATION OF EMPLOYMENT

17. Where a worker (other than a worker who normally works for the employer for less than 9 hours in a week) ceases to be employed by an employer after the provisions of this Schedule become effective the employer shall, immediately on the termination of the employment (hereinafter referred to as the "termination date"), pay to the worker as accrued holiday remuneration—

(1) in respect of employment in the 12 months up to 1st April immediately preceding the termination date, a sum equal to the holiday remuneration for any days of annual holiday for which he has qualified except days of annual holiday which he has been allowed or has become entitled to be allowed before leaving the employment; and

(2) in respect of any employment since 1st April immediately preceding the termination date, a sum equal to the holiday remuneration which would have been payable to him if he could have been allowed an annual holiday in respect of that employment at the time of leaving it:

Provided that—

(a) no worker shall be entitled to the payment by his employer of accrued holiday remuneration if he is dismissed on the grounds of misconduct and is so informed by the employer at the time of dismissal;

(*b*) where during the period or periods in respect of which the said accrued holiday remuneration is payable the worker has at his written request been allowed any day or days of holiday (other than days of holiday allowed by the employer under paragraph 12) for which he had not qualified under the provisions of this Schedule, any accrued holiday remuneration payable as aforesaid may be reduced by the amount of any sum paid by the employer to the worker in respect of such day or days of holiday ;

(*c*) where a worker is employed under a contract of service under which he is required to give not less than one week's notice before terminating his employment and the worker, without the consent of his employer, terminates his employment without having given not less than one week's notice or before one week has expired from the beginning of such notice, the amount of accrued holiday remuneration payable to the worker shall be the amount payable under the foregoing provisions of this paragraph less an amount equal to the statutory minimum remuneration which would be payable to him at the termination date for one week's work if working his normal working week and the normal number of daily hours worked by him.

CALCULATION OF EMPLOYMENT

18. For the purpose of calculating any period of employment qualifying a worker for an annual holiday or for any accrued holiday remuneration, the worker shall be treated as if he were employed for a month in respect of any month (as defined in paragraph 19) throughout which he has been in the employment of the employer.

Part III

GENERAL

DEFINITIONS

19. For the purposes of this Schedule—

"CARRYING CAPACITY" means the weight of the maximum load normally carried by the vehicle, and such carrying capacity when so established shall not be affected either by variations in the weight of the load resulting from collections or deliveries or emptying of containers during the course of the journey, or by the fact that on any particular journey a load greater or less than the established carrying capacity is carried.

"CASHIER" means a worker employed in a shop and engaged wholly or mainly in receiving cash or giving change.

"CENTRAL WAREHOUSE WORKER" means a worker wholly or mainly employed in a central warehouse, that is to say, a warehouse from which an undertaking in the retail drapery, outfitting and footwear trades supplies its branch shops.

"CLERK GRADE I" means a worker engaged wholly or mainly on clerical work which includes responsibility for maintaining ledgers or wages books or for preparing financial accounts of the undertaking or of a branch or department thereof.

"CLERK GRADE II" means a worker, other than a Clerk Grade I, engaged wholly or mainly on clerical work.

"CREDIT TRAVELLER" means a worker employed in an undertaking engaged in credit trading and wholly or mainly engaged in calling upon customers or prospective customers for the purpose of opening accounts, collecting payments or selling goods.

"CUSTOMARY HOLIDAY" means

(1) (*a*) In England and Wales—

(i) Christmas Day (or, if Christmas Day falls on a Sunday, such weekday as may be appointed by national proclamation, or, if none is so appointed, the next following Tuesday), Boxing Day, Good Friday, Easter Monday, Whit Monday (or where another day is substituted therefor by national proclamation, that day), August Bank Holiday and any day proclaimed as a public holiday throughout England and Wales ; and

(ii) one other day being a day on which the worker would normally work during the period commencing on the last day on which the worker would normally work before Christmas Day and ending on the next following 2nd January, to be fixed by the employer and notified to the worker not less than three weeks before the holiday ;

(*b*) In Scotland—

(i) New Year's Day (or, if New Year's Day falls on a Sunday, the following Monday) ;
the local Spring holiday ;
the local Autumn holiday ;
Christmas Day (or, if Christmas Day falls on a Sunday, the following Monday) ;

two other days being days on which the worker would normally work, in the course of a calendar year, to be fixed by the employer and notified to the worker not less than three weeks before the holiday, and any day proclaimed as a public holiday throughout Scotland ; and

(ii) one other day being a day on which the worker would normally work during the period commencing on the last day on which the worker would normally work before Christmas Day and ending on the next following 3rd January, to be fixed by the employer and notified to the worker not less than three weeks before the holiday ; or

(2) where in any undertaking it is not the custom or practice to observe such days as are specified in (1)(*a*)(i) or (1)(*b*)(i) above as holidays, such other days, not fewer in number, as may by agreement between the employer or his representative and the worker or his representative be substituted for the specified days.

"FULL-TIME WORKER" means a worker who normally works for the employer for at least 34 hours in the week on work to which this Schedule applies.

"MONTH" means the period commencing on a date of any number in one month and ending on the day before the date of the same number in the next month, or if the commencing date is the 29th, 30th or 31st day of a month, and there is no date of the same number in the next month, then on the last day of that month.

"NORMAL WORKING WEEK" means the number of days on which it has been usual for the worker to work in a week while in the employment of the employer during the 12 months immediately preceding the commencement of the holiday season, or, where accrued holiday remuneration is payable under (2) of paragraph 17, on the termination of the employment, during the 12 months immediately preceding the termination date:

Provided that—

(1) part of a day shall count as a day ;

(2) no account shall be taken of any week in which the worker did not perform any work for which statutory minimum remuneration has been fixed.

"ONE DAY'S HOLIDAY PAY" means the appropriate proportion of the remuneration which the worker would be entitled to receive from his employer at the date of the annual holiday (or where the holiday is taken in more than one period at the date of the first period) or at the termination date, as the case may be, for one week's work—

(1) if working his normal working week and the number of daily hours normally worked by him (exclusive of overtime),

(2) if the employer were not providing him with meals or board and lodging, and

(3) if paid at the appropriate rate of statutory minimum remuneration for work for which statutory minimum remuneration is payable and at the same rate for any work for the same employer for which such remuneration is not payable,

and in this definition "appropriate proportion" means—

where the worker's normal working week is	six days	.. one-sixth
„ „ „ „ „	five „	.. one-fifth
„ „ „ „ „	four „	.. one-quarter
„ „ „ „ „	three „	.. one-third
„ „ „ „ „	two „	.. one-half
„ „ „ „ „	one day	.. the whole.

"SALES ASSISTANT" means a worker who is wholly or mainly engaged in the serving of customers.

"SHOP MANAGER", "SHOP MANAGERESS" means a worker who is employed at, and is normally immediately in charge of the operation of, an undertaking or branch (but not of a department of an undertaking or branch), who has the custody of cash and stock, and who has immediate control of other workers (if any) employed at that undertaking or branch ; and for the purposes of this definition a worker shall not be deemed not to be immediately in charge of the operation of an undertaking or branch by reason only of being subject to the supervision of the employer or some person acting on his behalf, being in either case a person who is not normally, during the hours when the undertaking or branch is open to the public, wholly or mainly engaged in work at that undertaking or branch.

"STOCK HAND" means a worker employed in a shop, or in a warehouse operated in connection with a shop, and wholly or mainly engaged in the custody of goods or the receiving and checking of stock or the assembly of orders.

"TEMPORARY SHOP MANAGER", "TEMPORARY SHOP MANAGERESS" means a worker who during the absence of the shop manager or shop manageress performs all the duties of the shop manager or the shop manageress, whilst he is performing the said duties.

"TIME-AND-A-HALF" and "DOUBLE TIME" mean, respectively, one and a half times and twice the hourly rate obtained by dividing by 40 the minimum weekly remuneration to which the worker is entitled under the provisions of paragraph 3, 4 or 5.

"TRANSPORT WORKER" means a worker engaged wholly or mainly in driving a mechanically propelled or horse drawn road vehicle for the transport of goods and on work in connection with the vehicle and its load (if any) while on the road.

"WATCHMAN" means a worker wholly or mainly engaged in guarding the employer's premises for the prevention of theft, fire, damage or trespass.

"WEEK" means "pay week".

"WEEKLY SHORT DAY" means:

(1) that day in any week on which the worker is, in accordance with the provisions of section 17 of the Shops Act 1950, required not to be employed about the business of a shop after half-past one o'clock in the afternoon, or,

(2) where there is no such day, or where the day falls on a customary holiday, a working day in the week not being a customary holiday, fixed by the employer and notified to the worker not later than the Saturday preceding the week during which it is to have effect; or, failing such notification, the last working day in the week which is not a customary holiday:

Provided that where the day specified in (1) of this definition falls on Christmas Day or Boxing Day in England and Wales or Christmas Day or New Year's Day in Scotland the employer may fix as the weekly short day for that week a working day in the following week not being either a customary holiday or the weekly short day for that following week.

AREAS

20. In this Schedule:—

(1) "LONDON AREA" means the Metropolitan Police District, as defined in the London Government Act 1963(a), the City of London, the Inner Temple and the Middle Temple.

(2) "PROVINCIAL A AREA" means

    (a) In Scotland,

        (i) the following burghs:—

ABERDEEN COUNTY
Aberdeen (including part in Kincardine County)
Fraserburgh
Peterhead

ANGUS COUNTY
Arbroath
Brechin
Dundee
Forfar
Montrose

ARGYLL COUNTY
Dunoon

AYR COUNTY
Ardrossan
Ayr
Irvine
Kilmarnock
Largs
Prestwick
Saltcoats
Stevenston
Troon

DUNBARTON COUNTY
Bearsden
Clydebank
Dumbarton
Helensburgh
Kirkintilloch
Milngavie

EAST LOTHIAN COUNTY
North Berwick

FIFE COUNTY
Buckhaven and Methil
Burntisland
Cowdenbeath
Dunfermline
Kirkcaldy
Leven
Lochgelly
St. Andrews

INVERNESS COUNTY
Inverness

KINCARDINE COUNTY
Stonehaven

ORKNEY COUNTY
Kirkwall

PERTH COUNTY
Perth

RENFREW COUNTY
Barrhead
Gourock
Greenock
Johnstone
Paisley
Port Glasgow
Renfrew

ROSS AND CROMARTY COUNTY
Stornoway

ROXBURGH COUNTY
Hawick

SELKIRK COUNTY
Galashiels

(a) 1963 c. 33.

BANFF COUNTY
  Buckie

BUTE COUNTY
  Rothesay

CLACKMANNAN
  COUNTY
  Alloa

DUMFRIES COUNTY
  Dumfries

LANARK COUNTY
  Airdrie
  Coatbridge
  Glasgow
  Hamilton
  Lanark
  Motherwell and Wishaw
  Rutherglen

MIDLOTHIAN
  COUNTY
  Dalkeith
  Edinburgh
  Musselburgh

MORAY COUNTY
  Elgin

STIRLING COUNTY
  Denny and Dunipace
  Falkirk
  Grangemouth
  Kilsyth
  Stirling

WEST LOTHIAN
  COUNTY
  Armadale
  Bathgate
  Bo'ness

WIGTOWN COUNTY
  Stranraer

ZETLAND COUNTY
  Lerwick

  (ii) The following Special Lighting Districts, the boundaries of which have been defined, namely:—Vale of Leven and Renton in the County of Dunbarton ; and Larbert and Airth in the County of Stirling ; and

  (iii) The following areas, the boundaries of which were defined as Special Lighting Districts prior to 10th March 1943, namely:—Bellshill and Mossend, Blantyre, Cambuslang, Larkhall and Holytown, New Stevenston and Carfin, all in the County of Lanark.

  (b) In England and Wales, the areas administered by County Borough, Municipal Borough or Urban District Councils, except where they are included in the London area or are listed in (3)(b) of this paragraph.

(3) "PROVINCIAL B AREA" means

  (a) in Scotland, all areas other than those listed in (2)(a) of this paragraph ;

  (b) in England and Wales, all areas not included in the London area administered by Rural District Councils, and the areas administered by the following Municipal Borough and Urban District Councils:—

ENGLAND (excluding Monmouthshire)

BEDFORDSHIRE
  Ampthill
  Sandy

BERKSHIRE
  Wallingford
  Wantage

BUCKINGHAMSHIRE
  Buckingham
  Linslade
  Marlow
  Newport Pagnell

CHESHIRE
  Alsager
  Longdendale

DORSET
  Blandford Forum
  Lyme Regis
  Shaftesbury
  Sherborne
  Wareham
  Wimborne Minster

DURHAM
  Barnard Castle
  Tow Law

ELY, ISLE OF
  Chatteris

ESSEX
  Brightlingsea
  Burnham-on-Crouch
  Saffron Walden
  West Mersea
  Wivenhoe

LINCOLNSHIRE
  Alford
  Barton-upon-Humber
  Bourne
  Brigg
  Horncastle
  Mablethorpe and Sutton
  Market Rasen
  Woodhall Spa

NORFOLK
  Cromer
  Diss
  Downham Market
  Hunstanton
  North Walsham
  Sheringham
  Swaffham
  Thetford
  Wells-next-the-Sea
  Wymondham

CORNWALL
  Bodmin
  Bude Stratton
  Fowey
  Helston
  Launceston
  Liskeard
  Looe
  Lostwithiel
  Padstow
  Penryn
  St. Just
  Torpoint

DERBYSHIRE
  Bakewell
  Whaley Bridge
  Wirksworth

DEVON
  Ashburton
  Buckfastleigh
  Budleigh Salterton
  Crediton
  Dartmouth
  Great Torrington
  Holsworthy
  Honiton
  Kingsbridge
  Lynton
  Northam
  Okehampton
  Ottery St. Mary
  Salcombe
  Seaton
  South Molton
  Tavistock
  Totnes

GLOUCESTERSHIRE
  Nailsworth
  Tewkesbury

HEREFORDSHIRE
  Bromyard
  Kington
  Ledbury

HERTFORDSHIRE
  Baldock
  Chorleywood
  Royston
  Sawbridgeworth

HUNTINGDONSHIRE
  Huntingdon and
    Godmanchester
  Ramsey
  St. Ives
  St. Neots

KENT
  Lydd
  New Romney
  Queenborough
  Sandwich
  Tenterden

LANCASHIRE
  Carnforth
  Grange

NORTHAMPTON-
           SHIRE
  Brackley
  Burton Latimer
  Higham Ferrers
  Oundle

NORTHUMBERLAND
  Alnwick
  Amble

OXFORDSHIRE
  Bicester
  Chipping Norton
  Thame
  Woodstock

RUTLAND
  Oakham

SHROPSHIRE
  Bishop's Castle
  Church Stretton
  Ellesmere
  Market Drayton
  Newport
  Wem

SOMERSET
  Chard
  Crewkerne
  Glastonbury
  Ilminster
  Portishead
  Shepton Mallet
  Street
  Watchet
  Wellington

ENGLAND (excluding Monmouthshire)—*contd.*

SUFFOLK
  Aldeburgh
  Beccles
  Bungay
  Eye
  Hadleigh
  Halesworth
  Haverhill
  Leiston-cum-Sizewell
  Saxmundham
  Southwold
  Sudbury
  Stowmarket
  Woodbridge

SUSSEX
  Arundel
  Rye

WESTMORLAND
  Appleby
  Lakes

WILTSHIRE
  Bradford-on-Avon
  Calne
  Malmesbury
  Marlborough
  Melksham
  Westbury
  Wilton

WORCESTERSHIRE
  Bewdley
  Droitwich

YORKSHIRE
  Hedon
  Hornsea
  Malton
  Norton
  Pickering
  Richmond
  Tickhill
  Withernsea

WALES AND MONMOUTHSHIRE

ANGLESEY
Amlwch
Beaumaris
Llangefni
Menai Bridge

BRECONSHIRE
Builth Wells
Hay
Llanwrtyd Wells

CAERNARVONSHIRE
Bethesda
Betws-y-Coed
Criccieth
Llanfairfechan
Penmaenmawr
Portmadoc
Pwllheli

CARDIGANSHIRE
Aberayron
Cardigan
Lampeter
New Quay

CARMARTHENSHIRE
Cwmamman
Kidwelly
Llandeilo
Llandovery
Newcastle Emlyn

DENBIGHSHIRE
Llangollen
Llanrwst
Ruthin

FLINTSHIRE
Buckley
Mold

GLAMORGAN
Cowbridge

MERIONETHSHIRE
Bala
Barmouth
Dolgellau
Towyn

MONMOUTHSHIRE
Caerleon
Chepstow
Usk

MONTGOMERYSHIRE
Llanfyllin
Llanidloes
Machynlleth
Montgomery
Newtown and
 Llanllwchaiarn
Welshpool

PEMBROKESHIRE
Fishguard and
 Goodwick
Narberth
Neyland
Tenby

RADNORSHIRE
Knighton
Llandrindod Wells
Presteigne

(4) Any reference to a local government area shall be construed as a reference to that area as it was on 23rd April 1961, unless otherwise stated.

WORKERS TO WHOM THIS SCHEDULE APPLIES

21.—(1)—(i) Subject to the provisions of sub-paragraph (2) of this paragraph, the workers to whom this Schedule applies are all workers employed in Great Britain in any undertaking or any branch or department of an undertaking, being an undertaking, branch or department engaged—

(a) wholly or mainly in the retail drapery, outfitting and footwear trades ; or

(b) wholly or mainly in those trades and one or more of the groups of retail distributive trades set out in the Appendix to this paragraph, and to a greater extent in the retail drapery, outfitting and footwear trades than in any one of those groups:

Provided that if a branch or department of an undertaking is not so engaged this Schedule shall not apply to workers employed in that branch or department (notwithstanding that the undertaking as a whole is so engaged), except in the case of workers as respects their employment in a department of that branch if that department is so engaged.

(ii) For the purposes of this sub-paragraph

(a) in determining the extent to which an undertaking or branch or department of an undertaking is engaged in a group of trades, regard shall be had to the time spent in the undertaking, branch or department on work in that group of trades ;

(b) an undertaking or branch or department of an undertaking which is engaged in any operation in a group of trades shall be treated as engaged in that group of trades.

(2) This Schedule does not apply to any of the following workers in respect of their employment in any of the following circumstances, that is to say—

    (i) workers employed on the making, trimming, fitting, alteration or repair of wearing apparel ;

    (ii) workers in relation to whom the Road Haulage Wages Council operates in respect of any employment which is within the field of operation of that Council ;

    (iii) workers employed on post office business ;

    (iv) workers employed on the maintenance or repair of buildings, plant, equipment or vehicles (but not including workers employed as cleaners) ;

    (v) workers employed on the cutting, sewing, making up and fixing of blinds, curtains, pelmets and loose covers ;

    (vi) workers employed as watchmen.

(3) For the purpose of this Schedule the retail drapery, outfitting and footwear trades consist of

    (i) the sale by retail of

        (a) wearing apparel of all kinds (including footwear, headwear and hand-wear) and accessories, trimmings and adornments for wearing apparel (excluding jewellery and imitation jewellery) ;

        (b) haberdashery ;

        (c) textile fabrics in the piece, leather cloth, plastic cloth and oil cloth (but not including carpets, linoleum and other kinds of floor covering) ;

        (d) knitting, rug, embroidery, crochet and similar wools or yarns ;

        (e) made-up household textiles (but excluding mattresses and floor coverings) ;

        (f) umbrellas, sunshades, walking sticks, canes and similar articles ;

    (ii) operations in or about the shop or other place where any of the articles included in (i) of this sub-paragraph are sold by retail, being operations carried on for the purpose of such sale or otherwise in connection with such sale ;

    (iii) operations in connection with the warehousing or storing of any of the articles included in (i) of this sub-paragraph for the purpose of the sale thereof by retail, or otherwise in connection with such sale, where the warehousing or storing takes place at a warehouse or store carried on in conjunction with one or more shops or other places where the said articles are sold by retail ;

    (iv) operations in connection with the transport of any of the articles included in (i) of this sub-paragraph when carried on in conjunction with their sale by retail or with the warehousing or storing operations specified in (iii) of this sub-paragraph ; and

    (v) clerical or other office work carried on in conjunction with the sale by retail of any of the articles included in (i) of this sub-paragraph and relating to such sale or to any of the operations specified in (ii) to (iv) of this sub-paragraph ;

and for the purpose of this definition the sale by retail of any of the articles in (i) of this sub-paragraph includes the sale of that article to a person for use in connection with a trade or business carried on by him if such sale takes place at or in connection with a shop engaged in the retail sale to the general public of any of the articles included in (i) of this sub-paragraph.

APPENDIX TO PARAGRAPH 21

GROUPS OF RETAIL DISTRIBUTIVE TRADES

Group 1.—The Retail Food Trades, that is to say, the sale by retail of food or drink for human consumption and operations connected therewith including:—

(i) operations in or about the shop or other place where the food or drink aforesaid is sold, being operations carried on for the purpose of such sale or otherwise in connection with such sale ;

(ii) operations in connection with the warehousing or storing of such food or drink for the purpose of sale by retail, or otherwise in connection with such sale, where the warehousing or storing takes place at a warehouse or store carried on in conjunction with one or more shops or other places where such food or drink is sold by retail ;

(iii) operations in connection with the transport of such food or drink when carried on in conjunction with its sale by retail or with the warehousing or storing operations specified in (ii) above ; and

(iv) clerical or other office work carried on in conjunction with the sale by retail aforesaid and relating to such sale or to any of the operations in (i) to (iii) above ;

but not including

the sale by retail of bread, pastry or flour confectionery (other than biscuits or meat pastries) or the sale by retail of meat (other than bacon, ham, pressed beef, sausages or meat so treated as to be fit for human consumption without further preparation or cooking) or the sale by retail of milk (other than dried or condensed milk) or the sale by retail of ice-cream, aerated waters, chocolate confectionery or sugar confectionery, or the sale of food or drink for immediate consumption.

For the purpose of this definition "sale by retail" includes any sale of food or drink to a person for use in connection with a catering business carried on by him, when such sale takes place at or in connection with a shop engaged in the retail sale of food or drink to the general public.

Group 2.—The Retail Furnishing and Allied Trades, that is to say—

(1) the sale by retail of the following articles:—

(a) household and office furniture, including garden furniture, mattresses, floor coverings and mirrors, but excluding billiard tables, clocks, pianos, gramophones and pictures ;

(b) ironmongery, turnery and hardware, of kinds commonly used for household purposes, including gardening implements ;

(c) hand tools ;

(d) woodware, basketware, glassware, potteryware, chinaware, brassware, plasticware and ceramic goods, being articles or goods of kinds commonly used for household purposes or as household ornaments ;

(e) electrical and gas appliances and apparatus, of kinds commonly used for household purposes (excluding clocks), and accessories and component parts thereof ;

(f) heating, lighting and cooking appliances and apparatus, of kinds commonly used for household purposes, and accessories and component parts thereof ;

(g) radio and television sets and their accessories and component parts ;

(*h*) pedal cycles and their accessories and component parts ;

(*i*) perambulators, push chairs and invalid carriages ;

(*j*) toys, indoor games, requisites for outdoor games, gymnastics and athletics, but excluding billiard tables and sports clothing ;

(*k*) saddlery, leather goods (other than articles of wearing apparel), travel goods and ladies' handbags ;

(*l*) paint, distemper and wallpaper, and oils of kinds commonly used for household purposes (excluding petrol and lubricating oils) ;

(*m*) brushes, mops and brooms, used for household purposes, and similar articles ;

(*n*) disinfectants, chemicals, candles, soaps and polishes, of kinds commonly used for household purposes ;

(2) operations in or about the shop or other place where any of the articles specified in (1) above are sold by retail, being operations carried on for the purpose of such sale or otherwise in connection with such sale ;

(3) operations in connection with the warehousing or storing of any of the articles specified in (1) above for the purpose of the sale thereof by retail, or otherwise in connection with such sale, where the warehousing or storing takes place at a warehouse or store carried on in conjunction with one or more shops or other places where the said articles are sold by retail ;

(4) operations in connection with the transport of any of the articles specified in (1) above when carried on in conjunction with their sale by retail or with the warehousing or storing operations specified in (3) above ; and

(5) clerical or other office work carried on in conjunction with the sale by retail of any of the articles specified in (1) above and relating to such sale or to any of the operations specified in (2) to (4) above ;

and for the purpose of this definition the sale by retail of any of the articles specified in (1) above does not include sale by auction (except where the auctioneer

sells articles by retail which are his property or the property of his master) but includes the sale of any of the articles therein specified to a person for use in connection with a trade or business carried on by him if such sale takes place at or in connection with a shop engaged in the retail sale to the general public of any of the said articles.

Group 3.—The Retail Bookselling and Stationery Trades, that is to say—

(1) the sale by retail of the following articles : —

(*a*) books (excluding printed music and periodicals) ;

(*b*) all kinds of stationery including printed forms, note books, diaries and similar articles, and books of kinds used in an office or business for the purpose of record ;

(*c*) pens, pencils, ink, blotting paper and similar articles ;

(*d*) maps and charts ;

(*e*) wrapping and adhesive paper, string, paste and similar articles ;

(2) operations in or about the shop or other place where any of the articles specified in (1) above are sold by retail, being operations carried on for the purpose of such sale or otherwise in connection with such sale ;

(3) operations in connection with the warehousing or storing of any of the articles specified in (1) above for the purpose of the sale thereof by retail, or otherwise in connection with such sale, where the warehousing or storing takes place at a warehouse or store carried on in conjunction with one or more shops or other places where the said articles are sold by retail ;

(4) operations in connection with the transport of any of the articles specified in (1) above when carried on in conjunction with their sale by retail or with the warehousing or storing operations specified in (3) above ; and

(5) clerical or other office work carried on in conjunction with the sale by retail of any of the articles specified in (1) above and relating to such sale or to any of the operations specified in (2) to (4) above.

Group 4. The Retail Newsagency, Tobacco and Confectionery Trades, that is to say —

(1) the sale by retail of the following articles :—

    (a) newspapers, magazines and other periodicals ;

    (b) tobacco, cigars, cigarettes, snuff and smokers' requisites ;

    (c) articles of sugar confectionery and chocolate confectionery and ice-cream ;

(2) operations in or about the shop or other place where any of the articles specified in (1) above are sold by retail, being operations carried on for the purpose of such sale or otherwise in connection with such sale ;

(3) operations in connection with the warehousing or storing of any of the articles specified in (1) above for the purpose of the sale thereof by retail, or otherwise in connection with such sale, where the warehousing or storing takes place at a warehouse or store carried on in conjunction with one or more shops or other places where the said articles are sold by retail ;

(4) operations in connection with the transport of any of the articles specified in (1) above when carried on in conjunction with their sale by retail or with the warehousing or storing operations specified in (3) above ; and

(5) clerical or other office work carried on in conjunction with the sale by retail of any of the articles specified in (1) above and relating to such sale or to any of the operations specified in (2) to (4) above.

EXPLANATORY NOTE

(This Note is not part of the Order.)

This Order, which has effect from 9th October 1972, sets out the statutory minimum remuneration payable and the holidays to be allowed in substitution for the statutory minimum remuneration and holidays set out in the Wages Regulation (Retail Drapery, Outfitting and Footwear) Order 1972 (Order R.D.O. (60)), which Order is revoked.

New provisions are printed in italics.

STATUTORY INSTRUMENTS

1972 No. 1298

PENSIONS

The Pensions Increase (Annual Review) Order 1972

Made	-	-	-	*18th August* 1972
Laid before Parliament			*25th August* 1972
Coming into Operation			*1st December* 1972

Whereas the Minister for the Civil Service has, in accordance with the provisions of section 2 of the Pensions (Increase) Act 1971(**a**), as amended by section 25 of the Superannuation Act 1972(**b**), reviewed the rates of official pensions against the rise in the cost of living during the review period, that is to say, the period of fifteen months ending with 30th June 1972, and it has been found that in that period the cost of living has risen by 9·9 per cent.:

Now therefore the Minister for the Civil Service, in exercise of the powers conferred on him by sections 2 and 9(4) and (4A) of the said Act of 1971, as amended by section 25 of the said Act of 1972, and of all other powers enabling him in that behalf, hereby makes the following Order:—

Citation and commencement

1. This Order may be cited as the Pensions Increase (Annual Review) Order 1972, and shall come into operation on 1st December 1972.

Interpretation

2.—(1) In this Order—

"the 1971 Act" means the Pensions (Increase) Act 1971;

"basic rate" has the meaning given by section 17(1) of the 1971 Act;

"official pension" has the meaning given by section 5(1) of the 1971 Act;

"pension authority" has the meaning given by section 7(1) of the 1971 Act;

"qualifying condition" means one of the conditions laid down by section 3 of the 1971 Act.

(2) For the purposes of this Order the time when a pension "begins" is that stated in section 8(2) of the 1971 Act, and "beginning date" shall be construed accordingly.

(3) The Interpretation Act 1889(**c**) shall apply for the interpretation of this Order as it applies for the interpretation of an Act of Parliament.

Pension increases

3.—(1) The annual rate of an official pension may, if any qualifying condition is satisfied, be increased by the pension authority in respect of any period beginning on or after 1st December 1972, as follows: —

(**a**) 1971 c. 56. (**b**) 1972 c. 11. (**c**) 1889 c. 63.

(*a*) a pension beginning on or before 1st April 1971 may be increased by 9·9 per cent. of the basic rate as increased under section 1 of the 1971 Act;

(*b*) a pension beginning in the six months following 1st April 1971 may be increased by 11·0 per cent. of the basic rate;

(*c*) a pension beginning in the six months following 1st October 1971 may be increased by 5·6 per cent. of the basic rate;

(*d*) a pension beginning in the three months following 1st April 1972 may be increased by 3·5 per cent. of the basic rate.

(2) For the purpose of showing the cumulative effect of the increases payable under section 1 of the 1971 Act and under paragraph (1) above, that section, with the effect of paragraph (1) above incorporated in it, is set out in the Schedule to this Order.

Increases of certain lump sums

4.—(1) In respect of any lump sum or instalment of a lump sum which became payable in the six months ending with 1st April 1972, but for which the beginning date fell before 2nd October 1971, there may be paid an increase of 2·7 per cent. of the amount of the lump sum or instalment as increased by the amount of any increase under section 1 of the 1971 Act.

(2) In respect of any lump sum or instalment of a lump sum which became payable in the three months ending with 1st July 1972, but for which the beginning date fell before 2nd October 1971, there may be paid an increase of 5·4 per cent. of the amount of the lump sum or instalment as increased by the amount of any increase under section 1 of the 1971 Act.

(3) In respect of any lump sum or instalment of a lump sum which became payable in the three months ending with 1st July 1972, but for which the beginning date fell in the six months ending with 1st April 1972, there may be paid an increase of 2·6 per cent. of the amount of the lump sum or instalment.

Given under the official seal of the Minister for the Civil Service on 18th August 1972.

(L.S.)

A. W. Wyatt,
Authorised by the Minister
for the Civil Service.

SCHEDULE   Article 3(2)

Section 1 of the Pensions (Increase) Act 1971 reproduced with the effect of article 3(1) of this Order incorporated in it

1.—(1) Subject to the provisions of this Act, the annual rate of an official pension may, if any qualifying condition is satisfied, be increased by the pension authority in respect of any period beginning on or after 1st December 1972, as follows:—

(*a*) a pension beginning before the year 1969 may be increased by the amount necessary to bring the rate up to the 1969 standard, that is to say, to the rate arrived at by applying to the basic rate of pension the multiplier given in Schedule 1 for the year in which the pension began, and by a further 29·682 per cent. of the rate so increased;

(b) a pension beginning on or before 1st April 1969 but not earlier than that year may be increased by 29·682 per cent. of the basic rate;

(c) a pension beginning in the six months following 1st April 1969 may be increased by 27·484 per cent of the basic rate;

(d) a pension beginning in the six months following 1st October 1969 may be increased by 25·286 per cent. of the basic rate;

(e) a pension beginning in the six months following 1st April 1970 may be increased by 20·890 per cent. of the basic rate;

(f) a pension beginning in the six months following 1st October 1970 may be increased by 16·494 per cent. of the basic rate;

(g) a pension beginning in the six months following 1st April 1971 may be increased by 11 per cent. of the basic rate;

(h) a pension beginning in the six months following 1st October 1971 may be increased by 5·6 per cent. of the basic rate;

(i) a pension beginning in the three months following 1st April 1972 may be increased by 3·5 per cent. of the basic rate.

(2) In the case of a pension beginning before the year 1969 the increase authorised by subsection 1(a) above shall take the place of those authorised by the Pensions (Increase) Acts 1920 to 1969, but in the cases provided for by section 6 below shall be of the larger amount there specified by reference to increases that might have been made under those Acts together with a further increase of 29·682 per cent. of the pension as so increased.

EXPLANATORY NOTE

(*This Note is not part of the Order.*)

Under section 2 of the Pensions (Increase) Act 1971 (as amended by section 25 of the Superannuation Act 1972) the Minister for the Civil Service is required to conduct a review of rates of public service pensions against any rise in the cost of living during the review period. The Order provides for the payment, with effect from 1st December 1972, of the pension increases resulting from the 1972 review and based on the rise in the cost of living during the review period of fifteen months ending with 30th June 1972. To qualify for increase a person must satisfy one of the qualifying conditions specified in section 3 of the 1971 Act.

For pensions which began on or before 1st April 1971 the increase is of the percentage by which the cost of living rose during the review period (9·9%). For pensions which began in the six months following 1st April 1971, in the six months following 1st October 1971 or in the three months following 1st April 1972, the increases (11%, 5·6%, and 3·5% respectively) are of the percentage by which the cost of living at the end of the review period exceeded its mean level during the respective periods of six months ending 30th April 1971, six months ending 31st October 1971 and three months ending 1st February 1972.

The Order reproduces, in the Schedule, section 1 of the 1971 Act with the effect of the Order incorporated in it, so as to indicate the cumulative increases payable under the Act and the Order.

The Order also provides for the payment, as a result of the review, of increases on certain lump sums of which payment was deferred and which became payable in the nine months ending with 1st July 1972.

STATUTORY INSTRUMENTS

1972 No. 1299

PENSIONS

The Pensions Increase (Reduction of Qualifying Age) Order 1972

Made - - -	18*th August* 1972
Laid before Parliament	25*th August* 1972
Coming into Operation	1*st December* 1972

The Minister for the Civil Service, in exercise of the powers conferred on him by section 3(8) of the Pensions (Increase) Act 1971(**a**) and of all other powers enabling him in that behalf, hereby makes the following Order:—

1. This Order may be cited as the Pensions Increase (Reduction of Qualifying Age) Order 1972, and shall come into operation on 1st December 1972.

2. The Interpretation Act 1889(**b**) shall apply for the interpretation of this Order as it applies for the interpretation of an Act of Parliament.

3. The age of sixty years referred to in subsections (2)(*a*) and (3)(*a*) of section 3 of the Pensions (Increase) Act 1971 (which lay down qualifying conditions for increases of pensions) shall be reduced to the age of fifty-five years.

Given under the official seal of the Minister for the Civil Service on 18th August 1972.

(L.S.)

A. W. Wyatt,
Authorised by the Minister
for the Civil Service.

EXPLANATORY NOTE
(This Note is not part of the Order.)
This Order provides for the reduction from 60 to 55 of the age at which a public service pensioner (or a dependant, other than the widow, of such a pensioner) whose pension is in payment may qualify for an increase of pension under the Pensions (Increase) Act 1971.

(**a**) 1971 c.56.   (**b**) 1889 c. 63.

STATUTORY INSTRUMENTS

1972 No. 1300

SOCIAL SECURITY

The National Insurance (Mariners) Amendment Regulations 1972

Made - - - -	16*th August* 1972
Laid before Parliament	1*st September* 1972
Coming into Operation	2*nd October* 1972

The Secretary of State for Social Services, in exercise of his powers under sections 4(4), 4(7), 14(1)(*a*) and 100 of the National Insurance Act 1965**(a)** and of all other powers enabling him in that behalf, and in conjunction with the Treasury so far as relates to matters with regard to which they have so directed, hereby makes the following regulations, which contain no provisions other than such as are made in consequence of the National Insurance Act 1972**(b)** and which accordingly by virtue of section 6(5) of, and paragraph 2(1)(*a*) of Schedule 4 to, that Act are exempt from the requirements of section 108 of the said Act of 1965 (reference to the National Insurance Advisory Committee), and which are made in consequence of the said Act of 1972 and which accordingly by virtue of section 6(5) of, and paragraph 2(2)(*a*) of Schedule 4 to, that Act are exempt from the requirements of section 107(1) of the said Act of 1965 (no regulations to be made wholly or partly by virtue of the provisions of section 100 of that Act unless a draft of the regulations has been approved by resolution of each House of Parliament):—

Citation, interpretation and commencement

1. These regulations, which may be cited as the National Insurance (Mariners) Amendment Regulations 1972, shall be read as one with the National Insurance (Mariners) Regulations 1967**(c)**, as amended **(d)** (hereinafter referred to as "the principal regulations"), and shall come into operation on 2nd October 1972.

Amendment of regulation 5 of the principal regulations

2. In regulation 5 of the principal regulations (contributions of mariners employed as masters or members of the crews of any ships or vessels other than home-trade ships)—

(*a*) in paragraph (1)(*a*) for the sum "£0·089" there shall be substituted the sum "£0·105";

(a) 1965 c. 51.   (b) 1972 c. 57.
(c) S.I. 1967/386 (1967 I, p. 1294).
(d) S.I. 1967/594, 1969/1277, 1970/46, 507, 977, 1971/1420 (1967 I, p. 1801; 1969 III, p. 3811; 1970 I, p. 243, 1713, II, p. 3089; 1971 II, p. 3983).

(b) in paragraph (1)(b) for the sum "£0·041" there shall be substituted the sum "£0·059".

Amendment of regulation 21 of the principal regulations

3. In regulation 21(2)(a) of the principal regulations (annual maximum)—

(a) in sub-head (viii) for the words "which ends on or after" there shall be substituted the words "which ends on" and for the amounts "£78·41" and "£77·91" there shall be substituted the amounts "£88·67" and "£88·17" respectively;

(b) after sub-head (viii) there shall be added the following sub-head:—

"(ix) which ends on or after 5th April 1974, shall, if the graduated contributions so paid in that year amount to £98·55 or more, be £98·05."

Substitution of Schedules 5 and 6 to the principal regulations

4. For the provisions of Schedule 5 and Schedule 6 to the principal regulations there shall be substituted the provisions set out in Schedule 1 and Schedule 2 to these regulations.

Transitory provisions

5. The graduated contributions payable in respect of any payment of remuneration—

(a) in respect of a voyage commencing before 2nd October 1972, which ends before 2nd January 1973, or in respect of any period of leave on pay immediately following such a voyage; or

(b) in respect of such part of a voyage ending on or after 2nd January 1973, as occurs before 2nd October 1972;

shall be calculated as if these regulations had not been made.

Signed by authority of the Secretary of State for Social Services.

Paul Dean,
Parliamentary Under-Secretary of State,
Department of Health and Social Security.

15th August 1972.

V. H. Goodhew,
Oscar Murton,

Two of the Lords Commissioners
of Her Majesty's Treasury.

16th August 1972.

Regulation 4　　　　　　　　SCHEDULE 1

Provisions to be substituted for Schedule 5 to the principal regulations

Regulation 18　　　　　　　SCHEDULE 5

EMPLOYMENT WHICH IS NOT A NON-PARTICIPATING EMPLOYMENT

PART 1

SCALE FOR PAY PERIOD OF A WEEK OR FOR A VOYAGE PERIOD FOR WHICH NO OR ONE WEEKLY EMPLOYER'S CONTRIBUTION IS PAYABLE

Amount of payment (1)	Amount of contribution (2)
£	£
9·01	0·01
9·25	0·02
9·50	0·04
10·00	0·06
10·50	0·08
11·00	0·11
11·50	0·13
12·00	0·15
12·50	0·18
13·00	0·20
13·50	0·23
14·00	0·25
14·50	0·27
15·00	0·30
15·50	0·32
16·00	0·34
16·50	0·37
17·00	0·39
17·50	0·42
18·00	0·45
19·00	0·50
20·00	0·55
21·00	0·59
22·00	0·64
23·00	0·69
24·00	0·74
25·00	0·78
26·00	0·83
27·00	0·88
28·00	0·93
29·00	0·97
30·00	1·02
31·00	1·07
32·00	1·12
33·00	1·16
34·00	1·21
35·00	1·26
36·00	1·31
37·00	1·35
38·00	1·40

Amount of payment (1)	Amount of contribution (2)
£	£
39·00	1·45
40·00	1·50
41·00	1·54
42·00	1·59
43·00	1·64
44·00	1·69
45·00	1·73
46·00	1·78
47·00	1·83
48·00 or more	1·85

PART II

SCALE FOR PAY PERIOD OF ONE MONTH

Amount of payment (1)	Amount of contribution (2)
£	£
39·02	0·02
40·00	0·09
42·00	0·19
44·00	0·28
46·00	0·38
48·00	0·47
50·00	0·57
52·00	0·66
54·00	0·76
56·00	0·85
58·00	0·95
60·00	1·04
62·00	1·14
64·00	1·23
66·00	1·33
68·00	1·42
70·00	1·52
72·00	1·61
74·00	1·71
76·00	1·80
78·00	1·95
82·00	2·14
86·00	2·33
90·00	2·52

Amount of payment (1)	Amount of contribution (2)
£	£
94·00	2·71
98·00	2·90
102·00	3·09
106·00	3·28
110·00	3·47
114·00	3·66
118·00	3·85
122·00	4·04
126·00	4·23
130·00	4·42
134·00	4·61
138·00	4·80
142·00	4·99
146·00	5·18
150·00	5·37
154·00	5·56
158·00	5·75
162.00	5·94
166·00	6·13
170·00	6·32
174·00	6·51
178·00	6·70
182·00	6·89
186·00	7·08
190·00	7·27
194·00	7·46
198·00	7·65
202·00	7·84
206·00	7·98
208·00 or more	8·03

SCHEDULE 2   Regulation 4

Provisions to be substituted for Schedule 6 to the principal regulations

SCHEDULE 6   Regulation 18

NON-PARTICIPATING EMPLOYMENT

PART I

SCALE FOR PAY PERIOD OF A WEEK OR FOR A VOYAGE PERIOD FOR WHICH NO OR ONE WEEKLY
EMPLOYER'S CONTRIBUTION IS PAYABLE

Amount of payment (1)	Amount of contribution (2)
£	£
9·01	0·01
12·00	0·02
15·00	0·04
18·00	0·07
19·00	0·12
20·00	0·16
21·00	0·21
22·00	0·26
23·00	0·31
24·00	0·35
25·00	0·40
26·00	0·45
27·00	0·50
28·00	0·54
29·00	0·59
30·00	0·64
31·00	0·69
32·00	0·73
33·00	0·78
34·00	0·83
35·00	0·88
36·00	0·92
37·00	0·97
38·00	1·02
39·00	1·07
40·00	1·11
41·00	1·16
42·00	1·21
43·00	1·26
44·00	1·30
45·00	1·35
46·00	1·40
47·00	1·45
48·00 or more	1·47

Part II

SCALE FOR PAY PERIOD OF ONE MONTH

Amount of payment (1)	Amount of contribution (2)
£	£
39·01	0·01
40·00	0·03
50·00	0·08
60·00	0·13
70·00	0·17
78·00	0·29
82·00	0·48
86·00	0·67
90·00	0·86
94·00	1·05
98·00	1·24
102·00	1·43
106·00	1·62
110·00	1·81
114·00	2·00
118·00	2·19
122·00	2·38
126·00	2·57
130·00	2·76
134·00	2·95
138·00	3·14
142·00	3·33
146·00	3·52
150·00	3·71
154·00	3·90
158·00	4·09
162·00	4·28
166·00	4·47
170·00	4·66
174·00	4·85
178·00	5·04
182·00	5·23
186·00	5·42
190·00	5·61
194·00	5·80
198·00	5·99
202·00	6·18
206·00	6·32
208·00	6·37
or more	

EXPLANATORY NOTE
(This Note is not part of the Regulations.)

These Regulations contain no provisions other than such as are made in consequence of the National Insurance Act 1972 and accordingly, by virtue of paragraph 2 of Schedule 4 to that Act, no reference of them has been made to the National Insurance Advisory Committee, nor has a draft of the Regulations been laid before Parliament for approval by resolution of each House.

The Regulations amend the provisions of the National Insurance (Mariners) Regulations 1967 relating to reduction of flat-rate contributions payable in respect of certain mariners (regulation 2); relating to the annual maximum amount payable by way of graduated contributions (regulation 3); and relating to seamen's liability for graduated contributions and their assessment and calculation (regulation 4 and Schedules 1 and 2). The Regulations also contain a transitory provision relating to the calculation of graduated contributions (regulation 5).

STATUTORY INSTRUMENTS

1972 No. 1301

SOCIAL SECURITY

The National Insurance (Unemployment and Sickness Benefit and Miscellaneous Amendments) Regulations 1972

Made - - -	*16th August* 1972
Laid before Parliament	*1st September* 1972
Coming into Operation	*2nd October* 1972

The National Insurance Joint Authority, in exercise of powers conferred by section 20(2)(*a*) of the National Insurance Act 1965(**a**) as amended by section 14 of, and paragraph 3(*b*) of Schedule 5 to, the National Insurance Act 1971(**b**), and the Secretary of State for Social Services, in conjunction with the Treasury so far as relates to matters with regard to which the Treasury have so directed, in exercise of his powers under sections 48(1), 75(2) and 81(3) of the said Act of 1965 and section 11(1)(*a*)—(*d*) of the National Insurance Act 1966(**c**), as amended by section 6(1) of the National Insurance Act 1972(**d**), in each case in exercise of all other powers enabling them in that behalf, hereby make the following regulations which, as they are made before the expiration of six months beginning with the passing of the said Act of 1972 and contain no provisions other than such as are made in consequence of the said Act of 1972 or operate with reference to the amount of a person's earnings under section 20(2) of the said Act of 1965, are exempt from the requirements of section 108 of the said Act of 1965 (reference to the National Insurance Advisory Committee) by virtue of paragraph 2(1) of Schedule 4 to the said Act of 1972:—

Citation, commencement and interpretation

1.—(1) These regulations, which may be cited as the National Insurance (Unemployment and Sickness Benefit and Miscellaneous Amendments) Regulations 1972, shall come into operation on 2nd October 1972.

(**a**) 1965 c. 51.   (**b**) 1971 c. 50.
(**c**) 1966 c. 6.   (**d**) 1972 c. 57.

(2) The rules for construction of Acts of Parliament contained in the Interpretation Act 1889(a) shall apply in relation to this instrument and in relation to any revocation effected by it as if this instrument and the regulations revoked by it were Acts of Parliament and as if each revocation were a repeal.

Amendments of the National Insurance (Unemployment and Sickness Benefit) Regulations 1967

2. In regulation 7 of the National Insurance (Unemployment and Sickness Benefit) Regulations 1967(b), as amended (c) (days not to be treated as days of unemployment or incapacity for work),—

(*a*) in paragraph (1)(*h*) for the words "are ordinarily less than £2·00 a week" there shall be substituted the words "are ordinarily not more than £4·50 a week"; and

(*b*) in paragraph (1)(*i*) for the words "do not exceed 33½ new pence" there shall be substituted the words "do not exceed 75 pence".

Amendments of the National Insurance and Industrial Injuries (Miscellaneous and Consequential Provisions) Regulations 1966

3. In regulation 2 of the National Insurance and Industrial Injuries (Miscellaneous and Consequential Provisions) Regulations 1966(d), as amended (e) (forward allowances and disallowances of sickness benefit and injury benefit),—

(*a*) in paragraph (1)(*a*), after the words "sickness benefit" there shall be inserted the words "or invalidity benefit";

(*b*) in paragraphs (1)(*c*) and (2), after the words "sickness benefit" there shall be inserted the words "invalidity benefit"; and

(*c*) after paragraph (3) there shall be inserted the following paragraph:—

"(4) Where a claim for invalidity benefit is disallowed on the ground that—

(*a*) the contribution condition in section 3(2) of the National Insurance Act 1971(f) has not been satisfied, or

(*b*) the claimant has not been entitled to sickness benefit for 168 days in the relevant period of interruption of employment,

the decision disallowing that claim shall, subject to the provisions of section 72 of the Act (review of decisions of insurance officer, local tribunal or Commissioner), be treated as a decision disallowing any further claim (being a continuation claim within the meaning of paragraph 2(*c*) of column (1) of Schedule 2 to the National

---

(a) 1889 c. 63.　　　　　　　　　　(b) S.I. 1967/330 (1967 I, p. 1131).
(c) The relevant amending instrument is S.I. 1970/46 (1970 I, p. 243).
(d) S.I. 1966/1006 (1966 II, p. 2403).
(e) There is no amendment which relates expressly to the subject matter of these regulations.
(f) 1971 c. 50.

Insurance (Claims and Payments) Regulations 1971(**a**), as amended (**b**)) by that person for that benefit until the grounds for the original disallowance have ceased to exist.".

Amendment of the National Insurance (Determination of Claims and Questions) (No. 2) *Regulations* 1967

4. In regulation 15 of the National Insurance (Determination of Claims and Questions) (No. 2) Regulations 1967(**c**), as amended (**d**) (review of decisions involving payment or increase of benefit), for sub-paragraph (*d*) of paragraph (2) there shall be substituted the following sub-paragraph:—

"(*d*) The provisions of paragraph (2)(*a*) shall not apply to the review of a decision disallowing a claim for sickness benefit, invalidity benefit or unemployment benefit in so far as it is a decision which, under the provisions of regulation 2(3), regulation 2(4) or regulation 2A of the National Insurance and Industrial Injuries (Miscellaneous and Consequential Provisions) Regulations 1966, has been treated as a decision disallowing a further claim for any of those benefits."

Revocation of regulations

5. The regulations specified in column (1) of the Schedule to these regulations are hereby revoked to the extent mentioned in column (3) of that Schedule.

Given under the official seal of the National Insurance Joint Authority.

(L.S.)

F. B. Hindmarsh,
A person authorised by the
National Insurance Joint Authority
to act on behalf of the Secretary,
National Insurance Joint
Authority.

11th August 1972.

Keith Joseph,
Secretary of State for Social Services.

14th August 1972.

V. H. Goodhew,
Oscar Murton,
Two of the Lords Commissioners of
Her Majesty's Treasury.

16th August 1972.

(**a**) S.I. 1971/707 (1971 I, p. 1908).
(**b**) There is no amendment which relates expressly to the subject matter of these regulations.
(**c**) S.I. 1967/1570 (1967 III, p. 4350).
(**d**) The relevant amending instruments are S.I. 1971/1419, 1972/166, (1971 II, p. 3964; 1972 I, p. 588).

SCHEDULE   Regulation 5.

Regulations revoked (1)	Reference (2)	Extent of revocation (3)
The Family Allowances, National Insurance, Industrial Injuries and Miscellaneous Provisions (Decimalisation of the Currency) Regulations 1970.	S.I. 1970/46 (1970 I, p. 243).	Regulation 7(1).
The National Insurance (General Benefit and Claims and Payments) Amendment Regulations 1971.	S.I. 1971/1478 (1971 III, p. 4155).	The whole regulations.
The National Insurance (Claims and Payments and Miscellaneous Provisions) Regulations 1972.	S.I. 1972/166 (1972 I, p. 588).	Regulation 5.

EXPLANATORY NOTE

(This Note is not part of the Regulations.)

These Regulations, having been made before the expiration of six months beginning with the passing of the National Insurance Act 1972 and containing no provisions other than such as are made in consequence of the said Act of 1972 or operate with reference to the amount of a person's earnings under section 20(2) of the National Insurance Act 1965, are not required to be, and have not been, referred to the National Insurance Advisory Committee.

Regulation 1 is formal; regulation 2 amends regulation 7 of the National Insurance (Unemployment and Sickness Benefit) Regulations 1967 by increasing the unemployment benefit subsidiary occupation earnings limit and the earnings limit for permitted work for sickness and invalidity benefit purposes; regulation 3 amends regulation 2 of the National Insurance and Industrial Injuries (Miscellaneous and Consequential Provisions) Regulations 1966 making provision for claims and decisions relating to invalidity benefit to operate prospectively; regulation 4 amends regulation 15 of the National Insurance (Determination of Claims and Questions) (No. 2) Regulations 1967 (review of decisions involving payment or increase of benefit) in consequence of the amendment to the 1966 Regulations effected by regulation 3 of these Regulations; and regulation 5 and the Schedule relate to revocations of regulations.

STATUTORY INSTRUMENTS

1972 No. 1302

SOCIAL SECURITY

The National Insurance (Increase of Benefit and Miscellaneous Provisions) Regulations 1972

Made - - -	*16th August* 1972
Laid before Parliament	*1st September* 1972
Coming into Operation	*2nd October* 1972

The National Insurance Joint Authority, in exercise of powers conferred by sections 45 and 50(1)(*a*) of the National Insurance Act 1965(**a**), and the Secretary of State for Social Services, in exercise of his powers under section 49 of and paragraphs 17 and 18 of Schedule 11 to that Act, paragraph 3 of Schedule 6 to the National Insurance Act 1969(**b**) and section 1 of the National Insurance Act 1970(**c**), and of all other powers enabling them in that behalf, and in conjunction with the Treasury so far as relates to matters with regard to which the Treasury have so directed, hereby make the following regulations, which contain no provisions other than such as are made in consequence of the National Insurance Act 1972(**d**) and which accordingly, by virtue of paragraph 2(1)(*a*) of Part I of Schedule 4 to that Act, are exempt from the requirements of section 108 of the National Insurance Act 1965 (reference to the National Insurance Advisory Committee):—

Citation, commencement and interpretation

1.—(1) These regulations may be cited as the National Insurance (Increase of Benefit and Miscellaneous Provisions) Regulations 1972, and shall come into operation on 2nd October 1972.

(2) In these regulations, unless the context otherwise requires—

"the principal Act" means the National Insurance Act 1965;

"the Act of 1971" means the National Insurance Act 1971(**e**);

"the Act of 1972" means the National Insurance Act 1972;

and other expressions have the same meanings as in the principal Act.

(3) References in these regulations to any enactment or regulation shall, except in so far as the context otherwise requires, be construed as references to that enactment or regulation as amended or extended by or under any other enactment, order or regulation.

(4) The rules for the construction of Acts of Parliament contained in the Interpretation Act 1889(**f**) shall apply for the purpose of the interpretation of these regulations as they apply for the purpose of the interpretation of an Act of Parliament.

(**a**) 1965 c. 51.	(**b**) 1969 c. 44.
(**c**) 1970 c. 51.	(**d**) 1972 c. 57.
(**e**) 1971 c. 50.	(**f**) 1889 c. 63.

Higher rates and amounts of benefit payable under regulations

2. Subject to the provisions of regulations 5 and 6 of these regulations, as from the dates specified in Schedule A column 1 of these regulations there shall be substituted for each of the Tables mentioned in column 2 thereof the Table mentioned in the Schedule set opposite thereto in column 3.

Miscellaneous amendments relating to benefit and to contributions

3.—(1) As from the dates specified in Schedule J column 1 of these regulations, there shall in the regulations mentioned in column 2 thereof be made the amendments specified against those regulations mentioned in columns 3 and 4 thereof.

(2) As from 2nd October 1972, Schedule 2 to the National Insurance (New Entrants Transitional) Regulations 1949(**a**), as amended(**b**) (amounts payable, by way of refund of contributions, to persons entering insurance too late to be able to satisfy contribution conditions for widow's benefit or retirement pension), shall be amended by the addition thereto, at the end, of the provisions set out in Schedule K to these regulations.

Conditions relating to payment of additional benefit under awards made before the appointed or prescribed day

4. Where an award of any benefit under the principal Act has been made before the day appointed or prescribed for the payment of benefit of the description to which the award relates at a higher weekly rate by virtue of the Act of 1972 or of these regulations, paragraphs 2 and 3 of Schedule 6 to the National Insurance Act 1969(**c**) (effect of any such award) shall, if the period to which the award relates has not ended before that day, have effect subject to the condition that, if the award has not been made in accordance with the provisions of sub-paragraph (2) of the said paragraph 3 (which sub-paragraph authorises the making of such an award providing for the payment of the benefit at the higher weekly rate as from that day) and a question arises as to—

(*a*) the weekly rate at which the benefit is payable by virtue of the Act of 1972 or of these regulations, or

(*b*) whether the conditions for the receipt of the benefit at the higher weekly rate are satisfied,

the benefit shall be or continue to be payable at the weekly rate specified in the award until the said question shall have been determined in accordance with the provisions of the principal Act.

Persons not ordinarily resident in Great Britain

5.—(1) Notwithstanding the provisions of these or any other regulations, but subject to the provisions of this regulation, a person who is not ordinarily resident in Great Britain immediately before 2nd October 1972 (in this regulation referred to as "the said date") shall, unless and until that person becomes ordinarily resident in Great Britain, be disqualified for receiving—

(*a*) in the case of a woman who immediately before the said date is a married woman and had not retired from regular employment, any additional retirement pension by virtue of her husband's insurance, if the husband before the said date had retired from regular employment and was not ordinarily resident in Great Britain;

(*b*) in the case of a woman who immediately before the said date is a

---

(a) S.I. 1949/352 (1949 I, p. 2737).
(b) As last amended by S.I. 1971/1220 (1971 II, p. 3556).   (c) 1969 c. 44.

widow, any additional retirement pension by virtue of her husband's insurance, if her husband had died before the said date;

(c) in any other case, any additional retirement pension (not being additional retirement pension to which either of the two foregoing subparagraphs applies) if that person had retired from regular employment before the said date;

(d) any additional widow's benefit if her husband had died or retired before the said date;

(e) any additional child's special allowance if her former husband had died before the said date.

(2) Notwithstanding as aforesaid, if immediately before the said date a person is not ordinarily resident in Great Britain but that person has, or would, but for the absence of any child from Great Britain, have in his family immediately before the said date a child in relation to whom the conditions for guardian's allowance specified in section 29 of the principal Act are satisfied, that person and any other person who would otherwise be entitled to any additional guardian's allowance in respect of that child shall be disqualified for receiving any additional guardian's allowance in respect of that child unless and until the child becomes (or is) included in the family of a person who is ordinarily resident in Great Britain.

(3) The disqualifications for the receipt of additional benefit contained in this regulation shall not apply to a person for any period during which he is in Great Britain.

(4) For the purposes of this regulation references to additional benefit of any description are to be construed as referring to additional benefit of that description by virtue (either directly or indirectly) of any provision of the Act of 1972 or of these regulations.

(5) A widow who—

(a) is not ordinarily resident in Great Britain immediately before the said date, and was entitled to widow's benefit immediately before attaining pensionable age, or who would, but for any provision of the principal Act disqualifying her for the receipt of such benefit, have been so entitled; and

(b) is or becomes entitled to a retirement pension by virtue of her own insurance the right to which is calculated by taking into account under section 33 of the principal Act her husband's contributions;

shall be disqualified for receiving any additional retirement pension the right to which is so calculated unless and until she becomes ordinarily resident in Great Britain if—

(i) her husband died before the said date; or

(ii) before the said date he had retired from regular employment and was not ordinarily resident in Great Britain.

(6) The provisions of paragraph 3(1) of Part II of Schedule 6 to the National Insurance Act 1969(a) shall apply where, notwithstanding the foregoing provisions of this regulation, benefit of an amount higher than the amount awarded to a person has in fact been paid to him.

(7) The disqualification for the receipt of additional retirement pension contained in paragraph (1)(c) of this regulation shall not apply to a woman

---

(a) 1969 c. 44.

in relation to a retirement pension by virtue of her husband's insurance, if that husband had not retired from regular employment before the said date and either—

    (i) he was her husband immediately before that date; or

    (ii) she married him on or after that date.

Transitory provision

6. As respects the period beginning on 2nd October 1972 and ending on 4th October 1972, the rate of a person's unemployment or sickness benefit for any day in the said period payable by virtue of section 19(3) of the principal Act or invalidity pension payable by virtue of section 3(4) of the Act of 1971 (unemployment benefit, sickness benefit and invalidity pension for persons over pensionable age) shall be determined as if the day from which higher rates of retirement pension are payable by virtue of the foregoing provisions of these regulations were 5th October 1972.

Given under the official seal of the National Insurance Joint Authority.

(L.S.)

                        F. B. Hindmarsh,
           A person authorised by the
             National Insurance Joint
      Authority to act on behalf of the
        Secretary, National Insurance
              Joint Authority.

11th August 1972.

                        Keith Joseph,
    Secretary of State for Social Services.

14th August 1972.

                        V. H. Goodhew,
                    Oscar Murton,
      Two of the Lords Commissioners
        of Her Majesty's Treasury.

16th August 1972.

Regulation 2 SCHEDULE A

Date of operation	Existing table	Schedule containing substituted table
1	2	3
5th October 1972	The National Insurance (Unemployment and Sickness Benefit) Regulations 1967**(a)** Table contained in Schedule 2 as amended **(b)**	Schedule B
2nd October 1972	The National Insurance (Maternity Benefit and Miscellaneous Provisions) Regulations 1954**(c)** Table contained in regulation 13 as amended**(d)**	Schedule C
2nd October 1972	The National Insurance (Widow's Benefit and Retirement Pensions) Regulations 1972**(e)** Table contained in Schedule 1	Schedule D
2nd October 1972	The National Insurance (Pensions, Existing Beneficiaries and Other Persons) (Transitional) Regulations 1948**(f)** Table contained in Schedule 1 as amended**(g)**	Schedule E
	Table contained in Schedule 2 as amended**(h)**	Schedule F
	Table contained in Schedule 3 as amended**(i)**	Schedule G
2nd October 1972	The National Insurance (Pensions, Existing Contributors) (Transitional) Regulations 1948**(j)** Table contained in Schedule 2 as amended**(k)**	Schedule H
	Tables contained in Schedule 5 Part III as amended **(l)**	Schedule I

(a) S.I. 1967/330 (1967 I, p. 1131).
(b) As amended by reg. 2 of and Schedules A and B to S.I. 1971/1220 (1971 II, p.3556).
(c) S.I. 1954/189 (1954 I, p. 1387).
(d) As last amended by reg. 2 of and Schedules A and C to S.I. 1971/1220 (1971 II, p.3556).
(e) S.I. 1972/606 (1972 I, p. 2011).
(f) S.I. 1948/55 (Rev. XVI, p. 36: 1948 I, p. 2822).
(g) As last amended by reg. 2 of and Schedules A and E to S.I. 1971/1220 (1971 II, p.3556).
(h) As last amended by reg. 2 of and Schedules A and F to S.I. 1971/1220 (1971 II, p.3556).
(i) As last amended by reg. 2 of and Schedules A and G to S.I. 1971/1220 (1971 II, p.3556).
(j) S.I. 1948/612 (Rev. XVI, p. 18: 1948 I, p. 2834).
(k) As last amended by reg. 2 of and Schedules A and H to S.I. 1971/1220 (1971 II, p.3556).
(l) As last amended by reg. 2 of and Schedules A and I to S.I. 1971/1220 (1971 II, p.3556).

SCHEDULE B   Regulation 2

(1)	(2)	(3)	(4)	(5)
Number of contributions paid or credited in the relevant contribution year	Full weekly rate of benefit applicable under Schedule 3 to the Act			
	£ 6·75	£ 4·75	£ 4·15	£ 3·70
	Reduced rate at which benefit is payable			
	£	£	£	£
48—49	6·48	4·67	4·00	3·57
46—47	6·21	4·53	3·85	3·44
43—45	5·94	4·26	3·67	3·31
40—42	5·45	3·98	3·41	3·09
37—39	4·94	3·58	3·15	2·83
34—36	4·43	3·20	2·81	2·59
30—33	3·91	2·84	2·46	2·29
26—29	3·38	2·38	2·08	1·85

SCHEDULE C   Regulation 2

Numbers including the number of contributions paid or credited in respect of the relevant period	Weekly rate	
	Of maternity allowance without increase	Of increase in respect of adult dependant
1	2	3
	£	£
48—49	6·48	4·00
46—47	6·21	3·85
43—45	5·94	3·67
40—42	5·45	3·41
37—39	4·94	3·15
34—36	4·43	2·81
30—33	3·91	2·46
26—29	3·38	2·08

Regulation 2   SCHEDULE D

1	2	3	4
	Full weekly rate of benefit applicable under Schedule 3 to the National Insurance Act 1965		
Yearly average of contributions paid or credited	£ 9·45	£ 6·75	£ 4·15
	Reduced rate at which benefit payable		
	£	£	£
48—49	9·06	6·48	4·00
46—47	8·67	6·21	3·85
43—45	8·21	5·94	3·67
40—42	7·63	5·45	3·41
37—39	6·95	4·94	3·15
34—36	6·21	4·43	2·81
30—33	5·47	3·91	2·46
26—29	4·73	3·38	2·08
22—25	4·00	2·88	1·74
18—21	3·29	2·36	1·43
13—17	2·52	1·89	1·20

Regulation 2   SCHEDULE E

Rate of widow's basic pension or contributory old age pension by virtue of husband's insurance and rate (apart from additional allowance or increase) of widow's pension immediately before the appointed day 1	Corresponding rate of widowed mother's allowance, widow's pension or retirement pension for a widow by virtue of husband's insurance 2	Corresponding increased rate of widow's basic pension or of contributory old age pension by virtue of husband's insurance 3
s d	£	£
9 0	6·08	1·86
8 0	5·39	1·64
7 0	4·73	1·41
6 0	4·05	1·17
5 0	3·38	1·01
4 0	—	0·86
3 0	—	0·63
2 0	—	0·45

SCHEDULE F

Regulation 2

Rate of retirement pension 1	Corresponding rate of increase in respect of an adult dependant or of retirement pension for a wife 2
£	£
6·08	3·74
5·58	3·41
5·39	3·34
4·94	2·98
4·73	2·92
4·43	2·75
4·05	2·46
3·91	2·40
3·69	2·34
3·38	2·08
3·04	1·98
2·88	1·78
2·70	1·74
2·54	1·65
2·36	1·51
2·27	1·31
2·03	1·27
1·89	1·20
1·69	1·07
1·60	0·94
1·35	0·81
1·22	0·81
1·01	0·71
0·92	0·50
0·74	0·50
0·61	0·47
0·59	0·40

Regulation 2   SCHEDULE G

Rate at which an old age or widow's pension would, apart from the Increase of Pensions Regulations and but for the repeal of the Contributory Pensions Acts, have been payable	Rate of retirement pension (except in a case where column 4 applies) being the rate at which an old age or widow's pension would, but for the repeal of the Contributory Pensions Acts, have been payable	Corresponding increased rate of retirement pension	Rate of retirement pension for wife by virtue of husband's insurance, where he is alive, being the rate at which an old age pension would, but for the repeal of the Contributory Pensions Acts, have been payable	Corresponding increased rate of retirement pension
1	2	3	4	5
s. d.	£ s. d.	£	s. d.	£
9 0	1 3 0	6·08	14 0	3·74
8 3	1 1 0	5·58	12 6	3·41
8 0	1 0 0	5·39	12 0	3·34
7 3	18 6	4·94	11 0	2·98
7 0	18 0	4·73	11 0	2·92
6 6	16 6	4·43	10 0	2·75
6 0	15 0	4·05	9 0	2·46
5 9	14 6	3·91	9 0	2·40
5 6	14 0	3·69	8 6	2·34
5 0	13 0	3·38	8 0	2·08
4 6	11 6	3·04	7 0	1·98
4 3	11 0	2·88	6 6	1·78
4 0	10 0	2·70	6 0	1·74
3 9	9 6	2·54	6 0	1·65
3 6	9 0	2·36	5 6	1·51
3 3	8 6	2·27	5 0	1·31
3 0	8 0	2·03	5 0	1·27
2 9	7 0	1·89	4 6	1·20
2 6	6 6	1·69	4 0	1·07
2 3	6 0	1·60	3 6	0·94
2 0	5 0	1·35	3 0	0·81
1 9	4 6	1·22	3 0	0·81
1 6	4 0	1·01	2 6	0·71
1 3	3 6	0·92	2 0	0·50
1 0	3 0	0·74	2 0	0·50
9	2 0	0·61	1 6	0·47
6	1 6	0·59	1 0	0·40

SCHEDULE H   Regulation 2

Yearly average of contributions paid or credited 1	Reduced rate at which pension is payable 2
	£
48—49	1·94
46—47	1·86
43—45	1·78
40—42	1·64
37—39	1·48
34—36	1·33
30—33	1·17
26—29	1·01
22—25	0·86
18—21	0·71
13—17	0·57

SCHEDULE I   Regulation 2

TABLE 1

Rate at which an old age pension would, but for the repeal of the Contributory Pensions Acts, have been payable 1	Corresponding rate of retirement pension where pensionable age attained during period:—				
	From 5 July 1948 to 4 July 1949 2	From 5 July 1949 to 4 July 1950 3	From 5 July 1950 to 4 July 1951 4	From 5 July 1951 to 4 July 1952 5	From 5 July 1952 to 4 July 1953 6
£ s. d.	£	£	£	£	£
1 3 0	6·21	6·21	6·48	6·48	6·48
1 0 0	5·58	5·78	6·08	6·21	6·48
18 0	5·00	5·39	5·78	6·21	6·48
15 0	4·19	4·73	5·58	6·08	6·48
13 0	3·69	4·50	5·39	5·78	6·48
10 0	3·29	4·05	4·73	5·58	6·21
8 0	2·70	3·38	4·50	5·58	6·21
5 0	1·89	2·88	4·19	5·39	6·21
3 0	1·35	2·70	4·05	5·00	6·21
— —	0·74	2·03	3·38	4·73	6·08

TABLE 2

Corresponding rates of retirement pensions

Yearly average of contributions paid or credited																				
1	2	3	4	5	6	7	8	9	10	11	12	13	14	15	16	17	18	19	20	21
£	£	£	£	£	£	£	£	£	£	£	£	£	£	£	£	£	£	£	£	£
0·74	0·74	1·35	1·89	2·03	2·70	2·88	3·29	3·38	3·69	4·05	4·19	4·50	4·73	5·00	5·39	5·58	5·78	6·08	6·21	6·48
48–49	0·72	1·22	1·69	1·94	2·54	2·75	3·04	3·31	3·62	3·91	4·10	4·43	4·66	4·94	5·06	5·39	5·58	5·78	6·08	6·21
46–47	0·72	1·22	1·69	1·94	2·36	2·70	2·88	3·29	3·38	3·69	4·05	4·19	4·50	4·73	5·00	5·06	5·39	5·58	5·78	6·08
43–45	0·72	1·22	1·60	1·89	2·27	2·54	2·75	3·04	3·31	3·62	3·69	4·05	4·19	4·50	4·73	4·94	5·06	5·39	5·58	5·78
40–42	0·72	1·01	1·40	1·69	2·03	2·36	2·70	2·75	3·04	3·31	3·38	3·62	3·91	4·10	4·43	4·50	4·73	4·94	5·00	5·39
37–39	0·61	0·92	1·35	1·60	1·94	2·03	2·36	2·54	2·75	3·04	3·31	3·38	3·69	4·05	4·10	4·43	4·50	4·73	4·94	4·94
34–36	0·61	0·92	1·22	1·35	1·69	1·89	2·03	2·27	2·54	2·75	3·04	3·29	3·31	3·38	3·69	3·62	4·10	3·91	4·05	4·43
30–33	0·59	0·74	1·01	1·22	1·60	1·69	1·89	1·94	2·03	2·54	2·36	2·88	2·70	2·75	3·29	3·29	3·31	3·38	3·62	3·91
26–29	0·59	0·72	0·92	1·01	1·35	1·40	1·60	1·69	1·89	1·94	2·03	2·54	2·27	2·36	2·54	2·70	2·75	2·88	3·04	3·31
22–25	0·59	0·61	0·74	0·92	1·01	1·22	1·40	1·35	1·60	1·60	1·94	1·89	1·89	1·94	2·03	2·27	2·36	2·54	2·54	2·75
18–21	0·41	0·59	0·72	0·74	0·92	1·01	1·22	1·01	1·40	1·35	1·60	1·40	1·60	1·60	1·69	1·89	1·94	2·03	2·03	2·27
13–17	0·41	0·59	0·61	0·61	0·72	0·74	0·74	0·92	1·01	1·01	1·22	1·22	1·35	1·35	1·35	1·40	1·40	1·60	1·60	1·69

TABLE 3

Rate of retirement pension	Corresponding rate of increase in respect of an adult dependant or of retirement pension for a wife	Rate of retirement pension	Corresponding rate of increase in respect of an adult dependant or of retirement pension for a wife
1	2	3	4
£	£	£	£
6·48	4·00	3·04	1·98
6·21	3·80	2·88	1·78
6·08	3·74	2·75	1·78
5·78	3·61	2·70	1·74
5·58	3·41	2·54	1·65
5·39	3·34	2·36	1·51
5·06	3·15	2·27	1·31
5·00	3·08	2·03	1·27
4·94	2·98	1·94	1·20
4·73	2·92	1·89	1·20
4·66	2·81	1·69	1·07
4·50	2·75	1·60	0·94
4·43	2·75	1·40	0·94
4·19	2·51	1·35	0·81
4·10	2·51	1·22	0·81
4·05	2·46	1·01	0·71
3·91	2·40	0·92	0·50
3·69	2·34	0·74	0·50
3·62	2·14	0·72	0·47
3·38	2·08	0·61	0·47
3·31	2·02	0·59	0·40
3·29	2·02	0·41	0·34

SCHEDULE J   Regulation 3(1)

Date of operation	Regulations amended	Amendments	
		There shall be substituted for the expressions specified in column 3 (wherever they occur) the expressions specified in column 4	
1	2	3	4
1. 2nd October 1972	The National Insurance (Pensions, Existing Beneficiaries and Other Persons) (Transitional) Regulations 1948 regulations 9(3) and 10 as amended(a) (Rates of converted retirement pension for existing beneficiaries, of increase of retirement pension in respect of adult dependants, and of retirement pension for wives of certain existing beneficiaries)		

(a) The relevant amending instruments are S.I. 1951/1232, 1957/1950, 1965/40, 1969/1361, 1970/46, 1971/1220 (1951 I, p. 1457; 1957 I, p. 1704; 1965 I, p. 47; 1969 III, p. 4048; 1970 I, p. 243; 1971 II, p. 3556).

SCHEDULE J—(*continued*)

Date of operation	Regulations amended	Amendments	
		There shall be substituted for the expressions specified in column 3 (wherever they occur) the expressions specified in column 4	
1	2	3	4
	Regulation 9(3) proviso	20th September 1971 £6·00 £3·70	2nd October 1972 £6·75 £4·15
	Regulation 10(1)	£6·00	£6·75
	Regulation 10(2) proviso(a)	20th September 1971	2nd October 1972
2. 2nd October 1972	The National Insurance (Pensions, Existing Contributors) (Transitional) Regulations 1948 (Rates of benefit for certain widows over the age of 50 on the appointed day who are existing contributors)		
	Regulation 11(4)(*a*) as amended(a)	£6·00	£6·75
3. The date in relation to any benefit under the principal Act as from which the weekly rate of that benefit is increased by virtue of the Act of 1972 or of these Regulations	The National Insurance (Hospital In-Patients) Regulations 1972(b) regulations 3, 4, 5 and 7 (Reduction in certain circumstances of weekly rates of benefit in the case of hospital in-patients)		
	Regulation 3(3)	£1·45 £1·20	£1·60 £1·35
	Regulation 4	£1·20 £2·40	£1·35 £2·70
	Regulation 5(1)	£1·45 £1·20	£1·60 £1·35
	Regulation 5(2)	£2·65 £2·40 £1·20	£2·95 £2·70 £1·35
	Regulation 5(3)(*a*)	£2·40	£2·70
	Regulation 5(3)(*b*)	£3·85 £3·60	£4·30 £4·05
	Regulation 5(4)(*c*)	£1·45 £1·20	£1·60 £1·35
	Regulation 5(4)(*d*)	£3·50	£3·95

(a) As last amended by regulation 3(1) and Schedule J of S.I. 1971/1220 (1971 II, p. 3556).
(b) S.I. 1972/603 (1972 I, p. 1979).

SCHEDULE J—(*continued*)

Date of operation	Regulations amended	Amendments	
		There shall be substituted for the expressions specified in column 3 (wherever they occur) the expressions specified in column 4	
1	2	3	4
	Regulation 7(3) and (4)	£1·20 £1·45 £2·65 £2·40	£1·35 £1·60 £2·95 £2·70
4. 2nd October 1972	The National Insurance (Hospital In-Patients) Regulations 1972		
	(Benefit payable on discharge from a hospital or similar institution)		
	Regulation 8(2)	£9·00	£10·00
5. 2nd October 1972	The National Insurance (New Entrants Transitional Regulations 1949(a)		
	(Modification of provisions of the Act relating to retirement pensions in the case of certain widows)		
	Regulation 5(2)(*a*) as amended(b)	£6·00	£6·75
6. 2nd October 1972	The National Insurance (Old Persons' Pensions) Regulations 1970(c)		
	(Rates of benefit for or in respect of persons over pensionable age on 5th July 1948)		
	Regulation 7 as amended(d)	£3·60	£4·05

(a) S.I. 1949/352 (1949 I, p. 2737).
(b) As last amended by regulation 3(1) and Schedule J of S.I. 1971/1220 (1971 II, p. 3556).
(c) S.I. 1970/1280 (1970 II, p. 4168).
(d) The relevant amending instrument is S.I. 1971/1220 (1971 II, p. 3556).

SCHEDULE K

Regulation 3(2)

PROVISIONS TO BE ADDED TO SCHEDULE 2 TO THE NATIONAL INSURANCE (NEW ENTRANTS TRANSITIONAL) REGULATIONS 1949

10. Applicable (in substitution for the provisions of paragraph 9 of this Schedule) to contributions in respect of contribution weeks commencing on or after 2nd October 1972.

	MEN				WOMEN		
Age of man at expiration of period of currency of contribution card on which contribution was paid	Employed	Self-employed	Non-employed	Age of woman at expiration of period of currency of contribution card on which contribution was paid	Employed	Self-employed	Non-employed
	Portion of contribution to be refunded				Portion of contribution to be refunded		
	pence 47	pence 111	pence 111		pence 41	pence 83	pence 82
(1)	(2)	(3)	(4)	(5)	(6)	(7)	(8)
	Total number of pence to be refunded (including interest) in respect of each contribution				Total number of pence to be refunded (including interest) in respect of each contribution		
65 and over	48	112	112	60 and over	41	84	83
64	49	115	115	59	42	86	85
63	50	118	118	58	43	88	87
62	51	121	121	57	44	90	89
61	53	124	124	56	45	93	92
60	54	127	127	55	46	95	94
59	55	130	130	54	47	97	96
58	57	134	134	53	49	100	99

EXPLANATORY NOTE

(This Note is not part of the Regulations)

These regulations are, by virtue of paragraph 2(1)(*a*) of Part I of Schedule 4 to the National Insurance Act 1972, exempt from reference to the National Insurance Advisory Committee and no such reference has been made.

The regulations increase the rates of benefit payable under certain regulations made under the National Insurance Acts 1965 to 1971, or deemed by virtue of section 117 of the National Insurance Act 1965 to have been made under that Act, in order to bring them into conformity with the higher rates of benefit payable under that Act by virtue of the Act of 1972, and contain other provisions of a minor or consequential character.

STATUTORY INSTRUMENTS

1972 No. 1303

MERCHANDISE MARKS

The Motor Vehicles (Designation of Approval Marks) (No. 2) Regulations 1972

Made - - - -	*17th August* 1972
Laid before Parliament	*29th August* 1972
Coming into Operation	*19th September* 1972

The Secretary of State for the Environment (hereinafter referred to as "the Secretary of State"), in exercise of his powers under section 63(1) of the Road Traffic Act 1972**(a)** and of all other enabling powers, and after consultation with representative organisations in accordance with the provisions of section 199(2) of that Act, hereby makes the following Regulations:—

1.—(1) These Regulations shall come into operation on 19th September 1972 and may be cited as the Motor Vehicles (Designation of Approval Marks) (No. 2) Regulations 1972.

(2) In these Regulations the expression "the International Agreement of 1958" means the Agreement concerning the adoption of uniform conditions of approval and reciprocal recognition of approval for motor vehicle equipment and parts concluded at Geneva on 20th March 1958**(b)**, as amended **(c)**, to which the United Kingdom is a party **(d)**.

(3) The Interpretation Act 1889**(e)** shall apply for the interpretation of these Regulations as it applies for the interpretation of an Act of Parliament.

2.—(1) The Secretary of State hereby designates as an approval mark a marking which is in the same form as and of a size not less than the marking shown in the diagram in Part I of Schedule 1 to these Regulations subject, however, to the provisions of Part II of that Schedule, the said marking being one for which the International Agreement of 1958 by virtue of the Regulation specified in Part III of that Schedule, annexed to that Agreement, and dated 14th August 1970, and as amended by Corrigendum 1 dated 22nd April 1971, makes such provision as is mentioned in section 63(1)(*a*)(ii) and (*b*) of the Road Traffic Act 1972 in relation to a motor vehicle fitted with certain parts consisting of the seats and of their anchorages on the vehicle.

(a) 1972 c. 20. (b) Cmnd. 2535.
(c) Cmnd. 3562.
(d) By instrument of accession dated 14th January 1963 deposited with the Secretary-General of the United Nations on 15th January 1963.
(e) 1889 c. 63.

(2) The Secretary of State hereby designates as an approval mark a marking which is in the same form as and of a size not less than the marking shown in the diagram in Part I of Schedule 2 to these Regulations subject, however, to the provisions of Part II of that Schedule, the said marking being one for which the International Agreement of 1958 by virtue of the Regulation specified in Part III of that Schedule, annexed to that Agreement and dated 14th September 1970 makes such provision as is mentioned in section 63(1)(*a*)(ii) and (*b*) of the Road Traffic Act 1972 in relation to a motor vehicle fitted with a certain part consisting of a device for the protection of the vehicle against unauthorised use.

(3) The Secretary of State hereby designates as an approval mark a marking which is in the same form as and of a size not less than the marking shown in the diagram in Part I of Schedule 3 to these Regulations, subject, however, to the provisions of Part II of that Schedule, the said marking being one for which the International Agreement of 1958 by virtue of the Regulation specified in Part III of that Schedule, annexed to that Agreement and dated 11th March 1970 makes such provision as is mentioned in section 63(1)(*a*)(ii) and (*b*) of the Road Traffic Act 1972 in relation to a motor vehicle equipped with a positive-ignition engine with regard to the emission of gaseous pollutants by that engine.

Signed by authority of the Secretary of State.

17th August 1972.

John Peyton,
Minister for Transport Industries,
Department of the Environment.

SCHEDULE 1

PART I

Diagram showing marking

17R-2439

PART II

1. The number shown inside the circle in the marking in the above diagram will be varied, where appropriate, to be the number assigned to each Contracting State party to the International Agreement of 1958 and applying the Regulation specified in Part III of this Schedule.

2. The number which is shown outside the circle in the said marking will be varied, where appropriate, to be the number allotted by a competent authority to distinguish the manufacturer of the type of motor vehicle concerned, being a motor vehicle fitted with certain parts consisting of the seats and their anchorages on the vehicle.

PART III

Regulation No. 17

UNIFORM PROVISIONS CONCERNING THE APPROVAL OF VEHICLES WITH REGARD TO THE STRENGTH OF THE SEATS AND OF THEIR ANCHORAGES.

SCHEDULE 2

PART I

Diagram showing marking

18R-2439

PART II

1. The number shown inside the circle in the marking in the above diagram will be varied, where appropriate, to be the number assigned to each Contracting State party to the International Agreement of 1958 and applying the Regulation specified in Part III of this Schedule.

2. The number which is shown outside the circle in the said marking will be varied, where appropriate, to be the number allotted by a competent authority to distinguish the manufacturer of the type of motor vehicle concerned, being a motor vehicle fitted with a device for its protection against unauthorised use.

PART III

Regulation No. 18

UNIFORM PROVISIONS CONCERNING THE APPROVAL OF POWER-DRIVEN VEHICLES WITH REGARD TO THEIR PROTECTION AGAINST UNAUTHORISED USE.

SCHEDULE 3

PART I

Diagram showing marking

15R-2439

PART II

1. The number shown inside the circle in the marking in the above diagram will be varied, where appropriate, to be the number assigned to each Contracting State party to the International Agreement of 1958 and applying the Regulation specified in Part III of this Schedule.

2. The number which is shown outside the circle in the said marking will be varied, where appropriate, to be the number allotted by a competent authority to distinguish the manufacturer of the type of motor vehicle concerned, being a motor vehicle equipped with a positive-ignition engine with regard to the emission of gaseous pollutants by the engine.

PART III

Regulation No. 15

UNIFORM PROVISIONS CONCERNING THE APPROVAL OF VEHICLES EQUIPPED WITH A POSITIVE-IGNITION ENGINE WITH REGARD TO THE EMISSION OF GASEOUS POLLUTANTS BY THE ENGINE.

EXPLANATORY NOTE

(This Note is not part of the Regulations.)

Section 63(1) of the Road Traffic Act 1972 enacts, inter alia, that where any international agreement to which the United Kingdom is a party provides—

(*a*) for markings to be applied to a motor vehicle to indicate that the vehicle is fitted with motor vehicle parts of any description and either—

(i) that the parts conform with a type approved by any country; or

(ii) that the vehicle is such that as so fitted it conforms with a type so approved; and

(*b*) for motor vehicles bearing these markings to be recognised as complying with the requirements imposed by the law of another country,

the Secretary of State for the Environment may by regulations designate the markings as approval marks.

Section 63 of the Road Traffic Act 1972 also provides that any markings so designated shall be deemed for the purpose of the Trade Descriptions Act 1968 (c.29) to be a trade description and that it shall be an offence under that Act to apply an approval mark without proper authority.

These Regulations designate for the purposes of the said section 63 as approval marks, markings complying with the provisions of Schedule 1, 2 or 3 of these Regulations and in respect of which the International Agreement of 1958 (referred to in these Regulations) and the Regulation specified in Part III of each of the Schedules to these Regulations and annexed to that Agreement makes such provision as is mentioned in (*a*)(ii) and (*b*) above as respects motor vehicles fitted with motor vehicle parts. The motor vehicle parts concerned (in the case of a marking complying with the provisions of Schedule 1 to these Regulations) consist of the seats and their anchorages, (in the case of a marking complying with Schedule 2 to these Regulations) consist of a device for the protection of a vehicle against unauthorised use and (in the case of a marking complying with Schedule 3 to these Regulations) consist of a positive-ignition engine with regard to the emission of gaseous pollutants by that engine.

STATUTORY INSTRUMENTS

1972 No. 1304

MERCHANT SHIPPING

The Seamen's Savings Bank Regulations 1972

Made - - - -	18*th August* 1972
Laid before Parliament	25*th August* 1972
Coming into operation	1*st January* 1973

The Secretary of State, after consulting with the organisations referred to in section 99(2) of the Merchant Shipping Act 1970(**a**), in exercise of powers conferred by paragraph 3 of Schedule 4 to that Act and now vested in him(**b**) and of all other powers enabling him in that behalf, hereby makes the following Regulations—

Citation, commencement and interpretation

1.—(1) These Regulations may be cited as the Seamen's Savings Bank Regulations 1972 and shall come into operation on 1st January 1973.

(2) In these Regulations—

" deposit " means a deposit received at and not repaid by any seamen's savings bank referred to in section 148 of the Merchant Shipping Act 1894(**c**); and

" depositor " means the person appearing in the records of any such bank as the person entitled to a deposit.

(3) The Interpretation Act 1889(**d**) shall apply to the interpretation of these Regulations as it applies to the interpretation of an Act of Parliament.

Repayment of deposits

2. Notwithstanding the repeal of section 148 of the Merchant Shipping Act 1894, during the period beginning on the date on which these Regulations come into operation and ending on 20th May 1973, a deposit may be repaid to or to the order of the depositor.

Transfer to National Savings Bank

3. On 31st May 1973 the amount of all deposits (including interest to that date) shall be transferred to the National Savings Bank ; and the amount so transferred in respect of each depositor shall be treated as a deposit in the National Savings Bank in the name of the depositor.

Michael Heseltine,
Minister for Aerospace,
Department of Trade and Industry.

18th August 1972.

(**a**) 1970 c. 36.
(**b**) See S.I. 1970/1537 (1970 III, p. 5293).
(**c**) 57 & 58 Vict. c. 60.
(**d**) 52 & 53 Vict. c. 63.

EXPLANATORY NOTE
(This Note is not part of the Regulations.)

These Regulations make provision for the repayment of deposits in the Seamen's Savings Bank, which is to be closed, and for the transfer to the National Savings Bank of any deposits not repaid.

STATUTORY INSTRUMENTS

1972 No. 1306

LANDLORD AND TENANT

The Rent Regulation (Forms etc.) Regulations 1972

Made - - -	*21st August* 1972
Laid before Parliament	*25th August* 1972
Coming into Operation	*27th August* 1972

The Secretary of State for the Environment (as respects England, except Monmouthshire) in exercise of powers conferred by sections 37(1) and 50(1) (as read with section 114(1)) of the Rent Act 1968(**a**) and now vested in him(**b**) and in exercise of all other powers enabling him in that behalf, and the Secretary of State for Wales (as respects Wales and Monmouthshire) in exercise of the powers conferred by the said sections 37(1) and 50(1) (as read with the said section 114(1)) and of all other powers enabling him in that behalf, hereby make the following regulations:—

1. These regulations may be cited as the Rent Regulation (Forms etc.) Regulations 1972 and shall come into operation on 27th August 1972.

2.—(1) In these regulations "the Housing Finance Act" means the Housing Finance Act 1972(**c**).

(2) The Interpretation Act 1889(**d**) shall apply for the interpretation of these regulations as it applies for the interpretation of an Act of Parliament.

3. The form contained in Part I of the Schedule to these regulations, or a form substantially to the same effect, shall be the form to be used for the purpose of a notice of increase of rent under section 37(3) of the Housing Finance Act (increase of rent for improvements).

4. The form contained in Part II of the Schedule to these regulations, or a form substantially to the same effect, shall be the form of notice to be served by a local authority pursuant to section 28(3) of the Housing Finance Act (notice to tenant of landlord's application for qualification certificate) and such notice shall contain the information and explanation specified in that form.

(**a**) 1968 c. 23. (**b**) See S.I. 1970/1681 (1970 III, p. 5551).
(**c**) 1972 c. 47. (**d**) 1889 c. 63.

SCHEDULE
PART I

RENT ACT 1968

HOUSING FINANCE ACT 1972

Notice of Increase of Unregistered Rent under Regulated Tenancy on account of Improvement (Notes 1 & 2)

Housing
Finance Act
Section 37(3)

Date ....

To .... tenant of ....

I hereby give you notice that your rent will be increased as follows :-

Present rent	*Increase in rent*	*New rent*	*Date of new rent*
per	per....................	per	(Note 3)
£	£	£	*as from*

This increase represents an annual increase of 12½% of £   (Note 4) which is the amount spent on making the improvement (Note 5) described below. You have certain rights of appeal which are explained in Note 6 to this form.

Description of Improvement

Signature of [landlord] [agent authorised to serve this notice]................

[Name of landlord if notice served by agent............................]

Address of landlord ....

....

[Address of agent...................

..............................]

Strike out
words in
square
brackets if
they do not
apply.

NOTES

1. This Notice of Increase is for a tenancy—
   (a) which is regulated under the Rent Act 1968; and
   (b) for which a fair rent has not been registered under the Act; and
   (c) where improvement works have been completed.

2. This notice of increase cannot be used in a case where improvements have been made : —
   (a) with respect to which a grant under Part I of the Housing Act 1969 is payable, or has been paid, and
   (b) which were completed at a time when the tenancy was a regulated tenancy.

It can however be used, whether or not a grant is payable, where : —
      (i) the improvements were completed while the tenancy was controlled, and
      (ii) no notice of increase for the improvement was served during the controlled tenancy.

3. This Notice cannot be retrospective and the date to be inserted here should be a date after the date of the service of this Notice.

4. The sum to be inserted here must not include any part of the expenditure on the improvement which has been met by a local authority under Part I of the Housing Act 1969, section 12 of the Clean Air Act 1956 (Grants for smokeless fuel burning appliances); or by a local authority or the British Airports Authority under section 15 of the Airports Authority Act 1965 (Soundproofing Grants).

5. Improvements for this purpose include structural alterations, extensions and additions to the premises and the provision of additional fixtures or fittings; but they do not include anything done by way of decoration or repair.

Private street works carried out under sections 174, 189 or 190 of the Highways Act 1959 or any corresponding provision in any local Act also count as an improvement to any premises having access to the street. If other premises belonging to the landlord besides those occupied by the tenant benefit from street works, the landlord's expenditure must be apportioned by agreement in writing between the landlord and the tenant or be determined by the county court. Neither the necessity for the street works nor the amount of the landlord's expenditure in connection with them can be questioned by the tenant.

6. If the tenant claims that any improvement was unnecessary or that an unreasonable amount was spent on it, he can, not later than one month after the service of this Notice, or such longer time as the court may allow, apply to the county court for an order cancelling or reducing the increase of rent stated in this Notice.

No such application may be made in the following cases—

(a) where the improvement was made with the assistance of a grant under Part I of the Housing Act 1969; or

(b) where the improvement works consist of the soundproofing of a dwellinghouse near an aerodrome and a grant towards the works has been paid by the British Airports Authority or by a local authority acting on their behalf; or

(c) where the tenant has in writing consented to the improvement and acknowledged that the rent could be increased on account of it.

7. If this Notice is served while the regulated tenancy is still a contractual one and the landlord, by serving a notice to quit at the same time as this Notice, could bring the tenancy to an end before the date specified in this Notice for the increased rent to take effect, this Notice will operate to convert the tenancy into a statutory tenancy as from that date.

PART II

HOUSING FINANCE ACT 1972

NOTICE TO TENANT OF LANDLORD'S APPLICATION FOR QUALIFICATION CER- Section 28(3).
TIFICATE FOR DWELLING WITH STANDARD AMENITIES (NO GRANT PAYABLE
UNDER SECTIONS 2(1) OR 9(1) OF THE HOUSING ACT 1969).

. . . . .Council.

To. . . . .

. . . .

. . . .

(Name and address of tenant)

1. An application under section 28 of the Housing Finance Act 1972 has
been made to the Council by. . . . .
. . . .(name of landlord or landlord's agent)
for a qualification certificate in respect of the dwelling at. . . . .
. . . .

2. The attached copy of the application is sent to you as the person
named as the tenant of the above dwelling under a controlled tenancy.

3. You may, within 28 days of the service of this notice, make representations to the Council that the dwelling does not satisfy the qualifying conditions. (See paragraph 4 below). Any representations in writing should be
sent to . . . .

4. For a qualification certificate to be issued the following conditions,
known as the qualifying conditions, must be satisfied: —

      (i) the dwelling must be provided with all the standard amenities[1] for
         the exclusive use of its occupants.

     (ii) the dwelling must be in good repair, having regard to its age,
         character and locality and disregarding internal decorative repair.

    (iii) the dwelling must be in all other respects fit for human habita-
         tion.[2]

5. If a qualification certificate is issued, then, unless the dwelling is occupied partly for business and partly as living accommodation, the tenancy
will become a regulated tenancy on the issue of the certificate.

6. In the case of a dwelling occupied partly for business and partly as
living accommodation, the tenancy, instead of becoming regulated, would
have the protection of Part II of the Landlord and Tenant Act 1954 on the
issue of the qualification certificate.

7. Where improvement works have been carried out, the landlord will have
been entitled, on completion of the works, to increase the rent by an amount
which when expressed as an annual figure, is equal to $12\frac{1}{2}\%$ of the amount
(net of grant) spent by the landlord on the works. He will still be entitled
to charge this increase if he has not yet done so.

8. Once a controlled tenancy becomes a regulated tenancy, the landlord
may apply to the rent officer for the registration of a fair rent. You will
then be given an opportunity to make representations about the rent to be
registered. When the fair rent has been registered, then if this is higher

than the controlled rent (excluding rates but including any $12\frac{1}{2}\%$ increase to which the landlord is entitled—see the preceding paragraph), the increase in rent is subject to phasing as follows:—

(a) if improvement works started on or after 1st January 1972 and the $12\frac{1}{2}\%$ increase amounted to at least 50p per week, the rest of the increase up to the fair rent, if £1 per week or more, will be spread equally over two annual stages, the first being one year after the $12\frac{1}{2}\%$ increase so charged (but not earlier than the date of registration) or one year after registration if earlier, and the second being one year after the first; if the rest of the increase is less than £1 per week, the rent may be increased each year by not more than 50p per week until the fair rent is reached,

(b) in other cases, the increase up to the fair rent will, if the registration is made on or after 1st January 1973[3], be spread equally over three annual stages, unless it is less than £1·50 per week in which case the rent may be increased by not more than 50p per week each year until the fair rent is reached. If the registration is made more than three months after the application to the rent officer the second stage will be 15 months after that application, and the third stage (if any) will be 12 months after the second stage.

9. Instead of applying to the rent officer it is open to you and the landlord, at any time from 1st January 1973, to enter into an agreement yourselves. You will be free to agree not only the rent ultimately to be paid but also any phasing of the rent increase up to that rent. Particulars of any such agreement must however be entered on a prescribed form which must be deposited with the local authority. A leaflet is available free of charge at council offices, rent offices and Citizens' Advice Bureaux.

10. When a tenancy becomes a regulated tenancy the tenant still enjoys the wide measure of security of tenure given by the Rent Act 1968.

11. Any representations you make that the dwelling does not satisfy the qualifying conditions will be considered by the Council, who will notify you of their decision, whether they refuse the application or issue a qualification certificate.

Date   Signature of authorised officer.

---

[1]The standard amenities are:—

1) A fixed bath or shower which must be in a bathroom unless this is not reasonably practicable.

2) A wash-hand basin.

3) A sink.

4) A water closet which must be in, and accessible from within, the dwelling unless this is not reasonably practicable.

5) A hot and cold water supply at the fixed bath or shower, at the wash-hand basin and at the sink.

[2]The standard of fitness for human habitation is laid down in section 4 of the Housing Act 1957 as amended by section 71 of the Housing Act 1969. A dwelling is 'fit for human habitation' if it is reasonably suitable for occupation having regard to repairs, stability, freedom from damp, internal arrangement, natural lighting, ventilation, water supply, drainage and sanitary conveniences, and facilities for preparation and cooking of food and for the disposal of waste water.

³If the registration is made in November or December 1972, the increase in rent will be spread equally over three annual stages, beginning not earlier than 1 January 1973; except that if it is less than £1·50 per week the rent may be increased by not more than 50p per week in each calendar year, beginning not earlier than 1 January 1973, until the fair rent is reached.   If the registration is made before November 1972, the increase in rent will be spread as follows: the first increment cannot exceed one-fifth of the rent increase or 37½p per week, whichever is greater, and this is payable on or after registration; the second increment, payable one year later, cannot exceed (a) the amount needed to bring the first and second increments together up to three-fifths of the total rent increase, or (b) 50p per week, whichever is greater; and the remainder (if any) needed to bring the rent up to the registered fair rent can be charged one year after that.

Peter Walker,
Secretary of State for the Environment.

21st August 1972.

Peter Thomas,
Secretary of State for Wales.

18th August 1972.

EXPLANATORY NOTE

(This Note is not part of the Regulations.)

These Regulations, which apply throughout England and Wales, prescribe two forms to be used for the purposes of the Housing Finance Act 1972.

The first is the form of notice of increase of rent under section 37(3) of the Act. This section applies where a tenancy has been converted from control to regulation, and where the rent is less than it would have been if the landlord had, before the conversion, served all notices of increase of rent which he was entitled to serve; the section enables the landlord to increase the rent after the conversion by the amount of the difference.

The second is the form of notice to be served by a local authority on a tenant under a controlled tenancy pursuant to section 28(3) of the Act. The Regulations also prescribe the information and explanation which that notice shall contain. Section 28(3) relates to the notice to be served by the local authority on a controlled tenant where the landlord has applied to the authority for a qualification certificate; upon the issue of that certificate a tenancy is (with certain exceptions) converted from control to regulation under the provisions of Part III of the Act.

STATUTORY INSTRUMENTS

1972 No. 1307

LANDLORD AND TENANT

The Rent Regulation (Local Authority Applications) Regulations 1972

Made - - -		*21st August* 1972
Laid before Parliament		*25th August* 1972
Coming into Operation		*27th August* 1972

The Secretary of State for the Environment (as respects England, except Monmouthshire) and the Secretary of State for Wales (as respects Wales and Monmouthshire) in exercise of their powers under sections 44A(8) and 50(1) (as read with section 114(1)) of the Rent Act 1968(a) and of all other powers enabling them in that behalf, and in so far as the regulations relate to Rent Assessment Committees, after consultation with the Council on Tribunals, hereby make the following regulations:—

Citation and commencement

1. These regulations may be cited as the Rent Regulation (Local Authority Applications) Regulations 1972 and shall come into operation on 27th August 1972.

Interpretation

2.—(1) In these regulations, unless the context otherwise requires—

"the Act" means the Rent Act 1968;

"application" means an application which is made by a local authority to the rent officer under section 44A(1) of the Act;

"chairman" means the chairman of a rent assessment committee;

"committee" means a rent assessment committee constituted under Schedule 5 to the Act;

"hearing" has the meaning assigned to it by regulation 8(1) of these regulations;

"local authority" means the local authority who have made an application;

"parties" means the landlord and the tenant under the regulated tenancy of the dwelling-house to which an application relates;

"reference" has the meaning assigned to it by regulation 7(1) of these regulations.

(a) 1968 c. 23.

(2) Any reference to a party in regulations 11, 12 and 13 of these regulations shall be construed as including a reference to a person authorised by a party to make oral representations on his behalf pursuant to regulation 8 of these regulations.

(3) The Interpretation Act 1889(a) shall apply for the interpretation of these regulations as it applies for the interpretation of an Act of Parliament.

Procedure on application to rent officer

3.—(1) On receiving an application, the rent officer—

(*a*) may by notice in writing served on a party require him to give to the rent officer, within such period of not less than seven days from the service of the notice as may be specified in the notice, such information as he may reasonably require regarding the rent and the other terms of the tenancy and the dwelling-house; and

(*b*) shall serve on each of the parties a notice informing him of the application and specifying a period of not less than seven days from the service of the notice during which representations in writing may be made to the rent officer as to whether a rent for the dwelling-house should be registered in pursuance of section 44A(2) of the Act, and if so, what the amount of that rent should be.

(2) The rent officer shall make such inquiry, if any, as he thinks fit and consider any information supplied or representation made to him in pursuance of paragraph (1)(*a*) or paragraph (1)(*b*) above and—

(*a*) if the rent officer is satisfied that the rent, or the highest rent, payable for the dwelling-house does not exceed what in his opinion is a fair rent, he shall notify the parties and the local authority accordingly;

(*b*) if it appears to the rent officer that the rent, or the highest rent, payable for the dwelling-house may exceed what in his opinion would be a fair rent, he shall serve a notice under regulation 4 below.

Consultation and representation

4.—(1) A notice under this regulation shall be served on each of the parties informing him that the rent officer proposes, at a time (which shall not be earlier than seven days after the service of the notice) and place specified in the notice to consider in consultation with the parties, or such of them as may appear at that time and place, whether a rent should be registered in pursuance of section 44A(2) of the Act, and if so, what the amount of that rent should be.

(2) At any such consultation the parties may each be represented by a person authorised by him in that behalf, whether or not that person is of counsel or a solicitor.

Decision of rent officer

5.—(1) When, after such consideration as is mentioned in regulation 4 above, the rent officer has reached his decision, he shall notify each of the parties and the local authority whether he is not satisfied that the rent, or the highest rent, payable for the dwelling-house exceeds what in his opinion is a fair rent, or as the case may be, whether he has registered a rent pursuant to section 44A(2) of the Act and of the amount of the rent so registered.

(a) 1889 c. 63.

(2) When the rent officer registers a rent pursuant to section 44A(2) of the Act (registration of a rent if the rent, or the highest rent, payable for the dwelling-house exceeds a fair rent) the notification of that registration to be given to the parties pursuant to paragraph (1) above shall be given by a notice stating that if, within twenty-eight days of the service of the notice or such longer period as he or a committee may allow, an objection in writing is received by the rent officer from either of the parties the matter will be referred to a committee.

Reference to a committee

6.—(1) If such an objection as is mentioned in regulation 5(2) above is received, then—

> (a) if it is received within the period of twenty-eight days specified in that regulation or a committee so direct, the rent officer shall refer the matter to a committee;

> (b) if it is received after the expiry of that period the rent officer may either refer the matter to a committee or seek the directions of a committee whether so to refer it.

(2) The rent officer shall indicate in the register whether the matter has been referred to a committee in pursuance of this regulation.

Procedure on a reference

7.—(1) In these regulations "reference" means a matter referred to a committee in pursuance of regulation 6 above.

(2) The committee to whom a reference is made under regulation 6 above—

> (a) may by notice in writing served on a party require him to give to the committee, within such period of not less than fourteen days from the service of the notice as may be specified in the notice, such further information, in addition to any given to the rent officer in pursuance of regulation 3(1)(a) above, as they may reasonably require;

> (b) shall serve on each of the parties a notice specifying a period of not less than fourteen days from the service of the notice during which either representations in writing or a request to make oral representations may be made by him to the committee; and

> (c) shall make such further inquiry, if any, as they think fit.

The hearing and representation

8.—(1) In these regulations "hearing" means the meeting or meetings of a committee to hear oral representations in accordance with paragraph (2) below.

(2) Where, within the period specified in regulation 7 above or such further period as the committee may allow, either of the parties requests to make oral representations the committee shall give the parties an opportunity to be heard at a hearing.

(3) At a hearing the parties may each be heard either in person or by a person authorised by him in that behalf, whether or not that person is of counsel or a solicitor.

Documents

9.—(1) The committee shall, where the reference is to be subject to a hearing, take all reasonable steps to ensure that there is supplied to each of the parties before the date of the hearing—

(*a*) a copy of, or sufficient extracts from or particulars of, any document relevant to the reference which has been received from the rent officer or from a party (other than a document which is in the possession of such party, or of which he has previously been supplied with a copy by the rent officer); and

(*b*) a copy of any document which embodies the results of any inquiries made by or for the committee for the purposes of that reference, or which contains relevant information in relation to fair rents previously determined for other dwelling-houses and which has been prepared for the committee for the purposes of that reference.

(2) Where a reference is not to be subject to a hearing, the committee shall supply to each of the parties a copy of, or sufficient extracts from or particulars of, any such document as is mentioned in paragraph (1)(*a*) above (other than a document excepted from that paragraph) and a copy of any such document as is mentioned in paragraph (1)(*b*) above, and they shall not reach their decision until they are satisfied that each party has been given a sufficient opportunity of commenting upon any document of which a copy, or from which extracts or of which particulars, has or have been so supplied, and upon the other's case.

Time and place of hearing

10.—(1) A hearing shall be on such date and at such time and place as the committee shall appoint.

(2) Notices of such date, time and place shall be given by the committee, not less than 10 days before the said date, to each of the parties.

Procedure at hearing

11.—(1) A hearing shall be in public unless, for special reasons, the committee decide otherwise; but nothing in these regulations shall prevent a member of the Council on Tribunals in that capacity from attending any hearing.

(2) At the hearing—

(*a*) the parties shall be heard in such order, and, subject to the provisions of these regulations, the procedure shall be such as the committee shall determine;

(*b*) a party may call witnesses, give evidence on his own behalf and cross-examine any witnesses called by the other party.

(3) If a party does not appear at a hearing the committee, on being satisfied that the requirements of these regulations regarding the giving of notice of hearings have been duly complied with, may proceed to deal with the reference upon the representations of any party present and upon the documents and information which they may properly consider.

Inspection of dwelling-house

12.—(1) The committee may of their own motion, and shall at the request of one of the parties (subject in either case to any necessary consent being obtained) inspect the dwelling-house which is the subject of the reference.

(2) An inspection may be made before, during or after the close of the hearing, or at such stage in relation to the consideration of the representations in writing, as the committee shall decide, and the committee shall give to the parties and their representatives an opportunity to attend.

(3) Notice of an inspection shall be given as though it were notice of a hearing, save that the requirements for such notice may be dispensed with or relaxed in so far as the committee are satisfied that the parties have received sufficient notice.

(4) Where an inspection is made after the close of a hearing, the committee shall, if they consider that it is expedient to do so on account of any matter arising from the inspection, reopen the hearing; and if the hearing is to be reopened, regulation 10(2) above shall apply as it applied to the original hearing, save in so far as its requirements may be dispensed with or relaxed with the consent of the parties.

Adjournment

13.—(1) The committee at their discretion may of their own motion, or at the request of the parties, or one of them, at any time and from time to time postpone or adjourn a hearing.

(2) Where at any hearing—

    (i) any document relevant to the reference is not in the possession of a party present at that hearing; and

    (ii) that party has not been supplied with a copy of, or sufficient extracts from or particulars of, that document by the rent officer or by the committee in accordance with the provisions of regulation 9(1) above,

then unless—

    (*a*) that party consents to the continuation of the hearing; or

    (*b*) the committee consider that that party has a sufficient opportunity of dealing with that document without an adjournment of the hearing,

the committee shall adjourn the hearing for a period which they consider will afford that party a sufficient opportunity of dealing with that document.

(3) Such notice of any postponed or adjourned hearing as is reasonable in the circumstances shall be given to each of the parties by the committee.

Decision of committee

14.—(1) The committee shall consider any information supplied or representations made to them in pursuance of regulation 7 or regulation 8 above and, where there is a hearing, any evidence adduced at that hearing, and—

   (*a*) if it appears to them that the rent registered by the rent officer is a fair rent, they shall confirm that rent;

   (*b*) if it does not appear to them that that rent is a fair rent, they shall determine a fair rent for the dwelling-house.

(2) Where the committee confirm or determine a rent under this regulation they shall notify each of the parties and the rent officer accordingly.

(3) On receiving the notification, the rent officer shall, as the case may require, either indicate in the register that the rent has been confirmed or register the rent determined by the committee as the rent for the dwelling-house.

15.—(1) The decision of the committee upon a reference shall be recorded in a document signed by the chairman (or in the event of his absence or incapacity, by another member of the committee) which shall contain the reasons for the decision, but shall contain no reference to the decision being by a majority (if that be the case) or to any opinion of a minority.

(2) The chairman (or in the event of his absence or incapacity, either of the other members of the committee) shall have power, by certificate under his hand, to correct any clerical or accidental error or omission in the said document.

(3) A copy of the said document and of any such correction shall be sent by the committee to each of the parties and to the rent officer.

Giving of notices, etc.

16. Where any notice or other written matter is required under the provisions of regulation 9, 10, 12, 13 or 15 above to be given or supplied by the committee it shall be sufficient compliance with the regulations if such notice or matter is sent by post in a prepaid letter and addressed to the party for whom it is intended at his usual or last known address, or if that party has appointed an agent to act on his behalf in relation to the reference, to that agent at the address of the agent supplied to the committee.

Peter Walker,
Secretary of State for the Environment.

21st August 1972.

Peter Thomas,
Secretary of State for Wales.

18th August 1972.

EXPLANATORY NOTE

(This Note is not part of the Regulations.)

These Regulations prescribe the procedure to be followed when a local authority apply to the rent officer, under section 44A of the Rent Act 1968, for the consideration of the fair rent of a dwelling-house within their area for which a rent may be, or has been, registered under that Act.

In particular the Regulations provide that—

(*a*) on receiving the application, the rent officer is to notify the landlord and tenant, who may make representations in writing as to whether a rent should be registered (Reg. 3);

(*b*) if it appears to the rent officer that the rent, or the highest rent, payable for the dwelling-house may exceed a fair rent, then he is to hold a consultation, which the landlord and the tenant may attend, and at which they may each be represented (Reg. 4);

(*c*) if the rent officer registers a rent, the landlord or the tenant may have the matter referred to a rent assessment committee (Regs. 5 and 6);

(*d*) the committee to whom a matter is referred shall give the landlord and the tenant an opportunity of making representations, either in writing, or orally at a hearing at which they may each be represented (Regs. 7 and 8);

(*e*) if it does not appear to the committee to whom a matter is referred that the rent registered by the rent officer is a fair rent, then they shall determine a fair rent (Reg. 14).

STATUTORY INSTRUMENTS

1972 No. 1309 (S.95)

AGRICULTURE

LIVESTOCK INDUSTRIES

The Licensing of Bulls (Scotland) Regulations 1972

Made - - -	*11th August* 1972
Laid before Parliament	*30th August* 1972
Coming into Operation	*1st September* 1972

In exercise of the powers conferred upon me by sections 1, 2, 4, 5, 6, 10 and 11 of the Improvement of Live Stock (Licensing of Bulls) Act 1931(**a**), as amended by section 6 of the Agriculture (Miscellaneous Provisions) Act 1944(**b**) and extended by section 16(4) of the Agriculture (Miscellaneous Provisions) Act 1963(**c**), and as amended and extended by section 8 of, and Schedule 3 to, the Agriculture (Miscellaneous Provisions) Act 1972(**d**), and of all other powers enabling me in that behalf, and with the approval of the Treasury as to fees, and on the joint recommendation of the Royal College of Veterinary Surgeons and the British Veterinary Association as to regulation 13(2) hereof, I hereby make the following regulations: —

Citation, commencement and extent

1. These regulations, which may be cited as the Licensing of Bulls (Scotland) Regulations 1972, shall come into operation on 1st September 1972 and shall apply to Scotland.

Revocation

2. The Regulations specified in Schedule 2 to these regulations are hereby revoked, but such revocation shall not affect the validity of any notice duly served thereunder or any proceedings duly undertaken by virtue of those regulations, which shall have effect as if served under or undertaken by virtue of the corresponding provisions of these regulations.

Interpretation

3.—(1) In these regulations, unless the context otherwise requires—

"the Act" means the Improvement of Live Stock (Licensing of Bulls) Act 1931;

"general permit" means any permit other than a special permit;

"licence" means a licence under the Act to keep a bull for breeding purposes;

"a member of the Veterinary Panel" means a veterinary surgeon who is a member of a panel appointed for the purposes of Schedule 3 to the Agriculture (Miscellaneous Provisions) Act 1972 by the Royal College of Veterinary Surgeons and the British Veterinary Association acting jointly;

(**a**) 1931 c. 43.	(**b**) 1944 c. 28.
(**c**) 1963 c. 11.	(**d**) 1972 c. 62.

"the Minister" means the Minister of Agriculture, Fisheries and Food;

"permit" means a permit under the Act to keep a bull for any purpose other than breeding purposes;

"special permit" means a permit which, by virtue of the proviso to section 4(4) of the Act (which authorises the granting of permits in respect of bulls kept for zoological or experimental purposes), does not include a condition that the bull to which it relates shall not be allowed to serve a cow.

(2) Any reference in these regulations to a form denoted by a number shall be construed as a reference to the form so numbered in Schedule 1 to these regulations or a form substantially to the like effect.

(3) The Interpretation Act 1889(a) shall apply for the interpretation of these regulations as it applies for the interpretation of an Act of Parliament. and as though these regulations and the regulations hereby revoked were Acts of Parliament.

Prescribed age of bull

4. For the purposes of section 1 of the Act (which prohibits the keeping of a bull that has attained the prescribed age unless a licence or permit is in force in respect of it) the prescribed age shall be the age of ten months.

Applications for licences and permits

5. An application for a licence shall be in Form 1 and shall be accompanied by a certificate in Form 2 signed by a member of the Veterinary Panel and the application shall contain, in the case of a bull of the Friesian breed, a sketch plan of the natural markings of the bull showing separately the bull as viewed from the left hand and right hand sides and its head as viewed from the front. An application for a permit shall be in Form 3.

Time for making applications

6.—(1) Subject to the provisions of paragraph (2) hereof, the prescribed time for making an application for a licence or a permit shall be as follows:—

(*a*) in the case of a licence, not later than seven days before the bull attains the prescribed age;

(*b*) in the case of a permit, within such time as may be applicable according to the following Table—

Where a licence or permit in respect of the bull has not at any time been applied for.	Not later than twenty-eight days before the bull attains the prescribed age.
Where a licence in respect of the bull has been refused or revoked.	Before the expiration of fourteen days from the date of the refusal or revocation or, if a referee's inspection is duly applied for, within fourteen days after the Secretary of State notifies the applicant that he has confirmed the refusal or revocation in accordance with the referee's report.

(a) 1889 c. 63.

| Where a permit in respect of the bull has been granted and has not expired. | Not later than fourteen days before the expiry of that permit. |

(2) Notwithstanding the provisions of the foregoing paragraph, in the case of a bull which is or is to be imported or brought into Scotland and which at the date of entry into Scotland has attained or will have attained the prescribed age or will attain that age within twenty one days from that date, an application for a licence or permit shall be made not later than fourteen days after the date of entry.

Forms of licences and permits

7. A licence shall be in Form 4 and a permit shall be in Form 5.

Duplicate of licences and permits

8. Any application for a duplicate of a licence or permit that has been lost or destroyed shall be in Form 6.

Change of place at which permit bulls may be kept

9. Where it is a condition of a permit that the bull to which it relates shall be kept at a specified place, any application made under section 4(2) of the Act for the substitution in the permit of some other place for the place theretofore specified shall be made in writing by the owner of the bull.

Notice of suspension

10. Any notice of suspension served under section 4(3) of the Act (making it a condition of a licence that the bull to which it relates shall not for a specified period be allowed to serve a cow) shall be served on any person for the time being having the bull in his possession or custody.

Application for referee's inspection

11.—(1) Any application made under section 5(1) of the Act for a referee's inspection of a bull, consequent on the refusal or revocation of a licence or on the service of a notice of suspension as respects that bull, shall be in Form 7, and shall be made before the expiration of a period of fourteen days from the date of the refusal or revocation or the service of the notice, as the case may be.

(2) Any notice of the result of his application given to an applicant by the Secretary of State shall be given in writing.

Fees

12.—(1) Fees of the following amounts shall be payable to the Secretary of State in respect of licences, special permits, and inspections by referees—

(a) in respect of a licence to keep a bull (excluding the professional fees of the member of the Veterinary Panel for inspecting and certifying the bull payable by the applicant for a licence) ... ... £1·00

(b) in respect of a special permit ... ... £8·00

(c) in respect of a duplicate of any licence or permit ... £0·70 (*d*) in respect of an inspection by a referee—

    (i) except as otherwise prescribed below, for each bull   £22·00

    (ii) where two bulls owned by the same person are to be inspected by the same referee at the same premises at the same time, for each bull ...   .   £19·00

    (iii) where three or more bulls owned by the same person are to be so inspected at the same time, for each bull   £18·00

Provided that no fee shall be payable in respect of a licence or special permit to keep a bull where at the time of application therefor a licence or special permit issued by the Minister in respect of England and Wales is in force in relation to the bull.

(2) The prescribed fee shall be remitted direct to the Secretary of State with the corresponding application except in the case of application for a licence.

(3) If, before the inspection referred to in regulation 11(1) hereof takes place, the application for a referee's inspection is withdrawn by the applicant, the Secretary of State may return the fee to him.

Prescribed inspection marks

13.—(1) The provisions of paragraph 2 of this regulation shall have effect for the purposes of paragraph 1(2) of Schedule 3 to the Agriculture (Miscellaneous Provisions) Act 1972 (which provides for the marking of bulls by members of the Veterinary Panel with a prescribed mark and in a prescribed manner).

(2) The mark prescribed for a bull that is to be marked is the letter V inside a square and the bull shall be marked with it in or on the right ear, or if that is impracticable, on some other appropriate place.

Service of notices and other documents

14.—(1) Any notice required or authorised by or under the Act to be given or served by the Secretary of State may be given or served by delivering it to the person to or on whom it is to be given or served, or by sending it to him by post in a letter addressed to him at his last known place of abode or business.

(2) Any application, notice or other document required or authorised by or under the Act to be made, given or sent by any person to the Secretary of State shall be made, given, sent by post or otherwise delivered in a letter addressed to the Secretary, Department of Agriculture and Fisheries for Scotland, at any office of the Department in Scotland.

Prescribed mark for identification purposes

15.—(1) This regulation shall have effect for the purposes of section 10(1)(*b*) of the Act (which empowers an officer of the Secretary of State to mark any bull with a prescribed mark in a prescribed manner).

(2) If an officer of the Secretary of State has reason to suppose that any bull apparently over the prescribed age is unlicensed and not the subject of any special or general permit he may mark the bull with the identification mark prescribed in the following paragraph.

(3) The mark prescribed for a bull that is being marked by an officer of the Secretary of State for the purpose of identification shall be a combination of any two letters of the alphabet or a combination of figures or both such combinations and the bull shall be marked with that mark in or on one of its ears or, if that is impracticable, on some other appropriate place.

Transitional provisions

16.—(1) The following conditions shall apply to the inspection, marking, licensing or rejection of a bull in respect of which an application for a licence made to the Secretary of State before the date of commencement of the present regulations remains undetermined as at such date: —

(*a*) The bull shall be inspected by an officer of the Secretary of State and for this purpose the Secretary of State may require the owner of the bull to make it available for inspection at any place or time that has been notified to the owner, and the owner shall provide all reasonable facilities and assistance for the purpose of the inspection and marking of the bull:

Provided that a bull that has previously been inspected on behalf of the Secretary of State for any other purpose may, if the Secretary of State thinks fit, be exempted from the inspection prescribed by this regulation.

(*b*) If, after inspection, the bull is found suitable for a licence, it shall be marked by an officer of the Secretary of State with a design consisting of a thistle in or on its right ear, or, if that is impracticable, on some other appropriate place.

(*c*) If, after inspection, the bull is found unsuitable for a licence, it shall be marked by an officer of the Secretary of State with the letter R in or on its left ear or, if that is impracticable, on some other appropriate place.

(*d*) Any bull that has been inspected and marked pursuant to this article may also be marked by an officer of the Secretary of State for identification purposes with the identification mark prescribed in regulation 15(3) of these regulations.

(2) A licence granted under these transitional provisions shall be in Form 8. A licence granted as a result of a successful appeal against the refusal of the Secretary of State to grant a licence shall, if the appeal arose out of an application for a licence made before the present regulations came into force, also be in Form 8.

(3) An applicant for a licence whose application has been made before the date of commencement of the present regulations and whose bull has not been inspected by an officer of the Secretary of State may if he so desires withdraw his application, in which case the Secretary of State may refund the fee paid by the applicant. Such withdrawal shall be without prejudice to the applicant's right to apply for a licence under and subject to the conditions of these regulations.

Gordon Campbell,
One of Her Majesty's
Principal Secretaries of State.

St. Andrew's House,
Edinburgh,
9th August 1972.

We approve.

V. H. Goodhew,
Hugh Rossi,
Two of the Lords Commissioners
of Her Majesty's Treasury.

11th August 1972.

Regulation 3(2) SCHEDULE 1

Regulation 5 FORM 1

No.

DEPARTMENT OF AGRICULTURE AND FISHERIES FOR SCOTLAND

Improvement of Live Stock (Licensing of Bulls) Act 1931 (as amended)
Licensing of Bulls (Scotland) Regulations 1972

APPLICATION FOR A LICENCE TO KEEP A BULL

Date of birth   19 *Earmarks*
　　　　day　　month　　year Breed Society Mark

Breeding* Mark allotted or approved under
　　　　　　TB Order 1964

I hereby apply for a licence in respect of the bull described above, and I hereby certify the foregoing particulars to be correct.

I am the owner†/agent for the owner of the bull†.

FULL NAME OF APPLICANT (IN BLOCK LETTERS)

Address

Telephone Number

Date   Signature

*For a pure-bred enter breed. For a cross-bred enter "cross-bred" and give the genetic make up (e.g. ⅜ Charolais × ⅛ Friesan) insofar as this is known.

†Delete as appropriate.

Regulation 5 FORM 2

VETERINARY CERTIFICATE

1. I have inspected this bull and to the best of my knowledge and belief the particulars given in the attached application as to date of birth and breeding are correct.

2. I hereby certify that

(*a*) the earmarks quoted in the application are correct;

†(b) the markings on the bull are in accordance with the sketch plan contained in the application;

(c) this bull had not previously been marked with the inspection mark prescribed by the Secretary of State on the joint recommendation of the Royal College of Veterinary Surgeons and the British Veterinary Association;

(d) I have marked this bull with the prescribed inspection mark in the prescribed manner;

(e) I am a member of the panel appointed jointly by the Royal College of Veterinary Surgeons and the British Veterinary Association for the purposes of inspecting bulls under the Act;

3A*. In my professional opinion, at the time of examination this bull was suitable for a licence under the Act as it was not:

(a) of defective or inferior conformation and likely to beget defective or inferior progeny; or

(b) permanently affected with any contagious or infectious disease; or

(c) permanently affected with any other disease rendering the bull unsuitable for breeding purposes.

3B*. In my professional opinion this bull is not suitable for a licence under the Act for the following reasons:

Signed   Date

Veterinary Surgeon
FULL NAME (BLOCK LETTERS)
PRACTICE AND ADDRESS

†Delete if the bull is not of the Friesian breed.
*Delete paragraph 3A or 3B as appropriate.

FORM 3   Regulation 5
DEPARTMENT OF AGRICULTURE AND FISHERIES FOR SCOTLAND
Improvement of Live Stock (Licensing of Bulls) Act 1931 (as amended)
Licensing of Bulls (Scotland) Regulations 1972

APPLICATION FOR A PERMIT TO KEEP AN UNLICENSED BULL

Date of birth   19   *Earmarks*
        day month year   Breed Society Mark
Breeding (see Note 1)   Mark allotted or approved under
                                     TB Order 1964

Full postal address of premises
at which bull is to be kept

I hereby apply for a *special permit see Notes 1, 2 to keep the unlicensed bull des-
                      general
cribed above until   19   for the purpose of

I enclose *cheque/postal order/money order for £8 (see Note (3)) in payment of the prescribed fee.

I am the *owner/agent for the owner of the bull.

Full name of applicant (in BLOCK LETTERS)

Address

                                Telephone No.

Date   19 .   Signature

*Strike out words that do not apply.

NOTES:

1. The breeding of the bull need not be given when a permit is applied for except in a case where exemption from section 4(4) of the Improvement of Live Stock (Licensing of Bulls) Act 1931, i.e. where the bull is kept in a zoological collection or otherwise in the interests of the science of zoology and kept solely for experimental purposes, is to be given. In such a case when a special permit is applied for the breed of the bull should be entered if it is pure bred; for a cross-bred the word "cross-bred" should be entered and the genetic make up (e.g. ⅞ Charolais × ⅛ Friesian) should be given (insofar as this is known).

2. A general permit is a permit which includes a condition that the bull must not be allowed to serve any cow of heifer. This type of permit is issued when a bull is to be kept entire to be fattened for slaughter.

3. The prescribed fee for a special permit is £8. A fee is not required for a general permit.

4. This application should be returned to the Secretary, Department of Agriculture and Fisheries for Scotland, Livestock Improvement Branch, Chesser House, Gorgie Road, Edinburgh EH11 3AW.

Regulation 7

FORM 4

No.

DEPARTMENT OF AGRICULTURE AND FISHERIES FOR SCOTLAND

Improvement of Live Stock (Licensing of Bulls) Act 1931 (as amended) Licensing of Bulls (Scotland) Regulations 1972

BULL LICENCE

This is to certify that the bull described in the application attached is licensed under the Improvement of Live Stock (Licensing of Bulls) Act 1931 (as amended).

Date 19 . Assistant Secretary.

Regulation 7

FORM 5

No.

DEPARTMENT OF AGRICULTURE AND FISHERIES FOR SCOTLAND

Improvement of Live Stock (Licensing of Bulls) Act 1931 (as amended) Licensing of Bulls (Scotland) Regulations 1972

*SPECIAL/GENERAL PERMIT TO KEEP AN UNLICENSED BULL

Date of birth 19 . *Earmarks*
    day month year   Breed Society Mark

Breeding Mark allotted or approved under
TB Order 1964

The Secretary of State hereby permits the unlicensed bull described above belonging to

to be kept at

until

for the purpose of

subject to the following conditions:

Date 19 . Assistant Secretary.

*Strike out words that do not apply.

NOTE:

For general permits the breeding of the bull should not be quoted.

FORM 6 Regulation 8

DEPARTMENT OF AGRICULTURE AND FISHERIES FOR SCOTLAND

Improvement of Live Stock (Licensing of Bulls) Act 1931 (*as amended*)
Licensing of Bulls (Scotland) Regulations 1972

APPLICATION FOR A DUPLICATE OF A LICENCE OR PERMIT

Date of birth 19 . *Earmarks*
      day   month   year Breed Society Mark

Breeding* Mark allotted or approved under
TB Order 1964

Full name of applicant (in BLOCK LETTERS)

Full postal address

I certify that the †licence/permit numbered............................ and issued on or about .... to keep the bull described above has been lost or destroyed and I hereby apply for a duplicate.

I enclose †cheque/postal order/money order for 70p in payment of the prescribed fee.

Date 19 . Signature

*For a pure-bred bull enter breed. For a cross-bred bull enter "cross-bred" and give the genetic make-up (e.g. $\frac{7}{8}$ Charolais $\times$ $\frac{1}{8}$ Friesan) insofar as this is known.
†Strike out works that do not apply.
This application should be returned to the Secretary, Department of Agriculture and Fisheries for Scotland, Livestock Improvement Branch, Chesser House, Gorgie Road, Edinburgh EH11 3AW.

FORM 7 Regulation 11(1)

DEPARTMENT OF AGRICULTURE AND FISHERIES FOR SCOTLAND

Improvement of Live Stock (Licensing of Bulls) Act 1931 (*as amended*)
Licensing of Bulls (Scotland) Regulations 1972

APPLICATION FOR A REFEREE'S INSPECTION

Date of birth 19 . *Earmarks*
      day   month   year Breed Society Mark

Breeding† Mark allotted or approved under
TB Order 1964

Full name of applicant (in BLOCK LETTERS)
Full postal address

Whereas the Secretary of State has *refused to grant/revoked/served a notice of suspension of a licence to keep the bull described above, now therefore I require a referee's inspection of the bull in accordance with Section 5 of the Improvement of Live Stock (Licensing of Bulls) Act 1931.

The bull will be kept during the next 28 days at

I enclose *cheque/postal order/money order for $\left.\begin{array}{l} *£22\cdot00 \\ £19\cdot00 \\ £18\cdot00 \end{array}\right\}$ (see Note) in payment of the prescribed fee.‡

Date 19 . Signature

†For a pure-bred enter breed. For a cross-bred enter "cross-bred" and give the genetic make-up (e.g. $\frac{7}{8}$ Charolais $\times$ $\frac{1}{8}$ Friesan) insofar as this is known.
*Strike out words that do not apply.
‡This will be returned if the refusal, revocation or notice of suspension is not confirmed.

NOTE:

1. The prescribed fees payable for referee's inspection are:—

    (i) for the inspection of one bull ... ... £22·00

    (ii) for the inspection of two bulls in the same ownership, provided the inspection of each bull is to be carried out by the same referee on the same premises and at the same time, for each bull ... ... £19·00

    (iii) for the inspection of three or more bulls in the same ownership, provided the inspection of each bull is carried out by the same referee on the same premises and at the same time, for each bull ... ... £18·00

2. This application should be returned to:—
    The Secretary
    Department of Agriculture and Fisheries for Scotland
    Livestock Improvement Branch
    Chesser House
    Gorgie Road
    Edinburgh
    EH11 3AW.

Regulation 16   FORM 8

DEPARTMENT OF AGRICULTURE AND FISHERIES FOR SCOTLAND

Improvement of Live Stock (Licensing of Bulls) Act 1931 *(as amended)*
Licensing of Bulls (Scotland) Regulations 1972

BULL LICENCE   No.

Date of birth   19 .   *Earmarks*
              day   month   year
Breeding

This is to certify that the bull described above is licensed under the improvement of Live Stock (Licensing of Bulls) Act 1931.

Date   19 .   Assistant Secretary.

Regulation 2

SCHEDULE 2

Column 1 Regulations revoked	Column 2 References
The Licensing of Bulls (Scotland) Regulations 1952.	S.I. 1952/1046 (1952 I, p. 158).
The Improvement of Livestock (Licensing of Bulls) (Scotland) Amendment Regulations 1960.	S.I. 1960/579 (1960 I, p. 184).
The Improvement of Livestock (Licensing of Bulls) (Scotland) Amendment Regulations 1961.	S.I. 1961/2163 (1961 III, p. 3892).
The Improvement of Livestock (Licensing of Bulls) (Scotland) Amendment Regulations 1964.	S.I. 1964/122 (1964 I, p. 217).
The Improvement of Livestock (Licensing of Bulls) (Scotland) Amendment Regulations 1966.	S.I. 1966/728 (1966 II, p. 1690).
The Improvement of Livestock (Licensing of Bulls) (Scotland) Amendment Regulations 1969.	S.I. 1969/1154 (1969 II, p. 3418).

EXPLANATORY NOTE

(This Note is not part of the Regulations.)

By virtue of section 8 and of Schedule 3 to the Agriculture (Miscellaneous Provisions) Act 1972 licensing of bulls by reference to pedigree and certain other standards of suitability is abolished and the Secretary of State for Scotland is empowered to make Regulations requiring an application for a licence under the Improvement of Live Stock (Licensing of Bulls) Act 1931 to be accompanied by a veterinary certificate as to the bull's suitability for a licence on the basis of conformation and freedom from disease.

These Regulations therefore revoke previous Regulations governing the licensing of bulls in Scotland. Applications for a bull licence must now be accompanied by a veterinary certificate in the form prescribed by the Regulations. The veterinary surgeon who gives the certificate, must be a member of the panel defined in the Regulations and must also mark the bull with the prescribed inspection mark. The Regulations prescribe an identification mark with which an officer of the Secretary of State for Scotland can mark a bull if it is apparently over the prescribed age for licensing and unlicenced. To facilitate the licensing of bulls in respect of which applications made under the previous Regulations had not been determined at the date the present Regulations came into force, the Regulations contain transitional provisions. New forms of licence and application are prescribed. The Regulations also prescribe the fees payable in respect of applications made thereunder.

STATUTORY INSTRUMENTS

1972 No. 1310

CONSTABULARY, IRELAND

The Royal Irish Constabulary (Widows' Pensions) (Amendment) Regulations 1972

Made - - -	18*th August* 1972
Laid before Parliament	31*st August* 1972
Coming into Operation	2*nd October* 1972

In exercise of the powers conferred on me by section 1 of the Royal Irish Constabulary (Widows' Pensions) Act 1954(a) (read with Article 2(1) of the Minister for the Civil Service Order 1968(b)), I hereby, with the consent of the Minister for the Civil Service, make the following Regulations:—

1. These Regulations may be cited as the Royal Irish Constabulary (Widows' Pensions) (Amendment) Regulations 1972 and shall come into operation on 2nd October 1972.

2.—(1) For paragraph (1) of Regulation 3 of the Royal Irish Constabulary (Widows' Pensions) Regulations 1971(c) (interpretation) there shall be substituted the following provision:—

"(1) In these Regulations "the standard weekly rate" means the rate of £6.75 a week unless the widow is over the age of 80 years in which case it means the rate of £7.00 a week.".

(2) The reference in paragraph (4) of the said Regulation 3 to the Pensions (Increase) Act 1971(d) shall be construed as a reference to that Act as amended by the Superannuation Act 1972(e).

Robert Carr,
One of Her Majesty's Principal
Secretaries of State.

15th August 1972.

Consent of the Minister for the Civil Service given under his Official Seal on 18th August 1972.

(L.S.)

W. G. Bristow,
Authorised by the
Minister for the Civil Service.

(a) 1954 c. 17.   (b) S.I. 1968/1656 (1968 III, p. 4485).
(c) S.I. 1971/1469 (1971 III, p. 4147).   (d) 1971 c. 56.
(e) 1972 c. 11.

EXPLANATORY NOTE
(This Note is not part of the Regulations.)

Under the Royal Irish Constabulary (Widows' Pensions) Regulations 1971 there may be paid to certain widows of former members of the Royal Irish Constabulary a pension or an allowance supplementary to an existing pension. A pension or allowance is not payable under the 1971 Regulations unless the rate of any state insurance benefit received by the widow is less than the standard weekly rate of £6.00 or, where the widow is over the age of 80 years, of £6.25. Subject to a minimum rate of £0.25 a week in the case of a pension, such an award is to be at such rate as will secure that the combined rate of the Royal Irish Constabulary awards and the widow's state insurance benefit, if any, is equal to the standard weekly rate; for this purpose state insurance benefit means any benefit or pension under the National Insurance Act 1965 (c. 51) or the National Insurance (Industrial Injuries) Act 1965 (c. 52) or similar benefit or pension paid out of public funds in Northern Ireland, any of the Channel Islands, the Isle of Man or the Republic of Ireland.

The present Regulations increase the standard weekly rate to £6.75 a week in the case of a widow who is not over the age of 80 years and to £7.00 a week in the case of a widow who is over that age. They also provide that the reference in the 1971 Regulations to the Pensions (Increase) Act 1971 shall be construed as a reference to that Act as amended by the Superannuation Act 1972.

STATUTORY INSTRUMENTS

1972 No. 1312

WAGES COUNCILS

The Wages Regulation (Linen and Cotton Handkerchief etc.) Order 1972

Made - - -	*21st August* 1972
Coming into Operation	*13th September* 1972

Whereas the Secretary of State has received from the Linen and Cotton Handkerchief and Household Goods and Linen Piece Goods Wages Council (Great Britain) the wages regulation proposals set out in the Schedule hereto;

Now, therefore, the Secretary of State in exercise of powers conferred by section 11 of the Wages Councils Act 1959(**a**) and now vested in him (**b**), and of all other powers enabling him in that behalf, hereby makes the following Order: —

1. This Order may be cited as the Wages Regulation (Linen and Cotton Handkerchief etc.) Order 1972.

2.—(1) In this Order, the expression "the specified date" means the 13th September 1972, provided that where, as respects any worker who is paid wages at intervals not exceeding seven days, that date does not correspond with the beginning of the period for which the wages are paid, the expression "the specified date" means, as respects that worker, the beginning of the next such period following that date.

(2) The Interpretation Act 1889(**c**) shall apply to the interpretation of this Order as it applies to the interpretation of an Act of Parliament and as if this Order and the Order hereby revoked were Acts of Parliament.

3. The wages regulation proposals set out in the Schedule hereto shall have effect as from the specified date and as from that date the Wages Regulation (Linen and Cotton Handkerchief etc.) Order 1971(**d**) shall cease to have effect.

Signed by order of the Secretary of State.

21st August 1972.

R. R. D. McIntosh,
Deputy Secretary,
Department of Employment.

(**a**) 1959 c. 69.
(**b**) S.I. 1959/1769, 1968/729 (1959 I, 1795; 1968 II, p. 2108).
(**c**) 1889 c. 63.   (**d**) S.I. 1971/1454 (1971 III, p. 4123).

Article 3

SCHEDULE

The following minimum remuneration shall be substituted for the statutory minimum remuneration fixed by the Wages Regulation (Linen and Cotton Handerkchief etc.) Order 1971 (Order H.L. (77)).

STATUTORY MINIMUM REMUNERATION

PART I

GENERAL

1. The minimum remuneration payable to a worker to whom this Schedule applies for all work except work to which a minimum overtime rate applies under Part IV of this Schedule is:—

(1) in the case of a time worker, the hourly general minimum time rate payable to the worker under Part II of this Schedule;

(2) in the case of a male worker employed on piece work, piece rates each of which would yield, in the circumstances of the case, to an ordinary worker at least the same amount of money as the hourly general minimum time rate which would be payable to the worker under Part II of this Schedule if he were a time worker;

(3) in the case of a female worker employed on piece work, piece rates each of which would yield, in the circumstances of the case, to an ordinary worker at least the same amount of money as the hourly piece work basis time rate applicable to the worker under Part III of this Schedule.

PART II

GENERAL MINIMUM TIME RATES

2. The general minimum time rates are as follows:—

	Per hour p
(1) Male workers aged 18 years or over	
(a) up to and including 31st August 1973	
aged 19 years or over	$37\frac{1}{2}$
„ 18 and under 19 years	31
(b) from 1st September 1973 up to and including 31st August 1974	
aged 19 years or over	$37\frac{1}{2}$
„ 18 and under 19 years	34
(c) from 1st September 1974 up to and including 31st August 1975	
aged 19 years or over	$37\frac{1}{2}$
„ 18 and under 19 years	$35\frac{1}{2}$
(d) on and after 1st September 1975	
aged 18 years or over	$37\frac{1}{2}$
(2) Female workers aged 18 years or over	
(a) up to and including 31st August 1973	31
(b) from 1st September 1973 up to and including 31st August 1974 ...	34
(c) from 1st September 1974 up to and including 31st August 1975 ...	$35\frac{1}{2}$
(d) on and after 1st September 1975	$37\frac{1}{2}$

Provided that the general minimum time rates payable, during the first year's employment in the trade, to a female worker who enters, or has entered, the trade for the first time at or over the age of 18 years shall be:—

(*a*) up to and including 31st August 1973
during the first 3 months of such employment	22
during the second 3 months of such employemnt	23
during the third 3 months of such employment	25½
during the fourth 3 months of such employment	27½

(*b*) from 1st September 1973 up to and including 31st August 1974
during the first 3 months of such employment	24
during the second 3 months of such employment	25
during the third 3 months of such employment	28
during the fourth 3 months of such employment	30

(*c*) from 1st September 1974 up to and including 31st August 1975
during the first 3 months of such employment	25
during the second 3 months of such employment	26
during the third 3 months of such employment	29
during the fourth 3 months of such employment	31½

(*d*) on and after 1st September 1975
during the first 3 months of such employment	26½
during the second 3 months of such employment	27½
during the third 3 months of such employment	30½
during the fourth 3 months of such employment	33½

(3) All workers aged:—
17 and under 18 years	24
16 and under 17 years	19½
15 and under 16 years	15

PART III

PIECE WORK BASIS TIME RATES APPLICABLE TO FEMALE WORKERS

3. The piece work basis time rates applicable to female workers of any age employed on piece work are as follows:—

Per hour
p

(i) up to and including 31st August 1973	32
(ii) from 1st September 1973 up to and including 31st August 1974 ...	35
(iii) from 1st September 1974 up to and including 31st August 1975 ...	36½
(iv) from 1st September 1975	38½

PART IV

OVERTIME AND WAITING TIME
MINIMUM OVERTIME RATES

4.—(1) Minimum overtime rates are payable to any worker to whom this Schedule applies as follows:—

(*a*) on any day other than a Saturday or Sunday—

(i) for the first two hours worked in excess of 8 hours	time-and-a-quarter
(ii) thereafter	time-and-a-half

Provided that where the employer and the worker by agreement in writing fix in respect of each weekday the number of hours after which a minimum overtime rate shall be payable and the total number of such hours amounts to 40 weekly, the following minimum overtime rates shall be payable in substitution for those set out above—

    (i) for the first two hours worked in excess of the agreed
        number of hours ...   . time-and-a-quarter
    (ii) thereafter   ... ... time-and-a-half

(b) on a Saturday—
    (i) for the first two hours worked ... ... time-and-a-quarter
    (ii) thereafter ... ... time-and-a-half

(c) on a Sunday—
    for all time worked ... ... double time

(2) In this Part of this Schedule the expressions "time-and-a-quarter", "time-and-a-half" and "double time" mean, respectively, one and a quarter times, one and a half times and twice the minimum remuneration otherwise payable to the worker.

WAITING TIME

5.—(1) A worker is entitled to payment of the minimum remuneration specified in this Schedule for all time during which he is present on the premises of his employer, unless he is present thereon in any of the following circumstances:—

    (a) without the employer's consent, express or implied;

    (b) for some purpose unconnected with his work and other than that of waiting for work to be given to him to perform;

    (c) by reason only of the fact that he is resident thereon;

    (d) during the normal meal times in a room or place in which no work is being done, and he is not waiting for work to be given to him to perform.

(2) The minimum remuneration payable under sub-paragraph (1) of this paragraph to a piece worker when not engaged on piece work is that which would be payable if he were a time worker.

PART V

APPLICABILITY OF STATUTORY MINIMUM REMUNERATION

6. Subject to paragraph 7, this Schedule applies to workers in relation to whom the Linen and Cotton Handkerchief and Household Goods and Linen Piece Goods Wages Council (Great Britain) operates, that is to say, workers employed in Great Britain in the trade specified in the Regulations made by the Minister and dated 28th May 1920(a), with respect to the Constitution and Proceedings of the Trade Board for the Linen and Cotton Handkerchief and Household Goods and Linen Piece Goods Trade (Great Britain) namely:—

    . (1) The making of such articles as are specified in (a) and (b) below, from linen or cotton or mixed linen and cotton fabrics (excepting knitted fabrics), or from other textile fabrics when the work is carried on in establishments mainly engaged in the making of such articles from the before-mentioned fabrics, viz.:—

    (a) Handkerchiefs (including mufflers or flags when made in association or conjunction with handkerchiefs);

    (b) Bed-linen, towels, dusters, table-napery, bed-spreads, tea-cloths, table-centres, sideboard-covers, cushion-covers, or similar household articles; including all or any of the following operations:—

    (i) Hooking, cutting or tearing the material;

(a) S.R. & O. 1920/854 (1920 II, p. 854).

    (ii) Vice-folding;

    (iii) Machine hemming, hem-stitching, spoking, over-locking, tambouring, button-holing, and other plain or fancy machine stitching;

    (iv) All processes of embroidery or decorative needlework done by machine, whether before or after the making of the articles of the description specified above;

    (v) The following processes if done by machine—thread-drawing, thread-clipping, top-sewing, scalloping, nickelling and paring;

    (vi) All processes of laundering, smoothing, folding, ornamenting, boxing, finishing, warehousing, packing and other similar operations incidental to or appertaining to the making of the articles of the description specified above.

(2) The making up in linen warehouses or in establishments mainly engaged in linen lapping, of linen or mixed linen and cotton or other textile fabrics in the piece, or of linen or mixed linen and cotton or other textile articles cut from the piece, including—

    Measuring, cutting, lapping, ornamenting, boxing, warehousing, packing and similar operations.

7. Notwithstanding paragraph 6, this schedule does not apply to workers who are persons registered as handicapped by disablement in pursuance of the Disabled Persons (Employment) Acts 1944 and 1958(a), in respect of their employment by Remploy Limited.

EXPLANATORY NOTE

(This Note is not part of the Order.)

This Order, which has effect from 13th September 1972, sets out the statutory minimum remuneration payable in substitution for that fixed by the wages Regulation (Linen and Cotton Handkerchief etc.) Order 1971 (Order H.L. (77)), which Order is revoked.

New provisions are printed in italics.

(a) 1949 c. 10; 1958 c. 33.

STATUTORY INSTRUMENTS

1972 No. 1313

ACQUISITION OF LAND

The Compulsory Purchase of Land Regulations 1972

Made - - -	*21st August* 1972
Laid before Parliament	*4th September* 1972
Coming into Operation	*1st October* 1972

The Secretary of State for the Environment, in exercise of his powers under paragraphs 2, 3, 6, 13 and 18 of Schedule 1 to the Acquisition of Land (Authorisation Procedure) Act 1946(**a**) and sections 30 and 104 of, and paragraphs 1, 2 and 4 of Schedule 3 to, the Town and Country Planning Act 1968(**b**), and of all other powers enabling him in that behalf, hereby makes the following regulations: —

Title and commencement

1. These regulations may be cited as the Compulsory Purchase of Land Regulations 1972 and shall come into operation on 1st October 1972.

Interpretation

2.—(1) In these regulations—

"the Acquisition of Land Act" means the Acquisition of Land (Authorisation Procedure) Act 1946; and

"the Planning Act" means the Town and Country Planning Act 1971(**c**).

(2) In these regulations, any reference to a numbered form is a reference to the form bearing that number in the schedule hereto, or a form substantially to the like effect

(3) In these regulations, unless the context otherwise requires, references to any enactment shall be construed as references to that enactment as amended, extended or applied by or under any other enactment.

(4) The Interpretation Act 1889(**d**) shall apply for the interpretation of these regulations as it applies for the interpretation of an Act of Parliament.

Prescribed forms in connection with compulsory purchase

3. The prescribed forms for the undermentioned paragraphs of Schedule 1 to the Acquisition of Land Act (which sets out the procedure for authorising compulsory purchases) shall be as follows: —

    (*a*) for the purposes of paragraph 2, the form of compulsory purchase order shall be form 1, or if the order provides for the vesting of land given in exchange pursuant to paragraph 11, form 2 ;

(**a**) 1946 c. 49.	(**b**) 1968 c. 72.
(**c**) 1971 c. 78.	(**d**) 1889 c. 63.

(*b*) for the purposes of paragraph 3(1)(*a*), the form of newspaper notice concerning a compulsory purchase order shall be form 3 ;

(*c*) subject to the provisions of regulation 4 of these regulations, for the purposes of paragraph 3(1)(*b*) and (*c*), the form of notice to owners, lessees and occupiers of land comprised in a compulsory purchase order shall be form 4, or if the order is made on behalf of a parish council, form 5 ;

(*d*) for the purposes of paragraph 6, the form of notice of confirmation of a compulsory purchase order shall be form 6 ; but in relation to an order made by a Minister, that form shall have effect with the substitution for references to the confirmation of an order submitted of references to the making of the order ;

(*e*) for the purposes of paragraph 13, the form of newspaper notice stating that a certificate has been given under Part III of Schedule 1 to the Acquisition of Land Act shall be form 7.

Additional provisions with respect to listed buildings

4. Where a compulsory purchase order is made under section 114 of the Planning Act (which empowers the compulsory acquisition of listed buildings in need of repair), there shall be included in form 4, at the end of paragraph 2, the additional paragraphs set out after the notes on that form, as follows : —

(*a*) the additional paragraph numbered 3 shall be included in every case ;

(*b*) the additional paragraph numbered 4 shall be included in any case where the notice is required by section 117(3) of the Planning Act (which provides for minimum compensation in the case of a building deliberately left derelict) to include a statement that the authority or Minister has made application for a direction for minimum compensation ;

(*c*) the additional paragraph numbered 5 shall be included in every case ;

and the remaining paragraphs shall be re-numbered as necessary.

Prescribed forms in connection with general vesting declaration

5. The prescribed forms for the undermentioned paragraphs of Schedule 3 to the Town and Country Planning Act 1968 (which sets out the procedure for executing general vesting declarations for land compulsorily acquired) shall be as follows : —

(*a*) for the purposes of paragraph 1, the form of general vesting declaration shall be form 8 ;

(*b*) for the purposes of paragraph 2(1), the form of statement of the effect of paragraphs 1 to 8 shall be Part I of form 9 and the form for the giving of information to the authority shall be Part II of form 9 ;

(*c*) for the purposes of paragraph 4, the form of notice specifying the land and stating the effect of a general vesting declaration shall be form 10.

Revocations

6. The Compulsory Purchase of Land Regulations 1949(**a**) and the Compulsory Purchase of Land (General Vesting Declaration) Regulations 1969(**b**) are hereby revoked ; but this revocation shall not affect the validity of any order, notice, advertisement, declaration or other document made, executed or issued before the commencement of these regulations in a form prescribed by any of the revoked regulations.

(**a**) S.I. 1949/507 (1949 I, p. 2379).   (**b**) S.I. 1969/425 (1969 I, p. 1213).

SCHEDULE

Contents

Regulation 3(a)   FORM 1

COMPULSORY PURCHASE ORDER

The   Act   (a)
and the Acquisition of Land (Authorisation Procedure) Act 1946

―――――――――――――――――――――――――

[The   Act(s)   ]
The   hereby make the following order:—

1. Subject to the provisions of this order, the said   are, under
section   of the   Act   , hereby authorised to purchase compulsorily [on behalf of the parish council of   ]
for the purpose of   (b) the land which is described
in the schedule hereto and is delineated and shown
(c) on the map prepared in duplicate, sealed with the common seal of the said
                      and marked "Map referred to in the
Compulsory Purchase Order 19   ".   One duplicate of the map is deposited in the
offices of the said   and the other is deposited in the offices of the
                              (d).

[2. (e) Section 27 of the Compulsory Purchase Act 1965 shall not apply in
relation to the purchase of land authorised by this order.]

[3. (f) In relation to the foregoing purchase section 77 of the Railways Clauses
Consolidation Act 1845 [and sections 78 to 85 of that Act excluding any amendment
thereof by section 15 of the Mines (Working Facilities and Support) Act 1923]
[is] [are] hereby incorporated with the enactment under which the said purchase is
authorised, subject to the modifications that (g)   ].

4. This order may be cited as the   Compulsory
Purchase Order 19 .

Schedule

Number on map	Extent, description and situation of the land (j)	Owners or reputed owners	Lessees or reputed lessees	Occupiers (other than tenants for a month or less)
(1)	(2)	(3)	(4)	(5)

(k)

[(l) The order includes land falling within special categories to which Part III of
Schedule 1 to the Acquisition of Land (Authorisation Procedure) Act 1946
applies, namely—

Number on map	Description	]

Date (m)

―――――――――――――――――――――――――

For notes see after Form 2.

FORM 2   Regulation 3(a)

COMPULSORY PURCHASE ORDER

(Providing for the vesting of exchange land)

The   Act   (a)

and the Acquisition of Land (Authorisation Procedure) Act 1946

[The   Act(s)]

The   hereby make the following order:—

1. Subject to the provisions of this order, the said
are, under section   of the   Act   ,
hereby authorised to purchase compulsorily [on behalf of the parish council of
      ] for the purpose of   (b) the land which is
described in schedule 1 hereto and is delineated and shown
(c) on the map prepared in duplicate, sealed with the common seal of the said
          and marked "Map referred to in the
Compulsory Purchase Order 19   ".   One duplicate of the map is deposited in the
offices of the said   and the other is deposited in the
offices of the   (d).

[2. (e) Section 27 of the Compulsory Purchase Act 1965 shall not apply in relation
to the purchase of land authorised by this order.]

[3. (f) In relation to the foregoing purchase section 77 of the Railways Clauses
Consolidation Act 1845 [and sections 78 to 85 of that Act excluding any amendment
thereof by section 15 of the Mines (Working Facilities and Support) Act 1923] [is]
[are] hereby incorporated with the enactment under which the said purchase is authorised, subject to the modifications that (g)   ].

4.—(1) In this article "the order land" means (h) [the land referred to in article 1
hereof] [the land described as   in schedule 1 hereto]
and "the exchange land" means the land which is described in schedule 2 hereto and is
delineated and shown   (c) on the said map.

(2) As from the date on which this order becomes operative or the date on which the
order land, or any of it, is vested in the said   (whichever is the
later), the exchange land shall vest in the persons in whom the order land was vested
immediately before that date, subject to the like rights, trusts and incidents as attached
thereto; and the order land shall thereupon be discharged from all rights, trusts and
incidents to which it was previously subject.

5. This order may be cited as the   Compulsory Purchase
Order 19   .

Schedule 1

Land to be purchased

Number on map	Extent, description and situation of the land (j)	Owners or reputed owners	Lessees or reputed lessees	Occupiers (other than tenants for a month or less)
(1)	(2)	(3)	(4)	(5)

(k)

[(*l*) The order includes land falling within special categories to which Part III of Schedule 1 to the Acquisition of Land (Authorisation Procedure) Act 1946 applies, namely—

Number on map	*Description*	]

Schedule 2
Exchange land

Date (*m*)

NOTES TO FORMS 1 AND 2

(*a*) Insert the title of the Act authorising compulsory purchase. If the purpose of acquisition as stated in article 1 of the order is contained in some other Act, the title of that Act (or a collective title) should be added as a sub-heading.

(*b*) Describe the purpose in precise terms, using, where practicable, the words of the relevant Act.

(*c*) Describe the colouring or other method used to identify the land on the map. The boundaries of each parcel of land separately numbered in the schedule to the order should be clearly delineated. Also, the map itself should contain sufficient topographical detail to enable the situation of the land to be readily identified and should normally be on a scale of 1/500 or 1/1250.

(*d*) Insert the name of the confirming authority.

(*e*) This article should be omitted in the case of an order under the Housing Act 1957 and is optional in other cases.

(*f*) This article may be omitted, or may be inserted with or without reference to sections 78 to 85.

(*g*) Insert any consequential modifications required—e.g. "references in the said [section] [sections] to the company shall be construed as references to the said . . . . . . and references to the [railway or] works shall be construed as references to the land authorised to be purchased and any buildings or works constructed or to be constructed thereon".

(*h*) Use the first alternative if the whole of the land referred to in article 1 falls within paragraph 11 of Schedule 1 to the Act of 1946. Otherwise, use the second alternative and specify the parcel number(s) of the land which does fall within paragraph 11.

(*j*) This column should contain sufficient detail to tell the reader approximately where the land is situated, without reference to the map.

In describing the land regard should be had (where appropriate) to note (*l*) below.

(*k*) Col. (1) need not be completed where the order relates only to one parcel of land. Where there are two or more parcels they should be numbered 1, 2, etc. on the map and referred to accordingly in column (1). Columns (3) to (5) need not be completed in the case of any land in respect of which the confirming authority has dispensed with service on owners, lessees and occupiers under paragraph 3(1)(*b*) of Schedule 1 to the Acquisition of Land (Authorisation Procedure) Act 1946.

(*l*) The compulsory acquisition of land—

(*i*) which is the property of a local authority;

(*ii*) which has been acquired by statutory undertakers for the purposes of their undertaking;

(*iii*) forming part of a common, open space or fuel or field garden allotment;

(*iv*) held inalienably by the National Trust; or

(*v*) being, or being the site of, an ancient monument or other object of archæological interest,

is subject to Part III of Schedule 1 to the Act of 1946 and consequently may be subject to Special Parliamentary Procedure in certain circumstances.

The column 'Description' need only refer to the special category into which the relevant parcel of land falls.

(*m*) The order should be made under seal, duly authenticated.

FORM 3   Regulation 3(b)

NEWSPAPER NOTICE CONCERNING A COMPULSORY PURCHASE ORDER

COMPULSORY PURCHASE OF LAND IN   (a)

Notice is hereby given that the
                    have made the
Compulsory Purchase Order 19   under the   Act   (b)
They are about to submit this order to
          for confirmation, and if confirmed, the order will authorise them to purchase
compulsorily the land described below for the purpose of   (c)

A copy of the order and of the accompanying map may be seen at all reasonable
hours at   (d)

Any objection to the order must be made in writing to   (e)
before   (f) and should state the grounds of objection.

DESCRIPTION OF LAND
(g)
[Date and signature]

NOTES

(a) Insert the name of the area in which the land concerned is situated.

(b) Insert the title of the Act authorising compulsory purchase.   The Acquisition of Land
    (Authorisation Procedure) Act 1946 need not be mentioned.

(c) Insert the purpose as stated in the order.

(d) The place of deposit must be "within the locality".   It should therefore be within
    relatively easy reach of persons living in the area affected.

(e) Insert name and address of the confirming authority.

(f) Insert a date at least 21 clear days from the date of first publication of the notice
    (i.e. 21 days excluding the date of first publication).

(g) Insert description of all the land described in the order.   This need not repeat the
    schedule to the order, but must be in terms which enable the reader to appreciate what
    land is included.

Regulation 3(c)   FORM 4

NOTICE TO OWNERS, LESSEES AND OCCUPIERS OF LAND COMPRISED IN A COMPULSORY
PURCHASE ORDER

The   Act   (a)
and the Acquisition of Land (Authorisation Procedure) Act 1946

[The   Act(s)   ]

1. Take notice that the   ,
in exercise of their powers under the above Acts, on
19   made the   Compulsory Purchase Order 19   ,
which is about to be submitted to the   for confirmation.
The order, if confirmed, will authorise the   to purchase
compulsorily, for the purpose of   (b), the land described below.

2. A copy of the order and of the map referred to therein have been deposited at
(c) and may be seen there at all reasonable hours.

3. If no objection is duly made by an owner, lessee or occupier (except a tenant
for a month or less), or if all objections so made are withdrawn, or if the confirming
authority is satisfied that every objection so made (d) [either] relates exclusively to
matters of compensation which can be dealt with by the Lands Tribunal [or amounts
in substance to an objection to the provisions of the development plan defining the
proposed use of the land comprised in the order or any other land] [or amounts in
substance to an objection to the   Scheme/Order
19   ], the confirming authority may confirm the order with or without modifications.

4. In any other case where an objection has been made by an owner, lessee or
occupier (except a tenant for a month or less), the confirming authority is required,
before confirming the order, either to cause a public local inquiry to be held or to
afford to the objector an opportunity of appearing before and being heard by a person
appointed by the confirming authority for the purpose, and may then, after considering
the objection and the report of the person who held the inquiry or hearing, confirm
the order with or without modifications.

5. Any objection to the order must be made in writing to   (e)
before   (f), and should state the grounds of objection.

Description of land
(g)

[Date and signature]

NOTES

(a) The heading and any sub-heading should be the same as in the order.
(b) Insert the purpose as stated in the order.
(c) The place of deposit must be "within the locality". It should therefore be within
relatively easy reach of persons living in the area affected.
(d) The words in square brackets containing the reference to the development plan are
required only where the order is made under sections 112 and 113 of the Town and
Country Planning Act 1971. The words in square brackets containing the reference
to the..........................Scheme/Order 19...... are required only when the order is
made under highway land acquisition powers (as defined in section 47(2) of the Highways Act 1971) and the circumstances specified in section 54(1) of the Highways
Act 1971 apply. In all other cases the bracketed words should be omitted.
(e) Insert name and address of confirming authority.
(f) Insert a date at least 21 clear days from the date of service of the notice (i.e. 21 days
excluding the date of service).
(g) Insert description of all the land comprised in the order. This need not repeat the
schedule to the order, but must be in terms from which persons interested can readily
see how their land is affected.

Additional provisions in relation to compulsory purchase orders made under section 114 *of the Town and Country Planning Act* 1971

3. Under section 114 of the Town and Country Planning Act 1971, any person having an interest in a listed building which it is proposed to acquire compulsorily under that section may, within 28 days after the service of this notice, apply to the magistrates' court for an order staying further proceedings on the compulsory purchase order; and, if the court is satisfied that reasonable steps have been taken for properly preserving the building, the court must make an order accordingly.

4. The   (*a*) have made application in the order for a direction for minimum compensation (the meaning of which is explained   (*b*)). Under section 117 of the Town and Country Planning Act 1971, any person having an interest in the building may, within 28 days after the service of this notice, apply to the magistrates' court for an order that the application be refused; and if the court is satisfied that the building has not been deliberately allowed to fall into disrepair for the purpose of justifying its demolition and the development or re-development of the site or any adjoining site, the court must make the order applied for.

5. Subject to any action taken under the 1971 Act (which also provides for appeals against decisions of the court) the position with respect to this order is as set out below.

NOTES
(*a*) Insert the name of the acquiring authority. If the acquiring authority is a Minister, the paragraph should begin "The   has included in the draft order a direction for minimum compensation...............".

(*b*) Insert a reference to the place where the meaning of "direction for minimum compensation" is explained—eg "below" or "on the attached note". (This explanation is required by section 117(3) of the Town and Country Planning Act 1971 in any case where an application is made for such a direction; and it should normally include the text of section 117(4)).

Regulation 3(c)   FORM 5

NOTICE TO OWNERS, LESSEES AND OCCUPIERS OF LAND COMPRISED IN A COMPULSORY
PURCHASE ORDER MADE ON BEHALF OF A PARISH COUNCIL

The Local Government Act 1933
and
The Acquisition of Land (Authorisation Procedure) Act 1946

[The   Act(s)   (a)]

1. Take notice that the county council of   ,
in exercise of their powers under the above Acts, on
19   made the   Compulsory Purchase Order 19   , which
is about to be submitted to the Secretary of State for the Environment (b) for confirmation.   The order, if confirmed, will authorise the council to purchase compulsorily,
on behalf of the parish council of   , for the purpose of
(c), the land described below.

2. A copy of the order and the map referred to therein have been deposited at
(d) and may be seen there at all reasonable hours.

3. If no objection is duly made by any of the owners, lessees and occupiers of the
land in question, or if all objections so made are withdrawn, or if the Secretary of State
is satisfied that the objection relates exclusively to matters of compensation which can
be dealt with by the Lands Tribunal, the Secretary of State is required to confirm the
order with or without modification.

4. In any other case, the Secretary of State is required, before confirming the order,
either to cause a public local inquiry to be held or to afford to the objector an opportunity of appearing before and being heard by a person appointed by the Secretary of
State for the purpose, and may then, after considering the objection and the report of
the person who held the inquiry or hearing, confirm the order with or without modifications.

5. Any objection to the order must be made in writing to the Secretary of State for
the Environment, 2 Marsham Street, London, SW1P 3EB before
(e), and should state the grounds of objection.

Description of land
(f)
[Date and signature]

NOTES

(a) Any sub-heading should be the same as the sub-heading in the order.

(b) If the order relates to a parish council in Wales or Monmouthshire, it should refer
instead to the Secretary of State for Wales, whose address should be given in paragraph
5 as the Welsh Office, Cathays Park, Cardiff, CF1 3NQ.

(c) Insert the purpose as stated in the order.

(d) The place of deposit must be "within the locality".   It should therefore be within
relatively easy reach of persons living in the area affected.

(e) Insert a date at least 21 clear days from the date of service of the notice (ie 21 days
excluding the date of service).

(f) Insert description of all the land comprised in the order.   This need not repeat the
schedule to the order, but must be in terms from which persons interested can readily
see how their land is affected.

Form 6   Regulation 3(d)

Notice of Confirmation of a Compulsory Purchase Order

The   Act   (a)
and the Acquisition of Land (Authorisation Procedure) Act 1946

[The   Act(s)]

1. Notice is hereby given that the   , in exercise of [his] powers
under the above Acts, on   confirmed [with modifications]
the   Compulsory Purchase Order 19   submitted by the
                                                    [on behalf of the
parish council of   ].

2. The order as confirmed provides for the purchase for the purpose of
              (b) of the land described in [the] schedule [1] hereto. [By a
direction given under section 132 of the Town and Country Planning Act 1971,
consideration of the order, so far as it relates to the land described in schedule 2, has
been postponed until   ] (c). [By a direction given under
section 55 of the Highways Act 1971 consideration of the order, so far as it relates to the
land described in Schedule 2, has been postponed until   ](d).

3. A copy of the order as confirmed by the
and of the map referred to therein have been deposited at   (e)
and may be seen there at all reasonable hours.

4. (f) The order as confirmed becomes operative on the date on which this notice is
first published; but a person aggrieved by the order may, by application to the High
Court within 6 weeks from that date, question its validity on the grounds (i) that the
authorisation granted by the order is not empowered to be granted or (ii) that his
interests have been substantially prejudiced by failure to comply with any statutory
requirement relating to the order.

OR

4. The order as confirmed is subject to special parliamentary procedure and will
become operative as provided by the Statutory Orders (Special Procedure) Act 1945.
Unless the order is confirmed by Act of Parliament under section 6 of that Act, a
person aggrieved by the order may, by application to the High Court within 6 weeks
from the operative date, question its validity on the ground (i) that the authorisation
granted by the order is not empowered to be granted or (ii) that his interests have been
substantially prejudiced by failure to comply with any statutory requirement relating
to the order.

SCHEDULE [1]
Land comprised in the order as confirmed

[SCHEDULE 2
Land in respect of which consideration has been postponed]

(g)

[Date and signature]

Notes

(a) The heading and any sub-heading should be the same as in the order as confirmed.

(b) Insert the purpose as stated in the order.

(c) & (d) Omit the passages in square brackets where inappropriate.

(e) The place of desposit should be "within the locality". It should therefore be within
relatively easy reach of persons living in the area affected.

(f) Leave standing whichever alternative is appropriate.

(g) Where this form is to include a statement concerning general vesting declarations, the
statement should be included at this point.

Regulation 3(e)   FORM 7

NOTICE OF THE GIVING OF A CERTIFICATE UNDER PART III OF SCHEDULE 1 TO THE
ACQUISITION OF LAND (AUTHORISATION PROCEDURE) ACT 1946

The Acquisition of Land (Authorisation Procedure) Act 1946

1. The   Compulsory Purchase Order 19   , which has
been [submitted by   to the   for confirmation]
[prepared in draft by   ], includes the land described in the
schedule hereto.

2. (*a*) This land was acquired by   for the
purposes of their undertaking and the Secretary of State is satisfied that [it is used]
[an interest is held in it] for the purposes of the carrying on of their undertaking.

OR

This land [is] [forms part of] [a common] [an open space] [a fuel or field garden
allotment].

OR

This land [is] [forms part of] [is the site of] an ancient monument or other object of
archaeological interest.

3. Notice is hereby given that the Secretary of State, in exercise of his powers under
paragraph [10] [11] [12] of Part III of Schedule 1 to the above-mentioned Act, has
certified (*b*)

4. A map showing the land to which the certificate relates [and the land proposed to
be given in exchange] may be inspected at (*c*)   at all reasonable
hours.

5. The certificate becomes operative on the date on which this notice is first published;
but a person aggrieved by the certificate may, by application to the High Court within
6 weeks from that date, question its validity on the ground that his interests have been
substantially prejudiced by failure to comply with any statutory requirement relating
to the certificate.

SCHEDULE
(*d*)

[Date and signature]

NOTES

(*a*) Delete as appropriate.

(*b*) Insert the terms of the certificate.

(*c*) The place of deposit should be "within the locality". It should therefore be within
relatively easy reach of persons living in the area affected.

(*d*) Insert description of the land to which the certificate relates.

FORM 8 Regulation 5(a)

GENERAL VESTING DECLARATION

This GENERAL VESTING DECLARATION is made the day
of 19 by (*a*) (hereinafter
called "the Authority").
WHEREAS:

(1) On 19 an order entitled the
was [made] [confirmed] by (*b*)
under the powers conferred on [him] [them] by the
Act (*c*) authorising the Authority to acquire certain land
specified in the Schedule hereto.

(2) Notice of the [making] [confirmation] of the order was first published in accordance with [paragraph 6 of Schedule 1 to the Acquisition of Land (Authorisation Procedure) Act 1946 (*d*)] on 19 .

(3) (*e*) The said notice included a statement and a notification complying with paragraph 2(1) of Schedule 3 to the Town and Country Planning Act 1968.

OR

(3) A subsequent notice given on 19 before the service of any notice to treat in respect of any of the land described in the Schedule hereto included a statement and a notification complying with paragraph 2(1) of Schedule 3 to the Town and Country Planning Act 1968.

(4) (*e*) The said [subsequent] notice did not specify any period longer than two months beginning with the date of the first publication thereof as the period before the end of which this general vesting declaration could not be executed.

OR

(4) The said [subsequent] notice specified the period of months beginning with the date of the first publication thereof as the period before the end of which the general vesting declaration could not be executed.

OR

(4) The consent in writing of every occupier of any of the land described in the Schedule hereto was obtained for the execution on the date above mentioned of this general vesting declaration.

NOW THIS DEED WITNESSETH that in exercise of the powers conferred on them by section 30 of the Town and Country Planning Act 1968 (hereinafter called "the Act") the Authority hereby declare as follows:

1. The land described in [Part I of(*f*)] the Schedule hereto (being [the whole] [part] of the land authorised to be acquired by the order) and more particularly delineated on the plan annexed hereto together with the right to enter upon and take possession of the same shall vest in the Authority as from the end of the period of [insert period of 28 days or longer] from the date on which the service of notices required by paragraph 4 of Schedule 3 to the Act is completed.

2. For the purposes of paragraph 16(1) of Schedule 3 to the Act (which defines "long tenancy which is about to expire" in relation to a general vesting declaration as meaning a tenancy granted for an interest greater than a minor tenancy as therein defined but having at the date of the declaration a period still to run which is not more than the specified period, that is to say, such period, longer than one year, as may be specified in the declaration in relation to the land in which the tenancy subsists) the Authority hereby specify that [in relation to the land comprised in this declaration that period shall be years and months] [in relation to each area of land specified in column 1 of Part II of the Schedule hereto that period shall be the period stated with respect to that area in column 2 thereof].

THE SCHEDULE

(*g*) Date

NOTES

(a) Insert the name of the acquiring authority.

(b) Insert the name of the confirming authority or, where the order was made by a Minister, that Minister.

(c) Insert the title of the Act authorising compulsory purchase.

(d) Where the notice was published under a procedure prescribed by some enactment other than the Acquisition of Land (Authorisation Procedure) Act 1946, refer instead to the relevant provision of that enactment.

(e) Delete any alternative which does not apply.

(f) The Schedule should be divided into Part I and Part II where Part II is required for the purpose of the final sentence of paragraph 2 of the declaration.

(g) The declaration should be made under seal, duly authenticated.

Form 9   Regulation 5(b)

STATEMENT CONCERNING GENERAL VESTING DECLARATIONS

Part 1 below contains a statement of the effect of paragraphs 1 to 8 of Schedule 3 to the Town and Country Planning Act 1968 and Part II contains a form for giving information.

PART I

Power to make general vesting declaration

1. The   (hereinafter called   )
(*a*) may acquire any of the land described in [the] schedule [1] [above] [below] [hereto] (*b*) by making a general vesting declaration under section 30 of the Town and Country Planning Act 1968 which has the effect, subject to paragraph 4 below, of vesting the land in the   (*a*) at the end of the period mentioned in paragraph 2 below.   Generally a declaration may not be made before the end of a period of two months from the order becoming operative except with the consent of every occupier of the land affected.

Notices concerning general vesting declaration

2. Before the   (*a*) make a general vesting declaration, they must serve notice of it on every occupier of any of the land affected (except land where there is one of the short tenancies described in paragraph 3) and on every person who gives them information relating to the land in pursuance of the invitation contained in this or any similar notice.   When the service of notices of the general vesting declaration is completed, an intermediate period before vesting begins to run.   This period, which must not be less than 28 days, will be specified in the declaration.   At the end of this period the land described in the declaration will, subject to what is said in paragraph 4, vest in the   (*a*) together with the right to enter on the land and take possession of it.   At the same time every person on whom the   (*a*) could have served a notice to treat in respect of his interest in the land (other than a tenant under one of the short tenancies described in paragraph 3) will be entitled to compensation for the acquisition of his interest in the land and to interest on the compensation from the date of vesting.

Tenancies with only a short time to run

3. Where a person's interest arises under a tenancy which has only a short time to run, the position stated above is subject to modifications.   For the modifications to apply the tenancy must be either a "minor tenancy", i.e. a tenancy for a year or a yearly tenancy or a tenancy for a lesser interest, or "a long tenancy which is about to expire".   The latter expression means a tenancy granted for an interest greater than a minor tenancy but having at the date of the general vesting declaration a period still to run which is not more than the period specified in the declaration for this purpose (which must be more than a year).   In calculating how long a tenancy has to run, where any option to renew or to terminate it is available to either party, it is assumed that the landlord will take every opportunity open to him to terminate the tenancy while the tenant will use every opportunity to retain or extend his interest.

Notice of entry

4. The   (*a*) may not exercise the right of entry referred to in paragraph 2 in respect of land subject to one of the short tenancies described in paragraph 3 unless they first serve notice to treat in respect of the tenancy and then serve every occupier of the land with a notice of their intention to enter and take possession after the period (not less than 14 days) specified in the notice.   The right of entry will be exercisable at the end of that period.   The effect of the general vesting declaration will be subject to the tenancy until it comes to an end.

[Schedule] (*b*)

PART II (*c*)

Form for giving information

The   Compulsory Purchase Order 19

To: (*a*)

[I] [We] being [a person] who, if a general vesting declaration were made under paragraph 1 of Schedule 3 to the Town and Country Planning Act 1968 in respect of all the land comprised in the compulsory purchase order cited above in respect of which notice to treat has not been given, would be entitled to claim compensation in respect of [all] [part of] that land, hereby give you the following information, pursuant to the provisions of paragraph 2(1)(*b*) of the said Schedule.

1. Name and address of claimant(s) (i)..
....

2. Land in which an interest is held by claimant(s) (ii)..
....

3. Nature of interest (iii)...
        Signed...
        [on behalf of..].
        Date..

    (i) In the case of a joint interest insert the names and addresses of all the claimants.

   (ii) The land should be described concisely.

 (iii) If the interest is leasehold, the date of commencement and length of term should be given. If the land is subject to a mortgage or other incumbrance, details should be given, e.g. name of building society and roll number.

NOTES

(*a*) Insert the name of the acquiring authority, and define them by an appropriate term. Thereafter rely on the definition wherever "(*a*)" appears in the text.

(*b*) If this notice is served separately from the notice of confirmation (Form 6), insert a description of the land in a schedule following paragraph 4. Otherwise delete square brackets and preceding words as appropriate.

(*c*) The acquiring authority are obliged by paragraph 2(1)(*b*) of Schedule 3 to the Act to include in the notice of confirmation (Form 6) or a subsequent notice:—

   (i) a statement of the effect of paragraphs 1 to 8 of that Schedule in a prescribed form (ie this form); and

  (ii) a notification to the effect that every person who, if a general vesting declaration were made in respect of all the land comprised in the order in respect of which notice to treat has not been given, would be entitled to claim compensation in respect of any such land is invited to give information to the authority making the declaration in the prescribed form with respect to his name and address and the land in question.

The acquiring authority may find it convenient to include this notification immediately before the form of invitation, which may then be introduced by such words as "The relevant prescribed form is [attached separately] [in these terms]".

NOTICE STATING EFFECT OF GENERAL VESTING DECLARATION
TOWN AND COUNTRY PLANNING ACT 1968

The   Compulsory Purchase Order 19

To:

of:

NOTICE IS HEREBY GIVEN that the   (hereinafter called
"the   ") (a) on   19   made a general vesting
declaration under section 30 of the Town and Country Planning Act 1968 (hereinafter
called "the Act") vesting the land described in the schedule to this notice (hereinafter
called "the said land") in themselves as from the end of the period of......days from
the date on which the service of the notices required by paragraph 4 of Schedule 3
to the Act is completed.

Paragraph 4 of Schedule 3 to the Act requires notices to be served on every occupier
of any of the land specified in the declaration (other than land in which there subsists
a "minor tenancy" or a "long tenancy which is about to expire"—these expressions
are defined in Appendix A to this notice)—and on every other person who has given
information to the   (a) with respect to any of that
land in pursuance of the invitation published and served under paragraph 2(1) of
Schedule 3 to the Act.

The   (a) will in due course specify in a certificate the
date on which the service of the said notices is completed.

The effect of the general vesting declaration is as follows.

On the date of vesting (as determined in accordance with the first paragraph of this
notice) the said land, together with the right to enter upon and take possession of it,
will vest in the   (a) as if the   (a)
had on that date exercised their powers to execute a deed poll under Part I of the
Compulsory Purchase Act 1965.

Also, on the date of vesting, the Acts providing for compensation will apply as if,
on the date on which the general vesting declaration was made (namely,
19   ), a notice to treat had been served on every person on whom the   (a)
could have served such a notice (other than any person entitled to an interest in the
land in respect of which such a notice had actually been served before the date of
vesting and any person entitled to a minor tenancy or a long tenancy which is about
to expire).

If the land includes any land in which there is a minor tenancy or a long tenancy
which is about to expire, the right of entry will not be exercisable in respect of that
land unless, after serving a notice to treat in respect of that tenancy, the
              (a) have served on every occupier of any of the land in which the tenancy
subsists a notice stating that, at the end of a specified period (at least 14 days from the
date of the service of the notice, i.e. 14 days excluding the date of first publication)
they intend to enter upon and take possession of the land specified in the notice, and
that period has expired: the vesting of the land will then be subject to the tenancy
until that period expires, or the tenancy comes to an end, whichever happens first.

Schedule 3A to the Act (as enacted in Appendix A of Schedule 2 to the Land Commission (Dissolution) Act 1971) contains supplementary provisions as to general
vesting declarations.   These provisions are set out in Appendix B to this notice.

A copy of the general vesting declaration to which this notice refers and of the
plan annexed to the declaration can be inspected at   (b) and may be
seen at all reasonable hours.

SCHEDULE

[Description of the land vested in the   (a) by the general
vesting declaration].

APPENDIX A

[Here set out paragraph 16 of Schedule 3 to the Act]

APPENDIX B

[Here set out Schedule 3A to the Act]

[Date and signature]

NOTES

(a) Insert the name of the authority, and define them by an appropriate term.   Thereafter
rely on that definition wherever "(a)" appears in the text.

(b) Insert address of the authority's office, as appropriate.

P. Walker,
Secretary of State for the Environment.

21st August 1972.

EXPLANATORY NOTE
(*This Note is not part of the Regulations.*)

These Regulations consolidate with amendments the previous Regulations
which prescribe forms for use in connection with—

(a) compulsory purchase of land under the procedure of the Acquisition
of Land (Authorisation Procedure) Act 1946 and

(b) general vesting declarations, following a compulsory purchase order.

The forms prescribed by these Regulations include—

(i) the compulsory purchase order itself.   This contains extended
requirements concerning the description of the land ;

(ii) the preliminary notices—i.e. the newspaper notice and the personal
notice to owners, lessees and occupiers, describing the effect of
the order and specifying how objections can be made.   The former is a revised and simplified notice ;

(iii) the notice of confirmation ;

(iv) the notice that a certificate has been given under Part III of
Schedule 1 to the Act of 1946 ;

(v) the general vesting declaration itself ;

(vi) the statement of the effect of the statutory provisions relating to
a general vesting declaration ;

(vii) the notice that such a declaration has been made, and explaining
the effect.

Apart from the changes noted above, the changes of substance from the
previous Regulations are necessitated by other legislation—e.g. the omission
of material relevant only to the Land Commission.   Otherwise the changes
are relatively minor, being verbal changes.

STATUTORY INSTRUMENTS

1972 No. 1314 (C.32)

TOWN AND COUNTRY PLANNING,

ENGLAND AND WALES

The Town and Country Planning Act 1971
(Commencement No. 5) (West Midlands) Order 1972

Made - - - *21st August* 1972

The Secretary of State for the Environment in exercise of the power conferred on him by section 21 of the Town and Country Planning Act 1971(a) hereby makes the following order: —

1.—(1) This order may be cited as the Town and Country Planning Act 1971 (Commencement No. 5) (West Midlands) Order 1972.

(2) In this order: —

"the Act" means the Town and Country Planning Act 1971; and

"the Order area" means the area described in Schedule 1 to this order.

2. The provisions of the Act specified in the first column of Schedule 2 hereto (which relate to the matters specified in the second column of the said Schedule) shall come into operation in the Order area on 11th September 1972.

SCHEDULE 1

THE ORDER AREA

The county boroughs of Birmingham, Burton upon Trent, Coventry, Dudley, Solihull, Stoke-on-Trent, Walsall, Warley, West Bromwich, Wolverhampton and Worcester.

The administrative counties of Herefordshire, Salop, Warwickshire and Worcestershire.

In the administrative county of Staffordshire:—

The boroughs of Lichfield, Newcastle-under-Lyme, Stafford and Tamworth.

The urban districts of Aldridge-Brownhills, Biddulph, Cannock, Kidsgrove, Leek, Rugeley, Stone and Uttoxeter.

The rural districts of Cannock, Lichfield, Newcastle-under-Lyme, Seisdon, Stafford, Stone, Tutbury and Uttoxeter.

In the rural district of Cheadle, the whole of the following parishes:—

Alton
Caverswall
Cheadle
Checkley
Cheddleton
Consall
Cotton
Dilhorne
Draycott in the Moors
Farley

(a) 1971 c. 78.

Forsbrook
Ipstones
Kingsley
Oakamoor

Those parts of the parishes of Blore with Swinscoe and Waterhouses which lie outside the area included in the Peak District National Park (Designation) Order 1951, and which are more particularly delineated on the map annexed hereto and thereon hatched black.

In the rural district of Leek, the whole of the following parishes:—

Bagnall
Bradnop
Brown Edge
Endon and Stanley
Horton
Longsdon
Rushton
Tittesworth

Those parts of the parishes of Heaton, Onecote and Leekfrith which lie outside the area included in the Peak District National Park (Designation) Order 1951, and which are more particularly delineated on the said map and thereon hatched black.

SCHEDULE 2

PROVISIONS COMING INTO OPERATION IN THE ORDER AREA ON 11th September 1972

provisions of the Act	Subject matter of provisions
In Part II: section 9(3) and (5) to (8)	Amended provisions relating to approval of structure plans by Secretary of State.
section 10A	Provision for joint surveys, reports and structure plans.
section 10B	Provision for withdrawal of structure plans, and as to effect of steps taken in connection with plans withdrawn or not submitted.
section 14(4)	Provisions relating to approval of local plans submitted to the Secretary of State.

P. Walker,
Secretary of State for the Environment.

21st August 1972.

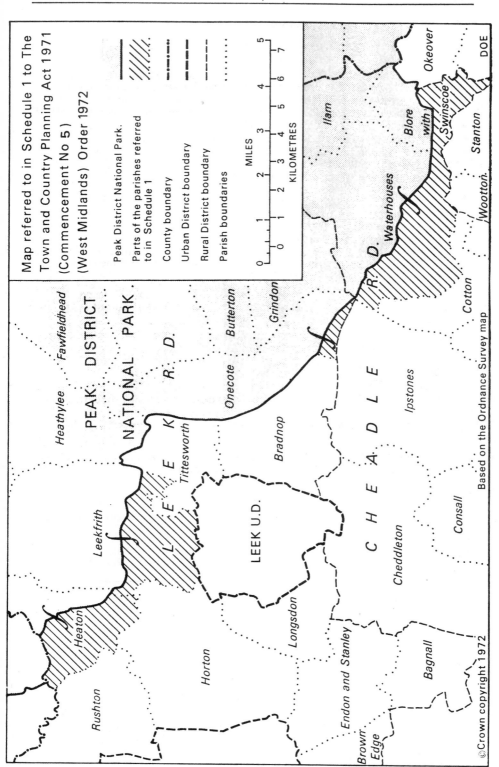

Map referred to in Schedule 1 to The Town and Country Planning Act 1971 (Commencement No 5) (West Midlands) Order 1972

Peak District National Park.

Parts of the parishes referred to in Schedule 1

County boundary

Urban District boundary

Rural District boundary

Parish boundaries

MILES

KILOMETRES

© Crown copyright 1972

Based on the Ordnance Survey map

DOE

EXPLANATORY NOTE

(This Note is not part of the Order.)

This Order brings into force for the area of the West Midlands as described in Schedule 1 to the Order those provisions of Part II of the Town and Country Planning Act 1971 which were inserted into that Act by sections 1, 2 and 3 of the Town and Country Planning (Amendment) Act 1972 (1972 c. 42) and which are set out in Schedule 2 to the Order.   By virtue of the Town and Country Planning Act 1971 (Commencement No. 1) (West Midlands) Order 1972 (S.I. 1972/1060 (C.18)), the remaining provisions of Part II of the Act, which relate to structure and local plans were brought into force in the area concerned on 25th July 1972.

The provisions which are brought into force by the present Order are—

(*a*) new substantive provisions empowering any two or more local planning authorities, with the consent of the Secretary of State, to carry out their duties under Part II of the Act of 1971 to institute surveys, prepare reports and prepare and submit structure plans for their areas by instituting a joint survey, preparing a joint report and preparing and submitting a joint structure plan for a combined area consisting of their areas or any part of their areas;

(*b*) new substantive provisions for the withdrawal of structure plans after submission to the Secretary of State;

(*c*) provisions specifying an amended procedure for the consideration and approval by the Secretary of State of structure plans and proposals for the amendment of structure plans (under this new procedure, the Secretary of State will no longer be required to afford objectors to the structure plan or to the proposals an opportunity of being heard at an inquiry but he will still be required to consider all valid objections and will, in addition, be required to hold an examination in public of matters affecting his consideration of the plan or proposals);

(*d*) the provisions now set out in section 14(4) of the Act of 1971 for the procedure to be adopted where the Secretary of State has directed that a local plan be submitted to him for approval.

STATUTORY INSTRUMENTS

1972 No. 1315

THERAPEUTIC SUBSTANCES

The Therapeutic Substances (Sulphanilamide Derivatives) (Supply of Eye Drops and Eye Ointments) Regulations 1972

Made - - -	*22nd August* 1972
Laid before Parliament	*31st August* 1972
Coming into Operation	*1st October* 1972

The Secretary of State for Social Services, the Secretary of State for Wales, the Secretary of State for Scotland and the Secretary of State for Northern Ireland, acting jointly, in exercise of their powers under section 9 of the Therapeutic Substances Act 1956(a), as amended by Article 2(2) of, and Schedule 1 to, the Transfer of Functions (Wales) Order 1969(b) and as having effect subject to the provisions of section 1(1)(a) of the Northern Ireland (Temporary Provisions) Act 1972(c) and of all other powers enabling them in that behalf, after consultation with the Medical Research Council, hereby make the following regulations:--

Citation and commencement

1. These regulations may be cited as the Therapeutic Substances (Sulphanilamide Derivatives) (Supply of Eye Drops and Eye Ointments) Regulations 1972, and shall come into operation on 1st October 1972.

Interpretation

2.—(1) In these regulations, unless the context otherwise requires—

"eye drops" means sterile aqueous or oily solutions or suspensions for instillation into the eye;

"eye ointment" means any sterile ointment for application to the conjunctival sac or lid margin of the eye;

"ophthalmic optician" means a person registered in either of the registers kept under section 2 of the Opticians Act 1958(d) of ophthalmic opticians or a body corporate enrolled in the list kept under section 4 of that Act of such bodies carrying on business as ophthalmic opticians.

(2) The Interpretation Act 1889(e) applies for the purpose of the interpretation of these regulations as it applies for the purpose of the interpretation of an Act of Parliament.

Sale or supply without prescription

3. Section 9(1) of the Therapeutic Substances Act 1956 (control of sale and supply of substances to which Part II of that Act applies) shall not apply to the sale or supply of:—

(a) 1956 c. 25. (b) S.I. 1969/388 (1969 I, p. 1070). (c) 1972 c. 22.
(d) 1958 c. 32. (e) 1889 c. 63.

(a) sulphacetamide sodium contained in any eye ointment when the sale or supply is to a person who requires it for the purpose of enabling him to comply with any requirements made by or in pursuance of any enactment with respect to the provision of first-aid rooms or first-aid boxes or cases, or

(b) sulphacetamide sodium or sulphafurazole diethanolamine contained in any eye ointment or eye drops when the sale or supply is to an ophthalmic optician for the purpose of his profession or business.

Keith Joseph,
Secretary of State for Social Services.

8th August 1972.

Peter Thomas,
Secretary of State for Wales.

18th August 1972.

Gordon Campbell,
Secretary of State for Scotland.

22nd August 1972.

Signed by authority of the Secretary of State for Northern Ireland.

P. Channon,
Minister of State,
Northern Ireland Office.

14th August 1972.

EXPLANATORY NOTE

(This Note is not part of the Regulations.)

The Therapeutic Substances (Control of Sale and Supply) (No. 2) Regulations 1971 (S.I. 1971/459) bring within the scope of Part II of the Therapeutic Substances Act 1956 various substances including sulphanilamide and certain of its derivatives. The effect of these regulations is to permit the sale and supply without prescription of eye ointments containing sulphacetamide sodium to persons under statutory obligations with respect to first-aid rooms or first-aid boxes or cases and of eye ointments or eye drops containing sulphacetamide sodium or sulphafurazole diethanolamine to ophthalmic opticians for the purposes of their profession.

STATUTORY INSTRUMENTS

1972 No. 1326

SUGAR

The Sugar (Distribution Payments) (No. 17) Order 1972

Made - - - -	*23rd August* 1972
Laid before Parliament	*24th August* 1972
Coming into Operation	*25th August* 1972

The Minister of Agriculture, Fisheries and Food, in exercise of the powers conferred upon him by sections 14(5) and 33(4) of the Sugar Act 1956(**a**), having effect subject to the provisions of section 3 of, and Part II of Schedule 5 to, the Finance Act 1962(**b**), section 22 of the Finance Act 1964(**c**) and section 52 of the Finance Act 1966(**d**) and of all other powers enabling him in that behalf, with the concurrence of the Treasury, and on the advice of the Sugar Board hereby makes the following order:—

1.—(1) This order may be cited as the Sugar (Distribution Payments) (No. 17) Order 1972, and shall come into operation on 25th August 1972.

(2) The Interpretation Act 1889(**e**) shall apply for the interpretation of this order as it applies for the interpretation of an Act of Parliament.

2. Notwithstanding the provisions of article 2 of the Sugar (Distribution Payments) (No. 16) Order 1972(**f**), the rates of distribution payments payable under and in accordance with the provisions of section 14 of the Sugar Act 1956, having effect as aforesaid, in respect of sugar and invert sugar imported or home produced or used in the manufacture of imported composite sugar products shall on and after 25th August 1972 be those rates specified in the Schedule to this order; and section 10 of the Finance Act 1901(**g**) (which relates to new or altered customs or excise duties and their effect upon contracts) shall apply accordingly.

In Witness whereof the Official Seal of the Minister of Agriculture, Fisheries and Food is hereunto affixed on 21st August 1972.

(L.S.)

E. J. G. Smith,
Authorised by the Minister.

We concur.
23rd August 1972.

Anthony Barber,
V. H. Goodhew,
Two of the Lords Commissioners of
Her Majesty's Treasury.

(**a**) 1956 c. 48.   (**b**) 1962 c. 44.   (**c**) 1964 c. 49.   (**d**) 1966 c. 18.
(**e**) 1889 c. 63. (**f**) S.I. 1972/1252 (1972 II, p. 3758). (**g**) 1901 c. 7.

SCHEDULE
PART I
RATES OF DISTRIBUTION PAYMENT FOR SUGAR

Polarisation	Rate of Distribution Payment per ton
Exceeding:—	£
99°	14·000
98° but not exceeding 99°	13·202
97° ,, ,, ,, 98°	12·880
96° ,, ,, ,, 97°	12·544
95° ,, ,, ,, 96°	12·208
94° ,, ,, ,, 95°	11·872
93° ,, ,, ,, 94°	11·536
92° ,, ,, ,, 93°	11·200
91° ,, ,, ,, 92°	10·864
90° ,, ,, ,, 91°	10·528
89° ,, ,, ,, 90°	10·192
88° ,, ,, ,, 89°	9·856
87° ,, ,, ,, 88°	9·576
86° ,, ,, ,, 87°	9·296
85° ,, ,, ,, 86°	9·044
84° ,, ,, ,, 85°	8·792
83° .. ,, ,, 84°	8·540
82° ,, ,, ,, 83°	8·288
81° ,, ,, ,, 82°	8·064
80° ,, ,, ,, 81°	7·840
79° ,, ,, ,, 80°	7·616
78° ,, ,, ,, 79°	7·392
77° ,, ,, ,, 78°	7·168
76° ,, ,, ,, 77°	6·944
Not exceeding 76°	6·720

PART II
RATES OF DISTRIBUTION PAYMENT FOR INVERT SUGAR

Sweetening matter content by weight	Rate of Distribution Payment per cwt.
	£
70 per cent. or more	0·44
Less than 70 per cent. and more than 50 per cent.	0·31
Not more than 50 per cent.	0·15

EXPLANATORY NOTE
(This Note is not part of the Order.)

This order provides for increases equivalent to £8 per ton of refined sugar in the rates of distribution payment in respect of sugar and invert sugar which become eligible for such payments on and after 25th August 1972.

STATUTORY INSTRUMENTS

1972 No. 1327

SUGAR

The Sugar (Distribution Repayments) (Amendment) (No. 16) Order 1972

Made - - - -	23rd *August* 1972
Laid before Parliament	24th *August* 1972
Coming into Operation	25th *August* 1972

The Minister of Agriculture, Fisheries and Food, in exercise of the powers conferred upon him by sections 15 and 33(4) of the Sugar Act 1956(**a**), having effect subject to the provisions of section 3 of, and Part II of Schedule 5 to, the Finance Act 1962(**b**), section 22 of the Finance Act 1964(**c**) and section 52 of the Finance Act 1966(**d**) and of all other powers enabling him in that behalf, an order(**e**) having been made under section 14 of the said Act, hereby makes the following order:—

1.—(1) This order may be cited as the Sugar (Distribution Repayments) (Amendment) (No. 16) Order 1972, and shall come into operation on 25th August 1972.

(2) The Interpretation Act 1889(**f**) shall apply for the interpretation of this order as it applies for the interpretation of an Act of Parliament.

2.—(1) Notwithstanding the provisions of article 2(1) of the Sugar (Distribution Repayments) (Amendment) (No. 15) Order 1972(**g**) the amount of distribution repayment payable in respect of invert sugar, if the relevant drawback is payable thereon as being invert sugar produced in the United Kingdom from materials on which sugar duty has been paid on or after 25th August 1972, shall be calculated thereon at the rate applicable to the invert sugar in accordance with the rates prescribed in the Schedule to this order.

(2) Article 2(1) of the Sugar (Distribution Repayments) Order 1972(**h**) shall apply for the interpretation of this article.

In Witness whereof the Official Seal of the Minister of Agriculture, Fisheries and Food is hereunto affixed on 23rd August 1972.

(L.S.)

E. J. G. Smith,
Authorised by the Minister.

(**a**) 1956 c. 48. (**b**) 1962 c. 44. (**c**) 1964 c. 49.
(**d**) 1966 c. 18. (**e**) S.I. 1972/1326 (1972 II, p. 4003). (**f**) 1889 c. 63.
(**g**) S.I. 1972/1253 (1972 II, p. 3760). (**h**) S.I. 1972/67 (1972 I, p. 162).

THE SCHEDULE

RATES OF DISTRIBUTION REPAYMENT FOR INVERT SUGAR

Sweetening matter content by weight	Rate of Distribution Repayment per cwt.
	£
More than 80 per cent.	0·52
More than 70 per cent. but not more than 80 per cent.	0·44
More than 60 per cent. but not more than 70 per cent.	0·31
More than 50 per cent. but not more than 60 per cent.	0·25
Not more than 50 per cent. and the invert sugar not being less in weight than 14 lb. per gallon	0·15

EXPLANATORY NOTE

(This Note is not part of the Order.)

This order, which is consequent upon the Sugar (Distribution Payments) (No. 17) Order 1972 (S.I. 1972/1326), provides for increases equivalent to £8 per ton of refined sugar in the rates of distribution repayment, in respect of sugar and invert sugar produced in the United Kingdom from materials which become eligible for distribution payments on or after 25th August 1972.

STATUTORY INSTRUMENTS

1972 No. 1328

SUGAR

The Composite Sugar Products (Distribution Payments—Average Rates) (No. 17) Order 1972

Made - - - -	23*rd August* 1972	
Laid before Parliament	24*th August* 1972	
Coming into Operation	25*th August* 1972	

Whereas the Minister of Agriculture, Fisheries and Food (hereinafter called " the Minister ") has on the recommendation of the Sugar Board made an order(a) pursuant to the powers conferred upon him by section 9(1) of the Sugar Act 1956(b) having effect subject to section 14(8) of that Act and to the provisions of section 3 of, and Part II of Schedule 5 to, the Finance Act 1962(c), section 22 of the Finance Act 1964(d) and section 52 of the Finance Act 1966(e), providing that in the case of certain descriptions of composite sugar products distribution payments shall be calculated on the basis of an average quantity of sugar or invert sugar taken to have been used in the manufacture of the products and that certain other descriptions shall be treated as not containing any sugar or invert sugar:

And whereas the Minister has by the Sugar (Distribution Payments) (No. 17) Order 1972(f) provided for a change in the rates of distribution payments in respect of sugar and invert sugar which became eligible for such payments on and after 25th August 1972.

Now, therefore, the Minister on the recommendation of the Sugar Board, and in exercise of the powers conferred upon him by sections 9(1) and 33(4) of the Sugar Act 1956, having effect as aforesaid, and of all other powers enabling him in that behalf, hereby makes the following order:—

1.—(1) This order may be cited as the Composite Sugar Products (Distribution Payments—Average Rates) (No. 17) Order 1972, and shall come into operation on 25th August 1972.

(2) The Interpretation Act 1889(g) shall apply to the interpretation of this order as it applies to the interpretation of an Act of Parliament.

2. Distribution payments payable on or after 25th August 1972 under and in accordance with section 14 of the Sugar Act 1956, having effect as aforesaid, in respect of sugar and invert sugar used in the manufacture of the descriptions of imported composite sugar products specified in the second column of Schedule 1 to this order, being goods which are classified in the tariff headings indicated in relation to them in the first column of the said Schedule shall, notwithstanding the provisions of the Sugar (Distribution Payments) (No. 17) Order 1972 and the Composite Sugar Products (Distribution Payments—Average Rates) (No. 16) Order 1972(a) be calculated by reference to the weight of the products and the rates specified in relation thereto in the third column of the said Schedule.

3. Imported composite sugar products other than those of a description specified in Schedules 1 and 2 to this order shall be treated as not containing any sugar or invert sugar for the purposes of distribution payments.

(a) S.I. 1972/1254 (1972 II, p. 3762). (b) 1956 c. 48. (c) 1962 c. 44. (d) 1964 c. 49.
  (e) 1966 c. 18. (f) S.I. 1972/1326 (1972 II, p. 4003). (g) 1889 c. 63.

In Witness whereof the Official Seal of the Minister of Agriculture, Fisheries and Food is hereunto affixed on 23rd August 1972.

(L.S.)

E. J. G. Smith,
Authorised by the Minister.

SCHEDULE 1

In this Schedule:—

" Tariff heading " means a heading or, where the context so requires, a subheading of the Customs Tariff 1959 (see paragraph (1) of Article 2 of the Import Duties (General) (No. 7) Order 1971)(a).

Tariff heading	Description of Composite Sugar Products	Rate of Distribution Payment
		Per cwt. £
04.02 ..	Milk and cream, preserved, concentrated or sweetened, containing more than 10 per cent. by weight of added sugar	0·31
17.02 (B) (2) and 17.05 (B)	Syrups containing sucrose sugar, whether or not flavoured or coloured, but not including fruit juices containing added sugar in any proportion:—	
	Containing 70 per cent. or more by weight of sweetening matter	0·44
	Containing less than 70 per cent., and more than 50 per cent. by weight of sweetening matter	0·31
	Containing not more than 50 per cent. by weight of sweetening matter	0·15
17.02 (F) ..	Caramel:—	
	Solid	0·70
	Liquid	0·48
17.04 ..	Sugar confectionery, not containing cocoa ..	0·56
18.06 ..	Chocolate and other food preparations containing cocoa and added sugar:—	
	Chocolate couverture not prepared for retail sale; chocolate milk crumb, liquid ..	0·31
	Chocolate milk crumb, solid	0·38
	Solid chocolate bars or blocks, milk or plain with or without fruit or nuts; other chocolate confectionery consisting wholly of chocolate or of chocolate and other ingredients not containing added sugar ..	0·31
	Other	0·40

(a) S.I. 1971/1971 (1971 III, p. 5330).

SCHEDULE 1—*continued*

Tariff heading	Description of Composite Sugar Products	Rate of Distribution Payment
		Per cwt. £
19.08 ..	Pastry, biscuits, cakes and other fine bakers' wares containing added sugar:—	
	Biscuits, wafers and rusks containing more than 12½ per cent. by weight of added sugar, and other biscuits, wafers and rusks included in retail packages with such goods.. ..	0·17
	Cakes with covering or filling containing added sugar; meringues	0·23
	Other	0·08
20.01 ..	Vegetables and fruit, prepared or preserved by vinegar or acetic acid, containing added sugar:—	
	Containing 10 per cent. or more by weight of added sugar	0·24
	Other	0·05
20.03 ..	Fruit preserved by freezing, containing added sugar	0·08
20.04 ..	Fruit, fruit-peel and parts of plants, preserved by sugar (drained, glacé or crystallised)	0·46
20.05 ..	Jams, fruit jellies, marmalade, fruit puree and fruit pastes, being cooked preparations, containing added sugar	0·43
20.06 ..	Fruit otherwise prepared or preserved, containing added sugar:—	
	Ginger	0·35
	Other	0·08

SCHEDULE 2

Tariff heading	Description of Composite Sugar Products
17.05 (A) and (B)	Sugar and invert sugar, flavoured or coloured.

EXPLANATORY NOTE

(This Note is not part of the Order.)

This order provides for increases in the average rates of distribution payments payable in respect of imported composite sugar products of the descriptions specified in Schedule 1 on and after 25th August 1972. These correspond to increases in the rates of distribution payment effected by the Sugar (Distribution Payments) (No. 17) Order 1972 (S.I. 1972/1326). Provision is also made for certain imported composite sugar products to be treated as not containing any sugar or invert sugar.

STATUTORY INSTRUMENTS

1972 No. 1329

ANIMALS

DISEASES OF ANIMALS

The Brucellosis (Beef Incentives) Payments Scheme 1972

Made - - -	*22nd August* 1972
Laid before Parliament	*31st August* 1972
Coming into Operation	*30th September* 1972

The Minister of Agriculture, Fisheries and Food and the Secretaries of State for Scotland and Wales respectively, acting jointly, in pursuance of subsections (1), (9) and (10) of section 106 of the Agriculture Act 1970(**a**) and of all their other enabling powers, with the consent of the Treasury, hereby make the following scheme:

Citation, commencement and extent

1. This scheme, which may be cited as the Brucellosis (Beef Incentives) Payments Scheme 1972, shall come into operation on 30th September 1972 and shall apply to the United Kingdom.

Interpretation

2.—(1) In this scheme, unless the context otherwise requires—

"accredited herd" means a herd of cattle in Great Britain which, to the satisfaction of the appropriate Minister, either—

(*a*) has been found to be free from brucellosis by means of a series of diagnostic tests carried out by him or on his behalf and has been, since the date of commencement of such tests, the subject of adequate precautions against the introduction or re-introduction and consequent spreading of brucellosis, or

(*b*) has been wholly constituted by the transfer of animals from other accredited herds in Great Britain or from such similar herds outside Great Britain as the Minister of Agriculture, Fisheries and Food, in relation to herds in England and Wales, or the Secretary of State, in relation to herds in Scotland, may either generally or in any special case allow, and has been, since being so constituted, the subject of such precautions as aforesaid;

and "accreditation" shall be construed accordingly;

"the appropriate Minister" means the Minister of Agriculture, Fisheries and Food or, in relation to herds kept in Scotland, the Secretary of State, and "the Ministry" means the Ministry of Agriculture for Northern Ireland;

(**a**) 1970 c. 40.

"beef cow scheme" means a scheme made under section 12 of the Agriculture Act 1967(a);

"brucellosis incentives agreement" means a voluntary arrangement between the appropriate Minister and the owner of a herd providing for the eradication of brucellosis from the herd upon terms which include the slaughter by the owner of any reactors found in the herd, without compensation, the making of payments to the owner in respect of a period commencing not earlier than the date of the final test as a result of which it becomes an accredited herd or, if there is no such test, the date on which the constitution of the herd is commenced and the taking by him of precautions against the introduction or re-introduction and consequent spreading of brucellosis;

"certified herd" means a herd of cattle in Northern Ireland in respect of which the Ministry has issued a Brucellosis Certificate in accordance with the provisions of an order made under the Diseases of Animals Act (Northern Ireland) 1958(b) in connection with the eradication of that disease, being an order which provides for such certificates to be issued only in respect of herds—

(a) which have been officially tested by the Ministry for the presence of brucella infection with negative results, or

(b) have been wholly constituted by the transfer of animals from other certified herds or from similar herds in the Republic of Ireland;

and "certification" shall be construed accordingly;

"hill cattle scheme" means a scheme made under section 13(1)(b) of the Hill Farming Act 1946(c);

"incentive payments" has the meaning assigned to it by paragraph 3 of this scheme;

"prescribed date" means a prescribed date for the purposes of a beef cow scheme;

"qualifying day" means a qualifying day for the purposes of a hill cattle scheme;

"reactor" means an animal which, when tested for brucellosis by or on behalf of the appropriate Minister, gives rise to a reaction consistent with its being affected with that disease;

'test" means a test by or on behalf of the appropriate Minister or the Ministry for the purpose of determining whether brucellosis is present in a herd.

(2) For the purposes of this scheme the date of a test is the date when samples are first taken from cattle for use in the test.

(3) The Interpretation Act 1889(d) applies to the interpretation of this scheme as it applies to the interpretation of an Act of Parliament.

Incentive payments for the eradication of brucellosis

3.—(1) Payments, to be known as incentive payments, may be made by the appropriate Minister in accordance with the provisions of this scheme in connection with the eradication of brucellosis from herds of cattle.

(2) Such incentive payments shall be made by way of supplement to subsidy payments under a hill cattle or beef cow scheme, and shall be subject to

(a) 1967 c. 22.　　　　　　　　(b) 1958 c. 13 (N.I.).
(c) 1946 c. 73.　　　　　　　　(d) 1889 c. 63.

the terms and conditions governing the subsidy payments to which they are supplemental.

(3) Subject to sub-paragraph (5) below, incentive payments under this scheme may be made in respect of a herd when a qualifying day for the purposes of a hill cattle scheme or a prescribed date for the purpose of a beef cow scheme, as the case may be, falls within the appropriate qualifying period specified in paragraph 4 or paragraph 5 below, and on that qualifying day or prescribed date—

 (*a*) in the case of a herd in Great Britain, the herd is the subject of a brucellosis incentives agreement and either is an accredited herd or has undergone a final test as a result of which it subsequently becomes an accredited herd;

 (*b*) in the case of a herd in Northern Ireland, the herd is a certified herd or is to the satisfaction of the Ministry fully qualified for certification.

(4) The amount of any such incentive payment shall be £5 for each animal which qualifies for the subsidy payment to which the incentive payment is supplemental.

(5) No payment shall be made under this scheme—

 (*a*) in respect of a herd which for the time being qualifies for incentive payments under the Brucellosis Payments Scheme 1971(**a**), or

 (*b*) by way of supplement to subsidy payments under a hill cattle scheme which is in force on the date on which this scheme is made, or

 (*c*) in relation to a qualifying day or prescribed date before 1st January 1972.

Qualifying period for incentive payments in Great Britain

4.—(1) Subject to sub-paragraphs (2) and (3) below, the qualifying period for incentive payments in respect of a herd in Great Britain shall commence—

 (*a*) in the case of such a herd as is referred to under head (*a*) of the definition of an accredited herd in paragraph 2 above, on the date of the final test as a result of which it has first become an accredited herd;

 (*b*) in the case of such a herd as is referred to under head (*b*) of that definition, on the date on which the first animal to be comprised in the herd has been moved on to the premises where the herd is to be kept;

and shall end five years after it has commenced or on 31st March 1976, whichever is the later.

(2) Where in relation to a qualifying day or prescribed date a herd has not been in existence long enough to qualify for subsidy payments under a hill cattle scheme or a beef cow scheme, as the case may be, the qualifying period for the herd shall not commence earlier than one month after that qualifying day or prescribed date.

(3) Where during the qualifying period the making either of incentive payments under this scheme or of equivalent increases in subsidy payments under a beef cow or hill cattle scheme has been temporarily interrupted, or the commencement of such payments or increases has been delayed, as a

<hr>

(**a**) S.I. 1971/1967 (1971 III, p. 5311).

result of a break in accreditation or in the operation of a brucellosis incentives agreement or other special circumstances, the appropriate Minister may if he thinks fit extend the period by not more than the length of the interruption or delay.

Qualifying period for incentive payments in Northern Ireland

5.—(1) Subject to sub-paragraph (2) below, the qualifying period for incentive payments in respect of a herd in Northern Ireland shall commence—

(*a*) in the case of such a herd as is referred to under head (*a*) of the definition of a certified herd in paragraph 2 above, on the date of the final test as a result of which it has become a certified herd, except where on 1st September 1970 the Ministry was satisfied that the herd was reinfected with brucellosis, in which case the period shall commence with the date on which the herd is subsequently found to the satisfaction of the Ministry to be free from that reinfection;

(*b*) in the case of such a herd as is referred to under head (*b*) of that definition, on the date on which, to the satisfaction of the Ministry, the herd has become fully qualified for certification;

and shall end two years after it has commenced or on 31st March 1973, whichever is the later.

(2) The qualifying period for a herd, if it continues until 31st March 1974, shall then come to an end, unless on 31st March 1972—

(*a*) the herd was already in being and was not a certified herd, and

(*b*) the last test as a result of which it became a certified herd had not been made,

or unless on 1st September 1970 the herd was a certified herd as to which the Ministry was satisfied that it was reinfected with brucellosis.

Supplementary hill cattle and beef cow payments for animals slaughtered in the course of brucellosis eradication

6.—(1) Where on a qualifying day for the purposes of a hill cattle scheme or a prescribed date for the purposes of a beef cow scheme, as the case may be, the number of cows eligible for subsidy payments under that scheme in a herd to which this paragraph applies is reduced as a result of animals in the herd being slaughtered in the course of the eradication of brucellosis, supplementary payments may be made by the appropriate Minister under this scheme to the person entitled to subsidy payments under that scheme equal to the difference between the payment to which he would in the opinion of the appropriate Minister have been entitled under that scheme in respect of the herd if the animals had not been slaughtered and the payment to which he is actually so entitled.

(2) It shall be a condition of payment under this paragraph that any animals in respect of which payment is made shall be replaced as soon after slaughter as appears to the appropriate Minister to be reasonably practicable, but he may nevertheless make such a payment before replacement of the animals if he is satisfied that suitable arrangements have been made for repayment in the event of the animals not being so replaced.

(3) This paragraph applies to herds which are on the qualifying day or prescribed date, as the case may be, either—

(*a*) accredited herds, or

(*b*) certified herds, or

(*c*) herds which are undergoing a programme of testing, voluntary or compulsory, for the presence of brucellosis, carried out by or under the direction of the appropriate Minister or the Ministry, for the purpose of enabling them to qualify as accredited or certified herds, or

(*d*) herds in Northern Ireland which have been wholly constituted by the transfer of animals from other certified herds or from similar herds in the Republic of Ireland and which are, to the satisfaction of the Ministry, fully qualified for certification.

(4) For the purposes of this paragraph subsidy payments under a hill cattle or beef cow scheme shall include any payments made by way of supplement to those subsidy payments either under paragraph 3 of this scheme or under paragraph 4 of the Brucellosis Payments Scheme 1971.

In Witness whereof the Official Seal of the Minister of Agriculture, Fisheries and Food is hereunto affixed on 10th August 1972.

J. M. L. Prior,
Minister of Agriculture, Fisheries and Food.

(L.S.)

Gordon Campbell,
Secretary of State for Scotland.

15th August 1972.

Given under my hand on 15th August 1972.

Peter Thomas,
Secretary of State for Wales.

We approve,
22nd August 1972.

V. H. Goodhew,
Oscar Murton,
Two of the Lords Commissioners of
Her Majesty's Treasury.

EXPLANATORY NOTE

(This Note is not part of the scheme.)

This scheme, which is made under section 106(1) of the Agriculture Act 1970, enables incentive payments to be made in connection with the eradication of brucellosis from beef herds in the United Kingdom, both inside and outside eradication areas.

The payments will take the place of the differential payments hitherto made under hill cattle and beef cow schemes, as these latter expire. They will be supplemental to payments under the new hill cattle and beef cow schemes, and there is no change in either the amounts or the terms of the incentive payments. This scheme does however define the periods for which incentive payments may be made, i.e. for approximately five years following accreditation in Great Britain and for approximately two years following certification in Northern Ireland.

The scheme does not apply to herds eligible for incentive payments under the Brucellosis Payments Scheme 1971, by which the owner of a herd in an eradication area in Great Britain can receive payments from the commencement of eradication until approximately one year after accreditation.

The scheme also enables the appropriate Minister to make up hill cattle and beef cow subsidy payments which are reduced as a result of animals being slaughtered for brucellosis and not replaced by the date on which they would have qualified. Consequential reductions in incentive payments made under this scheme or under the Brucellosis Payments Scheme 1971 can also be made good.

STATUTORY INSTRUMENTS

1972 No. 1330 (S.98)

CLEAN AIR

The Alkali, &c., Works (Scotland) Order 1972

Made - - -	21*st August* 1972
Laid before Parliament	31*st August* 1972
Coming into Operation	1*st November* 1972

In exercise of the powers conferred on me by section 1 of the Alkali, &c., Works Regulation (Scotland) Act 1951(**a**) and of all other powers enabling me in that behalf, after holding an inquiry and after consultation with the local authorities and other interests appearing to me to be concerned, I hereby make the following order: —

1. This order may be cited as the Alkali, &c., Works (Scotland) Order 1972 and shall come into operation on 1st November 1972.

2.—(1) The Interpretation Act 1889(**b**) applies for the interpretation of this order as it applies for the interpretation of an Act of Parliament.

(2) In this order—

(*a*) "the Act of 1906" means the Alkali, &c., Works Regulation Act 1906(**c**); and

"the order of 1965" means the Alkali, &c., Works (Scotland) Order 1965(**d**),

(*b*) any reference to a British Standard or to a British Standard Code of Practice in any such British Standard referred to, shall be construed as a reference to a British Standard Specification or a British Standard Code of Practice published under authority of the General Council of the British Standards Institution and where a British Standard referred to, itself refers to a British Standard or to a British Standard Code of Practice, the reference to such British Standard or to such British Standard Code of Practice shall be taken to be a reference to the latest edition thereof as at 31st December 1970 including any amendments thereto published at that date.

3. The list of noxious or offensive gases mentioned in section 27 of the Act of 1906 as extended and amended by the order of 1965 shall be further extended and amended to read as set out in Schedule 1 to this order.

(**a**) 1951 c. 21. (**b**) 1889 c. 63.
(**c**) 1906 c. 14. (**d**) S.I. 1965/478 (1965 I, p. 1215).

4. The list of works mentioned in the First Schedule to the Act of 1906 as extended and amended by the order of 1965 shall be further extended and amended to read as set out in Schedule 2 to this order.

5. The order of 1965 is hereby revoked.

Gordon Campbell,
One of Her Majesty's Principal
Secretaries of State.

St. Andrew's House,
Edinburgh.
21st August 1972.

Article 3

SCHEDULE 1

SECTION 27 OF THE ACT OF 1906 CONTAINING THE LIST OF NOXIOUS OR OFFENSIVE
GASES AS EXTENDED AND AMENDED

The expression "noxious or offensive gas" includes the following gases and fumes:—

Acetic acid or its anhydride;
Acetylene;
Acrylates;
Aldehydes;
Amines;
Ammonia or its compounds;
Arsenic or its compounds;
Bisulphide of carbon;
Bromine or its compounds;
Carbon monoxide;
Chlorine or its compounds;
Cyanogen compounds;
Di-isocyanates;
Fluorine or its compounds;
Fumaric acid;
Fumes containing aluminium, antimony, arsenic, beryllium, cadmium, calcium, chlorine, chromium, copper, iron, lead, magnesium, manganese, mercury, molybdenum, phosphorus, potassium, selenium, silicon, sodium, titanium, tungsten, uranium, vanadium, zinc or their compounds;
Fumes from benzene works, cement works, paraffin oil works, petroleum works, or tar works;
Hydrogen chloride;
Hydrogen sulphide;
Iodine or its compounds;
Maleic acid or its anhydride;
Nitric acid or oxides of nitrogen;
Nitriles;
Phthalic acid or its anhydride;
Picolines;
Products containing hydrogen from the partial oxidation of hydrocarbons;
Pyridine;
Sulphuric acid or its anhydride;
Sulphurous acid or its anhydride, except that arising solely from the combustion of coal;
Volatile organic sulphur compounds;

Article 4

SCHEDULE 2

FIRST SCHEDULE TO THE ACT OF 1906 AS EXTENDED AND AMENDED
LIST OF WORKS

(1) Sulphuric acid works, that is to say, works in which the manufacture of sulphuric acid is carried on by the lead chamber process, namely, the process by which sulphurous acid is converted into sulphuric acid by the agency of oxides of nitrogen and by the use of a lead chamber or by any other process involving the use of oxides of nitrogen.

(2) Sulphuric acid (Class II) works, that is to say, works in which the manufacture of sulphuric acid is carried on by any process other than the lead chamber process, and works for the concentration or distillation of sulphuric acid.

(3) Chemical manure works, that is to say, works in which the manufacture of chemical manure is carried on, and works in which any mineral phosphate is subjected to treatment involving chemical change through the application or use of any acid and works for the granulating of chemical manures involving the evolution of any noxious or offensive gas.

(4) Gas liquor works, that is to say, works (not being sulphate of ammonia works or chloride of ammonia works as defined in paragraph (6) of this schedule) in which hydrogen sulphide or any other noxious or offensive gas is evolved by the use of ammoniacal liquor in any manufacturing process, and works in which any such liquor is desulphurised by the application of heat in any process connected with the purification of gas.

(5) Nitric acid works, that is to say, works in which the manufacture of nitric acid is carried on and works in which nitric acid is recovered from oxides of nitrogen and works where in the manufacture of any product any acid-forming oxide of nitrogen is evolved.

(6) Sulphate of ammonia works and chloride of ammonia works, that is to say, works in which the manufacture of sulphate of ammonia or of chloride of ammonia is carried on.

(7) Chlorine works, that is to say, works in which chlorine is made or used in any manufacturing process.

(8) Hydrochloric acid works, that is to say—

(a) hydrochloric acid works, or works (not being alkali works as defined in section 27(1) of this Act) where hydrogen chloride is evolved either during the preparation of liquid hydrochloric acid or for use in any manufacturing process or as the result of the use of chlorides in a chemical process;

(b) tin plate flux works, that is to say, works in which any residue or flux from tin plate works is calcined for the utilisation of such residue or flux, and in which hydrogen chloride is evolved; and

(c) salt works, that is to say, works (not being works in which salt is produced by refining rock salt otherwise than by the dissolution of rock salt at the place of deposit) in which the extraction of salt from brine is carried on, and in which hydrogen chloride is evolved.

(9) Sulphide works, that is to say, works in which hydrogen sulphide is evolved by the decomposition of metallic sulphides, or in which hydrogen sulphide is used in the production of such sulphides, or any works in which hydrogen sulphide is evolved as part of a chemical process.

(10) Alkali waste works, that is to say, works in which alkali waste or the drainage therefrom is subjected to any chemical process for the recovery of sulphur or for the utilisation of any constituent of such waste or drainage.

(11) Venetian red works, that is to say, works for the manufacture of Venetian red, crocus, or polishing powder, by heating sulphate or some other salt of iron.

(12) Lead deposit works, that is to say, works in which the sulphate of lead deposit from sulphuric acid chambers is dried or smelted.

(13) Arsenic works, that is to say, works for the preparation of arsenious acid, or where nitric acid or a nitrate is used in the manufacture of arsenic acid or an arsenate and works in which any volatile compound of arsenic is evolved in any manufacturing process and works in which arsenic is made.

(14) Nitrate and chloride of iron works, that is to say, works in which nitric acid or a nitrate is used in the manufacture of nitrate or chloride of iron.

(15) Bisulphide of carbon works, that is to say, works for the manufacture, use or recovery of bisulphide of carbon.

(16) Sulphocyanide works, that is to say, works in which the manufacture of any sulphocyanide is carried on by the reaction of bisulphide of carbon upon ammonia or any of its compounds.

(17) Picric acid works, that is to say, works in which nitric acid or a nitrate is used in the manufacture of picric acid.

(18) Paraffin oil works, that is to say, works in which crude shale oil is produced or refined, and works in which—

(a) any product of the refining of crude shale oil is treated so as to cause the evolution of gases containing any sulphur compound; or

(b) any such product as aforesaid is used in any subsequent chemical manufacturing process.

(19) Bisulphite works, that is to say, works in which sulphurous acid is used in the manufacture of acid sulphites of the alkalis or alkaline earths and works for the manufacture of liquid sulphur dioxide or of sulphurous acid or of any sulphite and works (not being smelting works as defined in section 8(1) of this Act or other works defined elsewhere in this schedule) in which oxides of sulphur are evolved in any chemical manufacturing process.

(20) Tar works, that is to say, works where gas tar or coal tar is distilled or is heated in any manufacturing process and works in which any product of the distillation of gas tar or coal tar is distilled or is heated in any manufacturing operation involving the evolution of any noxious or offensive gas.

(21) Zinc works, that is to say, works in which, by the application of heat, zinc is extracted from the ore, or from any residue containing that metal, and works in which compounds of zinc are made by dry processes giving rise to fume.

(22) Benzene works, that is to say, works (not being tar works as defined in paragraph (20) of this schedule) in which—

(a) any wash oil used for the scrubbing of coal gas is distilled; or

(b) any crude benzol is distilled.

(23) Pyridine works, that is to say, works in which pyridine or picolines is or are made or recovered.

(24) Bromine works, that is to say, works in which bromine is made or used in any manufacturing operation.

(25) Hydrofluoric acid works, that is to say, works in which hydrofluoric acid is evolved in the manufacture of liquid hydrofluoric acid or its compounds.

(26) Cement production works, that is to say, works in which—

(a) argillaceous and calcareous materials are used in the production of cement clinker; or

(b) cement clinker is handled and ground; or

(c) cement is packed.

(27) Lead works, that is to say, works (not being works for the recovery of lead from scrap by direct liquation) in which—

(a) by the application of heat, lead is extracted from any material containing lead or its compounds; or

(b) compounds of lead are manufactured from metallic lead or its compounds by dry processes which give rise to dust or fume.

(28) Fluorine works, that is to say, works in which fluorine or its compounds with other halogens are made or used in any manufacturing process, and works for the manufacture of fluorides, borofluorides or silicofluorides.

(29) Acid sludge works, that is to say, works in which acid sludge produced in the refining of coal tar, petroleum or other hydrocarbon derivatives is treated in such manner as to cause the evolution of any noxious or offensive gas.

(30) Iron works and steel works, that is to say, works in which—

(a) iron or ferro-alloys are produced in a blast furnace; or

(b) raw materials for use in blast furnaces are handled or prepared; or

(c) iron ores for use in blast furnaces are calcined or sintered; or

(d) iron or steel is melted in cupolas employing a heated air blast, or in electric arc furnaces; or

(e) steel is produced, melted or refined in Bessemer, Tropenas, open hearth or electric arc furnaces; or

(f) oxygen or air enriched with oxygen is used for the refining of iron or for the production, shaping or finishing of steel; or

(g) ferro-alloys are made by processes giving rise to fume.

(31) Copper works, that is to say, works in which—

(a) by the application of heat—

(i) copper is extracted from any ore or concentrate or from any material containing copper or its compounds; or

(ii) molten copper is refined; or

(iii) copper or copper alloy swarf is degreased; or

(iv) copper alloys are recovered from scrap fabricated metal, swarf or residues by processes designed to reduce the zinc content; or

(b) copper or copper alloy is melted and cast in moulds the internal surfaces of which have been coated with grease-bound or oil-bound dressings:

Provided that sub-paragraph (b) of this paragraph shall not apply to works in which the aggregate casting capacity does not exceed ten tons per day.

(32) Aluminium works, that is to say, works in which—

(a) aluminium is extracted from any material containing aluminium by a process evolving any noxious or offensive gases; or

(b) oxide of aluminium is extracted from any ore; or

(c) aluminium swarf is degreased by the application of heat; or (*d*) aluminium or aluminium alloys are recovered from aluminium or aluminium alloy scrap fabricated metal, swarf, skimmings, drosses or other residues by melting but not including works in which aluminium or aluminium alloys are separated from ferrous metals by liquation in sloping hearth furnaces; or

(*e*) aluminium is recovered from slag; or

(*f*) molten aluminium or aluminium alloys are treated by any process involving the evolution of chlorine or its compounds; or

(*g*) materials used in the above processes or the products thereof are treated or handled by methods which cause noxious or offensive gases to be evolved.

(33) Electricity works, that is to say, works in which—

(*a*) solid or liquid fuel is burned to raise steam for the generation of electricity for distribution to the general public or for purposes of public transport; or

(*b*) liquid fuel is burned in an internal combustion engine (other than a compression ignition engine burning fuel with a sulphur content not exceeding that specified for fuel within Class A2 referred to in British Standard 2869 : 1970, and tested in accordance with British Standard 4384 : 1969) for the generation of electricity for distribution to the general public; or

(*c*) boilers having an aggregate maximum continuous rating of not less than 450,000 lb of steam per hour and normally fired by solid or liquid fuel are used to produce steam for the generation of electricity for purposes other than those referred to in sub-paragraph (*a*) of this paragraph.

(34) Producer gas works, that is to say, works in which producer gas is made from coal and in which raw producer gas is transmitted or used.

(35) Gas and coke works, that is to say, works (not being producer gas works as defined in paragraph (34) of this schedule) in which—

(*a*) coal, oil or mixtures of coal or oil with other carbonaceous materials or products of petroleum refining or natural gas or methane from coal mines or gas derived from fermentation of carbonaceous materials, are handled or prepared for carbonisation or gasification or reforming and in which these materials are subsequently carbonised or gasified or reformed; or

(*b*) water gas is produced or purified; or

(*c*) coke or semi-coke is produced and quenched, cut, crushed or graded; or

(*d*) gases derived from any process referred to in sub-paragraph (*a*) of this paragraph are subjected to purification processes.

(36) Ceramic works, that is to say, works in which—

(*a*) pottery products (including domestic earthenware and china, sanitary ware, electrical porcelain, glazed tiles and teapots) are made in intermittent kilns fired by coal or oil; or

(*b*) heavy clay or refractory goods are fired—

 (i) by coal or oil in intermittent kilns; or

 (ii) by coal or oil in continuous grate-fired kilns, not being tunnel kilns; or

 (iii) in any kiln in which a reducing atmosphere is essential; or

(*c*) salt glazing of any earthenware or clay material is carried on.

(37) Lime works, that is to say, works in which calcium carbonate or calcium-magnesium carbonate is burnt through the agency of coal or oil.

(38) Sulphate reduction works, that is to say, works in which metallic sulphates are reduced to the corresponding sulphides by heating with carbonaceous matter.

(39) Caustic soda works, that is to say, works in which—

    (*a*) either concentrated solutions of caustic soda or fused caustic soda are produced in vessels heated by coal; or

    (*b*) black liquor produced in the manufacture of paper is calcined in the recovery of caustic soda.

(40) Chemical incineration works, that is to say, works for the destruction by burning of wastes produced in the course of organic chemical reactions which occur during the manufacture of materials for the fabrication of plastics and fibres, and works for the destruction by burning of chemical wastes containing combined chlorine, fluorine, nitrogen, phosphorus or sulphur.

(41) Uranium works, that is to say, works (not being works licensed under the Nuclear Installations Acts 1965(**a**) and 1969(**b**) and not being nuclear reactors or works involving the processing of irradiated fuel therefrom for the purpose of removing fission products) in which—

    (*a*) any ore or concentrate or any material containing uranium or its compounds is treated for the production of uranium or its alloys or its compounds; or

    (*b*) any volatile compounds of uranium are manufactured or used; or

    (*c*) uranium or its compounds are manufactured, fashioned or fabricated by any dry process giving rise to dust or fume.

(42) Beryllium works, that is to say, works in which—

    (*a*) any ore or concentrate or any material containing beryllium or its compounds is treated for the production of beryllium or its alloys or its compounds; or

    (*b*) any material containing beryllium or its alloys or its compounds is treated, processed or fabricated in any manner giving rise to dust or fume.

(43) Selenium works, that is to say, works in which—

    (*a*) any ore or concentrate or any material containing selenium or its compounds is treated for the production of selenium or its alloys or its compounds; or

    (*b*) any material containing selenium or its alloys or its compounds other than as colouring matter, is treated, processed or fabricated in any manner giving rise to dust or fume.

(44) Phosphorus works, that is to say, works in which—

    (*a*) phosphorus is made; or

    (*b*) yellow phosphorus is used in any chemical or metallurgical process.

(45) Ammonia works, that is to say, works in which ammonia is—

    (*a*) made; or

    (*b*) used in the ammonia-soda process; or

    (*c*) used in the manufacture of carbonate, nitrate or phosphate of ammonia or urea or nitriles.

(46) Hydrogen cyanide works, that is to say, works in which hydrogen cyanide is made or is used in any chemical manufacturing process.

(47) Acetylene works, that is to say, works in which acetylene is made and used in any chemical manufacturing process.

(48) Amine works, that is to say, works in which methylamines or ethylamines are made or used in any chemical process.

    (**a**) 1965 c. 57.   (**b**) 1969 c. 18.

(49) Calcium carbide works, that is to say, works in which calcium carbide is made.

(50) Aldehyde works, that is to say, works in which formaldehyde, acetaldehyde or acrolein or the methyl, ethyl or propyl derivatives of acrolein are made.

(51) Anhydride works, that is to say, works in which acetic, maleic or phthalic anhydrides or the corresponding acids are made.

(52) Chromium works, that is to say, works in which any chrome ore or concentrate is treated for the production therefrom of chromium compounds or chromium metal is made by dry processes giving rise to fume.

(53) Magnesium works, that is to say, works in which magnesium or any compound of magnesium is made by dry processes giving rise to fume.

(54) Cadmium works, that is to say, works in which metallic cadmium is recovered or cadmium alloys are made or any compound of cadmium is made by dry processes giving rise to fume.

(55) Manganese works, that is to say, works in which manganese or its alloys or any compound of manganese is made by dry processes giving rise to fume.

(56) Metal recovery works, that is to say, works in which metal is recovered from scrap cable by burning the insulation.

(57) Petroleum works, that is to say, works in which—
 (a) crude petroleum is handled or stored; or
 (b) crude petroleum is refined by any operation carried out at petroleum refineries to convert crude petroleum into saleable products; or
 (c) any product of such refining is subjected to further refining; or
 (d) natural gas is refined; or
 (e) any product of any of the foregoing refining operations is used, except as a solvent, in any subsequent chemical manufacturing process, not being a chemical manufacturing process defined in any other paragraph of this schedule; or
 (f) used lubricating oil is prepared for re-use by any thermal process.

(58) Acrylate works, that is to say, works in which acrylates are—
 (a) made or purified; or
 (b) (i) made; or
 (ii) purified;
 and polymerised.

(59) Di-isocyanate works, that is to say, works in which di-isocyanates are—
 (a) made; or
 (b) partly polymerised; or
 (c) used in the manufacture of expanded plastics.

(60) Mineral works, that is to say, works in which—
 (a) (i) metallurgical slags; or
 (ii) pulverised fuel ash; or
 (iii) minerals other than—
     (A) moulding sand in foundries; or
     (B) coal
 are subjected to any size reduction, grading or heating by processes giving rise to dust; and
 (b) any product of any of the processes referred to in sub-paragraph (a) of this paragraph is handled.

EXPLANATORY NOTE

(This Note is not part of the Order.)

The Alkali, &c., Works Regulation Act 1906 as extended by section 11 of the Clean Air Act 1968 (c.62) brings under control the discharge of certain listed noxious or offensive gases, and of smoke, grit and dust from certain listed types of work. The Alkali, &c., Works Regulation (Scotland) Act 1951 empowers the Secretary of State to make orders extending or amending both the list of gases and the list of works. The existing list of gases is set out in section 27 of the 1906 Act as extended and amended by the Alkali &c., Works (Scotland) Order 1965, and the existing list of works is set out in the First Schedule to the 1906 Act also as extended and amended by the 1965 Order. This Order further extends and amends both these lists and consolidates the original lists set out in the 1906 Act, the extensions and amendments made in the 1965 Order which is revoked and the extensions and amendments made in this Order.

Copies of British Standards and British Standard Codes of Practice referred to in this Order may be purchased from British Standards Institution, British Standards House, 2 Park Street, London W1Y 4AA.

STATUTORY INSTRUMENTS

1972 No. 1333 (S. 99)

LANDLORD AND TENANT

RENT CONTROL, ETC. (SCOTLAND)

The Rent Book (Scotland) Regulations 1972

Made - - -	*21st August* 1972
Laid before Parliament	*1st September* 1972
Coming into Operation	*25th September* 1972

In exercise of the powers conferred upon me by section 35(1)(c) of the Rent (Scotland) Act 1971(**a**), as inserted by section 47 of the Housing (Financial Provisions) (Scotland) Act 1972(**b**), and by sections 68(1) and 99(1)(d) of the said Act of 1971, and of all other powers enabling me in that behalf, I hereby make the following regulations:—

1. These regulations may be cited as the Rent Book (Scotland) Regulations 1972 and shall come into operation on 25th September 1972.

2.—(1) In these regulations—
"the Act" means the Rent (Scotland) Act 1971;
"the Regulations of 1965" means the Rent Book (Forms of Notice) (Scotland) Regulations 1965(**c**); and
"the Regulations of 1968" means the Rent Book (Forms of Notice) (Scotland) Regulations 1968(**d**).

(2) The Interpretation Act 1889(**e**) shall apply for the interpretation of these regulations as it applies for the interpretation of an Act of Parliament.

3.—(1) The Regulations of 1965 and the Regulations of 1968 are hereby revoked.

(2) Section 38 of the Interpretation Act 1889 shall apply as if these regulations were an Act of Parliament and as if the regulations hereby revoked by these regulations were Acts of Parliament repealed by an Act of Parliament.

4.—(1) Every rent book or similar document provided by a landlord for use in respect of a dwellinghouse, which is let on or subject to a regulated tenancy, shall contain a notice to the tenant in the form set out in Schedule 1 to these regulations, or in a form substantially to the like effect, of all the matters referred to in the said form:
Provided that a notice in the form prescribed by regulation 4 of the Regulations of 1965, or in a form substantially to the like effect, shall be sufficient compliance with the provisions of this regulation until 1st November 1972.

(**a**) 1971 c. 28.
(**c**) S.I. 1965/2043 (1965 III, p. 6043).
(**e**) 1889 c. 63.

(**b**) 1972 c. 46.
(**d**) S.I. 1968/145 (1968 I, p. 384).

(2) Any expression used in this regulation or in Schedule 1 to these regulations which is also used in Parts III and IV of the Act, shall, unless the context otherwise requires, have the same meaning as in those Parts.

5.—(1) Every rent book or similar document provided by a landlord for use in respect of a dwellinghouse, which is let on or subject to a controlled tenancy, shall contain a notice to the tenant in the form set out in Schedule 2 to these regulations, or in a form substantially to the like effect, of all the matters referred to in the said form:

Provided that a notice in the form prescribed by regulation 3 of the Regulations of 1965, or in a form substantially to the like effect, shall be sufficient compliance with the provisions of this regulation until 1st November 1972.

(2) Any expression used in this regulation or in Schedule 2 to these regulations, which is also used in Part V of the Act, shall, unless the context otherwise requires, have the same meaning as in that Part.

6.—(1) Every rent book or similar document, required by section 98(1) of the Act to be provided by a lessor for use in respect of a dwellinghouse under a contract to which Part VII of the Act applies, shall be in the form set out in Schedule 3 to these regulations, or in a form substantially to the like effect, and shall contain the information referred to in the said form:

Provided that a notice in the form prescribed by regulation 5 of the Regulations of 1968, as read with regulation 3 of the Regulations of 1965, or in a form substantially to the like effect, shall be sufficient compliance with the provisions of this regulation until 1st November 1972.

(2) Any expression used in this regulation or in Schedule 3 to these regulations, which is also used in Part VII of the Act, shall, unless the context otherwise requires, have the same meaning as in that Part.

Gordon Campbell,
One of Her Majesty's Principal
Secretaries of State.

St. Andrew's House,
Edinburgh.
21st August 1972.

Regulation 4

SCHEDULE 1

Form of notice to be inserted in every rent book or similar
document used in respect of a dwellinghouse let on or subject
to a regulated tenancy.

INFORMATION FOR TENANT

GENERAL

1. Address of the dwellinghouse..

2. Name and address of landlord and of his agents (if any)..

3. The following particulars of the tenancy:—

(a) The rent payable under the tenancy £.................... per ...., exclusive/ inclusive of rates borne by the landlord;

(b) The nature of the tenancy, that is, whether it is a contractual or a statutory tenancy;

(c) The date of commencement of the contractual/statutory tenancy;

(d) The duration of the contractual tenancy;

(e) The rental period;

(f) Any services or furniture provided by the landlord and the amount (if any) of the rent which is apportioned to them under the tenancy agreement; and

(g) The respective liability of the landlord and tenant for the maintenance and repair of the dwellinghouse.

4. Rateable value of the dwellinghouse on 23rd March 1965 (or upon such later date as its rateable value was first shown on the valuation roll).

5. If the tenancy became a regulated tenancy by conversion from being a controlled tenancy, state the date of conversion and the method by which the tenancy became a regulated tenancy.

6. In general, the fact that the tenancy is a regulated tenancy affects the rent which may be lawfully recovered for the dwellinghouse and imposes restrictions upon the landlord's right to recover possession of the dwellinghouse.

RENT LAWFULLY RECOVERABLE

7. The amount of the maximum rent which the landlord may lawfully recover from you depends initially upon whether or not a fair rent has been registered for the dwellinghouse. A fair rent is determined by an independent official—the rent officer—or, on appeal, by an independent committee—the rent assessment committee—and either the tenant or the landlord or both acting jointly may apply to the rent officer for the registration of such a rent for the dwellinghouse.

Where no rent is registered

8. The Rent Act 1965(a) (now re-enacted in the Rent (Scotland) Act 1971) provided that, whatever might be the rent agreed to be payable, the landlord could not recover from his tenant more than—

(a) in the case of a tenancy beginning before 8th December 1965, the rent payable on that date, and

(b) in the case of a tenancy beginning on or after that date, the rent payable for the last rental period of the last previous regulated tenancy, if there had been one within the previous three years, or, if not, the rent payable under the tenancy agreement.

The only sums which could be added to this "frozen" rent were increases in respect of rates borne by the landlord, increases in the cost of services provided by the landlord, and $12\frac{1}{2}\%$ per annum of the landlord's expenditure on certain improvements.

9. As from 1st January 1973, however, it will be possible for the "frozen" rent to be increased by a written agreement between you and the landlord. The agreement must contain a statutory statement to the effect that your security of tenure will not be affected if you refuse to enter into the agreement and that entry into the agreement will not deprive you or the landlord of the right to apply at any time for the registration of a fair rent. Additional information is required to be given in the agreement if the increase in rent agreed upon is wholly or partly to take account of works in respect of which an improvement or standard grant has been approved. There are also special provisions to protect the tenant where an agreement is entered into after the tenancy has become converted into a regulated tenancy and such an agreement cannot take effect until the rent officer has been consulted to ensure that the agreed rent does not exceed a fair rent for the dwellinghouse.

(a) 1965 c. 75.

*10. If no rent is registered for the dwellinghouse, state—

    (*a*) the amount of rent lawfully recoverable by the landlord—£................ per ....;

    (*b*) how that amount has been arrived at; and

    (*c*) the amount (if any) of the rates payable by the landlord included in the rent—£................ per ....

Where a rent is registered

*11. A rent of £................ per .... (exclusive of rates) was registered for the dwellinghouse on................

(The word "variable" should be added after the amount of the registered rent if the entry in the register permits the landlord to vary the rent to take account of changes in the cost of providing services or of maintaining or repairing the dwellinghouse in accordance with the terms shown in the register, without having to get a new rent registered.)

12. The landlord may not charge more than the registered rent and, if the registered rent is higher than the amount previously recoverable, then, unless the terms of the tenancy entitle him to do so, the landlord cannot increase the rent up to the amount registered for any rental period of the contractual tenancy. He may, however, do so for any rental period of the statutory tenancy by serving the appropriate notice of increase.

13. Where the registration is the first after the tenancy has become converted into a regulated tenancy (except upon the death of a first successor) or after the completion, during the existence of the regulated tenancy, of grant-aided improvements, the landlord's right to serve such a notice of increase is restricted and he may only increase the rent, by such a notice, up to the amount of the registered rent in annual instalments as follows:—

    From (date)................................by (amount of the increase) £................ per ....
      to £................ per ....

    From (date)................................by (amount of the increase) £................ per ....
      to £................ per ....

    From (date)................................by (amount of the increase) £................ per ....
      to £................ per ....
    etc.

*14. If the register shows that the rates in respect of the dwellinghouse are borne by the landlord, the landlord may charge the following additional amount by way of rates:—

                                      £................ per ....
    From (date)................................ £................ per ....
    From (date)................................ £................ per ....
    etc.

15. The registered rent cannot be changed without applying to the rent officer. For three years after the registration took effect, no application for the registration of a different rent can be made except by you and the landlord acting jointly or where there has been a change in circumstances taken into account when the rent was registered. At the expiry of that three-year period, if you and the landlord have entered into a rent agreement, you may both apply to the rent officer for the cancellation of the registration, but the rent officer will only cancel it, if he is satisfied that the agreed rent does not exceed a fair rent.

16. Further information about rents of regulated tenancies is set out in booklets available free of charge at the offices of the rent officer, the Citizens' Advice Bureau, and the local authority. If you think that your landlord is not entitled to the rent being charged or that he is making an increase which is not permitted, you should consult a solicitor or a Citizens' Advice Bureau.

---

*These entries must be kept up to date.

SECURITY OF TENURE

17. If your landlord terminates the contractual tenancy by serving a notice to quit upon you, then, so long as you continue to retain possession of the dwellinghouse without being entitled to do so under a contractual tenancy, you will be regarded as occupying your dwellinghouse under a statutory tenancy. Upon your death, your widow, or any member of your family, who had been residing with you at the time of and for a period of six months immediately before your death, may be entitled to succeed to the tenancy. It is possible for the tenancy to be transmitted twice in this way after the death of the person who had been the original tenant.

18. Your landlord cannot evict you from the dwellinghouse without a decree from the sheriff which, except in certain cases, will be granted only if he thinks it reasonable to do so and either there is suitable alternative accommodation available for you or if one of a limited number of conditions is satisfied (for example, if you have failed to pay the rent lawfully due or if you or your family have been a nuisance or annoyance to neighbours).

19. It is a criminal offence for the landlord or for anyone else to try to make you leave by using force, by threatening you or your family, by withdrawing services or by interfering with your home or your possessions, unless authorised by the sheriff. If anyone does this, you should complain to the police.

SUB-LETTING

20. If you sub-let the dwellinghouse and you are not permitted to do so under your tenancy agreement, your landlord may apply to the sheriff for an order for possession of the dwellinghouse.

21. If you sub-let any part of the dwellinghouse on a regulated tenancy—

(a) you must give the landlord, within 14 days, a statement in writing of the sub-letting, giving particulars of occupancy, including the rent charged. The penalty for failing to do this without reasonable excuse or for giving false particulars, is a fine not exceeding £10. When you have once given the landlord the particulars, you need not do so again if the only change is a change of sub-tenant; and

(b) if you overcharge your sub-tenant, the landlord may apply to the sheriff for an order for possession of the dwellinghouse.

RENT ALLOWANCES

22. If you consider that you cannot afford the rent which is charged, you may apply to the local authority for a rent allowance. Every local authority is obliged to bring into operation, not later than 1st January 1973, a rent allowance scheme and your landlord will be under a duty to furnish you with information about this scheme after it has been made. You will also be able to obtain information about the scheme from your local authority's offices.

ADVICE

23. If you are in doubt as to your rights and obligations as a tenant, you may seek advice from your local authority, a Citizens' Advice Bureau or a solicitor.

Regulation 5

SCHEDULE 2

Form of notice to be inserted in every rent book or similar document used in respect of a dwellinghouse let on or subject to a controlled tenancy.

INFORMATION FOR TENANT

GENERAL

1. Address of the dwellinghouse...

2. Name and address of landlord and of his agents (if any)...

3. The following particulars of the tenancy:—

    (*a*) The rent payable under the tenancy £............... per .... exclusive/ inclusive of rates borne by the landlord;

    (*b*) The nature of the tenancy, that is, whether it is a contractual or a statutory tenancy;

    (*c*) The date of commencement of the contractual/statutory tenancy;

    (*d*) The duration of the contractual tenancy;

    (*e*) The rental period;

    (*f*) Any services or furniture provided by the landlord and the amount (if any) of the rent which is apportioned to them under the tenancy agreement; and

    (*g*) The respective liability of the landlord and tenant for the maintenance and repair of the dwellinghouse.

4. In general, the fact that the tenancy is a controlled tenancy restricts the rent which may be lawfully recovered for the dwellinghouse and imposes restrictions upon the landlord's right to recover possession of the dwellinghouse.

RENT LAWFULLY RECOVERABLE

*5. The amount of the maximum rent which the landlord may lawfully recover from you is £............... per ...., exclusive/inclusive of rates borne by the landlord.

*6. If the rent is inclusive of rates, the amount of rates included in the rent is:—

From (date)..   £............... per ....

From (date)..   £............... per ....
etc.

7. If you think that your landlord is not entitled to the rent being charged or that he is making an increase which is not permitted, you should consult a solicitor or a Citizens' Advice Bureau and either you or the landlord can apply to the sheriff to determine the matter.

†[8. The rent includes £............... per .... in respect of—

    (*a*) [the repairs increase permitted by section 49 of the Rent (Scotland) Act 1971] [the increase permitted by section 50 of the Rent (Scotland) Act 1971];

    (*b*) the passing on to the tenant by the landlord of a [repairs increase] [section 50 increase] payable by the landlord to his landlord or passed on to him by that landlord.

9. If you consider that the dwellinghouse is not in good and tenantable repair or that it is in any other respect unfit for human habitation, you may apply to your local authority for a certificate of disrepair.

10. If the local authority grant this certificate, the landlord is not entitled to any of the above increases so long as the certificate remains in force and you are entitled to deduct from your rent the fee of 5p which you have to pay to the local authority when applying for the certificate. If you have already paid any such increases of rent between the date when you applied to the local authority for the certificate and the date of the certificate, you may deduct the amount paid from any payments of rent within the following two years.

11. If, however, the landlord considers that the certificate of disrepair ought not to have been granted or that any disrepair was your fault, he can appeal to the sheriff within 21 days after the service of the copy of the certificate on him, and, on any such appeal, the sheriff may revoke the certificate. If the certificate is revoked by the sheriff, you will become liable to pay any increase in rent which you may have withheld from the date on which you applied to the local authority for the certificate.

---

*These entries must be kept up to date.

†Delete words in square brackets if they do not apply.

12. If, after the local authority have granted a certificate of disrepair, the landlord carries out the necessary repairs, the local authority will revoke the certificate. The increase of rent will then become payable as from the date of revocation of the certificate.

13. If, after the local authority has refused to grant a certificate of disrepair, your landlord raises a Court action against you for the recovery of the above increases and you satisfy the Court that, during the period in respect of which the proceedings were brought, the dwellinghouse was not in good repair, then no sum is recoverable in respect of any of these increases of rent for that period.]

SECURITY OF TENURE

14. If your landlord terminates the contractual tenancy by serving a notice to quit upon you, then so long as you continue to retain possession of the dwellinghouse without being entitled to do so under a contractual tenancy, you will be regarded as occupying the dwellinghouse by virtue of a statutory tenancy. Upon your death, your widow, or any member of your family, who had been residing with you at the time of and for a period of six months immediately before your death, may be entitled to succeed to the tenancy. It is possible for the tenancy to be transmitted twice in this way after the death of the person who had been the original tenant, but, on a second succession, the tenancy is converted into a regulated tenancy.

15. Your landlord cannot evict you from the dwellinghouse without a decree from the sheriff which will be granted only if he thinks it reasonable to do so and either there is suitable alternative accommodation available for you or if one of a limited number of conditions is satisfied (for example, if you have failed to pay the rent lawfully due or if you or your family have been a nuisance or annoyance to neighbours).

16. It is a criminal offence for the landlord or for anyone else to try to make you leave by using force, by threatening you or your family, by withdrawing services or by interfering with your home or your possessions, unless authorised by the sheriff. If anyone does this, you should complain to the police.

SUB-LETTING

17. If you sub-let the dwellinghouse and you are not permitted to do so under your tenancy agreement, your landlord may apply to the sheriff for an order for possession of the dwellinghouse.

18. If you sub-let part of the dwellinghouse on a protected tenancy,

(a) you must give the landlord, within 14 days, a statement in writing of the sub-letting, giving particulars of occupancy, including the rent charged. The penalty for failing to do this without reasonable excuse or for giving false particulars, is a fine not exceeding £10. When you have once given the landlord the particulars, you need not do so again if the only change is a change of sub-tenant;

(b) if you overcharge your sub-tenant, the landlord may apply to the sheriff for an order for possession of the dwellinghouse; and

(c) where the sheriff has already determined the recoverable rent for the sub-let part of the dwellinghouse and you overcharge your sub-tenant, you may be liable to a fine of £100.

RENT ALLOWANCES

19. If you consider that you cannot afford the rent which is charged, you may apply to the local authority for a rent allowance. Every local authority is obliged to bring into operation, not later than 1st January 1973, a rent allowance scheme and your landlord will be under a duty to furnish you with information about this scheme after it has been made. You will also be able to obtain information about the scheme from your local authority's offices.

CONVERSION INTO REGULATION

20. The tenancy will cease to be controlled and will become a regulated tenancy—

    (*a*) upon a second succession to the tenancy (see paragraph 14 above); or

    (*b*) if the local authority, upon application by the landlord, issue a qualification certificate certifying that the dwellinghouse has all the standard amenities, meets the tolerable standard and is in good repair; or

    (*c*) on the date of conversion applicable to the dwellinghouse. This depends upon the rateable value of the dwellinghouse on 27th August 1972, as follows:—

Rateable Value	Date of Conversion
£50 or more	1st January 1973
£25—£49	1st January 1974
Less than £25	1st January 1975

(The Secretary of State has power, by order, to advance or retard the relevant date of conversion.)

When your tenancy is converted into a regulated tenancy, your security of tenure is not affected but your rent may be increased. Further information is set out in booklets on this subject available free of charge at the offices of the rent officer, the Citizens' Advice Bureau, and the local authority.

ADVICE

21. If you are in doubt as to your rights and obligations as a tenant, you may seek advice from your local authority, a Citizens' Advice Bureau or a solicitor.

Regulation 6

SCHEDULE 3

The form of, and the information to be contained in, every rent book or similar document required by section 98(1) of the Act to be provided for use in respect of a dwellinghouse under a contract to which Part VII of the Act applies.

INFORMATION FOR TENANT

GENERAL

1. Address of the dwellinghouse...

2. Name and address of the lessor (the landlord) and of his agents (if any)

....

3. The following particulars of the contract:—

    (*a*) The rent payable under the contract is £.............. per week;

    (*b*) The date of commencement and duration of the tenancy;

    (*c*) The furniture or services provided by the lessor and the amount (if any) of the rent which is apportioned to them under the contract;

    (*d*) The amount (if any) of the rates borne by the lessor included in the rent; and

    (*e*) The respective liability of the lessor and lessee for the maintenance and repair of the dwellinghouse.

RENT LAWFULLY RECOVERABLE

4. Either you or the lessor under the contract, or the local authority, may refer the contract to a rent tribunal. On such a reference, the rent tribunal may approve the rent payable under the contract or may reduce the rent to such sum as they consider reasonable. The case may again be referred to the rent tribunal for reconsideration of the rent approved or reduced on the ground of change of circumstances, and, upon any such reconsideration, the rent tribunal has power to increase the rent payable. Any approval, reduction or increase may be limited to the rent payable in respect of a particular period.

5. The rent determined by the rent tribunal is registered and it then becomes a criminal offence for any person to require or receive, on account of rent for that dwellinghouse under any furnished contract, payment of any amount in excess of the registered rent and the amount of any excess may be recovered by the person by whom it is paid.

*6. State the amount (if any) of the rent which has been registered—£.................... per week.

SECURITY OF TENURE

7. If, after the contract has been referred to a rent tribunal, the lessor serves a notice to quit upon you at any time before the decision of the rent tribunal is given or within a period of 6 months thereafter, then the notice may not take effect before the expiry of that period, except in certain circumstances. Unless the rent tribunal directs that a shorter period than 6 months should be substituted, you may apply for a renewal of this security of tenure, before the period expires, for periods of up to 6 months at a time.

8. Where a notice to quit has been served and the contract has not been referred to a rent tribunal, you may still refer the contract to the rent tribunal provided you do so before the notice to quit takes effect, and at the same time you may apply for a postponement of the operation of the notice for up to 6 months. You may apply for the renewal of this security of tenure, before the period expires, for periods of up to 6 months at a time.

9. If you have been granted security by a rent tribunal and you fail to comply with the terms of the contract or cause a nuisance or annoyance to adjoining neighbours or cause the condition of the dwellinghouse to deteriorate, the lessor may apply to the rent tribunal for a reduction of the period of security which has been afforded to you.

10. When the notice to quit takes effect (that is, after any period of suspension which may have been granted by the rent tribunal) the lessor is entitled, if you do not leave voluntarily, to obtain an order for possession of the dwellinghouse from the sheriff. He cannot evict you from the dwellinghouse without a decree from the sheriff and it is a criminal offence for him or for anyone to try to make you leave by using force, by threatening you or your family, by withdrawing services or by interfering with your home or your possessions, unless authorised by the sheriff. If anyone does this, you should complain to the police.

ADVICE

11. If you are in doubt as to your rights and obligations as a lessee under the contract, you may seek advice from the rent tribunal, the local authority, a Citizens' Advice Bureau or a solicitor.

DETAILS OF WEEKLY PAYMENTS OF RENT

(Here insert the dates upon which the weekly payments of rent are made and the amount of rent which is paid.)

---

*This entry must be kept up to date.

EXPLANATORY NOTE

(This Note is not part of the Regulations.)

These regulations supersede the Rent Book (Forms of Notice) (Scotland) Regulations 1965 and the Rent Book (Forms of Notice) (Scotland) Regulations 1968, but they provide that the forms of notice prescribed by those regulations may still be used until 1st November 1972.

The regulations revise the form of notice to be inserted in every rent book or similar document provided by a landlord for use in respect of a dwellinghouse let on or subject to a regulated or a controlled tenancy.

They also prescribe the form of, and the information to be contained in, every rent book or similar document which is required, by section 98(1) of the Rent (Scotland) Act 1971, to be provided by a lessor for use in respect of a dwellinghouse under a contract to which Part VII of that Act applies where the rent is payable weekly.

STATUTORY INSTRUMENTS

1972 No. 1336

NATIONAL HEALTH SERVICE, ENGLAND AND WALES

The National Health Service (General Dental Services) Amendment (No. 2) Regulations 1972

Made - - - -	*22nd August* 1972
Laid before Parliament	*1st September* 1972
Coming into Operation	*1st October* 1972

The Secretary of State for Social Services, in exercise of his powers under section 40 of the National Health Service Act 1946**(a)**, as amended by section 11 of the National Health Service (Amendment) Act 1949**(b)** and now vested in him by the Secretary of State for Social Services Order 1968**(c)** hereby makes the following regulations:—

1.—(1) These regulations may be cited as the National Health Service (General Dental Services) Amendment (No. 2) Regulations 1972 and shall come into operation on 1st October 1972.

(2) In these regulations:

"the principal regulations" means the National Health Service (General Dental Services) Regulations 1967**(d)** as amended **(e)**; and

"regulation 28" means regulation 28 of the principal regulations as amended by regulation 2(4) of the National Health Service (General Dental Services) Amendment Regulations 1972**(f)** (which provided for a new scale of fees for treatment).

(3) The Interpretation Act 1889**(g)** applies to the interpretation of these regulations as it applies to the interpretation of an Act of Parliament.

2. The principal regulations shall be further amended as follows:—

(1) In paragraph 8(2)(*a*) of Schedule 1 Part I to the principal regulations (which deals with "occasional treatment") for the amount of £2·30 there shall be substituted the amount £2·60.

(2) For Parts I to VI of Schedule 5 to the principal regulations (which set out the scale of fees for dental treatment) there shall be substituted the following:—

(a) 1946 c. 81.   (b) 1949 c. 93.
(c) S.I. 1968/1699 (1968 III, p. 4585).   (d) S.I. 1967/937 (1967 II, p. 2816).
(e) The relevant amending instruments are S.I. 1968/443, 1969/217, 1969/399, 1970/899, 1970/1329, 1970/1407, 1971/984, 1972/82 (1968 I, p. 1152; 1969 I, p. 605; 1969 I, p. 1118; 1970 II, p. 2831; 1970 III, p. 4432; 1970 III, p. 4651; 1971 II, p. 2858; 1972 I, p. 226).
(f) S.I. 1972/82 (1972 I, p. 226).   (g) 1889 c. 63.

"SCHEDULE 5

SCALE OF FEES FOR DENTAL TREATMENT AND CONDITIONS WITH RESPECT TO MATERIALS

PART I DIAGNOSIS

1. Clinical examination and report   ...   £0·74
   Provided that—

   (1) only one fee shall be payable during a course of treatment;

   (2) no fee shall be payable for:—

   (a) an examination in respect of repairs to dentures for edentulous patients,

   (b) a group examination in schools or institutions,

   (c) an examination of a person aged 21 years or over if the same practitioner† has been paid or is entitled to be paid for an examination and report on that person made at any time during any of the 5 months preceding the month during which a further examination is made,

   (d) an examination of a person under 21 years of age if the same practitioner† has been paid or is entitled to be paid for an examination and report on that person made on or after the preceding 1st March, 1st July or 1st November, whichever of these dates last occurred;

   (3) in the case of a woman who is or has been pregnant and who is not edentulous, in addition to the examinations for which payment may otherwise be made under this item, a fee shall be payable for one examination during the antenatal and postnatal period and all such examinations may be carried out at any time during that period.‡

2. Radiological examination and report:

   Fees per course of treatment—

   (a) Intra-oral films:
   1 film ...   .   £0·50
   2 films   ...   .   £0·60

---

†Reference in this scale of fees to dental treatment by the same practitioner shall include also dental treatment by his principal or the partner of either or by the assistant of any of them, and where the practitioner is employed by a body corporate shall include treatment by another employee of that body.
‡The antenatal and postnatal period is the period of pregnancy and the 12 months subsequent to the date of confinement.

*3 films	...	...	...	...	£0·70
*each additional film			...	...	£0·18 up to a maximum of £2·32

(b) Extra-oral films:

1 film ...	...	...	...	...	£0·80
*each additional film			...	...	£0·46 up to a maximum of £1·72

Provided that a fee shall not be payable in cases in which the Board have required the submission of the films, or in which the Board's prior approval was required, unless the films or duplicates therefore are submitted to the Board.

PART II CONSERVATIVE TREATMENT

A. *Periodontal Treatment*

3. Scaling, including the removal of calculus and other deposits from the teeth, the provision of prophylactic or other necessary treatment for all ordinary or simple disorders of the gums and any necessary oral hygiene instruction, for persons aged 16 or over at the beginning of a course of treatment:—

    (a) Scaling and gum treatment (except cases under (b))   ...   . £1·10

    *(b) Scaling and gum treatment to be followed by extraction of the teeth charted for scaling, gum treatment and extraction during the same course of treatment ...   . Such fee as the Board may approve, not exceeding £0·90

*Provided that no fee shall be payable where the last course of treatment in respect of which provision was made for payment under item 3(a) or (b) to the same practitioner† commenced at any time during any of the 5 months preceding the month in which the further treatment is to be done, unless the prior approval of the Board has been obtained.

4. Treatment urgently required for acute infective conditions of the gingivae/oral mucosa, including any necessary oral hygiene instruction:
Fee per course of treatment   ...   ... £0·58

*5. Other periodontal treatment including any necessary oral hygiene instruction, periodontal surgery and protracted scaling (estimates to include an outline of proposed treatment):

    (a) with periodontal surgery   ...   ... Such fee as the Board may approve.

    (b) without periodontal surgery   ... Such fee as the Board may approve up to a maximum of £6·50

B. *Restorative Treatment*

6. Fillings (including any dressings, pulp capping and other necessary preparatory treatment), except fillings in deciduous

---

*See schedule 2 for treatment requiring prior approval.

†Reference in this scale of fees to dental treatment by the same practitioner shall include also dental treatment by his principal or the partner of either or by the assistant of any of them, and where the practitioner is employed by a body corporate shall include treatment by another employee of that body.

teeth of children under 16 years. The fillings to which this scale applies shall be permanent in character.

Fee per filling:—

(a) amalgam filling in:

(i) a single surface cavity ...   ...   £0·94 with a maximum of £0·94 for 2 or more such fillings in any one surface of a tooth and a maximum of £1·30 for 2 or more such fillings per tooth not all in one surface.

(ii) a mesial-occlusal-distal cavity inclusive of any extension of such a cavity in a molar or pre-molar tooth   ...   .   £2·00

(iii) a mesial-occlusal or distal-occlusal cavity inclusive of any extension of such a cavity into the lingual or buccal surfaces or both in a molar or pre-molar tooth   ...   .   £1·60 with a maximum for a combination of such fillings of £2·00 per tooth

(iv) a compound cavity other than a cavity covered by (ii) or (iii) above   ...   .   £1·30 with a maximum of £1·70 for 2 or more such fillings per tooth.

*(v) additional fee for pin or screw retention   ...   .   £0·80

(b) (i) silicate, silico-phosphate or synthetic resin filling   ...   ...   £1·22 with a maximum for 2 or more such fillings per tooth of £1·76

*(ii) additional fee for pin or screw retention   ...   .   £0·80

Provided that—

(a) for combinations of the types of fillings set out below in the same tooth no fee shall be payable in excess of the amount shown opposite:—

1 or more of (a)(i) with 1 of (a)(iii)   ...   .   £1·90
1 or more of (a)(i) with 1 of (a)(iv)   ...   .   £1·50
1 or more of (a)(i) with 2 or more of (a)(iv)   ...   .   £1·90
1 of (a)(iii) with 1 or more of (a)(iv)   ...   .   £1·90

*(b) no fee in excess of £2·60 shall be payable for any combination of any types of filling in one tooth, except where pin or screw retention is used when the maximum shall be   ...   £3·20

*See schedule 2 for treatment requiring prior approval.

7. Root treatment of permanent teeth, including all attention in connection therewith except for the provision of X-rays or the insertion of any filling in the crown of the tooth:—

    (*a*) treatment comprising either the devitalization of the pulp of the tooth and the subsequent removal of the pulp followed by the necessary treatment and filling of each root canal of the tooth, or the treatment of septic root canals and the subsequent filling of each canal—

        (i) root filling following extirpation of vital pulp in a single-rooted tooth ... ... £2·70 per tooth.

        (ii) all other root fillings ... ... £5·30 per tooth.

    (*b*) vital pulpotomy consisting of removal of the coronal portion of the pulp, including any necessary dressing—

        Fee per tooth ... ... £2·40

    (*c*) (i) apicectomy, fee per tooth ... £4·70

        (ii) apicectomy with retrograde root filling, fee per tooth ... ... £5·90

*8. Gold fillings (other than inlays) ... ... £4·50 per filling with a maximum for 2 or more such fillings per tooth of £6·20

9. Inlays (including any dressings):

	A	B
*(a) metal inlay	Alloys containing 60 per cent or more fine gold.	Any other alloys.
(i) a single surface cavity	£6·40	£5·40
(ii) a compound cavity	£8·70	£7·40
(iii) a compound cavity involving the incisal angle	£8·50	£7·40
(iv) a confluent compound cavity ...	£12·80	£10·50

*(b) fused porcelain inlay ... ... Such fee as the Board may approve within a range of £7·00 to £11·00

*(c) provision or renewal of a facing of silicate or synthetic resin ... ... £1·00 per inlay.

(*d*) refixing or recementing an inlay ... £1·00 per inlay.

*(e) renewal or replacement by another inlay ... ... The fee for a new inlay of the type being provided.

*See schedule 2 for treatment requiring prior approval.

10. Crowning of permanent teeth, including any dressings but excluding root treatment:—

   *(a) Full veneer or jacket crown, cast (on a vital or non-vital tooth):

      (i) gold ... ... £14·40

      (ii) gold with facing of silicate or synthetic resin ... ... £15·40

   *(b) Three-quarter crown gold, cast (on a vital or non-vital tooth) ... ... £12·80

   *(c) Full veneer or jacket crown:

      (i) synthetic resin on a vital tooth... £8·00

      (ii) synthetic resin on a non-vital tooth ... ... £7·00

      (iii) synthetic resin constructed on a cast gold core or thimble on a vital tooth ... ... £10·00

   *(d) Full veneer or jacket crown:

      (i) porcelain on a vital tooth ... £13·00

      (ii) porcelain on a non-vital tooth ... £10·80

      (iii) porcelain constructed on a cast gold core or thimble on a vital tooth ... ... £15·00

   *(e) Full veneer or jacket crown:

      (i) synthetic resin constructed on a cast gold core and post ... £11·60

      (ii) porcelain constructed on a cast gold core and post ... ... £14·80

   *(f) Synthetic resin post or dowel crown:

      (i) without diaphragm ... ... £6·20

      (ii) with gold post and diaphragm ... £9·50

      (iii) with gold post, diaphragm and backing ... ... £11·60

   *(g) Modifications to the above crowns, and other forms of crown not in the opinion of the Board included in the above items ... ... Such fee as the Board may approve not exceeding £17·00

   (h) Refixing or recementing a crown ... £1·00 per crown.

   *(i) Repair of a crown:

      (i) Renewal of the coronal portion only of a post or dowel crown appropriate to item 10(f)(i) or 10(f)(ii) ... ... £4·80

*See schedule 2 for treatment requiring prior approval.

(ii) Other repair of a crown   ...   Such fee as the Board may approve not exceeding 70% of the fee for a new crown of the type being repaired.

*(j) Renewal by a similar type of crown   The fee for a new crown of the type being provided.

*(k) Replacement by a different type of crown ...   .   The fee for a new crown of the type being provided.

Provided that, where the Board approve the use of a special bonding technique in connection with a porcelain crown, the Board may increase the fee by an amount not exceeding £7·30.

PART III SURGICAL TREATMENT

*11. Extractions:

Fee per course of treatment:—

1 tooth	£1·00 ⎫
2 teeth	£1·10 ⎪
3, 4 or 5 teeth	£1·20 ⎪
6, 7 or 8 teeth	£1·40 ⎪ With an additional fee of
9, 10 or 11 teeth	£1·60 ⎬ £0·10 for each quadrant of
12, 13 or 14 teeth	£1·80 ⎪ the mouth involved other
15, 16 or 17 teeth	£2·00 ⎪ than the first.
18, 19 or 20 teeth	£2·20 ⎪
Over 20 teeth	£2·40 ⎭

Provided that where an exceptional number of visits is necessary because of the abnormal medical condition of the patient the Board may allow an additional fee not exceeding £2·70 per course of treatment.

*12. (a) Alveolectomy, in either upper or lower jaw   ...   .   Such fee as the Board may approve up to a maximum of £5·50 (or such higher fee as they may in special circumstances approve).

(b) Removal of cyst, buried root, impacted tooth or grossly exostosed tooth or other similar operation, including all necessary attention in connection therewith other than abnormal post-operative haemorrhage necessitating an additional visit other than for the removal of sutures   ...   Such fee as the Board may approve up to a maximum of £11·50 (or such higher fee as they may in special circumstances approve).

(c) Surgery on soft tissue, other than periodontal surgery appropriate to item 5   ...   .   Such fee as the Board may approve up to a maximum of £2·50 (or such higher fee as they may in special circumstances approve).

*See schedule 2 for treatment requiring prior approval.

13. Administration of a general anaesthetic:

    (*a*) In connection with treatment under item 11

        (i) where a doctor or dentist other than the dentist carrying out the extraction administers the anaesthetic:

        Fee per visit—

1 to 3 teeth extracted	£1·20
4 to 11 teeth extracted ...	£1·70
12 to 19 teeth extracted ...	£2·30
20 teeth or over extracted ...	£2·90

        (ii) where the anaesthetic is administered by the dentist carrying out the extraction:

        Fee per patient per course of treatment   ...   .   £0·42

    *(iii) where the Board are satisfied that the anaesthetist would be faced with special difficulties owing to the medical condition of the patient and the anaesthetic is to be administered by a doctor or dentist other than the dentist carrying out the extraction ... ... Such fee as the Board may approve not exceeding £6·20 per course of treatment.

Provided that no fee exceeding £2·90 per course of treatment shall be payable under (i) or under (i) and (ii) combined, and no fee exceeding £7·30 per course of treatment shall be payable for any combination of (iii) with (i), or with both (i) and (ii).

    *(*b*) In connection with treatment under items 5, 7(*c*) and 12 where a doctor or dentist other than the dentist carrying out the treatment administers the anaesthetic   ...   .   Such fee as the Board may approve not exceeding £2·90

Provided that in cases presenting special clinical difficulty the fee will be such fee as the Board may approve not exceeding £6·20.

PART IV DENTURES, BRIDGES AND SPECIAL APPLIANCES OTHER THAN ORTHODONTIC APPLIANCES

A. *Dentures*

Fees for the provision of dentures cover the provision of all necessary clasps, rests and strengtheners and all adjustments needed within a reasonable period of time after completion.

*14. Dentures in synthetic resin:

    (*a*) full upper and full lower dentures ... £16·50

---

*See schedule 2 for treatment requiring prior approval.

(*b*) denture bearing 1, 2 or 3 teeth   ...   £7·50
denture bearing 4 to 8 teeth   ...   £8·90
denture bearing 9 to 14 teeth   ...   £10·00

Provided that no fee for upper and lower dentures shall exceed £16·50

(*c*) additional fee for lingual or palatal bar—

    (i) stainless steel   ...   .   £1·36

    (ii) gold or other approved material   Such fee as the Board may approve not exceeding £5·00

(*d*) additional fee for the provision of a soft lining or soft partial lining where this is required on account of the abnormal anatomical condition of the patient's alveolus   ...   ...   £2·34 per denture.

15. Relining or rebasing of dentures, or provision of soft linings to existing dentures, including all adjustments needed within a reasonable period of time after completion:

(*a*) relining or rebasing a denture—

    (i) not accompanied by repairs and/or additions   ...   ...   £3·60 per denture.

    *(ii) accompanied by repairs and/or additions ...   .   Such fee per denture as the Board may approve.

*(*b*) provision or renewal of soft lining or soft partial lining to an existing denture where it is required on account of the abnormal anatomical condition of the patient's alveolus

    (i) not accompanied by repairs and/or additions   ...   ...   £4·30 per denture.

    (ii) accompanied by repairs and/or additions ...   .   Such fee per denture as the Board may approve.

16. Repairs (except repairs which are appropriate to item 15(*a*)(ii) or item 15(*b*)(ii)):

(*a*) (i) repairing a crack or fracture (including provision of any strengthener)   ...   .   £1·00

    (ii) refixing a tooth or providing and fixing a replacement tooth (including any gum associated therewith)   ...   .   £0·94

    (iii) refixing a clasp (including any gum associated therewith)   ...   £0·94

    (iv) providing and fixing a replacement clasp (including any gum associated therewith)   ...   ...   £1·70

    (v) covering exposed pins   ...   ...   £0·50

---

*See schedule 2 for treatment requiring prior approval.

(*b*) each additional repair under (*a*)

(i)—(v)　　...　　...　　...　　...　　£0·32

(*c*) renewal of gum not associated with repair under (*a*)　　...　　...　　...　　£1·00

Provided that no fee in excess of £2·60 per denture shall be payable under item 16.

17. Additions (except additions which are appropriate to item 15(*a*)(ii) or item 15(*b*)(ii)):

(*a*) addition of a clasp or tooth (including any gum associated therewith) ...　　£2·60

(*b*) addition of new gum not associated with addition under item 17(*a*)　　...　　£2·60 per denture.

Provided that no fee in excess of £3·60 per denture shall be payable under item 17 or for any combination of treatment under items 16 and 17.

*18. Backing and tagging of teeth on non-metallic based dentures:

Fee per tooth in addition to the appropriate fee for a non-metallic based denture:—

(i) stainless steel　　...　　...　　...　　£1·00

(ii) chrome cobalt or a precious metal alloy containing less than 60 per cent fine gold　　...　　...　　£1·90

(iii) precious metal alloy containing 60 per cent or more fine gold　　...　　£2·50

*19. Metal based dentures. These dentures may not be provided until such period after extraction (normally not less than three months) as the dentist thinks fit:

(*a*) Fee per denture in—

	A Stainless steel	B Chrome cobalt
(i) Base metal alloys:		
partial denture bearing 1, 2 or 3 teeth　...　...　...　...	£14·00	£17·00
partial denture bearing 4, 5 or 6 teeth　...　...　...　...	£15·00	£17·50
partial denture bearing 7, 8 or 9 teeth　...　...　...　...	£16·00	£18·00
partial denture bearing 10 or more teeth　...　...　...	£16·00	£19·00
full denture　...　...　...　...	£14·00	£17·50
additional fee where teeth are backed in any metal ...　...	£1·70 per tooth up to a maximum of £6·80 per denture.	£1·10 per tooth up to a maximum of £4·40 per denture.

*See schedule 2 for treatment requiring prior approval.

	A	B
(ii) Precious metal alloys:	Containing less than 60 per cent fine gold.	Containing 60 per cent or more fine gold.

partial denture bearing 1, 2 or 3
   teeth ... ...   £18·00
partial denture bearing 4, 5 or 6
   teeth ... ...   £20·00
partial denture bearing 7, 8 or 9
   teeth ... ...   £21·00
partial denture bearing 10 or
   more teeth ... ...   £22·00
full denture ... ...   £19·00
additional fee where teeth are
   backed in any metal   ... £2·00 per tooth up to a maximum of £8·00 per denture.

Such fee as the Board may approve.

(*b*) Repairs ... ...
and
(*c*) Additions ... ...

Fee appropriate to similar treatment to synthetic resin dentures as covered by items 16 and/or 17 together with such additional fee, if any, as the Board may approve.

B. *Bridges and Special Appliances*
*20. Bridges:

(*a*) Provision of a bridge ... ... Such fee as the Board may approve.

(*b*) Repairing a bridge ... ... Such fee as the Board may approve.

(*c*) Re-cementing a bridge ... ... £1·60

*21. (*a*) Obturators, fee per case in addition to appropriate denture fee ... ... Such fee as the Board may approve within a range of £5·20 to £8·80 or such additional fee as may be approved in special circumstances.

(*b*) Repairs to obturators ... ... Such fee as the Board may approve.

(*c*) Treatment involving splints or other appliances (other than in connection with periodontal treatment) ... Such fee as the Board may approve.

Part V Treatment Special to Children

*22. Conservative treatment of deciduous teeth of children under 16 years at the beginning of a course of treatment:

(*a*) by filling (including any dressings, pulp-capping and other necessary preparatory treatment)—

   (i) with amalgam, one surface ... £0·90 per tooth.

---

*See schedule 2 for treatment requiring prior approval.

(ii) with amalgam, more than one surface ... ...   £1·30 per tooth.

(iii) with any other filling material ...   £0·56 per tooth.

(b) by conservation of a molar with a preformed metal cap ... ...   £1·50 per tooth.

Provided that no fee in excess of £1·50 shall be payable for any combination of the above types of conservation necessary in one tooth.

(c) by conservation by other means—

(i) by preparing self-cleansing areas followed by applications of silver nitrate or similar medicaments

per tooth ... ...   £0·44
maximum per patient ...   £1·10

*Provided that no fee shall be payable under (i) where the treatment occurs within 12 months of similar treatment to the same surface by the same practitioner† unless, in exceptional circumstances, the approval of the Board is first obtained.

(ii) by topical applications of obtundents and coagulants

per patient ... ...   £0·40

*Provided that no fee shall be payable under (ii) where the treatment occurs within 12 months of similar treatment by the same practitioner† unless, in exceptional circumstances, the approval of the Board is first obtained.

(d) by vital pulpotomy, including any necessary dressing, per tooth ...   £0·80

23.   (a) Removal of calculus and other deposits from the teeth of children under 16 years at the beginning of a course of treatment and the provision of necessary treatment for all ordinary or simple disorders of the gums ... ...   £0·44

*Provided that no fee shall be payable under item 23(a)—

(i) where the last course of treatment in respect of which provision was made for payment under item 23(a) or (b) to the same practitioner† commenced at any time during any of the 5 months preceding the month in which the further treatment is to be done;

---

*See schedule 2 for treatment requiring prior approval.
†Reference in this scale of fees to dental treatment by the same practitioner shall include also dental treatment by his principal or the partner of either or by the assistant of any of them, and where the practitioner is employed by a body corporate shall include treatment by another employee of that body.

(ii) in respect of a patient under 9 years at the beginning of a course of treatment,

unless the prior approval of the Board has been obtained.

*(b) Removal of calculus, where in exceptional cases calculus is present to an abnormal degree, from the teeth of children under 16 years at the beginning of a course of treatment, and the provision of necessary treatment for all ordinary or simple disorders of the gums   ...   .   £1·10

(c) Removal of stain including any necessary polishing   ...   .   £0·40

Provided that no fee shall be payable under item 23(c)—

*(i) where the last course of treatnent in respect of which provision was made for payment under item 23(c) to the same practitioner† commenced at any time during any of the 11 months preceding the month in which the further treatment is to be done unless the prior approval of the Board has been obtained;

(ii) during a course of treatment where a fee is paid under item 23(a) or (b).

24.   *(a) Orthodontic treatment of children and young persons under 18 years at the beginning of a course of treatment   ...   .   Such fee as the Board may approve.

(b) Repairs to orthodontic appliances   Such fee as the Board may approve.

Part VI General Items

25. Dressing of teeth in respect of a casual patient:

Fee for one tooth   ...   .   £0·56
Fee for two or more teeth   ...   ...   £0·80

26. Domiciliary visits where a patient's condition so requires:

Fee per visit to one or more patients at one address   ...   .   £1·70

27. Treatment of sensitive cementum or dentine:

Fee per course   ...   .   £0·40

---

†Reference in this scale of fees to dental treatment by the same practitioner shall include also dental treatment by his principal or the partner of either or by the assistant of any of them, and where the practitioner is employed by a body corporate shall include treatment by another employee of that body.
*See schedule 2 for treatment requiring prior approval.

28. Taking of material for pathological or bacteriological examination, etc.:

Fee per course ... ... £0·60

29. Treatment for arrest of abnormal haemorrhage, including abnormal haemorrhage following dental treatment provided otherwise than as part of general dental services:

Fee per visit for arrest of bleeding or for administration of associated after-care £1·40

Provided that—

(i) the same practitioner† who arrests bleeding may not also be paid for the administration of after-care;

(ii) where the treatment consists solely of the removal of plugs and/or stitches the fee shall be only £0·70

(iii) the maximum fee per course of treatment shall be £3·30 or such higher sum as the Board may in special circumstances approve.

*30. Fee for any other treatment not included in this scale ... ... Such fee as the Board may approve."

3.—(1) Subject to the following provisions of this regulation, these regulations shall not apply to general dental services provided under a contract or arrangement entered into or made before 1st October 1972 and such services shall continue to be subject to the provisions of the regulations in force immediately before that date other than the provisions thereof ceasing to have effect by virtue of regulation 4 hereof.

(2) In respect of an advice of payment from the Board to a Council dated during the period beginning with 1st April 1972 and ending with 30th September 1972 the Council shall pay to the practitioner an additional sum equal to 10·8 per cent of the amounts authorised for payment.

(3) Where an advice of payment from the Board to a Council dated on or after 1st October 1972 is in respect of a contract or arrangement entered into or made on or after 1st March 1972 and before 1st October 1972 the Council shall pay to a practitioner in addition to the fees authorised under regulation 28 a sum equal to 10·8 per cent of the amount of these fees.

(4) Where an advice of payment from the Board to a Council dated on or after 1st October 1972 is in respect of a contract or arrangement entered into or made on or after 1st October 1970 and before 1st March 1972 the Council shall pay to a practitioner in addition to the fees authorised under regulation 28 a sum equal to 17·2 per cent of the amount of these fees.

---

*See schedule 2 for treatment requiring prior approval.

†Reference in this scale of fees to dental treatment by the same practitioner shall include also dental treatment by his principal or the partner of either or by the assistant of any of them, and where the practitioner is employed by a body corporate shall include treatment by another employee of that body.

(5) Where an advice of payment from the Board to a Council dated on or after 1st October 1972 is in respect of a contract or arrangement entered into or made before 1st October 1970 the Council shall pay to a practitioner in addition to the fees authorised under regulation 28 a sum equal to 40·5 per cent of the amount of these fees.

4. Regulation 3 of the National Health Service (General Dental Services) Amendment Regulations 1972**(a)** shall cease to have effect.

5. For paragraphs 1 and 3 of Schedule 6 to the principal regulations there shall be respectively substituted the following paragraphs:—

"1. Rates applicable to whole time employment at a health centre.

GRADE   SCALE OF REMUNERATION

I   Commencing at £3,336 per annum rising to £4,191 per annum by annual increments as follows:—

£
3,336
3,453
3,576
3,699
3,822
3,942
4,062
4,191

II   Commencing at £2,448 per annum rising to £3,534 per annum by annual increments as follows:—

£
2,448
2,538
2,643
2,748
2,853
2,958
3,063
3,168
3,285
3,405
3,534

In addition, London Weighting at the following rates shall be payable to salaried Dental Practitioners employed at health centres within the Metropolitan Police District as defined by section 76 of the London Government Act, 1963**(b)**.

(i) Inner Zone Allowance

Practitioners employed at health centres within the administrative boundaries of the following eight London Borough Councils: Camden, Hackney, Islington, Kensington and Chelsea, Lambeth, Southwark, Tower Hamlets, Westminster ...   £144 per annum.

(a) S.I. 1972/82 (1972 I, p. 226).   **(b)** 1963 c. 33.

(ii) Outer Zone Allowance

Practitioners employed at health centres within the Metropolitan Police District as defined by section 76 of the London Government Act, 1963, but excluding the areas referred to
in (i) above   ...   .   £105 per annum

3. Rates of sessional remuneration

GRADE	FEES PER SESSION OF 3 HOURS
I	£8·50
II	£6·80"

Keith Joseph,
Secretary of State for Social Services.

22nd August 1972.

EXPLANATORY NOTE

(This Note is not part of the Regulations.)

These Regulations further amend the National Health Service (General Dental Services) Regulations 1967 by providing for a new scale of fees and for certain additional payments for practitioners, other than salaried practitioners, providing general dental services. The Regulations also provide for a new scale of remuneration for salaried dental practitioners.

STATUTORY   INSTRUMENTS

1972 No. 1338 (S.100)

CROFTERS, COTTARS AND SMALL LANDHOLDERS, SCOTLAND

The Crofting Counties Agricultural Grants (Scotland) (No. 2) Scheme 1972

Made - - -	*17th August* 1972
Laid before Parliament	*4th September* 1972
Coming into Operation	*25th September* 1972

In exercise of the powers conferred on me by section 22(1) of the Crofters (Scotland) Act 1955(a) and section 14(1) of the Crofters (Scotland) Act 1961(b), and of all other powers enabling me in that behalf and after consultation with the Crofters Commission and with the approval of the Treasury, I hereby make the following scheme:—

Citation and commencement

1. This scheme may be cited as the Crofting Counties Agricultural Grants (Scotland) (No. 2) Scheme 1972 and shall come into operation on 25th September 1972.

Interpretation

2.—(1) In this scheme, unless the context otherwise requires, the expressions "breeding cow", "eligible occupier" and "qualifying day" have the same meanings as in the Hill Cattle (Scotland) Scheme 1968(c) as amended, (d) (hereinafter referred to as "the Hill Cattle Scheme").

(2) The Interpretation Act 1889(e) shall apply for the interpretation of this Scheme as it applies for the interpretation of an Act of Parliament.

Grants to be made

3.—(1) Subject to the provisions of this scheme, the Secretary of State may in respect of the year 1972 make a grant under this scheme in relation to any breeding cow, being a breeding cow to which this scheme applies, in respect of which a subsidy payment at the reduced rate has been or falls to be made under the Hill Cattle Scheme in respect of that year as being a breeding cow on the qualifying day in that year (which payment is hereinafter referred to as "the subsidy payment").

(2) In this paragraph the expression "subsidy payment at the reduced rate" means a subsidy payment reduced in accordance with the provisions of paragraph 4(2) of the Hill Cattle Scheme.

(a) 3 & 4 Eliz. 2. c. 21.   (b) 1961 c. 58.   (c) S.I. 1968/981 (1968 II, p. 2590).
(d) The relevant amending instruments are
  S.I. 1970/1648, S.I. 1972/725 (1970 III, p. 5423, 1972 II, p. 2288).   (e) 1889 c. 63.

Breeding cow to which this scheme applies

4.—(1) This scheme applies to any breeding cow—

(*a*) which is grazed and maintained on land comprising or forming part of a qualified croft or holding, being a croft or holding occupied by a person as a crofter or as an eligible occupier, or

(*b*) which is grazed and maintained on common grazings or common pasture to which the Crofters (Scotland) Acts 1955 and 1961 apply by a crofter or eligible occupier in exercise of a right to share in the common grazings or common pasture deemed to form part of a qualified croft or holding of which he is the occupier,

being in either case a cow in respect of which the subsidy payment has been or falls to be made to that crofter or eligible occupier as the person maintaining the cow or to such a person as is mentioned in paragraph 6(2) of the Hill Cattle Scheme.

(2) In this paragraph, the expression "qualified croft or holding", in relation to the year 1972, means a croft or holding in respect of which no grant under the Crofting Counties Agricultural Grants (Scotland) Scheme 1972(**a**) for the cropping of marginal land in that year has been paid and in respect of which, in the opinion of the Secretary of State, no such grant is payable.

Person to whom grant is to be made

5.—(1) Subject to the following provisions of this paragraph a grant under this scheme in respect of any breeding cow shall be payable to the person to whom the subsidy payment has been or falls to be made in respect of that cow.

(2) Where payment of grant under this scheme is made to such a person as is mentioned in paragraph 6(2) of the Hill Cattle Scheme, paragraph 5(2) of that scheme shall apply to the payment of such grant as it applies to the subsidy payment.

Application for grant

6. Any person who desires to obtain a grant under this scheme shall make an application for a grant in such form and at such time as the Secretary of State may direct and shall furnish such information as the Secretary of State may require and such application may, if the Secretary of State thinks fit, be combined with an application for a subsidy payment under the Hill Cattle Scheme.

Amount of grant

7. The amount of any grant which may be made under this scheme in respect of any breeding cow to which this scheme applies as being a breeding cow on the qualifying day in the year 1972 shall be £5·75.

Prohibition against assignation of grant

8. Paragraph 14 of the Hill Cattle Scheme shall apply to any grant falling to be paid under this scheme as it applies to a subsidy payment falling to be paid under that scheme.

(**a**) S.I. 1972/407 (1972 I, p. 1499).

Gordon Campbell,
One of Her Majesty's Principal
Secretaries of State.

St. Andrew's House,
Edinburgh, 1.

11th August 1972.

We approve.

V. H. Goodhew,

Oscar Murton,

Two of the Lords Commissioners of
Her Majesty's Treasury.

17th August 1972.

EXPLANATORY NOTE

(This Note is not part of the Scheme.)

This Scheme enables the Secretary of State to make grants to crofters and certain other occupiers of land in the seven crofting counties of Scotland for the year 1972 in supplement of the subsidy payment made in respect of that year under the Hill Cattle (Scotland) Scheme 1968. This supplement, at the increased rate of £5·75 announced in the Annual Review and Determination of Guarantees 1972, is payable only where no grant under the Crofting Counties Agricultural Grants (Scotland) Scheme 1972 for the cropping of marginal land in 1972 has been paid in respect of the croft, holding or grazings on which the cow is maintained and in the opinion of the Secretary of State no such grant is payable. The provisions of this scheme under which persons may qualify for a payment are the same as the provisions of the Crofting Counties Agricultural Grants (Scotland) (No. 2) Scheme 1968 (S.I. 1968/1496) in terms of which a supplement at the rate of £5 was payable.

STATUTORY INSTRUMENTS

1972 No. 1339

NATIONAL HEALTH SERVICE, ENGLAND AND WALES

The National Health Service (Superannuation) (Amendment) Regulations 1972

Made - - - -	*25th August* 1972
Laid before Parliament	*6th September* 1972
Coming into Operation	*1st October* 1972

The Secretary of State for Social Services in exercise of his powers under section 10 of the Superannuation Act 1972**(a)** and of any other powers enabling him in that behalf, after consulting representatives of persons likely to be affected by these regulations, and with the consent of the Minister for the Civil Service, hereby makes the following regulations:—

Citation and commencement

1.—(1) These regulations may be cited as the National Health Service (Superannuation) (Amendment) Regulations 1972 and shall come into operation on 1st October 1972.

(2) The National Health Service (Superannuation) Regulations 1961**(b)**, the National Health Service (Superannuation) (Amendment) Regulations 1966**(c)** and these regulations may be cited together as the National Health Service (Superannuation) Regulations 1961 to 1972.

Interpretation

2.—(1) In these regulations "the principal regulations" means the National Health Service (Superannuation) Regulations 1961 as amended by the National Health Service (Superannuation) (Amendment) Regulations 1966 and other words and expressions used have the same meaning as in the principal regulations.

(2) The Interpretation Act 1889**(d)** applies to the interpretation of these regulations as it applies to the interpretation of an Act of Parliament.

(a) 1972 c. 11.
(c) S.I. 1966/1523 (1966 III, p. 4309).
(b) S.I. 1961/1441 (1961 II, p. 2824).
(d) 1889 c. 63.

Contributions

3. The rates of contribution specified in paragraphs (*a*) and (*b*) of, and the proviso to regulation 7(1) of the principal regulations (amount of contributions to be paid by the officer and by the employing authority) shall be increased by three-quarters of one per cent. of the officer's remuneration which is for the time being taken into account for the purpose of the said regulation, being remuneration which is paid or deemed to have been paid on or after 1st October 1972.

Keith Joseph,
Secretary of State for Social Services.

22nd August 1972.

Consent of the Minister for the Civil Service given under his Official Seal on 25th August 1972.

(L.S.)

K. H. McNeill,
Authorised by the Minister for the Civil Service.

EXPLANATORY NOTE

(This Note is not part of the Regulations.)

These Regulations increase the rates of contribution payable under the National Health Service superannuation scheme.

STATUTORY INSTRUMENTS

1972 No. 1340

SUGAR

The Sugar (Distribution Payments) (No. 18) Order 1972

Made - - - -	29th August 1972
Laid before Parliament	30th August 1972
Coming into Operation	31st August 1972

The Minister of Agriculture, Fisheries and Food, in exercise of the powers conferred upon him by sections 14(5) and 33(4) of the Sugar Act 1956(a), having effect subject to the provisions of section 3 of, and Part II of Schedule 5 to, the Finance Act 1962(b), section 22 of the Finance Act 1964(c) and section 52 of the Finance Act 1966(d) and of all other powers enabling him in that behalf, with the concurrence of the Treasury, and on the advice of the Sugar Board hereby makes the following order:—

1.—(1) This order may be cited as the Sugar (Distribution Payments) (No. 18) Order 1972, and shall come into operation on 31st August 1972.

(2) The Interpretation Act 1889(e) shall apply for the interpretation of this order as it applies for the interpretation of an Act of Parliament.

2. Notwithstanding the provisions of article 2 of the Sugar (Distribution Payments) (No. 17) Order 1972(f), the rates of distribution payments payable under and in accordance with the provisions of section 14 of the Sugar Act 1956, having effect as aforesaid, in respect of sugar and invert sugar imported or home produced or used in the manufacture of imported composite sugar products shall on and after 31st August 1972 be those rates specified in the Schedule to this order; and section 10 of the Finance Act 1901(g) (which relates to new or altered customs or excise duties and their effect upon contracts) shall apply accordingly.

In Witness whereof the Official Seal of the Minister of Agriculture, Fisheries and Food is hereunto affixed on 24th August 1972.

(L.S.)

Basil Engholm,
Secretary.

We concur.
29th August 1972.

Anthony Barber,
Tim Fortescue,
Two of the Lords Commissioners of
Her Majesty's Treasury.

(a) 1956 c. 48.   (b) 1962 c. 44.   (c) 1964 c. 49.   (d) 1966 c. 18.
(e) 1889 c. 63.   (f) S.I. 1972/1326 (1972 II, p. 4003). (g) 1901 c. 7.

SCHEDULE

PART I

RATES OF DISTRIBUTION PAYMENT FOR SUGAR

Polarisation	Rate of Distribution Payment per ton
	£
Exceeding—	
99°	22 ·000
98° but not exceeding 99°	20 ·746
97° ,, ,, ,, 98°	20 ·240
96° ,, ,, ,, 97°	19 ·712
95° ,, ,, ,, 96°	19 ·184
94° ,, ,, ,, 95°	18 ·656
93° ,, ,, ,, 94°	18 ·128
92° ,, ,, ,, 93°	17 ·600
91° ,, ,, ,, 92°	17 ·072
90° ,, ,, ,, 91°	16 ·544
89° ,, ,, ,, 90°	16 ·016
88° ,, ,, ,, 89°	15 ·488
87° ,, ,, ,, 88°	15 ·048
86° ,, ,, ,, 87°	14 ·608
85° ,, ,, ,, 86°	14 ·212
84° ,, ,, ,, 85°	13 ·816
83° ,, ,, ,, 84°	13 ·420
82° ,, ,, ,, 83°	13 ·024
81° ,, ,, ,, 82°	12 ·672
80° ,, ,, ,, 81°	12 ·320
79° ,, ,, ,, 80°	11 ·968
78° ,, ,, ,, 79°	11 ·616
77° ,, ,, ,, 78°	11 ·264
76° ,, ,, ,, 77°	10 ·912
Not exceeding 76°	10 ·560

PART II

RATES OF DISTRIBUTION PAYMENT FOR INVERT SUGAR

Sweetening matter content by weight	Rate of Distribution Payment per cwt.
	£
70 per cent. or more	0 ·69
Less than 70 per cent. and more than 50 per cent.	0 ·50
Not more than 50 per cent.	0 ·24

EXPLANATORY NOTE

(This Note is not part of the Order.)

This order provides for increases equivalent to £8 per ton of refined sugar in the rates of distribution payment in respect of sugar and invert sugar which become eligible for such payments on and after 31st August 1972.

STATUTORY INSTRUMENTS

1972 No. 1341

SUGAR

The Sugar (Distribution Repayments) (Amendment) (No. 17) Order 1972

Made - - - -	29*th August* 1972
Laid before Parliament	30*th August* 1972
Coming into Operation	31*st August* 1972

The Minister of Agriculture, Fisheries and Food, in exercise of the powers conferred upon him by sections 15 and 33(4) of the Sugar Act 1956(a), having effect subject to the provisions of section 3 of, and Part II of Schedule 5 to, the Finance Act 1962(b), section 22 of the Finance Act 1964(c) and section 52 of the Finance Act 1966(d) and of all other powers enabling him in that behalf, an order(e) having been made under section 14 of the said Act, hereby makes the following order:—

1.—(1) This order may be cited as the Sugar (Distribution Repayments) (Amendment) (No. 17) Order 1972, and shall come into operation on 31st August 1972.

(2) The Interpretation Act 1889(f) shall apply for the interpretation of this order as it applies for the interpretation of an Act of Parliament.

2.—(1) Notwithstanding the provisions of article 2(1) of the Sugar (Distribution Repayments) (Amendment) (No. 16) Order 1972(g) the amount of distribution repayment payable in respect of invert sugar, if the relevant drawback is payable thereon as being invert sugar produced in the United Kingdom from materials on which sugar duty has been paid on or after 31st August 1972, shall be calculated thereon at the rate applicable to the invert sugar in accordance with the rates prescribed in the Schedule to this order.

(2) Article 2(1) of the Sugar (Distribution Repayments) Order 1972(h) shall apply for the interpretation of this article.

In Witness whereof the Official Seal of the Minister of Agriculture, Fisheries and Food is hereunto affixed on 29th August 1972.

(L.S.)

Basil Engholm,
Secretary.

(a) 1956 c. 48.   (b) 1962 c. 44.   (c) 1964 c. 49.
(d) 1966 c. 18.   (e) S.I. 1972/1340 (1972 II, p. 4056).   (f) 1889 c. 63.
(g) S.I. 1972/1327 (1972 II, p. 4005).   (h) S.I. 1972/67 (1972 I, p. 162).

THE SCHEDULE

RATES OF DISTRIBUTION REPAYMENT FOR INVERT SUGAR

Sweetening matter content by weight	Rate of Distribution Repayment per cwt.
	£
More than 80 per cent.	0·82
More than 70 per cent. but not more than 80 per cent.	0·69
More than 60 per cent. but not more than 70 per cent.	0·50
More than 50 per cent. but not more than 60 per cent.	0·39
Not more than 50 per cent. and the invert sugar not being less in weight than 14 lb. per gallon	0·24

EXPLANATORY NOTE

(*This Note is not part of the Order.*)

This order, which is consequent upon the Sugar (Distribution Payments) (No. 18) Order 1972 (S.I. 1972/1340), provides for increases equivalent to £8 per ton of refined sugar in the rates of distribution repayment, in respect of sugar and invert sugar produced in the United Kingdom from materials which become eligible for distribution payments on or after 31st August 1972.

STATUTORY INSTRUMENTS

1972 No. 1342

SUGAR

The Composite Sugar Products (Distribution Payments— Average Rates) (No. 18) Order 1972

Made - - - -	*29th August* 1972
Laid before Parliament	*30th August* 1972
Coming into Operation	*31st August* 1972

Whereas the Minister of Agriculture, Fisheries and Food (hereinafter called " the Minister ") has on the recommendation of the Sugar Board made an order(a) pursuant to the powers conferred upon him by section 9(1) of the Sugar Act 1956(b) having effect subject to section 14(8) of that Act and to the provisions of section 3 of, and Part II of Schedule 5 to, the Finance Act 1962(c), section 22 of the Finance Act 1964(d) and section 52 of the Finance Act 1966(e), providing that in the case of certain descriptions of composite sugar products distribution payments shall be calculated on the basis of an average quantity of sugar or invert sugar taken to have been used in the manufacture of the products and that certain other descriptions shall be treated as not containing any sugar or invert sugar:

And whereas the Minister has by the Sugar (Distribution Payments) (No. 18) Order 1972(f) provided for a change in the rates of distribution payments in respect of sugar and invert sugar which became eligible for such payments on and after 31st August 1972.

Now, therefore, the Minister on the recommendation of the Sugar Board, and in exercise of the powers conferred upon him by sections 9(1) and 33(4) of the Sugar Act 1956, having effect as aforesaid, and of all other powers enabling him in that behalf, hereby makes the following order:—

1.—(1) This order may be cited as the Composite Sugar Products (Distribution Payments—Average Rates) (No. 18) Order 1972, and shall come into operation on 31st August 1972.

(2) The Interpretation Act 1889(g) shall apply to the interpretation of this order as it applies to the interpretation of an Act of Parliament.

2. Distribution payments payable on or after 31st August 1972 under and in accordance with section 14 of the Sugar Act 1956, having effect as aforesaid, in respect of sugar and invert sugar used in the manufacture of the descriptions of imported composite sugar products specified in the second column of Schedule 1 to this order, being goods which are classified in the tariff headings indicated in relation to them in the first column of the said Schedule shall, notwithstanding the provisions of the Sugar (Distribution Payments) (No. 18) Order 1972 and the Composite Sugar Products (Distribution Payments—Average Rates) (No. 17) Order 1972(a) be calculated by reference to the weight of the products and the rates specified in relation thereto in the third column of the said Schedule.

3. Imported composite sugar products other than those of a description specified in Schedules 1 and 2 to this order shall be treated as not containing any sugar or invert sugar for the purposes of distribution payments.

(a) S.I. 1972/1328 (1972 II, p. 4007).   (b) 1956 c. 48.   (c) 1962 c. 44.   (d) 1964 c. 49.   (e) 1966 c. 18.   (f) S.I. 1972/1340 (1972 II, p. 4056).   (g) 1889 c. 63.

In Witness whereof the Official Seal of the Minister of Agriculture, Fisheries and Food is hereunto affixed on 29th August 1972.

(L.S.)

Basil Engholm,
Secretary.

SCHEDULE 1

In this Schedule:—

" Tariff heading " means a heading or, where the context so requires, a subheading of the Customs Tariff 1959 (see paragraph (1) of Article 2 of the Import Duties (General) (No. 7) Order 1971(a)).

Tariff heading	Description of Composite Sugar Products	Rate of Distribution Payment
		Per cwt. £
04.02 ..	Milk and cream, preserved, concentrated or sweetened, containing more than 10 per cent. by weight of added sugar	0·48
17.02 (B) (2) and 17.05 (B)	Syrups containing sucrose sugar, whether or not flavoured or coloured, but not including fruit juices containing added sugar in any proportion:—	
	Containing 70 per cent. or more by weight of sweetening matter	0·69
	Containing less than 70 per cent., and more than 50 per cent. by weight of sweetening matter	0·50
	Containing not more than 50 per cent. by weight of sweetening matter	0·24
17.02 (F) ..	Caramel:—	
	Solid	1·10
	Liquid	0·76
17.04 ..	Sugar confectionery, not containing cocoa ..	0·89
18.06 ..	Chocolate and other food preparations containing cocoa and added sugar:—	
	Chocolate couverture not prepared for retail sale; chocolate milk crumb, liquid ..	0·48
	Chocolate milk crumb, solid	0·60
	Solid chocolate bars or blocks, milk or plain with or without fruit or nuts; other chocolate confectionery consisting wholly of chocolate or of chocolate and other ingredients not containing added sugar ..	0·49
	Other	0·63

(a) S.I. 1971/1971 (1971 III, p. 5330).

SCHEDULE 1—*continued*

Tariff heading	Description of Composite Sugar Products	Rate of Distribution Payment
		Per cwt. £
19.08 ..	Pastry, biscuits, cakes and other fine bakers' wares containing added sugar:—	
	Biscuits, wafers and rusks containing more than $12\frac{1}{2}$ per cent. by weight of added sugar, and other biscuits, wafers and rusks included in retail packages with such goods.. ..	0·27
	Cakes with covering or filling containing added sugar; meringues	0·36
	Other	0·13
20.01 ..	Vegetables and fruit, prepared or preserved by vinegar or acetic acid, containing added sugar:—	
	Containing 10 per cent. or more by weight of added sugar	0·38
	Other	0·08
20.03 ..	Fruit preserved by freezing, containing added sugar	0·13
20.04 ..	Fruit, fruit-peel and parts of plants, preserved by sugar (drained, glacé or crystallised)	0·72
20.05 ..	Jams, fruit jellies, marmalades, fruit puree and fruit pastes, being cooked preparations, containing added sugar	0·69
20.06 ..	Fruit otherwise prepared or preserved, containing added sugar:—	
	Ginger	0·55
	Other	0·13

SCHEDULE 2

Tariff heading	Description of Composite Sugar Products
17.05 (A) and (B)	Sugar and invert sugar, flavoured or coloured.

EXPLANATORY NOTE

(This Note is not part of the Order.)

This order provides for increases in the average rates of distribution payments payable in respect of imported composite sugar products of the descriptions specified in Schedule 1 on and after 31st August 1972. These correspond to increases in the rates of distribution payment effected by the Sugar (Distribution Payments) (No. 18) Order 1972 (S.I. 1972/1340). Provision is also made for certain imported composite sugar products to be treated as not containing any sugar or invert sugar.

STATUTORY INSTRUMENTS

1972 No. 1344

VALUE ADDED TAX

The Value Added Tax Tribunals Rules 1972

Made - - - -	*30th August* 1972
Laid before the House of Commons	*8th September* 1972
Coming into Operation	*1st October* 1972

ARRANGEMENT OF RULES

The Commissioners of Customs and Excise, in exercise of the powers conferred on them by Schedule 6 to the Finance Act 1972**(a)**, and after consultation with the Council on Tribunals, hereby make the following Rules:—

Citation and commencement

1. These Rules may be cited as the Value Added Tax Tribunals Rules 1972 and shall come into operation on 1st October 1972.

Interpretation

2.—(1) In these Rules, unless the context otherwise requires—

"the Act" means the Finance Act 1972;

"appellant" means a person who brings an appeal under Section 40 of the Act;

"chairman" has the same meaning as in Schedule 6 to the Act, and includes the President and any Vice-President;

"the Commissioners" means the Commissioners of Customs and Excise;

"costs" includes fees, charges, disbursements, expenses and remuneration;

"disputed decision" means the decision of the Commissioners against which an appellant or intending appellant appeals or desires to appeal to a tribunal;

"the President" means the President of Value Added Tax Tribunals or the person nominated by the Lord Chancellor to discharge for the time being the functions of the President;

"proper officer" means a member of the administrative staff of the value added tax tribunals appointed by a chairman to perform the duties of a proper officer under these Rules;

"tribunal" means a value added tax tribunal constituted in accordance with the provisions of Schedule 6 to the Act;

"tribunal centre" means an administrative office of the value added tax tribunals;

"the appropriate tribunal centre" means the tribunal centre for the time being appointed by the President for the area in which is situated the address to which the disputed decision was sent by the Commissioners or the tribunal centre to which an appeal or an application under Rule 20 in relation to the disputed decision may be transferred under these Rules;

"Vice-President" means a Vice-President of Value Added Tax Tribunals.

(2) The Interpretation Act 1889**(b)** shall apply to the interpretation of these Rules as it applies to the interpretation of an Act of Parliament.

Method of appealing

3.—(1) An appeal to a tribunal shall be brought by a notice of appeal served at the appropriate tribunal centre.

(2) A notice of appeal shall be signed by or on behalf of the appellant and shall—

   (*a*) state the name and the business address or, if he has no business address, the address of the appellant,

   (*b*) state the address of the office of the Commissioners from which the disputed decision was sent,

---

(a) 1972 c. 41.   **(b)** 1889 c. 63.

(*c*) state the date of the letter from the Commissioners containing the disputed decision,

(*d*) set out, or have attached thereto a document containing, the grounds of the appeal, and

(*e*) have attached thereto a copy of any letter from the Commissioners continuing his time to appeal against the disputed decision and of any letter from the Commissioners notifying to the appellant a date, later than the date of the letter containing the disputed decision, from which his time to appeal against the disputed decision shall run.

(3) Subject to Rule 11, the parties to an appeal shall be the appellant and the Commissioners.

Time for appealing

4. Subject to Rule 18 a notice of appeal shall be served at the appropriate tribunal centre before the expiration of 30 days after the date of the letter from the Commissioners containing the disputed decision: Provided that if, during such period of 30 days, the Commissioners shall have notified the appellant in writing that his time to appeal against the disputed decision should continue until the expiration of 21 days after a date set out in such letter or to be set out in a further letter, a notice of appeal may be served at the appropriate tribunal centre at any time before the expiration of 21 days after such date.

Acknowledgement of notice of appeal and notification to the Commissioners

5. A proper officer shall send—

(*a*) an acknowledgement of the service of a notice of appeal at the appropriate tribunal centre to the appellant, and

(*b*) a copy of such notice of appeal and any document attached thereto to the Commissioners

and the acknowledgement and the copy of the notice of appeal shall state the date of service of the notice of appeal.

Statement of case by the Commissioners

6.—(1) The Commissioners shall, within 21 days of the date of service of a notice of appeal or application under Rule 20, and within 14 days after the date of service of a notice of application for an extension of time to appeal or to apply under Rule 20, serve at the appropriate tribunal centre a copy of the disputed decision and

(*a*) in relation to an appeal, a document stating their grounds for the disputed decision and any further grounds they may wish to advance in support thereof,

(*b*) in relation to an application under Rule 20, a document stating whether or not they wish to oppose the application and their grounds for any such opposition, and

(*c*) in relation to an application for an extension of time, a document stating whether or not they wish to oppose the application and their grounds for any such opposition,

and a proper officer shall send a copy of such document to the appellant or applicant.

(2) Where the Commissioners contend that an appeal does not lie to, or cannot be entertained by, a tribunal they shall serve a notice to that effect containing the grounds for such contention at the appropriate tribunal centre as soon as practicable after the receipt of the copy of the notice of appeal or application, and a proper officer shall send a copy of the notice to the other party to the appeal or application.

Disclosure, inspection and production of documents

7.—(1) A party to an appeal or application under Rule 20 shall, within 21 days of the date of service of the notice of appeal or application, serve at the appropriate tribunal centre a list of the documents in his possesion, custody and power which he proposes to produce at the hearing of the appeal or application and shall in such list indicate a reasonable period (commencing not earlier than 7 days and ending not later than 14 days after the date of such list) during which, and a reasonable place at which, the other party may inspect and take copies of such documents.

(2) A proper officer shall send a copy of any list of documents served at the appropriate tribunal centre to the other party to the appeal or application.

(3) A party shall be entitled to inspect and take copies of any document set out in the list of documents served by the other party during the period and at the place specified by such other party in his list of documents and during such period and at such place as a tribunal may direct.

(4) Unless a tribunal shall otherwise direct, a party shall produce any document set out in his list of documents at the hearing of the appeal or application and at the hearing of any application therein when called upon so to do by the other party.

Witness statements

8.—(1) A party to an appeal may, within 21 days after the date of service of the notice of appeal, serve at the appropriate tribunal centre a statement in writing (in these Rules called "a witness statement") containing evidence proposed to be given by any person at the hearing of the appeal.

(2) A witness statement shall contain the name, address and description of the person proposing to give the evidence contained therein and shall be signed by him.

(3) A proper officer shall send a copy of a witness statement served at the appropriate tribunal centre to the other party to the appeal and such copy shall state the date of service and shall contain a note to the effect that unless a notice of objection thereto is served in accordance with paragraph (4) of this Rule, the witness statement may be read at the hearing of the appeal as evidence of the facts stated therein without the person who made the witness statement giving oral evidence thereat.

(4) If a party objects to a witness statement being admitted in evidence on the hearing of the appeal as evidence of any fact stated therein he shall serve a notice of objection to such witness statement at the appropriate tribunal centre not later than 14 days after the date of the service of such witness statement at the appropriate tribunal centre whereupon a proper officer shall send a copy of the notice of objection to the other party and the witness statement shall not be read or admitted in evidence at such hearing but the person who signed such witness statement may give evidence orally at the hearing.

(5) Subject to paragraph (4) of this Rule, unless a tribunal shall otherwise direct, a statement contained in a witness statement signed by any person and duly served under this Rule shall be admissible in evidence at the hearing of the appeal as evidence of any fact stated therein of which direct oral evidence by him would be admissible.

Witness summonses

9.—(1) Where a witness is required by any party to an appeal or application to attend the hearing of the appeal or application to give oral evidence or to produce any document in his possession, custody or power necessary for the purpose of that hearing, a tribunal shall, upon the application of such party, issue a summons requiring the attendance of such witness at such hearing and, where appropriate, the production of the document, wherever such witness may be within the United Kingdom.

(2) A summons issued under this Rule shall be signed by a chairman and must be served personally upon the witness thereby required to attend the hearing by leaving a copy of the summons with him and showing him the original thereof not less than 4 days before the day on which the attendance of the witness is thereby required.

(3) A summons issued under this Rule and duly served shall have effect until the conclusion of the hearing at which the attendance of the witness is thereby required.

(4) No person shall be required to attend to give evidence or to produce any document at any hearing which he could not be required to give or produce on the trial of an action in a court of law.

(5) No person upon whom a summons shall be served under this Rule shall be required to attend to give evidence or to produce any document at the hearing therein specified unless, upon such service, he is paid or tendered a sum sufficient to cover his reasonable expenses of travelling to and from, and his attendance at, such hearing.

(6) A tribunal may, upon the application of any person served at the appropriate tribunal centre, set aside a summons served upon him under this Rule.

Partners

10. Partners in a firm which is not a legal person distinct from the partners of whom it is composed may appeal, or apply to a tribunal to entertain an appeal, against a decision of the Commissioners relating to the business of the firm in the name of the firm and, unless a tribunal shall otherwise direct, the proceedings shall be carried on in the name of the firm, but with the same consequences as would have ensued if the appeal or application had been brought in the names of the partners.

Death or bankruptcy of an appellant or applicant

11. Where, at any stage in the proceedings in an appeal or application under Rule 20, the liability or interest of the appellant or applicant, by reason of his death or bankruptcy or for any other reason whatsoever, is assigned or transmitted to or devolves upon some other person, the appeal or application shall not abate or determine, but a tribunal, on the application of the Commissioners or such other person, may direct that such other person be made a party to the appeal or application, and the appeal or application be carried on as if such other person had been substituted for the appellant or applicant.

Amendments

12.—(1) For the purposes of determining the real question in dispute or of correcting an error or defect in an appeal or application or any proceedings therein, a tribunal may at any time, either of its own motion or on the application of any party to the appeal or application, or other person interested, direct that a notice of appeal, notice of application or other document in any proceedings be amended in such manner as may be specified in such direction on such terms as it may think fit.

(2) This Rule shall not apply to a decision of a tribunal.

Transfer between tribunal centres

13.—(1) A tribunal on the application of a party to an appeal or application under Rule 20 may direct that the appeal or application and all proceedings relating to the disputed decision (including, in the case of an application under Rule 20, any appeal to a tribunal against the disputed decision) be transferred to such tribunal centre as may be specified in such direction whereupon, for the purposes of these Rules, the tribunal centre specified in such direction shall be the appropriate tribunal centre for such appeal or application and all proceedings relating to the disputed decision, without prejudice to the power of a tribunal to give a further direction relating thereto under this Rule.

(2) This Rule shall not apply to an application under Rule 21.

Withdrawal of an appeal or application

14. An appellant or applicant may at any time withdraw his appeal or application by serving at the appropriate tribunal centre a notice of withdrawal signed by him or on his behalf, and a proper officer shall send a copy thereof to the Commissioners.

Appeal or application allowed by consent

15. Where the parties to an appeal or application have agreed upon the terms of any decision or direction to be given by a tribunal, particulars of the terms so agreed signed by or on behalf of the parties may be served at the appropriate tribunal centre whereupon a tribunal may give a decision or direction in accordance with these terms without a hearing.

Incompetent appeal or application

16.—(1) A tribunal shall—

    (*a*) strike out an appeal or application under Rule 20 where no appeal against the disputed decision lies to a tribunal, and

    (*b*) dismiss an appeal where the appeal cannot be entertained by a tribunal.

(2) Except in accordance with Rule 15, no appeal or application under Rule 20 shall be struck out or dismissed under this Rule without a hearing but any such hearing may be adjourned in accordance with Rule 31(2).

Powers of a tribunal to give directions

17.—(1) A tribunal may, either of its own motion or on the application of any party to an appeal or application under Rule 20 or other person interested, give any direction as to the conduct of, or as to any matter in connection with, an appeal or application which it may think necessary or expedient.

(2) If any party to an appeal or application or other person shall refuse or fail to comply with any direction of a tribunal, a tribunal may allow or dismiss the appeal or application (as the case may require) but a tribunal may, on the further application of any such party or other person served at the appropriate tribunal centre, within 14 days after the date of the document containing the decision allowing or dismissing the appeal or application, direct that such appeal or application be reinstated on such terms as it may think just.

Power of a tribunal to extend time

18. A tribunal may extend the time within which any party to an appeal or application or other person is required or authorised by or pursuant to these Rules or any decision or direction of a tribunal to do anything in relation to an appeal or application, whether or not the period has expired, on such terms as it may think just; and may, of its own motion, extend any period (including the period for service of a notice of appeal or a notice of an application under Rule 20) without prior notice or reference to any person and without a hearing.

Method of applying for a direction, or for the issue or setting aside the issue of a witness summons

19.—(1) An application to a tribunal for a direction or for the issue of a witness summons made otherwise than at a hearing shall be made by a notice served at the appropriate tribunal centre.

(2) An application to set aside the issue of a witness summons shall be made by a notice served at the appropriate tribunal centre before the day on which the attendance of the witness is thereby required.

(3) A notice under this Rule shall—

(*a*) state the name and business address or, if he has no business address, the address of the applicant,

(*b*) state the direction required or details of the witness summons thereby sought to be issued or set aside, and

(*c*) set out, or have attached thereto a document containing, the grounds of the application.

(4) This Rule shall not apply to an application under Rule 20 or Rule 21.

Method of applying for an appeal to be entertained without payment or deposit of tax

20.—(1) An application to a tribunal to entertain an appeal without payment or deposit with the Commissioners of any tax shall be made by a notice served at the appropriate tribunal centre.

(2) Subject to Rule 18 a notice under this rule shall be served before the expiration of 14 days after the date of the letter from the Commissioners containing the disputed decision or before the expiration of 14 days after any later date notified by the Commissioners to the applicant under the proviso to Rule 4.

(3) A notice under this Rule shall be signed by or on behalf of the applicant and shall—

(*a*) state the name and the business address or, if he has no business address, the address of the applicant to which the disputed decision was sent,

(*b*) state the address of the office of the Commissioners from which the disputed decision was sent,

(*c*) state the date of the letter from the Commissioners containing the disputed decision,

(*d*) set out, or have attached thereto a document containing, the grounds of the application, and

(*e*) have attached thereto a copy of any letter from the Commissioners continuing his time to appeal against the disputed decision and of any letter from the Commissioners notifying to the appellant a date, later than the date of the letter containing the disputed decision, from which his time to appeal against the disputed decision shall run.

(4) Subject to Rule 11, the parties to an application under this Rule shall be the applicant and the Commissioners.

Applications for leave to make an assessment

21.—(1) An application by the Commissioners for leave of a tribunal to make an assessment shall be made by a notice of application signed by a representative of the Commissioners and served at any tribunal centre which shall thereupon be deemed to be the appropriate tribunal centre for the purposes of such application and the proceedings therein, but a tribunal may direct that an application under this Rule be transferred to such other tribunal centre as may be specified in such direction which shall then be deemed to be the appropriate tribunal centre for the purposes of such application and the proceedings therein without prejudice to the power of a tribunal to give a further direction relating thereto under this Rule.

(2) A notice under this Rule shall—

(*a*) state the address of the office of the Commissioners from which it is sent, and

(*b*) set out, or have attached thereto a document containing, the grounds of the application.

(3) Nothing in this Rule or in any direction of a tribunal under this Rule shall affect the appropriate tribunal centre for the purposes of any appeal against a decision of the Commissioners made by leave of a tribunal.

(4) No person other than the Commissioners shall be a party to any application under this Rule which shall be heard without notice to any person other than the Commissioners.

Acknowledgement of notice of an application and notification

22. A proper officer shall send an acknowledgement of the service of a notice of application at the appropriate tribunal centre to the applicant and shall send a copy thereof and any document attached thereto—

(*a*) to the Commissioners, in the case of an application for an appeal to be entertained without payment or deposit of any tax, or for an extension of the applicant's time for appealing against a decision of the Commissioners, or for an extension of the applicant's time for applying under Rule 20, and

(*b*) to the other party to the appeal or application, in the case of an application for a direction in an appeal or application under Rule 20 (not being an application for the issue, or to set aside the issue, of a witness summons or an application by a person who is not a party to the appeal or application), and

(*c*) to the party who obtained the issue of such witness summons, in the case of an application to set aside the issue of a witness summons, and

(*d*) to the parties to the appeal or application, in the case of an application by a person who is not a party to the appeal or application and which is not an application to set aside the issue of a witness summons, and

(*e*) to the parties to the appeal or application sought to be reinstated, in the case of an application for the reinstatement of an appeal or application.

Notice of a hearing

23.—(1) A proper officer shall send to the parties to an appeal or application made under Rule 20 a notice stating the date and time when, and place where, such appeal or application will be heard not less than 14 days before such date.

(2) Unless a tribunal otherwise directs, an application made at a hearing shall be heard forthwith, and no notice thereof shall be sent to the parties thereto.

(3) Subject to paragraphs (1) and (2) of this Rule, a proper officer shall send a notice stating the date and time when, and the place where, an application will be heard not less than 7 days before such date

    (*a*) in the case of an application made under Rule 21 or any application in such proceedings, to the Commissioners, and

    (*b*) in the case of an application for the issue of a witness summons, to the applicant, and

    (*c*) in the case of any other application, to the applicant and the person or persons to whom a copy of the notice of application is required to be sent under Rule 22.

(4) Any person to whom a notice of the hearing of an application is required to be sent under paragraph (3) of this Rule shall, for the purposes of these Rules, be a party to such application.

Hearings in public or in private

24.—(1) The hearing of an appeal shall be in public unless a tribunal, on the application of a party thereto, directs that the hearing or any part of the hearing shall take place in private.

(2) Unless a tribunal otherwise directs, the hearing of any application made otherwise than at the hearing of an appeal shall take place in private.

(3) Any member of the Council on Tribunals or the Scottish Committee of the Council on Tribunals in his capacity as such a member may attend the hearing of any appeal or application notwithstanding that such appeal or application is in private.

Representation at a hearing

25. At the hearing of an appeal or application—

    (*a*) any party to the appeal or application (other than the Commissioners) may conduct his case himself or may be represented by any person whom he may appoint for the purpose, and

    (*b*) the Commissioners may, except in the case of an application to which they are not parties, be represented by any person whom they may appoint for the purpose.

Failure to appear at a hearing

26.—(1) If, when an appeal or application is called on for hearing, no party thereto appears in person or by his representative, a tribunal may dismiss the appeal or application, but a tribunal may, on the application of either party or any person interested served at the appropriate tribunal centre within 14 days after the date of the document containing the decision of the tribunal, reinstate such appeal or application on such terms as it may think just.

(2) If, when an appeal or application is called on for hearing, one party does not appear in person or by his representative, the tribunal may proceed in the absence of that party, but any decision or direction given in the absence of one party may, on the application of such party or other person interested served at the appropriate tribunal centre within 14 days after the date of the document containing the decision or direction be set aside by a tribunal on such terms as it may think just.

Procedure at a hearing

27.—(1) At the hearing of an appeal or application the tribunal shall allow—

(a) the appellant or applicant or his representative to address the tribunal,

(b) the appellant or applicant to give evidence in support of his appeal or application and to produce documentary evidence,

(c) the appellant or applicant or his representative to call other witnesses,

(d) the appellant or applicant or his representative to make a second address closing his case, and

(e) the appellant or applicant or his representative to cross-examine any witness called by or on behalf of the other party to the appeal or application (including the other party to the appeal or application if he gives evidence).

(2) At the hearing of an appeal or application the tribunal shall also allow—

(a) the other party to the appeal or application or his representative to address the tribunal,

(b) the other party to give evidence in opposition to the appeal or application and to produce documentary evidence,

(c) the other party or his representative to call other witnesses,

(d) the other party or his representative to make a second address closing his case, and

(e) the other party or his representative to cross-examine any witness called by or on behalf of the appellant or applicant (including the appellant or applicant if he gives evidence).

(3) At the hearing of an appeal or application the chairman and any other member of the tribunal may put any questions to any witness called by or on behalf of the appellant or applicant (including the appellant or applicant if he gives evidence) and any witness called by or on behalf of the other party to the appeal or application (including such other party if he gives evidence).

(4) Subject to the provisions of these Rules a tribunal may regulate its own procedure as it may think fit.

Evidence at a hearing

28.—(1) Subject to paragraphs (4) and (5) of Rule 8, a tribunal may direct or allow evidence of any fact to be given in any manner it may think fit and shall not refuse evidence tendered to it on the grounds only that such evidence would be inadmissible in a court of law.

(2) A tribunal may require oral evidence of a witness (including a party to an appeal or application) to be given on oath or affirmation and for that purpose a chairman and any member of the administrative staff of the tribunals on the direction of a chairman shall have power to administer oaths or take affirmations.

(3) At the hearing of an appeal or application the tribunal shall allow a party to produce any document set out in his list of documents served under Rule 7 and unless a tribunal otherwise directs—

    (*a*) any document contained in such a list of documents which appears to be an original document shall be deemed to be an original document printed, written, signed or executed as it respectively appears to have been, and

    (*b*) any document contained in such a list of documents which appears to be a copy shall be deemed to be a true copy.

Decision or direction at a hearing

29.—(1) At the conclusion of a hearing the decision or direction of the tribunal may be announced by the chairman, but in any event the decision or direction shall be recorded in a document signed by a chairman and dated when so signed and which shall contain all findings of fact by the tribunal and the reasons for the decision or direction.

(2) A proper officer shall send a copy of the decision or direction of the tribunal (including any decision or direction given by consent under Rule 15) to each party to the appeal or application.

(3) A chairman may correct any error in any document containing the decision or direction of a tribunal, but if a chairman corrects any such document after a copy thereof has been sent to any party, a proper officer shall, as soon as practicable thereafter, send a copy of such corrected document to such party.

(4) Where a copy of a document containing a decision or direction of a tribunal dismissing an appeal or application is sent to a person entitled under Rule 17(2) or Rule 26(1) or Rule 26(2) to apply to have the appeal or application reinstated, the copy shall contain a note to that effect.

Award of costs

30.—(1) A tribunal may direct that a party or applicant shall pay to the other party to the appeal or application within such period as the tribunal may specify such sum as it may determine on account of the costs of such other party of and incidental to the appeal or application.

(2) Any costs awarded by a tribunal under this Rule shall be recoverable as a civil debt.

Miscellaneous powers of a tribunal

31.—(1) A chairman may postpone the hearing of any appeal or application.

(2) A tribunal may adjourn the hearing of an appeal or application on such terms as it may think just.

(3) A tribunal may at any time direct a party to an appeal or application under Rule 20 to serve further particulars of his case at the appropriate tribunal centre within such period from the date of such direction (not being less than 7 days from such date) as may be specified therein, and a proper officer shall send a copy of any further particulars served at the appropriate tribunal centre to the other party to the appeal or application.

(4) A tribunal may, of its own motion or on the application of any party to an appeal or application, waive any breach or non-observance of any provision of these Rules or any decision or direction of a tribunal on such terms as it may think just.

Service at a Tribunal centre

32.—(1) Service of a notice of appeal, notice of application or other document at a tribunal centre shall be effected by the same being handed to a proper officer at such tribunal centre or by the same being received by post at such tribunal centre.

(2) Any notice of appeal, notice of application or other document handed in, or received at a tribunal centre other than the appropriate tribunal centre may be sent by post in a letter addressed to the proper officer at the appropriate tribunal centre or handed back to the person from whom it was received or sent by post in a letter addressed to the person from whom it appears to have been received or by whom it appears to have been sent.

The sending of documents to the parties

33.—(1) Any document authorised or required to be sent to the Commissioners may be sent to them by post in a letter addressed to them at the address of their office from which the disputed decision or the application appears to have been sent or at such other address as the Commissioners may from time to time by notice served at the appropriate tribunal centre specify.

(2) Any document authorised or required to be sent to any party to an appeal or application other than the Commissioners may be sent by post in a letter addressed to him at his address stated in his notice of appeal or application or sent by post in a letter addressed to any person named in his notice of appeal or application as having been instructed to act for him in connection therewith or sent by post in a letter addressed to such person and at such address as he may from time to time by notice served at the appropriate tribunal centre specify: Provided that where partners appeal or apply to a tribunal in the name of their firm any document sent by post in a letter addressed to the firm at the address of the firm stated in the notice of appeal or notice of application or such other address as such partners may from time to time by notice served at the appropriate tribunal centre specify shall be deemed to have been duly sent to all such partners.

(3) Subject to the foregoing provisions of this Rule, any document authorised or required to be sent to any party to an appeal or application or other person may be sent by post in a letter addressed to him at his usual or last known address or addressed to him or such other person and at such address as he may from time to time by notice served at the appropriate tribunal centre specify.

Dorothy Johnstone,
Commissioner of Customs and Excise.

30th August 1972.

King's Beam House,
Mark Lane,
London EC3R 7HE.

EXPLANATORY NOTE

(This Note is not part of the Rules.)

These Rules (which have been prepared in consultation with the Council on Tribunals) set out the procedure to be followed when an appeal is made to a value added tax tribunal under section 40 of the Finance Act 1972 against a decision of the Commissioners of Customs and Excise, or when the Commissioners apply to a tribunal under section 31(4) of that Act for leave to make an assessment.

Provision is made for the serving of a notice of appeal at the appropriate tribunal centre and for limiting the time within which appeals are to be brought, although such time may be extended by the tribunal, as may any other time limit. Provision is also made for the exchange of documents (Rule 7); the use of witness statements (Rule 8); the summoning of witnesses (Rule 9); the procedure at the hearing (Rule 27); the methods of proof which will be acceptable to the tribunal (Rule 28); and the award of costs (Rule 30).

STATUTORY INSTRUMENTS

1972 No. 1345

CAR TAX

The Car Tax Regulations 1972

Made - - -	*30th August* 1972
Laid before the House of Commons	*8th September* 1972

Coming into operation—

Regulations 1, 2, 6	*1st October* 1972
Remainder	*1st April* 1973

The Commissioners of Customs and Excise, in exercise of the powers conferred upon them by paragraph 26 of Schedule 7 to the Finance Act 1972(a) and of all other powers enabling them in that behalf, hereby make the following Regulations:—

Citation, Commencement and Interpretation

1.—(1) These Regulations may be cited as the Car Tax Regulations 1972.

(2) Regulations 1, 2 and 6 of these Regulations shall come into operation on 1st October 1972 and the remaining Regulations on 1st April 1973.

(3) In these Regulations—

"the Act" means the Finance Act 1972;

"registered", in relation to a vehicle shall have the same meaning as in section 52 of the Act;

"registered person" means a person registered pursuant to paragraph 15 of Schedule 7 to the Act;

"tax" means car tax.

(4) The Interpretation Act 1889(b) shall apply for the interpretation of these Regulations as it applies for the interpretation of an Act of Parliament.

Notification of Liability to be Registered

2. The following particulars shall be contained in any notification under paragraph 15(2) of Schedule 7 to the Act (under which persons liable to be registered are required to notify the Commissioners of that fact)—

(*a*) the name and address of the person liable to be registered and the name in which he carries on business;

(*b*) the number of chargeable vehicles made or imported by him in the course of his business during the calendar year in which the notification is made and in the preceding calendar year; and

(*c*) the address of all places in the United Kingdom used by him in the course of his business for making or storing chargeable vehicles, and where the main records and accounts of his business are kept.

(a) 1972 c. 41.   (b) 1889 c. 63.

Registered Persons

3. Unless the Commissioners otherwise direct, every registered person shall keep the following records and accounts and shall preserve them for a period of not less than three years—

(a) a record of every chargeable vehicle made or imported by him, with sufficient particulars to identify each vehicle including the make, model and colour and the serial numbers of the chassis and engine and showing the date when the vehicle was made or imported;

(b) in the case of a vehicle appropriated to his own use, a record of the date when tax in respect of it became due by reason of the appropriation and the amount of that tax;

(c) in the case of a vehicle delivered under an agreement providing for its sale or return—

(i) a record showing the name and address of the person to whom it was so delivered, the date when it was so delivered, the date when tax in respect of it became due by reason of it ceasing to be his property or being treated for the purposes of the tax as ceasing to be his property and the amount of that tax;

(ii) a copy of the agreement and of any documents applying the agreement to the vehicle, and

(iii) any notice received by him that the vehicle has ceased to be his property or is to be treated for the purpose of the tax as ceasing to be his property;

(d) in any other case—

(i) a record showing the date when the vehicle was sent out from his premises, the name and address of the person to whom it was sent out, and the amount of tax due in respect of it;

(ii) a copy of any invoice, delivery note or like document issued by him in respect of the vehicle;

(e) copies of all certificates furnished by him pursuant to Regulation 5 of these Regulations;

(f) all statements furnished to him pursuant to Regulation 7(2) of these Regulations.

4.—(1) Every registered person shall in every year furnish the Commissioners with returns in the form numbered 1 in the Schedule to these Regulations showing the amount of tax due from him in respect of each of the three-monthly periods ending on and including the last day of February, the last day of May, the last day of August and the last day of November and containing full information in respect of all other matters to which the said form relates and a declaration that the return is correct and complete and shall furnish such return not later than the last day of the month next following the end of the period to which it relates provided that—

(a) where the Commissioners are satisfied that in order to meet the circumstances of any particular case it is necessary to vary the date on which any such period as aforesaid begins or ends or the date on which any such return as aforesaid shall be furnished they may give to a registered person such directions as they think fit;

(*b*) the first such return to be furnished after the beginning of April 1973 shall show the amount of tax due in respect of a period of five months ending on and including the last day of August 1973;

(*c*) for the security of the revenue the Commissioners may direct a registered person to furnish such a return—

(i) in respect of the period from the beginning of any such three-monthly period as aforesaid to such date as they direct, and to furnish it within seven days of that date, or

(ii) in respect of monthly periods beginning on the first day and ending on the last day of each month, and to furnish it not later than seven days after the end of the month.

(2) Any person to whom the Commissioners give any direction in pursuance of paragraph (*a*) or (*c*) of the proviso to paragraph (1) of this Regulation shall comply therewith.

(3) Any registered person who ceases to be liable to be registered during any such period as aforesaid shall, after so ceasing, furnish the Commissioners with a return in respect of that part of the period during which he was so liable.

(4) The tax due from a registered person shall be paid to the Commissioners when he furnishes a return in accordance with the provisions of this Regulation and in any event not later than the last day provided for by this Regulation for furnishing that return.

5.—(1) Unless the Commissioners otherwise allow, every registered person shall furnish to any person receiving from him a chargeable vehicle which has not yet been registered a certificate that tax due in respect of the vehicle has been or will be paid and shall furnish such certificate when the tax becomes due.

(2) Every certificate required under paragraph (1) of this Regulation shall, unless the Commissioners otherwise direct—

(*a*) be in the form numbered 2 in the Schedule to these Regulations;

(*b*) be numbered and issued consecutively; .

(*c*) be signed by the registered person or by a person authorised by him in writing so to do.

(3) Unless the Commissioners otherwise direct no registered person shall issue more than one such certificate in respect of any one vehicle.

6.—(1) If a registered person dies or becomes bankrupt or otherwise incapacitated the Commissioners may, from the date on which he died or became bankrupt or otherwise incapacitated until some other person is registered in his stead or the incapacity ceases, as the case may be, treat as a registered person any person acting or purporting to act as a personal representative, trustee, receiver or committee; and the provisions of the Act and of these Regulations shall apply to any person so treated as though he were a registered person.

(2) Any person acting or purporting to act as aforesaid shall, within twenty-one days of being appointed, or of commencing, so to act, whichever is the earlier, inform the Commissioners in writing of the date of the death or of the nature of the incapacity and the date on which it began.

Records and returns by persons to whom chargeable vehicles are delivered on sale or return

7.—(1) Every person who in the course of a business carried on by him has chargeable vehicles on which tax has not been paid delivered to him under an agreement providing for their sale or return shall—

(a) keep a separate record in respect of each registered person from whom such vehicles are so delivered showing the date when each such vehicle—

(i) was delivered from that registered person, and

(ii) was returned to that registered person, or

(iii) ceased to be the property of that registered person, or is treated for the purpose of the tax as having ceased to be his property

and preserve such records for not less than three years, and

(b) furnish to the registered person from whom such vehicles were so delivered statements in respect of the period of five months ending on and including the last day of August 1973 and thereafter in each year in respect of the three-monthly periods ending on and including the last day of February, the last day of May, the last day of August and the last day of November showing the date when each such vehicle ceased to be the property of that registered person or is treated for the purpose of the tax as having ceased to be his property, and shall furnish each such statement not later than fourteen days after the expiration of the period to which it relates.

(2) Every record required to be kept and every statement required to be furnished by paragraph (1) of this Regulation shall contain sufficient particulars to identify each vehicle to which it relates including the make, model and colour, and the serial numbers of the chassis and engine.

Commissioners' Certificates

8. The Commissioners may issue a certificate in respect of any chargeable vehicle stating that tax on that vehicle has been paid or remitted.

Statement to accompany certain untaxed vehicles

9.—(1) Every person, not being a registered person, who makes or imports a chargeable vehicle shall furnish to any person acquiring from him any such vehicle before tax in respect of it has been paid a statement in writing that the vehicle is a chargeable vehicle on which tax will be payable before it is registered.

(2) Every such statement shall be furnished at the time the vehicle is acquired from the person furnishing it and shall show his name and address, a description of the vehicle with sufficient particulars to identify it including the approximate year of manufacture, the make, model and colour and serial numbers of the chassis and engine and any registration mark.

Remission of tax on vehicles used outside the United Kingdom

10.—(1) The Commissioners may remit tax on any chargeable vehicle which is payable by a person who for the purposes of the registration of the vehicle is treated as the person keeping the vehicle, if he is a person entering the United Kingdom and imports the vehicle, whether or not at the same time, on condition that—

(*a*) at the time he enters the United Kingdom he intends to remain in the United Kingdom for not less than twelve months from that time;

(*b*) the vehicle is intended solely for his own personal use and that of his dependants during the period specified in paragraph (3) of this Regulation, and

(*c*) he has both owned and used the vehicle outside the United Kingdom for periods together amounting to not less than twelve months and he has himself been outside the United Kingdom throughout those periods of ownership and use.

(2) Where the vehicle referred to in the foregoing paragraph is imported by the husband or wife of the person there referred to, the period or periods of ownership and use outside the United Kingdom shall be such period or periods as the Commissioners may in any particular case allow.

(3) The following conditions shall be complied with in relation to the vehicle referred to in paragraph (1) of this Regulation, namely, it shall not be, or be offered, exposed or advertised to be, lent, hired, pledged, given away, exchanged, sold or otherwise disposed of in the United Kingdom within a period of two years from the date on which such relief was afforded.

Distress

11.—(1) If upon demand made by a Collector of Customs and Excise a person neglects or refuses to pay tax which he is required to pay under the Act or any Regulation made thereunder, the Collector may distrain on the goods and chattels of that person and by warrant signed by him direct any authorised person to levy such distress, provided that where an amount of tax is due under paragraph 17 of Schedule 7 to the Act no distress shall be levied until twenty-one days after that amount became due.

(2) For the purpose of levying any such distress an authorised person may after obtaining a warrant for the purpose signed by a Collector of Customs and Excise break open, in the daytime, any house or premises.

(3) A levy or warrant to break open shall be executed by or under the direction of, and in the presence of, the authorised person.

(4) A distress levied by the authorised person shall be kept for five days, at the costs and charges of the person neglecting or refusing to pay.

(5) If the person aforesaid does not pay the sum due, together with the costs and charges, within the said five days, the distress shall be independently appraised and shall be sold by public auction by the authorised person for payment of the sums due and all costs and charges; and costs and charges of taking, keeping and selling the distress shall be retained by the authorised person, and any surplus remaining after the deduction of the costs and charges and of the sum due shall be restored to the owner of the goods distrained.

Diligence

12. In Scotland, the following provisions shall have effect—

(*a*) Upon certificate made to him by a Collector of Customs and Excise that any tax is due under the Act or under Regulations made thereunder and has not been paid the sheriff or sheriff substitute for the county shall issue a warrant for the Collector recovering the said tax by poinding the goods and effects of any person entered in the certificate as being a defaulter.

(*b*) The warrant shall be executed by the sheriff officers of the county.

(*c*) The goods and effects so poinded shall be detained and kept on the ground, or at the house where the same were poinded, or in such other place of which the owner shall have notice, near to the said ground or house, as the officer so poinding the same shall think proper, for the space of five days, during which time the said goods and effects shall remain in the custody of the said officer, and liable to the payment of the whole tax in arrear and to the costs to be paid to the officer who poinded the same as hereinafter directed, unless the owner from whom the same were poinded shall redeem the same, within the said space of five days, by payment to the officer of the said tax in arrear and costs, to be settled in the same manner as if the said goods and effects had been sold as hereinafter directed.

(*d*) The goods and effects so poinded shall, after the expiration of the said five days, be valued and appraised by any two persons to be appointed by the officer and shall be sold and disposed of, at a sum not less than the value, by the officer who does poind the same.

(*e*) The value shall be applied, in the first place to the satisfaction and payment of the tax owing by the person whose goods are so poinded, and, in the second place, to the payment for the trouble of the officer so poinding, at the rate of 10 new pence per pound of the tax for which the goods shall be so poinded unless the owner from whom the same were poinded shall redeem the same by payment of the appraised value, within the space of five days after the valuation, to the officer who poinded the same.

(*f*) In case any surplus remains of the price of value, after payment of the said tax, and after payment of what is allowed to be retained by the officer in manner herein directed, such surplus shall be returned to the owner from whom the goods were poinded.

(*g*) In case no purchaser appears at the said sale, then the said goods and effects, so poinded, shall be consigned and lodged in the hands of the sheriff of the county, or his substitute, and if not redeemed by the owner within the space of five days after the consignment in the hands of the said sheriff or sheriff substitute, the same shall be rouped, sold, and disposed of by order of the sheriff, in such manner, and at such time and place, as he shall appoint, he always being liable to the payment of the tax to the authorised person, and to payment to the officer who shall have poinded the same, for his trouble and expense, as before stated, and to the fees due to the officer, and being, in the third place, entitled to 5 new pence per pound of the value of the goods so disposed of, for his own pains and trouble, after preference and allowance of the said tax, and of what is appointed to be paid to the officer for his trouble.

(*h*) There shall also be allowed, to the officer so poinding, the expense of maintaining and preserving the said goods and effects from the time of poinding the same, during the period allowed to the owner to redeem them, and also the expense of the sale; and in like manner the expense shall be allowed to the sheriff or sheriff substitute, for maintaining or preserving the goods poinded, during the period that the owner is allowed to redeem, after consignment in his hands, and until the sale thereof, and also the expense of the sale.

(*i*) Every auctioneer, or seller by commission, selling by auction, in Scotland, any goods or effects whatsoever by any mode of sale at auction, shall, at least three days before he begins any sale by way of auction, deliver or cause to be delivered to the authorised person a notice in writing, signed by such auctioneer or seller by auction, specifying therein the particular day when such sale is to begin, and the name and surname of the person whose goods and effects are to be sold, with his place of residence.

13. For the purposes of paragraph 12(1) of Schedule 7 to the Act (determination of disputes as to wholesale value) the prescribed period shall be a period of fourteen days.

30th August 1972.

Dorothy Johnstone,
Commissioner of Customs and Excise.

King's Beam House,
Mark Lane,
London EC3R 7HE.

SCHEDULE

Form No. 1 Regulation 4

Return of Car Tax to be furnished by Registered Persons

Name ....

Address ....

Return for period... to...................................

PART I

1. Amount of car tax due on vehicles appropriated to
my own use (if none, please write "NONE") ....

2. Amount of car tax due on other vehicles (if none,
please write "NONE") ....

3. Underpayment (if any) of tax due in previous periods
(if none, please write "NONE") ....

4. Total tax due ....

PART 2

In the period specified above,

(*a*) Have you begun to use or ceased to use any
premises in connection with your business of
manufacturing or importing chargeable vehicles
including premises where vehicles or materials
used for making them are stored? ....

Particulars of changes (if any) ....

....

(*b*) Has any change occurred in the name, consti-
tution or ownership of your business? ....

Particulars of changes (if any) ....

....

(*c*) Has any change occurred in the activity of your
business in connection with chargeable vehicles? ....

Particulars of changes (if any) ....

....

(*d*) Has any other change occurred in the circumstances of the business (eg death, incapacity, or
insolvency of the registered person) such as may
necessitate alteration of the registration? ....

Particulars of changes (if any) ....

....

PART 3

Declaration by Signatory

I,..., declare

(Insert FULL name of signatory in BLOCK CAPITALS)

> (*a*) That the information given in Part I of this return is a full and true account of car tax due for the period specified in respect of the business carried on by the above-named registered person(s) of making or importing chargeable vehicles;

> (*b*) That the rate and amounts payable have been computed in accordance with the statutory provisions and the directions of the Commissioners of Customs and Excise, and

> (*c*) That the information given in Part 2 of this return is true and complete.

Dated   Signed   Proprietor
                                                                       Partner
                                                                       Director
                                                                       Secretary

Form No. 2   Regulation 5

Certificate for Car Tax

"I .... being duly authorised to give this certificate on behalf of *... a person registered pursuant to paragraph 15 of Schedule 7 to the Finance Act 1972 hereby certify that car tax due on the vehicle described below has been or will be paid by *...

> Make of vehicle

> Model of vehicle

> Colour

> Chassis No.

> Engine No.

*insert name of registered person.

Dated..   Signed.......................................

EXPLANATORY NOTE

(This Note is not part of the Regulations.)

These Regulations are made under Schedule 7 to the Finance Act 1972. They regulate generally the administration and collection of the car tax, with particular reference to such matters as registration for tax, the keeping of records and furnishing of returns of tax, payment of tax and issue of certificates of tax payment, remission of tax on vehicles used outside the United Kingdom, and recovery by distress of unpaid tax.

The provision in Regulation 2 relating to the particulars required for notification of liability to be registered comes into effect from 1st October 1972 and the keeping of records and other requirements are brought into effect on 1st April 1973 when the car tax commences to be chargeable.

STATUTORY INSTRUMENTS

1972 No. 1347 (S.102)

NATIONAL ASSISTANCE SERVICES

The National Assistance (Charges for Accommodation) (Scotland) Regulations 1972

Made - - -	*28th August* 1972
Laid before Parliament	*7th September* 1972
Coming into Operation	*2nd October* 1972

In exercise of the powers conferred on me by section 22 of the National Assistance Act 1948(**a**) as read with section 87(3) and (4) of the Social Work (Scotland) Act 1968(**b**), and of all other powers enabling me in that behalf, I hereby make the following regulations:—

1. These regulations may be cited as the National Assistance (Charges for Accommodation) (Scotland) Regulations 1972, and shall come into operation on 2nd October 1972.

2.—(1) In these regulations, unless the context otherwise requires—

"the Act of 1948" means the National Assistance Act 1948;

"the Act of 1970" means the National Insurance (Old persons' and widows' pensions and attendance allowance) Act 1970(**c**);

"Personal Injuries Scheme", "Service Pensions Instrument" and "1914-18 War Injuries Scheme" have the same meanings as in the National Insurance (Overlapping Benefits) Regulations 1972(**d**).

(2) Any reference in these regulations to the provisions of any enactment or instrument shall be construed, unless the context otherwise requires, as a reference to those provisions as amended by any subsequent enactment or instrument.

(3) The Interpretation Act 1889(**e**) shall apply for the interpretation of these regulations as it applies to the interpretation of an Act of Parliament, and as if these regulations and the regulations hereby revoked were Acts of Parliament.

3. The National Assistance (Charges for Accommodation) (Scotland) Regulations 1971(**f**) are hereby revoked.

4. For the purposes of section 22(3) of the Act of 1948 (which relates to charges to be made for accommodation provided under Part III of the Act) the liability of a person to pay for accommodation provided in premises managed by a local authority shall in no case be reduced below the sum of £5·40 per week.

(**a**) 1948 c. 29. (**b**) 1968 c. 49. (**c**) 1970 c. 51.
(**d**) S.I. 1972/604 (1972 I, p. 1994). (**e**) 1889 c. 63.
(**f**) S.I. 1971/1500 (1971 III. p. 4197).

5. Where accommodation is provided for a child accompanied by a person over the age of 16, the liability of that person under section 22(7) of the Act of 1948 to pay for the accommodation of that child shall in no case be reduced below such of the following sums as is appropriate, that is to say—

(*a*) in respect of a child under 5 years of age, the sum of £1·90 per week;

(*b*) in respect of a child aged 5 years or over but less than 11 years, the sum of £2·25 per week;

(*c*) in respect of a child aged 11 years or over but less than 13 years, the sum of £2·75 per week;

(*d*) in respect of a child aged 13 years or over but less than 16 years, the sum of £3·40 per week.

6. For the purposes of section 22(4) of the Act of 1948 a local authority shall assume that a person to whom section 22(3) of the Act of 1948 applies will need for his personal requirements the sum of £1·35 per week:

Provided that if that person is someone to whom there is payable attendance allowance under the provisions of section 4(2) of the Act of 1970 as amended by section 14 of and paragraph 12(2) of Schedule 5 to the National Insurance Act 1971(**a**) or constant attendance allowance under any Personal Injuries Scheme, Service Pensions Instrument or any 1914-18 War Injuries Scheme, the aforementioned sum assumed to be needed for his personal requirements shall be increased by the amount of such attendance allowance or constant attendance allowance.

Gordon Campbell,
One of Her Majesty's Principal
Secretaries of State.

St. Andrew's House,
Edinburgh.
28th August 1972.

EXPLANATORY NOTE

(This Note is not part of the Regulations.)

These Regulations replace the National Assistance (Charges for Accommodation) (Scotland) Regulations 1971. The minimum weekly amount which a person is required to pay for accommodation provided for him under the Social Work (Scotland) Act 1968 (which by virtue of section 87(3) of that Act is to be regarded for purposes of charges as accommodation provided under Part III of the National Assistance Act 1948) is increased from £4·80 to £5·40. In the case of a person accompanied by a child, the weekly amounts payable in respect of the child are increased from £1·70 to £1·90 when the

---

(**a**) 1971 c. 50.

child is under 5 years, from £2 to £2·25 when the child is aged 5 years or over but less than 11 years, from £2·45 to £2·75 when the child is aged 11 years or over but less than 13 years, and from £3 to £3·40 when the child is aged 13 years or over but less than 16 years. The weekly sum for personal requirements which (unless in special circumstances the local authority considers a different sum appropriate) the local authority shall allow in assessing a person's ability to pay for accommodation is increased from £1·20 to £1·35 but if the person is one to whom there is payable attendance allowance under the National Insurance (Old persons' and widows' pensions and attendance allowance) Act 1970 as amended or constant attendance allowance under any Personal Injuries Scheme, Service Pensions Instrument or any 1914-18 War Injuries Scheme, the weekly sum for personal requirements shall be increased by that amount.

S T A T U T O R Y   I N S T R U M E N T S

1972 No. 1348 (S.103)

NATIONAL HEALTH SERVICE, SCOTLAND

The National Health Service (General Dental Services) (Scotland) Amendment (No. 2) Regulations 1972

Made - - - -	*28th August* 1972
Laid before Parliament	*1st September* 1972
Coming into Operation	*1st October* 1972

In exercise of the powers conferred on me by section 39 of the National Health Service (Scotland) Act 1947(a), as amended by section 11 of the National Health Service (Amendment) Act 1949(b), and of all other powers enabling me in that behalf, I hereby make the following regulations:—

1.—(1) These regulations may be cited as the National Health Service (General Dental Services) (Scotland) Amendment (No. 2) Regulations 1972 and shall come into operation on 1st October 1972.

(2) In these regulations:—

"the principal regulations" means the National Health Service (General Dental Services) (Scotland) Regulations 1966(c) as amended (d); and

"regulation 27" means regulation 27 of the principal regulations as amended by regulation 3(5) of the National Health Service (General Dental Services) (Scotland) Amendment Regulations 1972(e) (which provided for a new scale of fees for treatment).

(3) The Interpretation Act 1889(f) shall apply for the interpretation of these regulations as it applies for the interpretation of an Act of Parliament, and as if these regulations were an Act of Parliament.

2.—Regulation 4 of the National Health Service (General Dental Services) (Scotland) Amendment Regulations 1972 shall cease to have effect.

3.—The principal regulations shall be amended as follows:—

(1) In regulation 29 (which provides for additional remuneration for the provision of treatment elsewhere than at the practitioner's surgery) for the amount of £1·50 in paragraph (1) there shall be substituted the amount of £1·70, and for the amount of 30p there shall be substituted the amount of 34p.

(a) 1947 c. 27. (b) 1949 c. 93.
(c) S.I. 1966/1449 (1966 III, p. 3802).
(d) The relevant amending instruments are S.I. 1969/436, 1970/924, 1340, 1972/96 (1969 I, p. 1276; 1970 II p. 2888; III p. 4486; 1972 I, p. 265).
(e) S.I. 1972/96 (1972, I, p. 265). (f) 1889 c. 63.

(2) In paragraph 3(2)(*b*) of Part I of Schedule 1 (which deals with limited treatment) for the amount of £2·30 there shall be substituted the amount of £2·60.

(3) For Parts I to VI of Schedule 5 (which sets out the scale of fees for treatment) there shall be substituted the provisions set out in the Schedule to these regulations.

4.—(1) Subject to the following provisions of this regulation, these regulations shall not apply to general dental services provided under a contract or arrangement entered into or made before 1st October 1972 and such services shall continue to be subject to the provisions of the regulations in force immediately before that date, other than the provisions thereof ceasing to have effect by virtue of regulation 2 hereof.

(2) In respect of an advice of payment from the Board to a Council dated during the period beginning with 1st April 1972 and ending with 30th September 1972, the Council shall pay to a practitioner an additional sum equal to 10·8 per cent of the amounts authorised for payment.

(3) Where an advice of payment from the Board to a Council dated on or after 1st October 1972 is in respect of a contract or arrangement entered into or made on or after 1st March 1972 and before 1st October 1972 the Council shall pay to a practitioner in addition to the fees authorised under regulation 27 a sum equal to 10·8 per cent of the amount of these fees.

(4) Where an advice of payment from the Board to a Council dated on or after 1st October 1972 is in respect of a contract or arrangement entered into or made on or after 1st October 1970 and before 1st March 1972 the Council shall pay to a practitioner in addition to the fees authorised under regulation 27 a sum equal to 17·2 per cent of the amount of these fees.

(5) Where an advice of payment from the Board to a Council dated on or after 1st October, 1972 is in respect of a contract or arrangement entered into or made before 1st October 1970 the Council shall pay to a practitioner in addition to the fees authorised under regulation 27 a sum equal to 40·5 per cent of the amount of these fees.

Gordon Campbell,
One of Her Majesty's Principal
Secretaries of State.

St. Andrew's House,
Edinburgh.
28th August 1972.

SCHEDULE

Part I—Diagnosis

1. Clinical examination and report ...   ...   £0·74
Provided that—
    (1) only one fee shall be payable during
    a course of treatment;
    (2) no fee shall be payable for:—
      (*a*) an examination in respect of
        repairs to dentures for edentu-
        lous patients,
        (*b*) a group examination in schools
        or institutions,

(c) an examination of a person aged 21 years or over if the same practitioner† has been paid or is entitled to be paid for an examination and report on that person made at any time during any of the 5 months preceding the month during which a further examination is made,

(d) an examination of a person under 21 years of age if the same practitioner† has been paid or is entitled to be paid for an examination and report on that person made within the preceding three months;

(3) in the case of a woman who is or has been pregnant and who is not edentulous, in addition to the examinations for which payment may otherwise be made under this item, a fee shall be payable for one examination during the antenatal and postnatal period and all such examinations may be carried out at any time during that period.‡

2. Radiological examination and report: Fees per course of treatment—

(a) Intra-oral films:

1 film	£0·50
2 films	£0·60
*3 films	£0·70
*each additional film	£0·18 up to a maximum of £2·32

(b) Extra-oral films:

1 film	£0·80
*each additional film	£0·46 up to a maximum of £1·72.

Provided that a fee shall not be payable in cases in which the Board have required the submission of the films, or in which the Board's prior approval was required, unless the films or duplicates thereof are submitted to the Board.

PART II. CONSERVATIVE TREATMENT

A. *Periodontal Treatment*

3. Scaling, including the removal of calculus and other deposits from the teeth, the provision of prophylactic or other necessary treatment for all ordinary or simple disorders of the gums and any necessary

---

†Reference in this scale of fees to dental treatment by the same practitioner shall include also dental treatment by his principal or the partner of either or by the assistant of any of them, and where the practitioner is employed by a body corporate shall include treatment by another employee of that body.

‡The antenatal and postnatal period is the period of pregnancy and the 12 months subsequent to the date of confinement.

*See schedule 2 for treatment requiring prior approval.

oral hygiene instruction, for persons aged 16 or over at the beginning of a course of treatment:—

(a) Scaling and gum treatment (except cases under (b)) ... ... £1·10

*(b) Scaling and gum treatment to be followed by extraction of the teeth charted for scaling, gum treatment and extraction during the same course of treatment ... ... Such fee as the Board may approve, not exceeding £0·90

*Provided that no fee shall be payable where the last course of treatment in respect of which provision was made for payment under item 3(a) or (b) to the same practitioner† commenced at any time during any of the 5 months preceding the month in which the further treatment is to be done, unless the prior approval of the Board has been obtained.

4. Treatment urgently required for acute infective conditions of the gingivae/oral mucosa, including any necessary oral hygiene instruction:
Fee per course of treatment ... ... £0·58

*5. Other periodontal treatment including any necessary oral hygiene instruction, periodontal surgery and protracted scaling (estimates to include an outline of proposed treatment):

(a) with periodontal surgery ... ... Such fee as the Board may approve.

(b) without periodontal surgery ... Such fee as the Board may approve up to a maximum of £6·50.

B. *Restorative Treatment*

6. Fillings (including any dressings, pulp capping and other necessary preparatory treatment), except fillings in deciduous teeth of children under 16 years. The fillings to which this scale applies shall be permanent in character. Fee per filling:—

(a) amalgam filling in:

(i) a single surface cavity ... ... £0·94 with a maximum of £0·94 for 2 or more such fillings in any one surface of a tooth and a maximum of £1·30 for 2 or more such fillings per tooth not all in one surface.

(ii) a mesial-occlusal-distal cavity inclusive of any extension of such a cavity in a molar or pre-molar tooth ... ... £2·00.

(iii) a mesial-occlusal or distal-occlusal cavity inclusive of any extension of such a cavity into the lingual or buccal surfaces or both in a molar or pre-molar

*See schedule 2 for treatment requiring prior approval.
†Reference in this scale of fees to dental treatment by the same practitioner shall include also dental treatment by his principal or the partner of either or by the assistant of any of them, and where the practitioner is employed by a body corporate shall include treatment by another employee of that body.

tooth ... ... £1·60 with a maximum for a combination of such fillings of £2·00 per tooth.

 (iv) a compound cavity other than a cavity covered by (ii) or (iii) above ... ... £1·30 with a maximum of £1·70 for 2 or more such fillings per tooth.

* (v) additional fee for pin or screw retention ... ... £0·80.

(b) (i) silicate, silico-phosphate or synthetic resin filling ... ... £1·22 with a maximum for 2 or more such fillings per tooth of £1·76.

 *(ii) additional fee for pin or screw retention ... ... £0·80

Provided that—

(a) for combinations of the types of fillings set out below in the same tooth no fee shall be payable in excess of the amount shown opposite:—

1 or more of (a)(i) with 1 of (a)(iii)   £1·90
1 or more of (a)(i) with 1 of (a)(iv)   £1·50
1 or more of (a)(i) with 2 or more of (a)(iv) ... ...   £1·90
1 of (a)(iii) with 1 or more of (a) (iv) ... ...   £1·90

*(b) no fee in excess of £2·60 shall be payable for any combination of any types of filling in one tooth, except where pin or screw retention is used when the maximum shall be ... ... £3·20

7. Root treatment of permanent teeth, including all attention in connection therewith except for the provision of x-rays or the insertion of any filling in the crown of the tooth:—

(a) treatment comprising either the devitalization of the pulp of the tooth and the subsequent removal of the pulp followed by the necessary treatment and filling of each root canal of the tooth, or the treatment of septic root canals and the subsequent filling of each canal—

 (i) root filling following extirpation of vital pulp in a single-rooted tooth ... ... £2·70 per tooth.

 (ii) all other root fillings ... ... £5·30 per tooth.

(b) vital pulpotomy consisting of removal of the coronal portion of the pulp, including any necessary dressing—

Fee per tooth ... ... £2·40

(c) (i) apicectomy, fee per tooth ... £4·70
 (ii) apicectomy with retrograde root filling, fee per tooth ... ... £5·90

*See schedule 2 for treatment requiring prior approval.

*8. Gold fillings (other than inlays) ...   ...   £4·50 per filling with a maximum for 2 or more such fillings per tooth of £6·20

9. Inlays (including any dressings):

	A	B
*(a) metal inlay	Alloys containing 60 per cent or more fine gold.	Any other alloys.
(i) a single surface cavity	£6·40	£5·40
(ii) a compound cavity	£8·70	£7·40
(iii) a compound cavity involving the incisal angle	£8·50	£7·40
(iv) a confluent compound cavity ...	£12·80	£10·50

*(b) fused porcelain inlay   ...   ...   Such fee as the Board may approve within a range of £7·00 to £11·00

*(c) provision or renewal of a facing of silicate or synthetic resin   ...   ...   £1·00 per inlay.

(d) refixing or recementing an inlay ...   £1·00 per inlay.

*(e) renewal or replacement by another inlay ...   .   The fee for a new inlay of the type being provided.

10. Crowning of permanent teeth, including any dressings but excluding root treatment:—

*(a) Full veneer or jacket crown, cast (on a vital or non-vital tooth):
  (i) gold   ...   .   £14·40
  (ii) gold with facing of silicate or synthetic resin ...   .   £15·40

*(b) Three-quarter crown gold, cast (on a vital or non-vital tooth) ...   ...   £12·80

*(c) Full veneer or jacket crown:
  (i) synthetic resin on a vital tooth ...   £8·00
  (ii) synthetic resin on a non-vital tooth ...   .   £7·00
  (iii) synthetic resin constructed on a cast gold core or thimble on a vital tooth   ...   .   £10·00

*(d) Full veneer or jacket crown:
  (i) porcelain on a vital tooth   ...   £13·00
  (ii) porcelain on a non-vital tooth ...   £10·80
  (iii) porcelain constructed on a cast gold core or thimble on a vital tooth   ...   .   £15·00

*(e) Full veneer or jacket crown:
  (i) synthetic resin constructed on a cast gold core and post ...   ...   £11·60
  (ii) porcelain constructed on a cast gold core and post   ...   ...   £14·80

*See schedule 2 for treatment requiring prior approval.

*(f) Synthetic resin post or dowel crown:

    (i) without diaphragm   ...   ...   £6·20

    (ii) with gold post and diaphragm ...   £9·50

    (iii) with gold post, diaphragm and backing   ...   .   £11·60

*(g) Modifications to the above crowns, and other forms of crown not in the opinion of the Board included in the above items   ...   .   Such fee as the Board may approve not exceeding £17·00

(h) Refixing or recementing a crown ...   £1·00 per crown.

*(i) Repair of a crown:

    (i) Renewal of the coronal portion only of a post or dowel crown appropriate to item 10(f)(i) or 10(f)(ii)   ...   .   £4·80

    (ii) Other repair of a crown   ...   Such fee as the Board may approve not exceeding 70% of the fee for a new crown of the type being repaired.

*(j) Renewal by a similar type of crown   The fee for a new crown of the type being provided.

*(k) Replacement by a different type of crown ...   .   The fee for a new crown of the type being provided.

Provided that, where the Board approve the use of a special bonding technique in connection with a porcelain crown, the Board may increase the fee by an amount not exceeding £7·30.

PART III. SURGICAL TREATMENT

*11. Extractions:

Fee per course of treatment:—

1 tooth ...	...	...	...	...	£1·00
2 teeth ...	...	...	...	...	£1·10
3, 4 or 5 teeth ...	...	...	...	£1·20
6, 7 or 8 teeth ...	...	...	...	£1·40
9, 10 or 11 teeth	...	...	...	£1·60
12, 13 or 14 teeth	...	...	...	£1·80
15, 16 or 17 teeth	...	...	...	£2·00
18, 19 or 20 teeth	...	...	...	£2·20
Over 20 teeth	...	...	...	...	£2·40

With an additional fee of £0·10 for each quadrant of the mouth involved other than the first.

Provided that where an exceptional number of visits is necessary because of the abnormal medical condition of the patient the Board may allow an additional fee not exceeding £2·70 per course of treatment.

*12.   (a) Alveolectomy, in either upper or lower jaw   ...   .   Such fee as the Board may approve up to a maximum of £5·50 (or such higher fee as they may in special circumstances approve).

    (b) Removal of cyst, buried root, impacted tooth or grossly exostosed

*See schedule 2 for treatment requiring prior approval.

tooth or other similar operation, including all necessary attention in connection therewith other than abnormal post-operative haemorrhage necessitating an additional visit other than for the removal of sutures ... Such fee as the Board may approve up to a maximum of £11·50 (or such higher fee as they may in special circumstances approve).

(c) Surgery on soft tissue, other than periodontal surgery appropriate to item 5 ... ... Such fee as the Board may approve up to a maximum of £2·50 (or such higher fee as they may in special circumstances approve).

13. Administration of a general anaesthetic:

(a) In connection with treatment under item 11,

(i) where a doctor or dentist other than the dentist carrying out the extraction administers the anaesthetic:

Fee per visit—

1 to 3 teeth extracted ...	£1·20
4 to 11 teeth extracted ...	£1·70
12 to 19 teeth extracted ...	£2·30
20 teeth or over extracted ...	£2·90

(ii) where the anaesthetic is administered by the dentist carrying out the extraction:

Fee per patient per course of treatment ... ... £0·42

*(iii) where the Board are satisfied that the anaesthetist would be faced with special difficulties owing to the medical condition of the patient and the anaesthetic is to be administered by a doctor or dentist other than the dentist carrying out the extraction ... ... Such fee as the Board may approve not exceeding £6·20 per course of treatment.

Provided that no fee exceeding £2·90 per course of treatment shall be payable under (i) or under (i) and (ii) combined, and no fee exceeding £7·30 per course of treatment shall be payable for any combination of (iii) with (i), or with both (i) and (ii).

*(b) In connection with treatment under items 5, 7(c) and 12 where a doctor or dentist other than the dentist carrying out the treatment administers the anaesthetic ... ... Such fee as the Board may approve not exceeding £2·90

Provided that in cases presenting special clinical difficulty the fee will be such fee as the Board may approve not exceeding £6·20.

*See schedule 2 for treatment requiring prior approval.

PART IV. DENTURES, BRIDGES AND SPECIAL APPLIANCES OTHER THAN
ORTHODONTIC APPLIANCES

A. *Dentures*

Fees for the provision of dentures cover the provision of all necessary clasps, rests and strengtheners and all adjustments needed within a reasonable period of time after completion.

*14. Dentures in synthetic resin:

    (*a*) full upper and full lower dentures ...   £16·50

    (*b*) denture bearing 1, 2 or 3 teeth ... £7·50
    denture bearing 4 to 8 teeth   ... £8·90
    denture bearing 9 to 14 teeth ... £10·00

Provided that no fee for upper and lower dentures shall exceed £16·50

    (*c*) additional fee for lingual or palatal bar—

      (i) stainless steel ... ... £1·36

      (ii) gold or other approved material   Such fee as the Board may approve not exceeding £5·00

    (*d*) additional fee for the provision of a soft lining or soft partial lining where this is required on account of the abnormal anatomical condition of the patient's alveolus ... ... £2·34 per denture.

15. Relining or rebasing of dentures, or provision of soft linings to existing dentures, including all adjustments needed within a reasonable period of time after completion:

    (*a*) relining or rebasing a denture—

      (i) not accompanied by repairs and/or additions ... ... £3·60 per denture.

    *(ii) accompanied by repairs and/or additions ... ... Such fee per denture as the Board may approve.

    *(*b*) provision or renewal of soft lining or soft partial lining to an existing denture where it is required on account of the abnormal anatomical condition of the patient's alveolus. ...

      (i) not accompanied by repairs and/or additions ... ... £4·30 per denture.

      (ii) accompanied by repairs and/or additions ... ... Such fee per denture as the Board may approve.

16. Repairs (except repairs which are appropriate to item 15(*a*)(ii) or item 15(*b*) (ii)):

    (*a*) (i) repairing a crack or fracture (including provision of any strengthener) ... ... £1·00

      (ii) refixing a tooth or providing and fixing a replacement tooth (including any gum associated therewith) ... ... £0·94

*See schedule 2 for treatment requiring prior approval.

(iii) refixing a clasp (including any gum associated therewith) ... £0·94

(iv) providing and fixing a replacement clasp (including any gum associated therewith) ... ... £1·70

(v) covering exposed pins ... ... £0·50

(b) each additional repair under (a) (i)—(v) ... ... £0·32

(c) renewal of gum not associated with repair under (a) ... ... £1·00

Provided that no fee in excess of £2·60 per denture shall be payable under item 16.

17. Additions (except additions which are appropriate to item 15(a)(ii) or item 15(b)(ii)):

(a) addition of a clasp or tooth (including any gum associated therewith) ... £2·60

(b) addition of new gum not associated with addition under item 17(a) ... £2·60 per denture.

Provided that no fee in excess of £3·60 per denture shall be payable under item 17 or for any combination of treatment under items 16 and 17.

*18. Backing and tagging of teeth on non-metallic based dentures:

Fee per tooth in addition to the appropriate fee for a non-metallic based denture:—

(i) stainless steel ... ... £1·00

(ii) chrome cobalt or a precious metal alloy containing less than 60 per cent fine gold ... ... £1·90

(iii) precious metal alloy containing 60 per cent or more fine gold ... £2·50

*19. Metal based dentures. These dentures may not be provided until such period after extraction (normally not less than three months) as the dentist thinks fit:

(a) Fee per denture in—

	A Stainless steel.	B Chrome cobalt.
(i) Base metal alloys: partial denture bearing 1, 2 or 3 teeth	£14·00	£17·00
partial denture bearing 4, 5 or 6 teeth	£15·00	£17·50
partial denture bearing 7, 8 or 9 teeth	£16·00	£18·00
partial denture bearing 10 or more teeth	£16·00	£19·00
full denture	£14·00	£17·50
additional fee where teeth are backed in any metal	£1·70 per tooth up to a maximum of £6·80 per denture.	£1·10 per tooth up to a maximum of £4·40 per denture.
(ii) Precious metal alloys: ...	Containing less than 60 per cent fine gold.	Containing 60 per cent or more fine gold.

*See schedule 2 for treatment requiring prior approval.

partial denture bearing 1, 2 or 3 teeth	£18·00	
partial denture bearing 4, 5 or 6 teeth	£20·00	
partial denture bearing 7, 8 or 9 teeth	£21·00	Such fee as the Board may approve.
partial denture bearing 10 or more teeth	£22·00	
full denture	£19·00	
additional fee where teeth are backed in any metal	£2·00 per tooth up to a maximum of £8·00 per denture.	

(b) Repairs and

(c) Additions

Fee appropriate to similar treatment to synthetic resin dentures as covered by items 16 and/or 17 together with such additional fee, if any, as the Board may approve.

B. *Bridges and Special Appliances*

*20. Bridges:

    (a) Provision of a bridge ... ... Such fee as the Board may approve.

    (b) Repairing a bridge ... ... Such fee as the Board may approve.

    (c) Re-cementing a bridge ... ... £1·60

*21. (a) Obturators, fee per case in addition to appropriate denture fee ... ... Such fee as the Board may approve within a range of £5·20 to £8·80 or such additional fee as may be approved in special circumstances.

    (b) Repairs to obturators ... ... Such fee as the Board may approve.

    (c) Treatment involving splints or other appliances (other than in connection with periodontal treatment) ... ... Such fee as the Board may approve.

Part V. Treatment Special to Children

*22. Conservative treatment of deciduous teeth of children under 16 years at the beginning of a course of treatment:

    (a) by filling (including any dressings, pulp-capping and other necessary preparatory treatment)—

        (i) with amalgam, one surface ... £0·90 per tooth.

        (ii) with amalgam, more than one surface ... ... £1·30 per tooth.

        (iii) with any other filling material ... £0·56 per tooth.

    (b) by conservation of a molar with a preformed metal cap ... ... £1·50 per tooth.

    Provided that no fee in excess of £1·50 shall be payable for any combination of the above types of conservation necessary in one tooth.

*See schedule 2 for treatment requiring prior approval.

    (c) by conservation by other means—

        (i) by preparing self-cleansing areas followed by applications of silver nitrate or similar medicaments

per tooth	£0·44
maximum per patient ...	£1·10

        *Provided that no fee shall be payable under (i) where the treatment occurs within 12 months of similar treatment to the same surface by the same practitioner† unless, in exceptional circumstances, the approval of the Board is first obtained.

        (ii) by topical applications of obtundents and coagulants

            per patient ... ... £0·40

        *Provided that no fee shall be payable under (ii) where the treatment occurs within 12 months of similar treatment by the same practitioner† unless, in exceptional circumstances, the approval of the Board is first obtained.

    (d) by vital pulpotomy, including any necessary dressing, per tooth ... £0·80

23.   (a) Removal of calculus and other deposits from the teeth of children under 16 years at the beginning of a course of treatment and the provision of necessary treatment for all ordinary or simple disorders of the gums ... ... £0·44

*Provided that no fee shall be payable under item 23(a)—

        (i) where the last course of treatment in respect of which provision was made for payment under item 23(a) or (b) to the same practitioner† commenced at any time during any of the 5 months preceding the month in which the further treatment is to be done;

        (ii) in respect of a patient under 9 years at the beginning of a course of treatment,

unless the prior approval of the Board has been obtained.

    *(b) Removal of calculus, where in exceptional cases calculus is present to an abnormal degree, from the teeth of children under 16 years at the beginning of a course of treatment, and the provision of necessary treatment for all ordinary or simple disorders of the gums ... ... £1·10

---

*See schedule 2 for treatment requiring prior approval.
†Reference in this scale of fees to dental treatment by the same practitioner shall include also dental treatment by his principal or the partner of either or by the assistant of any of them, and where the practitioner is employed by a body corporate shall include treatment by another employee of that body.

(c) Removal of stain including any necessary polishing ... ... £0·40

Provided that no fee shall be payable under item 23(c)—

*(i) where the last course of treatment in respect of which provision was made for payment under item 23(c) to the same practitioner† commenced at any time during any of the 11 months preceding the month in which the further treatment is to be done unless the prior approval of the Board has been obtained;

(ii) during a course of treatment where a fee is paid under item 23(a) or (b).

24. *(a) Orthodontic treatment of children and young persons under 18 years at the beginning of a course of treatment ... ... Such fee as the Board may approve.

(b) Repairs to orthodontic appliances Such fee as the Board may approve.

PART VI. GENERAL ITEMS

25. Dressing of teeth in respect of a casual patient:

Fee for one tooth ... ... £0·56

Fee for two or more teeth ... ... £0·80

26. Treatment of sensitive cementum or dentine:

Fee per course ... ... £0·40

27. Taking of material for pathological or bacteriological examination, etc.:

Fee per course ... ... £0·60

28. Treatment for arrest of abnormal haemorrhage, including abnormal haemorrhage following dental treatment provided otherwise than as part of general dental services:

Fee per visit for arrest of bleeding or for administration of associated after-care ... ... £1·40.

Provided that—

(i) the same practitioner† who arrests bleeding may not also be paid for the administration of after-care;

(ii) where the treatment consists solely of the removal of plugs and/or stitches the fee shall be only £0·70.

---

*See schedule 2 for treatment requiring prior approval.

†Reference in this scale of fees to dental treatment by the same practitioner shall include also dental treatment by his principal or the partner of either or by the assistant of any of them, and where the practitioner is employed by a body corporate shall include treatment by another employee of that body.

       (iii) the maximum fee per course of
             treatment shall be £3·30 or such
             higher sum as the Board may in
             special circumstances approve.

*29. Fee for any other treatment not included
     in this scale   ...   .   Such fee as the Board may approve.

  *See schedule 2 for treatment requiring prior approval.

EXPLANATORY NOTE

(This Note is not part of the Regulations.)

    These Regulations further amend the National Health Service (General Dental Services) (Scotland) Regulations 1966 by providing for a new scale of fees and for certain additional payments for practitioners, other than salaried practitioners, providing general dental services.

STATUTORY INSTRUMENTS

1972 No. 1350

AGRICULTURE

The Price Stability of Imported Products (Rates of Levy) (Cereals) (No. 19) Order 1972

Made - - - - *31st August* 1972
Coming into Operation *1st September* 1972

The Minister of Agriculture, Fisheries and Food, in exercise of the powers conferred upon him by section 1(2), (4), (5), (6) and (7) of the Agriculture and Horticulture Act 1964(a) and of all other powers enabling him in that behalf, hereby makes the following order:—

1. This order may be cited as the Price Stability of Imported Products (Rates of Levy) (Cereals) (No. 19) Order 1972, and shall come into operation on 1st September 1972.

2.—(1) In this order—

" the Principal Order " means the Price Stability of Imported Products (Levy Arrangements) (Cereals) Order 1971(b), as amended by any subsequent order and if any such order is replaced by any subsequent order the expression shall be construed as a reference to such subsequent order;

AND other expressions have the same meaning as in the Principal Order.

(2) The Interpretation Act 1889(c) shall apply to the interpretation of this order as it applies to the interpretation of an Act of Parliament and as if this order and the order hereby revoked were Acts of Parliament.

3. In accordance with and subject to the provisions of Part II of the Principal Order (which provides for the charging of levies on imports of certain specified commodities) the rate of levy for such imports into the United Kingdom of any specified commodity as are described in column 2 of the Schedule to this order in relation to a tariff heading indicated in column 1 of that Schedule shall be the rate set forth in relation thereto in column 3 of that Schedule.

4. The Price Stability of Imported Products (Rates of Levy) (Cereals) (No. 18) Order 1972(d) is hereby revoked.

In Witness whereof the Official Seal of the Minister of Agriculture, Fisheries and Food is hereunto affixed on 31st August 1972.

(L.S.)

T. R. M. Sewell,
Assistant Secretary.

(a) 1964 c. 28. (b) S.I. 1971/631 (1971 I, p. 1660). (c) 1889 c. 63.
(d) S.I. 1972/1137 (1972 II, p. 3347).

SCHEDULE

1. Tariff Heading	2. Description of Imports	3. Rate of Levy
	Imports of:—	per ton £
10.01	Denatured wheat	3 ·00
	Wheat (other than denatured wheat)..	8 ·25
10.03	Barley other than barley having a potential diastatic activity of not less than 170 degrees	5 ·25
10.04	Oats	1 ·00
10.05	Maize (other than sweet corn on the cob)	4 ·50
10.07	Grain sorghum	3 ·50
11.02	Cereal groats, meals, kibbled or cut cereals, rolled, flaked, crushed or bruised cereals and other processed cereals—	
	of barley	4 ·50
	of maize	5 ·50

EXPLANATORY NOTE

(This Note is not part of the Order.)

This order, which comes into operation on 1st September 1972, supersedes the Price Stability of Imported Products (Rates of Levy) (Cereals) (No. 18) Order 1972.

It—

(a) reduces the rate of levy to be charged on imports of—

(i) denatured wheat to £3·00 per ton;

(ii) wheat (other than denatured wheat) to £8·25 per ton;

(iii) barley other than barley having a potential diastatic activity of not less than 170 degrees to £5·25 per ton;

(iv) oats, maize (other than sweet corn on the cob) and grain sorghum to £1·00, £4·50 and £3·50 per ton respectively; and

(b) reimposes unchanged the remaining rates of levy in force immediately before the commencement of the order.

1972 No. 1181

PARLIAMENT

Resolution of the House of Commons dated 1st August 1972 passed in pursuance of the House of Commons Members' Fund Act 1948, s.3 (11 and 12 Geo. 6 c. 36)

Resolved,

That in pursuance of the provisions of section 3 of the House of Commons Members' Fund Act 1948, the maximum annual amounts of the periodical payments which may be made out of the House of Commons Members' Fund under the House of Commons Members' Fund Act 1939(**a**) as amended by the said Act of 1948 and by the Resolutions of the House of 17th November 1955(**b**), 7th March 1957(**c**), 17th May 1961(**d**), 9th March 1965(**e**) and 4th May 1971(**f**), be varied as from 1st October 1972, as follows:

(*a*) for paragraph 1 of Schedule 1 to the said Act of 1939, as so amended, there shall be substituted the following paragraph:

'1. The annual amount of any periodical payment made to any person by virtue of his past membership of the House of Commons shall not exceed £660 or such sum as, in the opinion of the trustees, will bring his income up to £1,000 per annum, whichever is the less:

Provided that if, having regard to length of service and need, the trustees think fit, they may make a larger payment not exceeding £1,190, or such sum as, in their opinion, will bring his income up to £1,500 per annum, whichever is the less';

(*b*) for paragraph 2 of the said Schedule there shall be substituted the following paragraph: —

'2. The annual amount of any periodical payment to any person by virtue of her being a widow of a past Member of the House of Commons shall not exceed £375 or such sum as, in the opinion of the trustees, will bring her income up to £750 per annum, whichever is the less:

Provided that if, having regard to her husband's length of service or to her need, the trustees think fit, they may make a larger payment not exceeding £595 or such sum as, in the opinion of the trustees, will bring her income up to £925 per annum, whichever is the less';

(*c*) in paragraph 2A of the said Schedule for the words 'the annual amount of any periodical payment' to the end of the paragraph, there shall be substituted the words: —

'the annual amount of any periodical payment made to any such widower shall not exceed £375 or such sum as, in the opinion of the trustees, will bring his income up to £750 per annum whichever is the less:

Provided that if, having regard to his wife's length of service or to his needs the trustees think fit, they may make a larger payment not exceeding £595 or such sum as, in the opinion of the trustees, will bring his income up to £925 per annum, whichever is the less'.

(**a**) 2 & 3 Geo. 6. c. 49.
(**c**) S.I. 1957/388 (1957 II, p. 3068).
(**e**) S.I. 1965/718 (1965 I, p. 2567).
(**b**) S.I. 1956/1668 (1956 II, p. 2993).
(**d**) S.I. 1961/958 (1961 II, p. 3345).
(**f**) S.I. 1971/770 (1971 II, p. 4028).

APPENDIX
OF CERTAIN INSTRUMENTS
NOT REGISTERED AS S. I.

Orders in Council,
Letters Patent
and Royal Instructions

relating to the Constitutions etc. of
Overseas Territories or to appeals to the Judicial
Committee,

Royal Proclamations, etc.

HONG KONG

The Hong Kong Additional Instructions 1972

Dated: the 28th June 1972.   *ELIZABETH* R.

ADDITIONAL INSTRUCTIONS to Our Governor and Commander-in-Chief in and over Our Colony of Hong Kong and its Dependencies or other Officer for the time being Administering the Government of Our said Colony and its Dependencies.

We do hereby direct and enjoin and declare Our will and pleasure as follows:—

Citation, construction and commencement.
1.—(1) These Instructions may be cited as the Hong Kong Additional Instructions 1972 and shall be construed as one with the Hong Kong Royal Instructions 1917 as amended (hereinafter called " the principal Instructions ").

(2) The Hong Kong Royal Instructions 1917 to 1970 and these Instructions may be cited together as the Hong Kong Royal Instructions 1917 to 1972.

Amendment of clause XIII of principal Instructions.
2. Clause XIII of the principal Instructions is amended by substituting for the word " eight " the word " ten ", and for the word " thirteen " the word " fifteen ".

Given at Our Court at St. James's this twenty-eighth day of June 1972 in the Twenty-first year of Our Reign.

MATRIMONIAL CAUSES

The Matrimonial Causes (Decree Absolute) General Order 1972

> *Made -   -   -   -*   20*th July* 1972
> *Coming into Operation*   1*st September* 1972

Whereas it is provided by sections 5(7) and 10 of the Matrimonial Causes Act 1965(**a**) that no decree nisi of divorce or nullity of marriage shall be made absolute before the expiration of six months from its grant unless the court by general or special order from time to time fixes a shorter period:

And whereas by the Matrimonial Causes (Decree Absolute) General Order 1957 it was ordered that the said period of six months should be reduced to three months:

And whereas it is expedient that for the said period of three months there should be substituted a period of six weeks:

Now, therefore, in exercise of the powers conferred by the said sections 5(7) and 10, the court makes the following Order:—

1.—(1) This Order may be cited as the Matrimonial Causes (Decree Absolute) General Order 1972 and shall come into operation on 1st September 1972.

(2) In this Order a decree means a decree of divorce or nullity of marriage.

2. In relation to any decree nisi granted after the coming into operation of this Order the period of six months specified in section 5(7) of the Matrimonial Causes Act 1965 shall be reduced to six weeks and accordingly the decree shall not be made absolute until the expiration of six weeks from its grant unless the court by special order fixes a shorter period.

Dated 20th July 1972.

Signed for and on behalf of the High Court of Justice:

Hailsham of St. Marylebone, C.
Lord Chancellor,
President of the High Court of Justice.

George Baker, P.
President of the Family Division.

(**a**) 1965 c. 72.

EXPLANATORY NOTE

(This Note is not part of the Order.)

This Order reduces from three months to six weeks the normal period after which a decree nisi of divorce or nullity of marriage can be made absolute.

CARIBBEAN AND NORTH ATLANTIC TERRITORIES

The Cayman Islands Royal Instructions 1972

Dated: the 26th July 1972.   *ELIZABETH* R.

INSTRUCTIONS to Our Governor of Our Cayman Islands or other Officer for the time being Administering the Government of Our said Islands.

We do hereby direct and enjoin and declare our will and pleasure as follows:—

PART I

Introductory

1.—(1) These Instructions may be cited as the Cayman Islands Royal Instructions 1972. *Citation, commencement, publication, and revocation.*

(2) These Instructions shall be published in such manner as the Governor shall think fit, and shall come into operation on the date of the next dissolution of the Legislative Assembly of the Cayman Islands after the date of these Instructions.

(3) The Cayman Islands Royal Instructions 1962(**a**) are revoked.

2. The provisions of section 50 of the Constitution of the Cayman Islands contained in Schedule 2 to the Cayman Islands (Constitution) Order 1972 (hereinafter referred to as " the Constitution ") shall apply to the interpretation of these Instructions as they apply to the interpretation of the Constitution. *Interpretation.*

3.—(1) These Instructions, so far as they are applicable to any functions to be performed by a deputy to the Governor appointed under section 4 of the Constitution, shall be deemed to be addressed to and shall be observed by such deputy. *Instructions to be observed by deputy.*

(2) Any such deputy may, if he thinks fit, apply to Us through a Secretary of State for instructions in any matter ; but he shall forthwith transmit to the Governor a copy of every despatch or other communication by which he applies for any such instructions.

4. The Governor shall forthwith communicate to the Executive Council these Instructions and all such others as he may from time to time find it convenient for Our service to impart to them. *Governor to communicate Instructions to Executive Council.*

PART II

The Governor

5. Except in circumstances in which he is not regarded as absent from the Islands for the purposes of section 3 of the Constitution the Governor shall not quit the Islands without first having obtained Our permission through a Secretary of State. *Leave of absence for Governor*

6. The Governor shall correspond with a Secretary of State on all subjects connected with his office, shall transmit to a Secretary of State all reports and information touching his office, and shall apply to a Secretary of State for all such instructions as he may require for his guidance. *Governor to correspond with Secretary of State.*

(**a**) S.I. 1962 II, p. 2403

Part III

Legislation

Rules for the enactment of laws.

7. In the making of laws the Legislature of the Islands shall observe, as far as practicable, the following rules:—

(*a*) All Laws shall be styled " Laws " and the words of enactment shall be " Enacted by the Legislature of the Cayman Islands ".

(*b*) All Laws shall be distinguished by titles, and shall be divided into successive sections consecutively numbered, and to every section there shall be annexed in the margin a short indication of its contents.

(*c*) The Laws enacted in each year shall be distinguished by consecutive numbers, commencing in each year with the number one.

(*d*) Matters having no proper relation to each other shall not be provided for by the same Law ; no Law shall contain anything foreign to what the title of the Law imports ; and no provision having indefinite duration shall be included in any Law expressed to have limited duration.

(*e*) All Laws shall be published by Government Notice in the Islands.

(*f*) Copies of all Laws shall be printed, and shall bear the following:—

(i) particulars of the days on which each Law was enacted and published by Government Notice ; and

(ii) particulars of the day on which each Law came into operation or, if that day has not been determined, a reference to any provision in the Law whereby it may be determined.

Certain Bills not to be assented to without Instructions.

8. The Governor shall not, without having previously obtained Our Instructions through a Secretary of State, assent to any Bill within any of the following classes, unless the Bill contains a clause suspending its operation until the signification of Our pleasure thereon, that is to say:—

(*a*) any Bill for the divorce of married persons ;

(*b*) any Bill whereby any grant of land or money or other donation may be made to himself ;

(*c*) any Bill affecting the currency of the Islands or relating to the issue of bank notes ;

(*d*) any Bill establishing any banking association or altering the constitution, rights or duties of any banking association ;

(*e*) any Bill imposing differential duties ;

(*f*) any Bill the provisions of which shall appear to him to be inconsistent with obligations imposed upon Us by treaty ;

(*g*) any Bill interfering with the discipline or control of Our forces by land, sea or air ;

(*h*) any Bill whereby persons of any community or religion may either—

(i) be subjected or made liable to disabilities or restrictions to which persons of other communities or religions are not subjected or made liable ; or

(ii) be granted advantages which are not enjoyed by persons of other communities or religions ;

(*i*) any Bill of an extraordinary nature and importance whereby Our prerogative, or the rights or property of Our subjects not residing in the Islands, or the trade, transport or communications of any part of Our dominions or any territory in which We may for the time being have jurisdiction may be adversely affected ;

(*j*) any Bill containing provisions to which Our assent has once been refused or which has been disallowed by Us:

Provided that, if the Governor is satisfied that urgent necessity requires that any Bill falling within any of the classes described in this clause (other than a Bill appearing to him to be inconsistent with obligations imposed upon Us by treaty) be brought into immediate operation, he may assent to the Bill without such Instructions as aforesaid and although the Bill contains no such clause as aforesaid, but he shall, at the earliest opportunity, transmit the Bill to Us together with his reasons for so assenting.

9.—(1) Every Bill, not being a Government measure, intended to Private Bills. affect or favour a particular person, association or corporate body, shall contain a provision saving the rights of Us, Our Heirs and Successors, all bodies politic and corporate, and all others except such as are mentioned in the Bill and those claiming by, from or under them.

(2) (*a*) No such Bill shall be introduced into the Legislature of the Islands until due notice has been given by not less than three successive publications of the Bill by Government Notice in the Islands ; and the Governor shall not assent to the Bill unless it has been so published.

(*b*) A certificate under the hand of the Governor signifying that such publication has been made shall be transmitted to Us when the Bill or Law is forwarded in pursuance of these Instructions.

10. When any Law has been enacted or any Bill has been reserved, Laws and the Governor shall forthwith transmit to Us, through a Secretary of reserved Bills State, for the signification of Our pleasure, a transcript in duplicate to be sent of the Law or of the Bill, duly authenticated under the Public Seal Secretary of and by his own signature, together with an explanation of the reasons State. and occasion for the enactment of the Law or for the passing of the Bill.

11. As soon as practicable after the commencement of each year Laws to be the Governor shall cause a complete collection of all Laws enacted published. in the Islands during the preceding year to be published for general information.

PART IV

Miscellaneous

12.—(1) Before disposing of any land or buildings belonging to Us Disposition in the Islands the Governor shall cause it to be surveyed and such of Crown reservations to be made thereout as he may think necessary for any lands. public purpose.

(2) The Governor shall not, either directly or indirectly, purchase for himself any land or building belonging to Us in the Islands without Our special permission given through a Secretary of State.

Power of pardon in capital cases.

13.—(1) Whenever any offender has been condemned by any civil court in the Islands to suffer death, the Governor shall cause a written report of the case of that offender from the judge who tried the case, together with such other information derived from the record of the case or elsewhere as the Governor may require, to be taken into consideration at a meeting of the Executive Council.

(2) The Governor shall not pardon or reprieve the offender unless it appears to him expedient to do so, upon receiving the advice of the Executive Council thereon ; but he is to decide either to extend or to withhold a pardon or reprieve according to his own deliberate judgment, whether the members of the Council concur therein or not ; causing, nevertheless, to be entered in the minutes of the Council a statement of his reasons, in case he should decide any such question in opposition to the judgment of the majority of the members thereof.

Governor may require oath of allegiance.

14. The Governor may, whenever he thinks fit, require any person holding public office to make an oath of allegiance in the form set out in the Schedule to the Constitution, and shall either administer the oath or cause it to be administered by some other person holding public office.

Given at Our Court at St. James's this 26th day of July in the Twenty-first year of Our Reign.

PENSIONS

At the Court at Buckingham Palace, the 26th day of July 1972

Present,

The Queen's Most Excellent Majesty in Council.

WHEREAS by section 3 of the Naval and Marine Pay and Pensions Act 1865(**a**) it is enacted that all pay, wages, pensions, bounty money, grants or other allowances in the nature thereof, payable in respect of services in Her Majesty's naval or marine force to a person being or having been an officer, seaman or marine, or to the widow or any relative of a deceased officer, seaman or marine, shall be paid in such manner and subject to such restrictions, conditions and provisions, as are from time to time directed by Order in Council:

AND WHEREAS Her Majesty deems it expedient to amend the Order in Council dated 25th September 1964, as amended (**b**), concerning pensions and other grants in respect of disablement or death due to service in the naval forces during the 1914 World War and after 2nd September 1939 (hereinafter referred to as " the 1964 Order "):

NOW, THEREFORE, Her Majesty, in exercise of the powers conferred upon Her as aforesaid and of all other powers whatsoever Her thereunto enabling, is pleased, by and with the advice of Her Privy Council, to order, and it is hereby ordered that, notwithstanding anything in the 1964 Order, the following provisions of this Order shall take effect accordingly and, except in the cases stated in the Order in Council of 19th December 1881, and except as otherwise provided by statute, shall be established and obeyed as the sole authority in the matters herein treated of.

Substitution of Schedules to the 1964 Order

1. For Schedules 2, 3 (other than Part II of Table 3 thereof), 4, 6 and 7 to the 1964 Order (rates of pensions and other grants payable in respect of disablement or death due to service in the naval forces during the 1914 World War and after 2nd September 1939) there shall be substituted the Schedules set out in Part I of the Appendix hereto and numbered 2, 3, 4, 6 and 7 respectively.

Amendment of Articles of the 1964 Order

2. In Articles 5 (entitlement where a claim is made in respect of a disablement, or death occurs, more than 7 years after the termination of service), 17 (unemployability allowances), 21 (treatment allowances), 31

(**a**) 28 & 29 Vict. c. 73.
(**b**) The relevant amending Orders are the Orders of 22nd December 1964, 24th February 1966, 9th June 1966, 23rd August 1967, 26th July 1968, 31st July 1969 and 28th July 1971.

(rent allowance to widows, and unmarried dependants who lived as wives, who have children) and 71 (commencement and application of the Order, amendment and revocation of previous Orders, and transitional provisions) of the 1964 Order there shall be made the amendments set out in Part II of the Appendix hereto.

Substitution of Article 57 of the 1964 Order

3. For Article 57 of the 1964 Order (pensioners admitted to institutions) there shall be substituted the Article set out in Part III of the Appendix hereto.

Commencement

4.—(1) Subject to the following provisions of this Article, this Order shall come into operation on 2nd October 1972 so, however, that in relation to any award payable weekly the foregoing reference to 2nd October 1972, where this is not the normal weekly pay day for that award, shall be construed as a reference to the first normal weekly pay day for that award following 2nd October 1972.

(2) Article 1 shall come into operation in relation to an officer on 1st October 1972.

(3) In so far as Article 1 substitutes the higher maximum rate of allowance for part-time treatment specified in paragraph 10 of Schedule 6 in Part I of the Appendix hereto, it shall be deemed to have come into operation on 3rd November 1971.

W. G. Agnew.

WAR PENSIONS 4117

APPENDIX

PART I

Schedules to be substituted in the 1964 Order by
Article 1 of this Order

SCHEDULE 2
TABLE 1
YEARLY RATES OF RETIRED PAY AND PENSIONS FOR DISABLED OFFICERS AND NURSES

A.—*Male Officers, and Women Officers under Article 1 (35) (a)*

Rank*

(1) Degree of disablement	(2) Rear-Admiral. *Major-General*	(3) Commodore 1st or 2nd Class, Captain with 6 or more years seniority whose service terminated on or after 1st April 1970. *Colonel-Commandant, Colonel whose service terminated on or after 1st April 1970*	(4) Captain of less than 6 years seniority or whose service terminated before 1st April 1970. *Colonel 2nd Commandant, Colonel whose service terminated before 1st April 1970. Lieutenant Colonel†* and corresponding Ranks	(5) Commander. *Major†* and corresponding Ranks	(6) Lieutenant-Commander. *Captain†* and corresponding Ranks	(7) Lieutenant. *Lieutenant with 4 years commissioned service or over*	(8) Sub-Lieutenant, Acting Sub-Lieutenant, Senior Commissioned Officer (Branch List), Commissioned Officer from Warrant Rank, Midshipman (A) or Cadet. *Lieutenant with under 4 years commissioned service, 2nd Lieutenant, Senior Commissioned Officer (Branch List), Commissioned Officer from Warrant Rank* and corresponding Ranks	(9) Commissioned Officer (Branch List), Warrant Officer, Midshipman, Cadet after completion of shore training where, in the case of any of these ranks, service terminated before 1st January 1957, Naval Cadet (serving with the Fleet). *Commissioned Officer (Branch List), Warrant Officer* and corresponding Ranks	(10) Additional Retired Pay under paragraphs (1), (2) and (5) of the proviso to Article 1 of the 1921 (Officers) Order and paragraphs (1), (2), (3) and (6) of Article 1 of the 1921 (Warrant Officers) Order. All Ranks
Per cent.	£	£	£	£	£	£	£	£	£
100 ...	889·00	844·00	799·00	769·00	739·00	709·00	679·00	649·00	619·00
90 ...	800·10	759·60	719·10	692·10	665·10	638·10	611·10	584·10	557·10
80 ...	711·20	675·20	639·20	615·20	591·20	567·20	543·20	519·20	495·20
70 ...	622·30	590·80	559·30	538·30	517·30	496·30	475·30	454·30	433·30
60 ...	533·40	506·40	479·40	461·40	443·40	425·40	407·40	389·40	371·40
50 ...	444·50	422·00	399·50	384·50	369·50	354·50	339·50	324·50	309·50
40 ...	355·60	337·60	319·60	307·60	295·60	283·60	271·60	259·60	247·60
30 ...	266·70	253·20	239·70	230·70	221·70	212·70	203·70	194·70	185·70
20 ...	177·80	168·80	159·80	153·80	147·80	141·80	135·80	129·80	123·80

* Ranks in the Royal Marines are given in italics.   † Temporary Marine Officer relinquishing commission, etc., prior to 1st April 1919, to come under succeeding column.

B.—Women Officers (other than those under Article 1 (35) (a)), and Nurses

Degree of disablement	Rank				Addition to Service Retired Pay. All Ranks
	Superintendent. Member with status of Captain, R.N. or above	Chief Officer. Member with status of Commander, R.N.	First Officer. Member with status of Lieutenant-Commander, R.N.	Second Officer, Third Officer. Member with status of Lieutenant, R.N. or below	
(1)	(2)	(3)	(4)	(5)	(6)
	£	£	£	£	£
Per cent.					
100	739·00	704·00	674·00	644·00	594·00
90	665·10	633·60	606·60	579·60	534·60
80	591·30	563·20	539·20	515·20	475·20
70	517·30	492·80	471·80	450·80	415·80
60	443·40	422·40	404·40	386·40	356·40
50	369·50	352·00	337·00	322·00	297·00
40	295·60	281·60	269·60	257·60	237·60
30	221·70	211·20	202·20	193·20	178·20
20	147·80	140·80	134·80	128·80	118·80

SCHEDULE 2

TABLE 2

WEEKLY RATES OF PENSIONS

A.—Disabled Ratings—Men*

Degree of disable-ment	Fleet Chief Petty Officer. Regimental Sergeant-Major	Quarter-master Sergeant	Chief Petty Officer. Colour Sergeant	Petty Officer. Sergeant	Leading Rating. Corporal	A.B. Rating, Ordinary Rating, Boy. Marine
(1)	(2)	(3)	(4)	(5)	(6)	(7)
Per cent.	£	£	£	£	£	£
100 ...	12·04	11·87	11·70	11·54	11·37	11·20
90 ...	10·83	10·68	10·53	10·38	10·23	10·08
80 ...	9·63	9·50	9·36	9·23	9·10	8·96
70 ...	8·43	8·31	8·19	8·08	7·96	7·84
60 ...	7·22	7·12	7·02	6·92	6·82	6·72
50 ...	6·02	5·94	5·85	5·77	5·69	5·60
40 ...	4·82	4·75	4·68	4·62	4·55	4·48
30 ...	3·61	3·56	3·51	3·46	3·41	3·36
20 ...	2·41	2·38	2·34	2·31	2·28	2·24

* Ranks in the Royal Marines are given in italics.

B.—Disabled Ratings—Women

Degree of disable-ment	Member of a Voluntary Aid Detachment serving as an un-certificated Nurse, Grade 1	Fleet Chief Wren	Chief Wren	Petty Officer Wren	Leading Wren	Wren
(1)	(2)	(3)	(4)	(5)	(6)	(7)
Per cent.	£	£	£	£	£	£
100 ...	11·79	11·62	11·45	11·37	11·29	11·20
90 ...	10·61	10·46	10·31	10·23	10·16	10·08
80 ...	9·43	9·30	9·16	9·10	9·03	8·96
70 ...	8·25	8·14	8·02	7·96	7·90	7·84
60 ...	7·07	6·97	6·87	6·82	6·77	6·72
50 ...	5·90	5·81	5·73	5·69	5·65	5·60
40 ...	4·72	4·65	4·58	4·55	4·52	4·48
30 ...	3·54	3·49	3·44	3·41	3·39	3·36
20 ...	2·36	2·33	2·29	2·28	2·26	2·24

SCHEDULE 3

TABLE 1

Gratuities Payable for Specified Minor Injuries

Description of Injury	Officers	Other Members
	£	£
For the loss of:		
A. FINGERS:		
Index finger—		
Whole	615	585
2 phalanges	490	465
1 phalanx	411	391
Guillotine amputation of tip without loss of bone ...	256	246
Middle finger—		
Whole	537	512
2 phalanges	411	391
1 phalanx	332	317
Guillotine amputation of tip without loss of bone ...	206	196
Ring or little finger—		
Whole	332	317
2 phalanges	287	272
1 phalanx	256	246
Guillotine amputation of tip without loss of bone ...	130	125
B. TOES:		
Great toe—		
through metatarso-phalangeal joint	615	585
part, with some loss of bone	179	174
1 other toe—		
through metatarso-phalangeal joint	179	174
part, with some loss of bone	80	75
2 toes, excluding great toe—		
through metatarso-phalangeal joint	256	246
part, with some loss of bone	130	125
3 toes, excluding great toe—		
through metatarso-phalangeal joint	287	272
part, with some loss of bone	179	174
4 toes, excluding great toe—		
through metatarso-phalangeal joint	411	391
part, with some loss of bone	179	174

SCHEDULE 3

TABLE 2

GRATUITIES PAYABLE TO OFFICERS FOR DISABLEMENT ASSESSED AT LESS THAN 20 PER CENT., NOT BEING A MINOR INJURY SPECIFIED IN TABLE 1

A.—Male Officers, and Women Officers under Article 1 (35) (*a*)

Rank*	Temporary less than a year Per cent.			Temporary more than a year Per cent.			Indeterminate Per cent.		
	1–5	6–14	15–19	1–5	6–14	15–19	1–5	6–14	15–19
	£	£	£	£	£	£	£	£	£
Rear-Admiral. *Major-General*...	45	99	172	88	197	344	265	590	1,032
Commodore 1st or 2nd Class, Captain with 6 or more years seniority whose service terminated on or after 1st April 1970. *Colonel-Commandant, Colonel whose service terminated on or after 1st April* 1970	43	94	165	84	188	328	253	563	985
Captain of less than 6 years seniority or whose service terminated before 1st April 1970. *Colonel 2nd Commandant, Colonel whose service terminated before 1st April* 1970, *Lieutenant-Colonel* ...	41	90	157	80	179	312	241	536	938
Commander. *Major*	39	87	151	78	173	302	233	518	906
Lieutenant-Commander. *Captain*	38	84	146	75	167	291	225	500	875
Lieutenant, Sub-Lieutenant, Acting Sub-Lieutenant, Senior Commissioned Officer (Branch List), Midshipman (A), and, where service terminated on or after 1st January 1957, Midshipman or Cadet. *Lieutenant, 2nd Lieutenant, Senior Commissioned Officer (Branch List)*	36	79	138	71	158	275	213	473	828
Commissioned Officer (Branch List), Midshipman, Cadet after completion of shore training, where, in the case of any of these ranks, service terminated before 1st January 1957. *Commissioned Officer (Branch List)*	34	75	130	67	149	260	201	446	780

* Ranks in the Royal Marines are given in italics.

B.—Women Officers (other than those under Article 1(35)(*a*))

Rank	Estimated duration of the disablement within the degree referred to								
	Temporary less than a year			Temporary more than a year			Indeterminate		
	Per cent.			Per cent.			Per cent.		
	1–5	6–14	15–19	1–5	6–14	15–19	1–5	6–14	15–19
	£	£	£	£	£	£	£	£	£
Superintendent. Member with status of Captain, R.N. or above	38	84	146	75	167	291	225	500	875
Chief Officer. Member with status of Commander, R.N.	36	80	140	72	160	279	215	479	838
First Officer. Member with status of Lieutenant-Commander, R.N.	35	77	135	69	154	268	207	461	807
Second Officer, Third Officer. Member with status of Lieutenant, R.N. or below ...	34	74	130	66	148	258	199	443	775

SCHEDULE 3

TABLE 3

PART 1

GRATUITIES PAYABLE TO RATINGS FOR DISABLEMENT ASSESSED AT LESS THAN 20 PER CENT., NOT BEING A MINOR INJURY SPECIFIED IN TABLE 1

Ratings*	Estimated duration of the disablement within the degree referred to								
	Temporary less than a year			Temporary more than a year			Indeterminate		
	Per cent.			Per cent.			Per cent.		
	1–5	6–14	15–19	1–5	6–14	15–19	1–5	6–14	15–19
	£	£	£	£	£	£	£	£	£
A.—Men									
Fleet Chief Petty Officer. *Regimental Sergeant-Major*...	33	72	126	65	144	252	194	432	756
Quartermaster Sergeant ...	33	71	125	64	143	249	192	427	747
Chief Petty Officer. *Colour Sergeant*	32	71	123	63	141	246	190	422	738
Petty Officer. *Sergeant* ...	32	70	122	63	139	243	188	417	730
Leading Rating. *Corporal* ...	31	69	120	62	138	240	185	412	721
A.B. Rating, Ordinary Rating, Boy. *Marine*	31	68	119	61	136	237	183	407	712
B.—Women									
Member of a Voluntary Aid Detachment serving as an uncertificated Nurse, Grade 1	33	71	125	64	143	249	192	427	747
Fleet Chief Wren	32	70	123	63	140	245	189	420	735
Chief Wren	32	69	121	62	139	242	187	415	726
Petty Officer Wren	31	69	120	62	138	240	185	412	721
Leading Wren	31	69	120	61	137	239	184	410	717
Wren	31	68	119	61	136	237	183	407	712

* Ranks in the Royal Marines are given in italics.

SCHEDULE 4

TABLE 1

YEARLY RATES OF PENSIONS FOR WIDOWS OF OFFICERS

*A.—Pensions other than pensions awarded under Article 11(1) or (2) of the 1921
(Officers) Order or Article 11(1) of the 1921 (Warrant Officers) Order*

Rank* (1)	(2)	(3)
	£	£
Admiral of the Fleet	1,069	1,069
Admiral. *General*	909	909
Vice-Admiral. *Lieutenant-General*	809	809
Rear-Admiral. *Major General*	719	719
Commodore, Commodore 1st or 2nd Class, Captain with 6 or more years seniority whose service terminated on or after 1st April 1970. *Brigadier-General, Colonel-Commandant, Colonel whose service terminated on or after 1st April 1970*	659	659
Captain of less than 6 years seniority or whose service terminated before 1st April 1970. *Colonel 2nd Commandant, Colonel whose service terminated before 1st April 1970, Lieutenant-Colonel*	599	599
Commander. *Major*	579	579
Lieutenant-Commander. *Captain*	549	170
Lieutenant. *Lieutenant with 4 years commissioned service or over*	534	150
Sub-Lieutenant, Acting Sub-Lieutenant, Senior Commissioned Officer (Branch List), Commissioned Officer from Warrant rank, Midshipman (A) and, where service terminated on or after 1st January 1957, Midshipman or Cadet. *Lieutenant with less than 4 years commissioned service, 2nd Lieutenant, Senior Commissioned Officer (Branch List), Commissioned Officer from Warrant rank, Quartermaster*	519	130
Commissioned Officer (Branch List), Midshipman, Cadet where, in the case of any of these ranks, service terminated before 1st January 1957, Warrant Officer. *Commissioned Officer (Branch List), Warrant Officer*	494	105

*B.—Pensions awarded under Article 11(1) or (2) of the 1921 (Officers) Order or
Article 11(1) of the 1921 (Warrant Officers) Order*

Rank* (1)	(2)
	£
Admiral of the Fleet	1,169
Admiral. *General*	969
Vice-Admiral. *Lieutenant-General*	869
Rear-Admiral. *Major-General*	769
Commodore. *Brigadier-General*	689
Captain. *Colonel, Lieutenant-Colonel*	609
Commander. *Major*	585
Lieutenant-Commander. *Captain*	549
Lieutenant. *Lieutenant with over 4 years commissioned service*	534
Sub-Lieutenant, Commissioned Officer from Warrant rank. *Lieutenant with less than 4 years commissioned service, 2nd Lieutenant, Quartermaster, Commissioned Officer from Warrant rank*	519
Warrant Officer. *Warrant Officer*	494

* Ranks in the Royal Marines are given in italics.

TABLE 2

WEEKLY RATES OF PENSIONS FOR WIDOWS OF RATINGS

Rating (or equivalent rating)*		
(1)	(2)	(3)
	£	£
Fleet Chief Petty Officer. *Regimental Sergeant-Major or Marine Warrant Officer, Class 1*	9·05	2·28
Quartermaster Sergeant or Marine Warrant Officer, Class II ...	9·00	2·23
Chief Petty Officer. *Colour Sergeant or Staff Sergeant*	8·95	2·18
Petty Officer, First Class Petty Officer (O.S.), Petty Officer (N.S.). *Sergeant*	8·90	2·13
Second Class Petty Officer, Leading Rating. *Corporal*	8·85	2·08
A.B. Rating, Ordinary Rating. *Marine*	8·80	2·03

TABLE 3

MAXIMUM YEARLY RATES OF PENSIONS FOR OTHER RELATIVES OF 1914 WORLD WAR OFFICERS

Rank*		
(1)	(2)	(3)
	£	£
Admiral of the Fleet	1,169	1,069
Admiral. *General*	969	909
Vice-Admiral. *Lieutenant-General*	869	809
Rear-Admiral. *Major-General*	769	719
Commodore. *Brigadier-General*	669	659
Captain. *Colonel, Lieutenant-Colonel*	599	599
Commander. *Major*	579	579
Lieutenant-Commander. *Captain*	170	170
Lieutenant. *Lieutenant with over 4 years commissioned service*	150	150
Sub-Lieutenant, Commissioned Officer from Warrant rank. *Lieutenant with less than 4 years commissioned service, 2nd Lieutenant, Quartermaster, Commissioned Officer from Warrant rank*	130	130
Warrant Officer. *Warrant Officer*	105	—

* Ranks in the Royal Marines are given in italics.

SCHEDULE 6

RATES OF ALLOWANCES PAYABLE IN RESPECT OF DISABLEMENT

Description of Allowance	Rate	
	Officers and Nurses	Ratings
1. Education allowance under Article 13 ...	£120·00 per annum (maximum)	£120·00 per annum (maximum)
2. Constant attendance allowance—		
(a) under the proviso to Article 14 ...	£468·00 per annum (maximum)	£9·00 per week (maximum)
(b) in any other case under that Article	£234·00 per annum (maximum)	£4·50 per week (maximum)
2A. Exceptionally severe disablement allowance under Article 14A	£234·00 per annum	£4·50 per week
3. Severe disablement occupational allowance under Article 15	£104·00 per annum	£2·00 per week
4. Allowance for wear and tear of clothing—		
(a) under Article 16(1)(a)	£12·00 per annum	£12·00 per annum
(b) under Article 16(1)(b) and 16(2) ...	£19·00 per annum	£19·00 per annum
5. Unemployability allowances—		
(a) personal allowance under Article 17(1)(i)	£382·20 per annum	£7·35 per week
(b) additional allowances for dependants by way of—		
(i) increase or further increase of allowance in respect of a wife, husband or unmarried dependant living as a wife, under Article 17(4)(c)	£179·80 per annum (maximum)	£3·65 per week (maximum)
(ii) allowance in respect of an adult dependant under Article 17(4)(d)	£215·80 per annum (maximum)	£4·15 per week (maximum)
(iii) increased allowance under Article 17(4)(f)—		
(a) in respect of the child, or the elder or eldest of the children, of a member	£171·60 per annum	£3·30 per week
(b) in respect of the second child of a member	£124·80 per annum	£2·40 per week
(c) in respect of each other child of a member	£119·60 per annum	£2·30 per week
5A. Invalidity allowance under Article 17A—		
(a) if on the relevant date the member was under the age of 35, or if that date fell before 5th July 1948	£59·80 per annum	£1·15 per week
(b) if head (a) does not apply and on the relevant date the member was under the age of 45	£36·40 per annum	£0·70 per week
(c) if heads (a) and (b) do not apply, and on the relevant date the member was a man under the age of 60, or a woman under the age of 55	£18·20 per annum	£0·35 per week
6. Comforts allowance—		
(a) under Article 18(1)(a)	£88·40 per annum	£1·70 per week
(b) under Article 18(1)(b)	£44·20 per annum	£0·85 per week
7. Allowance for lowered standard of occupation under Article 19	£232·96 per annum (maximum)	£4·48 per week (maximum)

Description of Allowance	Rate	
	Officers and Nurses	Ratings
8. Age allowance under Article 20 where the degree of pensioned disablement is—		
(a) 40 to 50 per cent.	£28·60 per annum	£0·55 per week
(b) over 50 per cent. but not exceeding 70 per cent.	£41·60 per annum	£0·80 per week
(c) over 70 per cent. but not exceeding 90 per cent.	£59·80 per annum	£1·15 per week
(d) over 90 per cent.	£83·20 per annum	£1·60 per week
9. Treatment allowances—		
(a) increase of personal allowance under Article 21(2)	£83·20 per annum (maximum)	£1·60 per week (maximum)
(b) increase of personal allowance under Article 21(3)—		
(i) under sub-paragraph (a) ...	£6·75 per week	£6·75 per week
(ii) under sub-paragraph (c)—		
(a) if on the relevant date the member was under the age of 35 or if that date fell before 5th July 1948	£59·80 per annum	£1·15 per week
(b) if head (a) does not apply and on the relevant date the member was under the age of 45	£36·40 per annum	£0·70 per week
(c) if heads (a) and (b) do not apply and on the relevant date the member was a man under the age of 60, or a woman under the age of 55 ...	£18·20 per annum	£0·35 per week
(c) increased additional allowance under Article 21(4) proviso (a)	£215·80 per annum	£4·15 per week
(d) increased additional allowance under Article 21(4) proviso (b)—		
(i) in respect of the child, or the elder of the children, of a member	£109·20 per annum	£2·10 per week
(ii) in respect of the second child of a member	£62·40 per annum	£1·20 per week
(iii) in respect of each other child of a member	£57·20 per annum	£1·10 per week
(e) higher rate of additional allowance under Article 21(4A)—		
(i) in respect of the child, or the elder or eldest of the children, of a member	£171·60 per annum	£3·30 per week
(ii) in respect of the second child of a member	£124·80 per annum	£2·40 per week
(iii) in respect of each other child of a member	£119·60 per annum	£2·30 per week
(f) additional allowance under Article 21(5)	£215·80 per annum	£4·15 per week
10. Part-time treatment allowance under Article 23	£4·75 per day (maximum)	£4·75 per day (maximum)

SCHEDULE 7

RATES OF PENSIONS, OTHER THAN WIDOWS' PENSIONS, AND ALLOWANCES PAYABLE IN RESPECT OF DEATH

Description of Pension or Allowance	Rate	
	Officers and Nurses	Ratings
1. Pension under Article 30 to unmarried dependant who lived as wife	£458·50 per annum (maximum)	£8·30 per week (maximum)
2. Rent allowance under Article 31 ...	£3·40 per week (maximum)	£3·40 per week (maximum)
3. Allowance under Article 32 to elderly widow or unmarried dependant who lived as wife—		
(a) if age 65 but under 70	£26·00 per annum	£0·50 per week
(b) if age 70 or over	£52·00 per annum	£1·00 per week
4. Pension to widower under Article 34 ...	£464·00 per annum (maximum)	£8·80 per week (maximum)
5. Allowances in respect of children— (a) under Article 35(1)— (i) in respect of the child, or the elder or eldest of the children, of a member	(i) Commissioned Officer* or Nurse— £190·10 per annum (ii) Warrant Officer† —£184·10 per annum	£3·50 per week
(ii) in respect of each other child of a member— (a) where the child qualifies for a family allowance under the Family Allowances Act 1965 or under any legislation in Northern Ireland or the Isle of Man corresponding to that Act	(i) Commissioned Officer* or Nurse— £164·10 per annum (ii) Warrant Officer† —£158·10 per annum	£3·00 per week
(b) where the child does not so qualify...	(i) Commissioned Officer* or Nurse— £182·30 per annum (ii) Warrant Officer† —£176·30 per annum	£3·35 per week

* Commissioned Officer includes Acting Sub-Lieutenant and Senior Commissioned Officer (Branch List).
† Warrant Officer includes Commissioned Officer (Branch List), Midshipman and Cadet.

Description of Pension or Allowance	Rate	
	Officers and Nurses	Ratings
5. Allowances in respect of children, *cont*— (*b*) under Article 35(3)—	(i) Commissioned Officer*— £269·30 per annum (maximum) (ii) Warrant Officer†— (*a*) where the child is under 15 years of age— £190·10 per annum (maximum) (*b*) where the child is 15 years of age or over— £261·30 per annum (maximum)	where the child is 15 years of age or over— £5·00 per week (maximum)
6. Pension under Article 36 to a motherless or fatherless child— (*a*) in respect of the child, or the elder or eldest of the children, of a member, and in respect of each other child of a member who does not qualify for a family allowance as aforesaid ...	(i) Commissioned Officer* or Nurse— £269·30 per annum (ii) Warrant Officer†— (*a*) where the child is under 15 years of age— £190·10 per annum (*b*) where the child is 15 years of age or over— £261·30 per annum	(i) where the child is under 15 years of age— £3·50 per week (ii) where the child is 15 years of age or over— £5·00 per week
(*b*) in respect of each other child of a member who qualifies for a family allowance as aforesaid	(i) Commissioned Officer* or Nurse— £243·30 per annum (ii) Warrant Officer†— (*a*) where the child is under 15 years of age— £164·10 per annum (*b*) where the child is 15 years of age or over— £235·30 per annum	(i) where the child is under 15 years of age— £3·00 per week (ii) where the child is 15 years of age or over— £4·50 per week
7. Pension or allowance under Article 37(3) to or in respect of a child over the age limit	£351·00 per annum (maximum)	£6·75 per week (maximum)

* Commissioned Officer includes Acting Sub-Lieutenant and Senior Commissioned Officer (Branch List).

† Warrant Officer includes Commissioned Officer (Branch List), Midshipman and Cadet.

Description of Pension or Allowance	Rate	
	Officers and Nurses	Ratings
8. Education allowance under Article 38 ...	£120·00 per annum (maximum)	£120·00 per annum (maximum)
9. Pensions to parents— (a) minimum rate under Article 40(4) ...	£15·00 per annum	£0·25 per week
(b) under paragraphs (a) and (b) of Article 40(4)— (i) where there is only one eligible parent	(i) Commissioned Officer*— £75·00 per annum (maximum) (ii) Warrant Officer†— £60·00 per annum (maximum)	£1·00 per week (maximum)
(ii) where there is more than one eligible parent	(i) Commissioned Officer*— £100·00 per annum (maximum) (ii) Warrant Officer†— £85·00 per annum (maximum)	£1·38 per week (maximum)
(c) increase under the proviso to Article 40(4)	£20·00 per annum (maximum)	(i) where there is only one eligible parent— £0·38 per week (maximum) (ii) where there is more than one eligible parent— £0·62 per week (maximum)
(d) under paragraph (c) of Article 40(5)	—	£1·00 per week (maximum)
10. Pensions to other dependants— (a) under Article 41(2)	£54·00 per annum (maximum)	£1·00 per week (maximum)
(b) for each juvenile dependant under Article 41(3)	(i) Commissioned Officer*— £26·00 per annum (maximum) (ii) Warrant Officer†— £20·00 per annum (maximum)	£0·30 per week (maximum)
(c) aggregate rate under Article 41(3) ...	(i) Commissioned Officer*— £75·00 per annum (maximum) (ii) Warrant Officer†— £65·00 per annum (maximum)	£1·00 per week (maximum)

* Commissioned Officer includes Acting Sub-Lieutenant and Senior Commissioned Officer (Branch List).
† Warrant Officer includes Commissioned Officer (Branch List), Midshipman and Cadet.

PART II

Amendment of Articles of the 1964 Order

1. In Article 5 (entitlement where a claim is made in respect of a disablement, or death occurs, more than 7 years after the termination of service) in paragraph (1) the words " and he was at the time of his death, or at any time previously thereto had been, in receipt of a pension awarded by the Minister under this Order or any previous Order " shall be omitted, and paragraph (6) is hereby revoked.

2. In Article 17 (unemployability allowances) in paragraph (2) for the words " £104 a year " there shall be substituted the words " £234 a year ".

3. In Article 21 (treatment allowances) for paragraph (4A) there shall be substituted the following paragraph: —

" (4A) The rate of an additional allowance awarded under paragraph (4) of this Article in respect of a child or children of a member may be further increased to the appropriate rate specified in Schedule 6 paragraph 9(*e*) if the member—

(*a*) is in receipt of an increase of his personal allowance under paragraph (3)(*c*) of this Article or, but for his age on the relevant date, would be in receipt of such an increase ; or

(*b*) is in receipt of an allowance under Article 17(1)(i) ; or

(*c*) having reached the age of 65 years or, in the case of a woman member, 60 years is not eligible for retirement pension under the National Insurance Acts 1965 to 1972, or any benefit similar thereto as is referred to in paragraph (6) of this Article, solely by reason of his failure to satisfy any contribution conditions.".

4. In Article 31 (rent allowance to widows, and unmarried dependants who lived as wives, who have children) in paragraph (1) for the words " having regard to the amount by which her weekly rent and rates exceed 6s." there shall be substituted the words " having regard to her weekly rent and rates ".

5. In Article 71 (commencement and application of this Order, amendment and revocation of previous Orders, and transitional provisions) at the end of paragraph (7) there shall be added the words " and as if any requirement thereof that the member had been at the time of his death in receipt of retired pay, pension or allowance in respect of disablement, was satisfied in every case.".

PART III

Substitution of Article 57 of the 1964 Order

For Article 57 (pensioners admitted to institutions) there shall be substituted the following Article: —

" 57. *Maintenance in hospital or an institution.*—(1) Where any person to or in respect of whom a pension or gratuity may be or has been awarded is receiving or has received free in-patient treatment, or is being or has been maintained in an institution (otherwise than for the purpose of undergoing medical or other treatment) which is supported wholly or partly out of public funds, or in which he is being or has been maintained pursuant to arrangements made by the Secretary of State, the Secretary of State may deduct such amount as he may think fit having regard to all the circumstances of the case from the pension or gratuity payable in respect of the period during which such treatment is received or during which the person is being so maintained, as the case may be, and may apply the amount so deducted, or any part thereof, in such proportions and subject to such conditions as he may determine having regard to all the circumstances of the case, in a payment or payments to the person upon his discharge following a period of free in-patient treatment, or in or towards paying or repaying the cost of maintaining the person incurred by any appropriate authority.

(2) For the purposes of this Article, a person shall be regarded as receiving or having received free in-patient treatment for any period for which he is or has been maintained free of charge while undergoing medical or other treatment as an in-patient—

(a) in a hospital or similar institution maintained or administered under the National Health Service Acts 1946 to 1968, the National Health Service (Scotland) Acts 1947 to 1968 or the Health Services Act (Northern Ireland) 1971, or by or on behalf of the Secretary of State, or by or on behalf of the Defence Council ; or

(b) pursuant to arrangements made by the Secretary of State or by a Hospital Board or a Regional Hospital Board constituted under the National Health Service Acts 1946 to 1968, the National Health Service (Scotland) Acts 1947 to 1968 or the Health Services Act (Northern Ireland) 1971 in a hospital or similar institution not so maintained or administered ;

and, for this purpose, a person shall only be regarded as not being maintained free of charge in a hospital or similar institution for any period if he is paying or has paid, in respect of maintenance, charges which are designed to cover the whole cost of the accommodation or services (other than services by way of treatment) provided for him in the hospital or similar institution for that period.".

EXPLANATORY NOTE

(This Note is not part of the Order.)

This Order further amends the Order of 25th September 1964.

Article 1 substitutes new Tables for those contained in Schedules 2, 3, 4, 6 and 7 to the 1964 Order and has the effect of increasing—

Disablement pensions and allowances

(a) the rates of pensions in respect of 100 per cent. disablement by £62·00 a year in the case of officers and £1·20 a week in the case of ratings and the rates of pensions for lower degrees of disablement and awards for cases of minor injuries and other cases of less than 20 per cent. disablement proportionately ;

(b) the maximum rates of disablement addition on a pension basis payable to certain officers in receipt of service retired pay by £62·00 a year ;

(c) the normal maximum rate of an allowance payable for constant attendance from £208·00 a year to £234·00 a year in the case of officers and from £4·00 a week to £4·50 a week in the case of ratings, and the maximum rate for exceptional cases of very severe disablement from £416·00 a year to £468·00 a year in the case of officers and from £8·00 a week to £9·00 a week in the case of ratings;

(d) the exceptionally severe disablement allowance from £208·00 a year to £234·00 a year in the case of officers and from £4·00 a week to £4·50 a week in the case of ratings;

(e) the allowance for unemployable pensioners from £340·60 a year to £382·20 a year in the case of officers and from £6·55 a week to £7·35 a week in the case of ratings;

(f) the total additional allowance payable in respect of the wife or adult dependant of an unemployable pensioner and of a pensioner receiving treatment as defined in Article 21(8) from £192·40 a year to £215·80 a year in the case of officers and from £3·70 a week to £4·15 a week in the case of ratings;

(g) the allowances payable in respect of children of unemployable pensioners in respect of the first or only child from £153·40 a year to £171·60 a year in the case of officers and from £2·95 a week to £3·30 a week in the case of ratings, in respect of the second child from £106·60 a year to £124·80 a year in the case of officers and from £2·05 a week to £2·40 a week in the case of ratings and in respect of any other child from £101·40 a year to £119·60 a year in the case of officers and from £1·95 a week to £2·30 a week in the case of ratings;

(h) the maximum allowance for lowered standard of occupation from £208·00 a year to £232·96 a year in the case of officers and from £4·00 a week to £4·48 a week in the case of ratings;

(i) the allowances payable to pensioners who have attained the age of 65 and whose pensioned disablement is assessed at 40 per cent or over from between £26·00 a year and £72·80 a year to between £28·60 a year and £83·20 a year in the case of officers and from between £0·50 a week and £1·40 a week to between £0·55 a week and £1·60 a week in the case of ratings;

(j) the allowances payable in respect of children of pensioners receiving treatment as defined in Article 21(8) in respect of the first or only child from £96·20 a year to £109·20 a year in the case of officers and from £1·85 a week to £2·10 a week in the case of ratings, in respect of the second child from £49·40 a year to £62·40 a year in the case of officers and from £0·95 a week to £1·20 a week in the case of ratings, and in respect of any other child from £44·20 a year to £57·20 a year in the case of officers and from £0·85 a week to £1·10 a week in the case of ratings, and to further increase those allowances where the said pensioners are not entitled to invalidity pension and allowance under national insurance provisions solely because of failure to satisfy the contribution conditions to £171·60 a year; £3·30 a week; £124·80 a year; £2·40 a week; £119·60 a year and £2·30 a week respectively;

(*k*) the maximum of the additional personal treatment allowance payable to a pensioner who is not entitled to full sickness benefit or invalidity pension and allowance under national insurance provisions from £6·00 a week to £6·75 a week ;

Widows' benefits

(*l*) the rates of pensions for certain widows by £52·00 a year in the case of officers and by £1·00 a week in the case of ratings ;

(*m*) the maximum pensions payable to unmarried dependants who lived as wives of deceased members of the naval forces from £406·50 a year to £458·50 a year in the case of officers and from £7·30 a week to £8·30 a week in the case of ratings ;

(*n*) the maximum rent allowance payable to certain widows from £3·00 a week to £3·40 a week ;

(*o*) the allowances payable to widows in respect of children for the first or only child from £171·90 a year to £190·10 a year in the case of officers and from £3·15 a week to £3·50 a week in the case of ratings, and in respect of each other child from £145·90 a year to £164·10 a year in the case of officers and from £2·65 a week to £3·00 a week in the case of ratings, where the child qualifies for a family allowance, and from £164·10 a year to £182·30 a year in the case of officers and from £3·00 a week to £3·35 a week in the case of ratings where the child does not so qualify ;

Other benefits

(*p*) the maximum pensions payable to certain widowers from £412·00 a year to £464·00 a year in the case of officers and from £7·80 a week to £8·80 a week in the case of ratings ;

(*q*) the rates of pensions and allowances payable to or in respect of the children of deceased members of the naval forces (such children having become motherless or having ceased to be under the control of their mothers) in respect of the first or only child or any other child who does not qualify for a family allowance from £251·10 a year to £269·30 a year in the case of children of officers and from £3·15 or £4·65 a week to £3·50 or £5·00 a week (according to the age of the child) in the case of children of ratings, and in respect of each other child who qualifies for a family allowance from £225·10 a year to £243·30 a year in the case of children of officers and from £2·65 or £4·15 a week to £3·00 or £4·50 a week (according to the age of the child) in the case of children of ratings ;

(*r*) the maximum rates of pensions payable to motherless or fatherless children who, having attained the age of 18 years, are incapable of self-support by reason of infirmity which arose before they attained the normal age limit for pension purposes, from £312·00 a year to £351·00 a year in the case of children of officers and from £6·00 a week to £6·75 a week in the case of children of ratings.

Article 2 makes amendments to the 1964 Order, the effects of which are:—

(*a*) to remove a restriction under which no award could be made in respect of the death of a member, occurring more than 7 years after the termination of his service, unless he had been in receipt of a pension in respect of disablement;

(*b*) to raise the maximum amount of earnings which may be received by a member while deemed to be unemployable for the purposes of an award of unemployability allowance from £104 a year to £234 a year;

(*c*) to enable the maximum rate of additional allowances payable in respect of the children of a member receiving treatment as defined in Article 21(8) to be awarded in cases where the member would not otherwise qualify for such an award solely by reason of his age, in cases where the member is in receipt of an unemployability allowance and in certain cases where the member is not eligible for retirement pension;

(*d*) to enable the rate of rent allowance to be determined by reference to the amount of weekly rent and rates instead of as hitherto the amount by which the weekly rent and rates exceeds 30p.

Article 3 extends the Secretary of State's discretionary power to make deductions from awards in respect of maintenance in an institution supported out of public funds to all cases where the pensioner is maintained free of charge in a National Health Service hospital or similar institution for the purpose of receiving treatment and provides for payments out of such deductions to be made to the pensioner for his resettlement following a period of such treatment.

PENSIONS

ROYAL WARRANT

To amend the Royal Warrant of 19th September 1964, concerning pensions and other grants in respect of disablement or death due to service in the military forces during the 1914 World War and after 2nd September 1939.

Preamble

WHEREAS We deem it expedient to amend Our Warrant of 19th September 1964(**a**), as amended(**b**), concerning pensions and other grants in respect of disablement or death due to service in the military forces during the 1914 World War and after 2nd September 1939 (hereinafter referred to as " the 1964 Warrant "):

Our Will and Pleasure is that, notwithstanding anything in the 1964 Warrant, the following provisions of this Our Warrant shall take effect accordingly and, except in the cases stated in the Warrant of Her Majesty Queen Victoria of 27th October 1884, and except as otherwise provided by statute, shall be established and obeyed as the sole authority in the matters herein treated of.

Substitution of Schedules to the 1964 Warrant

1. For Schedules 2, 3 (other than Part II of Table 3 thereof), 4, 6 and 7 to the 1964 Warrant (rates of pensions and other grants payable in respect of disablement or death due to service in the military forces during the 1914 World War and after 2nd September 1939) there shall be substituted the Schedules set out in Part I of the Appendix hereto and numbered 2, 3, 4, 6 and 7 respectively.

Amendment of Articles of the 1964 Warrant

2. In Articles 5 (entitlement where a claim is made in respect of a disablement, or death occurs, more than 7 years after the termination of service), 17 (unemployability allowances), 21 (treatment allowances), 31 (rent allowance to widows, and unmarried dependants who lived as wives, who have children) and 71 (commencement and application of the Warrant, amendment and revocation of previous Warrants, and transitional provisions) of the 1964 Warrant there shall be made the amendments set out in Part II of the Appendix hereto.

Substitution of Article 57 of the 1964 Warrant

3. For Article 57 of the 1964 Warrant (pensioners admitted to institutions) there shall be substituted the Article set out in Part III of the Appendix hereto.

(**a**) Cmnd. 2467.
(**b**) The relevant amending Warrants are Cmnd. 2553, 2926, 3023, 3385, 3728, 4134, 4742.

Commencement

4.—(1) Subject to the following provisions of this Article, this Our Warrant shall come into operation on 2nd October 1972 so, however, that in relation to any award payable weekly the foregoing reference to 2nd October 1972, where this is not the normal weekly pay day for that award, shall be construed as a reference to the first normal weekly pay day for that award following 2nd October 1972.

(2) Article 1 shall come into operation in relation to an officer on 1st October 1972.

(3) In so far as Article 1 substitutes the higher maximum rate of allowance for part-time treatment specified in paragraph 10 of Schedule 6 in Part I of the Appendix hereto, it shall be deemed to have come into operation on 3rd November 1971.

Given at Our Court at St. James's, this twenty-seventh day of July 1972, in the 21st Year of Our Reign.

By Her Majesty's Command.

Keith Joseph.

APPENDIX

Part I

Schedules to be substituted in the 1964 Warrant by Article 1 of this Our Warrant

SCHEDULE 2

TABLE 1

Yearly Rates of Retired Pay and Pensions for Disabled Officers and Nurses

A.—Male Officers, and Women Officers under Article 1(35)(b)

Degree of disablement	Rank								Additional Retired Pay under paragraphs (1), (2) and (5) of the proviso to Article 1 of the 1920 Warrant All Ranks
	Major-General	Brigadier-General	Brigadier	Colonel	Lieutenant-Colonel	Major	Captain	Lieutenant* or Second-Lieutenant	
(1)	(2)	(3)	(4)	(5)	(6)	(7)	(8)	(9)	(10)
Per cent.	£	£	£	£	£	£	£	£	£
100	889·00	859·00	844·00	799·00	769·00	739·00	709·00	679·00	619·00
90	800·10	773·10	759·60	719·10	692·10	665·10	638·10	611·10	557·10
80	711·20	687·20	675·20	639·20	615·20	591·20	567·20	543·20	495·20
70	622·30	601·30	590·80	559·30	538·30	517·30	496·30	475·30	433·30
60	533·40	515·40	506·40	479·40	461·40	443·40	425·40	407·40	371·40
50	444·50	429·50	422·00	399·50	384·50	369·50	354·50	339·50	309·50
40	355·60	343·60	337·60	319·60	307·60	295·60	283·60	271·60	247·60
30	266·70	257·70	253·20	239·70	230·70	221·70	212·70	203·70	185·70
20	177·80	171·80	168·80	159·80	153·80	147·80	141·80	135·80	123·80

* Quartermasters, Assistant Paymasters and Inspectors of Army Schools may be treated as Lieutenants.

B.—Women Officers (other than those under Article 1(35)(b)) and Nurses

Degree of disablement (1)	Colonel or above, Senior Controller, Controller. Member with status of Colonel or above. (2) £	Lieutenant-Colonel, Chief Commander. Member with status of Lieutenant-Colonel. (3) £	Rank — Major, Senior Commander. Member with status of Major. (4) £	Captain, Lieutenant, Second Lieutenant, Junior Commander, Subaltern, Second Subaltern. Member with status of Captain or below. (5) £	Addition to Service Retired Pay All Ranks (6) £
Per cent.					
100	739·00	704·00	674·00	644·00	594·00
90	665·10	633·60	606·60	579·60	534·60
80	591·20	563·20	539·20	515·20	475·20
70	517·30	492·80	471·80	450·80	415·80
60	443·40	422·40	404·40	386·40	356·40
50	369·50	352·00	337·00	322·00	297·00
40	295·60	281·60	269·60	257·60	237·60
30	221·70	211·20	202·20	193·20	178·20
20	147·80	140·80	134·80	128·80	118·80

SCHEDULE 2

TABLE 2

WEEKLY RATES OF PENSIONS

A.—Disabled Other Ranks—Men

Degree of disable-ment	Rank (or equivalent rank)					
	Warrant Officer Class I	Warrant Officer Class II or N.C. Officer Class I	Staff Serjeant or N.C. Officer Class II	Serjeant or N.C. Officer Class III	Corporal or N.C. Officer Class IV	Private etc. Class V
Per cent.	£	£	£	£	£	£
100 ...	12·04	11·87	11·70	11·54	11·37	11·20
90 ...	10·83	10·68	10·53	10·38	10·23	10·08
80 ...	9·63	9·50	9·36	9·23	9·10	8·96
70 ...	8·43	8·31	8·19	8·08	7·96	7·84
60 ...	7·22	7·12	7·02	6·92	6·82	6·72
50 ...	6·02	5·94	5·85	5·77	5·69	5·60
40 ...	4·82	4·75	4·68	4·62	4·55	4·48
30 ...	3·61	3·56	3·51	3·46	3·41	3·36
20 ...	2·41	2·38	2·34	2·31	2·28	2·24

B.—Disabled Other Ranks—Women

Degree of disable-ment	Rank (or equivalent rank or status)					
	Warrant Officer Class I	Warrant Officer Class II	Staff Serjeant	Serjeant	Corporal	Private
Per cent.	£	£	£	£	£	£
100 ...	11·62	11·54	11·45	11·37	11·29	11·20
90 ...	10·46	10·38	10·31	10·23	10·16	10·08
80 ...	9·30	9·23	9·16	9·10	9·03	8·96
70 ...	8·14	8·08	8·02	7·96	7·90	7·84
60 ...	6·97	6·92	6·87	6·82	6·77	6·72
50 ...	5·81	5·77	5·73	5·69	5·65	5·60
40 ...	4·65	4·62	4·58	4·55	4·52	4·48
30 ...	3·49	3·46	3·44	3·41	3·39	3·36
20 ...	2·33	2·31	2·29	2·28	2·26	2·24

SCHEDULE 3

TABLE 1

GRATUITIES PAYABLE FOR SPECIFIED MINOR INJURIES

Description of Injury	Officers	Other Ranks
	£	£
For the loss of:—		
A. FINGERS:—		
Index finger—		
Whole	615	585
2 phalanges	490	465
1 phalanx	411	391
Guillotine amputation of tip without loss of bone ...	256	246
Middle finger—		
Whole	537	512
2 phalanges	411	391
1 phalanx	332	317
Guillotine amputation of tip without loss of bone ...	206	196
Ring or little finger—		
Whole	332	317
2 phalanges	287	272
1 phalanx	256	246
Guillotine amputation of tip without loss of bone ...	130	125
B. TOES:—		
Great toe—		
through metatarso-phalangeal joint	615	585
part, with some loss of bone	179	174
1 other toe—		
through metatarso-phalangeal joint	179	174
part, with some loss of bone	80	75
2 toes, excluding great toe—		
through metatarso-phalangeal joint	256	246
part, with some loss of bone	130	125
3 toes, excluding great toe—		
through metatarso-phalangeal joint	287	272
part, with some loss of bone	179	174
4 toes, excluding great toe—		
through metatarso-phalangeal joint	411	391
part, with some loss of bone	179	174

SCHEDULE 3

TABLE 2

GRATUITIES PAYABLE TO OFFICERS FOR DISABLEMENT ASSESSED AT LESS THAN 20 PER CENT., NOT BEING A MINOR INJURY SPECIFIED IN TABLE 1

Rank	Estimated duration of the disablement within the degree referred to								
	Temporary less than a year			Temporary more than a year			Indeterminate		
	Per cent.			Per cent.			Per cent.		
	1–5	6–14	15–19	1–5	6–14	15–19	1–5	6–14	15–19
	£	£	£	£	£	£	£	£	£
A.—Male Officers, and Women Officers under Article 1(35)(*b*).									
Major-General	45	99	172	88	197	344	265	590	1,032
Brigadier...	43	94	165	84	188	328	253	563	985
Colonel	41	90	157	80	179	312	241	536	938
Lieutenant-Colonel ...	39	87	151	78	173	302	233	518	906
Major	38	84	146	75	167	291	225	500	875
Captain or Subaltern ...	36	79	138	71	158	275	213	473	828
B.—Women Officers (*other than those under Article* 1(35)(*b*)).									
Colonel or above, Senior Controller, Controller. Member with status of Colonel or above ...	38	84	146	75	167	291	225	500	875
Lieutenant-Colonel, Chief Commander. Member with status of Lieutenant-Colonel ...	36	80	140	72	160	279	215	479	838
Major, Senior Commander. Member with status of Major ...	35	77	135	69	154	268	207	461	807
Captain, Lieutenant, Second Lieutenant, Junior Commander, Subaltern, Second Subaltern. Member with status of Captain or below	34	74	130	66	148	258	199	443	775

SCHEDULE 3

TABLE 3

PART I

GRATUITIES PAYABLE TO OTHER RANKS FOR DISABLEMENT ASSESSED AT LESS THAN 20 PER CENT., NOT BEING A MINOR INJURY SPECIFIED IN TABLE 1

Rank	Estimated duration of the disablement within the degree referred to								
	Temporary less than a year			Temporary more than a year			Indeterminate		
	Per cent.			Per cent.			Per cent.		
	1–5	6–14	15–19	1–5	6–14	15–19	1–5	6–14	15–19
	£	£	£	£	£	£	£	£	£
A.—Men									
Warrant Officer, Class I	33	72	126	65	144	252	194	432	756
Warrant Officer, Class II	33	71	125	64	143	249	192	427	747
Staff Serjeant	32	71	123	63	141	246	190	422	738
Serjeant	32	70	122	63	139	243	188	417	730
Corporal	31	69	120	62	138	240	185	412	721
Private	31	68	119	61	136	237	183	407	712
B.—Women									
Warrant Officer, Class I	32	70	123	63	140	245	189	420	735
Warrant Officer, Class II	32	70	122	63	140	243	188	418	731
Staff Serjeant	32	69	121	62	139	242	187	415	726
Serjeant	31	69	120	62	138	240	185	412	721
Corporal	31	69	120	61	137	239	184	410	717
Private	31	68	119	61	136	237	183	407	712

SCHEDULE 4

TABLE 1

YEARLY RATES OF PENSIONS FOR WIDOWS OF OFFICERS

A.—Pensions other than pensions awarded under Article 11(1) *of the* 1920 *Warrant*

Rank (1)								(2)	(3)
								£	£
Field Marshal	...	...	...	...	...	...	...	1,069	1,069
General	...	...	...	...	...	...	...	909	909
Lieutenant-General	...	...	...	...	...	...	809	809
Major-General	...	...	...	...	...	...	719	719
Brigadier-General or Brigadier	...	...	...	...	...	659	659
*Colonel	...	...	...	...	...	...	...	599	599
†Lieutenant-Colonel	...	...	...	...	...	...	579	579
Major	...	...	...	...	...	...	...	549	170
Captain	...	...	...	...	...	...	...	534	150
‡Lieutenant ...	...	...	...	...	...	...	519	130
Second Lieutenant	...	...	...	...	...	...	519	130

B.—Pensions awarded under Article 11(1) *of the* 1920 *Warrant*

Rank (1)									(2)
									£
Field Marshal	...	...	...	...	...	...	...	...	1,169
General	...	...	...	...	...	...	...	...	969
Lieutenant-General	...	...	...	...	...	...	...	869
Major-General	...	...	...	...	...	...	...	769
Brigadier-General ...	...	...	...	...	...	...	689
*Colonel	...	...	...	...	...	...	...	609
†Lieutenant-Colonel	...	... '	...	...	...	...	585
Major	...	...	...	...	...	...	...	549
Captain	...	...	...	...	...	...	...	534
‡Lieutenant ...	...	...	...	...	...	...	519
Second Lieutenant	...	...	...	...	...	...	519

NOTE: Where the death is due to service during the 1914 World War—

* Colonel means a Colonel who has been employed as a substantive Colonel if a combatant officer, or in the rank of Colonel if a medical, veterinary or departmental officer.

† Including a Colonel not employed as above.

‡ Quartermasters, Assistant Paymasters and Inspectors of Army Schools not holding permanent commissions in the Regular Forces may be treated as Lieutenants.

TABLE 2

WEEKLY RATES OF PENSIONS FOR WIDOWS OF SOLDIERS

Rank (or equivalent rank) (1)	(2)	(3)
	£	£
Warrant Officer, Class I	9·05	2·28
Warrant Officer, Class II or Non-Commissioned Officer, Class I	9·00	2·23
Staff Serjeant or Non-Commissioned Officer, Class II	8·95	2·18
Serjeant or Non-Commissioned Officer, Class III	8·90	2·13
Corporal or Non-Commissioned Officer, Class IV	8·85	2·08
Private, etc., Class V	8·80	2·03

TABLE 3

MAXIMUM YEARLY RATES OF PENSIONS FOR RELATIVES OF 1914 WORLD WAR OFFICERS

Rank (1)	(2)	(3)
	£	£
Field Marshal	1,169	1,069
General	969	909
Lieutenant-General	869	809
Major-General	769	719
Brigadier-General	669	659
	£	
*Colonel	599	
†Lieutenant-Colonel	579	
Major	170	
Captain	150	
‡Lieutenant	130	
Second-Lieutenant	130	

NOTE: Where the death is due to service during the 1914 World War—

* Colonel means a Colonel who has been employed as a substantive Colonel if a combatant officer, or in the rank of Colonel if a medical, veterinary or departmental officer.

† Including a Colonel not employed as above.

‡ Quartermasters, Assistant Paymasters and Inspectors of Army Schools not holding permanent commissions in the Regular Forces may be treated as Lieutenants.

SCHEDULE 6

RATES OF ALLOWANCES PAYABLE IN RESPECT OF DISABLEMENT

Description of Allowance	Rate	
	Officers and Nurses	Soldiers
1. Education allowance under Article 13 ...	£120·00 per annum (maximum)	£120·00 per annum (maximum)
2. Constant attendance allowance—		
(a) under the proviso to Article 14 ...	£468·00 per annum (maximum)	£9·00 per week (maximum)
(b) in any other case under that Article	£234·00 per annum (maximum)	£4·50 per week (maximum)
2A. Exceptionally severe disablement allowance under Article 14A	£234·00 per annum	£4·50 per week
3. Severe disablement occupational allowance under Article 15	£104·00 per annum	£2·00 per week
4. Allowance for wear and tear of clothing—		
(a) under Article 16(1)(a)	£12·00 per annum	£12·00 per annum
(b) under Article 16(1)(b) and 16(2) ...	£19·00 per annum	£19·00 per annum
5. Unemployability allowances—		
(a) personal allowance under Article 17(1)(i)	£382·20 per annum	£7·35 per week
(b) additional allowances for dependants by way of—		
(i) increase or further increase of allowance in respect of a wife, husband or unmarried dependant living as a wife, under Article 17(4)(c)	£179·80 per annum (maximum)	£3·65 per week (maximum)
(ii) allowance in respect of an adult dependant under Article 17(4)(d)	£215·80 per annum (maximum)	£4·15 per week (maximum)
(iii) increased allowance under Article 17(4)(f)—		
(a) in respect of the child, or the elder or eldest of the children, of a member	£171·60 per annum	£3·30 per week
(b) in respect of the second child of a member	£124·80 per annum	£2·40 per week
(c) in respect of each other child of a member	£119·60 per annum	£2·30 per week
5A. Invalidity allowance under Article 17A—		
(a) if on the relevant date the member was under the age of 35, or if that date fell before 5th July 1948 ...	£59·80 per annum	£1·15 per week
(b) if head (a) does not apply and on the relevant date the member was under the age of 45	£36·40 per annum	£0·70 per week
(c) if heads (a) and (b) do not apply, and on the relevant date the member was a man under the age of 60, or a woman under the age of 55 ...	£18·20 per annum	£0·35 per week
6. Comforts allowance—		
(a) under Article 18(1)(a)	£88·40 per annum	£1·70 per week
(b) under Article 18(1)(b)	£44·20 per annum	£0·85 per week
7. Allowance for lowered standard of occupation under Article 19	£232·96 per annum (maximum)	£4·48 per week (maximum)
8. Age allowance under Article 20 where the degree of pensioned disablement is—		
(a) 40 to 50 per cent.	£28·60 per annum	£0·55 per week
(b) over 50 per cent. but not exceeding 70 per cent.	£41·60 per annum	£0·80 per week

Description of Allowance	Rate	
	Officers and Nurses	Soldiers
(c) over 70 per cent. but not exceeding 90 per cent.	£59·80 per annum	£1·15 per week
(d) over 90 per cent.	£83·20 per annum	£1·60 per week
9. Treatment allowances—		
(a) increase of personal allowance under Article 21(2)	£83·20 per annum (maximum)	£1·60 per week (maximum)
(b) increase of personal allowance under Article 21(3)—		
(i) under sub-paragraph (a) ...	£6·75 per week	£6·75 per week
(ii) under sub-paragraph (c)—		
(a) if on the relevant date the member was under the age of 35 or if that date fell before 5th July 1948	£59·80 per annum	£1·15 per week
(b) if head (a) does not apply and on the relevant date the member was under the age of 45	£36·40 per annum	£0·70 per week
(c) if heads (a) and (b) do not apply and on the relevant date the member was a man under the age of 60, or a woman under the age of 55 ...	£18·20 per annum	£0·35 per week
(c) increased additional allowance under Article 21(4) proviso (a)	£215·80 per annum	£4·15 per week
(d) increased additional allowance under Article 21(4) proviso (b)—		
(i) in respect of the child, or the elder or eldest of the children, of a member	£109·20 per annum	£2·10 per week
(ii) in respect of the second child of a member	£62·40 per annum	£1·20 per week
(iii) in respect of each other child of a member	£57·20 per annum	£1·10 per week
(e) higher rate of additional allowance under Article 21(4A)—		
(i) in respect of the child, or the elder or eldest of the children, of a member	£171·60 per annum	£3·30 per week
(ii) in respect of the second child of a member	£124·80 per annum	£2·40 per week
(iii) in respect of each other child of a member	£119·60 per annum	£2·30 per week
(f) additional allowance under Article 21(5)	£215·80 per annum	£4·15 per week
10. Part-time treatment allowance under Article 23	£4·75 per day (maximum)	£4·75 per day (maximum)

SCHEDULE 7

RATES OF PENSIONS, OTHER THAN WIDOWS' PENSIONS, AND ALLOWANCES
PAYABLE IN RESPECT OF DEATH

Description of Pension or Allowance	Rate	
	Officers and Nurses	Soldiers
1. Pension under Article 30 to unmarried dependant who lived as wife	£458·50 per annum (maximum)	£8·30 per week (maximum)
2. Rent allowance under Article 31 ...	£3·40 per week (maximum)	£3·40 per week (maximum)
3. Allowance under Article 32 to elderly widow or unmarried dependant who lived as wife—		
(a) if age 65 but under 70	£26·00 per annum	£0·50 per week
(b) if age 70 or over	£52·00 per annum	£1·00 per week
4. Pension to widower under Article 34 ...	£464·00 per annum (maximum)	£8·80 per week (maximum)
5. Allowances in respect of children— (a) under Article 35(1)—		
(i) in respect of the child, or the elder or eldest of the children, of a member	£190·10 per annum	£3·50 per week
(ii) in respect of each other child of a member—		
(a) where the child qualifies for a family allowance under the Family Allowances Act 1965 or under any legislation in Northern Ireland or the Isle of Man corresponding to that Act	£164·10 per annum	£3·00 per week
(b) where the child does not so qualify...	£182·30 per annum	£3·35 per week
(b) under Article 35(3)	£269·30 per annum (maximum)	where the child is 15 years of age or over—£5·00 per week (maximum)
6. Pension under Article 36 to a motherless or fatherless child— (a) in respect of the child, or the elder or eldest of the children, of a member, and in respect of each other child of a member who does not qualify for a family allowance as aforesaid ...	£269·30 per annum	(i) where the child is under 15 years of age— £3·50 per week (ii) where the child is 15 years of age or over— £5·00 per week
(b) in respect of each' other child of a member who qualifies for a family allowance as aforesaid	£243·30 per annum	(i) where the child is under 15 years of age— £3·00 per week (ii) where the child is 15 years of age or over— £4·50 per week

Description of Pension or Allowance	Rate	
	Officers and Nurses	Soldiers
7. Pension or allowance under Article 37(3) to or in respect of a child over the age limit	£351·00 per annum (maximum)	£6·75 per week (maximum)
8. Education allowance under Article 38 ...	£120·00 per annum (maximum)	£120·00 per annum (maximum)
9. Pensions to parents—		
(a) minimum rate under Article 40(4) ...	£15·00 per annum	£0·25 per week
(b) under paragraphs (a) and (b) of Article 40(4)—		
(i) where there is only one eligible parent	£75·00 per annum (maximum)	£1·00 per week (maximum)
(ii) where there is more than one eligible parent	£100·00 per annum (maximum)	£1·38 per week (maximum)
(c) increase under the proviso to Article 40(4)	£20·00 per annum (maximum)	(i) where there is only one eligible parent— £0·38 per week (maximum) (ii) where there is more than one eligible parent— £0·62 per week (maximum)
(d) under paragraph (b) of Article 40(5)...	—	£1·00 per week (maximum)
10. Pensions to other dependants—		
(a) under Article 41(2)	£54·00 per annum (maximum)	£1·00 per week (maximum)
(b) for each juvenile dependant under Article 41(3)	£26·00 per annum (maximum)	£0·30 per week (maximum)
(c) aggregate rate under Article 41(3) ...	£75·00 per annum (maximum)	£1·00 per week (maximum)

PART II

Amendment of Articles of the 1964 Warrant

1. In Article 5 (entitlement where a claim is made in respect of a disablement, or death occurs, more than 7 years after the termination of service) in paragraph (1) the words " and he was at the time of his death, or at any time previously thereto had been, in receipt of a pension awarded by the Minister under this Our Warrant or any previous Warrant " shall be omitted, and paragraph (6) is hereby revoked.

2. In Article 17 (unemployability allowances) in paragraph (2) for the words " £104 a year " there shall be substituted the words " £234 a year ".

3. In Article 21 (treatment allowances) for paragraph (4A) there shall be substituted the following paragraph : —

" (4A) The rate of an additional allowance awarded under paragraph (4) of this Article in respect of a child or children of a member may be further increased to the appropriate rate specified in Schedule 6 paragraph 9(*e*) if the member—

    (*a*) is in receipt of an increase of his personal allowance under paragraph (3)(*c*) of this Article or, but for his age on the relevant date, would be in receipt of such an increase ; or

    (*b*) is in receipt of an allowance under Article 17(1)(i) ; or

    (*c*) having reached the age of 65 years or, in the case of a woman member, 60 years is not eligible for retirement pension under the National Insurance Acts 1965 to 1972, or any benefit similar thereto as is referred to in paragraph (6) of this Article, solely by reason of his failure to satisfy any contribution conditions.".

4. In Article 31 (rent allowance to widows, and unmarried dependants who lived as wives, who have children) in paragraph (1) for the words " having regard to the amount by which her weekly rent and rates exceed 6s." there shall be substituted the words " having regard to her weekly rent and rates ".

5. In Article 71 (commencement and application of this Warrant, amendment and revocation of previous Warrants, and transitional provisions) at the end of paragraph (7) there shall be added the words " and as if any requirement thereof that the member had been at the time of his death in receipt of retired pay, pension or allowance in respect of disablement, was satisfied in every case.".

PART III

Substitution of Article 57 of the 1964 Warrant

For Article 57 (pensioners admitted to institutions) there shall be substituted the following Article : —

" 57. *Maintenance in hospital or an institution*.—(1) Where any person to or in respect of whom a pension or gratuity may be or has been awarded is receiving or has received free in-patient treatment, or is being or has been maintained in an institution (otherwise than for the purpose of undergoing medical or other treatment) which is supported wholly or partly out of public funds, or in which he is being or has been maintained pursuant to arrangements made by the Secretary of State, the Secretary of State may deduct such amount as he may think fit having regard to all the circumstances of the case from the pension or gratuity payable in respect of the period during which such treatment is received or during which the person is being so maintained, as the case may be, and may apply the amount so deducted, or any part thereof, in such proportions and subject to such conditions as he may determine having regard to all the circumstances of the case, in a payment or payments to the person upon his discharge following a period of free in-patient treatment, or in or towards paying or repaying the cost of maintaining the person incurred by any appropriate authority.

(2) For the purposes of this Article, a person shall be regarded as receiving or having received free in-patient treatment for any period for which he is or has been maintained free of charge while undergoing medical or other treatment as an in-patient—

(a) in a hospital or similar institution maintained or administered under the National Health Service Acts 1946 to 1968, the National Health Service (Scotland) Acts 1947 to 1968 or the Health Services Act (Northern Ireland) 1971, or by or on behalf of the Secretary of State, or by or on behalf of the Defence Council ; or

(b) pursuant to arrangements made by the Secretary of State or by a Hospital Board or a Regional Hospital Board constituted under the National Health Service Acts 1946 to 1968, the National Health Service (Scotland) Acts 1947 to 1968 or the Health Services Act (Northern Ireland) 1971 in a hospital or similar institution not so maintained or administered ;

and, for this purpose, a person shall only be regarded as not being maintained free of charge in a hospital or similar institution for any period if he is paying or has paid, in respect of his maintenance, charges which are designed to cover the whole cost of the accommodation or services (other than services by way of treatment) provided for him in the hospital or similar institution for that period."

EXPLANATORY NOTE

(This Note is not part of the Royal Warrant.)

This Royal Warrant further amends the Royal Warrant of 19th September 1964.

Article 1 substitutes new Tables for those contained in Schedules 2, 3, 4, 6 and 7 to the 1964 Warrant and has the effect of increasing—

Disablement pensions and allowances

(a) the rates of pensions in respect of 100 per cent. disablement by £62·00 a year in the case of officers and by £1·20 a week in the case of other ranks and the rates of pensions for lower degrees of disablement and awards for cases of minor injuries and other cases of less than 20 per cent. disablement proportionately ;

(b) the maximum rates of disablement addition on a pension basis payable to certain officers in receipt of service retired pay by £62·00 a year ;

(c) the normal maximum rate of an allowance payable for constant attendance from £208·00 a year to £234·00 a year in the case of officers and from £4·00 a week to £4·50 a week in the case of other ranks, and the maximum rate for exceptional cases of very severe disablement from £416·00 a year to £468·00 a year in the case of officers and from £8·00 a week to £9·00 a week in the case of other ranks ;

(d) the exceptionally severe disablement allowance from £208·00 a year to £234·00 a year in the case of officers and from £4·00 a week to £4·50 a week in the case of other ranks ;

(e) the allowance for unemployable pensioners from £340·60 a year to £382·20 a year in the case of officers and from £6·55 a week to £7·35 a week in the case of other ranks ;

(f) the total additional allowance payable in respect of the wife or adult dependant of an unemployable pensioner and of a pensioner receiving treatment as defined in Article 21(8) from £192·40 a year to £215·80 a year in the case of officers and from £3·70 a week to £4·15 a week in the case of other ranks ;

(g) the allowances payable in respect of children of unemployable pensioners in respect of the first or only child from £153·40 a year to £171·60 a year in the case of officers and from £2·95 a week to £3·30 a week in the case of other ranks, in respect of the second child from £106·60 a year to £124·80 a year in the case of officers and from £2·05 a week to £2·40 a week in the case of other ranks and in respect of any other child from £101·40 a year to £119·60 a year in the case of officers and from £1·95 a week to £2·30 a week in the case of other ranks ;

(h) the maximum allowance for lowered standard of occupation from £208·00 a year to £232·96 a year in the case of officers and from £4·00 a week to £4·48 a week in the case of other ranks ;

(i) the allowances payable to pensioners who have attained the age of 65 and whose pensioned disablement is assessed at 40 per cent. or over from between £26·00 a year and £72·80 a year to between £28·60 a year and £83·20 a year in the case of officers and from between £0·50 a week and £1·40 a week to between £0·55 a week and £1·60 a week in the case of other ranks ;

(j) the allowances payable in respect of children of pensioners receiving treatment as defined in Article 21(8) in respect of the first or only child from £96·20 a year to £109·20 a year in the case of officers and from £1·85 a week to £2·10 a week in the case of other ranks, in respect of the second child from £49·40 a year to £62·40 a year in the case of officers and from £0·95 a week to £1·20 a week in the case of other ranks, and in respect of any other child from £44·20 a year to £57·20 a year in the case of officers and from £0·85 a week to £1·10 a week in the case of other ranks, and to further increase those allowances where the said pensioners are not entitled to invalidity pension and allowance under national insurance provisions solely because of failure to satisfy the contribution conditions, to £171·60 a year; £3·30 a week; £124·80 a year; £2·40 a week; £119·60 a year and £2·30 a week respectively;

(k) the maximum of the additional personal treatment allowance payable to a pensioner who is not entitled to full sickness benefit or invalidity pension and allowance under national insurance provisions from £6·00 a week to £6·75 a week;

Widows' benefits

(l) the rates of pensions for certain widows by £52·00 a year in the case of officers and by £1·00 a week in the case of other ranks;

(m) the maximum pensions payable to unmarried dependants who lived as wives of deceased members of the military forces from £406·50 a year to £458·50 a year in the case of officers and from £7·30 a week to £8·30 a week in the case of other ranks;

(n) the maximum rent allowance payable to certain widows from £3·00 a week to £3·40 a week;

(o) the allowances payable to widows in respect of children for the first or only child from £171·90 a year to £190·10 a year in the case of officers and from £3·15 a week to £3·50 a week in the case of other ranks, and in respect of each other child from £145·90 a year to £164·10 a year in the case of officers and from £2·65 a week to £3·00 a week in the case of other ranks, where the child qualifies for a family allowance, and from £164·10 a year to £182·30 a year in the case of officers and from £3·00 a week to £3·35 a week in the case of other ranks where the child does not so qualify;

Other benefits

(p) the maximum pensions payable to certain widowers from £412·00 a year to £464·00 a year in the case of officers and from £7·80 a week to £8·80 a week in the case of other ranks;

(q) the rates of pensions and allowances payable to or in respect of the children of deceased members of the military forces (such children having become motherless or having ceased to be under the control of their mothers) in respect of the first or only child or any other child who does not qualify for a family allowance from £251·10 a year to £269·30 a year in the case of children of officers and from £3·15 or £4·65 a week to £3·50 or £5·00 a week (according to the age of the child) in the case of children of other ranks, and in respect of each other child who qualifies for a family allowance from £225·10 a year to £243·30 a year in the case of children of officers and from £2·65 or £4·15 a week to £3·00 or £4·50 a week (according to the age of the child) in the case of children of other ranks;

(r) the maximum rates of pensions payable to motherless or fatherless after the termination of his service, unless he had been in receipt of self-support by reason of infirmity which arose before they attained the normal age limit for pension purposes, from £312·00 a year to £351·00 a year in the case of children of officers and from £6·00 a week to £6·75 a week in the case of children of other ranks.

Article 2 makes amendments to the 1964 Warrant, the effects of which are : —

    (a) to remove a restriction under which no award could be made in respect of the death of a member, occurring more than 7 years after the termination of his service, unless he had been in receipt of a pension in respect of disablement ;

    (b) to raise the maximum amount of earnings which may be received by a member while deemed to be unemployable for the purposes of an award of unemployability allowance from £104 a year to £234 a year ;

    (c) to enable the maximum rate of additional allowances payable in respect of the children of a member receiving treatment as defined in Article 21(8) to be awarded in cases where the member would not otherwise qualify for such an award solely by reason of his age, in cases where the member is in receipt of an unemployability allowance and in certain cases where the member is not eligible for retirement pension ;

    (d) to enable the rate of rent allowance to be determined by reference to the amount of weekly rent and rates instead of as hitherto the amount by which the weekly rent and rates exceed 30p.

Article 3 extends the Secretary of State's discretionary power to make deductions from awards in respect of maintenance in an institution supported out of public funds to all cases where the pensioner is maintained free of charge in a National Health Service hospital or similar institution for the purpose of receiving treatment and provides for payments out of such deductions to be made to the pensioner for his resettlement following a period of such treatment.

PENSIONS
ORDER BY HER MAJESTY

To amend the Order of 24th September 1964, concerning pensions and other grants in respect of disablement or death due to service in the air forces during the 1914 World War and after 2nd September 1939.

ELIZABETH R.

Preamble

WHEREAS by Section 2 of the Air Force (Constitution) Act 1917(**a**) it is provided that it shall be lawful for Her Majesty, by order signified under the hand of a Secretary of State, to make orders with respect to the government, discipline, pay, allowances and pensions of the Air Force, and with respect to all other matters and things relating to the Air Force, including any matter by that Act authorised to be prescribed or expressed to be subject to orders or regulations:

AND WHEREAS Her Majesty deems it expedient to amend the Order dated 24th September 1964(**b**), as amended(**c**), concerning pensions and other grants in respect of disablement or death due to service in the air forces during the 1914 World War and after 2nd September 1939 (hereinafter referred to as " the 1964 Order "):

NOW, THEREFORE, Her Majesty, in exercise of the powers conferred upon Her as aforesaid and of all other powers whatsoever Her thereunto enabling, is pleased to order, and it is hereby ordered that, notwithstanding anything in the 1964 Order, the following provisions of this Order shall take effect accordingly and, except in the cases stated in the Order by His Majesty King George V of 13th January 1922, and except as otherwise provided by statute, shall be established and obeyed as the sole authority in the matters herein treated of.

Substitution of Schedules to the 1964 Order

1. For Schedules 2, 3 (other than Part II of Table 3 thereof), 4, 6 and 7 to the 1964 Order (rates of pensions and other grants payable in respect of disablement or death due to service in the air forces during the 1914 World War and after 2nd September 1939) there shall be substituted the Schedules set out in Part I of the Appendix hereto and numbered 2, 3, 4, 6 and 7 respectively.

Amendment of Articles of the 1964 Order

2. In Articles 5 (entitlement where a claim is made in respect of a disablement, or death occurs, more than 7 years after the termination of service), 17 (unemployability allowances), 21 (treatment allowances), 31 (rent allowance to widows, and unmarried dependants who lived as wives, who have children) and 71 (commencement and application of the Order, amendment and revocation of previous Orders, and transitional provisions) of the 1964 Order there shall be made the amendments set out in Part II of the Appendix hereto.

(**a**) 7 & 8 Geo. 5 c. 51.　　　　　(**b**) Cmnd. 2472.
(**c**) The relevant amending Orders are Cmnd. 2554, 2927, 3024, 3384, 3729, 4135, 4743.

Substitution of Article 57 of the 1964 Order

3. For Article 57 of the 1964 Order (pensioners admitted to institutions) there shall be substituted the Article set out in Part III of the Appendix hereto.

Commencement

4.—(1) Subject to the following provisions of this Article, this Order shall come into operation on 2nd October 1972 so, however, that in relation to any award payable weekly the foregoing reference to 2nd October 1972, where this is not the normal weekly pay day for that award, shall be construed as a reference to the first normal weekly pay day for that award following 2nd October 1972.

(2) Article 1 shall come into operation in relation to an officer on 1st October 1972.

(3) In so far as Article 1 substitutes the higher maximum rate of allowance for part-time treatment specified in paragraph 10 of Schedule 6 in Part I of the Appendix hereto, it shall be deemed to have come into operation on 3rd November 1971.

By Her Majesty's Command.

Keith Joseph,
Secretary of State for Social Services.

31st July 1972.

APPENDIX

Part I

*Schedules to be substituted in the 1964 Order by Article 1
of this Order*

SCHEDULE 2

TABLE 1

YEARLY RATES OF RETIRED PAY AND PENSIONS FOR DISABLED OFFICERS AND NURSES

A.—Male Officers, and Women Officers under Article 1(35)(b)

Degree of disablement (1)	Air Vice-Marshal (2)	Air Commodore* (3)	Air Commodore (4)	Group Captain (5)	Wing Commander (6)	Squadron Leader (7)	Flight Lieutenant (8)	Flying Officer, Pilot Officer or Acting Pilot Officer (9)	Additional Retired Pay under paragraphs (1), (2) and (5) of the proviso to Article 1 of the 1921 Order. All Ranks (10)
	£	£	£	£	£	£	£	£	£
Per cent.									
100	889·00	859·00	844·00	799·00	769·00	739·00	709·00	679·00	619·00
90	800·10	773·10	759·60	719·10	692·10	665·10	638·10	611·10	557·10
80	711·20	687·20	675·20	639·20	615·20	591·20	567·20	543·20	495·20
70	622·30	601·30	590·80	559·30	538·30	517·30	496·30	475·30	433·30
60	533·40	515·40	506·40	479·40	461·40	443·40	425·40	407·40	371·40
50	444·50	429·50	422·00	399·50	384·50	369·50	354·50	339·50	309·50
40	355·60	343·60	337·60	319·60	307·60	295·60	283·60	271·60	247·60
30	266·70	257·70	253·20	239·70	230·70	221·70	212·70	203·70	185·70
20	177·80	171·80	168·80	159·80	153·80	147·80	141·80	135·80	123·80

* Disabled as a result of service during the 1914 World War.

SCHEDULE 2

TABLE 1—continued

B.—Women Officers (other than those under Article 1(35)(b)) and Nurses

Degree of disablement	Rank				Addition to Service Retired Pay. All ranks
	Air Commandant, Group Officer. Member with status of Group Captain or above	Wing Officer. Member with status of Wing Commander	Squadron Officer. Member with status of Squadron Leader	Flying Officer, Pilot Officer, Acting Pilot Officer, Flight Officer, Section Officer, Assistant Section Officer. Member with status of Flying Officer or below	
(1)	(2)	(3)	(4)	(5)	(6)
	£	£	£	£	£
Per cent.					
100	739·00	704·00	674·00	644·00	594·00
90	665·10	633·60	606·60	579·60	534·60
80	591·20	563·20	539·20	515·20	475·20
70	517·30	492·80	471·80	450·80	415·80
60	443·40	422·40	404·40	386·40	356·40
50	369·50	352·00	337·00	322·00	297·00
40	295·60	281·60	269·60	257·60	237·00
30	221·70	211·20	202·20	193·20	178·20
20	147·80	140·80	134·80	128·80	118·80

SCHEDULE 2

TABLE 2

WEEKLY RATES OF PENSIONS

A.—Disabled Airmen

Degree of disablement	Rank (or equivalent rank)					
	Warrant Officer or Airman, Class A	Warrant Officer 2nd Class or Airman, Class B	Flight Sergeant or Airman, Class C	Sergeant or Airman, Class D	Corporal or Airman, Class E	Leading or Senior Aircraftman and Aircraftman or Airman, Class F
Per cent.	£	£	£	£	£	£
100 ...	12·04	11·87	11·70	11·54	11·37	11·20
90 ...	10·83	10·68	10·53	10·38	10·23	10·08
80 ...	9·63	9·50	9·36	9·23	9·10	8·96
70 ...	8·43	8·31	8·19	8·08	7·96	7·84
60 ...	7·22	7·12	7·02	6·92	6·82	6·72
50 ...	6·02	5·94	5·85	5·77	5·69	5·60
40 ...	4·82	4·75	4·68	4·62	4·55	4·48
30 ...	3·61	3·56	3·51	3·46	3·41	3·36
20 ...	2·41	2·38	2·34	2·31	2·28	2·24

B.—Disabled Airwomen

Degree of disablement	Rank (or equivalent rank or status)					
	Member of a Voluntary Aid Detachment serving as an uncertificated Nurse, Grade I	Warrant Officer	Flight Sergeant	Sergeant	Corporal	Leading or Senior Aircraftwoman and Aircraftwoman
Per cent.	£	£	£	£	£	£
100 ...	11·79	11·62	11·45	11·37	11·29	11·20
90 ...	10·61	10·46	10·31	10·23	10·16	10·08
80 ...	9·43	9·30	9·16	9·10	9·03	8·96
70 ...	8·25	8·14	8·02	7·96	7·90	7·84
60 ...	7·07	6·97	6·87	6·82	6·77	6·72
50 ...	5·90	5·81	5·73	5·69	5·65	5·60
40 ...	4·72	4·65	4·58	4·55	4·52	4·48
30 ...	3·54	3·49	3·44	3·41	3·39	3·36
20 ...	2·36	2·33	2·29	2·28	2·26	2·24

SCHEDULE 3

TABLE 1

GRATUITIES PAYABLE FOR SPECIFIED MINOR INJURIES

Description of Injury	Officers	Airmen (Airwomen)
	£	£
For the loss of:—		
A. FINGERS:—		
Index finger—		
Whole	615	585
2 phalanges	490	465
1 phalanx	411	391
Guillotine amputation of tip without loss of bone ...	256	246
Middle finger—		
Whole	537	512
2 phalanges	411	391
1 phalanx	332	317
Guillotine amputation of tip without loss of bone ...	206	196
Ring or little finger—		
Whole	332	317
2 phalanges	287	272
1 phalanx	256	246
Guillotine amputation of tip without loss of bone ...	130	125
B. TOES:—		
Great toe—		
through metatarso-phalangeal joint	615	585
part, with some loss of bone	179	174
1 other toe—		
through metatarso-phalangeal joint	179	174
part, with some loss of bone	80	75
2 toes, excluding great toe—		
through metatarso-phalangeal joint	256	246
part, with some loss of bone	130	125
3 toes, excluding great toe—		
through metatarso-phalangeal joint	287	272
part, with some loss of bone	179	174
4 toes, excluding great toe—		
through metatarso-phalangeal joint	411	391
part, with some loss of bone	179	174

SCHEDULE 3

TABLE 2

Gratuities Payable to Officers for Disablement Assessed at less than 20 per cent., not being a Minor Injury Specified in Table 1

Rank	Estimated duration of the disablement within the degree referred to								
	Temporary less than a year			Temporary more than a year			Indeterminate		
	Per cent.			Per cent.			Per cent.		
	1–5	6–14	15–19	1–5	6–14	15–19	1–5	6–14	15–19
	£	£	£	£	£	£	£	£	£
A.—Male Officers, and Women Officers under Article 1(35)(b).									
Air Vice-Marshal ...	45	99	172	88	197	344	265	590	1,032
Air Commodore ...	43	94	165	84	188	328	253	563	985
Group Captain	41	90	157	80	179	312	241	536	938
Wing Commander ...	39	87	151	78	173	302	233	518	906
Squadron Leader ...	38	84	146	75	167	291	225	500	875
Flight Lieutenant, Flying Officer, Pilot Officer or Acting Pilot Officer ...	36	79	138	71	158	275	213	473	828
B.—Women Officers (other than those under Article 1(35)(b)).									
Air Commandant, Group Officer. Member with status of Group Captain or above ...	38	84	146	75	167	291	225	500	875
Wing Officer. Member with status of Wing Commander	36	80	140	72	160	279	215	479	838
Squadron Officer. Member with status of Squadron Leader ...	35	77	135	69	154	268	207	461	807
Flying Officer, Pilot Officer, Acting Pilot Officer, Flight Officer, Section Officer, Assistant Section Officer. Member with status of Flying Officer or below	34	74	130	66	148	258	199	443	775

SCHEDULE 3

TABLE 3

PART I

GRATUITIES PAYABLE TO AIRMEN (AIRWOMEN) FOR DISABLEMENT ASSESSED AT LESS THAN 20 PER CENT., NOT BEING A MINOR INJURY SPECIFIED IN TABLE 1

Rank	Estimated duration of the disablement within the degree referred to								
	Temporary less than a year			Temporary more than a year			Indeterminate		
	Per cent.			Per cent.			Per cent.		
	1–5	6–14	15–19	1–5	6–14	15–19	1–5	6–14	15–19
	£	£	£	£	£	£	£	£	£
A.—Men									
Warrant Officer ...	33	72	126	65	144	252	194	432	756
Warrant Officer, 2nd Class	33	71	125	64	143	249	192	427	747
Flight Sergeant	32	71	123	63	141	246	190	422	738
Sergeant	32	70	122	63	139	243	188	417	730
Corporal	31	69	120	62	138	240	185	412	721
Leading or Senior Aircraftman and Aircraftman	31	68	119	61	136	237	183	407	712
B.—Women									
Member of a Voluntary Aid Detachment serving as an uncertificated Nurse, Grade I ...	33	71	125	64	143	249	192	427	747
Warrant Officer	32	70	123	63	140	245	189	420	735
Flight Sergeant	32	69	121	62	139	242	187	415	726
Sergeant	31	69	120	62	138	240	185	412	721
Corporal	31	69	120	61	137	239	184	410	717
Leading or Senior Aircraftwoman and Aircraftwoman	31	68	119	61	136	237	183	407	712

SCHEDULE 4

TABLE 1

YEARLY RATES OF PENSIONS FOR WIDOWS OF OFFICERS

A.—Pensions other than pensions awarded under Article 11(1) *of the* 1921 *Order*

Rank (1)	(2)	(3)
	£	£
Marshal of the Royal Air Force or Marshal of the Air ...	1069	1069
Air Chief Marshal	909	909
Air Marshal	809	809
Air Vice-Marshal	719	719
Air Commodore	659	659
Group Captain	599	599
Wing Commander	579	579
Squadron Leader	549	170
Flight Lieutenant	534	150
Flying (or Observer) Officer	519	130
Pilot Officer	} 519	130
Acting Pilot Officer		

B.—Pensions awarded under Article 11(1) *of the* 1921 *Order*

Rank (1)	(2)
	£
Marshal of the Air	1169
Air Chief Marshal	969
Air Marshal	869
Air Vice-Marshal	769
Air Commodore	689
Group Captain	609
Wing Commander	585
Squadron Leader	549
Flight Lieutenant	534
Flying (or Observer) Officer	519
Pilot Officer	519

TABLE 2

WEEKLY RATES OF PENSIONS FOR WIDOWS OF AIRMEN

Rank (or equivalent rank) (1)	(2)	(3)
	£	£
Warrant Officer or Airman, Class A	9·05	2·28
Warrant Officer, 2nd Class or Airman, Class B	9·00	2·23
Flight Sergeant or Airman, Class C	8·95	2·18
Sergeant or Airman, Class D	8·90	2·13
Corporal or Airman, Class E	8·85	2·08
Leading or Senior Aircraftman, Aircraftman or Airman, Class F	8·80	2·03

TABLE 3

MAXIMUM YEARLY RATES OF PENSIONS FOR RELATIVES OF 1914 WORLD WAR OFFICERS

Rank (1)	(2)	(3)
	£	£
Marshal of the Air	1169	1069
Air Chief Marshal	969	909
Air Marshal	869	809
Air Vice-Marshal	769	719
Air Commodore	669	659
	£	
Group Captain	599	
Wing Commander	579	
Squadron Leader	170	
Flight Lieutenant	150	
Flying (or Observer) Officer	130	
Pilot Officer	130	

SCHEDULE 6

RATES OF ALLOWANCES PAYABLE IN RESPECT OF DISABLEMENT

Description of Allowance	Rate	
	Officers and Nurses	Airmen (Airwomen)
1. Education allowance under Article 13 ...	£120·00 per annum (maximum)	£120·00 per annum (maximum)
2. Constant attendance allowance—		
(a) under the proviso to Article 14 ...	£468·00 per annum (maximum)	£9·00 per week (maximum)
(b) in any other case under that Article	£234·00 per annum (maximum)	£4·50 per week (maximum)
2A. Exceptionally severe disablement allowance under Article 14A ...	£234·00 per annum	£4·50 per week
3. Severe disablement occupational allowance under Article 15	£104·00 per annum	£2·00 per week
4. Allowance for wear and tear of clothing—		
(a) under Article 16(1)(a)	£12·00 per annum	£12·00 per annum
(b) under Article 16(1)(b) and 16(2) ...	£19·00 per annum	£19·00 per annum
5. Unemployability allowances—		
(a) personal allowance under Article 17(1)(i)	£382·20 per annum	£7·35 per week
(b) additional allowances for dependants by way of—		
(i) increase or further increase of allowance in respect of a wife, husband, or unmarried dependant living as a wife, under Article 17(4)(c)	£179·80 per annum (maximum)	£3·65 per week (maximum)
(ii) allowance in respect of an adult dependant under Article 17(4)(d)	£215·80 per annum (maximum)	£4·15 per week (maximum)
(iii) increased allowance under Article 17(4)(f)—		
(a) in respect of the child, or the elder or eldest of the children, of a member	£171·60 per annum	£3·30 per week
(b) in respect of the second child of a member	£124·80 per annum	£2·40 per week
(c) in respect of each other child of a member	£119·60 per annum	£2·30 per week
5A. Invalidity allowance under Article 17A—		
(a) if on the relevant date the member was under the age of 35, or if that date fell before 5th July 1948	£59·80 per annum	£1·15 per week
(b) if head (a) does not apply and on the relevant date the member was under the age of 45	£36·40 per annum	£0·70 per week
(c) if heads (a) and (b) do not apply, and on the relevant date the member was a man under the age of 60, or a woman under the age of 55 ...	£18·20 per annum	£0·35 per week
6. Comforts allowance—		
(a) under Article 18(1)(a)	£88·40 per annum	£1·70 per week
(b) under Article 18(1)(b)	£44·20 per annum	£0·85 per week
7. Allowance for lowered standard of occupation under Article 19	£232·96 per annum (maximum)	£4·48 per week (maximum)
8. Age allowance under Article 20 where the degree of pensioned disablement is—		
(a) 40 to 50 per cent.	£28·60 per annum	£0·55 per week

Description of Allowance	Rate	
	Officers and Nurses	Airmen (Airwomen)
(b) over 50 per cent. but not exceeding 70 per cent.	£41·60 per annum	£0·80 per week
(c) over 70 per cent. but not exceeding 90 per cent.	£59·80 per annum	£1·15 per week
(d) over 90 per cent.	£83·20 per annum	£1·60 per week
9. Treatment allowances—		
(a) increase of personal allowance under Article 21(2)	£83·20 per annum (maximum)	£1·60 per week (maximum)
(b) increase of personal allowance under Article 21(3)—		
(i) under sub-paragraph (a) ...	£6·75 per week	£6·75 per week
(ii) under sub-paragraph (c)—		
(a) if on the relevant date the member was under the age of 35 or if that date fell before 5th July 1948	£59·80 per annum	£1·15 per week
(b) if head (a) does not apply and on the relevant date the member was under the age of 45	£36·40 per annum	£0·70 per week
(c) if heads (a) and (b) do not apply and on the relevant date the member was a man under the age of 60, or a woman under the age of 55	£18·20 per annum	£0·35 per week
(c) increased additional allowance under Article 21(4) proviso (a)	£215·80 per annum	£4·15 per week
(d) increased additional allowance under Article 21(4) proviso (b)—		
(i) in respect of the child, or the elder or eldest of the children, of a member	£109·20 per annum	£2·10 per week
(ii) in respect of the second child of a member	£62·40 per annum	£1·20 per week
(iii) in respect of each other child of a member	£57·20 per annum	£1·10 per week
(e) higher rate of additional allowance under Article 21(4A)—		
(i) in respect of the child, or the elder or eldest of the children, of a member	£171·60 per annum	£3·30 per week
(ii) in respect of the second child of a member	£124·80 per annum	£2·40 per week
(iii) in respect of each other child of a member	£119·60 per annum	£2·30 per week
(f) additional allowance under Article 21(5)	£215·80 per annum	£4·15 per week
10. Part-time treatment allowance under Article 23	£4·75 per day (maximum)	£4·75 per day (maximum)

SCHEDULE 7

RATES OF PENSIONS, OTHER THAN WIDOWS' PENSIONS, AND ALLOWANCES
PAYABLE IN RESPECT OF DEATH

Description of Pension or Allowance	Rate	
	Officers and Nurses	Airmen (Airwomen)
1. Pension under Article 30 to unmarried dependant who lived as wife	£458·50 per annum (maximum)	£8·30 per week (maximum)
2. Rent allowance under Article 31 ...	£3·40 per week (maximum)	£3·40 per week (maximum)
3. Allowance under Article 32 to elderly widow or unmarried dependant who lived as wife—		
(a) if age 65 but under 70	£26·00 per annum	£0·50 per week
(b) if age 70 or over	£52·00 per annum	£1·00 per week
4. Pension to widower under Article 34 ...	£464·00 per annum (maximum)	£8·80 per week (maximum)
5. Allowances in respect of children— (a) under Article 35(1)— (i) in respect of the child, or the elder or eldest of the children, of a member	£190·10 per annum	£3·50 per week
(ii) in respect of each other child of a member— (a) where the child qualifies for a family allowance under the Family Allowances Act 1965 or under any legislation in Northern Ireland or the Isle of Man corresponding to that Act	£164·10 per annum	£3·00 per week
(b) where the child does not so qualify...	£182·30 per annum	£3·35 per week
(b) under Article 35(3)	£269·30 per annum (maximum)	where the child is 15 years of age or over —£5·00 per week (maximum)
6. Pension under Article 36 to a motherless or fatherless child— (a) in respect of the child, or the elder or eldest of the children, of a member, and in respect of each other child of a member who does not qualify for a family allowance as aforesaid ...	£269·30 per annum	(i) where the child is under 15 years of age— £3·50 per week (ii) where the child is 15 years of age or over— £5·00 per week
(b) in respect of each other child of a member who qualifies for a family allowance as aforesaid	£243·30 per annum	(i) where the child is under 15 years of age— £3·00 per week (ii) where the child is 15 years of age or over— £4·50 per week

Description of Pension or Allowance	Rate	
	Officers and Nurses	Airmen (Airwomen)
7. Pension or allowance under Article 37(3) to or in respect of a child over the age limit	£351·00 per annum (maximum)	£6·75 per week (maximum)
8. Education allowance under Article 38 ...	£120·00 per annum (maximum)	£120·00 per annum (maximum)
9. Pensions to parents— (a) minimum rate under Article 40(4) ...	£15·00 per annum	£0·25 per week
(b) under paragraphs (a) and (b) of Article 40(4)— (i) where there is only one eligible parent	£75·00 per annum (maximum)	£1·00 per week (maximum)
(ii) where there is more than one eligible parent	£100·00 per annum (maximum)	£1·38 per week (maximum)
(c) increase under the proviso to Article 40(4)	£20·00 per annum (maximum)	(i) where there is only one eligible parent— £0·38 per week (maximum) (ii) where there is more than one eligible parent— £0·62 per week (maximum)
(d) under paragraph (b) of Article 40(5)	—	£1·00 per week (maximum)
10. Pensions to other dependants— (a) under Article 41(2)	£54·00 per annum (maximum)	£1·00 per week (maximum)
(b) for each juvenile dependant under Article 41(3)	£26·00 per annum (maximum)	£0·30 per week (maximum)
(c) aggregate rate under Article 41(3) ...	£75·00 per annum (maximum)	£1·00 per week (maximum)

Part II

Amendment of Articles of the 1964 Order

1. In Article 5 (entitlement where a claim is made in respect of a disablement, or death occurs, more than 7 years after the termination of service) in paragraph (1) the words " and he was at the time of his death, or at any time previously thereto had been, in receipt of a pension awarded by the Minister under this Order or any previous Order " shall be omitted, and paragraph (6) is hereby revoked.

2. In Article 17 (unemployability allowances) in paragraph (2) for the words " £104 a year " there shall be substituted the words " £234 a year ".

3. In Article 21 (treatment allowances) for paragraph (4A) there shall be substituted the following paragraph: —

" (4A) The rate of an additional allowance awarded under paragraph (4) of this Article in respect of a child or children of a member may be further increased to the appropriate rate specified in Schedule 6 paragraph 9(*e*) if the member—

(*a*) is in receipt of an increase of his personal allowance under paragraph (3)(*c*) of this Article or, but for his age on the relevant date, would be in receipt of such an increase ; or

(*b*) is in receipt of an allowance under Article 17(1)(i) ; or

(*c*) having reached the age of 65 years or, in the case of a woman member, 60 years is not eligible for retirement pension under the National Insurance Acts 1965 to 1972, or any benefit similar thereto as is referred to in paragraph (6) of this Article, solely by reason of his failure to satisfy any contribution conditions.".

4. In Article 31 (rent allowance to widows, and unmarried dependants who lived as wives, who have children) in paragraph (1) for the words " having regard to the amount by which her weekly rent and rates exceed 6s." there shall be substituted the words " having regard to her weekly rent and rates ".

5. In Article 71 (commencement and application of this Order, amendment and revocation of previous Orders, and transitional provisions) at the end of paragraph (7) there shall be added the words " and as if any requirement thereof that the member had been at the time of his death in receipt of retired pay, pension or allowance in respect of disablement, was satisfied in every case.".

Part III

Substitution of Article 57 of the 1964 Order

For Article 57 (pensioners admitted to institutions) there shall be substituted the following Article: —

" 57. *Maintenance in hospital or an institution.*—(1) Where any person to or in respect of whom a pension or gratuity may be or has been awarded is receiving or has received free in-patient treatment, or is being or has been maintained in an institution (otherwise than for the purpose of undergoing medical or other treatment) which is supported wholly or partly out of public funds, or in which he is being or has been maintained pursuant to arrangements made by the Secretary of State, the Secretary of State may deduct such amount as he may think fit having regard to all the circumstances of the case from the pension or gratuity payable in respect of the period during which such treatment is received or during which the person is being so maintained, as the case may be, and may apply the amount so deducted, or any part thereof, in such proportions and subject to such conditions as he may determine having regard to all the circumstances of the case, in a payment or payments to the person upon his discharge following a period of free in-patient treatment, or in or towards paying or repaying the cost of maintaining the person incurred by any appropriate authority.

(2) For the purposes of this Article, a person shall be regarded as receiving or having received free in-patient treatment for any period for which he is or has been maintained free of charge while undergoing medical or other treatment as an in-patient—

(a) in a hospital or similar institution maintained or administered under the National Health Service Acts 1946 to 1968, the National Health Service (Scotland) Acts 1947 to 1968 or the Health Services Act (Northern Ireland) 1971, or by or on behalf of the Secretary of State, or by or on behalf of the Defence Council ; or

(b) pursuant to arrangements made by the Secretary of State or by a Hospital Board or a Regional Hospital Board constituted under the National Health Service Acts 1946 to 1968, the National Health Service (Scotland) Acts 1947 to 1968 or the Health Services Act (Northern Ireland) 1971 in a hospital or similar institution not so maintained or administered ;

and, for this purpose, a person shall only be regarded as not being maintained free of charge in a hospital or similar institution for any period if he is paying or has paid, in respect of his maintenance, charges which are designed to cover the whole cost of the accommodation or services (other than services by way of treatment) provided for him in the hospital or similar institution for that period.".

EXPLANATORY NOTE

(This Note is not part of the Order.)

This Order further amends the Order of 24th September 1964.

Article 1 substitutes new Tables for those contained in Schedules 2, 3, 4, 6 and 7 to the 1964 Order and has the effect of increasing—

Disablement pensions and allowances

(a) the rates of pensions in respect of 100 per cent. disablement by £62·00 a year in the case of officers and by £1·20 a week in the case of airmen and the rates of pensions for lower degrees of disablement and awards for cases of minor injuries and other cases of less than 20 per cent. disablement proportionately ;

(b) the maximum rates of disablement addition on a pension basis payable to certain officers in receipt of service retired pay by £62·00 a year ;

(c) the normal maximum rate of an allowance payable for constant attendance from £208·00 a year to £234·00 a year in the case of officers and from £4·00 a week to £4·50 a week in the case of airmen, and the maximum rate for exceptional cases of very severe disablement from £416·00 a year to £468·00 a year in the case of officers and from £8·00 a week to £9·00 a week in the case of airmen ;

(d) the exceptionally severe disablement allowance from £208·00 a year to £234·00 a year in the case of officers and from £4·00 a week to £4·50 a week in the case of airmen ;

(e) the allowance for unemployable pensioners from £340·60 a year to £382·20 a year in the case of officers and from £6·55 a week to £7·35 a week in the case of airmen ;

(f) the total additional allowance payable in respect of the wife or adult dependant of an unemployable pensioner and of a pensioner receiving treatment as defined in Article 21(8) from £192·40 a year to £215·80 a year in the case of officers and from £3·70 a week to £4·15 a week in the case of airmen ;

(g) the allowances payable in respect of children of unemployable pensioners in respect of the first or only child from £153·40 a year to £171·60 a year in the case of officers and from £2·95 a week to £3·30 a week in the case of airmen, in respect of the second child from £106·60 a year to £124·80 a year in the case of officers and from £2·05 a week to £2·40 a week in the case of airmen and in respect of any other child from £101·40 a year to £119·60 a year in the case of officers and from £1·95 a week to £2·30 a week in the case of airmen ;

(h) the maximum allowance for lowered standard of occupation from £208·00 a year to £232·96 a year in the case of officers and from £4·00 a week to £4·48 a week in the case of airmen ;

(i) the allowances payable to pensioners who have attained the age of 65 and whose pensioned disablement is assessed at 40 per cent. or over from between £26·00 a year and £72·80 a year to between £28·60 a year and £83·20 a year in the case of officers and from between £0·50 a week and £1·40 a week to between £0·55 a week and £1·60 a week in the case of airmen ;

(j) the allowances payable in respect of children of pensioners receiving treatment as defined in Article 21(8) in respect of the first or only child from £96·20 a year to £109·20 a year in the case of officers and from £1·85 a week to £2·10 a week in the case of airmen, in respect of the second child from £49·40 a year to £62·40 a year in the case of officers and from £0·95 a week to £1·20 a week in the case of airmen, and in respect of any other child from £44·20 a year to £57·20 a year in the case of officers and from £0·85 a week to £1·10 a week in the case of airmen, and to further increase those allowances where the said pensioners are not entitled to invalidity pension and allowance under national insurance provisions solely because of failure to satisfy the contribution conditions, to £171·60 a year ; £3·30 a week ; £124·80 a year ; £2·40 a week ; £119·60 a year and £2·30 a week respectively ;

(k) the maximum of the additional personal treatment allowance payable to a pensioner who is not entitled to full sickness benefit or invalidity pension and allowance under national insurance provisions from £6·00 a week to £6·75 a week ;

Widows' benefits

(l) the rates of pensions for certain widows by £52·00 a year in the case of officers and by £1·00 a week in the case of airmen ;

(m) the maximum pensions payable to unmarried dependants who lived as wives of deceased members of the air forces from £406·50 a year to £458·50 a year in the case of officers and from £7·30 a week to £8·30 a week in the case of airmen ;

(n) the maximum rent allowance payable to certain widows from £3·00 a week to £3·40 a week ;

(o) the allowances payable to widows in respect of children for the first or only child from £171·90 a year to £190·10 a year in the case of officers and from £3·15 a week to £3·50 a week in the case of airmen, and in respect of each other child from £145·90 a year to £164·10 a year in the case of officers and from £2·65 a week to £3·00 a week in the case of airmen, where the child qualifies for a family allowance, and from £164·10 a year to £182·30 a year in the case of officers and from £3·00 a week to £3·35 a week in the case of airmen where the child does not so qualify ;

Other benefits

(p) the maximum pensions payable to certain widowers from £412·00 a year to £464·00 a year in the case of officers and from £7·80 a week to £8·80 a week in the case of airmen ;

(q) the rates of pensions and allowances payable to or in respect of the children of deceased members of the air forces (such children having become motherless or having ceased to be under the control of their mothers) in respect of the first or only child or any other child who does not qualify for a family allowance from £251·10 a year to £269·30 a year in the case of children of officers and from £3·15 or £4·65 a week to £3·50 or £5·00 a week (according to the age of the child) in the case of children of airmen, and in respect of each other child who qualifies for a family allowance from £225·10 a year to £243·30 a year in the case of children of officers and from £2·65 or £4·15 a week to £3·00 or £4·50 a week (according to the age of the child) in the case of children of airmen ;

(r) the maximum rates of pensions payable to motherless or fatherless children who, having attained the age of 18 years, are incapable of self-support by reason of infirmity which arose before they attained the normal age limit for pension purposes, from £312·00 a year to £351·00 a year in the case of children of officers and from £6·00 a week to £6·75 a week in the case of children of airmen.

Article 2 makes amendments to the 1964 Order, the effects of which are :—

(*a*) to remove a restriction under which no award could be made in respect of the death of a member, occurring more than 7 years after the termination of his service, unless he had been in receipt of a pension in respect of disablement ;

(*b*) to raise the maximum amount of earnings which may be received by a member while deemed to be unemployable for the purposes of an award of unemployability allowance from £104 a year to £234 a year ;

(*c*) to enable the maximum rate of additional allowances payable in respect of the children of a member receiving treatment as defined in Article 21(8) to be awarded in cases where the member would not otherwise qualify for such an award solely by reason of his age, in cases where the member is in receipt of an unemployability allowance and in certain cases where the member is not eligible for retirement pension ;

(*d*) to enable the rate of rent allowance to be determined by reference to the amount of weekly rent and rates instead of as hitherto the amount by which the weekly rent and rates exceed 30p.

Article 3 extends the Secretary of State's discretionary power to make deductions from awards in respect of maintenance in an institution supported out of public funds to all cases where the pensioner is maintained free of charge in a National Health Service hospital or similar institution for the purpose of receiving treatment and provides for payments out of such deductions to be made to the pensioner for his resettlement following a period of such treatment.

BY THE QUEEN

A PROCLAMATION

ELIZABETH R.

Whereas by section 1 of the Emergency Powers Act 1920(**a**), as amended by the Emergency Powers Act 1964(**b**), it is enacted that if it appears to Us that there have occurred or are about to occur events of such a nature as to be calculated, by interfering with the supply and distribution of food, water, fuel or light, or with the means of locomotion, to deprive the community, or any substantial portion of the community, of the essentials of life, We may, by Proclamation, declare that a state of emegency exists:

And whereas the present stoppage of work among persons employed in the ports does, in Our opinion, constitute a state of emergency within the meaning of the said Act of 1920, as so amended:

Now, therefore, in pursuance of the said Act of 1920, as so amended, We do, by and with the advice of Our Privy Council, hereby declare that a state of emergency exists.

Given at Our Court at H.M. Yacht Britannia this third day of August in the year of our Lord nineteen hundred and seventy-two, and in the twenty-first year of Our Reign.

GOD SAVE THE QUEEN

(**a**) 1920 c. 55.   (**b**) 1964 c. 38.

Modifications to Legislation

Year and Number (or date)	Act or instrument	How affected
1853	London Hackney Carriage Act 1853 (c. 33)	ss. 7, 17(2) **am.**, 1972/1047
1855	Places of Worship Registration Act 1855 (c.81)	s. 5 **am.**, 1972/911
1882	Corn Returns Act 1882 (c. 37)	ss. 8, 9(6) **am.**, (E. and W.) 1972/1244; (S.) 1972/1274
Aug.	Solicitors' Remuneration O. 1883 (Rev. XXI, p. 205)	**r.**, 1972/1139
1887	Savings Banks Act 1887 (c. 40)	s. 10 **am.**, 1972/911
1896	Friendly Societies Act 1896 (c. 25)	ss. 97(1) **am.**, 1972/911 97(2) **r.** (S.) 1972/890; (E. and W.), 1972/911
1897 708	Judicial Trustee Rules 1897 (Rev. XII, p. 911)	**r.**, 1972/1096
1899 315	Judicial Trustees Act 1896—Addnl. Rule 1899 (Rev. XII, p. 922)	**r.**, 1972/1096
1900 332	Judicial Trustee Rule (April) 1900 (Rev. XII, p. 923)	**r.**, 1972/1096
1901 599	Merchant Shipping (Mercantile Marine Fund) Act 1898, sch. 2—Amdg. O. in C. 1901 (Rev. XIV, p. 676)	**r.**, 1972/456
1902 623	Felt Hats Manufacture involving use of inflammable Solvent — Regs. 1902 (Rev. VII, p. 316)	**r.** (21.6.73), 1972/917

Year and Number (or date)	Act or instrument	How affected
1906	Alkali, &c., Works Regulation Act 1906 (c. 14)	s. 27, sch. 1 **am.**, 1972/1330
1907 1020	Limited Partnerships Rules 1907 (Rev. XVII, p. 15)	**am.**, 1972/1040
1908 558	Merchant Shipping (Mercantile Marine Fund) Act 1898 sch. 2, alteration of exemptions—O. in C. 1908 (Rev. XIV, p. 678)	**r.**, 1972/456
1910 1180	Licensing Rules 1910 (Rev. XI, p. 10)	**am.**, 1972/44
1919 1108	Merchant Shipping Light dues, scale, rules and exemption—Amdg. O. in C. 1919 (Rev. XIV, p. 679)	**r.**, 1972/456
1925	Administration of Estates Act 1925 (c. 23)	s. 46(1) **am.**, 1972/916
2	Solicitors' Remuneration (Registered Land) O. 1925 (Rev. XXI, p. 221)	**r.**, 1972/1139
755	Solicitors' Remuneration Act General O. 1925 (Rev. XXI, p. 213)	**r.**, 1972/1139
1926 25 Feb.	Air Navigation (Investigation of Accidents) Regs., application to Jersey and Guernsey—O. in C. 1926 (Rev. I, p. 1320)	sch. Pt. II **r.**, 1972/962
1929 1048	Trustee Savings Bank Regs. 1929 (Rev. XX, p. 584)	**r.**, 1972/583
1933 1149	Savings Certificates Regs. 1933 (Rev. XV, p. 309)	**r.**, 1972/641
1934 990	Cellulose Solutions Regs. 1934 (Rev. VII, p. 241)	**am.**, 1972/917
1321	Public Service Vehicles (Drivers' and Conductors' Licences) Regs. 1934 (Rev. XX, p. 403)	**am.**, 1972/1061

Year and Number (or date)	Act or instrument	How affected
1935		
803	Merchant Shipping (Light Dues) O. 1935 (Rev. XIV, p. 680)	**r.,** 1972/456
1936		
326	Solicitors' Remuneration O. 1936 (Rev. XXI, p. 215)	**r.,** 1972/1139
327	Solicitors' Remuneration (Registered Land) O. 1936 (1936 II, p. 2513)	**r.,** 1972/1139
626	County Ct. Rules 1936 (1936 I, p. 282)	**am.,** 1972/208, 1156
1937		
785	Savings Certificates (Amdt.) Regs. 1937 (Rev. XV, p. 309)	**r.,** 1972/641
1938	Young Persons (Employment) Act 1938 (c. 69)	s. 5 **am.,** 1972/911
1939	House of Commons Members' Fund Act 1939 (c. 49)	sch. 1 **am.,** 1972/1181
1940		
1998	Land Charges Rules 1940 (Rev. XI, p. 812)	**r.,** 1972/50
2195	Land Charges (No. 2) Rules 1940 (Rev. XI, p. 813)	**r.,** 1972/50
1943		
683	Welsh Cts. (Oaths and Interpreters) Rules 1943 (Rev. XVI, p. 1107)	**am.,** 1972/97
1944	Education Act 1944 (c. 31)	s. 35 **am.,** 1972/444 s. 94(1) **am.,** 1972/911
203	Solicitors' Remuneration O. 1944 (Rev. XXI, p. 217)	**r.,** 1972/1139
1946		
2105	Is. of Scilly (Housing) O. 1946 (Rev. XII, p. 572)	**r.,** 1972/1204
1947	Exchange Control Act 1947 (c. 14) ...	sch. 1 **am.,** 1972/386, 930
1	Statutory Instruments Regs. 1947 (Rev. XXI, p. 498)	**am.,** 1972/1205
1659	Police Grant (S.) O. 1947 (Rev. XVIII, p. 189)	**am.,** 1972/24

Year and Number (or date)	Act or instrument	How affected
1948	Companies Act 1948 (c. 38)	ss. 92(2)(*h*), 102A(2)(*d*) **am.**, 1972/1268
	Industrial Assurance and Friendly Societies Act 1948 (c. 39)	sch. 1 para. 7 **am.**, 1972/911
1259	National Health Service (Medical and Pharmaceutical Service Ctees. and Tribunal (S.) Regs. 1948 (Rev. XV, p. 887)	**am.**, 1972/827
1261	National Insurance (Widow's Benefit and Retirement Pensions) Regs. 1948 (Rev. XVI, p. 207)	**r.**, 1972/606
1274	National Insurance and Industrial Injuries (Collection of Contributions) Regs. 1948 (Rev. XVI, p. 148)	**am.**, 1972/1287
1390	National Health Service (Appointment of Medical and Dental Officers) (S.) Regs. 1948 (Rev. XV, p. 854)	**r.**, 1972/467
1411	Civil Aviation (Births, Deaths and Missing Persons) Regs. 1948 (Rev. I, p. 1302)	**am.**, 1972/323
1425	National Insurance (Classification) Regs. 1948 (Rev. XVI, p. 95)	**r.**, 1972/555
1451	National Health Service (Tribunal for Supplementary Ophthalmic Services) (S.) Regs. 1948 (Rev. XV, p. 975)	**r.**, 1972/827
1452	National Health Service (Joint Ophthalmic Services Ctees.) (S.) O. 1948 (Rev. XV, p. 977)	**r.**, 1972/828
1470	National Insurance (Married Women) Regs. 1948 (Rev. XVI, p. 123)	**am.**, 1972/1150
1471	National Insurance (Industrial Injuries) (Mariners) Regs. 1948 (Rev. XVI, p. 432)	**am.**, 1972/1276
2573	Falkland Is. (Legislative Council) O. in C. 1948 (Rev. VII, p. 591)	**am.**, 1972/668
2711	National Insurance (Overlapping Benefits) Regs. 1948 (Rev. XVI, p. 196)	**r.**, 1972/604
1949	Marriage Act 1949 (c. 76)	ss. 27(6), 32(5), 41(6), 51, 57(4), 63(1), 64(2), 65(2) **am.**, 1972/911
86	National Insurance (Classification) Amdt. Regs. 1949 (1949 I, p. 2705)	**r.**, 1972/555
507	Compulsory Purchase of Land Regs. 1949 (1949 I, p. 2379)	**r.**, 1972/1313

Year and Number (or date)	Act or instrument	How affected
1949		
790	Gas (Meter) Regs. 1949 (1949 I, p. 1985)	**am.,** 1972/695
1461	National Insurance (Hospital In-Patients) Regs. 1949 (1949 I, p. 2718)	**r.,** 1972/603
1518	National Insurance (Classification) Amdt. (No. 2) Regs. 1949 (1949 I, p. 2706)	**r.,** 1972/555
1950	Shops Act 1950 (c. 28)	s. 35 **am.,** 1972/911
765	National Insurance (Classification) Amdt. (No. 2) Regs. 1950 (1950 II, p. 10)	**r.,** 1972/555
830	National Insurance (Classification) Amdt. (No. 3) Regs. 1950 (1950 II, p. 12)	**r.,** 1972/555
862	Defence (Finance) Regs. 1939 reg. 2A, applying to Hong Kong—Treas. Direction 1950 (1950 III, p. 415)	**r.,** 1972/982
1951		
165	National Health Service (Joint Ophthalmic Services Ctees. (S.) Amdt. O. 1951 (1951 I, p. 1420)	**r.,** 1972/828
353	National Health Service (Joint Ophthalmic Service Ctees.) (S.) Amdt. (No. 2) O. 1951 (1951 I, p. 1423)	**r.,** 1972/828
993	National Insurance (Classification) Amdt. Regs. 1951 (1951 I, p. 1454)	**r.,** 1972/555
1232	National Insurance (Increase of Benefit, Re-entry into Regular Employment and Miscellaneous Provns.) Regs. 1951 (1951 I, p. 1457)	**am.,** 1972/603, 604, 606
1952		
422	National Insurance (Overlapping Benefits) Amdt. Regs. 1952 (1952 II, p. 2194)	**r.,** 1972/604
494	National Insurance (Classification) Amdt. Regs. 1952 (1952 II, p. 2136)	**r.,** 1972/555
526	National Insurance (Overlapping Benefits) Amdt. (No. 2) Regs. (1952 II, p. 2196)	**r.,** 1972/604
559	Public Rights of Way (Applications to Quarter Sessions) Regs. 1952 (1952 II, p. 2318)	**am.,** 1972/93

Year and Number (or date)	Act or instrument	How affected
1952		
1024	National Insurance (Classification) Amdt. (No. 2) Regs. 1952 (1952 II, p. 2137)	**r.,** 1972/555
1046	Licensing of Bulls (S.) Regs. 1952 (1952 I, p. 158)	**r.,** 1972/1309
1432	Detention Centre Rules 1952 (1952 I, p. 787)	**am.,** 1972/1012
1454	National Insurance (Classification) Amdt. (No. 3) Regs. 1952 (1952 II, p. 2139)	**r.,** 1972/555
2113	Bankruptcy Rules 1952 (1952 I, p. 213)	**am.,** 1972/529
2144	National Insurance (Increase of Benefit and Miscellaneous Provns.) Regs. 1952 (1952 II, p. 2154)	**am.,** 1972/606
2179	National Insurance (Hospitals In-Patients) Amdt. Regs. 1952 (1952 II, p. 2147)	**r.,** 1972/603
1953	Births and Deaths Registration Act 1953 (c. 20)	ss. 13(2), 30(2), 31(2), 32, 33(1) **am.,** 1972/911
	Marshall Aid Commemoration Act 1953 (c. 39)	s. 1 **am.,** 1972/961
117	Solicitors' Remuneration O. 1953 (1953 II, p. 1946)	**r.,** 1972/1139
118	Solicitors' Remuneration (Registered Land) O. 1953 (II, p. 1951)	**r.,** 1972/1139
392	Merchant Shipping (Light Dues) O. 1953 (1953 I, p. 1065)	**r.,** 1972/456
756	National Insurance (Overlapping Benefits) Amdt. Regs. 1953 (1953 I, p. 1367)	**r.,** 1972/604
979	National Insurance (Widow's Benefit and Retirement Pensions) Amdt. Regs. 1953 (1953 I, p. 1368)	**r.,** 1972/606
1954		
189	National Insurance (Maternity Benefit and Miscellaneous Provns.) Regs. 1954 (1954 I, p. 1387)	**am.,** 1972/604
585	National Insurance (Classification) Amdt. Regs. 1954 (1954 I, p. 1407)	**r.,** 1972/555
853	Importation of Carcases and Animal Products O. 1954 (1954 I, p. 136)	**r.,** 1972/287
898	British Transport Commission (Male Wages Grades Pensions) Regs. 1954 (1954 I, p. 175)	**am.,** 1972/51

Year and Number (or date)	Act or instrument	How affected
1955		
255	Ironstone Restoration Fund (Standard Rate) O. 1955 (1955 I, p. 1183)	**r.,** 1971/211
493	National Insurance (Increase of Benefit and Miscellaneous Provns.) Regs. 1955 (1955 II, p. 1586)	**am.,** 1972/606
1363	Road Vehicles Lighting (Standing Vehicles) (Exemption) (London) Regs. 1955 (1955 II, p. 2324)	**r.,** 1972/557
1956		
142	Agricultural Goods and Services Scheme (E. and W.) O. 1956 (1956 I, p. 134)	**r.,** 1972/704
162	Rules of Procedure (Army) 1956 (1956 I, p. 213)	**r.,** 1972/316
163	Rules of Procedure (Air Force) 1956 (1956 II, p. 2020)	**r.,** 1972/419
580	Certificates of Arrest and Surrender of Deserters and Absentees (Air Force) Regs. 1956 (1956 II, p. 2172)	**r.,** 1972/286
630	Bd. of Inquiry (Army) Rules 1956 (1956 I, p. 207)	**am.,** 1972/847
657	Certificates of Arrest and Surrender of Deserters and Absentees (Army) Regs. 1956 (1956 I, p. 363)	**r.,** 1972/318
741	Road Vehicles Lighting (Standing Vehicles) (Exemption) (General) Regs. 1956 (1956 II, p. 2007)	**r.,** 1972/557
894	Schools (S.) Code 1956 (1956 I, p. 735)	**am.,** 1972/776
1066	Trustee Savings Banks (Amdt.) Regs. 1956 (1956 II, p. 2194)	**r.,** 1972/583
1136	Savings Certificates (Amdt.) (No. 2) Regs. 1956 (1956 I, p. 1503)	**r.,** 1972/641
1179	Trustee Savings Banks (Amdt.) (No. 2) Regs. 1956 (1956 II, p. 2195)	**r.,** 1972/583
1199	National Insurance (Widow's Benefit and Miscellaneous Provns.) Regs. 1956 (1956 I, p. 1625)	**am.,** 1972/606
1403	Distress for Rates O. 1956 (1956 I, p. 687)	**r.,** 1972/820
1655	Registration of Restrictive Trading Agreements (Fees) Regs. 1956 (1956 II, p. 1988)	**r.,** 1972/196
1657	Premium Savings Bonds Regs. 1956 (1956 I, p. 1489)	**r.,** 1972/765
1827	Premium Savings Bonds (Channel Is.) Regs. 1956 (1956 I, p. 1501)	**r.,** 1972/765

Year and Number (or date)	Act or instrument	How affected
1956		
2050	Premium Savings Bonds (Is. of Man) Regs. 1956 (1956 I, p. 1502)	**r.,** 1972/765
1957		
223	Increase of Pensions (India, Pakistan and Burma) Rules 1957 (1957 II, p. 1821)	**superseded,** 1972/990
488	National Health Service (Designation of London Teaching Hospitals) O. 1957 (1957 I, p. 1452)	**am.,** 1972/60, 474, 475
1309	National Insurance (Widow's Benefit and Retirement Pensions) Amdt. Regs. 1957 (1957 I, p. 1615)	**r.,** 1972/606
1542	Agricultural Goods and Services Scheme (E. and W.) (Amdt.) O. 1957 (1957 I, p. 99)	**r.,** 1972/704
1733	Premium Savings Bonds (Amdt.) Regs. 1957 (1957 I, p. 1449)	**r.,** 1972/765
1734	Savings Certificates (Amdt.) Regs. 1957 (1957 I, p. 1450)	**r.,** 1972/641
1835	National Insurance (Child's Special Allowance) Regs. 1957 (1957 I, p. 1523)	**am.,** 1972/603, 604
1849	National Insurance (Hospital In-Patients) Amdt. Regs. 1957 (1957 I, p. 1546)	**r.,** 1972/603
1889	National Insurance (Overlapping Benefits) Amdt. Regs. 1957 (1957 I, p. 1603)	**r.,** 1972/604
1949	National Insurance (Widow's Benefit and Retirement Pensions) Amdt. (No. 2) Regs. 1957 (1957 I, p. 1620)	**r.,** 1972/606
2077	National Insurance (Increase of Benefit and Misc. Provns.) Regs. 1957 (1957 I, p. 1556)	**am.,** 1972/603, 604, 606
2175	National Insurance (Classification) Amdt. Regs. 1957 (1957 I, p. 1623)	**r.,** 1972/555
2225	Naval Cts.-Martial (Procedure) O. 1957 (1957 II, p. 2198)	**am.,** 1972/966
1958		
473	Public Service Vehicles (Conditions of Fitness) Regs. 1958 (1958 II, p. 2014)	**r.,** 1972/751
519	Independent Schools Tribunal Rules 1958 (1958 I, p. 1006)	**am.,** 1972/42
561	Certificate of Arrest and Surrender of Deserters and Absentees (Navy) Regs. 1958 (1958 II, p. 2121)	**r.,** 1972/430

Year and Number (or date)	Act or instrument	How affected
1958		
926	Public Service Vehicles (Equipment and and Use) Regs. 1958 (1958 II, p. 2036)	**r.,** 1972/751
1172	Agriculture Goods and Services Scheme (E. and W.) (Amdt.) O. 1958 (1958, I, p. 100)	**r.,** 1972/704
1208	Control of Borrowing (Amdt.) O. 1958 (1958 I, p. 203)	**am.,** 1972/1218
1220	Thermal Insulation (Industrial Build-ings) Regs. 1958 (1958 I, p. 1130)	**r.,** 1972/87
1959	County Cts. Act 1959 (c. 22)	s. 148(1)(3) **am.,** 1972/1103
81	Agricultural Land Tribunals and Notices to Quit O. 1959 (1959 I, p. 91)	**am.,** 1972/1207
82	Agricultural (Control of Notices to Quit) (Service Men) O., 1959 (1959 I, p. 121)	**r.,** 1972/1207
382	Public Services Vehicles (Conditions of Fitness) (Amdt.) Regs. 1959 (1959 II, p. 2236)	**r.,** 1972/751
467	National Insurance (Industrial Injuries) (Prescribed Diseases) Regs. 1959 (1959 II, p. 1943)	**am.,** 1972/910, 1258
890	Standards for School Premises Regs. 1959 (1959 I, p. 1006)	**am.,** 1972/1255
1290	National Insurance (Overlapping Bene-fits) Amdt. Regs. 1959 (1959 II, p. 1873)	**r.,** 1972/604
1341	Agricultural Goods and Services Scheme (E. and W.) (Amdt.) O. 1959 (1959 I, p. 130)	**r.,** 1972/704
1507	Welsh Cts. (Interpreters) Rules 1959 (1959 II, p. 2575)	**superseded,** 1972/97
1542	Increase of Pensions (India, Pakistan and Burma) Regs. 1959 (1959 II, p. 2060)	**superseded,** 1972/990
1861	National Insurance (Non-participation —Benefits and Schemes) Regs. 1959 (1959 II, p. 1865)	**am.,** 1972/428, 1031
2255	Commissioners for Oaths (Fees) O. 1959 (1959 II, p. 1977)	**r.,** 1972/1188
1960	Road Traffic Act 1960 (c. 16) ...	ss. 127, 134, 144 **mod.,** 1972/341
	Local Employment Act 1960 (c. 18)	s. 19(2) **am.,** 1972/903, 996

Year and Number (or date)	Act or instrument	How affected
1960		
250	Cycle Racing on Highways Regs. 1960 (1960 III, p. 3047)	**am.**, 1972/336
579	Improvement of Livestock (Licensing of Bulls) (S.) Amdt. Regs. 1960 (1960 I, p. 184)	**r.**, 1972/1309
827	National Insurance (Classification Amdt. Regs. 1960 (1960 II, p. 2208)	**r.**, 1972/555
1210	National Insurance (Graduated Contributions and Non-participating Employments—Miscellaneous Provns.) Regs. 1960 (1960 II, p. 2234)	**am.**, 1972/555, 606.
1238	Agricultural Goods and Services Scheme (E. and W.) (Amdt.) O. 1960 (1960 I, p. 105)	**r.**, 1972/704
1283	National Insurance (Hospital In-Patients) Amdt. Regs. 1960 (1960 II, p. 2163)	**r.**, 1972/603
1306	Premium Savings Bonds (Amdt.) Regs. 1960 (1960 I, p. 409)	**r.**, 1972/765
1981	Savings Certificates (Amdt.) (No. 2) Regs. 1960 (1960 I, p. 414)	**r.**, 1972/641
1982	Premium Savings Bonds (Amdt.) (No. 2) Regs. 1960 (1960 I, p. 411)	**r.**, 1972/765
2094	Importation of Carcases and Animal Products (Amdt.) O. 1960 (1960 I, p. 298)	**r.**, 1972/287
2335	Trustee Savings Banks (Amdt.) Regs. 1960 (1960 III, p. 3065)	**r.**, 1972/583
2422	National Insurance (Increase of Benefit and Miscellaneous Provns.) Regs. 1960 (1960 II, p. 2169)	**am.**, 1972/606
1961	Diplomatic Immunities (Conferences with Commonwealth Countries and the Republic of Ireland) Act 1961 (c. 11)	s. 1 **am.**, 1972/114
	Factories Act 1961 (c. 34)	s. 178(1) **am.**, 1972/911
136	Is. of Scilly (Housing) O. 1961 ...	**r.**, 1972/1204
329	Importation of Carcases and Animal Products (Amdt.) O. 1961	**r.**, 1972/287
420	National Insurance (Classification) Amdt. Regs. 1961	**r.**, 1972/555
557	National Insurance (Graduated Retirement Benefit and Consequential Provns.) Regs. 1961	**am.**, 1972/604
1198	International Tin Council (Immunities and Privileges) O. 1961	**r.**, 1972/120

Year and Number (or date)	Act or instrument	How affected
1961		
1441	National Health Service (Superannuation) Regs. 1961	**am.**, 1972/1339
1528	Savings Certificates (Amdt.) Regs. 1961	**r.**, 1972/641
1837	Certificates of Arrest and Surrender of Deserters and Absentees (Air Force) (Amdt.) Regs. 1961	**r.**, 1972/286
2009	Certificates of Arrest and Surrender of Deserters and Absentees (Army) (Amdt.) Regs. 1961	**r.**, 1972/318
2152	Rules of Procedure (Air Force) (Amdt.) Rules 1961	**r.**, 1972/419
2163	Improvement of Livestock (Licensing of Bulls) (S.) Amdt. Regs. 1961	**r.**, 1972/1309
2223	Rules of Procedure (Army) (Amdt.) Rules 1961	**r.**, 1972/316
2316	Colonial Air Navigation O. 1961 ...	**am.**, 1972/445
2414	Trustee Savings Banks (Amdt.) Regs. 1961	**r.**, 1972/583
1962		
	Education (S.) Act 1962 (c. 47) ...	s. 32(1) **am.**, 1972/59
12	National Insurance (Consequential Provns.) Regs. 1962	**am.**, 1972/604, 606
163	Judicial Trustee (Amdt.) Rules 1962 ...	**r.**, 1972/1096
864	Superannuation (Teaching and N.I. Civil Service) Interchange (S.) Rules 1962	**r.**, 1972/532
2466	Parochial Fees O. 1962	**r.**, 1972/177
1963	British Museum Act 1963 (c. 24) ...	sch. 3 Pt. I **am.**, 1972/653
394	National Insurance (Increase of Benefit and Miscellaneous Provns.) Regs. 1963	**am.**, 1972/606
881	Increase of Pensions (India, Pakistan and Burma) Regs. 1963	**superseded**, 1972/990
911	Importation of Carcases and Animal Products (Amdt.) O. 1963	**r.**, 1972/287
936	Savings Certificates (Amdt.) (No. 2) Regs. 1963	**r.**, 1972/641
1101	Sugar (Distribution Payments and Re-payments) Regs. 1963	**r.**, 1972/69
1571	Milk (Special Designation) Regs. 1963	**am.**, 1972/1117
1665	Public Service Vehicles (Conditions of Fitness) (Amdt.) Regs. 1963	**r.**, 1972/751
1710	Weights and Measures Regs. 1963 ...	**am.**, 1972/767
1713	Diseases of Animals (Misc. Fees) O. 1963	**r.**, 1972/863
1722	Is. of Scilly (Housing) (Amdt.) O. 1963	**r.**, 1972/1204

Year and Number (or date)	Act or instrument	How affected
1964		
22	National Health Service (Joint Ophthalmic Services Ctees.) (S.) Amdt. O. 1964	**r.**, 1972/828
64	Diseases of Animals (Misc. Fees) O. 1964	**r.**, 1972/863
73	National Insurance (Industrial Injuries) (Claims and Payments) Regs. 1964	**am.**, 1972/375, 1231
122	Improvement of Livestock (Licensing of Bulls) (S.) Amdt. Regs. 1964	**r.**, 1972/1309
297	National Insurance (Widow's Benefit and Miscellaneous Provns.) Regs. 1964	**am.**, 1972/603, 604, 606
489	Defence (Transfer of Functions) (No. 2) O. 1964	**am.**, 1972/316, 419
504	National Insurance (Industrial Injuries) (Benefit) Regs. 1964	**am.**, 1972/393, 1231
690	Copyright (International Conventions) O. 1964	**r.**, 1972/673
706	Agriculture (Notices to Remedy and Notices to Quit) O. 1964	**am.**, 1972/1207
1006	Rules of Procedure (Army) (Amdt.) Rules 1964	**r.**, 1972/316
1089	Importation of Carcases and Animal Products (Amdt.) O. 1964	**r.**, 1972/287
1150	Tuberculosis (Compensation) O. 1964	**am.**, 1972/814
1152	Tuberculosis (Compensation) (S.) O. 1964	**am.**, 1972/825
1194	Copyright (International Conventions) (Amdt.) O. 1964	**r.**, 1972/673
1282	Rules of Procedure (Air Forces) (Amdt.) Rules 1964	**r.**, 1972/419
1454	National Health Service (Appointment of Medical and Dental Officers) (S.) Amdt. Regs. 1964	**r.**, 1972/467
1651	Copyright (International Conventions) (Amdt. No. 2) O. 1964	**r.**, 1972/673
1854	Rules of Procedure (Air Force) (Second Amdt.) Rules 1964	**r.**, 1972/419
1864	Rules of Procedure (Army) (Second Amdt.) Rules 1964	**r.**, 1972/316
2001	National Insurance (Widow's Benefit and Consequential Provns.) Regs. 1964	**r.**, 1972/606
2007	Pensions (Polish Forces) Scheme 1964	**am.**, 1972/95
2077	Personal Injuries (Civilians) Scheme 1964	**am.**, 1972/1177

Year and Number (or date)	Act or instrument	How affected
1965	National Insurance Act 1965 (c. 51) ...	s. 49(4) **am.**, 1972/166, 91(2) **am.**, 1972/911
	Coal Industry Act 1965 (c. 82) ...	s. 1(4) **am.**, 1972/469
40	National Insurance (Increase of Benefit and Miscellaneous Provns.) Regs. 1965	**am.**, 1972/606
321	A.S. (Rules of Ct., consolidation and amdt.) 1965	**am.**, 1972/164
478	Alkali, &c., Works (S.) O. 1965 ...	**r.**, 1972/1330
516	Income Tax (Employments) Regs. 1965	**am.**, 1972/552, 1186
573	Trustee Savings Banks (Amdt.) Regs. 1965	**r.**, 1972/583
577	Fire Services (Appointments and Promotion) Regs. 1965	**am.**, 1972/932
722	Probation (Conditions of Service) Rules 1965	**am.**, 1972/803
723	Probation Rules 1965	**am.**, 1972/1208
1046	Merchant Shipping (Pilot Ladders) Rules 1965	**am.**, 1972/531
1050	Purchase Tax Regs. 1965	**am.**, 1972/1146
1067	Merchant Shipping (Dangerous Goods) Rules 1965	**am.**, 1972/666
1157	Industrial Tribunals (S.) Regs. 1965 ...	**am.**, 1972/638
1303	Copyright (International Conventions) (Amdt.) O. 1965	**r.**, 1972/673
1373	Building Regs. 1965	**r.**, 1972/317
1467	Common Investment Funds Scheme 1965	**am.**, 1972/528
1500	County Ct. Funds Rules 1965 ...	**am.**, 1972/334
1776	Rules of the Supreme Ct. 1965 ...	**am.**, 1972/813, 1194
1857	Copyright (International Conventions) (Amdt. No. 2) O. 1965	**r.**, 1972/673
1860	Cayman Is. (Constitution) O. 1965 ...	**r.**, 1972/1101
2043	Rent Book (Forms of Notice) (S.) Regs. 1965	**r.**, 1972/1333
2159	Copyright (International Conventions) (Amdt. No. 3) O. 1965	**r.**, 1972/673
1966	Rating Act 1966 (c. 9)	s. 7(4) **am.**, 1972/112
	Ministry of Social Security Act 1966 (c. 20)	sch. 2 Pt. II paras. 9, 10 **replaced**, 12A **am.** (4.6.73), 12B **inserted**, 17 **am.**, 1972/1145
37	Importation of Carcases and Animal Products (Amdt.) O. 1966	**r.**, 1972/287
164	Pneumoconiosis, Byssinosis and Misc. Diseases Benefit Scheme 1966	**am.**, 1972/1289

Year and Number (or date)	Act or instrument	How affected
1966		
165	Workmen's Compensation (Supplementation) Scheme 1966	am., 1972/1288
216	Savings Certificates (Amdt.) Regs. 1966	r., 1972/641
253	Housing (Prescribed Forms) Regs. 1966	r., 1972/253
446	Increase of Pensions (India, Pakistan and Burma) Regs. 1966	superseded, 1972/990
579	Local Land Charges Rules 1966 ...	am., 1972/690
667	Origin of Goods (Republic of Ireland) Regs. 1966	am., 1972/338
675	Public Service Vehicles (Conditions of Fitness) (Amdt.) Regs. 1966	r., 1972/751
676	Public Service Vehicles (Equipment and Use) (Amdt.) Regs. 1966	r., 1972/751
684	Copyright (International Conventions) (Amdt.) O. 1966	r., 1972/673
689	Air Navigation (Guernsey) O. 1966 ...	r., 1972/453
690	Air Navigation (Jersey) O. 1966 ...	r., 1972/452
727	Post Office Savings Bank Regs. 1966...	r., 1972/764
728	Improvement of Livestock (Licensing of Bulls) (S.) Amdt. Regs. 1966	r., 1972/1309
916	Air Navigation (General) (Guernsey) Regs. 1966	r., 1972/486
917	Air Navigation (General) (Jersey) Regs. 1966	r., 1972/487
945	Copyright (Gibraltar: Protection of Foreign Broadcasts) O. 1966	r., 1972/673
959	National Insurance (Earnings-related Benefit) Regs. 1966	am., 1972/909
970	National Insurance (Overlapping Benefits and Hospital In-Patients) Amdt. Regs. 1966	r., 1972/603, 604
1006	National Insurance and Industrial Injuries (Misc. and Consequential Provisions) Regs. 1966	am., 1972/166, 1301
1065	Supplementary Benefit (General) Regs. 1966	am., 1972/330
1144	Building (Second Amdt.) Regs. 1966...	r., 1972/317
1185	Copyright (International Conventions) (Amdt. No. 2) O. 1966	r., 1972/673
1409	Copyright (International Conventions) (Amdt. No. 3) O. 1966	r., 1972/673
1449	National Health Service (General Dental Services) (S.) Regs. 1966	am., 1972/96, 1348
1967	General Rate Act 1967 (c. 9)	sch. 9 paras. 12, 13 am., 1972/81
	Road Traffic Regulation Act 1967 (c. 76)	s. 81 mod., 1972/540

Year and Number (or date)	Act or instrument	How affected
1967		
46	Rules of Procedure (Army) (Amdt.) Rules 1967	**r.**, 1972/316
62	Rules of Procedure (Air Force) (Amdt.) Rules 1967	**r.**, 1972/419
172	Merchant Shipping (Tonnage) Regs. 1967	**am.**, 1972/656
225	Antigua Constitution O. 1967... ...	**am.**, 1972/301
293	Pensions (Polish Forces) Scheme (Extension) O. 1967	**superseded,** 1972/95
313	Industrial Tribunals (Dock Work) Regs. 1967	**r.** (saving), 1972/38
314	Industrial Tribunals (Dock Work) (S.) Regs. 1967	**r.** (saving), 1972/39
330	National Insurance (Unemployment and Sickness Benefit) Regs. 1967	**am.**, 1972/166, 1301
359	Industrial Tribunals (Redundancy Payments) Regs. 1967	**r.** (saving), 1972/38
360	Industrial Tribunals (Redundancy Payments) (S.) Regs. 1967	**r.** (saving), 1972/39
361	Industrial Tribunals (Employment and Compensation) Regs. 1967	**r.** (saving), 1972/38
362	Industrial Tribunals (Employment and Compensation) (S.) O. 1967	**r.** (saving), 1972/39
385	Food (Control of Irradiation) Regs. 1967	**am.**, 1972/205
386	National Insurance (Mariners) Regs. 1967	**am.**, 1972/1300
388	Food (Control of Irradiation) (S.) Regs. 1967	**am.**, 1972/307
489	Teachers' Superannuation Regs. 1967	**am.**, 1972/1092
512	New Street Byelaws (Ext. of Operation) O. 1967	**superseded,** 1972/595
562	National Insurance (Overlapping Benefits) Amdt. Regs. 1967	**r.**, 1972/604
606	Importation of Carcases and Animal Products (Amdt.) O. 1967	**r.**, 1972/287
709	Oil in Navigable Waters (Prohibited Sea Areas) O. 1967	**am.**, 1972/676
715	Rate Support Grant (S.) Regs. 1967 ...	**am.**, 1972/1090
743	Rules of Procedure (Army) (Second Amdt.) Rules 1967	**r.**, 1972/316
844	National Insurance (Assessment of Graduated Contributions) Regs. 1967	**am.**, 1972/235, 1259
846	Parliamentary Commissioner's Pension Regs. 1967	**am.**, 1972/494
877	Copyright (International Conventions) (Amdt.) O. 1967	**r.**, 1972/673

Year and Number (or date)	Act or instrument	How affected
1967		
937	National Health Service (General Dental Services) Regs. 1967	**am.,** 1972/82, 1336
970	Cayman Is. (Constitution) (Amdt.) O. 1967	**r.,** 1972/1101
976	Carriage by Air (Parties to Convention) O. 1967	**superseded,** 1972/970
1018	Army Terms of Service Regs. 1967 ...	**am.,** 1972/517
1021	Police (Discipline) (S.) Regs. 1967 ...	**am.,** 1972/777
1151	Copyright (International Conventions) (Amdt. No. 2) O. 1967	**r.,** 1972/673
1163	Electricity Bds. (Standard Amount) (S.) O. 1967	**r.,** 1972/1138
1175	British Railways Bd. (Amdt. of Certified Amount) (S.) O. 1967	**superseded,** 1972/1237
1265	National Insurance (Increase of Benefit and Miscellaneous Provns.) Regs. 1967	**am.,** 1972/606
1269	Public Service Vehicles (Conditions of Fitness) (Amdt.) Regs. 1967	**r.,** 1972/751
1466	Rules of Procedure (Air Force) (Second Amdt.) Rules 1967	**r.,** 1972/419
1469	Rules of Procedure (Army) (Third Amdt.) Rules 1967	**r.,** 1972/316
1570	National Insurance (Determination of Claims and Questions) (No. 2) Regs. 1967	**am.,** 1972/166, 1301
1572	Family Allowances (Determination of Claims and Questions) (No. 2) Regs. 1967	**am.,** 1972/167
1645	Building (Third Amdt.) Regs. 1967 ...	**r.,** 1972/317
1725	Merchant Shipping (Limitation of Liability) (Sterling Equivalents) O. 1967	**r.,** 1972/734
1767	Exchange Control (Scheduled Territories) O. 1967	**r.,** 1972/386
1793	Importation of Carcases and Animal Products (Amdt.) (No. 2) O. 1967	**r.,** 1972/287
1805	Importation of Carcases and Animal Products (Amdt.) (No. 3) O. 1967	**r.,** 1972/287
1821	Royal Navy Terms of Service Regs. 1967	**am.,** 1972/558
1842	Rules of Procedure (Army) (Fourth Amdt.) Rules 1967	**r.,** 1972/316
1845	Rules of Procedure (Air Force) (Third Amdt.) Rules 1967	**r.,** 1972/419

Year and Number (or date)	Act or instrument	How affected
1967		
1882	Superannuation (Teaching and N.I. Local Government) Interchange (S.) Rules 1967	**r.** (saving), 1972/328
1968	Industrial Expansion Act 1968 (c. 32)	s. 8(3) **am.**, 1972/1243
	Overseas Aid Act 1968 (c. 57) ...	s. 3(2) **am.**, 1972/1046
25	Police Cadets Regs. 1968	**am.**, 1972/706
145	Rent Books (Forms of Notice) (S.) Regs. 1968	**r.**, 1972/1333
208	Police Cadets (S.) Regs. 1968	**am.**, 1972/778
225	National Health Service (Appointment of Medical and Dental Officers) (S.) Amdt. Regs. 1968	**r.**, 1972/467
333	Exchange Control (Scheduled Territories) (Amdt.) O. 1968	**r.**, 1972/386
524	Family Allowances, National Insurance and Industrial Injuries (Consequential) Regs. 1968	**am.**, 1972/606
619	Plant Breeders' Rights (Fees) Regs. 1968	**r.**, 1972/506
716	Police (S.) Regs. 1968	**r.**, 1972/777
717	Police (Promotion) (S.) Regs. 1968 ...	**am.**, 1972/777
824	Public Service Vehicles (Conditions of Fitness) (Amdt.) Regs. 1968	**r.**, 1972/751
826	Public Service Vehicles (Equipment and Use) (Amdt.) Regs. 1968	**r.**, 1972/751
981	Hill Cattle (S.) Scheme 1968	**am.**, 1972/725
987	Redundant Mineworkers (Payments Scheme) O. 1968	**am.**, 1972/335
994	Premium Savings Bonds (Amdt.) Regs. 1968	**r.**, 1972/765
995	Savings Certificates (Amdt.) No. 2 Regs. 1968	**r.**, 1972/641
1064	Post Office Savings Bank Amdt. (No. 1) Regs. 1968	**r.**, 1972/764
1066	Rate Rebates (Limits of Income) O. 1968	**superseded,** 1972/81
1071	Cts.-Martial Appeal Rules 1968 ...	**am.**, 1972/798
1173	Rules of Procedure (Air Force) (Amdt.) Rules 1968	**r.**, 1972/419
1177	Registration of Births, Deaths and Marriages (Fees) (S.) O. 1968	**r.**, 1972/890
1180	Rules of Procedure (Army) (Amdt.) Rules 1968	**r.**, 1972/316
1242	Registration of Births, Deaths and Marriages (Fees) O. 1968	**am.**, 1972/911
1399	Exchange Control (Scheduled Territories) (Amdt.) (No. 2) O. 1968	**r.**, 1972/386

Year and Number (or date)	Act or instrument	How affected
1968		
1443	Premium Savings Bonds (Amdt.) (No. 2) Regs. 1968	r., 1972/765
1444	Savings Certificates (Amdt.) (No. 3) Regs. 1968	r., 1972/641
1526	Public Service Vehicles (Conditions of Fitness) (Amdt.) (No. 2) Regs. 1968	r., 1972/751
1561	Customs Duty (Personal Reliefs) (No. 4) O. 1968	am., 1972/872
1684	National Insurance (Classification) Amdt. Regs. 1968	r., 1972/555
1714	Motor Vehicles (Tests) Regs. 1968 ...	am., 1972/898
1763	Industrial Training (Footwear, Leather and Fur Skin Bd.) O. 1968	am., 1972/597
1801	Armed Forces (Discharge by Purchase) Regs. 1968	am., 1972/8
1858	Copyright (International Conventions) (Amdt.) O. 1968	r., 1972/673
1862	Inter-Governmental Maritime Consultative Organisations (Immunities and Privileges) O. 1968	am., 1972/118
1898	Rules of Procedure (Army) (Second Amdt.) Rules 1968	r., 1972/316
1921	Rules of Procedure (Air Force) (Second Amdt.) Rules 1968	r., 1972/419
1954	Building Societies (Accounts and Annual Return etc.) Regs. 1968	r., 1972/70
1963	Police (S.) Amdt. (No. 2) Regs. 1968...	r., 1972/777
2003	Probation (Conditions of Service) (Amdt. No. 2) Rules 1968	superseded, 1972/803
2077	Plant Breeders' Rights (Applications in Designated Countries) O. 1968	am., 1972/403
1969	Housing Act 1969 (c. 33)	s. 37(4) am., 1972/440, 21(7) am., 1972/953
	Housing (S.) Act 1969 (c. 34)	s. 59(4) am., 1972/457
	Trustee Savings Banks Act 1969 (c. 50)	ss. 75(1) am., 75(3) inserted, 77(1) am., 1972/1029 75, 77 mod., 1972/1278
1969		
81	Weights and Measures (Amdt.) Regs. 1969	r., 1972/767
150	Aircraft (Exemption from Seizure on Patent Claims) O. 1969	r., 1972/969
168	Police (S.) Amdt. Regs. 1969	r., 1969/777
200	Motor Vehicles (Designation of Approval Marks) Regs. 1969	r., 1972/577

Year and Number (or date)	Act or instrument	How affected
1969		
233	Rate Support Grant (S.) O. 1969 ...	**am.,** 1972/262
257	National Health Service (Appointment of Medical and Dental Officers) (S.) Amdt. Regs. 1969	**r.,** 1972/467
321	Motor Vehicles (Construction and Use) Regs. 1969	**am.,** 1972/805, 843, 987
386	Merchant Shipping (Light Dues) O. 1969	**r.,** 1972/456
425	Compulsory Purchase of Land (General Vesting Declaration) Regs. 1969	**r.,** 1972/1313
483	Provision of Milk and Meals Regs. 1969	**am.,** 1972/1098
505	Police (S.) Amdt. (No. 2) Regs. 1969...	**r.,** 1972/777
519	Companies (Bd. of Trade) Fees O. 1969	**am.,** 1972/1055
595	Air Navigation (Isle of Man) O. 1969	**r.,** 1972/454
637	Is. of Scilly (Housing) (Amdt.) O. 1969	**r.,** 1972/1204
638	Is. of Scilly (Housing) O. 1969 ...	**r.,** 1972/1204
639	Building (Fourth Amdt.) Regs. 1969...	**r.,** 1972/317
679	Rules of Procedure (Air Force) (Amdt.) Rules 1969	**r.,** 1972/419
680	Rules of Procedure (Army) (Amdt.) Rules 1969	**r.,** 1972/316
732	Increase of Pensions (India, Pakistan and Burma) Regs. 1969	**superseded,** 1972/990
743	Copyright (Bermuda: Protection of Foreign Broadcasts) O. 1969	**r.,** 1972/673
841	Education Authy. Bursaries (S.) Regs. 1969	**am.,** 1972/844
879	Industrial Training (Road Transport Bd.) O. 1969	**r.,** 1972/772
915	Equine Animals (Importation) O. 1969	**am.,** 1972/761
927	Police (S.) Amdt. (No. 3) Regs. 1969...	**r.,** 1972/777
997	Superannuation (Local Govt. and Approved Employment) Interchange Rules 1969	**am.,** 1972/933
1015	White Fish and Herring Subsidies (U.K.) Scheme 1969	**r.,** 1972/1171
1021	Plant Breeders' Rights Regs. 1969 ...	**am.,** 1972/84
1022	Plant Breeders' Rights (Fees) (Amdt.) Regs. 1969	**r.,** 1972/506
1027	Plant Varieties (Index) Regs. 1969 ...	**r.,** 1972/507
1028	Plant Varieties (Performance Trials) Regs. 1969	**am.,** 1972/647
1038	Food (Control of Irradiation) (S.) Amdt. Regs. 1969	**r.,** 1972/307
1039	Food (Control of Irradiation) (Amdt.) Regs. 1969	**r.,** 1972/205

Year and Number (or date)	Act or instrument	How affected
1969		
1135	Family Allowances, National Insurance and Industrial Injuries (Post Office Act 1969) Consequential Regs. 1969	am., 1972/555
1139	Licensing of Bulls (E. and W.) Regs. 1969	r., 1972/1261
1154	Improvement of Livestock (Licensing of Bulls) (S.) Amdt. Regs. 1969	r., 1972/1309
1211	Governor's Pensions (Maximum Amounts) O. 1969	r., 1972/229
1333	Premium Savings Bonds (Amdt.) Regs. 1969	r., 1972/765
1334	Savings Certificates (Amdt.) (No. 2) Regs. 1969	r., 1972/641
1335	Post Office Savings Bank (Amdt.) Regs. 1969	r., 1972/764
1361	National Insurance (Increase of Benefit and Miscellaneous Provns.) Regs. 1969	am., 1972/606
1362	National Insurance and Industrial Injuries (Classification and Collection of Contributions) Amdt. Regs. 1969	am., 1972/555
1419	Rent Regulation (Forms etc.) (S.) Regs. 1969	r. (saving), 1972/1221
1532	Town and Country Planning (Control of Advertisements) Regs. 1969	am., 1972/489
1586	Police (S.) Amdt. (No. 4) Regs. 1969...	r., 1972/777
1587	Building Societies (Accounts and Annual Return etc.) (Amdt.) Regs. 1969	r., 1972/70
1632	Police (Appeals) (S.) Rules 1969 ...	am., 1972/777
1634	Industrial Training (Hairdressing and Allied Services Bd.) O. 1969	r., 1972/895
1696	National Insurance (Contributions) Regs. 1969	am., 1972/166
1700	Trustee Savings Banks (Amdt.) Regs. 1969	r., 1972/583
1704	Agriculture (Calculation of Value for Compensation) Regs. 1969	am., 1972/864
1713	Remuneration of Teachers (Further Education) O. 1969	r., 1972/255
1740	Wages Regulation (Sack and Bag) (Holidays) O. 1969	am., 1972/854
1746	Civil Aviation (Documentary Evidence) Regs. 1969	r., 1972/187

Year and Number (or date)	Act or instrument	How affected
1969		
1758	Post Office Savings Bank (Amdt.) (No. 2) Regs. 1969	**r.**, 1972/764
1780	Remuneration of Teachers (Farm Institutes) O. 1969	**r.**, 1972/276
1822	Foreign Sea-Fishery Officers (North-East Atlantic Fisheries Commission Scheme) O. 1969	**am.**, 1972/758
1837	Hong Kong (Non-Domiciled Parties) Divorce Rules 1969	**am.**, 1972/774
1845	Winter Keep (S.) Scheme 1969 ...	**am.**, 1972/861
1846	Rent Regulation (Forms etc.) (S.) (Amdt.) Regs. 1969	**r.** (saving), 1972/1221
1869	Supreme Ct. (Non-Contentious Probate) Fees O. 1969	**am.**, 1972/1191
1871	Industrial Training (Road Transport Bd.) O. 1969 (Amdt.) O. 1969	**r.**, 1972/772
1970	Finance Act 1970 (c. 24)	s. 35(2) **am.**, 1972/92
	Family Income Supplements Act 1970 (c. 55)	ss. 2, 3 **am.**, 1972/135
46	Family Allowances, National Insurance, Industrial Injuries and Miscellaneous Provns. (Decimalisation of the Currency) Regs. 1970	**am.**, 1972/603, 604, 606, 1301
109	Building (Fifth Amdt.) Regs. 1970 ...	**r.**, 1972/317
110	Wages Regulation (Unlicensed Place of Refreshment) O. 1970	**r.**, 1972/264
124	Plant Varieties (Index) (Amdt.) Regs. 1970	**r.**, 1972/507
144	Drivers' Hours (Goods Vehicles) (Exemptions) Regs. 1970	**r.**, 1972/574
198	Fixed Penalty (Procedure) Regs. 1970	**am.**, 1972/333
202	Goods Vehicles (Operators' Licences) (Temporary Use in G.B.) Regs. 1970	**r.**, 1972/716
217	National Insurance (Classification) Amdt. Regs. 1970	**r.**, 1972/555
264	Rules of Procedure (Army) (Amdt.) Rules 1970	**r.**, 1972/316
281	Fiduciary Note Issue (Extension of Period) O. 1970	**r.**, 1972/154
290	Copyright (International Conventions) (Amdt.) O. 1970	**r.**, 1972/673
332	Sugar Beet (Research and Education) (Increase of Contributions) O. 1970	**superseded**, 1972/105
336	Rate Rebates (Limits of Income) (S.) O. 1970	**superseded**, 1972/112

Year and Number (or date)	Act or instrument	How affected
1970		
359	Price Stability of Imported Products (Levy Arrangements) (Eggs) O. 1970	**am.,** 1972/620
422	Rules of Procedure (Air Force) (Amdt.) Rules 1970	**r.,** 1972/419
425	Police (S.) Amdt. Regs. 1970	**r.,** 1972/777
453	Plant Varieties (Index) (Amdt. No. 2) Regs. 1970	**r.,** 1972/507
454	Plant Breeders' Rights (Fees) (Amdt.) Regs. 1970	**r.,** 1972/506
467	General Medical Council (Registration (Fees) Regs.) O. of C. 1970	**r.,** 1972/429
482	British Solomon Is. O. 1970	**am.,** 1972/959
558	Customs Duty (Personal Reliefs) O. 1970	**am.,** 1972/838
612	Public Service Vehicles (International Circulation) Regs. 1970	**r.,** 1972/341
637	Copyright (International Conventions) (Amdt. No. 2) O. 1970	**r.,** 1972/673
639	Merchant Shipping (Light Dues) O. 1970	**r.,** 1972/456
666	Income Tax (Employments) (No. 5) Regs. 1970	**superseded,** 1972/552
703	Wages Regulation (Keg and Drum) (Holidays) O. 1970	**r.,** 1972/819
740	Remuneration of Teachers (Farm Institutes) (Amdt.) O. 1970	**r.,** 1972/276
741	Remuneration of Teachers (Further Education) (Amdt.) O. 1970	**r.,** 1972/255
748	Exchange Control (Scheduled Territories) (Amdt.) O. 1970	**r.,** 1972/386
789	Exchange Control (Purchase of Foreign Currency) O. 1970	**am.,** 1972/137
823	Air Navigation (Noise Certification) O. 1970	**am.,** 1972/455
847	Rate Rebates (Limits of Income) O. 1970	**superseded,** 1972/81
862	Teachers' Superannuation (Family Benefits) Regs. 1970	**am.,** 1972/360, 1092
954	Air Navigation O. 1970	**r.,** 1972/129
977	Family Allowances, National Insurance, Industrial Injuries and Miscellaneous Provisions (Decimalisation of the Currency) Amdt. (No. 2) Regs. 1970	**am.,** 1972/555
1021	Superannuation (Judicial Offices) Rules 1970	**am.,** 1972/1277

Year and Number (or date)	Act or instrument	How affected
1970		
1032	Wages Regulation (Perambulator and Invalid Carriage) O. 1970	r., 1972/16
1040	Offices, Shops and Railway Premises Act 1963 (Exemption No. 9) O. 1970	r., 1972/1086
1047	Corn Returns Regs. 1970	am., 1972/1245
1056	Trustee Savings Banks (Pensions) O. 1970	r., 1972/1029
1081	Air Navigation (General) Regs. 1970	r., 1972/322
1082	Rules of the Air and Air Traffic Control Regs. 1970	r., 1972/321
1083	Air Navigation (Restriction of Flying) Regs. 1970	r., 1972/320
1089	Plant Varieties (Index) (Amdt. No. 3) Regs. 1970	r., 1972/507
1099	Corn Returns (S.) Regs. 1970 ...	am., 1972/1275
1129	Wages Regulation (Lace Finishing) O. 1970	r., 1972/1223
1130	Wages Regulation (Lace Finishing) (Holidays) O. 1970	r., 1972/1224
1142	Income Tax (Employments) (No. 6) (Seamen) Regs. 1970	am., 1972/1186
1209	Fixed Penalty (Procedure) (Amdt.) (No. 4) Regs. 1970	r., 1972/333
1268	Wages Regulation (Road Haulage) O. 1970	r., 1972/581
1288	Export of Goods (Control) O. 1970 ...	am., 1972/89, 266, 938
1329	National Health Service (General Dental Services) Amdt. (No. 2) Regs. 1970	r., 1972/82
1335	Building (Sixth Amdt.) Regs. 1970 ...	r., 1972/317
1340	National Health Service (General Dental Services) (S.) Amdt. (No. 2) Regs. 1970	am., 1972/96
1372	Diseases of Animals (Approved Disinfectants) O. 1970	am., 1972/242
1392	Diseases of Animals (Misc. Fees) O. 1970	r., 1972/863
1441	County Cts. (Administration Order Jurisdiction) O. 1970	superseded, 1972/1103
1442	Air Navigation (Amdt.) O. 1970 ...	r., 1972/129
1447	Wages Regulation (Licensed Residential Establishment and Licensed Restaurant) O. 1970	r., 1972/757
1448	Rules of the Air and Air Traffic Control (Amdt.) Regs. 1970	r., 1972/321
1449	Air Navigation (General) (Amdt.) Regs. 1970	r., 1972/322

Year and Number (or date)	Act or instrument	How affected
1970		
1455	Exchange Control (Scheduled Territories) (Amdt. No. 2) O. 1970	**r.,** 1972/386
1463	Police (S.) Amdt. (No. 2) Regs. 1970...	**r.,** 1972/777
1495	Wages Regulation (Industrial and Staff Canteen) O. 1970	**r.,** 1972/869
1580	National Insurance (Widow's Pensions and Miscellaneous Provns.) Regs. 1970	**am.,** 1972/604, 606
1599	Wages Regulation (Ostrich and Fancy Feathers and Artificial Flowers) O. 1970	**r.,** 1972/9
1700	Motor Vehicles (Rear Markings) Regs. 1970	**am.,** 1972/842
1704	National Insurance (Classification) (Amdt.) (No. 2) Regs. 1970	**r.,** 1972/555
1731	Rules of Procedure (Air Force) (Second Amdt.) Rules 1970	**r.,** 1972/419
1732	Rules of Procedure (Army) (Second Amdt.) Rules 1970	**r.,** 1972/316
1737	Nurses (S.) Rules 1970	**am.,** 1972/879
1759	Farm Capital Grant Scheme 1970 ...	**am.,** 1972/368
1798	Goods Vehicles (Operators' Licences) (Temporary Use in G.B.) (Amdt.) Regs. 1970	**r.,** 1972/716
1805	Farm Capital Grant (S.) Scheme 1970	**am.,** 1972/362
1849	Town and Country Planning (Industrial Development Certificates: Exemption) O. 1970	**r.,** 1972/903, 996
1853	Superannuation (Local Govt. and Approved Employment) Interchange (S.) Rules 1970	**am.,** 1972/63
1870	Supreme Ct. Fees O. 1970	**am.,** 1972/1190
1950	Judges' Remuneration (No. 2) O. 1970	**r.,** 1972/1104
1951	Air Navigation (Second Amdt.) O. 1970	**r.,** 1972/129
1958	Functions of Traffic Wardens O. 1970	**am.,** 1972/540
1968	Judicial Offices (Salaries) O. 1970 ...	**r.,** 1972/1078
1981	National Insurance (General Benefit) Regs. 1970	**am.,** 1972/166, 394
1986	General Medical Council (Registration (Fees) (Amdt.) Regs. O. of C. 1970	**r.,** 1972/429
1995	Air Navigation (General) (Second Amdt.) Regs. 1970	**r.,** 1972/322
2007	Bankruptcy Fees O. 1970	**am.,** 1972/1054, 1189
2014	Drivers' Hours (Goods Vehicles) (Exemptions) (Amdt.) (No. 3) Regs. 1970	**r.,** 1972/574
2021	Solicitors' Remuneration O. 1970 ...	**r.,** 1972/1139
2022	Solicitors' Remuneration (Registered Land) O. 1970	**r.,** 1972/1139

Year and Number (or date)	Act or instrument	How affected
1971	Pensions (Increase) Act 1971 (c. 56) ...	s. 3(2)(*a*) (3)(*a*) **am.,** 1972/1299
	Town and Country Planning Act 1971 (c. 78)	s. 68(1) **am.,** 1972/903, 996
87	Wages Regulation (Dressmaking and Women's Light Clothing) (S.) O. 1971	**r.,** 1972/207
102	Matrimonial Causes Fees O. 1971 ...	**r.** (saving), 1972/194
107	Witnesses' Allowances Regs. 1971 ...	**am.,** 1972/49
108	Coroners (Fees and Allowances) Rules 1971	**am.,** 1972/980
136	Jurors' Allowances Regs. 1971 ...	**r.,** 1972/1001
145	Firemen's Pension Scheme 1971 ...	**am.,** 1972/522
156	Police Regs. 1971	**am.,** 1972/74, 339, 1195
196	Police (S.) Amdt. Regs. 1971	**r.,** 1972/777
207	Wages Regulation (Sack and Bag) O. 1971	**r.,** 1972/854
222	Approved Schools and Classifying Centres (Contributions by Local Authies.) Regs. 1971	**r.,** 1972/241
226	Family Income Supplements (General) Regs. 1971	**am.,** 1972/14, 1282
227	Family Income Supplements (Claims and Payments) Regs. 1971	**am.,** 1972/1282
249	Residential Establishments (Payments by Local Authies.) (S.) O. 1971	**am.,** 1972/466
271	Air Navigation (General) (Third Amdt.) Regs. 1971	**r.,** 1972/322
274	Import Duty Drawbacks (No. 1) O. 1971	**am.,** 1972/406
304	Therapeutic Substances (Supply of Antibiotics and Chemotherapeutic Substances for Agricultural Purposes) Regs. 1971	**am.,** 1972/190
308	Wages Regulation (Dressmaking and Women's Light Clothing) (E. and W.) O. 1971	**r.,** 1972/168
352	Goods Vehicles (Plating and Testing) Regs. 1971	**am.,** 1972/195, 806
353	Goods Vehicles (Operators' Licences) (Temporary Use in G.B.) (Amdt.) Regs. 1971	**r.,** 1972/716
367	Sugar Beet (Research and Education) O. 1971	**superseded,** 1972/224
374	Functions of Traffic Wardens (S.) O. 1971	**am.,** 1972/540
383	Merchant Shipping (Tonnage) (Overseas Territories) O. 1971	**am.,** 1972/447

Year and Number (or date)	Act or instrument	How affected
1971		
384	Foreign Compensation (Financial Provisions) O. 1971	**superseded,** 1972/302
469	Rate Support Grant (S.) O. 1971 ...	**am.,** 1972/263
470	Rate Support Grant (Increase) (S.) O. 1971	**superseded,** 1972/262
475	Eggs (Protection of Guarantees) O. 1971	**r.,** 1972/492
477	Exchange Control (Authorised Dealers and Depositaries) O. 1971	**r.,** 1972/132
479	Fixed Penalty (Procedure) (Amdt.) Regs. 1971	**r.,** 1972/333
510	Royal Air Force Terms of Service Regs. 1971	**am.,** 1972/355
517	Royal Navy Terms of Service (Amdt.) Regs. 1971	**superseded,** 1972/558
549	Savings Certificates (Amdt.) Regs. 1971	**r.,** 1971/641
550	Premium Savings Bonds (Amdt.) Regs. 1971	**r.,** 1972/765
562	Non-Residents' Transitional Relief from Income Tax on Dividends (Extension of Period) O. 1971	**superseded,** 1972/465
563	Transitional Relief for Interest and Royalties paid to Non-Residents (Extension of Period) O. 1971	**superseded,** 1972/464
621	National Insurance (Attendance Allowance) Regs. 1971	**am.,** 1972/664, 1232
683	Police (S.) Amdt. (No. 2) Regs. 1971...	**r.,** 1972/777
702	Family Income Supplements (Computation) Regs. 1971	**r.,** 1972/135
707	National Insurance (Claims and Payments) Regs. 1971	**am.,** 1972/166
724	Merchant Shipping (Pilot Ladders) (Amdt.) Rules 1971	**r.,** 1972/531
750	Wages Regulation (Rope, Twine and Net) O. 1971	**r.,** 1972/782
770	Resolution of the H. of C. dated 4th May, 1971 passed in pursuance of the H. of C. Members' Fund Act 1948, s. 3 (11 & 12 Geo. 6. c. 36) (1971 II, p. 4028)	**superseded,** 1972/1181
804	Police Cadets (Amdt.) (No. 2) Regs. 1971	**superseded,** 1972/706
830	Wages Regulation (Retail Bespoke Tailoring) (E. and W.) O. 1971	**r.,** 1972/680
845	Wages Regulation (Retail Drapery, Outfitting and Footwear) O. 1971	**r.,** 1972/35
855	Price Stability of Imported Products (Minimum Import Price Levels) (Beef and Veal) O. 1971	**r.,** 1972/254

Year and Number (or date)	Act or instrument	How affected
1971		
857	Price Stability of Imported Products (Minimum Import Price Levels) (Milk and Milk Products) O. 1971	**am.,** 1972/652
868	Wages Regulation (Pin, Hook and Eye, and Snap Fastener) O. 1971	**r.,** 1972/718
885	Wages Regulation (Keg and Drum) O. 1971	**r.,** 1972/818
953	Matrimonial Causes Rules 1971 ...	**am.,** 1972/1095
972	Medicines (Standard Provisions for Licences and Certificates) Regs. 1971	**am.,** 1972/1226
973	Medicines (Applications for Product Licences and Clinical Trial and Animal Test Certificates) Regs. 1971	**am.,** 1972/1201
990	Wages Regulation (Retail Food) (E. and W.) O. 1971	**r.,** 1972/153
991	Wages Regulation (Licensed Non-residential Establishment) O. 1971	**r.,** 1972/943
992	Wages Regulation (Licensed Non-residential Establishment) (Managers and Club Stewards) O. 1971	**r.,** 1972/944
1023	Wages Regulation (Retail Food) (S.) O. 1971	**r.,** 1972/165
1028	Exchange Control (Authorised Dealers and Depositaries) (Amdt.) O. 1971	**r.,** 1972/132
1037	Milk (N.I.) O. 1971	**am.,** 1972/366
1038	Milk (G.B.) O. 1971	**am.,** 1972/367
1088	Wages Regulation (Stamped or Pressed Metal-Wares) O. 1971	**r.,** 1972/1087
1089	Wages Regulation (Stamped or Pressed Metal-Wares) (Holidays) O. 1971	**r.,** 1972/1088
1102	Plant Breeders' Rights (Fees) (Amdt.) Regs. 1971	**r.,** 1972/506
1103	Foreign Sea-Fishery Officers (International Commn. for the Northwest Atlantic Fisheries Scheme) O. 1971	**am.,** 1972/868
1109	Town and Country Planning (Structure and Local Plans) Regs. 1971	**r.,** 1972/1154
1135	Civil Aviation (Navigation Services Charges) Regs. 1971	**am.,** 1972/188
1203	Police (S.) Amdt. (No. 3) Regs. 1971...	**r.,** 1972/777
1220	National Insurance (Increase of Benefit and Miscellaneous Provns.) Regs. 1971	**am.,** 1972/603, 606
1257	Bd. of Inquiry (Army) (Amdt.) Rules 1971	**superseded,** 1972/847
1287	Diseases of Animals (Approved Disinfectants) (Amdt.) O. 1971	**r.,** 1972/242
1297	Awards (First Degree, etc. Courses) Regs. 1971	**am.,** 1972/1124

Year and Number (or date)	Act or instrument	How affected
1971		
1370	Exchange Control (Authorised Dealers and Depositaries) (Amdt.) (No. 2) O. 1971	r., 1972/132
1404	National Assistance (Charges for Accommodation) Regs. 1971	r., 1972/1240
1406	Exchange Control (Scheduled Territories) (Amdt.) O. 1971	r., 1972/386
1415	Wages Regulation (Flax and Hemp) O. 1971	r., 1972/928
1419	National Insurance (Miscellaneous Amdts.) Regs. 1971	am., 1972/603, 604, 606
1421	National Insurance and Industrial Injuries (Classification, Contributions and Collection of Contributions) Amdt. Regs. 1971	am., 1972/555
1426	Remuneration of Teachers (Further Education) (Amdt.) O. 1971	r., 1972/255
1440	National Insurance (Industrial Injuries) (Hospital In-Patients) Regs. 1971	am., 1972/605
1450	Medicines (Exemption from Licences) (Special and Transitional Cases) O. 1971	am., 1972/1200
1454	Wages Regulation (Linen and Cotton Handkerchief etc.) O. 1971	r., 1972/1312
1469	Royal Irish Constabulary (Widows' Pensions) Regs. 1971	am., 1972/1310
1478	National Insurance (General Benefit and Claims and Payments) Amdt. Regs. 1971	r., 1972/1301
1492	Disabled Persons (Badges for Motor Vehicles) Regs. 1971	am., 1972/906
1500	National Assistance (Charges for Accommodation) (S.) Regs. 1971	r., 1972/1347
1505	Fixed Penalty (Procedure) (Amdt.) (No. 2) Regs. 1971	r., 1972/333
1518	Wages Regulation (Retail Furnishing and Allied Trades) O. 1971	r., 1972/1116
1531	Wages Regulation (Milk Distributive) (S.) O. 1971	r., 1972/1279
1537	Milk and Meals (Education) (S.) Regs. 1971	am., 1972/1220
1539	Remuneration of Teachers (Primary and Secondary Schools) O. 1971	r., 1972/1082
1551	Opencast Coal (Rate of Interest on Compensation) (No. 2)	r., 1972/373
1556	Exchange Control (Scheduled Territories) (Amdt.) (No. 2) O. 1971	r., 1972/386

Year and Number (or date)	Act or instrument	How affected
1971		
1566	Exchange Control (Authorised Dealers and Depositaries) (Amdt.) (No. 3) O. 1971	r., 1972/132
1600	Building (Seventh Amdt.) Regs. 1971	r., 1972/317
1628	Road Vehicles (Excise) (Prescribed Particulars) Regs. 1971	r., 1972/850
1631	Wages Regulation (Retail Drapery, Outfitting and Footwear) (Amdt.) O. 1971	r., 1972/35
1633	National Insurance (Miscellaneous Amdts.) (No. 2) Regs. 1971	am., 1972/604
1686	Civil Aviation (Notices) Regs. 1971 ...	am., 1972/431
1698	Wages Regulation (Milk Distribution) (E. and W.) O. 1971	am., 1972/482
1708	Dutch Elm Disease (Local Authies.) O. 1971	am., 1972/1242
1715	Civil Aviation (Route Charges for Navigation Services) Regs. 1971	am., 1972/108, 905
1717	Brucellosis (Area Eradication) (E. and W.) O. 1971	am., 1972/1173
1728	National Insurance (Classification) Amdt. Regs. 1971	r., 1972/555
1733	Air Navigation (Third Amdt.) O. 1971	r., 1972/129
1737	Cayman Is. (Constitution) (Amdt.) O. 1971	r., 1972/1101
1750	Air Navigation (General) (Fourth Amdt.) Regs. 1971	r., 1972/322
1751	Rules of the Air and Air Traffic Control (Second Amdt.) Regs. 1971	r., 1972/321
1752	Brucellosis (Area Eradication) (S.) O. 1971	am., 1972/738, 1219
1775	Teachers Superannuation (Family Benefits) (S.) Regs. 1971	am., 1972/442, 1239
1839	Diseases of Animals (Approved Disinfectants) (Amdt.) (No. 2) O. 1971	r., 1972/242
1850	Copyright (International Conventions) (Amdt.) O. 1971	r., 1972/673
1870	Premium Savings Bonds (Amdt.) (No. 2) Regs. 1971	r., 1972/765
1938	Price Stability of Imported Products (Rates of Levy) (Eggs) (No. 28) O. 1971	r., 1972/21
1971	Import Duties (General) (No. 7) O. 1971	am., 1972/52, 226, 569, 648, 677, 1021, 1048
1972	Rules of the Air and Air Traffic Control (Third Amdt.) Regs. 1971	r., 1972/321
1987	Injuries in War (Shore Employments) Compensation (Amdt.) Scheme 1971	superseded, 1972/1280

Year and Number (or date)	Act or instrument	How affected
1971		
1993	Acquisition of Land (Rate of Interest after Entry) (No. 4) Regs. 1971	**r.,** 1972/949
1994	Acquisition of Land (Rate of Interest after Entry) (S.) (No. 4) Regs. 1971	**r.,** 1972/950
2002	Exchange Control (Scheduled Territories) (Amdt.) (No. 3) O. 1971	**r.,** 1972/386
2034	Exchange Control (Authorised Dealers and Depositaries) (Amdt.) (No. 4) O. 1971	**r.,** 1972/132
2082	Sugar (Rates of Surcharge and Surcharge Repayments) (No. 10) O. 1971	**superseded,** 1972/1
2083	Composite Sugar Products (Surcharge and Surcharge Repayments—Average Rates) (No. 10) O. 1971	**superseded,** 1972/2
2100	Cayman Is. (Legislative Assembly—Extension of Duration) O. 1971	**r.,** 1972/1101
2102	Extradition (Hijacking) O. 1971 ...	**am.,** 1972/1102
2103	Extradition (Tokyo Convention) O. 1971	**am.,** 1972/960
2154	Price Stability of Imported Products (Rates of Levy) (Cereals) (No. 14) O. 1971	**r.,** 1972/15
1972		
15	Price Stability of Imported Products (Rates of Levy) (Cereals) (No. 1) O. 1972	**r.,** 1972/57
21	Price Stability of Imported Products (Rates of Levy) (Eggs) (No. 1) O. 1972	**r.,** 1972/58
25	Price Stability of Imported Products (Rates of Levy) (Eggs) (No. 2) O. 1972	**r.,** 1972/58
35	Wages Regulation (Retail Drapery, Outfitting and Footwear O. 1972	**r.,** 1972/1297
57	Price Stability of Imported Products (Rates of Levy) (Cereals) (No. 2) O. 1972	**r.,** 1972/83
58	Price Stability of Imported Products (Rates of Levy) (Eggs) (No. 3) O. 1972	**r.,** 1972/193
66	Sugar (Distribution Payments) O. 1972	**am.,** 1972/356
67	Sugar (Distribution Repayments) O. 1972	**am.,** 1972/357
68	Composite Sugar Products (Distribution Payments—Average Rates) O. 1972	**superseded,** 1972/358

Year and Number (or date)	Act or instrument	How affected
1972		
72	National Health Service (General Dental Services) Amdt. Regs. 1972	am., 1972/1336
83	Price Stability of Imported Products (Rates of Levy) (Cereals) (No. 3) O. 1972	r., 1972/94
94	Price Stability of Imported Products (Rates of Levy) (Cereals) (No. 4) O. 1972	r., 1972/149
96	National Health Service (General Dental Services) (S.) Amdt. Regs. 1972	am., 1972/1348
129	Air Navigation O. 1972	am., 1972/672, 1266
132	Exchange Control (Authorised Dealers and Depositaries) O. 1972	am., 1972/556
136	Police (S.) Amdt. Regs. 1972	r., 1972/777
146	Exchange Control (Scheduled Territories) (Amdt.) O. 1972	r., 1972/386
149	Price Stability of Imported Products (Rates of Levy) (Cereals) (No. 5) O. 1972	r., 1972/170
150	Civil Aviation Authority (Charges) Regs. 1972	am., 1972/1272
160	Electricity (Advertising, Display and Flood Lighting) (Restriction) O. 1972	am., 1972/273
166	National Insurance (Claims and Payments and Misc. Provisions) Regs. 1972	am., 1972/1301
169	Electricity (Non-Domestic Heating) (Restriction) O. 1972	r., 1972/306
170	Price Stability of Imported Products (Rates of Levy) (Cereals) (No. 6) O. 1972	r., 1972/215
176	Road Vehicles Lighting (Standing Vehicles) (Exemption) (General) Regs. 1972	r., 1972/557
193	Price Stability of Imported Products (Rates of Levy) (Eggs) (No. 4) O. 1972	r., 1972/277
215	Price Stability of Imported Products (Rates of Levy) (Cereals) (No. 7) O. 1972	r., 1972/230
225	Electricity (Directions) O. 1972 ...	r., 1972/305
230	Price Stability of Imported Products (Rates of Levy) (Cereals) (No. 8) O. 1972	r., 1972/299
239	Electricity (Non-Domestic Heating) (Restriction) Amdt. O. 1972	r., 1972/306

Year and Number (or date)	Act or instrument	How affected
1972		
240	Electricity (Directions) No. 2 O. 1972	r., 1972/305
245	Electricity (Directions) No. 3 O. 1972	r., 1972/305
255	Remuneration of Teachers (Further Education) O. 1972	r., 1972/683
265	Electricity (Directions) No. 4 O. 1972	r., 1972/305
266	Export of Goods (Control) (Amdt. No. 2) O. 1972	r., 1972/938
273	Electricity (Restrictions) Amdt. O. 1972	r., 1972/306
276	Remuneration of Teachers (Farm Institutes) O. 1972	r., 1972/771
277	Price Stability of Imported Products (Rates of Levy) (Eggs) (No. 5) O. 1972	r., 1972/399
299	Price Stability of Imported Products (Rates of Levy) (Cereals) (No. 9) O. 1972	r., 1972/347
320	Air Navigation (Restriction of Flying) Regs. 1972	am., 1972/1066
321	Rules of the Air and Air Traffic Control Regs. 1972	am., 1972/699, 1233
347	Price Stability of Imported Products (Rates of Levy) (Cereals) (No. 10) O. 1972	r., 1972/372
356	Sugar (Distribution Payments) (No. 2) O. 1972	superseded, 1972/432
357	Sugar (Distribution Repayments) (Amdt.) O. 1972	superseded, 1972/433
358	Composite Sugar Products (Distribution Payments—Average Rates) (No. 2) O. 1972	superseded, 1972/434
372	Price Stability of Imported Products (Rates of Levy) (Cereals) (No. 11) O. 1972	r., 1972/488
373	Opencast Coal (Rate of Interest on Compensation) O. 1972	r., 1972/1216
386	Exchange Control (Scheduled Territories) O. 1972	r., 1972/930
394	National Insurance (General Benefit and Miscellaneous Amdts.) Regs. 1972	am., 1972/603, 604
399	Price Stability of Imported Products (Rates of Levy) (Eggs) (No. 6) O. 1972	r., 1972/609
400	Price Stability of Imported Products (Rates of Levy) (Cereals) (No. 12) O. 1972	r., 1972/488

Year and Number (or date)	Act or instrument	How affected
1972		
421	Intermediate Area and Derelict Land Clearance Area O. 1972	**am.**, 1972/585
428	National Insurance (Non-participation —Benefit and Schemes) Amdt. Provisional Regs. 1972	**r.**, 1972/1031
432	Sugar (Distribution Payments) (No. 3) O. 1972	**superseded**, 1972/578
433	Sugar (Distribution Repayments) (Amdt.) (No. 2) O. 1972	**superseded**, 1972/579
434	Composite Sugar Products (Distribution Payments—Average Rates) (No. 3) O. 1972	**superseded**, 1972/580
488	Price Stability of Imported Products (Rates of Levy) (Cereals) (No. 13) O. 1972	**r.**, 1972/530
495	Trustee Savings Banks (Pensions) (Amdt.) O. 1972	**r.**, 1972/1029
530	Price Stability of Imported Products (Rates of Levy) (Cereals) (No. 14) O. 1972	**r.**, 1972/678
551	Teachers' Superannuation (Financial Provns.) (S.) Regs. 1972	**am.**, 1972/1239
555	National Insurance (Classification) Regs. 1972	**am.**, 1972/1287
568	Teachers' Superannuation (Financial Provns.) Regs. 1972	**am.**, 1972/1092
578	Sugar (Distribution Payments) (No. 4) O. 1972	**superseded**, 1972/598
579	Sugar (Distribution Repayments) (Amdt.) (No. 3) O. 1972	**superseded**, 1972/599
580	Composite Sugar Products (Distribution Payments—Average Rates) (No. 4) O. 1972	**superseded**, 1972/600
598	Sugar (Distribution Payments) (No. 5) O. 1972	**superseded**, 1972/649
599	Sugar (Distribution Repayments) (Amdt.) (No. 4) O. 1972	**superseded**, 1972/650
600	Composite Sugar Products (Distribution Payments—Average Rates) (No. 5) O. 1972	**superseded**, 1972/651
609	Price Stability of Imported Products (Rates of Levy) (Eggs) (No. 7) O. 1972	**r.**, 1972/790
649	Sugar (Distribution Payments) (No. 6) O. 1972	**superseded**, 1972/659
650	Sugar (Distribution Repayments) (Amdt.) (No. 5) O. 1972	**superseded**, 1972/660

Year and Number (or date)	Act or instrument	How affected
1972		
651	Composite Sugar Products (Distribution Payments—Average Rates) (No. 6) O. 1972	**superseded,** 1972/661
659	Sugar (Distribution Payments) (No. 7) O. 1972	**superseded,** 1972/735
660	Sugar (Distribution Repayments) (Amdt.) (No. 6) O. 1972	**superseded,** 1972/736
661	Composite Sugar Products (Distribution Payments—Average Rates) (No. 7) O. 1972	**superseded,** 1972/737
678	Price Stability of Imported Products (Rates of Levy) (Cereals) (No. 15) O. 1972	**r.,** 1972/824
735	Sugar (Distribution Payments) (No. 8) O. 1972	**superseded,** 1972/753
736	Sugar (Distribution Repayments) (Amdt.) (No. 7) O. 1972	**superseded,** 1972/754
737	Composite Sugar Products (Distribution Payments—Average Rates) (No. 8) O. 1972	**superseded,** 1972/755
753	Sugar (Distribution Payments) (No. 9) O. 1972	**superseded,** 1972/799
754	Sugar (Distribution Repayments) (Amdt.) (No. 8) O. 1972	**superseded,** 1972/800
755	Composite Sugar Products (Distribution Payments—Average Rates) (No. 9) O. 1972	**superseded,** 1972/801
777	Police (S.) Regs. 1972	**am.,** 1972/1206
790	Price Stability of Imported Products (Rates of Levy) (Eggs) (No. 8) O. 1972	**r.,** 1972/851
799	Sugar (Distribution Payments) (No. 10) O. 1972	**superseded,** 1972/821
800	Sugar (Distribution Repayments) (Amdt.) (No. 9) O. 1972	**superseded,** 1972/822
801	Composite Sugar Products (Distribution Payments—Average Rates) (No. 10) O. 1972	**superseded,** 1972/823
808	Cayman Is. Constitution (Amdt.) O. 1972	**r.,** 1972/1101
821	Sugar (Distribution Payments) (No. 11) O. 1972	**superseded,** 1972/976
822	Sugar (Distribution Repayments) (Amdt.) (No. 10) O. 1972	**superseded,** 1972/977
823	Composite Sugar Products (Distribution Payments—Average Rates) (No. 11) O. 1972	**superseded,** 1972/978

Year and Number (or date)	Act or instrument	How affected
1972		
824	Price Stability of Imported Products (Rates of Levy) (Cereals) (No. 16) O. 1972	**r.**, 1972/991
851	Price Stability of Imported Products (Rates of Levy) (Eggs) (No. 9) O. 1972	**r.**, 1972/998
903	Town and Country Planning (Industrial Development Certificates: Exemption) O. 1972	**r.**, 1972/996
949	Acquisition of Land (Rate of Interest after Entry) Regs. 1972	**r.**, 1972/1126
950	Acquisition of Land (Rate of Interest after Entry) (S.) Regs. 1972	**r.**, 1972/1127
976	Sugar (Distribution Payments) (No. 12) O. 1972	**superseded,** 1972/1043
977	Sugar (Distribution Repayments) (Amdt.) (No. 11) O. 1972	**superseded,** 1972/1044
978	Composite Sugar Products (Distribution Payments—Average Rates) (No. 12) O. 1972	**superseded,** 1972/1045
991	Price Stability of Imported Products (Rates of Levy) (Cereals) (No. 17) O. 1972	**r.**, 1972/1137
1043	Sugar (Distribution Payments) (No. 13) O. 1972	**superseded,** 1972/1079
1044	Sugar (Distribution Repayments) (Amdt.) (No. 12) O. 1972	**superseded,** 1972/1080
1045	Composite Sugar Products (Distribution Payments—Average Rates) (No. 13) O. 1972	**superseded,** 1972/1081
1079	Sugar (Distribution Payments) (No. 14) O. 1972	**superseded,** 1972/1134
1080	Sugar (Distribution Repayments) (Amdt.) (No. 13) O. 1972	**superseded,** 1972/1135
1081	Composite Sugar Products (Distribution Payments—Average Rates) (No. 14) O. 1972	**superseded,** 1972/1136
1134	Sugar (Distribution Payments) (No. 15) O. 1972	**superseded,** 1972/1252
1135	Sugar (Distribution Repayments) (Amdt.) (No. 14) O. 1972	**superseded,** 1972/1253
1136	Composite Sugar Products (Distribution Payments—Average Rates) (No. 15) O. 1972	**superseded,** 1972/1254
1137	Price Stability of Imported Products (Rates of Levy) (Cereals) (No. 18) O. 1972	**r.**, 1972/1350

Year and Number (or date)	Act or instrument	How affected
1972		
1252	Sugar (Distribution Payments) (No. 16) O. 1972	**superseded,** 1972/1326
1253	Sugar (Distribution Repayments) (Amdt.) (No.15) O. 1972	**superseded,** 1972/1327
1254	Composite Sugar Products (Distribution Payments—Average Rates) (No. 16) O. 1972	**superseded,** 1972/1328
1326	Sugar (Distribution Payments) (No. 17) O. 1972	**superseded,** 1972/1340
1327	Sugar (Distribution Repayments) (Amdt.) (No. 16) O. 1972	**superseded,** 1972/1341
1328	Composite Sugar Products (Distribution Payments—Average Rates) (No. 17) O. 1972	**superseded,** 1972/1342

Index to Part II

SBN 11 840113 0*